LP	Liquidity premium
M	Maturity value of a bond
M/B	Market-to-book ratio
MCC	Marginal cost of capital
MIRR	Modified internal rate of return
MRP	Maturity risk premium
MVA	Market value added
N	Calculator key denoting number of periods
n	(1) Life of a project or investment
	(2) Number of shares outstanding
NPV	Net present value
NOWC	Net operating working capital
P	(1) Price of a share of stock; P_0 = price of the stock today
	(2) Sales price per unit of product sold
P_f	Price of good in foreign country
P_h	Price of good in home country
P_N	A stock's horizon, or terminal, value
P/E	Price/earnings ratio
PMT	Payment of an annuity
PPP	Purchasing power parity
PV	Present value
PVA_n	Present value of an annuity for n years
PVIF	Present value interest factor for a lump sum
PVIFA	Present value interest factor for an annuity
Q	Quantity produced or sold
r	Correlation coefficient
ROA	Return on assets
ROE	Return on equity
RP	Risk premium
RP_M	Market risk premium
RR	Retention rate
S	Sales
SML	Security Market Line
Σ	Summation sign (capital sigma)
σ	Standard deviation (lowercase sigma)
σ^2	Variance
t	Time period
T	Marginal income tax rate
TIE	Times-interest-earned ratio
V	Variable cost per unit
V_B	Bond value
VC	Total variable costs
WACC	Weighted average cost of capital
YTC	Yield to call
YTM	Yield to maturity

FUNDAMENTALS OF FINANCIAL MANAGEMENT

CONCISE THIRD EDITION

FUNDAMENTALS OF FINANCIAL MANAGEMENT

CONCISE THIRD EDITION

EUGENE F. BRIGHAM
UNIVERSITY OF FLORIDA

JOEL F. HOUSTON
UNIVERSITY OF FLORIDA

SOUTH-WESTERN
™
THOMSON LEARNING

Australia • Canada • Mexico • Singapore • Spain • United Kingdom • United States

Publisher:	Mike Roche
Executive Editor:	Mike Reynolds
Market Strategist:	Charles Stutesman
Developmental Editor:	Elizabeth Thomson
Project Manager:	Barrett Lackey

Cover Image: Copyright © 2000 Bruce Rogovin

ISBN: 0-03-032101-8 (text) + 0-03-032162-X (CD) = 0-03-033263-X (Pkg)
Library of Congress Catalog Card Number: 00-111720

For more information contact South-Western, 5191 Natorp Boulevard, Mason, Ohio, 45040 or find us on the Internet at http://www.swcollege.com
For permission to use material from this text or product, contact us by

- telephone: 1-800-730-2214
- fax: 1-800-730-2215
- web: http://www.thomsonrights.com

Printed in the United States of America

2 3 4 5 6 7 8 9 0   048   9 8 7 6 5 4 3 2 1

FUNDAMENTALS OF FINANCIAL MANAGEMENT

CONCISE THIRD EDITION

Fundamentals of Financial Management: Concise Third Edition continues to offer the most complete and integrated teaching system available.

When *Fundamentals of Financial Management* was first published more than 25 years ago, our intent was to write an introductory finance text that students could truly understand. Today, nine editions later, *Fundamentals* has become the leading undergraduate finance text. We have always tried to reflect changes in the world of finance, along with the latest innovations in education and publishing. Our goal with each new edition is to produce a book and ancillary package that set yet another new standard for finance textbooks.

The many changes we made over time resulted in a better, more complete textbook, but one that is much longer than it was originally. Indeed, despite the continued success of *Fundamentals*, we often heard the comment that it was difficult to cover the entire book in a single term.

When we first became aware of this situation, we turned to students and other professors for advice. Some students and professors advised us not to worry about the size issue. They argued that a larger, more complete textbook is better because it provides professors more flexibility in designing their courses, is a better reference for students after they complete the course, and allows interested students to read chapters not covered in the course on their own. Others took a different position, arguing that as a textbook gets larger, it becomes increasingly difficult to develop a manageable syllabus, and that many students buy a larger, more expensive text than they want or need. In the end, we concluded that both arguments have merit, so we decided six years ago to create the first edition of *Fundamentals of Financial Management: The Concise Edition* for those who like *Fundamentals* but think a smaller, more concise textbook would better serve their needs.

The response to *Concise* has been overwhelmingly positive. As teachers and authors, we have always tried to incorporate current innovations in the field of finance, in education, and in publishing into our books and their related ancillaries. The third edition of *Concise* has a new look and new ancillary items that provide the most complete and integrated teaching package available. Of course, our commitment to quality, accuracy, and student accessibility remains as strong as ever.

RELATIONSHIP TO *FUNDAMENTALS*

When we first created *Concise*, we debated streamlining the book either by covering all the topics in less depth or by covering fewer topics but maintaining the depth and rigor of *Fundamentals*. We chose to retain the depth and level while eliminating some less essential topics. While the omitted topics are interesting and important, they are not critical for students who do not major in finance, and finance majors will study them anyway in subsequent courses.

Concise is significantly different than *Fundamentals* primarily because it is shorter. Consequently, most of the chapters will be familiar to users of *Fundamentals*. So, while *Concise* can be viewed as a streamlined edition of *Fundamentals*, the third edition maintains a thorough discussion of such basic core topics as the time value of money, the relationship between risk and return, the financial environment, financial statements, stock and bond valuation, and capital budgeting.

INTENDED MARKET

All chapters are written in a flexible, modular format.

Like *Fundamentals*, *Concise* is primarily intended for the introductory finance course. Unlike *Fundamentals*, it is possible to cover all of the chapters in *Concise* in a single term, and perhaps even to supplement it with a few outside readings or cases. *Concise* may also be used in courses in which the material is covered in two terms, allowing professors the flexibility to assign even more additional cases, readings, and exercises.

Although the chapters in *Concise* are sequenced logically, they are written in a flexible, modular format, which will help instructors cover the material in a different sequence should they choose to do so.

OUTLINE OF THE THIRD EDITION

Finance is an exciting, challenging, and ever-changing discipline. Changing technology and increased globalization are dramatically transforming financial practices and markets. In this third edition we strive to communicate the excitement and to demonstrate how these changes are affecting finance and other aspects of business.

Changing technology has affected not only *what* we teach but also *how* we teach. More and more, we find ourselves using computer spreadsheets and the Internet to supplement our classroom lectures. With this in mind, we developed a set of integrated spreadsheets and Internet exercises and placed them (as appropriate) throughout the book and ancillaries. These items, which are available both on a CD-ROM and via the Internet, will make it easier for instructors to teach and for students to learn the fundamentals of financial management.

In developing and improving *Concise*, we tried to convey the excitement and ever-changing nature of finance and to make students realize its importance and relevance. More often than not, students discover that finance is more interesting and relevant than they had anticipated. Nevertheless, finance remains a challenging subject for many students, and we kept this in mind as we developed the text and its supporting materials.

Of course, an introductory finance course should be more than just a series of topics—students must understand not only the basic concepts but also how they fit together. With this in mind, *Concise* begins with a discussion of financial objectives, where we show how managers and investors use financial statements to determine how well firms are meeting those objectives. We also discuss how incentive compensation, along with the threat of takeovers, motivates managers to improve performance and how that benefits both stockholders and society at large. We also describe early on the financial environment, financial forecasting, the fundamental trade-off between risk and return, and the time value of money. Then we build on these basic concepts to explain how stock and bond prices are determined.

Building on this background, subsequent chapters explain the financial tools and techniques that are used to help firms maximize value by improving decisions. Included here are capital budgeting techniques, procedures for determining the capital structure, working capital management, and multinational financial management.

Our organization has four important advantages:

Four important advantages of the third edition's organization.

1. Explaining early on how accounting data are used, how pro forma financial statements are projected, how financial markets operate, and how security prices are determined helps students understand how financial management affects stock prices. Also, the early coverage of risk analysis, time value of money, and valuation techniques permits us to use and reinforce those concepts throughout the remainder of the book.

2. Structuring the book around markets and valuation enhances continuity and helps students see how the various topics are related to one another.

3. Most students—even those who do not plan to major in finance—are interested in stock and bond values, rates of return, and the like. Because one's ability to learn a topic is a function of his or her interest and motivation, and because *Concise* covers securities and security markets early, our organization is pedagogically sound.

4. Once the basic concepts have been established, it is easier for students to understand how and why corporations make specific investment and financing decisions and how they develop and execute their working capital policies.

Analyzing Financial Decisions with Spreadsheets
Spreadsheet programs such as *Microsoft Excel* are ideally suited for analyzing many financial issues, and a knowledge of spreadsheets is rapidly becoming essential for people in business. Therefore, we "modernized" the book by indicating how spreadsheets are used to deal with the issues discussed in the text.

In the text chapters, we discuss finance concepts, provide examples of the concepts, and explain how the analysis necessary to make optimal financial decisions is done. Where the analysis involves arithmetic, we assume that students are using calculators to do the math. However, if the problem is one that could be solved more efficiently with a computer, we state this and briefly describe how the computer would be used. These explanations are short, easy to follow, and can be skipped without loss of continuity. Thus, students will get an idea of how they could go from calculators to spreadsheets, but they can stop at that point. However, if instructors want to emphasize computers in the course, or if individual students want to learn more about spreadsheets on their own, the text itself and a spreadsheet ancillary make that relatively easy. We developed a spreadsheet model for each chapter in the book except Chapter 1. These models show exactly how the decisions dealt with in the chapter can be analyzed with an *Excel* spreadsheet. Therefore, our models include a good bit of explanation and serve both as an *Excel* tutorial and as a template for analyzing whatever financial issues are covered in the particular chapter.

The models are contained on a CD-ROM that accompanies each textbook, and they are also accessible from the Harcourt College web site. As noted above, the models are not necessary for going through the book and learning the essential financial concepts. However, if a student wants to learn how these concepts are implemented in the real world, and thus get a leg up in the job market, the disk and the models will be a big help. And, of course, if an instructor wants to build spreadsheet analysis into the course, our models will provide an excellent platform.

A New Chapter Focusing on Multinational Financial Management It has become a cliché to argue that world capital markets have become increasingly integrated and that investors should think globally when they make important financial decisions. Like most clichés, this one is true, but even so, many introductory finance textbooks have not paid sufficient attention to international issues. With this in mind, three years ago in the second edition of *Concise* we added a new series of boxes called "Global Perspectives," which look at issues covered in the chapters from a global viewpoint. In this third edition of *Concise*, we have taken the additional step of adding a new chapter that is dedicated to multinational financial management.

Consolidated Coverage of Working Capital Management Given the addition of a new chapter on international finance, we looked for places to streamline the text in order to keep *Concise* succinct. Based on our own classroom experiences and the feedback that we have received from other professors, we decided to consolidate the two chapters, "Managing Current Assets" and "Financing Current Assets," into a single new chapter entitled "Working Capital Management." At first we were concerned that we might be giving insufficient attention to this important topic. However, after reworking these chapters, we are convinced that the new consolidated chapter presents all of the key ideas of working capital management in a clear and straightforward manner.

Increased Emphasis on Cash Flow and Economic Value The third edition includes an expanded discussion on moving beyond accounting statements to cash flows and economic value. These concepts are integrated throughout the book.

Relocation of Chapter on Financial Forecasting The chapter on financial forecasting (formerly Chapter 14) has been moved up to Chapter 4 so that it now follows financial statement analysis. Introducing forecasting earlier enables us to show more clearly how one uses historical data to help develop plans for future improvements and also how forecasted cash flows affect stock and bond valuation and capital budgeting decisions.

Revised Discussion of the Term Structure of Interest Rates   We simplified and modernized the term structure discussion in Chapter 5. We eliminated much of the arcane term structure theory and instead make a smooth transition from our earlier discussion of interest rate levels to a discussion of the factors that influence the shape and level of the yield curve.

Free Cash Flow Approach to Stock Valuation   We discuss the standard dividend growth model for stock valuation, but because that model is inadequate for many purposes, we added a section on the free cash flow approach to corporate valuation. This approach is particularly useful when dealing with newly formed companies, with divisions of large corporations, and with firms that are being evaluated as part of a merger analysis.

Reorganized Capital Budgeting Coverage   More attention is devoted to estimating project risk. To help students better understand how risk affects the capital budgeting decision, we now include sensitivity and scenario analysis as part of the chapter on estimating cash flows.

Changes to Capital Structure Chapter   The third edition more clearly describes how changes in capital structure affect the costs of debt and equity. The Hamada equation is introduced into the analysis to provide students with a more direct way to estimate optimal capital structure.

As always, we updated and clarified both the text and the end-of-chapter problems, and we made numerous improvements in the pedagogy. In particular, the book's new four-color design leads to a more exciting presentation. In addition, we updated the real-world examples and pointed out recent developments in the financial environment. We also removed some of the more technical appendixes from the text and have instead included them as part of our newly designed web site. Finally, we expanded the coverage of certain topics whose importance has increased, and we deleted redundant and less important material to streamline the discussion and improve the flow. Some of the more important changes are noted in the following table:

CONTENTS

■ A new "Technology Matters" box discusses how electronic commerce is changing the way firms operate.

■ Added a discussion of EBITDA and a section on "Modifying Accounting Data for Managerial Decisions." Updated federal tax section.

■ Added EBITDA coverage and price/cash flow ratios to reflect analysts' increased focus on these items.

■ Financial forecasting has been moved up from Chapter 14 to follow the financial statement analysis chapter. New section on strategic plans discusses mission statements, corporate scope, corporate objectives, and corporate strategies. New sections on operating plans and financial plans.

■ Updated to reflect important changes in the financial environment. Simplified and modernized the term structure discussion. New "Industry Practice" box describes the various stock market indexes.

■ Added discussion on calculating investment returns and the implications of a changing stock market risk premium.

■ Added spreadsheets as a solution method for TVM problems. The spreadsheet discussions occur throughout the chapter and where relevant in other parts of the text. New "Technology Matters" box on how to use the Internet for financial planning.

■ Added spreadsheet solution method to solve bond problems.

■ Added discussion of alternative approaches for valuing common stocks, including a new valuation method based on free cash flows.

■ Simplified the breakpoint discussion. A new "Industry Practice" box discusses special types of preferred stock, and a new "Technology Matters" box discusses cost of capital estimation for Internet companies.

■ We now illustrate how spreadsheets are used in capital budgeting.

■ Sensitivity analysis and scenario analysis are now included as part of the chapter on estimating cash flows. This new approach allows students to see how risk affects capital budgeting decisions. We built inflation directly into cash flows and reduced discussion of replacement projects.

■ Hamada equation is introduced to quantify how changing the capital structure might affect the firm's cost of capital.

■ A new "Industry Practice" box discusses the effect of stock repurchases on dividend yields.

■ We consolidated the prior edition's two working capital chapters and streamlined the discussion of working capital management.

■ We expanded the discussion of the costs and benefits of multinational investment. More emphasis is given on how the cost of capital varies for domestic and international projects. A "Global Perspectives" box gives a detailed discussion of the EMU and the euro and its impact on Americans.

NEW AND IMPROVED PEDAGOGY

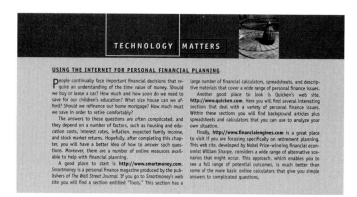

NEW! "Technology Matters" boxes illustrate how innovations in technology are changing the world of financial management.

NEW! We developed a **spreadsheet model** for each chapter in the book except Chapter 1. These models show exactly how the problems dealt with in the chapter can be solved with an *Excel* spreadsheet. In addition, **spreadsheet problems** that require students to use the spreadsheet model can be found with the end-of-chapter pedagogy. Electronic versions of the models are available on the text's companion web site and are included on the student CD-ROM that is packaged with every copy of the text.

4. Spreadsheet Solution

	A	B	C	D	E	F	G
1	Interest rate	0.05					
2	Time	0	1	2	3	4	5
3	Cash flow		0	0	0	0	127.63
4	Present value	100					

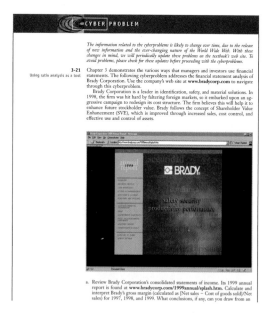

NEW! Cyberproblems — these end-of-chapter exercises plug students into the Internet, allowing them to hone their web research skills to solve financial problems. Additional cyberproblems are found on the companion web site for *Concise* at **http://www. harcourtcollege.com/finance/concise3e**. The cyberproblems were developed by Steven Bouchard and Christopher Buzzard.

TRIED AND TRUE PEDAGOGY

Other pedagogical elements and supporting materials have helped make *Concise* so successful. Included are the following:

Each chapter opens with a **vignette** describing how an actual corporation has contended with the issues discussed in the chapter. These vignettes heighten students' interest by pointing out the real-world relevance and applicability of what might otherwise seem to be dry, technical material.

Throughout the book there are **"Industry Practice," "Global Perspectives,"** and **"Small Business"** boxes that provide real-world illustrations of how financial concepts are applied in practice.

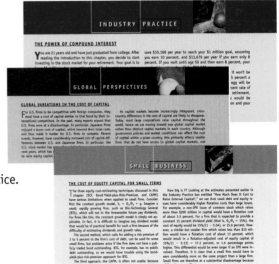

chases of raw materials, and those larger purchases will spontaneously lead to a higher level of accounts payable. For Allied, the 2001 ratio of accounts payable to sales is $60/$3,000 = 0.02 = 2%. Allied's managers assume that their payables policy will not change, so the forecasted accounts payable for 2002 is 0.02($3,300) = $66 million.

More sales will require more labor, and higher sales should also result in higher taxable income and thus taxes. Therefore, accrued wages and taxes will both increase. For Allied, the 2001 ratio of accruals to sales is $140/$3,000 = 0.0467 = 4.67%. If this ratio does not change, then the forecasted level of accruals for 2002 will be 0.0467($3,300) = $154 million.

Retained earnings will also increase, but not at the same rate as sales: The new balance for retained earnings will be the old level plus the addition to retained earnings, which we calculated in Step 1. Also, notes payable, long-term bonds, preferred stock, and common stock will not rise spontaneously with sales — rather, the projected levels of these accounts will depend on financing decisions, as we discuss later.

In summary, (1) higher sales must be supported by additional assets, (2) some of the asset increases can be financed by spontaneous increases in accounts payable and accruals, and by retained earnings, but (3) any shortfall must be financed from external sources, using some combination of debt, preferred stock, and common stock.

The spontaneously increasing liabilities (accounts payable and accruals) are forecasted and shown in Column 3 of Table 4-4, the first-pass forecast. Then, those liability and equity accounts whose values reflect conscious management decisions — notes payable, long-term bonds, preferred stock, and common stock — are initially set at their 2001 levels. Thus, 2002 notes payable are initially set at $110 million, the long-term bond level is forecasted at $754 million, and so on. The 2002 value for the retained earnings (RE) account is obtained by adding the projected addition to retained earnings as developed in the 2002 income statement (see Table 4-3) to the 2001 ending balance:

$$2002 \text{ RE} = 2001 \text{ RE} + 2002 \text{ forecasted addition to RE}$$
$$= \$766 + \$68 = \$834 \text{ million.}$$

The forecast of total assets as shown in Column 3 (first-pass forecast) of Table 4-4 is $2,200 million, which indicates that Allied must add $200 million of new assets in 2002 to support the higher sales level. However, the forecasted liability and equity accounts as shown in the lower portion of Column 3 rise by only $88 million, to $2,088 million. Since the balance sheet must balance, Allied must raise an additional $2,200 − $2,088 = $112 million, which we define as **Additional Funds Needed (AFN).** The AFN will be raised by some combination of borrowing from the bank as notes payable, issuing long-term bonds, and selling new common stock.

Funds Needed

firm must raise
rough borrowing or
w common or
ck.

STEP 3. RAISING THE ADDITIONAL FUNDS NEEDED

Allied's financial staff will raise the needed funds based on several factors, including the effect of the firm's target capital structure, the effect of short-term borrowing on the current ratio, conditions in the debt and equity markets, and restrictions

Throughout the book, key terms are highlighted in the text and defined in the margins. These **marginal glossaries** enable students to quickly find and review the key topics covered in the chapter.

Self-Test Questions, which serve as checkpoints for students to test their understanding, follow each major section of the chapters.

The detailed spreadsheet model is not provided in the text, but its key outputs were shown in the "Model Outputs" section back in Table 4-5. We see that before the operating changes Allied forecasted a slight increase in NOPAT (net operating profit after taxes), but it projected a very large increase in net operating working capital and in total operating capital. The net result is a very low level of free cash flow, only $7.3 million. Although we do not show projections of the full financial statements for all eight years of the explicit forecast horizon, here are the initially projected free cash flows (FCFs):

YEARS	2002	2003	2004	2005	2006	2007	2008	2009
FCF	7.3	8.4	8.9	9.8	14.6	63.7	96.9	103.7

As we will see in Chapter 9, investors and financial managers use such forecasts to estimate the firm's stock price. Thus, this model helps managers measure the expected changes in the determinants of value under different strategic and operating alternatives.

SELF-TEST QUESTIONS

What is the AFN, and how is the percent of sales method used to estimate it?

Why do accounts payable and accruals provide "spontaneous funds" to a growing firm?

Would payables and accruals provide spontaneous funds to a no-growth firm? One that is declining?

Why do retained earnings not grow at the same rate as sales? In answering this question, think about a firm whose sales are not growing (g = 0%), but that is profitable and does not pay out all of its earnings as dividends.

THE AFN FORMULA

Most firms forecast their capital requirements by constructing pro forma income statements and balance sheets as described above. However, if the ratios are expected to remain constant, then the following formula can be used to forecast financial requirements. Here we apply the formula to Allied based on the 2001 data, not the revised data, as the revised data do not assume constant ratios.

$$
\begin{array}{rcl}
\text{Additional} & \text{Required} & \text{Spontaneous} & \text{Increase in} \\
\text{funds} &=& \text{increase} &-& \text{increase in} &-& \text{retained} \\
\text{needed} && \text{in assets} && \text{liabilities} && \text{earnings} \\
\text{AFN} &=& (A^*/S_0)\Delta S &-& (L^*/S_0)\Delta S &-& MS_1(RR). & (4\text{-}1)
\end{array}
$$

Here

AFN = additional funds needed.

A* = assets that are tied directly to sales, hence which must increase if sales are to increase. Note that A designates total assets and A* designates those assets that must increase if sales are to increase. When the firm

Web addresses are included in each chapter to give students access to additional information about the companies and government agencies discussed in the text.

Are you interested in learning more about the history of accounting? If so, take a tour through the "Virtual History of Accounting" organized by the Association of Chartered Accountants in the United States and located at **http://www.acaus.org/history/index.html.**

The **end-of-chapter materials** contain a large number of Questions, Self-Test Problems, Starter Problems, Exam-Type Problems, Problems, and Spreadsheet Problems. The problems vary in level of difficulty yet cover all the topics discussed in the chapter.

An **Integrated Case,** which is generally related to the vignette, appears at the end of each chapter. These "mini-cases" both illustrate and tie together the key topics covered in the chapter, hence, provide an ideal platform for lectures that systematically cover the key materials in the chapter.

INTEGRATED CASE

D'LEON INC., PART I

2-26 SECTION I: Financial Statements Donna Jamison, a 1996 graduate of the University of Florida with four years of banking experience, was recently brought in as assistant to the chairman of the board of D'Leon Inc., a small food producer that operates in north Florida and whose specialty is high-quality pecan and other nut products sold in the snack-foods market. D'Leon's president, Al Watkins, decided in 2000 to undertake a major expansion and to "go national" in competition with Frito-Lay, Eagle, and other major snack-food companies. Watkins felt that D'Leon's products were of a higher quality than the competition's, that this quality differential would enable it to charge a premium price, and that the end result would be greatly increased sales, profits, and stock price.

Campo, a retired banker who was D'Leon's chɑ... largest stockholder. Campo agreed to give up a golfing days and to help nurse the company bacl with Jamison's help.

Jamison began by gathering the financial state other data given in Tables IC2-1, IC2-2, IC2-3, Assume that you are Jamison's assistant, and you her answer the following questions for Campo. will continue with this case in Chapter 3, and yo more comfortable with the analysis there, but these questions will help prepare you for Chapter clear explanations, not just yes or no answers!)

a. What effect did the expansion have on sales, ing profit after taxes (NOPAT), net operatir capital (NOWC), total investor-supplied ope ital, and net income?

THE INSTRUCTIONAL PACKAGE:
AN INTEGRATED SYSTEM

Concise now offers an even more innovative, technologically advanced ancillary package to enhance students' learning and to make it easier for instructors to prepare for and conduct classes. The integrated package includes many outstanding resources, all of which have been revised and updated for the new third edition.

ESSENTIAL COURSE MANAGEMENT TOOLS FOR THE INSTRUCTOR

- **NEW! Instructor's Resource CD-ROM** — This innovative instructor's resource system includes electronic versions of the *Instructor's Manual*, *Word Test Bank*, spreadsheet models, solutions to spreadsheet problems, and *PowerPoint* presentations. It is laid out so as to maximize accessibility and minimize search time.

- **NEW!** *Concise* **Online Course** — Delivered via the WebCT platform, this integrated web-based learning environment combines the textbook and ancillary package with the vast resources of the Internet and the convenience of anytime learning. Extremely user friendly, the powerful customization features of the WebCT framework enable instructors to customize this online course to their own unique teaching styles and their students' individual needs. Course features include content keyed to the third edition, self-tests and online exams, Internet activities and links to related resources, a suggested course syllabus, student and instructor materials, free technical support for instructors, and much more.

- *Instructor's Manual* — This comprehensive manual contains answers to all text questions and problems, plus detailed solutions to the integrated cases. A computerized version in *Microsoft Word* is also available on the Instructor's Resource CD-ROM and on the Instructor's Web Site. This digital version of the *Instructor's Manual* is available for posting on an instructor's password-protected web site.

- *PowerPoint* **Lecture Presentation** — Prepared in *Microsoft PowerPoint*, this computer graphics slide show covers all the essential issues presented in each chapter. Graphs, tables, lists, and calculations are developed sequentially, much as one might develop them on a blackboard. The new and improved slides are even more crisp, colorful, and professor friendly. The slides, if used with the student's *Blueprints* supplement, facilitate student note taking. Instructors can, of course, modify or delete our slides, or add some of their own. The slides can be found on the Student CD-ROM, the Instructor's Resource CD-ROM, and the companion web site.

- *Test Bank* — This large *Test Bank* contains more than 1,200 class-tested questions and problems and is available both in printed and electronic form. Information regarding the topics, degree of difficulty, and the correct answers, along with complete solutions for all numerical problems, is provided with each question.

- *Computerized Test Bank* — This software has many features that make test preparation, scoring, and grade recording easy. Also, the *Computer-*

ized Test Bank allows automatic conversion of multiple-choice questions and problems into free-response questions. In addition, questions can be altered to make different versions of a given test, and the software makes it easy to add to or edit the existing test items, or to compile a test that covers specific topics.

- **IMPROVED! Web Site for *Concise*, Third Edition** — Designed to be both a teaching and learning tool, the *Concise* web site, at **http://www.harcourtcollege.com/finance/concise3e** has separate areas for instructors and students. In the instructor's password-protected area, a number of the *Concise* ancillaries can be downloaded, and instructors also have access to NewsWire articles, chapter-specific finance links, data files for companies featured in opening vignettes, spreadsheet problems, online quizzing, and many more financial resources.

- *Technology Supplement* — The *Technology Supplement* contains tutorials for five commonly used financial calculators, for *Microsoft Excel*, and for *PowerPoint* presentation software. The calculator tutorials cover everything a student needs to know about the calculator to work the problems in the text.

- **Finance NewsWire** — Adopters of *Concise* will have access to a password-protected portion of the Harcourt College Finance web site, where they will be provided with summaries of recent articles in *The Wall Street Journal*, *Business Week*, or another major business publication, along with discussion questions and references to the text. These summaries, written by Emery Trahan and Paul Bolster of Northeastern University, facilitate incorporating late-breaking news into classroom discussions.

SUPERIOR STUDENT ANCILLARY PACKAGE

- **NEW!** *Excel* **Student CD-ROM** — Packaged with each copy of the text, the spreadsheet models illustrate how concepts covered in the text are implemented in the real world, giving students a significant advantage in the job market. The models include thorough explanations and serve both as an *Excel* tutorial and as a template for solving financial problems for each chapter of the book. This CD-ROM also includes the PowerPoint presentations and practice problems for each chapter.

- *Study Guide* — This supplement lists the key learning objectives for each chapter, outlines the key sections, provides self-test questions, and provides a set of problems similar to those in the text and the *Test Bank*, but with fully worked-out solutions.

- *Blueprints* — This supplement, which is based on the end-of-chapter Integrated Cases and keyed to the *PowerPoint* presentation, was developed (1) to help guide students through the chapter in a systematic manner and (2) to help students listen to lectures and also take good notes. Each chapter of the *Blueprints* begins with the case itself and is then followed by copies of each slide, along with space for notes and comments.

- **NEW!** *Finance Interactive* — This supplement is an online interactive tutorial that helps students practice calculations and definitions. *Finance Interactive* provides a chapter-by-chapter review of topics covered in

Concise, with approximately 500 questions and many straightforward examples.

- **IMPROVED! Student Web Site for *Concise*, Third Edition** — This site serves as both a resource and review tool for students taking the introductory finance course. It contains links to relevant finance sites keyed to chapters in the text, archived news summaries tied to chapters in the text, and finance career opportunities. Students can also test their understanding of material with self-grading chapter quizzes, cyberproblems, and *Excel* spreadsheet problems. The site can be found at **http://www.harcourtcollege.com/finance/concise3e.**

- **Spreadsheet Books** — Harcourt College Publishers has published several books on spreadsheets, including both *Microsoft Excel* and *Lotus 1-2-3*. Included are *Financial Analysis with Microsoft Excel*, second edition, and *Financial Analysis with Lotus 1-2-3*, both by Timothy R. Mayes and Todd M. Shank.

- **NEW!** *Effective Use of a Financial Calculator* — Written by Pamela Hall, this handbook is designed to help increase students' understanding of both finance and financial calculators, enabling them to work problems more quickly and effectively.

- *Digital Finance Case Library* — More than 100 cases written by Eugene Brigham and Linda Klein are now available via Harcourt College's Cases in Financial Management web site. This customized case database allows instructors to select cases and create their own customized casebooks. These cases can be used as supplements to illustrate the various topics covered in the textbook.

ACKNOWLEDGMENTS

This textbook reflects the efforts of a great many people, both those who have worked on *Concise* and our related books over a number of years, as well as those who worked specifically on this third edition. First, we would like to thank Dana Aberwald Clark, who worked closely with us at every stage of the revision—her assistance was absolutely invaluable. Second, Christopher Buzzard did an outstanding job helping us develop the *Excel* models, the web site, and the *PowerPoint* presentations.

Our colleagues Lou Gapenski, Andy Naranjo, M. Nimalendran, Jay Ritter, Mike Ryngaert, Craig Tapley, and Carolyn Takeda gave us many useful suggestions regarding the ancillaries and many parts of the book, including the integrated cases. Also, we benefitted from the work of Mike Ehrhardt and Phillip Daves of the University of Tennessee, who worked on two companion books. Next, we would like to thank the following professors, who reviewed this edition in detail and provided many useful comments and suggestions: James Bennett, University of Massachusetts–Boston; John R. Blease, University of Oregon; Raj K. Kohli, Indiana University–South Bend; Gayle A. Russell, Eastern Connecticut State University; Lifan Wu, California State University–Los Angeles; Marcelo Eduardo, Mississippi College; and Mark Correll, University of Colorado.

We would also like to thank the following professors, whose reviews and comments on our earlier books have contributed to this edition: Robert Adams, Mike Adler, Sharif Ahkam, Syed Ahmad, Ed Altman, Bruce Anderson, Ron Anderson, Tom Anderson, John Andrews, Bob Angell, Vince Apilado, Harvey Arbalaez, Kavous Ardalan, Henry Arnold, Bob Aubey, Gil Babcock, Peter Bacon, Kent Baker, Robert Balik, Tom Bankston, Babu Baradwaj, Sam Basu, Les Barenbaum, Charles Barngrover, Greg Bauer, Bill Beedles, Brian Belt, Moshe Ben-Horim, Bill Beranek, Tom Berry, Will Bertin, Scott Besley, Dan Best, Roger Bey, Gilbert W. Bickum, Dalton Bigbee, John Bildersee, Laurence E. Blose, Russ Boisjoly, Bob Boldin, Keith Boles, Michael Bond, Geof Booth, Waldo Born, Rick Boulware, Kenneth Boudreaux, Helen Bowers, Oswald Bowlin, Don Boyd, G. Michael Boyd, Pat Boyer, Joe Brandt, Elizabeth Brannigan, Mary Broske, Christopher Brown, David T. Brown, Kate Brown, Larry Brown, Bill Brueggeman, Paul Bursik, Bill Campsey, Bob Carlson, Severin Carlson, David Cary, Steve Celec, Mary Chaffin, Don Chance, Antony Chang, Susan Chaplinsky, K. C. Chen, Jay Choi, S. K. Choudhary, Lal Chugh, Maclyn Clouse, Bruce Collins, Mitch Conover, Margaret Considine, Phil Cooley, Joe Copeland, David Cordell, Marsha Cornett, M. P. Corrigan, John Cotner, Charles Cox, David Crary, John Crockett, Jr., Roy Crum, Brent Dalrymple, Bill Damon, Joel Dauten, Steve Dawson, Sankar De, Fred Dellva, Chad Denson, James Desreumaux, Bodie Dickerson, Bernard Dill, Gregg Dimkoff, Les Dlabay, James D'Mello, Mark Dorfman, Tom Downs, Frank Draper, Gene Drzycimski, Dean Dudley, David Durst, Ed Dyl, Fred J. Ebeid, Daniel Ebels, Richard Edelman, Charles Edwards, U. Elike, John Ellis, George Engler, Suzanne Erickson, Dave Ewert, John Ezzell, L. Franklin Fant, Richard J. Fendler, Michael Ferri, Jim Filkins, John Finnerty, Robert Fiore, Susan Fischer, Peggy Fletcher, Steven Flint, Russ Fogler, Jennifer Frazier, Dan French, Michael Garlington, David Garraty, Sharon Garrison, Jim Garven, Adam Gehr, Jr., Jim Gentry, Wafica Ghoul, Armand Gilinsky, Jr., Philip Glasgo, Rudyard Goode, Raymond Gorman, Walt Goulet, Bernie Grablowsky, Theoharry Grammatikos, Owen Gregory, Ed Grossnickle, John Groth, Alan Grunewald, Manak Gupta, Darryl Gurley, Sam Hadaway, Don Hakala, Gerald Hamsmith, William Hardin, John Harris, Paul Hastings, Bob Haugen, Stevenson Hawkey, Del Hawley, Eric M. Haye, Robert Hehre, Kath Henebry, David Heskel, George Hettenhouse, Hans Heymann, Kendall Hill, Roger Hill, Tom Hindelang, Linda Hittle, Ralph Hocking, J. Ronald Hoffmeister, Robert Hollinger, Jim Horrigan, John Houston, John Howe, Keith Howe, Steve Isberg, Jim Jackson, Vahan Janjigian, Narayanan Jayaraman, Zhenhn Jin, Kose John, Craig Johnson, Keith Johnson, Ramon Johnson, Steven Johnson, Ray Jones, Frank Jordan, Manuel Jose, Sally Joyner, Alfred Kahl, Gus Kalogeras, Rajiv Kalra, Ravi Kamath, John Kaminarides, Michael Keenan, Bill Kennedy, Peppi M. Kenny, James Keys, Carol Kiefer, Joe Kiernan, Richard Kish, Robert Kleiman, Erich Knehans, Don Knight, Ladd Kochman, Dorothy Koehl, Jaroslaw Komarynsky, Duncan Kretovich, Harold Krogh, Charles Kroncke, Don Kummer, Robert A. Kunkel, Reinhold Lamb, Joan Lamm, Larry Lang, David Lange, P. Lange, Howard Lanser, Edward Lawrence, Martin Lawrence, Wayne Lee, Jim LePage, David E. LeTourneau, Jules Levine, John Lewis, Jason Lin, Chuck Linke, Bill Lloyd, Susan Long, Judy Maese, Bob Magee, Ileen Malitz, Bob Malko, Phil Malone, Abbas Mamoozadeh, Terry Maness, Chris Manning, Surendra Mansinghka, Timothy Manuel, Brian Maris, Terry Martell, David Martin, D. J. Masson, John

Mathys, Ralph May, John McAlhany, Andy McCollough, Ambrose McCoy, Thomas McCue, Bill McDaniel, John McDowell, Charles McKinney, Robyn McLaughlin, James McNulty, Jeanette Medewitz-Diamond, Jamshid Mehran, Larry Merville, Rick Meyer, Jim Millar, Ed Miller, John Miller, John Mitchell, Carol Moerdyk, Bob Moore, Scott Moore, Barry Morris, Gene Morris, Dianne R. Morrison, Chris Muscarella, David Nachman, Tim Nantell, Don Nast, Edward Nelling, Bill Nelson, Bob Nelson, William Nelson, Bob Niendorf, Bruce Niendorf, Ben Nunnally, Jr., Tom O'Brien, William O'Connell, Dennis O'Connor, John O'Donnell, Jim Olsen, Robert Olsen, Dean Olson, Jim Pappas, Stephen Parrish, Helen Pawlowski, Barron Peake, Michael Pescow, Glenn Petry, Jim Pettijohn, Rich Pettit, Dick Pettway, Aaron Phillips, Hugo Phillips, H. R. Pickett, John Pinkerton, Gerald Pogue, Eugene Poindexter, R. Potter, Franklin Potts, R. Powell, Dianna Preece, Chris Prestopino, John Primus, Jerry Prock, Howard Puckett, Herbert Quigley, George Racette, Bob Radcliffe, Allen Rappaport, Bill Rentz, Ken Riener, Charles Rini, John Ritchie, Pietra Rivoli, Antonio Rodriguez, James Rosenfeld, Stuart Rosenstein, E. N. Roussakis, Dexter Rowell, Marjorie Rubash, Bob Ryan, Jim Sachlis, Abdul Sadik, Thomas Scampini, Kevin Scanlon, Frederick Schadeler, Patricia L. Schaeff, David Schalow, Mary Jane Scheuer, David Schirm, Robert Schwebach, Carol Schweser, John Settle, Alan Severn, James Sfiridis, Sol Shalit, Frederic Shipley, Dilip Shome, Ron Shrieves, Neil Sicherman, J. B. Silvers, Clay Singleton, Joe Sinkey, Stacy Sirmans, Jaye Smith, Patricia Smith, Patricia Matisz Smith, Don Sorensen, David Speairs, Ken Stanley, Ed Stendardi, Alan Stephens, Don Stevens, Jerry Stevens, Glen Strasburg, David Suk, Katherine Sullivan, Timothy Sullivan, Philip Swensen, Bruce Swenson, Ernest Swift, Paul Swink, Eugene Swinnerton, Gary Tallman, Dular Talukdar, Dennis Tanner, Russ Taussig, Richard Teweles, Ted Teweles, Madeline Thimmes, Francis D. Thomas, Andrew Thompson, John Thompson, Arlene Thurman, Dogan Tirtirogu, Janet Todd, Holland J. Toles, William Tozer, Emery Trahan, George Trivoli, George Tsetsekos, David Upton, Howard Van Auken, Pretorious Van den Dool, Pieter Vandenberg, Paul Vanderheiden, David Vang, JoAnn Vaughan, Jim Verbrugge, Patrick Vincent, Steve Vinson, Susan Visscher, John Wachowicz, Joe Walker, Mike Walker, Sam Weaver, Marsha Weber, Al Webster, Kuo-Chiang Wei, Bill Welch, Fred Weston, Richard Whiston, Norm Williams, Tony Wingler, Ed Wolfe, Criss Woodruff, Don Woods, Robert Wyatt, Steve Wyatt, Michael Yonan, John Zietlow, Dennis Zocco, and Kent Zumwalt.

Special thanks are due to Chris Barry, Texas Christian University, and Shirley Love, Idaho State University, who wrote the boxes relating to small-business issues; to Steven Bouchard, Goldey Beacom College, who helped develop the cyberproblems; to Emery Trahan and Paul Bolster, Northeastern University, who developed and wrote the summaries and questions for the Finance NewsWire; to Dilip Shome, Virginia Polytechnic Institute, who helped greatly with the capital structure chapter; to Dave Brown and Mike Ryngaert, University of Florida, who helped us with the bankruptcy material; to Roy Crum, Andy Naranjo, and Subu Venkataraman, who worked with us on the international materials; to Scott Below, East Carolina University, who developed the web site information and references; to Laurie and Stan Eakins of East Carolina, who developed the materials on *Microsoft Excel* for the *Technology Supplement*; and to Larry Wolken, Texas A&M University, who offered his hard work and advice for the development of the *Lecture Presentation Software*. Susan Whitman typed and helped proof the various manuscripts. Finally, the

Harcourt College Publishers and Elm Street Publishing Services staffs, especially Sue Nodine, Mike Reynolds, Charlie Stutesman, and Elizabeth Thomson, helped greatly with all phases of the textbook's development and production.

ERRORS IN THE TEXTBOOK

At this point, most authors make a statement like this: "We appreciate all the help we received from the people listed above, but any remaining errors are, of course, our own responsibility." And generally there are more than enough remaining errors! Having experienced difficulties with errors ourselves, both as students and instructors, we resolved to avoid this problem in *Concise*. As a result of our detection procedures, we are convinced that this book is relatively free of significant errors, meaning those that either confuse or distract readers.

Partly because of our confidence that few such errors remain, but primarily because we want very much to detect any errors that may have slipped by to correct them in subsequent printings, we decided to offer a reward of $10 per error to the first person who reports it to us. For purpose of this reward, errors are defined as misspelled words, nonrounding numerical errors, incorrect statements, and any other error that inhibits comprehension. Typesetting problems such as irregular spacing and differences of opinion regarding grammatical or punctuation conventions do not qualify for this reward. Given the ever-changing nature of the World Wide Web, changes in web addresses also do not qualify as errors, although we would like to learn about them. Finally, any qualifying error that has follow-through effects is counted as two errors only. Please report any errors to Joel Houston either through e-mail at **clarkda@dale.cba.ufl.edu** or by regular mail at the address below.

CONCLUSION

Finance is, in a real sense, the cornerstone of the enterprise system—good financial management is vitally important to the economic health of business firms, hence, to the nation and the world. Because of its importance, finance should be widely and thoroughly understood, but this is easier said than done. The field is relatively complex, and it is undergoing constant change in response to shifts in economic conditions. All of this makes finance stimulating and exciting, but also challenging and sometimes perplexing. We sincerely hope that this third edition of *Concise* will meet its own challenge by contributing to a better understanding of our financial system.

EUGENE F. BRIGHAM
JOEL F. HOUSTON
P.O. Box 117168
College of Business Administration
University of Florida
Gainesville, Florida 32611-7168

June 2001

BRIEF CONTENTS

CONTENTS

PART III
FINANCIAL ASSETS 346

Chapter 8 Bonds and Their Valuation 348

Chapter 9 Stocks and Their Valuation 406

Appendixes

 PART

INTRODUCTION TO FINANCIAL MANAGEMENT

An Overview of Financial Management

SOURCE: Courtesy BEN & JERRY'S HOMEMADE, INC. www.benjerry.com

$

BEN & JERRY'S

For many companies, the decision would have been an easy "yes." However, Ben & Jerry's Homemade Inc. has always taken pride in doing things differently. Its profits had been declining, but in 1995 the company was offered an opportunity to sell its premium ice cream in the lucrative Japanese market. However, Ben & Jerry's turned down the business because the Japanese firm that would have distributed their product had failed to develop a reputation for promoting social causes! Robert Holland Jr., Ben & Jerry's CEO at the time, commented that, "The only reason to take the opportunity was to make money." Clearly, Holland, who resigned from the company in late 1996, thought there was more to running a business than just making money.

The company's cofounders, Ben Cohen and Jerry Greenfield, opened the first Ben & Jerry's ice cream shop in 1978 in a vacant Vermont gas station with just $12,000 of capital plus a commitment to run the business in a manner consistent with their underlying values. Even though it is more expensive, the company only buys milk and cream from small local farms in Vermont. In addition, 7.5 percent of the company's before-tax income is donated to charity, and each of the company's 750 employees receives three free pints of ice cream each day.

Many argue that Ben & Jerry's philosophy and commitment to social causes compromises its ability to make money. For example, in a recent article in *Fortune* magazine, Alex Taylor III commented that, "Operating a business is tough enough. Once you add social goals to the demands of serving customers, making a profit, and returning value to shareholders, you tie yourself up in knots."

Ben & Jerry's financial performance has had its ups and downs. While the company's stock grew by leaps and bounds through the early 1990s, problems began to arise in 1993. These problems included increased competition in the premium ice cream market, along with a leveling off of sales in that market, plus their own inefficiencies and sloppy, haphazard product development strategy.

The company lost money for the first time in 1994, and as a result, Ben Cohen stepped down as CEO. Bob Holland, a former consultant for McKinsey & Co. with a reputation as a turnaround specialist, was tapped as Cohen's replacement. The company's stock price rebounded in 1995, as the market responded positively to the steps made by Holland to right the company. The stock price, however, floundered toward the end of 1996, following Holland's resignation.

Over the last few years, Ben & Jerry's has had a new resurgence. Holland's replacement, Perry Odak, has done a number of things to improve the company's financial performance, and its reputation among Wall Street's analysts and institutional investors has benefited. Odak quickly brought in a new management team to rework the company's production and sales operations, and he aggressively opened new stores and franchises both in the United States and abroad.

In April 2000, Ben & Jerry's took a more dramatic step to benefit its shareholders. It agreed to be acquired by Unilever, a large Anglo-Dutch conglomerate that owns a host of major brands including Dove Soap, Lipton Tea, and Breyers Ice Cream. Unilever agreed to pay $43.60 for each share of Ben & Jerry's stock—a 66 percent increase over the price the stock traded at just before takeover rumors first surfaced in December 1999. The total price tag for Ben & Jerry's was $326 million.

While the deal clearly benefited Ben & Jerry's shareholders, some observers believe that the company "sold out" and abandoned its original mission. In response to these concerns, Ben & Jerry's will retain its Vermont headquarters and its separate board, and its social missions will remain intact. Others have suggested that Ben & Jerry's philosophy may even induce Unilever to increase its own corporate philanthropy. Despite these assurances, it still remains to be seen whether Ben & Jerry's vision can be maintained within the confines of a large conglomerate.

As you will see throughout the book, many of today's companies face challenges similar to those of Ben & Jerry's. Every day, corporations struggle with decisions such as these: Is it fair to our labor force to shift production overseas? What is the appropriate level of compensation for senior management? Should we increase, or decrease, our charitable contributions? In general, how do we balance social concerns against the need to create shareholder value? ∎

PUTTING THINGS IN PERSPECTIVE

See **http://www.benjerry.com/mission.html** for Ben & Jerry's interesting mission statement. It might be a good idea to print it out and take it to class for discussion.

The purpose of this chapter is to give you an idea of what financial management is all about. After you finish the chapter, you should have a reasonably good idea of what finance majors might do after graduation. You should also have a better understanding of (1) some of the forces that will affect financial management in the future; (2) the place of finance in a firm's organization; (3) the relationships between financial managers and their counterparts in the accounting, marketing, production, and personnel departments; (4) the goals of a firm; and (5) the way financial managers can contribute to the attainment of these goals. ∎

CAREER OPPORTUNITIES IN FINANCE

Information on finance careers, additional chapter links, and practice quizzes are available on the web site to accompany this text: **http://www.harcourtcollege.com/finance/concise3e.**

Finance consists of three interrelated areas: (1) *money and capital markets*, which deals with securities markets and financial institutions; (2) *investments*, which focuses on the decisions made by both individual and institutional investors as they choose securities for their investment portfolios; and (3) *financial management*, or "business finance," which involves decisions within firms. The career opportunities within each field are many and varied, but financial managers must have a knowledge of all three areas if they are to do their jobs well.

MONEY AND CAPITAL MARKETS

Many finance majors go to work for financial institutions, including banks, insurance companies, mutual funds, and investment banking firms. For success here, one needs a knowledge of valuation techniques, the factors that cause interest rates to rise and fall, the regulations to which financial institutions are subject, and the various types of financial instruments (mortgages, auto loans, certificates of deposit, and so on). One also needs a general knowledge of all aspects of business administration, because the management of a financial institution involves accounting, marketing, personnel, and computer systems, as well as financial management. An ability to communicate, both orally and in writing, is important, and "people skills," or the ability to get others to do their jobs well, are critical.

INVESTMENTS

Consult **http:// www.careers-in- business.com** for an excellent site containing information on a variety of business career areas, listings of current jobs, and a variety of other reference materials.

Finance graduates who go into investments often work for a brokerage house such as Merrill Lynch, either in sales or as a security analyst. Others work for banks, mutual funds, or insurance companies in the management of their investment portfolios; for financial consulting firms advising individual investors or pension funds on how to invest their capital; for investment banks whose primary function is to help businesses raise new capital; or as financial planners whose job is to help individuals develop long-term financial goals and portfolios. The three main functions in the investments area are sales, analyzing individual securities, and determining the optimal mix of securities for a given investor.

FINANCIAL MANAGEMENT

Financial management is the broadest of the three areas, and the one with the most job opportunities. Financial management is important in all types of businesses, including banks and other financial institutions, as well as industrial and retail firms. Financial management is also important in governmental operations, from schools to hospitals to highway departments. The job opportunities in financial management range from making decisions regarding plant expansions to choosing what types of securities to issue when financing expansion. Financial managers also have the responsibility for deciding the credit terms under which customers may buy, how much inventory the firm should carry, how much cash to keep on hand, whether to acquire other firms (merger analysis), and how much of the firm's earnings to plow back into the business versus pay out as dividends.

Regardless of which area a finance major enters, he or she will need a knowledge of all three areas. For example, a bank lending officer cannot do his or her job well without a good understanding of financial management, because he or she must be able to judge how well a business is being operated. The same thing holds true for Merrill Lynch's security analysts and stockbrokers, who must have an understanding of general financial principles if they are to give their customers intelligent advice. Similarly, corporate financial managers need to know what their bankers are thinking about, and they also need to know how investors judge a firm's performance and thus determine its stock price. So, if you decide to make finance your career, you will need to know something about all three areas.

But suppose you do not plan to major in finance. Is the subject still important to you? Absolutely, for two reasons: (1) You need a knowledge of finance to make many personal decisions, ranging from investing for your retirement to deciding whether to lease versus buy a car. (2) Virtually all important business decisions have financial implications, so important decisions are generally made by teams from the accounting, finance, legal, marketing, personnel, and production departments. Therefore, if you want to succeed in the business arena, you must be highly competent in your own area, say, marketing, but you must also have a familiarity with the other business disciplines, including finance.

Thus, there are financial implications in virtually all business decisions, and nonfinancial executives simply must know enough finance to work these implications into their own specialized analyses.[1] Because of this, every student of business, regardless of his or her major, should be concerned with financial management.

SELF-TEST QUESTIONS

What are the three main areas of finance?

If you have definite plans to go into one area, why is it necessary that you know something about the other areas?

Why is it necessary for business students who do not plan to major in finance to understand the basics of finance?

FINANCIAL MANAGEMENT IN THE NEW MILLENNIUM

When financial management emerged as a separate field of study in the early 1900s, the emphasis was on the legal aspects of mergers, the formation of new firms, and the various types of securities firms could issue to raise capital. During the Depression of the 1930s, the emphasis shifted to bankruptcy and reorganization, corporate liquidity, and the regulation of security markets. During the 1940s and early 1950s, finance continued to be taught as a descriptive, institutional subject, viewed more from the standpoint of an outsider rather than that of a manager. However, a movement toward theoretical analysis began during the late 1950s, and the focus shifted to managerial decisions designed to maximize the value of the firm.

---

[1] It is an interesting fact that the course "Financial Management for Nonfinancial Executives" has the highest enrollment in most executive development programs.

The focus on value maximization continues as we begin the 21st century. However, two other trends are becoming increasingly important: (1) the globalization of business and (2) the increased use of information technology. Both of these trends provide companies with exciting new opportunities to increase profitability and reduce risks. However, these trends are also leading to increased competition and new risks. To emphasize these points throughout the book, we regularly profile how companies or industries have been affected by increased globalization and changing technology. These profiles are found in the boxes labeled "Global Perspectives" and "Technology Matters."

GLOBALIZATION OF BUSINESS

Many companies today rely to a large and increasing extent on overseas operations. Table 1-1 summarizes the percentage of overseas revenues and profits for 10 well-known corporations. Very clearly, these 10 "American" companies are really international concerns.

Check out **http://www.nummi.com/home.htm** to find out more about New United Motor Manufacturing, Inc. (NUMMI), the joint venture between Toyota and General Motors. Read about NUMMI's history and organizational goals.

Four factors have led to the increased globalization of businesses: (1) Improvements in transportation and communications lowered shipping costs and made international trade more feasible. (2) The increasing political clout of consumers, who desire low-cost, high-quality products. This has helped lower trade barriers designed to protect inefficient, high-cost domestic manufacturers and their workers. (3) As technology has become more advanced, the costs of developing new products have increased. These rising costs have led to joint ventures between such companies as General Motors and Toyota, and to global operations for many firms as they seek to expand markets and thus spread development costs over higher unit sales. (4) In a world populated with multinational firms able to shift production to wherever costs are lowest, a firm whose manufacturing operations are restricted to one country cannot compete unless costs in its home country happen to be low, a condition that does not

TABLE 1-1	Percentage of Revenue and Net Income from Overseas Operations for 10 Well-Known Corporations

COMPANY	PERCENTAGE OF REVENUE ORIGINATED OVERSEAS	PERCENTAGE OF NET INCOME GENERATED OVERSEAS
Chase Manhattan	23.9	21.9
Coca-Cola	61.2	65.1
Exxon Mobil	71.8	62.7
General Electric	31.7	22.8
General Motors	26.3	55.3
IBM	57.5	49.6
McDonald's	61.6	60.9
Merck	21.6	43.4
Minn. Mining & Mfg.	52.1	27.2
Walt Disney	15.4	16.6

SOURCE: *Forbes* Magazine's 1999 Ranking of the 100 Largest U.S. Multinationals; *Forbes*, July 24, 2000, 335–338.

COKE RIDES THE GLOBAL ECONOMY WAVE

During the past 20 years, Coca-Cola has created tremendous value for its shareholders. A $10,000 investment in Coke stock in January 1980 would have grown to nearly $600,000 by mid-1998. A large part of that impressive growth was due to Coke's overseas expansion program. Today nearly 75 percent of Coke's profit comes from overseas, and Coke sells roughly half of the world's soft drinks.

More recently, Coke has discovered that there are also risks when investing overseas. Indeed, between mid-1998 and January 2001, Coke's stock fell by roughly a third—which means that the $600,000 stock investment decreased in value to $400,000 in about 2.5 years. Coke's poor performance during this period was due in large part to troubles overseas. Weak economic conditions in Brazil, Germany, Japan, Southeast Asia, Venezuela, Colombia, and Russia, plus a quality scare in Belgium and France, hurt the company's bottom line.

Despite its recent difficulties, Coke remains committed to its global vision. Coke is also striving to learn from these difficulties. The company's leaders have acknowledged that Coke may have become overly centralized. Centralized control enabled Coke to standardize quality and to capture operating efficiencies, both of which initially helped to establish its brand name throughout the world. More recently, however, Coke has become concerned that too much centralized control has made it slow to respond to changing circumstances and insensitive to differences among the various local markets it serves.

Coke's CEO, Douglas N. Daft, reflected these concerns in a recent editorial that was published in the March 27, 2000, edition of *Financial Times*. Daft's concluding comments appear below:

So overall, we will draw on a long-standing belief that Coca-Cola always flourishes when our people are allowed to use their insight to build the business in ways best suited to their local culture and business conditions.

We will, of course, maintain clear order. Our small corporate team will communicate explicitly the clear strategy, policy, values, and quality standards needed to keep us cohesive and efficient. But just as important, we will also make sure we stay out of the way of our local people and let them do their jobs. That will enhance significantly our ability to unlock growth opportunities, which will enable us to consistently meet our growth expectations.

In our recent past, we succeeded because we understood and appealed to global commonalties. In our future, we'll succeed because we will also understand and appeal to local differences. The 21st century demands nothing less.

For more information about the Coca-Cola Company, go to **http://www.thecoca-colacompany.com/world/index.html**, where you can find profiles of Coca-Cola's presence in foreign countries. You may follow additional links to Coca-Cola web sites in foreign countries.

necessarily exist for many U.S. corporations. As a result of these four factors, survival requires that most manufacturers produce and sell globally.

Service companies, including banks, advertising agencies, and accounting firms, are also being forced to "go global," because these firms can best serve their multinational clients if they have worldwide operations. There will, of course, always be some purely domestic companies, but the most dynamic growth, and the best employment opportunities, are often with companies that operate worldwide.

Even businesses that operate exclusively in the United States are not immune to the effects of globalization. For example, the costs to a homebuilder in rural Nebraska are affected by interest rates and lumber prices — both of which are determined by worldwide supply and demand conditions. Furthermore, demand for the homebuilder's houses is influenced by interest rates and also by conditions in the local farm economy, which depend to a large extent on foreign demand for wheat. To operate efficiently, the Nebraska builder must be able to forecast the demand for houses, and that demand depends on worldwide events. So, at least some knowledge of global economic conditions is important to virtually everyone, not just to those involved with businesses that operate internationally.

INFORMATION TECHNOLOGY

As we advance into the new millennium, we will see continued advances in computer and communications technology, and this will continue to revolutionize the way financial decisions are made. Companies are linking networks of personal

eTOYS TAKES ON TOYS "Я" US

The toy market illustrates how electronic commerce is changing the way firms operate. Over the past decade, this market has been dominated by Toys "Я" Us, although Toys "Я" Us has faced increasing competition from retail chains such as Wal-Mart, Kmart, and Target. Then, in 1997, Internet startup eToys Inc. began selling and distributing toys through the Internet.

When eToys first emerged, many analysts believed that the Internet provided toy retailers with a sensational opportunity. This point was made amazingly clear in May 1999 when eToys issued stock to the public in an initial public offering (IPO). The stock immediately rose from its $20 offering price to $76 per share, and the company's market capitalization (calculated by multiplying stock price by the number of shares outstanding) was a mind-blowing $7.8 billion.

To put this valuation in perspective, eToys' market value at the time of the offering ($7.8 billion) was 35 percent greater than that of Toys "Я" Us ($5.7 billion). eToys' valuation was particularly startling given that the company had yet to earn a profit. (It lost $73 million in the year ending March 1999.) Moreover, while Toys "Я" Us had nearly 1,500 stores and revenues in excess of $11 billion, eToys had no stores and revenues of less than $35 million.

Investors were clearly expecting that an increasing number of toys will be bought over the Internet. One analyst estimated at the time of the offering that eToys would be worth $10 billion within a decade. His analysis assumed that in 10 years the toy market would total $75 billion, with $20 billion coming from online sales. Indeed, online sales do appear to be here to stay. For many customers, online shopping is quicker and more convenient, particularly for working parents of young children, who purchase the lion's share of toys. From the company's perspective, Internet commerce has a number of other advantages. The costs of maintaining a web site and distributing toys online may be smaller than the costs of maintaining and managing 1,500 retail stores.

Not surprisingly, Toys "Я" Us did not sit idly by — it recently announced plans to invest $64 million in a separate online subsidiary, Toysrus.com. The company also announced an online partnership with Internet retailer Amazon.com. In addition, Toys "Я" Us is redoubling its efforts to make traditional store shopping more enjoyable and less frustrating.

While the Internet provides toy companies with new and interesting opportunities, these companies also face tremendous risks as they try to respond to the changing technology. Indeed, in the months following eToys' IPO, Toys "Я" Us' stock fell sharply, and by January 2000, its market value was only slightly above $2 billion. Since then, Toys "Я" Us stock has rebounded, and its market capitalization was once again approaching $5 billion. The shareholders of eToys were less fortunate. Concerns about inventory management during the 1999 holiday season and the collapse of many Internet stocks spurred a tremendous collapse in eToys' stock — its stock fell from a post–IPO high of $76 a share to $0.31 a share in January 2001. Two months later, eToys declared bankruptcy.

computers to one another, to the firms' own mainframe computers, to the Internet and the World Wide Web, and to their customers' and suppliers' computers. Thus, financial managers are increasingly able to share information and to have "face-to-face" meetings with distant colleagues through video teleconferencing. The ability to access and analyze data on a real-time basis also means that quantitative analysis is becoming more important, and "gut feel" less sufficient, in business decisions. As a result, the next generation of financial managers will need stronger computer and quantitative skills than were required in the past.

Changing technology provides both opportunities and threats. Improved technology enables businesses to reduce costs and expand markets. At the same time, however, changing technology can introduce additional competition, which may reduce profitability in existing markets.

The banking industry provides a good example of the double-edged technology sword. Improved technology has allowed banks to process information much more efficiently, which reduces the costs of processing checks, providing credit, and identifying bad credit risks. Technology has also allowed banks to serve customers better. For example, today bank customers use automatic teller machines (ATMs) everywhere, from the supermarket to the local mall. Today, many banks also offer products that allow their customers to use the Internet to manage their accounts and to pay bills. However, changing technology also threatens banks' profitability. Many customers no longer feel compelled to use a local bank, and the Internet allows them to shop worldwide for the best deposit and loan rates. An even greater threat is the continued development of electronic commerce. Electronic commerce allows customers and businesses to transact directly, thus reducing the need for intermediaries such as commercial banks. In the years ahead, financial managers will have to continue to keep abreast of technological developments, and they must be prepared to adapt their businesses to the changing environment.

SELF-TEST QUESTIONS

What two key trends are becoming increasingly important in financial management today?

How has financial management changed from the early 1900s to the present?

How might a person become better prepared for a career in financial management?

THE FINANCIAL STAFF'S RESPONSIBILITIES

The financial staff's task is to acquire and then help operate resources so as to maximize the value of the firm. Here are some specific activities:

1. **Forecasting and planning.** The financial staff must coordinate the planning process. This means they must interact with people from other departments as they look ahead and lay the plans that will shape the firm's future.

2. **Major investment and financing decisions.** A successful firm usually has rapid growth in sales, which requires investments in plant, equipment, and inventory. The financial staff must help determine the optimal sales growth rate, help decide what specific assets to acquire, and then choose the best way to finance those assets. For example, should the firm finance with debt, equity, or some combination of the two, and if debt is used, how much should be long term and how much short term?

3. **Coordination and control.** The financial staff must interact with other personnel to ensure that the firm is operated as efficiently as possible. All business decisions have financial implications, and all managers — financial and otherwise — need to take this into account. For example, marketing decisions affect sales growth, which in turn influences investment requirements. Thus, marketing decision makers must take account of how their actions affect and are affected by such factors as the availability of funds, inventory policies, and plant capacity utilization.

4. **Dealing with the financial markets.** The financial staff must deal with the money and capital markets. As we shall see in Chapter 5, each firm affects and is affected by the general financial markets where funds are

raised, where the firm's securities are traded, and where investors either make or lose money.

5. **Risk management.** All businesses face risks, including natural disasters such as fires and floods, uncertainties in commodity and security markets, volatile interest rates, and fluctuating foreign exchange rates. However, many of these risks can be reduced by purchasing insurance or by hedging in the derivatives markets. The financial staff is responsible for the firm's overall risk management program, including identifying the risks that should be managed and then managing them in the most efficient manner.

In summary, people working in financial management make decisions regarding which assets their firms should acquire, how those assets should be financed, and how the firm should conduct its operations. If these responsibilities are performed optimally, financial managers will help to maximize the values of their firms, and this will also contribute to the welfare of consumers and employees.

┌─────────────────────────┐
│ **SELF-TEST QUESTION** │
└─────────────────────────┘

What are some specific activities with which a firm's finance staff is involved?

ALTERNATIVE FORMS OF BUSINESS ORGANIZATION

There are three main forms of business organization: (1) sole proprietorships, (2) partnerships, and (3) corporations, plus several hybrid forms. In terms of numbers, about 80 percent of businesses are operated as sole proprietorships, while most of the remainder are divided equally between partnerships and corporations. Based on the dollar value of sales, however, about 80 percent of all business is conducted by corporations, about 13 percent by sole proprietorships, and about 7 percent by partnerships and hybrids. Because most business is conducted by corporations, we will concentrate on them in this book. However, it is important to understand the differences among the various forms.

SOLE PROPRIETORSHIP

Sole Proprietorship
An unincorporated business owned by one individual.

A **sole proprietorship** is an unincorporated business owned by one individual. Going into business as a sole proprietor is easy — one merely begins business operations. However, even the smallest businesses normally must be licensed by a governmental unit.

The proprietorship has three important advantages: (1) It is easily and inexpensively formed, (2) it is subject to few government regulations, and (3) the business avoids corporate income taxes.

The proprietorship also has three important limitations: (1) It is difficult for a proprietorship to obtain large sums of capital; (2) the proprietor has unlimited personal liability for the business's debts, which can result in losses that exceed the money he or she has invested in the company; and (3) the life of a business organized as a proprietorship is limited to the life of the individual who created it. For these three reasons, sole proprietorships are used primarily for small-business operations. However, businesses are frequently started as proprietorships and then converted to corporations when their growth causes the disadvantages of being a proprietorship to outweigh the advantages.

PARTNERSHIP

Partnership
An unincorporated business owned by two or more persons.

A **partnership** exists whenever two or more persons associate to conduct a noncorporate business. Partnerships may operate under different degrees of formality, ranging from informal, oral understandings to formal agreements filed with the secretary of the state in which the partnership was formed. The major advantage of a partnership is its low cost and ease of formation. The disadvantages are similar to those associated with proprietorships: (1) unlimited liability, (2) limited life of the organization, (3) difficulty of transferring ownership, and (4) difficulty of raising large amounts of capital. The tax treatment of a partnership is similar to that for proprietorships, which is often an advantage, as we demonstrate in Chapter 2.

Regarding liability, the partners can potentially lose all of their personal assets, even assets not invested in the business, because under partnership law, each partner is liable for the business's debts. Therefore, if any partner is unable to meet his or her pro rata liability in the event the partnership goes bankrupt, the remaining partners must make good on the unsatisfied claims, drawing on their personal assets to the extent necessary. The partners of the national accounting firm Laventhol and Horwath, a huge partnership that went bankrupt as a result of suits filed by investors who relied on faulty audit statements, learned all about the perils of doing business as a partnership. Thus, a Texas partner who audits a business that goes under can bring ruin to a millionaire New York partner who never went near the client company.

The first three disadvantages — unlimited liability, impermanence of the organization, and difficulty of transferring ownership — lead to the fourth, the difficulty partnerships have in attracting substantial amounts of capital. This is generally not a problem for a slow-growing business, but if a business's products or services really catch on, and if it needs to raise large amounts of capital to capitalize on its opportunities, the difficulty in attracting capital becomes a real drawback. Thus, growth companies such as Hewlett-Packard and Microsoft generally begin life as a proprietorship or partnership, but at some point their founders find it necessary to convert to a corporation.

CORPORATION

Corporation
A legal entity created by a state, separate and distinct from its owners and managers, having unlimited life, easy transferability of ownership, and limited liability.

A **corporation** is a legal entity created by a state, and it is separate and distinct from its owners and managers. This separateness gives the corporation three major advantages: (1) *Unlimited life*. A corporation can continue after its original owners and managers are deceased. (2) *Easy transferability of ownership interest*. Ownership interests can be divided into shares of stock, which, in turn, can be transferred far more easily than can proprietorship or partnership interests. (3) *Limited liability*. Losses are limited to the actual funds invested. To illustrate limited liability, suppose you invested $10,000 in a partnership that then went bankrupt, owing $1 million. Because the owners are liable for the debts of a partnership, you could be assessed for a share of the company's debt, and you could be held liable for the entire $1 million if your partners could not pay their shares. Thus, an investor in a partnership is exposed to unlimited liability. On the other hand, if you invested $10,000 in the stock of a corporation that then went bankrupt, your potential loss on the investment would be limited to your $10,000 investment.[2] These three factors — unlimited life, easy transferability of ownership interest, and limited liability — make it much easier for corporations than for proprietorships or partnerships to raise money in the capital markets.

The corporate form offers significant advantages over proprietorships and partnerships, but it also has two disadvantages: (1) Corporate earnings may be subject to double taxation — the earnings of the corporation are taxed at the corporate level, and then any earnings paid out as dividends are taxed again as income to the stockholders. (2) Setting up a corporation, and filing the many required state and federal reports, is more complex and time-consuming than for a proprietorship or a partnership.

A proprietorship or a partnership can commence operations without much paperwork, but setting up a corporation requires that the incorporators prepare a charter and a set of bylaws. Although personal computer software that creates charters and bylaws is now available, a lawyer is required if the fledgling corporation has any nonstandard features. The *charter* includes the following information: (1) name of the proposed corporation, (2) types of activities it will pursue, (3) amount of capital stock, (4) number of directors, and (5) names and addresses of directors. The charter is filed with the secretary of the state in which the firm will be incorporated, and when it is approved, the corporation is officially in existence.[3] Then, after the corporation is in operation, quarterly and annual employment, financial, and tax reports must be filed with state and federal authorities.

The *bylaws* are a set of rules drawn up by the founders of the corporation. Included are such points as (1) how directors are to be elected (all elected each year, or perhaps one-third each year for three-year terms); (2) whether the existing stockholders will have the first right to buy any new shares the firm issues; and (3) procedures for changing the bylaws themselves, should conditions require it.

The value of any business other than a very small one will probably be maximized if it is organized as a corporation for the following three reasons:

1. Limited liability reduces the risks borne by investors, and, other things held constant, *the lower the firm's risk, the higher its value.*

2. A firm's value is dependent on its *growth opportunities*, which in turn are dependent on the firm's ability to attract capital. Since corporations can attract capital more easily than can unincorporated businesses, they are better able to take advantage of growth opportunities.

---

[2] In the case of small corporations, the limited liability feature is often a fiction, because bankers and other lenders frequently require personal guarantees from the stockholders of small, weak businesses.

[3] Note that more than 60 percent of major U.S. corporations are chartered in Delaware, which has, over the years, provided a favorable legal environment for corporations. It is not necessary for a firm to be headquartered, or even to conduct operations, in its state of incorporation.

3. The value of an asset also depends on its *liquidity*, which means the ease of selling the asset and converting it to cash at a "fair market value." Since an investment in the stock of a corporation is much more liquid than a similar investment in a proprietorship or partnership, this too enhances the value of a corporation.

As we will see later in the chapter, most firms are managed with value maximization in mind, and this, in turn, has caused most large businesses to be organized as corporations.

Hybrid Forms of Organization

Limited Partnership
A hybrid form of organization consisting of general partners, who have unlimited liability for the partnership's debts, and limited partners, whose liability is limited to the amount of their investment.

Although the three basic types of organization — proprietorships, partnerships, and corporations — dominate the business scene, several hybrid forms are gaining popularity. For example, there are some specialized types of partnerships that have somewhat different characteristics than the "plain vanilla" kind. First, it is possible to limit the liabilities of some of the partners by establishing a **limited partnership,** wherein certain partners are designated *general partners* and others *limited partners*. In a limited partnership, the limited partners are liable only for the amount of their investment in the partnership, while the general partners have unlimited liability. However, the limited partners typically have no control, which rests solely with the general partners, and their returns are likewise limited. Limited partnerships are common in real estate, oil, and equipment leasing ventures. However, they are not widely used in general business situations because no one partner is usually willing to be the general partner and thus accept the majority of the business's risk, while would-be limited partners are unwilling to give up all control.

Limited Liability Partnership (Limited Liability Company)
A hybrid form of organization in which all partners enjoy limited liability for the business's debts. It combines the limited liability advantage of a corporation with the tax advantages of a partnership.

The **limited liability partnership (LLP),** sometimes called a **limited liability company (LLC),** is a relatively new type of partnership that is now permitted in many states. In both regular and limited partnerships, at least one partner is liable for the debts of the partnership. However, in an LLP, all partners enjoy limited liability with regard to the business's liabilities, and, in that regard, they are similar to shareholders in a corporation. In effect, the LLP form of organization combines the limited liability advantage of a corporation with the tax advantages of a partnership. Of course, those who do business with an LLP as opposed to a regular partnership are aware of the situation, which increases the risk faced by lenders, customers, and others who deal with the LLP.

Professional Corporation (Professional Association)
A type of corporation common among professionals that provides most of the benefits of incorporation but does not relieve the participants of malpractice liability.

There are also several different types of corporations. One type that is common among professionals such as doctors, lawyers, and accountants is the **professional corporation (PC),** or in some states, the **professional association (PA).** All 50 states have statutes that prescribe the requirements for such corporations, which provide most of the benefits of incorporation but do not relieve the participants of professional (malpractice) liability. Indeed, the primary motivation behind the professional corporation was to provide a way for groups of professionals to incorporate and thus avoid certain types of unlimited liability, yet still be held responsible for professional liability.

Finally, note that if certain requirements are met, particularly with regard to size and number of stockholders, one (or more) individual can establish a corporation but elect to be taxed as if the business were a proprietorship or partnership. Such firms, which differ not in organizational form but only in how their owners are taxed, are called *S corporations*. Although S corporations are similar in many ways to limited liability partnerships, LLPs frequently offer more flexibility and benefits to their owners — so many that large numbers of S corporation businesses are converting to this relatively new organizational form.

SELF-TEST QUESTIONS

What are the key differences between sole proprietorships, partnerships, and corporations?

Why will the value of any business other than a very small one probably be maximized if it is organized as a corporation?

FINANCE IN THE ORGANIZATIONAL STRUCTURE OF THE FIRM

Organizational structures vary from firm to firm, but Figure 1-1 presents a fairly typical picture of the role of finance within a corporation. The chief financial officer (CFO) generally has the title of vice-president: finance, and he

FIGURE 1-1	Role of Finance in a Typical Business Organization

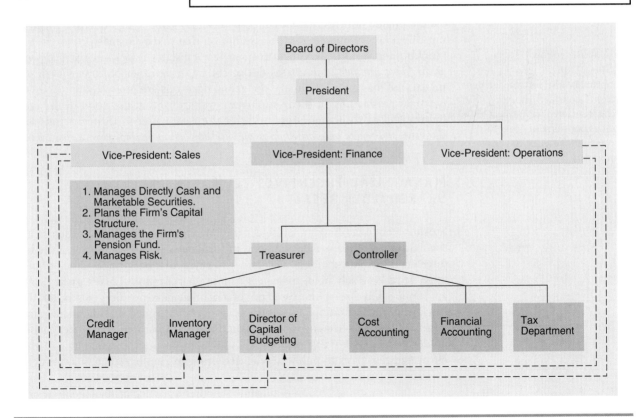

or she reports to the president. The financial vice-president's key subordinates are the treasurer and the controller. In most firms the treasurer has direct responsibility for managing the firm's cash and marketable securities, for planning its capital structure, for selling stocks and bonds to raise capital, for overseeing the corporate pension plan, and for managing risk. The treasurer also supervises the credit manager, the inventory manager, and the director of capital budgeting (who analyzes decisions related to investments in fixed assets). The controller is typically responsible for the activities of the accounting and tax departments.

SELF-TEST QUESTION

Identify the two primary subordinates who report to the firm's chief financial officer, and indicate the primary responsibilities of each.

THE GOALS OF THE CORPORATION

Shareholders are the owners of a corporation, and they purchase stocks because they are looking for a financial return. In most cases, shareholders elect directors, who then hire managers to run the corporation on a day-to-day basis. Since managers are working on behalf of shareholders, it follows that they should pursue policies that enhance shareholder value. Consequently, throughout this book we operate on the assumption that management's primary goal is **stockholder wealth maximization,** which translates into *maximizing the price of the firm's common stock.* Firms do, of course, have other objectives — in particular, the managers who make the actual decisions are interested in their own personal satisfaction, in their employees' welfare, and in the good of the community and of society at large. Still, for the reasons set forth in the following sections, *stock price maximization is the most important goal for most corporations.*

Stockholder Wealth Maximization
The primary goal for management decisions; considers the risk and timing associated with expected earnings per share in order to maximize the price of the firm's common stock.

MANAGERIAL INCENTIVES TO MAXIMIZE SHAREHOLDER WEALTH

Stockholders own the firm and elect the board of directors, which then selects the management team. Management, in turn, is supposed to operate in the best interests of the stockholders. We know, however, that because the stock of most large firms is widely held, managers of large corporations have a great deal of autonomy. This being the case, might not managers pursue goals other than stock price maximization? For example, some have argued that the managers of large, well-entrenched corporations could work just hard enough to keep stockholder returns at a "reasonable" level and then devote the remainder of their effort and resources to public service activities, to employee benefits, to higher executive salaries, or to golf.

It is almost impossible to determine whether a particular management team is trying to maximize shareholder wealth or is merely attempting to keep stockholders satisfied while managers pursue other goals. For example, how can we tell whether employee or community benefit programs are in the long-run best interests of the stockholders? Similarly, are huge executive salaries really necessary to attract and retain excellent managers, or are they just another example of managers taking advantage of stockholders?

It is impossible to give definitive answers to these questions. However, we do know that the managers of a firm operating in a competitive market will be forced to undertake actions that are reasonably consistent with shareholder wealth maximization. If they depart from that goal, they run the risk of being removed from their jobs, either by the firm's board of directors or by outside forces. We will have more to say about this in a later section.

SOCIAL RESPONSIBILITY

Social Responsibility
The concept that businesses should be actively concerned with the welfare of society at large.

Another issue that deserves consideration is **social responsibility:** Should businesses operate strictly in their stockholders' best interests, or are firms also responsible for the welfare of their employees, customers, and the communities in which they operate? Certainly firms have an ethical responsibility to provide a safe working environment, to avoid polluting the air or water, and to produce safe products. However, socially responsible actions have costs, and not all businesses would voluntarily incur all such costs. If some firms act in a socially responsible manner while others do not, then the socially responsible firms will be at a disadvantage in attracting capital. To illustrate, suppose all firms in a given industry have close to **"normal" profits** and **rates of return on investment,** that is, close to the average for all firms and just sufficient to attract capital. If one company attempts to exercise social responsibility, it will have to raise prices to cover the added costs. If other firms in its industry do not follow suit, their costs and prices will be lower. The socially responsible firm will not be able to compete, and it will be forced to abandon its efforts. Thus, any voluntary socially responsible acts that raise costs will be difficult, if not impossible, in industries that are subject to keen competition.

Normal Profits and Rates of Return
Those profits and rates of return that are close to the average for all firms and are just sufficient to attract capital.

What about oligopolistic firms with profits above normal levels — cannot such firms devote resources to social projects? Undoubtedly they can, and many large, successful firms do engage in community projects, employee benefit programs, and the like to a greater degree than would appear to be called for by pure profit or wealth maximization goals.[4] Furthermore, many such firms contribute large sums to charities. Still, publicly owned firms are constrained by capital market forces. To illustrate, suppose a saver who has funds to invest is considering two alternative firms. One devotes a substantial part of its resources to social actions, while the other concentrates on profits and stock prices. Many investors would shun the socially oriented firm, thus putting it at a disadvantage in the capital market. After all, why should the stockholders of one corporation subsidize society to a greater extent than those of other businesses? For this reason, even highly profitable firms (unless they are closely

---

[4] Even firms like these often find it necessary to justify such projects at stockholder meetings by stating that these programs will contribute to long-run profit maximization.

held rather than publicly owned) are generally constrained against taking unilateral cost-increasing social actions.

Does all this mean that firms should not exercise social responsibility? Not at all. But it does mean that most significant cost-increasing actions will have to be put on a *mandatory* rather than a voluntary basis to ensure that the burden falls uniformly on all businesses. Thus, such social benefit programs as fair hiring practices, minority training, product safety, pollution abatement, and antitrust actions are most likely to be effective if realistic rules are established initially and then enforced by government agencies. Of course, it is critical that industry and government cooperate in establishing the rules of corporate behavior, and that the costs as well as the benefits of such actions be estimated accurately and then taken into account.

In spite of the fact that many socially responsible actions must be mandated by government, in recent years numerous firms have voluntarily taken such actions, especially in the area of environmental protection, because they helped sales. For example, many detergent manufacturers now use recycled paper for their containers, and food companies are packaging more and more products in materials that consumers can recycle or that are biodegradable. To illustrate, McDonald's replaced its styrofoam boxes, which take years to break down in landfills, with paper wrappers that are less bulky and decompose more rapidly. Some companies, such as The Body Shop and Ben & Jerry's Ice Cream, go to great lengths to be socially responsible. According to the president of The Body Shop, the role of business is to promote the public good, not just the good of the firm's shareholders. Furthermore, she argues that it is impossible to separate business from social responsibility. For some firms, socially responsible actions may not de facto be costly—the companies heavily advertise their actions, and many consumers prefer to buy from socially responsible companies rather than from those that shun social responsibility.

 Go to **http://www.the-body-shop.com/usa/aboutus/values.html** to see the corporate values The Body Shop embraces.

STOCK PRICE MAXIMIZATION AND SOCIAL WELFARE

If a firm attempts to maximize its stock price, is this good or bad for society? In general, it is good. Aside from such illegal actions as attempting to form monopolies, violating safety codes, and failing to meet pollution control requirements, *the same actions that maximize stock prices also benefit society.* First, note that stock price maximization requires efficient, low-cost businesses that produce high-quality goods and services at the lowest possible cost. Second, stock price maximization requires the development of products and services that consumers want and need, so the profit motive leads to new technology, to new products, and to new jobs. Finally, stock price maximization necessitates efficient and courteous service, adequate stocks of merchandise, and well-located business establishments—these are the factors that lead to sales, which in turn are necessary for profits. Therefore, most actions that help a firm increase the price of its stock also benefit society at large. This is why profit-motivated, free-enterprise economies have been so much more successful than socialistic and communistic economic systems. Since financial management plays a crucial role in the operations of successful firms, and since successful firms are absolutely necessary for a healthy,

LEVI STRAUSS TRIES TO BLEND PROFITS WITH SOCIAL ACTIVISM

Levi Strauss & Company has been around for nearly 150 years. Well known for its Dockers and 501 jeans, the firm has also been recognized for its commitment to social values. Indeed, when Levi Strauss first issued stock to the public in 1971, it took the unusual step of warning potential investors that the company's dedication to social activism was so deep that it might compromise corporate profits.

Levi Strauss' words and actions continually reflect this strong devotion to social causes. In 1987, CEO Bob Haas developed the company's Mission and Aspiration Statement, which highlighted an emphasis on diversity, teamwork, and integrity. A few years later, the company created a 10-day course for employees that focused on ethical decision making. As one of the course developers put it: "It was about asking, 'How do I find meaning in the workplace?' It was about seeing that work is noble, that we're more than getting pants out the door."

Moreover, the company's philosophy had a profound effect on its business decisions. For example, it withdrew its investments in China to protest human rights violations. This action contrasted sharply with those of most other companies, which continued making investments in China in order to enhance shareholder value.

Levi Strauss has received considerable praise and numerous awards for its vision, and until recently, the company was able to practice social activism while maintaining strong profitability. However, the company's profitability has fallen recently, causing many to argue that it must rethink its vision if it is to survive. In the face of huge losses, it is not surprising that tension has arisen between the conflicting goals of social activism and profitability. Peter Jacobi, who recently retired as president of Levi Strauss, summarized this tension when he was quoted in a recent *Fortune* magazine article:

The problem is [that] some people thought the values were an end in themselves. You have some people who say, "Our objective is to be the most enlightened work environment in the world." And then you have others that say, "Our objective is to make a lot of money." The value-based [socially oriented] people look at the commercial folks as heathens; the commercial people look at the values people as wusses getting in the way.

Despite these concerns, Levi Strauss' recent problems may not be solely or even predominantly attributed to its social activism. The company has been slow to respond to fashion trends and to changing distribution system technology. Despite large investments, the company is still way behind its competitors in managing inventory and getting product to market.

To be sure, all is not completely bleak for Levi Strauss. The company still has a very strong brand name, and it still continues to generate a lot of cash. For example, in 1998, the company generated cash flow of $1.1 billion, more than either Gap or Nike.

One factor that makes Levi Strauss unique is its ownership structure. The Haas family has long controlled the company. Moreover, after completing a leveraged buyout in 1996, the company is once again privately held. As part of the buyout agreement, investors who wanted to maintain their ownership stake had to grant complete power for 15 years to four family members led by Bob Haas. This ownership structure has enabled Levi Strauss to pursue its social objectives without facing the types of pressure that a more shareholder-oriented company would face. Arguably, however, the lack of external pressure helps explain why the company has been so slow to adapt to changing technology and market conditions.

SOURCE: "How Levi's Trashed a Great American Brand," *Fortune*, April 12, 1999, 82–90.

Go to http://www.levistrauss.com/index_about.html to take a look at Levi Strauss & Co.'s vision statement, history, other general information about the company, and its ideals.

productive economy, it is easy to see why finance is important from a social welfare standpoint.[5]

---

[5] People sometimes argue that firms, in their efforts to raise profits and stock prices, increase product prices and gouge the public. In a reasonably competitive economy, which we have, prices are constrained by competition and consumer resistance. If a firm raises its prices beyond reasonable levels, it will simply lose its market share. Even giant firms such as General Motors lose business to the Japanese and German automakers, as well as to Ford, if they set prices above levels necessary to cover production costs plus a "normal" profit. Of course, firms *want* to earn more, and they constantly try to cut costs, to develop new products, and so on, and thereby to earn above-normal profits. Note, though, that if they are indeed successful and do earn above-normal profits, those very profits will attract competition, which will eventually drive prices down, so again the main long-term beneficiary is the consumer.

BUSINESS ETHICS

Business Ethics
A company's attitude and conduct toward its employees, customers, community, and stockholders.

The word *ethics* is defined in Webster's dictionary as "standards of conduct or moral behavior." **Business ethics** can be thought of as a company's attitude and conduct toward its employees, customers, community, and stockholders. High standards of ethical behavior demand that a firm treat each party that it deals with in a fair and honest manner. A firm's commitment to business ethics can be measured by the tendency of the firm and its employees to adhere to laws and regulations relating to such factors as product safety and quality, fair employment practices, fair marketing and selling practices, the use of confidential information for personal gain, community involvement, bribery, and illegal payments to obtain business.

Most firms today have in place strong codes of ethical behavior, and they also conduct training programs designed to ensure that employees understand the correct behavior in different business situations. However, it is imperative that top management — the chairman, president, and vice-presidents — be openly committed to ethical behavior, and that they communicate this commitment through their own personal actions as well as through company policies, directives, and punishment/reward systems.

When conflicts arise between profits and ethics, sometimes the ethical considerations are so strong that they clearly dominate. However, in many cases the choice between ethics and profits is not clear cut. For example, suppose Norfolk Southern's managers know that its coal trains are polluting the air along its routes, but the amount of pollution is within legal limits and preventive actions would be costly. Are the managers ethically bound to reduce pollution? Similarly, suppose a medical products company's own research indicates that one of its new products may cause problems. However, the evidence is relatively weak, other evidence regarding benefits to patients is strong, and independent government tests show no adverse effects. Should the company make the potential problem known to the public? If it does release the negative (but questionable) information, this will hurt sales and profits, and possibly keep some patients who would benefit from the new product from using it. There are no obvious answers to questions such as these, but companies must deal with them on a regular basis, and a failure to handle the situation properly can lead to huge product liability suits, which could push a firm into bankruptcy.

How would you define "business ethics"?

Is "being ethical" good for profits in the long run? In the short run?

AGENCY RELATIONSHIPS

It has long been recognized that managers may have personal goals that compete with shareholder wealth maximization. Managers are empowered by the owners of the firm — the shareholders — to make decisions, and that creates a potential conflict of interest known as *agency theory*.

An *agency relationship* arises whenever one or more individuals, called *principals*, hire another individual or organization, called an *agent*, to perform some service and delegate decision-making authority to that agent. In financial management, the primary agency relationships are those between (1) stockholders and managers and (2) managers and debtholders.[6]

STOCKHOLDERS VERSUS MANAGERS

Agency Problem
A potential conflict of interests between the agent (manager) and (1) the outside stockholders or (2) the creditors (debtholders).

A potential **agency problem** arises whenever the manager of a firm owns less than 100 percent of the firm's common stock. If the firm is a proprietorship managed by its owner, the owner-manager will presumably operate so as to maximize his or her own welfare, with welfare measured in the form of increased personal wealth, more leisure, or perquisites.[7] However, if the owner-manager incorporates and then sells some of the stock to outsiders, a potential conflict of interests immediately arises. Now the owner-manager may decide to lead a more relaxed lifestyle and not work as strenuously to maximize shareholder wealth, because less of this wealth will accrue to him or her. Also, the owner-manager may decide to consume more perquisites, because some of those costs will be borne by the outside shareholders. In essence, the fact that the owner-manager will neither gain all the benefits of the wealth created by his or her efforts nor bear all of the costs of perquisites will increase the incentive to take actions that are not in the best interests of other shareholders.

In most large corporations, potential agency conflicts are important, because large firms' managers generally own only a small percentage of the stock. In this situation, shareholder wealth maximization could take a back seat to any number of conflicting managerial goals. For example, people have argued that some managers' primary goal seems to be to maximize the size of their firms. By creating a large, rapidly growing firm, managers (1) increase their job security, because a hostile takeover is less likely; (2) increase their

---

[6] The classic work on the application of agency theory to financial management was by Michael C. Jensen and William H. Meckling, "Theory of the Firm, Managerial Behavior, Agency Costs, and Ownership Structure," *Journal of Financial Economics*, October 1976, 305–360.

[7] *Perquisites* are fringe benefits such as luxurious offices, executive assistants, expense accounts, limousines, corporate jets, generous retirement plans, and the like.

INDUSTRY | PRACTICE

ARE CEOs OVERPAID?

Business Week's annual survey of executive compensation recently reported that the average large-company CEO made $12.4 million in 1999, up from $2 million in 1990. This dramatic increase can be attributed to the fact that CEOs increasingly receive most of their compensation in the form of stock and stock options, which skyrocketed in value because of a strong stock market in the 1990s.

Heading the pack on the *Business Week* list was Computer Associates International Inc.'s Charles Wang, who in 1999 made $655.4 million, mostly from stock options. Rounding out the top five were L. Dennis Kozlowski of Tyco International ($170.0 million), David Pottruck of Charles Schwab ($127.9 million), John Chambers of Cisco Systems ($121.7 million), and Stephen Case of America Online ($117.0 million). It is worth noting that these payouts occurred in large part because the executives exercised stock options granted in earlier years. Thus, their 1999 reported compensation overstated their average compensation over time. More importantly, note that their stock options provided these CEOs with an incentive to raise their companies' stock prices. Indeed, most observers believe there is a strong causal relationship between CEO compensation procedures and stock price performance.

However, some critics argue that although performance incentives are entirely appropriate as a method of compensation, the overall level of CEO compensation is just too high. The critics ask such questions as these: Would these CEOs have been unwilling to take their jobs if they had been offered only half as many stock options? Would they have put forth less effort, and would their firms' stock prices have not gone up as much? It is hard to say. Other critics lament that the exercise of stock options has dramatically increased the compensation of not only truly excellent CEOs, but it has also dramatically increased the compensation of some pretty average CEOs, who were lucky enough to have had the job during a stock market boom that raised the stock prices of even companies with rather poor performance. Another problem is that the huge CEO salaries are widening the gap between top executives and middle manager salaries. This is leading to employee discontent and a decrease in employee morale and loyalty.

own power, status, and salaries; and (3) create more opportunities for their lower- and middle-level managers. Furthermore, since the managers of most large firms own only a small percentage of the stock, it has been argued that they have a voracious appetite for salaries and perquisites, and that they generously contribute corporate dollars to their favorite charities because they get the glory but outside stockholders bear the cost.[8]

Managers can be encouraged to act in stockholders' best interests through incentives that reward them for good performance but punish them for poor performance. Some specific mechanisms used to motivate managers to act in shareholders' best interests include (1) managerial compensation, (2) direct intervention by shareholders, (3) the threat of firing, and (4) the threat of takeover.

1. **Managerial compensation.** Managers obviously must be compensated, and the structure of the compensation package can and should be designed to meet two primary objectives: (a) to attract and retain able managers and (b) to align managers' actions as closely as possible with the

---

[8] An excellent article that reviews the effectiveness of various mechanisms for aligning managerial and shareholder interests is Andrei Shleifer and Robert Vishny, "A Survey of Corporate Governance," *Journal of Finance*, June 1997, 737–783. Another paper that looks at managerial stockholding worldwide is Rafael La Porta, Florencio Lopez-De-Silanes, and Andrei Shleifer, "Corporate Ownership Around the World," *Journal of Finance*, April 1999, 471–517.

interests of stockholders, who are primarily interested in stock price maximization. Different companies follow different compensation practices, but a typical senior executive's compensation is structured in three parts: (a) a specified annual salary, which is necessary to meet living expenses; (b) a bonus paid at the end of the year, which depends on the company's profitability during the year; and (c) options to buy stock, or actual shares of stock, which reward the executive for long-term performance.

Performance Shares
Stock that is awarded to executives on the basis of the company's performance.

Managers are more likely to focus on maximizing stock prices if they are themselves large shareholders. Often, companies grant senior managers **performance shares,** where the executive receives a number of shares dependent upon the company's actual performance and the executive's continued service. For example, in 1991 Coca-Cola granted one million shares of stock worth $81 million to its CEO at the time, the late Roberto Goizueta. The award was based on Coke's performance under Goizueta's leadership, but it also stipulated that Goizueta would receive the shares only if he stayed with the company for the remainder of his career.

Executive Stock Option
An option to buy stock at a stated price within a specified time period that is granted to an executive as part of his or her compensation package.

Most large corporations also provide **executive stock options,** which allow managers to purchase stock at some future time at a given price. Obviously, a manager who has an option to buy, say, 10,000 shares of stock at a price of $10 during the next 5 years will have an incentive to help raise the stock's value to an amount greater than $10.

The number of performance shares or options awarded is generally based on objective criteria. Years ago, the primary criteria were accounting measures such as earnings per share (EPS) and return on equity (ROE). Today, though, the focus is more on the market value of the firm's shares or, better yet, on the performance of its shares relative to other stocks in its industry. Various procedures are used to structure compensation programs, and good programs are relatively complicated. Still, it has been thoroughly established that a well-designed compensation program can do wonders to improve a company's financial performance.

2. **Direct intervention by shareholders.** Years ago most stock was owned by individuals, but today the majority is owned by institutional investors such as insurance companies, pension funds, and mutual funds. Therefore, the institutional money managers have the clout, if they choose to use it, to exercise considerable influence over most firms' operations. First, they can talk with a firm's management and make suggestions regarding how the business should be run. In effect, institutional investors act as lobbyists for the body of stockholders. Second, any shareholder who has owned at least $2,000 of a company's stock for one year can sponsor a proposal that must be voted on at the annual stockholders' meeting, even if the proposal is opposed by management. Although shareholder-sponsored proposals are nonbinding and are limited to issues outside of day-to-day operations, the results of such votes are clearly heard by top management.[9]

3. **The threat of firing.** Until recently, the probability of a large firm's management being ousted by its stockholders was so remote that it posed

---

[9] A recent article that provides a detailed investigation of shareholder proposals during 1997 is Cynthia J. Campbell, Stuart L. Gillan, and Cathy M. Niden, "Current Perspectives on Shareholder Proposals: Lessons from the 1997 Proxy Season," *Financial Management,* Spring 1999, 89–98.

little threat. This situation existed because the shares of most firms were so widely distributed, and management's control over the voting mechanism was so strong, that it was almost impossible for dissident stockholders to get the votes needed to overthrow a management team. However, as noted above, that situation is changing.

Consider the case of Eckhard Pfeiffer, who recently lost his job as CEO of Compaq Computer Corporation. Under Pfeiffer's leadership, Compaq became the world's largest computer manufacturer. However, the company has struggled in recent years to maintain profitability in a time of rapidly falling computer prices. Soon after Compaq announced another sub-par quarterly earnings report for the first quarter of 1999, the board of directors told Pfeiffer that they wanted new leadership. Pfeiffer resigned the following day.

Indeed, in recent years the top executives at Mattel, Coca-Cola, Lucent, Gillette, Procter & Gamble, Maytag, and Xerox have resigned or been fired after serving as CEO only a short period of time. Most of these departures were no doubt due to their companies' poor performance.

Hostile Takeover
The acquisition of a company over the opposition of its management.

4. **The threat of takeovers. Hostile takeovers** (when management does not want the firm to be taken over) are most likely to occur when a firm's stock is undervalued relative to its potential because of poor management. In a hostile takeover, the managers of the acquired firm are generally fired, and any who manage to stay on lose status and authority. Thus, managers have a strong incentive to take actions designed to maximize stock prices. In the words of one company president, "If you want to keep your job, don't let your stock sell at a bargain price."

STOCKHOLDERS (THROUGH MANAGERS) VERSUS CREDITORS

In addition to conflicts between stockholders and managers, there can also be conflicts between creditors and stockholders. Creditors have a claim on part of the firm's earnings stream for payment of interest and principal on the debt, and they have a claim on the firm's assets in the event of bankruptcy. However, stockholders have control (through the managers) of decisions that affect the profitability and risk of the firm. Creditors lend funds at rates that are based on (1) the riskiness of the firm's existing assets, (2) expectations concerning the riskiness of future asset additions, (3) the firm's existing capital structure (that is, the amount of debt financing used), and (4) expectations concerning future capital structure decisions. These are the primary determinants of the riskiness of a firm's cash flows, hence the safety of its debt issues.

Now suppose stockholders, acting through management, cause a firm to take on a large new project that is far riskier than was anticipated by the creditors. This increased risk will cause the required rate of return on the firm's debt to increase, and that will cause the value of the outstanding debt to fall. If the risky project is successful, all the benefits go to the stockholders, because creditors' returns are fixed at the old, low-risk rate. However, if the project is unsuccessful, the bondholders may have to share in the losses. From the stockholders' point of view, this amounts to a game of "heads I win, tails you lose," which is obviously not good for the creditors. Similarly, suppose its managers borrow additional funds and use the proceeds to repurchase some of the firm's outstanding stock in an effort to "leverage up" stockholders' return on equity. The value of the debt will probably decrease, because more debt will have a claim against the firm's cash flows and assets. In both the riskier asset and the increased leverage situations, stockholders tend to gain at the expense of creditors.

Can and should stockholders, through their managers/agents, try to expropriate wealth from creditors? In general, the answer is no, for unethical behavior is penalized in the business world. First, creditors attempt to protect themselves against stockholders by placing restrictive covenants in debt agreements. Moreover, if creditors perceive that a firm's managers are trying to take advantage of them, they will either refuse to deal further with the firm or else will charge a higher-than-normal interest rate to compensate for the risk of possible exploitation. Thus, firms that deal unfairly with creditors either lose access to the debt markets or are saddled with high interest rates and restrictive covenants, all of which are detrimental to shareholders.

In view of these constraints, it follows that to best serve their shareholders in the long run, managers must play fairly with creditors. As agents of both shareholders and creditors, managers must act in a manner that is fairly balanced between the interests of the two classes of security holders. Similarly, because of other constraints and sanctions, management actions that would expropriate wealth from any of the firm's other *stakeholders*, including its employees, customers, suppliers, and community, will ultimately be to the detriment of its shareholders. In our society, stock price maximization requires fair treatment for all parties whose economic positions are affected by managerial decisions.

SELF-TEST QUESTIONS

What are agency costs, and who bears them?

What are some mechanisms that encourage managers to act in the best interests of stockholders? To not take advantage of bondholders?

Why should managers not take actions that are unfair to any of the firm's stakeholders?

MANAGERIAL ACTIONS TO MAXIMIZE SHAREHOLDER WEALTH

What types of actions can managers take to maximize the price of a firm's stock? To answer this question, we first need to ask, "What factors determine the price of a company's stock?" While we will address this issue in detail in

Chapter 9, we can lay out three basic facts here. (1) Any financial asset, including a company's stock, is valuable only to the extent that the asset generates cash flows. (2) The timing of the cash flows matters—cash received sooner is better, because it can be reinvested to produce additional income. (3) Investors are generally averse to risk, so all else equal, they will pay more for a stock whose cash flows are relatively certain than for one with relatively risky cash flows. Because of these three factors, managers can enhance their firms' value (and the stock price) by increasing expected cash flows, speeding them up, and reducing their riskiness.

Within the firm, managers make investment decisions regarding the types of products or services produced, as well as the way goods and services are produced and delivered. Also, managers must decide *how to finance the firm*—what mix of debt and equity should be used, and what specific types of debt and equity securities should be issued? In addition, the financial manager must decide what percentage of current earnings to pay out as dividends rather than retain and reinvest; this is called the **dividend policy decision.** Each of these investment and financing decisions is likely to affect the level, timing, and riskiness of the firm's cash flows, and therefore the price of its stock. Naturally, managers should make investment and financing decisions designed to maximize the firm's stock price.

Although managerial actions affect the value of a firm's stock, stock prices are also affected by such external factors as legal constraints, the general level of economic activity, tax laws, interest rates, and conditions in the stock market. Figure 1-2 diagrams these general relationships. Working within the set of external constraints shown in the box at the extreme left, management makes a set of long-run strategic policy decisions that chart a future course for the firm. These policy decisions, along with the general level of economic activity and the level of corporate income taxes, influence the firm's expected cash flows, their timing, their eventual payment to stockholders as dividends, and their

Dividend Policy Decision
The decision as to how much of current earnings to pay out as dividends rather than retain for reinvestment in the firm.

FIGURE 1-2   **Summary of Major Factors Affecting Stock Prices**

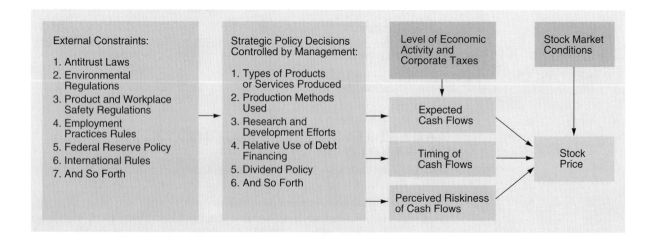

---

riskiness. These factors all affect the price of the stock, but so does another factor, conditions in the stock market as a whole.

SELF-TEST QUESTION

Identify some factors beyond a firm's control that influence its stock price.

DOES IT MAKE SENSE TO TRY TO MAXIMIZE EARNINGS PER SHARE?

Profit Maximization
The maximization of the firm's net income.

Earnings Per Share (EPS)
Net income divided by the number of shares of common stock outstanding.

In arguing that managers should take steps to maximize the firm's stock price, we have said nothing about the traditional objective, **profit maximization,** or the maximization of **earnings per share (EPS).** However, while a growing number of analysts rely on cash flow projections to assess performance, at least as much attention is still paid to accounting measures, especially EPS. The traditional accounting performance measures are appealing because (1) they are easy to use and understand; (2) they are calculated on the basis of more or less standardized accounting practices, which reflect the accounting profession's best efforts to measure financial performance on a consistent basis both across firms and over time; and (3) net income is supposed to be reflective of the firm's potential to produce cash flows over time.

Generally, there is a high correlation between EPS, cash flow, and stock price, and all of them generally rise if a firm's sales rise. Nevertheless, as we will see in subsequent chapters, stock prices depend not just on today's earnings and cash flows—future cash flows and the riskiness of the future earnings stream also affect stock prices. Some actions may increase earnings and yet reduce stock price, while other actions may boost stock price but reduce earnings. For example, consider a company that undertakes large expenditures today that are designed to improve future performance. These expenditures will likely reduce earnings per share, yet the stock market may respond positively if it believes that these expenditures will significantly enhance future earnings. By contrast, a company that undertakes actions today to enhance its earnings may see a drop in its stock price, if the market believes that these actions compromise future earnings and/or dramatically increase the firm's risk.

Even though the level and riskiness of current and future cash flows ultimately determine stockholder value, financial managers cannot ignore the effects of their decisions on reported EPS, because earnings announcements send messages to investors. Say, for example, a manager makes a decision that will ultimately enhance cash flows and stock price, yet the short-run effect is to lower this year's profitability and EPS. Such a decision might be a change in inventory accounting policy that increases reported expenses but also increases cash flow because it reduces current taxes. In this case, it makes sense for the manager to adopt the policy because it generates additional cash, even though it reduces reported profits. Note, though, that management must communicate the reason for the earnings decline, for otherwise the company's stock price will probably decline after the lower earnings are reported.

Is profit maximization an appropriate goal for financial managers?

Should financial managers concentrate strictly on cash flow and ignore the impact of their decisions on EPS?

ORGANIZATION OF THE BOOK

The primary goal of all managers is to maximize the value of the firm. To achieve this goal, all managers must have a general understanding of how businesses are organized, how financial markets operate, how interest rates are determined, how the tax system operates, and how accounting data are used to evaluate a business's performance. In addition, managers must have a good understanding of such fundamental concepts as the time value of money, risk measurement, asset valuation, and evaluation of specific investment opportunities. This background information is essential for *anyone* involved with the kinds of decisions that affect the value of a firm's securities.

The organization of this book reflects these considerations, so the five chapters of Part I present some important background material. Chapter 1 discusses the goals of the firm and the "philosophy" of financial management. Chapter 2 describes the key financial statements, discusses what they are designed to do, and then explains how our tax system affects earnings, cash flows, stock prices, and managerial decisions. Chapter 3 shows how financial statements are analyzed, while Chapter 4 develops techniques for forecasting financial statements. Chapter 5 discusses how financial markets operate and how interest rates are determined.

Part II considers two of the most fundamental concepts in financial management. First, Chapter 6 explains how risk is measured and how it affects security prices and rates of return. Next, Chapter 7 discusses the time value of money and its effects on asset values and rates of return.

Part III covers the valuation of stocks and bonds. Chapter 8 focuses on bonds, and Chapter 9 considers stocks. Both chapters describe the relevant institutional details, then explain how risk and time value jointly determine stock and bond prices.

Part IV, "Investing in Long-Term Assets: Capital Budgeting," applies the concepts covered in earlier chapters to decisions related to fixed asset investments. First, Chapter 10 explains how to measure the cost of the funds used to acquire assets, or the cost of capital. Next, Chapter 11 shows how this information is used to evaluate potential capital investments by answering this question: Can we expect a project to provide a higher rate of return than the cost of the funds used to finance it? Only if the expected return exceeds the cost of capital will accepting a project increase stockholders' wealth. Chapter 12 goes into more detail on capital budgeting decisions, looking at relevant cash flows, new (expansion) projects, and project risk analysis.

Part V discusses how firms should finance their long-term assets. First, Chapter 13 examines capital structure theory, or the issue of how much debt versus equity the firm should use. Then, Chapter 14 considers dividend policy, or the decision to retain earnings versus paying them out as dividends.

In Part VI, our focus shifts from long-term, strategic decisions to short-term, day-to-day operating decisions and multinational financial management. In Chapter 15, we see how cash, inventories, and accounts receivable are managed and the best way of financing these current assets. Chapter 16 discusses multinational financial management issues such as exchange rates, exchange rate risk, and political risk.

It is worth noting that some instructors may choose to cover the chapters in a different sequence from their order in the book. The chapters are written to a large extent in a modular, self-contained manner, so such reordering should present no major difficulties.

TYING IT ALL TOGETHER

This chapter has provided an overview of financial management. The key concepts covered are listed below.

- Finance consists of three interrelated areas: (1) **money and capital markets,** (2) **investments,** and (3) **financial management.**

- In recent years the two most important trends in finance have been the **increased globalization of business** and the growing use of **computers and information technology.** These trends are likely to continue in the future.

- The **financial staff's** task is to **obtain** and **use funds** so as to **maximize the value of the firm.**

- The three main forms of business organization are the **sole proprietorship,** the **partnership,** and the **corporation.**

- Although each form of organization offers advantages and disadvantages, **most business is conducted by corporations because this organizational form maximizes larger firms' values.**

- The primary goal of management should be to **maximize stockholders' wealth,** and this means **maximizing the firm's stock price.** Note, though, that actions that maximize stock prices also increase social welfare.

- An **agency problem** is a potential conflict of interests that can arise between a principal and an agent. Two important agency relationships are (1) those between the owners of the firm and its management and (2) those between the managers, acting for stockholders, and the debtholders.

- There are a number of ways to **motivate managers to act in the best interests of stockholders,** including (1) properly structured **managerial compensation,** (2) **direct intervention by stockholders,** (3) the **threat of firing,** and (4) the **threat of takeovers.**

- The **price of a firm's stock** depends on the **cash flows paid to shareholders,** the **timing of the cash flows,** and their **riskiness.** The level and riskiness of cash flows are affected by the **financial environment** as well as by **investment, financing,** and **dividend policy decisions** made by financial managers.

QUESTIONS

1-1 What are the three principal forms of business organization? What are the advantages and disadvantages of each?

1-2 Would the "normal" rate of return on investment be the same in all industries? Would "normal" rates of return change over time? Explain.

1-3 Would the role of a financial manager be likely to increase or decrease in importance relative to other executives if the rate of inflation increased? Explain.

1-4 Should stockholder wealth maximization be thought of as a long-term or a short-term goal — for example, if one action would probably increase the firm's stock price from a current level of $20 to $25 in 6 months and then to $30 in 5 years but another action would probably keep the stock at $20 for several years but then increase it to $40 in 5 years, which action would be better? Can you think of some specific corporate actions that might have these general tendencies?

1-5 Drawing on your background in accounting, can you think of any accounting differences that might make it difficult to compare the relative performance of different firms?

1-6 Would the management of a firm in an oligopolistic or in a competitive industry be more likely to engage in what might be called "socially conscious" practices? Explain your reasoning.

1-7 What's the difference between stock price maximization and profit maximization? Under what conditions might profit maximization *not* lead to stock price maximization?

1-8 If you were the president of a large, publicly owned corporation, would you make decisions to maximize stockholders' welfare or your own personal interests? What are some actions stockholders could take to ensure that management's interests and those of stockholders coincided? What are some other factors that might influence management's actions?

1-9 The president of Southern Semiconductor Corporation (SSC) made this statement in the company's annual report: "SSC's primary goal is to increase the value of the common stockholders' equity over time." Later on in the report, the following announcements were made:
  a. The company contributed $1.5 million to the symphony orchestra in Birmingham, Alabama, its headquarters city.
  b. The company is spending $500 million to open a new plant in Mexico. No revenues will be produced by the plant for 4 years, so earnings will be depressed during this period versus what they would have been had the decision not been made to open the new plant.
  c. The company is increasing its relative use of debt. Whereas assets were formerly financed with 35 percent debt and 65 percent equity, henceforth the financing mix will be 50-50.
  d. The company uses a great deal of electricity in its manufacturing operations, and it generates most of this power itself. Plans are to utilize nuclear fuel rather than coal to produce electricity in the future.
  e. The company has been paying out half of its earnings as dividends and retaining the other half. Henceforth, it will pay out only 30 percent as dividends.
  Discuss how each of these actions would be reacted to by SSC's stockholders and customers, and then how each action might affect SSC's stock price.

1-10 Assume that you are serving on the board of directors of a medium-sized corporation and that you are responsible for establishing the compensation policies of senior management. You believe that the company's CEO is very talented, but your concern is that she is always looking for a better job and may want to boost the company's short-run performance (perhaps at the expense of long-run profitability) to make herself more marketable to other corporations. What effect would these concerns have on the compensation policy you put in place?

1-11   If the overall stock market is extremely volatile, and if many analysts foresee the possibility of a stock market crash, how might these factors influence the way corporations choose to compensate their senior executives?

1-12   Teacher's Insurance and Annuity Association–College Retirement Equity Fund (TIAA–CREF) is the largest institutional shareholder in the United States. Traditionally, TIAA–CREF has acted as a passive investor. However, TIAA–CREF announced a tough new corporate governance policy begninning October 5, 1993.

In a statement mailed to all 1,500 companies in which it invests, TIAA–CREF outlined a policy designed to improve corporate performance, including a goal of higher stock prices for the $52 billion in stock assets it holds, and to encourage corporate boards to have a majority of independent (outside) directors. TIAA–CREF wants to see management more accountable to shareholder interests, as evidenced by its statement that the fund will vote against any director "where companies don't have an effective, independent board which can challenge the CEO."

Historically, TIAA–CREF did not quickly sell poor-performing stocks. In addition, the fund invested a large part of its assets to match performance of the major market indexes locking TIAA–CREF into ownership of certain companies. Further complicating the problem, TIAA–CREF owns stakes of from 1 percent to 10 percent in several companies, and selling such large blocks of stock would depress their prices.

Common stock ownership confers a right to sponsor initiatives to shareholders regarding the corporation. A corresponding voting right exists for shareholders.
a. Is TIAA–CREF an ordinary shareholder?
b. Due to its asset size, TIAA–CREF assumes large positions with which it plans to actively vote. However, who owns TIAA–CREF?
c. Should the investment managers of a fund like TIAA–CREF determine the voting practices of the fund's shares, or should the voting rights be passed on to TIAA–CREF's stakeholders?

1-13   The senior managers of Hancock Oil are evaluating a new oil exploration project. The project requires a large amount of capital and is quite risky, but it has the possibility of being extremely profitable. In a separate action, the company's managers are also considering increasing Hancock's dividend payout ratio. The proposed project and proposed dividend increase are both expected to increase the company's stock price.
a. How would the proposed exploration project affect Hancock's outstanding bondholders?
b. How would the proposed dividend increase affect Hancock's outstanding bondholders?
c. Should Hancock's managers go ahead with the proposed project and dividend increase?
d. What steps can bondholders take to protect themselves against managerial decisions that reduce the value of their bonds?

1-14   Stewart Web Design currently operates an unincorporated partnership with 75 employees. The partners are contemplating organizing as a corporation. How might each of the following actions affect the firm's decision to incorporate?
a. Congress is considering a tax bill that would reduce individual tax rates but increase corporate tax rates.
b. Congress is considering a bill that would extend the coverage of a large number of environmental and labor regulations to now include companies that have more than 50 employees. Presently, companies with fewer than 200 employees are excluded from these regulations.

1-15   Edmund Enterprises recently made a large investment in upgrading its technology. While the technology improvements will not have much of an impact on performance in the short run, they are expected to produce significant cost savings over the next several years. What impact will this investment have on Edmund Enterprises' earnings per share this year? What impact might this investment have on the company's stock price?

ST-1

Key terms

Define each of the following terms:
a. Sole proprietorship; partnership; corporation
b. Limited partnership; limited liability partnership; professional corporation
c. Stockholder wealth maximization
d. Social responsibility; business ethics
e. Normal profits; normal rate of return
f. Agency problem
g. Performance shares; executive stock options
h. Hostile takeover
i. Profit maximization
j. Earnings per share
k. Dividend policy decision

CYBER PROBLEM

The information related to the cyberproblems is likely to change over time, due to the release of new information and the ever-changing nature of the World Wide Web. With these changes in mind, we will periodically update these problems on the textbook's web site. To avoid problems, please check for these updates before proceeding with the cyberproblems.

1-1

Overview of financial management

Management's primary goal is to maximize stockholder wealth. Firms often award stock options and bonuses on the basis of management performance, thus linking management's personal wealth with the firm's financial performance. The better the job managers do in maximizing share price, the greater their compensation.

Walt Disney's CEO, Michael Eisner, draws a compensation package in part based on the net income and return on shareholder equity of The Walt Disney Company. In 1994, he attracted a lot of attention when he exercised stock options on 5.4 million Disney shares for a net profit (after taxes and brokerage expenses) of around $127

million. At the time, he had also earned another 8 million stock options, then valued at about $161 million. Year after year, Eisner ranks among the most highly compensated CEOs in America. In 1999, Michael Eisner's total compensation from Walt Disney Co. totaled $50.7 million in salary and exercised stock options.

Let's see if Mr. Eisner deserves such generous bonuses and stock options. Look at Disney's 1999 Annual Report on the web at **http://disney.go.com/investors/annual99/index.html** to answer the following questions:

a. Click on the page and then click on Financial Review. Describe how Disney's three main business segments have been divided into five distinct operating segments. What percentage of operating income did each contribute to the firm?

b. If on November 30, 1984, you invested $1,000 in Disney stock and reinvested all your dividends, how much would you have had on November 30, 1999?

c. How does the compound annual return on your Disney stock during this 15-year period compare to the return earned on the S&P 500 during this same period?

d. If you had purchased 100 shares of Disney stock for $2,500 in the company's initial public offering 59 years ago and had purchased no additional Disney shares, how many shares would you have, and how much would they be worth, as of November 30, 1999?

e. What is the compound annual growth rate of the stock's value over this 59-year period?

f. On the basis of the company's performance through 1999, do you think that Mr. Eisner and his management team have done a good job? Has this impression changed based on the company's recent performance?

INTEGRATED CASE

TAKE A DIVE

1-2 Financial Management Overview Kato Summers opened Take A Dive 17 years ago; the store is located in Malibu, California, and sells surfing-related equipment. Today, Take a Dive has 50 employees including Kato and his daughter Amber, who works part time in the store to help pay for her college education.

Kato's business has boomed in recent years, and he is looking for new ways to take advantage of his increasing business opportunities. Although Kato's formal business training is limited, Amber will soon graduate with a degree in finance. Kato has offered her the opportunity to join the business as a full-fledged partner. Amber is interested, but she is also considering other career opportunities in finance.

Right now, Amber is leaning toward staying with the family business, partly because she thinks it faces a number of interesting challenges and opportunities. Amber is particularly interested in further expanding the business and then incorporating it. Kato is intrigued by her ideas, but he is also concerned that her plans might change the way in which he does business. In particular, Kato has a strong commitment to social activism, and he has always tried to strike a balance between work and pleasure. He is worried that these goals will be compromised if the company incorporates and brings in outside shareholders.

Amber and Kato plan to take a long weekend off to sit down and think about all of these issues. Amber, who is highly organized, has outlined a series of questions for them to address:

a. What kinds of career opportunities are open to finance majors?

b. What are the primary responsibilities of a corporate financial staff?

c. What are the most important financial management issues today?

d. (1) What are the alternative forms of business organization?
   (2) What are their advantages and disadvantages?

e. What is the primary goal of the corporation?
   (1) Do firms have any responsibilities to society at large?
   (2) Is stock price maximization good or bad for society?
   (3) Should firms behave ethically?

f. What is an agency relationship?
   (1) What agency relationships exist within a corporation?
   (2) What mechanisms exist to influence managers to act in shareholders' best interests?
   (3) Should shareholders (through managers) take actions that are detrimental to bondholders?

g. Is maximizing stock price the same thing as maximizing profit?

h. What factors affect stock prices?

i. What factors affect the level and riskiness of cash flows?

2

Financial Statements, Cash Flow, and Taxes

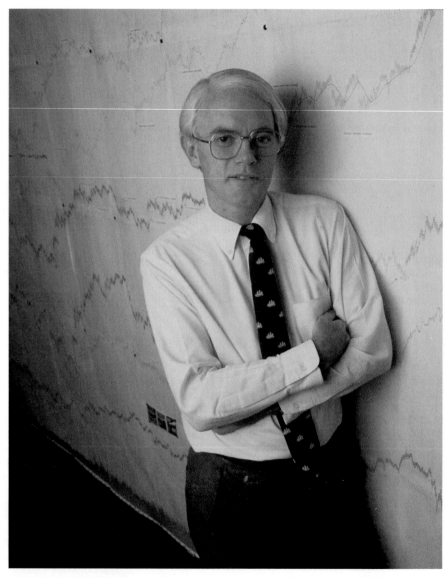

SOURCE: © Bill O'Connell/Black Star

DOING YOUR HOMEWORK WITH FINANCIAL STATEMENTS

$

Suppose you are a small investor who knows a little about finance and accounting. Could you compete successfully against large institutional investors with armies of analysts, high-powered computers, and state-of-the-art trading strategies?

The answer, according to one Wall Street legend, is a resounding yes! Peter Lynch, who had an outstanding track record as manager of the $10 billion Fidelity Magellan fund and then went on to become the best-selling author of *One Up on Wall Street* and *Beating the Street,* has long argued that small investors can beat the market by using common sense and information available to all of us as we go about our day-to-day lives.

For example, a college student may be more adept at scouting out the new and interesting products that will become tomorrow's success stories than is an investment banker who works 75 hours a week in a New York office. Parents of young children are likely to know which baby foods will succeed, or which diapers are best. Couch potatoes may have the best feel for which tortilla chips have the brightest future, or whether a new remote control is worth its price.

The trick is to find a product that will boom, yet whose manufacturer's stock is undervalued. If this sounds too easy, you are right. Lynch argues that once you have discovered a good product, there is still much homework to be done. This involves combing through the vast amount of financial information that is regularly provided by companies. It also requires taking a closer and more critical look at how the company conducts its business — Lynch refers to this as "kicking the tires."

To illustrate his point, Lynch relates his experience with Dunkin' Donuts. As a consumer, Lynch was impressed with the quality of the product. This impression led him to take a closer look at the company's financial statements and operations. He liked what he saw, and Dunkin' Donuts became one of the best investments in his portfolio.

The next two chapters discuss what financial statements are and how they are analyzed. Once you have identified a good product as a possible investment, the principles discussed in these chapters will help you "kick the tires." ■

A manager's primary goal is to maximize the value of his or her firm's stock. Value is based on the stream of cash flows the firm will generate in the future. But how does an investor go about estimating future cash flows, and how does a manager decide which actions are most likely to increase cash flows? The answers to both questions lie in a study of the financial statements that publicly traded firms must provide to investors. Here "investors" include both institutions (banks, insurance companies, pension funds, and the like) and individuals. Thus, this chapter begins with a discussion of what the basic financial statements are, how they are used, and what kinds of financial information users need.

The value of any business asset — whether it is a *financial asset* such as a stock or a bond, or a *real (physical) asset* such as land, buildings, and equipment — depends on the usable, after-tax cash flows the asset is expected to produce. Therefore, the chapter also explains the difference between accounting income and cash flow. Finally, since it is *after-tax* cash flow that is important, the chapter provides an overview of the federal income tax system.

Much of the material in this chapter reviews concepts covered in basic accounting courses. However, the information is important enough to go over again. Accounting is used to "keep score," and if a firm's managers do not know the score, they won't know if their actions are appropriate. If you took midterm exams but were not told how you were doing, you would have a difficult time improving your grades. The same thing holds in business. If a firm's managers — whether they are in marketing, personnel, production, or finance — do not understand financial statements, they will not be able to judge the effects of their actions, and the firm will not be successful. Although only accountants need to know how to *make* financial statements, everyone involved with business needs to know how to *interpret* them. ∎

A BRIEF HISTORY OF ACCOUNTING AND FINANCIAL STATEMENTS

Are you interested in learning more about the history of accounting? If so, take a tour through the "Virtual History of Accounting" organized by the Association of Chartered Accountants in the United States and located at **http://www.acaus.org/history/index.html.**

Financial statements are pieces of paper with numbers written on them, but it is important to also think about the real assets that underlie the numbers. If you understand how and why accounting began, and how financial statements are used, you can better visualize what is going on, and why accounting information is so important.

Thousands of years ago, individuals (or families) were self-contained in the sense that they gathered their own food, made their own clothes, and built their own shelters. Then specialization began — some people became good at making pots, others at making arrowheads, others at making clothing, and so on.

As specialization began, so did trading, initially in the form of barter. At first, each artisan worked alone, and trade was strictly local. Eventually, though, master craftsmen set up small factories and employed workers, money (in the form of clamshells) began to be used, and trade expanded beyond the local area. As these developments occurred, a primitive form of banking began, with wealthy merchants lending profits from past dealings to enterprising factory owners who needed capital to expand or to young traders who needed money to buy wagons, ships, and merchandise.

When the first loans were made, lenders could physically inspect borrowers' assets and judge the likelihood of the loan's being repaid. Eventually, though, lending became more complex — borrowers were developing larger factories, traders were acquiring fleets of ships and wagons, and loans were being made to develop distant mines and trading posts. At that point, lenders could no longer personally inspect the assets that backed their loans, and they needed some way of summarizing borrowers' assets. Also, some investments were made on a share-of-the-profits basis, and this meant that profits (or income) had to be determined. At the same time, factory owners and large merchants needed reports to see how effectively their own enterprises were being run, and governments needed information for use in assessing taxes. For all these reasons, a need arose for financial statements, for accountants to prepare those statements, and for auditors to verify the accuracy of the accountants' work.

The economic system has grown enormously since its beginning, and accounting has become more complex. However, the original reasons for financial statements still apply: Bankers and other investors need accounting information to make intelligent decisions, managers need it to operate their businesses efficiently, and taxing authorities need it to assess taxes in a reasonable way.

It should be intuitively clear that it is not easy to translate physical assets into numbers, which is what accountants do when they construct financial statements. The numbers shown on balance sheets generally represent the historical costs of assets. However, inventories may be spoiled, obsolete, or even missing; fixed assets such as machinery and buildings may have higher or lower values than their historical costs; and accounts receivable may be uncollectable. Also, some liabilities such as obligations to pay retirees' medical costs may not even show up on the balance sheet. Similarly, some costs reported on the income statement may be understated, as would be true if a plant with a useful life of 10 years were being depreciated over 40 years. When you examine a set of financial statements, you should keep in mind that a physical reality lies behind the numbers, and you should also realize that the translation from physical assets to "correct" numbers is far from precise.

As mentioned previously, it is important for accountants to be able to generate financial statements, while others involved in the business need to know how to interpret them. Particularly, financial managers must have a working knowledge of financial statements and what they reveal to be effective. Spreadsheets provide financial managers with a powerful and reliable tool to conduct financial analysis, and several different types of spreadsheet models are provided with the text. These models demonstrate how financial principles taught in this book are applied in practice. Readers are encouraged to use these models to gain further insights into various concepts and procedures.

FINANCIAL STATEMENTS AND REPORTS

Annual Report
A report issued annually by a corporation to its stockholders. It contains basic financial statements, as well as management's analysis of the past year's operations and opinions about the firm's future prospects.

For an excellent example of a corporate annual report, take a look at 3M's annual report found at **http://www.mmm.com/about3M/index.jhtml**. Then, click on investor relations and annual reports on the left-hand side of your screen. Here you can find several recent annual reports in Adobe Acrobat format.

Of the various reports corporations issue to their stockholders, the **annual report** is probably the most important. Two types of information are given in this report. First, there is a verbal section, often presented as a letter from the chairman, that describes the firm's operating results during the past year and discusses new developments that will affect future operations. Second, the annual report presents four basic financial statements—the *balance sheet*, the *income statement*, the *statement of retained earnings*, and the *statement of cash flows*. Taken together, these statements give an accounting picture of the firm's operations and financial position. Detailed data are provided for the two or three most recent years, along with historical summaries of key operating statistics for the past 5 or 10 years.[1]

The quantitative and verbal materials are equally important. The financial statements report *what has actually happened* to assets, earnings, and dividends over the past few years, whereas the verbal statements attempt to explain why things turned out the way they did.

For illustrative purposes, we shall use data taken from Allied Food Products, a processor and distributor of a wide variety of staple foods, to discuss the basic financial statements. Formed in 1978 when several regional firms merged, Allied has grown steadily, and it has earned a reputation for being one of the best firms in its industry. Allied's earnings dropped a bit in 2001, to $113.5 million versus $117.8 million in 2000. Management reported that the drop resulted from losses associated with a drought and from increased costs due to a three-month strike. However, management then went on to paint a more optimistic picture for the future, stating that full operations had been resumed, that several unprofitable businesses had been eliminated, and that 2002 profits were expected to rise sharply. Of course, an increase in profitability may not occur, and

---

[1] Firms also provide quarterly reports, but these are much less comprehensive. In addition, larger firms file even more detailed statements, giving breakdowns for each major division or subsidiary, with the Securities and Exchange Commission (SEC). These reports, called *10-K reports*, are made available to stockholders upon request to a company's corporate secretary. Finally, many larger firms also publish *statistical supplements*, which give financial statement data and key ratios going back 10 to 20 years, and their reports are available on the World Wide Web.

analysts should compare management's past statements with subsequent results. In any event, *the information contained in an annual report is used by investors to help form expectations about future earnings and dividends.* Therefore, the annual report is obviously of great interest to investors.

SELF-TEST QUESTIONS

What is the annual report, and what two types of information are given in it?

What four types of financial statements are typically included in the annual report?

Why is the annual report of great interest to investors?

THE BALANCE SHEET

Balance Sheet
A statement of the firm's financial position at a specific point in time.

The left-hand side of Allied's year-end 2001 and 2000 **balance sheets,** which are given in Table 2-1, shows the firm's assets, while the right-hand side shows the liabilities and equity, or the claims against these assets. The assets are listed in order of their "liquidity," or the length of time it typically takes to convert them to cash. The claims are listed in the order in which they must be paid: Accounts payable must generally be paid within 30 days, notes payable within 90

TABLE 2-1	Allied Food Products: December 31 Balance Sheets (Millions of Dollars)				
ASSETS	**2001**	**2000**	**LIABILITIES AND EQUITY**	**2001**	**2000**
Cash and marketable securities	$ 10	$ 80	Accounts payable	$ 60	$ 30
Accounts receivable	375	315	Notes payable	110	60
Inventories	615	415	Accruals	140	130
Total current assets	$1,000	$ 810	Total current liabilities	$ 310	$ 220
Net plant and equipment	1,000	870	Long-term bonds	754	580
			Total debt	$1,064	$ 800
			Preferred stock (400,000 shares)	40	40
			Common stock (50,000,000 shares)	130	130
			Retained earnings	766	710
			Total common equity	$ 896	$ 840
Total assets	$2,000	$1,680	Total liabilities and equity	$2,000	$1,680

NOTE: The bonds have a sinking fund requirement of $20 million a year. Sinking funds are discussed in Chapter 8, but in brief, a sinking fund simply involves the repayment of long-term debt. Thus, Allied was required to pay off $20 million of its mortgage bonds during 2001. The current portion of the long-term debt is included in notes payable here, although in a more detailed balance sheet it would be shown as a separate item under current liabilities.

days, and so on, down to the stockholders' equity accounts, which represent ownership and need never be "paid off."

Some additional points about the balance sheet are worth noting:

1. **Cash versus other assets.** Although the assets are all stated in terms of dollars, only cash represents actual money. (Marketable securities can be converted to cash within a day or two, so they are almost like cash and are reported with cash on the balance sheet.) Receivables are bills others owe Allied. Inventories show the dollars the company has invested in raw materials, work-in-process, and finished goods available for sale. And net plant and equipment reflect the amount of money Allied paid for its fixed assets when it acquired those assets in the past, less accumulated depreciation. Allied can write checks for a total of $10 million (versus current liabilities of $310 million due within a year). The noncash assets should produce cash over time, but they do not represent cash in hand, and the amount of cash they would bring if they were sold today could be higher or lower than the values at which they are carried on the books.

2. **Liabilities versus stockholders' equity.** The claims against assets are of two types — liabilities (or money the company owes) and the stockholders' ownership position.[2] The **common stockholders' equity,** or **net worth,** is a residual. For example, at the end of 2001,

$$\text{Assets} - \text{Liabilities} - \text{Preferred stock} = \frac{\text{Common}}{\text{stockholder's equity}}$$
$$\$2{,}000{,}000{,}000 - \$1{,}064{,}000{,}000 - \$40{,}000{,}000 = \$896{,}000{,}000$$

Suppose assets decline in value; for example, suppose some of the accounts receivable are written off as bad debts. Liabilities and preferred stock remain constant, so the value of the common stockholders' equity must decline. Therefore, the risk of asset value fluctuations is borne by the common stockholders. Note, however, that if asset values rise (perhaps because of inflation), these benefits will accrue exclusively to the common stockholders.

3. **Preferred versus common stock.** Preferred stock is a hybrid, or a cross between common stock and debt. In the event of bankruptcy, preferred stock ranks below debt but above common stock. Also, the preferred dividend is fixed, so preferred stockholders do not benefit if the company's earnings grow. Finally, many firms do not use any preferred stock, and those that do generally do not use much of it. Therefore, when the term "equity" is used in finance, we generally mean "common equity" unless the word "total" is included.

4. **Breakdown of the common equity accounts.** The common equity section is divided into two accounts — "common stock" and "retained earn-

---

Common Stockholders' Equity (Net Worth)
The capital supplied by common stockholders — common stock, paid-in capital, retained earnings, and, occasionally, certain reserves. *Total equity* is common equity plus preferred stock.

---

[2] One could divide liabilities into (1) debts owed to someone and (2) other items, such as deferred taxes, reserves, and so on. Because we do not make this distinction, the terms *debt* and *liabilities* are used synonymously. It should be noted that firms occasionally set up reserves for certain contingencies, such as the potential costs involved in a lawsuit currently in the courts. These reserves represent an accounting transfer from retained earnings to the reserve account. If the company wins the suit, retained earnings will be credited, and the reserve will be eliminated. If it loses, a loss will be recorded, cash will be reduced, and the reserve will be eliminated.

ings." The **retained earnings** account is built up over time as the firm "saves" a part of its earnings rather than paying all earnings out as dividends. The common stock account arises from the issuance of stock to raise capital, as discussed in Chapter 9.

The breakdown of the common equity accounts is important for some purposes but not for others. For example, a potential stockholder would want to know whether the company actually earned the funds reported in its equity accounts or whether the funds came mainly from selling stock. A potential creditor, on the other hand, would be more interested in the total equity the owners have in the firm and would be less concerned with the source of the equity. In the remainder of this chapter, we generally aggregate the two common equity accounts and call this sum *common equity* or *net worth*.

5. **Inventory accounting.** Allied uses the FIFO (first-in, first-out) method to determine the inventory value shown on its balance sheet ($615 million). It could have used the LIFO (last-in, first-out) method. During a period of rising prices, by taking out old, low-cost inventory and leaving in new, high-cost items, FIFO will produce a higher balance sheet inventory value but a lower cost of goods sold on the income statement. (This is strictly accounting; companies actually use older items first.) Since Allied uses FIFO, and since inflation has been occurring, (a) its balance sheet inventories are higher than they would have been had it used LIFO, (b) its cost of goods sold is lower than it would have been under LIFO, and (c) its reported profits are therefore higher. In Allied's case, if the company had elected to switch to LIFO in 2001, its balance sheet figure for inventories would have been $585,000,000 rather than $615,000,000, and its earnings (which will be discussed in the next section) would have been reduced by $18,000,000. Thus, the inventory valuation method can have a significant effect on financial statements. This is important when an analyst is comparing different companies.

6. **Depreciation methods.** Most companies prepare two sets of financial statements — one for tax purposes and one for reporting to stockholders. Generally, they use the most accelerated method permitted under the law to calculate depreciation for tax purposes, but they use straight line, which results in a lower depreciation charge, for stockholder reporting. However, Allied has elected to use rapid depreciation for both stockholder reporting and tax purposes. Had Allied elected to use straight line depreciation for stockholder reporting, its 2001 depreciation expense would have been $25,000,000 less, so the $1 billion shown for "net plant" on its balance sheet would have been $25,000,000 higher. Its net income and its retained earnings would also have been higher.

7. **The time dimension.** The balance sheet may be thought of as a snapshot of the firm's financial position *at a point in time* — for example, on December 31, 2000. Thus, on December 31, 2000, Allied had $80 million of cash and marketable securities, but this account had been reduced to $10 million by the end of 2001. The balance sheet changes every day as inventories are increased or decreased, as fixed assets are added or retired, as bank loans are increased or decreased, and so on. Companies whose businesses are seasonal have especially large changes in their balance sheets. Allied's inventories are low just before the harvest season, but

they are high just after the fall crops have been brought in and processed. Similarly, most retailers have large inventories just before Christmas but low inventories and high accounts receivable just after Christmas. Therefore, firms' balance sheets change over the year, depending on when the statement is constructed.

> **SELF-TEST QUESTIONS**
>
> What is the balance sheet, and what information does it provide?
>
> How is the order of the information shown on the balance sheet determined?
>
> Why might a company's December 31 balance sheet differ from its June 30 balance sheet?

THE INCOME STATEMENT

Income Statement
A statement summarizing the firm's revenues and expenses over an accounting period, generally a quarter or a year.

Depreciation
The charge to reflect the cost of assets used up in the production process. Depreciation is not a cash outlay.

Tangible Assets
Physical assets such as plant and equipment.

Amortization
A noncash charge similar to depreciation except that it is used to write off the costs of intangible assets.

Intangible Assets
Assets such as patents, copyrights, trademarks, and goodwill.

EBITDA
Earnings before interest, taxes, depreciation, and amortization.

Table 2-2 gives the 2001 and 2000 **income statements** for Allied Food Products. Net sales are shown at the top of each statement, after which various costs are subtracted to obtain the net income available to common shareholders, which is generally referred to as net income. These costs include operating costs, interest costs, and taxes. A report on earnings and dividends per share is given at the bottom of the income statement. Earnings per share (EPS) is called "the bottom line," denoting that of all the items on the income statement, EPS is the most important. Allied earned $2.27 per share in 2001, down from $2.36 in 2000, but it still raised the dividend from $1.06 to $1.15.[3]

Taking a closer look at the income statement, we see that depreciation and amortization are important components of total operating costs. Depreciation and amortization are similar in that both represent allocations of the costs of assets over their useful lives; however, there are some important distinctions. Recall from accounting that **depreciation** is an annual charge against income that reflects the estimated dollar cost of the capital equipment used up in the production process. Depreciation applies to **tangible assets,** such as plant and equipment, whereas **amortization** applies to **intangible assets** such as patents, copyrights, trademarks, and goodwill. Some companies use amortization to write off research and development costs, or the accounting goodwill that is recorded when one firm purchases another for more than its book value. Since they are similar, depreciation and amortization are often lumped together on the income statement.

Managers, security analysts, and bank loan officers often calculate **EBITDA,** which is defined as earnings before interest, taxes, depreciation, and amorti-

---

[3] Effective after December 15, 1997, companies must report "comprehensive income" as well as net income. Comprehensive income is equal to net income plus several comprehensive income items. One example of comprehensive income is the unrealized gain or loss that occurs when a marketable security, classified as available for sale, is marked-to-market. For our purposes, in this introductory finance text, we will assume that there are no comprehensive income items, so we will present only basic income statements throughout the text.

TABLE 2-2

Allied Food Products: Income Statements for Years Ending December 31 (Millions of Dollars, Except for Per-Share Data)

	2001	2000
Net sales	$3,000.0	$2,850.0
Operating costs excluding depreciation and amortization	2,616.2	2,497.0
Earnings before interest, taxes, depreciation, and amortization (EBITDA)	$ 383.8	$ 353.0
Depreciation	100.0	90.0
Amortization	0.0	0.0
Depreciation and amortization	$ 100.0	$ 90.0
Earnings before interest and taxes (EBIT, or operating income)	$ 283.8	$ 263.0
Less interest	88.0	60.0
Earnings before taxes (EBT)	$ 195.8	$ 203.0
Taxes (40%)	78.3	81.2
Net income before preferred dividends[b]	$ 117.5	$ 121.8
Preferred dividends	4.0	4.0
Net income	$ 113.5	$ 117.8
Common dividends	$ 57.5	$ 53.0
Addition to retained earnings	$ 56.0	$ 64.8
Per-share data:		
Common stock price	$23.00	$26.00
Earnings per share (EPS)[a]	$ 2.27	$ 2.36
Dividends per share (DPS)[a]	$ 1.15	$ 1.06
Book value per share (BVPS)[a]	$17.92	$16.80
Cash flow per share (CFPS)[a]	$ 4.27	$ 4.16

[a] There are 50,000,000 shares of common stock outstanding. Note that EPS is based on earnings after preferred dividends — that is, on net income available to common stockholders. Calculations of EPS, DPS, BVPS, and CFPS for 2001 are as follows:

$$\text{Earnings per share} = \text{EPS} = \frac{\text{Net income}}{\text{Common shares outstanding}} = \frac{\$113,500,000}{50,000,000} = \$2.27.$$

$$\text{Dividends per share} = \text{DPS} = \frac{\text{Dividends paid to common stockholders}}{\text{Common shares outstanding}} = \frac{\$57,500,000}{50,000,000} = \$1.15.$$

$$\text{Book value per share} = \text{BVPS} = \frac{\text{Total common equity}}{\text{Common shares outstanding}} = \frac{\$896,000,000}{50,000,000} = \$17.92.$$

$$\text{Cash flow per share} = \text{CFPS} = \frac{\text{Net income} + \text{Depreciation} + \text{Amortization}}{\text{Common shares outstanding}} = \frac{\$213,500,000}{50,000,000} = \$4.27.$$

[b] On a typical firm's income statement, this line would be labeled "net income" rather than "net income before preferred dividends." However, when we use the term net income in this text, we mean net income available to common shareholders. To simplify the terminology, we refer to net income available to common shareholders as simply net income. Students should understand that when they review annual reports, firms use the term net income to mean income after taxes but before preferred and common dividends.

zation. Allied currently has no amortization charges, so the depreciation and amortization on its income statement comes solely from depreciation. In 2001, Allied's EBITDA was $383.8 million. Subtracting the $100 million of depreciation expense from its EBITDA leaves the company with $283.8 million in operating income (EBIT). After subtracting $88 million in interest expense and $78.3 million in taxes, we obtain net income before preferred dividends of $117.5 million. Finally, we subtract out $4 million in preferred dividends, which leaves Allied with $113.5 million in net income available to common stockholders. When analysts refer to a company's net income, they generally mean net income available to common shareholders. Likewise, throughout this book unless otherwise indicated, net income means net income available to common stockholders.

While the balance sheet can be thought of as a snapshot in time, the income statement reports on operations *over a period of time*, for example, during the calendar year 2001. During 2001 Allied had sales of $3 billion, and its net income available to common stockholders was $113.5 million. Income statements can cover any period of time, but they are usually prepared monthly, quarterly, or annually. Of course, sales, costs, and profits will be larger the longer the reporting period, and the sum of the last 12 monthly (or 4 quarterly) income statements should equal the values shown on the annual income statement.

For planning and control purposes, management generally forecasts monthly (or perhaps quarterly) income statements, and it then compares actual results to the budgeted statements. If revenues are below and costs above the forecasted levels, then management should take corrective steps before the problem becomes too serious.

SELF-TEST QUESTIONS

What is an income statement, and what information does it provide?

Why is earnings per share called "the bottom line"?

Differentiate between amortization and depreciation.

What is EBITDA?

Regarding the time period reported, how does the income statement differ from the balance sheet?

STATEMENT OF RETAINED EARNINGS

Statement of Retained Earnings
A statement reporting how much of the firm's earnings were retained in the business rather than paid out in dividends. The figure for retained earnings that appears here is the sum of the annual retained earnings for each year of the firm's history.

Changes in retained earnings between balance sheet dates are reported in the **statement of retained earnings.** Table 2-3 shows that Allied earned $113.5 million during 2001, paid out $57.5 million in common dividends, and plowed $56 million back into the business. Thus, the balance sheet item "Retained earnings" increased from $710 million at the end of 2000 to $766 million at the end of 2001.

Note that "Retained earnings" represents a *claim against assets*, not assets per se. Moreover, firms retain earnings primarily to expand the business, and this means investing in plant and equipment, in inventories, and so on, *not* piling up cash in a bank account. Changes in retained earnings occur because

TECHNOLOGY MATTERS

FINANCIAL ANALYSIS ON THE INTERNET

A wide range of valuable financial information is available on the Internet. With just a couple of clicks, an investor can easily find the key financial statements for most publicly traded companies.

Say, for example, you are thinking about buying Disney stock, and you are looking for financial information regarding the company's recent performance. Here's a partial (but by no means a complete) list of places you can go to get started:

- One source is Yahoo's finance web site, **finance.yahoo.com.**[a] Here you will find updated market information along with links to a variety of interesting research sites. Enter a stock's ticker symbol, click on Get Quotes, and you will see the stock's current price, along with recent news about the company. Click on Profile (under More Info) and you will find a report on the company's key financial ratios. Links to the company's income statement, balance sheet, and statement of cash flows can also be found. The Yahoo site also has a list of insider transactions, so you can tell if a company's CEO and other key insiders are buying or selling their company's stock. In addition, there is a message board where investors share opinions about the company, and there is a link to the company's filings with the Securities and Exchange Commission (SEC). Note that, in most cases, a more complete list of the SEC filings can be found at **www.sec.gov** or at **www.edgar-online.com.**

- Other sources for up-to-date market information are **cnnfn.com** and **cbs.marketwatch.com.** Each also has an area where you can obtain stock quotes along with company financials, links to Wall Street research, and links to SEC filings.
- Another good source is **www.quicken.com.** Enter the ticker symbol in the area labeled quotes and research. The site will take you to an area where you can find a link to the company's financial statements, along with analysts' earnings estimates and SEC filings. This site also has a section where you can estimate the stock's intrinsic value. (In Chapter 9 we will discuss various methods for calculating intrinsic value.)
- If you are looking for charts of key accounting variables (for example, sales, inventory, depreciation and amortization, and reported earnings), along with the financial statements, take a look at **www.smartmoney.com.**
- Another good place to look is **www.marketguide.com.** Here you find links to analysts' research reports along with the key financial statements.
- Two other places to consider: **www.hoovers.com** and **my.zacks.com.** Each has free research available along with more detailed information provided to subscribers.

Once you have accumulated all of this information, you may be looking for sites that provide opinions regarding the direction of the overall market and views regarding individual stocks. Two popular sites in this category are The Motley Fool's web site, **www.fool.com**, and the web site for The Street.com, **www.thestreet.com.**

Keep in mind that this list is just a small subset of the information available online. You should also realize that a lot of these sites change their content over time, and new and interesting sites are always being added to the Internet.

---

[a]To avoid redundancy, we have intentionally left off **http://** in all web addresses given here. A quick way to change an address is to highlight the portion of the address that is different and type in the appropriate letters of the new address. Once you're finished just press Enter.

TABLE 2-3 | **Allied Food Products: Statement of Retained Earnings for Year Ending December 31, 2001 (Millions of Dollars)**

Balance of retained earnings, December 31, 2000	$710.0
Add: Net income, 2001	113.5
Less: Dividends to common stockholders	(57.5)[a]
Balance of retained earnings, December 31, 2001	$766.0

[a] Here, and throughout the book, parentheses are used to denote negative numbers.

ANALYSTS ARE INCREASINGLY RELYING ON CASH FLOW TO VALUE STOCKS

Tokyo-based Softbank recently acquired several Internet-related businesses, including Ziff-Davis Inc., which publishes more than 80 magazines including *PC Week* and *PC Magazine*. Ziff-Davis also provides training courses in computer technology, and it distributes information through the Internet and computer trade shows.

In an article on Softbank, *Barron's* indicated that Ziff-Davis has been "losing money," and a quick look at the company's recent income statements confirms that it had losses in 1998 and the first quarter of 1999. Despite the company's negative reported earnings, the company's chief financial officer, Timothy O'Brien, took exception with the notion that Ziff-Davis was "losing money." So, he sent *Barron's* the following response:

To the Editor:

In his discussion of Softbank, Neil Martin (*International Trader,* June 14) referred to Ziff-Davis as "losing money." In fact, Ziff-Davis continues to generate significant positive cash flow.

We are a diversified media company. Analysts measure our strength and stability relative to our ability to generate EBITDA (earnings before interest, taxes, depreciation, and amortization). Analysts project that we will generate EBITDA of approximately $220 million in 1999, and that takes into account our substantial investment in ZDTV, the company's 24-hour cable network devoted to computing and the Internet.

Ziff-Davis did report a net loss for 1998 and for the first quarter of 1999. However, this loss was due to noncash expenses, primarily the amortization of approximately $120 million in goodwill per year. Even with continuing investments in our key businesses, Ziff-Davis has the financial flexibility to continue to repay indebtedness with free cash flow.

Timothy C. O'Brien,
Chief Financial Officer, Ziff-Davis

Cash-flow measures such as EBITDA have long been popular with bankers and other short-term lenders, who focus more on borrowers' ability to generate cash to pay off loans than on accounting earnings. In the past, these measures were less popular with stock analysts, who focused on reported earnings and price earnings ratios. However, today more and more Wall Street analysts are siding with Tim O'Brien, arguing that cash flow measures such as EBITDA often provide a better indication of true value than do earnings per share.

These analysts note that the DA part of EBITDA reduces reported profits but not cash, so EBITDA reflects the cash available to a firm better than accounting profits. It is logical that credit analysts interested in a company's ability to repay its loans focus heavily on EBITDA, but what about equity analysts, who are seeking to find a firm's value to its stockholders? First, most analysts agree that a firm's value depends on its ability to generate cash flows over the long run. If depreciation and amortization (DA) charges truly reflect a decline in the assets used to produce cash flows, then the DA will have to be reinvested in the business if cash flows are to continue. The DA may reflect "available cash" in the short run, but it is not truly

common stockholders allow the firm to reinvest funds that otherwise could be distributed as dividends. *Thus, retained earnings as reported on the balance sheet do not represent cash and are not "available" for the payment of dividends or anything else.*[4]

---

[4] The amount reported in the retained earnings account is *not* an indication of the amount of cash the firm has. Cash (as of the balance sheet date) is found in the cash account, an asset account. A positive number in the retained earnings account indicates only that in the past the firm has earned some income, but its dividends have been less than its earnings. Even though a company reports record earnings and shows an increase in the retained earnings account, it still may be short of cash.

The same situation holds for individuals. You might own a new BMW (no loan), lots of clothes, and an expensive stereo, hence have a high net worth, but if you had only 23 cents in your pocket plus $5 in your checking account, you would still be short of cash.

available to investors because it will have to be reinvested if the business is to continue to operate.

So, analysts must consider the nature of the D and A charges. If depreciation is related to essential assets, as it usually is, then it is a cost that should be deducted to get an idea of the firm's long-run cash generating potential. Amortization is analyzed similarly, but here there is more ambiguity, because amortization is related to two primary types of write-offs: (1) amortization of research and development costs associated with products such as airplanes, computers, software, and pharmaceutical drugs, and (2) amortization of merger-related goodwill, which reflects the difference between the price a company pays when it acquires another company and the book value of the acquired company. Both types of amortization can be huge, so there can be huge differences between EBIT and EBITDA.

The key question then becomes, "Will the company be required to reinvest the cash flow reflected in the DA part of EBITDA if it is to continue to generate cash flow on into the future?" If the answer is yes, then the DA component is not "free cash flow" that is available to investors, and it should be deducted when determining the firm's long-run earning power. If the answer is no, then DA does represent free cash flow and is available to investors.

The situation where all this is most important is when mergers occur and large amounts of goodwill are created. Consider two examples. First, suppose Microsoft acquires a small software company whose owner developed and patented a new type of mouse. Microsoft paid $3.1 million for the company, whose book value was $100,000, so $3 million of goodwill was created. The mouse will help Microsoft for three years, after which it will be obsolete. Here it would be appropriate for Microsoft to amortize the goodwill at the rate of $1 million per year; this $1 million would need to be reinvested to maintain Microsoft's cash flow, and this $1 million of its EBITDA would not represent long-run earning potential.

Now consider the case of Softbank's acquisition of Ziff-Davis. Softbank paid far more for Ziff-Davis than Ziff-Davis' accounting value as reflected on its balance sheet, and that difference was recorded as goodwill. Softbank paid the high price because Ziff-Davis was earning an abnormally high rate of return on its book assets, and it was expected to earn high returns on into the future because it had created a niche in the publishing industry that would be hard for a new competitor to overcome. Here, because the above-normal earning power is likely to be sustained over time, EBITDA is more reflective of long-run cash flow potential than is accounting profit.

Amortization will be high in an industry if patents are important, as is the case in the pharmaceutical industry, or if mergers are producing a lot of goodwill, as has been the case with high-tech and financial services firms. This was spelled out in a recent "Heard on the Street" column in *The Wall Street Journal*, which noted that cash flow valuations are now in vogue in the cable, high-tech, Internet, pharmaceutical, and financial services sectors.

SOURCES: *Barron's*, July 19, 1999, 54; and "Analysts Increasingly Favor Using Cash Flow Over Reported Earnings in Stock Valuations," Heard on The Street, *The Wall Street Journal*, April 1, 1999, C2.

SELF-TEST QUESTIONS

What is the statement of retained earnings, and what information does it provide?

Why do changes in retained earnings occur?

Explain why the following statement is true: "Retained earnings as reported on the balance sheet do not represent cash and are not 'available' for the payment of dividends or anything else."

STATEMENT OF RETAINED EARNINGS   47

NET CASH FLOW

When you studied income statements in accounting, the emphasis was probably on the firm's net income. In finance, however, we focus on **net cash flow.** The value of an asset (or a whole firm) is determined by the cash flow it generates. The firm's net income is important, but cash flow is even more important because dividends must be paid in cash and because cash is necessary to purchase the assets required to continue operations.

As we discussed in Chapter 1, the firm's goal should be to maximize its stock price. Since the value of any asset, including a share of stock, depends on the cash flow produced by the asset, managers should strive to maximize the cash flow available to investors over the long run. A business's *net cash flow* generally differs from its **accounting profit** because some of the revenues and expenses listed on the income statement were not paid in cash during the year. The relationship between net cash flow and net income can be expressed as follows:

$$\text{Net cash flow} = \text{Net income} - \text{Noncash revenues} + \text{Noncash charges}. \quad (2\text{-}1)$$

The primary examples of noncash charges are depreciation and amortization. These items reduce net income but are not paid out in cash, so we add them back to net income when calculating net cash flow. Another example of a noncash charge is deferred taxes. In some instances, companies are allowed to defer tax payments to a later date even though the tax payment is reported as an expense on the income statement. Therefore, deferred tax payments would be added to net income when calculating net cash flow.[5] At the same time, some revenues may not be collected in cash during the year, and these items must be subtracted from net income when calculating net cash flow.

Typically, depreciation and amortization are by far the largest noncash items, and in many cases the other noncash items roughly net out to zero. For this reason, many analysts assume that net cash flow equals net income plus depreciation and amortization:

$$\text{Net cash flow} = \text{Net income} + \text{Depreciation and amortization}. \quad (2\text{-}2)$$

To keep things simple, we will generally assume Equation 2-2 holds. However, you should remember that Equation 2-2 will not accurately reflect net cash flow in those instances where there are significant noncash items beyond depreciation and amortization.

We can illustrate Equation 2-2 with 2001 data for Allied taken from Table 2-2:

$$\text{Net cash flow} = \$113.5 + \$100.0 = \$213.5 \text{ million}.$$

To illustrate depreciation itself, suppose a machine with a life of five years and a zero expected salvage value was purchased in 2000 for $100,000 and placed into service in 2001. This $100,000 cost is not expensed in the purchase year; rather, it is charged against production over the machine's five-year depreciable life. If the depreciation expense were not taken, profits would be overstated, and taxes would be too high. So, the annual depreciation charge is deducted from sales revenues, along with such other costs as labor and raw ma-

---

[5] Deferred taxes may arise, for example, if a company uses accelerated depreciation for tax purposes but straight-line depreciation for reporting its financial statements to investors.

IN VALUING STOCKS, IS IT EARNINGS OR CASH FLOW THAT MATTERS?

When it comes to valuing a company's stock, what's more important: cash flow or earnings? Analysts often disagree, and the measure used often depends on the industry. For example, analysts have traditionally emphasized cash flow rather than earnings when valuing cable stocks. This distinction has been important because, traditionally, cable companies have had to make large capital expenditures. These expenditures generate large depreciation expenses, which depress reported earnings. However, since depreciation is a noncash expense, cable companies often continue to show strong cash flows, even when earnings are declining or even negative.

For example, in recent years leading cable companies such as Tele-Communications Inc., Cox Communications, and Comcast Corporation have all reported low or negative earnings. Nevertheless, over the past five years cable stocks have outperformed the overall market, generating an average annual return in excess of 30 percent. One reason for this strong performance is that each of these companies has generated a strong cash flow.

Besides their growth in cash flow, there are at least two other reasons cable stocks have performed so well despite weak earnings. First, many believe that the cable companies will be-

come the dominant providers of Internet service, which if true will lead to much higher growth in the future. Second, in recent years cable companies have become acquisition targets. For example, AT&T recently acquired cable giant Tele-Communications Inc. and Media One. This takeover activity has helped bid up the prices of all cable stocks.

To be sure, many analysts take a more sanguine view of the cable industry's future prospects. Cable companies continue to face increased competition from digital satellite companies, and other technologies are emerging to compete with cable for providing high-speed Internet access. Finally, despite their growth potential, it is clear that to compete in the years ahead the cable companies will have to continue making large capital expenditures. As a result, much of the cash flow will not be available to pay dividends to shareholders — rather, it will be required for investments that are necessary to maintain existing revenues. So, while cash flow will probably continue to be an important determinant of cable stock values, more and more analysts are insisting that these companies must also begin to generate positive earnings.

terials, to determine income. However, because the $100,000 was actually expended back in 2000, the depreciation charged against income in 2001 and subsequent years is not a cash outlay, as are labor or raw materials charges. *Depreciation is a noncash charge, so it must be added back to net income to obtain the net cash flow.* If we assume that all other noncash items (including amortization) sum to zero, then net cash flow is simply equal to net income plus depreciation.

SELF-TEST QUESTIONS

Differentiate between net cash flow and accounting profit.

In accounting, the emphasis is on net income. What is emphasized in finance, and why is that item emphasized?

Assuming that depreciation is its only noncash cost, how can someone calculate a business's cash flow?

STATEMENT OF CASH FLOWS

Net cash flow represents the amount of cash a business generates for its shareholders in a given year. However, the fact that a company generates high cash flow does not necessarily mean that the *amount of cash* reported on its balance sheet will also be high. The cash flow may be used in a variety of ways. For example, the firm may use its cash flow to pay dividends, to increase inventories, to finance accounts receivable, to invest in fixed assets, to reduce debt, or to buy back common stock. Indeed, the company's cash position as reported on the balance sheet is affected by a great many factors, including the following:

1. **Cash flow.** Other things held constant, a positive net cash flow will lead to more cash in the bank. However, as we discuss below, other things are generally not held constant.

2. **Changes in working capital.** Net working capital, which is discussed in detail in Chapter 15, is defined as current assets minus current liabilities. Increases in current assets other than cash, such as inventories and accounts receivable, decrease cash, whereas decreases in these accounts increase cash. For example, if inventories are to increase, the firm must use some of its cash to buy the additional inventory, whereas if inventories decrease, this generally means the firm is selling off inventories and not replacing them, hence generating cash. On the other hand, increases in current liabilities such as accounts payable increase cash, whereas decreases in these accounts decrease it. For example, if payables increase, the firm has received additional credit from its suppliers, which saves cash, but if payables decrease, this means the firm has used cash to pay off its suppliers.

3. **Fixed assets.** If a company invests in fixed assets, this will reduce its cash position. On the other hand, the sale of fixed assets will increase cash.

4. **Security transactions.** If a company issues stock or bonds during the year, the funds raised will enhance its cash position. On the other hand, if it uses cash to buy back outstanding debt or equity, or pays dividends to its shareholders, this will reduce cash.

Statement of Cash Flows
A statement reporting the impact of a firm's operating, investing, and financing activities on cash flows over an accounting period.

Each of the above factors is reflected in the **statement of cash flows,** which summarizes the changes in a company's cash position. The statement separates activities into three categories:

1. *Operating activities*, which includes net income, depreciation, and changes in current assets and current liabilities other than cash and short-term debt.

2. *Investing activities*, which includes investments in or sales of fixed assets.

3. *Financing activities*, which includes cash raised during the year by issuing short-term debt, long-term debt, or stock. Also, since dividends paid or cash used to buy back outstanding stock or bonds reduces the company's cash, such transactions are included here.

Accounting texts explain how to prepare the statement of cash flows, but the statement is used to help answer questions such as these: Is the firm generating enough cash to purchase the additional assets required for growth? Is the firm generating any extra cash that can be used to repay debt or to invest in new products? Will inadequate cash flows force the company to issue more stock? Such information is useful both for managers and investors, so the statement of cash flows is an important part of the annual report. Financial managers generally use this statement, along with the cash budget, when forecasting their companies' cash positions. This issue is considered in more detail in Chapter 15.

Table 2-4 is Allied's statement of cash flows as it would appear in the company's annual report. The top part of the table shows cash flows generated by and used in operations — for Allied, operations provided net cash flows of *minus* $2.5 million. The operating cash flows are generated in the normal course of business, and this amount is determined by adjusting the net income figure to account for depreciation and amortization plus other cash flows related to operations. Allied's day-to-day operations in 2001 provided $257.5 million; however, the increase in receivables and inventories more than offset this amount, resulting in a *negative* $2.5 million cash flow from operations.

The second section shows long-term fixed-assets investing activities. Allied purchased fixed assets totaling $230 million; this was the only long-term investment it made during 2001.

TABLE 2-4	Allied Food Products: Statement of Cash Flows for 2001 (Millions of Dollars)

OPERATING ACTIVITIES	
Net income before preferred dividends	$117.5
Additions (Sources of Cash)	
Depreciation and amortization[a]	100.0
Increase in accounts payable	30.0
Increase in accruals	10.0
Subtractions (Uses of Cash)	
Increase in accounts receivable	(60.0)
Increase in inventories	(200.0)
Net cash provided by operating activities	($ 2.5)
LONG-TERM INVESTING ACTIVITIES	
Cash used to acquire fixed assets[b]	($230.0)
FINANCING ACTIVITIES	
Increase in notes payable	$ 50.0
Increase in bonds	174.0
Payment of common and preferred dividends	(61.5)
Net cash provided by financing activities	$162.5
Net decrease in cash and marketable securities	($ 70.0)
Cash and securities at beginning of year	80.0
Cash and securities at end of year	$ 10.0

[a] Depreciation and amortization are noncash expenses that were deducted when calculating net income. They must be added back to show the actual cash flow from operations.

[b] The net increase in fixed assets is $130 million; however, this net amount is after deducting the year's depreciation expense. Depreciation expense must be added back to find the actual expenditures on fixed assets. From the company's income statement, we see that the 2001 depreciation expense is $100 million; thus, expenditures on fixed assets were actually $230 million.

Allied's financing activities, shown in the third section, include borrowing from banks (notes payable), selling new bonds, and paying dividends on its common and preferred stock. Allied raised $224 million by borrowing, but it paid $61.5 million in preferred and common dividends, so its net inflow of funds from financing activities was $162.5 million.

When all of the sources and uses of cash are totaled, we see that Allied's cash outflows exceeded its cash inflows by $70 million during 2001. It met that shortfall by drawing down its cash and marketable securities holdings by $70 million, as confirmed by Table 2-1, the firm's balance sheet.

Allied's statement of cash flows should be worrisome to its managers and to outside analysts. The company had a $2.5 million cash shortfall from operations, it spent $230 million on new fixed assets, and it paid out another $61.5 million in dividends. It covered these cash outlays by borrowing heavily and by selling off most of its marketable securities. Obviously, this situation cannot continue year after year, so something will have to be done. In Chapter 3, we will consider some of the actions Allied's financial staff might recommend to ease the cash flow problem.

SELF-TEST QUESTIONS

What is the statement of cash flows, and what types of questions does it answer?

Identify and briefly explain the three different categories of activities shown in the statement of cash flows.

MODIFYING ACCOUNTING DATA FOR MANAGERIAL DECISIONS

Thus far in the chapter we have focused on financial statements as they are prepared by accountants and presented in the annual report. However, these statements are designed more for use by creditors and tax collectors than for managers and equity (stock) analysts. Therefore, certain modifications are used for corporate decision making and stock valuation purposes. In the following sections we discuss how financial analysts combine stock prices and accounting data to evaluate and reward managerial performance.

OPERATING ASSETS AND OPERATING CAPITAL

Different firms have different financial structures, different tax situations, and different amounts of nonoperating assets. These differences affect traditional accounting measures such as the rate of return on equity. They can cause two firms, or two divisions within a single firm, that actually have similar operations to appear to be operated with different efficiency. This is important, because if managerial compensation systems are to function properly, operating managers must be judged and compensated for those things that are under their control, not on the basis of things outside their control. Therefore, to judge managerial performance, we need to compare managers' ability to generate *operating income* (or *EBIT*) with the *operating assets* under their control.

The first step in modifying the traditional accounting framework is to divide total assets into two categories, **operating assets,** which consist of the cash and marketable securities, accounts receivable, inventories, and fixed assets necessary to operate the business, and **nonoperating assets,** which would include cash and marketable securities above the level required for normal operations, investments in subsidiaries, land held for future use, and the like. Moreover, operating assets are further divided into *working capital* and fixed assets such as plant and equipment. Obviously, if a manager can generate a given amount of profits and cash flows with a relatively small investment in operating assets, that reduces the amount of capital investors must put up and thus increases the rate of return on that capital.

The primary source of capital for business is investors—stockholders, bondholders, and lenders such as banks. Investors must be paid for the use of their money, with payment coming as interest in the case of debt and as dividends plus capital gains in the case of stock. So, if a company acquires more assets than it actually needs, and thus raises too much capital, then its capital costs will be unnecessarily high.

Must all of the capital used to acquire assets be obtained from investors? The answer is no, because some of the funds will come from suppliers and be reported as *accounts payable*, while other funds will come as *accrued wages and accrued taxes*, which amount to short-term loans from workers and tax authorities. Generally, both accounts payable and accruals are "free" in the sense that no explicit fee is charged for their use. Therefore, if a firm needs $100 million of current assets, but it has $10 million of accounts payable and another $10 million of accrued wages and taxes, then its *investor-supplied capital* would be only $80 million.

Those current assets used in operations are called **operating working capital,** and operating working capital less accounts payable and accruals is called **net operating working capital.** Therefore, net operating working capital is the working capital acquired with investor-supplied funds.[6] Here is a workable definition in equation form:

$$\text{Net operating working capital} = \text{All current assets} - \begin{array}{c}\text{All current}\\\text{liabilities that do}\\\text{not charge interest}\end{array} \quad \textbf{(2-3)}$$

---

[6] Note that the term "capital" can be given two meanings. First, when accountants use the term "capital," they typically mean the sum of long-term debt, preferred stock, and common equity, or perhaps those items plus interest-bearing short-term debt. However, when economists use the term, they generally mean assets used in production, as in "labor plus capital." If all funds were raised from long-term sources, and if all assets were operating assets, then money capital would equal operating assets, and the accountants' capital would always equal the economists' capital. When you encounter the term "capital" in the business and financial literature, it can mean either asset capital or money capital. For example, in Coca-Cola's operating manuals, which explain to its employees how Coke wants the company to be operated, capital means "assets financed by investor-supplied capital." However, in most accounting and finance textbooks, and in the traditional finance literature, "capital" means investor-supplied capital, not assets. It might be easier if we picked one meaning and then used it consistently in this book. However, that would be misleading, because both meanings are encountered in practice. Therefore, we shall use the term "capital" in both ways. However, you should be able to figure out which definition is implied from the context in which the term is used.

Operating Assets
The cash and marketable securities, accounts receivable, inventories, and fixed assets necessary to operate the business.

Nonoperating Assets
Cash and marketable securities above the level required for normal operations, investments in subsidiaries, land held for future use, and other nonessential assets.

Operating Working Capital
Current assets used in operations.

Net Operating Working Capital
Operating working capital less accounts payable and accruals. It is the working capital acquired with investor-supplied funds.

Now think about how these concepts can be used in practice. First, all companies must carry some cash to "grease the wheels" of their operations. Companies continuously cash checks from customers and write checks to suppliers, employees, and so on. Because inflows and outflows do not coincide perfectly, a company must keep some cash and marketable securities in its bank account. In other words, some cash and marketable securities is required to conduct operations. The same is true for most other current assets, such as inventory and accounts receivable, which are required for normal operations. Our measure of operating working capital assumes that cash and marketable securities on the balance sheet represent the amount that is required under normal operations. However, in some instances companies have large holdings of cash and marketable securities that they are holding as a reserve for some contingency, or as a "parking place" for funds prior to an acquisition, a major captial investment program, or the like. In such instances, the excess cash and marketable securities should not be viewed as part of operating working capital.

Looking at the other side of the balance sheet, some current liabilities — especially accounts payable and accruals — arise in the normal course of operations. Moreover, each dollar of these current liabilities is a dollar that the company does not have to raise from investors to acquire current assets. Therefore, when finding the net operating working capital, we deduct these current liabilities from the operating current assets. Other current liabilities that charge interest, such as notes payable to banks, are treated as investor-supplied capital and thus are not deducted when calculating net operating working capital.

We can apply these definitions to Allied, using the balance sheet data given back in Table 2-1. Here is the net operating working capital for 2001:

$$\text{Net operating working capital} = \left(\text{Cash and marketable securities} + \text{Accounts receivable} + \text{Inventories} \right) - \left(\text{Accounts payable} + \text{Accruals} \right)$$

$$= (\$10 + \$375 + \$615) - (\$60 + \$140)$$

$$= \$800 \text{ million.}$$

Allied's total operating capital for 2001 was

$$\text{Total operating capital} = \text{Net operating working capital} + \text{Net fixed assets} \tag{2-4}$$

$$= \$800 + \$1,000$$

$$= \$1,800 \text{ million.}$$

Now note that Allied's net operating working capital a year earlier, at year-end 2000, was

$$\text{Net operating working capital} = (\$80 + \$315 + \$415) - (\$30 + \$130)$$

$$= \$650 \text{ million,}$$

and, since it had $870 million of fixed assets, its total operating capital was

$$\text{Total operating capital} = \$650 + \$870$$

$$= \$1,520 \text{ million.}$$

Therefore, Allied increased its operating capital from $1,520 to $1,800 million, or by $280 million, during 2001. Furthermore, most of this increase went into working capital, which rose by $150 million. This 23 percent increase in net operating working capital, when sales only rose 5 percent (from $2,850 to

$3,000 million), should set off warning bells in your head: What caused Allied to tie up so much additional cash in working capital? Are inventories not moving? Are receivables not being collected and thus building up? We will address these questions in detail later in the chapter.

NET OPERATING PROFIT AFTER TAXES (NOPAT)

Net Operating Profit After Taxes (NOPAT)
The profit a company would generate if it had no debt and held no nonoperating assets.

If two companies have different amounts of debt, hence different interest charges, they could have identical operating performances but different net incomes — the one with more debt would have a lower net income. Net income is certainly important, but as the example below shows, net income does not always reflect the true performance of a company's operations or the effectiveness of its operating managers and employees. A better measurement for comparing managers' performance is **net operating profit after taxes,** or **NOPAT,** which is the amount of profit a company would generate if it had no debt and held no nonoperating assets. NOPAT is defined as follows:[7]

$$\text{NOPAT} = \text{EBIT}(1 - \text{Tax rate}). \qquad (2\text{-}5)$$

Using data from the income statement in Table 2-2, Allied's 2001 NOPAT was

$$\text{NOPAT} = \$283.8(1 - 0.4) = \$283.8(0.6) = \$170.3 \text{ million}.$$

Thus, Allied generated an after-tax profit of $170.3 million from its operations. This was a little better than the 2000 NOPAT of $263(0.6) = $157.8 million. However, the income statements in Table 2-2 show that Allied's earnings per share declined from 2000 to 2001. This decrease in EPS was caused by an increase in interest expense, not by a decrease in operating profit. See Table 2-2. Moreover, the balance sheets in Table 2-1 show that debt increased from 2000 to 2001. But why did Allied increase its debt? The reason was that Allied's investment in operating capital increased dramatically from 2000 to 2001, and that increase was financed primarily with debt.

FREE CASH FLOW

Free Cash Flow
The cash flow actually available for distribution to all investors (stockholders and debtholders) after the company has made all the investments in fixed assets, new products, and working capital necessary to sustain ongoing operations.

Earlier in the chapter we defined net cash flow as being equal to net income plus noncash adjustments, typically net income plus depreciation and amortization. Note, though, that cash flows cannot be maintained over time unless depreciating fixed assets are replaced and new products are developed, so management is not completely free to use cash flows however it chooses. Therefore, we now define another term, **free cash flow,** which is the cash flow actually available for distribution to all investors (stockholders and debtholders) *after the company has made all the investments in fixed assets, new products, and working capital necessary to sustain ongoing operations.*

---

[7] For firms with a more complicated tax situation, it is better to define NOPAT as follows: NOPAT = (Net income before preferred dividends) + (Net interest expense)(1 − Tax rate). Also, if firms are able to defer paying some of their taxes, perhaps by the use of accelerated depreciation, then NOPAT should be adjusted to reflect the taxes that the company actually paid on its operating income. For additional information see Tom Copeland, Tim Koller, and Jack Murrin, *Valuation: Measuring and Managing the Value of Companies,* 3rd edition (New York: John Wiley & Sons, Inc., 2000); and G. Bennett Stewart III, *The Quest for Value* (New York: HarperCollins Publishers, Inc., 1991).

When you studied income statements in accounting, the emphasis probably was on the firm's net income, which is its accounting profit. However, we began this chapter by telling you that the value of a company's operations is determined by the stream of cash flows that the operations will generate now and in the future. As the statement of cash flows shows, accounting profit and cash flow can be quite different.

To be more specific, the value of a company's operations depends on all the future expected free cash flows (FCF), defined as after-tax operating profit minus the amount of investment in working capital and fixed assets necessary to sustain the business. Thus, free cash flow represents the cash that is actually available for distribution to investors. Therefore, the way for managers to make their companies more valuable is to increase their free cash flow.

CALCULATING FREE CASH FLOW

Operating Cash Flow
Equal to NOPAT plus any noncash adjustments, calculated on an after-tax basis.

As shown earlier in the chapter, Allied had a 2001 NOPAT of $170.3 million. Its **operating cash flow** is NOPAT plus any noncash adjustments as shown on the statement of cash flows. For Allied, where depreciation is the only noncash charge, the 2001 operating cash flow is[8]

$$\text{Operating cash flow} = \text{NOPAT} + \text{Depreciation} \qquad (2\text{-}6)$$
$$= \$170.3 + \$100$$
$$= \$270.3 \text{ million.}$$

Please note that this definition of operating cash flow is calculated on an after-tax basis. As shown earlier in the chapter, Allied had $1,520 million of operating assets, or operating capital, at the end of 2000, but $1,800 million at the end of 2001. Therefore, during 2001 it made a *net investment in operating capital* of

$$\text{Net investment in operating capital} = \$1,800 - \$1,520 = \$280 \text{ million.}$$

Fixed assets rose from $870 to $1,000 million, or by $130 million. However, Allied took $100 million of depreciation, so its gross investment in fixed assets was $130 + $100 = $230 million for the year. With this background, we find the *gross investment in operating capital* as follows:

$$\text{Gross investment} = \text{Net investment} + \text{Depreciation}$$
$$= \$280 + \$100 = \$380 \text{ million.}$$

Allied's free cash flow in 2001 was

$$\text{FCF} = \text{Operating cash flow} - \text{Gross investment in operating capital} \qquad (2\text{-}7)$$
$$= \$270.3 - \$380$$
$$= -\$109.7 \text{ million.}$$

---

[8] In those instances in which operating costs include an amortization expense, operating cash flow would also need to include an adjustment for the amortization charge. However, in practice, only a small percentage of firms report amortization expenses on their income statements. Moreover, the accounting and tax treatments of amortization charges are often quite complex. For these reasons, we have chosen to disregard amortization expenses when calculating operating cash flow and free cash flow. See Copeland, Koller, and Murrin, *Valuation: Measuring and Managing the Value of Companies*, for a more detailed discussion of how to incorporate amortization expenses into the calculation of free cash flow.

If we subtract depreciation from both operating cash flow and gross investment in operating capital in Equation 2-7, we obtain the following algebraically equivalent expression for free cash flow:

$$FCF = NOPAT - \text{Net investment in operating capital} \qquad (2\text{-}7a)$$
$$= \$170.3 - \$280$$
$$= -\$109.7 \text{ million.}$$

Even though Allied had a positive NOPAT, its very high investment in operating capital resulted in a negative free cash flow. Since free cash flow is what is available for distribution to investors, not only was there nothing for investors, but investors actually had to provide *more* money to Allied to keep the business going. Investors provided most of the required new money as debt.

Is a negative free cash flow always bad? The answer is, "Not necessarily. It depends on *why* the free cash flow was negative." If FCF was negative because NOPAT was negative, this is bad, because the company is probably experiencing operating problems. Exceptions to this might be startup companies, or companies that are incurring significant current expenses to launch a new product line. Also, many high-growth companies have positive NOPAT but negative free cash flow due to investments in operating assets needed to support growth. There is nothing wrong with profitable growth, even if it causes negative cash flows in the short term.

SELF-TEST QUESTIONS

What is net operating working capital?

What is total operating capital?

What is NOPAT? Why might it be a better performance measure than net income?

What is free cash flow? Why is free cash flow the most important determinant of a firm's value?

MVA AND EVA

Neither traditional accounting data nor the modified data discussed in the preceding section bring in stock prices. Since the primary goal of management is to maximize the firm's stock price, we need to bring stock prices into the picture. Financial analysts have therefore developed two new performance measures, MVA, or Market Value Added, and EVA, or Economic Value Added. These concepts are discussed in this section.[9]

---

[9] The concepts of EVA and MVA were developed by Joel Stern and Bennett Stewart, co-founders of the consulting firm Stern Stewart & Company. Stern Stewart copyrighted the terms "EVA" and "MVA," so other consulting firms have given other names to these values. Still, EVA and MVA are the terms most commonly used in practice.

MARKET VALUE ADDED (MVA)

Market Value Added (MVA)
The difference between the market value of the firm's stock and the amount of equity capital investors have supplied.

The primary goal of most firms is to maximize shareholders' wealth. This goal obviously benefits shareholders, but it also helps to ensure that scarce resources are allocated efficiently, which benefits the economy. Shareholder wealth is maximized by maximizing the *difference* between the market value of the firm's stock and the amount of equity capital that was supplied by shareholders. This difference is called the **Market Value Added (MVA):**

$$\text{MVA} = \text{Market value of stock} - \text{Equity capital supplied by shareholders}$$
$$= (\text{Shares outstanding})(\text{Stock price}) - \text{Total common equity.} \quad (2\text{-}8)$$

To illustrate, consider our illustrative company, Allied Food Products. In 2001, its total market equity value was $1,150 million, while its balance sheet showed that stockholders had put up only $896 million. Thus, Allied's MVA was $1,150 − $896 = $254 million. This $254 million represents the difference between the money that Allied's stockholders have invested in the corporation since its founding — including retained earnings — versus the cash they could get if they sold the business. The higher its MVA, the better the job management is doing for the firm's shareholders.

ECONOMIC VALUE ADDED (EVA)

Economic Value Added (EVA)
Value added to shareholders by management during a given year.

Whereas MVA measures the effects of managerial actions since the very inception of a company, **Economic Value Added (EVA)** focuses on managerial effectiveness in a given year. The basic formula for EVA is as follows:

$$\text{EVA} = \text{Net operating profit after taxes, or NOPAT}$$
$$\qquad - \text{After-tax dollar cost of capital used to support operations}$$
$$= \text{EBIT}(1 - \text{Corporate tax rate})$$
$$\qquad - (\text{Total investor-supplied operating capital})(\text{After-tax percentage cost of capital}). \quad (2\text{-}9)$$

Total investor-supplied operating capital is the sum of the interest-bearing debt, preferred stock, and common equity used to acquire the company's net operating assets, that is, its net operating working capital plus net plant and equipment.

EVA is an estimate of a business's true economic profit for the year, and it differs sharply from accounting profit.[10] EVA represents the residual income that remains after the cost of *all* capital, including equity capital, has been deducted, whereas accounting profit is determined without imposing a charge for equity capital. As we will discuss more completely in Chapter 10, equity capital has a cost, because funds provided by shareholders could have been invested elsewhere where they would have earned a return. Shareholders give up the opportunity to invest funds elsewhere when they provide capital to the firm. The return they could earn elsewhere in investments of equal risk represents the cost of equity capital. This cost is an *opportunity cost* rather than an *accounting cost*, but it is quite real nevertheless.

Note that when calculating EVA we do not add back depreciation. Although it is not a cash expense, depreciation is a cost, and it is therefore deducted when

---

[10] The most important reason EVA differs from accounting profit is that the cost of equity capital is deducted when EVA is calculated. Other factors that could lead to differences include adjustments that might be made to depreciation, to research and development costs, to inventory valuations, and so on. See Stewart, *The Quest for Value.*

determining both net income and EVA. Our calculation of EVA assumes that the true economic depreciation of the company's fixed assets exactly equals the depreciation used for accounting and tax purposes. If this were not the case, adjustments would have to be made to obtain a more accurate measure of EVA.

EVA provides a good measure of the extent to which the firm has added to shareholder value. Therefore, if managers focus on EVA, this will help to ensure that they operate in a manner that is consistent with maximizing shareholder wealth. Note too that EVA can be determined for divisions as well as for the company as a whole, so it provides a useful basis for determining managerial compensation at all levels. As a result of all this, EVA is being used by an increasing number of firms as the primary basis for determining managerial compensation.

Table 2-5 shows how Allied's MVA and EVA are calculated. The stock price was $23 per share at year-end 2001, down from $26 per share at the end of 2000; its percentage after-tax cost of capital was 10.3 percent in 2000 and 10.0 percent in 2001, and its tax rate was 40 percent. Other data in Table 2-5 were given in the basic financial statements provided earlier in the chapter.

Note first that the lower stock price and the higher book value of equity (due to retaining earnings during 2001) combined to reduce the MVA. The 2001 MVA is still positive, but $460 − $254 = $206 million of stockholders' value was lost during 2001.

EVA for 2000 was just barely positive, and in 2001 it was negative. Operating income (NOPAT) rose, but EVA still declined, primarily because the amount of capital rose more sharply than NOPAT — by about 18 percent versus 8 percent — and the cost of this increased capital pulled EVA down.

Recall also that net income fell somewhat from 2000 to 2001, but not nearly so dramatically as the decline in EVA. Net income does not reflect the amount

TABLE 2-5   **MVA and EVA for Allied (Millions of Dollars)**

	2001	2000
MVA CALCULATION		
Price per share	$23.0	$26.0
Number of shares (millions)	50	50
Market value of equity	$1,150.0	$1,300.0
Book value of equity	896.0	840.0
MVA = Market value − Book value	$ 254.0	$ 460.0
EVA CALCULATION		
EBIT	$283.8	$263.0
Tax rate	40%	40%
NOPAT = EBIT (1 − T)	$170.3	$157.8
Total investor-supplied operating capital[a]	$1,800.0	$1,520.0
After-tax cost of capital (%)	10.0%	10.3%
Dollar cost of capital	$180.0	$156.6
EVA = NOPAT − Capital cost	($9.7)	$1.2

[a] Investor-supplied operating capital equals the sum of notes payable, long-term debt, preferred stock, and common equity. It could also be calculated as total liabilities and equity minus accounts payable and accruals.

MANY FIRMS ADOPT EVA IN AN ATTEMPT TO ENHANCE SHAREHOLDER WEALTH

According to *Fortune* magazine, "Economic Value Added (EVA)" is today's hottest financial idea. Developed and popularized by the consulting firm Stern Stewart & Co., EVA helps managers ensure that a given business unit is adding to stockholder value, while investors can use it to spot stocks that are likely to increase in value. Right now, relatively few managers and investors are using EVA, so those who do use it have a competitive advantage. However, *Fortune* thinks this situation won't last long, as more managers and investors are catching the EVA fever every day.

What exactly is EVA? EVA is a way to measure an operation's true profitability. The cost of debt capital (interest expense) is deducted when calculating net income, but no cost is deducted to account for the cost of common equity. Therefore, in an economic sense, net income overstates "true" income. EVA overcomes this flaw in conventional accounting.

EVA is found by taking the after-tax operating profit and subtracting the annual cost of *all* the capital a firm uses. Such highly successful giants as Coca-Cola, AT&T, Quaker Oats, Briggs & Stratton, and CSX have jumped on the EVA bandwagon and attribute much of their success to its use. According to AT&T financial executive William H. Kurtz, EVA played a major role in AT&T's decision to acquire McCaw Cellular. In addition, AT&T made EVA the primary measure of its business unit managers' performance.

Surprisingly, many corporate executives have no idea how much capital they are using or what that capital costs. The cost of debt capital is easy to determine because it shows up in financial statements as interest expense; however, the cost of equity capital, which is actually much larger than the cost of debt capital, does not appear in financial statements. As a result, managers often regard equity as free capital, even though it actually has a high cost. So, until a management team determines its cost of capital, it cannot know whether it is covering all costs and thereby adding value to the firm.

Although EVA is perhaps the most widely discussed concept in finance today, it is not completely new; the need to earn more than the cost of capital is actually one of the oldest ideas in business. However, the idea is often lost because of a misguided focus on conventional accounting.

One of EVA's greatest virtues is its direct link to stock prices. AT&T found an almost perfect correlation between its EVA and its stock price. Moreover, security analysts have found that stock prices track EVA far more closely than other factors such as earnings per share, operating margin, or return on equity. This correlation occurs because EVA is what investors really care about, namely, the net cash return on their capital. Therefore, more and more security analysts are calculating companies' EVAs and using them to help identify good buys in the stock market.

SOURCES: "The Real Key to Creating Wealth," *Fortune,* September 20, 1993, 38–44; and "America's Wealth Creators," *Fortune,* November 22, 1999, 275.

of equity capital employed, but EVA does. Because of this omission, net income is not as useful as EVA for setting corporate goals and measuring managerial performance.

We will have more to say about both MVA and EVA later in the book, but we can close this section with two observations. First, there is a relationship between MVA and EVA, but it is not a direct one. If a company has a history of negative EVAs, then its MVA will probably be negative, and vice versa if it has a history of positive EVAs. However, the stock price, which is the key ingredient in the MVA calculation, depends more on expected future performance than on historical performance. Therefore, a company with a history of negative EVAs could have a positive MVA, provided investors expect a turnaround in the future.

The second observation is that when EVAs or MVAs are used to evaluate managerial performance as part of an incentive compensation program, EVA is the measure that is typically used. The reasons are (1) EVA shows the value added during a given year, whereas MVA reflects performance over the company's entire life, perhaps even including times before the current managers were born, and (2) EVA can be applied to individual divisions or other units of a large corporation, whereas MVA must be applied to the entire corporation.

For these reasons, MVA is used primarily to evaluate top corporate officers over periods of five to 10 years, or longer.

SELF-TEST QUESTIONS

Define the terms "Market Value Added (MVA)" and "Economic Value Added (EVA)."

How does EVA differ from accounting profit?

THE FEDERAL INCOME TAX SYSTEM

 A web site of interest concerning federal tax law is **http:// www.taxsites.com/ federal.html.** From this home page one can visit other sites that provide summaries of recent tax legislation or current information on corporate and individual tax rates.

The value of any financial asset (including stocks, bonds, and mortgages), as well as most real assets such as plants or even entire firms, depends on the stream of cash flows produced by the asset. Cash flows from an asset consist of *usable* income plus depreciation, and usable income means income *after taxes.*

Our tax laws can be changed by Congress, and in recent years changes have occurred frequently. Indeed, a major change has occurred, on average, every three to four years since 1913, when our federal income tax system began. Further, certain parts of our tax system are tied to the inflation rate, so changes occur automatically each year, depending on the rate of inflation during the previous year. Therefore, although this section will give you a good background on the basic nature of our tax system, you should consult current rate schedules and other data published by the Internal Revenue Service (available in U.S. post offices) before you file your personal or business tax returns.

Currently (2001), federal income tax rates for individuals go up to 39.6 percent, and, when Social Security, Medicare, and state and city income taxes are included, the marginal tax rate on an individual's income can easily exceed 50 percent. Business income is also taxed heavily. The income from partnerships and proprietorships is reported by the individual owners as personal income and, consequently, is taxed at federal-plus-state rates going up to 50 percent or more. Corporate profits are subject to federal income tax rates of up to 39 percent, plus state income taxes. Furthermore, corporations pay taxes and then distribute after-tax income to their stockholders as dividends, which are also taxed. So, corporate income is really subject to double taxation. *Because of the magnitude of the tax bite, taxes play a critical role in many financial decisions.*

As this text is being written, a Republican Congress and administration continue to debate the merits of different changes in the tax laws. Even in the unlikely event that no explicit changes are made in the tax laws, changes will still occur because certain aspects of the tax calculation are tied to the inflation rate. Thus, by the time you read this chapter, tax rates and other factors will almost certainly be different from those we provide. Still, if you understand this section, you will understand the basics of our tax system, and you will know how to operate under the revised tax code.

Taxes are so complicated that university law schools offer master's degrees in taxation to lawyers, many of whom are also CPAs. In a field complicated enough to warrant such detailed study, only the highlights can be covered in a book such as this. This is really enough, though, because business managers and investors should and do rely on tax specialists rather than trusting their own limited knowledge. Still, it is important to know the basic elements of the tax system as a starting point for discussions with tax experts.

INDIVIDUAL INCOME TAXES

Individuals pay taxes on wages and salaries, on investment income (dividends, interest, and profits from the sale of securities), and on the profits of propri-

| TABLE 2-6 | Individual Tax Rates in April 2001 |

Single Individuals

IF YOUR TAXABLE INCOME IS	YOU PAY THIS AMOUNT ON THE BASE OF THE BRACKET	PLUS THIS PERCENTAGE ON THE EXCESS OVER THE BASE	AVERAGE TAX RATE AT TOP OF BRACKET
Up to $26,250	$ 0	15.0%	15.0%
$26,250–$63,550	3,937.50	28.0	22.6
$63,550–$132,600	14,381.50	31.0	27.0
$132,600–$288,350	35,787.00	36.0	31.9
Over $288,350	91,857.00	39.6	39.6

Married Couples Filing Joint Returns

IF YOUR TAXABLE INCOME IS	YOU PAY THIS AMOUNT ON THE BASE OF THE BRACKET	PLUS THIS PERCENTAGE ON THE EXCESS OVER THE BASE	AVERAGE TAX RATE AT TOP OF BRACKET
Up to $43,850	$ 0	15.0%	15.0%
$43,850–$105,950	6,577.50	28.0	22.6
$105,950–$161,450	23,965.50	31.0	25.5
$161,450–$288,350	41,170.50	36.0	30.1
Over $288,350	86,854.50	39.6	39.6

NOTES:

a. These are the tax rates in April 2001. The income ranges at which each tax rate takes effect, as well as the ranges for the additional taxes discussed below, are indexed with inflation each year, so they will change from those shown in the table.

b. The average tax rate approaches 39.6 percent as taxable income rises without limit. At $1 million of taxable income, the average tax rates for single individuals and married couples filing joint returns are 37.4 percent and 36.9 percent, respectively, while at $10 million they are 39.4 and 39.3 percent, respectively.

c. In 2000, a *personal exemption* of $2,800 per person or dependent could be deducted from gross income to determine taxable income. Thus, a husband and wife with two children would have a 2000 exemption of 4 × $2,800 = $11,200. The amount of the exemption is scheduled to increase with inflation. However, if gross income exceeds certain limits ($193,400 for joint returns and $128,950 for single individuals in 2000), the exemption is phased out, and this has the effect of raising the effective tax rate on incomes over the specified limit by about 0.5 percent per family member, or 2.0 percent for a family of four. In addition, taxpayers can claim *itemized deductions* for charitable contributions and certain other items, but these deductions are reduced if the gross income exceeds $128,950 (for both single individuals and joint returns), and this raises the effective tax rate for high-income taxpayers by another 1 percent or so. The combined effect of the loss of exemptions and the reduction of itemized deductions is about 3 percent, so the marginal federal tax rate for high-income individuals goes up to about 42.6 percent.

In addition, there is the Social Security tax, which amounts to 6.2 percent (12.4 percent for a self-employed person) on up to $76,200 of earned income, plus a 1.45 percent Medicare payroll tax (2.9 percent for self-employed individuals) on *all* earned income. Finally, older high-income taxpayers who receive Social Security payments must pay taxes on 85 percent of their Social Security receipts, up from 50 percent in 1994. All of this pushes the effective tax rate up even further.

Progressive Tax

A tax system where the tax rate is higher on higher incomes. The personal income tax in the United States, which goes from 0 percent on the lowest increments of income to 39.6 percent, is progressive.

Taxable Income

Gross income minus exemptions and allowable deductions as set forth in the Tax Code.

Marginal Tax Rate

The tax rate applicable to the last unit of a person's income.

Average Tax Rate

Taxes paid divided by taxable income.

Bracket Creep

A situation that occurs when progressive tax rates combine with inflation to cause a greater portion of each taxpayer's real income to be paid as taxes.

etorships and partnerships. Our tax rates are **progressive** — that is, the higher one's income, the larger the percentage paid in taxes. Table 2-6 gives the tax rates for single individuals and married couples filing joint returns under the rate schedules that were in effect in April 2001.

1. **Taxable income** is defined as gross income less a set of exemptions and deductions that are spelled out in the instructions to the tax forms individuals must file. When filing a tax return in 2001 for the tax year 2000, each taxpayer received an exemption of $2,800 for each dependent, including the taxpayer, which reduces taxable income. However, this exemption is indexed to rise with inflation, and the exemption is phased out (taken away) for high-income taxpayers. Also, certain expenses including mortgage interest paid, state and local income taxes paid, and charitable contributions, can be deducted and thus be used to reduce taxable income, but again, high-income taxpayers lose most of these deductions.

2. The **marginal tax rate** is defined as the tax rate on the last unit of income. Marginal rates begin at 15 percent and rise to 39.6 percent. Note, though, that when consideration is given to the phase-out of exemptions and deductions, to Social Security and Medicare taxes, and to state taxes, the marginal tax rate can actually exceed 50 percent.

3. One can calculate **average tax rates** from the data in Table 2-6. For example, if Jill Smith, a single individual, had taxable income of $35,000, her tax bill would be $3,937.50 + ($35,000 − $26,250)(0.28) = $3,937.50 + $2,450 = $6,387.50. Her *average tax rate* would be $6,387.50/$35,000 = 18.25% versus a *marginal rate* of 28 percent. If Jill received a raise of $1,000, bringing her income to $36,000, she would have to pay $280 of it as taxes, so her after-tax raise would be $720. In addition, her Social Security and Medicare taxes would increase by $76.50, which would cut her net raise to $643.50.

4. As indicated in the notes to the table, the tax code indexes tax brackets to inflation to avoid the **bracket creep** that occurred several years ago and that in reality raised tax rates substantially.[11]

Taxes on Dividend and Interest Income

Dividend and interest income received by individuals from corporate securities is added to other income and thus is taxed at rates going up to about 50 percent.[12] Since corporations pay dividends out of earnings that have already been

---

[11] For example, if you were single and had a taxable income of $26,250, your tax bill would be $3,937.50. Now suppose inflation caused prices to double and your income, being tied to a cost-of-living index, rose to $52,500. Because our tax rates are progressive, if tax brackets were not indexed, your taxes would jump to $11,287.50. Your after-tax income would thus increase from $22,312.50 to $41,212.50, but, because prices have doubled, your real income would *decline* from $22,312.50 to $20,606.25 (calculated as one-half of $41,212.50). You would be in a higher tax bracket, so you would be paying a higher percentage of your real income in taxes. If this happened to everyone, and if Congress failed to change tax rates sufficiently, real disposable incomes would decline because the federal government would be taking a larger share of the national product. This is called the federal government's "inflation dividend." However, since tax brackets are now indexed, if your income doubled due to inflation, your tax bill would double, but your after-tax real income would remain constant at $22,312.50. Bracket creep was a real problem until the 1980s, when indexing put an end to it.

[12] You do not pay Social Security and Medicare taxes on interest, dividends, and capital gains, only on earned income, but state taxes are generally imposed on dividends, interest, and capital gains.

taxed, there is *double taxation* of corporate income — income is first taxed at the corporate rate, and when what is left is paid out as dividends, it is taxed again at the personal rate.

It should be noted that under U.S. tax laws, interest on most state and local government bonds, called *municipals* or *"munis,"* is not subject to federal income taxes. Thus, investors get to keep all of the interest received from most municipal bonds but only a fraction of the interest received from bonds issued by corporations or by the U.S. government. This means that a lower-yielding muni can provide the same after-tax return as a higher-yielding corporate bond. For example, a taxpayer in the 39.6 percent marginal tax bracket who could buy a muni that yielded 5.5 percent would have to receive a before-tax yield of 9.11 percent on a corporate or U.S. Treasury bond to have the same after-tax income:

$$\text{Equivalent pre-tax yield on taxable bond} = \frac{\text{Yield on muni}}{1 - \text{Marginal tax rate}}$$

$$= \frac{5.5\%}{1 - 0.396} = 9.11\%.$$

If we know the yield on the taxable bond, we can use the following equation to find the equivalent yield on a muni:

$$\text{Equivalent yield on muni} = \left(\begin{array}{c} \text{Pre-tax yield} \\ \text{on taxable} \\ \text{bond} \end{array} \right)(1 - \text{Marginal tax rate})$$

$$= 9.11\% (1 - 0.396) = 9.11\%(0.604) = 5.5\%.$$

The exemption from federal taxes stems from the separation of federal and state powers, and its primary effect is to help state and local governments borrow at lower rates than they otherwise could.

Munis always yield less than corporate bonds with similar risk, maturity, and liquidity. Because of this, it would make no sense for someone in a zero or very low tax bracket to buy munis. Therefore, most munis are owned by high-bracket investors.

Capital Gains versus Ordinary Income

Capital Gain or Loss
The profit (loss) from the sale of a capital asset for more (less) than its purchase price.

Assets such as stocks, bonds, and real estate are defined as *capital assets.* If you buy a capital asset and later sell it for more than your purchase price, the profit is called a **capital gain;** if you suffer a loss, it is called a **capital loss.** An asset sold within one year of the time it was purchased produces a *short-term gain or loss* and one held for more than a year produces a *long-term gain or loss.* Thus, if you buy 100 shares of Disney stock for $42 per share and sell it for $52 per share, you make a capital gain of 100 × $10, or $1,000. However, if you sell the stock for $32 per share, you will have a $1,000 capital loss. Depending on how long you held the stock, you will have a short-term or long-term gain or loss.[13] If you sell the stock for exactly $42 per share, you make neither a gain nor a loss; you simply get your $4,200 back, and no tax is due.

---

[13] If you have a net capital loss (capital losses exceed capital gains) for the year, you can currently deduct only up to $3,000 of this loss against your other income (for example, salary, interest, and dividends). This $3,000 loss limitation is not applicable to losses on the sale of business assets, which by definition are not capital assets.

Short-term capital gains are added to such ordinary income as wages, dividends, and interest and then are taxed at the same rate as ordinary income. However, long-term capital gains are taxed differently. The top rate on long-term gains is 20 percent. Thus, if in 2000 you were in the 39.6 percent tax bracket, any short-term gains you earned would be taxed just like ordinary income, but your long-term gains would be taxed at 20 percent. Thus, capital gains on assets held for more than 12 months are better than ordinary income for many people because the tax bite is smaller.[14]

Capital gains tax rates have varied over time, but they have generally been lower than rates on ordinary income. The reason is simple — Congress wants the economy to grow, for growth we need investment in productive assets, and low capital gains tax rates encourage investment. To see why, suppose you owned a company that earned $1 million after corporate taxes. Because it is your company, you could have it pay out the entire $1 million profit as dividends, or you could have it retain and reinvest all or part of the income to expand the business. If it paid dividends, they would be taxable to you at a rate of 39.6 percent. However, if the company reinvests its income, that reinvestment should cause the company's earnings and stock price to increase. Then, if you wait for one year and then sell some of your stock at a now-higher price, you will have earned capital gains, but they will be taxed at only 20 percent. Further, you can postpone the capital gains tax indefinitely by simply not selling the stock.

It should be clear that a lower tax rate on capital gains will encourage investment. The owners of small businesses will want to reinvest income to get capital gains, as will stockholders in large corporations. Individuals with money to invest will understand the tax advantages associated with investing in newly formed companies versus buying bonds, so new ventures will have an easier time attracting equity capital. All in all, lower capital gains tax rates stimulate capital formation and investment.[15]

CORPORATE INCOME TAXES

The corporate tax structure, shown in Table 2-7, is relatively simple. To illustrate, if a firm had $65,000 of taxable income, its tax bill would be

$$\text{Taxes} = \$7,500 + 0.25(\$15,000)$$
$$= \$7,500 + \$3,750 = \$11,250,$$

---

[14] The Tax Code governing capital gains is very complex, and we have illustrated only the most common provision.

[15] Fifty percent of any capital gains on the newly issued stock of certain small companies is excluded from taxation, provided the small-company stock is held for five years or longer. The remaining 50 percent of the gain is taxed at a rate of 20 percent for most taxpayers. Thus, if one bought newly issued stock from a qualifying small company and held it for at least five years, any capital gains would be taxed at a maximum rate of 10 percent for most taxpayers. This provision was designed to help small businesses attract equity capital.

TABLE 2-7 | Corporate Tax Rates as of January 2001

IF A CORPORATION'S TAXABLE INCOME IS	IT PAYS THIS AMOUNT ON THE BASE OF THE BRACKET	PLUS THIS PERCENTAGE ON THE EXCESS OVER THE BASE	AVERAGE TAX RATE AT TOP OF BRACKET
Up to $50,000	$ 0	15%	15.0%
$50,000–$75,000	7,500	25	18.3
$75,000–$100,000	13,750	34	22.3
$100,000–$335,000	22,250	39	34.0
$335,000–$10,000,000	113,900	34	34.0
$10,000,000–$15,000,000	3,400,000	35	34.3
$15,000,000–$18,333,333	5,150,000	38	35.0
Over $18,333,333	6,416,667	35	35.0

and its average tax rate would be $11,250/$65,000 = 17.3%. Note that corporate income above $18,333,333 has an average and marginal tax rate of 35 percent.[16]

Interest and Dividend Income Received by a Corporation

Interest income received by a corporation is taxed as ordinary income at regular corporate tax rates. *However, 70 percent of the dividends received by one corporation from another is excluded from taxable income, while the remaining 30 percent is*

---

[16] Prior to 1987, many large, profitable corporations such as General Electric and Boeing paid no income taxes. The reasons for this were as follows: (1) expenses, especially depreciation, were defined differently for calculating taxable income than for reporting earnings to stockholders, so some companies reported positive profits to stockholders but losses — hence no taxes — to the Internal Revenue Service; and (2) some companies that did have tax liabilities used various tax credits to offset taxes that would otherwise have been payable. This situation was effectively eliminated in 1987.

The principal method used to eliminate this situation is the Alternative Minimum Tax (AMT). Under the AMT, both corporate and individual taxpayers must figure their taxes in two ways, the "regular" way and the AMT way, and then pay the higher of the two. The AMT is calculated as follows: (1) Figure your regular taxes. (2) Take your taxable income under the regular method and then add back certain items, especially income on certain municipal bonds, depreciation in excess of straight-line depreciation, certain research and drilling costs, itemized or standard deductions (for individuals), and a number of other items. (3) The income determined in (2) is defined as AMT income, and it must then be multiplied by the AMT tax rate to determine the tax due under the AMT system. An individual or corporation must then pay the higher of the regular tax or the AMT tax. In 2000, there were two AMT tax rates for individuals (26 percent and 28 percent, depending on the level of AMT income and filing status). Most corporations have an AMT of 20 percent. However, there is no AMT for very small companies, defined as those that have had average sales of less than $5 million for the last three years and whose average sales continue to be less than $7.5 million.

taxed at the ordinary tax rate.[17] Thus, a corporation earning more than $18,333,333 and paying a 35 percent marginal tax rate would pay only $(0.30)(0.35) = 0.105 = 10.5\%$ of its dividend income as taxes, so its effective tax rate on dividends received would be 10.5 percent. If this firm had $10,000 in pre-tax dividend income, its after-tax dividend income would be $8,950:

$$\begin{aligned}
\frac{\text{After-tax}}{\text{income}} &= \text{Before-tax income} - \text{Taxes} \\
&= \text{Before-tax income} - (\text{Before-tax income})(\text{Effective tax rate}) \\
&= \text{Before-tax income}(1 - \text{Effective tax rate}) \\
&= \$10,000\,[1 - (0.30)(0.35)] \\
&= \$10,000(1 - 0.105) = \$10,000(0.895) = \$8,950.
\end{aligned}$$

If the corporation pays its own after-tax income out to its stockholders as dividends, the income is ultimately subjected to *triple taxation:* (1) the original corporation is first taxed, (2) the second corporation is then taxed on the dividends it received, and (3) the individuals who receive the final dividends are taxed again. This is the reason for the 70 percent exclusion on intercorporate dividends.

If a corporation has surplus funds that can be invested in marketable securities, the tax factor favors investment in stocks, which pay dividends, rather than in bonds, which pay interest. For example, suppose GE had $100,000 to invest, and it could buy either bonds that paid interest of $8,000 per year or preferred stock that paid dividends of $7,000. GE is in the 35 percent tax bracket; therefore, its tax on the interest, if it bought bonds, would be $0.35(\$8,000) = \$2,800$, and its after-tax income would be $5,200. If it bought preferred (or common) stock, its tax would be $0.35[(0.30)(\$7,000)] = \$735$, and its after-tax income would be $6,265. Other factors might lead GE to invest in bonds, but the tax factor certainly favors stock investments when the investor is a corporation.[18]

Interest and Dividends Paid by a Corporation

A firm's operations can be financed with either debt or equity capital. If it uses debt, it must pay interest on this debt, whereas if it uses equity, it is expected to

---

[17] The size of the dividend exclusion actually depends on the degree of ownership. Corporations that own less than 20 percent of the stock of the dividend-paying company can exclude 70 percent of the dividends received; firms that own more than 20 percent but less than 80 percent can exclude 80 percent of the dividends; and firms that own more than 80 percent can exclude the entire dividend payment. We will, in general, assume a 70 percent dividend exclusion.

[18] This illustration demonstrates why corporations favor investing in lower-yielding preferred stocks over higher-yielding bonds. When tax consequences are considered, the yield on the preferred stock, $[1 - 0.35(0.30)](7.0\%) = 6.265\%$, is higher than the yield on the bond, $(1 - 0.35)(8.0\%) = 5.200\%$. Also, note that corporations are restricted in their use of borrowed funds to purchase other firms' preferred or common stocks. Without such restrictions, firms could engage in *tax arbitrage*, whereby the interest on borrowed funds reduces taxable income on a dollar-for-dollar basis, but taxable income is increased by only $0.30 per dollar of dividend income. Thus, current tax laws reduce the 70 percent dividend exclusion in proportion to the amount of borrowed funds used to purchase the stock.

pay dividends to the equity investors (stockholders). The interest *paid* by a corporation is deducted from its operating income to obtain its taxable income, but dividends paid are not deductible. Therefore, a firm needs $1 of pre-tax income to pay $1 of interest, but if it is in the 40 percent federal-plus-state tax bracket, it must earn $1.67 of pre-tax income to pay $1 of dividends:

$$\frac{\text{Pre-tax income needed}}{\text{to pay \$1 of dividends}} = \frac{\$1}{1 - \text{Tax rate}} = \frac{\$1}{0.60} = \$1.67.$$

Working backward, if a company has $1.67 in pre-tax income, it must pay $0.67 in taxes [(0.4)($1.67) = $0.67]. This leaves it with after-tax income of $1.00.

Table 2-8 shows the situation for a firm with $10 million of assets, sales of $5 million, and $1.5 million of earnings before interest and taxes (EBIT). As shown in Column 1, if the firm were financed entirely by bonds, and if it made interest payments of $1.5 million, its taxable income would be zero, taxes would be zero, and its investors would receive the entire $1.5 million. (The term *investors* includes both stockholders and bondholders.) However, as shown in Column 2, if the firm had no debt and was therefore financed only by stock, all of the $1.5 million of EBIT would be taxable income to the corporation, the tax would be $1,500,000(0.40) = $600,000, and investors would receive only $0.9 million versus $1.5 million under debt financing. The rate of return to investors on their $10 million investment is therefore much higher if debt is used.

Of course, it is generally not possible to finance exclusively with debt capital, and the risk of doing so would offset the benefits of the higher expected income. *Still, the fact that interest is a deductible expense has a profound effect on the way businesses are financed — our corporate tax system favors debt financing over equity financing.* This point is discussed in more detail in Chapters 10 and 13.

Corporate Capital Gains

Before 1987, corporate long-term capital gains were taxed at lower rates than corporate ordinary income, so the situation was similar for corporations and

TABLE 2-8	Returns to Investors under Bond and Stock Financing

	USE BONDS (1)	USE STOCK (2)
Sales	$5,000,000	$5,000,000
Operating costs	3,500,000	3,500,000
Earnings before interest and taxes (EBIT)	$1,500,000	$1,500,000
Interest	1,500,000	0
Taxable income	$ 0	$1,500,000
Federal-plus-state taxes (40%)	0	600,000
After-tax income	$ 0	$ 900,000
Income to investors	$1,500,000	$ 900,000
Rate of return on $10 million of assets	15.0%	9.0%

individuals. Under current law, however, corporations' capital gains are taxed at the same rates as their operating income.

Corporate Loss Carry-Back and Carry-Forward

Ordinary corporate operating losses can be carried back **(carry-back)** to each of the preceding 2 years and forward **(carry-forward)** for the next 20 years and used to offset taxable income in those years. For example, an operating loss in 2002 could be carried back and used to reduce taxable income in 2000 and 2001, and forward, if necessary, and used in 2003, 2004, and so on, to the year 2022. The loss is typically applied first to the earliest year, then to the next earliest year, and so on, until losses have been used up or the 20-year carry-forward limit has been reached.

To illustrate, suppose Apex Corporation had $2 million of *pre-tax* profits (taxable income) in 2000 and 2001, and then, in 2002, Apex lost $12 million. Also, assume that Apex's federal-plus-state tax rate is 40 percent. As shown in Table 2-9, the company would use the carry-back feature to recompute its taxes for 2000, using $2 million of the 2002 operating losses to reduce the 2000 pre-tax profit to zero. This would permit it to recover the taxes paid in 2000. Therefore, in 2002 Apex would receive a refund of its 2000 taxes be-cause of the loss experienced in 2002. Because $10 million of the unrecovered losses would still be available, Apex would repeat this procedure for 2001. Thus, in 2002 the company would pay zero taxes for 2002 and also would re-ceive a refund for taxes paid in 2000 and 2001. Apex would still have $8 mil-lion of unrecovered losses to carry forward, subject to the 20-year limit. This $8 million could be used until the entire $12 million loss had been used to offset taxable income. The purpose of permitting this loss treatment is to avoid penalizing corporations whose incomes fluctuate substantially from year to year.

TABLE 2-9	Apex Corporation: Calculation of Loss Carry-Back and Carry-Forward for 2000–2001 Using a $12 Million 2002 Loss	

	2000	2001
Original taxable income	$2,000,000	$2,000,000
Carry-back credit	− 2,000,000	− 2,000,000
Adjusted profit	$ 0	$ 0
Taxes previously paid (40%)	800,000	800,000
Difference = Tax refund	$ 800,000	$ 800,000

Total refund check received in 2003: $800,000 + $800,000 = $1,600,000

Amount of loss carry-forward available for use in 2003–2022:

2002 loss		$12,000,000
Carry-back losses used		4,000,000
Carry-forward losses still available		$ 8,000,000

Many multinational corporations have found an interesting but controversial way to reduce their tax burdens: By shifting some of their operations to countries with low or nonexistent taxes, they can significantly reduce their total tax bills. Over the years, several countries have passed tax laws that make the countries *tax havens* designed to attract foreign investment. Notable examples include the Bahamas, Grand Cayman, and the Netherlands Antilles.

Rupert Murdoch, chairman of global media giant News Corporation, has in some years paid virtually no taxes on his U.S. businesses, despite the fact that these businesses represent roughly 70 percent of his total operating profit. How has Murdoch been able to reduce his tax burden? By shifting profits to a News Corp. subsidiary that is incorporated in the Netherlands Antilles. As Murdoch puts it, "Moving assets around like that is one of the advantages of being global."

While activities such as Murdoch's are legal, some have questioned their ethics. Clearly, shareholders want corporations to take legal steps to reduce taxes. Indeed, many argue that managers have a fiduciary responsibility to take such actions whenever they are cost effective. Moreover, citizens of the various tax havens benefit from foreign investment. Who loses? Obviously, the United States loses tax revenue whenever a domestic corporation establishes a subsidiary in a tax haven. Ultimately, this loss of tax revenue either reduces services or raises the tax burden on other corporations and individuals. Nevertheless, even the U.S. government is itself somewhat ambivalent about the establishment of off-shore subsidiaries — it does not like to lose tax revenues, but it does like to encourage foreign investment.

To learn more about tax havens, check out **http://www.escapeartist.com** for an in-depth analysis into tax havens, including country profiles and indexes of offshore banks and foreign markets.

Improper Accumulation
Retention of earnings by a business for the purpose of enabling stockholders to avoid personal income taxes.

Improper Accumulation to Avoid Payment of Dividends

Corporations could refrain from paying dividends and thus permit their stockholders to avoid personal income taxes on dividends. To prevent this, the Tax Code contains an **improper accumulation** provision that states that earnings accumulated by a corporation are subject to penalty rates *if the purpose of the accumulation is to enable stockholders to avoid personal income taxes.* A cumulative total of $250,000 (the balance sheet item "retained earnings") is by law exempted from the improper accumulation tax for most corporations. This is a benefit primarily to small corporations.

The improper accumulation penalty applies only if the retained earnings in excess of $250,000 are *shown by the IRS to be unnecessary to meet the reasonable needs of the business.* A great many companies do indeed have legitimate reasons for retaining more than $250,000 of earnings. For example, earnings may be retained and used to pay off debt, to finance growth, or to provide the corporation with a cushion against possible cash drains caused by losses. How much a firm should properly accumulate for uncertain contingencies is a matter of judgment. We shall consider this matter again in Chapter 14, which deals with corporate dividend policy.

Consolidated Corporate Tax Returns

If a corporation owns 80 percent or more of another corporation's stock, it can aggregate income and file one consolidated tax return; thus, the losses of one company can be used to offset the profits of another. (Similarly, one division's losses can be used to offset another division's profits.) No business ever wants to incur losses (you can go broke losing $1 to save 35¢ in taxes), but tax offsets do help make it more feasible for large, multidivisional corporations to undertake risky new ventures or ventures that will suffer losses during a developmental period.

TAXATION OF SMALL BUSINESSES: S CORPORATIONS

S Corporation
A small corporation that, under Subchapter S of the Internal Revenue Code, elects to be taxed as a proprietorship or a partnership yet retains limited liability and other benefits of the corporate form of organization.

The Tax Code provides that small businesses that meet certain restrictions as spelled out in the code may be set up as corporations and thus receive the benefits of the corporate form of organization — especially limited liability — yet still be taxed as proprietorships or partnerships rather than as corporations. These corporations are called **S corporations.** ("Regular" corporations are called C corporations.) If a corporation elects S corporation status for tax purposes, all of the business's income is reported as personal income by its stockholders, on a pro rata basis, and thus is taxed at the rates that apply to individuals. This is an important benefit to the owners of small corporations in which all or most of the income earned each year will be distributed as dividends, because then the income is taxed only once, at the individual level.

SELF-TEST QUESTIONS

Explain what is meant by this statement: "Our tax rates are progressive."

Are tax rates progressive for all income ranges?

Explain the difference between marginal tax rates and average tax rates.

What is a "municipal bond," and how are these bonds taxed?

What are capital gains and losses, and how are they taxed relative to ordinary income?

How does the federal income tax system treat corporate dividends received by a corporation versus those received by an individual? Why is this distinction made?

What is the difference in the tax treatment of interest and dividends paid by a corporation? Does this difference favor debt or equity financing?

Briefly explain how tax loss carry-back and carry-forward procedures work.

DEPRECIATION

Depreciation plays an important role in income tax calculations — the larger the depreciation, the lower the taxable income, the lower the tax bill, hence the higher the cash flow from operations. Congress specifies, in the Tax Code, both the life over which assets can be depreciated for tax purposes and the methods of depreciation that can be used. We will discuss in detail how depreciation is calculated, and how it affects income and cash flows, when we take up capital budgeting in Chapters 11 and 12.

The primary purposes of this chapter were (1) to describe the basic financial statements, (2) to present some background information on cash flows, and (3) to provide an overview of the federal income tax system. The key concepts covered are listed below.

- The four basic statements contained in the **annual report** are the balance sheet, the income statement, the statement of retained earnings, and the statement of cash flows. Investors use the information provided in these statements to form expectations about the future levels of earnings and dividends, and about the firm's riskiness.

- The **balance sheet** shows assets on the left-hand side and liabilities and equity, or claims against assets, on the right-hand side. The balance sheet may be thought of as a snapshot of the firm's financial position at a particular point in time.

- The **income statement** reports the results of operations over a period of time, and it shows earnings per share as its "bottom line."

- The **statement of retained earnings** shows the change in retained earnings between the balance sheet dates. Retained earnings represent a claim against assets, not assets per se.

- The **statement of cash flows** reports the impact of operating, investing, and financing activities on cash flows over an accounting period.

- **Net cash flow** differs from **accounting profit** because some of the revenues and expenses reflected in accounting profits may not have been received or paid out in cash during the year. Depreciation is typically the largest noncash item, so net cash flow is often expressed as net income plus depreciation. Investors are at least as interested in a firm's projected net cash flow as in reported earnings because it is cash, not paper profit, that is paid out as dividends and plowed back into the business to produce growth.

- **Net operating working capital** is defined as the difference between the current assets necessary to operate the business and those current liabilities on which no interest is charged (generally, accounts payable and accruals). Thus, net operating working capital is the working capital acquired with investor-supplied funds.

- **Operating assets** are the cash and marketable securities, accounts receivable, inventories, and fixed assets necessary to operate the business.

- **NOPAT** is net operating profit after taxes. It is the after-tax profit a company would have if it had no debt and no investments in nonoperating assets. Since it excludes the effects of financial decisions, it is a better measure of operating performance than is net income.

- **Operating cash flow** arises from normal operations, and it is the difference between cash revenues and cash costs, including taxes on operating income. Operating cash flow differs from net cash flow because operating cash flow does not include either interest income or interest expense. It is equal to NOPAT plus any noncash adjustments.

- **Free cash flow (FCF)** is the amount of cash flow remaining after a company makes the asset investments necessary to support operations. In other words, FCF is the amount of cash flow available for distribution to investors, *so the value of a company is directly related to its ability to generate free cash flow.*
- **Market Value Added (MVA)** represents the difference between the market value of a firm's stock and the amount of equity its investors have supplied.
- **Economic Value Added (EVA)** is the difference between after-tax operating profit and the total cost of capital, including the cost of equity capital. EVA is an estimate of the value created by management during the year, and it differs substantially from accounting profit because no charge for the use of equity capital is reflected in accounting profit.
- The value of any asset depends on the stream of **after-tax cash flows** it produces. Tax rates and other aspects of our tax system are changed by Congress every year or so.
- In the United States, tax rates are **progressive** — the higher one's income, the larger the percentage paid in taxes.
- Assets such as stocks, bonds, and real estate are defined as **capital assets.** If a capital asset is sold for more than its cost, the profit is called a **capital gain.** If the asset is sold for a loss, it is called a **capital loss.** Assets held for more than a year provide **long-term** gains or losses.
- Operating income paid out as dividends is subject to **double taxation:** the income is first taxed at the corporate level, and then shareholders must pay personal taxes on their dividends.
- Interest income received by a corporation is taxed as **ordinary income;** however, 70 percent of the dividends received by one corporation from another are excluded from **taxable income.** The reason for this exclusion is that corporate dividend income is ultimately subjected to **triple taxation**.
- Because interest paid by a corporation is a **deductible** expense while dividends are not, our tax system favors debt over equity financing.
- Ordinary corporate operating losses can be **carried back** to each of the preceding 2 years and **forward** for the next 20 years and used to offset taxable income in those years.
- **S corporations** are small businesses that have the limited-liability benefits of the corporate form of organization yet are taxed as a partnership or a proprietorship.

QUESTIONS

2-1 What four statements are contained in most annual reports?

2-2 If a "typical" firm reports $20 million of retained earnings on its balance sheet, could its directors declare a $20 million cash dividend without any qualms whatsoever?

2-3 Explain the following statement: "While the balance sheet can be thought of as a snapshot of the firm's financial position *at a point in time*, the income statement reports on operations *over a period of time.*"

2-4 Differentiate between accounting income and net cash flow. Why might these two numbers differ?

2-5 Differentiate between operating cash flow and net cash flow. Why might these two numbers differ?

2-6 What do the numbers on financial statements actually represent?

2-7 Who are some of the basic users of financial statements, and how do they use them?

2-8 What is operating capital, and why is it important?

2-9 Explain the difference between NOPAT and net income. Which is a better measure of the performance of a company's operations?

2-10 What is free cash flow? Why is it the most important measure of cash flow?

2-11 In what way does the Tax Code discourage corporations from paying high dividends to their shareholders?

2-12 What does *double taxation of corporate income* mean?

2-13 If you were starting a business, what tax considerations might cause you to prefer to set it up as a proprietorship or a partnership rather than as a corporation?

2-14 Explain how the federal income tax structure affects the choice of financing (use of debt versus equity) of U.S. business firms.

2-15 For someone planning to start a new business, is the average or the marginal tax rate more relevant?

2-16 How might it be possible for a company to generate positive net accounting income yet have a negative EVA?

SELF-TEST PROBLEMS (SOLUTIONS APPEAR IN APPENDIX B)

ST-1
Key terms
Define each of the following terms:
a. Annual report; balance sheet; income statement
b. Common stockholders' equity, or net worth; retained earnings
c. Statement of retained earnings; statement of cash flows
d. Depreciation; tangible assets; amortization; intangible assets; EBITDA
e. Accounting profit; net cash flow; operating cash flow
f. Operating assets; nonoperating assets
g. Operating working capital; net operating working capital
h. Net operating profit after taxes (NOPAT); free cash flow
i. Market Value Added (MVA); Economic Value Added (EVA)
j. Progressive tax; taxable income
k. Marginal and average tax rates
l. Bracket creep
m. Capital gain or loss
n. Tax loss carry-back and carry-forward
o. Improper accumulation
p. S corporation

ST-2
Net income, cash flow, and EVA
Last year Rattner Robotics had $5 million in operating income (EBIT). The company had a net depreciation expense of $1 million and an interest expense of $1 million; its corporate tax rate was 40 percent. The company has $14 million in current assets and $4 million in non-interest-bearing current liabilities; it has $15 million in net plant and equipment. It estimates that it has an after-tax cost of capital of 10 percent. Assume that Rattner's only noncash item was depreciation.
a. What was the company's net income for the year?
b. What was the company's net cash flow?
c. What was the company's net operating profit after taxes (NOPAT)?
d. What was the company's operating cash flow?
e. If operating capital in the previous year was $24 million what was the company's free cash flow (FCF) for the year?
f. What was the company's Economic Value Added (EVA)?

ST-3
Effect of form of organization on taxes
Mary Henderson is planning to start a new business, MH Enterprises, and she must decide whether to incorporate or to do business as a sole proprietorship. Under either form, Henderson will initially own 100 percent of the firm, and tax considerations are important to her. She plans to finance the firm's expected growth by drawing a salary

just sufficient for her family living expenses, which she estimates will be about $40,000, and by retaining all other income in the business. Assume that as a married woman with one child, she files a joint return. She has income tax exemptions of 3 × $2,800 = $8,400, and she estimates that her itemized deductions for each of the 3 years will be $9,700. She expects MH Enterprises to grow and to earn income of $52,700 in 2002, $90,000 in 2003, and $150,000 in 2004. Which form of business organization will allow Henderson to pay the lowest taxes (and retain the most income) during the period from 2002 to 2004? Assume that the tax rates given in the chapter are applicable for all future years. (Social Security taxes would also have to be paid, but ignore them.)

STARTER PROBLEMS

2-1
Income statement

Little Books Inc. recently reported net income of $3 million. Its operating income (EBIT) was $6 million, and the company pays a 40 percent tax rate. What was the company's interest expense for the year? [Hint: Divide $3 million by $(1 - T) = 0.6$ to find taxable income.]

2-2
Net cash flow

Kendall Corners Inc. recently reported net income of $3.1 million. The company's depreciation expense was $500,000. What is the company's approximate net cash flow? Assume the firm has no amortization expense.

2-3
After-tax yield

An investor recently purchased a corporate bond that yields 9 percent. The investor is in the 36 percent tax bracket. What is the bond's after-tax yield?

2-4
Personal taxes

Joe and Jane Keller are a married couple who file a joint income tax return. The couple's taxable income was $102,000. How much federal taxes did they owe? Use the tax tables given in the chapter.

2-5
After-tax yield

Corporate bonds issued by Johnson Corporation currently yield 8 percent. Municipal bonds of equal risk currently yield 6 percent. At what tax rate would an investor be indifferent between these two bonds?

2-6
EVA

Kordell Company recently reported $170,000 in operating income (EBIT). The company's total operating capital is $800,000. The company's after-tax cost of that capital is 11.625 percent, and the company is in the 40 percent tax bracket. What is Kordell's EVA?

2-7
Statement of retained earnings

In its most recent financial statements, Newhouse Inc. reported $50 million of net income and $810 million of retained earnings. The previous year, its balance sheet showed $780 million of retained earnings. What were the total dividends paid to shareholders during the most recent year?

2-8
Income statement

Pearson Brothers recently reported an EBITDA of $7.5 million and $1.8 million of net income. The company has $2.0 million of interest expense and the corporate tax rate is 40 percent. What was the company's depreciation and amortization expense?

EXAM-TYPE PROBLEMS

The problems included in this section are set up in such a way that they could be used as multiple-choice exam problems.

2-9
Corporate tax liability

The Talley Corporation had a 2001 taxable income of $365,000 from operations after all operating costs but before (1) interest charges of $50,000, (2) dividends received of $15,000, (3) dividends paid of $25,000, and (4) income taxes. What is the firm's income tax liability and its after-tax income? What are the company's marginal and average tax rates on taxable income?

2-10
Corporate tax liability

The Wendt Corporation had $10.5 million of taxable income from operations in 2001.
a. What is the company's federal income tax bill for the year?
b. Assume the firm receives an additional $1 million of interest income from some bonds it owns. What is the tax on this interest income?

c. Now assume that Wendt does not receive the interest income but does receive an additional $1 million as dividends on some stock it owns. What is the tax on this dividend income?

2-11
After-tax yield
The Shrieves Corporation has $10,000 that it plans to invest in marketable securities. It is choosing between AT&T bonds, which yield 7.5 percent, state of Florida muni bonds, which yield 5 percent, and AT&T preferred stock, with a dividend yield of 6 percent. Shrieves' corporate tax rate is 35 percent, and 70 percent of the dividends received are tax exempt. Assuming that the investments are equally risky and that Shrieves chooses strictly on the basis of after-tax returns, which security should be selected? What is the after-tax rate of return on the highest-yielding security?

2-12
After-tax yield
Your personal tax rate is 36 percent. You can invest in either corporate bonds that yield 9 percent or municipal bonds (of equal risk) that yield 7 percent. Which investment should you choose? (Ignore state income taxes.)

2-13
Cash flow
The Klaven Corporation has operating income (EBIT) of $750,000. The company's depreciation expense is $200,000. Klaven is 100 percent equity financed, and it faces a 40 percent tax rate. What are its net income, its net cash flow, and its operating cash flow?

2-14
Balance sheet
Which of the following actions will, all else equal, increase the amount of cash on a company's balance sheet?
a. The company issues $2 million in new common stock.
b. The company invests $3 million in new plant and equipment.
c. The company generates negative net income and negative net cash flow during the year.
d. The company increases the dividend paid on its common stock.

2-15
Cash flow
Bailey Corporation recently reported the following income statement (dollars are in thousands):

Sales	$14,000,000
Operating costs excluding depreciation and amortization	7,000,000
EBITDA	$ 7,000,000
Depreciation and amortization	3,000,000
EBIT	$ 4,000,000
Interest	1,500,000
EBT	$ 2,500,000
Taxes (40%)	1,000,000
Net income	$ 1,500,000

Bailey's total operating capital is $20 billion and its after-tax cost of capital is 10 percent. Therefore, Bailey's total after-tax dollar cost of operating capital is $2 billion. During the past year, Bailey made a $1.3 billion net investment in its operating captial.
a. What is Bailey's NOPAT for the year?
b. What is Bailey's net cash flow for the year?
c. What is Bailey's operating cash flow for the year?
d. What is Bailey's free cash flow for the year?
e. What is Bailey's EVA for the year?

PROBLEMS

Note: By the time this book is published, Congress might have changed rates and/or other provisions of current tax law — as noted in the chapter, such changes occur fairly often. Work all problems on the assumption that the information in the chapter is applicable.

The Smythe-Davidson Corporation just issued its annual report. The current year's balance sheet and income statement as they appeared in the annual report are given below. Answer the questions that follow based on information given in the financial statements.

Smythe-Davidson Corporation: Balance Sheet as of December 31, 2001 (Millions of Dollars)

ASSETS		LIABILITIES AND EQUITY	
Cash and marketable securities	$ 15	Accounts payable	$ 120
Accounts receivable	515	Notes payable	220
Inventories	880	Accruals	280
Total current assets	$1,410	Total current liabilities	$ 620
Net plant and equipment	2,590	Long-term bonds	1,520
		Total debt	$2,140
		Preferred stock (800,000 shares)	80
		Common stock (100 million shares)	260
		Retained earnings	1,520
		Common equity	$1,780
Total assets	$4,000	Total liabilities and equity	$4,000

Smythe-Davidson Corporation: Income Statement for Year Ending December 31, 2001 (Millions of Dollars)

Sales	$6,250
Operating costs excluding depreciation	5,230
EBITDA	$1,020
Depreciation	220
EBIT	$ 800
Less: Interest	180
EBT	$ 620
Taxes (40%)	248
Net income before preferred dividends	$ 372
Preferred dividends	8
Net income available to common stockholders	$ 364
Common dividends paid	$ 146
Earnings per share	$3.64

a. Assume that all of the firm's revenues were received in cash during the year and that all costs except depreciation were paid in cash during the year. What is the firm's net cash flow available to common stockholders for the year? How is this number different from the accounting profit reported by the firm?

b. Construct the firm's Statement of Retained Earnings for December 31, 2001.

c. How much money has the firm reinvested in itself over the years instead of paying out dividends?

d. At the present time, how large a check could the firm write without it bouncing?

e. How much money must the firm pay its current creditors within the next year?

2-17

Income and cash flow analysis

The Menendez Corporation expects to have sales of $12 million in 2002. Costs other than depreciation are expected to be 75 percent of sales, and depreciation is expected to be $1.5 million. All sales revenues will be collected in cash, and costs other than depreciation must be paid for during the year. Menendez's federal-plus-state tax rate is 40 percent.

a. Set up an income statement. What is Menendez's expected net cash flow?

b. Suppose Congress changed the tax laws so that Menendez's depreciation expenses doubled. No changes in operations occurred. What would happen to reported profit and to net cash flow?

c. Now suppose that Congress, instead of doubling Menendez's depreciation, reduced it by 50 percent. How would profit and net cash flow be affected?

d. If this were your company, would you prefer Congress to cause your depreciation expense to be doubled or halved? Why?

e. In the situation in which depreciation doubled, would this possibly have an adverse effect on the company's stock price and on its ability to borrow money?

2-18

Income statement

Last year Martin Motors reported the following income statement:

Sales	$2,000,000
Cost of goods sold	1,200,000
EBITDA	$ 800,000
Depreciation	500,000
Operating income (EBIT)	$ 300,000
Interest expense	100,000
Taxable income (EBT)	$ 200,000
Taxes (40%)	80,000
Net income	$ 120,000

The company's CEO, Joe Lawrence, was unhappy with the firm's performance. This year, he would like to see net income doubled to $240,000. Depreciation, interest expense, and the tax rate will all remain constant, and the cost of goods sold will also remain at 60 percent of sales. How much sales revenue must the company generate to achieve the CEO's net income target?

2-19

Free cash flow

You have just obtained financial information for the past 2 years for Powell Panther Corporation. Answer the following questions.

Powell Panther Corporation: Income Statements for Year Ending December 31 (Millions of Dollars)

	2001	2000
Sales	$1,200.0	$1,000.0
Operating costs excluding depreciation	1,020.0	850.0
EBITDA	$ 180.0	$ 150.0
Depreciation	30.0	25.0
Earnings before interest and taxes	$ 150.0	$ 125.0
Less: Interest	21.7	20.2
Earnings before taxes	$ 128.3	$ 104.8
Taxes (40%)	51.3	41.9
Net income available to common stockholders	$ 77.0	$ 62.9
Common dividends	$ 60.5	$ 46.4

Powell Panther Corporation: Balance Sheets as of December 31 (Millions of Dollars)

	2001	2000
ASSETS		
Cash and marketable securities	$ 12.0	$ 10.0
Accounts receivable	180.0	150.0
Inventories	180.0	200.0
Total current assets	$372.0	$360.0
Net plant and equipment	300.0	250.0
Total assets	$672.0	$610.0
LIABILITIES AND EQUITY		
Accounts payable	$108.0	$ 90.0
Notes payable	67.0	51.5
Accruals	72.0	60.0
Total current liabilities	$247.0	$201.5
Long-term bonds	150.0	150.0
Total debt	$397.0	$351.5
Common stock (50 million shares)	50.0	50.0
Retained earnings	225.0	208.5
Common equity	$275.0	$258.5
Total liabilities and equity	$672.0	$610.0

a. What is the net operating profit after taxes (NOPAT) for 2001?
b. What are the amounts of net operating working capital for 2000 and 2001?
c. What are the amounts of total operating capital for 2000 and 2001?
d. What is the free cash flow for 2001?
e. How can you explain the large increase in dividends in 2001?

2-20
Loss carry-back, carry-forward

The Herrmann Company has made $150,000 before taxes during each of the last 15 years, and it expects to make $150,000 a year before taxes in the future. However, in 2001 the firm incurred a loss of $650,000. The firm will claim a tax credit at the time it files its 2001 income tax return, and it will receive a check from the U.S. Treasury. Show how it calculates this credit, and then indicate the firm's tax liability for each of the next 5 years. Assume a 40 percent tax rate on *all* income to ease the calculations.

2-21
Loss carry-back, carry-forward

The projected taxable income of the McAlhany Corporation, formed in 2002, is indicated in the table below. (Losses are shown in parentheses.) What is the corporate tax liability for each year? Assume a constant federal-plus-state tax rate of 40 percent.

YEAR	TAXABLE INCOME
2002	($ 95,000,000)
2003	70,000,000
2004	55,000,000
2005	80,000,000
2006	(150,000,000)

2-22
Form of organization

Susan Visscher has operated her small restaurant as a sole proprietorship for several years, but projected changes in her business's income have led her to consider incorporating. Visscher is married and has two children. Her family's only income, an annual salary of $52,000, is from operating the business. (The business actually earns more than $52,000, but Susan reinvests the additional earnings in the business.) She itemizes deductions, and she is able to deduct $8,600. These deductions, combined with her four personal exemptions for 4 × $2,800 = $11,200, give her a taxable income of $52,000 −

$8,600 − $11,200. (Assume the personal exemption remains at $2,800.) Of course, her actual taxable income, if she does not incorporate, would be higher by the amount of reinvested income. Visscher estimates that her business earnings before salary and taxes for the period 2002 to 2004 will be:

YEAR	EARNINGS BEFORE SALARY AND TAXES
2002	$ 70,000
2003	$ 95,000
2004	$110,000

a. What would her total taxes (corporate plus personal) be in each year under
  (1) A non-S corporate form of organization? (2002 tax = $7,530.)
  (2) A proprietorship? (2002 tax = $8,356.)
b. Should Visscher incorporate? Discuss.

2-23
Personal taxes

Mary Jarvis, a single individual, has this situation for the year 2001: salary of $82,000; dividend income of $12,000; interest on Disney bonds of $5,000; interest on state of Florida municipal bonds of $10,000; proceeds of $22,000 from the sale of Disney stock purchased in 1999 at a cost of $9,000; and proceeds of $22,000 from the November 2001 sale of Disney stock purchased in October 2001 at a cost of $21,000. Jarvis gets one exemption ($2,800), and she has allowable itemized deductions of $6,000; these amounts will be deducted from her gross income to determine her taxable income.
a. What is Jarvis's federal tax liability for 2001?
b. What are her marginal and average tax rates?
c. If she had $5,000 to invest and was offered a choice of either state of Florida bonds with a yield of 6 percent or more Disney bonds with a yield of 8 percent, which should she choose, and why?
d. At what marginal tax rate would Jarvis be indifferent in her choice between the Florida and Disney bonds?

SPREADSHEET PROBLEM

2-24
Financial statements, EVA, and MVA

Laiho Industries' 2000 and 2001 balance sheets (in thousands of dollars) are shown below:

	2001	2000
Cash	$102,850	$ 89,725
Accounts receivable	103,365	85,527
Inventories	38,444	34,982
Total current assets	$244,659	$210,234
Net fixed assets	67,165	42,436
Total assets	$311,824	$252,670
Accounts payable	$ 30,761	$ 23,109
Accruals	30,477	22,656
Notes payable	16,717	14,217
Total current liabilities	$ 77,955	$ 59,982
Long-term debt	76,264	63,914
Total liabilities	$154,219	$123,896
Common stock	100,000	90,000
Retained earnings	57,605	38,774
Total common equity	$157,605	$128,774
Total liabilities and equity	$311,824	$252,670

a. The company's sales for 2001 were $455,150,000, and EBITDA was 15 percent of sales. Furthermore, depreciation amounted to 11 percent of net fixed assets, interest charges were $8,575,000, the state-plus-federal corporate tax rate was 40 percent, and Laiho pays 40 percent of its net income out in dividends. Given this information, construct Laiho's 2001 income statement. (Hint: You might find it easiest to select the balance sheets, then copy them, and then paste them to an *Excel* worksheet. You might have to move the data around some in the worksheet to get things lined up properly.)

b. Next, construct the firm's statement of retained earnings for the year ending December 31, 2001, and then its 2001 statement of cash flows.

c. Calculate net operating working capital, total operating capital, net operating profit after taxes, operating cash flow, and free cash flow for 2001.

d. Calculate the firm's EVA and MVA for 2001. Assume that Laiho had 10 million shares outstanding, that the year-end closing stock price was $17.25 per share, and its after-tax cost of capital was 12 percent.

CYBER PROBLEM

The information related to the cyberproblems is likely to change over time, due to the release of new information and the ever-changing nature of the World Wide Web. With these changes in mind, we will periodically update these problems on the textbook's web site. To avoid problems, please check for these updates before proceeding with the cyberproblems.

2-25

Financial statements, cash flow, and taxes

A manager's primary goal is to maximize the value of his or her firm's stock. The stock's value is calculated as the present value of the firm's future cash flow stream. A study of a firm's financial statements provides clues to its past, present, and likely future performance. Managers must understand financial statements because their actions have a direct impact on them. Managers and investors alike need to know how to read and interpret financial statements.

Let's examine Minnesota Mining and Manufacturing (otherwise known as 3M) Company's financial statements as reported in its 1999 annual report, which can be found at **www.mmm.com/profile/finance/report.html.**

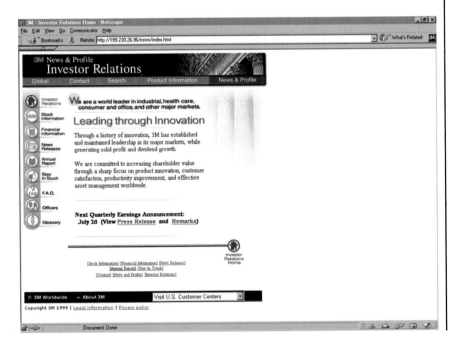

a. Look at 3M's consolidated balance sheet. Did 3M have more or less cash on December 31, 1999, than it did on December 31, 1998? How does this affect the firm's liquidity?

b. What was 3M's method for valuing inventory in fiscal year 1999? Refer to the "notes to consolidated financial statements" where the firm's accounting policies are discussed.

c. What is 3M's total common equity or net worth as of year-end 1999? Is this amount larger or smaller than year-end 1998? (Note that as of December 31, 1999, 3M had no preferred stock.)

d. Look at 3M's consolidated statement of income, which appears before its balance sheet in the annual report. What was 3M's operating income in 1999? Did operating income increase in 1999 when compared against 1998?

e. What was 3M's net income available to common stockholders for fiscal years 1997, 1998, and 1999?

f. What was 3M's reported "basic" and "diluted" earnings per common share (after the extraordinary loss) in 1998 and 1999? (Note that "basic" EPS uses the average number of shares actually outstanding in the EPS calculation, whereas "diluted" EPS assumes that all warrants issued with bonds and all convertibles are exercised and converted into common stock. Warrants and convertibles are discussed briefly in Chapter 8.)

INTEGRATED CASE

D'LEON INC., PART I

2-26 SECTION I: Financial Statements Donna Jamison, a 1996 graduate of the University of Florida with four years of banking experience, was recently brought in as assistant to the chairman of the board of D'Leon Inc., a small food producer that operates in north Florida and whose specialty is high-quality pecan and other nut products sold in the snack-foods market. D'Leon's president, Al Watkins, decided in 2000 to undertake a major expansion and to "go national" in competition with Frito-Lay, Eagle, and other major snack-food companies. Watkins felt that D'Leon's products were of a higher quality than the competition's, that this quality differential would enable it to charge a premium price, and that the end result would be greatly increased sales, profits, and stock price.

The company doubled its plant capacity, opened new sales offices outside its home territory, and launched an expensive advertising campaign. D'Leon's results were not satisfactory, to put it mildly. Its board of directors, which consisted of its president and vice-president plus its major stockholders (who were all local business people), was most upset when directors learned how the expansion was going. Suppliers were being paid late and were unhappy, and the bank was complaining about the deteriorating situation and threatening to cut off credit. As a result, Watkins was informed that changes would have to be made, and quickly, or he would be fired. Also, at the board's insistence Donna Jamison was brought in and given the job of assistant to Fred Campo, a retired banker who was D'Leon's chairman and largest stockholder. Campo agreed to give up a few of his golfing days and to help nurse the company back to health, with Jamison's help.

Jamison began by gathering the financial statements and other data given in Tables IC2-1, IC2-2, IC2-3, and IC2-4. Assume that you are Jamison's assistant, and you must help her answer the following questions for Campo. (Note: We will continue with this case in Chapter 3, and you will feel more comfortable with the analysis there, but answering these questions will help prepare you for Chapter 3. Provide clear explanations, not just yes or no answers!)

a. What effect did the expansion have on sales, net operating profit after taxes (NOPAT), net operating working capital (NOWC), total investor-supplied operating capital, and net income?

b. What effect did the company's expansion have on its net cash flow, operating cash flow, and free cash flow?

c. Jamison also has asked you to estimate D'Leon's EVA. She estimates that the after-tax cost of capital was 10 percent in 2000 and 13 percent in 2001.

d. Looking at D'Leon's stock price today, would you conclude that the expansion increased or decreased MVA?

e. D'Leon purchases materials on 30-day terms, meaning that it is supposed to pay for purchases within 30 days of receipt. Judging from its 2001 balance sheet, do you think D'Leon pays suppliers on time? Explain. If not, what problems might this lead to?

Balance Sheets

	2001	2000
ASSETS		
Cash	$ 7,282	$ 57,600
Accounts receivable	632,160	351,200
Inventories	1,287,360	715,200
Total current assets	$1,926,802	$1,124,000
Gross fixed assets	1,202,950	491,000
Less accumulated depreciation	263,160	146,200
Net fixed assets	$ 939,790	$ 344,800
Total assets	$2,866,592	$1,468,800
LIABILITIES AND EQUITY		
Accounts payable	$ 524,160	$ 145,600
Notes payable	636,808	200,000
Accruals	489,600	136,000
Total current liabilities	$1,650,568	$ 481,600
Long-term debt	723,432	323,432
Common stock (100,000 shares)	460,000	460,000
Retained earnings	32,592	203,768
Total equity	$ 492,592	$ 663,768
Total liabilities and equity	$2,866,592	$1,468,800

f. D'Leon spends money for labor, materials, and fixed assets (depreciation) to make products, and still more money to sell those products. Then, it makes sales that result in receivables, which eventually result in cash inflows. Does it appear that D'Leon's sales price exceeds its costs per unit sold? How does this affect the cash balance?

g. Suppose D'Leon's sales manager told the sales staff to start offering 60-day credit terms rather than the 30-day terms now being offered. D'Leon's competitors react by offering similar terms, so sales remain constant. What effect would this have on the cash account? How would the cash account be affected if sales doubled as a result of the credit policy change?

h. Can you imagine a situation in which the sales price exceeds the cost of producing and selling a unit of output, yet a dramatic increase in sales volume causes the cash balance to decline?

i. Did D'Leon finance its expansion program with internally generated funds (additions to retained earnings plus depreciation) or with external capital? How does the choice of financing affect the company's financial strength?

j. Refer to Tables IC2-2 and IC2-4. Suppose D'Leon broke even in 2001 in the sense that sales revenues

equaled total operating costs plus interest charges. Would the asset expansion have caused the company to experience a cash shortage that required it to raise external capital?

k. If D'Leon started depreciating fixed assets over 7 years rather than 10 years, would that affect (1) the physical stock of assets, (2) the balance sheet account for fixed assets, (3) the company's reported net income, and (4) its cash position? Assume the same depreciation method is used for stockholder reporting and for tax calculations, and the accounting change has no effect on assets' physical lives.

l. Explain how earnings per share, dividends per share, and book value per share are calculated, and what they mean. Why does the market price per share *not* equal the book value per share?

m. The 2001 income statement shows negative taxes, that is, a tax credit. Given the tax refund received in 2001, what can you conclude about the amount of taxes paid in the previous 2 years?

SECTION II: Taxes

n. Working with Jamison has required you to put in a lot of overtime, so you have had very little time to spend on

Income Statements

	2001	2000
Sales	$6,034,000	$3,432,000
Cost of goods sold	5,528,000	2,864,000
Other expenses	519,988	358,672
Total operating costs excluding depreciation	$6,047,988	$3,222,672
EBITDA	($13,988)	$ 209,328
Depreciation	116,960	18,900
EBIT	($ 130,948)	$ 190,428
Interest expense	136,012	43,828
EBT	($ 266,960)	$ 146,600
Taxes (40%)	(106,784)[a]	58,640
Net income	($ 160,176)	$ 87,960
EPS	($ 1.602)	$ 0.880
DPS	$ 0.110	$ 0.220
Book value per share	$ 4.926	$ 6.638
Stock price	$ 2.25	$ 8.50
Shares outstanding	100,000	100,000
Tax rate	40.00%	40.00%
Lease payments	40,000	40,000
Sinking fund payments	0	0

[a]The firm had sufficient taxable income in 1999 and 2000 to obtain its full tax refund in 2001.

Statement of Retained Earnings, 2001

Balance of retained earnings, 12/31/00	$203,768
Add: Net income, 2001	(160,176)
Less: Dividends paid	(11,000)
Balance of retained earnings, 12/31/01	$ 32,592

your private finances. It's now April 1, and you have only two weeks left to file your income tax return. You have managed to get all the information together that you will need to complete your return. D'Leon paid you a salary of $45,000, and you received $3,000 in dividends from common stock that you own. You are single, so your personal exemption is $2,800, and your itemized deductions are $5,150.

(1) On the basis of the information above and the April 2001 individual tax rate schedule, what is your tax liability?

(2) What are your marginal and average tax rates?

OPERATING ACTIVITIES	
Net income	($ 160,176)
Additions (Sources of Cash)	
Depreciation	116,960
Increase in accounts payable	378,560
Increase in accruals	353,600
Subtractions (Uses of Cash)	
Increase in accounts receivable	(280,960)
Increase in inventories	(572,160)
Net cash provided by operating activities	($ 164,176)
LONG-TERM INVESTING ACTIVITIES	
Cash used to acquire fixed assets	($ 711,950)
FINANCING ACTIVITIES	
Increase in notes payable	$ 436,808
Increase in long-term debt	400,000
Payment of cash dividends	(11,000)
Net cash provided by financing activities	$ 825,808
Sum: net decrease in cash	($ 50,318)
Plus: cash at beginning of year	57,600
Cash at end of year	$ 7,282

o. Assume that a corporation has $100,000 of taxable income from operations plus $5,000 of interest income and $10,000 of dividend income. What is the company's tax liability?

p. Assume that after paying your personal income tax as calculated in part n, you have $5,000 to invest. You have narrowed your investment choices down to California bonds with a yield of 7 percent or equally risky Exxon Mobil bonds with a yield of 10 percent. Which one should you choose and why? At what marginal tax rate would you be indifferent to the choice between California and Exxon Mobil bonds?

3 Analysis of Financial Statements

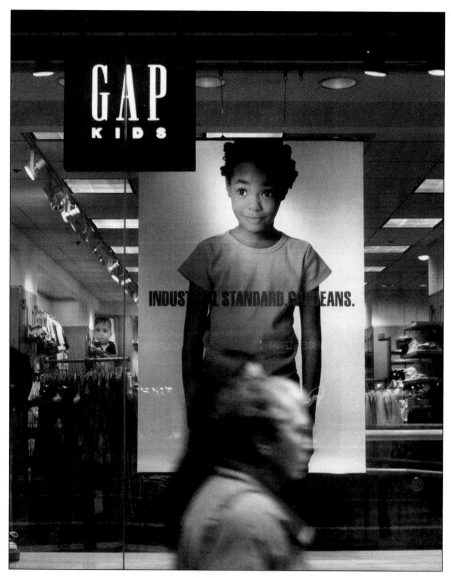

SOURCE: Jerry Arcieri/SABA

NOTE: We have covered this chapter both early in the course and toward the end. Early coverage gives students an overview of how financial decisions affect financial statements and results, and thus of what financial management is all about. Later coverage, after students have an understanding of stock valu-

THE GAP WARNS WALL STREET

GAP INC.

$

S hortly after the markets closed on August 30, 2000, Gap Inc. reported a 14 percent decline in its monthly same-store sales. The markets responded quickly, and Gap's stock price fell sharply in overnight trading. At the end of the following trading day, the stock's price was $22 per share, almost a 60 percent decline from its 52-week high of $53.75.

While the opening of new stores enabled Gap to report a 6 percent increase in overall sales, the market clearly focused on the disappointing decline in same-store sales. Analysts pouring over the company's financial data were also concerned about a weakening economy, the company's recent difficulties in managing its inventory, and the possibility that higher distribution costs and increased competition might lower future operating margins. An even closer look at the data showed that declines in same-store sales occurred at not only the flagship stores but also at the company's Banana Republic and Old Navy units. The more than 20 percent drop in same-store sales for Old Navy was particularly alarming, since analysts had assumed that Old Navy would be a major contributor to the company's future growth. Adding more fuel to the fire, the company indicated that distribution problems would limit the inventory that Old Navy stores would have for their back-to-school sales. Thus, the company cautioned investors that future sales and earnings might be weaker than expected.

Until this recent decline, Gap stock had performed quite well — shareholders have realized a 387 percent cumulative return over the past five years. Following this report, many analysts announced that they were downgrading their opinion of Gap stock. However, other analysts argued that Gap might still be an attractive investment for long-term investors due to its long-term track record and its ability in the past to recover from slumping sales.

Wall Street's response to Gap's announcement brings home several important points. First, investors and others outside the company use reported earnings and other financial statement data to determine a company's value. Second, analysts are primarily concerned about *future* performance — past performance is useful only to the extent that it provides information about the company's future. Finally, analysts go beyond reported profits and dig into the details of the financial statements.

So, while many people regard financial statements as "just accounting," they really are much more. As you will see in this chapter, the statements provide a wealth of information that is used for a wide variety of purposes by managers, investors, lenders, customers, suppliers, and regulators. An analysis of its statements can highlight a company's strengths and shortcomings,

ation, risk analysis, capital budgeting, capital structure, and working capital management, helps students appreciate why ratios are the way they are, and how they are used for different purposes. Depending on students' backgrounds, instructors may want to cover the chapter early or late.

and this information can be used by management to improve performance and by others to forecast future results. As you will see both here and in Chapter 4, financial analysis can be used to predict how such strategic decisions as the sale of a division, a major marketing program, or a plant expansion are likely to affect future financial performance. ■

PUTTING THINGS IN PERSPECTIVE

The primary goal of financial management is to maximize the stock price, not to maximize accounting measures such as net income or EPS. However, accounting data do influence stock prices, and to understand why a company is performing the way it is and to forecast where it is heading, one needs to evaluate the accounting information reported in the financial statements. Chapter 2 described the primary financial statements and showed how they change as a firm's operations undergo change. Now, in Chapter 3, we show how financial statements are used by managers to improve performance, by lenders to evaluate the likelihood of collecting on loans, and by stockholders to forecast earnings, dividends, and stock prices.

If management is to maximize a firm's value, it must take advantage of the firm's strengths and correct its weaknesses. Financial statement analysis involves (1) comparing the firm's performance with that of other firms in the same industry and (2) evaluating trends in the firm's financial position over time. These studies help management identify deficiencies and then take actions to improve performance. In this chapter, we focus on how financial managers (and investors) evaluate a firm's current financial position. Then, in the remaining chapters, we examine the types of actions management can take to improve future performance and thus increase its stock price.

This chapter should, for the most part, be a review of concepts you learned in accounting. However, accounting focuses on how financial statements are *made*, whereas our focus is on how they are *used* by management to improve the firm's performance and by investors when they set values on the firm's stock and bonds. Like Chapter 2, a spreadsheet model accompanies this chapter. You are encouraged to use the model and follow along with the textbook examples. ■

RATIO ANALYSIS

Financial statements report both on a firm's position at a point in time and on its operations over some past period. However, the real value of financial statements lies in the fact that they can be used to help predict future earnings and dividends. From an investor's standpoint, *predicting the future is what financial statement analysis is all about*, while from management's standpoint, *financial statement analysis is useful both to help anticipate future conditions and, more important, as a starting point for planning actions that will improve the firm's future performance.*

Financial ratios are designed to help one evaluate a financial statement. For example, Firm A might have debt of $5,248,760 and interest charges of $419,900, while Firm B might have debt of $52,647,980 and interest charges of $3,948,600. Which company is stronger? The burden of these debts, and the companies' ability to repay them, can best be evaluated (1) by comparing each firm's debt to its assets and (2) by comparing the interest it must pay to the income it has available for payment of interest. Such comparisons are made by *ratio analysis.*

In the paragraphs that follow, we will calculate the Year 2001 financial ratios for Allied Food Products, using data from the balance sheets and income statements given in Tables 2-1 and 2-2 back in Chapter 2. We will also evaluate the ratios in relation to the industry averages.[1] Note that all dollar amounts in the ratio calculations are in millions.

LIQUIDITY RATIOS

Liquid Asset
An asset that can be converted to cash quickly without having to reduce the asset's price very much.

A **liquid asset** is one that trades in an active market and hence can be quickly converted to cash at the going market price, and a firm's "liquidity position" deals with this question: Will the firm be able to pay off its debts as they come due over the next year or so? As shown in Table 2-1 in Chapter 2, Allied has debts totaling $310 million that must be paid off within the coming year. Will it have trouble satisfying those obligations? A full liquidity analysis requires the use of cash budgets, but by relating the amount of cash and other current assets to current obligations, ratio analysis provides a quick, easy-to-use measure of liquidity. Two commonly used **liquidity ratios** are discussed in this section.

Liquidity Ratios
Ratios that show the relationship of a firm's cash and other current assets to its current liabilities.

---

[1] In addition to the ratios discussed in this section, financial analysts also employ a tool known as *common size* balance sheets and income statements. To form a common size balance sheet, one simply divides each asset and liability item by total assets and then expresses the result as a percentage. The resultant percentage statement can be compared with statements of larger or smaller firms, or with those of the same firm over time. To form a common size income statement, one simply divides each income statement item by sales. With a spreadsheet, this is trivially easy.

ABILITY TO MEET SHORT-TERM OBLIGATIONS: THE CURRENT RATIO

Current Ratio
This ratio is calculated by dividing current assets by current liabilities. It indicates the extent to which current liabilities are covered by those assets expected to be converted to cash in the near future.

The **current ratio** is calculated by dividing current assets by current liabilities:

$$\text{Current ratio} = \frac{\text{Current assets}}{\text{Current liabilities}}$$

$$= \frac{\$1,000}{\$310} = 3.2 \text{ times.}$$

Industry average = 4.2 times.

Current assets normally include cash, marketable securities, accounts receivable, and inventories. Current liabilities consist of accounts payable, short-term notes payable, current maturities of long-term debt, accrued taxes, and other accrued expenses (principally wages).

If a company is getting into financial difficulty, it begins paying its bills (accounts payable) more slowly, borrowing from its bank, and so on. If current liabilities are rising faster than current assets, the current ratio will fall, and this could spell trouble. Because the current ratio provides the best single indicator of the extent to which the claims of short-term creditors are covered by assets that are expected to be converted to cash fairly quickly, it is the most commonly used measure of short-term solvency.

Allied's current ratio is well below the average for its industry, 4.2, so its liquidity position is relatively weak. Still, since current assets are scheduled to be converted to cash in the near future, it is highly probable that they could be liquidated at close to their stated value. With a current ratio of 3.2, Allied could liquidate current assets at only 31 percent of book value and still pay off current creditors in full.[2]

Although industry average figures are discussed later in some detail, it should be noted at this point that an industry average is not a magic number that all firms should strive to maintain — in fact, some very well-managed firms will be above the average while other good firms will be below it. However, if a firm's ratios are far removed from the averages for its industry, an analyst should be concerned about why this variance occurs. Thus, a deviation from the industry average should signal the analyst (or management) to check further.

QUICK, OR ACID TEST, RATIO

Quick (Acid Test) Ratio
This ratio is calculated by deducting inventories from current assets and dividing the remainder by current liabilities.

The **quick,** or **acid test, ratio** is calculated by deducting inventories from current assets and then dividing the remainder by current liabilities:

$$\text{Quick, or acid test, ratio} = \frac{\text{Current assets} - \text{Inventories}}{\text{Current liabilities}}$$

$$= \frac{\$385}{\$310} = 1.2 \text{ times.}$$

Industry average = 2.1 times.

---

[2] $1/3.2 = 0.31$, or 31 percent. Note that $0.31(\$1,000) = \$310$, the amount of current liabilities.

Inventories are typically the least liquid of a firm's current assets, hence they are the assets on which losses are most likely to occur in the event of liquidation. Therefore, a measure of the firm's ability to pay off short-term obligations without relying on the sale of inventories is important.

The industry average quick ratio is 2.1, so Allied's 1.2 ratio is low in comparison with other firms in its industry. Still, if the accounts receivable can be collected, the company can pay off its current liabilities without having to liquidate its inventory.

SELF-TEST QUESTIONS

Identify two ratios that are used to analyze a firm's liquidity position, and write out their equations.

What are the characteristics of a liquid asset? Give some examples.

Which current asset is typically the least liquid?

ASSET MANAGEMENT RATIOS

Asset Management Ratios
A set of ratios that measure how effectively a firm is managing its assets.

The second group of ratios, the **asset management ratios**, measures how effectively the firm is managing its assets. These ratios are designed to answer this question: Does the total amount of each type of asset as reported on the balance sheet seem reasonable, too high, or too low in view of current and projected sales levels? When they acquire assets, Allied and other companies must borrow or obtain capital from other sources. If a firm has too many assets, its cost of capital will be too high, hence its profits will be depressed. On the other hand, if assets are too low, profitable sales will be lost. Ratios that analyze the different types of assets are described in this section.

EVALUATING INVENTORIES: THE INVENTORY TURNOVER RATIO

Inventory Turnover Ratio
This ratio is calculated by dividing sales by inventories.

The **inventory turnover ratio** is defined as sales divided by inventories:

$$\text{Inventory turnover ratio} = \frac{\text{Sales}}{\text{Inventories}}$$

$$= \frac{\$3,000}{\$615} = 4.9 \text{ times.}$$

$$\text{Industry average} = 9.0 \text{ times.}$$

As a rough approximation, each item of Allied's inventory is sold out and restocked, or "turned over," 4.9 times per year. "Turnover" is a term that originated many years ago with the old Yankee peddler, who would load up his wagon with goods, then go off on his route to peddle his wares. The merchandise was called "working capital" because it was what he actually sold, or "turned over," to produce his profits, whereas his "turnover" was the number of trips he took each year. Annual sales divided by inventory equaled turnover, or trips per year. If he made 10 trips per year, stocked 100 pans, and made a gross profit of $5 per pan, his annual gross profit would be $(100)(\$5)(10) = \$5,000$. If he went faster and made 20 trips per year, his gross profit would double, other things held constant. So, his turnover directly affected his profits.

Allied's turnover of 4.9 times is much lower than the industry average of 9 times. This suggests that Allied is holding too much inventory. Excess inventory is, of course, unproductive, and it represents an investment with a low or zero rate of return. Allied's low inventory turnover ratio also makes us question the current ratio. With such a low turnover, we must wonder whether the firm is actually holding obsolete goods not worth their stated value.[3]

Note that sales occur over the entire year, whereas the inventory figure is for one point in time. For this reason, it is better to use an average inventory measure.[4] If the firm's business is highly seasonal, or if there has been a strong upward or downward sales trend during the year, it is especially useful to make some such adjustment. To maintain comparability with industry averages, however, we did not use the average inventory figure.

EVALUATING RECEIVABLES: THE DAYS SALES OUTSTANDING

Days Sales Outstanding (DSO)
This ratio is calculated by dividing accounts receivable by average sales per day; indicates the average length of time the firm must wait after making a sale before it receives cash.

Days sales outstanding (DSO), also called the "average collection period" (ACP), is used to appraise accounts receivable, and it is calculated by dividing accounts receivable by average daily sales to find the number of days' sales that are tied up in receivables. Thus, the DSO represents the average length of time that the firm must wait after making a sale before receiving cash, which is the average collection period. Allied has 46 days sales outstanding, well above the 36-day industry average:

$$\text{DSO} = \begin{matrix}\text{Days}\\\text{sales}\\\text{outstanding}\end{matrix} = \frac{\text{Receivables}}{\text{Average sales per day}} = \frac{\text{Receivables}}{\text{Annual sales}/365}$$

$$= \frac{\$375}{\$3,000/365} = \frac{\$375}{\$8.2192} = 45.625 \text{ days} \approx 46 \text{ days.}$$

$$\text{Industry average} = 36 \text{ days.}$$

---

[3] A problem arises calculating and analyzing the inventory turnover ratio. Sales are stated at market prices, so if inventories are carried at cost, as they generally are, the calculated turnover overstates the true turnover ratio. Therefore, it would be more appropriate to use cost of goods sold in place of sales in the formula's numerator. However, established compilers of financial ratio statistics such as Dun & Bradstreet use the ratio of sales to inventories carried at cost. To develop a figure that can be compared with those published by Dun & Bradstreet and similar organizations, it is necessary to measure inventory turnover with sales in the numerator, as we do here.

[4] Preferably, the average inventory value should be calculated by summing the monthly figures during the year and dividing by 12. If monthly data are not available, one can add the beginning and ending figures and divide by 2. Both methods adjust for growth but not for seasonal effects.

Note that in this calculation we used a 365-day year. Other analysts use a 360-day year for this calculation. If Allied had calculated its DSO using a 360-day year, its DSO would have been reduced slightly to 45 days.[5]

The DSO can also be evaluated by comparison with the terms on which the firm sells its goods. For example, Allied's sales terms call for payment within 30 days, so the fact that 46 days' sales, not 30 days', are outstanding indicates that customers, on the average, are not paying their bills on time. This deprives Allied of funds that it could use to invest in productive assets. Moreover, in some instances the fact that a customer is paying late may signal that the customer is in financial trouble, in which case Allied may have a hard time ever collecting the receivable. Therefore, if the trend in DSO over the past few years has been rising, but the credit policy has not been changed, this would be strong evidence that steps should be taken to expedite the collection of accounts receivable.

EVALUATING FIXED ASSETS: THE FIXED ASSETS TURNOVER RATIO

Fixed Assets Turnover Ratio
The ratio of sales to net fixed assets.

The **fixed assets turnover ratio** measures how effectively the firm uses its plant and equipment. It is the ratio of sales to net fixed assets:

$$\text{Fixed assets turnover ratio} = \frac{\text{Sales}}{\text{Net fixed assets}}$$

$$= \frac{\$3,000}{\$1,000} = 3.0 \text{ times.}$$

Industry average = 3.0 times.

Allied's ratio of 3.0 times is equal to the industry average, indicating that the firm is using its fixed assets about as intensively as are other firms in its industry. Therefore, Allied seems to have about the right amount of fixed assets in relation to other firms.

A potential problem can exist when interpreting the fixed assets turnover ratio. Recall from accounting that fixed assets reflect the historical costs of the assets. Inflation has caused the value of many assets that were purchased in the past to be seriously understated. Therefore, if we were comparing an old firm that had acquired many of its fixed assets years ago at low prices with a new company that had acquired its fixed assets only recently, we would probably find that the old firm had the higher fixed assets turnover ratio. However, this would be more reflective of the difficulty accountants have in dealing with inflation than of any inefficiency on the part of the new firm. The accounting profession is trying to devise ways of making financial statements reflect current values rather than historical values. If balance sheets were actually stated on a current value basis, this would help us make better comparisons, but at the

---

[5] It would be better to use *average* receivables, either an average of the monthly figures or (Beginning receivables + Ending receivables)/2 = ($315 + $375)/2 = $345 in the formula. Had the annual average receivables been used, Allied's DSO on a 365-day basis would have been $345.00/$8.2192 = 41.975 days, or approximately 42 days. The 42-day figure is the more accurate one, but because the industry average was based on year-end receivables, we used 46 days for our comparison. The DSO is discussed further in Chapter 15.

moment the problem still exists. Since financial analysts typically do not have the data necessary to make adjustments, they simply recognize that a problem exists and deal with it judgmentally. In Allied's case, the issue is not a serious one because all firms in the industry have been expanding at about the same rate, hence the balance sheets of the comparison firms are reasonably comparable.[6]

EVALUATING TOTAL ASSETS: THE TOTAL ASSETS TURNOVER RATIO

Total Assets Turnover Ratio
This ratio is calculated by dividing sales by total assets.

The final asset management ratio, the **total assets turnover ratio**, measures the turnover of all the firm's assets; it is calculated by dividing sales by total assets:

$$\text{Total assets turnover ratio} = \frac{\text{Sales}}{\text{Total assets}}$$

$$= \frac{\$3,000}{\$2,000} = 1.5 \text{ times.}$$

$$\text{Industry average} = 1.8 \text{ times.}$$

Allied's ratio is somewhat below the industry average, indicating that the company is not generating a sufficient volume of business given its total assets investment. Sales should be increased, some assets should be disposed of, or a combination of these steps should be taken.

SELF-TEST QUESTIONS

Identify four ratios that are used to measure how effectively a firm is managing its assets, and write out their equations.

How might rapid growth distort the inventory turnover ratio?

What potential problem might arise when comparing different firms' fixed assets turnover ratios?

DEBT MANAGEMENT RATIOS

Financial Leverage
The use of debt financing.

The extent to which a firm uses debt financing, or **financial leverage**, has three important implications: (1) By raising funds through debt, stockholders can maintain control of a firm while limiting their investment. (2) Creditors look to the equity, or owner-supplied funds, to provide a margin of safety, so the higher the proportion of the total capital that was provided by stockholders, the less the risk faced by creditors. (3) If the firm earns more on investments financed with borrowed funds than it pays in interest, the return on the owners' capital is magnified, or "leveraged."

---

[6] See FASB #89, *Financial Reporting and Changing Prices* (December 1986), for a discussion of the effects of inflation on financial statements.

To understand better how financial leverage affects risk and return, consider Table 3-1. Here we analyze two companies that are identical except for the way they are financed. Firm U (for "unleveraged") has no debt, whereas Firm L (for "leveraged") is financed with half equity and half debt that costs 15 percent. Both companies have $100 of assets and $100 of sales, and their expected operating income (also called earnings before interest and taxes, or EBIT) is $30. Thus, both firms *expect* to earn $30, before taxes, on their assets. Of course, things could turn out badly, in which case EBIT would be lower. Thus, in the

TABLE 3-1	Effects of Financial Leverage on Stockholders' Returns

FIRM U (UNLEVERAGED)

Current assets	$ 50	Debt	$ 0
Fixed assets	50	Common equity	100
Total assets	$100	Total liabilities and equity	$100

	EXPECTED CONDITIONS (1)	BAD CONDITIONS (2)
Sales	$100.00	$82.50
Operating costs	70.00	80.00
Operating income (EBIT)	$ 30.00	$ 2.50
Interest	0.00	0.00
Earnings before taxes (EBT)	$ 30.00	$ 2.50
Taxes (40%)	12.00	1.00
Net income (NI)	$ 18.00	$ 1.50
ROE_U = NI/Common equity = NI/$100 =	18.00%	1.50%

FIRM L (LEVERAGED)

Current assets	$ 50	Debt (interest = 15%)	$ 50
Fixed assets	50	Common equity	50
Total assets	$100	Total liabilities and equity	$100

	EXPECTED CONDITIONS (1)	BAD CONDITIONS (2)
Sales	$100.00	$82.50
Operating costs	70.00	80.00
Operating income (EBIT)	$ 30.00	$ 2.50
Interest (15%)	7.50	7.50
Earnings before taxes (EBT)	$ 22.50	($ 5.00)
Taxes (40%)	9.00	(2.00)
Net income (NI)	$ 13.50	($ 3.00)
ROE_L = NI/Common equity = NI/$50 =	27.00%	(6.00%)

second column of the table, we show EBIT declining from $30 to $2.50 under bad conditions.

Even though both companies' assets produce the same expected EBIT, under normal conditions Firm L should provide its stockholders with a return on equity of 27 percent versus only 18 percent for Firm U. This difference is caused by Firm L's use of debt, which "leverages up" its expected rate of return to stockholders. There are two reasons for the leveraging effect: (1) Since interest is deductible, the use of debt lowers the tax bill and leaves more of the firm's operating income available to its investors. (2) If operating income as a percentage of assets exceeds the interest rate on debt, as it generally does, then a company can use debt to acquire assets, pay the interest on the debt, and have something left over as a "bonus" for its stockholders. For our hypothetical firms, these two effects combine to push Firm L's expected rate of return on equity up far above that of Firm U. Thus, debt can "leverage up" the rate of return on equity.

However, financial leverage can cut both ways. As we show in Column 2, if sales are lower and costs are higher than were expected, the return on assets will also be lower than was expected. Under these conditions, the leveraged firm's return on equity falls especially sharply, and losses occur. Under the "bad conditions" in Table 3-1, the debt-free firm still shows a profit, but Firm L shows a loss and thus has a negative return on equity. This occurs because Firm L needs cash to service its debt, while Firm U does not. Firm U, because of its strong balance sheet, could ride out the recession and be ready for the next boom. Firm L, on the other hand, must pay interest of $7.50 regardless of its level of sales. Since in the recession its operations do not generate enough income to meet the interest payments, cash would be depleted, and the firm probably would need to raise additional funds. Because it would be running a loss, Firm L would have a hard time selling stock to raise capital, and its losses would cause lenders to raise the interest rate, increasing L's problems still further. As a result, Firm L just might not survive to enjoy the next boom.

We see, then, that firms with relatively high debt ratios have higher expected returns when the economy is normal, but they are exposed to risk of loss when the economy goes into a recession. Therefore, decisions about the use of debt require firms to balance higher expected returns against increased risk. Determining the optimal amount of debt is a complicated process, and we defer a discussion of this topic until Chapter 13. For now, we simply look at two procedures analysts use to examine the firm's debt: (1) They check the balance sheet to determine the proportion of total funds represented by debt, and (2) they review the income statement to see how well fixed charges are covered by operating profits.

HOW THE FIRM IS FINANCED: TOTAL DEBT TO TOTAL ASSETS

Debt Ratio
The ratio of total debt to total assets.

The ratio of total debt to total assets, generally called the **debt ratio**, measures the percentage of funds provided by creditors:

$$\text{Debt ratio} = \frac{\text{Total debt}}{\text{Total assets}}$$

$$= \frac{\$310 + \$754}{\$2,000} = \frac{\$1,064}{\$2,000} = 53.2\%.$$

$$\text{Industry average} = 40.0\%.$$

Total debt includes both current liabilities and long-term debt. Creditors prefer low debt ratios because the lower the ratio, the greater the cushion against creditors' losses in the event of liquidation. Stockholders, on the other hand, may want more leverage because it magnifies expected earnings.

Allied's debt ratio is 53.2 percent, which means that its creditors have supplied more than half the total financing. As we will discuss in Chapter 13, there are a variety of factors that determine a company's optimal debt ratio. Nevertheless, the fact that Allied's debt ratio exceeds the industry average raises a red flag and may make it costly for Allied to borrow additional funds without first raising more equity capital. Creditors may be reluctant to lend the firm more money, and management would probably be subjecting the firm to the risk of bankruptcy if it sought to increase the debt ratio any further by borrowing additional funds.[7]

ABILITY TO PAY INTEREST: TIMES-INTEREST-EARNED RATIO

Times-Interest-Earned (TIE) Ratio
The ratio of earnings before interest and taxes (EBIT) to interest charges; a measure of the firm's ability to meet its annual interest payments.

The **times-interest-earned (TIE) ratio** is determined by dividing earnings before interest and taxes (EBIT in Table 2-2) by the interest charges:

$$\text{Times-interest-earned (TIE) ratio} = \frac{\text{EBIT}}{\text{Interest charges}}$$

$$= \frac{\$283.8}{\$88} = 3.2 \text{ times.}$$

$$\text{Industry average} = 6.0 \text{ times.}$$

The TIE ratio measures the extent to which operating income can decline before the firm is unable to meet its annual interest costs. Failure to meet this obligation can bring legal action by the firm's creditors, possibly resulting in bankruptcy. Note that earnings before interest and taxes, rather than net income, is used in the numerator. Because interest is paid with pre-tax dollars, the firm's ability to pay current interest is not affected by taxes.

Allied's interest is covered 3.2 times. Since the industry average is 6 times, Allied is covering its interest charges by a relatively low margin of safety. Thus, the TIE ratio reinforces the conclusion from our analysis of the debt ratio that Allied would face difficulties if it attempted to borrow additional funds.

ABILITY TO SERVICE DEBT: EBITDA COVERAGE RATIO

The TIE ratio is useful for assessing a company's ability to meet interest charges on its debt, but this ratio has two shortcomings: (1) Interest is not the only fixed financial charge — companies must also reduce debt on schedule, and many firms lease assets and thus must make lease payments. If they fail to repay debt or meet lease payments, they can be forced into bankruptcy.

---

[7] The ratio of debt to equity is also used in financial analysis. The debt-to-assets (D/A) and debt-to-equity (D/E) ratios are simply transformations of each other:

$$D/E = \frac{D/A}{1 - D/A}, D/A = \frac{D/E}{1 + D/E}.$$

(2) EBIT does not represent all the cash flow available to service debt, especially if a firm has high depreciation and/or amortization charges. To account for these deficiencies, bankers and others have developed the **EBITDA coverage ratio,** defined as follows:[8]

$$\text{EBITDA coverage ratio} = \frac{\text{EBITDA} + \text{Lease payments}}{\text{Interest} + \text{Principal payments} + \text{Lease payments}}$$

$$= \frac{\$283.8 + \$100 + \$28}{\$88 + \$20 + \$28} = \frac{\$411.8}{\$136} = 3.0 \text{ times.}$$

Industry average = 4.3 times.

Allied had $283.8 million of operating income (EBIT), presumably all cash. Noncash charges of $100 million for depreciation and amortization (the DA part of EBITDA) were deducted in the calculation of EBIT, so they must be added back to find the cash flow available to service debt. Also, lease payments of $28 million were deducted before getting the $283.8 million of EBIT.[9] That $28 million was available to meet financial charges, hence it must be added back, bringing the total available to cover fixed financial charges to $411.8 million. Fixed financial charges consisted of $88 million of interest, $20 million of sinking fund payments, and $28 million for lease payments, for a total of $136 million.[10] Therefore, Allied covered its fixed financial charges by 3.0 times. However, if operating income declines, the coverage will fall, and operating income certainly can decline. Moreover, Allied's ratio is well below the industry average, so again, the company seems to have a relatively high level of debt.

The EBITDA coverage ratio is most useful for relatively short-term lenders such as banks, which rarely make loans (except real estate-backed loans) for longer than about five years. Over a relatively short period, depreciation-generated funds can be used to service debt. Over a longer time, those funds must be reinvested to maintain the plant and equipment or else the company cannot remain in business. Therefore, banks and other relatively short-term lenders focus on the EBITDA coverage ratio, whereas long-term bondholders focus on the TIE ratio.

---

[8] Different analysts define the EBITDA coverage ratio in different ways. For example, some would omit the lease payment information, and others would "gross up" principal payments by dividing them by (1 − T) because these payments are not tax deductions, hence must be made with after-tax cash flows. We included lease payments because, for many firms, they are quite important, and failing to make them can lead to bankruptcy just as surely as can failure to make payments on "regular" debt. We did not gross up principal payments because, if a company is in financial difficulty, its tax rate will probably be zero, hence the gross up is not necessary whenever the ratio is really important.

[9] Lease payments are included in the numerator because, unlike interest, they were deducted when EBITDA was calculated. We want to find *all* the funds that were available to service debt, so lease payments must be added to the EBIT and DA to find the funds that could be used to service debt and meet lease payments. To illustrate this, suppose EBIT before lease payments was $100, lease payments were $100, and DA was zero. After lease payments, EBIT would be $100 − $100 = $0. Yet lease payments of $100 were made, so obviously there was cash to make those payments. The available cash was the reported EBIT of $0 plus the $100 of lease payments.

[10] A sinking fund is a required annual payment designed to reduce the balance of a bond or preferred stock issue. A sinking fund payment is like the principal repayment portion of the payment on an amortized loan, but sinking funds are used for publicly traded bond issues, whereas amortization payments are used for bank loans and other private loans.

PROFITABILITY RATIOS

Profitability Ratios
A group of ratios that show the combined effects of liquidity, asset management, and debt on operating results.

Profitability is the net result of a number of policies and decisions. The ratios examined thus far provide useful clues as to the effectiveness of a firm's operations, but the **profitability ratios** show the combined effects of liquidity, asset management, and debt on operating results.

PROFIT MARGIN ON SALES

Profit Margin on Sales
This ratio measures net income per dollar of sales; it is calculated by dividing net income by sales.

The **profit margin on sales,** calculated by dividing net income by sales, gives the profit per dollar of sales:

$$\text{Profit margin on sales} = \frac{\text{Net income available to common stockholders}}{\text{Sales}}$$

$$= \frac{\$113.5}{\$3,000} = 3.8\%.$$

$$\text{Industry average} = 5.0\%.$$

Allied's profit margin is below the industry average of 5 percent. This sub-par result occurs because costs are too high. High costs, in turn, generally occur because of inefficient operations. However, Allied's low profit margin is also a result of its heavy use of debt. Recall that net income is income *after interest.* Therefore, if two firms have identical operations in the sense that their sales, operating costs, and EBIT are the same, but if one firm uses more debt than the other, it will have higher interest charges. Those interest charges will pull net income down, and since sales are constant, the result will be a relatively low profit margin. In such a case, the low profit margin would not indicate an operating problem, just a difference in financing strategies. Thus, the firm with the low profit margin might end up with a higher rate of return on its stockholders' investment due to its use of financial leverage. We will see exactly how profit margins and the use of debt interact to affect stockholder returns shortly, when we examine the Du Pont model.

INTERNATIONAL ACCOUNTING DIFFERENCES CREATE HEADACHES FOR INVESTORS

You must be a good financial detective to analyze financial statements, especially if the company operates overseas. Despite attempts to standardize accounting practices, there are many differences in the way financial information is reported in different countries, and these differences create headaches for investors trying to make cross-border company comparisons.

A study by two Rider College accounting professors demonstrated that huge differences can exist. The professors developed a computer model to evaluate the net income of a hypothetical but typical company operating in different countries. Applying the standard accounting practices of each country, the hypothetical company would have reported net income of $34,600 in the United States, $260,600 in the United Kingdom, and $240,600 in Australia.

Such variances occur for a number of reasons. In most countries, including the United States, an asset's balance sheet value is reported at original cost less any accumulated depreciation. However, in some countries, asset values are adjusted to reflect current market prices. Also, inventory valuation methods vary from country to country, as does the treatment of goodwill. Other differences arise from the treatment of leases, research and development costs, and pension plans.

These differences arise from a variety of legal, historical, cultural, and economic factors. For example, in Germany and Japan large banks are the key source of both debt and equity capital, whereas in the United States public capital markets are most important. As a result, U.S. corporations disclose a great deal of information to the public, while German and Japanese corporations use very conservative accounting practices that appeal to the banks.

The accounting profession has long recognized that international accounting differences exist, and it has taken steps toward making international comparisons easier. The International Accounting Standards Committee (IASC) was formed for the purpose of bringing financial accounting and reporting standards into closer conformity on a global basis. This committee, whose recognition and acceptance is growing, is currently working on projects to produce the first globally recognized accounting standards. A global accounting structure would enable investors and practitioners around the world to read and understand financial reports produced anywhere in the world. So, as you can see, the IASC's task is a very important one. It remains to be seen whether the IASC's lofty goal will be achieved.

SOURCE: "All Accountants Soon May Speak the Same Language," *The Wall Street Journal*, August 29, 1995, A15.

BASIC EARNING POWER (BEP)

Basic Earning Power (BEP) Ratio
This ratio indicates the ability of the firm's assets to generate operating income; calculated by dividing EBIT by total assets.

The **basic earning power (BEP) ratio** is calculated by dividing earnings before interest and taxes (EBIT) by total assets:

$$\text{Basic earning power ratio (BEP)} = \frac{\text{EBIT}}{\text{Total assets}}$$

$$= \frac{\$283.8}{\$2,000} = 14.2\%.$$

$$\text{Industry average} = 17.2\%.$$

This ratio shows the raw earning power of the firm's assets, before the influence of taxes and leverage, and it is useful for comparing firms with different tax situations and different degrees of financial leverage. Because of its low turnover ratios and low profit margin on sales, Allied is not earning as high a return on its assets as is the average food-processing company.[11]

RETURN ON TOTAL ASSETS

Return on Total Assets (ROA)
The ratio of net income to total assets.

The ratio of net income to total assets measures the **return on total assets (ROA)** after interest and taxes:

$$\begin{array}{l}\text{Return on} \\ \text{total assets}\end{array} = \text{ROA} = \dfrac{\begin{array}{c}\text{Net income available to}\\ \text{common stockholders}\end{array}}{\text{Total assets}}$$

$$= \frac{\$113.5}{\$2,000} = 5.7\%.$$

Industry average = 9.0%.

Allied's 5.7 percent return is well below the 9 percent average for the industry. This low return results from (1) the company's low basic earning power plus (2) high interest costs resulting from its above-average use of debt, both of which cause its net income to be relatively low.

RETURN ON COMMON EQUITY

Return on Common Equity (ROE)
The ratio of net income to common equity; measures the rate of return on common stockholders' investment.

Ultimately, the most important, or "bottom line," accounting ratio is the ratio of net income to common equity, which measures the **return on common equity (ROE):**

$$\begin{array}{l}\text{Return on} \\ \text{common equity}\end{array} = \text{ROE} = \dfrac{\begin{array}{c}\text{Net income available to}\\ \text{common stockholders}\end{array}}{\text{Common equity}}$$

$$= \frac{\$113.5}{\$896} = 12.7\%.$$

Industry average = 15.0%.

Stockholders invest to get a return on their money, and this ratio tells how well they are doing in an accounting sense. Allied's 12.7 percent return is below the 15 percent industry average, but not as far below as the return on total assets. This somewhat better result is due to the company's greater use of debt, a point that is analyzed in detail later in the chapter.

---

[11] Notice that EBIT is earned throughout the year, whereas the total assets figure is an end-of-the-year number. Therefore, it would be conceptually better to calculate this ratio as EBIT/Average assets = EBIT/[(Beginning assets + Ending assets)/2]. We have not made this adjustment because the published ratios used for comparative purposes do not include it. However, when we construct our own comparative ratios, we do make the adjustment. Incidentally, the same adjustment would also be appropriate for the next two ratios, ROA and ROE.

SELF-TEST QUESTIONS

Identify and write out the equations for four ratios that show the combined effects of liquidity, asset management, and debt management on profitability.

Why is the basic earning power ratio useful?

Why does the use of debt lower the ROA?

What does ROE measure? Since interest expense lowers profits, does using debt lower ROE?

MARKET VALUE RATIOS

Market Value Ratios
A set of ratios that relate the firm's stock price to its earnings, cash flow, and book value per share.

A final group of ratios, the **market value ratios,** relates the firm's stock price to its earnings, cash flow, and book value per share. These ratios give management an indication of what investors think of the company's past performance and future prospects. If the liquidity, asset management, debt management, and profitability ratios all look good, then the market value ratios will be high, and the stock price will probably be as high as can be expected.

PRICE/EARNINGS RATIO

Price/Earnings (P/E) Ratio
The ratio of the price per share to earnings per share; shows the dollar amount investors will pay for $1 of current earnings.

The **price/earnings (P/E) ratio** shows how much investors are willing to pay per dollar of reported profits. Allied's stock sells for $23, so with an EPS of $2.27 its P/E ratio is 10.1:

$$\text{Price/earnings (P/E) ratio} = \frac{\text{Price per share}}{\text{Earnings per share}}$$

$$= \frac{\$23.00}{\$2.27} = 10.1 \text{ times.}$$

Industry average = 12.5 times.

As we will see in Chapter 9, P/E ratios are higher for firms with strong growth prospects, other things held constant, but they are lower for riskier firms. Since Allied's P/E ratio is below the average for other food processors, this suggests that the company is regarded as being somewhat riskier than most, as having poorer growth prospects, or both.

PRICE/CASH FLOW RATIO

Price/Cash Flow Ratio
The ratio of price per share divided by cash flow per share; shows the dollar amount investors will pay for $1 of cash flow.

In some industries, stock price is tied more closely to cash flow rather than net income. Consequently, investors often look at the **price/cash flow ratio:**

$$\text{Price/cash flow} = \frac{\text{Price per share}}{\text{Cash flow per share}}$$

$$= \frac{\$23.00}{\$4.27} = 5.4 \text{ times.}$$

Industry average = 6.8 times.

The calculation for cash flow per share was shown in Chapter 2, but just to refresh your memory, cash flow per share is calculated as net income plus depreciation and amortization divided by common shares outstanding.

Allied's price/cash flow ratio is also below the industry average, once again suggesting that its growth prospects are below average, its risk is above average, or both.

Note that some analysts look at multiples beyond just the price/earnings and the price/cash flow ratios. For example, depending on the industry, some may look at measures such as price/sales, price/customers, or price/EBITDA per share. Ultimately, though, value depends on earnings and cash flows, so if these "exotic" ratios do not forecast future EPS and cash flow, they may turn out to be misleading.

MARKET/BOOK RATIO

The ratio of a stock's market price to its book value gives another indication of how investors regard the company. Companies with relatively high rates of return on equity generally sell at higher multiples of book value than those with low returns. First, we find Allied's book value per share:

$$\text{Book value per share} = \frac{\text{Common equity}}{\text{Shares outstanding}}$$

$$= \frac{\$896}{50} = \$17.92.$$

Market/Book (M/B) Ratio
The ratio of a stock's market price to its book value.

Now we divide the market price per share by the book value to get a **market/book (M/B) ratio** of 1.3 times:

$$\text{Market/book ratio} = \text{M/B} = \frac{\text{Market price per share}}{\text{Book value per share}}$$

$$= \frac{\$23.00}{\$17.92} = 1.3 \text{ times.}$$

Industry average = 1.7 times.

Investors are willing to pay less for a dollar of Allied's book value than for one of an average food-processing company.

The average company followed by the *Value Line Investment Survey* had a market/book ratio of about 4.28 in early 2001. Since M/B ratios typically exceed 1.0, this means that investors are willing to pay more for stocks than their accounting book values. This situation occurs primarily because asset values, as reported by accountants on corporate balance sheets, do not reflect either inflation or "goodwill." Thus, assets purchased years ago at preinflation prices are carried at their original costs, even though inflation might have caused their actual values to rise substantially, and successful going concerns have a value greater than their historical costs.

If a company earns a low rate of return on its assets, then its M/B ratio will be relatively low versus an average company. Thus, some airlines, which have not fared well in recent years, sell at M/B ratios below 1.0, while very successful

eBAY'S FINANCIAL STATEMENTS

If you examine the financial statements of a typical Internet retailer, you will quickly see that these companies are very different from their traditional "bricks and mortar" counterparts. For example, look at the 1998 year-end balance sheet of the online auctioneer, eBay Inc., shown in millions of dollars:

ASSETS:

Cash and marketable securities	$72.1
Accounts receivable	6.4
Other current assets	4.8
Total current assets	$83.3
Net property and equipment	7.8
Other assets	1.3
Total assets	$92.4

LIABILITIES AND EQUITY:

Total current liabilities	$ 8.0
Total shareholders' equity	84.4
Total liabilities and shareholders' equity	$92.4

During the year ending March 31, 1999, eBay generated net income of $8.15 million. At first glance, eBay may look like a somewhat sleepy company with modest profitability (ROE less than 10 percent), a strong balance sheet (lots of cash and little debt), and limited growth opportunities (because the company does not have much plant and equipment that can be used to generate future sales). However, midway through 1999, eBay's market capitalization (its stock price multiplied by the number of shares outstanding) was a whopping $17.6 billion! What makes this even more incredible is the fact that eBay's market capitalization had fallen dramatically from a high of $30 billion just two months earlier.

Why does the market value eBay so highly? Clearly, the market is forecasting that eBay will have phenomenal growth over the next several years. Many believe that online auctions will continue to grow, and eBay's costs should grow more slowly than its revenues. This should translate into strong earnings growth. Moreover, many proponents of eBay argue that the company is unlikely to face much in the way of serious competition, because it has the advantage of being the first major player in this market. After all, if you want to auction off that old baseball card, wouldn't you want to use the company that has the longest track record and the most potential bidders?

Critics suggest that while eBay is a great company, its price has gotten way ahead of its value, and it is due for a fall once the hype dies down. These critics also contend that it is foolish to think that eBay won't face serious competition. For example, Internet retailer Amazon.com has already leapt into the online auction market, and it threatens to be a serious competitor in the years ahead.

Over 18 months later in mid-2000, eBay's total assets had increased more than ten-fold to just over $1 billion, yet its market capitalization had fallen to $13 billion. Here are some key items from eBay's mid-2000 balance sheet, shown again in millions of dollars:

ASSETS:

Total current assets	$ 369.2
Net property and equipment	123.5
Other assets	579.0
Total assets	$1,071.7

LIABILITIES AND EQUITY:

Total current liabilities	$ 111.1
Long-term debt and leases	14.7
Other liabilities and minority interests	20.7
Total shareholders' equity	925.2
Total liabilities and shareholders' equity	$1,071.7

The more recent balance sheet numbers confirm that eBay has grown tremendously in a short period of time and that the company's operations are transforming over time. These changes will undoubtedly continue in the future.

firms such as Microsoft (which makes the operating systems for virtually all PCs) achieve high rates of return on their assets, causing their market values to be well in excess of their book values. In February 2001, Microsoft's book value per share was $8.71 versus a market price of $64.69, so its market/book ratio was $64.69/$8.71 = 7.43 times.

TREND ANALYSIS

Trend Analysis
An analysis of a firm's financial ratios over time; used to estimate the likelihood of improvement or deterioration in its financial condition.

It is important to analyze trends in ratios as well as their absolute levels, for trends give clues as to whether a firm's financial condition is likely to improve or to deteriorate. To do a **trend analysis**, one simply plots a ratio over time, as shown in Figure 3-1. This graph shows that Allied's rate of return on common equity has been declining since 1998, even though the industry average has been relatively stable. All the other ratios could be analyzed similarly.

FIGURE 3-1	Rate of Return on Common Equity, 1997–2001

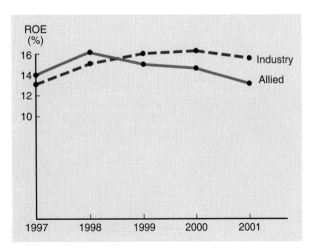

How does one do a trend analysis?

What important information does a trend analysis provide?

TYING THE RATIOS TOGETHER: THE DU PONT CHART AND EQUATION

Du Pont Chart
A chart designed to show the relationships among return on investment, asset turnover, profit margin, and leverage.

Table 3-2 summarizes Allied's ratios, and Figure 3-2 shows how the return on equity is affected by asset turnover, the profit margin, and leverage. The chart depicted in Figure 3-2 is called a modified **Du Pont chart** because that company's managers developed this approach for evaluating performance. Working from the bottom up, the left-hand side of the chart develops the *profit margin on sales*. The various expense items are listed and then summed to obtain Allied's total cost, which is subtracted from sales to obtain the company's net income. When we divide net income by sales, we find that 3.8 percent of each sales dollar is left over for stockholders. If the profit margin is low or trending down, one can examine the individual expense items to identify and then correct problems.

The right-hand side of Figure 3-2 lists the various categories of assets, totals them, and then divides sales by total assets to find the number of times Allied "turns its assets over" each year. The company's total assets turnover ratio is 1.5 times.

Du Pont Equation
A formula which shows that the rate of return on assets can be found as the product of the profit margin times the total assets turnover.

The profit margin times the total assets turnover is called the **Du Pont equation,** and it gives the rate of return on assets (ROA):

$$\text{ROA} = \text{Profit margin} \times \text{Total assets turnover}$$
$$= \frac{\text{Net income}}{\text{Sales}} \times \frac{\text{Sales}}{\text{Total assets}} \qquad (3\text{-}1)$$
$$= 3.8\% \times 1.5 = 5.7\%.$$

Allied made 3.8 percent, or 3.8 cents, on each dollar of sales, and assets were "turned over" 1.5 times during the year. Therefore, the company earned a return of 5.7 percent on its assets.

If the company were financed only with common equity, the rate of return on assets (ROA) and the return on equity (ROE) would be the same because total assets would equal common equity:

$$\text{ROA} = \frac{\text{Net income}}{\text{Total assets}} = \frac{\text{Net income}}{\text{Common equity}} = \text{ROE}.$$

This equality holds if and only if Total assets = Common equity, that is, if the company uses no debt. Allied does use debt, so its common equity is less than total assets. Therefore, the return to the common stockholders (ROE) must be greater than the ROA of 5.7 percent. Specifically, the rate of return on assets

TABLE 3-2

Allied Food Products: Summary of Financial Ratios (Millions of Dollars)

RATIO	FORMULA FOR CALCULATION	CALCULATION	RATIO	INDUSTRY AVERAGE	COMMENT
LIQUIDITY					
Current	$\dfrac{\text{Current assets}}{\text{Current liabilities}}$	$\dfrac{\$1{,}000}{\$310}$	= 3.2×	4.2×	Poor
Quick, or acid, test	$\dfrac{\text{Current assets} - \text{Inventories}}{\text{Current liabilities}}$	$\dfrac{\$385}{\$310}$	= 1.2×	2.1×	Poor
ASSET MANAGEMENT					
Inventory turnover	$\dfrac{\text{Sales}}{\text{Inventories}}$	$\dfrac{\$3{,}000}{\$615}$	= 4.9×	9.0×	Poor
Days sales outstanding (DSO)	$\dfrac{\text{Receivables}}{\text{Annual sales}/365}$	$\dfrac{\$375}{\$8.2192}$	= 46 days	36 days	Poor
Fixed assets turnover	$\dfrac{\text{Sales}}{\text{Net fixed assets}}$	$\dfrac{\$3{,}000}{\$1{,}000}$	= 3.0×	3.0×	OK
Total assets turnover	$\dfrac{\text{Sales}}{\text{Total assets}}$	$\dfrac{\$3{,}000}{\$2{,}000}$	= 1.5×	1.8×	Somewhat low
DEBT MANAGEMENT					
Total debt to total assets	$\dfrac{\text{Total debt}}{\text{Total assets}}$	$\dfrac{\$1{,}064}{\$2{,}000}$	= 53.2%	40.0%	High (risky)
Times-interest-earned (TIE)	$\dfrac{\text{Earnings before interest and taxes (EBIT)}}{\text{Interest charges}}$	$\dfrac{\$283.8}{\$88}$	= 3.2×	6.0×	Low (risky)
EBITDA coverage	$\dfrac{\text{EBITDA} + \text{Lease payments}}{\text{Interest} + \text{Principal payments} + \text{Lease payments}}$	$\dfrac{\$411.8}{\$136}$	= 3.0×	4.3×	Low (risky)
PROFITABILITY					
Profit margin on sales	$\dfrac{\text{Net income available to common stockholders}}{\text{Sales}}$	$\dfrac{\$113.5}{\$3{,}000}$	= 3.8%	5.0%	Poor
Basic earning power (BEP)	$\dfrac{\text{Earnings before interest and taxes (EBIT)}}{\text{Total assets}}$	$\dfrac{\$283.8}{\$2{,}000}$	= 14.2%	17.2%	Poor
Return on total assets (ROA)	$\dfrac{\text{Net income available to common stockholders}}{\text{Total assets}}$	$\dfrac{\$113.5}{\$2{,}000}$	= 5.7%	9.0%	Poor
Return on common equity (ROE)	$\dfrac{\text{Net income available to common stockholders}}{\text{Common equity}}$	$\dfrac{\$113.5}{\$896}$	= 12.7%	15.0%	Poor
MARKET VALUE					
Price/earnings (P/E)	$\dfrac{\text{Price per share}}{\text{Earnings per share}}$	$\dfrac{\$23.00}{\$2.27}$	= 10.1×	12.5×	Low
Price/cash flow	$\dfrac{\text{Price per share}}{\text{Cash flow per share}}$	$\dfrac{\$23.00}{\$4.27}$	= 5.4×	6.8×	Low
Market/book (M/B)	$\dfrac{\text{Market price per share}}{\text{Book value per share}}$	$\dfrac{\$23.00}{\$17.92}$	= 1.3×	1.7×	Low

FIGURE 3-2

Modified Du Pont Chart for Allied Food Products (Millions of Dollars)

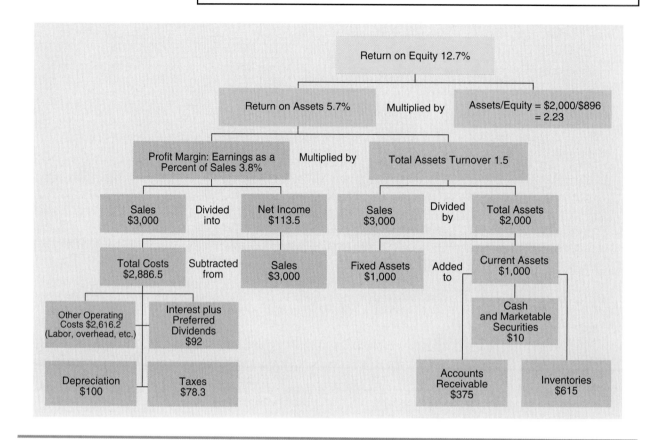

(ROA) can be multiplied by the *equity multiplier*, which is the ratio of assets to common equity:

$$\text{Equity multiplier} = \frac{\text{Total assets}}{\text{Common equity}}.$$

Firms that use a large amount of debt financing (more leverage) will necessarily have a high equity multiplier — the more the debt, the less the equity, hence the higher the equity multiplier. For example, if a firm has $1,000 of assets and is financed with $800, or 80 percent debt, then its equity will be $200, and its equity multiplier will be $1,000/$200 = 5. Had it used only $200 of debt, then its equity would have been $800, and its equity multiplier would have been only $1,000/$800 = 1.25.[12]

---

[12] Expressed algebraically,

$$\text{Debt ratio} = \frac{D}{A} = \frac{A - E}{A} = \frac{A}{A} - \frac{E}{A} = 1 - \frac{1}{\text{Equity multiplier}}.$$

Here D is debt, E is equity, A is total assets, and A/E is the equity multiplier. This equation ignores preferred stock.

Allied's return on equity (ROE) depends on its ROA and its use of leverage:[13]

$$\text{ROE} = \text{ROA} \times \text{Equity multiplier}$$

$$= \frac{\text{Net income}}{\text{Total assets}} \times \frac{\text{Total assets}}{\text{Common equity}} \qquad (3\text{-}2)$$

$$= 5.7\% \times \$2{,}000/\$896$$

$$= 5.7\% \times 2.23$$

$$= 12.7\%.$$

Now we can combine Equations 3-1 and 3-2 to form the *Extended Du Pont Equation*, which shows how the profit margin, the assets turnover ratio, and the equity multiplier combine to determine the ROE:

$$\text{ROE} = (\text{Profit margin})\,(\text{Total assets turnover})\,(\text{Equity multiplier})$$

$$= \frac{\text{Net income}}{\text{Sales}} \times \frac{\text{Sales}}{\text{Total assets}} \times \frac{\text{Total assets}}{\text{Common equity}}. \qquad (3\text{-}3)$$

For Allied, we have

$$\text{ROE} = (3.8\%)\,(1.5)\,(2.23)$$

$$= 12.7\%.$$

The 12.7 percent rate of return could, of course, be calculated directly: both Sales and Total assets cancel, leaving Net income/Common equity = $113.5/ $896 = 12.7%. However, the Du Pont equation shows how the profit margin, the total assets turnover, and the use of debt interact to determine the return on equity.[14]

Allied's management can use the Du Pont system to analyze ways of improving performance. Focusing on the left, or "profit margin," side of its modified Du Pont chart, Allied's marketing people can study the effects of raising sales prices (or lowering them to increase volume), of moving into new products or markets with higher margins, and so on. The company's cost accountants can study various expense items and, working with engineers, purchasing agents, and other operating personnel, seek ways to hold down costs. On the "turnover" side, Allied's financial analysts, working with both production and marketing people, can investigate ways to reduce the investment in

---

[13] Note that we could also find the ROE by "grossing up" the ROA, that is, by dividing the ROA by the common equity fraction: ROE = ROA/Equity fraction = 5.7%/0.448 = 12.7%. The two procedures are algebraically equivalent.

[14] Another frequently used ratio is the following:

$$\text{Rate of return on investors' capital} = \frac{\text{Net income} + \text{Interest}}{\text{Debt} + \text{Equity}}.$$

The numerator shows the dollar returns to investors, the denominator shows the total amount of money investors have put up, and the ratio itself shows the rate of return on all investors' capital. This ratio is especially important in the public utility industries, where regulators are concerned about the companies' using their monopoly positions to earn excessive returns on investors' capital. In fact, regulators try to set utility prices (service rates) at levels that will force the return on investors' capital to equal a company's cost of capital as defined in Chapter 10.

various types of assets. At the same time, the treasury staff can analyze the effects of alternative financing strategies, seeking to hold down interest expense and the risk of debt while still using leverage to increase the rate of return on equity.

As a result of such an analysis, Ellen Jackson, Allied's president, recently announced a series of moves designed to cut operating costs by more than 20 percent per year. Jackson and Allied's other executives have a strong incentive for improving the company's financial performance, because their compensation is based to a large extent on how well the company does. Allied's executives receive a salary that is sufficient to cover their living costs, but their compensation package also includes "performance shares" that will be awarded if and only if the company meets or exceeds target levels for earnings and the stock price. These target levels are based on Allied's performance relative to other food companies. So, if Allied does well, then Jackson and the other executives — and the stockholders — will also do well. But if things deteriorate, Jackson could be looking for a new job.

SELF-TEST QUESTIONS

Explain how the extended, or modified, Du Pont equation and chart can be used to reveal the basic determinants of ROE.

What is the equity multiplier?

How can management use the Du Pont system to analyze ways of improving the firm's performance?

COMPARATIVE RATIOS AND "BENCHMARKING"

Benchmarking
The process of comparing a particular company with a group of "benchmark" companies.

Ratio analysis involves comparisons — a company's ratios are compared with those of other firms in the same industry, that is, to industry average figures. However, like most firms, Allied's managers go one step further — they also compare their ratios with those of a smaller set of leading food companies. This technique is called **benchmarking,** and the companies used for the comparison are called *benchmark companies*. Allied's management benchmarks against Campbell Soup, a leading manufacturer of canned soups; Dean Foods, a processor of canned and frozen vegetables; Dole Food Company, a processor of fruits and vegetables; H.J. Heinz, which makes ketchup and other products; Flowers Industries, a producer of bakery and snack-food goods; Sara Lee, a manufacturer of baked goods; and Hershey Foods Corp., a producer of chocolates, nonchocolate confectionary products, and pasta. Ratios are calculated for each company. Then the ratios are listed in descending order, as shown below for the profit margin on sales (as reported on the firms' latest quarterly financial statements for 2000 by *Hoover's Online*):

	PROFIT MARGIN
Campbell Soup	10.0%
Sara Lee	6.0
Hershey Foods	4.8
Allied Food Products	**3.8**
Heinz	3.8
Dole Food Company	3.5
Dean Foods	2.6
Flowers Industries	0.6

The benchmarking setup makes it easy for Allied's management to see exactly where the company stands relative to its competition. As the data show, Allied is in the middle of its benchmark group with respect to its profit margin, so the company has room for improvement. Other ratios are analyzed similarly.

Comparative ratios are available from a number of sources, including *Value Line*. Table 3-3 presents a list of key ratios for a variety of industries covered by *Value Line*. Useful ratios are also compiled by Dun and Bradstreet (D&B) and the *Annual Statement Studies* published by Robert Morris Associates, which is the national association of bank loan officers. Also, financial statement data for thousands of publicly owned corporations are available on magnetic tapes and diskettes, and since brokerage houses, banks, and other financial institutions have access to these data, security analysts can and do generate comparative ratios tailored to their specific needs.

Each of the data-supplying organizations uses a somewhat different set of ratios designed for its own purposes. For example, D&B deals mainly with small firms, many of which are proprietorships, and it sells its services primarily to banks and other lenders. Therefore, D&B is concerned largely with the creditor's viewpoint, and its ratios emphasize current assets and liabilities, not market value ratios. So, when you select a comparative data source, you should be sure that your emphasis is similar to that of the agency whose ratios you plan to use. Additionally, there are often definitional differences in the ratios presented by different sources, so before using a source, be sure to verify the exact definitions of the ratios to ensure consistency with your own work.

SELF-TEST QUESTIONS

Differentiate between trend analysis and comparative ratio analysis.

Why is it useful to do a comparative ratio analysis?

What is benchmarking?

T A B L E 3 - 3   Key Financial Ratios for Selected Industries[a]

INDUSTRY NAME	CURRENT RATIO	QUICK RATIO	INVENTORY TURNOVER[b]	FIXED ASSETS TURNOVER	TOTAL ASSETS TURNOVER	DEBT RATIO[c]	DAYS SALES OUTSTANDING[d]	PROFIT MARGIN	RETURN ON ASSETS	RETURN ON EQUITY
Advertising	1.22	1.49	137.62	9.62	1.23	72.97%	166.81	6.16%	6.08%	7.67%
Aerospace/defense	1.77	1.04	7.16	8.90	1.17	51.09	69.39	4.96	5.58	16.78
Auto and truck	1.50	1.28	13.47	5.09	0.96	63.49	121.84	3.58	3.54	18.94
Beverage (soft drink)	1.08	0.85	19.40	6.02	0.98	69.87	39.88	4.30	4.00	30.18
Drug	3.26	2.47	9.93	3.24	0.67	36.46	76.22	−8.71	4.15	15.85
Educational services	1.66	1.22	61.66	5.83	1.25	31.35	48.39	11.48	12.42	18.97
Electronics	2.40	1.52	8.61	13.40	1.43	47.06	72.75	4.59	5.71	−14.55
Environmental	1.44	1.28	44.08	4.52	0.60	46.56	77.42	7.84	4.69	12.68
Food processing	1.64	0.99	12.00	4.79	1.55	51.50	34.47	5.28	6.98	46.67
Food wholesalers	1.42	0.70	16.88	15.62	4.19	63.15	17.52	1.00	4.01	11.98
Grocery	1.43	0.63	13.72	5.43	2.70	50.02	6.75	2.37	5.95	1.66
Homebuilding	2.79	0.43	2.39	66.18	1.13	59.58	26.13	6.35	5.67	17.50
Hotel/gaming	2.20	1.36	67.68	1.86	0.66	47.92	10.44	8.62	6.13	19.50
Medical services	1.81	1.77	53.93	13.45	1.11	53.89	70.79	6.15	4.36	20.30
Newspaper	1.21	1.13	78.22	3.16	0.72	44.13	51.86	9.01	6.77	18.64
Paper and forest products	1.62	0.96	9.40	1.26	0.76	47.64	40.00	3.36	2.34	7.74
Precision instruments	2.57	1.87	9.07	5.22	0.96	43.22	80.88	6.30	6.21	16.98
Railroad	0.79	0.68	35.15	0.60	0.40	42.67	46.08	10.92	4.20	11.46
Recreation	1.69	1.22	19.15	5.88	1.19	45.63	46.29	8.19	7.50	15.60
Restaurant	1.13	0.84	74.75	2.27	1.45	37.97	14.75	5.90	7.45	10.79
Retail store	1.98	0.69	6.17	5.19	2.00	50.71	41.21	3.36	6.42	14.88
Telecommunications equipment	3.35	2.71	8.98	5.70	0.93	27.16	71.23	5.30	5.11	6.46
Textile	2.53	1.31	6.25	2.94	1.15	64.18	45.76	2.72	2.91	6.90
Tobacco	1.50	0.55	6.46	11.66	1.59	60.72	23.21	9.84	14.52	208.83
Water utilities	0.76	0.70	66.24	0.29	0.24	45.14	42.55	15.16	3.49	11.65

[a] The ratios presented are averages for each industry. Ratios for the individual companies are also available.

[b] The inventory turnover ratio in this table is calculated as sales divided by inventory.

[c] The debt ratio in this table is calculated as the sum of all debt (current liabilities, deferred taxes, long-term debt, and preferred stock) divided by total assets.

[d] The days sales outstanding ratio in this table is calculated assuming a 365-day accounting year.

SOURCE: *Value Line*, July 2000.

USES AND LIMITATIONS OF RATIO ANALYSIS

To find quick information about a company, link to **http://www.marketguide.com.** Here you can find company profiles, stock price and share information, and several key ratios.

As noted earlier, ratio analysis is used by three main groups: (1) *managers*, who employ ratios to help analyze, control, and thus improve their firms' operations; (2) *credit analysts*, including bank loan officers and bond rating analysts, who analyze ratios to help ascertain a company's ability to pay its debts; and (3) *stock analysts*, who are interested in a company's efficiency, risk, and growth prospects. In later chapters we will look more closely at the basic factors that underlie each ratio, which will give you a better idea about how to interpret and use ratios. Note, though, that while ratio analysis can provide useful information concerning a company's operations and financial condition, it does have limitations that necessitate care and judgment. Some potential problems are listed below:

1. Many large firms operate different divisions in different industries, and for such companies it is difficult to develop a meaningful set of industry averages. Therefore, ratio analysis is more useful for small, narrowly focused firms than for large, multidivisional ones.

2. Most firms want to be better than average, so merely attaining average performance is not necessarily good. As a target for high-level performance, it is best to focus on the industry leaders' ratios. Benchmarking helps in this regard.

3. Inflation may have badly distorted firms' balance sheets — recorded values are often substantially different from "true" values. Further, since inflation affects both depreciation charges and inventory costs, profits are also affected. Thus, a ratio analysis for one firm over time, or a comparative analysis of firms of different ages, must be interpreted with judgment.

4. Seasonal factors can also distort a ratio analysis. For example, the inventory turnover ratio for a food processor will be radically different if the balance sheet figure used for inventory is the one just before versus just after the close of the canning season. This problem can be minimized by using monthly averages for inventory (and receivables) when calculating turnover ratios.

"Window Dressing" Techniques
Techniques employed by firms to make their financial statements look better than they really are.

5. Firms can employ **"window dressing" techniques** to make their financial statements look stronger. To illustrate, a Chicago builder borrowed on a two-year basis on December 29, 2001, held the proceeds of the loan as cash for a few days, and then paid off the loan ahead of time on January 2, 2002. This improved his current and quick ratios, and made his year-end 2001 balance sheet look good. However, the improvement was strictly window dressing; a week later the balance sheet was back at the old level.

6. Different accounting practices can distort comparisons. As noted earlier, inventory valuation and depreciation methods can affect financial statements and thus distort comparisons among firms. Also, if one firm leases a substantial amount of its productive equipment, then its assets may appear low relative to sales because leased assets often do not appear on the balance sheet. At the same time, the liability associated with the lease

obligation may not be shown as a debt. Therefore, leasing can artificially improve both the turnover and the debt ratios. However, the accounting profession has taken steps to reduce this problem.

7. It is difficult to generalize about whether a particular ratio is "good" or "bad." For example, a high current ratio may indicate a strong liquidity position, which is good, or excessive cash, which is bad (because excess cash in the bank is a nonearning asset). Similarly, a high fixed assets turnover ratio may denote either a firm that uses its assets efficiently or one that is undercapitalized and cannot afford to buy enough assets.

8. A firm may have some ratios that look "good" and others that look "bad," making it difficult to tell whether the company is, on balance, strong or weak. However, statistical procedures can be used to analyze the *net effects* of a set of ratios. Many banks and other lending organizations use such procedures to analyze firms' financial ratios, and then to classify them according to their probability of getting into financial trouble.[15]

Ratio analysis is useful, but analysts should be aware of these problems and make adjustments as necessary. Ratio analysis conducted in a mechanical, unthinking manner is dangerous, but used intelligently and with good judgment, it can provide useful insights into a firm's operations. Your judgment in interpreting a set of ratios is bound to be weak at this point, but it will improve as you go through the remainder of the book.

SELF-TEST QUESTIONS

List three types of users of ratio analysis. Would the different users emphasize the same or different types of ratios? Explain.

List several potential problems with ratio analysis.

PROBLEMS WITH ROE

In Chapter 1 we said that managers should strive to maximize shareholder wealth. If a firm takes steps to improve its ROE, does it mean that shareholder wealth will also increase? Not necessarily, for despite its widespread use and the fact that ROE and shareholder wealth are often highly correlated, some problems can arise when firms use ROE as the sole measure of performance.

First, ROE does not consider risk. While shareholders clearly care about returns, they also care about risk. To illustrate this point, consider two divisions

---

[15] The technique used is discriminant analysis. For a detailed discussion, see Edward I. Altman, "Financial Ratios, Discriminant Analysis, and the Prediction of Corporate Bankruptcy," *Journal of Finance*, September 1968, 589–609. For a summary, see Eugene F. Brigham and Phillip R. Daves, *Intermediate Financial Management*, 7th ed. (Fort Worth, TX: Harcourt College Publishers, 2002), Chapter 24 Extensions.

CALCULATING EVA

To better understand the idea behind EVA and how it is connected to ROE, let's look at Keller Electronics. Keller has $100,000 in investor-supplied operating capital, which, in turn, consists of $50,000 of long-term debt and $50,000 of common equity. The company has no preferred stock or notes payable. The long-term debt has a 10 percent interest rate. However, since the company is in the 40 percent tax bracket and interest expense is tax deductible, the after-tax cost of debt is only 6 percent. On the basis of their assessment of the company's risk, shareholders require a 14 percent return. This 14 percent return is what shareholders could expect to earn if they were to take their money elsewhere and invest in stocks that have the same risk as Keller. Keller's overall cost of capital is a weighted average of the cost of debt and equity, and it is 10 percent, found as 0.50(6%) + 0.50(14%) = 10%. The total dollar cost of capital per year is 0.10($100,000) = $10,000.

Now let's look at Keller's income statement. Its operating income, EBIT, is $20,000, and its interest expense is 0.10($50,000) = $5,000. Therefore, its taxable income is $20,000 − $5,000 = $15,000. Taxes equal 40 percent of taxable income, or 0.4($15,000) = $6,000, so the firm's net income is $9,000, and its return on equity, ROE, is $9,000/$50,000 = 18%.

Now what is Keller's EVA? Recall from Chapter 2 that the basic formula for EVA is:

$$\text{EVA} = \text{EBIT } (1 - \text{Corporate tax rate}) - (\text{Total investor-supplied operating capital})(\text{After-tax percentage cost of capital})$$

$$= \$20,000 \ (1 - 0.40) - (\$100,000)(0.10) = \$2,000.$$

This $2,000 EVA indicates that Keller provided its shareholders with $2,000 more than they could have earned elsewhere by investing in other stocks with the same risk as Keller's stock. To see where this $2,000 comes from, let's trace what happens to the money:

- The firm generates $20,000 in operating income.
- $6,000 goes to the government to pay taxes, leaving $14,000.
- $5,000 goes to the bondholders in the form of interest payments, thus leaving $9,000.
- $7,000 is what Keller's shareholders expected to earn: 0.14($50,000) = $7,000. Note that this $7,000 payment is not a requirement to stay in business — companies can stay in business as long as they pay their bills and their taxes. However, this $7,000 is what shareholders *expected to earn,* and it is the amount the firm *must earn* if it is to avoid reducing shareholder wealth.

- What's left over, the $2,000, is EVA. In this case, Keller's management created wealth because it provided shareholders with a return greater than what they presumably would have earned on alternative investments with the same risk as Keller's stock.

SOME ADDITIONAL POINTS

- In practice, it is often necessary to make several adjustments in order to arrive at a "better" measure of EVA. The adjustments deal with leased assets, depreciation, and other accounting details.
- Shareholders may not immediately receive the $9,000 that Keller made for them this year (the $7,000 that shareholders expected plus the $2,000 of EVA). Keller can either pay its earnings out as dividends or keep them in the firm as retained earnings. In either event, the $9,000 is shareholders' money. The factors influencing the dividend payout decision are discussed in Chapter 14.

THE CONNECTION BETWEEN ROE AND EVA

We said that EVA is different from the traditional accounting measure of profit in that EVA explicitly considers not just the interest cost of debt but also the cost of equity. Indeed, using the simple example above, we could also express EVA as net income minus the dollar cost of equity:

$$\text{EVA} = \text{Net income} - [(\text{Equity capital})(\text{Cost of equity capital})]$$

$$= \$9,000 - [(\$50,000)(0.14)]$$

$$= \$2,000.$$

Note that this is the same number we calculated before when we used the other formula for calculating EVA. Note also that the expression above could be rewritten as follows:

$$\text{EVA} = (\text{Equity capital})[\text{Net income/Equity capital} - \text{Cost of equity capital}],$$

or simply as:

$$\text{EVA} = (\text{Equity capital})(\text{ROE} - \text{Cost of equity capital}).$$

This last expression implies that EVA depends on three factors: rate of return, as reflected in ROE; risk, which affects the cost of equity; and size, which is measured by the amount of equity capital employed. Recall that earlier in this chapter we said that shareholder value depends on risk, return, and the amount of capital invested. This final equation illustrates this point.

within the same firm. Division S has very stable cash flows and a predictable 15 percent ROE. Division R, on the other hand, has a 16 percent expected ROE, but its cash flows are very risky, so the expected ROE may not materialize. If managers were compensated solely on the basis of ROE, and if the expected ROEs were actually achieved, then Division R's manager would receive a higher bonus than Division S's manager, even though Division S may actually create more value for shareholders as a result of its lower risk.

Second, ROE does not consider the amount of invested capital. To illustrate this point, let's consider a rather extreme example. A large company has $1 invested in Project A, which has an ROE of 50 percent, and $1 million invested in Project B, which has a 40 percent ROE. The projects are equally risky, and the two returns are both well above the cost the company had to pay for the capital invested in the projects. In this example, Project A has a higher ROE, but since it is so small, it does little to enhance shareholder wealth. Project B, on the other hand, has the lower ROE, but it adds much more to shareholder value.

Consider one last problem with ROE. Assume that you manage a division of a large firm. The firm uses ROE as the sole measure of performance, and it determines bonuses on the basis of ROE. Toward the end of the fiscal year, your division's ROE is an impressive 45 percent. Now you have an opportunity to invest in a large, low-risk project that has an estimated ROE of 35 percent, which is well above the cost of the capital you need to make the investment. Even though this project is profitable, you might be reluctant to make the investment because it would reduce your division's average ROE, and therefore reduce the size of your year-end bonus.

These three examples suggest that a project's return must be combined with its risk and size to determine its effect on shareholder value. To the extent that ROE focuses only on rate of return, increasing ROE may in some cases be inconsistent with increasing shareholder wealth. With this in mind, academics, practitioners, and consultants have tried to develop alternative measures that overcome ROE's potential problems when it is used as the sole gauge of performance. One such measure is Economic Value Added (EVA). In Chapter 2, we showed how to calculate EVA. For a discussion of the connection between ROE and EVA, see the accompanying box, "Calculating EVA."

SELF-TEST QUESTION

If a firm takes steps to improve its ROE, does this mean that shareholder wealth will also increase? Explain.

LOOKING BEYOND THE NUMBERS

Students might want to refer to AAII's educational web site at **http://www.aaii.org.** The site provides information on investing basics, financial planning, portfolio management, and the like, so individuals can manage their own assets more effectively.

Hopefully, working through this chapter has helped your understanding of financial statements and improved your ability to interpret accounting numbers. These important and basic skills are necessary when making business decisions, when evaluating performance, and when forecasting likely future developments.

Sound financial analysis involves more than just calculating numbers — good analysis requires that certain qualitative factors be considered when eval-

FINANCIAL ANALYSIS IN THE SMALL FIRM

Financial ratio analysis is especially useful for small businesses, and readily available sources provide comparative data by firm size. For example, Robert Morris Associates provides comparative ratios for a number of small-firm classes, down to a size range of zero to $250,000 in annual sales. Nevertheless, analyzing a small firm's statements presents some unique problems. We examine here some of those problems from the standpoint of a bank loan officer, one of the most frequent users of ratio analysis.

When evaluating a small-business credit prospect, a banker is essentially making a prediction about the company's ability to repay its debt. In making this prediction, the banker will be especially concerned about indicators of liquidity and about continuing prospects for profitability. Bankers like to do business with a new customer if it appears that loans can be paid off on time and that the company will remain in business and therefore continue to be a customer for some years to come. Thus, both short-run and long-run viability are of interest to the banker. Note too that the banker's perceptions about the business are important to the owner-manager, because the bank will probably be the firm's primary source of funds.

The first problem the banker is likely to encounter is that, unlike the bank's bigger customers, the small firm may not have audited financial statements. Further, the statements that are available may have been produced on an irregular basis (for example, in some months or quarters but not in others). If the firm is young, it may have historical financial statements for only one year, or perhaps none at all. Also, the financial statements may not have been produced by a reputable accounting firm but by the owner's brother-in-law.

The poor quality of its financial data may therefore be a hindrance for a small business that is attempting to establish a banking relationship. This could keep the firm from getting credit even though it is really on solid financial ground. Therefore, it is in the owner's interest to make sure that the firm's financial data are credible, even if it is more expensive to do so. Furthermore, if the banker is uncomfortable with the data, the firm's management should also be uncomfortable: Because many managerial decisions depend on the numbers in the firm's accounting statements, those numbers should be as accurate as possible.

For a given set of financial ratios, a small firm may be riskier than a larger one. Small firms often produce a single product, rely heavily on a single customer, or both. For example, several years ago a company called Yard Man Inc. manufactured and sold lawn equipment. Most of Yard Man's sales were to Sears, so most of its revenues and profits were due to its Sears account. When Sears decided to drop Yard Man as a supplier, the company was left without its most important customer. Yard Man is no longer in business. Because large firms typically have a broad customer base, they are not as exposed to the sudden loss of a large portion of their business.

A similar danger applies to a single-product company. Just as the loss of a key customer can be disastrous for a small business, so can a shift in the tides of consumer interest in a particular fad. For example, Coleco manufactured and sold the extremely popular Cabbage Patch dolls. The phenomenal popularity of the dolls was a great boon for Coleco. However, the public is fickle — one can never predict when such a fad will die out, leaving the company with a great deal of capacity to make a product that no one will buy, and with a large amount of overvalued inventory. Exactly that situation hit Coleco, and it was forced into bankruptcy.

Extending credit to a small company, especially to a small owner-managed company, often involves yet another risk that is less of a problem for larger firms — dependence on a single key individual whose unexpected death could cause the company to fail. Similarly, if the company is family owned and managed, there is typically one key decision maker, even though several other family members may be involved in helping to manage the company. In the case of the family business, the loss of the top person may not wipe out the company, but it often creates the serious problem of who will assume the leadership role. The loss of a key family member is often a highly emotional event, and it is not at all unusual for it to be followed by an ugly and protracted struggle for control of the business. It is in the family's interest, and certainly in the creditors' interests, to see that a plan of management succession is clearly specified before trouble arises. If no good plan can be worked out, perhaps the firm should be forced to carry "key person insurance," payable to the bank and used to retire the loan in the event of the key person's death.

In summary, to determine the creditworthiness of a small firm, the financial analyst must "look beyond the ratios" and analyze the viability of the firm's products, customers, management, and market. Still, ratio analysis is the first step in such a credit analysis.

uating a company. These factors, as summarized by the American Association of Individual Investors (AAII), include the following:

1. *Are the company's revenues tied to one key customer?* If so, the company's performance may decline dramatically if the customer goes elsewhere. On the other hand, if the relationship is firmly entrenched, this might actually stabilize sales.

2. *To what extent are the company's revenues tied to one key product?* Companies that rely on a single product may be more efficient and focused, but a lack of diversification increases risk. If revenues come from several different products, the overall bottom line will be less affected by a drop in the demand for any one product.

3. *To what extent does the company rely on a single supplier?* Depending on a single supplier may lead to unanticipated shortages, which investors and potential creditors should consider.

4. *What percentage of the company's business is generated overseas?* Companies with a large percentage of overseas business are often able to realize higher growth and larger profit margins. However, firms with large overseas operations find that the value of their operations depends in large part on the value of the local currency. Thus, fluctuations in currency markets create additional risks for firms with large overseas operations. Also, the potential stability of the region is important.

5. *Competition.* Generally, increased competition lowers prices and profit margins. In forecasting future performance, it is important to assess both the likely actions of the current competition and the likelihood of new competitors in the future.

6. *Future prospects.* Does the company invest heavily in research and development? If so, its future prospects may depend critically on the success of new products in the pipeline. For example, the market's assessment of a computer company depends on how next year's products are shaping up. Likewise, investors in pharmaceutical companies are interested in knowing whether the company has developed any potential blockbuster drugs that are doing well in the required tests.

7. *Legal and regulatory environment.* Changes in laws and regulations have important implications for many industries. For example, when forecasting the future of tobacco companies, it is crucial to factor in the effects of proposed regulations and pending or likely lawsuits. Likewise, when assessing banks, telecommunications firms, and electric utilities, analysts need to forecast both the extent to which these industries will be regulated in the future, and the ability of individual firms to respond to changes in regulation.

SELF-TEST QUESTION

What are some qualitative factors analysts should consider when evaluating a company's likely future financial performance?

The primary purpose of this chapter was to discuss techniques used by investors and managers to analyze financial statements. The key concepts covered are listed below.

- **Financial statement analysis** generally begins with a set of **financial ratios** designed to reveal the strengths and weaknesses of a company as compared with other companies in the same industry, and to show whether its financial position has been improving or deteriorating over time.

- **Liquidity ratios** show the relationship of a firm's current assets to its current liabilities, and thus its ability to meet maturing debts. Two commonly used liquidity ratios are the **current ratio** and the **quick, or acid test, ratio.**

- **Asset management ratios** measure how effectively a firm is managing its assets. These ratios include **inventory turnover, days sales outstanding, fixed assets turnover,** and **total assets turnover.**

- **Debt management ratios** reveal (1) the extent to which the firm is financed with debt and (2) its likelihood of defaulting on its debt obligations. They include the **debt ratio, times-interest-earned ratio,** and **EBITDA coverage ratio.**

- **Profitability ratios** show the combined effects of liquidity, asset management, and debt management policies on operating results. They include the **profit margin on sales,** the **basic earning power ratio,** the **return on total assets,** and the **return on common equity.**

- **Market value ratios** relate the firm's stock price to its earnings, cash flow, and book value per share, thus giving management an indication of what investors think of the company's past performance and future prospects. These include the **price/earnings ratio, price/cash flow ratio,** and the **market/book ratio.**

- **Trend analysis,** where one plots a ratio over time, is important, because it reveals whether the firm's condition is improving or deteriorating over time.

- The **Du Pont system** is designed to show how the profit margin on sales, the assets turnover ratio, and the use of debt interact to determine the rate of return on equity. The firm's management can use the Du Pont system to analyze ways of improving the firm's performance.

- **Benchmarking** is the process of comparing a particular company with a group of "benchmark" companies.

- ROE is important, but it does not take account of either the amount of investment or risk. **Economic Value Added (EVA)** adds these factors to the analysis.

- In analyzing a small firm's financial position, ratio analysis is a useful starting point. However, the analyst must also (1) examine the **quality of the financial data,** (2) ensure that the firm is **sufficiently diversified** to withstand shifts in customers' buying habits, and (3) determine whether the firm has a **plan for the succession of its management.**

Ratio analysis has limitations, but used with care and judgment, it can be very helpful.

QUESTIONS

3-1 Financial ratio analysis is conducted by four groups of analysts: managers, equity investors, long-term creditors, and short-term creditors. What is the primary emphasis of each of these groups in evaluating ratios?

3-2 Why would the inventory turnover ratio be more important when analyzing a grocery chain than an insurance company?

3-3 Over the past year, M. D. Ryngaert & Co. has realized an increase in its current ratio and a drop in its total assets turnover ratio. However, the company's sales, quick ratio, and fixed assets turnover ratio have remained constant. What explains these changes?

3-4 Profit margins and turnover ratios vary from one industry to another. What differences would you expect to find between a grocery chain such as Safeway and a steel company? Think particularly about the turnover ratios, the profit margin, and the Du Pont equation.

3-5 How does inflation distort ratio analysis comparisons, both for one company over time (trend analysis) and when different companies are compared? Are only balance sheet items or both balance sheet and income statement items affected?

3-6 If a firm's ROE is low and management wants to improve it, explain how using more debt might help.

3-7 How might (a) seasonal factors and (b) different growth rates distort a comparative ratio analysis? Give some examples. How might these problems be alleviated?

3-8 Why is it sometimes misleading to compare a company's financial ratios with other firms that operate in the same industry?

3-9 Indicate the effects of the transactions listed in the following table on total current assets, current ratio, and net income. Use (+) to indicate an increase, (−) to indicate a decrease, and (0) to indicate either no effect or an indeterminate effect. Be prepared to state any necessary assumptions, and assume an initial current ratio of more than 1.0. (Note: A good accounting background is necessary to answer some of these questions; if yours is not strong, just answer the questions you can handle.)

	TOTAL CURRENT ASSETS	CURRENT RATIO	EFFECT ON NET INCOME
a. Cash is acquired through issuance of additional common stock.	_____	_____	_____
b. Merchandise is sold for cash.	_____	_____	_____
c. Federal income tax due for the previous year is paid.	_____	_____	_____
d. A fixed asset is sold for less than book value.	_____	_____	_____
e. A fixed asset is sold for more than book value.	_____	_____	_____
f. Merchandise is sold on credit.	_____	_____	_____
g. Payment is made to trade creditors for previous purchases.	_____	_____	_____
h. A cash dividend is declared and paid.	_____	_____	_____
i. Cash is obtained through short-term bank loans.	_____	_____	_____
j. Short-term notes receivable are sold at a discount.	_____	_____	_____
k. Marketable securities are sold below cost.	_____	_____	_____
l. Advances are made to employees.	_____	_____	_____
m. Current operating expenses are paid.	_____	_____	_____
n. Short-term promissory notes are issued to trade creditors in exchange for past due accounts payable.	_____	_____	_____

	TOTAL CURRENT ASSETS	CURRENT RATIO	EFFECT ON NET INCOME
o. Ten-year notes are issued to pay off accounts payable.	____	____	____
p. A fully depreciated asset is retired.	____	____	____
q. Accounts receivable are collected.	____	____	____
r. Equipment is purchased with short-term notes.	____	____	____
s. Merchandise is purchased on credit.	____	____	____
t. The estimated taxes payable are increased.	____	____	____

3-10 Johnson Electric doubled its EVA last year, yet its return on equity declined. What could explain these changes?

SELF-TEST PROBLEMS (SOLUTIONS APPEAR IN APPENDIX B)

ST-1
Key terms
Define each of the following terms:
a. Liquidity ratios: current ratio; quick, or acid test, ratio
b. Asset management ratios: inventory turnover ratio; days sales outstanding (DSO); fixed assets turnover ratio; total assets turnover ratio
c. Financial leverage: debt ratio; times-interest-earned (TIE) ratio; EBITDA coverage ratio
d. Profitability ratios: profit margin on sales; basic earning power (BEP) ratio; return on total assets (ROA); return on common equity (ROE)
e. Market value ratios: price/earnings (P/E) ratio; price/cash flow ratio; market/book (M/B) ratio
f. Trend analysis; comparative ratio analysis; benchmarking
g. Du Pont chart; Du Pont equation; book value per share
h. "Window dressing"; seasonal effects on ratios

ST-2
Debt ratio
K. Billingsworth & Co. had earnings per share of $4 last year, and it paid a $2 dividend. Total retained earnings increased by $12 million during the year, while book value per share at year-end was $40. Billingsworth has no preferred stock, and no new common stock was issued during the year. If Billingsworth's year-end debt (which equals its total liabilities) was $120 million, what was the company's year-end debt/assets ratio?

ST-3
Ratio analysis
The following data apply to A.L. Kaiser & Company (millions of dollars):

Cash and marketable securities	$100.00
Fixed assets	$283.50
Sales	$1,000.00
Net income	$50.00
Quick ratio	2.0×
Current ratio	3.0×
DSO[a]	40.55 days
ROE	12%

[a]Calculation is based on a 365-day year.

Kaiser has no preferred stock — only common equity, current liabilities, and long-term debt.
a. Find Kaiser's (1) accounts receivable (A/R), (2) current liabilities, (3) current assets, (4) total assets, (5) ROA, (6) common equity, and (7) long-term debt.
b. In part a, you should have found Kaiser's accounts receivable (A/R) = $111.1 million. If Kaiser could reduce its DSO from 40.55 days to 30.4 days while holding other things constant, how much cash would it generate? If this cash were used to buy back common stock (at book value), thus reducing the amount of common equity, how would this affect (1) the ROE, (2) the ROA, and (3) the total debt/total assets ratio?

STARTER PROBLEMS

3-1
Liquidity ratios
Ace Industries has current assets equal to $3 million. The company's current ratio is 1.5, and its quick ratio is 1.0. What is the firm's level of current liabilities? What is the firm's level of inventories?

3-2
Days sales outstanding
Baker Brothers has a DSO of 40 days. The company's annual sales are $7,300,000. What is the level of its accounts receivable? Assume there are 365 days in a year.

3-3
Debt ratio
Bartley Barstools has an equity multiplier of 2.4. The company's assets are financed with some combination of long-term debt and common equity. What is the company's debt ratio?

3-4
Du Pont analysis
Doublewide Dealers has an ROA of 10 percent, a 2 percent profit margin, and a return on equity equal to 15 percent. What is the company's total assets turnover? What is the firm's equity multiplier?

3-5
Market to book ratio
Jaster Jets has $10 billion in total assets. The left side of its balance sheet consists of $1 billion in current liabilities, $3 billion in long-term debt, and $6 billion in common equity. The company has 800 million shares of common stock outstanding, and its stock price is $32 per share. What is Jaster's market/book ratio?

EXAM-TYPE PROBLEMS

The problems included in this section are set up in such a way that they could be used as multiple-choice exam problems.

3-6
Ratio calculations
Graser Trucking has $12 billion in assets, and its tax rate is 40 percent. The company's basic earning power (BEP) ratio is 15 percent, and its return on assets (ROA) is 5 percent. What is Graser's times-interest-earned (TIE) ratio?

3-7
Ratio calculations
Assume you are given the following relationships for the Brauer Corporation:

Sales/total assets	1.5×
Return on assets (ROA)	3%
Return on equity (ROE)	5%

Calculate Brauer's profit margin and debt ratio.

3-8
Liquidity ratios
The Petry Company has $1,312,500 in current assets and $525,000 in current liabilities. Its initial inventory level is $375,000, and it will raise funds as additional notes payable and use them to increase inventory. How much can Petry's short-term debt (notes payable) increase without pushing its current ratio below 2.0? What will be the firm's quick ratio after Petry has raised the maximum amount of short-term funds?

3-9
Ratio calculations
The Kretovich Company had a quick ratio of 1.4, a current ratio of 3.0, an inventory turnover of 6 times, total current assets of $810,000, and cash and marketable securities of $120,000 in 2001. What were Kretovich's annual sales and its DSO for that year? Assume there are 365 days in a year.

3-10
Times-interest-earned ratio
The H.R. Pickett Corporation has $500,000 of debt outstanding, and it pays an interest rate of 10 percent annually. Pickett's annual sales are $2 million, its average tax rate is 30 percent, and its net profit margin on sales is 5 percent. If the company does not maintain a TIE ratio of at least 5 times, its bank will refuse to renew the loan, and bankruptcy will result. What is Pickett's TIE ratio?

3-11
EBITDA coverage ratio
Willis Publishing has $30 billion in total assets. The company's basic earning power (BEP) ratio is 20 percent, and its times-interest-earned ratio is 8.0. Willis' depreciation and amortization expense totals $3.2 billion. It has $2 billion in lease payments and $1 billion must go toward principal payments on outstanding loans and long-term debt. What is Willis' EBITDA coverage ratio?

3-12
Return on equity
Midwest Packaging's ROE last year was only 3 percent, but its management has developed a new operating plan designed to improve things. The new plan calls for a total debt ratio of 60 percent, which will result in interest charges of $300,000 per year. Management projects an EBIT of $1,000,000 on sales of $10,000,000, and it expects to have

a total assets turnover ratio of 2.0. Under these conditions, the tax rate will be 34 percent. If the changes are made, what return on equity will the company earn?

3-13
Return on equity

Central City Construction Company, which is just being formed, needs $1 million of assets, and it expects to have a basic earning power ratio of 20 percent. Central City will own no securities, so all of its income will be operating income. If it chooses to, Central City can finance up to 50 percent of its assets with debt, which will have an 8 percent interest rate. Assuming a 40 percent federal-plus-state tax rate on all taxable income, what is the *difference* between its expected ROE if Central City finances with 50 percent debt versus its expected ROE if it finances entirely with common stock?

3-14
Conceptual: Return on equity

Which of the following statements is most correct? (Hint: Work Problem 3-13 before answering 3-14, and consider the solution setup for 3-13 as you think about 3-14.)

a. If a firm's expected basic earning power (BEP) is constant for all of its assets and exceeds the interest rate on its debt, then adding assets and financing them with debt will raise the firm's expected rate of return on common equity (ROE).

b. The higher its tax rate, the lower a firm's BEP ratio will be, other things held constant.

c. The higher the interest rate on its debt, the lower a firm's BEP ratio will be, other things held constant.

d. The higher its debt ratio, the lower a firm's BEP ratio will be, other things held constant.

e. Statement a is false, but statements b, c, and d are all true.

3-15
Return on equity

Lloyd and Daughters Inc. has sales of $200,000, a net income of $15,000, and the following balance sheet:

Cash	$ 10,000	Accounts payable	$ 30,000
Receivables	50,000	Other current liabilities	20,000
Inventories	150,000	Long-term debt	50,000
Net fixed assets	90,000	Common equity	200,000
Total assets	$300,000	Total liabilities and equity	$300,000

a. The company's new owner thinks that inventories are excessive and can be lowered to the point where the current ratio is equal to the industry average, $2.5\times$, without affecting either sales or net income. If inventories are sold off and not replaced so as to reduce the current ratio to $2.5\times$, if the funds generated are used to reduce common equity (stock can be repurchased at book value), and if no other changes occur, by how much will the ROE change?

b. Now suppose we wanted to take this problem and modify it for use on an exam, that is, to create a new problem that you have not seen to test your knowledge of this type of problem. How would your answer change if (1) We doubled all the dollar amounts? (2) We stated that the target current ratio was $3\times$? (3) We stated that the target was to achieve an inventory turnover ratio of $2\times$ rather than a current ratio of $2.5\times$? (Hint: Compare the ROE obtained with an inventory turnover ratio of $2\times$ to the original ROE obtained before any changes are considered.) (4) We said that the company had 10,000 shares of stock outstanding, and we asked how much the change in part a would increase EPS? (5) What would your answer to (4) be if we changed the original problem to state that the stock was selling for twice book value, so common equity would not be reduced on a dollar-for-dollar basis?

c. Now explain how we could have set the problem up to have you focus on changing accounts receivable, or fixed assets, or using the funds generated to retire debt (we would give you the interest rate on outstanding debt), or how the original problem could have stated that the company needed *more* inventories and it would finance them with new common equity or with new debt.

PROBLEMS

3-16
Balance sheet analysis

Complete the balance sheet and sales information in the table that follows for Hoffmeister Industries using the following financial data:

Debt ratio: 50%

Quick ratio: 0.80×

Total assets turnover: 1.5×

Days sales outstanding: 36.5 days[a]

Gross profit margin on sales: (Sales − Cost of goods sold)/Sales = 25%

Inventory turnover ratio: 5×

[a] Calculation is based on a 365-day year.

BALANCE SHEET

Cash	_____	Accounts payable	_____
Accounts receivable	_____	Long-term debt	60,000
Inventories	_____	Common stock	_____
Fixed assets	_____	Retained earnings	97,500
Total assets	$300,000	Total liabilities and equity	_____
Sales	_____	Cost of goods sold	_____

3-17
Ratio analysis

Data for Barry Computer Company and its industry averages follow.
a. Calculate the indicated ratios for Barry.
b. Construct the extended Du Pont equation for both Barry and the industry.
c. Outline Barry's strengths and weaknesses as revealed by your analysis.
d. Suppose Barry had doubled its sales as well as its inventories, accounts receivable, and common equity during 2001. How would that information affect the validity of your ratio analysis? (Hint: Think about averages and the effects of rapid growth on ratios if averages are not used. No calculations are needed.)

Barry Computer Company: Balance Sheet as of December 31, 2001 (In Thousands)

Cash	$ 77,500	Accounts payable	$ 129,000
Receivables	336,000	Notes payable	84,000
Inventories	241,500	Other current liabilities	117,000
Total current assets	$ 655,000	Total current liabilities	$ 330,000
Net fixed assets	292,500	Long-term debt	256,500
		Common equity	361,000
Total assets	$ 947,500	Total liabilities and equity	$ 947,500

Barry Computer Company: Income Statement for Year Ended December 31, 2001 (In Thousands)

Sales		$1,607,500
Cost of goods sold		
Materials	$717,000	
Labor	453,000	
Heat, light, and power	68,000	
Indirect labor	113,000	
Depreciation	41,500	1,392,500
Gross profit		$ 215,000
Selling expenses		115,000
General and administrative expenses		30,000
Earnings before interest and taxes (EBIT)		$ 70,000

Interest expense		24,500
Earnings before taxes (EBT)	$	45,500
Federal and state income taxes (40%)		18,200
Net income	$	27,300

RATIO	BARRY	INDUSTRY AVERAGE
Current assets/current liabilities	_____	2.0×
Days sales outstanding[a]	_____	35 days
Sales/inventories	_____	6.7×
Sales/total assets	_____	3.0×
Net income/sales	_____	1.2%
Net income/total assets	_____	3.6%
Net income/common equity	_____	9.0%
Total debt/total assets	_____	60.0%

[a] Calculation is based on a 365-day year.

3-18
Du Pont analysis

The Ferri Furniture Company, a manufacturer and wholesaler of high-quality home furnishings, has been experiencing low profitability in recent years. As a result, the board of directors has replaced the president of the firm with a new president, Helen Adams, who has asked you to make an analysis of the firm's financial position using the Du Pont chart. In addition to the information given below, you have been informed by the new president that the firm has no lease payments but has a $2 million sinking fund payment on its debt. The most recent industry average ratios, and Ferri's financial statements, are as follows:

INDUSTRY AVERAGE RATIOS

Current ratio	2×	Sales/fixed assets	6×
Debt/total assets	30%	Sales/total assets	3×
Times interest earned	7×	Profit margin on sales	3%
EBITDA coverage	9×	Return on total assets	9%
Sales/inventory	10×	Return on common equity	12.9%
Days sales outstanding[a]	24 days		

[a] Calculation is based on a 365-day year.

Ferri Furniture Company: Balance Sheet as of December 31, 2001 (Millions of Dollars)

Cash	$ 45	Accounts payable	$ 45
Marketable securities	33	Notes payable	45
Net receivables	66	Other current liabilities	21
Inventories	159	Total current liabilities	$111
Total current assets	$303	Long-term debt	24
		Total liabilities	$135
Gross fixed assets	225		
Less depreciation	78	Common stock	114
Net fixed assets	$147	Retained earnings	201
		Total stockholders' equity	$315
Total assets	$450	Total liabilities and equity	$450

Ferri Furniture Company: Income Statement for Year Ended December 31, 2001 (Millions of Dollars)

Net sales	$795.0
Cost of goods sold	660.0
Gross profit	$135.0
Selling expenses	73.5
EBITDA	$ 61.5
Depreciation expense	12.0
Earnings before interest and taxes (EBIT)	$ 49.5
Interest expense	4.5
Earnings before taxes (EBT)	$ 45.0
Taxes (40%)	18.0
Net income	$ 27.0

a. Calculate those ratios that you think would be useful in this analysis.
b. Construct an extended Du Pont equation for Ferri, and compare the company's ratios to the industry average ratios.
c. Do the balance sheet accounts or the income statement figures seem to be primarily responsible for the low profits?
d. Which specific accounts seem to be most out of line in relation to other firms in the industry?
e. If Ferri had a pronounced seasonal sales pattern, or if it grew rapidly during the year, how might that affect the validity of your ratio analysis? How might you correct for such potential problems?

3-19
Ratio analysis
The Corrigan Corporation's forecasted 2002 financial statements follow, along with some industry average ratios.
a. Calculate Corrigan's 2002 forecasted ratios, compare them with the industry average data, and comment briefly on Corrigan's projected strengths and weaknesses.
b. What do you think would happen to Corrigan's ratios if the company initiated cost-cutting measures that allowed it to hold lower levels of inventory and substantially decreased the cost of goods sold? No calculations are necessary. Think about which ratios would be affected by changes in these two accounts.

Corrigan Corporation: Forecasted Balance Sheet as of December 31, 2002

Cash	$ 72,000
Accounts receivable	439,000
Inventories	894,000
Total current assets	$1,405,000
Land and building	238,000
Machinery	132,000
Other fixed assets	61,000
Total assets	$1,836,000
Accounts and notes payable	$ 432,000
Accruals	170,000
Total current liabilities	$ 602,000
Long-term debt	404,290
Common stock	575,000
Retained earnings	254,710
Total liabilities and equity	$1,836,000

Corrigan Corporation: Forecasted Income Statement for Year Ended December 31, 2002

Sales	$4,290,000
Cost of goods sold	3,580,000
Gross operating profit	$ 710,000
General administrative and selling expenses	236,320
Depreciation	159,000
Miscellaneous	134,000
Earnings before taxes (EBT)	$ 180,680
Taxes (40%)	72,272
Net income	$ 108,408

PER-SHARE DATA

EPS	$4.71
Cash dividends	$0.95
Market price (average)	$23.57
P/E ratio	5×
Number of shares outstanding	23,000

INDUSTRY FINANCIAL RATIOS (2002)[a]

Quick ratio	1.0×
Current ratio	2.7×
Inventory turnover[b]	7.0×
Days sales outstanding[c]	32 days
Fixed assets turnover[b]	13.0×
Total assets turnover[b]	2.6×
Return on assets	9.1%
Return on equity	18.2%
Debt ratio	50.0%
Profit margin on sales	3.5%
P/E ratio	6.0×
Price/cash flow ratio	3.5×

[a] Industry average ratios have been constant for the past 4 years.

[b] Based on year-end balance sheet figures.

[c] Calculation is based on a 365-day year.

SPREADSHEET PROBLEM

3-20
Ratio analysis

This problem requires you to analyze the financial data given back in the spreadsheet problem for Chapter 2.

Laiho Industries' common stock has increased in price from $14.75 to $17.25 from the end of 2000 to the end of 2001, and its shares outstanding increased from 9 to 10 million shares during that same period. Laiho has annual lease payments of $75,000 (which are included in operating costs on the income statement), but no sinking fund payments are required. Now answer the following questions.

Using Laiho Industries' financial statements as given in the Chapter 2 spreadsheet problem, perform a ratio analysis for 2000 and 2001. Consider its liquidity, asset management, debt management, profitability, and market value ratios. (Hint: If you worked the Chapter 2 problem and saved your file, you can rename that file something like

Prob-03 and then perform the necessary calculations with the data generated for Chapter 2. This will save you from having to re-enter data.)

a. Has Laiho's liquidity position improved or worsened? Explain.
b. Has Laiho's ability to manage its assets improved or worsened? Explain.
c. How has Laiho's profitability changed during the last year?
d. Perform an extended Du Pont analysis for Laiho for 2000 and 2001.

CYBER PROBLEM

The information related to the cyberproblems is likely to change over time, due to the release of new information and the ever-changing nature of the World Wide Web. With these changes in mind, we will periodically update these problems on the textbook's web site. To avoid problems, please check for these updates before proceeding with the cyberproblems.

3-21

Using ratio analysis as a tool

Chapter 3 demonstrates the various ways that managers and investors use financial statements. The following cyberproblem addresses the financial statement analysis of Brady Corporation. Use the company's web site at **www.bradycorp.com** to navigate through this cyberproblem.

Brady Corporation is a leader in identification, safety, and material solutions. In 1998, the firm was hit hard by faltering foreign markets, so it embarked upon an aggressive campaign to redesign its cost structure. The firm believes this will help it to enhance future stockholder value. Brady follows the concept of Shareholder Value Enhancement (SVE), which is improved through increased sales, cost control, and effective use and control of assets.

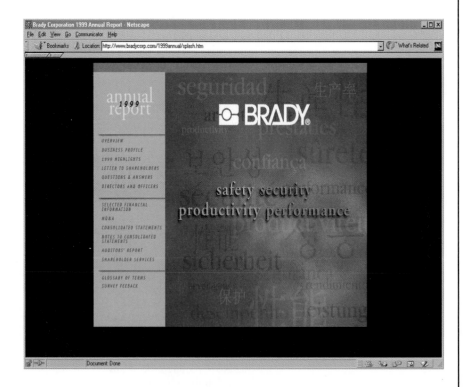

a. Review Brady Corporation's consolidated statements of income. Its 1999 annual report is found at **www.bradycorp.com/1999annual/splash.htm.** Calculate and interpret Brady's gross margin (calculated as [Net sales − Cost of goods sold]/Net sales) for 1997, 1998, and 1999. What conclusions, if any, can you draw from an-

alyzing these gross margins? (Hint: Have manufacturing costs as a percentage of sales increased, decreased, or remained level during this period?)
b. Calculate and interpret the firm's profit margin for 1997, 1998, and 1999. Has the firm's profit margin improved or worsened during this period? Why?
c. Calculate Brady's TIE ratio for 1997, 1998, and 1999, and interpret your results.
d. Look at Brady's balance sheets for 1998 and 1999. Calculate the firm's current and quick ratios, and comment on any changes in its liquidity position.
e. Using both the income statements and balance sheets, calculate Brady's total assets turnover for 1998 and 1999, and interpret your results.

INTEGRATED CASE

D'LEON INC., PART II

3-22 Financial Statement Analysis   Part I of this case, presented in Chapter 2, discussed the situation that D'Leon Inc., a regional snack-foods producer, was in after an expansion program. D'Leon had increased plant capacity and undertaken a major marketing campaign in an attempt to "go

national." Thus far, sales have not been up to the forecasted level, costs have been higher than were projected, and a large loss occurred in 2001 rather than the expected profit. As a result, its managers, directors, and investors are concerned about the firm's survival.

Donna Jamison was brought in as assistant to Fred Campo, D'Leon's chairman, who had the task of getting the

TABLE IC3-1	Balance Sheets			
		2002E	2001	2000
ASSETS				
Cash		$ 85,632	$ 7,282	$ 57,600
Accounts receivable		878,000	632,160	351,200
Inventories		1,716,480	1,287,360	715,200
Total current assets		$2,680,112	$1,926,802	$1,124,000
Gross fixed assets		1,197,160	1,202,950	491,000
Less accumulated depreciation		380,120	263,160	146,200
Net fixed assets		$ 817,040	$ 939,790	$ 344,800
Total assets		$3,497,152	$2,866,592	$1,468,800
LIABILITIES AND EQUITY				
Accounts payable		$ 436,800	$ 524,160	$ 145,600
Notes payable		300,000	636,808	200,000
Accruals		408,000	489,600	136,000
Total current liabilities		$1,144,800	$1,650,568	$ 481,600
Long-term debt		400,000	723,432	323,432
Common stock		1,721,176	460,000	460,000
Retained earnings		231,176	32,592	203,768
Total equity		$1,952,352	$ 492,592	$ 663,768
Total liabilities and equity		$3,497,152	$2,866,592	$1,468,800

NOTE: "E" indicates estimated. The 2002 data are forecasts.

company back into a sound financial position. D'Leon's 2000 and 2001 balance sheets and income statements, together with projections for 2002, are given in Tables IC3-1 and IC3-2. In addition, Table IC3-3 gives the company's 2000 and 2001 financial ratios, together with industry average data. The 2002 projected financial statement data represent Jamison's and Campo's best guess for 2002 results, assuming that some new financing is arranged to get the company "over the hump."

Jamison examined monthly data for 2001 (not given in the case), and she detected an improving pattern during the year. Monthly sales were rising, costs were falling, and large losses in the early months had turned to a small profit by December. Thus, the annual data look somewhat worse than final monthly data. Also, it appears to be taking longer for the advertising program to get the message across, for the new sales offices to generate sales, and for the new manufacturing facilities to operate efficiently. In other words, the lags between spending money and deriving benefits were longer than D'Leon's managers had anticipated. For these reasons, Jamison and Campo see hope for the company — provided it can survive in the short run.

Jamison must prepare an analysis of where the company is now, what it must do to regain its financial health, and what actions should be taken. Your assignment is to help her answer the following questions. Provide clear explanations, not yes or no answers.

a. Why are ratios useful? What are the five major categories of ratios?
b. Calculate D'Leon's 2002 current and quick ratios based on the projected balance sheet and income statement data. What can you say about the company's liquidity position in 2000, 2001, and as projected for 2002? We often think of ratios as being useful (1) to managers to help run the business, (2) to bankers for credit analysis, and (3) to stockholders for stock valuation. Would these different types of analysts have an equal interest in the liquidity ratios?
c. Calculate the 2002 inventory turnover, days sales outstanding (DSO), fixed assets turnover, and total assets turnover. How does D'Leon's utilization of assets stack up against other firms in its industry?
d. Calculate the 2002 debt, times-interest-earned, and EBITDA coverage ratios. How does D'Leon compare

TABLE IC3-2	Income Statements		
	2002E	**2001**	**2000**
Sales	$7,035,600	$6,034,000	$3,432,000
Cost of goods sold	5,875,992	5,528,000	2,864,000
Other expenses	550,000	519,988	358,672
Total operating costs excluding depreciation	$6,425,992	$6,047,988	$3,222,672
EBITDA	$ 609,608	($ 13,988)	$ 209,328
Depreciation	116,960	116,960	18,900
EBIT	$ 492,648	($ 130,948)	$ 190,428
Interest expense	70,008	136,012	43,828
EBT	$ 422,640	($ 266,960)	$ 146,600
Taxes (40%)	169,056	(106,784)[a]	58,640
Net income	$ 253,584	($ 160,176)	$ 87,960
EPS	$1.014	($1.602)	$0.880
DPS	$0.220	$0.110	$0.220
Book value per share	$7.809	$4.926	$6.638
Stock price	$12.17	$2.25	$8.50
Shares outstanding	250,000	100,000	100,000
Tax rate	40.00%	40.00%	40.00%
Lease payments	40,000	40,000	40,000
Sinking fund payments	0	0	0

NOTE: "E" indicates estimated. The 2002 data are forecasts.
[a]The firm had sufficient taxable income in 1999 and 2000 to obtain its full tax refund in 2001.

with the industry with respect to financial leverage? What can you conclude from these ratios?

e. Calculate the 2002 profit margin, basic earning power (BEP), return on assets (ROA), and return on equity (ROE). What can you say about these ratios?

f. Calculate the 2002 price/earnings ratio, price/cash flow ratio, and market/book ratio. Do these ratios indicate that investors are expected to have a high or low opinion of the company?

g. Use the extended Du Pont equation to provide a summary and overview of D'Leon's financial condition as projected for 2002. What are the firm's major strengths and weaknesses?

h. Use the following simplified 2002 balance sheet to show, in general terms, how an improvement in the DSO would tend to affect the stock price. For example, if the company could improve its collection procedures and thereby lower its DSO from 45.6 days to the 32-day industry average without affecting sales, how would that change "ripple through" the financial statements (shown in thousands below) and influence the stock price?

Accounts receivable	$ 878	Debt	$1,545
Other current assets	1,802		
Net fixed assets	817	Equity	1,952
Total assets	$3,497	Liabilities plus equity	$3,497

i. Does it appear that inventories could be adjusted, and, if so, how should that adjustment affect D'Leon's profitability and stock price?

j. In 2001, the company paid its suppliers much later than the due dates, and it was not maintaining financial ratios at levels called for in its bank loan agreements. Therefore, suppliers could cut the company off, and its bank could refuse to renew the loan when it comes due in 90 days. On the basis of data provided, would you, as a credit manager, continue to sell to D'Leon on credit? (You could demand cash on delivery, that is, sell on terms of COD, but that might cause D'Leon to stop buying from your company.) Similarly, if you were the bank loan officer, would you recommend renewing the loan or demand its repayment? Would your actions be influenced if, in early 2002, D'Leon showed you its 2002 projections plus proof that it was going to raise over $1.2 million of new equity capital?

k. In hindsight, what should D'Leon have done back in 2000?

l. What are some potential problems and limitations of financial ratio analysis?

m. What are some qualitative factors analysts should consider when evaluating a company's likely future financial performance?

Ratio Analysis

	2002E	2001	2000	INDUSTRY AVERAGE
Current	1.2×	2.3×	2.7×
Quick	0.4×	0.8×	1.0×
Inventory turnover	4.7×	4.8×	6.1×
Days sales outstanding (DSO)[a]	38.2	37.4	32.0
Fixed assets turnover	6.4×	10.0×	7.0×
Total assets turnover	2.1×	2.3×	2.6×
Debt ratio	82.8%	54.8%	50.0%
TIE	−1.0×	4.3×	6.2×
EBITDA coverage	0.1×	3.0×	8.0×
Profit margin	−2.7%	2.6%	3.5%
Basic earning power	−4.6%	13.0%	19.1%
ROA	−5.6%	6.0%	9.1%
ROE	−32.5%	13.3%	18.2%
Price/earnings	−1.4×	9.7×	14.2×
Price/cash flow	−5.2×	8.0×	11.0×
Market/book	0.5×	1.3×	2.4×
Book value per share	$4.93	$6.64	n.a.

NOTE: "E" indicates estimated. The 2002 data are forecasts.

[a] Calculation is based on a 365-day year.

4

Financial Planning and Forecasting

SOURCE: © Silver Image.

FORECASTING DISNEY'S FUTURE

WALT DISNEY CO.

In early 1998, corporations were reporting earnings for 1997. Simultaneously, security analysts were issuing their forecasts of earnings for 1998. Stock prices were extremely volatile, moving up with a good earnings surprise — that is, where reported EPS was higher than analysts had been expecting—and down with unpleasant surprises. Corporate executives know that these reactions will occur, so they generally try to give analysts early warnings when unpleasant surprises are likely to occur. The logic is that unpleasant surprises increase uncertainty about the future, so a stock will react less negatively to low earnings if the drop is anticipated than if it is a complete surprise.

Corporate finance staffs also review their own internal plans and forecasts during the first part of the year. Firms' formal plans are generally completed in the fall and then go into effect at the start of the year, so early in the year information starts coming in that indicates how the year is shaping up.

For executives at Walt Disney Co., 1998 was a particularly difficult year. After several years of outstanding performance, Disney's earnings fell, causing a sharp drop in its stock price. Trying to address investors' concerns, Disney's Chairman and Chief Executive, Michael Eisner, began his annual letter to shareholders with the following words:

To Disney Owners and Fellow Cast Members:

I am looking out the window and can see the seasons change (yes, the seasons do change in Los Angeles — the eucalyptus leaves droop more and the sprinklers go on less often). I am reminded that our rhythms are set by the seasons and that any number of human endeavors are ruled by the calendar. Such as this annual report. Every 12 months we compile it, and every 12 months I sit down to write you this letter.

There's just one problem with this annual exercise: It implies that businesses can be run in neat 12-month chunks of time. Unfortunately, the business cycle has its own seasons, which are not ruled by the orderly and predictable orbit of the earth around the sun. Indeed, at Disney we live by a 60-month calendar. We set our goals over rolling five-year timelines. In this context, each year is more like a season. Some are sunny and some are overcast, but each is merely a period of passage and not a destination. Our five-year calendars force us to think long-term. They make us devise strategies that add value, not squeeze profits.

Eisner went on to tell shareholders that the company's long-run forecast remained promising. After acknowledging that Disney had problems in its entertainment and broadcasting divisions, he went on to state that the company was taking steps to cut costs and to improve operations. Eisner also stated that Disney's earnings had been hampered because it had begun a series of expensive new projects, including Disney's Animal Kingdom, its Cruise Line, the launching of *ESPN Magazine,* and the renovation of Anaheim Stadium. However, he argued that they were laying the groundwork for future profitability.

In the two years that have followed since Eisner wrote this letter, Disney continued to have its ups and downs. Its stock price struggled throughout most of 1999, but it rebounded a bit in early 2001. In his most recent letter to shareholders, Eisner spoke optimistically about the company's future. However, in spite of Eisner's assurances, many analysts are still lukewarm about Disney's future prospects. Many others, though, are betting that the company's stock will continue to rebound. Unfortunately, no crystal ball exists for predicting the future. Instead, both corporate insiders and investors must base decisions on their own financial forecasts. While forecasting is necessarily somewhat subjective, we discuss in this chapter some basic principles that will improve financial forecasts. By the time you finish the chapter, you will have a good idea about how to forecast future results for Disney or any other company. ■

SOURCE: Walt Disney Co.'s 1998 and 1999 Annual Reports.

PUTTING THINGS IN PERSPECTIVE

Chapters 2 and 3 described what financial statements are and showed how both managers and investors analyze them to evaluate a firm's past performance. While this is clearly important, it is even more important to look ahead and to anticipate what is likely to happen in the future. So, both managers and investors need to understand how to forecast future results.

Pro Forma (Projected) Financial Statements
Financial statements that forecast the company's financial position and performance over a period of years.

Managers make **pro forma,** or **projected, financial statements** and then use them in four ways: (1) By looking at projected statements, they can assess whether the firm's anticipated performance is in line with the firm's own general targets and with investors' expectations. For example, if the projected financial statements indicate that the forecasted return on equity is well below the industry average, managers should investigate the cause and then seek a remedy. (2) Pro forma statements can be used to estimate the effect of proposed operating changes. Therefore, financial managers spend a lot of time doing "what if" analyses. (3) Managers use pro forma statements to anticipate the firm's future financing needs. (4) Projected financial statements are used to estimate future free cash flows, which determine the company's overall value. Thus, managers forecast free cash flows under different operating plans, forecast their capital requirements, and then choose the plan that maximizes shareholder value.

Security analysts make the same types of projections, forecasting future earnings, cash flows, and stock prices. Of course, managers have more information about the company than security analysts, and managers are the ones who make the decisions that determine the future. However, analysts influence investors, and investors determine the future of managers. To illustrate, suppose an influential analyst at a firm such as Goldman Sachs concludes, on the basis of a comparative financial analysis, that a particular firm's managers are less effective than others in the industry. The analyst's negative report could lead stockholders to revolt and replace management. Or, the report might lead a firm that specializes in taking over underperforming firms to buy stock in the company and then launch a hostile takeover designed to change management, improve cash flows, and make a large capital gain.

We will have more to say about investors' and analysts' use of projections in Chapter 9, when we discuss how stock prices are determined. First, though, in this chapter we explain how to create and use pro forma financial statements. We begin with the strategic plan, which provides a foundation for pro forma statements. ■

STRATEGIC PLANS

Our primary objective in this book is to explain what managers can do to make their companies more valuable. Managers must understand how investors determine the values of stocks and bonds if they are to identify, evaluate, and implement projects that meet or exceed investor expectations. However, value creation is impossible unless the company has a well-articulated plan. As Yogi Berra once said, "You've got to be careful if you don't know where you're going, because you might not get there."

Mission Statement
A condensed version of a firm's strategic plan.

Companies begin with a **mission statement,** which is in many ways a condensed version of their strategic plan. Figure 4-1 shows the mission statement of Coca-Cola, which we use to illustrate some of the key elements of strategic plans.

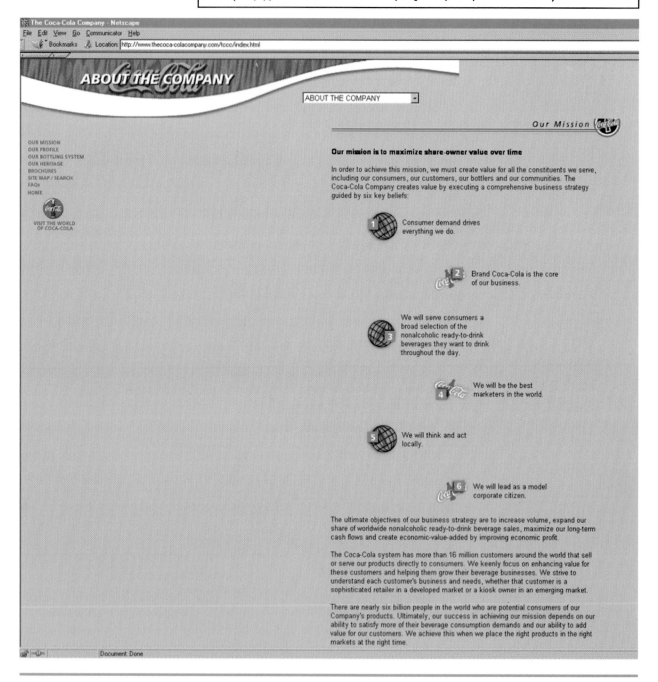

FIGURE 4-1 The Mission Statement of the Coca-Cola Company (http://www.thecoca-colacompany.com/tccc/mission.html)

CORPORATE PURPOSE

Both mission statements and strategic plans usually begin with a statement of the overall *corporate purpose*. Coca-Cola is very clear about its corporate purpose: ". . . maximize share-owner value over time."

This same corporate purpose is increasingly common for U.S. companies, but that has not always been the case. For example, Varian Associates, Inc., a New York Stock Exchange company with sales of almost $2 billion, was, in 1990, regarded as one of the most technologically advanced electronics companies. However, Varian's management was more concerned with developing new technology than with marketing it, and its stock price was lower than it had been 10 years earlier. Some of the larger stockholders were intensely unhappy with the state of affairs, and management was faced with the threat of a proxy fight or forced merger. In 1991, management announced a change in policy and stated that it would, in the future, emphasize both technological excellence *and* profitability, rather than focusing primarily on technology. Earnings improved dramatically, and the stock price rose from $6.75 to more than $60 within four years of that change in corporate purpose.

A corporate focus on creating wealth for the company's owners is not yet as common abroad as it is in the United States. For example, Veba AG, one of Germany's largest companies, created a stir in 1996 when it stated in its annual report that "Our commitment is to create value for you, our shareholders." This was quite different from the usual German model, in which companies have representatives from labor on their boards of directors and which explicitly state their commitments to a variety of stakeholders. As one might expect, Veba's stock has consistently outperformed the average German stock. As the trend in international investing continues, more and more non-U.S. companies are adopting a corporate purpose similar to that of Coke and Veba.

CORPORATE SCOPE

Its *corporate scope* defines a firm's lines of business and geographic area of operations. As Coca-Cola's mission statement indicates, the company limits its products to soft drinks, but on a global geographic scale. Pepsi-Cola recently followed Coke's lead — it restricted its scope by spinning off its food service businesses.

Several recent studies have found that the market tends to value focused firms more highly than it does diversified firms.[1] Nokia is an example of a company that has taken steps in recent years to sharpen its corporate focus. While most investors think of Nokia as a company that specializes in the wireless phone market, it has actually been around for more than 135 years, and until recently, Nokia was involved in a wide range of different industries. However, over the past decade, the Finnish conglomerate has sold off many of its less productive divisions. Investors have generally applauded the company's more focused strategy — Nokia's stock has risen nearly 2,000 percent over the past five years, and the company currently has a $200 billion market capitalization.

---

[1] See, for example, Philip G. Berger and Eli Ofek, "Diversification's Effect on Firm Value," *Journal of Financial Economics*, Vol. 37, No. 1, 39–66 (1995); and Larry Lang and René Stulz, "Tobin's Q, Corporate Diversification, and Firm Performance," *Journal of Political Economy*, Vol. 102, Issue 6, 1248–1280 (1994).

It is important to recognize that when it comes to corporate scope, one size doesn't fit all. For example, General Electric has investments in a large number of different areas, yet it is widely recognized as one of the best-managed and highly-valued industrial companies in the world.

CORPORATE OBJECTIVES

The corporate purpose states the general philosophy of the business, but it does not provide managers with operational objectives. The *statement of corporate objectives* sets forth specific goals to guide management. Most organizations have both qualitative and quantitative objectives. For example, Coca-Cola's mission statement lists six corporate objectives, including becoming "the best marketers in the world" and "leading as a model corporate citizen." However, these statements are qualitative, hence hard to measure, so the objectives need to be restated in quantitative terms, such as attaining a 50 percent market share, a 20 percent ROE, a 10 percent earnings growth rate, or a $100 million economic value added (EVA). Coca-Cola doesn't list its quantitative objectives in its mission statement, but it has them in its detailed strategic plan. Moreover, executive bonuses are based on achieving the quantitative objectives.

CORPORATE STRATEGIES

Once a firm has defined its purpose, scope, and objectives, it must develop a strategy for achieving its goals. *Corporate strategies* are broad approaches rather than detailed plans. For example, one airline may have a strategy of offering no-frills service between a limited number of cities, while another's strategy may be to offer "staterooms in the sky." Broadly speaking, a company's strategy often has several dimensions including whether (1) to invest overseas, (2) to invest in new lines of business and new technologies, and/or (3) to focus on a broad or narrow portion of the customer market. In any event, strategies should be both attainable and compatible with the firm's purpose, scope, and objectives.

SELF-TEST QUESTIONS

What are pro forma financial statements?

What are four ways that pro forma financial statements are used by managers?

Briefly describe the nature and use of the following corporate planning terms: (1) corporate purpose, (2) corporate scope, (3) corporate objectives, and (4) corporate strategies.

TABLE 4-1

Allied Food Products: Annual Planning Schedule

MONTHS	ACTION
April–May	Planning department analyzes general economic and industry factors. Marketing department prepares sales forecast for each product group.
June–July	Engineering department prepares cost estimates for new processing/distribution facilities and plant modernization programs.
August–September	Financial analysts evaluate proposed capital expenditures, divisional operating plans, and proposed sources and uses of funds.
October–November	Five-year plan is finalized by planning department, reviewed by divisional officers, and put into "semifinal" form.
December	Five-year plan is approved by the executive committee and then submitted to the board of directors for final approval.

OPERATING PLANS

Operating plans provide detailed implementation guidance, based on the corporate strategy, to help meet the corporate objectives. These plans can be developed for any time horizon, but like Disney, most companies use a five-year horizon. A five-year plan is most detailed for the first year, with each succeeding year's plan becoming less specific. The plan explains in considerable detail who is responsible for each particular function, when specific tasks are to be accomplished, sales and profit targets, and the like.

Table 4-1 summarizes the annual planning schedule of Allied Food Products. This schedule illustrates the fact that for larger companies, the planning process is essentially continuous. Next, Table 4-2 outlines the key elements of Allied's five-year plan. A full outline would require several pages, but Table 4-2 does provide insights into the format and content of a five-year plan. It should be noted that large, multidivisional companies such as General Electric break down their operating plans by divisions. Thus, each division has its own goals, mission, and plan for meeting its objectives, and these plans are then consolidated to form the corporate plan.[2]

SELF-TEST QUESTIONS

What is the purpose of a firm's operating plan?

What is the most common time horizon for operating plans?

Briefly describe the contents of a typical operating plan.

---

[2] For more on the corporate planning process, see Benton E. Gup, *Guide to Strategic Planning* (New York: McGraw-Hill, 1980).

TABLE 4-2   **Allied Food Products: Five-Year Operating Plan Outline**

Part 1. Corporate purpose

Part 2. Corporate scope

Part 3. Corporate objectives

Part 4. Projected business environment

Part 5. Corporate strategies

Part 6. Summary of projected business results

Part 7. Product line plans and policies

    a. Marketing

    b. Processing/distribution

    c. Finance

        1. Working capital

           (a) Overall working capital policy

           (b) Cash and marketable securities

           (c) Inventory management

           (d) Credit policy and receivables management

        2. Dividend policy

        3. Capital structure policy

        4. Financial forecast

           (a) Capital budget

           (b) Cash budget

           (c) Pro forma financial statements

           (d) External financing requirements

           (e) Financial condition analysis

        5. Accounting plan

        6. Control plan

    d. Administrative and personnel

    e. Research and development

    f. New products

THE FINANCIAL PLAN

The financial planning process can be broken down into six steps:

1. Project financial statements and use these projections to analyze the effects of the operating plan on projected profits and various financial ratios. The projections can also be used to monitor operations after the plan has been finalized and put into effect. Rapid awareness of deviations from the plan is essential in a good control system, which, in turn, is essential to corporate success in a changing world.

2. Determine the funds needed to support the five-year plan. This includes funds for plant and equipment as well as for inventories and receivables, for R&D programs, and for major advertising campaigns.

3. Forecast funds availability over the next five years. This involves estimating the funds to be generated internally as well as those to be obtained from external sources. Any constraints on operating plans imposed by financial restrictions must be incorporated into the plan; constraints include restrictions on the debt ratio, the current ratio, and the coverage ratios.

4. Establish and maintain a system of controls to govern the allocation and use of funds within the firm. In essence, this involves making sure that the basic plan is carried out properly.

5. Develop procedures for adjusting the basic plan if the economic forecasts upon which the plan was based do not materialize. For example, if the economy turns out to be stronger than was forecasted, then these new conditions must be recognized and reflected in higher production schedules, larger marketing quotas, and the like, and as rapidly as possible. Thus, Step 5 is really a "feedback loop" that triggers modifications to the financial plan.

6. Establish a performance-based management compensation system. It is critically important that such a system rewards managers for doing what stockholders want them to do—maximize share prices.

In the remainder of this chapter, we discuss how firms use computerized financial planning models to implement the three key components of the financial plan: (1) the sales forecast, (2) pro forma financial statements, and (3) the external financing plan.

SELF-TEST QUESTION

What are the six steps of the financial planning process?

COMPUTERIZED FINANCIAL PLANNING MODELS

Although financial forecasting as described in this chapter can be done with a calculator, virtually all corporate forecasts are made using computerized forecasting models. Most forecasting models are based on a spreadsheet program such as *Microsoft Excel*. Spreadsheets have two major advantages over pencil-and-paper calculations. First, it is much faster to construct a spreadsheet model than to make a "by-hand" forecast if the forecast period extends beyond a year or two. Second, and more important, with a spreadsheet model you can change inputs and instantaneously recompute the projected financial statements and ratios, thus making it easy for managers to determine the effects of changes in variables such as unit sales, labor costs, and sales prices.

In this chapter, we developed forecasted financial statements for Allied Food Products with an *Excel* model. The model is provided on the CD-ROM for the book, under the filename 04MODEL.xls. You do not have to understand the model to understand the chapter, but working through the model will give you a better feel for the forecasting process.[3]

> **SELF-TEST QUESTION**
>
> What are the two major advantages of spreadsheet models over pencil-and-paper calculations?

SALES FORECASTS

Sales Forecast
A forecast of a firm's unit and dollar sales for some future period; it is generally based on recent sales trends plus forecasts of the economic prospects for the nation, region, industry, and so forth.

The **sales forecast** generally starts with a review of sales during the past five to ten years, expressed in a graph such as that in Figure 4-2. The first part of the graph shows five years of historical sales for Allied. The graph could have contained 10 years of sales data, but Allied focuses on sales figures for the latest five years because the firm's studies have shown that its future growth is more closely related to recent events than to the distant past.

Allied had its ups and downs during the period from 1997 to 2001. In 1999, poor weather in California's fruit-producing regions resulted in low production, which caused 1999 sales to fall below the 1998 level. Then, a bumper crop in 2000 pushed sales up by 15 percent, an unusually high growth rate for a mature food processor. Based on a regression analysis, Allied's forecasters determined that the average annual growth rate in sales over the past five years was 9.1 percent. On the basis of this historical sales trend, on planned new-product introductions, and on Allied's forecast for the economy, the firm's planning committee projects a 10 percent sales growth rate during 2002, to sales of $3,300 million. Here are some of the factors Allied considered in developing its sales forecast:

1. Allied Food Products is divided into three divisions: canned foods, frozen foods, and packaged foods such as dried fruits. Sales growth is seldom the same for each of the divisions, so to begin the forecasting process, divisional projections are made on the basis of historical growth, and then the divisional forecasts are combined to produce a "first approximation" corporate sales forecast.

2. Next, the level of economic activity in each of the company's marketing areas is forecasted—for example, how strong will the economies be in each of Allied's six domestic and two foreign distribution territories, and what population changes are forecasted in each area?

3. Allied's planning committee also looks at the firm's probable market share in each distribution territory. Consideration is given to such factors as the firm's production and distribution capacity, its competitors' capacities,

---

[3] There are small rounding differences between "by-hand" answers and those obtained using the spreadsheet. The spreadsheet carries calculations out to more decimal places and thus is somewhat more accurate than "by-hand" calculations.

FIGURE 4-2

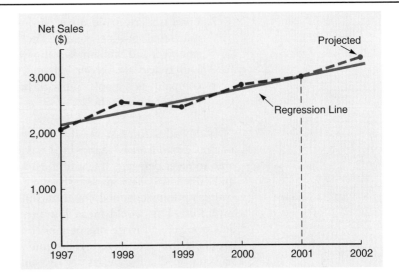

YEAR	SALES
1997	$2,058
1998	2,534
1999	2,472
2000	2,850
2001	3,000
2002	3,300 (Projected)

new-product introductions that are planned by Allied or its competitors, and potential changes in shelf-space allocations, which are vital for food sales. Pricing strategies are also considered—for example, does the company have plans to raise prices to boost margins, or to lower prices to increase market share and take advantage of economies of scale? Obviously, such factors could greatly affect future sales.

4. Allied's foreign sales present unique forecasting problems. In particular, its planners must consider how exchange rate fluctuations would affect sales. Allied must also consider the effects of trade agreements, governmental policies, and the like.

5. Allied's planners must also consider the effects of inflation on prices. Over the next five years, the inflation rate for food products is expected to average 3 to 4 percent, and Allied plans to increase prices, on average, by a like amount. In addition, the firm expects to expand its market share in certain products, resulting in a 4 percent growth rate in unit sales. The combination of unit sales growth and increases in sales prices has resulted in historical revenue growth rates in the 8 to 10 percent range, and this same situation is expected in the future.

6. Advertising campaigns, promotional discounts, credit terms, and the like also affect sales, so probable developments for these items are also factored in.

7. Forecasts are made for each division, both in the aggregate and on an individual product basis. The individual product sales forecasts are summed, and this sum is compared with the aggregated division forecasts. Differences are reconciled, and the end result is a sales forecast for the company as a whole but with breakdowns by the three divisions and by individual products.

If the sales forecast is off, the consequences can be serious. First, if the market expands *more* than Allied has geared up for, the company will not be able to meet demand. Its customers will end up buying competitors' products, and Allied will lose market share. On the other hand, if its projections are overly optimistic, Allied could end up with too much plant, equipment, and inventory. This would mean low turnover ratios, high costs for depreciation and storage, and write-offs of spoiled inventory. All of this would result in low profits, a low rate of return on equity, and a depressed stock price. If Allied had financed an unnecessary expansion with debt, high interest charges would compound its problems. Thus, an accurate sales forecast is critical to the firm's well-being.[4]

SELF-TEST QUESTIONS

List some factors that should be considered when developing a sales forecast.

Explain why an accurate sales forecast is critical to profitability.

FINANCIAL STATEMENT FORECASTING: THE PERCENT OF SALES METHOD

Percent of Sales Method
A method of forecasting future financial statements that expresses each account as a percentage of sales. These percentages can be constant, or they can change over time.

Once sales have been forecasted, we must forecast future balance sheets and income statements. The most commonly used technique is the **percent of sales method,** which begins with the sales forecast, expressed as an annual growth rate in dollar sales revenues. Although we showed only one year in our earlier example, Allied's managers actually forecasted sales for eight years, with these results:

YEAR	2002	2003	2004	2005	2006	2007	2008	2009
Growth rate in sales	10%	10%	10%	10%	9%	8%	7%	7%

This eight-year period is called the *explicit forecast period*, with the eighth year being the *forecast horizon*.

---

[4] A sales forecast is actually the *expected value of a probability distribution*, so there are many possible levels of sales. Because any sales forecast is subject to uncertainty, financial planners are just as interested in the degree of uncertainty inherent in the sales forecast, as measured by the standard deviation, as in the expected level of sales.

The initially forecasted growth rate is 10 percent, but high growth attracts competitors, and eventually the market becomes saturated. Therefore, population growth and inflation determine the *long-term sales growth rate* for most companies. Reasonable values for the long-term sales growth rate are from 5 to 7 percent for companies in mature industries. Allied's managers believe that a long-term sales growth rate of 7 percent is reasonable. Its managers also believe that competition will drive their growth rate down to this level within seven or eight years, so they have chosen an eight-year forecast period.

Companies often have what is called a *competitive advantage period*, during which they can grow at rates higher than the long-term growth rate. For companies with proprietary technology or strong brand identities, such as Microsoft or Coca-Cola, the competitive advantage period might be as long as 20 years. For companies that produce commodities or that are in highly competitive industries, the competitive advantage period might be as short as two or three years, or even be nonexistent.

To summarize, most financial plans have a forecast period of at least 5 years, with 5 to 15 years, depending on the expected length of the competitive advantage period, being most common.

Many items on the income statement and balance sheet are often assumed to increase proportionally with sales. For example, the inventories-to-sales ratio might increase 20 percent, receivables/sales might increase 15 percent, variable costs might increase 60 percent of sales, and so forth. Then, as sales increase, items that are tied to sales also increase, and the values of those items for a particular year are estimated as percentages of the forecasted sales for that year. The remaining items on the forecasted statements — items that are not tied directly to sales — are set at "reasonable" levels.

Note that if the forecasted percentage of sales for each item is the same as the percentage for the prior year, then each item will grow at the same rate as sales. While the financial statement forecasting method often begins by assuming that many key items will grow at the same rate as projected sales, it is important to recognize that this method can be easily adjusted to allow different income statement and balance sheet items to grow at different rates. This process is particularly straightforward whenever a spreadsheet is used to develop the forecast. With this understanding in mind, we explain in the following section how to use this method to forecast Allied's financial statements.

STEP 1. FORECASTED INCOME STATEMENT

First, we forecast the income statement for the coming year. This statement is needed to estimate both income and the addition to retained earnings. Table 4-3 shows the forecast for 2002. Sales are forecasted to grow by 10 percent. The forecast of sales for 2002, shown in Row 1 of Column 3, is calculated by multiplying the 2001 sales, shown in Column 1, by (1 + growth rate) = 1.1. The result is a 2002 forecast of $3,300 million.

The percent of sales method assumes initially that all costs except depreciation are a specified percentage of sales. For 2001, Allied's ratio of costs to sales is 87.2 percent ($2,616/$3,000 = 0.872). Thus, for each dollar of sales in 2001, Allied incurred 87.2 cents of costs. Initially, the company's managers assume that the cost structure will remain unchanged in 2002. Later in the chapter we explore the impact of an improvement in the cost structure, but for now we assume that costs will equal 87.2 percent of sales. See Column 3, Row 2.

TABLE 4-3

Allied Food Products: Actual 2001 and Projected 2002 Income Statements (Millions of Dollars)

	ACTUAL 2001[a] (1)	FORECAST BASIS (2)	2002 FORECAST (3)
1. Sales	$3,000	1.1 × 2001 Sales =	$3,300
2. Costs except depreciation	2,616	0.872 × 2002 Sales =	2,878
3. Depreciation	100	0.1 × 2002 Net plant =	110
4. Total operating costs	$2,716		$2,988
5. EBIT	$ 284		$ 312
6. Interest	88	⟶	88[b]
7. Earnings before taxes (EBT)	$ 196		$ 224
8. Taxes (40%)	78		89
9. NI before preferred dividends	$ 118		$ 135
10. Dividends to preferred	4	⟶	4[b]
11. NI available to common	$ 114		$ 131
12. Dividends to common	$ 58		$ 63[c]
13. Addition to retained earnings	$ 56		$ 68

[a] To reduce clutter, the income statement as shown previously in Chapter 2 is rounded to whole numbers.

[b] Indicates a 2001 amount carried over for the 2002 forecast. Indicated in Column 2 by an arrow.

[c] See the text for explanation of dividends.

Allied's managers assume that depreciation will be a fixed percentage of net plant and equipment. For 2001, the ratio of depreciation to net plant and equipment is 10 percent ($100/$1,000 = 0.10), and Allied's managers believe that this is a good estimate of future depreciation. As we discuss in the next section, the forecasted net plant and equipment for 2002 is $1,100. Therefore, the forecasted depreciation for 2002 is 0.10($1,100) = $110.

Total operating costs, shown in Row 4, are the sum of costs and depreciation. EBIT is found by subtraction, while the interest charges in Column 3 are simply carried over from Column 1.

Earnings before taxes (EBT) is then calculated, as is net income before preferred dividends. Preferred dividends are carried over from the 2001 column, and they will remain constant unless Allied decides to issue additional preferred stock. Net income available to common is then calculated, after which the 2002 dividends are forecasted as follows. The 2001 dividend per share is $1.15, and this dividend is expected to increase by about 8 percent, to $1.25. Since there are 50 million shares outstanding, the projected dividends are $1.25(50) = $62.5 million, rounded to $63 million.

To complete the forecasted income statement, the $63 million of projected dividends are subtracted from the $131 million projected net income, and the result is the first-pass projection of the addition to retained earnings, $131 − $63 = $68 million.

STEP 2. FORECAST THE BALANCE SHEET

The assets shown on Allied's balance sheet must increase if sales are to increase. For example, companies such as Allied write and deposit checks every day. Because they don't know exactly when all of these checks will clear, they can't predict exactly what the balance in their checking accounts will be on any given day. Therefore, they must maintain a balance of cash and marketable securities to avoid overdrawing their accounts. We discuss cash management in more detail in Chapter 15, but for now we simply assume that the cash required to support the company's operations is proportional to its sales. Allied's 2001 ratio of cash to sales was approximately 0.33 percent ($10/$3,000 = 0.003333), and its managers believe this ratio will remain constant in 2002. Therefore, the forecasted cash balance for 2002, shown in Column 3 of Table 4-4, is 0.003333($3,300) = $11 million.

Unless a company changes its credit policy or has a change in its types of customers, accounts receivable will increase proportionately with sales. Allied's 2001 ratio of accounts receivable to sales was $375/$3,000 = 0.125 = 12.5%. Later, we examine the effect of a change in credit policy, but for now we assume a constant credit policy and customer base. Therefore, the forecasted accounts receivable for 2002 is 0.125($3,300) = $412.5 million, rounded to $412 million as shown in Column 3 of Table 4-4.

As sales increase, companies generally need more inventory. For Allied, the 2001 ratio of inventory to sales is $615/$3,000 = 20.5%. Assuming no change in Allied's inventory management, the forecasted inventory for 2002 is 0.205($3,300) = $676.5 million, rounded to $677 million as shown in Column 3 of Table 4-4.

It might be reasonable to assume that cash, accounts receivable, and inventory grow proportionally with sales, but will the amount of net plant and equipment go up and down as sales go up and down? The correct answer could be yes or no. When companies acquire plant and equipment, they often install greater capacity than they currently need, due to economies of scale. For example, it was economically better for GM to build the Saturn automobile plant with a capacity of about 320,000 cars per year than to build the plant with a capacity of only 50,000 cars per year and then add capacity each year. Saturn's sales were far below 320,000 units for the first few years of production, so it was possible to increase sales during those years without also increasing plant and equipment. Even if a factory is at its maximum rated capacity, most companies can produce additional units by reducing the amount of downtime due to scheduled maintenance, by running machinery at a higher than optimal speed, or by running a second (or third) shift. Therefore, there is not necessarily a close relationship between sales and net plant and equipment in the short term.

However, for some companies there is a fixed relationship between sales and plant and equipment, even in the short term. For example, new stores in many retail chains achieve the same sales during their first year as the chain's existing stores. The only way these retailers can grow is by adding new stores, which results in a strong proportional relationship between fixed assets and sales.

In the long run, there is a relatively close relationship between sales and fixed assets for all companies: No company can continue to increase sales unless it eventually adds capacity. Therefore, as a first approximation it is reasonable to assume that the long-term ratio of net plant and equipment to sales will be constant.

TABLE 4-4

Allied Food Products: Actual 2001 and Projected 2002 Balance Sheets (Millions of Dollars)

	ACTUAL 2001 (1)	FORECAST BASIS (2)	2002 FORECAST		
			FIRST PASS (3)	AFN[a] (4)	SECOND PASS (5)
Cash and marketable securities	$ 10	0.33% × 2002 Sales =	$ 11	⟶	$ 11
Accounts receivable	375	12.5% × 2002 Sales =	412	⟶	412
Inventories	615	20.5% × 2002 Sales =	677	⟶	677
Total current assets	$1,000		$1,100		$1,100
Net plant and equipment	1,000	33.33% × 2002 Sales =	1,100	⟶	1,100
Total assets	$2,000		$2,200		$2,200
Accounts payable	$ 60	2% × 2002 Sales =	$ 66	⟶	$ 66
Notes payable	110	⟶	110[b]	+28	138
Accruals	140	4.67% × 2002 Sales =	154	⟶	154
Total current liabilities	$ 310		$ 330		$ 358
Long-term bonds	754	⟶	754[b]	+28	782
Total debt	$1,064		$1,084		$1,140
Preferred stock	40	⟶	40[b]	⟶	40
Common stock	130	⟶	130[b]	+56	186
Retained earnings	766	+68[c]	834	⟶	834
Total common equity	$ 896		$ 964		$1,020
Total liabilities and equity	$2,000		$2,088	+112	$2,200
Additional funds needed (AFN)			$ 112		

[a] AFN stands for "Additional Funds Needed." This figure is determined at the bottom of Column 3. Then, Column 4 shows how the required $112 of AFN will be raised.

[b] Indicates a 2001 amount carried over as the first-pass forecast. Arrows also indicate items whose values are carried over from one pass to another.

[c] From Line 13 in Column 3 of Table 4-3.

For the first years of a forecast, managers generally use the actual planned dollars of investment in plant and equipment. If those estimates are not available, it is reasonable to assume an approximately constant ratio of net plant and equipment to sales. For Allied, the ratio of net plant and equipment to sales for 2001 is $1,000/$3,000 = 33.33%. Allied's net plant and equipment have grown fairly steadily in the past, and its managers expect steady future growth. Therefore, they forecast net plant and equipment for 2002 to be 0.3333($3,300) = $1,100 million.

Once the individual asset accounts have been forecasted, they can be summed to complete the asset section of the balance sheet. For Allied, the total current assets forecasted for 2002 are $11 + $412 + $677 = $1,100 million, and fixed assets add another $1,100 million. Therefore, as Table 4-4 shows, Allied will need total assets of $2,200 million to support $3,300 million of sales in 2002.

If Allied's assets are to increase, its liabilities and equity must also increase — the additional assets must be financed. Some items on the liability side can be

Spontaneously Generated Funds
Funds that are obtained automatically from routine business transactions.

expected to increase spontaneously with sales, producing what are called **spontaneously generated funds.** For example, as sales increase, so will Allied's purchases of raw materials, and those larger purchases will spontaneously lead to a higher level of accounts payable. For Allied, the 2001 ratio of accounts payable to sales is $60/$3,000 = 0.02 = 2%. Allied's managers assume that their payables policy will not change, so the forecasted accounts payable for 2002 is 0.02($3,300) = $66 million.

More sales will require more labor, and higher sales should also result in higher taxable income and thus taxes. Therefore, accrued wages and taxes will both increase. For Allied, the 2001 ratio of accruals to sales is $140/$3,000 = 0.0467 = 4.67%. If this ratio does not change, then the forecasted level of accruals for 2002 will be 0.0467($3,300) = $154 million.

Retained earnings will also increase, but not at the same rate as sales: The new balance for retained earnings will be the old level plus the addition to retained earnings, which we calculated in Step 1. Also, notes payable, long-term bonds, preferred stock, and common stock will not rise spontaneously with sales — rather, the projected levels of these accounts will depend on financing decisions, as we discuss later.

In summary, (1) higher sales must be supported by additional assets, (2) some of the asset increases can be financed by spontaneous increases in accounts payable and accruals, and by retained earnings, but (3) any shortfall must be financed from external sources, using some combination of debt, preferred stock, and common stock.

The spontaneously increasing liabilities (accounts payable and accruals) are forecasted and shown in Column 3 of Table 4-4, the first-pass forecast. Then, those liability and equity accounts whose values reflect conscious management decisions — notes payable, long-term bonds, preferred stock, and common stock — are initially set at their 2001 levels. Thus, 2002 notes payable are initially set at $110 million, the long-term bond account is forecasted at $754 million, and so on. The 2002 value for the retained earnings (RE) account is obtained by adding the projected addition to retained earnings as developed in the 2002 income statement (see Table 4-3) to the 2001 ending balance:

$$2002 \text{ RE} = 2001 \text{ RE} + 2002 \text{ forecasted addition to RE}$$
$$= \$766 + \$68 = \$834 \text{ million.}$$

The forecast of total assets as shown in Column 3 (first-pass forecast) of Table 4-4 is $2,200 million, which indicates that Allied must add $200 million of new assets in 2002 to support the higher sales level. However, the forecasted liability and equity accounts as shown in the lower portion of Column 3 rise by only $88 million, to $2,088 million. Since the balance sheet must balance, Allied must raise an additional $2,200 − $2,088 = $112 million, which we define as **Additional Funds Needed (AFN).** The AFN will be raised by some combination of borrowing from the bank as notes payable, issuing long-term bonds, and selling new common stock.

Additional Funds Needed (AFN)
Funds that a firm must raise externally through borrowing or by selling new common or preferred stock.

STEP 3. RAISING THE ADDITIONAL FUNDS NEEDED

Allied's financial staff will raise the needed funds based on several factors, including the firm's target capital structure, the effect of short-term borrowing on the current ratio, conditions in the debt and equity markets, and restrictions imposed by existing debt agreements. The financial staff, after considering all of the relevant factors, decided on the following financing mix to raise the needed $112 million:

	AMOUNT OF NEW CAPITAL		
	PERCENT	DOLLARS (MILLIONS)	INTEREST RATE
Notes payable	25%	$ 28	8%
Long-term bonds	25	28	10
Common stock	50	56	—
	100%	$112	

These amounts, which are shown in Column 4 of Table 4-4, are added to the initially forecasted account totals as shown in Column 3 to generate the second-pass balance sheet. Thus, in Column 5 the notes payable account increases to $110 + $28 = $138 million, long-term bonds rise to $754 + $28 = $782 million, and common stock increases to $130 + $56 = $186 million. Then, the balance sheet is in balance.

A COMPLICATION: FINANCING FEEDBACKS

Our projected financial statements are incomplete in one sense — they do not reflect the fact that interest must be paid on the debt used to help finance the AFN, and that dividends will be paid on the shares issued to raise the common stock portion of the AFN. Those payments would lower net income and retained earnings shown in the projected statements. One could take account of these *financing feedback effects* by adding columns to Tables 4-3 and 4-4 and then making further adjustments. The adjustments are not difficult, but they do involve a good bit of arithmetic. In view of the fact that all of the data are based on forecasts, and since the adjustments add substantially to the work but relatively little to the accuracy of the forecasts, we leave them to later finance courses.[5]

ANALYSIS OF THE FORECAST

The 2002 forecast as developed above is only the first part of Allied's total forecasting process. We must go on to analyze the projected statements to determine whether the forecast meets the firm's financial targets as set forth in the five-year financial plan. If the statements do not meet the targets, then elements of the forecast must be changed.

Table 4-5 shows Allied's actual ratios for 2001, its projected 2002 ratios, and the latest industry average ratios. (The table also shows a "Revised Forecast for 2002" column, which we will discuss later. Disregard the revised data for now.) The firm's financial condition at the close of 2001 was weak, with many ratios

---

[5] For a thorough discussion of financing feedbacks, see Eugene F. Brigham and Phillip R. Daves, *Intermediate Financial Management,* 7th ed. (Fort Worth, TX: Harcourt College Publishers, 2002), Chapter 8.

TABLE 4-5

TABLE 4-5   Model Inputs, AFN, and Key Ratios

	ACTUAL 2001 (1)	PRELIMINARY FORECAST FOR 2002 (2)	REVISED FORECAST FOR 2002[a] (3)	INDUSTRY AVERAGE 2001 (4)
MODEL INPUTS				
Costs (excluding depreciation) as percentage of sales	87.2%	87.2%	86.0%	87.1%
Accounts receivable as percentage of sales	12.5	12.5	11.8	10.0
Inventories as percentage of sales	20.5	20.5	16.7	11.1
MODEL OUTPUTS				
NOPAT (net operating profit after taxes)	$170.3	$187.3	$211.2	
Net operating working capital	$800.0	$880.0	$731.5	
Total operating capital	$1,800.0	$1,980.0	$1,831.5	
Free cash flow (FCF)	($109.7)	$7.3	$179.7	
AFN		$112	($60)	
KEY RATIOS				
Current ratio	3.2×	3.1×	3.5×	4.2×
Inventory turnover	4.9×	4.9×	6.0×	9.0×
Days sales outstanding (365-day basis)	45.6	45.6	43.1	36.0
Total assets turnover	1.5×	1.5×	1.6×	1.8×
Debt ratio	53.2%	51.8%	49.9%	40.0%
Profit margin	3.8%	4.0%	4.7%	5.0%
Return on assets	5.7%	5.9%	7.5%	9.0%
Return on equity	12.7%	12.8%	15.6%	15.0%
Return on invested capital (NOPAT/Total operating capital)	9.5%	9.5%	11.5%	11.4%

[a] The "Revised" data show ratios after policy changes related to asset levels, as discussed later, have been incorporated into the forecast. All of the surplus AFN is used to pay off notes payable.

well below the industry averages. For example, Allied's current ratio, based on Column 1 of Table 4-4, was only 3.2 versus 4.2 for an average food processor.

The "Inputs" section shown on the top three rows of the table provides data on three of the model's key drivers: (1) costs (excluding depreciation) as a percentage of sales, (2) accounts receivable as a percentage of sales, and (3) inventories as a percentage of sales. The preliminary forecast in Column 2 assumes these variables remain constant. While Allied's cost-to-sales ratio is only slightly worse than the industry average, its ratios of accounts receivable to sales and inventories to sales are significantly higher than those of its competitors. Its investment in inventories and receivables is too high, causing its returns on assets, equity, and invested capital as shown in the lower part of the table to be too low. Therefore, Allied should make operational changes designed to reduce its current assets.

The "Key Ratios" section of Table 4-5 for the forecast period provides more details regarding the firm's weaknesses. Allied's asset management ratios are much worse than the industry averages. For example, its total assets turnover ratio is 1.5 versus an industry average of 1.8. Its poor asset management ratios drag down the return on invested capital (9.5 percent for Allied versus 11.4 percent for the industry average). Furthermore, Allied must carry more than the average amount of debt to support its excessive assets, and the extra interest expense reduces its profit margin to 4.0 percent versus 5.0 percent for the industry. Much of the debt is short term, and this results in a current ratio of 3.1 versus the 4.2 industry average. These problems will persist unless management takes action to improve things.

After reviewing its preliminary forecast, management decided to take three steps to improve its financial condition: (1) It decided to lay off some workers and close certain operations. It forecasted that these steps would lower operating costs (excluding depreciation) from the current 87.2 to 86 percent of sales as shown in Column 3 of Table 4-5. (2) By screening credit customers more closely and by being more aggressive in collecting past-due accounts, the company believes it can reduce the ratio of accounts receivable-to-sales from 12.5 to 11.8 percent. (3) Finally, management thinks it can reduce the inventories-to-sales ratio from 20.5 to 16.7 percent through the use of tighter inventory controls.[6]

These projected operational changes were then used to create a revised set of forecasted statements for 2002. We do not show the new financial statements, but the revised ratios are shown in the third column of Table 4-5. You can see the details in the chapter spreadsheet model, 04MODEL.xls. Here are the highlights of the revised forecast:

1. The reduction in operating costs improved the 2002 NOPAT, or net operating profit after taxes, by $23.9 million. Even more impressive, the improvements in the receivables policy and in inventory management reduced receivables and inventories by $148.5 million. The net result of the increase in NOPAT and the reduction of current assets was a very large increase in free cash flow for 2002, from a previously estimated $7.3 million to $179.7 million. Although we do not show it, the improvements in operations also led to significantly higher free cash flow for each year in the whole forecast period.

2. The profit margin improved to 4.7 percent. However, the firm's profit margin still lagged the industry average because its high debt ratio results in higher-than-average interest payments.

3. The increase in the profit margin resulted in an increase in projected retained earnings. More importantly, by tightening inventory controls and reducing the days sales outstanding, Allied projected a reduction in inventories and receivables. Taken together, these actions resulted in a *negative* AFN of $60 million, which means that Allied would actually generate $60 million more from internal operations during 2002 than it needs for new assets. All of this $60 million of surplus funds would be used to reduce short-term debt, which would lead to a decrease in the forecasted debt ratio from 51.8 to 49.9 percent. The debt ratio would still be well above the industry average, but this is a step in the right direction.

4. The indicated changes would also affect Allied's current ratio, which would improve from 3.1 to 3.5.

---

[6] We will discuss receivables and inventory management in detail in Chapter 15.

5. These actions would also raise the rate of return on assets from 5.9 to 7.5 percent, and they would boost the return on equity from 12.8 to 15.6 percent, which is even higher than the industry average.

Although Allied's managers believe that the revised forecast is achievable, they are not sure of this. Accordingly, they wanted to know how variations in sales would affect the forecast. Therefore, a spreadsheet model was run using several different sales growth rates, and the results were analyzed to see how the ratios would change under different growth scenarios. To illustrate, if the sales growth rate increased from 10 to 20 percent, the additional funding requirement would change dramatically, from a $60 million *surplus* to an $87 million *shortfall*.

The spreadsheet model was also used to evaluate dividend policy. If Allied decided to reduce its dividend growth rate, then additional funds would be generated, and those funds could be invested in plant, equipment, and inventories; used to reduce debt; or used to repurchase stock.

The model was also used to evaluate financing alternatives. For example, Allied could use the forecasted $60 million of surplus funds to retire long-term bonds rather than to reduce short-term debt. Under this financing alternative, the current ratio would drop from 3.5 to 2.9, but the firm's interest coverage ratio would rise, assuming that the firm's long-term debt carries a higher interest rate than its notes payable.

We see, then, that forecasting is an iterative process, both in the way the financial statements are generated and the way the financial plan is developed. For planning purposes, the financial staff develops a preliminary forecast based on a continuation of past policies and trends. This provides a starting point, or "baseline" forecast. Next, the projections are modified to see what effects alternative operating plans would have on the firm's earnings and financial condition. This results in a revised forecast. Then alternative operating plans are examined under different sales growth scenarios, and the model is used to evaluate both dividend policy and capital structure decisions.

The spreadsheet model can be used to analyze alternative working capital policies—that is, to see the effects of changes in cash management, credit policy, inventory policy, and the use of different types of short-term credit. We will examine Allied's working capital policy within the framework of the company's financial model later, but in the remainder of this chapter, we consider some other aspects of the financial forecasting process.

FORECASTING FREE CASH FLOW

The spreadsheet model can also be used to estimate Allied's free cash flow. Recall from Chapter 2, Equation 2-7, that free cash flow is calculated as follows:

FCF = Operating cash flow − Gross investment in operating capital.

Alternatively, FCF can be calculated using Equation 2-7a:

FCF = NOPAT − Net investment in operating capital.

Recall also that free cash flow represents the amount of cash generated in a given year minus the amount of cash needed to finance the additional capital expenditures and operating working capital needed to support the firm's growth.

The detailed spreadsheet model is not provided in the text, but its key outputs were shown in the "Model Outputs" section back in Table 4-5. We see that before the operating changes Allied forecasted a slight increase in NOPAT (net operating profit after taxes), but it projected a very large increase in net operating working capital and in total operating capital. The net result is a very low level of free cash flow, only $7.3 million. Although we do not show projections of the full financial statements for all eight years of the explicit forecast horizon, here are the initially projected free cash flows (FCFs):

YEARS	2002	2003	2004	2005	2006	2007	2008	2009
FCF	7.3	8.4	8.9	9.8	34.6	63.7	96.9	103.7

As we will see in Chapter 9, investors and financial managers use such forecasts to estimate the firm's stock price. Thus, this model helps managers measure the expected changes in the determinants of value under different strategic and operating alternatives.

SELF-TEST QUESTIONS

What is the AFN, and how is the percent of sales method used to estimate it?

Why do accounts payable and accruals provide "spontaneous funds" to a growing firm?

Would payables and accruals provide spontaneous funds to a no-growth firm? One that is declining?

Why do retained earnings not grow at the same rate as sales? In answering this question, think about a firm whose sales are not growing (g = 0%), but that is profitable and does not pay out all of its earnings as dividends.

THE AFN FORMULA

Most firms forecast their capital requirements by constructing pro forma income statements and balance sheets as described above. However, if the ratios are expected to remain constant, then the following formula can be used to forecast financial requirements. Here we apply the formula to Allied based on the 2001 data, not the revised data, as the revised data do not assume constant ratios.

$$
\begin{array}{cccc}
\text{Additional} & \text{Required} & \text{Spontaneous} & \text{Increase in} \\
\text{funds} & = \text{increase} & - \text{increase in} & - \text{retained} \\
\text{needed} & \text{in assets} & \text{liabilities} & \text{earnings}
\end{array}
$$

$$\text{AFN} = (A^*/S_0)\Delta S - (L^*/S_0)\Delta S - MS_1(RR). \quad (4\text{-}1)$$

Here

AFN = additional funds needed.

A* = assets that are tied directly to sales, hence which must increase if sales are to increase. Note that A designates total assets and A* designates those assets that must increase if sales are to increase. When the firm is operating at full capacity, as is the case here, $A^* = A$. Often, though, A^* and A are not equal, and either the equation must be modified or we must use the projected financial statement method.

S_0 = sales during the last year.

A^*/S_0 = percentage of required assets to sales, which also shows the required dollar increase in assets per \$1 increase in sales. $A^*/S_0 = \$2,000/\$3,000 = 0.6667$ for Allied. Thus, for every \$1 increase in sales, assets must increase by about 67 cents.

L^* = liabilities that increase spontaneously. L^* is normally much less than total liabilities (L). Spontaneous liabilities include accounts payable and accruals, but not bank loans and bonds.

L^*/S_0 = liabilities that increase spontaneously as a percentage of sales, or spontaneously generated financing per \$1 increase in sales. $L^*/S_0 = (\$60 + \$140)/\$3,000 = 0.0667$ for Allied. Thus, every \$1 increase in sales generates about 7 cents of spontaneous financing.

S_1 = total sales projected for next year. Note that S_0 designates last year's sales, and $S_1 = \$3,300$ million for Allied.

ΔS = change in sales = $S_1 - S_0 = \$3,300$ million $- \$3,000$ million = \$300 million for Allied.

M = profit margin, or profit per \$1 of sales. $M = \$114/\$3,000 = 0.0380$ for Allied. So, Allied earns 3.8 cents on each dollar of sales.

RR = retention ratio, which is the percentage of net income that is retained. For Allied, $RR = \$56/\$114 = 0.491$. RR is also equal to $1 -$ payout ratio, since the retention ratio and the payout ratio must total to $1.0 = 100\%$.

Inserting values for Allied into Equation 4-1, we find the additional funds needed to be \$118 million:

$$
\begin{aligned}
\text{AFN} &= \begin{matrix} \text{Required} \\ \text{asset} \\ \text{increase} \end{matrix} \; - \; \begin{matrix} \text{Spontaneous} \\ \text{liability} \\ \text{increase} \end{matrix} \; - \; \begin{matrix} \text{Increase} \\ \text{in retained} \\ \text{earnings} \end{matrix} \\[6pt]
&= 0.667(\Delta S) - 0.067(\Delta S) - 0.038(S_1)(0.491) \\[4pt]
&= 0.667(\$300 \text{ million}) - 0.067(\$300 \text{ million}) \\
&\quad - 0.038(\$3,300 \text{ million})(0.491) \\[4pt]
&= \$200 \text{ million} - \$20 \text{ million} - \$62 \text{ million} \\[4pt]
&= \$118 \text{ million}.
\end{aligned}
$$

To increase sales by \$300 million, the formula suggests that Allied must increase assets by \$200 million. The \$200 million of new assets must be financed in some manner. Of the total, \$20 million will come from a spontaneous increase in liabilities, while another \$62 million will be obtained from retained earnings. The remaining \$118 million must be raised from external sources. This value is an approximation, but it is only slightly different from the initial AFN figure (\$112 million) we developed in Table 4-4.[7]

This equation shows that external financing requirements depend on five key factors:

---

[7] If Table 4-4 had been extended to include financing feedbacks, the forecasted AFN would have been \$119 million, which is very close to the formula AFN.

Capital Intensity Ratio
The amount of assets required per dollar of sales (A^*/S_0).

- *Sales growth (ΔS).* Rapidly growing companies require large increases in assets, other things held constant.

- *Capital intensity (A^*/S_0).* The amount of assets required per dollar of sales, A^*/S_0 in Equation 4-1, is called the **capital intensity ratio.** This ratio has a major effect on capital requirements. Companies with higher assets-to-sales ratios require more assets for a given increase in sales, hence a greater need for external financing.

- *Spontaneous liabilities-to-sales ratio (L^*/S_0).* Companies that spontaneously generate a large amount of liabilities from accounts payable and accruals will have a relatively small need for external financing.

- *Profit margin (M).* The higher the profit margin, the larger the net income available to support increases in assets, hence the lower the need for external financing.

- *Retention ratio (RR).* Companies that retain more of their earnings as opposed to paying them out as dividends will generate more retained earnings and thus have less need for external financing.

Note that Equation 4-1 provides an accurate forecast only for companies whose ratios are all expected to remain constant. It is useful to obtain a quick "back of the envelope" estimate of external financing requirements for nonconstant ratio companies, but in the planning process one should calculate the actual additional funds needed by the projected financial statement method.

SELF-TEST QUESTIONS

If all ratios are expected to remain constant, a formula can be used to forecast AFN. Give the formula and briefly explain it.

How do the following factors affect external capital requirements?

(1) Retention ratio.

(2) Capital intensity.

(3) Profit margin.

(4) Dividend payout ratio.

FORECASTING FINANCIAL REQUIREMENTS WHEN THE BALANCE SHEET RATIOS ARE SUBJECT TO CHANGE

Both the AFN formula and the projected financial statement method as we initially used it assume that the ratios of assets and liabilities to sales (A^*/S_0 and L^*/S_0) remain constant over time. This, in turn, requires the assumption that each "spontaneous" asset and liability item increases at the same rate as sales. In graph form, this implies the type of relationship shown in Panel a of Figure 4-3, a relationship that is (1) linear and (2) passes through the origin. Under those conditions, if the company's sales increase from $200 million to $400 million, or by 100 percent, inventory will also increase by 100 percent, from $100 million to $200 million.

FIGURE 4-3   Four Possible Ratio Relationships (Millions of Dollars)

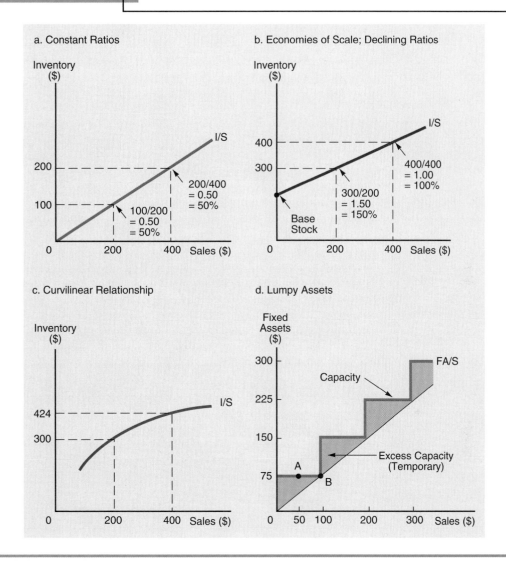

The assumption of constant ratios and identical growth rates is appropriate at times, but there are times when it is incorrect. Three such conditions are described in the following sections.

ECONOMIES OF SCALE

There are economies of scale in the use of many kinds of assets, and when economies occur, the ratios are likely to change over time as the size of the firm increases. For example, retailers often need to maintain base stocks of different inventory items, even if current sales are quite low. As sales expand, inventories may then grow less rapidly than sales, so the ratio of inventory to sales (I/S) declines. This situation is depicted in Panel b of Figure 4-3. Here we see that the inventory/sales ratio is 1.5, or 150 percent, when sales are $200 million, but the ratio declines to 1.0 when sales climb to $400 million.

The relationship in Panel b is linear, but nonlinear relationships often exist. Indeed, if the firm uses one popular model for establishing inventory levels (the EOQ model), its inventories will rise with the square root of sales. This situation is shown in Panel c of Figure 4-3, which shows a curved line whose slope decreases at higher sales levels. In this situation, very large increases in sales would require very little additional inventory.

LUMPY ASSETS

Lumpy Assets
Assets that cannot be acquired in small increments but must be obtained in large, discrete units.

In many industries, technological considerations dictate that if a firm is to be competitive, it must add fixed assets in large, discrete units; such assets are often referred to as **lumpy assets.** In the paper industry, for example, there are strong economies of scale in basic paper mill equipment, so when a paper company expands capacity, it must do so in large, lumpy increments. This type of situation is depicted in Panel d of Figure 4-3. Here we assume that the minimum economically efficient plant has a cost of $75 million, and that such a plant can produce enough output to reach a sales level of $100 million. If the firm is to be competitive, it simply must have at least $75 million of fixed assets.

Lumpy assets have a major effect on the fixed assets/sales (FA/S) ratio at different sales levels and, consequently, on financial requirements. At Point A in Panel d, which represents a sales level of $50 million, the fixed assets are $75 million, so the ratio FA/S = $75/$50 = 1.5. Sales can expand by $50 million, out to $100 million, with no additions to fixed assets. At that point, represented by Point B, the ratio FA/S = $75/$100 = 0.75. However, since the firm is operating at capacity (sales of $100 million), even a small increase in sales would require a doubling of plant capacity, so a small projected sales increase would bring with it a very large financial requirement.[8]

EXCESS ASSETS DUE TO FORECASTING ERRORS

Panels a, b, c, and d of Figure 4-3 all focus on target, or projected, relationships between sales and assets. Actual sales, however, are often different from projected sales, and the actual assets-to-sales ratio at a given time may be quite different from the planned ratio. To illustrate, the firm depicted in Panel b of

---

[8] Several other points should be noted about Panel d of Figure 4-3. First, if the firm is operating at a sales level of $100 million or less, any expansion that calls for a sales increase above $100 million would require a *doubling* of the firm's fixed assets. A much smaller percentage increase would be involved if the firm were large enough to be operating a number of plants. Second, firms generally go to multiple shifts and take other actions to minimize the need for new fixed asset capacity as they approach Point B. However, these efforts can only go so far, and eventually a fixed asset expansion will be required. Third, firms often make arrangements to share excess capacity with other firms in their industry. For example, the situation in the electric utility industry is very much like that depicted in Panel d. However, electric companies often build jointly owned plants, or else they "take turns" building plants, and then they buy power from or sell power to other utilities to avoid building new plants that would be underutilized.

Figure 4-3 might, when its sales are at $200 million and its inventories at $300 million, project a sales expansion to $400 million and then increase its inventories to $400 million in anticipation of the higher sales. However, suppose an unforeseen economic downturn held sales to only $300 million. Actual inventories would then be $400 million, but inventories of only $350 million would be needed to support actual sales of $300 million. Thus, inventories would be $50 million larger than needed. Then, when the firm makes its forecast for the following year, it must recognize that sales could expand by $100 million with no increase whatever in inventories, but that any sales expansion beyond $100 million would require additional financing to increase inventories.

SELF-TEST QUESTION

Describe three conditions under which the assumption that each "spontaneous" asset and liability item increases at the same rate as sales is *not* correct.

OTHER TECHNIQUES FOR FORECASTING FINANCIAL STATEMENTS

If any of the conditions noted above (economies of scale, excess capacity, or lumpy assets) apply, the A^*/S_0 ratio will not be a constant, and the constant growth forecasting methods as discussed thus far should not be used. Rather, other techniques must be used to forecast asset levels and additional financing requirements. Two of these methods — linear regression and excess capacity adjustments — are discussed in the following sections.

SIMPLE LINEAR REGRESSION

If we assume that the relationship between a certain type of asset and sales is linear, then we can use simple linear regression techniques to estimate the requirements for that type of asset for any given sales increase. For example, Allied's sales, inventories, and receivables during the last five years are shown in the lower section of Figure 4-4, and both current asset items are plotted in the upper section as a scatter diagram versus sales. Estimated regression equations, determined using a financial calculator or a spreadsheet, are also shown with each graph. For example, the estimated relationship between inventories and sales (in millions of dollars) is

$$\text{Inventories} = -\$35.7 + 0.186(\text{Sales}).$$

The plotted points are not very close to the regression line, which indicates that changes in inventory are affected by factors other than changes in sales. In fact, the correlation coefficient between inventories and sales is only 0.71, indicating that there is only a moderate linear relationship between these two

FIGURE 4-4

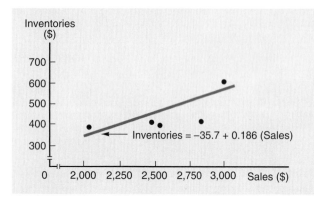

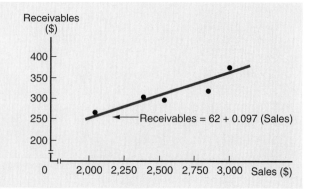

YEAR	SALES	INVENTORIES	ACCOUNTS RECEIVABLE
1997	$2,058	$387	$268
1998	2,534	398	297
1999	2,472	409	304
2000	2,850	415	315
2001	3,000	615	375

variables. Still, the regression relationship is strong enough to provide a reasonable basis for forecasting the target inventory level, as described below.

We can use the regression relationship between inventories and sales to forecast 2002 inventory levels. Since 2002 sales are projected at $3,300 million, 2002 inventories should be $578 million:

$$\text{Inventories} = -\$35.7 + 0.186(\$3,300) = \$578 \text{ million.}$$

This is $99 million less than the preliminary forecast based on the projected financial statement method. The difference occurs because the projected financial statement method assumed that the ratio of inventories to sales would remain constant, when in fact it will probably decline. Note also that although our graphs show linear relationships, we could have easily used a nonlinear regression model had such a relationship been indicated.

After analyzing the regression results, Allied's managers decided that a new forecast of AFN should be developed assuming a lower days sales outstanding and a higher inventory turnover ratio. Management recognized that the 2001 levels of these accounts were above the industry averages, hence that the preliminary results projected for 2002 back in Table 4-4 were unnecessarily high. When simple linear regression was used to forecast the receivables and inventories accounts, this caused the 2002 levels to reflect both the average relationships of these accounts to sales over the five-year period and the trend in the variables' values. In contrast, the projected financial statement method we developed earlier assumed that the nonoptimal 2001 relationships would remain constant in 2002 and beyond. These new assumptions were largely responsible for the improved forecasts shown in Column 3 of Table 4-5.

EXCESS CAPACITY ADJUSTMENTS

Consider again the Allied example set forth in Tables 4-3 and 4-4, but now assume that excess capacity exists in fixed assets. Specifically, assume that fixed assets in 2001 were being utilized to only 96 percent of capacity. If fixed assets had been used to full capacity, 2001 sales could have been as high as $3,125 million versus the $3,000 million in actual sales:

$$\begin{matrix} \text{Full} \\ \text{capacity} \\ \text{sales} \end{matrix} = \frac{\text{Actual sales}}{\begin{matrix}\text{Percentage of capacity} \\ \text{at which fixed assets} \\ \text{were operated}\end{matrix}} = \frac{\$3,000 \text{ million}}{0.96} = \$3,125 \text{ million}. \quad (4\text{-}2)$$

This suggests that Allied's target fixed assets/sales ratio should be 32 percent rather than 33.3 percent:

$$\text{Target fixed assets/Sales} = \frac{\text{Actual fixed assets}}{\text{Full capacity sales}} \quad (4\text{-}3)$$

$$= \frac{\$1,000}{\$3,125} = 0.32 = 32\%.$$

Therefore, if sales are to increase to $3,300 million, then fixed assets would have to increase to $1,056 million:

$$\begin{matrix}\text{Required level} \\ \text{of fixed assets}\end{matrix} = (\text{Target fixed assets/Sales})(\text{Projected sales}) \quad (4\text{-}4)$$

$$= 0.32(\$3,300) = \$1,056 \text{ million}.$$

We previously forecasted that Allied would need to increase fixed assets at the same rate as sales, or by 10 percent. That meant an increase from $1,000 million to $1,100 million, or by $100 million. Now we see that the actual required increase is only from $1,000 million to $1,056 million, or by $56 million. Thus, the capacity-adjusted forecast is $100 million − $56 million = $44 million less than the earlier forecast. With a smaller fixed asset requirement, the projected AFN would decline from an estimated $112 million to $112 million − $44 million = $68 million.

Note also that when excess capacity exists, sales can grow to the capacity sales as determined above with no increase whatever in fixed assets, but sales beyond that level will require fixed asset additions as calculated in our example. The same situation could occur with respect to inventories, and the required additions would be determined in exactly the same manner as for fixed assets. Theoretically, the same situation could occur with other types of assets. However, as a practical matter excess capacity normally exists only with respect to fixed assets and inventories.

SELF-TEST QUESTIONS

If sales are to double, would it be more important to use the regression method of forecasting asset requirements if the true situation were like that in Panel a or that in Panel b of Figure 4-3?

If excess capacity exists, how will that affect the AFN?

This chapter described techniques for forecasting financial statements, which is a crucial part of the financial planning process. As we will see throughout the rest of the book, both investors and corporations regularly use forecasting techniques to help value a company's stock, to estimate the benefits of potential projects, and to estimate how changes in capital structure, dividend policy, and working capital policy will influence shareholder value. The key concepts covered are listed below.

- To make their firms more valuable, managers must identify, evaluate, and implement projects that meet or exceed investor expectations. However, value creation for a firm is impossible unless a company has a well-articulated **strategic plan.**

- The firm's strategic plan begins with a **mission statement.**

- Key elements of a firm's strategic plan include **corporate purpose, corporate scope, corporate objectives,** and **corporate strategies.**

- **Operating plans** provide detailed implementation guidance to help meet corporate objectives.

- The **financial planning process** can be divided into six steps: (1) project financial statements and analyze them; (2) determine the funds needed to support the 5-year plan; (3) forecast funds availability over the next five years; (4) establish and maintain a system of controls for the allocation and use of funds; (5) develop procedures for adjusting the basic plan if the economic forecasts don't materialize; and (6) establish a performance-based management compensation system.

- Virtually all corporate forecasts are made using **computerized forecasting models** based on spreadsheet programs. Spreadsheets have two major advantages over pencil-and-paper calculations: (1) Spreadsheet models are faster than by-hand calculations and (2) models can be instantaneously recalculated making it easier to determine the effects of changes in variables.

- **Financial forecasting** generally begins with a forecast of the firm's sales, in terms of both units and dollars.

- Either the **projected,** or **pro forma, financial statement method** or the **AFN formula method** can be used to forecast financial requirements. The financial statement method is more reliable, and it also provides ratios that can be used to evaluate alternative business plans.

- A firm can determine its **additional funds needed (AFN)** by estimating the amount of new assets necessary to support the forecasted level of sales and then subtracting from that amount the spontaneous funds that will be generated from operations. The firm can then plan how to raise the AFN most efficiently.

- The **higher a firm's sales growth rate,** the **greater** will be its need for additional financing. In addition, the **greater the firm's capital intensity ratio,** the **greater** the need for external financing. Similarly, the **smaller its retention ratio,** the **greater** its need for additional funds. However, the **higher the profit margin,** the **lower** the need for external financing.

- Adjustments must be made if **economies of scale** exist in the use of assets, if **excess capacity** exists, or if assets must be added in **lumpy increments.**
- **Linear regression** and **excess capacity adjustments** can be used to forecast asset requirements in situations in which assets are not expected to grow at the same rate as sales.

The type of forecasting described in this chapter is important for several reasons. First, if the projected operating results are unsatisfactory, management can "go back to the drawing board," reformulate its plans, and develop more reasonable targets for the coming year. Second, it is possible that the funds required to meet the sales forecast simply cannot be obtained. If so, it is obviously better to know this in advance and to scale back the projected level of operations than to suddenly run out of cash and have operations grind to a halt. And third, even if the required funds can be raised, it is desirable to plan for their acquisition well in advance.

QUESTIONS

4-1 Certain liability and net worth items generally increase spontaneously with increases in sales. Put a check (✔) by those items that typically increase spontaneously:

Accounts payable	_____
Notes payable to banks	_____
Accrued wages	_____
Accrued taxes	_____
Mortgage bonds	_____
Common stock	_____
Retained earnings	_____

4-2 The following equation can, under certain assumptions, be used to forecast financial requirements:

$$AFN = (A^*/S_0)(\Delta S) - (L^*/S_0)(\Delta S) - MS_1(RR).$$

Under what conditions does the equation give satisfactory predictions, and when should it *not* be used?

4-3 Assume that an average firm in the office supply business has a 6 percent after-tax profit margin, a 40 percent debt/assets ratio, a total assets turnover of 2 times, and a dividend payout ratio of 40 percent. Is it true that if such a firm is to have *any* sales growth (g > 0), it will be forced either to borrow or to sell common stock (that is, it will need some nonspontaneous, external capital even if g is very small)?

4-4 Is it true that computerized corporate planning models were a fad during the 1990s but, because of a need for flexibility in corporate planning, they have been dropped by most firms in the millennium?

4-5 Suppose a firm makes the following policy changes. If the change means that external, nonspontaneous financial requirements (AFN) will increase, indicate this by a (+); indicate a decrease by a (−); and indicate indeterminate or no effect by a (0). Think in terms of the immediate, short-run effect on funds requirements.
a. The dividend payout ratio is increased. _____
b. The firm contracts to buy, rather than make, certain components used in its products. _____
c. The firm decides to pay all suppliers on delivery, rather than after a 30-day delay, to take advantage of discounts for rapid payment. _____
d. The firm begins to sell on credit (previously all sales had been on a cash basis). _____

e. The firm's profit margin is eroded by increased competition; sales are steady. _____
f. Advertising expenditures are stepped up. _____
g. A decision is made to substitute long-term mortgage bonds for short-term bank loans. _____
h. The firm begins to pay employees on a weekly basis (previously it had paid at the end of each month). _____

SELF-TEST PROBLEMS   (SOLUTIONS APPEAR IN APPENDIX B)

ST-1
Key terms
Define each of the following terms:
a. Mission statement
b. Sales forecast
c. Percent of sales method
d. Spontaneously generated funds
e. Pro forma financial statement
f. Additional funds needed (AFN); AFN formula
g. Capital intensity ratio
h. Lumpy assets

ST-2
Growth rate
Weatherford Industries Inc. has the following ratios: $A^*/S_0 = 1.6$; $L^*/S_0 = 0.4$; profit margin = 0.10; and retention ratio = 0.55, or 55 percent. Sales last year were $100 million. Assuming that these ratios will remain constant, use the AFN formula to determine the maximum growth rate Weatherford can achieve without having to employ nonspontaneous external funds.

ST-3
Additional funds needed
Suppose Weatherford's financial consultants report (1) that the inventory turnover ratio is sales/inventory = 3 times versus an industry average of 4 times and (2) that Weatherford could reduce inventories and thus raise its turnover to 4 without affecting sales, the profit margin, or the other asset turnover ratios. Under these conditions, use the AFN formula to determine the amount of additional funds Weatherford would require during each of the next 2 years if sales grew at a rate of 20 percent per year.

STARTER PROBLEMS

Carter Corporation's sales are expected to increase from $5 million in 2001 to $6 million in 2002, or by 20 percent. Its assets totaled $3 million at the end of 2001. Carter is at full capacity, so its assets must grow in proportion to projected sales. At the end of 2001, current liabilities are $1 million, consisting of $250,000 of accounts payable, $500,000 of notes payable, and $250,000 of accruals. The after-tax profit margin is forecasted to be 5 percent, and the forecasted retention ratio is 30 percent. Use this information to answer Problems 4-1, 4-2, and 4-3.

4-1
AFN formula
Use the AFN formula to forecast Carter's additional funds needed for the coming year.

4-2
AFN formula
What would the additional funds needed be if the company's year-end 2001 assets had been $4 million? Assume that all other numbers are the same. Why is this AFN different from the one you found in Problem 4-1? Is the company's "capital intensity" the same or different?

4-3
AFN formula
Return to the assumption that the company had $3 million in assets at the end of 2001, but now assume that the company pays no dividends. Under these assumptions, what would be the additional funds needed for the coming year? Why is this AFN different from the one you found in Problem 4-1?

4-4
Linear regression
Jasper Furnishings has $300 million in sales. The company expects that its sales will increase 12 percent this year. Jasper's CFO uses a simple linear regression to forecast the company's inventory level for a given level of projected sales. On the basis of re-

cent history, the estimated relationship between inventories and sales (in millions of dollars is

$$\text{Inventories} = \$25 + 0.125(\text{Sales}).$$

Given the estimated sales forecast and the estimated relationship between inventories and sales, what is your forecast of the company's year-end inventory turnover ratio?

4-5
Excess capacity

Walter Industries has $5 billion in sales and $1.7 billion in fixed assets. Currently, the company's fixed assets are operating at 90 percent of capacity.
a. What level of sales could Walter Industries have obtained if it had been operating at full capacity?
b. What is Walter's target fixed assets/sales ratio?
c. If Walter's sales increase 12 percent, how large of an increase in fixed assets would the company need in order to meet its target fixed assets/sales ratio?

4-6
Pro forma income statement

Austin Grocers recently reported the following income statement (in millions of dollars):

Sales	$700
Operating costs	500
EBIT	$200
Interest	40
EBT	$160
Taxes (40%)	64
Net income	$96
Dividends	$32
Addition to retained earnings	$64

This year the company is forecasting a 25 percent increase in sales, and it expects that its year-end operating costs will equal 70 percent of sales. Austin's tax rate, interest expense, and dividend payout ratio are all expected to remain constant.
a. What is Austin's projected 2002 net income?
b. What is the expected growth rate in Austin's dividends?

EXAM-TYPE PROBLEMS

The problems included in this section are set up in such a way that they could be used as multiple-choice exam problems.

4-7
Pro forma income statement

At the end of last year, Roberts Inc. reported the following income statement (in millions of dollars):

Sales	$3,000
Operating costs excluding depreciation	2,450
EBITDA	$ 550
Depreciation	250
EBIT	$ 300
Interest	125
EBT	$ 175
Taxes (40%)	70
Net income	$ 105

Looking ahead to the following year, the company's CFO has assembled the following information:

- Year-end sales are expected to be 10 percent higher than the $3 billion in sales generated last year.
- Year-end operating costs excluding depreciation are expected to equal 80 percent of year-end sales.
- Depreciation is expected to increase at the same rate as sales.
- Interest costs are expected to remain unchanged.
- The tax rate is expected to remain at 40 percent.

On the basis of this information, what will be the forecast for Roberts' year-end net income?

4-8
Pro forma statements and ratios

Adel Sporting Goods recently reported the following income statement and balance sheet.

INCOME STATEMENT	
Sales	$4,200
Operating costs	3,780
EBIT	$ 420
Interest	120
EBT	$ 300
Taxes (40%)	120
Net income	$ 180
Dividends paid	$ 0
Addition to retained earnings	$ 180
BALANCE SHEET	
Cash and marketable securities	$ 42
Accounts receivable	336
Inventories	441
Current assets	$ 819
Net fixed assets	2,562
Total assets	$3,381
Accounts payable and accruals	$ 168
Notes payable	250
Current liabilities	$ 418
Long-term debt	700
Common stock	400
Retained earnings	1,863
Total liabilities and equity	$3,381

In developing its forecast for the upcoming year, the company has assembled the following information:

- Sales are expected to increase 8 percent this upcoming year.
- Operating costs are expected to remain at 90 percent of sales.
- Cash and marketable securities are expected to remain at 1 percent of sales.
- Accounts receivable are expected to remain at 8 percent of sales.
- Due to excess capacity, the company expects that its year-end inventories will remain at current levels.
- Fixed assets are expected to remain at 61 percent of sales.

- Spontaneous liabilities (accounts payable and accruals) are expected to increase at the same rate as sales.
- The company will continue to pay a zero dividend, and its tax rate will remain at 40 percent.
- The company anticipates that any additional funds needed will be raised in the following manner: 25 percent notes payable, 25 percent long-term debt, and 50 percent common stock.

a. On the basis of the assumptions listed above, construct Adel's pro forma income statement and balance sheet. Assume that there are no financial feedback effects. (That is, assume interest will remain unchanged even though the company may increase its debt.)

b. On the basis of this forecast, describe changes from the prior year that Adel should expect in its return on equity, inventory turnover ratio, and profit margin.

4-9
Long-term financing needed
At year-end 2001, total assets for Ambrose Inc. were $1.2 million and accounts payable were $375,000. Sales, which in 2001 were $2.5 million, are expected to increase by 25 percent in 2002. Total assets and accounts payable are proportional to sales, and that relationship will be maintained. Ambrose typically uses no current liabilities other than accounts payable. Common stock amounted to $425,000 in 2001, and retained earnings were $295,000. Ambrose plans to sell new common stock in the amount of $75,000. The firm's profit margin on sales is 6 percent; 60 percent of earnings will be retained.

a. What was Ambrose's total debt in 2001?

b. How much new, long-term debt financing will be needed in 2002? (Hint: AFN − New stock = New long-term debt.)

4-10
Additional funds needed
The Flint Company's sales are forecasted to increase from $1,000 in 2001 to $2,000 in 2002. Here is the December 31, 2001, balance sheet:

Cash	$ 100	Accounts payable	$ 50
Accounts receivable	200	Notes payable	150
Inventories	200	Accruals	50
Total current assets	$ 500	Total current liabilities	$ 250
Net fixed assets	500	Long-term debt	400
		Common stock	100
		Retained earnings	250
Total assets	$1,000	Total liabilities and equity	$1,000

Flint's fixed assets were used to only 50 percent of capacity during 2001, but its current assets were at their proper levels. All assets except fixed assets increase in proportion to sales, and fixed assets would also increase proportionally with sales if the current excess capacity did not exist. Flint's after-tax profit margin is forecasted to be 5 percent, and its payout ratio will be 60 percent. What is Flint's additional funds needed (AFN) for the coming year?

4-11
Sales increase
Pierce Furnishings generated $2.0 million in sales during 2001, and its year-end total assets were $1.5 million. Also, at year-end 2001, current liabilities were $500,000, consisting of $200,000 of notes payable, $200,000 of accounts payable, and $100,000 of accruals. Looking ahead to 2002, the company estimates that its assets must increase by 75 cents for every $1 increase in sales. Pierce's profit margin is 5 percent, and its retention ratio is 40 percent. How large a sales increase can the company achieve without having to raise funds externally?

PROBLEMS

4-12
Pro forma statements and ratios
Tozer Computers makes bulk purchases of small computers, stocks them in conveniently located warehouses, and ships them to its chain of retail stores. Tozer's balance sheet as of December 31, 2001, is shown here (in millions of dollars):

Cash	$ 3.5	Accounts payable		$ 9.0
Receivables	26.0	Notes payable		18.0
Inventories	58.0	Accruals		8.5
Total current assets	$ 87.5	Total current liabilities		$ 35.5
Net fixed assets	35.0	Mortgage loan		6.0
		Common stock		15.0
		Retained earnings		66.0
Total assets	$122.5	Total liabilities and equity		$122.5

Sales for 2001 were $350 million, while net income for the year was $10.5 million. Tozer paid dividends of $4.2 million to common stockholders. The firm is operating at full capacity. Assume that all ratios remain constant.

a. If sales are projected to increase by $70 million, or 20 percent, during 2002, use the AFN equation to determine Tozer's projected external capital requirements.

b. Construct Tozer's pro forma balance sheet for December 31, 2002. Assume that all external capital requirements are met by bank loans and are reflected in notes payable.

c. Now calculate the following ratios, based on your projected December 31, 2002, balance sheet. Tozer's 2001 ratios and industry average ratios are shown here for comparison:

	TOZER COMPUTERS		INDUSTRY AVERAGE
	12/31/02	12/31/01	12/31/01
Current ratio	_____	2.5×	3×
Debt/total assets	_____	33.9%	30%
Rate of return on equity	_____	13.0%	12%

d. Now assume that Tozer grows by the same $70 million but that the growth is spread over 5 years—that is, that sales grow by $14 million each year.
(1) Calculate total additional financial requirements over the 5-year period. (Hint: Use 2001 ratios, $\Delta S = \$70$, but *total* sales for the 5-year period.)
(2) Construct a pro forma balance sheet as of December 31, 2006, using notes payable as the balancing item.
(3) Calculate the current ratio, total debt/total assets ratio, and rate of return on equity as of December 31, 2006. [Hint: Be sure to use *total sales*, which amount to $1,960 million, to calculate retained earnings, but 2006 profits to calculate the rate of return on equity—that is, return on equity = (2006 profits)/(12/31/06 equity).]

e. Do the plans outlined in parts b and/or d seem feasible to you? That is, do you think Tozer could borrow the required capital, and would the company be raising the odds on its bankruptcy to an excessive level in the event of some temporary misfortune?

4-13
Additional funds needed

Cooley Textile's 2001 financial statements are shown below.

Cooley Textile: Balance Sheet as of December 31, 2001 (Thousands of Dollars)

Cash	$ 1,080	Accounts payable	$ 4,320
Receivables	6,480	Accruals	2,880
Inventories	9,000	Notes payable	2,100
Total current assets	$16,560	Total current liabilities	$ 9,300
Net fixed assets	12,600	Mortgage bonds	3,500
		Common stock	3,500
		Retained earnings	12,860
Total assets	$29,160	Total liabilities and equity	$29,160

Cooley Textile: Income Statement for December 31, 2001 (Thousands of Dollars)

Sales	$36,000
Operating costs	32,440
Earnings before interest and taxes	$ 3,560
Interest	560
Earnings before taxes	$ 3,000
Taxes (40%)	1,200
Net income	$ 1,800
Dividends (45%)	$810
Addition to retained earnings	$990

Suppose 2002 sales are projected to increase by 15 percent over 2001 sales. Determine the additional funds needed. Assume that the company was operating at full capacity in 2001, that it cannot sell off any of its fixed assets, and that any required financing will be borrowed as notes payable. Also, assume that assets, spontaneous liabilities, and operating costs are expected to increase in proportion to sales. Use the projected financial statement method to develop a pro forma balance sheet and income statement for December 31, 2002. Use the pro forma income statement to determine the addition to retained earnings.

4-14 Krogh Lumber's 2001 financial statements are shown below.

Excess capacity

Krogh Lumber: Balance Sheet as of December 31, 2001 (Thousands of Dollars)

Cash	$ 1,800	Accounts payable	$ 7,200
Receivables	10,800	Notes payable	3,472
Inventories	12,600	Accruals	2,520
Total current assets	$25,200	Total current liabilities	$13,192
		Mortgage bonds	5,000
		Common stock	2,000
Net fixed assets	21,600	Retained earnings	26,608
Total assets	$46,800	Total liabilities and equity	$46,800

Krogh Lumber: Income Statement for December 31, 2001 (Thousands of Dollars)

Sales	$36,000
Operating costs	30,783
Earnings before interest and taxes	$ 5,217
Interest	1,017
Earnings before taxes	$ 4,200
Taxes (40%)	1,680
Net income	$ 2,520
Dividends (60%)	$1,512
Addition to retained earnings	1,008

a. Assume that the company was operating at full capacity in 2001 with regard to all items *except* fixed assets; fixed assets in 2001 were being utilized to only 75 percent of capacity. By what percentage could 2002 sales increase over 2001 sales without the need for an increase in fixed assets?

b. Now suppose 2002 sales increase by 25 percent over 2001 sales. How much additional external capital will be required? Assume that Krogh cannot sell any fixed assets. (Hint: Use the projected financial statement method to develop a pro forma income statement and balance sheet as in Tables 4-3 and 4-4.) Assume that any required financing is borrowed as notes payable. Use a pro forma income statement to determine the addition to retained earnings. (Another hint: Notes payable = $6,021.)

c. Suppose the industry average DSO and inventory turnover ratio are 90 days and 3.33, respectively, and that Krogh Lumber matches these figures in 2002 and then uses the funds released to reduce equity. (It pays a special dividend out of retained earnings.) What would this do to the rate of return on year-end 2002 equity? Use the balance sheet and income statement as developed in part b.

4-15
Additional funds needed

Morrissey Technologies Inc.'s 2001 financial statements are shown below.

Morrissey Technologies Inc.: Balance Sheet as of December 31, 2001

Cash	$ 180,000	Accounts payable	$ 360,000
Receivables	360,000	Notes payable	156,000
Inventories	720,000	Accruals	180,000
Total current assets	$1,260,000	Total current liabilities	$ 696,000
Fixed assets	1,440,000	Common stock	1,800,000
		Retained earnings	204,000
Total assets	$2,700,000	Total liabilities and equity	$2,700,000

Morrissey Technologies Inc.: Income Statement for December 31, 2001

Sales	$3,600,000
Operating costs	3,279,720
EBIT	$ 320,280
Interest	20,280
EBT	$ 300,000
Taxes (40%)	120,000
Net income	$ 180,000
PER SHARE DATA:	
Common stock price	$24.00
Earnings per share (EPS)	$ 1.80
Dividends per share (DPS)	$ 1.08

a. Suppose that in 2002 sales increase by 10 percent over 2001 sales and that 2002 DPS will increase to $1.12. Construct the pro forma financial statements using the projected financial statement method. Use AFN to balance the pro forma balance sheet. How much additional capital will be required? Assume the firm operated at full capacity in 2001.

b. If the profit margin were to remain at 5 percent and the dividend payout rate were to remain at 60 percent, at what growth rate in sales would the additional financing requirements be exactly zero? (Hint: Set AFN equal to zero and solve for g.)

The 2001 balance sheet and income statement for the Lewis Company are shown below.

Lewis Company: Balance Sheet as of December 31, 2001 (Thousands of Dollars)

Cash	$ 80	Accounts payable	$ 160
Accounts receivable	240	Accruals	40
Inventories	720	Notes payable	252
Total current assets	$1,040	Total current liabilities	$ 452
Fixed assets	3,200	Long-term debt	1,244
		Total debt	$1,696
		Common stock	1,605
		Retained earnings	939
Total assets	$4,240	Total liabilities and equity	$4,240

Lewis Company: Income Statement for December 31, 2001 (Thousands of Dollars)

Sales	$8,000
Operating costs	7,450
EBIT	$ 550
Interest	150
EBT	$ 400
Taxes (40%)	160
Net income	$ 240
PER SHARE DATA:	
Common stock price	$16.96
Earnings per share (EPS)	$ 1.60
Dividends per share (DPS)	$ 1.04

a. The firm operated at full capacity in 2001. It expects sales to increase by 20 percent during 2002 and expects 2002 dividends per share to increase to $1.10. Use the projected financial statement method to determine how much outside financing is required, developing the firm's pro forma balance sheet and income statement, and use AFN as the balancing item.
b. If the firm must maintain a current ratio of 2.3 and a debt ratio of 40 percent, how much financing will be obtained using notes payable, long-term debt, and common stock?

SPREADSHEET PROBLEM

Laiho Industries' financial planners must forecast the company's financial results for the coming year. The forecast will be based on the percent of sales method, and any additional funds needed will be obtained by using a mix of notes payable, long-term debt, and common stock. No preferred stock will be issued. Data for the problem, including Laiho Industries' balance sheet and income statement, can be found in the spreadsheet problem for Chapter 2. Use these data to answer the following questions.

a. Laiho Industries has had the following sales since 1996. Assuming the historical trend continues, what will sales be in 2002?

YEAR	SALES
1996	$129,215,000
1997	180,901,000
1998	235,252,000
1999	294,065,000
2000	396,692,000
2001	455,150,000

Base your forecast on a spreadsheet regression analysis of the 1996–2001 sales, and include the summary output of the regression in your answer. By what percentage are sales predicted to increase in 2002 over 2001? Is the sales growth rate increasing or decreasing?

b. Laiho's management believes that the firm will actually experience a 20 percent increase in sales during 2002. Use the Chapter 2 spreadsheet problem to obtain the company's 2001 financial statements, then use those statements to construct 2002 pro forma financial statements. Assume that any additional funds needed (AFN) will be raised as follows: notes payable, 25 percent; long-term debt, 50 percent; and new common stock, 25 percent.

c. Now create a graph that shows the sensitivity of AFN to the sales growth rate. To make this graph, compare the AFN at sales growth rates of 5, 10, 15, 20, 25, and 30 percent.

d. Calculate net operating working capital (NOWC), total operating capital, NOPAT, and operating cash flow (OCF) for 2001 and 2002. Also, calculate the free cash flow (FCF) for 2002.

e. Suppose Laiho's management does not believe that accounts receivable and inventories should remain as a constant percentage of sales. Rather, they think that current assets should be predicted by using a regression analysis of recent levels versus sales. Use the following data on accounts receivable, inventories, and sales to run regressions to estimate the necessary levels of accounts receivable and inventories for 2002.

YEAR	SALES[a]	INVENTORIES[a]	A/R[a]
1996	$129,215	$12,341	$ 24,764
1997	180,901	16,763	39,589
1998	235,252	20,564	53,764
1999	294,065	25,324	64,864
2000	396,692	35,997	98,568
2001	455,150	38,444	103,365

[a] In thousands of dollars.

CYBER PROBLEM

The information related to the cyberproblems is likely to change over time, due to the release of new information and the ever-changing nature of the World Wide Web. With these changes in mind, we will periodically update these problems on the textbook's web site. To avoid problems, please check for these updates before proceeding with the cyberproblems.

4-18
Financial forecasting—using analysts' reports

A sales forecast usually begins with a forecast of a firm's unit and dollar sales for some future period, and it is generally based on recent sales trends plus forecasts of the economic prospects for the nation, region, industry, and so forth. Analysts at

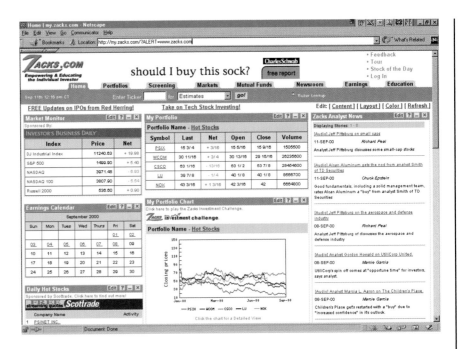

investment research firms also make forecasts of companies' current and likely future financial performances. These analysts must piece together information that includes forecasts of the overall economy and the level and direction of interest rates. Moreover, they must examine economic and competitive conditions in specific industries including sales, costs, margins, profits, and cash flows for specific firms. In this cyberproblem, you will look at analysts' forecasts of earnings and recommendations about the investment potential of specific firms based on their forecasts of the firms' performances. Use the Zacks Investment Research web site, which can be found at **my.zacks.com.**

a. Sun Microsystems has enjoyed dramatic increases in sales, earnings, and stock prices, and many employees and investors have become millionaires in a very short time. What were Sun Microsystems' actual earnings last quarter? Was there an earnings surprise? If so, what was it? What are the analysts' consensus estimates for the (1) current quarter, (2) current fiscal year, and (3) next fiscal year? What was the average broker recommendation for Sun Microsystems, and was there any change from the previous average recommendation? To answer this question, enter Sun Microsystems' stock symbol and request "All Reports." If you do not know Sun Microsystems' stock symbol, you can use Zack's "Ticker Lookup" function.

b. Access Sun Microsystems' company report, as prepared by Zacks. What percentage of Sun Microsystems' shareholders are institutional investors and insiders? What was the stock's 52-week high and low? What was the stock's price change during the past year?

c. Access Zack's long-term outlook of Sun Microsystems and discuss it.

d. Examine analysts' predictions about future earnings and investment potential for software companies Oracle and Microsoft. How do analysts generate earnings predictions and make recommendations?

NEW WORLD CHEMICALS INC.

4-19 Financial Forecasting Sue Wilson, the new financial manager of New World Chemicals (NWC), a California producer of specialized chemicals for use in fruit orchards, must prepare a financial forecast for 2002. NWC's 2001 sales were $2 billion, and the marketing department is forecasting a 25 percent increase for 2002.

Wilson thinks the company was operating at full capacity in 2001, but she is not sure about this. The 2001 financial statements, plus some other data, are given in Table IC4-1.

Assume that you were recently hired as Wilson's assistant, and your first major task is to help her develop the forecast.

TABLE IC4-1	Financial Statements and Other Data on NWC (Millions of Dollars)

A. 2001 BALANCE SHEET

Cash and securities	$ 20	Accounts payable and accruals	$ 100
Accounts receivable	240	Notes payable	100
Inventories	240	Total current liabilities	$ 200
Total current assets	$ 500	Long-term debt	100
Net fixed assets	500	Common stock	500
		Retained earnings	200
Total assets	$ 1,000	Total liabilities and equity	$1,000

B. 2001 INCOME STATEMENT

Sales	$2,000.00
Less: Variable costs	1,200.00
Fixed costs	700.00
Earnings before interest and taxes (EBIT)	$ 100.00
Interest	16.00
Earnings before taxes (EBT)	$ 84.00
Taxes (40%)	33.60
Net income	$ 50.40
Dividends (30%)	$ 15.12
Addition to retained earnings	$ 35.28

C. KEY RATIOS

	NWC	INDUSTRY	COMMENT
Basic earning power	10.00%	20.00%	
Profit margin	2.52	4.00	
Return on equity	7.20	15.60	
Days sales outstanding (365 days)	43.80 days	32.00 days	
Inventory turnover	8.33×	11.00×	
Fixed assets turnover	4.00	5.00	
Total assets turnover	2.00	2.50	
Debt/assets	30.00%	36.00%	
Times interest earned	6.25×	9.40×	
Current ratio	2.50	3.00	
Payout ratio	30.00%	30.00%	

She asked you to begin by answering the following set of questions.

a. Assume (1) that NWC was operating at full capacity in 2001 with respect to all assets, (2) that all assets must grow proportionally with sales, (3) that accounts payable and accruals will also grow in proportion to sales, and (4) that the 2001 profit margin and dividend payout will be maintained. Under these conditions, what will the company's financial requirements be for the coming year? Use the AFN equation to answer this question.

b. Now estimate the 2002 financial requirements using the projected financial statement approach. Disregard the assumptions in part a, and now assume (1) that each type of asset, as well as payables, accruals, and fixed and variable costs, grow in proportion to sales; (2) that NWC was operating at full capacity; (3) that the payout ratio is held constant at 30 percent; and (4) that external funds needed are financed 50 percent by notes payable and 50 percent by long-term debt. (No new common stock will be issued.)

c. Why do the two methods produce somewhat different AFN forecasts? Which method provides the more accurate forecast?

d. Calculate NWC's forecasted ratios, and compare them with the company's 2001 ratios and with the industry averages. How does NWC compare with the average firm in its industry, and is the company expected to improve during the coming year?

e. Calculate NWC's free cash flow for 2002.

f. Suppose you now learn that NWC's 2001 receivables and inventories were in line with required levels, given the firm's credit and inventory policies, but that excess capacity existed with regard to fixed assets. Specifically, fixed assets were operated at only 75 percent of capacity.

   (1) What level of sales could have existed in 2001 with the available fixed assets? What would the fixed assets-to-sales ratio have been if NWC had been operating at full capacity?

   (2) How would the existence of excess capacity in fixed assets affect the additional funds needed during 2002?

g. Without actually working out the numbers, how would you expect the ratios to change in the situation where excess capacity in fixed assets exists? Explain your reasoning.

h. On the basis of comparisons between NWC's days sales outstanding (DSO) and inventory turnover ratios with the industry average figures, does it appear that NWC is operating efficiently with respect to its inventories and accounts receivable? If the company were able to bring these ratios into line with the industry averages, what effect would this have on its AFN and its financial ratios? (Note: Inventories and receivables will be discussed in detail in Chapter 15.)

i. The relationship between sales and the various types of assets is important in financial forecasting. The financial statement method, under the assumption that each asset item grows proportionally with sales, leads to an AFN forecast that is reasonably close to the forecast using the AFN equation. Explain how each of the following factors would affect the accuracy of financial forecasts based on the AFN equation: (1) excess capacity; (2) base stocks of assets, such as shoes in a shoe store; (3) economies of scale in the use of assets; and (4) lumpy assets.

j. (1) How could regression analysis be used to detect the presence of the situations described above and then to improve the financial forecasts? Plot a graph of the following data, which is for a typical well-managed company in NWC's industry to illustrate your answer.

YEAR	SALES	INVENTORIES
1999	$1,280	$118
2000	1,600	138
2001	2,000	162
2002E	2,500	192

   (2) On the same graph that plots the above data, draw a line that shows how the regression line would have to appear to justify the use of the AFN formula and the projected financial statement forecasting method. As a part of your answer, show the growth rate in inventories that results from a 10 percent increase in sales from a sales level of (a) $200 and (b) $2,000 based on both the actual regression line and a *hypothetical* regression line, which is linear and which goes through the origin.

k. How would changes in these items affect the AFN? (1) The dividend payout ratio, (2) the profit margin, (3) the capital intensity ratio, and (4) if NWC begins buying from its suppliers on terms that permit it to pay after 60 days rather than after 30 days. (Consider each item separately and hold all other things constant.)

The Financial Environment: Markets, Institutions, and Interest Rates

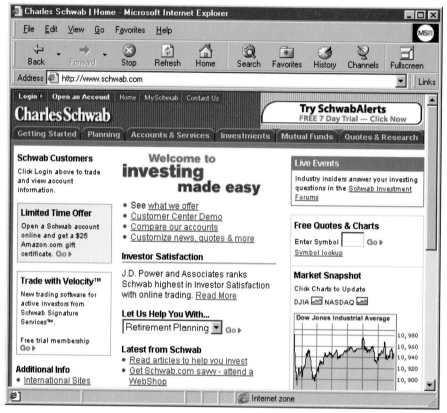

SOURCE: Accessed November 1999. © 1999 Charles Schwab & Co., Inc. www.schwab.com

To take a look at the online ventures of Charles Schwab and Merrill Lynch, check out their web sites at **http://www.schwab.com** and **http://askmerrill.ml.com.** You can test the Schwab customer experience or take a tour of Merrill Lynch Online.

CHARLES SCHWAB
AND MERRILL LYNCH

Financial managers and investors don't operate in a vacuum — they make decisions within a large and complex financial environment. This environment includes financial markets and institutions, tax and regulatory policies, and the state of the economy. The environment both defines the available financial alternatives and affects the outcomes of various decisions. Therefore, it is crucial that financial managers and investors have a good understanding of the environment in which they operate.

Good financial decisions require an understanding of the current direction of the economy, interest rates, and the stock market — but figuring out what's likely to happen is no trivial matter. Recently, the financial environment has been extraordinarily favorable to financial managers and investors: The economy has not seen a recession for nearly 10 years; interest rates and inflation have remained relatively low; and the stock market has boomed throughout most of the past decade. At the same time, the financial environment has undergone tremendous changes, presenting financial managers and investors with both opportunities and risks.

Consider Charles Schwab and Merrill Lynch. Benefiting from the strong stock market, traditional brokerage powerhouse Merrill Lynch has seen its stock rise more than 350 percent over the past five years. During this same period, Charles Schwab, the leader in online trading, has seen its stock rise by nearly 900 percent! The Internet has enabled online brokers such as Schwab, E*Trade, DLJDirect, and Datek to offer investors the opportunity to trade stocks at a small fraction of the price traditionally charged by full-service firms such as Merrill Lynch. While online trading was virtually nonexistent just a couple of years ago, there are now an estimated 160 online brokers serving more than 13 million customers. Some estimate that by 2003 there will be more than 40 million online accounts.

The same forces that dramatically affected the brokerage industry have had similar effects on other industries. Companies such as Barnes and Noble and Toys Я Us have been presented with new and aggressive competition from the likes of Amazon.com and eToys Inc. Likewise, changing technology has altered the way millions of consumers purchase airline tickets, hotel rooms, and automobiles. Consequently, financial managers must understand today's technological environment and be ready to change operations as the environment evolves. ■

In earlier chapters we discussed financial statements and showed how financial managers and others analyze them to see where their firms have been and are headed. Financial managers also need to understand the environment and markets within which businesses operate. Therefore, this chapter describes the markets where capital is raised, securities are traded, and stock prices are established, as well as the institutions that operate in these markets. In the process, we also explore the principal factors that determine the level of interest rates. ▪

THE FINANCIAL MARKETS

Businesses, individuals, and governments often need to raise capital. For example, suppose Carolina Power & Light (CP&L) forecasts an increase in the demand for electricity in North Carolina, and the company decides to build a new power plant. Because CP&L almost certainly will not have the $1 billion or so necessary to pay for the plant, the company will have to raise this capital in the financial markets. Or suppose Mr. Fong, the proprietor of a San Francisco hardware store, decides to expand into appliances. Where will he get the money to buy the initial inventory of TV sets, washers, and freezers? Similarly, if the Johnson family wants to buy a home that costs $100,000, but they have only $20,000 in savings, how can they raise the additional $80,000? If the city of New York wants to borrow $200 million to finance a new sewer plant, or the federal government needs money to meet its needs, they too need access to the capital markets.

On the other hand, some individuals and firms have incomes that are greater than their current expenditures, so they have funds available to invest. For example, Carol Hawk has an income of $36,000, but her expenses are only $30,000, and in 2000 Ford Motor Company had accumulated roughly $21 billion of cash and marketable securities, which it has available for future investments.

TYPES OF MARKETS

People and organizations wanting to borrow money are brought together with those having surplus funds in the *financial markets*. Note that "markets" is plural — there are a great many different financial markets in a developed economy such as ours. Each market deals with a somewhat different type of instrument in terms of the instrument's maturity and the assets backing it. Also, different markets serve different types of customers, or operate in different parts of the country. For these reasons it is often useful to classify markets along various dimensions:

1. **Physical asset vs. Financial asset markets.** *Physical asset markets* (also called "tangible" or "real" asset markets) are those for such products as

wheat, autos, real estate, computers, and machinery. *Financial asset markets*, on the other hand, deal with stocks, bonds, notes, mortgages, and other *claims on real assets*, as well as with *derivative securities* whose values are *derived* from changes in the prices of other assets.

Spot Markets
The markets in which assets are bought or sold for "on-the-spot" delivery.

Futures Markets
The markets in which participants agree today to buy or sell an asset at some future date.

Money Markets
The financial markets in which funds are borrowed or loaned for short periods (less than one year).

Capital Markets
The financial markets for stocks and for intermediate- or long-term debt (one year or longer).

Primary Markets
Markets in which corporations raise capital by issuing new securities.

Secondary Markets
Markets in which securities and other financial assets are traded among investors after they have been issued by corporations.

Initial Public Offering (IPO) Market
The market in which firms "go public" by offering shares to the public.

Private Markets
Markets in which transactions are worked out directly between two parties.

Public Markets
Markets in which standardized contracts are traded on organized exchanges.

2. **Spot vs. Futures markets. Spot markets** are markets in which assets are bought or sold for "on-the-spot" delivery (literally, within a few days). **Futures markets** are markets in which participants agree today to buy or sell an asset at some future date. For example, a farmer may enter into a futures contract in which he agrees today to sell 5,000 bushels of soybeans six months from now at a price of $5 a bushel. In contrast, an international food producer looking to buy soybeans in the future may enter into a futures contract in which it agrees to buy soybeans three months from now.

3. **Money vs. Capital markets. Money markets** are the markets for short-term, highly liquid debt securities. The New York and London money markets have long been the world's largest, but Tokyo is rising rapidly. **Capital markets** are the markets for intermediate- or long-term debt and corporate stocks. The New York Stock Exchange, where the stocks of the largest U.S. corporations are traded, is a prime example of a capital market. There is no hard and fast rule on this, but when describing debt markets, "short term" generally means less than one year, "intermediate term" means one to five years, and "long term" means more than five years.

4. **Primary vs. Secondary markets. Primary markets** are the markets in which corporations raise new capital. If Microsoft were to sell a new issue of common stock to raise capital, this would be a primary market transaction. The corporation selling the newly created stock receives the proceeds from the sale in a primary market transaction. **Secondary markets** are markets in which existing, already outstanding, securities are traded among investors. Thus, if Jane Doe decided to buy 1,000 shares of AT&T stock, the purchase would occur in the secondary market. The New York Stock Exchange is a secondary market, since it deals in outstanding, as opposed to newly issued, stocks and bonds. Secondary markets also exist for mortgages, various other types of loans, and other financial assets. The corporation whose securities are being traded is not involved in a secondary market transaction and, thus, does not receive any funds from such a sale.

The **initial public offering (IPO) market** is a subset of the primary market. Here firms "go public" by offering shares to the public for the first time. Microsoft had its IPO in 1986. Previously, Bill Gates and other insiders owned all the shares. In many IPOs, the insiders sell some of their shares plus the company sells new shares to raise additional capital.

5. **Private vs. Public markets. Private markets,** where transactions are worked out directly between two parties, are differentiated from **public markets,** where standardized contracts are traded on organized exchanges. Bank loans and private placements of debt with insurance companies are examples of private market transactions. Since these transactions are private, they may be structured in any manner that appeals to the two parties. By contrast, securities that are issued in public markets (for example, common stock and corporate bonds) are ultimately held by a large number of individuals. Public securities must have fairly standardized contractual

TABLE 5-1

Summary of Major Market Instruments, Market Participants, and Security Characteristics

INSTRUMENT (1)	MARKET (2)	MAJOR PARTICIPANTS (3)	SECURITY CHARACTERISTICS		
			RISKINESS (4)	ORIGINAL MATURITY (5)	INTEREST RATE ON 12/29/00[a] (6)
U.S. Treasury bills	Money	Sold by U.S. Treasury to finance federal expenditures	Default-free	91 days to 1 year	5.7%
Bankers' acceptances	Money	A firm's promise to pay, guaranteed by a bank	Low degree of risk if guaranteed by a strong bank	Up to 180 days	6.3
Commercial paper	Money	Issued by financially secure firms to large investors	Low default risk	Up to 270 days	6.4
Negotiable certificates of deposit (CDs)	Money	Issued by major money-center commercial banks to large investors	Default risk depends on the strength of the issuing bank	Up to 1 year	6.3
Money market mutual funds	Money	Invest in Treasury bills, CDs, and commercial paper; held by individuals and businesses	Low degree of risk	No specific maturity (instant liquidity)	6.0
Eurodollar market time deposits	Money	Issued by banks outside U.S.	Default risk depends on the strength of the issuing bank	Up to 1 year	6.3
Consumer credit loans	Money	Issued by banks/credit unions/finance companies to individuals	Risk is variable	Variable	Variable
U.S. Treasury notes and bonds	Capital	Issued by U.S. government	No default risk, but price will decline if interest rates rise	2 to 30 years	5.5

[a] The yields reported on money market mutual funds and bankers' acceptances are from *The Wall Street Journal*. All other data are from the *Federal Reserve Statistical Release*. Money market rates assume a 3-month maturity. The corporate bond rate is for AAA-rated bonds.

features, both to appeal to a broad range of investors and also because public investors cannot afford the time to study unique, nonstandardized contracts. Their diverse ownership also ensures that public securities are relatively liquid. Private market securities are, therefore, more tailor-made but less liquid, whereas public market securities are more liquid but subject to greater standardization.

Other classifications could be made, but this breakdown is sufficient to show that there are many types of financial markets. Also, note that the distinctions among markets are often blurred and unimportant, except as a general point of reference. For example, it makes little difference if a firm borrows for 11, 12, or 13 months, hence, whether we have a "money" or "capital" market transaction. You should recognize the big differences among types of markets, but don't get hung up trying to distinguish them at the boundaries.

A healthy economy is dependent on efficient transfers of funds from people who are net savers to firms and individuals who need capital. Without efficient

TABLE 5-1 continued

| | | | SECURITY CHARACTERISTICS | | |
INSTRUMENT (1)	MARKET (2)	MAJOR PARTICIPANTS (3)	RISKINESS (4)	ORIGINAL MATURITY (5)	INTEREST RATE ON 12/29/00[a] (6)
Mortgages	Capital	Borrowings from commercial banks and S&Ls by individuals and businesses	Risk is variable	Up to 30 years	7.1%
State and local government bonds	Capital	Issued by state and local governments to individuals and institutional investors	Riskier than U.S. government securities, but exempt from most taxes	Up to 30 years	5.1
Corporate bonds	Capital	Issued by corporations to individuals and institutional investors	Riskier than U.S. government securities, but less risky than preferred and common stocks; varying degree of risk within bonds depending on strength of issuer	Up to 40 years[b]	7.2
Leases	Capital	Similar to debt in that firms can lease assets rather than borrow and then buy the assets	Risk similar to corporate bonds	Generally 3 to 20 years	Similar to bond yields
Preferred stocks	Capital	Issued by corporations to individuals and institutional investors	Riskier than corporate bonds, but less risky than common stock	Unlimited	7 to 9%
Common stocks[c]	Capital	Issued by corporations to individuals and institutional investors	Risky	Unlimited	10 to 15%

[b] Just recently, a few corporations have issued 100-year bonds; however, the majority have issued bonds with maturities less than 40 years.

[c] Common stocks are expected to provide a "return" in the form of dividends and capital gains rather than interest. Of course, if you buy a stock, your *actual* return may be considerably higher or lower than your *expected* return. For example, Nasdaq stocks on average provided a negative return of 39.3 percent in 2000, but that was well below the return most investors expected.

Students can access current and historical interest rates and economic data as well as regional economic data for the states of Arkansas, Illinois, Indiana, Kentucky, Mississippi, Missouri, and Tennessee from the Federal Reserve Economic Data (FRED) site at **http://www.stls.frb.org/fred/**.

transfers, the economy simply could not function: Carolina Power & Light could not raise capital, so Raleigh's citizens would have no electricity; the Johnson family would not have adequate housing; Carol Hawk would have no place to invest her savings; and so on. Obviously, the level of employment and productivity, hence our standard of living, would be much lower. Therefore, it is absolutely essential that our financial markets function efficiently — not only quickly, but also at a low cost.[1]

Table 5-1 gives a listing of the most important instruments traded in the various financial markets. The instruments are arranged from top to bottom in

[1] As the countries of the former Soviet Union and other Eastern European nations move toward capitalism, just as much attention must be paid to the establishment of cost-efficient financial markets as to electrical power, transportation, communications, and other infrastructure systems. Economic efficiency is simply impossible without a good system for allocating capital within the economy.

ascending order of typical length of maturity. As we go through the book, we will look in much more detail at many of the instruments listed in Table 5-1. For example, we will see that there are many varieties of corporate bonds, ranging from "plain vanilla" bonds to bonds that are convertible into common stocks to bonds whose interest payments vary depending on the inflation rate. Still, the table gives an idea of the characteristics and costs of the instruments traded in the major financial markets.

RECENT TRENDS

Financial markets have experienced many changes during the last two decades. Technological advances in computers and telecommunications, along with the globalization of banking and commerce, have led to deregulation, and this has increased competition throughout the world. The result is a much more efficient, internationally linked market, but one that is far more complex than existed a few years ago. While these developments have been largely positive, they have also created problems for policy makers. At a recent conference, Federal Reserve Board Chairman Alan Greenspan stated that modern financial markets "expose national economies to shocks from new and unexpected sources, and with little if any lag." He went on to say that central banks must develop new ways to evaluate and limit risks to the financial system. Large amounts of capital move quickly around the world in response to changes in interest and exchange rates, and these movements can disrupt local institutions and economies.

With globalization has come the need for greater cooperation among regulators at the international level. Various committees are currently working to improve coordination, but the task is not easy. Factors that complicate coordination include (1) the differing structures among nations' banking and securities industries, (2) the trend in Europe toward financial service conglomerates, and (3) a reluctance on the part of individual countries to give up control over their national monetary policies. Still, regulators are unanimous about the need to close the gaps in the supervision of worldwide markets.

Derivative

Any financial asset whose value is derived from the value of some other "underlying" asset.

Another important trend in recent years has been the increased use of **derivatives**. A derivative is any security whose value is *derived* from the price of some other "underlying" asset. An option to buy IBM stock is a derivative, as is a contract to buy Japanese yen six months from now. The value of the IBM option depends on the price of IBM's stock, and the value of the Japanese yen "future" depends on the exchange rate between yen and dollars. The market for derivatives has grown faster than any other market in recent years, providing corporations with new opportunities but also exposing them to new risks.

Derivatives can be used either to reduce risks or to speculate. Suppose an importer's net income tends to fall whenever the dollar falls relative to the yen. That company could reduce its risk by purchasing derivatives that increase in value whenever the dollar declines. This would be called a *hedging operation*, and its purpose is to reduce risk exposure. Speculation, on the other hand, is done in the hope of high returns, but it raises risk exposure. For example, Procter & Gamble recently disclosed that it lost $150 million on derivative investments, and Orange County (California) went bankrupt as a result of its treasurer's speculation in derivatives.

The size and complexity of derivatives transactions concern regulators, academics, and members of Congress. Fed Chairman Greenspan noted that, in theory, derivatives should allow companies to manage risk better, but that it is not clear whether recent innovations have "increased or decreased the inherent stability of the financial system."

SELF-TEST QUESTIONS

Distinguish between physical asset markets and financial asset markets.

What is the difference between spot and futures markets?

Distinguish between money and capital markets.

What is the difference between primary and secondary markets?

Differentiate between private and public markets.

Why are financial markets essential for a healthy economy?

What is a derivative, and how is its value related to that of an "underlying asset"?

FINANCIAL INSTITUTIONS

Transfers of capital between savers and those who need capital take place in the three different ways diagrammed in Figure 5-1:

1. *Direct transfers* of money and securities, as shown in the top section, occur when a business sells its stocks or bonds directly to savers, without going through any type of financial institution. The business delivers its securities to savers, who in turn give the firm the money it needs.

2. As shown in the middle section, transfers may also go through an *investment banking house* such as Merrill Lynch, which *underwrites* the issue. An underwriter serves as a middleman and facilitates the issuance of securities. The company sells its stocks or bonds to the investment bank, which in turn sells these same securities to savers. The businesses' securities and the savers' money merely "pass through" the investment banking house. However, the investment bank does buy and hold the securities for a period of time, so it is taking a risk — it may not be able to resell them to savers for as much as it paid. Because new securities are involved and the corporation receives the proceeds of the sale, this is a primary market transaction.

3. Transfers can also be made through a *financial intermediary* such as a bank or mutual fund. Here the intermediary obtains funds from savers in exchange for its own securities. The intermediary then uses this money to purchase and then hold businesses' securities. For example, a saver might give dollars to a bank, receiving from it a certificate of deposit, and then the bank might lend the money to a small business in the form of a mortgage loan. Thus, intermediaries literally create new forms of capital — in this case, certificates of deposit, which are both safer and more liquid

FIGURE 5-1

Diagram of the Capital Formation Process

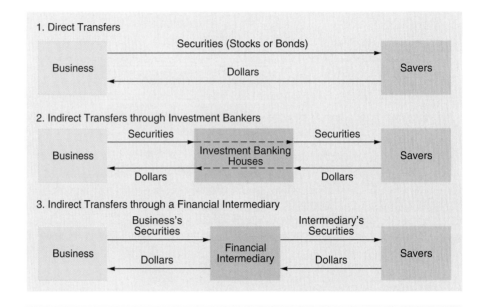

1. Direct Transfers

Business → Securities (Stocks or Bonds) → Savers
Business ← Dollars ← Savers

2. Indirect Transfers through Investment Bankers

Business → Securities → Investment Banking Houses → Securities → Savers
Business ← Dollars ← Investment Banking Houses ← Dollars ← Savers

3. Indirect Transfers through a Financial Intermediary

Business → Business's Securities → Financial Intermediary → Intermediary's Securities → Savers
Business ← Dollars ← Financial Intermediary ← Dollars ← Savers

---

than mortgages and thus are better securities for most savers to hold. The existence of intermediaries greatly increases the efficiency of money and capital markets.

In our example, we assume that the entity needing capital is a business, and specifically a corporation, but it is easy to visualize the demander of capital as a home purchaser, a government unit, and so on.

Direct transfers of funds from savers to businesses are possible and do occur on occasion, but it is generally more efficient for a business to enlist the services of an **investment banking house** such as Merrill Lynch, Salomon Smith Barney, Morgan Stanley Dean Witter, or Goldman Sachs. Such organizations (1) help corporations design securities with features that are currently attractive to investors, (2) then buy these securities from the corporation, and (3) resell them to savers. Although the securities are sold twice, this process is really one primary market transaction, with the investment banker acting as a facilitator to help transfer capital from savers to businesses.

The **financial intermediaries** shown in the third section of Figure 5-1 do more than simply transfer money and securities between firms and savers — they literally create new financial products. Since the intermediaries are generally large, they gain economies of scale in analyzing the creditworthiness of potential borrowers, in processing and collecting loans, and in pooling risks and thus helping individual savers diversify, that is, "not putting all their financial eggs in one basket." Further, a system of specialized intermediaries can enable savings to do more than just draw interest. For example, individuals can put money into banks and get both interest income and a convenient way of making payments (checking), or put money into life

Investment Banking House
An organization that underwrites and distributes new investment securities and helps businesses obtain financing.

Financial Intermediaries
Specialized financial firms that facilitate the transfer of funds from savers to demanders of capital.

insurance companies and get both interest income and protection for their beneficiaries.

In the United States and other developed nations, a set of specialized, highly efficient financial intermediaries has evolved. The situation is changing rapidly, however, and different types of institutions are performing services that were formerly reserved for others, causing institutional distinctions to become blurred. Still, there is a degree of institutional identity, and here are the major classes of intermediaries:

1. *Commercial banks*, the traditional "department stores of finance," serve a wide variety of savers and borrowers. Historically, commercial banks were the major institutions that handled checking accounts and through which the Federal Reserve System expanded or contracted the money supply. Today, however, several other institutions also provide checking services and significantly influence the money supply. Conversely, commercial banks are providing an ever-widening range of services, including stock brokerage services and insurance.

2. *Savings and loan associations (S&Ls)*, which have traditionally served individual savers and residential and commercial mortgage borrowers, take the funds of many small savers and then lend this money to home buyers and other types of borrowers. In the 1980s, the S&L industry experienced severe problems when (1) short-term interest rates paid on savings accounts rose well above the returns being earned on the existing mortgages held by S&Ls and (2) commercial real estate suffered a severe slump, resulting in high mortgage default rates. Together, these events forced many S&Ls to either merge with stronger institutions or close their doors.

3. *Mutual savings banks*, which are similar to S&Ls, operate primarily in the northeastern states, accept savings primarily from individuals, and lend mainly on a long-term basis to home buyers and consumers.

4. *Credit unions* are cooperative associations whose members are supposed to have a common bond, such as being employees of the same firm. Members' savings are loaned only to other members, generally for auto purchases, home improvement loans, and home mortgages. Credit unions are often the cheapest source of funds available to individual borrowers.

5. *Pension funds* are retirement plans funded by corporations or government agencies for their workers and administered primarily by the trust departments of commercial banks or by life insurance companies. Pension funds invest primarily in bonds, stocks, mortgages, and real estate.

6. *Life insurance companies* take savings in the form of annual premiums; invest these funds in stocks, bonds, real estate, and mortgages; and finally make payments to the beneficiaries of the insured parties. In recent years, life insurance companies have also offered a variety of tax-deferred savings plans designed to provide benefits to the participants when they retire.

7. *Mutual funds* are corporations that accept money from savers and then use these funds to buy stocks, long-term bonds, or short-term debt instruments issued by businesses or government units. These organizations pool funds and thus reduce risks by diversification. They also achieve economies of scale in analyzing securities, managing portfolios, and buying and selling securities. Different funds are designed to meet the objectives

Money Market Fund
A mutual fund that invests in short-term, low-risk securities and allows investors to write checks against their accounts.

of different types of savers. Hence, there are bond funds for those who desire safety, stock funds for savers who are willing to accept significant risks in the hope of higher returns, and still other funds that are used as interest-bearing checking accounts (the **money market funds**). There are literally thousands of different mutual funds with dozens of different goals and purposes.

Mutual funds have grown more rapidly than any other institution in recent years, in large part because of a change in the way corporations provide for employees' retirement. Before the 1980s, most corporations said, in effect, "Come work for us, and when you retire, we will give you a retirement income based on the salary you were earning during the last five years before you retired." The company was then responsible for setting aside funds each year to make sure that it had the money available to pay the agreed-upon retirement benefits. That situation is changing rapidly. Today, new employees are likely to be told, "Come work for us, and we will give you some money each payday that you can invest for your future retirement. You can't get the money until you retire (without paying a huge tax penalty), but if you invest wisely, you can retire in comfort." Most workers know they don't know how to invest wisely, so they turn their retirement funds over to a mutual fund. Hence, mutual funds are growing rapidly. Excellent information on the objectives and past performances of the various funds are provided in publications such as *Value Line Investment Survey* and *Morningstar Mutual Funds*, which are available in most libraries.

Financial institutions have historically been heavily regulated, with the primary purpose of this regulation being to ensure the safety of the institutions and thus to protect investors. However, these regulations — which have taken the form of prohibitions on nationwide branch banking, restrictions on the types of assets the institutions can buy, ceilings on the interest rates they can pay, and limitations on the types of services they can provide — have tended to impede the free flow of capital and thus have hurt the efficiency of our capital markets. Recognizing this fact, Congress has authorized some major changes, and more are on the horizon.

Financial Service Corporation
A firm that offers a wide range of financial services, including investment banking, brokerage operations, insurance, and commercial banking.

The result of the ongoing regulatory changes has been a blurring of the distinctions between the different types of institutions. Indeed, the trend in the United States today is toward huge **financial service corporations,** which own banks, S&Ls, investment banking houses, insurance companies, pension plan operations, and mutual funds, and which have branches across the country and around the world. Examples of financial service corporations, most of which started in one area but have now diversified to cover most of the financial spectrum, include Merrill Lynch, American Express, Citigroup, Fidelity, and Prudential.

Panel a of Table 5-2 lists the ten largest U.S. bank and thrift holding companies, and Panel b shows the leading world banking companies. Among the world's 10 largest, only two (Citigroup and Bank of America) are from the United States. While U.S. banks have grown dramatically as a result of recent mergers, they are still small by global standards. Panel c of the table lists the 10 leading underwriters in terms of dollar volume of new issues. Five of the top underwriters are also major commercial banks or are part of bank holding com-

TABLE 5-2

10 Largest U.S. Bank and Thrift Holding Companies and World Banking Companies and Top 10 Leading Underwriters

Panel a	Panel b	Panel c
U.S. BANK AND THRIFT HOLDING COMPANIES[a]	WORLD BANKING COMPANIES[b]	LEADING GLOBAL UNDERWRITERS[c]
Citigroup Inc.	Deutsche Bank AG (Frankfurt)	Merrill Lynch
Bank of America Corp.	Citigroup (New York)	Salomon Smith Barney
Chase Manhattan Corp.	BNP Paribas (Paris)	Morgan Stanley Dean Witter
Bank One Corp.	Bank of Tokyo-Mitsubishi Ltd. (Tokyo)	Credit Suisse First Boston
J. P. Morgan & Co.	Bank of America (Charlotte)	J. P. Morgan
First Union Corp.	UBS AG Group (Zurich)	Goldman Sachs
Wells Fargo & Co.	HSBC Holdings PLC (London)	Deutsche Bank
Washington Mutual Inc.	Fuji Bank Ltd. (Tokyo)	Lehman Brothers
Fleet Boston Financial Corp.	Sumitomo Bank Ltd. (Osaka)	UBS Warburg
SunTrust Banks Inc.	HypoVereinsbank AG (Munich)	Banc of America Securities

NOTES:

[a] Ranked by total assets as of June 30, 2000. SOURCE: Compiled by *American Banker* from bank and thrift holding company second quarter 2000 reports.

[b] Ranked by total assets as of December 31, 1999. SOURCE: "Top 50 World Banking Companies in Assets," *American Banker.com,* September 15, 2000.

[c] Ranked by dollar amount raised through new issues in 2000. For this ranking, the lead underwriter (manager) is given credit for the entire issue.

panies, which confirms the continued blurring of distinctions among different types of financial institutions.

SELF-TEST QUESTIONS

Identify three different ways capital is transferred between savers and borrowers.

What is the difference between a commercial bank and an investment bank?

Distinguish between investment banking houses and financial intermediaries.

List the major types of intermediaries and briefly describe the primary function of each.

THE STOCK MARKET

As noted earlier, secondary markets are those in which outstanding, previously issued securities are traded. By far the most active secondary market, and the most important one to financial managers, is the *stock market*, where the prices of firms' stocks are established. Since the primary goal of financial management is to maximize the firm's stock price, a knowledge of the stock market is important to anyone involved in managing a business.

While the two leading stock markets today are the New York Stock Exchange and the Nasdaq stock market, stocks are actually traded using a variety of market procedures. However, there are just two basic types of stock markets: (1) *physical location exchanges*, which include the New York Stock Exchange (NYSE), the American Stock Exchange (AMEX), and several regional stock exchanges, and (2) electronic dealer-based markets that include the Nasdaq stock market, the less formal over-the-counter market, and the recently developed electronic communications networks (ECNs). (See the Technology Matters box entitled, "Online Trading Systems.") Because the physical location exchanges are easier to describe and understand, we consider them first.

THE PHYSICAL LOCATION STOCK EXCHANGES

Physical Location Exchanges
Formal organizations having tangible physical locations that conduct auction markets in designated ("listed") securities.

The **physical location exchanges** are tangible physical entities. Each of the larger ones occupies its own building, has a limited number of members, and has an elected governing body — its board of governors. Members are said to have "seats" on the exchange, although everybody stands up. These seats, which are bought and sold, give the holder the right to trade on the exchange. There are currently 1,366 seats on the New York Stock Exchange, and on April 25, 2000, a seat on the NYSE sold for $1.7 million, which was down from the previous high of $2.6 million.

Most of the larger investment banking houses operate *brokerage departments*, and they own seats on the exchanges and designate one or more of their officers as members. The exchanges are open on all normal working days, with the members meeting in a large room equipped with telephones and other electronic equipment that enable each member to communicate with his or her firm's offices throughout the country.

 You can access the home pages of the major U.S. stock markets by typing **http://www.nyse.com** or **http://www.nasdaq.com**. These sites provide background information as well as the opportunity to obtain individual stock quotes.

Like other markets, security exchanges facilitate communication between buyers and sellers. For example, Merrill Lynch (the largest brokerage firm) might receive an order in its Atlanta office from a customer who wants to buy shares of AT&T stock. Simultaneously, Morgan Stanley Dean Witter's Denver office might receive an order from a customer wishing to sell shares of AT&T. Each broker communicates electronically with the firm's representative on the NYSE. Other brokers throughout the country are also communicating with their own exchange members. The exchange members with *sell orders* offer the shares for sale, and they are bid for by the members with *buy orders*. Thus, the exchanges operate as *auction markets*.[2]

---

[2] The NYSE is actually a modified auction market, wherein people (through their brokers) bid for stocks. Originally — about 200 years ago — brokers would literally shout, "I have 100 shares of Erie for sale; how much am I offered?" and then sell to the highest bidder. If a broker had a buy order, he or she would shout, "I want to buy 100 shares of Erie; who'll sell at the best price?" The same general situation still exists, although the exchanges now have members known as *specialists* who facilitate the trading process by keeping an inventory of shares of the stocks in which they specialize. If a buy order comes in at a time when no sell order arrives, the

(footnote continues)

TECHNOLOGY MATTERS

ONLINE TRADING SYSTEMS

The forces described in the vignette that led to online trading have also promoted online trading systems that bypass the traditional exchanges. These systems, known as electronic communications networks (ECNs), use technology to bring buyers and sellers together electronically. Bob Mazzarella, president of Fidelity Brokerage Services Inc., estimates that ECNs have already captured 20 to 35 percent of Nasdaq's trading volume. Instinet, the first and largest ECN, has a stake with Goldman Sachs, J. P. Morgan, and E*Trade in another network, Archipelago, which recently announced plans to form its own exchange. Likewise, Charles Schwab recently announced plans to join with Fidelity Investments, Donaldson, Lufkin & Jenrette, and Spear, Leeds & Kellogg to develop another ECN.

ECNs will accelerate the move toward 24-hour trading. Large clients who want to trade after the other markets have closed may utilize an ECN, bypassing the NYSE and Nasdaq. The move toward faster, cheaper, and continuous trading obviously benefits investors, but it does present regulators, who try to ensure that all investors have access to a "level playing field," with a number of headaches.

Because of the threat from ECNs and the need to raise capital and increase flexibility, both the NYSE and Nasdaq plan to convert from privately held, member-owned businesses to stockholder-owned, for-profit corporations. This suggests that the financial landscape will continue to undergo dramatic changes in the upcoming years.

SOURCES: Katrina Brooker, "Online Investing: It's Not Just for Geeks Anymore," *Fortune*, December 21, 1998, 89–98; and "Fidelity, Schwab Part of Deal to Create Nasdaq Challenger," *The Milwaukee Journal Sentinel*, July 22, 1999, 1.

THE OVER-THE-COUNTER AND THE NASDAQ STOCK MARKETS

Over-the-Counter Market
A large collection of brokers and dealers, connected electronically by telephones and computers, that provides for trading in unlisted securities.

While the stocks of most large companies trade on the NYSE, a larger number of stocks trade off the exchange in what has traditionally been referred to as the **over-the-counter market (OTC).** An explanation of the term "over-the-counter" will help clarify how this term arose. As noted earlier, the exchanges operate as auction markets — buy and sell orders come in more or less simultaneously, and exchange members match these orders. If a stock is traded infrequently, perhaps because the firm is new or small, few buy and sell orders come in, and matching them within a reasonable amount of time would be difficult. To avoid this problem, some brokerage firms maintain an inventory of such

---

(Footnote 2 continued)

specialist will sell off some inventory. Similarly, if a sell order comes in, the specialist will buy and add to inventory. The specialist sets a *bid price* (the price the specialist will pay for the stock) and an *asked price* (the price at which shares will be sold out of inventory). The bid and asked prices are set at levels designed to keep the inventory in balance. If many buy orders start coming in because of favorable developments or sell orders come in because of unfavorable events, the specialist will raise or lower prices to keep supply and demand in balance. Bid prices are somewhat lower than asked prices, with the difference, or *spread*, representing the specialist's profit margin.

Special facilities are available to help institutional investors such as mutual funds or pension funds sell large blocks of stock without depressing their prices. In essence, brokerage houses that cater to institutional clients will purchase blocks (defined as 10,000 or more shares) and then resell the stock to other institutions or individuals. Also, when a firm has a major announcement that is likely to cause its stock price to change sharply, it will ask the exchanges to halt trading in its stock until the announcement has been made and digested by investors. Thus, when Texaco announced that it planned to acquire Getty Oil, trading was halted for one day in both Texaco and Getty stocks.

stocks and stand prepared to make a market for these stocks. These "dealers" buy when individual investors want to sell, and then sell part of their inventory when investors want to buy. At one time, the inventory of securities was kept in a safe, and the stocks, when bought and sold, were literally passed over the counter.

Dealer Market
Includes all facilities that are needed to conduct security transactions not conducted on the physical location exchanges.

Today, these markets are often referred to as **dealer markets.** A dealer market is defined to include all facilities that are needed to conduct security transactions not made on the physical location exchanges. These facilities include (1) the relatively few *dealers* who hold inventories of these securities and who are said to "make a market" in these securities; (2) the thousands of brokers who act as *agents* in bringing the dealers together with investors; and (3) the computers, terminals, and electronic networks that provide a communication link between dealers and brokers. The dealers who make a market in a particular stock quote the price at which they will pay for the stock (the *bid price*) and the price at which they will sell shares (the *ask price*). Each dealer's prices, which are adjusted as supply and demand conditions change, can be read off computer screens all across the world. The *bid-ask spread*, which is the difference between bid and ask prices, represents the dealer's markup, or profit. The dealer's risk increases if the stock is more volatile, or if the stock trades infrequently. Generally, we would expect volatile, infrequently traded stocks to have wider spreads in order to compensate the dealers for assuming the risk of holding them in inventory.

Brokers and dealers who participate in the over-the-counter market are members of a self-regulatory body known as the *National Association of Securities Dealers (NASD)*, which licenses brokers and oversees trading practices. The computerized network used by the NASD is known as the NASD Automated Quotation System.

Nasdaq started as just a quotation system, but it has grown to become an organized securities market with its own listing requirements. Over the past decade the competition between the NYSE and Nasdaq has become increasingly fierce. In an effort to become more competitive with the NYSE and with international markets, the Nasdaq and the AMEX merged in 1998 to form the Nasdaq-Amex Market Group, which might best be referred to as an *organized investment network*. This investment network is often referred to as Nasdaq, but stocks continue to be traded and reported separately on the two markets. Increased competition among global stock markets assuredly will result in similar alliances among other exchanges and markets in the future.

Since most of the largest companies trade on the NYSE, the market capitalization of NYSE-traded stocks is much higher than for stocks traded on Nasdaq ($11.4 trillion compared with $3.6 trillion at year-end 2000). However, reported volume (number of shares traded) is often larger on Nasdaq, and more companies are listed on Nasdaq.[3]

Interestingly, many high-tech companies such as Microsoft and Intel have remained on Nasdaq even though they easily meet the listing requirements of the NYSE. At the same time, however, other high-tech companies such as Gateway 2000, America Online, and Iomega have left Nasdaq for the NYSE.

---

[3] One transaction on Nasdaq generally shows up as two separate trades (the buy and the sell). This "double counting" makes it difficult to compare the volume between stock markets.

INDUSTRY PRACTICE

A VERY EXPENSIVE BEER

A few summers ago, two professors met for a beer at an academic conference. During their conversation, the professors, William Christie of Vanderbilt University and Paul Schultz of Ohio State University, decided it would be interesting to see how prices are set for Nasdaq stocks. The results of their study were startling to many, and they produced a real firestorm in the investment community.

When looking through data on the bid/asked spreads set by Nasdaq market makers, Christie and Schultz found that the market makers routinely avoided posting quotes that had "odd-eighths fractions," that is, $\frac{1}{8}$, $\frac{3}{8}$, $\frac{5}{8}$, and $\frac{7}{8}$. For example, if a market maker were to use odd-eighths quotes, he might offer to buy a stock for $10\frac{1}{2}$ a share and sell it for $10\frac{5}{8}$, thus providing a "spread," or profit, of $\frac{1}{8}$ point ($10\frac{5}{8} - 10\frac{1}{2} = \frac{1}{8}$). The spread between the two prices is the market maker's compensation for providing a market and taking the risk associated with holding an inventory of a given stock. Note that if he or she avoided odd-eighths fractions, then the offer price would be $10\frac{3}{4}$ (which is $10\frac{6}{8}$), so the spread would be $10\frac{6}{8} - 10\frac{1}{2} = \frac{1}{4}$, or twice as high as if he or she made an odd-eighths quote.

What amazed Christie and Schultz was the fact that this practice was so widespread — even for widely followed stocks such as Apple Computer and Lotus Development. The professors concluded that the evidence strongly suggested that there had to be tacit collusion among Nasdaq dealers designed to keep spreads artificially high. The National Association of Securities Dealers (NASD) originally denied the accusations. Others have come forward to provide a justification for the practice.

The publicity surrounding the study led the Securities and Exchange Commission (SEC) to investigate. Without admitting guilt, the NASD settled with the SEC, and, as part of the agreement, the dealers agreed to spend $100 million during the next five years to improve their enforcement practices. These allegations have also led to a civil class-action suit. In a dramatic development, several of the nation's largest securities firms have reached an agreement to pay more than $1 billion in damages — which is believed to be the largest antitrust settlement in history. All of this explains why the professors' beers turned out to be so expensive.

SOURCES: William Christie, "An Expensive Beer for the N.A.S.D.," *The New York Times*, August 25, 1996, Sec. 3, 12; and Michael Rapoport, "Securities Firms' Settlement Wins Backing from Judge," *The Wall Street Journal Interactive Edition*, December 30, 1997.

Despite these defections, Nasdaq's growth over the past decade has been impressive. In the years ahead, the competition will no doubt remain fierce.

SELF-TEST QUESTIONS

What are the differences between the physical location exchanges and the Nasdaq stock market?

What is the bid-ask spread?

THE COST OF MONEY

Capital in a free economy is allocated through the price system. *The interest rate is the price paid to borrow debt capital. With equity capital, investors expect to receive dividends and capital gains, whose sum is the cost of equity money.* The factors that affect supply of and demand for investment capital, hence the cost of money, are discussed in this section.

MEASURING THE MARKET

A *stock index* is designed to show the performance of the stock market. The problem is that there are many stock indexes, and it is difficult to determine which index best reflects market actions. Some are designed to represent the whole equity market, some to track the returns of certain industry sectors, and others to track the returns of small-cap, mid-cap, or large-cap stocks. We discuss below three of the leading indexes.

DOW JONES INDUSTRIAL AVERAGE

Unveiled in 1896 by Charles H. Dow, the Dow Jones Industrial Average (DJIA) provided a benchmark for comparing individual stocks with the overall market and for comparing the market with other economic indicators. The industrial average began with just 10 stocks, was expanded in 1916 to 20 stocks, and then to 30 in 1928. Also, in 1928 *The Wall Street Journal* editors began adjusting it for stock splits, and making substitutions. Today, the DJIA still includes 30 companies. They represent almost a fifth of the market value of all U.S. stocks, and all are both leading companies in their industries and widely held by individual and institutional investors.

S&P 500 INDEX

Created in 1926, the S&P 500 Index is widely regarded as the standard for measuring large-cap U.S. stock market performance. The stocks in the S&P 500 are selected by the Standard & Poor's Index Committee for being the leading companies in the leading industries, and for accurately reflecting the U.S. stock market. It is value weighted, so the largest companies (in terms of value) have the greatest influence. The S&P 500 Index is used by 97 percent of all U.S. money managers and pension plan sponsors, and approximately $700 billion is managed so as to obtain the same performance as this index (that is, in indexed funds).

NASDAQ COMPOSITE INDEX

The Nasdaq Composite Index measures the performance of all common stocks listed on the Nasdaq stock market. Currently, it includes more than 5,000 companies, and because many of the technology-sectored companies are traded on the computer-based Nasdaq exchange, this index is generally regarded as an economic indicator of the high-tech industry. Microsoft, Intel, and Cisco Systems are the three largest Nasdaq companies, and they comprise a high percentage of the index's value-weighted market capitalization. For this reason, substantial movements in the same direction by these three companies can move the entire index.

RECENT PERFORMANCE

The accompanying figure plots the value that an investor would now have if he or she had invested $1.00 in each of the three indexes on August 31, 1979. The returns on the three indexes are compared to an investment strategy that only invests in T-bills. Every year, the proceeds from that T-bill investment are reinvested at the current one-year T-bill rate. Over the past 20 years each of these indexes has performed quite well, which reflects the spectacular rise in the stock market. During this pe-

Production Opportunities
The returns available within an economy from investments in productive (cash-generating) assets.

Time Preferences for Consumption
The preferences of consumers for current consumption as opposed to saving for future consumption.

Risk
In a financial market context, the chance that an investment will provide a low or negative return.

The four most fundamental factors affecting the cost of money are (1) **production opportunities,** (2) **time preferences for consumption,** (3) **risk,** and (4) **inflation**. To see how these factors operate, visualize an isolated island community where the people live on fish. They have a stock of fishing gear that permits them to survive reasonably well, but they would like to have more fish. Now suppose Mr. Crusoe had a bright idea for a new type of fishnet that would enable him to double his daily catch. However, it would take him a year to perfect his design, to build his net, and to learn how to use it efficiently, and Mr. Crusoe would probably starve before he could put his new net into operation. Therefore, he might suggest to Ms. Robinson, Mr. Friday, and several others that if they would give him one fish each day for a year, he would return two fish a day during all of the next year. If someone accepted the offer, then the fish that Ms. Robinson or one of the others gave to Mr. Crusoe would constitute *savings*; these savings would be *invested* in the fishnet; and the extra fish the net produced would constitute a *return on the investment*.

riod the average annualized returns of these indexes ranged from 12.0 percent for the S&P 500 to 13.5 percent for the Nasdaq. The Nasdaq's relatively strong performance occurred primarily after 1992, reflecting the fact that it includes a large number of technology stocks, a sector that has performed extraordinarily well in recent years.

Growth of a $1 Investment Made on August 31, 1979

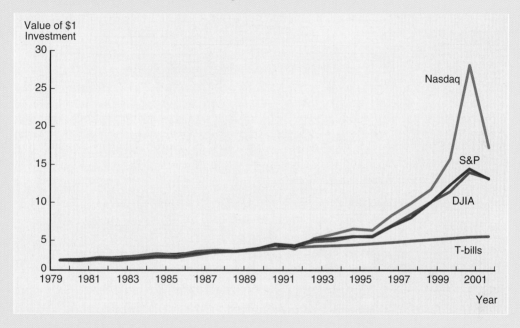

SOURCES: Yahoo! Finance, Nasdaq, and FRED Database.

Inflation
The amount by which prices increase over time.

Obviously, the more productive Mr. Crusoe thought the new fishnet would be, the more he could afford to offer potential investors for their savings. In this example, we assume that Mr. Crusoe thought he would be able to pay, and thus he offered, a 100 percent rate of return — he offered to give back two fish for every one he received. He might have tried to attract savings for less — for example, he might have decided to offer only 1.5 fish next year for every one he received this year, which would represent a 50 percent rate of return to Ms. Robinson and the other potential savers.

How attractive Mr. Crusoe's offer appeared to a potential saver would depend in large part on the saver's *time preference for consumption.* For example, Ms. Robinson might be thinking of retirement, and she might be willing to trade fish today for fish in the future on a one-for-one basis. On the other hand, Mr. Friday might have a wife and several young children and need his current fish, so he might be unwilling to "lend" a fish today for anything less than three fish next year. Mr. Friday would be said to have a high time preference for current consumption and Ms. Robinson a low time preference. Note also that if the entire population were living right at the subsistence level, time preferences for current consumption would necessarily be high, aggregate savings would be low, interest rates would be high, and capital formation would be difficult.

The *risk* inherent in the fishnet project, and thus in Mr. Crusoe's ability to repay the loan, would also affect the return investors would require: the higher the perceived risk, the higher the required rate of return. Also, in a more complex society there are many businesses like Mr. Crusoe's, many goods other than fish, and many savers like Ms. Robinson and Mr. Friday. Therefore, people use money as a medium of exchange rather than barter with fish. When money is used, its value in the future, which is affected by *inflation*, comes into play: the higher the expected rate of inflation, the larger the required return. We discuss this point in detail later in the chapter.

Thus, we see that the interest rate paid to savers depends in a basic way (1) on the rate of return producers expect to earn on invested capital, (2) on savers' time preferences for current versus future consumption, (3) on the riskiness of the loan, and (4) on the expected future rate of inflation. Producers' expected returns on their business investments set an upper limit on how much they can pay for savings, while consumers' time preferences for consumption establish how much consumption they are willing to defer, hence how much they will save at different rates of interest offered by producers.[4] Higher risk and higher inflation also lead to higher interest rates.

SELF-TEST QUESTIONS

What is the price paid to borrow money called?

What are the two items whose sum is the "price" of equity capital?

What four fundamental factors affect the cost of money?

INTEREST RATE LEVELS

Capital is allocated among borrowers by interest rates: Firms with the most profitable investment opportunities are willing and able to pay the most for capital, so they tend to attract it away from inefficient firms or from those whose products are not in demand. Of course, our economy is not completely free in the sense of being influenced only by market forces. Thus, the federal government has agencies that help designated individuals or groups obtain credit on favorable terms. Among those eligible for this kind of assistance are small businesses, certain minorities, and firms willing to build plants in areas with high unemployment. Still, most capital in the U.S. economy is allocated through the price system.

---

[4] The term "producers" is really too narrow. A better word might be "borrowers," which would include corporations, home purchasers, people borrowing to go to college, or even people borrowing to buy autos or to pay for vacations. Also, the wealth of a society and its demographics influence its people's ability to save and thus their time preferences for current versus future consumption.

FIGURE 5-2

Interest Rates as a Function of Supply and Demand for Funds

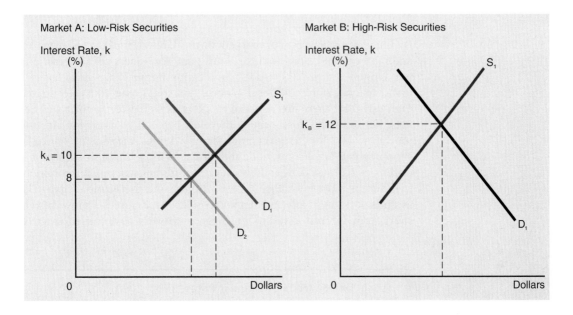

Figure 5-2 shows how supply and demand interact to determine interest rates in two capital markets. Markets A and B represent two of the many capital markets in existence. The going interest rate, which can be designated as either k or i, but for purposes of our discussion is designated as k, is initially 10 percent for the low-risk securities in Market A.[5] Borrowers whose credit is strong enough to borrow in this market can obtain funds at a cost of 10 percent, and investors who want to put their money to work without much risk can obtain a 10 percent return. Riskier borrowers must obtain higher-cost funds in Market B. Investors who are more willing to take risks invest in Market B, expecting to earn a 12 percent return but also realizing that they might actually receive much less.

If the demand for funds declines, as it typically does during business recessions, the demand curves will shift to the left, as shown in Curve D_2 in Market A. The market-clearing, or equilibrium, interest rate in this example declines to 8 percent. Similarly, you should be able to visualize what would happen if the Federal Reserve tightened credit: The supply curve, S_1, would shift to the left, and this would raise interest rates and lower the level of borrowing in the economy.

Capital markets are interdependent. For example, if Markets A and B were in equilibrium before the demand shift to D_2 in Market A, then investors were willing to accept the higher risk in Market B in exchange for a *risk premium* of $12\% - 10\% = 2\%$. After the shift to D_2, the risk premium would initially increase to $12\% - 8\% = 4\%$. Immediately, though, this much larger premium

---

[5] The letter "k" is the traditional symbol for interest rates and the cost of equity, but "i" is used frequently today because this term corresponds to the interest rate key on financial calculators. Therefore, in Chapter 7, when we discuss calculators, the term "i" will be used for the interest rate.

would induce some of the lenders in Market A to shift to Market B, which would, in turn, cause the supply curve in Market A to shift to the left (or up) and that in Market B to shift to the right. The transfer of capital between markets would raise the interest rate in Market A and lower it in Market B, thus bringing the risk premium back closer to the original 2 percent.

There are many capital markets in the United States. U.S. firms also invest and raise capital throughout the world, and foreigners both borrow and lend in the United States. There are markets for home loans; farm loans; business loans; federal, state, and local government loans; and consumer loans. Within each category, there are regional markets as well as different types of submarkets. For example, in real estate there are separate markets for first and second mortgages and for loans on single-family homes, apartments, office buildings, shopping centers, vacant land, and so on. Within the business sector there are dozens of types of debt and also several different markets for common stocks.

There is a price for each type of capital, and these prices change over time as shifts occur in supply and demand conditions. Figure 5-3 shows how long- and short-term interest rates to business borrowers have varied since the early

FIGURE 5-3   Long- and Short-Term Interest Rates, 1961-2000

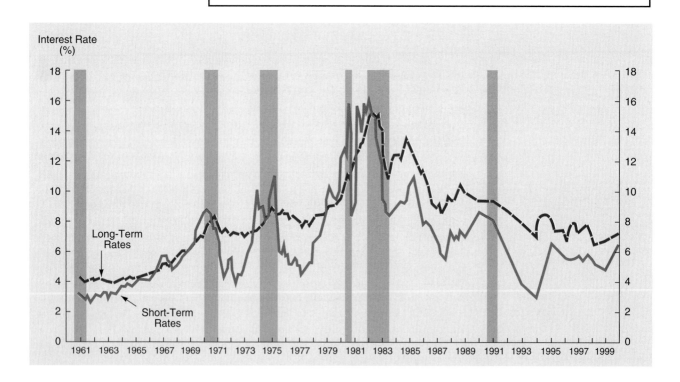

NOTES:

a. The shaded areas designate business recessions.

b. Short-term rates are measured by three- to six-month loans to very large, strong corporations, and long-term rates are measured by AAA corporate bonds.

SOURCE: *Federal Reserve Bulletin.*

1960s. Notice that short-term interest rates are especially prone to rise during booms and then fall during recessions. (The shaded areas of the chart indicate recessions.) When the economy is expanding, firms need capital, and this demand for capital pushes rates up. Also, inflationary pressures are strongest during business booms, and that also exerts upward pressure on rates. Conditions are reversed during recessions such as the one in 1990 and 1991. Slack business reduces the demand for credit, the rate of inflation falls, and the result is a drop in interest rates. Furthermore, the Federal Reserve deliberately lowers rates during recessions to help stimulate the economy.

These tendencies do not hold exactly — the period after 1984 is a case in point. The price of oil fell dramatically in 1985 and 1986, reducing inflationary pressures on other prices and easing fears of serious long-term inflation. Earlier, these fears had pushed interest rates to record levels. The economy from 1984 to 1987 was strong, but the declining fears of inflation more than offset the normal tendency of interest rates to rise during good economic times, and the net result was lower interest rates.[6]

The relationship between inflation and long-term interest rates is highlighted in Figure 5-4, which plots rates of inflation along with long-term interest rates. In the early 1960s, inflation averaged 1 percent per year, and interest rates on high-quality, long-term bonds averaged 4 percent. Then the Vietnam War heated up, leading to an increase in inflation, and interest rates began an upward climb. When the war ended in the early 1970s, inflation dipped a bit, but then the 1973 Arab oil embargo led to rising oil prices, much higher inflation rates, and sharply higher interest rates.

Inflation peaked at about 13 percent in 1980, but interest rates continued to increase into 1981 and 1982, and they remained quite high until 1985, because people were afraid inflation would start to climb again. Thus, the "inflationary psychology" created during the 1970s persisted to the mid-1980s.

Gradually, though, people began to realize that the Federal Reserve was serious about keeping inflation down, that global competition was keeping U.S. auto producers and other corporations from raising prices as they had in the past, and that constraints on corporate price increases were diminishing labor unions' ability to push through cost-increasing wage hikes. As these realizations set in, interest rates declined.

The gap between the current interest rate and the current inflation rate is defined as the "current real rate of interest." It is called the "real rate" because it shows how much investors really earned after taking out the effects of inflation. The real rate was extremely high during the mid-1980s, but it averaged about 4 percent during the 1990s.

In recent years, inflation has been running at about 3 percent a year. However, long-term interest rates have been volatile, because investors are not sure if inflation is truly under control or is getting ready to jump back to the higher levels of the 1980s. In the years ahead, we can be sure that the level of interest rates will vary (1) with changes in the current rate of inflation and (2) with changes in expectations about future inflation.

---

[6] Short-term rates are responsive to current economic conditions, whereas long-term rates primarily reflect long-run expectations for inflation. As a result, short-term rates are sometimes above and sometimes below long-term rates. The relationship between long-term and short-term rates is called the *term structure of interest rates*, and it is discussed later in the chapter.

FIGURE 5-4	Relationship between Annual Inflation Rates and Long-Term Interest Rates, 1961–2000

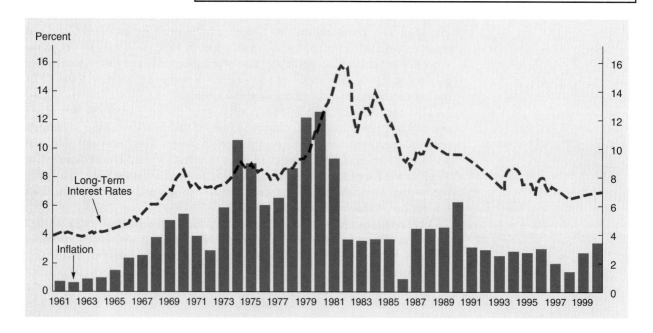

NOTES:

a. Interest rates are those on AAA long-term corporate bonds.

b. Inflation is measured as the annual rate of change in the Consumer Price Index (CPI).

SOURCE: *Federal Reserve Bulletin.*

SELF-TEST QUESTIONS

How are interest rates used to allocate capital among firms?

What happens to market-clearing, or equilibrium, interest rates in a capital market when the demand for funds declines? What happens when inflation increases or decreases?

Why does the price of capital change during booms and recessions?

How does risk affect interest rates?

THE DETERMINANTS OF MARKET INTEREST RATES

In general, the quoted (or nominal) interest rate on a debt security, k, is composed of a real risk-free rate of interest, k*, plus several premiums that reflect inflation, the riskiness of the security, and the security's marketability (or liquidity). This relationship can be expressed as follows:

$$\text{Quoted interest rate} = k = k^* + IP + DRP + LP + MRP. \quad (5\text{-}1)$$

Here

k = the quoted, or nominal, rate of interest on a given security.[7] There are many different securities, hence many different quoted interest rates.

k^* = the real risk-free rate of interest. k^* is pronounced "k-star," and it is the rate that would exist on a riskless security if zero inflation were expected.

k_{RF} = k^* + IP, and it is the quoted risk-free rate of interest on a security such as a U.S. Treasury bill, which is very liquid and also free of most risks. Note that k_{RF} includes the premium for expected inflation, because k_{RF} = k^* + IP.

IP = inflation premium. IP is equal to the average expected inflation rate over the life of the security. The expected future inflation rate is not necessarily equal to the current inflation rate, so IP is not necessarily equal to current inflation as reported in Figure 5-4.

DRP = default risk premium. This premium reflects the possibility that the issuer will not pay interest or principal at the stated time and in the stated amount. DRP is zero for U.S. Treasury securities, but it rises as the riskiness of issuers increases.

LP = liquidity, or marketability, premium. This is a premium charged by lenders to reflect the fact that some securities cannot be converted to cash on short notice at a "reasonable" price. LP is very low for Treasury securities and for securities issued by large, strong firms, but it is relatively high on securities issued by very small firms.

MRP = maturity risk premium. As we will explain later, longer-term bonds, even Treasury bonds, are exposed to a significant risk of price declines, and a maturity risk premium is charged by lenders to reflect this risk.

As noted above, since k_{RF} = k^* + IP, we can rewrite Equation 5-1 as follows:

$$\text{Nominal, or quoted, rate} = k = k_{RF} + DRP + LP + MRP.$$

We discuss the components whose sum makes up the quoted, or nominal, rate on a given security in the following sections.

THE REAL RISK-FREE RATE OF INTEREST, k^*

Real Risk-Free Rate of Interest, k^*
The rate of interest that would exist on default-free U.S. Treasury securities if no inflation were expected.

The **real risk-free rate of interest, k^*,** is defined as the interest rate that would exist on a riskless security if no inflation were expected, and it may be thought of as the rate of interest on *short-term* U.S. Treasury securities in an inflation-free world. The real risk-free rate is not static—it changes over time depending on economic conditions, especially (1) on the rate of return corporations and other borrowers expect to earn on productive assets and (2) on people's time preferences for current versus future consumption. Borrowers'

---

[7] The term *nominal* as it is used here means the *stated* rate as opposed to the *real* rate, which is adjusted to remove inflation effects. If you had bought a 10-year Treasury bond in February 2001, the quoted, or nominal, rate would be about 5.2 percent, but if inflation averages 2.5 percent over the next 10 years, the real rate would be about 5.2% − 2.5% = 2.7%.

expected returns on real asset investments set an upper limit on how much they can afford to pay for borrowed funds, while savers' time preferences for consumption establish how much consumption they are willing to defer, hence the amount of funds they will lend at different interest rates. It is difficult to measure the real risk-free rate precisely, but most experts think that k* has fluctuated in the range of 1 to 5 percent in recent years.[8] The best estimate of k* is the rate of return on indexed Treasury bonds, which are discussed in a box later in the chapter.

THE NOMINAL, OR QUOTED, RISK-FREE RATE OF INTEREST, k_{RF}

Nominal (Quoted) Risk-Free Rate, k_{RF}
The rate of interest on a security that is free of all risk; k_{RF} is proxied by the T-bill rate or the T-bond rate. k_{RF} includes an inflation premium.

The **nominal,** or **quoted, risk-free rate, k_{RF},** is the real risk-free rate plus a premium for expected inflation: $k_{RF} = k* + IP$. To be strictly correct, the risk-free rate should mean the interest rate on a totally risk-free security — one that has no risk of default, no maturity risk, no liquidity risk, no risk of loss if inflation increases, and no risk of any other type. There is no such security, hence there is no observable truly risk-free rate. However, there is one security that is free of most risks — an indexed U.S. Treasury security. These securities are free of default, maturity, and liquidity risks, and also of risk due to changes in the general level of interest rates.[9]

If the term "risk-free rate" is used without either the modifier "real" or the modifier "nominal," people generally mean the quoted (nominal) rate, and we will follow that convention in this book. Therefore, when we use the term risk-free rate, k_{RF}, we mean the nominal risk-free rate, which includes an inflation premium equal to the average expected inflation rate over the life of the security. In general, we use the T-bill rate to approximate the short-term risk-free rate, and the T-bond rate to approximate the long-term risk-free rate. So, whenever you see the term "risk-free rate," assume that we are referring either to the quoted U.S. T-bill rate or to the quoted T-bond rate.

INFLATION PREMIUM (IP)

Inflation has a major impact on interest rates because it erodes the purchasing power of the dollar and lowers the real rate of return on investments. To illus-

---

[8] The real rate of interest as discussed here is different from the *current* real rate as discussed in connection with Figure 5-4. The current real rate is the current interest rate minus the current (or latest past) inflation rate, while the real rate, without the word "current," is the current interest rate minus the *expected future* inflation rate over the life of the security. For example, suppose the current quoted rate for a one-year Treasury bill is 5 percent, inflation during the latest year was 2 percent, and inflation expected for the coming year is 4 percent. Then the *current* real rate would be 5% − 2% = 3%, but the *expected* real rate would be 5% − 4% = 1%. The rate on a 10-year bond would be related to the expected inflation rate over the next 10 years, and so on. In the press, the term "real rate" generally means the current real rate, but in economics and finance, hence in this book unless otherwise noted, the real rate means the one based on *expected* inflation rates.

[9] Indexed Treasury securities are the closest thing we have to a riskless security, but even they are not totally riskless, because k* itself can change and cause a decline in the prices of these securities. For example, between October 1998 and January 2000, the price of one indexed Treasury security declined from 98 to 89, or by almost 10 percent. The cause was an increase in the real rate on long-term securities from 3.7 percent to 4.4 percent. One year later, the real rate on long-term securities has dropped to 3.5 percent.

trate, suppose you saved $1,000 and invested it in a Treasury bill that matures in one year and pays a 5 percent interest rate. At the end of the year, you will receive $1,050 — your original $1,000 plus $50 of interest. Now suppose the inflation rate during the year is 10 percent, and it affects all items equally. If gas had cost $1 per gallon at the beginning of the year, it would cost $1.10 at the end of the year. Therefore, your $1,000 would have bought $1,000/$1 = 1,000 gallons at the beginning of the year, but only $1,050/$1.10 = 955 gallons at the end. In *real terms*, you would be worse off — you would receive $50 of interest, but it would not be sufficient to offset inflation. You would thus be better off buying 1,000 gallons of gas (or some other storable asset such as land, timber, apartment buildings, wheat, or gold) than buying the Treasury bill.

Investors are well aware of all this, so when they lend money, they build in an **inflation premium (IP)** equal to the average expected inflation rate over the life of the security. As discussed previously, for a short-term, default-free U.S. Treasury bill, the actual interest rate charged, $k_{\text{T-bill}}$, would be the real risk-free rate, k^*, plus the inflation premium (IP):

$$k_{\text{T-bill}} = k_{RF} = k^* + IP.$$

Inflation Premium (IP)
A premium equal to expected inflation that investors add to the real risk-free rate of return.

Therefore, if the real risk-free rate of interest were $k^* = 2.8\%$, and if inflation were expected to be 2 percent (and hence IP = 2%) during the next year, then the quoted rate of interest on one-year T-bills would be 2.8% + 2% = 4.8%. Indeed, in February 2001, the expected one-year inflation rate was about 2 percent, and the yield on one-year T-bills was about 4.8 percent, so the real risk-free rate on short-term securities at that time was 2.8 percent.

It is important to note that the inflation rate built into interest rates is the *inflation rate expected in the future*, not the rate experienced in the past. Thus, the latest reported figures might show an annual inflation rate of 3.3 percent, but that is for the *past* year. If people on the average expect a 6 percent inflation rate in the future, then 6 percent would be built into the current interest rate. Note also that the inflation rate reflected in the quoted interest rate on any security is the *average rate of inflation expected over the security's life*. Thus, the inflation rate built into a one-year bond is the expected inflation rate for the next year, but the inflation rate built into a 30-year bond is the average rate of inflation expected over the next 30 years.[10]

Expectations for future inflation are closely, but not perfectly, correlated with rates experienced in the recent past. Therefore, if the inflation rate reported for last month increased, people would tend to raise their expectations for future inflation, and this change in expectations would cause an increase in interest rates.

---

[10] To be theoretically precise, we should use a *geometric average*. Also, since millions of investors are active in the market, it is impossible to determine exactly the consensus expected inflation rate. Survey data are available, however, which give us a reasonably good idea of what investors expect over the next few years. For example, in 1980 the University of Michigan's Survey Research Center reported that people expected inflation during the next year to be 11.9 percent and that the average rate of inflation expected over the next 5 to 10 years was 10.5 percent. Those expectations led to record-high interest rates. However, the economy cooled in 1981 and 1982, and, as Figure 5-4 showed, actual inflation dropped sharply after 1980. This led to gradual reductions in the *expected future* inflation rate. In February 2001, as we write this, the expected inflation rate for the next year is about 2 percent, and the expected long-term inflation rate is about 2.5 percent. As inflationary expectations change, so do quoted market interest rates.

Note that Germany, Japan, and Switzerland have over the past 3.5 or so years had lower inflation rates than the United States, hence their interest rates have generally been lower than ours. Italy and most South American countries have experienced high inflation, and that is reflected in their interest rates.

DEFAULT RISK PREMIUM (DRP)

The risk that a borrower will *default* on a loan, which means not pay the interest or the principal, also affects the market interest rate on a security: the greater the default risk, the higher the interest rate. Treasury securities have no default risk, hence they carry the lowest interest rates on taxable securities in the United States. For corporate bonds, the higher the bond's rating, the lower its default risk, and, consequently, the lower its interest rate.[11] Here are some representative interest rates on long-term bonds during November 2000:

	RATE	DRP
U.S. Treasury	5.8%	—
AAA	7.5	1.7%
AA	7.8	2.0
A	8.1	2.3
BBB	8.3	2.5

Default Risk Premium (DRP)
The difference between the interest rate on a U.S. Treasury bond and a corporate bond of equal maturity and marketability.

The difference between the quoted interest rate on a T- bond and that on a corporate bond with similar maturity, liquidity, and other features is the **default risk premium (DRP).** Therefore, if the bonds listed above were otherwise similar, the default risk premium would be DRP = 7.5% − 5.8% = 1.7 percentage points for AAA corporate bonds, 7.8% − 5.8% = 2.0 percentage points for AA, 8.1% − 5.8% = 2.3 percentage points for A corporate bonds, and so forth. Default risk premiums vary somewhat over time, but the November 2000 figures are representative of levels in recent years.

LIQUIDITY PREMIUM (LP)

Liquidity Premium (LP)
A premium added to the equilibrium interest rate on a security if that security cannot be converted to cash on short notice and at close to "fair market value."

A "liquid" asset can be converted to cash quickly and at a "fair market value." Financial assets are generally more liquid than real assets. Because liquidity is important, investors include **liquidity premiums (LPs)** when market rates of securities are established. Although it is difficult to accurately measure liquidity premiums, a differential of at least two and probably four or five percentage points exists between the least liquid and the most liquid financial assets of similar default risk and maturity.

---

[11] Bond ratings, and bonds' riskiness in general, are discussed in detail in Chapter 8. For now, merely note that bonds rated AAA are judged to have less default risk than bonds rated AA, while AA bonds are less risky than A bonds, and so on. Ratings are designated AAA or Aaa, AA or Aa, and so forth, depending on the rating agency. In this book, the designations are used interchangeably.

MATURITY RISK PREMIUM (MRP)

Interest Rate Risk
The risk of capital losses to which investors are exposed because of changing interest rates.

Maturity Risk Premium (MRP)
A premium that reflects interest rate risk.

Reinvestment Rate Risk
The risk that a decline in interest rates will lead to lower income when bonds mature and funds are reinvested.

U.S. Treasury securities are free of default risk in the sense that one can be virtually certain that the federal government will pay interest on its bonds and will also pay them off when they mature. Therefore, the default risk premium on Treasury securities is essentially zero. Further, active markets exist for Treasury securities, so their liquidity premiums are also close to zero. Thus, as a first approximation, the rate of interest on a Treasury bond should be the risk-free rate, k_{RF}, which is equal to the real risk-free rate, k^*, plus an inflation premium, IP. However, an adjustment is needed for long-term Treasury bonds. The prices of long-term bonds decline sharply whenever interest rates rise, and since interest rates can and do occasionally rise, all long-term bonds, even Treasury bonds, have an element of risk called **interest rate risk.** As a general rule, the bonds of any organization, from the U.S. government to Continental Airlines, have more interest rate risk the longer the maturity of the bond.[12] Therefore, a **maturity risk premium (MRP),** which is higher the longer the years to maturity, must be included in the required interest rate.

The effect of maturity risk premiums is to raise interest rates on long-term bonds relative to those on short-term bonds. This premium, like the others, is difficult to measure, but (1) it varies somewhat over time, rising when interest rates are more volatile and uncertain, then falling when interest rates are more stable, and (2) in recent years, the maturity risk premium on 30-year T-bonds appears to have generally been in the range of one or two percentage points.[13]

We should mention that although long-term bonds are heavily exposed to interest rate risk, short-term bills are heavily exposed to **reinvestment rate risk.** When short-term bills mature and the funds are reinvested, or "rolled over," a decline in interest rates would necessitate reinvestment at a lower rate, and this would result in a decline in interest income. To illustrate, suppose you had $100,000 invested in one-year T-bills, and you lived on the income. In 1981, short-term rates were about 15 percent, so your income would have been about $15,000. However, your income would have declined to about $9,000 by 1983, and to just $4,800 by 2001. Had you invested your money in long-term T-bonds, your income (but not the value of the principal) would have been stable.[14] Thus, although "investing short" preserves one's principal, the interest income provided by short-term T-bills is less stable than the interest income on long-term bonds.

---

[12] For example, if someone had bought a 30-year Treasury bond for $1,000 in 1998, when the long-term interest rate was 5.25 percent, and held it until 2001, when long-term T-bond rates were about 5.5 percent, the value of the bond would have declined to about $965. That would represent a loss of 3.5 percent, and it demonstrates that long-term bonds, even U.S. Treasury bonds, are not riskless. However, had the investor purchased short-term T-bills in 1998 and subsequently reinvested the principal each time the bills matured, he or she would still have had $1,000. This point will be discussed in detail in Chapter 8.

[13] The MRP for long-term bonds has averaged 1.4 percent over the last 73 years. See *Stocks, Bonds, Bills, and Inflation: (Valuation Edition) 2000 Yearbook* (Chicago: Ibbotson Associates, 2000).

[14] Long-term bonds also have some reinvestment rate risk. If one is saving and investing for some future purpose, say, to buy a house or for retirement, then to actually earn the quoted rate on a long-term bond, the interest payments must be reinvested at the quoted rate. However, if interest rates fall, the interest payments must be reinvested at a lower rate; thus, the realized return would be less than the quoted rate. Note, though, that reinvestment rate risk is lower on a long-term bond than on a short-term bond because only the interest payments (rather than interest plus principal) on the long-term bond are exposed to reinvestment rate risk. Zero coupon bonds, which are discussed in Chapter 8, are completely free of reinvestment rate risk during their life.

A NEW, ALMOST RISKLESS TREASURY BOND

Investors who purchase bonds must constantly worry about inflation. If inflation turns out to be greater than expected, bonds will provide a lower-than-expected real return. To protect themselves against expected increases in inflation, investors build an inflation risk premium into their required rate of return. This raises borrowers' costs.

In order to provide investors with an inflation-protected bond, and also to reduce the cost of debt to the government, on January 29, 1997, the U.S. Treasury issued $7 billion of 10-year inflation-indexed bonds. These initial bonds paid an interest rate of 3.375 percent plus an additional amount to offset inflation. At the end of each six-month period, the principal (originally set at par, or $1,000) is adjusted by the inflation rate. For example, during the first six-month interest period, inflation (as measured by the CPI) was 1.085 percent. The inflation-adjusted principal was then calculated as $1,000(1 + inflation) = $1,000 \times 1.01085 = $1,010.85. So, on July 15, 1997, each bond paid interest of $0.03375/2 \times $1,010.85 = $17.06. Note that the interest rate is divided by two because interest is paid twice a year.

By January 15, 1998, a bit more inflation had occurred, and the inflation-adjusted principal was up to $1,019.69, so on January 15, 1998, each bond paid interest of $0.03375/2 \times $1,019.69 = $17.21. Thus, the total return during the first year consisted of $17.06 + $17.21 = $34.27 of interest and $1,019.69 - $1,000.00 = $19.69 of "capital gains," or $34.27 + $19.69 = $53.96 in total. Thus, the total return was $53.96/$1,000 = 5.396%.

This same adjustment process will continue each year until the bonds mature on January 15, 2007, at which time they will pay the adjusted maturity value. Thus, the cash income provided by the bonds rises by exactly enough to cover inflation, producing a real, inflation-adjusted rate of 3.375 percent. Further, since the principal also rises by the inflation rate, it too is protected from inflation. The accompanying table gives the inflation-adjusted principal and interest paid during the life of these 3⅜ percent coupon, 10-year, inflation-indexed bonds:

DATE	INFLATION-ADJUSTED PRINCIPAL	INTEREST PAID
7/15/97	$1,010.85	$17.06
1/15/98	1,019.69	17.21
7/15/98	1,026.51	17.32
1/15/99	1,035.12	17.47
7/15/99	1,049.01	17.70
1/15/00	1,061.92	17.92
7/15/00	1,080.85	18.24
1/15/01	1,098.52	18.54

SOURCE: Bureau of the Public Debt's Online, Historical Reference CPI Numbers and Daily Index Ratios for 3⅜%, 10-year note due January 15, 2007, at http://www.publicdebt.treas.gov/of/ofhiscpi.htm.

The Treasury regularly conducts auctions to issue indexed bonds. The 3.375 percent rate was based on the relative supply

SELF-TEST QUESTIONS

Write out an equation for the nominal interest rate on any debt security.

Distinguish between the *real* risk-free rate of interest, k^*, and the *nominal,* or *quoted,* risk-free rate of interest, k_{RF}.

How is inflation dealt with when interest rates are determined by investors in the financial markets?

Does the interest rate on a T-bond include a default risk premium? Explain.

Distinguish between liquid and illiquid assets, and identify some assets that are liquid and some that are illiquid.

Briefly explain the following statement: "Although long-term bonds are heavily exposed to interest rate risk, short-term bills are heavily exposed to reinvestment rate risk. The maturity risk premium reflects the net effects of these two opposing forces."

and demand for the issue, and it will remain constant over the life of the bond. However, new bonds are issued periodically, and their "coupon" real rates depend on the market at the time the bond is auctioned. In January 2001, 10-year indexed securities had a real rate of 3.5 percent.

Federal Reserve Board Chairman Greenspan lobbied in favor of the indexed bonds on the grounds that they would help him and the Fed make better estimates of investors' expectations about inflation. He did not explain his reasoning (to our knowledge), but it might have gone something like this:

- We know that interest rates in general are determined as follows:

$$k = k^* + IP + MRP + DRP + LP.$$

- For Treasury bonds, DRP and LP are essentially zero, so for a 10-year bond the rate is

$$k_{RF} = k^* + IP + MRP.$$

The reason the MRP is not zero is that if inflation increases, interest rates will rise and the price of the bonds will decline. Therefore, "regular" 10-year bonds are exposed to maturity risk, hence a maturity risk premium is built into their market interest rate.

- The indexed bonds are protected against inflation — if inflation increases, then so will their dollar returns, and as a result, their price will not decline in real terms. Therefore, indexed bonds should have no MRP, hence their market return is

$$k_{RF} = k^* + 0 + 0 = k^*.$$

In other words, the market rate on indexed bonds is the real rate.

- The difference between the yield on a regular 10-year bond and that on an indexed bond is the sum of the 10-year bonds' IP and MRP. The yield on regular 10-year bonds was 6.80 percent when the indexed bonds were issued, and the indexed bonds' yield was 3.375 percent. The difference, 3.425 percent, is the average expected inflation rate over the next 10 years plus the MRP for 10-year bonds.
- The 10-year MRP is about 1.0 percent, and it has been relatively stable in recent years. Therefore, the expected rate of inflation in January 1997 was about 2.425 percent (3.425% − 1.00% = 2.425%).

The interest received and the increase in principal are taxed each year as interest income, even though cash from the appreciation will not be received until the bond matures. Therefore, these bonds are especially suitable for individual retirement accounts (IRAs), which are not taxed until funds are withdrawn.

Keep in mind, though, that despite their protection against inflation, indexed bonds are not completely riskless. The real rate of interest can change, and if k* rises, the price of the indexed bonds will decline. This just confirms one more time that there is no such thing as a free lunch or a riskless security!

SOURCES: "Inflation Notes Will Offer Fed Forecast Tool," *The Wall Street Journal,* February 3, 1997, C1; and *The Wall Street Journal,* January 6, 2000, C21.

THE TERM STRUCTURE OF INTEREST RATES

Term Structure of Interest Rates
The relationship between bond yields and maturities.

Students can find current U.S. Treasury yield curve graphs and other global and domestic interest rate information at Bloomberg markets' site at **http://www. bloomberg.com/markets/index.html.**

The **term structure of interest rates** describes the relationship between long- and short-term rates. The term structure is important to corporate treasurers who must decide whether to borrow by issuing long- or short-term debt and to investors who must decide whether to buy long- or short-term bonds. Thus, it is important to understand (1) how long- and short-term rates relate to each other and (2) what causes shifts in their relative positions.

Interest rates for bonds with different maturities can be found in a variety of publications, including *The Wall Street Journal* and the *Federal Reserve Bulletin,* and on a number of web sites, including Bloomberg, Yahoo, and CNN Financial. From interest rate data obtained from these sources, we can construct the term structure at a given point in time. For example, the tabular section below Figure 5-5 presents interest rates for different maturities on three different

FIGURE 5-5

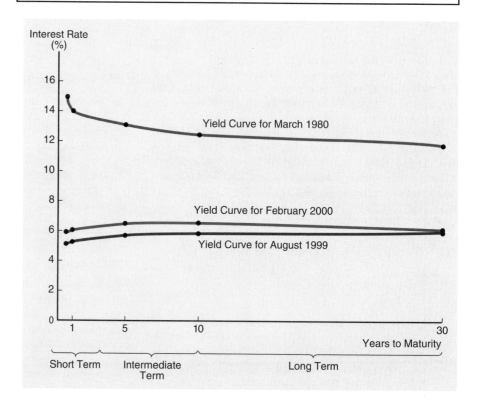

	INTEREST RATE		
TERM TO MATURITY	**MARCH 1980**	**AUGUST 1999**	**FEBRUARY 2000**
6 months	15.0%	5.1%	6.0%
1 year	14.0	5.2	6.2
5 years	13.5	5.8	6.7
10 years	12.8	5.9	6.7
30 years	12.3	6.0	6.3

Yield Curve

A graph showing the relationship between bond yields and maturities.

dates. The set of data for a given date, when plotted on a graph such as that in Figure 5-5 is called the **yield curve** for that date.

The yield curve changes both in position and in slope over time. In March 1980, all rates were relatively high, and since short-term rates were higher than long-term rates, the yield curve was *downward sloping*. However, by August 1999, all rates had fallen, and because short-term rates were lower than long-term rates, the yield curve was *upward sloping*. Six months later, in February 2000, all rates were higher, and the yield curve had become *humped*—medium-term rates were higher than both short- and long-term rates. If the current yield curve (February 2001) were graphed on Figure 5-5, it would be downward sloping for short-term securities but upward sloping for longer-term securities. The data points would plot close to the August 1999 yield curve.

Figure 5-5 shows yield curves for U.S. Treasury securities, but we could have constructed curves for corporate bonds issued by AT&T, IBM, Delta Airlines, or any other company that borrows money over a range of maturities. Had we constructed corporate curves and plotted them on Figure 5-5, they would have been above those for Treasury securities because corporate yields include default risk premiums. However, the corporate yield curves would have had the same general shape as the Treasury curves. Also, the riskier the corporation, the higher its yield curve, so Delta Airlines, which has a lower bond rating than either AT&T or IBM, would have a higher yield curve than those of AT&T and IBM.

Historically, in most years long-term rates have been above short-term rates, so the yield curve usually slopes upward. For this reason, people often call an upward-sloping yield curve a **"normal" yield curve** and a yield curve that slopes downward an **inverted,** or **"abnormal,"** curve. Thus, in Figure 5-5 the yield curve for March 1980 was inverted and the one for August 1999 was normal. However, the February 2000 curve was **humped**, which means that interest rates on medium-term maturities were higher than rates on both short- and long-term maturities. We explain in detail in the next section why an upward slope is the normal situation, but briefly, the reason is that short-term securities have less interest rate risk than longer-term securities, hence smaller MRPs. Therefore, short-term rates are normally lower than long-term rates.

"Normal" Yield Curve
An upward-sloping yield curve.

Inverted ("Abnormal") Yield Curve
A downward-sloping yield curve.

Humped Yield Curve
A yield curve where interest rates on medium-term maturities are higher than rates on both short- and long-term maturities.

SELF-TEST QUESTIONS

What is a yield curve, and what information would you need to draw this curve?

Distinguish among the shapes of a "normal" yield curve, an "abnormal" curve, and a "humped" curve.

WHAT DETERMINES THE SHAPE OF THE YIELD CURVE?

Since maturity risk premiums are positive, then if other things were held constant, long-term bonds would have higher interest rates than short-term bonds. However, market interest rates also depend on expected inflation, default risk, and liquidity, and each of these factors can vary with maturity.

Expected inflation has an especially important effect on the yield curve's shape. To see why, consider U.S. Treasury securities. Because Treasuries have essentially no default or liquidity risk, the yield on a Treasury bond that matures in t years can be found using the following equation:

$$k_T = k^*_t + IP_t + MRP_t.$$

While the real risk-free rate, k^*, may vary somewhat over time because of changes in the economy and demographics, these changes are random rather than predictable, so it is reasonable to assume that k^* will remain constant. However, the inflation premium, IP, does vary significantly over time, and in a somewhat predictable manner. Recall that the inflation premium is simply the

---

FIGURE 5-6   Illustrative Treasury Yield Curves

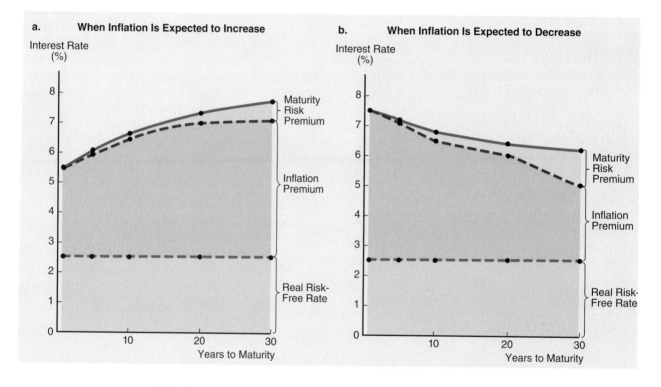

a. **When Inflation Is Expected to Increase**

b. **When Inflation Is Expected to Decrease**

	WITH INCREASING EXPECTED INFLATION					WITH DECREASING EXPECTED INFLATION			
MATURITY	k*	IP	MRP	YIELD	MATURITY	k*	IP	MRP	YIELD
1 year	2.50%	3.00%	0.00%	**5.50%**	1 year	2.50%	5.00%	0.00%	**7.50%**
5 years	2.50	3.40	0.18	**6.08**	5 years	2.50	4.60	0.18	**7.28**
10 years	2.50	4.00	0.28	**6.78**	10 years	2.50	4.00	0.28	**6.78**
20 years	2.50	4.50	0.42	**7.42**	20 years	2.50	3.50	0.42	**6.42**
30 years	2.50	4.67	0.53	**7.70**	30 years	2.50	3.33	0.53	**6.36**

---

average level of expected inflation over the life of the bond. Thus, if the market expects inflation to increase in the future, the inflation premium will be higher the longer the bond's maturity. On the other hand, if the market expects inflation to decline in the future, long-term bonds will have a smaller inflation premium than short-term bonds. Finally, if investors consider long-term bonds riskier than short-term bonds, the maturity risk premium will increase with maturity.

Panel a of Figure 5-6 shows the yield curve when inflation is expected to increase. Here long-term bonds have higher yields for two reasons: (1) Inflation is expected to be higher in the future, and (2) there is a positive maturity risk premium. Panel b of Figure 5-6 shows the yield curve when inflation is expected to decline, causing the yield curve to be downward sloping. Downward sloping yield curves often foreshadow an economic downturn, because weaker economic conditions tend to be correlated with declining inflation, which in turn leads to lower long-term rates.

Now let's consider the yield curve for corporate bonds. Recall that corporate bonds include a default-risk premium (DRP) and a liquidity premium (LP). Therefore, the yield on a corporate bond that matures in t years can be expressed as follows:

$$k_C = k^*_t + IP_t + MRP_t + DRP_t + LP_t.$$

A corporate bond's default and liquidity risks are affected by its maturity. For example, the default risk on Coca-Cola's short-term debt is very small, since there is almost no chance that Coca-Cola will go bankrupt over the next few years. However, Coke has some 100-year bonds, and while the odds of Coke defaulting on these bonds still might not be that high, the default risk on these bonds is considerably higher than that on its short-term debt.

Longer-term corporate bonds are also less liquid than shorter-term debt, hence the liquidity premium rises as maturity lengthens. The primary reason for this is that, for the reasons discussed earlier, short-term debt has less default risk, so a buyer can buy short-term debt without having to do as much credit checking as would be necessary for long-term debt. Thus, people can move into and out of short-term corporate debt much more rapidly than long-term debt. The end result is that short-term corporate debt is more liquid, hence has a smaller liquidity premium than the same company's long-term debt.

Figure 5-7 shows yield curves for two hypothetical corporate bonds, an AA-rated bond with minimal default risk and a BBB-rated bond with more default risk, along with the yield curve for Treasury securities as taken from Panel a of Figure 5-6. Here we assume that inflation is expected to increase, so the Treasury yield curve is upward sloping. Because of their additional default and liquidity risk, corporate bonds always trade at a higher yield than Treasury bonds with the same maturity, and BBB-rated bonds trade at higher yields than AA-rated bonds. Finally, note that the yield spread between corporate bonds and Treasury bonds is larger the longer the maturity. This occurs because longer-term corporate bonds have more default and liquidity risk than shorter-term bonds, and both of these premiums are absent in Treasury bonds.

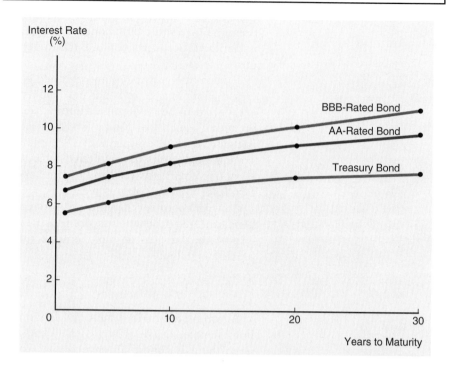

TERM TO MATURITY	INTEREST RATE		
	TREASURY BOND	AA-RATED BOND	BBB-RATED BOND
1 year	5.5%	6.7%	7.4%
5 years	6.1	7.4	8.1
10 years	6.8	8.2	9.1
20 years	7.4	9.2	10.2
30 years	7.7	9.8	11.1

SELF-TEST QUESTIONS

How do maturity risk premiums affect the yield curve?

If the rate of inflation is expected to increase, would this increase or decrease the slope of the yield curve?

If the rate of inflation is expected to remain constant in the future, would the yield curve slope up, down, or be horizontal?

Explain why corporate bonds' default and liquidity premiums are likely to increase with maturity.

Explain why corporate bonds always trade at higher yields than Treasury bonds and why BBB-rated bonds always trade at higher yields than AA-rated bonds.

USING THE YIELD CURVE TO ESTIMATE FUTURE INTEREST RATES[15]

In the last section we saw that the shape of the yield curve depends primarily on two factors: (1) expectations about future inflation and (2) the relative riskiness of securities with different maturities. We also saw how to calculate the yield curve, given inflation and maturity-related risks. In practice, this process often works in reverse: Investors and analysts plot the yield curve and then use information embedded in it to estimate the market's expectations regarding future inflation and risk.

This process of using the yield curve to estimate future expected interest rates is straightforward, provided (1) we focus on Treasury securities, and (2) we assume that all Treasury securities have the same risk; that is, there is no maturity risk premium. Some academics and practitioners contend that this second assumption is reasonable, at least as an approximation. They argue that the market is dominated by large bond traders who buy and sell securities of different maturities each day, that these traders focus only on short-term returns, and that they are not concerned with risk. According to this view, a bond trader is just as willing to buy a 30-year bond to pick up a short-term profit as he would be to buy a three-month security. Strict proponents of this view argue that the shape of the yield curve is therefore determined only by market expectations about future interest rates, thus their position has been called the *pure expectations theory* of the term structure of interest rates.

Expectations Theory
A theory which states that the shape of the yield curve depends on investors' expectations about future interest rates.

The pure **expectations theory** (which is sometimes simply referred to as the "expectations theory") assumes that investors establish bond prices and interest rates strictly on the basis of expectations for interest rates. This means that they are indifferent with respect to maturity in the sense that they do not view long-term bonds as being riskier than short-term bonds. If this were true, then the maturity risk premium (MRP) would be zero, and long-term interest rates would simply be a weighted average of current and expected future short-term interest rates. For example, if 1-year Treasury bills currently yield 7 percent, but 1-year bills were expected to yield 7.5 percent a year from now, investors would expect to earn an average of 7.25 percent over the next two years:[16]

$$\frac{7\% + 7.5\%}{2} = 7.25\%.$$

According to the expectations theory, this implies that a 2-year Treasury note purchased today should also yield 7.25 percent. Similarly, if 10-year bonds yield 9 percent today, and if 5-year bonds are expected to yield 7.5 percent 10 years from now, then investors should expect to earn 9 percent for 10 years

---

[15] This section is relatively technical, but instructors can omit it without loss of continuity.

[16] Technically, we should be using geometric averages rather than arithmetic averages, but the differences are not material in this example. For a discussion of this point, see Robert C. Radcliffe, *Investment: Concepts, Analysis, and Strategy*, 5th ed. (Reading, MA: Addison-Wesley, 1997), Chapter 5.

and 7.5 percent for 5 years, for an average return of 8.5 percent over the next 15 years:

$$\frac{9\% + 9\% + \cdots + 9\% + 7.5\% + \cdots + 7.5\%}{15} = \frac{10(9\%) + 5(7.5\%)}{15} = 8.5\%.$$

Consequently, a 15-year bond should yield this same return, 8.5 percent.

To understand the logic behind this averaging process, ask yourself what would happen if long-term yields were *not* an average of expected short-term yields. For example, suppose 2-year bonds yielded only 7 percent, not the 7.25 percent calculated above. Bond traders would be able to earn a profit by adopting the following trading strategy:

1. Borrow money for two years at a cost of 7 percent.
2. Invest the money in a series of 1-year bonds. The expected return over the 2-year period would be (7.0 + 7.5)/2 = 7.25%.

In this case, bond traders would rush to borrow money (demand funds) in the 2-year market and invest (or supply funds) in the 1-year market. Recall from Figure 5-2 that an increase in the demand for funds raises interest rates, whereas an increase in the supply of funds reduces interest rates. Therefore, bond traders' actions would push up the 2-year yield but reduce the yield on 1-year bonds. The net effect would be to bring about a market equilibrium in which 2-year rates were a weighted average of expected future 1-year rates.

Under these assumptions, we can "back out" of the yield curve the bond market's best guess about future interest rates. If, for example, you observe that Treasury securities with 1- and 2-year maturities yield 7 percent and 8 percent, respectively, this information can be used to calculate the market's forecast of what 1-year rates will yield one year from now. If the pure expectations theory is correct, the rate on 2-year bonds is the average of the current 1-year rate and the 1-year rate expected a year from now. Since the current 1-year rate is 7 percent, this implies that the 1-year rate one year from now is expected to be 9 percent:

$$2\text{-year yield} = 8\% = \frac{7\% + X\%}{2}$$

$$X = 16\% - 7\% = 9\% = 1\text{-year yield expected next year.}$$

The preceding analysis was based on the assumption that the maturity risk premium is zero. However, most evidence suggests that there is a positive maturity risk premium, so the MRP should be taken into account.

For example, assume once again that 1- and 2-year maturities yield 7 percent and 8 percent, respectively, but now assume that the maturity risk premium on the 2-year bond is 0.5 percent. This maturity risk premium implies that the expected return on 2-year bonds (8 percent) is 0.5 percent higher than the expected returns from buying a series of 1-year bonds (7.5 percent). With this background, we can use the following two-step procedure to back out X, the expected 1-year rate one year from now:

Step 1: 2-year yield − MRP on 2-year bond = 8.0% − 0.5% = 7.5%.

Step 2: 7.5% = (7.0% + X%)/2
$$X = 15.0\% - 7.0\% = 8.0\%.$$

Therefore, the yield next year on a 1-year T-bond should be 8 percent, up from 7 percent this year.

INVESTING OVERSEAS

Country Risk
The risk that arises from investing or doing business in a particular country.

Investors should consider additional risk factors before investing overseas. First there is **country risk**, which refers to the risk that arises from investing or doing business in a particular country. This risk depends on the country's economic, political, and social environment. Countries with stable economic, social, political, and regulatory systems provide a safer climate for investment, and therefore less country risk, than less stable nations. Examples of country risk include the risk associated with changes in tax rates, regulations, currency conversion, and exchange rates. Country risk also includes the risk that property will be expropriated without adequate compensation, as well as new host country stipulations about local production, sourcing or hiring practices, and damage or destruction of facilities due to internal strife.

A second point to keep in mind when investing overseas is that more often than not the security will be denominated in a currency other than the dollar, which means that the value of your investment will depend on what happens to exchange rates. This is known as **exchange rate risk.** For example, if a U.S. investor purchases a Japanese bond, interest will probably be paid in Japanese yen, which must then be converted into dollars if the investor wants to spend his or her money in the United States. If the yen weakens relative to the dollar, then it will buy fewer dollars, hence the investor will receive fewer dollars when it comes time to convert. Alternatively, if the yen strengthens relative to the dollar, the investor will earn higher dollar returns. It therefore follows that the effective rate of return on a foreign investment will depend on both the performance of the foreign security and on what happens to exchange rates over the life of the investment.

Exchange Rate Risk
The risk that exchange rate changes will reduce the number of dollars provided by a given amount of a foreign currency.

GLOBAL PERSPECTIVES

MEASURING COUNTRY RISK

Various forecasting services measure the level of country risk in different countries and provide indexes that measure factors such as each country's expected economic performance, access to world capital markets, political stability, and level of internal conflict. Country risk analysts use sophisticated models to measure it, thus providing corporate managers and overseas investors with a way to judge both the relative and absolute risk of investing in a given country. A sample of recent country risk estimates compiled by *Institutional Investor* is presented in the following table. The higher the country's score, the lower its estimated country risk. The maximum possible score is 100.

The countries with the least amount of country risk all have strong, market-based economies, ready access to worldwide capital markets, relatively little social unrest, and a stable political climate. Switzerland's top ranking may surprise you, but that country's ranking is the result of its strong economic performance. You may also be surprised that the United States was not ranked in the top five — it is ranked sixth.

Arguably, there are fewer surprises when looking at the bottom five. Each of these countries has considerable social and political unrest, and none has embraced a market-based economic system. Clearly, an investment in any of these countries is a risky proposition.

Top Five Countries (Least Amount of Country Risk)

RANK	COUNTRY	TOTAL SCORE (MAXIMUM POSSIBLE = 100)
1	Switzerland	95.6
2	Germany	94.6
3	Netherlands	94.5
4	Luxembourg	93.9
5	France	93.6

Bottom Five Countries (Greatest Amount of Country Risk)

RANK	COUNTRY	TOTAL SCORE (MINIMUM POSSIBLE = 0)
141	Sudan	8.7
142	Liberia	8.6
143	Afghanistan	6.5
144	Sierra Leone	6.4
145	North Korea	6.2

www

Students can access the home page of *Institutional Investor* magazine by typing **http://www.iimagazine.com.** Although the site requires users to register, the site is free to use. (Some data sets and articles are available only to subscribers.) The country risk rankings can be found by clicking on "Research and Rankings," shown on the top of the screen, and then clicking on "Country Credit" in the middle of the screen.

OTHER FACTORS THAT INFLUENCE INTEREST RATE LEVELS

In addition to inflationary expectations, other factors also influence both the general level of interest rates and the shape of the yield curve. The four most important factors are (1) Federal Reserve policy; (2) the federal budget deficit or surplus; (3) international factors, including the foreign trade balance and interest rates in other countries; and (4) the level of business activity.

FEDERAL RESERVE POLICY

 The home page for the Board of Governors of the Federal Reserve System can be found at **http://www.federalreserve.gov/**. You can access general information about the Federal Reserve, including press releases, speeches, and monetary policy.

As you probably learned in your economics courses, (1) the money supply has a major effect on both the level of economic activity and the inflation rate, and (2) in the United States, the Federal Reserve Board controls the money supply. If the Fed wants to stimulate the economy, as it did in 1995, it increases growth in the money supply. The initial effect of such an action is to cause interest rates to decline. However, a larger money supply may also lead to an increase in the expected inflation rate, which, in turn, could push interest rates up. The reverse holds if the Fed tightens the money supply.

To illustrate, in 1981 inflation was quite high, so the Fed tightened up the money supply. The Fed deals primarily in the short-term end of the market, so this tightening had the direct effect of pushing short-term rates up sharply. At the same time, the very fact that the Fed was taking strong action to reduce inflation led to a decline in expectations for long-run inflation, which led to a decline in long-term bond yields.

In 1991, the situation was just the reverse. To combat the recession, the Fed took steps to reduce interest rates. Short-term rates fell, and long-term rates also dropped, but not as sharply. These lower rates benefitted heavily indebted businesses and individual borrowers, and home mortgage refinancings put additional billions of dollars into consumers' pockets. Savers, of course, lost out, but the net effect of lower interest rates was a stronger economy. Lower rates encourage businesses to borrow for investment, stimulate the housing market, and bring down the value of the dollar relative to other currencies, which helps U.S. exporters and thus lowers the trade deficit.

During periods when the Fed is actively intervening in the markets, the yield curve may be temporarily distorted. Short-term rates will be temporarily "too low" if the Fed is easing credit, and "too high" if it is tightening credit. Long-term rates are not affected as much by Fed intervention. For example, the fear of rising inflation led the Federal Reserve to increase short-term interest rates six times during 1994. While short-term rates rose by nearly 4 percentage points, long-term rates increased by only 1.5 percentage points.

BUDGET DEFICITS OR SURPLUSES

If the federal government spends more than it takes in from tax revenues, it runs a deficit, and that deficit must be covered either by borrowing or by printing money (increasing the money supply). If the government borrows, this added demand for funds pushes up interest rates. If it prints money, this increases expectations for future inflation, which also drives up interest rates. Thus, the larger the federal deficit, other things held constant, the higher the level of interest rates. Whether long- or short-term rates are more affected depends on how the deficit is financed, so we cannot state, in general, how deficits will affect the slope of the yield curve.

Over the past several decades, the federal government routinely ran large budget deficits. However, in 1999, for the first time in recent memory, the government had a budget surplus, and further surpluses are projected on into the future. As a result, the government is buying back some of the outstanding Treasury securities. If these surpluses become a reality, the government would become a net supplier of funds rather than a net borrower of funds. All else equal, this would tend to reduce interest rates.

INTERNATIONAL FACTORS

Businesses and individuals in the United States buy from and sell to people and firms in other countries. If we buy more than we sell (that is, if we import more than we export), we are said to be running a *foreign trade deficit*. When trade deficits occur, they must be financed, and the main source of financing is debt. In other words, if we import $200 billion of goods but export only $100 billion, we run a trade deficit of $100 billion, and we would probably borrow the $100 billion.[17] Therefore, the larger our trade deficit, the more we must borrow, and as we increase our borrowing, this drives up interest rates. Also, foreigners are willing to hold U.S. debt if and only if the rate paid on this debt is competitive with interest rates in other countries. Therefore, if the Federal Reserve attempts to lower interest rates in the United States, causing our rates to fall below rates abroad, then foreigners will sell U.S. bonds, those sales will depress bond prices, and the result will be higher U.S. rates. Thus, if the trade deficit is large relative to the size of the overall economy, it may hinder the Fed's ability to combat a recession by lowering interest rates.

The United States has been running annual trade deficits since the mid-1970s, and the cumulative effect of these deficits is that the United States has become the largest debtor nation of all time. As a result, our interest rates are very much influenced by interest rates in other countries around the world (higher rates abroad lead to higher U.S. rates). Because of all this, U.S. corporate treasurers — and anyone else who is affected by interest rates — must keep up with developments in the world economy.

BUSINESS ACTIVITY

Figure 5-3, presented earlier, can be examined to see how business conditions influence interest rates. Here are the key points revealed by the graph:

1. Because inflation increased from 1961 to 1981, the general tendency during that period was toward higher interest rates. However, since the 1981 peak, the trend has generally been downward.

2. Until 1966, short-term rates were almost always below long-term rates. Thus, in those years the yield curve was almost always "normal" in the sense that it was upward sloping.

3. The shaded areas in the graph represent recessions, during which (1) both the demand for money and the rate of inflation tend to fall and (2) the Federal Reserve tends to increase the money supply in an effort to stimulate the economy. As a result, there is a tendency for interest

---

[17] The deficit could also be financed by selling assets, including gold, corporate stocks, entire companies, and real estate. The United States has financed its massive trade deficits by all of these means in recent years, but the primary method has been by borrowing from foreigners.

rates to decline during recessions. Currently, in early 2001, there are continued signs that the economy has begun to weaken. In response to these signs of economic weakness, the Federal Reserve has instituted a series of interest rate cuts. At the same time, there are also signs that inflation has begun to increase. These concerns about inflation may limit the Fed's ability to cut rates further.

4. During recessions, short-term rates decline more sharply than long-term rates. This occurs because (1) the Fed operates mainly in the short-term sector, so its intervention has the strongest effect there, and (2) long-term rates reflect the average expected inflation rate over the next 20 to 30 years, and this expectation generally does not change much, even when the current inflation rate is low because of a recession or high because of a boom. So, short-term rates are more volatile than long-term rates.

SELF-TEST QUESTIONS

Other than inflationary expectations, name some additional factors that influence interest rates, and explain the effects of each.

How does the Fed stimulate the economy? How does the Fed affect interest rates? Does the Fed have complete control over U.S. interest rates; that is, can it set rates at any level it chooses?

INTEREST RATES AND BUSINESS DECISIONS

The yield curve for August 1999, shown earlier in Figure 5-5, indicates how much the U.S. government had to pay in 1999 to borrow money for one year, five years, ten years, and so on. A business borrower would have had to pay somewhat more, but assume for the moment that we are back in August 1999 and that the yield curve for that year also applies to your company. Now suppose your company has decided (1) to build a new plant with a 30-year life that will cost $1 million and (2) to raise the $1 million by selling an issue of debt (or borrowing) rather than by selling stock. If you borrowed in 1999 on a short-term basis — say, for one year — your interest cost for that year would be only 5.2 percent, or $52,000. On the other hand, if you used long-term (30-year) financing, your cost would be 6.0 percent, or $60,000. Therefore, at first glance, it would seem that you should use short-term debt.

However, this could prove to be a horrible mistake. If you use short-term debt, you will have to renew your loan every year, and the rate charged on each new loan will reflect the then-current short-term rate. Interest rates could return to their previous highs, in which case you would be paying 14 percent, or $140,000, per year. Those high interest payments would cut into, and perhaps eliminate, your profits. Your reduced profitability could easily increase your firm's risk to the point where its bond rating would be lowered, causing lenders to increase the risk premium built into the interest rate they charge. That would force you to pay an even higher rate, which would further reduce your profitability, worrying lenders even more, and making them reluctant to renew your loan. If your lenders refused to renew the loan and demanded its repayment, as they would have every right to do, you might have to sell assets at a loss, which could lead to bankruptcy.

On the other hand, if you used long-term financing in 1999, your interest costs would remain constant at $60,000 per year, so an increase in interest rates in the economy would not hurt you. You might even be able to buy up some of your bankrupt competitors at bargain prices — bankruptcies increase dramatically when interest rates rise, primarily because many firms do use too much short-term debt.

Does all this suggest that firms should always avoid short-term debt? Not necessarily. If inflation falls over the next few years, so will interest rates. If you had borrowed on a long-term basis for 6.0 percent in August 1999, your company would be at a major disadvantage if it were locked into 6.0 percent debt while its competitors (who used short-term debt in 1999 and thus rode interest rates down in subsequent years) had a borrowing cost of only 3 or 4 percent.

Financing decisions would be easy if we could make accurate forecasts of future interest rates. Unfortunately, predicting interest rates with consistent accuracy is somewhere between difficult and impossible — people who make a living by selling interest rate forecasts say it is difficult, but many others say it is impossible.

Even if it is difficult to predict future interest rate *levels*, it is easy to predict that interest rates will *fluctuate* — they always have, and they always will. This being the case, sound financial policy calls for using a mix of long- and short-term debt, as well as equity, to position the firm so that it can survive in any interest rate environment. Further, the optimal financial policy depends in an important way on the nature of the firm's assets — the easier it is to sell off assets to generate cash, the more feasible it is to use large amounts of short-term debt. This makes it more feasible for a firm to finance its current assets such as inventories than its fixed assets such as buildings with short-term debt. We will return to this issue later in the book, when we discuss working capital policy.

Changes in interest rates also have implications for savers. For example, if you had a 401(k) plan — and someday you almost certainly will — you would probably want to invest some of your money in a bond mutual fund. You could choose a fund that had an average maturity of 25 years, 20 years, and so on, down to only a few months (a money market fund). How would your choice affect your investment results, hence your retirement income? First, your annual interest income would be affected. For example, if the yield curve were upward sloping, as it normally is, you would earn more interest if you choose a fund that held long-term bonds. Note, though, that if you choose a long-term fund and interest rates then rose, the market value of the bonds in the fund would decline. For example, as we will see in Chapter 8, if you had $100,000 in a fund whose average bond had a maturity of 25 years and a coupon rate of 6 percent, and if interest rates then rose from 6 percent to 10 percent, the market value of your fund would decline from $100,000 to about $64,000. On the other hand, if rates declined, your fund would increase in value. In any event, your choice of maturity would have a major effect on your investment performance, hence your future income.

If short-term interest rates are lower than long-term rates, why might a borrower still choose to finance with long-term debt?

Explain the following statement: "The optimal financial policy depends in an important way on the nature of the firm's assets."

TYING IT ALL TOGETHER

In this chapter, we discussed the nature of financial markets, the types of institutions that operate in these markets, how interest rates are determined, and some of the ways interest rates affect business decisions. In later chapters we will use this information to help value different investments, and to better understand corporate financing and investing decisions. The key concepts covered are listed below:

- There are many different types of **financial markets.** Each market serves a different region or deals with a different type of security.
- **Physical asset markets,** also called tangible or real asset markets, are those for such products as wheat, autos, and real estate.
- **Financial asset markets** deal with stocks, bonds, notes, mortgages, and other claims on real assets.
- **Spot markets** and **futures markets** are terms that refer to whether the assets are bought or sold for "on-the-spot" delivery or for delivery at some future date.
- **Money markets** are the markets for debt securities with maturities of less than one year.
- **Capital markets** are the markets for long-term debt and corporate stocks.
- **Primary markets** are the markets in which corporations raise new capital.
- **Secondary markets** are markets in which existing, already outstanding, securities are traded among investors.
- A **derivative** is a security whose value is derived from the price of some other "underlying" asset.
- Transfers of capital between borrowers and savers take place (1) by **direct transfers** of money and securities; (2) by transfers through **investment banking houses,** which act as middlemen; and (3) by transfers through **financial intermediaries,** which create new securities.
- Among the major classes of intermediaries are **commercial banks, savings and loan associations, mutual savings banks, credit unions, pension funds, life insurance companies,** and **mutual funds.**

- One result of ongoing regulatory changes has been a blurring of the distinctions between the different financial institutions. The trend in the United States has been toward **financial service corporations** that offer a wide range of financial services, including investment banking, brokerage operations, insurance, and commercial banking.

- The **stock market** is an especially important market because this is where stock prices (which are used to "grade" managers' performances) are established.

- There are two basic types of stock markets — the **physical location exchanges** (like the NYSE) and the **electronic dealer-based markets** (that include the Nasdaq and the over-the-counter market).

- Capital is allocated through the price system — a price must be paid to "rent" money. Lenders charge **interest** on funds they lend, while equity investors receive **dividends and capital gains** in return for letting firms use their money.

- Four fundamental factors affect the cost of money: (1) **production opportunities**, (2) **time preferences for consumption**, (3) **risk**, and (4) **inflation**.

- The **risk-free rate of interest, k_{RF},** is defined as the real risk-free rate, k^*, plus an inflation premium, IP, hence $k_{RF} = k^* + IP$.

- The **nominal** (or **quoted**) **interest rate** on a debt security, **k,** is composed of the real risk-free rate, k^*, plus premiums that reflect inflation (IP), default risk (DRP), liquidity (LP), and maturity risk (MRP):

$$k = k^* + IP + DRP + LP + MRP.$$

- If the **real risk-free rate of interest and the various premiums were constant over time,** interest rates would be stable. However, both the real rate and the premiums — especially the premium for expected inflation — **do change over time, causing market interest rates to change.** Also, Federal Reserve intervention to increase or decrease the money supply, as well as international currency flows, leads to fluctuations in interest rates.

- The relationship between the yields on securities and the securities' maturities is known as the **term structure of interest rates,** and the **yield curve** is a graph of this relationship.

- The shape of the yield curve depends on two key factors: (1) **expectations about future inflation** and (2) **perceptions about the relative riskiness of securities with different maturities.**

- The yield curve is normally **upward sloping** — this is called a **normal yield curve.** However, the curve can slope downward (an **inverted yield curve**) if the inflation rate is expected to decline. The yield curve can also be **humped,** which means that interest rates on medium-term maturities are higher than rates on both short- and long-term maturities.

- Because interest rate levels are difficult if not impossible to predict, **sound financial policy** calls for using a mix of short- and long-term debt, and also for positioning the firm to survive in any future interest rate environment.

QUESTIONS

5-1 What are financial intermediaries, and what economic functions do they perform?

5-2 Suppose interest rates on residential mortgages of equal risk were 7 percent in California and 9 percent in New York. Could this differential persist? What forces might tend to equalize rates? Would differentials in borrowing costs for businesses of equal risk located in California and New York be more or less likely to exist than differentials in residential mortgage rates? Would differentials in the cost of money for New York and California firms be more likely to exist if the firms being compared were very large or if they were very small? What are the implications of all this for the pressure now being put on Congress to permit banks to engage in nationwide branching?

5-3 What would happen to the standard of living in the United States if people lost faith in the safety of our financial institutions? Why?

5-4 How does a cost-efficient capital market help to reduce the prices of goods and services?

5-5 Which fluctuate more, long-term or short-term interest rates? Why?

5-6 Suppose you believe that the economy is just entering a recession. Your firm must raise capital immediately, and debt will be used. Should you borrow on a long-term or a short-term basis? Why?

5-7 Suppose the population of Area Y is relatively young while that of Area O is relatively old, but everything else about the two areas is equal.
   a. Would interest rates likely be the same or different in the two areas? Explain.
   b. Would a trend toward nationwide branching by banks and savings and loans, and the development of nationwide diversified financial corporations, affect your answer to part a?

5-8 Suppose a new process was developed that could be used to make oil out of seawater. The equipment required is quite expensive, but it would, in time, lead to very low prices for gasoline, electricity, and other types of energy. What effect would this have on interest rates?

5-9 Suppose a new and much more liberal Congress and administration were elected, and their first order of business was to take away the independence of the Federal Reserve System, and to force the Fed to greatly expand the money supply. What effect would this have
   a. On the level and slope of the yield curve immediately after the announcement?
   b. On the level and slope of the yield curve that would exist two or three years in the future?

5-10 It is a fact that the federal government (1) encouraged the development of the savings and loan industry; (2) virtually forced the industry to make long-term, fixed-interest-rate mortgages; and (3) forced the savings and loans to obtain most of their capital as deposits that were withdrawable on demand.
   a. Would the savings and loans have higher profits in a world with a "normal" or an inverted yield curve?
   b. Would the savings and loan industry be better off if the individual institutions sold their mortgages to federal agencies and then collected servicing fees or if the institutions held the mortgages that they originated?

5-11 Suppose interest rates on Treasury bonds rose from 7 to 14 percent as a result of higher interest rates in Europe. What effect would this have on the price of an average company's common stock?

5-12 What does it mean when it is said that the United States is running a trade deficit? What impact will a trade deficit have on interest rates?

5-13 What are the two leading stock exchanges in the United States today?

5-14 Differentiate between dealer markets and stock markets that have a physical location.

SELF-TEST PROBLEMS   (SOLUTIONS APPEAR IN APPENDIX B)

ST-1
Key terms
Define each of the following terms:
   a. Money market; capital market
   b. Primary market; secondary market; initial public offering (IPO) market
   c. Private markets; public markets
   d. Spot market; futures market

e. Derivatives
f. Investment banking house; financial service corporation
g. Financial intermediary
h. Mutual fund; money market fund
 i. Physical location exchanges; dealer market; over-the-counter market
 j. Production opportunities; time preferences for consumption; risk; inflation
k. Real risk-free rate of interest, k*; nominal (quoted) risk-free rate of interest, k_{RF}
 l. Inflation premium (IP)
m. Default risk premium (DRP)
n. Liquidity; liquidity premium (LP)
o. Interest rate risk; maturity risk premium (MRP)
p. Reinvestment rate risk; country risk
q. Term structure of interest rates; yield curve
 r. "Normal" yield curve; inverted ("abnormal") yield curve; humped yield curve
s. Expectations theory
 t. Foreign trade deficit; exchange rate risk

ST-2
Inflation rates

Assume that it is January 1, 2002. The rate of inflation is expected to be 4 percent throughout 2002. However, increased government deficits and renewed vigor in the economy are then expected to push inflation rates higher. Investors expect the inflation rate to be 5 percent in 2003, 6 percent in 2004, and 7 percent in 2005. The real risk-free rate, k*, is expected to remain at 2 percent over the next 5 years. Assume that no maturity risk premiums are required on bonds with 5 years or less to maturity. The current interest rate on 5-year T-bonds is 8 percent.
a. What is the average expected inflation rate over the next 4 years?
b. What should be the prevailing interest rate on 4-year T-bonds?
c. What is the implied expected inflation rate in 2006, or Year 5, given that Treasury bonds which mature in that year yield 8 percent?

STARTER PROBLEMS

5-1
Expected rate of interest

The real risk-free rate of interest is 3 percent. Inflation is expected to be 2 percent this year and 4 percent during the next 2 years. Assume that the maturity risk premium is zero. What is the yield on 2-year Treasury securities? What is the yield on 3-year Treasury securities?

5-2
Default risk premium

A Treasury bond that matures in 10 years has a yield of 6 percent. A 10-year corporate bond has a yield of 8 percent. Assume that the liquidity premium on the corporate bond is 0.5 percent. What is the default risk premium on the corporate bond?

5-3
Expected rate of interest

One-year Treasury securities yield 5 percent. The market anticipates that 1 year from now, 1-year Treasury securities will yield 6 percent. If the pure expectations theory is correct, what should be the yield today for 2-year Treasury securities?

5-4
Maturity risk premium

The real risk-free rate is 3 percent, and inflation is expected to be 3 percent for the next 2 years. A 2-year Treasury security yields 6.2 percent. What is the maturity risk premium for the 2-year security?

EXAM-TYPE PROBLEMS

The problems included in this section are set up in such a way that they could be used as multiple-choice exam problems.

5-5
Expected rate of interest

Interest rates on 1-year Treasury securities are currently 5.6 percent, while 2-year Treasury securities are yielding 6 percent. If the pure expectations theory is correct, what does the market believe will be the yield on 1-year securities 1 year from now?

5-6
Expected rate of interest

Interest rates on 4-year Treasury securities are currently 7 percent, while interest rates on 6-year Treasury securities are currently 7.5 percent. If the pure expectations theory is correct, what does the market believe that 2-year securities will be yielding 4 years from now?

5-7
Expected rate of interest

The real risk-free rate is 3 percent. Inflation is expected to be 3 percent this year, 4 percent next year, and then 3.5 percent thereafter. The maturity risk premium is estimated to be $0.0005 \times (t - 1)$, where t = number of years to maturity. What is the nominal interest rate on a 7-year Treasury note?

5-8
Expected rate of interest

Suppose the annual yield on a 2-year Treasury bond is 4.5 percent, while that on a 1-year bond is 3 percent. k* is 1 percent, and the maturity risk premium is zero.
  a. Using the expectations theory, forecast the interest rate on a 1-year bond during the second year. (Hint: Under the expectations theory, the yield on a 2-year bond is equal to the average yield on 1-year bonds in Years 1 and 2.)
  b. What is the expected inflation rate in Year 1? Year 2?

5-9
Expected rate of interest

Assume that the real risk-free rate is 2 percent and that the maturity risk premium is zero. If the nominal rate of interest on 1-year bonds is 5 percent and that on comparable-risk 2-year bonds is 7 percent, what is the 1-year interest rate that is expected for Year 2? What inflation rate is expected during Year 2? Comment on why the average interest rate during the 2-year period differs from the 1-year interest rate expected for Year 2.

5-10
Maturity risk premium

Assume that the real risk-free rate, k*, is 3 percent and that inflation is expected to be 8 percent in Year 1, 5 percent in Year 2, and 4 percent thereafter. Assume also that all Treasury bonds are highly liquid and free of default risk. If 2-year and 5-year Treasury bonds both yield 10 percent, what is the difference in the maturity risk premiums (MRPs) on the two bonds; that is, what is MRP_5 minus MRP_2?

5-11
Interest rates

Due to a recession, the inflation rate expected for the coming year is only 3 percent. However, the inflation rate in Year 2 and thereafter is expected to be constant at some level above 3 percent. Assume that the real risk-free rate is k* = 2% for all maturities and that the expectations theory fully explains the yield curve, so there are no maturity risk premiums. If 3-year Treasury bonds yield 2 percentage points more than 1-year bonds, what inflation rate is expected after Year 1?

PROBLEMS

5-12
Yield curves

Suppose you and most other investors expect the inflation rate to be 7 percent next year, to fall to 5 percent during the following year, and then to remain at a rate of 3 percent thereafter. Assume that the real risk-free rate, k*, will remain at 2 percent and that maturity risk premiums on Treasury securities rise from zero on very short-term bonds (those that mature in a few days) to a level of 0.2 percentage point for 1-year securities. Furthermore, maturity risk premiums increase 0.2 percentage point for each year to maturity, up to a limit of 1.0 percentage point on 5-year or longer-term T-bonds.
  a. Calculate the interest rate on 1-, 2-, 3-, 4-, 5-, 10-, and 20-year Treasury securities, and plot the yield curve.
  b. Now suppose Exxon Mobil, an AAA-rated company, had bonds with the same maturities as the Treasury bonds. As an approximation, plot an Exxon Mobil yield curve on the same graph with the Treasury bond yield curve. (Hint: Think about the default risk premium on Exxon Mobil's long-term versus its short-term bonds.)
  c. Now plot the approximate yield curve of Long Island Lighting Company, a risky nuclear utility.

5-13
Yield curves

The following yields on U.S. Treasury securities were taken from *The Wall Street Journal* in September 1999:

TERM	RATE
6 months	5.1%
1 year	5.5
2 years	5.6
3 years	5.7
4 years	5.8
5 years	6.0
10 years	6.1
20 years	6.5
30 years	6.3

Plot a yield curve based on these data.

5-14
Inflation and interest rates

In late 1980, the U.S. Commerce Department released new figures that showed that inflation was running at an annual rate of close to 15 percent. At the time, the prime rate of interest was 21 percent, a record high. However, many investors expected the new Reagan administration to be more effective in controlling inflation than the Carter administration had been. Moreover, many observers believed that the extremely high interest rates and generally tight credit, which resulted from the Federal Reserve System's attempts to curb the inflation rate, would shortly bring about a recession, which, in turn, would lead to a decline in the inflation rate and also in the interest rate. Assume that at the beginning of 1981, the expected inflation rate for 1981 was 13 percent; for 1982, 9 percent; for 1983, 7 percent; and for 1984 and thereafter, 6 percent.

a. What was the average expected inflation rate over the 5-year period 1981–1985? (Use the arithmetic average.)

b. What average *nominal* interest rate would, over the 5-year period, be expected to produce a 2 percent real risk-free rate of return on 5-year Treasury securities?

c. Assuming a real risk-free rate of 2 percent and a maturity risk premium that starts at 0.1 percent and increases by 0.1 percent each year, estimate the interest rate in January 1981 on bonds that mature in 1, 2, 5, 10, and 20 years, and draw a yield curve based on these data.

d. Describe the general economic conditions that could be expected to produce an upward-sloping yield curve.

e. If the consensus among investors in early 1981 had been that the expected inflation rate for every future year was 10 percent (that is, $I_t = I_{t+1} = 10\%$ for t = 1 to ∞), what do you think the yield curve would have looked like? Consider all the factors that are likely to affect the curve. Does your answer here make you question the yield curve you drew in part c?

SPREADSHEET PROBLEM

5-15
Analyzing interest rates

a. Suppose you are considering two possible investment opportunities: a 12-year Treasury bond and a 7-year, A-rated corporate bond. The current real risk-free rate is 4 percent, and inflation is expected to be 2 percent for the next two years, 3 percent for the following four years, and 4 percent thereafter. The maturity risk premium is estimated by this formula: MRP = 0.1%(t − 1). The liquidity premium for the corporate bond is estimated to be 0.7 percent. Finally, you may determine the default risk premium, given the company's bond rating, from the default risk premium table in the text. What yield would you predict for each of these two investments?

b. Given the following Treasury bond yield information from the September 27, 1999, *Wall Street Journal*, construct a graph of the yield curve as of that date.

MATURITY	YIELD
1 year	5.37%
2 years	5.47
3 years	5.65
4 years	5.71
5 years	5.64
10 years	5.75
20 years	6.33
30 years	5.94

c. Based on the information about the corporate bond that was given in part a, calculate yields and then construct a new yield curve graph that shows both the Treasury and the corporate bonds.

d. Using the Treasury yield information above, calculate the following forward rates:
(1) The 1-year rate, 1 year from now.
(2) The 5-year rate, 5 years from now.
(3) The 10-year rate, 10 years from now.
(4) The 10-year rate, 20 years from now.

The information related to the cyberproblems is likely to change over time, due to the release of new information and the ever-changing nature of the World Wide Web. With these changes in mind, we will periodically update these problems on the textbook's web site. To avoid problems, please check for these updates before proceeding with the cyberproblems.

5-16
Financial environment

The yield curve is a graph of the term structure of interest rates, which is the relationship of yield and maturity for securities of similar risk. When we think of the yield curve we typically think of the Treasury yield curve as found each day in financial publications such as *The Wall Street Journal.* The yield curve changes in both level and shape due to a variety of monetary, economic, and political factors that were discussed in Chapter 5. The Federal Reserve is a useful site for obtaining actual economic and monetary data. Along with other data, you can obtain historical interest rates at this site to construct a yield curve and analyze changes in interest rates.

To access information from the Federal Reserve, you will be using FRED (the Federal Reserve Economic Database). First, you must connect to the Federal Reserve Bank of St. Louis web site, which can be found at **www.stls.frb.org.** From this web page, click on data (near the bottom of the screen), and then select monthly interest rates from the list of database categories. On this page, you will find links to all of the information needed for this cyberproblem.

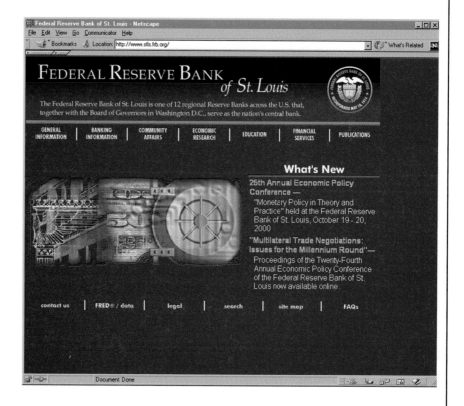

a. Construct four distinct Treasury yield curves using monthly interest rate data for February 1982, 1988, 1993, and 1998. Use the constant maturity interest rates for maturities of 3 months, 6 months, 1 year, 5 years, 10 years, and 30 years.
b. Examine the yield curves you have constructed. What could explain the large variation in the 3-month, risk-free rate over the different time periods?

c. (1) Contrast the slope of the February 1982 yield curve with that of February 1993. What do we call a yield curve that has the same shape as the 1982 yield curve? (2) Why might the 1982 yield curve be downward sloping? What does this indicate? (3) What does the 1993 yield curve illustrate about long-term versus short-term interest rates?

d. Contrast the yield curves of 1993 and 1998. Note that the 1998 yield curve is almost flat, while the 1993 yield curve has a very steep slope. What could account for this difference in slopes?

e. Pretend that you are an investor back in 1988, and you have no knowledge of future interest rates, except the information given in the yield curve. Use the 1988 yield curve to determine the expected yield on 5-year Treasury bonds five years from 1988 (or the 5-year bond rate in 1993). Then, compare that figure to the actual 5-year bond rate in 1993. Did investors under- or overestimate future inflation in 1988?

INTEGRATED CASE

SMYTH BARRY & COMPANY

5-17 Financial Markets, Institutions, and Interest Rates
Assume that you recently graduated with a degree in finance and have just reported to work as an investment advisor at the brokerage firm of Smyth Barry & Co. Your first assignment is to explain the nature of the U.S. financial markets to Michelle Varga, a professional tennis player who has just come to the United States from Mexico. Varga is a highly ranked tennis player who expects to invest substantial amounts of money through Smyth Barry. She is also very bright, and, therefore, she would like to understand in general terms what will happen to her money. Your boss has developed the following set of questions that you must ask and answer to explain the U.S. financial system to Varga.

a. What is a market? Differentiate between the following types of markets: physical asset vs. financial markets, spot vs. futures markets, money vs. capital markets, primary vs. secondary markets, and public vs. private markets.

b. What is an initial public offering (IPO) market?

c. If Apple Computer decided to issue additional common stock, and Varga purchased 100 shares of this stock from Merrill Lynch, the underwriter, would this transaction be a primary market transaction or a secondary market transaction? Would it make a difference if Varga purchased previously outstanding Apple stock in the dealer market?

d. Describe the three primary ways in which capital is transferred between savers and borrowers.

e. What are the two leading stock markets? Describe the two basic types of stock markets.

f. What do we call the price that a borrower must pay for debt capital? What is the price of equity capital? What are the four most fundamental factors that affect the cost

of money, or the general level of interest rates, in the economy?

g. What is the real risk-free rate of interest (k^*) and the nominal risk-free rate (k_{RF})? How are these two rates measured?

h. Define the terms inflation premium (IP), default risk premium (DRP), liquidity premium (LP), and maturity risk premium (MRP). Which of these premiums is included when determining the interest rate on (1) short-term U.S. Treasury securities, (2) long-term U.S. Treasury securities, (3) short-term corporate securities, and (4) long-term corporate securities? Explain how the premiums would vary over time and among the different securities listed above.

i. What is the term structure of interest rates? What is a yield curve?

j. Suppose most investors expect the inflation rate to be 5 percent next year, 6 percent the following year, and 8 percent thereafter. The real risk-free rate is 3 percent. The maturity risk premium is zero for bonds that mature in 1 year or less, 0.1 percent for 2-year bonds, and then the MRP increases by 0.1 percent per year thereafter for 20 years, after which it is stable. What is the interest rate on 1-year, 10-year, and 20-year Treasury bonds? Draw a yield curve with these data. What factors can explain why this constructed yield curve is upward sloping?

k. At any given time, how would the yield curve facing an AAA-rated company compare with the yield curve for U.S. Treasury securities? At any given time, how would the yield curve facing a BB-rated company compare with the yield curve for U.S. Treasury securities? Draw a graph to illustrate your answer.

l. What is the pure expectations theory? What does the pure expectations theory imply about the term structure of interest rates?

m. Suppose that you observe the following term structure for Treasury securities:

MATURITY	YIELD
1 year	6.0%
2 years	6.2
3 years	6.4
4 years	6.5
5 years	6.5

Assume that the pure expectations theory of the term structure is correct. (This implies that you can use the yield curve given above to "back out" the market's expectations about future interest rates.) What does the market expect will be the interest rate on 1-year securities one year from now? What does the market expect will be the interest rate on 3-year securities two years from now?

n. Finally, Varga is also interested in investing in countries other than the United States. Describe the various types of risks that arise when investing overseas.

PART **II**

FUNDAMENTAL CONCEPTS IN FINANCIAL MANAGEMENT

CHAPTER 6 Risk and Rates of Return

SOURCE: Beard, William Holbrook (1823–1900). New York Historical Society/The Bridgeman Art Library International, Ltd.

$

I f someone had invested $1,000 in a portfolio of large-company stocks in 1925 and then reinvested all dividends received, his or her investment would have grown to $2,845,697 by 1999. Over the same time period, a portfolio of small-company stocks would have grown even more, to $6,641,505. But if instead he or she had invested in long-term government bonds, the $1,000 would have grown to only $40,219, and to a measly $15,642 for short-term bonds.

Given these numbers, why would anyone invest in bonds? The answer is, "Because bonds are less risky." While common stocks have over the past 74 years produced considerably higher returns, (1) we cannot be sure that the past is a prologue to the future, and (2) stock values are more likely to experience sharp declines than bonds, so one has a greater chance of losing money on a stock investment. For example, in 1990 the average small-company stock lost 21.6 percent of its value, and large-company stocks also suffered losses. Bonds, though, provided positive returns that year, as they almost always do.

Of course, some stocks are riskier than others, and even in years when the overall stock market goes up, many individual stocks go down. Therefore, putting all your money into one stock is extremely risky. According to a *Business Week* article, the single best weapon against risk is diversification: "By spreading your money around, you're not tied to the fickleness of a given market, stock, or industry. . . . Correlation, in portfolio-manager speak, helps you diversify properly because it describes how closely two investments track each other. If they move in tandem, they're likely to suffer from the same bad news. So, you should combine assets with low correlations."

U.S. investors tend to think of "the stock market" as the U.S. stock market. However, U.S. stocks amount to only 35 percent of the value of all stocks. Foreign markets have been quite profitable, and they are not perfectly correlated with U.S. markets. Therefore, global diversification offers U.S. investors an opportunity to raise returns and at the same time reduce risk. However, foreign investing brings some risks of its own, most notably "exchange rate risk," which is the danger that exchange rate shifts will decrease the number of dollars a foreign currency will buy.

Although the central thrust of the *Business Week* article was on ways to measure and then reduce risk, it did point out that some recently created instruments that are actually extremely risky have been marketed as low-risk investments to naive investors. For example, several mutual funds have advertised that their portfolios "contain only securities backed by the U.S. government" but then failed to highlight that the funds themselves are using financial leverage, are investing in "derivatives," or are taking some other action that boosts current yields but exposes investors to huge risks.

When you finish this chapter, you should understand what risk is, how it is measured, and what actions can be taken to minimize it, or at least to ensure that you are adequately compensated for bearing it. ■

SOURCES: "Figuring Risk: It's Not So Scary," *Business Week,* November 1, 1993, 154–155; "T-Bill Trauma and the Meaning of Risk," *The Wall Street Journal,* February 12, 1993, C1; and *Stocks, Bonds, Bills, and Inflation: (Valuation Edition) 2000 Yearbook* (Chicago: Ibbotson Associates, 2000).

PUTTING THINGS IN PERSPECTIVE

In this chapter, we start from the basic premise that investors like returns and dislike risk. Therefore, people will invest in risky assets only if they expect to receive higher returns. We define precisely what the term *risk* means as it relates to investments, we examine procedures managers use to measure risk, and we discuss the relationship between risk and return. Then, in Chapters 7, 8, and 9, we extend these relationships to show how risk and return interact to determine security prices. Managers must understand these concepts and think about them as they plan the actions that will shape their firms' futures.

As you will see, risk can be measured in different ways, and different conclusions about an asset's riskiness can be reached depending on the measure used. Risk analysis can be confusing, but it will help if you remember the following:

1. All financial assets are expected to produce *cash flows,* and the riskiness of an asset is judged in terms of the riskiness of its cash flows.

2. The riskiness of an asset can be considered in two ways: (1) on a *stand-alone basis,* where the asset's cash flows are analyzed by themselves, or (2) in a *portfolio context,* where the cash flows from a number of assets are combined, and then the consolidated cash flows are analyzed.[1] There is an important difference between stand-alone and portfolio risk, and an asset that has a great deal of risk if held by itself may be much less risky if it is held as part of a larger portfolio.

3. In a portfolio context, an asset's risk can be divided into two components: (a) *diversifiable risk,* which can be diversified away and thus is of little con-

---

[1] A *portfolio* is a collection of investment securities. If you owned some General Motors stock, some Exxon Mobil stock, and some IBM stock, you would be holding a three-stock portfolio. Because diversification lowers risk, most stocks are held in portfolios.

cern to diversified investors, and (b) *market risk*, which reflects the risk of a general stock market decline and which cannot be eliminated by diversification, hence *does* concern investors. Only market risk is *relevant* — diversifiable risk is *irrelevant* to rational investors because it can be eliminated.

4. An asset with a high degree of relevant (market) risk must provide a relatively high expected rate of return to attract investors. Investors in general are *averse to risk,* so they will not buy risky assets unless those assets have high expected returns.

5. In this chapter, we focus on *financial assets* such as stocks and bonds, but the concepts discussed here also apply to *physical assets* such as computers, trucks, or even whole plants. ∎

INVESTMENT RETURNS

With most investments, an individual or business spends money today with the expectation of earning even more money in the future. The concept of *return* provides investors with a convenient way of expressing the financial performance of an investment. To illustrate, suppose you buy 10 shares of a stock for $1,000. The stock pays no dividends, but at the end of one year, you sell the stock for $1,100. What is the return on your $1,000 investment?

One way of expressing an investment return is in *dollar terms.* The dollar return is simply the total dollars received from the investment less the amount invested:

$$\text{Dollar return} = \text{Amount received} - \text{Amount invested}$$
$$= \$1,100 - \$1,000$$
$$= \$100.$$

If at the end of the year you had sold the stock for only $900, your dollar return would have been −$100.

Although expressing returns in dollars is easy, two problems arise: (1) To make a meaningful judgment about the return, you need to know the scale (size) of the investment; a $100 return on a $100 investment is a good return (assuming the investment is held for one year), but a $100 return on a $10,000 investment would be a poor return. (2) You also need to know the timing of the return; a $100 return on a $100 investment is a very good return if it occurs after one year, but the same dollar return after 20 years would not be very good.

The solution to the scale and timing problems is to express investment results as *rates of return*, or *percentage returns*. For example, the rate of return on the 1-year stock investment, when $1,100 is received after one year, is 10 percent:

$$\text{Rate of return} = \frac{\text{Amount received} - \text{Amount invested}}{\text{Amount invested}}$$
$$= \frac{\text{Dollar return}}{\text{Amount invested}} = \frac{\$100}{\$1,000}$$
$$= 0.10 = 10\%.$$

The rate of return calculation "standardizes" the return by considering the return per unit of investment. In this example, the return of 0.10, or 10 percent, indicates that each dollar invested will earn 0.10($1.00) = $0.10. If the rate of return had been negative, this would indicate that the original investment was not even recovered. For example, selling the stock for only $900 results in a −10 percent rate of return, which means that each dollar invested lost 10 cents.

Note also that a $10 return on a $100 investment produces a 10 percent rate of return, while a $10 return on a $1,000 investment results in a rate of return of only 1 percent. Thus, the percentage return takes account of the size of the investment.

Expressing rates of return on an annual basis, which is typically done in practice, solves the timing problem. A $10 return after one year on a $100 investment results in a 10 percent annual rate of return, while a $10 return after five years yields only a 1.9 percent annual rate of return. We will discuss all this in detail in Chapter 7, which deals with the time value of money.

Although we illustrated return concepts with one outflow and one inflow, in later chapters we demonstrate that rate of return concepts can easily be applied in situations where multiple cash flows occur over time. For example, when Intel makes an investment in new chip-making technology, the investment is made over several years and the resulting inflows occur over even more years. For now, it is sufficient to recognize that the rate of return solves the two major problems associated with dollar returns, size and timing. Therefore, the rate of return is the most common measure of investment performance.

> **SELF-TEST QUESTIONS**
>
> Differentiate between dollar return and rate of return.
>
> Why is the rate of return superior to the dollar return in terms of accounting for the size of investment and the timing of cash flows?

STAND-ALONE RISK

Risk
The chance that some unfavorable event will occur.

Risk is defined in *Webster's* as "a hazard; a peril; exposure to loss or injury." Thus, risk refers to the chance that some unfavorable event will occur. If you engage in skydiving, you are taking a chance with your life — skydiving is risky. If you bet on the horses, you are risking your money. If you invest in speculative stocks (or, really, *any* stock), you are taking a risk in the hope of making an appreciable return.

An asset's risk can be analyzed in two ways: (1) on a stand-alone basis, where the asset is considered in isolation, and (2) on a portfolio basis, where the asset is held as one of a number of assets in a portfolio. Thus, an asset's **stand-alone risk** is the risk an investor would face if he or she held only this one asset. Obviously, most assets are held in portfolios, but it is necessary to understand stand-alone risk in order to understand risk in a portfolio context.

Stand-Alone Risk
The risk an investor would face if he or she held only one asset.

To illustrate the riskiness of financial assets, suppose an investor buys $100,000 of short-term Treasury bills with an expected return of 5 percent. In this case, the rate of return on the investment, 5 percent, can be estimated quite precisely, and the investment is defined as being essentially *risk free*. However, if the $100,000 were invested in the stock of a company just being organized to prospect for oil in the mid-Atlantic, then the investment's return could not be estimated precisely. One might analyze the situation and conclude that the *expected* rate of return, in a statistical sense, is 20 percent, but the investor should also recognize that the *actual* rate of return could range from, say, +1,000 percent to −100 percent. Because there is a significant danger of actually earning much less than the expected return, the stock would be relatively risky.

No investment will be undertaken unless the expected rate of return is high enough to compensate the investor for the perceived risk of the investment. In our example, it is clear that few if any investors would be willing to buy the oil company's stock if its expected return were the same as that of the T-bill.

Risky assets rarely produce their expected rates of return — generally, risky assets earn either more or less than was originally expected. Indeed, if assets always produced their expected returns, they would not be risky. Investment risk, then, is related to the probability of actually earning a low or negative return — the greater the chance of a low or negative return, the riskier the investment. However, risk can be defined more precisely, and we do so in the next section.

PROBABILITY DISTRIBUTIONS

An event's *probability* is defined as the chance that the event will occur. For example, a weather forecaster might state, "There is a 40 percent chance of rain today and a 60 percent chance that it will not rain." If all possible events, or outcomes, are listed, and if a probability is assigned to each event, the listing is called a **probability distribution.** For our weather forecast, we could set up the following probability distribution:

Probability Distribution
A listing of all possible outcomes, or events, with a probability (chance of occurrence) assigned to each outcome.

OUTCOME (1)	PROBABILITY (2)	
Rain	0.4 =	40%
No rain	0.6 =	60
	1.0 =	100%

The possible outcomes are listed in Column 1, while the probabilities of these outcomes, expressed both as decimals and as percentages, are given in Column 2. Notice that the probabilities must sum to 1.0, or 100 percent.

Probabilities can also be assigned to the possible outcomes (or returns) from an investment. If you buy a bond, you expect to receive interest on the bond plus a return of your original investment, and those payments will provide you with a rate of return on your investment. The possible outcomes from this investment are (1) that the issuer will make the required payments or (2) that the issuer will default on the payments. The higher the probability of default, the riskier the bond, and the higher the risk, the higher the required rate of return. If you invest in a stock instead of buying a bond, you will again expect to earn a return on your money. A stock's return will come from dividends plus capital gains. Again, the riskier the stock — which means the higher the probability that the firm will fail to perform as you expected — the higher the expected return must be to induce you to invest in the stock.

With this in mind, consider the possible rates of return (dividend yield plus capital gain or loss) that you might earn next year on a $10,000 investment in the stock of either Martin Products Inc. or U.S. Water Company. Martin man-

DEMAND FOR THE COMPANY'S PRODUCTS	PROBABILITY OF THIS DEMAND OCCURRING	RATE OF RETURN ON STOCK IF THIS DEMAND OCCURS	
		MARTIN PRODUCTS	U.S. WATER
Strong	0.3	100%	20%
Normal	0.4	15	15
Weak	0.3	(70)	10
	1.0		

ufactures and distributes computer terminals and equipment for the rapidly growing data transmission industry. Because it faces intense competition, its new products may or may not be competitive in the marketplace, so its future earnings cannot be predicted very well. Indeed, some new company could develop better products and literally bankrupt Martin. U.S. Water, on the other hand, supplies an essential service, and because it has city franchises that protect it from competition, its sales and profits are relatively stable and predictable.

The rate-of-return probability distributions for the two companies are shown in Table 6-1. There is a 30 percent chance of strong demand, in which case both companies will have high earnings, pay high dividends, and enjoy capital gains. There is a 40 percent probability of normal demand and moderate returns, and there is a 30 percent probability of weak demand, which will mean low earnings and dividends as well as capital losses. Notice, however, that Martin Products' rate of return could vary far more widely than that of U.S. Water. There is a fairly high probability that the value of Martin's stock will drop substantially, resulting in a 70 percent loss, while there is no chance of a loss for U.S. Water.[2]

EXPECTED RATE OF RETURN

Expected Rate of Return, k̂
The rate of return expected to be realized from an investment; the weighted average of the probability distribution of possible results.

If we multiply each possible outcome by its probability of occurrence and then sum these products, as in Table 6-2, we have a *weighted average* of outcomes. The weights are the probabilities, and the weighted average is the **expected rate of return, k̂**, called "k-hat."[3] The expected rates of return for both Martin Products and U.S. Water are shown in Table 6-2 to be 15 percent. This type of table is known as a *payoff matrix*.

---

[2] It is, of course, completely unrealistic to think that any stock has no chance of a loss. Only in hypothetical examples could this occur. To illustrate, the price of Columbia Gas's stock dropped from $34.50 to $20.00 in just three hours a few years ago. All investors were reminded that any stock is exposed to some risk of loss, and those investors who bought Columbia Gas learned that lesson the hard way.

[3] In Chapters 8 and 9, we will use k_d and k_s to signify the returns on bonds and stocks, respectively. However, this distinction is unnecessary in this chapter, so we just use the general term, k, to signify the expected return on an investment.

TABLE 6-2   Calculation of Expected Rates of Return: Payoff Matrix

		MARTIN PRODUCTS		U.S. WATER	
DEMAND FOR THE COMPANY'S PRODUCTS (1)	PROBABILITY OF THIS DEMAND OCCURRING (2)	RATE OF RETURN IF THIS DEMAND OCCURS (3)	PRODUCT: (2) × (3) = (4)	RATE OF RETURN IF THIS DEMAND OCCURS (5)	PRODUCT: (2) × (5) = (6)
Strong	0.3	100%	30%	20%	6%
Normal	0.4	15	6	15	6
Weak	0.3	(70)	(21)	10	3
	1.0		$\hat{k} = 15\%$		$\hat{k} = 15\%$

The expected rate of return calculation can also be expressed as an equation that does the same thing as the payoff matrix table:[4]

$$\text{Expected rate of return} = \hat{k} = P_1 k_1 + P_2 k_2 + \cdots + P_n k_n$$

$$= \sum_{i=1}^{n} P_i k_i. \tag{6-1}$$

Here k_i is the *i*th possible outcome, P_i is the probability of the *i*th outcome, and n is the number of possible outcomes. Thus, $\hat{k}$ is a weighted average of the possible outcomes (the k_i values), with each outcome's weight being its probability of occurrence. Using the data for Martin Products, we obtain its expected rate of return as follows:

$$\hat{k} = P_1(k_1) + P_2(k_2) + P_3(k_3)$$
$$= 0.3(100\%) + 0.4(15\%) + 0.3(-70\%)$$
$$= 15\%.$$

U.S. Water's expected rate of return is also 15 percent:

$$\hat{k} = 0.3(20\%) + 0.4(15\%) + 0.3(10\%)$$
$$= 15\%.$$

We can graph the rates of return to obtain a picture of the variability of possible outcomes; this is shown in the Figure 6-1 bar charts. The height of each bar signifies the probability that a given outcome will occur. The range of probable returns for Martin Products is from −70 to +100 percent, with an expected return of 15 percent. The expected return for U.S. Water is also 15 percent, but its range is much narrower.

Thus far, we have assumed that only three situations can exist: strong, normal, and weak demand. Actually, of course, demand could range from a deep depression to a fantastic boom, and there are an unlimited number of possibilities

---

[4] The second form of the equation is simply a shorthand expression in which sigma (Σ) means "sum up," or add the values of n factors. If i = 1, then $P_i k_i = P_1 k_1$; if i = 2, then $P_i k_i = P_2 k_2$; and so on until i = n, the last possible outcome. The symbol $\sum_{i=1}^{n}$ simply says, "Go through the following process: First, let i = 1 and find the first product; then let i = 2 and find the second product; then continue until each individual product up to i = n has been found, and then add these individual products to find the expected rate of return."

FIGURE 6-1

**Probability Distributions of Martin Products'
and U.S. Water's Rates of Return**

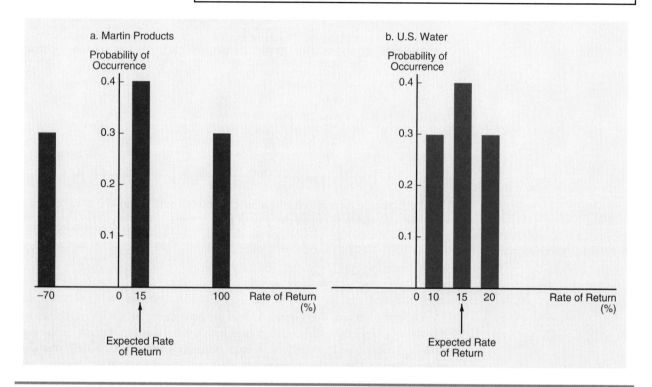

in between. Suppose we had the time and patience to assign a probability to each possible level of demand (with the sum of the probabilities still equaling 1.0) and to assign a rate of return to each stock for each level of demand. We would have a table similar to Table 6-1, except that it would have many more entries in each column. This table could be used to calculate expected rates of return as shown previously, and the probabilities and outcomes could be approximated by continuous curves such as those presented in Figure 6-2. Here we have changed the assumptions so that there is essentially a zero probability that Martin Products' return will be less than −70 percent or more than 100 percent, or that U.S. Water's return will be less than 10 percent or more than 20 percent, but virtually any return within these limits is possible.

The tighter, or more peaked, the probability distribution, the more likely it is that the actual outcome will be close to the expected value, and, consequently, the less likely it is that the actual return will end up far below the expected return. Thus, the tighter the probability distribution, the lower the risk assigned to a stock. Since U.S. Water has a relatively tight probability distribution, its *actual return* is likely to be closer to its 15 percent *expected return* than is that of Martin Products.

MEASURING STAND-ALONE RISK: THE STANDARD DEVIATION

Risk is a difficult concept to grasp, and a great deal of controversy has surrounded attempts to define and measure it. However, a common definition, and one that is satisfactory for many purposes, is stated in terms of probability distri-

FIGURE 6-2

**Continuous Probability Distributions of Martin Products'
and U.S. Water's Rates of Return**

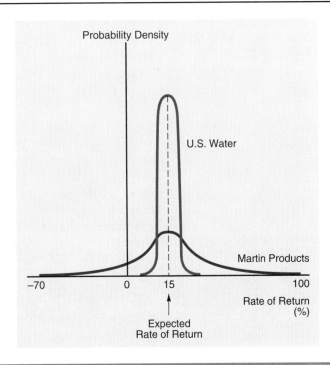

NOTE: The assumptions regarding the probabilities of various outcomes have been changed from those in Figure 6-1. There the probability of obtaining exactly 15 percent was 40 percent; here it is *much smaller* because there are many possible outcomes instead of just three. With continuous distributions, it is more appropriate to ask what the probability is of obtaining at least some specified rate of return than to ask what the probability is of obtaining exactly that rate. This topic is covered in detail in statistics courses.

butions such as those presented in Figure 6-2: *The tighter the probability distribution of expected future returns, the smaller the risk of a given investment.* According to this definition, U.S. Water is less risky than Martin Products because there is a smaller chance that its actual return will end up far below its expected return.

To be most useful, any measure of risk should have a definite value — we need a measure of the tightness of the probability distribution. One such measure is the **standard deviation**, the symbol for which is **σ**, pronounced "sigma." The smaller the standard deviation, the tighter the probability distribution, and, accordingly, the lower the riskiness of the stock. To calculate the standard deviation, we proceed as shown in Table 6-3, taking the following steps:

Standard Deviation, σ
A statistical measure of the variability of a set of observations.

1. Calculate the expected rate of return:

$$\text{Expected rate of return} = \hat{k} = \sum_{i=1}^{n} P_i k_i.$$

For Martin, we previously found $\hat{k} = 15\%$.

2. Subtract the expected rate of return ($\hat{k}$) from each possible outcome (k_i) to obtain a set of deviations about $\hat{k}$ as shown in Column 1 of Table 6-3:

$$\text{Deviation}_i = k_i - \hat{k}.$$

TABLE 6-3

	Calculating Martin Products' Standard Deviation	
$k_i - \hat{k}$ (1)	$(k_i - \hat{k})^2$ (2)	$(k_i - \hat{k})^2 P_i$ (3)
$100 - 15 = 85$	$7{,}225$	$(7{,}225)(0.3) = 2{,}167.5$
$15 - 15 = 0$	0	$(0)(0.4) = 0.0$
$-70 - 15 = -85$	$7{,}225$	$(7{,}225)(0.3) = \underline{2{,}167.5}$
		Variance $= \sigma^2 = \underline{\underline{4{,}335.0}}$

$$\text{Standard deviation} = \sigma = \sqrt{\sigma^2} = \sqrt{4{,}335} = 65.84\%.$$

Variance, σ^2
The square of the standard deviation.

3. Square each deviation, then multiply the result by the probability of occurrence for its related outcome, and then sum these products to obtain the **variance** of the probability distribution as shown in Columns 2 and 3 of the table:

$$\text{Variance} = \sigma^2 = \sum_{i=1}^{n} (k_i - \hat{k})^2 P_i. \tag{6-2}$$

4. Finally, find the square root of the variance to obtain the standard deviation:

$$\text{Standard deviation} = \sigma = \sqrt{\sum_{i=1}^{n} (k_i - \hat{k})^2 P_i}. \tag{6-3}$$

Wilshire Associates provides a download site for various returns series for indexes such as the Wilshire 5000 and the Wilshire 4500 at **http://www.wilshire.com/indexes/wilshire_indexes.htm** in Microsoft Excel™ format.

Thus, the standard deviation is essentially a weighted average of the deviations from the expected value, and it provides an idea of how far above or below the expected value the actual value is likely to be. Martin's standard deviation is seen in Table 6-3 to be $\sigma = 65.84\%$. Using these same procedures, we find U.S. Water's standard deviation to be 3.87 percent. Martin Products has the larger standard deviation, which indicates a greater variation of returns and thus a greater chance that the expected return will not be realized. Therefore, Martin Products is a riskier investment than U.S. Water when held alone.

If a probability distribution is normal, the *actual* return will be within ± 1 standard deviation of the *expected* return 68.26 percent of the time. Figure 6-3 illustrates this point, and it also shows the situation for $\pm 2\sigma$ and $\pm 3\sigma$. For Martin Products, $\hat{k} = 15\%$ and $\sigma = 65.84\%$, whereas $\hat{k} = 15\%$ and $\sigma = 3.87\%$ for U.S. Water. Thus, if the two distributions were normal, there would be a 68.26 percent probability that Martin's actual return would be in the range of 15 ± 65.84 percent, or from -50.84 to 80.84 percent. For U.S. Water, the 68.26 percent range is 15 ± 3.87 percent, or from 11.13 to 18.87 percent. With such a small σ, there is only a small probability that U.S. Water's return would be significantly less than expected, so the stock is not very risky. For the average firm listed on the New York Stock Exchange, σ has generally been in the range of 35 to 40 percent in recent years.[5]

---

[5] In the example, we described the procedure for finding the mean and standard deviation when the data are in the form of a known probability distribution. If only sample returns data over some past period are available, the standard deviation of returns can be estimated using this formula:

(footnote continues)

FIGURE 6-3

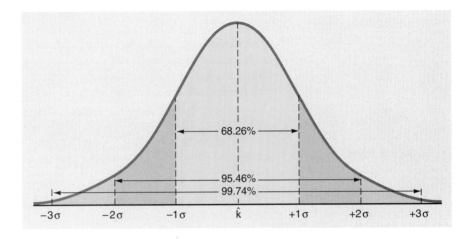

NOTES:
a. The area under the normal curve always equals 1.0, or 100 percent. *Thus, the areas under any pair of normal curves drawn on the same scale, whether they are peaked or flat, must be equal.*
b. Half of the area under a normal curve is to the left of the mean, indicating that there is a 50 percent probability that the actual outcome will be less than the mean, and half is to the right of k, indicating a 50 percent probability that it will be greater than the mean.
c. Of the area under the curve, 68.26 percent is within $\pm 1\sigma$ of the mean, indicating that the probability is 68.26 percent that the actual outcome will be within the range $k - 1\sigma$ to $k + 1\sigma$.
d. Procedures exist for finding the probability of other ranges. These procedures are covered in statistics courses.
e. For a normal distribution, the larger the value of σ, the greater the probability that the actual outcome will vary widely from, and hence perhaps be far below, the expected, or most likely, outcome. *Since the probability of having the actual result turn out to be far below the expected result is one definition of risk, and since σ measures this probability, we can use σ as a measure of risk.* This definition may not be a good one, however, if we are dealing with an asset held in a diversified portfolio. This point is covered later in the chapter.

(Footnote 5 continued)

$$\text{Estimated } \sigma = S = \sqrt{\frac{\sum_{t=1}^{n} (\bar{k}_t - \bar{k}_{Avg})^2}{n - 1}}. \tag{6-3a}$$

Here $\bar{k}_t$ ("k bar t") denotes the past realized rate of return in Period t, and $\bar{k}_{Avg}$ is the average annual return earned during the last n years. Here is an example:

YEAR	$\bar{k}_t$
1999	15%
2000	−5
2001	20

$$\bar{k}_{Avg} = \frac{(15 - 5 + 20)}{3} = 10.0\%.$$

$$\text{Estimated } \sigma \text{ (or S)} = \sqrt{\frac{(15 - 10)^2 + (-5 - 10)^2 + (20 - 10)^2}{3 - 1}}$$

$$= \sqrt{\frac{350}{2}} = 13.2\%.$$

(footnote continues)

MEASURING STAND-ALONE RISK: THE COEFFICIENT OF VARIATION

If a choice has to be made between two investments that have the same expected returns but different standard deviations, most people would choose the one with the lower standard deviation and, therefore, the lower risk. Similarly, given a choice between two investments with the same risk (standard deviation) but different expected returns, investors would generally prefer the investment with the higher expected return. To most people, this is common sense — return is "good," risk is "bad," and, consequently, investors want as much return and as little risk as possible. But how do we choose between two investments if one has the higher expected return but the other the lower standard deviation? To help answer this question, we use another measure of risk, the **coefficient of variation (CV)**, which is the standard deviation divided by the expected return:

Coefficient of Variation (CV)
Standardized measure of the risk per unit of return; calculated as the standard deviation divided by the expected return.

$$\text{Coefficient of variation} = \text{CV} = \frac{\sigma}{\hat{k}}. \qquad (6\text{-}4)$$

The coefficient of variation shows the risk per unit of return, and it provides a more meaningful basis for comparison when the expected returns on two alternatives are not the same. Since U.S. Water and Martin Products have the same expected return, the coefficient of variation is not necessary in this case. The firm with the larger standard deviation, Martin, must have the larger coefficient of variation when the means are equal. In fact, the coefficient of variation for Martin is 65.84/15 = 4.39 and that for U.S. Water is 3.87/15 = 0.26. Thus, Martin is almost 17 times riskier than U.S. Water on the basis of this criterion.

For a case where the coefficient of variation is necessary, consider Projects X and Y in Figure 6-4. These projects have different expected rates of return and different standard deviations. Project X has a 60 percent expected rate of return and a 15 percent standard deviation, while Project Y has an 8 percent expected return but only a 3 percent standard deviation. Is Project X riskier, on a relative basis, because it has the larger standard deviation? If we calculate the coefficients of variation for these two projects, we find that Project X has a coefficient of variation of 15/60 = 0.25, and Project Y has a coefficient of variation of 3/8 = 0.375. Thus, we see that Project Y actually has more risk per unit of return than Project X, in spite of the fact that X's standard deviation is larger. Therefore, even though Project Y has the lower standard deviation, according to the coefficient of variation it is riskier than Project X.

Project Y has the smaller standard deviation, hence the more peaked probability distribution, but it is clear from the graph that the chances of a really low

---

(Footnote 5 continued)

The historical σ is often used as an estimate of the future σ. Much less often, and generally incorrectly, $\bar{k}_{Avg}$ for some past period is used as an estimate of k, the expected future return. Because past variability is likely to be repeated, σ may be a good estimate of future risk, but it is much less reasonable to expect that the past *level* of return (which could have been as high as +100% or as low as −50%) is the best expectation of what investors think will happen in the future.

Equation 6-3a is built into all financial calculators, and it is very easy to use. We simply enter the rates of return and press the key marked S (or S_x) to get the standard deviation. Note, though, that calculators have no built-in formula for finding σ where probabilistic data are involved; there you must go through the process outlined in Table 6-3 and Equation 6-3. The same situation holds for computer spreadsheet programs.

FIGURE 6-4

Comparison of Probability Distributions and Rates of Return for Projects X and Y

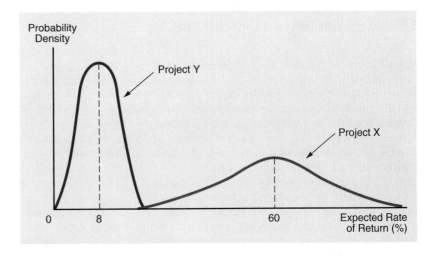

return are higher for Y than for X because X's expected return is so high. Because the coefficient of variation captures the effects of both risk and return, it is a better measure for evaluating risk in situations where investments have substantially different expected returns.

RISK AVERSION AND REQUIRED RETURNS

Suppose you have worked hard and saved $1 million, which you now plan to invest. You can buy a 5 percent U.S. Treasury note, and at the end of one year you will have a sure $1.05 million, which is your original investment plus $50,000 in interest. Alternatively, you can buy stock in R&D Enterprises. If R&D's research programs are successful, your stock will increase in value to $2.1 million. However, if the research is a failure, the value of your stock will go to zero, and you will be penniless. You regard R&D's chances of success or failure as being 50-50, so the expected value of the stock investment is 0.5($0) + 0.5($2,100,000) = $1,050,000. Subtracting the $1 million cost of the stock leaves an expected profit of $50,000, or an expected (but risky) 5 percent rate of return:

$$\text{Expected rate of return} = \frac{\text{Expected ending value} - \text{Cost}}{\text{Cost}}$$

$$= \frac{\$1,050,000 - \$1,000,000}{\$1,000,000}$$

$$= \frac{\$50,000}{\$1,000,000} = 5\%.$$

Thus, you have a choice between a sure $50,000 profit (representing a 5 percent rate of return) on the Treasury note and a risky expected $50,000 profit (also representing a 5 percent expected rate of return) on the R&D Enterprises stock. Which one would you choose? *If you choose the less risky investment, you are*

THE TRADE-OFF BETWEEN RISK AND RETURN

The table accompanying this box summarizes the historical trade-off between risk and return for different classes of investments from 1926 through 1999. As the table shows, those assets that produced the highest average returns also had the highest standard deviations and the widest ranges of returns. For example, small-company stocks had the highest average annual return, 17.6 percent, but their standard deviation of returns, 33.6 percent, was also the highest. By contrast, U.S. Treasury bills had the lowest standard deviation, 3.2 percent, but they also had the lowest average return, 3.8 percent.

When deciding among alternative investments, one needs to be aware of the trade-off between risk and return. While there is certainly no guarantee that history will repeat itself, returns observed in the past are a good starting point for estimating investments' returns in the future. Likewise, the standard deviations of past returns provide useful insights into the risks of different investments. For T-bills, however, the standard deviation needs to be interpreted carefully. Note that the table shows that Treasury bills have a positive standard deviation, which indicates some risk. However, if you invested in a one-year Treasury bill and held it for the full year, your realized return would be the same regardless of what happened to the economy that year, and thus the standard deviation of your return would be zero. So, why does the table show a 3.2 percent standard deviation for T-bills, which indicates some risk? In fact, a T-bill is riskless *if you hold it for one year*, but if you invest in a rolling portfolio of one-year T-bills and hold the portfolio for a number of years, your investment income will vary depending on what happens to the level of interest rates in each year. So, while you can be sure of the return you will earn on a T-bill in a given year, you cannot be sure of the return you will earn on a portfolio of T-bills over a period of time.

Selected Realized Returns, 1926–1999

	AVERAGE RETURN	STANDARD DEVIATION
Small-company stocks	17.6%	33.6%
Large-company stocks	13.3	20.1
Long-term corporate bonds	5.9	8.7
Long-term goverment bonds	5.5	9.3
U.S. Treasury bills	3.8	3.2

Source: Based on *Stocks, Bonds, Bills, and Inflation: (Valuation Edition) 2000 Yearbook* (Chicago: Ibbotson Associates, 2000), 14.

Risk Aversion
Risk-averse investors dislike risk and require higher rates of return as an inducement to buy riskier securities.

risk averse. Most investors are indeed risk averse, and certainly the average investor is risk averse with regard to his or her "serious money." Because this is a well-documented fact, we shall assume **risk aversion** *throughout the remainder of the book.*

What are the implications of risk aversion for security prices and rates of return? The answer is that, other things held constant, the higher a security's risk, the lower its price and the higher its required return. To see how risk aversion affects security prices, look back at Figure 6-2 and consider again U.S. Water and

Martin Products stocks. Suppose each stock sold for $100 per share and each had an expected rate of return of 15 percent. Investors are averse to risk, so under these conditions there would be a general preference for U.S. Water. People with money to invest would bid for U.S. Water rather than Martin stock, and Martin's stockholders would start selling their stock and using the money to buy U.S. Water. Buying pressure would drive up U.S. Water's stock, and selling pressure would simultaneously cause Martin's price to decline.

These price changes, in turn, would cause changes in the expected rates of return on the two securities. Suppose, for example, that U.S. Water's stock price was bid up from $100 to $150, whereas Martin's stock price declined from $100 to $75. This would cause U.S. Water's expected return to fall to 10 percent, while Martin's expected return would rise to 20 percent. The difference in returns, 20% − 10% = 10%, is a **risk premium, RP**, which represents the additional compensation investors require for assuming the additional risk of Martin stock.

Risk Premium, RP
The difference between the expected rate of return on a given risky asset and that on a less risky asset.

This example demonstrates a very important principle: *In a market dominated by risk-averse investors, riskier securities must have higher expected returns, as estimated by the marginal investor, than less risky securities. If this situation does not exist, buying and selling in the market will force it to occur.* We will consider the question of how much higher the returns on risky securities must be later in the chapter, after we see how diversification affects the way risk should be measured. Then, in Chapters 8 and 9, we will see how risk-adjusted rates of return affect the prices investors are willing to pay for different securities.

SELF-TEST QUESTIONS

What does "investment risk" mean?

Set up an illustrative probability distribution for an investment.

What is a payoff matrix?

Which of the two stocks graphed in Figure 6-2 is less risky? Why?

How does one calculate the standard deviation?

Which is a better measure of risk if assets have different expected returns: (1) the standard deviation or (2) the coefficient of variation? Why?

Explain the following statement: "Most investors are risk averse."

How does risk aversion affect rates of return?

RISK IN A PORTFOLIO CONTEXT

In the preceding section, we considered the riskiness of assets held in isolation. Now we analyze the riskiness of assets held in portfolios. As we shall see, an asset held as part of a portfolio is less risky than the same asset held in isolation. Accordingly, most financial assets are held as parts of portfolios. Banks, pension funds, insurance companies, mutual funds, and other financial institutions are required by law to hold diversified portfolios. Even individual investors — at least those whose security holdings constitute a significant part of their total wealth — generally hold portfolios, not the stock of only one firm. This being the case, from an investor's standpoint the fact that a particular stock goes up or down is not very important; *what is important is the return on his or her portfolio, and the portfolio's risk. Logically, then, the risk and return of an individual security should be analyzed in terms of how that security affects the risk and return of the portfolio in which it is held.*

To illustrate, Pay Up Inc. is a collection agency company that operates nationwide through 37 offices. The company is not well known, its stock is not very liquid, its earnings have fluctuated quite a bit in the past, and it doesn't pay a dividend. All this suggests that Pay Up is risky and that its required rate of return, k, should be relatively high. However, Pay Up's required rate of return in 2001, and all other years, was quite low in comparison to those of most other companies. This indicates that investors regard Pay Up as being a low-risk company in spite of its uncertain profits. The reason for this counterintuitive fact has to do with diversification and its effect on risk. Pay Up's earnings rise during recessions, whereas most other companies' earnings tend to decline when the economy slumps. It's like fire insurance — it pays off when other things go bad. Therefore, adding Pay Up to a portfolio of "normal" stocks tends to stabilize returns on the entire portfolio, thus making the portfolio less risky.

PORTFOLIO RETURNS

Expected Return on a Portfolio, $\hat{k}_p$
The weighted average of the expected returns on the assets held in the portfolio.

The **expected return on a portfolio, $\hat{k}_p$,** is simply the weighted average of the expected returns on the individual assets in the portfolio, with the weights being the fraction of the total portfolio invested in each asset:

$$\hat{k}_p = w_1\hat{k}_1 + w_2\hat{k}_2 + \cdots + w_n\hat{k}_n$$

$$= \sum_{i=1}^{n} w_i\hat{k}_i. \tag{6-5}$$

Here the $\hat{k}_i$'s are the expected returns on the individual stocks, the w_i's are the weights, and there are n stocks in the portfolio. Note (1) that w_i is the fraction of the portfolio's dollar value invested in Stock i (that is, the value of the investment in Stock i divided by the total value of the portfolio) and (2) that the w_i's must sum to 1.0.

Assume that in August 2001, a security analyst estimated that the following returns could be expected on the stocks of four large companies:

	EXPECTED RETURN, $\hat{k}$
Microsoft	12.0%
General Electric	11.5
Pfizer	10.0
Coca-Cola	9.5

If we formed a $100,000 portfolio, investing $25,000 in each stock, the expected portfolio return would be 10.75%:

$$\hat{k}_p = w_1\hat{k}_1 + w_2\hat{k}_2 + w_3\hat{k}_3 + w_4\hat{k}_4$$
$$= 0.25(12\%) + 0.25(11.5\%) + 0.25(10\%) + 0.25(9.5\%)$$
$$= 10.75\%.$$

Realized Rate of Return, $\bar{k}$
The return that was actually earned during some past period. The actual return ($\bar{k}$) usually turns out to be different from the expected return ($\hat{k}$) except for riskless assets.

Of course, after the fact and a year later, the actual **realized rates of return, $\bar{k}$**, on the individual stocks—the $\bar{k}_i$, or "k-bar," values—will almost certainly be different from their expected values, so $\bar{k}_p$ will be different from $\hat{k}_p = 10.75\%$. For example, Coca-Cola stock might double in price and provide a return of $+100\%$, whereas Microsoft stock might have a terrible year, fall sharply, and have a return of -75%. Note, though, that those two events would be somewhat offsetting, so the portfolio's return might still be close to its expected return, even though the individual stocks' actual returns were far from their expected returns.

PORTFOLIO RISK

As we just saw, the expected return on a portfolio is simply the weighted average of the expected returns on the individual assets in the portfolio. However, unlike returns, the riskiness of a portfolio, σ_p, is generally *not* the weighted average of the standard deviations of the individual assets in the portfolio; the portfolio's risk will be *smaller* than the weighted average of the assets' σ's. In fact, it is theoretically possible to combine stocks that are individually quite risky as measured by their standard deviations and to form a portfolio that is completely riskless, with $\sigma_p = 0$.

To illustrate the effect of combining assets, consider the situation in Figure 6-5. The bottom section gives data on rates of return for Stocks W and M individually, and also for a portfolio invested 50 percent in each stock. The three top graphs show plots of the data in a time series format, and the lower graphs show the probability distributions of returns, assuming that the future is expected to be like the past. The two stocks would be quite risky if they were held in isolation, but when they are combined to form Portfolio WM, they are not risky at all. (Note: These stocks are called W and M because the graphs of their returns in Figure 6-5 resemble a W and an M.)

The reason Stocks W and M can be combined to form a riskless portfolio is that their returns move countercyclically to each other—when W's returns fall, those of M rise, and vice versa. The tendency of two variables to move together is called **correlation**, and the **correlation coefficient, r**, measures this tendency.[6] In statistical terms, we say that the returns on Stocks W and M are *perfectly negatively correlated*, with $r = -1.0$.

Correlation
The tendency of two variables to move together.

Correlation Coefficient, r
A measure of the degree of relationship between two variables.

The opposite of perfect negative correlation, with $r = -1.0$, is *perfect positive correlation*, with $r = +1.0$. Returns on two perfectly positively correlated stocks

---

[6] The *correlation coefficient*, *r*, can range from $+1.0$, denoting that the two variables move up and down in perfect synchronization, to -1.0, denoting that the variables always move in exactly opposite directions. A correlation coefficient of zero indicates that the two variables are not related to each other — that is, changes in one variable are *independent* of changes in the other.

It is easy to calculate correlation coefficients with a financial calculator. Simply enter the returns on the two stocks and then press a key labeled "r." For W and M, $r = -1.0$.

FIGURE 6-5

Rate of Return Distributions for Two Perfectly Negatively Correlated Stocks (r = −1.0) and for Portfolio WM

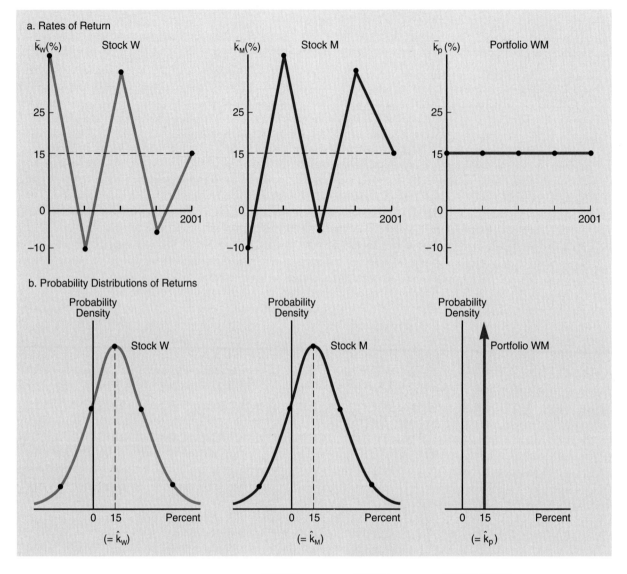

a. Rates of Return

b. Probability Distributions of Returns

YEAR	STOCK W ($\bar{k}_W$)	STOCK M ($\bar{k}_M$)	PORTFOLIO WM ($\bar{k}_p$)
1997	40.0%	(10.0%)	15.0%
1998	(10.0)	40.0	15.0
1999	35.0	(5.0)	15.0
2000	(5.0)	35.0	15.0
2001	15.0	15.0	15.0
Average return	15.0%	15.0%	15.0%
Standard deviation	22.6%	22.6%	0.0%

(M and M') would move up and down together, and a portfolio consisting of two such stocks would be exactly as risky as the individual stocks. This point is illustrated in Figure 6-6, where we see that the portfolio's standard deviation is equal to that of the individual stocks. *Thus, diversification does nothing to reduce risk if the portfolio consists of perfectly positively correlated stocks.*

Figures 6-5 and 6-6 demonstrate that when stocks are perfectly negatively correlated (r = −1.0), all risk can be diversified away, but when stocks are perfectly positively correlated (r = +1.0), diversification does no good whatsoever. In reality, most stocks are positively correlated, but not perfectly so. On average, the correlation coefficient for the returns on two randomly selected stocks would be about +0.6, and for most pairs of stocks, r would lie in the range of +0.5 to +0.7. *Under such conditions, combining stocks into portfolios reduces risk but does not eliminate it completely.* Figure 6-7 illustrates this point with two stocks whose correlation coefficient is r = +0.67. The portfolio's average return is 15 percent, which is exactly the same as the average return for each of the two stocks, but its standard deviation is 20.6 percent, which is less than the standard deviation of either stock. Thus, the portfolio's risk is *not* an average of the risks of its individual stocks — diversification has reduced, but not eliminated, risk.

From these two-stock portfolio examples, we have seen that in one extreme case (r = −1.0), risk can be completely eliminated, while in the other extreme case (r = +1.0), diversification does nothing to limit risk. The real world lies between these extremes, so in general combining two stocks into a portfolio reduces, but does not eliminate, the riskiness inherent in the individual stocks.

What would happen if we included more than two stocks in the portfolio? *As a rule, the riskiness of a portfolio will decline as the number of stocks in the portfolio increases.* If we added enough partially correlated stocks, could we completely eliminate risk? In general, the answer is no, but the extent to which adding stocks to a portfolio reduces its risk depends on the *degree of correlation* among the stocks: The smaller the positive correlation coefficients, the lower the risk in a large portfolio. If we could find a set of stocks whose correlations were zero or negative, all risk could be eliminated. *In the real world, where the correlations among the individual stocks are generally positive but less than +1.0, some, but not all, risk can be eliminated.*

To test your understanding, would you expect to find higher correlations between the returns on two companies in the same or in different industries? For example, would the correlation of returns on Ford's and General Motors' stocks be higher, or would the correlation coefficient be higher between either Ford or GM and AT&T, and how would those correlations affect the risk of portfolios containing them?

Answer: Ford's and GM's returns have a correlation coefficient of about 0.9 with one another because both are affected by auto sales, but their correlation is only about 0.6 with AT&T.

Implications: A two-stock portfolio consisting of Ford and GM would be less well diversified than a two-stock portfolio consisting of Ford or GM, plus AT&T. Thus, to minimize risk, portfolios should be diversified across industries.

Before leaving this section we should issue a warning — in the real world, it is *impossible* to find stocks like W and M, whose returns are expected to be perfectly negatively correlated. *Therefore, it is impossible to form completely riskless stock portfolios.* Diversification can reduce risk, but it cannot eliminate it. The real world is closer to the situation depicted in Figure 6-7.

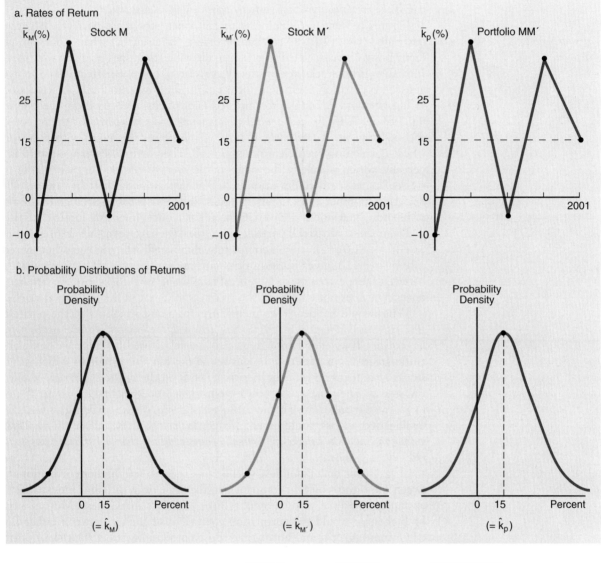

FIGURE 6-6 Rate of Return Distributions for Two Perfectly Positively Correlated Stocks (r = +1.0) and for Portfolio MM′

a. Rates of Return

b. Probability Distributions of Returns

YEAR	STOCK M ($\bar{k}_M$)	STOCK M′ ($\bar{k}_M'$)	PORTFOLIO MM′ ($\bar{k}_p$)
1997	(10.0%)	(10.0%)	(10.0%)
1998	40.0	40.0	40.0
1999	(5.0)	(5.0)	(5.0)
2000	35.0	35.0	35.0
2001	15.0	15.0	15.0
Average return	15.0%	15.0%	15.0%
Standard deviation	22.6%	22.6%	22.6%

FIGURE 6-7

Rate of Return Distributions for Two Partially Correlated Stocks (r = +0.67) and for Portfolio WY

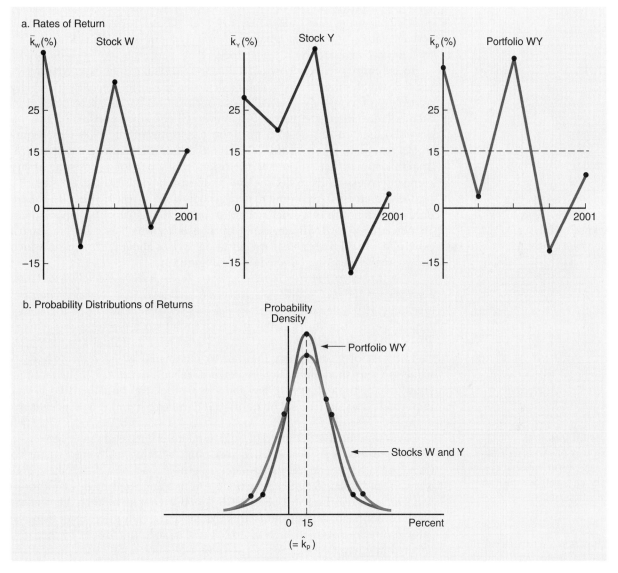

a. Rates of Return

b. Probability Distributions of Returns

YEAR	STOCK W ($\bar{k}_W$)	STOCK Y ($\bar{k}_Y$)	PORTFOLIO WY ($\bar{k}_p$)
1997	40.0%	28.0%	34.0%
1998	(10.0)	20.0	5.0
1999	35.0	41.0	38.0
2000	(5.0)	(17.0)	(11.0)
2001	15.0	3.0	9.0
Average return	15.0%	15.0%	15.0%
Standard deviation	22.6%	22.6%	20.6%

DIVERSIFIABLE RISK VERSUS MARKET RISK

As noted above, it is difficult if not impossible to find stocks whose expected returns are negatively correlated — most stocks tend to do well when the national economy is strong and badly when it is weak.[7] Thus, even very large portfolios end up with a substantial amount of risk, but not as much risk as if all the money were invested in only one stock.

To see more precisely how portfolio size affects portfolio risk, consider Figure 6-8, which shows how portfolio risk is affected by forming larger and larger portfolios of randomly selected New York Stock Exchange (NYSE) stocks. Standard deviations are plotted for an average one-stock portfolio, a two-stock portfolio, and so on, up to a portfolio consisting of all 2,000-plus common stocks that were listed on the NYSE at the time the data were graphed. The graph illustrates that, in general, the riskiness of a portfolio consisting of large-company stocks tends to decline and to approach some limit as the size of the portfolio increases. According to data accumulated in recent years, σ_1, the standard deviation of a one-stock portfolio (or an average stock), is approximately 35 percent. A portfolio consisting of all stocks, which is called the **market portfolio**, would have a standard deviation, σ_M, of about 20.4 percent, which is shown as the horizontal dashed line in Figure 6-8.

Thus, almost half of the riskiness inherent in an average individual stock can be eliminated if the stock is held in a reasonably well-diversified portfolio, which is one containing 40 or more stocks. Some risk always remains, however, so it is virtually impossible to diversify away the effects of broad stock market movements that affect almost all stocks.

The part of a stock's risk that *can* be eliminated is called *diversifiable risk*, while the part that *cannot* be eliminated is called *market risk*.[8] The fact that a large part of the riskiness of any individual stock can be eliminated is vitally important, because rational investors *will* eliminate it and thus render it irrelevant.

Diversifiable risk is caused by such random events as lawsuits, strikes, successful and unsuccessful marketing programs, winning or losing a major contract, and other events that are unique to a particular firm. Since these events are random, their effects on a portfolio can be eliminated by diversification — bad events in one firm will be offset by good events in another. **Market risk,** on the other hand, stems from factors that systematically affect most firms: war, inflation, recessions, and high interest rates. Since most stocks are negatively affected by these factors, market risk cannot be eliminated by diversification.

We know that investors demand a premium for bearing risk; that is, the higher the riskiness of a security, the higher its expected return must be to induce investors to buy (or to hold) it. However, if investors are primarily concerned with the riskiness of their *portfolios* rather than the riskiness of the indi-

---

Market Portfolio
A portfolio consisting of all stocks.

Diversifiable Risk
That part of a security's risk associated with random events; it *can* be eliminated by proper diversification.

Market Risk
That part of a security's risk that *cannot* be eliminated by diversification.

---

[7] It is not too hard to find a few stocks that happened to have risen because of a particular set of circumstances in the past while most other stocks were declining, but it is much harder to find stocks that could logically be *expected* to go up in the future when other stocks are falling.

[8] Diversifiable risk is also known as *company-specific*, or *unsystematic*, risk. Market risk is also known as *nondiversifiable*, or *systematic*, or *beta*, risk; it is the risk that remains after diversification.

FIGURE 6-8

Effects of Portfolio Size on Portfolio Risk for Average Stocks

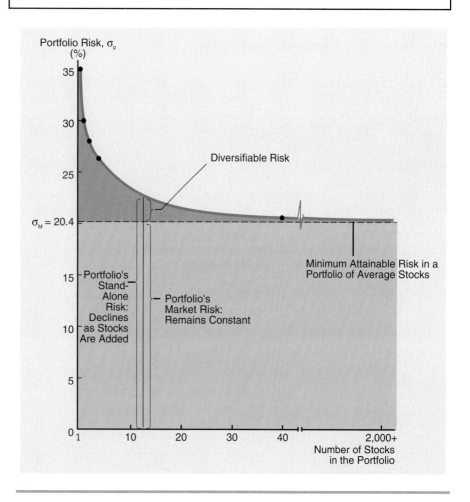

Capital Asset Pricing Model (CAPM)

A model based on the proposition that any stock's required rate of return is equal to the risk-free rate of return plus a risk premium that reflects only the risk remaining after diversification.

vidual securities in the portfolio, how should the riskiness of an individual stock be measured? One answer is provided by the **Capital Asset Pricing Model (CAPM)**, an important tool used to analyze the relationship between risk and rates of return.[9] The primary conclusion of the CAPM is this: *The relevant riskiness of an individual stock is its contribution to the riskiness of a well-diversified portfolio.* In other words, the riskiness of General Electric's stock to a doctor who

[9] Indeed, the 1990 Nobel Prize was awarded to the developers of the CAPM, Professors Harry Markowitz and William F. Sharpe. The CAPM is a relatively complex subject, and only its basic elements are presented in this text. For a more detailed discussion, see any standard investments textbook.

The basic concepts of the CAPM were developed specifically for common stocks, and, therefore, the theory is examined first in this context. However, it has become common practice to extend CAPM concepts to capital budgeting and to speak of firms having "portfolios of tangible assets and projects." Capital budgeting is discussed in Chapters 11 and 12.

has a portfolio of 40 stocks or to a trust officer managing a 150-stock portfolio is the contribution the GE stock makes to the portfolio's riskiness. The stock might be quite risky if held by itself, but if half of its risk can be eliminated by diversification, then its **relevant risk**, which is *its contribution to the portfolio's risk*, is much smaller than its stand-alone risk.

Relevant Risk
The risk of a security that cannot be diversified away, or its *market risk*. This reflects a security's contribution to the riskiness of a portfolio.

A simple example will help make this point clear. Suppose you are offered the chance to flip a coin once. If a head comes up, you win $20,000, but if a tail comes up, you lose $16,000. This is a good bet — the expected return is $0.5(\$20,000) + 0.5(-\$16,000) = \$2,000$. However, it is a highly risky proposition, because you have a 50 percent chance of losing $16,000. Thus, you might well refuse to make the bet. Alternatively, suppose you were offered the chance to flip a coin 100 times, and you would win $200 for each head but lose $160 for each tail. It is possible that you would flip all heads and win $20,000, and it is also possible that you would flip all tails and lose $16,000, but the chances are very high that you would actually flip about 50 heads and about 50 tails, winning a net of about $2,000. Although each individual flip is a risky bet, collectively you have a low-risk proposition because most of the risk has been diversified away. This is the idea behind holding portfolios of stocks rather than just one stock, except that with stocks all of the risk cannot be eliminated by diversification — those risks related to broad, systematic changes in the stock market will remain.

Are all stocks equally risky in the sense that adding them to a well-diversified portfolio would have the same effect on the portfolio's riskiness? The answer is no. Different stocks will affect the portfolio differently, so different securities have different degrees of relevant risk. How can the relevant risk of an individual stock be measured? As we have seen, all risk except that related to broad market movements can, and presumably will, be diversified away. After all, why accept risk that can be easily eliminated? *The risk that remains after diversifying is market risk, or the risk that is inherent in the market, and it can be measured by the degree to which a given stock tends to move up or down with the market.* In the next section, we develop a measure of a stock's market risk, and then, in a later section, we introduce an equation for determining the required rate of return on a stock, given its market risk.

The Concept of Beta

Beta Coefficient, b
A measure of market risk, which is the extent to which the returns on a given stock move with the stock market.

The tendency of a stock to move up and down with the market is reflected in its **beta coefficient, b**. Beta is a key element of the CAPM. An *average-risk stock* is *defined* as one that tends to move up and down in step with the general market as measured by some index such as the Dow Jones Industrials, the S&P 500, or the New York Stock Exchange Index. Such a stock will, *by definition*, be assigned a beta, b, of 1.0, which indicates that, in general, if the market moves up by 10 percent, the stock will also move up by 10 percent, while if the market falls by 10 percent, the stock will likewise fall by 10 percent. A portfolio of such b = 1.0 stocks will move up and down with the broad market averages, and it will be just as risky as the averages. If b = 0.5, the stock is only half as volatile as the market — it will rise and fall only half as much — and a portfolio of such stocks will be half as risky as a portfolio of b = 1.0 stocks. On the other hand, if b = 2.0, the stock is twice as volatile as an average stock, so a portfolio of such stocks will be twice as risky as an average portfolio. The value of such a portfolio could double — or halve — in a short time, and if you held such a portfolio, you could quickly go from millionaire to pauper.

Figure 6-9 graphs the relative volatility of three stocks. The data below the graph assume that in 1999 the "market," defined as a portfolio consisting of all stocks, had a total return (dividend yield plus capital gains yield) of $k_M = 10\%$, and Stocks H, A, and L (for High, Average, and Low risk) also all had returns of 10 percent. In 2000, the market went up sharply, and the return on the market portfolio was $\bar{k}_M = 20\%$. Returns on the three stocks also went up: H soared to 30 percent; A went up to 20 percent, the same as the market; and L only went up to 15 percent. Now suppose the market dropped in 2001, and the market return was $\bar{k}_M = -10\%$. The three stocks' returns also fell, H plunging to -30 percent, A falling to -10 percent, and L going down only to $\bar{k}_L = 0\%$. Thus, the three stocks all moved in the same direction as the market, but H was by far the most volatile; A was just as volatile as the market; and L was less volatile.

Beta measures a stock's volatility relative to an average stock, which by definition has $b = 1.0$, and a stock's beta can be calculated by plotting a line like those in Figure 6-9. The slopes of the lines show how each stock moves in response to a movement in the general market — *indeed, the slope coefficient of such a "regression line" is defined as a beta coefficient.* (Procedures for actually calculating betas are described in Appendix 6A.) Betas for literally thousands of companies are calculated and published by Merrill Lynch, Value Line, and numerous other organizations, and the beta coefficients of some well-known companies are shown in Table 6-4. Most stocks have betas in the range of 0.50 to 1.50, and the average for all stocks is 1.0 by definition.

Theoretically, it is possible for a stock to have a negative beta. In this case, the stock's returns would tend to rise whenever the returns on other stocks fall. In practice, we have never seen a stock with a negative beta. For example, *Value Line* follows more than 1,700 stocks, and not one has a negative beta. Keep in mind, though, that a stock in a given year may move counter to the overall market, even though the stock's beta is positive. If a stock has a positive beta, we would *expect* its return to increase whenever the overall stock market rises. However, company-specific factors may cause the stock's realized return to decline, even though the market's return is positive.

If a stock whose beta is greater than 1.0 is added to a $b = 1.0$ portfolio, then the portfolio's beta, and consequently its riskiness, will increase. Conversely, if a stock whose beta is less than 1.0 is added to a $b = 1.0$ portfolio, the portfolio's beta and risk will decline. *Thus, since a stock's beta measures its contribution to the riskiness of a portfolio, beta is the theoretically correct measure of the stock's riskiness.*

The preceding analysis of risk in a portfolio context is part of the Capital Asset Pricing Model (CAPM), and we can summarize our discussion to this point as follows:

1. A stock's risk consists of two components, market risk and diversifiable risk.

2. Diversifiable risk can be eliminated by diversification, and most investors do indeed diversify, either by holding large portfolios or by purchasing

GLOBAL PERSPECTIVES

THE BENEFITS OF DIVERSIFYING OVERSEAS

The size of the global stock market has grown steadily over the last several decades, and it passed the $15 trillion mark during 1995. U.S. stocks account for approximately 41 percent of this total, whereas the Japanese and European markets constitute roughly 25 and 26 percent, respectively. The rest of the world makes up the remaining 8 percent. Although the U.S. equity market has long been the world's biggest, its share of the world total has decreased over time.

The expanding universe of securities available internationally suggests the possibility of achieving a better risk-return trade-off than could be obtained by investing solely in U.S. securities. So, investing overseas might lower risk and simultaneously increase expected returns. The potential benefits of diversification are due to the facts that the correlation between the returns on U.S. and international securities is fairly low, and returns in developing nations are often quite high.

Figure 6-8, presented earlier, demonstrated that an investor can significantly reduce the risk of his or her portfolio by holding a large number of stocks. The figure accompanying this box suggests that investors may be able to reduce risk even further by holding a large portfolio of stocks from all around the world, given the fact that the returns of domestic and international stocks are not perfectly correlated.

Despite the apparent benefits from investing overseas, the typical U.S. investor still dedicates less than 10 percent of his or her portfolio to foreign stocks — even though foreign stocks represent roughly 60 percent of the worldwide equity market.

Researchers and practitioners alike have struggled to understand this reluctance to invest overseas. One explanation is that investors prefer domestic stocks because they have lower transaction costs. However, this explanation is not completely convincing, given that recent studies have found that investors buy and sell their overseas stocks more frequently than they trade their domestic stocks. Other explanations for the domestic bias focus on the additional risks from investing overseas (for example, exchange rate risk) or suggest that the typical U.S. investor is uninformed about international investments and/or views international investments as being extremely risky or uncertain. More recently, other analysts have argued that as world capital markets have become more integrated, the correlation of returns between different countries has increased, and hence the benefits from international diversification have declined. A third explanation is that U.S. corporations are themselves investing more internationally, hence U.S. investors are de facto obtaining international diversification.

Whatever the reason for the general reluctance to hold international assets, it is a safe bet that in the future U.S. investors will shift more and more of their assets to overseas investments.

SOURCE: Kenneth Kasa, "Measuring the Gains from International Portfolio Diversification," *Federal Reserve Bank of San Francisco Weekly Letter*, Number 94-14, April 8, 1994.

shares in a mutual fund. We are left, then, with market risk, which is caused by general movements in the stock market and which reflects the fact that most stocks are systematically affected by events like war, recessions, and inflation. Market risk is the only relevant risk to a rational, diversified investor because such an investor would eliminate diversifiable risk.

3. Investors must be compensated for bearing risk — the greater the riskiness of a stock, the higher its required return. However, compensation is required only for risk that cannot be eliminated by diversification. If risk premiums existed on stocks due to diversifiable risk, well-diversified investors would start buying those securities (which would not be especially risky to such investors) and bidding up their prices, and the stocks' final (equilibrium) expected returns would reflect only nondiversifiable market risk.

If this point is not clear, an example may help clarify it. Suppose half of Stock A's risk is market risk (it occurs because Stock A moves up and down with the market), while the other half of A's risk is diversifiable. You

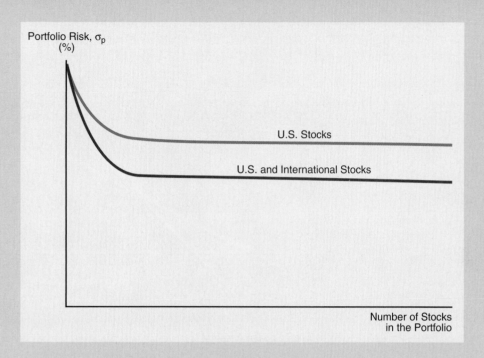

Portfolio Risk, σ_p (%)

U.S. Stocks

U.S. and International Stocks

Number of Stocks in the Portfolio

hold only Stock A, so you are exposed to all of its risk. As compensation for bearing so much risk, you want a risk premium of 8 percent over the 10 percent T-bond rate. Thus, your required return is $k_A = 10\% + 8\% = 18\%$. But suppose other investors, including your professor, are well diversified; they also hold Stock A, but they have eliminated its diversifiable risk and thus are exposed to only half as much risk as you. Therefore, their risk premium will be only half as large as yours, and their required rate of return will be $k_A = 10\% + 4\% = 14\%$.

If the stock were yielding more than 14 percent in the market, diversified investors, including your professor, would buy it. If it were yielding 18 percent, you would be willing to buy it, but well-diversified investors would bid its price up and its yield down, hence you could not buy it at a price low enough to provide you with an 18 percent return. In the end, you would have to accept a 14 percent return or else keep your money in the bank. Thus, risk premiums in a market populated by rational, diversified investors can reflect only market risk.

FIGURE 6-9

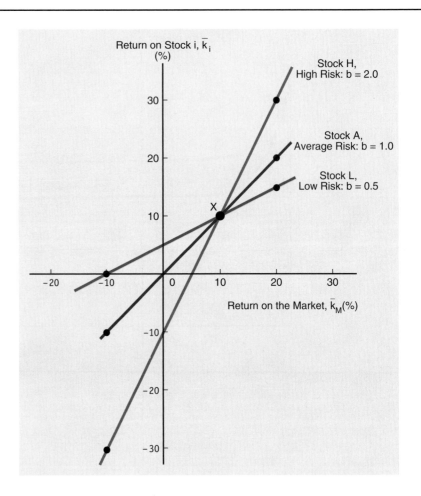

YEAR	$\bar{k}_H$	$\bar{k}_A$	$\bar{k}_L$	$\bar{k}_M$
1999	10%	10%	10%	10%
2000	30	20	15	20
2001	(30)	(10)	0	(10)

NOTE: These three stocks plot exactly on their regression lines. This indicates that they are exposed only to market risk. Mutual funds that concentrate on stocks with betas of 2, 1, and 0.5 would have patterns similar to those shown in the graph.

4. The market risk of a stock is measured by its beta coefficient, which is an index of the stock's relative volatility. Some benchmark betas follow:

b = 0.5: Stock is only half as volatile, or risky, as an average stock.
b = 1.0: Stock is of average risk.
b = 2.0: Stock is twice as risky as an average stock.

TABLE 6-4   Illustrative List of Beta Coefficients

STOCK	BETA
Merrill Lynch	1.85
America Online	1.60
General Electric	1.25
Microsoft Corp.	1.00
Coca-Cola	1.00
IBM	1.00
Procter & Gamble	0.85
Energen Corp.[a]	0.80
Heinz	0.70
Empire District Electric	0.45

[a] Energen is a gas distribution company. It has a monopoly in much of Alabama, and its prices are adjusted every three months so as to keep its profits relatively constant.

SOURCE: *Value Line,* September 2000, CD-ROM.

5. A portfolio consisting of low-beta securities will itself have a low beta, because the beta of a portfolio is a weighted average of its individual securities' betas:

$$b_p = w_1 b_1 + w_2 b_2 + \cdots + w_n b_n$$

$$= \sum_{i=1}^{n} w_i b_i. \qquad (6\text{-}6)$$

Here b_p is the beta of the portfolio, and it shows how volatile the portfolio is in relation to the market; w_i is the fraction of the portfolio invested in the ith stock; and b_i is the beta coefficient of the ith stock. For example, if an investor holds a \$100,000 portfolio consisting of \$33,333.33 invested in each of three stocks, and if each of the stocks has a beta of 0.7, then the portfolio's beta will be $b_p = 0.7$:

$$b_p = 0.3333(0.7) + 0.3333(0.7) + 0.3333(0.7) = 0.7.$$

Such a portfolio will be less risky than the market, so it should experience relatively narrow price swings and have relatively small rate-of-return fluctuations. In terms of Figure 6-9, the slope of its regression line would be 0.7, which is less than that for a portfolio of average stocks.

Now suppose one of the existing stocks is sold and replaced by a stock with $b_i = 2.0$. This action will increase the beta of the portfolio from $b_{p1} = 0.7$ to $b_{p2} = 1.13$:

$$b_{p2} = 0.3333(0.7) + 0.3333(0.7) + 0.3333(2.0)$$

$$= 1.13.$$

Had a stock with $b_i = 0.2$ been added, the portfolio beta would have declined from 0.7 to 0.53. Adding a low-beta stock, therefore, would reduce the riskiness of the portfolio. Consequently, adding new stocks to a portfolio can change the riskiness of that portfolio.

6. *Since a stock's beta coefficient determines how the stock affects the riskiness of a diversified portfolio, beta is the most relevant measure of any stock's risk.*

SELF-TEST QUESTIONS

Explain the following statement: "An asset held as part of a portfolio is generally less risky than the same asset held in isolation."

What is meant by *perfect positive correlation, perfect negative correlation,* and *zero correlation?*

In general, can the riskiness of a portfolio be reduced to zero by increasing the number of stocks in the portfolio? Explain.

What is an average-risk stock? What will be its beta?

Why is beta the theoretically correct measure of a stock's riskiness?

If you plotted the returns on a particular stock versus those on the Dow Jones Index over the past five years, what would the slope of the regression line you obtained indicate about the stock's market risk?

THE RELATIONSHIP BETWEEN RISK AND RATES OF RETURN

In the preceding section, we saw that under the CAPM theory, beta is the appropriate measure of a stock's relevant risk. Now we must specify the relationship between risk and return: For a given level of risk as measured by beta, what rate of return will investors require to compensate them for bearing that risk? To begin, let us define the following terms:

$\hat{k}_i$ = *expected* rate of return on the ith stock.

k_i = *required* rate of return on the ith stock. Note that if $\hat{k}_i$ is less than k_i, you would not purchase this stock, or you would sell it if you owned it. If $\hat{k}_i$ were greater than k_i, you would want to buy the stock, because it looks like a bargain. You would be indifferent if $\hat{k}_i = k_i$.

$\bar{k}$ = realized, after-the-fact return. One obviously does not know $\bar{k}$ at the time he or she is considering the purchase of a stock.

k_{RF} = risk-free rate of return. In this context, k_{RF} is generally measured by the return on long-term U.S. Treasury bonds.

IS THE DOW JONES HEADING TO 36,000?

In the 18-year period since 1982, the Dow Jones Industrial Average has risen from 777 to over 10,526, or an increase of approximately 1,255 percent! Although millions of investors have profited from this increase, many analysts believe that stocks are now overvalued. These analysts point to record P/E ratios as an indication that stock prices are too high. Federal Reserve Chairman Alan Greenspan made the same point, warning about the dangers of "irrational exuberance."

In sharp contrast to this bearish perspective, James Glassman and Kevin Hassett, co-authors of a book, *Dow 36,000*, make the following argument:

> Using sensible assumptions, we are comfortable with stock prices rising to three or four times their current levels. Our calculations show that with earnings growing at the same rate as the gross domestic product and Treasury bond yields below 6 percent, a perfectly reasonable level for the Dow would be 36,000 — tomorrow, not 10 or 20 years from now.

How do Glassman and Hassett reach this conclusion? They claim that the market risk premium ($k_M - k_{RF}$) has declined, and that it will continue to decline in the future. Investors require a risk premium for bearing risk, and the size of that premium depends on the average investor's degree of risk aversion. From 1926 through 1999, large-company stocks have produced average annual returns of 13.3 percent, while the returns on long-term government bonds have averaged 5.5 percent, suggesting a risk premium of 13.3% − 5.5% = 7.8%. However, Glassman and Hassett make the following assertion:

> What has happened since 1982, and especially during the past four years, is that investors have become calmer and smarter. They are requiring a much smaller extra return, or "risk premium," from stocks to compensate for their fear. That premium, which has averaged about 7 percent in modern history, is now around 3 percent. We believe that it is headed for its proper level: zero. That means that stock prices should rise accordingly.

A declining risk premium leads to a lower required return on stocks. This, in turn, implies that stock prices should rise because the same cash flows will then be discounted at a lower rate. To support their argument, Glassman and Hassett cite research by Jeremy Siegel of the University of Pennsylvania's Wharton School. In his best-selling book, *Stocks for the Long Run*, Siegel documents that over the long run stocks have not been riskier than bonds. Indeed, based on his research, Siegel concludes that, "The safest long-term investment for the preservation of purchasing power has clearly been stocks, not bonds."

Siegel acknowledges that stocks are riskier for short-term investors. This point is confirmed when we compare the average annual standard deviation of stock market returns (20 percent) with that of bonds (9 percent). The higher volatility of stocks occurs because stocks get hit harder than bonds in the short run when the economy weakens or inflation increases. However, stocks have always eventually recovered, and over longer periods they have outperformed bonds.

Glassman and Hassett contend that more and more investors are viewing stocks as long-term investments, and they are convinced that the long-run risk of stocks is fairly low. This has led investors to put increasing amounts of money in the stock market, pushing up stock prices and driving stocks' returns even higher. These positive results, in turn, lower the perceived riskiness of stocks, and that leads to still more buying and further stock market gains.

To put all of this in perspective, we need to address three important points. First, the relevant market risk premium is forward looking — it is based on investors' perceptions of the relative riskiness of stocks versus bonds in the future, and it will change over time. Most analysts acknowledge that the risk premium has fallen, but few agree with Glassman and Hassett that it is or should be zero. Most believe that investors require a premium in the neighborhood of at least 3 to 5 percent as an inducement for holding stocks. Moreover, the risk premium would probably rise sharply if something led to a sustained market decline.

Second, if the risk premium were to stabilize at a relatively low level, then investors would receive low stock returns in the future. For example, if the T-bond yield were 5 percent and the market risk premium were 3 percent, then the required return on the market would be 8 percent. In this situation, it would be unreasonable to expect stock returns of 12 to 13 percent in the future.

Third, investors should be concerned with real returns, which take inflation into account. For example, suppose the risk-free nominal rate of return were 5.5 percent and the market risk premium were 3 percent. Here, the expected nominal return on an average stock would be 8.5 percent. If inflation were 3.5 percent, the real return would be only 5.0 percent. Correctly looking at things in terms of real returns suggests that with low market risk premiums, stocks will have a hard time competing with inflation-indexed Treasury securities, which currently provide investors with only a slightly lower real return with considerably less risk.

SOURCE: James K. Glassman and Kevin A. Hassett, "Stock Prices Are Still Far Too Low," *The Wall Street Journal*, March 17, 1999, A26.

$$RP_M = (k_M - k_{RF}) =$$

b_i = beta coefficient of the ith stock. The beta of an average stock is $b_A = 1.0$.

k_M = required rate of return on a portfolio consisting of all stocks, which is called the *market portfolio*. k_M is also the required rate of return on an average ($b_A = 1.0$) stock.

$RP_M = (k_M - k_{RF})$ = risk premium on "the market," and also on an average ($b = 1.0$) stock. This is the additional return over the risk-free rate required to compensate an average investor for assuming an average amount of risk. Average risk means a stock whose $b_i = b_A = 1.0$.

$RP_i = (k_M - k_{RF})b_i = (RP_M)b_i$ = risk premium on the ith stock. The stock's risk premium will be less than, equal to, or greater than the premium on an average stock, RP_M, depending on whether its beta is less than, equal to, or greater than 1.0. If $b_i = b_A = 1.0$, then $RP_i = RP_M$.

Market Risk Premium, RP$_M$
The additional return over the risk-free rate needed to compensate investors for assuming an average amount of risk.

The **market risk premium, RP$_M$,** shows the premium investors require for bearing the risk of an average stock. The size of this premium depends on the perceived risk of the stock market and investors' degree of risk aversion. Let us assume that at the current time Treasury bonds yield $k_{RF} = 6\%$ and an average share of stock has a required rate of return of $k_M = 11\%$. Therefore, the market risk premium is 5 percent calculated as:

$$RP_M = k_M - k_{RF} = 11\% - 6\% = 5\%.$$

It should be noted that the risk premium of an average stock, $k_M - k_{RF}$, is hard to measure because it is impossible to obtain precise estimates of the expected future return of the market, k_M.[10] Given the difficulty of estimating future market returns, analysts often look to historical data to estimate the market risk premium. Historical data suggest that the market risk premium varies somewhat from year to year, and it has generally ranged from 4 to 8 percent.

While historical estimates might be a good starting point for estimating the market risk premium, historical estimates may be misleading if investors' attitudes toward risk change considerably over time. (See the Industry Practice Box entitled "Estimating the Market Risk Premium.") Indeed, many analysts have argued that the market risk premium has fallen in recent years because an increasing number of investors have been willing to bear the risks of the stock market. If this claim is correct, the market risk premium may be considerably lower than what would be implied using historical data. (See the Industry Practice Box entitled "Is the Dow Jones Heading to 36,000?" for a discussion of

---

[10] This concept, as well as other aspects of the CAPM, is discussed in more detail in Chapter 3 of Eugene F. Brigham and Phillip R. Daves, *Intermediate Financial Management*, 7th ed. (Fort Worth, TX: Harcourt College Publishers, 2002). Chapter 3 of *Intermediate Financial Management* also discusses the assumptions embodied in the CAPM framework. Some of these are unrealistic, and because of this the theory does not hold exactly.

how changes in investor risk aversion may have influenced the market risk premium and stock returns in recent years.)

While the market risk premium represents the risk premium for the entire stock market, the risk premium on individual stocks will vary. For example, if one stock were twice as risky as another, its risk premium would be twice as high, while if its risk were only half as much, its risk premium would be half as large. Further, we can measure a stock's relative riskiness by its beta coefficient. If we know the market risk premium, RP_M, and the stock's risk as measured by its beta coefficient, b_i, we can find the stock's risk premium as the product $(RP_M)b_i$. For example, if $b_i = 0.5$ and $RP_M = 5\%$, then RP_i is 2.5 percent:

$$\text{Risk premium for Stock i} = RP_i = (RP_M)b_i \qquad (6\text{-}7)$$
$$= (5\%)(0.5)$$
$$= 2.5\%.$$

As the discussion in Chapter 5 implied, the required return for any investment can be expressed in general terms as

$$\text{Required return} = \text{Risk-free return} + \text{Premium for risk.}$$

Here the risk-free return includes a premium for expected inflation, and we assume that the assets under consideration have similar maturities and liquidity. Under these conditions, the required return for Stock i can be written as follows:

$$\text{SML Equation: } \begin{pmatrix} \text{Required return} \\ \text{on Stock i} \end{pmatrix} = \begin{pmatrix} \text{Risk-free} \\ \text{rate} \end{pmatrix} + \begin{pmatrix} \text{Market risk} \\ \text{premium} \end{pmatrix}\begin{pmatrix} \text{Stock i's} \\ \text{beta} \end{pmatrix}$$

$$k_i = k_{RF} + (k_M - k_{RF})b_i \qquad (6\text{-}8)$$
$$= k_{RF} + (RP_M)b_i$$
$$= 6\% + (11\% - 6\%)(0.5)$$
$$= 6\% + 5\%(0.5)$$
$$= 8.5\%.$$

Equation 6-8 is called the Security Market Line (SML).

If some other Stock j were riskier than Stock i and had $b_j = 2.0$, then its required rate of return would be 16 percent:

$$k_j = 6\% + (5\%)2.0 = 16\%.$$

An average stock, with $b = 1.0$, would have a required return of 11 percent, the same as the market return:

$$k_A = 6\% + (5\%)1.0 = 11\% = k_M.$$

Security Market Line (SML)
The line on a graph that shows the relationship between risk as measured by beta and the required rate of return for individual securities. Equation 6-8 is the equation for the SML.

As noted above, Equation 6-8 is called the **Security Market Line (SML)** equation, and it is often expressed in graph form, as in Figure 6-10, which shows the SML when $k_{RF} = 6\%$ and $k_M = 11\%$. Note the following points:

1. Required rates of return are shown on the vertical axis, while risk as measured by beta is shown on the horizontal axis. This graph is quite different from the one shown in Figure 6-9, where the returns on individual stocks were plotted on the vertical axis and returns on the market index were shown on the horizontal axis. The slopes of the

INDUSTRY PRACTICE

ESTIMATING THE MARKET RISK PREMIUM

The Capital Asset Pricing Model (CAPM) is more than just a theory describing the trade-off between risk and return. The CAPM is also widely used in practice. As we will see in Chapter 9, investors use the CAPM to determine the discount rate for valuing stocks. Later, in Chapter 10, we will also see that corporate managers use the CAPM to estimate the cost of equity financing.

The market risk premium is an important component of the CAPM. In practice, what we would ideally like to use in the CAPM is the *expected* market risk premium, which gives an indication of investors' future returns. Unfortunately, we cannot direcly observe investors' expectations. Instead, academicians and practitioners often use an historical estimate of the market risk premium as a proxy for the expected risk premium.

Historical premiums are found by taking the differences between actual returns of the overall stock market and the risk-free rate. Ibbotson Associates provide perhaps the most comprehensive estimates of historical risk premiums. Their estimates indicate that the equity risk premium has averaged about 8 percent a year over the past 75 years.

Analysts have pointed out some of the shortcomings of using an historical estimate as a proxy for the expected risk premium. First, historical estimates may be very misleading at times when the market risk premium is changing. As we mentioned in an earlier box entitled "Is the Dow Jones Heading to 36,000?," many analysts believe that the expected risk premium has fallen in recent years. It is important to recognize that a sharp drop in the expected risk premium (perhaps because of lower perceived risk and/or declining risk aversion) pushes up stock prices, and that ironically *increases* the observed (histor-

ical) risk premium. In this situation, an analyst would be seriously missing the boat if he used the historical risk premium to approximate the expected risk premium. To further illustrate this point, the strong performance in the stock market over the past several years has produced high historical premiums — indeed, Ibbotson Associates estimate that the market risk premium averaged 22.3 percent a year during the period between 1995 and 1999. Nobody would seriously suggest that future investors require a 22.3 percent premium to invest in the stock market! Given these concerns, Ibbotson and others suggest that historical estimates are more reliable if estimated over longer time intervals.

A second concern is that historical estimates may be biased upward because they only include the returns of firms that have survived and do not take into account the performances of failing firms. Stephen Brown, William Goetzmann, and Stephen Ross discussed the implications of this "survivorship bias" in a 1995 *Journal of Finance* article. Putting these ideas into practice, Tom Copeland, Tim Koller, and Jack Murrin have recently suggested that this "survivorship bias" increases historical returns by 1½ to 2 percent a year. For that reason, they suggest that practitioners trying to estimate a forward-looking expected risk premium subtract 1½ to 2 percent from their historical risk premium estimates.

SOURCES: *Stocks, Bonds, Bills, and Inflation: (Valuation Edition) 2000 Yearbook* (Chicago: Ibbotson Associates, 2000); Stephen J. Brown, William N. Goetzmann, and Stephen A. Ross, "Survival," *The Journal of Finance,* Vol. 50, No. 3, July 1995, 853–873; and Tom Copeland, Tim Koller, and Jack Murrin, *Valuation: Measuring and Managing the Value of Companies, 3rd edition,* (New York: McKinsey & Company, 2000).

three lines in Figure 6-9 were used to calculate the three stocks' betas, and those betas were then plotted as points on the horizontal axis of Figure 6-10.

2. Riskless securities have $b_i = 0$; therefore, k_{RF} appears as the vertical axis intercept in Figure 6-10. If we could construct a portfolio that had a beta of zero, it would have an expected return equal to the risk-free rate.

3. The slope of the SML (5% in Figure 6-10) reflects the degree of risk aversion in the economy — the greater the average investor's aversion to risk, then (a) the steeper the slope of the line, (b) the greater the

FIGURE   6 - 1 0   The Security Market Line (SML)

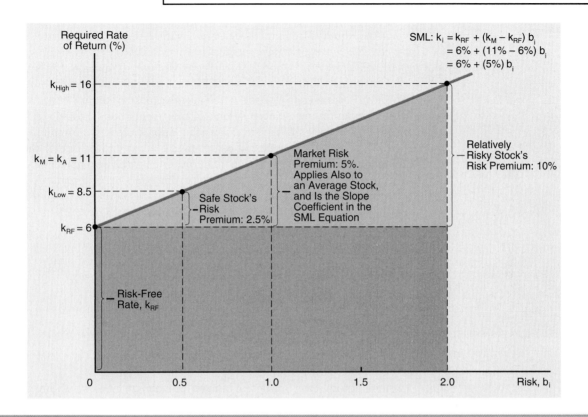

risk premium for all stocks, and (c) the higher the required rate of return on all stocks.[11] These points are discussed further in a later section.

4. The values we worked out for stocks with $b_i = 0.5$, $b_i = 1.0$, and $b_i = 2.0$ agree with the values shown on the graph for k_{Low}, k_A, and k_{High}.

Both the Security Market Line and a company's position on it change over time due to changes in interest rates, investors' aversion to risk, and individual companies' betas. Such changes are discussed in the following sections.

---

[11] Students sometimes confuse beta with the slope of the SML. This is a mistake. The slope of any straight line is equal to the "rise" divided by the "run," or $(Y_1 - Y_0)/(X_1 - X_0)$. Consider Figure 6-10. If we let $Y = k$ and $X = beta$, and we go from the origin to $b = 1.0$, we see that the slope is $(k_M - k_{RF})/(b_M - b_{RF}) = (11\% - 6\%)/(1 - 0) = 5\%$. Thus, the slope of the SML is equal to $(k_M - k_{RF})$, the market risk premium. In Figure 6-10, $k_i = 6\% + 5\%b_i$, so a doubling of beta (for example, from 1.0 to 2.0) would produce a 5 percentage point increase in k_i.

THE IMPACT OF INFLATION

As we learned in Chapter 5, interest amounts to "rent" on borrowed money, or the price of money. Thus, k_{RF} is the price of money to a riskless borrower. We also learned that the risk-free rate as measured by the rate on U.S. Treasury securities is called the *nominal*, or *quoted*, *rate*, and it consists of two elements: (1) a *real inflation-free rate of return*, k^*, and (2) an *inflation premium*, *IP*, equal to the anticipated rate of inflation.[12] Thus, $k_{RF} = k^* + IP$. The real rate on long-term Treasury bonds has historically ranged from 2 to 4 percent, with a mean of about 3 percent. Therefore, if no inflation were expected, long-term Treasury bonds would yield about 3 percent. However, as the expected rate of inflation increases, a premium must be added to the real risk-free rate of return to compensate investors for the loss of purchasing power that results from inflation. Therefore, the 6 percent k_{RF} shown in Figure 6-10 might be thought of as consisting of a 3 percent real risk-free rate of return plus a 3 percent inflation premium: $k_{RF} = k^* + IP = 3\% + 3\% = 6\%$.

If the expected inflation rate rose by 2 percent, to $3\% + 2\% = 5\%$, this would cause k_{RF} to rise to 8 percent. Such a change is shown in Figure 6-11. Notice that under the CAPM, the increase in k_{RF} leads to an *equal* increase in the rate of return on all risky assets, because the same inflation premium is built into the required rate of return of both riskless and risky assets.[13] For example, the rate of return on an average stock, k_M, increases from 11 to 13 percent. Other risky securities' returns also rise by two percentage points.

CHANGES IN RISK AVERSION

The slope of the Security Market Line reflects the extent to which investors are averse to risk — the steeper the slope of the line, the greater the average investor's risk aversion. Suppose investors were indifferent to risk; that is, they were not risk averse. If k_{RF} were 6 percent, then risky assets would also provide an expected return of 6 percent, because if there were no risk aversion, there would be no risk premium, and the SML would graph as a horizontal line. As risk aversion increases, so does the risk premium, and this causes the slope of the SML to become steeper.

Figure 6-12 illustrates an increase in risk aversion. The market risk premium rises from 5 to 7.5 percent, causing k_M to rise from $k_{M1} = 11\%$ to $k_{M2} = 13.5\%$. The returns on other risky assets also rise, and the effect of this shift in risk aversion is more pronounced on riskier securities. For example, the required return on a stock with $b_i = 0.5$ increases by only 1.25 percentage points, from 8.5 to 9.75 percent, whereas that on a stock with $b_i = 1.5$ increases by 3.75 percentage points, from 13.5 to 17.25 percent.

---

[12] Long-term Treasury bonds also contain a maturity risk premium, MRP. Here we include the MRP in k^* to simplify the discussion.

[13] Recall that the inflation premium for any asset is equal to the average expected rate of inflation over the asset's life. Thus, in this analysis we must assume either that all securities plotted on the SML graph have the same life or else that the expected rate of future inflation is constant.

It should also be noted that k_{RF} in a CAPM analysis can be proxied by either a long-term rate (the T-bond rate) or a short-term rate (the T-bill rate). Traditionally, the T-bill rate was used, but in recent years there has been a movement toward use of the T-bond rate because there is a closer relationship between T-bond yields and stocks than between T-bill yields and stocks. See *Stocks, Bonds, Bills, and Inflation: (Valuation Edition) 2000 Yearbook* (Chicago: Ibbotson Associates, 2000) for a discussion.

FIGURE 6-11   Shift in the SML Caused by an Increase in Inflation

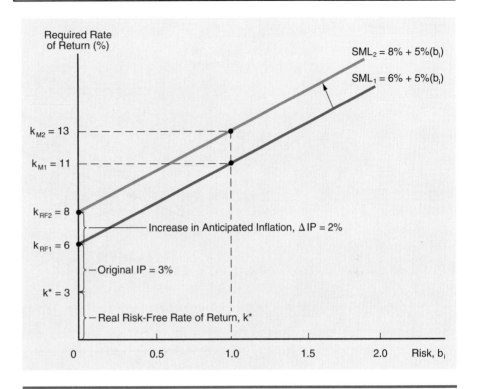

CHANGES IN A STOCK'S BETA COEFFICIENT

As we shall see later in the book, a firm can influence its market risk, hence its beta, through changes in the composition of its assets and also through its use of debt. A company's beta can also change as a result of external factors such as increased competition in its industry, the expiration of basic patents, and the like. When such changes occur, the required rate of return also changes, and, as we shall see in Chapter 9, this will affect the firm's stock price. For example, consider Allied Food Products, with a beta of 1.40. Now suppose some action occurred that caused Allied's beta to increase from 1.40 to 2.00. If the conditions depicted in Figure 6-10 held, Allied's required rate of return would increase from 13 to 16 percent:

$$k_1 = k_{RF} + (k_M - k_{RF})b_i$$
$$= 6\% + (11\% - 6\%)1.40$$
$$= 13\%$$

to

$$k_2 = 6\% + (11\% - 6\%)2.0$$
$$= 16\%.$$

As we shall see in Chapter 9, this change would have a dramatic impact on Allied's stock price.

FIGURE 6-12

Shift in the SML Caused by Increased Risk Aversion

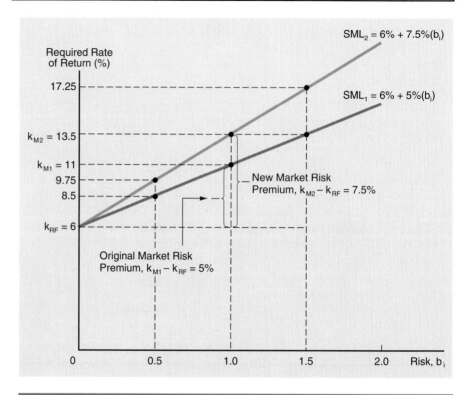

SELF-TEST QUESTIONS

Differentiate among the expected rate of return $(\hat{k})$, the required rate of return (k), and the realized, after-the-fact return $(\overline{k})$ on a stock. Which would have to be larger to get you to buy the stock, $\hat{k}$ or k? Would $\hat{k}$, k, and $\overline{k}$ typically be the same or different? Explain.

What are the differences between the relative volatility graph (Figure 6-9), where "betas are made," and the SML graph (Figure 6-10), where "betas are used"? Discuss both how the graphs are constructed and the information they convey.

What happens to the SML graph in Figure 6-10 when inflation increases or decreases?

What happens to the SML graph when risk aversion increases or decreases? What would the SML look like if investors were indifferent to risk, that is, if they had zero risk aversion?

How can a firm influence its market risk as reflected in its beta?

PHYSICAL ASSETS VERSUS SECURITIES

In a book on financial management for business firms, why do we spend so much time discussing the riskiness of stocks? Why not begin by looking at the riskiness of such business assets as plant and equipment? *The reason is that, for a management whose primary goal is stock price maximization, the overriding consideration is the riskiness of the firm's stock, and the relevant risk of any physical asset must be measured in terms of its effect on the stock's risk as seen by investors.* For example, suppose Goodyear Tire Company is considering a major investment in a new product, recapped tires. Sales of recaps, hence earnings on the new operation, are highly uncertain, so on a stand-alone basis the new venture appears to be quite risky. However, suppose returns in the recap business are negatively correlated with Goodyear's regular operations—when times are good and people have plenty of money, they buy new tires, but when times are bad, they tend to buy more recaps. Therefore, returns would be high on regular operations and low on the recap division during good times, but the opposite would occur during recessions. The result might be a pattern like that shown earlier in Figure 6-5 for Stocks W and M. Thus, what appears to be a risky investment when viewed on a stand-alone basis might not be very risky when viewed within the context of the company as a whole.

This analysis can be extended to the corporation's stockholders. Because Goodyear's stock is owned by diversified stockholders, the real issue each time management makes an asset investment is this: How will this investment affect the risk of our stockholders? Again, the stand-alone risk of an individual project may look quite high, but viewed in the context of the project's effect on stockholders' risk, it may not be very large. We will address this issue again in Chapter 10, where we examine the effects of capital budgeting on companies' beta coefficients and thus on stockholders' risks.

SELF-TEST QUESTIONS

Explain the following statement: "The stand-alone risk of an individual project may be quite high, but viewed in the context of a project's effect on stockholders' risk, the project's true risk may not be very large."

How would the correlation between returns on a project and returns on the firm's other assets affect the project's risk?

SOME CONCERNS ABOUT BETA AND THE CAPM

The Capital Asset Pricing Model (CAPM) is more than just an abstract theory described in textbooks—it is also widely used by analysts, investors, and corporations. However, despite the CAPM's intuitive appeal, a number of recent studies have raised concerns about its validity. In particular, a recent study by Eugene Fama of the University of Chicago and Kenneth French of Yale found no historical relationship between stocks' returns and their market betas, confirming a position long held by a number of professors and stock market analysts.[14]

If beta does not determine returns, what does? Fama and French found two variables that are consistently related to stock returns: (1) the firm's size and (2) its market/book ratio. After adjusting for other factors, they found that smaller firms have provided relatively high returns, and that returns are higher on stocks with low market/book ratios. By contrast, they found no relationship between a stock's beta and its return.

As an alternative to the traditional CAPM, researchers and practitioners have begun to look to more general multi-beta models that encompass the CAPM and address its shortcomings. The multi-beta model is an attractive generalization of the traditional CAPM model's insight that market risk—risk that cannot be diversified away—underlies the pricing of assets. In the multi-beta model, market risk is measured relative to a set of risk factors that determine the behavior of asset returns, whereas the CAPM gauges risk only relative to the market return. It is important to note that the risk factors in the multi-beta model are all nondiversifiable sources of risk. Empirical research investigating the relationship between economic risk factors and security returns is ongoing, but it has discovered several systematic empirical risk factors, including the bond default premium, the bond term structure premium, and inflation.

Practitioners and academicians have long recognized the limitations of the CAPM, and they are constantly looking for ways to improve it. The multi-beta model is a potential step in that direction. Although the CAPM represents a significant step forward in security pricing theory, it does have some deficiencies when applied in practice, hence estimates of k_i found through use of the SML may be subject to considerable error.

SELF-TEST QUESTION

Are there any reasons to question the validity of the CAPM? Explain.

VOLATILITY VERSUS RISK

Before closing this chapter, we should note that volatility does not necessarily imply risk. For example, suppose a company's sales and earnings fluctuate widely from month to month, from year to year, or in some other manner. Does this imply that the company is risky in either the stand-alone or portfolio sense? If the fluctuations follow seasonal or cyclical patterns, as for an ice cream distributor or a steel company, they can be predicted, hence volatility would not signify much in the way of risk. If the ice cream company's earnings dropped about as much as they normally did in the winter, this would not concern in-

---

[14] See Eugene F. Fama and Kenneth R. French, "The Cross-Section of Expected Stock Returns," *Journal of Finance*, Vol. 47, 1992, 427–465; and Eugene F. Fama and Kenneth R. French, "Common Risk Factors in the Returns on Stocks and Bonds," *Journal of Financial Economics*, Vol. 33, 1993, 3–56.

vestors, so the company's stock price would not be affected. Similarly, if the steel company's earnings fell during a recession, this would not be a surprise, so the company's stock price would not fall nearly as much as its earnings. Therefore, earnings volatility does not necessarily imply investment risk.

Now consider some other company, say, Wal-Mart. In 1995 Wal-Mart's earnings declined for the first time in its history. That decline worried investors — they were concerned that Wal-Mart's era of rapid growth had ended. The result was that Wal-Mart's stock price declined more than its earnings. Again, we conclude that while a downturn in earnings does not necessarily imply risk, it could, depending on conditions.

Now let's consider stock price volatility as opposed to earnings volatility. Is stock price volatility more likely to imply risk than earnings volatility? The answer is a loud yes! Stock prices vary because investors are uncertain about the future, especially about future earnings. So, if you see a company whose stock price fluctuates relatively widely (which will result in a high beta), you can bet that its future earnings are relatively unpredictable. Thus, biotech companies have less predictable earnings than utilities, biotechs' stock prices are volatile, and they have relatively high betas.

To conclude, keep two points in mind: (1) Earnings volatility does not necessarily signify risk — you have to think about the cause of the volatility before reaching any conclusion as to whether earnings volatility indicates risk. (2) Stock price volatility *does* signify risk.

SELF-TEST QUESTIONS

Does earnings volatility necessarily imply risk? Explain.

Why is stock price volatility more likely to imply risk than earnings volatility?

TYING IT ALL TOGETHER

In this chapter, we described the trade-off between risk and return. We began by discussing how to calculate risk and return for both individual assets and portfolios. In particular, we differentiated between stand-alone risk and risk in a portfolio context, and we explained the benefits of diversification. Finally, we developed the CAPM, which explains how risk affects rates of return. In the chapters that follow, we will give you the tools to estimate the required rates of return for bonds, preferred stock, and common stock, and we will explain how firms use these returns to develop their costs of capital. As you will see, the cost of capital is an important element in the firm's capital budgeting process. The key concepts covered in this chapter are listed below.

- **Risk** can be defined as the chance that some unfavorable event will occur.

- The riskiness of an asset's cash flows can be considered on a **stand-alone basis** (each asset by itself) or in a **portfolio context**, where the investment is combined with other assets and its risk is reduced through **diversification**.

- Most rational investors hold **portfolios of assets,** and they are more concerned with the riskiness of their portfolios than with the riskiness of individual assets.

- The **expected return** on an investment is the mean value of its probability distribution of returns.

- The **greater the probability** that the actual return will be far below the expected return, the **greater the stand-alone risk** associated with an asset. Two measures of stand-alone risk are the **standard deviation** and the **coefficient of variation.**

- The average investor is **risk averse**, which means that he or she must be compensated for holding risky assets. Therefore, riskier assets have higher required returns than less risky assets.

- An asset's risk consists of (1) **diversifiable risk**, which can be eliminated by diversification, plus (2) **market risk**, which cannot be eliminated by diversification.

- The **relevant risk** of an individual asset is its contribution to the riskiness of a well-diversified **portfolio,** which is the asset's **market risk**. Since market risk cannot be eliminated by diversification, investors must be compensated for bearing it.

- The **Capital Asset Pricing Model** is a model based on the proposition that any stock's required rate of return is equal to the risk-free rate of return plus a risk premium that reflects only the risk remaining after diversification.

- A stock's **beta coefficient, b**, is a measure of its market risk. Beta measures the extent to which the stock's returns move relative to the market.

- A **high-beta stock** is more volatile than an average stock, while a **low-beta stock** is less volatile than an average stock. An average stock has b = 1.0.

- The **beta of a portfolio** is a **weighted average** of the betas of the individual securities in the portfolio.

- The **Security Market Line (SML)** equation shows the relationship between a security's market risk and its required rate of return. The return required for any security i is equal to the **risk-free rate** plus the **market risk premium** times the security's beta: $k_i = k_{RF} + (k_M - k_{RF})b_i$.

- Even though the expected rate of return on a stock is generally equal to its required return, a number of things can happen to cause the required rate of return to change: (1) **the risk-free rate can change** because of changes in either real rates or anticipated inflation, (2) **a stock's beta can change**, and (3) **investors' aversion to risk can change**.

- Because returns on assets in different countries are not perfectly correlated, **global diversification** may result in lower risk for multinational companies and globally diversified portfolios.

In the next three chapters, we will see how a security's rate of return affects its value. Then, in the remainder of the book, we will examine the ways in which a firm's management can influence a stock's riskiness and hence its price.

QUESTIONS

6-1 The probability distribution of a less risky expected return is more peaked than that of a riskier return. What shape would the probability distribution have for (a) completely certain returns and (b) completely uncertain returns?

6-2 Security A has an expected return of 7 percent, a standard deviation of expected returns of 35 percent, a correlation coefficient with the market of -0.3, and a beta coefficient of -0.5. Security B has an expected return of 12 percent, a standard deviation of returns of 10 percent, a correlation with the market of 0.7, and a beta coefficient of 1.0. Which security is riskier? Why?

6-3 Suppose you owned a portfolio consisting of $250,000 worth of long-term U.S. government bonds.
  a. Would your portfolio be riskless?
  b. Now suppose you hold a portfolio consisting of $250,000 worth of 30-day Treasury bills. Every 30 days your bills mature, and you reinvest the principal ($250,000) in a new batch of bills. Assume that you live on the investment income from your portfolio and that you want to maintain a constant standard of living. Is your portfolio truly riskless?
  c. Can you think of any asset that would be completely riskless? Could someone develop such an asset? Explain.

6-4 A life insurance policy is a financial asset. The premiums paid represent the investment's cost.
  a. How would you calculate the expected return on a life insurance policy?
  b. Suppose the owner of a life insurance policy has no other financial assets — the person's only other asset is "human capital," or lifetime earnings capacity. What is the correlation coefficient between returns on the insurance policy and returns on the policyholder's human capital?
  c. Life insurance companies have to pay administrative costs and sales representatives' commissions; hence, the expected rate of return on insurance premiums is generally low, or even negative. Use the portfolio concept to explain why people buy life insurance in spite of negative expected returns.

6-5 If investors' aversion to risk increased, would the risk premium on a high-beta stock increase more or less than that on a low-beta stock? Explain.

6-6 If a company's beta were to double, would its expected return double?

6-7 Is it possible to construct a portfolio of stocks that has an expected return equal to the risk-free rate?

6-8 A stock had a 12 percent return last year, a year in which the overall stock market declined in value. Does this mean that the stock has a negative beta?

SELF-TEST PROBLEMS (SOLUTIONS APPEAR IN APPENDIX B)

ST-1
Key terms
Define the following terms, using graphs or equations to illustrate your answers wherever feasible:
  a. Stand-alone risk; risk; probability distribution
  b. Expected rate of return, $\hat{k}$
  c. Continuous probability distribution
  d. Standard deviation, σ; variance, σ^2; coefficient of variation, CV
  e. Risk aversion; realized rate of return, $\bar{k}$
  f. Risk premium for Stock i, RP_i; market risk premium, RP_M
  g. Capital Asset Pricing Model (CAPM)

h. Expected return on a portfolio, $\hat{k}_p$; market portfolio
i. Correlation coefficient, r; correlation
j. Market risk; diversifiable risk; relevant risk
k. Beta coefficient, b; average stock's beta, b_A
l. Security Market Line (SML); SML equation
m. Slope of SML as a measure of risk aversion

ST-2
Realized rates of return

Stocks A and B have the following historical returns:

YEAR	STOCK A'S RETURNS, k_A	STOCK B'S RETURNS, k_B
1997	(10.00%)	(3.00%)
1998	18.50	21.29
1999	38.67	44.25
2000	14.33	3.67
2001	33.00	28.30

a. Calculate the average rate of return for each stock during the period 1997 through 2001. Assume that someone held a portfolio consisting of 50 percent of Stock A and 50 percent of Stock B. What would have been the realized rate of return on the portfolio in each year from 1997 through 2001? What would have been the average return on the portfolio during this period?
b. Now calculate the standard deviation of returns for each stock and for the portfolio. Use Equation 6-3a in Footnote 5.
c. Looking at the annual returns data on the two stocks, would you guess that the correlation coefficient between returns on the two stocks is closer to 0.9 or to −0.9?
d. If you added more stocks at random to the portfolio, which of the following is the most accurate statement of what would happen to σ_p?
  (1) σ_p would remain constant.
  (2) σ_p would decline to somewhere in the vicinity of 21 percent.
  (3) σ_p would decline to zero if enough stocks were included.

ST-3
Beta and required rate of return

ECRI Corporation is a holding company with four main subsidiaries. The percentage of its business coming from each of the subsidiaries, and their respective betas, are as follows:

SUBSIDIARY	PERCENTAGE OF BUSINESS	BETA
Electric utility	60%	0.70
Cable company	25	0.90
Real estate	10	1.30
International/special projects	5	1.50

a. What is the holding company's beta?
b. Assume that the risk-free rate is 6 percent and the market risk premium is 5 percent. What is the holding company's required rate of return?
c. ECRI is considering a change in its strategic focus; it will reduce its reliance on the electric utility subsidiary, so the percentage of its business from this subsidiary will be 50 percent. At the same time, ECRI will increase its reliance on the international/ special projects division, so the percentage of its business from that subsidiary will rise to 15 percent. What will be the shareholders' required rate of return if ECRI adopts these changes?

6-1
Expected return

A stock's expected return has the following distribution:

DEMAND FOR THE COMPANY'S PRODUCTS	PROBABILITY OF THIS DEMAND OCCURRING	RATE OF RETURN IF THIS DEMAND OCCURS
Weak	0.1	(50%)
Below average	0.2	(5)
Average	0.4	16
Above average	0.2	25
Strong	0.1	60
	1.0	

Calculate the stock's expected return, standard deviation, and coefficient of variation.

6-2
Portfolio beta

An individual has $35,000 invested in a stock that has a beta of 0.8 and $40,000 invested in a stock with a beta of 1.4. If these are the only two investments in her portfolio, what is her portfolio's beta?

6-3
Expected and required rates of return

Assume that the risk-free rate is 5 percent and the market risk premium is 6 percent. What is the expected return for the overall stock market? What is the required rate of return on a stock that has a beta of 1.2?

6-4
Required rate of return

Assume that the risk-free rate is 6 percent and the expected return on the market is 13 percent. What is the required rate of return on a stock that has a beta of 0.7?

6-5
Beta and required rate of return

A stock has a required return of 11 percent. The risk-free rate is 7 percent, and the market risk premium is 4 percent.
a. What is the stock's beta?
b. If the market risk premium increases to 6 percent, what will happen to the stock's required rate of return? Assume the risk-free rate and the stock's beta remain unchanged.

EXAM-TYPE PROBLEMS

The problems included in this section are set up in such a way that they could be used as multiple-choice exam problems.

6-6
Expected returns

The market and Stock J have the following probability distributions:

PROBABILITY	k_M	k_J
0.3	15%	20%
0.4	9	5
0.3	18	12

a. Calculate the expected rates of return for the market and Stock J.
b. Calculate the standard deviations for the market and Stock J.
c. Calculate the coefficients of variation for the market and Stock J.

6-7
Expected returns

Stocks X and Y have the following probability distributions of expected future returns:

PROBABILITY	X	Y
0.1	(10%)	(35%)
0.2	2	0
0.4	12	20
0.2	20	25
0.1	38	45

a. Calculate the expected rate of return, $\hat{k}$, for Stock Y. ($\hat{k}_X$ = 12%.)

b. Calculate the standard deviation of expected returns for Stock X. (That for Stock Y is 20.35 percent.) Now calculate the coefficient of variation for Stock Y. Is it possible that most investors might regard Stock Y as being *less* risky than Stock X? Explain.

6-8
Required rate of return

Suppose k_{RF} = 5%, k_M = 10%, and k_A = 12%.

a. Calculate Stock A's beta.

b. If Stock A's beta were 2.0, what would be A's new required rate of return?

6-9
Required rate of return

Suppose k_{RF} = 9%, k_M = 14%, and b_i = 1.3.

a. What is k_i, the required rate of return on Stock i?

b. Now suppose k_{RF} (1) increases to 10 percent or (2) decreases to 8 percent. The slope of the SML remains constant. How would this affect k_M and k_i?

c. Now assume k_{RF} remains at 9 percent but k_M (1) increases to 16 percent or (2) falls to 13 percent. The slope of the SML does not remain constant. How would these changes affect k_i?

6-10
Portfolio beta

Suppose you hold a diversified portfolio consisting of a $7,500 investment in each of 20 different common stocks. The portfolio beta is equal to 1.12. Now, suppose you have decided to sell one of the stocks in your portfolio with a beta equal to 1.0 for $7,500 and to use these proceeds to buy another stock for your portfolio. Assume the new stock's beta is equal to 1.75. Calculate your portfolio's new beta.

6-11
Portfolio required return

Suppose you are the money manager of a $4 million investment fund. The fund consists of 4 stocks with the following investments and betas:

STOCK	INVESTMENT	BETA
A	$ 400,000	1.50
B	600,000	(0.50)
C	1,000,000	1.25
D	2,000,000	0.75

If the market's required rate of return is 14 percent and the risk-free rate is 6 percent, what is the fund's required rate of return?

6-12
Portfolio beta

You have a $2 million portfolio consisting of a $100,000 investment in each of 20 different stocks. The portfolio has a beta equal to 1.1. You are considering selling $100,000 worth of one stock that has a beta equal to 0.9 and using the proceeds to purchase another stock that has a beta equal to 1.4. What will be the new beta of your portfolio following this transaction?

6-13
Required rate of return

Stock R has a beta of 1.5, Stock S has a beta of 0.75, the expected rate of return on an average stock is 13 percent, and the risk-free rate of return is 7 percent. By how much does the required return on the riskier stock exceed the required return on the less risky stock?

6-14
Evaluating risk and return

Stock X has an expected return of 10 percent, a beta coefficient of 0.9, and a standard deviation of expected returns of 35 percent. Stock Y has an expected return of 12.5 percent, a beta coefficient of 1.2, and a standard deviation of expected returns of 25 percent. The risk-free rate is 6 percent, and the market risk premium is 5 percent.

a. Calculate each stock's coefficient of variation.

b. Which stock is riskier for diversified investors?

c. Calculate each stock's required rate of return.

d. On the basis of the two stocks' expected and required returns, which stock would be most attractive to a diversified investor?

e. Calculate the required return of a portfolio that has $7,500 invested in Stock X and $2,500 invested in Stock Y.

f. If the market risk premium increased to 6 percent, which of the two stocks would have the largest increase in their required return?

PROBLEMS

6-15

Expected returns

Suppose you won the Florida lottery and were offered (1) $0.5 million or (2) a gamble in which you would receive $1 million if a head were flipped but zero if a tail came up.
  a. What is the expected value of the gamble?
  b. Would you take the sure $0.5 million or the gamble?
  c. If you choose the sure $0.5 million, are you a risk averter or a risk seeker?
  d. Suppose you actually take the sure $0.5 million. You can invest it in either a U.S. Treasury bond that will return $537,500 at the end of a year or a common stock that has a 50-50 chance of being either worthless or worth $1,150,000 at the end of the year.
    (1) What is the expected dollar profit on the stock investment? (The expected profit on the T-bond investment is $37,500.)
    (2) What is the expected rate of return on the stock investment? (The expected rate of return on the T-bond investment is 7.5 percent.)
    (3) Would you invest in the bond or the stock?
    (4) Exactly how large would the expected profit (or the expected rate of return) have to be on the stock investment to make *you* invest in the stock, given the 7.5 percent return on the bond?
    (5) How might your decision be affected if, rather than buying one stock for $0.5 million, you could construct a portfolio consisting of 100 stocks with $5,000 invested in each? Each of these stocks has the same return characteristics as the one stock — that is, a 50-50 chance of being worth either zero or $11,500 at year-end. Would the correlation between returns on these stocks matter?

6-16

Security Market Line

The Kish Investment Fund, in which you plan to invest some money, has total capital of $500 million invested in five stocks:

STOCK	INVESTMENT	STOCK'S BETA COEFFICIENT
A	$160 million	0.5
B	120 million	2.0
C	80 million	4.0
D	80 million	1.0
E	60 million	3.0

The beta coefficient for a fund like Kish Investment can be found as a weighted average of the fund's investments. The current risk-free rate is 6 percent, whereas market returns have the following estimated probability distribution for the next period:

PROBABILITY	MARKET RETURN
0.1	7%
0.2	9
0.4	11
0.2	13
0.1	15

  a. What is the estimated equation for the Security Market Line (SML)? (Hint: First determine the expected market return.)
  b. Calculate the fund's required rate of return for the next period.
  c. Suppose Bridget Nelson, the president, receives a proposal for a new stock. The investment needed to take a position in the stock is $50 million, it will have an expected

return of 15 percent, and its estimated beta coefficient is 2.0. Should the new stock be purchased? At what expected rate of return should the fund be indifferent to purchasing the stock?

6-17
Realized rates of return

Stocks A and B have the following historical returns:

YEAR	STOCK A'S RETURNS, k_A	STOCK B'S RETURNS, k_B
1997	(18.00%)	(14.50%)
1998	33.00	21.80
1999	15.00	30.50
2000	(0.50)	(7.60)
2001	27.00	26.30

a. Calculate the average rate of return for each stock during the period 1997 through 2001.
b. Assume that someone held a portfolio consisting of 50 percent of Stock A and 50 percent of Stock B. What would have been the realized rate of return on the portfolio in each year from 1997 through 2001? What would have been the average return on the portfolio during this period?
c. Calculate the standard deviation of returns for each stock and for the portfolio.
d. Calculate the coefficient of variation for each stock and for the portfolio.
e. If you are a risk-averse investor, would you prefer to hold Stock A, Stock B, or the portfolio? Why?

6-18
Financial calculator needed; Expected and required rates of return

You have observed the following returns over time:

YEAR	STOCK X	STOCK Y	MARKET
1997	14%	13%	12%
1998	19	7	10
1999	−16	−5	−12
2000	3	1	1
2001	20	11	15

Assume that the risk-free rate is 6 percent and the market risk premium is 5 percent.
a. What are the betas of Stocks X and Y? (Hint: See Appendix 6A.)
b. What are the required rates of return for Stocks X and Y?
c. What is the required rate of return for a portfolio consisting of 80 percent of Stock X and 20 percent of Stock Y?
d. If Stock X's expected return is 22 percent, is Stock X under- or overvalued?

SPREADSHEET PROBLEM

6-19
Evaluating risk and return

Bartman Industries' stock prices and dividends, along with the Wilshire 5000 Index, are shown below for the period 1995-2000. The Wilshire 5000 data are adjusted to include dividends.

	BARTMAN INDUSTRIES		REYNOLDS INCORPORATED		WILSHIRE 5000
YEAR	STOCK PRICE	DIVIDEND	STOCK PRICE	DIVIDEND	INCLUDES DIVS.
2000	$17.250	$1.15	$48.750	$3.00	11,663.98
1999	14.750	1.06	52.300	2.90	8,785.70
1998	16.500	1.00	48.750	2.75	8,679.98
1997	10.750	0.95	57.250	2.50	6,434.03
1996	11.375	0.90	60.000	2.25	5,602.28
1995	7.625	0.85	55.750	2.00	4,705.97

a. Use the data given to calculate annual returns for Bartman, Reynolds, and the Wilshire 5000 Index, and then calculate average returns over the 5-year period. (Hint: Remember, returns are calculated by subtracting the beginning price from the ending price to get the capital gain or loss, adding the dividend to the capital gain or loss, and dividing the result by the beginning price. Assume that dividends are already included in the index. Also, you cannot calculate the rate of return for 1995 because you do not have 1994 data.)

b. Calculate the standard deviations of the returns for Bartman, Reynolds, and the Wilshire 5000. (Hint: Use the sample standard deviation formula given in Footnote 5 to this chapter, which corresponds to the STDEV function in *Excel*.)

c. Now calculate the coefficients of variation for Bartman, Reynolds, and the Wilshire 5000.

d. Construct a scatter diagram graph that shows Bartman's and Reynolds' returns on the vertical axis and the market index's returns on the horizontal axis.

e. Estimate Bartman's and Reynolds' betas by running regressions of their returns against the Wilshire 5000's returns. Are these betas consistent with your graph?

f. The risk-free rate on long-term Treasury bonds is 6.04 percent. Assume that the average annual return on the Wilshire 5000 is *not* a good estimate of the market's required return — it is too high, so use 11 percent as the expected return on the market. Now use the SML equation to calculate the two companies' required returns.

g. If you formed a portfolio that consisted of 50 percent of Bartman stock and 50 percent of Reynolds stock, what would be the beta and the required return for the portfolio?

h. Suppose an investor wants to include Bartman Industries' stock in his or her portfolio. Stocks A, B, and C are currently in the portfolio, and their betas are 0.769, 0.985, and 1.423, respectively. Calculate the new portfolio's required return if it consists of 25 percent of Bartman, 15 percent of Stock A, 40 percent of Stock B, and 20 percent of Stock C.

CYBER PROBLEM

The information related to the cyberproblems is likely to change over time, due to the release of new information and the ever-changing nature of the World Wide Web. With these changes in mind, we will periodically update these problems on the textbook's web site. To avoid problems, please check for these updates before proceeding with the cyberproblems.

6-20
Risk and rates of return

The tendency of a stock's price to move up and down with the market is reflected in its beta coefficient. Therefore, beta is a measure of an investment's market risk and is a key element of the CAPM.

In this exercise you will find betas using Yahoo!Finance, located at **http://finance.yahoo.com**. To find a company's beta, enter the desired stock symbol and request a basic quote. Once you have the basic quote, select the "Profile" option in the "More Info" section of the basic quote screen. Scroll down this page to find the stock's beta.

a. According to Yahoo!Finance, what is the beta for a company called ELXSI, whose stock symbol is ELXS?

b. From Yahoo!Finance obtain a report on MBNA America Bank's holding company, KRB, whose stock symbol is KRB. What is KRB's beta?

c. Obtain and view a report for Exxon Mobil Corporation and identify its beta. Use Yahoo!Finance's look-up feature to obtain Exxon Mobil's trading symbol. To do this, click on *symbol lookup*, type part of the company name, say Exxon, and then click on Lookup. (Hint: You should find that the company's stock symbol is XOM.)

d. Obtain and view a report on Ford Motor Company, and identify its beta. Use Yahoo!Finance's look-up feature to obtain Ford's trading symbol.

e. If you made an equal dollar investment in each of the four stocks above, ELXSI, KRB, Exxon Mobil, and Ford Motor Company, what would be your portfolio's beta?

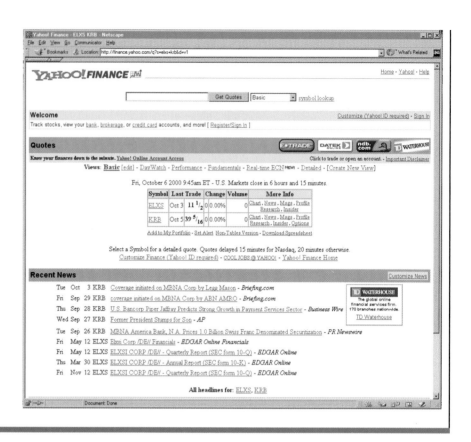

INTEGRATED CASE

MERRILL FINCH INC.

6-21 Risk and Return Assume that you recently graduated
with a major in finance, and you just landed a job as a financial
planner with Merrill Finch Inc., a large financial services corporation. Your first assignment is to invest $100,000 for a client.
Because the funds are to be invested in a business at the end of 1
year, you have been instructed to plan for a 1-year holding period. Further, your boss has restricted you to the following investment alternatives in the table below, shown with their
probabilities and associated outcomes. (Disregard for now the
items at the bottom of the data; you will fill in the blanks later.)

Merrill Finch's economic forecasting staff has developed
probability estimates for the state of the economy, and its security analysts have developed a sophisticated computer program, which was used to estimate the rate of return on each
alternative under each state of the economy. High Tech Inc.
is an electronics firm; Collections Inc. collects past-due
debts; and U.S. Rubber manufactures tires and various other
rubber and plastics products. Merrill Finch also maintains a
"market portfolio" that owns a market-weighted fraction of
all publicly traded stocks; you can invest in that portfolio,
and thus obtain average stock market results. Given the situation as described, answer the following questions.

a. (1) Why is the T-bill's return independent of the state of
the economy? Do T-bills promise a completely risk-free
return? (2) Why are High Tech's returns expected to
move with the economy whereas Collections' are expected to move counter to the economy?
b. Calculate the expected rate of return on each alternative
and fill in the blanks on the row for $\hat{k}$ in the table below.
c. You should recognize that basing a decision solely on expected returns is only appropriate for risk-neutral individuals. Since your client, like virtually everyone, is risk
averse, the riskiness of each alternative is an important
aspect of the decision. One possible measure of risk is
the standard deviation of returns. (1) Calculate this value
for each alternative, and fill in the blank on the row for
σ in the table below. (2) What type of risk is measured
by the standard deviation? (3) Draw a graph that shows
roughly the shape of the probability distributions for
High Tech, U.S. Rubber, and T-bills.
d. Suppose you suddenly remembered that the coefficient
of variation (CV) is generally regarded as being a better
measure of stand-alone risk than the standard deviation
when the alternatives being considered have widely differing expected returns. Calculate the missing CVs, and

STATE OF THE ECONOMY	PROBABILITY	T-BILLS	HIGH TECH	COLLECTIONS	U.S. RUBBER	MARKET PORTFOLIO	2-STOCK PORTFOLIO
				ESTIMATED RATE OF RETURN			
Recession	0.1	8.0%	(22.0%)	28.0%	10.0%*	(13.0%)	3.0%
Below average	0.2	8.0	(2.0)	14.7	(10.0)	1.0	
Average	0.4	8.0	20.0	0.0	7.0	15.0	10.0
Above average	0.2	8.0	35.0	(10.0)	45.0	29.0	
Boom	0.1	8.0	50.0	(20.0)	30.0	43.0	15.0
$\hat{k}$				1.7%	13.8%	15.0%	
σ		0.0		13.4	18.8	15.3	3.3
CV				7.9	1.4	1.0	0.3
b				−0.87	0.89		

* Note that the estimated returns of U.S. Rubber do not always move in the same direction as the overall economy. For example, when the economy is below average, consumers purchase fewer tires than they would if the economy was stronger. However, if the economy is in a flat-out recession, a large number of consumers who were planning to purchase a new car may choose to wait and instead purchase new tires for the car they currently own. Under these circumstances, we would expect U.S. Rubber's stock price to be higher if there is a recession than if the economy was just below average.

fill in the blanks on the row for CV in the table above. Does the CV produce the same risk rankings as the standard deviation?

e. Suppose you created a 2-stock portfolio by investing $50,000 in High Tech and $50,000 in Collections. (1) Calculate the expected return ($\hat{k}_p$), the standard deviation (σ_p), and the coefficient of variation (CV_p) for this portfolio and fill in the appropriate blanks in the table above. (2) How does the riskiness of this 2-stock portfolio compare with the riskiness of the individual stocks if they were held in isolation?

f. Suppose an investor starts with a portfolio consisting of one randomly selected stock. What would happen (1) to the riskiness and (2) to the expected return of the portfolio as more and more randomly selected stocks were added to the portfolio? What is the implication for investors? Draw a graph of the two portfolios to illustrate your answer.

g. (1) Should portfolio effects impact the way investors think about the riskiness of individual stocks? (2) If you decided to hold a 1-stock portfolio, and consequently were exposed to more risk than diversified investors, could you expect to be compensated for all of your risk; that is, could you earn a risk premium on that part of your risk that you could have eliminated by diversifying?

h. The expected rates of return and the beta coefficients of the alternatives as supplied by Merrill Finch's computer program are as follows:

SECURITY	RETURN ($\hat{k}$)	RISK (BETA)
High Tech	17.4%	1.30
Market	15.0	1.00
U.S. Rubber	13.8	0.89
T-bills	8.0	0.00
Collections	1.7	(0.87)

(1) What is a beta coefficient, and how are betas used in risk analysis? (2) Do the expected returns appear to be related to each alternative's market risk? (3) Is it possible to choose among the alternatives on the basis of the information developed thus far? Use the data given at the start of the problem to construct a graph that shows how the T-bill's, High Tech's, and Collections' beta coefficients are calculated. Then discuss what betas measure and how they are used in risk analysis.

i. The yield curve is currently flat, that is, long-term Treasury bonds also have an 8 percent yield. Consequently, Merrill Finch assumes that the risk-free rate is 8 percent. (1) Write out the Security Market Line (SML) equation, use it to calculate the required rate of return on each alternative, and then graph the relationship between the expected and required rates of return. (2) How do the expected rates of return compare with the required rates of return? (3) Does the fact that Collections has an expected return that is less than the T-bill rate make any sense? (4) What would be the market risk and the required return of a 50-50 portfolio of High Tech and Collections? Of High Tech and U.S. Rubber?

j. (1) Suppose investors raised their inflation expectations by 3 percentage points over current estimates as reflected in the 8 percent risk-free rate. What effect would higher inflation have on the SML and on the returns required on high- and low-risk securities? (2) Suppose instead that investors' risk aversion increased enough to cause the market risk premium to increase by 3 percentage points. (Inflation remains constant.) What effect would this have on the SML and on returns of high- and low-risk securities?

CALCULATING BETA COEFFICIENTS

The CAPM is an *ex ante* model, which means that all of the variables represent before-the-fact, *expected* values. In particular, the beta coefficient used in the SML equation should reflect the expected volatility of a given stock's return versus the return on the market during some *future* period. However, people generally calculate betas using data from some *past* period, and then assume that the stock's relative volatility will be the same in the future as it was in the past.

To illustrate how betas are calculated, consider Figure 6A-1. The data at the bottom of the figure show the historical realized returns for Stock J and for the market over the last five years. The data points have been plotted on the scatter diagram, and a regression line has been drawn. If all the data points had fallen on a straight line, as they did in Figure 6-9 in Chapter 6, it would be easy to draw an accurate line. If they do not, as in Figure 6A-1, then you must fit the line either "by eye" as an approximation or with a calculator.

Recall what the term *regression line*, or *regression equation*, means: The equation $Y = a + bX + e$ is the standard form of a simple linear regression. It states that the dependent variable, Y, is equal to a constant, a, plus b times X, where b is the slope coefficient and X is the independent variable, plus an error term, e. Thus, the rate of return on the stock during a given time period (Y) depends on what happens to the general stock market, which is measured by $X = \bar{k}_M$.

Once the data have been plotted and the regression line has been drawn on graph paper, we can estimate its intercept and slope, the a and b values in $Y = a + bX$. The intercept, a, is simply the point where the line cuts the vertical axis. The slope coefficient, b, can be estimated by the "rise-over-run" method. This involves calculating the amount by which $\bar{k}_J$ increases for a given increase in $\bar{k}_M$. For example, we observe in Figure 6A-1 that $\bar{k}_J$ increases from -8.9 to $+7.1$ percent (the rise) when $\bar{k}_M$ increases from 0 to 10.0 percent (the run). Thus, b, the beta coefficient, can be measured as follows:

$$b = \text{Beta} = \frac{\text{Rise}}{\text{Run}} = \frac{\Delta Y}{\Delta X} = \frac{7.1 - (-8.9)}{10.0 - 0.0} = \frac{16.0}{10.0} = 1.6.$$

Note that rise over run is a ratio, and it would be the same if measured using any two arbitrarily selected points on the line.

The regression line equation enables us to predict a rate of return for Stock J, given a value of $\bar{k}_M$. For example, if $\bar{k}_M = 15\%$, we would predict $\bar{k}_J = -8.9\% + 1.6(15\%) = 15.1\%$. However, the actual return would probably differ from the predicted return. This deviation is the error term, e_J, for the year, and it varies randomly from year to year depending on company-specific factors. Note, though, that the higher the correlation coefficient, the closer the points lie to the regression line, and the smaller the errors.

In actual practice, monthly, rather than annual, returns are generally used for $\bar{k}_J$ and $\bar{k}_M$, and five years of data are often employed; thus, there would be

Calculating Beta Coefficients

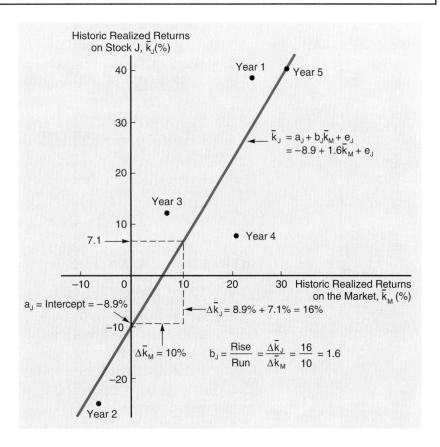

YEAR	MARKET ($\bar{k}_M$)	STOCK J ($\bar{k}_J$)
1	23.8%	38.6%
2	(7.2)	(24.7)
3	6.6	12.3
4	20.5	8.2
5	30.6	40.1
Average $\bar{k}$	14.9%	14.9%
$\sigma_{\bar{k}}$	15.1%	26.5%

$5 \times 12 = 60$ data points on the scatter diagram. Also, in practice one would use the *least squares method* for finding the regression coefficients a and b. This procedure minimizes the squared values of the error terms, and it is discussed in statistics courses.

The least squares value of beta can be obtained quite easily with a financial calculator. The procedures that follow explain how to find the values of beta and the slope using either a Texas Instruments, a Hewlett-Packard, or a Sharp financial calculator.

Texas Instruments BA, BA-II, or MBA Calculator

1. Press [2nd] [Mode] until "STAT" shows in the display.
2. Enter the first X value ($\bar{k}_M = 23.8$ in our example), press [x ⇄ y], and then enter the first Y value ($\bar{k}_J = 38.6$) and press [Σ+].
3. Repeat Step 2 until all values have been entered.
4. Press [2nd] [b/a] to find the value of Y at X = 0, which is the value of the Y intercept (a), −8.9219, and then press [x ⇄ y] to display the value of the slope (beta), 1.6031.
5. You could also press [2nd] [Corr] to obtain the correlation coefficient, r, which is 0.9134.

Putting it all together, you should have this regression line:

$$\bar{k}_J = -8.92 + 1.60\bar{k}_M$$
$$r = 0.9134.$$

Hewlett-Packard 10B[1]

1. Press [■] [Clear all] to clear your memory registers.
2. Enter the first X value ($\bar{k}_M = 23.8$ in our example), press [INPUT], and then enter the first Y value ($\bar{k}_J = 38.6$) and press [Σ+]. Be *sure* to enter the X variable first.
3. Repeat Step 2 until all values have been entered.
4. To display the vertical axis intercept, press 0 [■] [ŷ,m]. Then −8.9219 should appear.
5. To display the beta coefficient, b, press [■] [SWAP]. Then 1.6031 should appear.
6. To obtain the correlation coefficient, press [■] [x̂,r] and then [■] [SWAP] to get r = 0.9134.

Putting it all together, you should have this regression line:

$$\bar{k}_J = -8.92 + 1.60\bar{k}_M$$
$$r = 0.9134.$$

Sharp EL-733

1. Press [2nd F] [Mode] until "STAT" shows in the lower right corner of the display.
2. Press [2nd F] [CA] to clear all memory registers.
3. Enter the first X value ($\bar{k}_M = 23.8$ in our example) and press [(x,y)]. (This is the RM key; do not press the second F key at all.) Then enter the first Y value ($\bar{k}_J = 38.6$), and press [DATA]. (This is the M+ key; again, do not press the second F key.)

---

[1] The Hewlett-Packard 17B calculator is even easier to use. If you have one, see Chapter 9 of the *Owner's Manual*.

4. Repeat Step 3 until all values have been entered.

5. Press `2nd F` `a` to find the value of Y at X = 0, which is the value of the Y intercept (a), −8.9219, and then press `2nd F` `b` to display the value of the slope (beta), 1.6031.

6. You can also press `2nd F` `r` to obtain the correlation coefficient, r, which is 0.9134.

Putting it all together, you should have this regression line:

$$\bar{k}_J = -8.92 + 1.60\bar{k}_M$$

$$r = 0.9134.$$

Beta coefficients can also be calculated with spreadsheet programs such as *Excel.* Simply input the returns data and then use the spreadsheet's regression routine to calculate beta. The model on the file named 06MODEL.xls calculates beta for our illustrative Stock J, and it produces exactly the same results as with the calculator. However, the spreadsheet is more flexible. First, the file can be retained, and when new data become available, they can be added and a new beta can be calculated quite rapidly. Second, the regression output can include graphs and statistical information designed to give us an idea of how stable the beta coefficient is. In other words, while our beta was calculated to be 1.60, the "true beta" might actually be higher or lower, and the regression output can give us an idea of how large the error might be. Third, the spreadsheet can be used to calculate returns data from historical stock price and dividend information, and then the returns can be fed into the regression routine to calculate the beta coefficient. This is important, because stock market data are generally provided in the form of stock prices and dividends, making it necessary to calculate returns. This can be a big job if a number of different companies and a number of time periods are involved.

PROBLEMS

6A-1

Beta coefficients and rates of return

You are given the following set of data:

	HISTORICAL RATES OF RETURN ($\bar{k}$)	
YEAR	STOCK Y ($\bar{k}_Y$)	NYSE ($\bar{k}_M$)
1	3.0%	4.0%
2	18.2	14.3
3	9.1	19.0
4	(6.0)	(14.7)
5	(15.3)	(26.5)
6	33.1	37.2
7	6.1	23.8
8	3.2	(7.2)
9	14.8	6.6
10	24.1	20.5
11	18.0	30.6
Mean	9.8%	9.8%
$\sigma_{\bar{k}}$	13.8	19.6

a. Construct a scatter diagram graph (*on graph paper*) showing the relationship between returns on Stock Y and the market as in Figure 6A-1; then draw a freehand approximation of the regression line. What is the approximate value of the beta coefficient? (If you have a calculator with statistical functions, use it to calculate beta.)

b. Give a verbal interpretation of what the regression line and the beta coefficient show about Stock Y's volatility and relative riskiness as compared with other stocks.

c. Suppose the scatter of points had been more spread out but the regression line was exactly where your present graph shows it. How would this affect (1) the firm's risk if the stock were held in a 1-asset portfolio and (2) the actual risk premium on the stock if the CAPM held exactly? How would the degree of scatter (or the correlation coefficient) affect your confidence that the calculated beta will hold true in the years ahead?

d. Suppose the regression line had been downward sloping and the beta coefficient had been negative. What would this imply about (1) Stock Y's relative riskiness and (2) its probable risk premium?

e. Construct an illustrative probability distribution graph of returns (see Figure 6-7) for portfolios consisting of (1) only Stock Y, (2) 1 percent each of 100 stocks with beta coefficients similar to that of Stock Y, and (3) all stocks (that is, the distribution of returns on the market). Use as the expected rate of return the arithmetic mean as given previously for both Stock Y and the market, and assume that the distributions are normal. Are the expected returns "reasonable" — that is, is it reasonable that $\hat{k}_Y = \bar{k}_M = 9.8\%$?

f. Now, suppose that in the next year, Year 12, the market return was 27 percent, but Firm Y increased its use of debt, which raised its perceived risk to investors. Do you think that the return on Stock Y in Year 12 could be approximated by this historical characteristic line?

$$\hat{k}_Y = 3.8\% + 0.62(\hat{k}_M) = 3.8\% + 0.62(27\%) = 20.5\%.$$

g. Now, suppose $\bar{k}_Y$ in Year 12, after the debt ratio was increased, had actually been 0 percent. What would the new beta be, based on the most recent 11 years of data (that is, Years 2 through 12)? Does this beta seem reasonable — that is, is the change in beta consistent with the other facts given in the problem?

6A-2
Security Market Line
You are given the following historical data on market returns, $\bar{k}_M$, and the returns on Stocks A and B, $\bar{k}_A$ and $\bar{k}_B$:

YEAR	$\bar{k}_M$	$\bar{k}_A$	$\bar{k}_B$
1	29.00%	29.00%	20.00%
2	15.20	15.20	13.10
3	(10.00)	(10.00)	0.50
4	3.30	3.30	7.15
5	23.00	23.00	17.00
6	31.70	31.70	21.35

k_{RF}, the risk-free rate, is 9 percent. Your probability distribution for k_M for next year is as follows:

PROBABILITY	k_M
0.1	(14%)
0.2	0
0.4	15
0.2	25
0.1	44

a. Determine graphically the beta coefficients for Stocks A and B.

b. Graph the Security Market Line, and give its equation.

c. Calculate the required rates of return on Stocks A and B.

d. Suppose a new stock, C, with $\hat{k}_C = 18$ percent and $b_C = 2.0$, becomes available. Is this stock in equilibrium; that is, does the required rate of return on Stock C equal its expected return? Explain. If the stock is not in equilibrium, explain how equilibrium will be restored.

CHAPTER 7

Time Value of Money[1]

SOURCE: © Zigy Kaluzny/Tony Stone Images.

[1] This chapter was written on the assumption that most students will have financial calculators. Calculators are relatively inexpensive, and students who cannot use them run the risk of being deemed obsolete and uncompetitive before they even graduate. Therefore, the chapter has been written to include a discussion of financial calculator solutions along with the regular calculator, and tabular and spreadsheet solutions. Those sections that require the use of financial calculators, are identified, and instructors may choose to permit students to skip them.

Your reaction to the question in the title of this vignette is probably, "First things first! I'm worried about getting a job, not retiring!" However, an awareness of the retirement situation could help you land a job because (1) this is an important issue today, (2) employers prefer to hire people who know the issues, and (3) professors often test students on time value of money with problems related to saving for some future purpose, including retirement. So read on.

A recent *Fortune* article began with some interesting facts: (1) The U.S. savings rate is the lowest of any industrial nation. (2) The ratio of U.S. workers to retirees, which was 17 to 1 in 1950, is now down to 3.2 to 1, and it will decline to less than 2 to 1 after 2020. (3) With so few people paying into the Social Security System, and so many drawing funds out, Social Security may soon be in serious trouble. The article concluded that even people making $85,000 per year will have trouble maintaining a reasonable standard of living after they retire, and many of today's college students will have to support their parents.

If Ms. Jones, who earns $85,000, retires in 2001, expects to live for another 20 years after retirement, and needs 80 percent of her pre-retirement income, she would require $68,000 during 2001. However, if inflation amounts to 5 percent per year, her income requirement would increase to $110,765 in 10 years and to $180,424 in 20 years. If inflation were 7 percent, her Year 20 requirement would jump to $263,139! How much wealth would Ms. Jones need at retirement to maintain her standard of living, and how much would she have had to save during each working year to accumulate that wealth?

The answer depends on a number of factors, including the rate she could earn on her savings, the inflation rate, and when her savings program began. Also, the answer would depend on how much she will receive from Social Security and from her corporate retirement plan, if she has one. (She might not receive much from Social Security unless she is really down and out.) Note, too, that her plans could be upset if the inflation rate increased, if the return on her savings changed, or if she lived beyond 20 years.

Fortune and other organizations have done studies relating to the retirement issue, using the tools and techniques described in this chapter. The general conclusion is that most Americans have been putting their heads in the sand — many of us have been ignoring what is almost certainly going to be a huge personal and social problem. But if you study this chapter carefully, you can avoid the trap that seems to be catching so many people. ■

Note also that tutorials on how to use several Hewlett-Packard, Texas Instruments, and Sharp calculators are provided in the *Technology Supplement* to this book, which is available to adopting instructors. We also discuss spreadsheets briefly in the chapter, and a more complete discussion is contained in the file 07MODEL.xls on the CD-ROM that accompanies the book. The spreadsheet material is also set up so that it can be either covered or skipped.

PUTTING THINGS IN PERSPECTIVE

Excellent retirement calculators are available at **http://www.sovereignbank.com/calculate/index.html**. You will need to scroll down the page until you see retirement calculators — there are 17 of them, each designed to answer a different question. Each one provides results, graphs, and explanations.

In Chapter 1, we saw that the primary goal of financial management is to maximize the value of the firm's stock. We also saw that stock values depend in part on the timing of the cash flows investors expect to receive from an investment — a dollar expected soon is worth more than a dollar expected in the distant future. Therefore, it is essential for financial managers to have a clear understanding of the time value of money and its impact on stock prices. These concepts are discussed in this chapter, where we show how the timing of cash flows affects asset values and rates of return.

The principles of time value analysis have many applications, ranging from setting up schedules for paying off loans to decisions about whether to acquire new equipment. *In fact, of all the concepts used in finance, none is more important than the time value of money, also called discounted cash flow (DCF) analysis.* Since this concept is used throughout the remainder of the book, it is vital that you understand the material in this chapter before you move on to other topics. ■

TIME LINES

Time Line
An important tool used in time value of money analysis; it is a graphical representation used to show the timing of cash flows.

One of the most important tools in time value analysis is the **time line,** which is used by analysts to help visualize what is happening in a particular problem and then to help set up the problem for solution. To illustrate the time line concept, consider the following diagram:

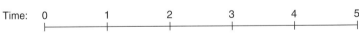

Time 0 is today; Time 1 is one period from today, or the end of Period 1; Time 2 is two periods from today, or the end of Period 2; and so on. Thus, the numbers above the tick marks represent end-of-period values. Often the periods are years, but other time intervals such as semiannual periods, quarters, months, or even days can be used. If each period on the time line represents a year, the interval from the tick mark corresponding to 0 to the tick mark corresponding to 1 would be Year 1, the interval from 1 to 2 would be Year 2, and so on. Note that each tick mark corresponds to the end of one period as well as the beginning of the next period. In other words, the tick mark at Time 1 represents the *end* of Year 1, and it also represents the *beginning* of Year 2 because Year 1 has just passed.

Cash flows are placed directly below the tick marks, and interest rates are shown directly above the time line. Unknown cash flows, which you are trying to find in the analysis, are indicated by question marks. Now consider the following time line:

Time: 0   5%   1   2   3
         |----------|---------|---------|
Cash flows: −100   ?

Here the interest rate for each of the three periods is 5 percent; a single amount (or lump sum) cash **outflow** is made at Time 0; and the Time 3 value is an unknown **inflow**. Since the initial $100 is an outflow (an investment), it has a minus sign. Since the Period 3 amount is an inflow, it does not have a minus sign, which implies a plus sign. Note that no cash flows occur at Times 1 and 2. Note also that we generally do not show dollar signs on time lines to reduce clutter.

Now consider a different situation, where a $100 cash outflow is made today, and we will receive an unknown amount at the end of Time 2:

         0   5%   1   10%   2
         |----------|---------|
        −100   ?

Here the interest rate is 5 percent during the first period, but it rises to 10 percent during the second period. If the interest rate is constant in all periods, we show it only in the first period, but if it changes, we show all the relevant rates on the time line.

Time lines are essential when you are first learning time value concepts, but even experts use time lines to analyze complex problems. We will be using time lines throughout the book, and you should get into the habit of using them when you work problems.

SELF-TEST QUESTION

Draw a three-year time line to illustrate the following situation: (1) An outflow of $10,000 occurs at Time 0. (2) Inflows of $5,000 then occur at the end of Years 1, 2, and 3. (3) The interest rate during all three years is 10 percent.

FUTURE VALUE

A dollar in hand today is worth more than a dollar to be received in the future because, if you had it now, you could invest it, earn interest, and end up with more than one dollar in the future. The process of going from today's values, or present values (PVs), to future values (FVs) is called **compounding**. To illustrate, suppose you deposit $100 in a bank that pays 5 percent interest each year. How much would you have at the end of one year? To begin, we define the following terms:

PV = present value, or beginning amount, in your account. Here PV = $100.

i = interest rate the bank pays on the account per year. The interest earned is based on the balance at the beginning of each year, and we assume that it is paid at the end of the year. Here i = 5%, or, expressed as a decimal, i = 0.05. Throughout this chapter, we designate the interest rate as i (or I) because that symbol is used on most financial calculators. Note, though, that in later chapters we use the symbol k to denote interest rates because k is used more often in the financial literature.

INT = dollars of interest you earn during the year = Beginning amount × i. Here INT = $100(0.05) = $5.

FV_n = future value, or ending amount, of your account at the end of n years. Whereas PV is the value now, or the *present value*, FV_n is the value n years into the *future*, after the interest earned has been added to the account.

n = number of periods involved in the analysis. Here n = 1.

In our example, n = 1, so FV_n can be calculated as follows:

$$FV_n = FV_1 = PV + INT$$
$$= PV + PV(i)$$
$$= PV(1 + i)$$
$$= \$100(1 + 0.05) = \$100(1.05) = \$105.$$

Future Value (FV)
The amount to which a cash flow or series of cash flows will grow over a given period of time when compounded at a given interest rate.

Thus, the **future value (FV)** at the end of one year, FV_1, equals the present value multiplied by 1 plus the interest rate, so you will have $105 after one year.

What would you end up with if you left your $100 in the account for five years? Here is a time line set up to show the amount at the end of each year:

	0	5%	1	2	3	4	5
Initial deposit:	−100		FV_1 = ?	FV_2 = ?	FV_3 = ?	FV_4 = ?	FV_5 = ?
Interest earned:			5.00	5.25	5.51	5.79	6.08
Amount at the end of each period = FV_n:			105.00	110.25	115.76	121.55	**127.63**

Note the following points: (1) You start by depositing $100 in the account — this is shown as an outflow at t = 0. (2) You earn $100(0.05) = $5 of interest during the first year, so the amount at the end of Year 1 (or t = 1) is $100 + $5 = $105. (3) You start the second year with $105, earn $5.25 on the now larger amount, and end the second year with $110.25. Your interest during Year 2, $5.25, is higher than the first year's interest, $5, because you earned $5(0.05) = $0.25 interest on the first year's interest. (4) This process continues, and because the beginning balance is higher in each succeeding year, the annual interest earned increases. (5) The total interest earned, $27.63, is reflected in the final balance at t = 5, $127.63.

Note that the value at the end of Year 2, $110.25, is equal to

$$FV_2 = FV_1(1 + i)$$
$$= PV(1 + i)(1 + i)$$
$$= PV(1 + i)^2$$
$$= \$100(1.05)^2 = \$110.25.$$

Continuing, the balance at the end of Year 3 is

$$FV_3 = FV_2(1 + i)$$
$$= PV(1 + i)^3$$
$$= \$100(1.05)^3 = \$115.76,$$

and

$$FV_5 = \$100(1.05)^5 = \$127.63.$$

In general, the future value of an initial lump sum at the end of n years can be found by applying Equation 7-1:

$$FV_n = PV(1 + i)^n. \qquad (7\text{-}1)$$

Equation 7-1 and most other time value of money equations can be solved in four ways: numerically with a regular calculator, with interest tables, with a financial calculator, or with a computer spreadsheet program. Most advanced work in financial management will be done with a financial calculator or on a computer, but when learning basic concepts it is best to work through all the methods.

Numerical Solution

One can use a regular calculator and either multiply $(1 + i)$ by itself $n - 1$ times or else use the exponential function to raise $(1 + i)$ to the nth power. With most calculators, you would enter $1 + i = 1.05$ and multiply it by itself four times, or else enter 1.05, then press the y^x (exponential) function key, and then enter 5. In either case, your answer would be 1.2763 (if you set your calculator to display four decimal places), which you would multiply by \$100 to get the final answer, \$127.6282, which would be rounded to \$127.63.

In certain problems, it is extremely difficult to arrive at a solution using a regular calculator. We will tell you this when we have such a problem, and in these cases we will not show a numerical solution. Also, at times we show the numerical solution just below the time line, as a part of the diagram, rather than in a separate section.

Interest Tables (Tabular Solution)

Future Value Interest Factor for i and n (FVIF$_{i,n}$)
The future value of \$1 left on deposit for n periods at a rate of i percent per period.

The **Future Value Interest Factor for i and n (FVIF$_{i,n}$)** is defined as $(1 + i)^n$, and these factors can be found by using a regular calculator as discussed above and then put into tables. Table 7-1 is illustrative, while Table A-3 in Appendix A at the back of the book contains FVIF$_{i,n}$ values for a wide range of i and n values.

Since $(1 + i)^n = FVIF_{i,n}$, Equation 7-1 can be rewritten as follows:

$$FV_n = PV(FVIF_{i,n}). \qquad (7\text{-}1a)$$

To illustrate, the FVIF for our five-year, 5 percent interest problem can be found in Table 7-1 by looking down the first column to Period 5, and then looking across that row to the 5 percent column, where we see that FVIF$_{5\%,5} = 1.2763$. Then, the value of \$100 after five years is found as follows:

$$FV_n = PV(FVIF_{i,n})$$
$$= \$100(1.2763) = \$127.63.$$

TABLE 7-1

PERIOD (n)	0%	5%	10%	15%
Future Value Interest Factors: $FVIF_{i,n} = (1 + i)^n$				
1	1.0000	1.0500	1.1000	1.1500
2	1.0000	1.1025	1.2100	1.3225
3	1.0000	1.1576	1.3310	1.5209
4	1.0000	1.2155	1.4641	1.7490
5	1.0000	**1.2763**	1.6105	2.0114
6	1.0000	1.3401	1.7716	2.3131
7	1.0000	1.4071	1.9487	2.6600
8	1.0000	1.4775	2.1436	3.0590
9	1.0000	1.5513	2.3579	3.5179
10	1.0000	1.6289	2.5937	4.0456

Before financial calculators became readily available (in the 1980s), such tables were used extensively, but they are rarely used today in the real world.

Financial Calculator Solution

Equation 7-1 and a number of other equations have been programmed directly into financial calculators, and these calculators can be used to find future values. Note that calculators have five keys that correspond to the five most commonly used time value of money variables:

Here

    N = the number of periods. Some calculators use n rather than N.
     I = interest rate per period. Some calculators use i or I/YR rather than I.
   PV = present value.
 PMT = payment. This key is used only if the cash flows involve a series of equal, or constant, payments (an annuity). If there are no periodic payments in a particular problem, then PMT = 0.
   FV = future value.

On some financial calculators, these keys are actually buttons on the face of the calculator, while on others they are shown on a screen after going into the time value of money (TVM) menu.

    In this chapter, we deal with equations involving only four of the variables at any one time — three of the variables are known, and the calculator then solves for the fourth (unknown) variable. In the next chapter, when we deal with bonds, we will use all five variables in the bond valuation equation.[2]

---

[2] The equation programmed into the calculators actually has five variables, one for each key. In this chapter, the value of one of the variables is always zero. It is a good idea to get into the habit of inputting

(footnote continues)

To find the future value of $100 after five years at 5 percent using a financial calculator, note that we must solve Equation 7-1:

$$FV_n = PV(1 + i)^n. \qquad \text{(7-1)}$$

The equation has four variables, FV_n, PV, i, and n. If we know any three, we can solve for the fourth. In our example, we enter N = 5, I = 5, PV = 100, and PMT = 0. Then, when we press the FV key, we get the answer, FV = 127.63 (rounded to two decimal places).[3]

Many financial calculators require that all cash flows be designated as either inflows or outflows, with outflows being entered as negative numbers. In our illustration, you deposit, or put in, the initial amount (which is an outflow to you) and you take out, or receive, the ending amount (which is an inflow to you). If your calculator requires that you follow this sign convention, the PV would be entered as −100. Enter the −100 by keying in 100 and then pressing the "change sign" or +/− key. (If you entered 100, then the FV would appear as −127.63.) Also, on some calculators you are required to press a "Compute" key before pressing the FV key.

Sometimes the convention of changing signs can be confusing. For example, if you have $100 in the bank now and want to find out how much you will have after five years if your account pays 5 percent interest, the calculator will give you a negative answer, in this case −127.63, because the calculator assumes you are going to withdraw the funds. This sign convention should cause you no problem if you think about what you are doing.

We should also note that financial calculators permit you to specify the number of decimal places that are displayed. Twelve significant digits are actually used in the calculations, but we generally use two places for answers when working with dollars or percentages and four places when working with decimals. The nature of the problem dictates how many decimal places should be displayed.

Spreadsheet Solution

As noted back in Chapter 2, spreadsheet programs are ideally suited for solving many financial problems, including time value of money problems.[4] With very little effort, the spreadsheet itself becomes a time line. Here is how the problem would look in a spreadsheet:

(Footnote 2 continued)

a zero for the unused variable (whose value is automatically set equal to zero when you clear the calculator's memory); if you forget to clear your calculator, inputting a zero will help you avoid trouble.

[3] Here we assume that compounding occurs once each year. Most calculators have a setting that can be used to designate the number of compounding periods per year. For example, the HP-10B comes preset with payments at 12 per year. You would need to change it to 1 per year to get FV = 127.63. With the HP-10B, you would do this by typing 1, pressing the gold key, and then pressing the P/YR key.

[4] In this section, and in other sections and chapters, we discuss spreadsheet solutions to various financial problems. If a reader is not familiar with spreadsheets and has no interest in them, then these sections can be omitted. For those who are interested, 07MODEL.xls is the *Excel* file on the CD-ROM for this chapter that does the various calculations in the chapter. If you have the time, we *highly recommend* that you go through the models. This will give you practice with *Excel*, which will help tremendously in later courses, in the job market, and in the workplace. Also, going through the models will enhance your understanding of financial concepts.

	A	B	C	D	E	F	G
1	Interest rate	0.05					
2	Time	0	1	2	3	4	5
3	Cash flow	−100					
4	Future value		105.00	110.25	115.76	121.55	**127.63**

Cell B1 shows the interest rate, entered as a decimal number, 0.05. Row 2 shows the periods for the time line. With *Microsoft Excel*, you could enter **0** in Cell B2, then the formula **=B2+1** in Cell C2, and then copy this formula into Cells D2 through G2 to produce the time periods shown on Row 2. Note that if your time line had many years, say, 50, you would simply copy the formula across more columns. Other procedures could also be used to enter the periods.

Row 3 shows the cash flows. In this case, there is only one cash flow, shown in Cell B3. Row 4 shows the future value of this cash flow at the end of each year. Cell C4 contains the formula for Equation 7-1. The formula could be written as **=−$B$3*(1+.05)^C2**, but we wrote it as **=−$B$3*(1+$B$1)^C2**, which gives us the flexibility to change the interest rate in Cell B1 to see how the future value changes with changes in interest rates. Note that the formula has a minus sign for the PV (which is in Cell B3) to account for the minus sign of the cash flow. This formula was then copied into Cells D4 through G4. As Cell G4 shows, the value of $100 compounded for five years at 5 percent per year is $127.63.

You could also find the FV by putting the cursor on Cell G4, then clicking the function wizard, then Financial, then scrolling down to FV, and then clicking OK to bring up the FV dialog box. Then enter B1 or 0.05 for Rate, G2 or 5 for Nper, 0 or leave blank for Pmt because there are no periodic payments, B3 or −100 for PV, and 0 or leave blank for Type to indicate that payments occur at the end of the period. Then, when you click OK, you get the future value, $127.63.

Note that the dialog box prompts you to fill in the arguments in an equation. The equation itself, in *Excel* format, is FV(Rate,Nper,Pmt,PV,Type) = FV(0.05,5,0,−100,0). Rather than insert numbers, you could input cell references for Rate, Nper, Pmt, and PV. Either way, when Excel sees the equation, it knows to use our Equation 7-1 to fill in the specified arguments, and to deposit the result in the cell where the cursor was located when you began the process. If someone *really* knows what they are doing and has memorized the formula, they can skip both the time line and the function wizard and just insert data into the formula to get the answer. But until you become an expert, we recommend that you use time lines to visualize the problem and the function wizard to complete the formula.

COMPARING THE FOUR PROCEDURES

The first step in solving any time value problem is to understand the verbal description of the problem well enough to diagram it on a time line. Woody Allen said that 90 percent of success is just showing up. With time value problems, 90 percent of success is correctly setting up the time line.

After you diagram the problem on a time line, your next step is to pick an approach to solve the problem. Which of the four approaches should you use

— numerical, tabular, financial calculator, or spreadsheet? In general, you should use the easiest approach. But which is easiest? The answer depends on the particular situation.

First, we would never recommend the tabular approach — it went out when calculators were invented some 20 years ago. Second, all business students should know Equation 7-1 by heart and should also know how to use a financial calculator. So, for simple problems such as finding the future value of a single payment, it is probably easiest and quickest to use either the numerical approach or a financial calculator.

For problems with more than a couple of cash flows, the numerical approach is usually too time consuming, so here either the calculator or spreadsheet approaches would generally be used. Calculators are portable and quick to set up, but if many calculations of the same type must be done, or if you want to see how changes in an input such as the interest rate affect the future value, the spreadsheet approach is generally more efficient. If the problem has many irregular cash flows, or if you want to analyze many scenarios with different cash flows, then the spreadsheet approach is definitely the most efficient. The important point is that you understand the various approaches well enough to make a rational choice, given the nature of the problem and the equipment you have available. In any event, you must understand the concepts behind the calculations and know how to set up time lines in order to work complex problems. This is true for stock and bond valuation, capital budgeting, lease analysis, and many other important types of problems.

PROBLEM FORMAT

To help you understand the various types of time value problems, we generally use a standard format. First, we state the problem in words. Next, we diagram the problem on a time line. Then, beneath the time line, we show the equation that must be solved. Finally, we present four alternative procedures for solving the equation to obtain the answer: (1) use a regular calculator to obtain a numerical solution, (2) use the tables, (3) use a financial calculator, or (4) use a spreadsheet program. For some of the very easy problems, we will not show a spreadsheet solution, and for some difficult problems, we will not show numerical or tabular solutions because they are simply too inefficient.

To illustrate the format, consider again our five-year, 5 percent example:

Time Line:

```
0    5%    1         2         3         4         5
|----------+---------+---------+---------+---------|
-100                                            FV=?
```

Equation:

$$FV_n = PV(1 + i)^n = \$100(1.05)^5.$$

1. Numerical Solution

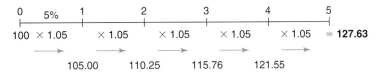

```
0      5%    1         2         3         4         5
|------------+---------+---------+---------+---------|
100 × 1.05     × 1.05    × 1.05    × 1.05    × 1.05   = 127.63

           105.00    110.25    115.76    121.55
```

Using a regular calculator, raise 1.05 to the 5th power and multiply by $100 to get $FV_5 = \$127.63$.

2. Tabular Solution

Look up $FVIF_{5\%,5}$ in Table 7-1 or Table A-3 at the end of the book, and then multiply by $100:

$$FV_5 = \$100(FVIF_{5\%,5}) = \$100(1.2763) = \$127.63.$$

3. Financial Calculator Solution

Inputs:	5	5	−100	0	
	N	I	PV	PMT	FV
Output:					= 127.63

Note that the calculator diagram tells you to input N = 5, I = 5, PV = −100, and PMT = 0, and then to press the FV key to get the answer, 127.63. Interest rates are entered as percentages (5), not decimals (0.05). Also, note that in this particular problem, the PMT key does not come into play, as no constant series of payments is involved.[5] Finally, you should recognize that small rounding differences will often occur among the various solution methods because tables use fewer significant digits (4) than do calculators (12), and also because rounding sometimes is done at intermediate steps in long problems.

4. Spreadsheet Solution

	A	B	C	D	E	F	G
1	Interest rate	0.05					
2	Time	0	1	2	3	4	5
3	Cash flow	−100					
4	Future value		105.00	110.25	115.76	121.55	127.63

Cell G4 contains the formula for Equation 7-1: **=−$B$3*(1+$B$1)^G2** or **=−$B$3*(1+.05)^G2**. You could also use *Excel's* FV function to find the $127.63, following the procedures described in the previous section.

GRAPHIC VIEW OF THE COMPOUNDING PROCESS: GROWTH

Figure 7-1 shows how $1 (or any other lump sum) grows over time at various interest rates. The data used to plot the curves could be obtained from Table

---

[5] We input PMT = 0, but if you cleared the calculator before you started, the PMT register would already have been set to 0.

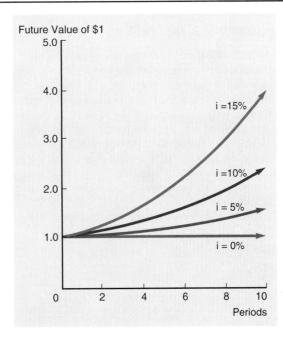

A-3, but we generated the data and then made the graph with a spreadsheet model. See 07MODEL.xls. The higher the rate of interest, the faster the rate of growth. The interest rate is, in fact, a growth rate: If a sum is deposited and earns 5 percent interest, then the funds on deposit will grow at a rate of 5 percent per period. Note also that time value concepts can be applied to anything that is growing—sales, population, earnings per share, your future salary, or whatever.

SELF-TEST QUESTIONS

Explain what is meant by the following statement: "A dollar in hand today is worth more than a dollar to be received next year."

What is compounding? Explain why earning "interest on interest" is called "compound interest."

Explain the following equation: $FV_1 = PV + INT$.

Set up a time line that shows the following situation: (1) Your initial deposit is $100. (2) The account pays 5 percent interest annually. (3) You want to know how much money you will have at the end of three years.

Write out an equation that could be used to solve the preceding problem.

What are the five TVM (time value of money) input keys on a financial calculator? List them (horizontally) in the proper order.

INDUSTRY PRACTICE

THE POWER OF COMPOUND INTEREST

You are 21 years old and have just graduated from college. After reading the introduction to this chapter, you decide to start investing in the stock market for your retirement. Your goal is to have $1 million when you retire at age 65. Assuming you earn a 10 percent annual rate on your stock investments, how much must you invest at the end of each year in order to reach your goal?

The answer is $1,532.24, but this amount depends critically on the return earned on your investments. If returns drop to 8 percent, your required annual contributions would rise to $2,801.52, while if returns rise to 12 percent, you would only need to put away $825.21 per year.

What if you are like most of us and wait until later to worry about retirement? If you wait until age 40, you will need to

save $10,168 per year to reach your $1 million goal, assuming you earn 10 percent, and $13,679 per year if you earn only 8 percent. If you wait until age 50 and then earn 8 percent, the required amount will be $36,830 per year.

While $1 million may seem like a lot of money, it won't be when you get ready to retire. If inflation averages 5 percent a year over the next 44 years, your $1 million nest egg will be worth only $116,861 in today's dollars. At an 8 percent rate of return, and assuming you live for 20 years after retirement, your annual retirement income in today's dollars would be only $11,903 before taxes. So, after celebrating graduation and your new job, start saving!

PRESENT VALUE

Opportunity Cost Rate
The rate of return on the best available alternative investment of equal risk.

Suppose you have some extra cash, and you have a chance to buy a low-risk security that will pay $127.63 at the end of five years. Your local bank is currently offering 5 percent interest on five-year certificates of deposit (CDs), and you regard the security as being exactly as safe as a CD. The 5 percent rate is defined as your **opportunity cost rate,** or the rate of return you could earn on an alternative investment of similar risk. How much should you be willing to pay for the security?

Present Value (PV)
The value today of a future cash flow or series of cash flows.

From the future value example presented in the previous section, we saw that an initial amount of $100 invested at 5 percent per year would be worth $127.63 at the end of five years. As we will see in a moment, you should be indifferent between $100 today and $127.63 at the end of five years. The $100 is defined as the **present value,** or **PV,** of $127.63 due in five years when the opportunity cost rate is 5 percent. If the price of the security were less than $100, you should buy it, because its price would then be less than the $100 you would have to spend on a similar-risk alternative to end up with $127.63 after five years. Conversely, if the security cost more than $100, you should not buy it, because you would have to invest only $100 in a similar-risk alternative to end up with $127.63 after five years. If the price were exactly $100, then you should be indifferent — you could either buy the security or turn it down. Therefore, $100 is defined as the security's **fair,** or **equilibrium, value.**

Fair (Equilibrium) Value
The price at which investors are indifferent between buying or selling a security.

In general, *the present value of a cash flow due n years in the future is the amount which, if it were on hand today, would grow to equal the future amount.* Since $100 would grow to $127.63 in five years at a 5 percent interest rate, $100 is the present value of $127.63 due in five years when the opportunity cost rate is 5 percent.

Discounting
The process of finding the present value of a cash flow or a series of cash flows; discounting is the reverse of compounding.

Finding present values is called **discounting,** and it is simply the reverse of compounding — if you know the PV, you can compound to find the FV, while if you know the FV, you can discount to find the PV. When discounting, you would follow these steps:

Time Line:

PV = ? 127.63

Equation:

To develop the discounting equation, we begin with the future value equation, Equation 7-1:

$$FV_n = PV(1 + i)^n = PV(FVIF_{i,n}). \qquad (7\text{-}1)$$

Next, we solve it for PV in several equivalent forms:

$$PV = \frac{FV_n}{(1 + i)^n} = FV_n\left(\frac{1}{1 + i}\right)^n = FV_n(PVIF_{i,n}). \qquad (7\text{-}2)$$

The last form of Equation 7-2 recognizes that the interest factor $PVIF_{i,n}$ is equal to the term in parentheses in the second version of the equation.

1. Numerical Solution

0	5%	1	2	3	4	5
−**100** =	←	105.00 ←	110.25 ←	115.76 ←	121.55 ←	127.63
		÷ 1.05	÷ 1.05	÷ 1.05	÷ 1.05	÷ 1.05

Divide $127.63 by 1.05 five times, or by $(1.05)^5$, to find PV = $100.

2. Tabular Solution

Present Value Interest Factor for i and n ($PVIF_{i,n}$)
The present value of $1 due n periods in the future discounted at i percent per period.

The term in parentheses in Equation 7-2 is called the **Present Value Interest Factor for i and n,** or **$PVIF_{i,n}$,** and Table A-1 in Appendix A contains present value interest factors for selected values of i and n. The value of $PVIF_{i,n}$ for i = 5% and n = 5 is 0.7835, so the present value of $127.63 to be received after five years when the appropriate interest rate is 5 percent is $100:

$$PV = \$127.63(PVIF_{5\%,5}) = \$127.63(0.7835) = \$100.$$

3. Financial Calculator Solution

Inputs: 5   5   0   127.63
          N   I   PV   PMT   FV
Output: = −100

Enter N = 5, I = 5, PMT = 0, and FV = 127.63, and then press PV to get PV = −100. This is the easy way!

4. Spreadsheet Solution

	A	B	C	D	E	F	G
1	Interest rate	0.05					
2	Time	0	1	2	3	4	5
3	Cash flow		0	0	0	0	127.63
4	Present value	100					

You could enter the spreadsheet version of Equation 7-2 in Cell B4, **=127.63/(1+0.05)^5**, but you could also use the built-in spreadsheet PV function. In *Excel*, you would put the cursor on Cell B4, then click the function wizard, indicate that you want a Financial function, scroll down, and double click PV. Then, in the dialog box, enter B1 or 0.05 for Rate, G2 or 5 for Nper, 0 for Pmt (because there are no annual payments), G3 or 127.63 for FV, and 0 (or leave blank) for Type because the cash flow occurs at the end of the year. Then, press OK to get the answer, PV = $100.00.

GRAPHIC VIEW OF THE DISCOUNTING PROCESS

Figure 7-2 shows how the present value of $1 (or any other sum) to be received in the future diminishes as the years to receipt and the interest rate increase. Again, the data used to plot the curves could be obtained with a calculator, but we used a spreadsheet to calculate the data and make the graph. See 07MODEL.xls. The graph shows (1) that the present value of a sum to be received at some future date decreases and approaches zero as the payment date is extended further into the future, and (2) that the rate of decrease is greater the higher the interest (discount) rate. At relatively high interest rates, funds due in the future are worth very little today, and even at a relatively low discount rate, the present value of a sum due in the very distant future is quite small. For example, at a 20 percent discount rate, $1 million due in 100 years is worth approximately 1 cent today. (However, 1 cent would grow to almost $1 million in 100 years at 20 percent.)

SELF-TEST QUESTIONS

What is meant by the term "opportunity cost rate"?

What is discounting? How is it related to compounding?

How does the present value of an amount to be received in the future change as the time is extended and as the interest rate increases?

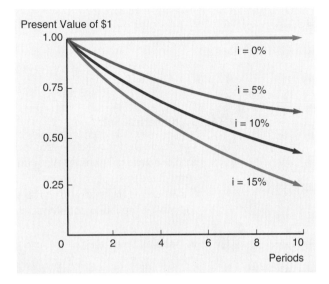

SOLVING FOR INTEREST RATE AND TIME

At this point, you should realize that compounding and discounting are related, and that we have been dealing with one equation that can be solved for either the FV or the PV.

FV Form:

$$FV_n = PV(1 + i)^n. \qquad (7\text{-}1)$$

PV Form:

$$PV = \frac{FV_n}{(1 + i)^n} = FV_n\left(\frac{1}{1 + i}\right)^n. \qquad (7\text{-}2)$$

There are four variables in these equations—PV, FV, i, and n—and if you know the values of any three, you can find the value of the fourth. Thus far, we have always given you the interest rate (i) and the number of years (n), plus either the PV or the FV. In many situations, though, you will need to solve for either i or n, as we discuss below.

SOLVING FOR i

Suppose you can buy a security at a price of $78.35, and it will pay you $100 after five years. Here you know PV, FV, and n, and you want to find i, the interest rate you would earn if you bought the security. Problems such as this are solved as follows:

Time Line:

```
0    i = ?   1        2        3        4        5
|-----------|--------|--------|--------|--------|
-78.35                                          100
```

Equation:

$$FV_n = PV(1 + i)^n \tag{7-1}$$

$$\$100 = \$78.35(1 + i)^5. \text{ Solve for i.}$$

1. Numerical Solution

Go through a trial-and-error process in which you insert different values of i into Equation 7-1 until you find a value that "works" in the sense that the right-hand side of the equation equals $100. The solution value is i = 0.05, or 5 percent. The trial-and-error procedure is extremely tedious and inefficient for most time value problems, so no one in the real world uses it.

2. Tabular Solution

$$FV_n = PV(1 + i)^n = PV(FVIF_{i,n})$$

$$\$100 = \$78.35(FVIF_{i,5})$$

$$FVIF_{i,5} = \$100/\$78.35 = 1.2763.$$

Find the value of the FVIF as shown above, and then look across the Period 5 row in Table A-3 until you find FVIF = 1.2763. This value is in the 5% column, so the interest rate at which $78.35 grows to $100 over five years is 5 percent. This procedure can be used only if the interest rate is in the table; therefore, it will not work for fractional interest rates or where n is not a whole number. Approximation procedures can be used, but they are laborious and inexact.

3. Financial Calculator Solution

Inputs:	5		-78.35	0	100
	N	**I**	**PV**	**PMT**	**FV**
Output:		= 5.0			

Enter N = 5, PV = -78.35, PMT = 0, and FV = 100, and then press I to get I = 5%. This procedure is easy, and it can be used for any interest rate or for any value of n, including fractional values.

4. Spreadsheet Solution

	A	B	C	D	E	F	G
1	Time	0	1	2	3	4	5
2	Cash flow	-78.35	0	0	0	0	100
3	Interest rate	5%					

Most spreadsheets have a built-in function to find the interest rate. In *Excel*, you would put the cursor on Cell B3, then click the function wizard, indicate that you want a Financial function, scroll down to Rate, and click OK. Then, in the dialog box, enter G1 or 5 Nper, 0 for Pmt because there are no periodic payments, B2 or −78.35 for PV, G2 or 100 for FV, 0 for type, and leave "Guess" blank to let *Excel* decide where to start its iterations. Then, when you click OK, *Excel* solves for the interest rate, 5.00 percent. *Excel* also has other procedures that could be used to find the 5 percent, but for this problem the Rate function is easiest to apply.

Solving for n

Suppose you know that a security will provide a return of 5 percent per year, that it will cost $78.35, and that you will receive $100 at maturity, but you do not know when the security matures. Thus, you know PV, FV, and i, but you do not know n, the number of periods. Here is the situation:

Time Line:

Equation:

$$FV_n = PV(1 + i)^n \qquad (7\text{-}1)$$

$$\$100 = \$78.35(1.05)^n. \text{ Solve for n.}$$

1. Numerical Solution

Again, you could go through a trial-and-error process wherein you substitute different values for n into the equation. You would find (eventually) that n = 5 "works," so 5 is the number of years it takes for $78.35 to grow to $100 if the interest rate is 5 percent.

2. Tabular Solution

$$FV_n = PV(1 + i)^n = PV(FVIF_{i,n})$$

$$\$100 = \$78.35(FVIF_{5\%,n})$$

$$FVIF_{5\%,n} = \$100/\$78.35 = 1.2763.$$

Now look down the 5% column in Table A-3 until you find FVIF = 1.2763. This value is in Row 5, which indicates that it takes five years for $78.35 to grow to $100 at a 5 percent interest rate.

3. Financial Calculator Solution

Inputs:		5		−78.35		0		100
	N		**I**		**PV**		**PMT**	**FV**

Output: = 5.0

Enter I = 5, PV = −78.35, PMT = 0, and FV = 100, and then press N to get N = 5.

4. Spreadsheet Solution

To solve this problem, starting with a new spreadsheet, you could enter the formula **=78.35*(1.05)^B2** in Cell B4 and then use the goal-seeking function on the Tools menu to find a value for B2 that causes the value in B4 to equal 100. The value is 5.00. You could also use the Solver function on the Tools menu to solve the equation.

SELF-TEST QUESTIONS

Assuming that you are given PV, FV, and the time period, n, write out an equation that can be used to determine the interest rate, i.

Assuming that you are given PV, FV, and the interest rate, i, write out an equation that can be used to determine the time period, n.

Explain how a financial calculator can be used to solve for i and n.

FUTURE VALUE OF AN ANNUITY

Annuity
A series of payments of an equal amount at fixed intervals for a specified number of periods.

Ordinary (Deferred) Annuity
An annuity whose payments occur at the *end* of each period.

Annuity Due
An annuity whose payments occur at the *beginning* of each period.

An **annuity** is a series of equal payments made at fixed intervals for a specified number of periods. For example, $100 at the end of each of the next three years is a three-year annuity. The payments are given the symbol PMT, and they can occur at either the beginning or the end of each period. If the payments occur at the *end* of each period, as they typically do, the annuity is called an **ordinary, or deferred, annuity.** Payments on mortgages, car loans, and student loans are typically set up as ordinary annuities. If payments are made at the *beginning* of each period, the annuity is an **annuity due.** Rental payments for an apartment, life insurance premiums, and lottery payoffs are typically set up as annuities due. Since ordinary annuities are more common in finance, when the term "annuity" is used in this book, you should assume that the payments occur at the end of each period unless otherwise noted.

ORDINARY ANNUITIES

An ordinary, or deferred, annuity consists of a series of equal payments made at the *end* of each period. If you deposit $100 at the end of each year for three years in a savings account that pays 5 percent interest per year, how much will you have at the end of three years? To answer this question, we must find the future value of the annuity, FVA_n. Each payment is compounded out to the end of Period n, and the sum of the compounded payments is the future value of the annuity, FVA_n.

FVA_n
The future value of an annuity over n periods.

Time Line:

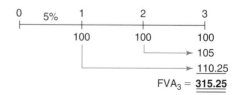

Here we show the regular time line as the top portion of the diagram, but we also show how each cash flow is compounded to produce the value FVA_n in the lower portion of the diagram.

Equation:

$$FVA_n = PMT(1 + i)^{n-1} + PMT(1 + i)^{n-2} + PMT(1 + i)^{n-3} + \cdots$$
$$+ PMT(1 + i)^0$$

$$= PMT \sum_{t=1}^{n} (1 + i)^{n-t} \tag{7-3}$$

$$= PMT(FVIFA_{i,n}).$$

The first line of Equation 7-3 represents the application of Equation 7-1 to each individual payment of the annuity. In other words, each term is the compounded amount of a single payment, with the superscript in each term indicating the number of periods during which the payment earns interest. For example, because the first annuity payment was made at the end of Period 1, interest would be earned in Periods 2 through n only, so compounding would be for n − 1 periods rather than n periods. Compounding for the second annuity payment would be for Period 3 through Period n, or n − 2 periods, and so on. The last annuity payment is made at the end of the annuity's life, so there is no time for interest to be earned. The second form of Equation 7-3 is just a shorthand version of the first. Finally, the third line shows the payment multiplied by the **Future Value Interest Factor for an Annuity (FVIFA_{i,n})**, which is the tabular approach.

1. Numerical Solution

The lower section of the time line shows the numerical solution, which involves using the first line of Equation 7-3. The future value of each cash flow is found, and those FVs are summed to find the FV of the annuity, $315.25. This is a tedious process for long annuities.

2. Tabular Solution

The summation term in Equation 7-3 is called the Future Value Interest Factor for an Annuity (FVIFA_{i,n}):[6]

$$FVIFA_{i,n} = \sum_{t=1}^{n} (1 + i)^{n-t}. \tag{7-3a}$$

FVIFAs have been calculated for various combinations of i and n, and Table A-4 in Appendix A contains a set of FVIFA factors. To find the answer to the

---

[6] Another form for Equation 7-3a is as follows:

$$FVIFA_{i,n} = \frac{(1 + i)^n - 1}{i}.$$

This form is found by applying the algebra of geometric progressions. This equation is useful in situations when the required values of i and n are not in the tables and no financial calculator or computer is available.

Future Value Interest Factor for an Annuity (FVIFA_{i,n})
The future value interest factor for an annuity of n periods compounded at i percent.

three-year, $100 annuity problem, first refer to Table A-4 and look down the 5% column to the third period; the FVIFA is 3.1525. Thus, the future value of the $100 annuity is $315.25:

$$FVA_n = PMT(FVIFA_{i,n})$$
$$FVA_3 = \$100(FVIFA_{5\%,3}) = \$100(3.1525) = \$315.25.$$

3. Financial Calculator Solution

Inputs: 3   5   0   − 100

| N | I | PV | PMT | FV |

Output: = 315.25

Note that in annuity problems, the PMT key is used in conjunction with the N and I keys, plus either the PV or the FV key, depending on whether you are trying to find the PV or the FV of the annuity. In our example, you want the FV, so press the FV key to get the answer, $315.25. Since there is no initial payment, we input PV = 0.

4. Spreadsheet Solution

	A	B	C	D	E
1	Interest rate	0.05			
2	Time	0	1	2	3
3	Cash flow		100	100	100
4	Future value				**315.25**

Most spreadsheets have a built-in function to find the future value of an annuity. In *Excel*, we could put the cursor on Cell E4, then click function wizard, Financial, FV, and OK to get the FV dialog box. Then, we would enter 0.05 or B1 for Rate, 3 or E2 for Nper, and −100 for Pmt. (Like the financial calculator approach, the payment is entered as a negative number to show that it is a cash outflow.) We would leave PV blank because there is no initial payment, and we would leave Type blank to signify that payments come at the end of the periods. Then, when we clicked OK, we would get the FV of the annuity, $315.25. Note that it isn't necessary to show the time line, since the FV function doesn't require you to input a range of cash flows. Still, the time line is useful to help visualize the problem.

ANNUITIES DUE

Had the three $100 payments in the previous example been made at the *beginning* of each year, the annuity would have been an *annuity due*. On the time line, each payment would be shifted to the left one year; therefore, each payment would be compounded for one extra year.

1. Time Line and Numerical Solution

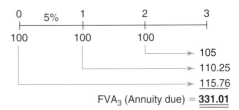

Again, the time line is shown at the top of the diagram, and the values as calculated with a regular calculator are shown under Year 3. The future value of each cash flow is found, and those FVs are summed to find the FV of the annuity due. The payments occur earlier, so more interest is earned. Therefore, the future value of the annuity due is larger — $331.01 versus $315.25 for the ordinary annuity.

2. Tabular Solution

In an annuity due, each payment is compounded for one additional period, so the future value of the entire annuity is equal to the future value of an ordinary annuity compounded for one additional period. Here is the tabular solution:

$$FVA_n \text{ (Annuity due)} = PMT(FVIFA_{i,n})(1 + i) \qquad (7\text{-}3b)$$

$$= \$100(3.1525)(1.05) = \$331.01.$$

3. Financial Calculator Solution

Most financial calculators have a switch, or key, marked "DUE" or "BEG" that permits you to switch from end-of-period payments (ordinary annuity) to beginning-of-period payments (annuity due). When the beginning mode is activated, the display will normally show the word "BEGIN." Thus, to deal with annuities due, switch your calculator to "BEGIN" and proceed as before:

BEGIN

Inputs:	3	5	0	−100	
	N	**I**	**PV**	**PMT**	**FV**
Output:					= 331.01

Enter N = 3, I = 5, PV = 0, PMT = −100, and then press FV to get the answer, $331.01. *Since most problems specify end-of-period cash flows, you should always switch your calculator back to "END" mode after you work an annuity due problem.*

4. Spreadsheet Solution

For the annuity due, proceed just as for the ordinary annuity except enter 1 for Type to indicate that we now have an annuity due. Then, when you click OK, the answer $331.01 will appear.

PRESENT VALUE OF AN ANNUITY

Suppose you were offered the following alternatives: (1) a three-year annuity with payments of $100 or (2) a lump sum payment today. You have no need for the money during the next three years, so if you accept the annuity, you would deposit the payments in a bank account that pays 5 percent interest per year. Similarly, the lump sum payment would be deposited into a bank account. How large must the lump sum payment today be to make it equivalent to the annuity?

ORDINARY ANNUITIES

If the payments come at the end of each year, then the annuity is an ordinary annuity, and it would be set up as follows:

Time Line:

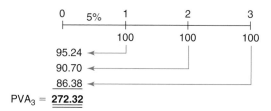

PVA_n
The present value of an annuity of n periods.

The regular time line is shown at the top of the diagram, and the numerical solution values are shown in the left column. The PV of the annuity, **PVA_n**, is $272.32.

Equation:

The general equation used to find the PV of an ordinary annuity is shown below:[7]

———————

[7] The summation term is called the PVIFA, and, using the geometric progression solution process, its value is found to be

$$PVIFA_{i,n} = \sum_{t=1}^{n}\left(\frac{1}{1+i}\right)^t = \frac{1 - \dfrac{1}{(1+i)^n}}{i} = \frac{1}{i} - \frac{1}{i(1+i)^n}.$$

(footnote continues)

$$PVA_n = PMT\left(\frac{1}{1+i}\right)^1 + PMT\left(\frac{1}{1+i}\right)^2 + \cdots + PMT\left(\frac{1}{1+i}\right)^n$$

$$= PMT \sum_{t=1}^{n} \left(\frac{1}{1+i}\right)^t. \tag{7-4}$$

1. Numerical Solution

The present value of each cash flow is found and then summed to find the PV of the annuity. This procedure is shown in the lower section of the time line diagram, where we see that the PV of the annuity is $272.32.

2. Tabular Solution

Present Value Interest Factor for an Annuity (PVIFA$_{i,n}$)
The present value interest factor for an annuity of n periods discounted at i percent.

The summation term in Equation 7-4 is called the **Present Value Interest Factor for an Annuity (PVIFA$_{i,n}$)**, and values for the term at different values of i and n are shown in Table A-2 at the back of the book. Here is the equation:

$$PVA_n = PMT(PVIFA_{i,n}). \tag{7-4a}$$

To find the answer to the three-year, $100 annuity problem, simply refer to Table A-2 and look down the 5% column to the third period. The PVIFA is 2.7232, so the present value of the $100 annuity is $272.32:

$$PVA_n = PMT(PVIFA_{i,n})$$
$$PVA_3 = \$100(PVIFA_{5\%,3}) = \$100(2.7232) = \$272.32.$$

3. Financial Calculator Solution

Inputs:	3	5		−100	0
	N	**I**	**PV**	**PMT**	**FV**
Output:			= 272.32		

Enter N = 3, I = 5, PMT = −100, and FV = 0, and then press the PV key to find the PV, $272.32.

4. Spreadsheet Solution

	A	B	C	D	E
1	Interest rate	0.05			
2	Time	0	1	2	3
3	Cash flow		100	100	100
4	Present value	$272.32			

(Footnote 7 continued)

This form of the equation is useful for dealing with annuities when the values for i and n are not in the tables and no financial calculator or computer is available.

In *Excel*, put the cursor on Cell B4 and then click the function wizard, Financial, PV, and OK. Then enter B1 or 0.05 for Rate, E2 or 3 for Nper, −100 for Pmt, 0 or leave blank for FV, and 0 or leave blank for Type. Then, when you click OK, you get the answer, $272.32.

One especially important application of the annuity concept relates to loans with constant payments, such as mortgages and auto loans. With such loans, called *amortized loans*, the amount borrowed is the present value of an ordinary annuity, and the payments constitute the annuity stream. We will examine constant payment loans in more depth in a later section of this chapter.

ANNUITIES DUE

Had the three $100 payments in the preceding example been made at the beginning of each year, the annuity would have been an *annuity due*. Each payment would be shifted to the left one year, so each payment would be discounted for one less year. Here is the time line setup:

1. Time Line and Numerical Solution

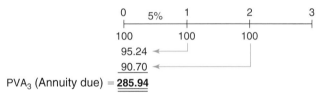

Again, we find the PV of each cash flow and then sum these PVs to find the PV of the annuity due. This procedure is illustrated in the lower section of the time line diagram. Since the cash flows occur sooner, the PV of the annuity due exceeds that of the ordinary annuity, $285.94 versus $272.32.

2. Tabular Solution

In an annuity due, each payment is discounted for one less period. Since its payments come in faster, an annuity due is more valuable than an ordinary annuity. This higher value is found by multiplying the PV of an ordinary annuity by $(1 + i)$:

$$PVA_n \text{ (Annuity due)} = PMT(PVIFA_{i,n})(1 + i) \tag{7-4b}$$

$$= \$100(2.7232)(1.05) = \$285.94.$$

3. Financial Calculator Solution

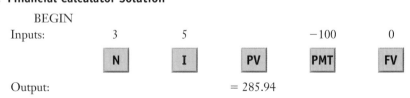

Switch to the beginning-of-period mode, and then enter N = 3, I = 5, PMT = −100, and FV = 0, and then press PV to get the answer, $285.94. *Again, since most problems deal with end-of-period cash flows, don't forget to switch your calculator back to the "END" mode.*

4. Spreadsheet Solution

For an annuity due, proceed exactly as for a regular annuity except enter 1 rather than 0 for Type to indicate that we now have an annuity due.

> **SELF-TEST QUESTIONS**
>
> Which annuity has the greater present value: an ordinary annuity or an annuity due? Why?
>
> Explain how financial calculators can be used to find the present value of annuities.

PERPETUITIES

Perpetuity
A stream of equal payments expected to continue forever.

Most annuities call for payments to be made over some finite period of time — for example, $100 per year for three years. However, some annuities go on indefinitely, or perpetually, and these are called **perpetuities.** The present value of a perpetuity is found by applying Equation 7-5.[8]

$$\text{PV(Perpetuity)} = \frac{\text{Payment}}{\text{Interest rate}} = \frac{\text{PMT}}{i}. \qquad (7\text{-}5)$$

Consol
A perpetual bond issued by the British government to consolidate past debts; in general, any perpetual bond.

Perpetuities can be illustrated by some British securities issued after the Napoleonic Wars. In 1815, the British government sold a huge bond issue and used the proceeds to pay off many smaller issues that had been floated in prior years to pay for the wars. Since the purpose of the bonds was to consolidate past debts, the bonds were called **consols.** Suppose each consol promised to pay $100 per year in perpetuity. (Actually, interest was stated in pounds.) What would each bond be worth if the opportunity cost rate, or discount rate, was 5 percent? The answer is $2,000:

$$\text{PV (Perpetuity)} = \frac{\$100}{0.05} = \$2,000 \text{ if } i = 5\%.$$

---

[8] The derivation of Equation 7-5 is given in the Web/CD Extension to Chapter 5 of Eugene F. Brigham and Phillip R. Daves, *Intermediate Financial Management,* 7th ed. (Fort Worth, TX: Harcourt College Publishers, 2002).

Suppose the interest rate rose to 10 percent; what would happen to the consol's value? The value would drop to $1,000:

$$PV \text{ (Perpetuity)} = \frac{\$100}{0.10} = \$1,000 \text{ at i} = 10\%.$$

We see that the value of a perpetuity changes dramatically when interest rates change. Perpetuities are discussed further in Chapter 9.

SELF-TEST QUESTIONS

What happens to the value of a perpetuity when interest rates increase? What happens when interest rates decrease?

UNEVEN CASH FLOW STREAMS

Uneven Cash Flow Stream
A series of cash flows in which the amount varies from one period to the next.

Payment (PMT)
This term designates *equal* cash flows coming at regular intervals.

Cash Flow (CF)
This term designates *uneven* cash flows.

The definition of an annuity includes the words *constant payment* — in other words, annuities involve payments that are equal in every period. Although many financial decisions do involve constant payments, other important decisions involve uneven, or nonconstant, cash flows; for example, common stocks typically pay an increasing stream of dividends over time, and fixed asset investments such as new equipment normally do not generate constant cash flows. Consequently, it is necessary to extend our time value discussion to include **uneven cash flow streams.**

Throughout the book, we will follow convention and reserve the term **payment (PMT)** for annuity situations where the cash flows are equal amounts, and we will use the term **cash flow (CF)** to denote uneven cash flows. Financial calculators are set up to follow this convention, so if you are dealing with uneven cash flows, you will need to use the "cash flow register."

PRESENT VALUE OF AN UNEVEN CASH FLOW STREAM

The PV of an uneven cash flow stream is found as the sum of the PVs of the individual cash flows of the stream. For example, suppose we must find the PV of the following cash flow stream, discounted at 6 percent:

```
      0   6%   1      2      3      4      5      6      7
PV = ?     100    200    200    200    200     0    1,000
```

The PV will be found by applying this general present value equation:

$$PV = CF_1\left(\frac{1}{1+i}\right)^1 + CF_2\left(\frac{1}{1+i}\right)^2 + \cdots + CF_n\left(\frac{1}{1+i}\right)^n$$

$$= \sum_{t=1}^{n} CF_t\left(\frac{1}{1+i}\right)^t = \sum_{t=1}^{n} CF_t(PVIF_{i,t}). \qquad (7\text{-}6)$$

We could find the PV of each individual cash flow using the numerical, tabular, financial calculator, or spreadsheet methods, and then sum these values to find the present value of the stream. Here is what the process would look like:

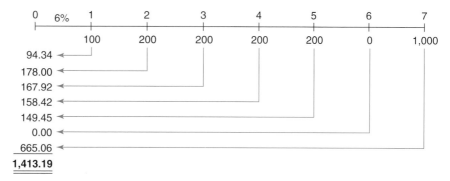

All we did was to apply Equation 7-6, show the individual PVs in the left column of the diagram, and then sum these individual PVs to find the PV of the entire stream.

The present value of a cash flow stream can always be found by summing the present values of the individual cash flows as shown above. However, cash flow regularities within the stream may allow the use of shortcuts. For example, notice that the cash flows in periods 2 through 5 represent an annuity. We can use that fact to solve the problem in a slightly different manner:

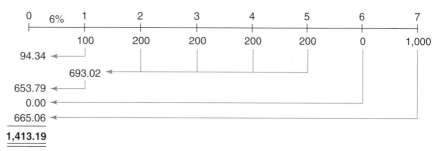

Cash flows during Years 2 to 5 represent an ordinary annuity, and we find its PV at Year 1 (one period before the first payment). This PV ($693.02) must then be discounted back one more period to get its Year 0 value, $653.79.

Problems involving uneven cash flows can be solved in one step with most financial calculators. First, you input the individual cash flows, in chronological order, into the cash flow register. Cash flows are usually designated CF_0, CF_1, CF_2, CF_3, and so on. Next, you enter the interest rate, I. At this point, you have substituted in all the known values of Equation 7-6, so you only need to press the NPV key to find the present value of the stream. The calculator has been programmed to find the PV of each cash flow and then to sum these values to find the PV of the entire stream. To input the cash flows for this problem, enter 0 (because $CF_0 = 0$), 100, 200, 200, 200, 200, 0, 1000 in that order into the cash flow register, enter I = 6, and then press NPV to obtain the answer, $1,413.19.

Two points should be noted. First, when dealing with the cash flow register, the calculator uses the term "NPV" rather than "PV." The N stands for "net," so NPV is the abbreviation for "Net Present Value," which is simply the net present value of a series of positive and negative cash flows. Our example has no negative cash flows, but if it did, we would simply input them with negative signs.[9]

The second point to note is that annuities can be entered into the cash flow register more efficiently by using the N_j key. (On some calculators, you are prompted to enter the number of times the cash flow occurs, and on still other calculators, the procedures for inputting data, as we discuss next, may be different. You should consult your calculator manual or our *Technology Supplement* to determine the appropriate steps for your specific calculator.) In this illustration, you would enter $CF_0 = 0$, $CF_1 = 100$, $CF_2 = 200$, $N_j = 4$ (which tells the calculator that the 200 occurs 4 times), $CF_6 = 0$, and $CF_7 = 1000$. Then enter $I = 6$ and press the NPV key, and 1,413.19 will appear in the display. Also, note that amounts entered into the cash flow register remain in the register until they are cleared. Thus, if you had previously worked a problem with eight cash flows, and then moved to a problem with only four cash flows, the calculator would simply add the cash flows from the second problem to those of the first problem. Therefore, you must be sure to clear the cash flow register before starting a new problem.

Spreadsheets are especially useful for solving problems with uneven cash flows. Just as with a financial calculator, you must enter the cash flows in the spreadsheet:

	A	B	C	D	E	F	G	H	I
1	Interest rate	0.06							
2	Time	0	1	2	3	4	5	6	7
3	Cash flow		100	200	200	200	200	0	1,000
4	Present value	1,413.19							

To find the PV of these cash flows with *Excel*, put the cursor on Cell B4, click the function wizard, click Financial, scroll down to NPV, and click OK to get the dialog box. Then enter B1 or 0.06 for Rate and the range of cells containing the cash flows, C3:I3, for Value 1. N stands for Net, so the NPV is the net present value of a stream of cash flows, some of which may be negative. Now, when you click OK, you get the PV of the stream, $1,413.19. Note that you use the PV function if the cash flows (or payments) are constant, but the NPV function if they are not constant. Note too that one of the advantages of spreadsheets over financial calculators is that you can see the cash flows, which makes it easy to spot any typing errors.

---

[9] To input a negative number, type in the positive number, then press the $+/-$ key to change the sign to negative. If you begin by typing the minus sign, you make the mistake of subtracting the negative number from the last number that was entered in the calculator.

FUTURE VALUE OF AN UNEVEN CASH FLOW STREAM

Terminal Value
The future value of an uneven cash flow stream.

The future value of an uneven cash flow stream (sometimes called the **terminal value**) is found by compounding each payment to the end of the stream and then summing the future values:

$$FV_n = CF_1(1 + i)^{n-1} + CF_2(1 + i)^{n-2} + \cdots + CF_n$$

$$= \sum_{t=1}^{n} CF_t(1 + i)^{n-t} = \sum_{t=1}^{n} CF_t(FVIF_{i,n-t}). \qquad (7\text{-}7)$$

The future value of our illustrative uneven cash flow stream is \$2,124.92:

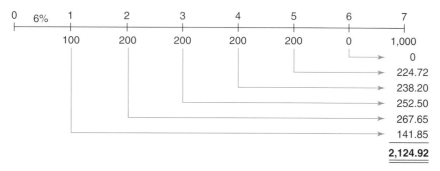

Some financial calculators have a net future value (NFV) key which, after the cash flows and interest rate have been entered, can be used to obtain the future value of an uneven cash flow stream. In any event, it is easy enough to compound the individual cash flows to the terminal year and then sum them to find the FV of the stream. Also, we are generally more interested in the present value of an asset's cash flow stream than in the future value because the present value represents today's value, which is used to find the fair value of the asset. Finally, note that the cash flow stream's net present value can be used to find its net future value: $NFV = NPV(1 + i)^n$. Thus, in our example, you could find the PV of the stream, then find the FV of that PV, compounded for n periods at i percent. In the illustrative problem, find PV = 1,413.19 using the cash flow register and I = 6. Then enter N = 7, I = 6, PV = −1413.19, and PMT = 0, and then press FV to find FV = 2,124.92, which equals the NFV shown on the time line above.

SOLVING FOR i WITH UNEVEN CASH FLOW STREAMS

It is relatively easy to solve for i numerically or with the tables when the cash flows are lump sums or annuities. However, it is *extremely difficult* to solve for i if the cash flows are uneven, because then you would have to go through many tedious trial-and-error calculations. With a spreadsheet program or a financial calculator, though, it is easy to find the value of i. Simply input the CF values into the cash flow register and then press the IRR key. IRR stands for "internal rate of return," which is the percentage return on an investment. We will defer further discussion of this calculation for now, but we will take it up later, in our discussion of capital budgeting methods in Chapter 11.[10]

---

[10] To obtain an IRR solution, at least one of the cash flows must have a negative sign, indicating that it is an investment. Since none of the CFs in our example were negative, the cash flow stream has no IRR. However, had we input a cost for CF_0, say, −\$1,000, we could have obtained an IRR, which would be the rate of return earned on the \$1,000 investment. Here IRR would be 13.96 percent.

Give two examples of financial decisions that would typically involve uneven cash flows. (Hint: Think about a bond or a stock that you plan to hold for five years.)

What is meant by the term "terminal value"?

SEMIANNUAL AND OTHER COMPOUNDING PERIODS

Annual Compounding
The arithmetic process of determining the final value of a cash flow or series of cash flows when interest is added *once* a year.

Semiannual Compounding
The arithmetic process of determining the final value of a cash flow or series of cash flows when interest is added *twice* a year.

In all of our examples thus far, we have assumed that interest is compounded once a year, or annually. This is called **annual compounding.** Suppose, however, that you put $100 into a bank which states that it pays a 6 percent annual interest rate but that interest is credited each six months. This is called **semiannual compounding.** How much would you have accumulated at the end of one year, two years, or some other period under semiannual compounding? Note that virtually all bonds pay interest semiannually, most stocks pay dividends quarterly, and most mortgages, student loans, and auto loans require monthly payments. Therefore, it is essential that you understand how to deal with nonannual compounding.

To illustrate semiannual compounding, assume that $100 is placed into an account at an interest rate of 6 percent and left there for three years. First, consider again what would happen under *annual* compounding:

```
0     6%    1         2         3
├───────────┼─────────┼─────────┤
-100                            FV=?
```

$$FV_n = PV(1 + i)^n = \$100(1.06)^3$$
$$= \$119.10.$$

We would, of course, get this same answer using the tables, a financial calculator, or a spreadsheet.

How would things change if interest were paid semiannually rather than annually? First, whenever payments occur more frequently than once a year, or when interest is stated to be compounded more than once a year, then you must (1) convert the stated interest rate to a "periodic rate," and (2) convert the number of years to "number of periods," as follows:

Periodic rate = Stated rate/Number of payments per year.

Number of periods = Number of years $\times$ Periods per year.

In our example, where we must find the value of $100 after three years when the stated interest rate is 6 percent, compounded semiannually (or twice a year), you would begin by making the following conversions:

Periodic rate = 6%/2 = 3%.

Periods = N = 3 $\times$ 2 = 6.

TECHNOLOGY MATTERS

USING THE INTERNET FOR PERSONAL FINANCIAL PLANNING

People continually face important financial decisions that require an understanding of the time value of money. Should we buy or lease a car? How much and how soon do we need to save for our children's education? What size house can we afford? Should we refinance our home mortgage? How much must we save in order to retire comfortably?

The answers to these questions are often complicated, and they depend on a number of factors, such as housing and education costs, interest rates, inflation, expected family income, and stock market returns. Hopefully, after completing this chapter, you will have a better idea of how to answer such questions. Moreover, there are a number of online resources available to help with financial planning.

A good place to start is **http://www.smartmoney.com**. *Smartmoney* is a personal finance magazine produced by the publishers of *The Wall Street Journal*. If you go to *Smartmoney*'s web site you will find a section entitled "Tools." This section has a number of financial calculators, spreadsheets, and descriptive materials that cover a wide range of personal finance issues.

Another good place to look is Quicken's web site, **http://www.quicken.com**. Here you will find several interesting sections that deal with a variety of personal finance issues. Within these sections you will find background articles plus spreadsheets and calculators that you can use to analyze your own situation.

Finally, **http://www.financialengines.com** is a great place to visit if you are focusing specifically on retirement planning. This web site, developed by Nobel Prize–winning financial economist William Sharpe, considers a wide range of alternative scenarios that might occur. This approach, which enables you to see a full range of potential outcomes, is much better than some of the more basic online calculators that give you simple answers to complicated questions.

In this situation, the investment will earn 3 percent every six months for six periods, not 6 percent per year for three years. As we shall see, there is a significant difference between these two procedures.

You should make the conversions as your first step when working on such a problem *because calculations must be done using the appropriate number of periods and periodic rate, not the number of years and stated rate.* Periodic rates and number of periods, not yearly rates and number of years, should normally be shown on time lines and entered into your calculator whenever you are dealing with nonannual compounding.[11]

With this background, we can now find the value of $100 after three years if it is held in an account that pays a stated rate of 6 percent, but with semiannual compounding. Here is the time line:

Time Line:

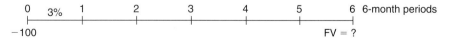

---

[11] With some financial calculators, you can enter the annual (nominal) rate and the number of compounding periods rather than make the conversion we recommend. We prefer making the conversion because it is easier to see the problem setup in a time line, and also because it is easy to forget to readjust your calculator after you change its settings and to then make an error on the next problem because of the incorrect setting.

1. Equation and Numerical Solution

$$FV_n = PV(1 + i)^n = \$100(1.03)^6$$
$$= \$100(1.1941) = \$119.41.$$

Here i = rate per period = annual rate/compounding periods per year = 6%/ 2 = 3%, and n = the total number of periods = years $\times$ periods per year = $3 \times 2 = 6$.

2. Tabular Solution

$$FV_6 = \$100(FVIF_{3\%,6}) = \$100(1.1941) = \$119.41.$$

Look up FVIF for 3%, 6 periods in Table A-3 and complete the arithmetic.

3. Financial Calculator Solution

Inputs:	6	3	− 100	0	
	N	**I**	**PV**	**PMT**	**FV**
Output:					= 119.41

Enter N = years $\times$ periods per year = $3 \times 2 = 6$, I = annual rate/periods per year = 6/2 = 3, PV = −100, and PMT = 0. Then press FV to find the answer, $119.41.

4. Spreadsheet Solution

The spreadsheet developed to find the future value of a lump sum under semi-annual compounding would look like the one for annual compounding, with two changes: The interest rate would be halved, and the time line would show twice as many periods. The future value under semiannual compounding, $119.41, would be larger than $119.10, the future value under annual compounding, because interest on interest is being earned more frequently.

Throughout the world economy, different compounding periods are used for different types of investments. For example, bank accounts generally pay interest daily; most bonds pay interest semiannually; and stocks generally pay dividends quarterly.[12] If we are to properly compare securities with different compounding periods, we need to put them on a common basis. This requires us to distinguish between **nominal,** or **quoted, interest rates** and **effective,** or **equivalent, annual rates.**[13]

The nominal, or quoted, or stated, interest rate in our example is 6 percent. *The effective (or equivalent) annual rate (EAR, also called EFF%) is defined as the*

Nominal (Quoted, or Stated) Interest Rate
The contracted, or quoted, or stated, interest rate.

Effective (Equivalent) Annual Rate (EFF% or EAR)
The annual rate of interest actually being earned, as opposed to the quoted rate. Also called the "equivalent annual rate."

---

[12] Some banks and savings and loans even pay interest compounded *continuously.* Continuous compounding is discussed in Appendix 7A.

[13] The term *nominal rate* as it is used here has a different meaning than the way it was used in Chapter 5. There, nominal interest rates referred to stated market rates as opposed to real (zero inflation) rates. In this chapter, the term *nominal rate* means the stated, or quoted, annual rate as opposed to the effective annual rate. In both cases, though, *nominal* means *stated,* or *quoted,* as opposed to some adjusted rate.

rate that would produce the same ending (future) value if annual compounding had been used. In our example, the effective annual rate is the once-a-year rate that would produce an FV of $119.41 at the end of Year 3. Here is a time line of the situation:

```
   0 EAR (or EFF%) 1              2              3   Years
   ├─────────────────┼──────────────┼──────────────┤
  -100                                          119.41
```

Our task now is to find the effective annual rate, EAR or EFF%, that is equivalent to 6 percent with semiannual compounding.

We can determine the effective annual rate, given the nominal rate and the number of compounding periods per year, by solving this equation:

$$\text{Effective annual rate} = \text{EAR (or EFF\%)} = \left(1 + \frac{i_{\text{Nom}}}{m}\right)^m - 1.0. \qquad (7\text{-}8)$$

Here i_{Nom} is the nominal, or quoted, interest rate, and m is the number of compounding periods per year. For example, to find the effective annual rate if the nominal rate is 6 percent and semiannual compounding is used, we have[14]

$$\begin{aligned}
\text{Effective annual rate} = \text{EAR (or EFF\%)} &= \left(1 + \frac{0.06}{2}\right)^2 - 1.0 \\
&= (1.03)^2 - 1.0 \\
&= 1.0609 - 1.0 = 0.0609 = 6.09\%.
\end{aligned}$$

The points made about semiannual compounding can be generalized as follows. When compounding occurs more frequently than once a year, we can use a modified version of Equation 7-1 to find the future value of any lump sum:

$$\text{Annual compounding: } FV_n = PV(1 + i)^n. \qquad \textbf{(7-1)}$$

$$\text{More frequent compounding: } FV_n = PV\left(1 + \frac{i_{\text{Nom}}}{m}\right)^{mn}. \qquad (7\text{-}9)$$

Here i_{Nom} is the nominal, or quoted, rate, m is the number of times compounding occurs per year, and n is the number of years. For example, when banks pay daily interest, the value of m is set at 365 and Equation 7-9 is applied.[15]

To illustrate further the effect of compounding monthly rather than annually, consider the interest rate charged on credit cards. Many banks charge 1.5 percent per month, and, in their advertising, they state that the **Annual Percentage Rate (APR)** is 1.5% × 12 = 18%. However, the "true" rate is the effective annual rate of 19.6 percent:

Annual Percentage Rate (APR)
The periodic rate × the number of periods per year.

---

[14] Most financial calculators are programmed to find the EAR or, given the EAR, to find the nominal rate. This is called "interest rate conversion," and you simply enter the nominal rate and the number of compounding periods per year and then press the EFF% key to find the effective annual rate.

[15] To illustrate, the future value of $1 invested at 10 percent for 1 year under daily compounding is $1.1052:

$$FV_n = \$1\left(1 + \frac{0.10}{365}\right)^{365(1)} = \$1(1.105156) = \$1.1052.$$

Note also that banks sometimes use 360 as the number of days per year for this and other calculations.

$$\text{Effective annual rate} = \text{EAR (or EFF\%)} = \left(1 + \frac{0.18}{12}\right)^{12} - 1.0$$
$$= (1.015)^{12} - 1.0$$
$$= 0.196 = 19.6\%.$$

Semiannual and other compounding periods can also be used for discounting, and for both lump sums and annuities. First, consider the case where we want to find the PV of an ordinary annuity of $100 per year for three years when the interest rate is 8 percent, *compounded annually:*

Time Line:

1. **Numerical Solution**

Find the PV of each cash flow and sum them. The PV of the annuity is $257.71.

2. **Tabular Solution**

$$\text{PVA}_n = \text{PMT}(\text{PVIFA}_{i,n})$$
$$= \$100(\text{PVIFA}_{8\%,3}) = \$100(2.5771) = \$257.71.$$

3. **Financial Calculator Solution**

Inputs: 3   8   100   0

N   I   PV   PMT   FV

Output: = −257.71

4. **Spreadsheet Solution**

A spreadsheet could be developed as we did earlier in the chapter in our discussion of the present value of an annuity. Rows would be set up to show the interest rate (8 percent), time (t = 0 through t = 3), and cash flows (100 at t = 1 through t = 3). Then the present value of the annuity, $257.71, could be determined using the *Excel* PV function.

Now, let's change the situation to *semiannual compounding*, where the annuity calls for payments of $50 each six months rather than $100 per year, and the rate is 8 percent, compounded semiannually. Here is the time line:

Time Line:

1. Numerical Solution

Find the PV of each cash flow by discounting at 4 percent. Treat each tick mark on the time line as a period, so there are six periods. The PV of the annuity is $262.11 versus $257.71 under annual compounding.

2. Tabular Solution

$$PVA_n = PMT(PVIFA_{i,n})$$
$$= \$50(PVIFA_{4\%,6}) = \$50(5.2421) = \$262.11.$$

3. Financial Calculator Solution

Inputs:	6	4		50	0
	N	**I**	**PV**	**PMT**	**FV**

Output: $= -262.11$

4. Spreadsheet Solution

The spreadsheet developed to find the present value of an annuity under semi-annual compounding would look like the one for annual compounding, but the interest rate and annuity payment would be halved, and the time line would have twice as many periods.

The annuity value with semiannual compounding is $262.11, which is greater than the annual annuity value. The reason is that the semiannual payments come in sooner, so the $50 semiannual annuity is more valuable than the $100 annual annuity.

SELF-TEST QUESTIONS

What changes must you make in your calculations to determine the future value of an amount that is being compounded at 8 percent semiannually versus one being compounded annually at 8 percent?

Why is semiannual compounding better than annual compounding from a saver's standpoint? What about a borrower's standpoint?

Define the terms "annual percentage rate," "effective (or equivalent) annual rate," and "nominal interest rate."

How does the term "nominal rate" as used in this chapter differ from the term as it was used in Chapter 5?

COMPARISON OF DIFFERENT TYPES OF INTEREST RATES

Finance deals with three types of interest rates: nominal rates, i_{Nom}; periodic rates, i_{PER}; and effective annual rates, EAR or EFF%. Therefore, it is essential that you understand what each one is and when it should be used.

1. **Nominal, or quoted, rate.** This is the rate that is quoted by banks, brokers, and other financial institutions. So, if you talk with a banker, broker, mortgage lender, auto finance company, or student loan officer about rates, the nominal rate is the one he or she will normally quote you. However, to be meaningful, the quoted nominal rate must also include the number of compounding periods per year. For example, a bank might offer 6 percent, compounded quarterly, on CDs, or a mutual fund might offer 5 percent, compounded monthly, on its money market account.

   The nominal rate on loans to consumers is also called the Annual Percentage Rate (APR). If a credit card issuer quotes an APR of 18 percent, monthly, this means an interest rate of 18%/12 = 1.5 percent per month.

   Nominal rates can be compared with one another, *but only if the instruments being compared use the same number of compounding periods per year.* Thus, you could compare the quoted yields on two bonds if they both pay interest semiannually. However, to compare a 6 percent, annual payment CD with a 5 percent, daily payment money market fund, we would need to put both instruments on an *effective (or equivalent) annual rate (EAR)* basis as discussed later in this section.

   Note that the nominal rate is never shown on a time line, and it is never used as an input in a financial calculator (unless compounding occurs only once a year, in which case i_{Nom} = periodic rate = EAR). If more frequent compounding occurs, you should use the periodic rate as discussed below.

2. **Periodic rate, i_{PER}.** This is the rate charged by a lender or paid by a borrower each period. It can be a rate per year, per six-month period, per quarter, per month, per day, or per any other time interval. For example, a bank might charge 1.5 percent per month on its credit card loans, or a finance company might charge 3 percent per quarter on installment loans. We find the periodic rate as follows:

$$\text{Periodic rate, } i_{PER} = i_{Nom}/m, \qquad (7\text{-}10)$$

which implies that

$$\text{Nominal annual rate} = i_{Nom} = (\text{Periodic rate})(m). \qquad (7\text{-}11)$$

Here i_{Nom} is the nominal annual rate and m is the number of compounding periods per year. To illustrate, consider a finance company loan at 3 percent per quarter:

$$\text{Nominal annual rate} = i_{Nom} = (\text{Periodic rate})(m) = (3\%)(4) = 12\%,$$

or

$$\text{Periodic rate} = i_{Nom}/m = 12\%/4 = 3\% \text{ per quarter.}$$

If there is only one payment per year, or if interest is added only once a year, then m = 1, and the periodic rate is equal to the nominal rate.

The periodic rate is the rate that is generally shown on time lines and used in calculations.[16] To illustrate use of the periodic rate, suppose you make the

---

[16] The only exception is in situations where (1) annuities are involved and (2) the payment periods do not correspond to the compounding periods. If an annuity is involved and if its payment periods do not correspond to the compounding periods — for example, if you are making quarterly payments into a bank account to build up a specified future sum, but the bank pays interest on a

(footnote continued)

following eight quarterly payments of $100 each into an account that pays a nominal rate of 12 percent, compounded quarterly. How much would you have after two years?

Time Line and Equation:

0	3%	1	2	3	4	5	6	7	8	Quarters

-100 -100 -100 -100 -100 -100 -100 -100

FV = ?

$$FVA_n = \sum_{t=1}^{n} PMT(1 + i)^{n-t} = \sum_{t=1}^{8} \$100(1.03)^{8-t}.$$

1. Numerical Solution

Compound each $100 payment at 12/4 = 3 percent for the appropriate number of periods, and then sum these individual FVs to find the FV of the payment stream, $889.23.

2. Tabular Solution

Look up FVIFA for 3%, 8 periods, in Table A-4, and complete the arithmetic:

$$FVA_n = PMT(FVIFA_{i,n})$$
$$= \$100(FVIFA_{3\%,8}) = \$100(8.8923) = \$889.23.$$

3. Financial Calculator Solution

Inputs: 8   3   0 -100

N	I	PV	PMT	FV

Output: = 889.23

Input N = 2 × 4 = 8, I = 12/4 = 3, PV = 0, and PMT = -100, and then press the FV key to get FV = $889.23.

4. Spreadsheet Solution

A spreadsheet could be developed as we did earlier in the chapter in our discussion of the future value of an annuity. Rows would be set up to show

---

(Footnote 16 continues)

daily basis — then the calculations are more complicated. For such problems, one can proceed in two alternative ways. (1) Determine the periodic (daily) interest rate by dividing the nominal rate by 360 (or 365 if the bank uses a 365-day year), then compound each payment over the exact number of days from the payment date to the terminal point, and then sum the compounded payments to find the future value of the annuity. This is what would generally be done in the real world, because with a computer, it would be a simple process. (2) Calculate the EAR based on daily compounding, then find the corresponding nominal rate based on quarterly compounding (because the annuity payments are made quarterly), then find the quarterly periodic rate, and then use that rate with standard annuity procedures. The second procedure is faster with a calculator, but hard to explain and generally not used in practice given the ready availability of computers.

the interest rate, time, cash flow, and future value of the annuity. The interest rate used in the spreadsheet would be the periodic interest rate (i_{Nom}/m) and the number of time periods shown would be $(m)(n)$.

3. **Effective (or equivalent) annual rate (EAR).** This is the annual rate that produces the same result as if we had compounded at a given periodic rate m times per year. The EAR is found as follows:

$$\text{EAR (or EFF\%)} = \left(1 + \frac{i_{Nom}}{m}\right)^m - 1.0. \qquad (7\text{-}8)$$

You could also use the interest conversion feature of a financial calculator.

In the EAR equation, i_{Nom}/m is the periodic rate, and m is the number of periods per year. For example, suppose you could borrow using either a credit card that charges 1 percent per month or a bank loan with a 12 percent quoted nominal interest rate that is compounded quarterly. Which should you choose? To answer this question, the cost rate of each alternative must be expressed as an EAR:

$$\text{Credit card loan: EAR} = (1 + 0.01)^{12} - 1.0 = (1.01)^{12} - 1.0$$
$$= 1.126825 - 1.0 = 0.126825 = 12.6825\%.$$
$$\text{Bank loan: EAR} = (1 + 0.03)^4 - 1.0 = (1.03)^4 - 1.0$$
$$= 1.125509 - 1.0 = 0.125509 = 12.5509\%.$$

Thus, the credit card loan is slightly more costly than the bank loan. This result should have been intuitive to you — both loans have the same 12 percent nominal rate, yet you would have to make monthly payments on the credit card versus quarterly payments under the bank loan.

The EAR rate is not used in calculations. However, it should be used to compare the effective cost or rate of return on loans or investments when payment periods differ, as in the credit card versus bank loan example.

SELF-TEST QUESTIONS

Define the nominal (or quoted) rate, the periodic rate, and the effective annual rate.

How are the nominal rate, the periodic rate, and the effective annual rate related?

What is the one situation where all three of these rates will be the same?

Which rate should be shown on time lines and used in calculations?

FRACTIONAL TIME PERIODS[17]

In all the examples used thus far in the chapter, we have assumed that payments occur at either the beginning or the end of periods, but not at some date *within* a period. However, we often encounter situations that require compounding or

---

[17] This section is relatively technical, but it can be omitted without loss of continuity.

discounting over fractional periods. For example, suppose you deposited $100 in a bank that adds interest to your account daily, that is, uses daily compounding, and pays a nominal rate of 10 percent with a 360-day year. How much will be in your account after nine months? The answer is $107.79:[18]

$$\text{Periodic rate} = i_{PER} = 0.10/360 = 0.00027778 \text{ per day.}$$
$$\text{Number of days} = 0.75(360) = 270.$$
$$\text{Ending amount} = \$100(1.00027778)^{270} = \$107.79.$$

Now suppose you borrow $100 from a bank that charges 10 percent per year "simple interest," which means annual rather than daily compounding, but you borrow the $100 for only 270 days. How much interest would you have to pay for the use of $100 for 270 days? Here we would calculate a daily interest rate, i_{PER}, as above, but multiply by 270 rather than use it as an exponent:

$$\text{Interest owed} = \$100(0.00027778)(270) = \$7.50 \text{ interest charged.}$$

You would owe the bank a total of $107.50 after 270 days. This is the procedure most banks actually use to calculate interest on loans, except that they generally require you to pay the interest on a monthly basis rather than after 270 days.

Finally, let's consider a somewhat different situation. Say an Internet access firm had 100 customers at the end of 2001, and its customer base is expected to grow steadily at the rate of 10 percent per year. What is the estimated customer base nine months into the new year? This problem would be set up exactly like the bank account with daily compounding, and the estimate would be 107.79 customers, rounded to 108.

The most important thing in problems like these, as in all time value problems, is to be careful! Think about what is involved in a logical, systematic manner, draw a time line if it would help you visualize the situation, and then apply the appropriate equations.

AMORTIZED LOANS

Amortized Loan
A loan that is repaid in equal payments over its life.

One of the most important applications of compound interest involves loans that are paid off in installments over time. Included are automobile loans, home mortgage loans, student loans, and most business loans other than very short-term loans and long-term bonds. If a loan is to be repaid in equal periodic amounts (monthly, quarterly, or annually), it is said to be an **amortized loan.**[19]

Table 7-2 illustrates the amortization process. A firm borrows $1,000, and the loan is to be repaid in three equal payments at the end of each of the next three years. (In this case, there is only one payment per year, so years = periods and the stated rate = periodic rate.) The lender charges a 6 percent

---

[18] Here we assumed a 360-day year, and we also assumed that the nine months all have 30 days. In real-world calculations, the bank's computer (and many financial calculators) would have a built-in calendar, and if you input the beginning and ending dates, the computer or calculator would tell you the exact number of days, taking account of 30-day months, 31-day months, and 28- or 29-day months.

[19] The word *amortized* comes from the Latin *mors*, meaning "death," so an amortized loan is one that is "killed off" over time.

	BEGINNING AMOUNT	PAYMENT	INTERESTª	REPAYMENT OF PRINCIPALᵇ	REMAINING BALANCE
YEAR	(1)	(2)	(3)	(2) − (3) = (4)	(1) − (4) = (5)
1	$1,000.00	$ 374.11	$ 60.00	$ 314.11	$685.89
2	685.89	374.11	41.15	332.96	352.93
3	352.93	374.11	21.18	352.93	0.00
		$1,122.33	$122.33	$1,000.00	

TABLE 7-2   Loan Amortization Schedule, 6 Percent Interest Rate

ªInterest is calculated by multiplying the loan balance at the beginning of the year by the interest rate. Therefore, interest in Year 1 is $1,000(0.06) = $60; in Year 2 it is $685.89(0.06) = $41.15; and in Year 3 it is $352.93(0.06) = $21.18.

ᵇRepayment of principal is equal to the payment of $374.11 minus the interest charge for each year.

interest rate on the loan balance that is outstanding at the beginning of each year. The first task is to determine the amount the firm must repay each year, or the constant annual payment. To find this amount, recognize that the $1,000 represents the present value of an annuity of PMT dollars per year for three years, discounted at 6 percent:

Time Line and Equation:

$$PV = \frac{PMT}{(1 + i)^1} + \frac{PMT}{(1 + i)^2} + \frac{PMT}{(1 + i)^3} = \sum_{t=1}^{3} \frac{PMT}{(1 + i)^t}$$

$$\$1,000 = \sum_{t=1}^{3} \frac{PMT}{(1.06)^t}.$$

Here we know everything except PMT, so we can solve the equation for PMT.

1. Numerical Solution

You could follow the trial-and-error procedure, inserting values for PMT in the equation until you found a value that "worked" and caused the right side of the equation to equal $1,000. This would be a tedious process, but you would eventually find PMT = $374.11.

2. Tabular Solution

Substitute in known values and look up PVIFA for 6%, 3 periods in Table A-2:

$$PVA_n = PMT(PVIFA_{i,n})$$
$$\$1,000 = PMT(PVIFA_{6\%,3}) = PMT(2.6730)$$
$$PMT = \$1,000/2.6730 = \$374.11.$$

3. Financial Calculator Solution

Inputs:	3	6	1000		0
	N	**I**	**PV**	**PMT**	**FV**

Output: = −374.11

Enter N = 3, I = 6, PV = 1000, and FV = 0, and then press the PMT key to find PMT = −$374.11.

4. Spreadsheet Solution

The spreadsheet is ideal for developing amortization tables. The setup is similar to Table 7-2, but you would want to include "input" cells for the interest rate, principal value, and the length of the loan. This would make the spreadsheet flexible in the sense that the loan terms could be changed and a new amortization table would be recalculated instantly. Then use the function wizard to find the payment. If you had I = 6% in B1, N = 3 in B2, and PV = 1000 in B3, then the function **=PMT(B1, B2, B3)** would find the payment, $374.11.

Amortization Schedule
A table showing precisely how a loan will be repaid. It gives the required payment on each payment date and a breakdown of the payment, showing how much is interest and how much is repayment of principal.

Therefore, the firm must pay the lender $374.11 at the end of each of the next three years, and the percentage cost to the borrower, which is also the rate of return to the lender, will be 6 percent. Each payment consists partly of interest and partly of repayment of principal. This breakdown is given in the **amortization schedule** shown in Table 7-2. The interest component is largest in the first year, and it declines as the outstanding balance of the loan decreases. For tax purposes, a business borrower or homeowner reports the interest component shown in Column 3 as a deductible cost each year, while the lender reports this same amount as taxable income.

Financial calculators are programmed to calculate amortization tables — you simply enter the input data, and then press one key to get each entry in Table 7-2. If you have a financial calculator, it is worthwhile to read the appropriate section of the calculator manual and learn how to use its amortization feature. As we show in the model for this chapter, with a spreadsheet such as *Excel*, it is easy to set up and print out a full amortization schedule.

SELF-TEST QUESTIONS

To construct an amortization schedule, how do you determine the amount of the periodic payments?

How do you determine the amount of each payment that goes to interest and to principal?

TYING IT ALL TOGETHER

Financial decisions often involve situations in which someone pays money at one point in time and receives money at some later time. Dollars paid or received at two different points in time are different, and this difference is recognized and accounted for by *time value of money (TVM) analysis.* We summarize below the types of TVM analysis and the key concepts covered in this chapter, using the data shown in Figure 7-3 to illustrate the various points. Refer to the figure constantly, and try to find in it an example of the points covered as you go through this summary.

- **Compounding** is the process of determining the **future value (FV)** of a cash flow or a series of cash flows. The compounded amount, or future value, is equal to the beginning amount plus the interest earned.

- Future value: $FV_n = PV(1 + i)^n = PV(FVIF_{i,n})$.
  (single payment)

  Example: $1,000 compounded for 1 year at 4 percent:

  $$FV_1 = \$1,000(1.04)^1 = \$1,040.$$

- **Discounting** is the process of finding the **present value (PV)** of a future cash flow or a series of cash flows; discounting is the reciprocal, or reverse, of compounding.

- Present value: $PV = \dfrac{FV_n}{(1 + i)^n} = FV_n\left(\dfrac{1}{1 + i}\right)^n = FV_n(PVIF_{i,n})$.
  (single payment)

  Example: $1,000 discounted back for 2 years at 4 percent:

  $$PV = \frac{\$1,000}{(1.04)^2} = \$1,000\left(\frac{1}{1.04}\right)^2 = \$1,000(0.9246) = \$924.60.$$

- An **annuity** is defined as a series of equal periodic payments (PMT) for a specified number of periods.

- Future value:
  (annuity)

  $$FVA_n = PMT(1+i)^{n-1} + PMT(1+i)^{n-2} + PMT(1+i)^{n-3} + \cdots + PMT(1+i)^0$$

  $$= PMT \sum_{t=1}^{n} (1 + i)^{n-t}$$

  $$= PMT(FVIFA_{i,n}).$$

FIGURE 7-3	**Illustration for Chapter Summary** **(i = 4%, Annual Compounding)**

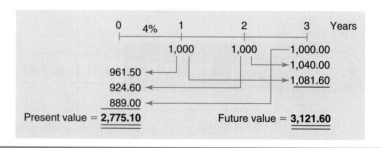

Present value = 2,775.10   Future value = 3,121.60

Example: FVA of 3 payments of $1,000 when i = 4%:

$$FVA_3 = \$1,000(3.1216) = \$3,121.60.$$

■ Present value: $PVA_n = \dfrac{PMT}{(1 + i)^1} + \dfrac{PMT}{(1 + i)^2} + \cdots + \dfrac{PMT}{(1 + i)^n}$
(annuity)

$$= PMT \sum_{t=1}^{n} \left[\frac{1}{1 + i}\right]^t$$

$$= PMT(PVIFA_{i,n}).$$

Example: PVA of 3 payments of $1,000 when i = 4% per period:

$$PVA_3 = \$1,000(2.7751) = \$2,775.10.$$

■ An annuity whose payments occur at the *end* of each period is called an **ordinary annuity.** The formulas above are for ordinary annuities.

■ If each payment occurs at the beginning of the period rather than at the end, then we have an **annuity due.** In Figure 7-3, the payments would be shown at Years 0, 1, and 2 rather than at Years 1, 2, and 3. The PV of each payment would be larger, because each payment would be discounted back one year less, so the PV of the annuity would also be larger. Similarly, the FV of the annuity due would also be larger because each payment would be compounded for an extra year. The following formulas can be used to convert the PV and FV of an ordinary annuity to an annuity due:

$$PVA \text{ (annuity due)} = PVA \text{ of an ordinary annuity} \times (1 + i).$$

Example: PVA of 3 beginning-of-year payments of $1,000 when i = 4%:

$$PVA \text{ (annuity due)} = \$1,000(2.7751)(1.04) = \$2,886.10.$$

Example: FVA of 3 beginning-of-year payments of $1,000 when i = 4%:

$$FVA \text{ (annuity due)} = FVA \text{ of an ordinary annuity} \times (1 + i).$$
$$FVA \text{ (annuity due)} = \$1,000(3.1216)(1.04) = \$3,246.46.$$

■ If the time line in Figure 7-3 were extended out forever so that the $1,000 payments went on forever, we would have a **perpetuity** whose value could be found as follows:

$$\text{Value of perpetuity} = \frac{PMT}{i} = \frac{\$1,000}{0.04} = \$25,000.$$

■ If the cash flows in Figure 7-3 were unequal, we could not use the annuity formulas. To find the PV or FV of an uneven series, find the PV or FV of each individual cash flow and then sum them. Note, though, that if some of the cash flows constitute an annuity, then the annuity formula can be used to calculate the present or future value of that part of the cash flow stream.

■ **Financial calculators** have built-in programs that perform all of the operations discussed in this chapter. It would be useful for you to buy such a calculator and to learn how to use it.

■ **Spreadsheet programs** are especially useful for problems with many uneven cash flows. They are also very useful if you want to solve a problem repeatedly with different inputs. See 07MODEL.xls on the CD-ROM that accompanies this text for spreadsheet models of the topics covered in this chapter.

■ TVM calculations generally involve equations that have four variables, and if you know three of the values, you (or your calculator) can solve for the fourth.

■ If you know the cash flows and the PV (or FV) of a cash flow stream, you can **determine the interest rate.** For example, in the Figure 7-3 illustration, if you were given the information that a loan called for 3 payments of $1,000 each, and that the loan had a value today of PV = $2,775.10, then you could find the interest rate that caused the sum of the PVs of the payments to equal $2,775.10. Since we are dealing with an annuity, you could proceed as follows:

a. With a financial calculator, enter N = 3, PV = 2775.10, PMT = −1000, FV = 0, and then press the I key to find I = 4%.

b. To use the tables, first recognize that PVA_n = $2,775.10 = $1,000($PVIFA_{i,3}$). Then solve for $PVIFA_{i,3}$:

$$PVIFA_{i,3} = \$2,775.10/\$1,000 = 2.7751.$$

Look up 2.7751 in Table A-2, in the third row. It is in the 4% column, so the interest rate must be 4 percent. If the factor did not appear in the table, this would indicate that the interest rate was not a whole number. In that case, you could not use this procedure to find the exact rate. In practice, though, this is not a problem, because in business people use financial calculators or computers to find interest rates.

■ Thus far in this section we have assumed that payments are made, and interest is earned, annually. However, many contracts call for more frequent payments; for example, mortgage and auto loans call for monthly payments, and most bonds pay interest semiannually. Similarly, most banks compute interest daily. When compounding occurs more frequently than once a year, this fact must be recognized. We can use the Figure 7-3 example to illustrate semiannual compounding. First, recognize that the 4 percent stated rate is a nominal rate that must be converted to a periodic rate, and the number of years must be converted to periods:

$$i_{PER} = \text{Stated rate/Periods per year} = 4\%/2 = 2\%.$$

$$\text{Periods} = \text{Years} \times \text{Periods per year} = 3 \times 2 = 6.$$

The periodic rate and number of periods would be used for calculations and shown on time lines.

If the $1,000 per-year payments were actually payable as $500 each 6 months, you would simply redraw Figure 7-3 to show 6 payments of $500 each, but you would also use a **periodic interest rate** of 4%/2 = 2% for determining the PV or FV of the payments.

■ If we are comparing the costs of loans that require payments more than once a year, or the rates of return on investments that pay interest more frequently, then the comparisons should be based on **equivalent (or effective) rates of return** using this formula:

$$\text{Effective annual rate} = \text{EAR (or EFF\%)} = \left(1 + \frac{i_{Nom}}{m}\right)^m - 1.0.$$

For semiannual compounding, the effective annual rate is 4.04 percent:

$$\left(1 + \frac{0.04}{2}\right)^2 - 1.0 = (1.02)^2 - 1.0 = 1.0404 - 1.0 = 0.0404 = 4.04\%.$$

- The general equation for finding the future value for any number of compounding periods per year is:

$$FV_n = PV\left(1 + \frac{i_{Nom}}{m}\right)^{mn},$$

where

i_{Nom} = quoted interest rate.
m = number of compounding periods per year.
n = number of years.

- An **amortized loan** is one that is paid off in equal payments over a specified period. An **amortization schedule** shows how much of each payment constitutes interest, how much is used to reduce the principal, and the unpaid balance at each point in time.

The concepts covered in this chapter will be used throughout the remainder of the book. For example, in Chapters 8 and 9, we apply present value concepts to find the values of bonds and stocks, and we see that the market prices of securities are established by determining the present values of the cash flows they are expected to provide. In later chapters, the same basic concepts are applied to corporate decisions involving expenditures on capital assets, to the types of capital that should be used to pay for assets, and so forth.

QUESTIONS

7-1 What is an *opportunity cost rate*? How is this rate used in time value analysis, and where is it shown on a time line? Is the opportunity rate a single number that is used in all situations?

7-2 An *annuity* is defined as a series of payments of a fixed amount for a specific number of periods. Thus, $100 a year for 10 years is an annuity, but $100 in Year 1, $200 in Year 2, and $400 in Years 3 through 10 does *not* constitute an annuity. However, the second series *contains* an annuity. Is this statement true or false?

7-3 If a firm's earnings per share grew from $1 to $2 over a 10-year period, the *total growth* would be 100 percent, but the *annual growth rate* would be *less than* 10 percent. True or false? Explain.

7-4 Would you rather have a savings account that pays 5 percent interest compounded semiannually or one that pays 5 percent interest compounded daily? Explain.

7-5 To find the present value of an uneven series of cash flows, you must find the PVs of the individual cash flows and then sum them. Annuity procedures can never be of use, even if some of the cash flows constitute an annuity (for example, $100 each for Years 3, 4, 5, and 6), because the entire series is not an annuity. Is this statement true or false? Explain.

7-6 The present value of a perpetuity is equal to the payment on the annuity, PMT, divided by the interest rate, i: PV = PMT/i. What is the *sum*, or future value, of a perpetuity of PMT dollars per year? (Hint: The answer is infinity, but explain why.)

ST-1
Key terms

Define each of the following terms:
a. PV; i; INT; FV_n; n; PVA_n; FVA_n; PMT; m; i_{Nom}
b. $FVIF_{i,n}$; $PVIF_{i,n}$; $FVIFA_{i,n}$; $PVIFA_{i,n}$
c. Opportunity cost rate; fair (equilibrium) value
d. Annuity; lump sum payment; cash flow; uneven cash flow stream
e. Ordinary (deferred) annuity; annuity due
f. Perpetuity; consol
g. Outflow; inflow; time line
h. Compounding; discounting
i. Annual, semiannual, quarterly, monthly, and daily compounding
j. Effective (equivalent) annual rate (EAR); nominal (quoted) interest rate; Annual Percentage Rate (APR); periodic rate
k. Amortization schedule; principal component versus interest component of a payment; amortized loan
l. Terminal value

ST-2
Future value

Assume that it is now January 1, 2002. On January 1, 2003, you will deposit $1,000 into a savings account that pays 8 percent.
a. If the bank compounds interest annually, how much will you have in your account on January 1, 2006?
b. What would your January 1, 2006, balance be if the bank used quarterly compounding rather than annual compounding?
c. Suppose you deposited the $1,000 in 4 payments of $250 each on January 1 of 2003, 2004, 2005, and 2006. How much would you have in your account on January 1, 2006, based on 8 percent annual compounding?
d. Suppose you deposited 4 equal payments in your account on January 1 of 2003, 2004, 2005, and 2006. Assuming an 8 percent interest rate, how large would each of your payments have to be for you to obtain the same ending balance as you calculated in part a?

ST-3
Time value of money

Assume that it is now January 1, 2002, and you will need $1,000 on January 1, 2006. Your bank compounds interest at an 8 percent annual rate.
a. How much must you deposit on January 1, 2003, to have a balance of $1,000 on January 1, 2006?
b. If you want to make equal payments on each January 1 from 2003 through 2006 to accumulate the $1,000, how large must each of the 4 payments be?
c. If your father were to offer either to make the payments calculated in part b ($221.92) or to give you a lump sum of $750 on January 1, 2003, which would you choose?
d. If you have only $750 on January 1, 2003, what interest rate, compounded annually, would you have to earn to have the necessary $1,000 on January 1, 2006?
e. Suppose you can deposit only $186.29 each January 1 from 2003 through 2006, but you still need $1,000 on January 1, 2006. What interest rate, with annual compounding, must you seek out to achieve your goal?
f. To help you reach your $1,000 goal, your father offers to give you $400 on January 1, 2003. You will get a part-time job and make 6 additional payments of equal amounts each 6 months thereafter. If all of this money is deposited in a bank that pays 8 percent, compounded semiannually, how large must each of the 6 payments be?
g. What is the effective annual rate being paid by the bank in part f?
h. *Reinvestment rate risk* was defined in Chapter 5 as being the risk that maturing securities (and coupon payments on bonds) will have to be reinvested at a lower rate of interest than they were previously earning. Is there a reinvestment rate risk involved in the preceding analysis? If so, how might this risk be eliminated?

ST-4
Effective annual rates

Bank A pays 8 percent interest, compounded quarterly, on its money market account. The managers of Bank B want its money market account to equal Bank A's effective annual rate, but interest is to be compounded on a monthly basis. What nominal, or quoted, rate must Bank B set?

STARTER PROBLEMS

7-1
Future value

If you deposit $10,000 in a bank account that pays 10 percent interest annually, how much money will be in your account after 5 years?

7-2
Present value

What is the present value of a security that promises to pay you $5,000 in 20 years? Assume that you can earn 7 percent if you were to invest in other securities of equal risk.

7-3
Financial calculator needed; Time for a lump sum to double

If you deposit money today into an account that pays 6.5 percent interest, how long will it take for you to double your money?

7-4
Financial calculator needed; Reaching a financial goal

John Roberts has $42,180.53 in a brokerage account, and he plans to contribute an additional $5,000 to the account at the end of every year. The brokerage account has an expected annual return of 12 percent. If John's goal is to accumulate $250,000 in the account, how many years will it take for John to reach his goal?

7-5
Effective rate of interest

Your parents are planning to retire in 18 years. They currently have $250,000, and they would like to have $1,000,000 when they retire. What annual rate of interest would they have to earn on their $250,000 in order to reach their goal, assuming they save no more money?

7-6
Future value of an annuity

What is the future value of a 5-year ordinary annuity that promises to pay you $300 each year? The rate of interest is 7 percent.

7-7
Future value of an annuity due

What is the future value of a 5-year annuity due that promises to pay you $300 each year? Assume that all payments are reinvested at 7 percent a year, until Year 5.

7-8
Future value of an annuity

What is the future value of a 5-year annuity due that promises to pay you $300 each year? Assume that all payments are reinvested at 7 percent a year, until Year 4.

7-9
Present and future value of a cash flow stream

An investment pays you $100 at the end of each of the next 3 years. The investment will then pay you $200 at the end of Year 4, $300 at the end of Year 5, and $500 at the end of Year 6. If the interest rate earned on the investment is 8 percent, what is its present value? What is its future value?

7-10
Comparison of interest rates

An investment pays you 9 percent interest, compounded quarterly. What is the periodic rate of interest? What is the nominal rate of interest? What is the effective rate of interest?

7-11
Loan amortization and effective interest rate

You are thinking about buying a car, and a local bank is willing to lend you $20,000 to buy the car. Under the terms of the loan, it will be fully amortized over 5 years (60 months), and the nominal rate of interest will be 12 percent, with interest paid monthly. What would be the monthly payment on the loan? What would be the effective rate of interest on the loan?

EXAM-TYPE PROBLEMS

The problems included in this section are set up in such a way that they could be used as multiple-choice exam problems.

7-12
Present value comparison

Which amount is worth more at 14 percent, compounded annually: $1,000 in hand today or $2,000 due in 6 years?

7-13
Growth rates

Shalit Corporation's 2001 sales were $12 million. Sales were $6 million 5 years earlier (in 1996).
a. To the nearest percentage point, at what rate have sales been growing?
b. Suppose someone calculated the sales growth for Shalit Corporation in part a as follows: "Sales doubled in 5 years. This represents a growth of 100 percent in 5 years, so, dividing 100 percent by 5, we find the growth rate to be 20 percent per year." Explain what is wrong with this calculation.

7-14
Expected rate of return

Washington-Atlantic invests $4 million to clear a tract of land and to set out some young pine trees. The trees will mature in 10 years, at which time Washington-Atlantic plans to sell the forest at an expected price of $8 million. What is Washington-Atlantic's expected rate of return?

7-15

Effective rate of interest

Your broker offers to sell you a note for $13,250 that will pay $2,345.05 per year for 10 years. If you buy the note, what interest rate (to the closest percent) will you be earning?

7-16

Effective rate of interest

A mortgage company offers to lend you $85,000; the loan calls for payments of $8,273.59 per year for 30 years. What interest rate is the mortgage company charging you?

7-17

Required lump sum payment

To complete your last year in business school and then go through law school, you will need $10,000 per year for 4 years, starting next year (that is, you will need to withdraw the first $10,000 one year from today). Your rich uncle offers to put you through school, and he will deposit in a bank paying 7 percent interest, compounded annually, a sum of money that is sufficient to provide the 4 payments of $10,000 each. His deposit will be made today.

a. How large must the deposit be?
b. How much will be in the account immediately after you make the first withdrawal? After the last withdrawal?

7-18

Repaying a loan

While you were a student in college, you borrowed $12,000 in student loans at an interest rate of 9 percent, compounded annually. If you repay $1,500 per year, how long, to the nearest year, will it take you to repay the loan?

7-19

Reaching a financial goal

You need to accumulate $10,000. To do so, you plan to make deposits of $1,250 per year, with the first payment being made a year from today, in a bank account that pays 12 percent interest, compounded annually. Your last deposit will be less than $1,250 if less is needed to round out to $10,000. How many years will it take you to reach your $10,000 goal, and how large will the last deposit be?

7-20

Present value of a cash flow stream

A rookie quarterback is in the process of negotiating his first contract. The team's general manager has offered him three possible contracts. Each of the contracts lasts for 4 years. All of the money is guaranteed and is paid at the end of each year. The terms of each of the contracts are listed below:

	CONTRACT 1 PAYMENTS	CONTRACT 2 PAYMENTS	CONTRACT 3 PAYMENTS
Year 1	$3 million	$2 million	$7 million
Year 2	3 million	3 million	1 million
Year 3	3 million	4 million	1 million
Year 4	3 million	5 million	1 million

The quarterback discounts all cash flows at 10 percent. Which of the three contracts offers him the most value?

7-21

Present value of a perpetuity

What is the present value of a perpetuity of $100 per year if the appropriate discount rate is 7 percent? If interest rates in general were to double and the appropriate discount rate rose to 14 percent, what would happen to the present value of the perpetuity?

7-22

Financial calculator needed; PV and effective annual rate

Assume that you inherited some money. A friend of yours is working as an unpaid intern at a local brokerage firm, and her boss is selling some securities that call for 4 payments, $50 at the end of each of the next 3 years, plus a payment of $1,050 at the end of Year 4. Your friend says she can get you some of these securities at a cost of $900 each. Your money is now invested in a bank that pays an 8 percent nominal (quoted) interest rate, but with quarterly compounding. You regard the securities as being just as safe, and as liquid, as your bank deposit, so your required effective annual rate of return on the securities is the same as that on your bank deposit. You must calculate the value of the securities to decide whether they are a good investment. What is their present value to you?

7-23

Loan amortization

Assume that your aunt sold her house on December 31, and that she took a mortgage in the amount of $10,000 as part of the payment. The mortgage has a quoted (or nominal) interest rate of 10 percent, but it calls for payments every 6 months, beginning on June 30, and the mortgage is to be amortized over 10 years. Now, one year later, your aunt must file Schedule B of her tax return with the IRS, informing them of the interest that was included in the 2 payments made during the year. (This interest will be income to your aunt and a deduction to the buyer of the house.) To the closest dollar, what is the total amount of interest that was paid during the first year?

7-24
Loan amortization

Your company is planning to borrow $1,000,000 on a 5-year, 15%, annual payment, fully amortized term loan. What fraction of the payment made at the end of the second year will represent repayment of principal?

7-25
Nonannual compounding

a. It is now January 1, 2002. You plan to make 5 deposits of $100 each, one every 6 months, with the first payment being made *today*. If the bank pays a nominal interest rate of 12 percent, but uses semiannual compounding, how much will be in your account after 10 years?

b. Ten years from today you must make a payment of $1,432.02. To prepare for this payment, you will make 5 equal deposits, beginning today and for the next 4 quarters, in a bank that pays a nominal interest rate of 12 percent, quarterly compounding. How large must each of the 5 payments be?

7-26
Nominal rate of return

As the manager of Oaks Mall Jewelry, you want to sell on credit, giving customers 3 months in which to pay. However, you will have to borrow from the bank to carry the accounts receivable. The bank will charge a nominal 15 percent, but with monthly compounding. You want to quote a nominal rate to your customers (all of whom are expected to pay on time) that will exactly cover your financing costs. What nominal annual rate should you quote to your credit customers?

7-27
Financial calculator needed; Required annuity payments

Assume that your father is now 50 years old, that he plans to retire in 10 years, and that he expects to live for 25 years after he retires, that is, until he is 85. He wants a fixed retirement income that has the same purchasing power at the time he retires as $40,000 has today (he realizes that the real value of his retirement income will decline year by year after he retires). His retirement income will begin the day he retires, 10 years from today, and he will then get 24 additional annual payments. Inflation is expected to be 5 percent per year from today forward; he currently has $100,000 saved up; and he expects to earn a return on his savings of 8 percent per year, annual compounding. To the nearest dollar, how much must he save during each of the next 10 years (with deposits being made at the end of each year) to meet his retirement goal?

7-28
Value of an annuity

The prize in last week's Florida lottery was estimated to be worth $35 million. If you were lucky enough to win, the state will pay you $1.75 million per year over the next 20 years. Assume that the first installment is received immediately.

a. If interest rates are 8 percent, what is the present value of the prize?

b. If interest rates are 8 percent, what is the future value after 20 years?

c. How would your answers change if the payments were received at the end of each year?

7-29
Future value of an annuity

Your client is 40 years old and wants to begin saving for retirement. You advise the client to put $5,000 a year into the stock market. You estimate that the market's return will be, on average, 12 percent a year. Assume the investment will be made at the end of the year.

a. If the client follows your advice, how much money will she have by age 65?

b. How much will she have by age 70?

7-30
Present value

You are serving on a jury. A plaintiff is suing the city for injuries sustained after falling down an uncovered manhole. In the trial, doctors testified that it will be 5 years before the plaintiff is able to return to work. The jury has already decided in favor of the plaintiff, and has decided to grant the plaintiff an award to cover the following items:

(1) Recovery of 2 years of back-pay ($34,000 in 2000, and $36,000 in 2001). Assume that it is December 31, 2001, and that all salary is received at year end. This recovery should include the time value of money.

(2) The present value of 5 years of future salary (2002–2006). Assume that the plaintiff's salary would increase at a rate of 3 percent a year.

(3) $100,000 for pain and suffering.

(4) $20,000 for court costs.

Assume an interest rate of 7 percent. What should be the size of the settlement?

7-31
Future value

You just started your first job, and you want to buy a house within 3 years. You are currently saving for the down payment. You plan to save $5,000 the first year. You also anticipate that the amount you save each year will rise by 10 percent a year as your salary increases over time. Interest rates are assumed to be 7 percent, and all savings occur at year end. How much money will you have for a down payment in 3 years?

7-32
Required annuity payment

A 15-year security has a price of $340.4689. The security pays $50 at the end of each of the next 5 years, and then it pays a different fixed cash flow amount at the end of each of the following 10 years. Interest rates are 9 percent. What is the annual cash flow amount between Years 6 and 15?

7-33
Financial calculator needed;
Nonannual compounding An investment pays $20 semiannually for the next 2 years. The investment has a 7 percent nominal interest rate, and interest is compounded quarterly. What is the future value of the investment?

PROBLEMS

7-34
Present and future values
for different periods Find the following values, *using the equations,* and then work the problems using a financial calculator or the tables to check your answers. Disregard rounding differences. (Hint: If you are using a financial calculator, you can enter the known values, and then press the appropriate key to find the unknown variable. Then, without clearing the TVM register, you can "override" the variable that changes by simply entering a new value for it and then pressing the key for the unknown variable to obtain the second answer. This procedure can be used in parts b and d, and in many other situations, to see how changes in input variables affect the output variable.) Assume that compounding/discounting occurs once a year.
a. An initial $500 compounded for 1 year at 6 percent.
b. An initial $500 compounded for 2 years at 6 percent.
c. The present value of $500 due in 1 year at a discount rate of 6 percent.
d. The present value of $500 due in 2 years at a discount rate of 6 percent.

7-35
Present and future values
for different interest rates Use the tables or a financial calculator to find the following values. See the hint for Problem 7-34. Assume that compounding/discounting occurs once a year.
a. An initial $500 compounded for 10 years at 6 percent.
b. An initial $500 compounded for 10 years at 12 percent.
c. The present value of $500 due in 10 years at a 6 percent discount rate.
d. The present value of $1,552.90 due in 10 years at a 12 percent discount rate and at a 6 percent rate. Give a verbal definition of the term *present value,* and illustrate it using a time line with data from this problem. As a part of your answer, explain why present values are dependent upon interest rates.

7-36
Time for a lump sum to double To the closest year, how long will it take $200 to double if it is deposited and earns the following rates? [Notes: (1) See the hint for Problem 7-34. (2) This problem cannot be solved exactly with some financial calculators. For example, if you enter $PV = -200$, $FV = 400$, and $I = 7$ in an HP-12C, and then press the N key, you will get 11 years for part a. The correct answer is 10.2448 years, which rounds to 10, but the calculator rounds up. However, the HP-10B and HP-17B give the correct answer. You should look up $FVIF = \$400/\$200 = 2$ in the tables for parts a, b, and c, but figure out part d.] Assume that compounding occurs once a year.
a. 7 percent.
b. 10 percent.
c. 18 percent.
d. 100 percent.

7-37
Future value of an annuity Find the *future value* of the following annuities. The first payment in these annuities is made at the *end* of Year 1; that is, they are *ordinary annuities.* (Note: See the hint to Problem 7-34. Also, note that you can leave values in the TVM register, switch to "BEG," press FV, and find the FV of the annuity due.) Assume that compounding occurs once a year.
a. $400 per year for 10 years at 10 percent.
b. $200 per year for 5 years at 5 percent.
c. $400 per year for 5 years at 0 percent.
d. Now rework parts a, b, and c assuming that payments are made at the *beginning* of each year; that is, they are *annuities due.*

7-38
Present value of an annuity Find the *present value* of the following *ordinary annuities* (see note to Problem 7-37). Assume that discounting occurs once a year.
a. $400 per year for 10 years at 10 percent.
b. $200 per year for 5 years at 5 percent.
c. $400 per year for 5 years at 0 percent.
d. Now rework parts a, b, and c assuming that payments are made at the *beginning* of each year; that is, they are *annuities due.*

7-39
Uneven cash flow stream a. Find the present values of the following cash flow streams. The appropriate interest rate is 8 percent, compounded annually. (Hint: It is fairly easy to work this problem

dealing with the individual cash flows. However, if you have a financial calculator, read the section of the manual that describes how to enter cash flows such as the ones in this problem. This will take a little time, but the investment will pay huge dividends throughout the course. Note that if you do work with the cash flow register, you must enter $CF_0 = 0$.)

YEAR	CASH STREAM A	CASH STREAM B
1	$100	$300
2	400	400
3	400	400
4	400	400
5	300	100

b. What is the value of each cash flow stream at a 0 percent interest rate, compounded annually?

7-40
Effective rate of interest

Find the interest rates, or rates of return, on each of the following:
a. You *borrow* $700 and promise to pay back $749 at the end of 1 year.
b. You *lend* $700 and receive a promise to be paid $749 at the end of 1 year.
c. You borrow $85,000 and promise to pay back $201,229 at the end of 10 years.
d. You borrow $9,000 and promise to make payments of $2,684.80 per year for 5 years.

7-41
Future value for various compounding periods

Find the amount to which $500 will grow under each of the following conditions:
a. 12 percent compounded annually for 5 years.
b. 12 percent compounded semiannually for 5 years.
c. 12 percent compounded quarterly for 5 years.
d. 12 percent compounded monthly for 5 years.

7-42
Present value for various compounding periods

Find the present value of $500 due in the future under each of the following conditions:
a. 12 percent nominal rate, semiannual compounding, discounted back 5 years.
b. 12 percent nominal rate, quarterly compounding, discounted back 5 years.
c. 12 percent nominal rate, monthly compounding, discounted back 1 year.

7-43
Future value of an annuity for various compounding periods

Find the future values of the following ordinary annuities:
a. FV of $400 each 6 months for 5 years at a nominal rate of 12 percent, compounded semiannually.
b. FV of $200 each 3 months for 5 years at a nominal rate of 12 percent, compounded quarterly.
c. The annuities described in parts a and b have the same amount of money paid into them during the 5-year period, and both earn interest at the same nominal rate, yet the annuity in part b earns $101.75 more than the one in part a over the 5 years. Why does this occur?

7-44
Effective versus nominal interest rates

The First City Bank pays 7 percent interest, compounded annually, on time deposits. The Second City Bank pays 6 percent interest, compounded quarterly.
a. Based on effective, or equivalent, interest rates, in which bank would you prefer to deposit your money?
b. Could your choice of banks be influenced by the fact that you might want to withdraw your funds during the year as opposed to at the end of the year? In answering this question, assume that funds must be left on deposit during the entire compounding period in order for you to receive any interest.

7-45
Amortization schedule

a. Set up an amortization schedule for a $25,000 loan to be repaid in equal installments at the end of each of the next 5 years. The interest rate is 10 percent, compounded annually.
b. How large must each annual payment be if the loan is for $50,000? Assume that the interest rate remains at 10 percent, compounded annually, and that the loan is paid off over 5 years.
c. How large must each payment be if the loan is for $50,000, the interest rate is 10 percent, compounded annually, and the loan is paid off in equal installments at the end of each of the next 10 years? This loan is for the same amount as the loan in part b, but the payments are spread out over twice as many periods. Why are these payments not half as large as the payments on the loan in part b?

7-46
Financial calculator needed;
Amortization schedule

The Jackson family is interested in buying a home. The family is applying for a $125,000, 30-year mortgage. Under the terms of the mortgage, they will receive $125,000 today to help purchase their home. The loan will be fully amortized over the next 30 years. Current mortgage rates are 8 percent. Interest is compounded monthly and all payments are due at the end of the month.
a. What is the monthly mortgage payment?
b. What portion of the mortgage payments made during the first year will go toward interest?
c. What will be the remaining balance on the mortgage after 5 years?
d. How much could the Jacksons borrow today if they were willing to have a $1,200 monthly mortgage payment? (Assume that the interest rate and the length of the loan remain the same.)

7-47
Effective rates of return

Assume that AT&T's pension fund managers are considering two alternative securities as investments: (1) Security Z (for zero intermediate year cash flows), which costs $422.41 today, pays nothing during its 10-year life, and then pays $1,000 after 10 years or (2) Security B, which has a cost today of $1,000 and which pays $80 at the end of each of the next 9 years and then $1,080 at the end of Year 10.
a. What is the rate of return on each security?
b. Assume that the interest rate AT&T's pension fund managers can earn on the fund's money falls to 6 percent, compounded annually, immediately after the securities are purchased and is expected to remain at that level for the next 10 years. What would the price of each security change to, what would the fund's profit be on each security, and what would be the percentage profit (profit divided by cost) for each security?
c. Assuming that the cash flows for each security had to be reinvested at the new 6 percent market interest rate, (1) what would be the value attributable to each security at the end of 10 years and (2) what "actual, after-the-fact" rate of return would the fund have earned on each security? (Hint: The "actual" rate of return is found as the interest rate that causes the PV of the compounded Year 10 amount to equal the original cost of the security.)
d. Now assume all the facts as given in parts b and c, except assume that the interest rate *rose* to 12 percent rather than fell to 6 percent. What would happen to the profit figures as developed in part b and to the "actual" rates of return as determined in part c? Explain your results.

7-48
Required annuity payments

A father is planning a savings program to put his daughter through college. His daughter is now 13 years old. She plans to enroll at the university in 5 years, and it should take her 4 years to complete her education. Currently, the cost per year (for everything — food, clothing, tuition, books, transportation, and so forth) is $12,500, but a 5 percent annual inflation rate in these costs is forecasted. The daughter recently received $7,500 from her grandfather's estate; this money, which is invested in a bank account paying 8 percent interest, compounded annually, will be used to help meet the costs of the daughter's education. The remaining costs will be met by money the father will deposit in the savings account. He will make 6 equal deposits to the account, one deposit in each year from now until his daughter starts college. These deposits will begin today and will also earn 8 percent interest, compounded annually.
a. What will be the present value of the cost of 4 years of education at the time the daughter becomes 18? [Hint: Calculate the future value of the cost (at 5%) for each year of her education, then discount 3 of these costs back (at 8%) to the year in which she turns 18, then sum the 4 costs.]
b. What will be the value of the $7,500 that the daughter received from her grandfather's estate when she starts college at age 18? (Hint: Compound for 5 years at an 8 percent annual rate.)
c. If the father is planning to make the first of 6 deposits today, how large must each deposit be for him to be able to put his daughter through college? (Hint: An annuity due assumes interest is earned on all deposits; however, the 6th deposit earns no interest — therefore, the deposits are an ordinary annuity.)

SPREADSHEET PROBLEM

7-49
Time value of money

Answer the following questions, using a spreadsheet model to do the calculations.
a. Find the FV of $1,000 invested to earn 10 percent after 5 years. Answer this question by using a math formula and also by using the *Excel* function wizard.

b. Now create a table that shows the FV at 0 percent, 5 percent, and 20 percent for 0, 1, 2, 3, 4, and 5 years. Then create a graph with years on the horizontal axis and FV on the vertical axis to display your results.

c. Find the PV of $1,000 due in 5 years if the discount rate is 10 percent. Again, work the problem with a formula and also by using the function wizard.

d. A security has a cost of $1,000 and will return $2,000 after 5 years. What rate of return does the security provide?

e. Suppose California's population is 30 million people, and its population is expected to grow by 2 percent per year. How long would it take for the population to double?

f. Find the PV of an annuity that pays $1,000 at the end of each of the next 5 years if the interest rate is 15 percent. Then find the FV of that same annuity.

g. How would the PV and FV of the annuity change if it were an annuity due rather than an ordinary annuity?

h. What would the FV and the PV for parts a and c be if the interest rate were 10 percent with semiannual compounding rather than 10 percent with annual compounding?

i. Find the PV and the FV of an investment that makes the following end-of-year payments. The interest rate is 8 percent.

YEAR	PAYMENT
1	$100
2	200
3	400

j. Suppose you bought a house and took out a mortgage for $50,000. The interest rate is 8 percent, and you must amortize the loan over 10 years with equal end-of-year payments. Set up an amortization schedule that shows the annual payments and the amount of each payment that goes to pay off the principal and the amount that constitutes interest expense to the borrower and interest income to the lender.

   (1) Create a graph that shows how the payments are divided between interest and principal repayment over time.

   (2) Suppose the loan called for 10 years of monthly payments, with the same original amount and the same nominal interest rate. What would the amortization schedule show now?

k. Refer to Problem 7-48. Solve this problem using a spreadsheet model.

CYBER PROBLEM

The information related to the cyberproblems is likely to change over time, due to the release of new information and the ever-changing nature of the World Wide Web. With these changes in mind, we will periodically update these problems on the textbook's web site. To avoid problems, please check for these updates before proceeding with the cyberproblems.

7-50
Prepayment versus investment analysis

In managing one's own finances, as well as those of a business, there are numerous decision situations where applications of Time Value of Money (TVM) concepts and methods help one assess the financial consequences of alternative courses of action. One such situation is the decision to prepay part or all of one's mortgage or loan balance by making extra periodic principal payments. As one makes extra principal payments, the loan balance is reduced faster. This means you pay less interest over the life of the loan and the loan will be repaid earlier (that is, fewer payments). For example, a person might decide to pay $50 per month extra (that is, if their mortgage payment was $900 per month, they might pay $950 each month, $50 extra) on a mortgage loan. The extra payment of $50 would be applied each month to reduce the principal balance. However, there are important factors to consider before making this decision. For example, if the mortgage loan is on the person's primary residence, the interest on the loan may be tax deductible. As you know from previous text chapters, this reduces the net, after-tax cost of the loan.

To consider the financial consequences of this decision, visit the web site **www.interest.com/hugh/calc**, which offers various web calculators free, including a prepayment versus investment scenario analysis. Before using this web site, you will need to amortize the loan you will use as input data for the analysis.

Suppose you purchase a home for $150,000 and obtain a 90 percent mortgage loan, 30-year maturity, at a fixed annual interest rate of 8 percent, with deferred monthly payments. What is the monthly payment for principal and interest (P&I) on this loan?

The loan amount is $150,000 × 0.90 = $135,000. The calculator keystrokes follow. N = 360 (30 years × 12 months per year); I = 8.0/12 = 0.6667; PV = −135000; FV = 0 (the loan will be paid off at maturity); solve for PMT = $990.62. (Note: If you enter the interest rate at 0.6667 percent per month you get the payment above. If you carry full precision on your calculator, the PMT = $990.58.)

The data you will need for the prepayment scenario include the following.

Loan balance: $135,000

Current payment: $990.62

Additional payment: $50.00

Loan interest rate: 8.0%

Loan interest deductibility: Yes

Investment rate return: 6.00%*

Tax bracket: 30.00%

Investment type: After-tax

*The investment rate return is your opportunity cost estimate. It is the annual rate you think you can earn on the $50 extra principal payment if you did not make extra principal payments on your mortgage but instead, invested it.

Now visit the web site **www.interest.com/hugh/calc**, and select Prepayment versus Investment.

a. After 12 months of making extra payments, what will be the loan balance?
b. After 12 months of making the regular payment and investing the $50, what will be the loan balance?
c. Under the regular payment and investing option, excluding the tax due on the interest earned, what is the investment balance after 12 months?
d. Compare the scenarios of investment versus prepayment by examining the 60th payment, which occurs at the end of the 5th year. What is the difference between the (1) interest portion of that payment, (2) tax deduction for interest, and (3) principal balance? Finally, how much is in the investment account?

INTEGRATED CASE

FIRST NATIONAL BANK

7-51 **Time Value of Money Analysis** Assume that you are nearing graduation and that you have applied for a job with a local bank, First National Bank. As part of the bank's evaluation process, you have been asked to take an examination that covers several financial analysis techniques. The first section of the test addresses time value of money analysis. See how you would do by answering the following questions.

a. Draw time lines for (1) a $100 lump sum cash flow at the end of Year 2, (2) an ordinary annuity of $100 per year for 3 years, and (3) an uneven cash flow stream of −$50, $100, $75, and $50 at the end of Years 0 through 3.
b. (1) What is the future value of an initial $100 after 3 years if it is invested in an account paying 10 percent, annual compounding?

(2) What is the present value of $100 to be received in 3 years if the appropriate interest rate is 10 percent, annual compounding?

c. We sometimes need to find how long it will take a sum of money (or anything else) to grow to some specified amount. For example, if a company's sales are growing at a rate of 20 percent per year, how long will it take sales to double?

d. What is the difference between an ordinary annuity and an annuity due? What type of annuity is shown below? How would you change it to the other type of annuity?

e. (1) What is the future value of a 3-year ordinary annuity of $100 if the appropriate interest rate is 10 percent, annual compounding?
(2) What is the present value of the annuity?
(3) What would the future and present values be if the annuity were an annuity due?

f. What is the present value of the following uneven cash flow stream? The appropriate interest rate is 10 percent, compounded annually.

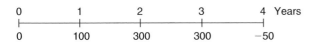

g. What annual interest rate will cause $100 to grow to $125.97 in 3 years?

h. A 20-year-old student wants to begin saving for her retirement. Her plan is to save $3 a day. Every day she places $3 in a drawer. At the end of each year, she invests the accumulated savings ($1,095) in an online stock account that has an expected annual return of 12 percent.
(1) If she keeps saving in this manner, how much will she have accumulated by age 65?
(2) If a 40-year-old investor began saving in this manner, how much would he have by age 65?

(3) How much would the 40-year-old investor have to save each year to accumulate the same amount at age 65 as the 20-year-old investor described above?

i. (1) Will the future value be larger or smaller if we compound an initial amount more often than annually, for example, every 6 months, or *semiannually*, holding the stated interest rate constant? Why?
(2) Define (a) the stated, or quoted, or nominal, rate, (b) the periodic rate, and (c) the effective annual rate (EAR).
(3) What is the effective annual rate corresponding to a nominal rate of 10 percent, compounded semiannually? Compounded quarterly? Compounded daily?
(4) What is the future value of $100 after 3 years under 10 percent semiannual compounding? Quarterly compounding?

j. When will the effective annual rate be equal to the nominal (quoted) rate?

k. (1) What is the value at the end of Year 3 of the following cash flow stream if the quoted interest rate is 10 percent, compounded semiannually?

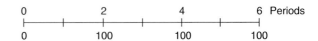

(2) What is the PV of the same stream?
(3) Is the stream an annuity?
(4) An important rule is that you should *never* show a nominal rate on a time line or use it in calculations unless what condition holds? (Hint: Think of annual compounding, when $i_{Nom} = EAR = i_{PER}$.) What would be wrong with your answer to parts k (1) and k (2) if you used the nominal rate, 10 percent, rather than the periodic rate, $i_{Nom}/2 = 10\%/2 = 5\%$?

l. (1) Construct an amortization schedule for a $1,000, 10 percent, annual compounding loan with 3 equal installments.
(2) What is the annual interest expense for the borrower, and the annual interest income for the lender, during Year 2?

CONTINUOUS COMPOUNDING AND DISCOUNTING

In Chapter 7 we dealt only with situations where interest is added at discrete intervals — annually, semiannually, monthly, and so forth. In some instances, though, it is possible to have instantaneous, or *continuous*, growth. In this appendix, we discuss present value and future value calculations when the interest rate is compounded continuously.

CONTINUOUS COMPOUNDING

Continuous Compounding
A situation in which interest is added continuously rather than at discrete points in time.

The relationship between discrete and **continuous compounding** is illustrated in Figure 7A-1. Panel a shows the annual compounding case, where interest is added once a year; Panel b shows the situation when compounding occurs twice a year; and Panel c shows interest being earned continuously. As the graphs show, the more frequent the compounding period, the larger the final compounded amount because interest is earned on interest more often.

Equation 7-9 in the chapter can be applied to any number of compounding periods per year:

$$\text{More frequent compounding: } FV_n = PV\left(1 + \frac{i_{Nom}}{m}\right)^{mn}. \qquad (7\text{-}9)$$

FIGURE 7A-1 Annual, Semiannual, and Continuous Compounding: Future Value with i = 25%

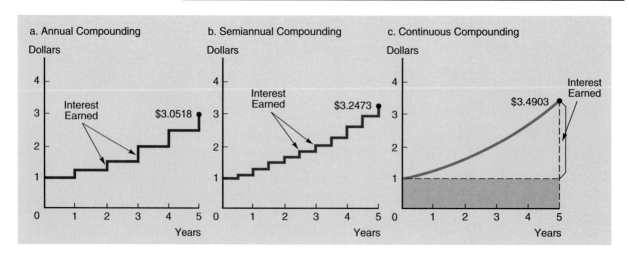

To illustrate, let PV = $100, i = 10%, and n = 5. At various compounding periods per year, we obtain the following future values at the end of five years:

$$\text{Annual: } FV_5 = \$100\left(1 + \frac{0.10}{1}\right)^{1(5)} = \$100(1.10)^5 = \$161.05.$$

$$\text{Semiannual: } FV_5 = \$100\left(1 + \frac{0.10}{2}\right)^{2(5)} = \$100(1.05)^{10} = \$162.89.$$

$$\text{Monthly: } FV_5 = \$100\left(1 + \frac{0.10}{12}\right)^{12(5)} = \$100(1.0083)^{60} = \$164.53.$$

$$\text{Daily: } FV_5 = \$100\left(1 + \frac{0.10}{365}\right)^{365(5)} = \$164.86.$$

We could keep going, compounding every hour, every minute, every second, and so on. At the limit, we could compound every instant, or *continuously*. The equation for continuous compounding is

$$FV_n = PV(e^{in}). \tag{7A-1}$$

Here e is the value 2.7183 . . . . . If $100 is invested for five years at 10 percent compounded continuously, then FV_5 is calculated as follows:[1]

$$\text{Continuous: } FV_5 = \$100[e^{0.10(5)}] = \$100(2.7183 \ . \ . \ .)^{0.5}$$
$$= \$164.87.$$

CONTINUOUS DISCOUNTING

Equation 7A-1 can be transformed into Equation 7A-2 and used to determine present values under continuous discounting:

$$PV = \frac{FV_n}{e^{in}} = FV_n(e^{-in}). \tag{7A-2}$$

Thus, if $1,649 is due in 10 years, and if the appropriate *continuous* discount rate, i, is 5 percent, then the present value of this future payment is

$$PV = \frac{\$1,649}{(2.7183 \ . \ . \ .)^{0.5}} = \frac{\$1,649}{1.649} = \$1,000.$$

---

[1] Calculators with exponential functions can be used to evaluate Equation 7A-1. For example, with an HP-10B you would type .5, then press the e^x key to get 1.6487, and then multiply by $100 to get $164.87.

PART **III**

FINANCIAL ASSETS

CHAPTER 8 — Bonds and Their Valuation

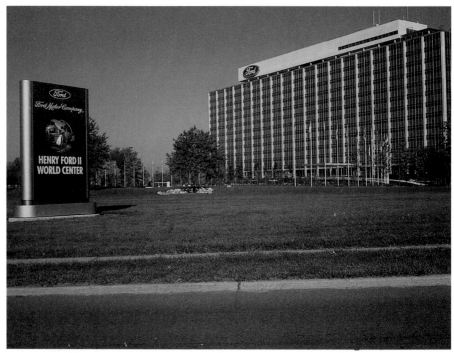

SOURCE: Courtesy of Ford Motor Company

FORD'S BOND ISSUE SETS A NEW RECORD

FORD MOTOR COMPANY

During the summer of 1999 the future course of interest rates was highly uncertain. Continued strength in the economy and growing fears of inflation had caused interest rates to rise, and many analysts were concerned that this trend would continue. However, others were forecasting declining rates — they saw no threat from inflation and were more concerned about the economy running out of gas. Because of this uncertainty, bond investors tended to wait on the sidelines for some definitive economic news. At the same time, companies tended to postpone bond issues out of fear that nervous investors would be unwilling to purchase them.

This is exactly the situation in which Ford Motor found itself in June 1999, when it decided to put a large debt issue on hold. However, after just three weeks, Ford sensed a shift in the investment climate, and it announced plans for an $8.6 billion bond issue. As shown in the following table, the Ford issue set a new record, surpassing an $8 billion AT&T issue that had taken place a few months earlier.

Ford's $8.6 billion issue actually consisted of four separate bonds. Ford Credit, a subsidiary that provides customer financing, borrowed $1.0 billion dollars at a two-year floating rate and another $1.8 billion at a three-year floating rate. Ford Motor itself borrowed $4 billion as five-year fixed-rate debt and another $1.8 billion at a 32-year fixed rate.

Top Ten U.S. Corporate Bond Financings as of July 1999

ISSUER	DATE	AMOUNT (BILLIONS OF DOLLARS)
Ford	July 9, 1999	$8.60
AT&T	March 23, 1999	8.00
RJR Holdings	May 12, 1989	6.11
WorldCom	August 6, 1998	6.10
Sprint	November 10, 1998	5.00
Assoc. Corp. of N. America	October 27, 1998	4.80
Norfolk Southern	May 14, 1997	4.30
US West	January 16, 1997	4.10
Conoco	April 15, 1999	4.00
Charter Communications	March 12, 1999	3.58

SOURCE: Thomson Financial Securities Data, Credit Suisse First Boston as reported in *The Wall Street Journal*, July 12, 1999, C1.

Most analysts agreed that these bonds had limited default risk. At the time, Ford held $24 billion in cash and had earned a record $2.5 billion during the second quarter of 1999. However, the auto industry faces some inherent risks. When all the risk factors were balanced, the issues all received a single-A rating. Much to the relief of the jittery bond market, the Ford issue was well received. Dave Cosper, Ford Credit's Treasurer, said "There was a lot of excitement, and demand exceeded our expectations."

The response to the Ford offering revealed that investors had a strong appetite for large bond issues with strong credit ratings. Larger issues are more liquid than smaller ones, and liquidity is particularly important to bond investors when the direction of the overall market is highly uncertain.

Interestingly, large investment-grade issues by well-known companies such as Ford are also helping to fill the vacuum created by the reduction in Treasury debt. The Federal government is forecasting future budget surpluses, and it plans to use a portion of the surplus to reduce its outstanding debt. As this occurs, Treasury bonds outstanding will decrease, forcing many Treasury investors into the corporate bond market, where they will look for investment-grade issues by companies such as Ford.

Already anticipating this demand, Ford is planning to regularly issue large blocks of debt in the global market. Seeing Ford's success, less than one month after the Ford issue, Wal-Mart entered the list of top ten U.S. corporate bond financings with a new $5 billion issue. Other large companies have subsequently followed suit. ■

SOURCE: Gregory Zuckerman, "Ford's Record Issue May Drive Imitators," *The Wall Street Journal*, July 12, 1999, C1.

PUTTING THINGS IN PERSPECTIVE

Bonds are one of the most important types of securities. If you skim through *The Wall Street Journal*, you will see references to a wide variety of these securities. This variety may seem confusing, but in actuality just a few characteristics distinguish the various types of bonds.

While bonds are often viewed as relatively safe investments, one can certainly lose money on them. Indeed, "riskless" long-term U.S. Treasury bonds have declined in value three of the last seven years. Note, though, that it is also possible to rack up impressive gains in the bond market. Long-term government bonds provided a total return of nearly 16 percent in 1997 and more than 30 percent in 1995.

In this chapter, we will discuss the types of bonds companies and government agencies issue, the terms that are contained in bond contracts, the types of risks to which both bond investors and issuers are exposed, and procedures for determining the values of and rates of return on bonds. ■

WHO ISSUES BONDS?

Bond
A long-term debt instrument.

A **bond** is a long-term contract under which a borrower agrees to make payments of interest and principal, on specific dates, to the holders of the bond. For example, on January 3, 2002, Allied Food Products borrowed $50 million by issuing $50 million of bonds. For convenience, we assume that Allied sold 50,000 individual bonds for $1,000 each. Actually, it could have sold one $50 million bond, 10 bonds with a $5 million face value, or any other combination that totals to $50 million. In any event, Allied received the $50 million, and in exchange it promised to make annual interest payments and to repay the $50 million on a specified maturity date.

Investors have many choices when investing in bonds, but bonds are classified into four main types: Treasury, corporate, municipal, and foreign. Each type differs with respect to expected return and degree of risk.

Treasury Bonds
Bonds issued by the federal government, sometimes referred to as government bonds.

Treasury bonds, sometimes referred to as government bonds, are issued by the federal government.[1] It is reasonable to assume that the federal government will make good on its promised payments, so these bonds have no default risk. However, Treasury bond prices decline when interest rates rise, so they are not free of all risks.

Corporate Bonds
Bonds issued by corporations.

Corporate bonds, as the name implies, are issued by corporations. Unlike Treasury bonds, corporate bonds are exposed to default risk—if the issuing company gets into trouble, it may be unable to make the promised interest and principal payments. Different corporate bonds have different levels of default risk, depending on the issuing company's characteristics and on the terms of the specific bond. Default risk is often referred to as "credit risk," and, as we saw in Chapter 5, the larger the default or credit risk, the higher the interest rate the issuer must pay.

Municipal Bonds
Bonds issued by state and local governments.

Municipal bonds, or "munis," are issued by state and local governments. Like corporate bonds, munis have default risk. However, munis offer one major advantage over all other bonds: As we discussed in Chapter 2, the interest earned on most municipal bonds is exempt from federal taxes and also from state taxes if the holder is a resident of the issuing state. Consequently, municipal bonds carry interest rates that are considerably lower than those on corporate bonds with the same default risk.

Foreign Bonds
Bonds issued by either foreign governments or foreign corporations.

Foreign bonds are issued by foreign governments or foreign corporations. Foreign corporate bonds are, of course, exposed to default risk, and so are some foreign government bonds. An additional risk exists if the bonds are denominated in a currency other than that of the investor's home currency. For example, if you purchase corporate bonds denominated in Japanese yen, you will lose money—even if the company does not default on its bonds—if the Japanese yen falls relative to the dollar.

---

[1] The U.S. Treasury actually calls its debt issues "bills," "notes," or "bonds." T-bills generally have maturities of 1 year or less at the time of issue, notes generally have original maturities of 2 to 7 years, and bond maturities extend out to 30 years. There are technical differences between bills, notes, and bonds, but they are not important for our purposes, so we generally call all Treasury securities "bonds." Note too that a 30-year T-bond at the time of issue becomes a 1-year bond 29 years later.

An excellent site for information on many types of bonds is Bonds Online, which can be found at **http://www. bondsonline.com**. The site has a great deal of information about corporates, municipals, treasuries, and bond funds. It includes free bond searches, through which the user specifies the attributes desired in a bond and then the search returns the publicly traded bonds meeting the criteria. The site also includes a downloadable bond calculator and an excellent glossary of bond terminology.

┌─────────────────────────────┐
│ **SELF-TEST QUESTIONS**   │
└─────────────────────────────┘

What is a bond?

What are the four main types of bonds?

Why are U.S. Treasury bonds not riskless?

To what types of risk are investors of foreign bonds exposed?

KEY CHARACTERISTICS OF BONDS

Although all bonds have some common characteristics, they do not always have the same contractual features. For example, most corporate bonds have provisions for early repayment (call features), but these provisions can be quite different for different bonds. Differences in contractual provisions, and in the underlying strength of the companies backing the bonds, lead to major differences in bonds' risks, prices, and expected returns. To understand bonds, it is important that you understand the following terms.

PAR VALUE

Par Value
The face value of a bond.

The **par value** is the stated face value of the bond; for illustrative purposes we generally assume a par value of $1,000, although any multiple of $1,000 (for example, $5,000) can be used. The par value generally represents the amount of money the firm borrows and promises to repay on the maturity date.

COUPON INTEREST RATE

Coupon Payment
The specified number of dollars of interest paid each period, generally each six months.

Coupon Interest Rate
The stated annual interest rate on a bond.

Allied's bonds require the company to pay a fixed number of dollars of interest each year (or, more typically, each six months). When this **coupon payment,** as it is called, is divided by the par value, the result is the **coupon interest rate.** For example, Allied's bonds have a $1,000 par value, and they pay $100 in interest each year. The bond's coupon interest is $100, so its coupon interest rate is $100/$1,000 = 10 percent. The $100 is the yearly "rent" on the $1,000 loan. This payment, which is fixed at the time the bond is issued, remains in force during the life of the bond.[2] Typically, at the time a bond is issued, its coupon payment is set at a level that will enable the bond to be issued at or near its par

---

[2] Incidentally, some time ago bonds literally had a number of small (1/2- by 2-inch), dated coupons attached to them, and on each interest payment date, the owner would clip off the coupon for that date and either cash it at his or her bank or mail it to the company's paying agent, who would then mail back a check for the interest. A 30-year, semiannual bond would start with 60 coupons, whereas a 5-year annual payment bond would start with only 5 coupons. Today, new bonds must be *registered* — no physical coupons are involved, and interest checks are mailed automatically to the registered owners of the bonds. Even so, people continue to use the terms *coupon* and *coupon interest rate* when discussing registered bonds.

value. Consequently, most of our examples and problems throughout this text will focus on bonds with fixed coupon rates.

In some cases, however, a bond's coupon payment will vary over time. These **floating rate bonds** work as follows. The coupon rate is set for, say, the initial six-month period, after which it is adjusted every six months based on some market rate. Some corporate issues are tied to the Treasury bond rate, while other issues are tied to other rates. Many additional provisions can be included in floating rate issues. For example, some are convertible to fixed rate debt, whereas others have upper and lower limits ("caps" and "floors") on how high or low the rate can go.

Floating rate debt is popular with investors who are worried about the risk of rising interest rates, since the interest paid increases whenever market rates rise. This causes the market value of the debt to be stabilized, and it also provides institutional buyers such as banks with income that is better geared to their own obligations. Banks' deposit costs rise with interest rates, so the income on floating rate loans that they have made rises at the same time their deposit costs are rising. The savings and loan industry was virtually destroyed as a result of their practice of making fixed rate mortgage loans but borrowing on floating rate terms. If you are earning 6 percent but paying 10 percent—which they were— you soon go bankrupt—which they did.

Moreover, floating rate debt appeals to corporations that want to issue long-term debt without committing themselves to paying an historically high interest rate for the entire life of the loan.

Some bonds pay no coupons at all, but are offered at a substantial discount below their par values and hence provide capital appreciation rather than interest income. These securities are called **zero coupon bonds** (*"zeros"*). Other bonds pay some coupon interest, but not enough to be issued at par. In general, any bond originally offered at a price significantly below its par value is called an **original issue discount (OID) bond.** Corporations first used zeros in a major way in 1981. In recent years IBM, Alcoa, JCPenney, ITT, Cities Service, GMAC, Lockheed Martin, and even the U.S. Treasury have used zeros to raise billions of dollars. Some of the details associated with issuing or investing in zero coupon bonds are discussed more fully in Appendix 8A.

MATURITY DATE

Bonds generally have a specified **maturity date** on which the par value must be repaid. Allied's bonds, which were issued on January 3, 2002, will mature on January 2, 2017; thus, they had a 15-year maturity at the time they were issued. Most bonds have **original maturities** (the maturity at the time the bond is issued) ranging from 10 to 40 years, but any maturity is legally permissible.[3] Of course, the effective maturity of a bond declines each year after it has been issued. Thus, Allied's bonds had a 15-year original maturity, but in 2003, a year later, they will have a 14-year maturity, and so on.

---

[3] In July 1993, Walt Disney Co., attempting to lock in a low interest rate, issued the first 100-year bonds to be sold by any borrower in modern times. Soon after, Coca-Cola became the second company to stretch the meaning of "long-term bond" by selling $150 million worth of 100-year bonds.

Floating Rate Bond
A bond whose interest rate fluctuates with shifts in the general level of interest rates.

Zero Coupon Bond
A bond that pays no annual interest but is sold at a discount below par, thus providing compensation to investors in the form of capital appreciation.

Original Issue Discount Bond
Any bond originally offered at a price below its par value.

Maturity Date
A specified date on which the par value of a bond must be repaid.

Original Maturity
The number of years to maturity at the time a bond is issued.

CALL PROVISIONS

Call Provision

A provision in a bond contract that gives the issuer the right to redeem the bonds under specified terms prior to the normal maturity date.

Most corporate bonds contain a **call provision,** which gives the issuing corporation the right to call the bonds for redemption.[4] The call provision generally states that the company must pay the bondholders an amount greater than the par value if they are called. The additional sum, which is termed a *call premium*, is often set equal to one year's interest if the bonds are called during the first year, and the premium declines at a constant rate of INT/N each year thereafter, where INT = annual interest and N = original maturity in years. For example, the call premium on a $1,000 par value, 10-year, 10 percent bond would generally be $100 if it were called during the first year, $90 during the second year (calculated by reducing the $100, or 10 percent, premium by one-tenth), and so on. However, bonds are often not callable until several years (generally 5 to 10) after they were issued. This is known as a *deferred call*, and the bonds are said to have *call protection.*

Suppose a company sold bonds when interest rates were relatively high. Provided the issue is callable, the company could sell a new issue of low-yielding securities if and when interest rates drop. It could then use the proceeds of the new issue to retire the high-rate issue and thus reduce its interest expense. This process is called a *refunding operation.*

The call privilege is valuable to the firm but potentially detrimental to the investor, especially if the bonds were issued in a period when interest rates were cyclically high. Accordingly, the interest rate on a new issue of callable bonds will exceed that on a new issue of noncallable bonds. For example, on August 30, 2001, Pacific Timber Company sold a bond issue yielding 9.5 percent; these bonds were callable immediately. On the same day, Northwest Milling Company sold an issue of similar risk and maturity yielding 9.2 percent; its bonds were noncallable for 10 years. Investors were willing to accept a 0.3 percent lower interest rate on Northwest's bonds for the assurance that the 9.2 percent interest rate would be earned for at least 10 years. Pacific, on the other hand, had to incur a 0.3 percent higher annual interest rate to obtain the option of calling the bonds in the event of a decline in rates.

SINKING FUNDS

Sinking Fund Provision

A provision in a bond contract that requires the issuer to retire a portion of the bond issue each year.

Some bonds also include a **sinking fund provision** that facilitates the orderly retirement of the bond issue. On rare occasions the firm may be required to deposit money with a trustee, which invests the funds and then uses the accumulated sum to retire the bonds when they mature. Usually, though, the sinking fund is used to buy back a certain percentage of the issue each year. A failure to meet the sinking fund requirement causes the bond to be thrown into default, which may force the company into bankruptcy. Obviously, a sinking fund can constitute a significant cash drain on the firm.

In most cases, the firm is given the right to handle the sinking fund in either of two ways:

---

[4] A majority of municipal bonds also contain call provisions. Call provisions have been included with Treasury bonds, although this occurs less frequently.

1. The company can call in for redemption (at par value) a certain percentage of the bonds each year; for example, it might be able to call 5 percent of the total original amount of the issue at a price of $1,000 per bond. The bonds are numbered serially, and those called for redemption are determined by a lottery administered by the trustee.
2. The company may buy the required number of bonds on the open market.

The firm will choose the least-cost method. If interest rates have risen, causing bond prices to fall, it will buy bonds in the open market at a discount; if interest rates have fallen, it will call the bonds. Note that a call for sinking fund purposes is quite different from a refunding call as discussed above. A sinking fund call typically requires no call premium, but only a small percentage of the issue is normally callable in any one year.[5]

Although sinking funds are designed to protect bondholders by ensuring that an issue is retired in an orderly fashion, you should recognize that sinking funds can work to the detriment of bondholders. For example, suppose the bond carries a 10 percent interest rate, but yields on similar bonds have fallen to 7.5 percent. A sinking fund call at par would require an investor to give up a bond that pays $100 of interest and then to reinvest in a bond that pays only $75 per year. This obviously disadvantages those bondholders whose bonds are called. On balance, however, bonds that have a sinking fund are regarded as being safer than those without such a provision, so at the time they are issued sinking fund bonds have lower coupon rates than otherwise similar bonds without sinking funds.

OTHER FEATURES

Convertible Bond
A bond that is exchangeable, at the option of the holder, for common stock of the issuing firm.

Warrant
A long-term option to buy a stated number of shares of common stock at a specified price.

Income Bond
A bond that pays interest only if the interest is earned.

Indexed (Purchasing Power) Bond
A bond that has interest payments based on an inflation index so as to protect the holder from inflation.

Several other types of bonds are used sufficiently often to warrant mention. First, **convertible bonds** are bonds that are convertible into shares of common stock, at a fixed price, at the option of the bondholder. Convertibles have a lower coupon rate than nonconvertible debt, but they offer investors a chance for capital gains in exchange for the lower coupon rate. Bonds issued with **warrants** are similar to convertibles. Warrants are options that permit the holder to buy stock for a stated price, thereby providing a capital gain if the price of the stock rises. Bonds that are issued with warrants, like convertibles, carry lower coupon rates than straight bonds.

Another type of bond is an **income bond**, which pays interest only if the interest is earned. Thus, these securities cannot bankrupt a company, but from an investor's standpoint they are riskier than "regular" bonds. Yet another bond is the **indexed**, or **purchasing power, bond,** which first became popular in Brazil, Israel, and a few other countries plagued by high inflation rates. The interest rate paid on these bonds is based on an inflation index such as the consumer price index, so the interest paid rises automatically when the inflation rate rises, thus protecting the bondholders against inflation. In January 1997, the U.S. Treasury began issuing indexed bonds, and 10-year indexed bonds currently pay a real rate that is roughly 3.5 percent plus the rate of inflation.

---

[5] Some sinking funds require the issuer to pay a call premium.

Define floating rate bonds and zero coupon bonds.

What problem was solved by the introduction of long-term floating rate debt, and how is the rate on such bonds determined?

Why is a call provision advantageous to a bond issuer? When will the issuer initiate a refunding call? Why?

What are the two ways a sinking fund can be handled? Which method will be chosen by the firm if interest rates have risen? If interest rates have fallen?

Are securities that provide for a sinking fund regarded as being riskier than those without this type of provision? Explain.

What is the difference between a call for sinking fund purposes and a refunding call?

Define convertible bonds, bonds with warrants, income bonds, and indexed bonds.

Why do bonds with warrants and convertible bonds have lower coupons than similarly rated bonds that do not have these features?

BOND VALUATION

The value of any financial asset — a stock, a bond, a lease, or even a physical asset such as an apartment building or a piece of machinery — is simply the present value of the cash flows the asset is expected to produce.

The cash flows from a specific bond depend on its contractual features as described above. For a standard coupon-bearing bond such as the one issued by Allied Foods, the cash flows consist of interest payments during the 15-year life of the bond, plus the amount borrowed (generally the $1,000 par value) when the bond matures. In the case of a floating rate bond, the interest payments vary over time. In the case of a zero coupon bond, there are no interest payments, only the face amount when the bond matures. For a "regular" bond with a fixed coupon rate, here is the situation:

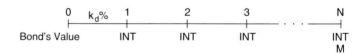

Here

k_d = the bond's market rate of interest = 10%. This is the discount rate that is used to calculate the present value of the bond's cash flows. Note that k_d is *not* the coupon interest rate, and it is equal to the coupon rate only if (as in this case) the bond is selling at par. Generally, most coupon bonds are issued at par, which implies that the coupon rate is set at k_d. Thereafter, interest rates as measured by k_d will fluctuate, but the coupon rate is fixed, so k_d will equal the coupon rate only by chance.

We used the term "i" or "I" to designate the interest rate in Chapter 7 because those terms are used on financial calculators, but "k," with the subscript "d" to designate the rate on a debt security, is normally used in finance.[6]

N = the number of years before the bond matures = 15. Note that N declines each year after the bond has been issued, so a bond that had a maturity of 15 years when it was issued (original maturity = 15) will have N = 14 after one year, N = 13 after two years, and so on. Note also that at this point we assume that the bond pays interest once a year, or annually, so N is measured in years. Later on, we will deal with semiannual payment bonds, which pay interest each six months.

INT = dollars of interest paid each year = Coupon rate × Par value = 0.10($1,000) = $100. In calculator terminology, INT = PMT = 100. If the bond had been a semiannual payment bond, the payment would have been $50 each six months. The payment would be zero if Allied had issued zero coupon bonds, and it would vary if the bond was a "floater."

M = the par, or maturity, value of the bond = $1,000. This amount must be paid off at maturity.

We can now redraw the time line to show the numerical values for all variables except the bond's value:

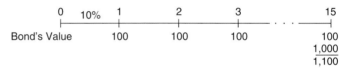

The following general equation can be solved to find the value of any bond:

$$\text{Bond's value} = V_B = \frac{INT}{(1 + k_d)^1} + \frac{INT}{(1 + k_d)^2} + \cdots + \frac{INT}{(1 + k_d)^N} + \frac{M}{(1 + k_d)^N}$$

$$= \sum_{t=1}^{N} \frac{INT}{(1 + k_d)^t} + \frac{M}{(1 + k_d)^N}. \qquad (8\text{-}1)$$

Equation 8-1 can also be rewritten for use with the tables:

$$V_B = INT(PVIFA_{k_d,N}) + M(PVIF_{k_d,N}). \qquad (8\text{-}2)$$

Inserting values for our particular bond, we have

$$V_B = \sum_{t=1}^{15} \frac{\$100}{(1.10)^t} + \frac{\$1,000}{(1.10)^{15}}$$

$$= \$100(PVIFA_{10\%,15}) + \$1,000(PVIF_{10\%,15}).$$

Note that the cash flows consist of an annuity of N years plus a lump sum payment at the end of Year N, and this fact is reflected in Equations 8-1 and 8-2. Further, Equation 8-1 can be solved by the four procedures discussed in

---

[6] The appropriate interest rate on debt securities was discussed in Chapter 5. The bond's riskiness, liquidity, and years to maturity, as well as supply and demand conditions in the capital markets, all influence the interest rate on bonds.

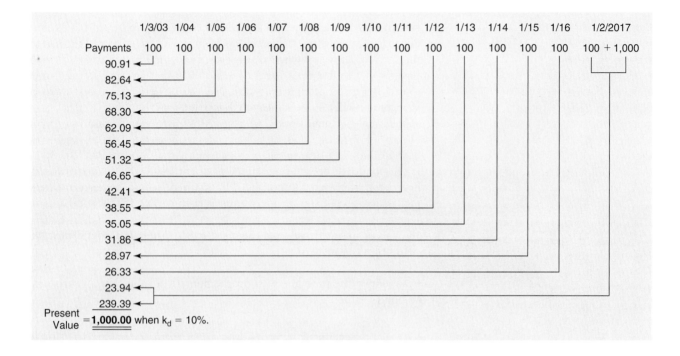

Chapter 7: (1) numerically, (2) using the tables, (3) with a financial calculator, and (4) with a spreadsheet.

Numerical Solution

Simply discount each cash flow back to the present and sum these PVs to find the bond's value; see Figure 8-1 for an example. This procedure is not very efficient, especially if the bond has many years to maturity.

Tabular Solution

Simply look up the appropriate PVIFA and PVIF values in Tables A-1 and A-2 at the end of the book, insert them into the equation, and complete the arithmetic:

$$V_B = \$100(7.6061) + \$1,000(0.2394)$$
$$= \$760.61 + \$239.40 \approx \$1,000.$$

There is a one cent rounding error, which results from the fact that the tables only go to four decimal places.

Financial Calculator Solution

In Chapter 7, we worked problems where only four of the five time value of money (TVM) keys were used. However, all five keys are used with bonds. Here is the setup:

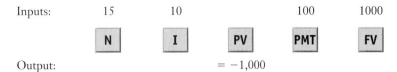

		Inputs:	15	10		100	1000

N	I	PV	PMT	FV

Output: $= -1{,}000$

Simply input N = 15, I = k = 10, INT = PMT = 100, M = FV = 1000, and then press the PV key to find the value of the bond, $1,000. Since the PV is an outflow to the investor, it is shown with a negative sign. The calculator is programmed to solve Equation 8-1: It finds the PV of an annuity of $100 per year for 15 years, discounted at 10 percent, then it finds the PV of the $1,000 maturity payment, and then it adds these two PVs to find the value of the bond.

Spreadsheet Solution

	A	B	C	D	E	F	G	H	I	J	K	L	M	N	O	P	Q
1	Spreadsheet for bond value calculation																
2				Going rate, or yield													
3	Coupon rate	10%				10%											
4																	
5	Time	0	1	2	3	4	5	6	7	8	9	10	11	12	13	14	15
6	Interest Pmt		100	100	100	100	100	100	100	100	100	100	100	100	100	100	100
7	Maturity Pmt																1000
8	Total CF		100	100	100	100	100	100	100	100	100	100	100	100	100	100	1100
9																	
10	PV of CF	1000															

Here we want to find the PV of the cash flows, so we would use the PV function. Put the cursor on Cell B10, click the function wizard, then Financial, PV, and OK. Then fill in the dialog box with Rate = 0.1 or F3, Nper = 15 or Q5, Pmt =100 or C6, FV = 1000 or Q7, and Type = 0 or leave it blank. Then, when you click OK, you will get the value of the bond, $1,000.

An alternative, and in this case somewhat easier procedure given that the time line has been created, is to use the NPV function. Click the function wizard, then Financial, NPV, and OK. Then input Rate = 0.1 or F3 and Value 1 = C8:Q8. Then click OK to get the answer, $1,000.

Note that by changing the interest rate in F3, we can instantly find the value of the bond at any going interest rate. Note also that *Excel* and other spreadsheet software packages provide specialized functions for bond prices. For example, in *Excel* you could use the function wizard to enter this formula:

=PRICE(Date(2002,1,3),Date(2017,1,3),10%,10%,100,1,0).

The first two arguments in the function give the current and maturity dates. The next argument is the bond's coupon rate, followed by the current market interest rate, or yield. The fifth argument, 100, is the redemption value of the bond at maturity, expressed as a percent of the face value. The sixth argument is the number of payments per year, and the last argument, 0, tells the program to use the U.S. convention for counting days, which is to assume 30 days per month and 360 days per year. This function produces the value 100, which is the current price expressed as a percent of the bond's par value, which is $1,000. Therefore, you can multiply $1,000 by 100 percent to get the current price, which is $1,000. This function is essential if a bond is being evaluated between coupon payment dates.

CHANGES IN BOND VALUES OVER TIME

At the time a coupon bond is issued, the coupon is generally set at a level that will cause the market price of the bond to equal its par value. If a lower coupon were set, investors would not be willing to pay $1,000 for the bond, while if a higher coupon were set, investors would clamor for the bond and bid its price up over $1,000. Investment bankers can judge quite precisely the coupon rate that will cause a bond to sell at its $1,000 par value.

A bond that has just been issued is known as a *new issue*. (Investment bankers classify a bond as a new issue for about one month after it has first been issued.) Once the bond has been on the market for a while, it is classified as an *outstanding bond*, also called a *seasoned issue*. Newly issued bonds generally sell very close to par, but the prices of seasoned bonds vary widely from par. Except for floating rate bonds, coupon payments are constant, so when economic conditions change, a bond with a $100 coupon that sold at par when it was issued will sell for more or less than $1,000 thereafter.

Allied's bonds with a 10 percent coupon rate were originally issued at par. If k_d remained constant at 10 percent, what would the value of the bond be one year after it was issued? Now the term to maturity is only 14 years — that is, N = 14. With a financial calculator, just override N = 15 with N = 14, press the PV key, and you find a value of $1,000. If we continued, setting N = 13, N = 12, and so forth, we would see that the value of the bond will remain at $1,000 as long as the going interest rate remains constant at the coupon rate, 10 percent.[7]

Now suppose interest rates in the economy fell after the Allied bonds were issued, and, as a result, k_d *fell below the coupon rate*, decreasing from 10 to 5 percent. Both the coupon interest payments and the maturity value remain con-

---

[7] The bond prices quoted by brokers are calculated as described. However, if you bought a bond between interest payment dates, you would have to pay the basic price plus accrued interest. Thus, if you purchased an Allied bond six months after it was issued, your broker would send you an invoice stating that you must pay $1,000 as the basic price of the bond plus $50 interest, representing one-half the annual interest of $100. The seller of the bond would receive $1,050. If you bought the bond the day before its interest payment date, you would pay $1,000 + (364/365)($100) = $1,099.73. Of course, you would receive an interest payment of $100 at the end of the next day. See Self-Test Problem 2 for a detailed discussion of bond quotations between interest payment dates.

Throughout the chapter, we assume that bonds are being evaluated immediately after an interest payment date. The more expensive financial calculators such as the HP-17B have a built-in calendar that permits the calculation of exact values between interest payment dates, as do spreadsheet programs.

stant, but now 5 percent values for PVIF and PVIFA would have to be used in Equation 8-2. The value of the bond at the end of the first year would be $1,494.96:

$$V_B = \$100(\text{PVIFA}_{5\%,14}) + \$1,000(\text{PVIF}_{5\%,14})$$
$$= \$100(9.8986) + \$1,000(0.5051)$$
$$= \$989.86 + \$505.10$$
$$= \$1,494.96.$$

With a financial calculator, just change $k_d = I$ from 10 to 5, and then press the PV key to get the answer, $1,494.93. Thus, if k_d fell *below* the coupon rate, the bond would sell above par, or at a *premium*.

The arithmetic of the bond value increase should be clear, but what is the logic behind it? The fact that k_d has fallen to 5 percent means that if you had $1,000 to invest, you could buy new bonds like Allied's (every day some 10 to 12 companies sell new bonds), except that these new bonds would pay $50 of interest each year rather than $100. Naturally, you would prefer $100 to $50, so you would be willing to pay more than $1,000 for an Allied bond to obtain its higher coupons. All investors would react similarly, and as a result, the Allied bonds would be bid up in price to $1,494.93, at which point they would provide the same rate of return to a potential investor as the new bonds, 5 percent.

Assuming that interest rates remain constant at 5 percent for the next 14 years, what would happen to the value of an Allied bond? It would fall gradually from $1,494.93 at present to $1,000 at maturity, when Allied will redeem each bond for $1,000. This point can be illustrated by calculating the value of the bond 1 year later, when it has 13 years remaining to maturity. With a financial calculator, merely input the values for N, I, PMT, and FV, now using N = 13, and press the PV key to find the value of the bond, $1,469.68. Thus, the value of the bond will have fallen from $1,494.93 to $1,469.68, or by $25.25. If you were to calculate the value of the bond at other future dates, the price would continue to fall as the maturity date approached.

Notice that if you purchased the bond at a price of $1,494.93 and then sold it one year later with k_d still at 5 percent, you would have a capital loss of $25.25, or a total return of $100.00 − $25.25 = $74.75. Your percentage rate of return would consist of an *interest yield* (also called a *current yield*) plus a *capital gains yield*, calculated as follows:

$$\text{Interest, or current, yield} = \$100/\$1,494.93 = 0.0669 = 6.69\%$$
$$\text{Capital gains yield} = -\$25.25/\$1,494.93 = -0.0169 = \underline{-1.69\%}$$
$$\text{Total rate of return, or yield} = \$74.75/\$1,494.93 = 0.0500 = \underline{\underline{5.00\%}}$$

Had interest rates risen from 10 to 15 percent during the first year after issue rather than fallen from 10 to 5 percent, then you would enter N = 14, I = 15, PMT = 100, and FV = 1000, and then press the PV key to find the value of the bond, $713.78. In this case, the bond would sell at a *discount* of $286.22 below its par value:

$$\text{Discount} = \text{Price} - \text{Par value} = \$713.78 - \$1,000.00$$
$$= -\$286.22.$$

The total expected future return on the bond would again consist of a current yield and a capital gains yield, but now the capital gains yield would be *positive*. The total return would be 15 percent. To see this, calculate the price of the bond with 13 years left to maturity, assuming that interest rates remain at 15 percent. With a calculator, enter N = 13, I = 15, PMT = 100, and FV = 1000, and then press PV to obtain the bond's value, $720.84.

Notice that the capital gain for the year is the difference between the bond's value at Year 2 (with 13 years remaining) and the bond's value at Year 1 (with 14 years remaining), or $720.84 − $713.78 = $7.06. The interest yield, capital gains yield, and total yield are calculated as follows:

$$\text{Interest, or current, yield} = \$100/\$713.78 = 0.1401 = 14.01\%$$
$$\text{Capital gains yield} = \$7.06/\$713.78 = 0.0099 = \underline{0.99\%}$$
$$\text{Total rate of return, or yield} = \$107.06/\$713.78 = 0.1500 = \underline{\underline{15.00\%}}$$

Figure 8-2 graphs the value of the bond over time, assuming that interest rates in the economy (1) remain constant at 10 percent, (2) fall to 5 percent and then remain constant at that level, or (3) rise to 15 percent and remain constant

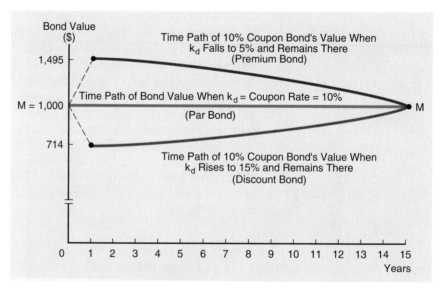

FIGURE 8-2 **Time Path of the Value of a 10% Coupon, $1,000 Par Value Bond When Interest Rates Are 5%, 10%, and 15%**

YEAR	$k_d = 5\%$	$k_d = 10\%$	$k_d = 15\%$
0	—	$1,000	—
1	$1,494.93	1,000	$ 713.78
.	.	.	.
.	.	.	.
.	.	.	.
15	1,000	1,000	1,000

NOTE: The curves for 5% and 15% have a slight bow.

at that level. Of course, if interest rates do *not* remain constant, then the price of the bond will fluctuate. However, regardless of what future interest rates do, the bond's price will approach $1,000 as it nears the maturity date (barring bankruptcy, in which case the bond's value might fall dramatically).

Figure 8-2 illustrates the following key points:

1. Whenever the going rate of interest, k_d, is equal to the coupon rate, a *fixed-rate* bond will sell at its par value. Normally, the coupon rate is set equal to the going rate when a bond is issued, causing it to sell at par initially.

2. Interest rates do change over time, but the coupon rate remains fixed after the bond has been issued. Whenever the going rate of interest *rises above* the coupon rate, a fixed-rate bond's price will fall *below* its par value. Such a bond is called a **discount bond.**

3. Whenever the going rate of interest *falls below* the coupon rate, a fixed-rate bond's price will rise *above* its par value. Such a bond is called a **premium bond.**

4. Thus, an *increase* in interest rates will cause the prices of outstanding bonds to *fall*, whereas a *decrease* in rates will cause bond prices to *rise*.

5. The market value of a bond will always approach its par value as its maturity date approaches, provided the firm does not go bankrupt.

Discount Bond
A bond that sells below its par value; occurs whenever the going rate of interest is *above* the coupon rate.

Premium Bond
A bond that sells above its par value; occurs whenever the going rate of interest is *below* the coupon rate.

These points are very important, for they show that bondholders may suffer capital losses or make capital gains, depending on whether interest rates rise or fall after the bond was purchased. And, as we saw in Chapter 5, interest rates do indeed change over time.

SELF-TEST QUESTIONS

Explain, verbally, the following equation:

$$V_B = \sum_{t=1}^{N} \frac{INT}{(1 + k_d)^t} + \frac{M}{(1 + k_d)^N}.$$

What is meant by the terms "new issue" and "seasoned issue"?

Explain what happens to the price of a fixed-rate bond if (1) interest rates rise above the bond's coupon rate or (2) interest rates fall below the bond's coupon rate.

Why do the prices of fixed-rate bonds fall if expectations for inflation rise?

What is a "discount bond"? A "premium bond"?

BOND YIELDS

If you examine the bond market table of *The Wall Street Journal* or a price sheet put out by a bond dealer, you will typically see information regarding each bond's maturity date, price, and coupon interest rate. You will also see the bond's reported yield. Unlike the coupon interest rate, which is fixed, the bond's yield varies from day to day depending on current market conditions. Moreover, the yield can be calculated in three different ways, and three "answers" can be obtained. These different yields are described in the following sections.

YIELD TO MATURITY

Yield to Maturity (YTM)
The rate of return earned on a bond if it is held to maturity.

Suppose you were offered a 14-year, 10 percent annual coupon, $1,000 par value bond at a price of $1,494.93. What rate of interest would you earn on your investment if you bought the bond and held it to maturity? This rate is called the bond's **yield to maturity (YTM),** and it is the interest rate generally discussed by investors when they talk about rates of return. The yield to maturity is generally the same as the market rate of interest, k_d, and to find it, all you need to do is solve Equation 8-1 for k_d:

$$V_B = \$1,494.93 = \frac{\$100}{(1 + k_d)^1} + \cdots + \frac{\$100}{(1 + k_d)^{14}} + \frac{\$1,000}{(1 + k_d)^{14}}.$$

You could substitute values for k_d until you find a value that "works" and forces the sum of the PVs on the right side of the equation to equal $1,494.93.

Finding k_d = YTM by trial-and-error would be a tedious, time-consuming process, but as you might guess, it is easy with a financial calculator.[8] Here is the setup:

Inputs:	14		−1494.93	100	1000
	N	**I**	**PV**	**PMT**	**FV**
Output:		= 5			

Simply enter N = 14, PV = −1494.93, PMT = 100, and FV = 1000, and then press the I key. The answer, 5 percent, will then appear.

The yield to maturity is identical to the total rate of return discussed in the preceding section. The yield to maturity can also be viewed as the bond's *promised rate of return*, which is the return that investors will receive if all the promised payments are made. However, the yield to maturity equals the *expected rate of return* only if (1) the probability of default is zero and (2) the bond cannot be called. If there is some default risk, or if the bond may be called, then there is some probability that the promised payments to maturity will not be received, in which case the calculated yield to maturity will differ from the expected return.

The YTM for a bond that sells at par consists entirely of an interest yield, but if the bond sells at a price other than its par value, the YTM will consist of

---

[8] You could also find the YTM with a spreadsheet. In *Excel*, you would use the Rate function, inputting Nper = 14, Pmt = 100, PV = −1494.93, FV = 1000, 0 for Type, and leave Guess blank. Also, you could use the compound interest tables at the back of this book (Tables A-1 and A-2) to find PVIF and PVIFA factors that force the following equation to an equality:

$$V_B = \$1,494.93 = \$100(\text{PVIFA}_{k_d,14}) + \$1,000(\text{PVIF}_{k_d,14}).$$

Factors for 5 percent would "work," indicating that 5 percent is the bond's YTM. This procedure can be used only if the YTM works out to a whole number percentage.

the interest yield plus a positive or negative capital gains yield. Note also that a bond's yield to maturity changes whenever interest rates in the economy change, and this is almost daily. One who purchases a bond and holds it until it matures will receive the YTM that existed on the purchase date, but the bond's calculated YTM will change frequently between the purchase date and the maturity date.

YIELD TO CALL

If you purchased a bond that was callable and the company called it, you would not have the option of holding the bond until it matured. Therefore, the yield to maturity would not be earned. For example, if Allied's 10 percent coupon bonds were callable, and if interest rates fell from 10 percent to 5 percent, then the company could call in the 10 percent bonds, replace them with 5 percent bonds, and save $100 − $50 = $50 interest per bond per year. This would be beneficial to the company, but not to its bondholders.

Yield to Call (YTC)
The rate of return earned on a bond if it is called before its maturity date.

If current interest rates are well below an outstanding bond's coupon rate, then a callable bond is likely to be called, and investors will estimate its expected rate of return as the **yield to call (YTC)** rather than as the yield to maturity. To calculate the YTC, solve this equation for k_d:

$$\text{Price of bond} = \sum_{t=1}^{N} \frac{\text{INT}}{(1 + k_d)^t} + \frac{\text{Call price}}{(1 + k_d)^N}. \tag{8-3}$$

Here N is the number of years until the company can call the bond; call price is the price the company must pay in order to call the bond (it is often set equal to the par value plus one year's interest); and k_d is the YTC.

To illustrate, suppose Allied's bonds had a provision that permitted the company, if it desired, to call the bonds 10 years after the issue date at a price of $1,100. Suppose further that interest rates had fallen, and one year after issuance the going interest rate had declined, causing the price of the bonds to rise to $1,494.93. Here is the time line and the setup for finding the bond's YTC with a financial calculator:

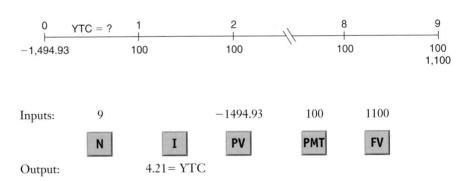

The YTC is 4.21 percent — this is the return you would earn if you bought the bond at a price of $1,494.93 and it was called nine years from today. (The bond could not be called until 10 years after issuance, and one year has gone by, so there are nine years left until the first call date.)

GLOBAL PERSPECTIVES

DRINKING YOUR COUPONS

Chateau Teyssier, an English vineyard, was looking for some cash to purchase some additional vines and to modernize its production facilities. Their solution? With the assistance of a leading underwriter, Matrix Securities, the vineyard recently issued 375 bonds, each costing 2,650 British pounds. The issue raised nearly 1 million pounds, which, at the time, was worth roughly $1.5 million.

What makes these bonds interesting is that, instead of getting paid with something boring like money, these bonds pay their investors back with wine. Each June until 2002, when the bond matures, investors will receive their "coupons." Between

1997 and 2001, each bond will provide six cases of the vineyard's rose or claret. Starting in 1998 and continuing through maturity in 2002, investors will also receive four cases of its prestigious Saint Emilion Grand Cru. Then, in 2002, they will get their money back.

The bonds are not without risk. The vineyard's owner, Jonathan Malthus, acknowledges that the quality of the wine, "is at the mercy of the gods."

SOURCE: Steven Irvine, "My Wine Is My Bond, and I Drink My Coupons," *Euromoney*, July 1996, 7. Used with permission.

Do you think Allied *will* call the bonds when they become callable? Allied's action would depend on what the going interest rate is when the bonds become callable. If the going rate remains at $k_d = 5\%$, then Allied could save 10% − 5% = 5%, or $50 per bond per year, by calling them and replacing the 10 percent bonds with a new 5 percent issue. There would be costs to the company to refund the issue, but the interest savings would probably be worth the cost, so Allied would probably refund the bonds. Therefore, you would probably earn YTC = 4.21% rather than YTM = 5% if you bought the bonds under the indicated conditions.

In the balance of this chapter, we assume that bonds are not callable unless otherwise noted, but some of the end-of-chapter problems deal with yield to call.

CURRENT YIELD

Current Yield
The annual interest payment on a bond divided by the bond's current price.

If you examine brokerage house reports on bonds, you will often see reference to a bond's **current yield.** The current yield is the annual interest payment divided by the bond's current price. For example, if Allied's bonds with a 10 percent coupon were currently selling for $985, the bond's current yield would be 10.15 percent ($100/$985).

Unlike the yield to maturity, the current yield does not represent the return that investors should expect to receive from holding the bond. The current yield provides information regarding the amount of cash income that a bond will generate in a given year, but since it does not take account of capital gains or losses that will be realized if the bond is held until maturity (or call), it does not provide an accurate measure of the bond's total expected return.

The fact that the current yield does not provide an accurate measure of a bond's total return can be illustrated with a zero coupon bond. Since zeros pay no annual income, they always have a current yield of zero. This indicates that the bond will not provide any cash interest income, but since the bond will appreciate in value over time, its total rate of return clearly exceeds zero.

Describe the difference between the yield to maturity and the yield to call.

How does a bond's current yield differ from its total return?

Could the current yield exceed the total return?

BONDS WITH SEMIANNUAL COUPONS

Although some bonds pay interest annually, the vast majority actually pay interest semiannually. To evaluate semiannual payment bonds, we must modify the valuation models (Equations 8-1 and 8-2) as follows:

1. Divide the annual coupon interest payment by 2 to determine the dollars of interest paid each six months.
2. Multiply the years to maturity, N, by 2 to determine the number of semiannual periods.
3. Divide the nominal (quoted) interest rate, k_d, by 2 to determine the periodic (semiannual) interest rate.

By making these changes, we obtain the following equation for finding the value of a bond that pays interest semiannually:

$$V_B = \sum_{t=1}^{2N} \frac{INT/2}{(1 + k_d/2)^t} + \frac{M}{(1 + k_d/2)^{2N}}. \qquad (8\text{-}1a)$$

To illustrate, assume now that Allied Food Products' bonds pay $50 interest each six months rather than $100 at the end of each year. Thus, each interest payment is only half as large, but there are twice as many of them. The coupon rate is thus "10 percent, semiannual payments." This is the nominal, or quoted, rate.[9]

When the going (nominal) rate of interest is 5 percent with semiannual compounding, the value of this 15-year bond is found as follows:

Inputs:	30	2.5		50	1000
	N	**I**	**PV**	**PMT**	**FV**
Output:			= −1,523.26		

---

[9] In this situation, the nominal coupon rate of "10 percent, semiannually," is the rate that bond dealers, corporate treasurers, and investors generally would discuss. Of course, the *effective annual rate* would be higher than 10 percent at the time the bond was issued:

$$EAR = EFF\% = \left(1 + \frac{k_{Nom}}{m}\right)^m - 1 = \left(1 + \frac{0.10}{2}\right)^2 - 1 = (1.05)^2 - 1 = 10.25\%.$$

Note also that 10 percent with annual payments is different than 10 percent with semiannual payments. Thus, we have assumed a change in effective rates in this section from the situation in the preceding section, where we assumed 10 percent with annual payments.

Enter N = 30, k = I = 2.5, PMT = 50, FV = 1000, and then press the PV key to obtain the bond's value, $1,523.26. The value with semiannual interest payments is slightly larger than $1,518.98, the value when interest is paid annually. This higher value occurs because interest payments are received somewhat faster under semiannual compounding.

SELF-TEST QUESTION

Describe how the annual bond valuation formula is changed to evaluate semiannual coupon bonds. Then, write out the revised formula.

ASSESSING THE RISKINESS OF A BOND

INTEREST RATE RISK

Interest Rate Risk
The risk of a decline in a bond's price due to an increase in interest rates.

As we saw in Chapter 5, interest rates go up and down over time, and an increase in interest rates leads to a decline in the value of outstanding bonds. This risk of a decline in bond values due to rising interest rates is called **interest rate risk.** To illustrate, suppose you bought some 10 percent Allied bonds at a price of $1,000, and interest rates in the following year rose to 15 percent. As we saw before, the price of the bonds would fall to $713.78, so you would have a loss of $286.22 per bond.[10] Interest rates can and do rise, and rising rates cause a loss of value for bondholders. Thus, people or firms who invest in bonds are exposed to risk from changing interest rates.

One's exposure to interest rate risk is higher on bonds with long maturities than on those maturing in the near future.[11] This point can be demonstrated by showing how the value of a 1-year bond with a 10 percent annual coupon fluctuates with changes in k_d, and then comparing these changes with those on a 14-year bond as calculated previously. The 1-year bond's values at different interest rates are shown below:

---

[10] You would have an *accounting* (and tax) loss only if you sold the bond; if you held it to maturity, you would not have such a loss. However, even if you did not sell, you would still have suffered a *real economic loss in an opportunity cost sense* because you would have lost the opportunity to invest at 15 percent and would be stuck with a 10 percent bond in a 15 percent market. In an economic sense, "paper losses" are just as bad as realized accounting losses.

[11] Actually, a bond's maturity and coupon rate both affect interest rate risk. Low coupons mean that most of the bond's return will come from repayment of principal, whereas on a high coupon bond with the same maturity, more of the cash flows will come in during the early years due to the relatively large coupon payments. A measurement called "duration," which finds the average number of years the bond's PV of cash flows remain outstanding, has been developed to combine maturity and coupons. A zero coupon bond, which has no interest payments and whose payments all come at maturity, has a duration equal to the bond's maturity. Coupon bonds all have durations that are shorter than maturity, and the higher the coupon rate, the shorter the duration. Bonds with longer duration are exposed to more interest rate risk. A discussion of duration would go beyond the scope of this book, but see any investments text for a discussion of the concept.

Value at $k_d = 5\%$:

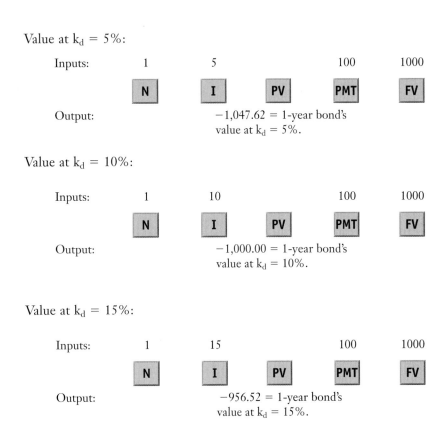

Value at $k_d = 10\%$:

Value at $k_d = 15\%$:

You would obtain the first value with a financial calculator by entering N = 1, I = 5, PMT = 100, and FV = 1000, and then pressing PV to get $1,047.62. With everything still in your calculator, enter I = 10 to override the old I = 5, and press PV to find the bond's value at k_d = I = 10; it is $1,000. Then enter I = 15 and press the PV key to find the last bond value, $956.52.

The values of the 1-year and 14-year bonds at several current market interest rates are summarized and plotted in Figure 8-3. Note how much more sensitive the price of the 14-year bond is to changes in interest rates. At a 10 percent interest rate, both the 14-year and the 1-year bonds are valued at $1,000. When rates rise to 15 percent, the 14-year bond falls to $713.78, but the 1-year bond only falls to $956.52.

For bonds with similar coupons, this differential sensitivity to changes in interest rates always holds true — the longer the maturity of the bond, the more its price changes in response to a given change in interest rates. Thus, even if the risk of default on two bonds is exactly the same, the one with the longer maturity is typically exposed to more risk from a rise in interest rates.[12]

---

[12]If a 10-year bond were plotted in Figure 8-3, its curve would lie between those of the 14-year bond and the 1-year bond. The curve of a 1-month bond would be almost horizontal, indicating that its price would change very little in response to an interest rate change, but a 100-year bond (or a perpetuity) would have a very steep slope. Also, zero coupon bond prices are quite sensitive to interest rate changes, and the longer the maturity of the zero, the greater its price sensitivity. Therefore, 30-year zero coupon bonds have a huge amount of interest rate risk.

FIGURE 8-3

Value of Long- and Short-Term 10% Annual Coupon Bonds at Different Market Interest Rates

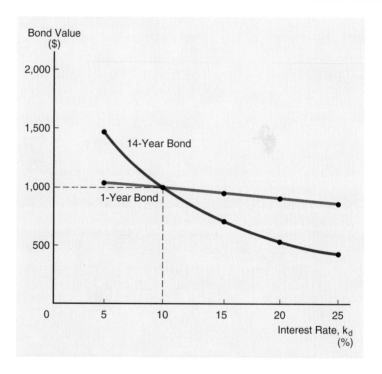

CURRENT MARKET INTEREST RATE, k_d	VALUE OF	
	1-YEAR BOND	14-YEAR BOND
5%	$1,047.62	$1,494.93
10	1,000.00	1,000.00
15	956.52	713.78
20	916.67	538.94
25	880.00	426.39

NOTE: Bond values were calculated using a financial calculator assuming annual, or once-a-year, compounding.

The logical explanation for this difference in interest rate risk is simple. Suppose you bought a 14-year bond that yielded 10 percent, or $100 a year. Now suppose interest rates on comparable-risk bonds rose to 15 percent. You would be stuck with only $100 of interest for the next 14 years. On the other hand, had you bought a 1-year bond, you would have a low return for only 1 year. At the end of the year, you would get your $1,000 back, and you could then reinvest it and receive 15 percent, or $150 per year, for the next 13 years.

Thus, interest rate risk reflects the length of time one is committed to a given investment.

REINVESTMENT RATE RISK

As we saw in the preceding section, an *increase* in interest rates will hurt bond-holders because it will lead to a decline in the value of a bond portfolio. But can a *decrease* in interest rates also hurt bondholders? The answer is yes, because if interest rates fall, a bondholder will probably suffer a reduction in his or her income. For example, consider a retiree who has a portfolio of bonds and lives off the income they produce. The bonds, on average, have a coupon rate of 10 percent. Now suppose interest rates decline to 5 percent. Many of the bonds will be called, and as calls occur, the bondholder will have to replace 10 percent bonds with 5 percent bonds. Even bonds that are not callable will mature, and when they do, they will have to be replaced with lower-yielding bonds. Thus, our retiree will suffer a reduction of income.

Reinvestment Rate Risk
The risk that a decline in interest rates will lead to a decline in income from a bond portfolio.

The risk of an income decline due to a drop in interest rates is called **reinvestment rate risk,** and its importance has been demonstrated to all bond-holders in recent years as a result of the sharp drop in rates since the mid-1980s. Reinvestment rate risk is obviously high on callable bonds. It is also high on short maturity bonds, because the shorter the maturity of a bond, the fewer the years when the relatively high old interest rate will be earned, and the sooner the funds will have to be reinvested at the new low rate. Thus, retirees whose primary holdings are short-term securities, such as bank CDs and short-term bonds, are hurt badly by a decline in rates, but holders of long-term bonds continue to enjoy their old high rates.

COMPARING INTEREST RATE AND REINVESTMENT RATE RISK

Note that interest rate risk relates to the *value* of the bonds in a portfolio, while reinvestment rate risk relates to the *income* the portfolio produces. If you hold long-term bonds, you will face interest rate risk, that is, the value of your bonds will decline if interest rates rise, but you will not face much reinvestment rate risk, so your income will be stable. On the other hand, if you hold short-term bonds, you will not be exposed to much interest rate risk, so the value of your portfolio will be stable, but you will be exposed to reinvestment rate risk, and your income will fluctuate with changes in interest rates.

Investment Horizon
The period of time an investor plans to hold a particular investment.

It is important to recognize that a bond's risk depends critically on how long the investor plans to hold the bond — this is often referred to as the **investment horizon.** To illustrate the connection between risk and the investment horizon, consider first an investor that has a relatively short, one-year investment horizon. Reinvestment rate risk is of minimal concern to this investor, since there is little time for reinvestment. This investor could also eliminate his interest rate risk by buying a one-year Treasury security, since he is assured that he will receive the face value of the bond one year from now (which is also his investment horizon). However, if this investor were to buy a long-term Treasury security, he would bear a considerable amount of interest rate risk.

Since the investor plans to hold the security for only one year, he will have to sell the security one year from now, and the price he will receive will depend on what happens to interest rates during the next year. As we demonstrated earlier, even a small change in interest rates can have a large effect on the prices of long-term securities. Consequently, investors with shorter investment horizons view long-term bonds as risky investments.

By contrast, short-term bonds tend to be riskier than long-term bonds for investors who have longer investment horizons. Consider an investor who is saving to accumulate a large amount of money by the date of her retirement, which is anticipated to be in 25 years. If she buys a series of short-term bonds over the next 25 years, all of the coupons and principal payments must be reinvested until the date of her planned retirement. Since there is uncertainty today about the rates that will be earned on these reinvested cash flows, long-term investors who buy a series of short-term bonds face a substantial amount of reinvestment rate risk. If she instead buys a longer-term bond today, this reinvestment rate risk will be smaller because there will be fewer maturity payments to reinvest.

One simple way to minimize interest rate and reinvestment rate risk is to buy a zero coupon Treasury security with a maturity that equals your investment horizon. For example, assume your investment horizon is 10 years. If you buy a 10-year zero, you will receive a guaranteed payment in 10 years that equals the bond's face value. Moreover, since there are no coupons to reinvest, there is no reinvestment rate risk. This feature explains why many investors find zero coupon bonds so attractive.

Nevertheless, two words of caution are in order. First, as we show in Appendix 8A, investors in zeros have to pay taxes each year on their amortized gain in value, even though the bonds don't produce any cash until the bond matures or is sold — a feature that some investors find unattractive. Second, buying a zero coupon with a maturity equal to your investment horizon enables you to lock in nominal cash flow, but the value of that cash flow will still depend on what happens to inflation during your investment horizon.

The connection between investment horizon and risk also has implications for the maturity risk premium. While the maturity risk premium cannot be directly observed, most estimates indicate that there is a positive maturity risk premium.[13] Recall from Chapter 5 that a positive maturity risk premium suggests that investors believe that long-term bonds are riskier than short-term bonds. A positive maturity risk premium would suggest that a majority of bond investors have short-term investment horizons.

SELF-TEST QUESTIONS

Differentiate between interest rate risk and reinvestment rate risk.

To which type of risk are holders of long-term bonds more exposed? Short-term bondholders?

---

[13] The maturity risk premium for long-term bonds has averaged 1.4 percent over the last 73 years. See *Stocks, Bonds, Bills, and Inflation: (Valuation Edition) 2000 Yearbook* (Chicago: Ibbotson Associates, 2000).

DEFAULT RISK

Another important risk associated with bonds is default risk. If the issuer defaults, investors receive less than the promised return on the bond. Therefore, investors need to assess a bond's default risk before making a purchase. Recall from Chapter 5 that the quoted interest rate includes a default risk premium — the greater the default risk, the higher the bond's yield to maturity. The default risk on Treasury securities is zero, but default risk can be substantial for corporate and municipal bonds.

Suppose two bonds have the same promised cash flows, coupon rate, maturity, liquidity, and inflation exposure, but one bond has more default risk than the other. Investors will naturally pay less for the bond with the greater chance of default. As a result, bonds with higher default risk will have higher interest rates: $k_d = k^* + IP + DRP + LP + MRP$.

If its default risk changes, this will affect the price of a bond. For example, if the default risk of the Allied bonds increases, the bonds' price will fall and the yield to maturity ($YTM = k_d$) will increase.

In this section we consider some issues related to default risk. First, we show that corporations can influence the default risk of their bonds by changing the types of bonds they issue. Second, we discuss bond ratings, which are used to measure default risk. Third, we describe the "junk bond market," which is the market for bonds with a relatively high probability of default. Finally, we consider bankruptcy and reorganization, which affect how much an investor will recover if a default occurs.

Various Types of Corporate Bonds

Default risk is influenced by both the financial strength of the issuer and the terms of the bond contract, especially whether collateral has been pledged to secure the bond. Some types of bonds are described below.

Mortgage Bonds

Mortgage Bond
A bond backed by fixed assets. *First mortgage bonds* are senior in priority to claims of *second mortgage bonds.*

Under a **mortgage bond,** the corporation pledges certain assets as security for the bond. To illustrate, in 2001, Billingham Corporation needed $10 million to build a major regional distribution center. Bonds in the amount of $4 million, secured by a *first mortgage* on the property, were issued. (The remaining $6 million was financed with equity capital.) If Billingham defaults on the bonds, the bondholders can foreclose on the property and sell it to satisfy their claims.

If Billingham chose to, it could issue *second mortgage bonds* secured by the same $10 million of assets. In the event of liquidation, the holders of these second mortgage bonds would have a claim against the property, but only after the first mortgage bondholders had been paid off in full. Thus, second mortgages are sometimes called *junior mortgages,* because they are junior in priority to the claims of *senior mortgages,* or *first mortgage bonds.*

Indenture

A formal agreement between the issuer of a bond and the bondholders.

All mortgage bonds are subject to an **indenture,** which is a legal document that spells out in detail the rights of both the bondholders and the corporation. The indentures of many major corporations were written 20, 30, 40, or more years ago. These indentures are generally "open ended," meaning that new bonds can be issued from time to time under the same indenture. However, the amount of new bonds that can be issued is virtually always limited to a specified percentage of the firm's total "bondable property," which generally includes all land, plant, and equipment.

For example, in the past Savannah Electric Company had provisions in its bond indenture that allowed it to issue first mortgage bonds totaling up to 60 percent of its fixed assets. If its fixed assets totaled $1 billion, and if it had $500 million of first mortgage bonds outstanding, it could, by the property test, issue another $100 million of bonds (60% of $1 billion = $600 million).

At times, Savannah Electric was unable to issue any new first mortgage bonds because of another indenture provision: its times-interest-earned (TIE) ratio was below 2.5, the minimum coverage that it must have if it sells new bonds. Thus, although Savannah Electric passed the property test, it failed the coverage test, so it could not issue any more first mortgage bonds. Savannah Electric then had to finance with junior bonds. Since first mortgage bonds carried lower rates of interest than junior long-term debt, this restriction was a costly one.

Savannah Electric's neighbor, Georgia Power Company, had more flexibility under its indenture — its interest coverage requirement was only 2.0. In hearings before the Georgia Public Service Commission, it was suggested that Savannah Electric should change its indenture coverage to 2.0 so that it could issue more first mortgage bonds. However, this was simply not possible — the holders of the outstanding bonds would have to approve the change, and it is inconceivable that they would vote for a change that would seriously weaken their position.

Debentures

Debenture

A long-term bond that is not secured by a mortgage on specific property.

A **debenture** is an unsecured bond, and as such it provides no lien against specific property as security for the obligation. Debenture holders are, therefore, general creditors whose claims are protected by property not otherwise pledged. In practice, the use of debentures depends both on the nature of the firm's assets and on its general credit strength. Extremely strong companies such as AT&T often use debentures; they simply do not need to put up property as security for their debt. Debentures are also issued by weak companies that have already pledged most of their assets as collateral for mortgage loans. In this latter case, the debentures are quite risky, and they will bear a high interest rate.

Subordinated Debentures

Subordinated Debentures

A bond having a claim on assets only after the senior debt has been paid off in the event of liquidation.

The term *subordinate* means "below," or "inferior to," and, in the event of bankruptcy, subordinated debt has claims on assets only after senior debt has been paid off. **Subordinated debentures** may be subordinated either to designated notes payable (usually bank loans) or to all other debt. In the event of liquida-

S&P DEVELOPS CRITERIA TO DETERMINE BOND RATINGS FOR INTERNET FIRMS

Determining credit quality is always difficult, and this is particularly true for Internet firms. In a recent report, Standard and Poor's (S&P) highlighted some of the special challenges these firms pose. First, many Internet firms are emphasizing long-term growth as opposed to current profitability. While this focus may be desirable for shareholders, the lack of profitability creates additional risk for bondholders, which is a negative for bond ratings. On the other hand, many Internet firms have cash-rich balance sheets as a result of high IPO prices, and this cash can be used as a cushion to pay bills and meet interest payments.

S&P's report outlines other factors on which it focuses when evaluating Internet firms. Here is a partial list:

■ *Brand recognition:* Companies with well-established brand names are more likely to survive, hence they receive higher ratings.

■ *Revenue diversity:* Companies whose revenues are not tied to a single idea or product generally have less risk and better ratings.

■ *Potential competition:* S&P attempts to evaluate potential entrants into the company's line of business. Those with loyal customers and fewer outside threats receive higher ratings.

■ *Long-run sustainability of the basic business model:* This is the most important factor, but the hardest to estimate.

SOURCE: "New Ratings Criteria for Internet Firms," *Standard & Poor's CreditWeek,* June 23, 1999, 22–25.

---

tion or reorganization, holders of subordinated debentures cannot be paid until all senior debt, as named in the debentures' indenture, has been paid. Precisely how subordination works, and how it strengthens the position of senior debtholders, is explained in detail in Appendix 8B.

BOND RATINGS

Investment Grade Bonds
Bonds rated triple-B or higher; many banks and other institutional investors are permitted by law to hold only investment grade bonds.

Junk Bond
A high-risk, high-yield bond.

Since the early 1900s, bonds have been assigned quality ratings that reflect their probability of going into default. The three major rating agencies are Moody's Investors Service (Moody's), Standard & Poor's Corporation (S&P), and Fitch Investors Service. Moody's and S&P's rating designations are shown in Table 8-1.[14] The triple- and double-A bonds are extremely safe. Single-A and triple-B bonds are also strong enough to be called **investment grade bonds,** and they are the lowest-rated bonds that many banks and other institutional investors are permitted by law to hold. Double-B and lower bonds are speculative, or **junk bonds.** These bonds have a significant probability of going into default. A later section discusses junk bonds in more detail.

---

[14] In the discussion to follow, reference to the S&P rating is intended to imply the Moody's and Fitch's ratings as well. Thus, triple-B bonds mean both BBB and Baa bonds; double-B bonds mean both BB and Ba bonds; and so on.

TABLE 8-1   Moody's and S&P Bond Ratings

	INVESTMENT GRADE				JUNK BONDS			
Moody's	Aaa	Aa	A	Baa	Ba	B	Caa	C
S&P	AAA	AA	A	BBB	BB	B	CCC	D

NOTE: Both Moody's and S&P use "modifiers" for bonds rated below triple-A. S&P uses a plus and minus system; thus, A+ designates the strongest A-rated bonds and A− the weakest. Moody's uses a 1, 2, or 3 designation, with 1 denoting the strongest and 3 the weakest; thus, within the double-A category, Aa1 is the best, Aa2 is average, and Aa3 is the weakest.

Bond Rating Criteria

Bond ratings are based on both qualitative and quantitative factors, some of which are listed below:

1. Various ratios, including the debt ratio and the times-interest-earned ratio. The better the ratios, the higher the rating.
2. Mortgage provisions: Is the bond secured by a mortgage? If it is, and if the property has a high value in relation to the amount of bonded debt, the bond's rating is enhanced.
3. Subordination provisions: Is the bond subordinated to other debt? If so, it will be rated at least one notch below the rating it would have if it were not subordinated. Conversely, a bond with other debt subordinated to it will have a somewhat higher rating.
4. Guarantee provisions: Some bonds are guaranteed by other firms. If a weak company's debt is guaranteed by a strong company (usually the weak company's parent), the bond will be given the strong company's rating.
5. Sinking fund: Does the bond have a sinking fund to ensure systematic repayment? This feature is a plus factor to the rating agencies.
6. Maturity: Other things the same, a bond with a shorter maturity will be judged less risky than a longer-term bond, and this will be reflected in the ratings.
7. Stability: Are the issuer's sales and earnings stable?
8. Regulation: Is the issuer regulated, and could an adverse regulatory climate cause the company's economic position to decline? Regulation is especially important for utilities and telephone companies.
9. Antitrust: Are any antitrust actions pending against the firm that could erode its position?
10. Overseas operations: What percentage of the firm's sales, assets, and profits are from overseas operations, and what is the political climate in the host countries?
11. Environmental factors: Is the firm likely to face heavy expenditures for pollution control equipment?
12. Product liability: Are the firm's products safe? The tobacco companies today are under pressure, and so are their bond ratings.

13. Pension liabilities: Does the firm have unfunded pension liabilities that could pose a future problem?

14. Labor unrest: Are there potential labor problems on the horizon that could weaken the firm's position? As this is written, a number of airlines face this problem, and it has caused their ratings to be lowered.

15. Accounting policies: If a firm uses relatively conservative accounting policies, its reported earnings will be of "higher quality" than if it uses less conservative procedures. Thus, conservative accounting policies are a plus factor in bond ratings.

Representatives of the rating agencies have consistently stated that no precise formula is used to set a firm's rating; all the factors listed, plus others, are taken into account, but not in a mathematically precise manner. Statistical studies have borne out this contention, for researchers who have tried to predict bond ratings on the basis of quantitative data have had only limited success, indicating that the agencies use subjective judgment when establishing a firm's rating.[15]

Nevertheless, as we see in Table 8-2, there is a strong correlation between bond ratings and many of the ratios that we described in Chapter 3. Not surprisingly, companies with lower debt ratios, higher free cash flow to debt, higher returns on invested capital, higher EBITDA coverage ratios, and higher times-interest-earned (TIE) ratios typically have higher bond ratings.

Importance of Bond Ratings

Bond ratings are important both to firms and to investors. First, because a bond's rating is an indicator of its default risk, the rating has a direct, measurable influence on the bond's interest rate and the firm's cost of debt. Second,

---

[15] See Ahmed Belkaoui, *Industrial Bonds and the Rating Process* (London: Quorum Books, 1983).

TABLE 8-2	Bond Rating Criteria; Three-Year (1997–1999) Median Financial Ratios for Different Bond Rating Classifications						
	AAA	AA	A	BBB	BB	B	CCC
Times-interest-earned (EBIT/Interest)	17.5×	10.8×	6.8×	3.9×	2.3×	1.0×	0.2×
EBITDA interest coverage (EBITDA/Interest)	21.8	14.6	9.6	6.1	3.8	2.0	1.4
Net cash flow/Total debt	105.8%	55.8%	46.1%	30.5%	19.2%	9.4%	5.8%
Free cash flow/Total debt	55.4	24.6	15.6	6.6	1.9	(4.5)	(14.0)
Return on capital	28.2	22.9	19.9	14.0	11.7	7.2	0.5
Operating income/Sales[a]	29.2	21.3	18.3	15.3	15.4	11.2	13.6
Long-term debt/Total capital	15.2	26.4	32.5	41.0	55.8	70.7	80.3
Total debt/Total capital	26.9	35.6	40.1	47.4	61.3	74.6	89.4

NOTE:
[a]Operating income here is defined as sales minus cost of goods manufactured (before depreciation and amortization), selling, general and administrative, and research and development costs.

SOURCE: "Adjusted Key U.S. Industrial Financial Ratios," *Standard & Poor's CreditWeek*, September 20, 2000, 39–44.

most bonds are purchased by institutional investors rather than individuals, and many institutions are restricted to investment-grade securities. Thus, if a firm's bonds fall below BBB, it will have a difficult time selling new bonds because many potential purchasers will not be allowed to buy them.

As a result of their higher risk and more restricted market, lower-grade bonds have higher required rates of return, k_d, than high-grade bonds. Figure 8-4 illustrates this point. In each of the years shown on the graph, U.S. government bonds have had the lowest yields, AAAs have been next, and BBB bonds have had the highest yields. The figure also shows that the gaps between yields on the three types of bonds vary over time, indicating that the cost differentials, or risk premiums, fluctuate from year to year. This point is highlighted in Figure 8-5, which gives the yields on the three types of bonds and the risk premiums for AAA and BBB bonds in June 1963 and September 2000.[16] Note first that the risk-free rate, or vertical axis intercept, rose 1.8 percentage points from 1963 to 2000, primarily reflecting the increase in realized and anticipated inflation. Second, the slope of the line has increased since 1963, indicating an increase in investors' risk aversion. Thus, the penalty for having a low credit rating varies over time. Occasionally, as in 1963, the penalty is quite small, but at other times it is large. These slope differences reflect investors' aversion to risk.

Changes in Ratings

Changes in a firm's bond rating affect both its ability to borrow long-term capital and the cost of that capital. Rating agencies review outstanding bonds on a periodic basis, occasionally upgrading or downgrading a bond as a result of its issuer's changed circumstances. For example, the September 13, 2000, issue of *Standard & Poor's CreditWeek* reported that Michaels Stores Inc.'s senior unsecured debt had been raised from BB− to BB. Michaels is the leading retailer of arts and crafts, and the rating upgrade reflects its improving performance measures and captial structure resulting from the redemption of $96.9 million convertible subordinated notes. The September 27, 2000, issue reported the downgrade of Loews Cineplex Entertainment Corp.'s bank loan and corporate credit ratings from B to CCC+. This downgrade reflects the company's weak operating performance, deteriorating credit measures, and an announcement that it was in violation of certain financial covenants. The firm is in the process of negotiating with its bank group to resolve the covenant violation, and it is seeking additional capital to meet financing commitments.

---

[16] The term *risk premium* ought to reflect only the difference in expected (and required) returns between two securities that results from differences in their risk. However, the differences between *yields to maturity* on different types of bonds consist of (1) a true risk premium; (2) a liquidity premium, which reflects the fact that U.S. Treasury bonds are more readily marketable than most corporate bonds; (3) a call premium, because most Treasury bonds are not callable whereas corporate bonds are; and (4) an expected loss differential, which reflects the probability of loss on the corporate bonds. As an example of the last point, suppose the yield to maturity on a BBB bond was 8.4 percent versus 5.8 percent on government bonds, but there was a 5 percent probability of total default loss on the corporate bond. In this case, the expected return on the BBB bond would be 0.95(8.4%) + 0.05(0%) = 8.0%, and the risk premium would be 2.2 percent, not the full 2.6 percentage points difference in "promised" yields to maturity. Because of all these points, the risk premiums given in Figure 8-5 overstate somewhat the true (but unmeasurable) theoretical risk premiums.

FIGURE 8-4

Yields on Selected Long-Term Bonds, 1960–2000

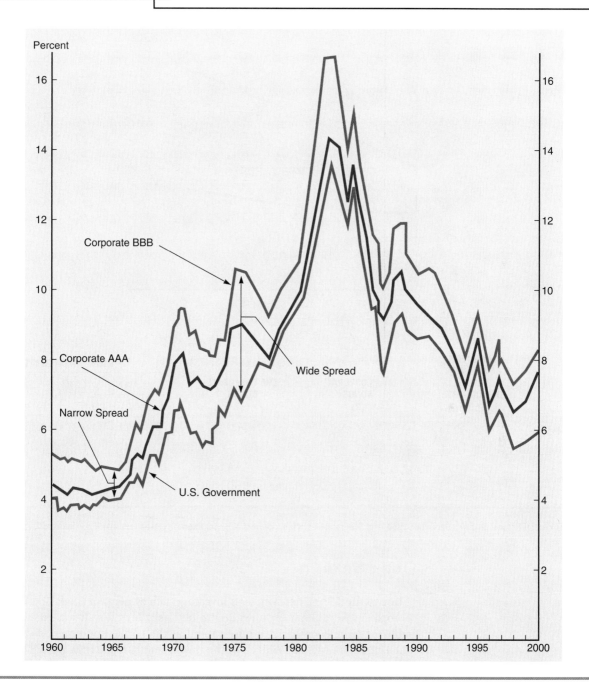

SOURCES: Federal Reserve Board, *Historical Chart Book,* 1983, and *Federal Reserve Bulletin,* various issues.

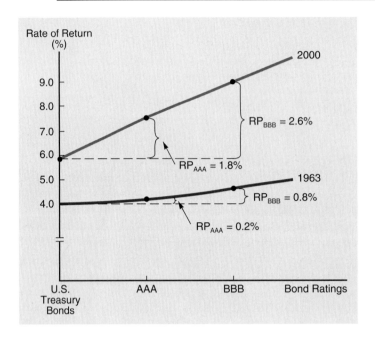

	LONG-TERM GOVERNMENT BONDS (DEFAULT-FREE) (1)	AAA CORPORATE BONDS (2)	BBB CORPORATE BONDS (3)	RISK PREMIUMS	
				AAA (4) = (2) − (1)	BBB (5) = (3) − (1)
June 1963	4.0%	4.2%	4.8%	0.2%	0.8%
September 2000	5.8	7.6	8.4	1.8	2.6

RP_{AAA} = risk premium on AAA bonds.
RP_{BBB} = risk premium on BBB bonds.

SOURCES: *Federal Reserve Bulletin,* December 1963, and Federal Reserve Bank of St. Louis, Selected Interest Rates and U.S. Financial Data.

JUNK BONDS

Prior to the 1980s, fixed-income investors such as pension funds and insurance companies were generally unwilling to buy risky bonds, so it was almost impossible for risky companies to raise capital in the public bond markets. Then, in the late 1970s, Michael Milken of the investment banking firm Drexel Burnham Lambert, relying on historical studies which showed that risky bonds yielded more than enough to compensate for their risk, began to convince institutional investors of the merits of purchasing risky debt. Thus was born the "junk bond," a high-risk, high-yield bond issued to finance a leveraged buyout, a merger, or a troubled company.[17] For example, Public Service of New Hampshire financed

---

[17] Another type of junk bond is one that was highly rated when it was issued but whose rating has fallen because the issuing corporation has fallen on hard times. Such bonds are called "fallen angels."

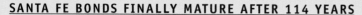

SANTA FE BONDS FINALLY MATURE AFTER 114 YEARS

In 1995, Santa Fe Pacific Company made the final payment on some outstanding bonds that were originally issued in 1881! While the bonds were paid off in full, their history has been anything but routine.

Since the bonds were issued in 1881, investors have seen Santa Fe go through two bankruptcy reorganizations, two depressions, several recessions, two world wars, and the collapse of the gold standard. Through it all, the company remained intact, although ironically it did agree to be acquired by Burlington Northern just prior to the bonds' maturity.

When the bonds were issued in 1881, they had a 6 percent coupon. After a promising start, competition in the railroad business, along with the Depression of 1893, dealt a crippling one-two punch to the company's fortunes. After two bankruptcy reorganizations — and two new management teams — the company got back on its feet, and in 1895 it replaced the original bonds with new 100-year bonds. The new bonds, sanctioned by the Bankruptcy Court, matured in 1995 and carried a 4 percent coupon. However, they also had a wrinkle that was in effect until 1900 — the company could skip the coupon payment if, in management's opinion, earnings were not sufficiently high to service the debt. After 1900, the company could no longer just ignore the coupon, but it did have the option of deferring the payments if management deemed deferral necessary. In the late 1890s, Santa Fe did skip the interest, and the bonds sold at an all-time low of $285 (28.5% of par) in 1896. The bonds reached a peak in 1946, when they sold for $1,312.50 in the strong, low interest rate economy after World War II.

Interestingly, the bonds' principal payment was originally pegged to the price of gold, meaning that the principal received at maturity would increase if the price of gold increased. This type of contract was declared invalid in 1933 by President Roosevelt and Congress, and the decision was upheld by the Supreme Court in a 5–4 vote. If just one Supreme Court justice had gone the other way, then, due to an increase in the price of gold, the bonds would have been worth $18,626 rather than $1,000 when they matured in 1995!

In many ways, the saga of the Santa Fe bonds is a testament to the stability of the U.S. financial system. On the other hand, it illustrates the many types of risks that investors face when they purchase long-term bonds. Investors in the 100-year bonds issued by Disney and Coca-Cola, among others, should perhaps take note.

construction of its troubled Seabrook nuclear plant with junk bonds, and junk bonds were used by Ted Turner to finance the development of CNN and Turner Broadcasting. In junk bond deals, the debt ratio is generally extremely high, so the bondholders must bear as much risk as stockholders normally would. The bonds' yields reflect this fact — a promised return of 25 percent per annum was required to sell the Public Service of New Hampshire bonds.

The emergence of junk bonds as an important type of debt is another example of how the investment banking industry adjusts to and facilitates new developments in capital markets. In the 1980s, mergers and takeovers increased dramatically. People like T. Boone Pickens and Henry Kravis thought that certain old-line, established companies were run inefficiently and were financed too conservatively, and they wanted to take these companies over and restructure them. Michael Milken and his staff at Drexel Burnham Lambert began an active campaign to persuade certain institutions (often S&Ls) to purchase high-yield bonds. Milken developed expertise in putting together deals that were attractive to the institutions yet feasible in the sense that projected cash flows were sufficient to meet the required interest payments. The fact that interest on the bonds was tax deductible, combined with the much higher debt ratios of the restructured firms, also increased after-tax cash flows and helped make the deals feasible.

The development of junk bond financing has done much to reshape the U.S. financial scene. The existence of these securities contributed to the loss of independence of Gulf Oil and hundreds of other companies, and it led to major shake-ups in such companies as CBS, Union Carbide, and USX (formerly U.S.

Steel). It also caused Drexel Burnham Lambert to leap from essentially nowhere in the 1970s to become the most profitable investment banking firm during the 1980s.

The phenomenal growth of the junk bond market was impressive, but controversial. In 1989, Drexel Burnham Lambert was forced into bankruptcy, and "junk bond king" Michael Milken, who had earned $500 million two years earlier, was sent to jail. Those events led to the collapse of the junk bond market in the early 1990s. Since then, however, the junk bond market has rebounded, and junk bonds are here to stay as an important form of corporate financing.

BANKRUPTCY AND REORGANIZATION

During recessions, bankruptcies normally rise, and the most recent recession (in 1991–1992) was no exception. The 1991–1992 casualties included Pan Am, Carter Hawley Hale Stores, Continental Airlines, R. H. Macy & Company, Zale Corporation, and McCrory Corporation. Because of its importance, at least a brief discussion of bankruptcy is warranted within the chapter, and a more detailed discussion is presented in Appendix 8B.

When a business becomes *insolvent*, it does not have enough cash to meet its interest and principal payments. A decision must then be made whether to dissolve the firm through *liquidation* or to permit it to *reorganize* and thus stay alive. These issues are addressed in Chapters 7 and 11 of the federal bankruptcy statutes, and the final decision is made by a federal bankruptcy court judge.

The decision to force a firm to liquidate versus permit it to reorganize depends on whether the value of the reorganized firm is likely to be greater than the value of the firm's assets if they are sold off piecemeal. In a reorganization, the firm's creditors negotiate with management on the terms of a potential reorganization. The reorganization plan may call for a *restructuring* of the firm's debt, in which case the interest rate may be reduced, the term to maturity lengthened, or some of the debt may be exchanged for equity. The point of the restructuring is to reduce the financial charges to a level that the firm's cash flows can support. Of course, the common stockholders also have to give up something — they often see their position diluted as a result of additional shares being given to debtholders in exchange for accepting a reduced amount of debt principal and interest. A trustee may be appointed by the court to oversee the reorganization, but generally the existing management is allowed to retain control.

Liquidation occurs if the company is deemed to be too far gone to be saved — if it is worth more dead than alive. If the bankruptcy court orders a liquidation, assets are sold off and the cash obtained is distributed as specified in Chapter 7 of the Bankruptcy Act. Here is the priority of claims:

1. Secured creditors are entitled to the proceeds from the sale of the specific property that was used to support their loans.
2. The trustee's costs of administering and operating the bankrupt firm are next in line.
3. Expenses incurred after bankruptcy was filed come next.

4. Wages due workers, up to a limit of $2,000 per worker, follow.

5. Claims for unpaid contributions to employee benefit plans are next. This amount, together with wages, cannot exceed $2,000 per worker.

6. Unsecured claims for customer deposits up to $900 per customer are sixth in line.

7. Federal, state, and local taxes due come next.

8. Unfunded pension plan liabilities are next. (Limitations exist as specified in Appendix 8B.)

9. General unsecured creditors are ninth on the list.

10. Preferred stockholders come next, up to the par value of their stock.

11. Common stockholders are finally paid, if anything is left, which is rare.

Appendix 8B provides an illustration of how a firm's assets are distributed after it has been liquidated. For now, you should know (1) that the federal bankruptcy statutes govern both reorganization and liquidation, (2) that bankruptcies occur frequently, and (3) that a priority of the specified claims must be followed when distributing the assets of a liquidated firm.

SELF-TEST QUESTIONS

Differentiate between mortgage bonds and debentures.

Name the major rating agencies, and list some factors that affect bond ratings.

Why are bond ratings important both to firms and to investors?

For what purposes have junk bonds typically been used?

Differentiate between a Chapter 7 liquidation and a Chapter 11 reorganization. When would each be used?

List the priority of claims for the distribution of a liquidated firm's assets.

BOND MARKETS

Corporate bonds are traded primarily in the over-the-counter market. Most bonds are owned by and traded among the large financial institutions (for example, life insurance companies, mutual funds, and pension funds, all of which deal in very large blocks of securities), and it is relatively easy for the over-the-counter bond dealers to arrange the transfer of large blocks of bonds among the relatively few holders of the bonds. It would be much more difficult to conduct similar operations in the stock market among the literally millions of large and small stockholders, so a higher percentage of stock trades occur on the exchanges.

Information on bond trades in the over-the-counter market is not published, but a representative group of bonds is listed and traded on the bond division of

FIGURE 8-6   NYSE Bond Market Transactions, October 10, 2000

CORPORATION BONDS				
VOLUME $8,119,000				
BONDS	CUR YLD	VOL	CLOSE	NET CHG.
BellsoT $6\frac{1}{4}$03	6.4	10	$98\frac{3}{8}$	$-\frac{3}{8}$
BellsoT $6\frac{3}{8}$04	6.5	25	$98\frac{3}{4}$	$+\frac{3}{4}$
BellsoT $5\frac{7}{8}$09	6.5	20	$90\frac{5}{8}$	$-\frac{1}{2}$
BellsoT 7s25	7.5	50	$93\frac{1}{4}$	$-\frac{1}{2}$
BellsoT $8\frac{1}{4}$32	8.2	20	101	$\cdots$
BellsoT $7\frac{1}{2}$33	8.1	30	93	$+\frac{7}{8}$

SOURCE: *The Wall Street Journal,* October 11, 2000, C13.

the NYSE. Figure 8-6 gives a section of the bond market page of *The Wall Street Journal* for trading on October 10, 2000. A total of 146 issues were traded on that date, but we show only the bonds of BellSouth Telecommunications. Note that BellSouth Telecommunications had six different bonds that were traded on October 10. The company actually had more than 10 bond issues outstanding, but several of them did not trade on that date.

The bonds of BellSouth and other companies can have various denominations, but for convenience we generally think of each bond as having a par value of $1,000 — this is how much per bond the company borrowed and how much it must someday repay. However, since other denominations are possible, for trading and reporting purposes bonds are quoted as percentages of par. Looking at the fourth bond listed in the data in Figure 8-6, we see that there is a 7 just after the company's name; this indicates that the bond is of the series that pays 7 percent interest, or 0.07($1,000) = $70.00 of interest per year. The 7 percent is the bond's *coupon rate*. The BellSouth Telecommunications bonds, and all the others listed in the *Journal*, pay interest semiannually, so all rates are nominal, not EAR rates. The 25 which comes next indicates that this bond matures and must be repaid in the year 2025; it is not shown in the figure, but this bond was issued in 1995, so it had a 30-year original maturity. The 7.5 in the second column is the bond's current yield: Current yield = $70.00/$932.50 = 7.51%, rounded to 7.5 percent. The 50 in the third column indicates that 50 of these bonds were traded on October 10, 2000. Since the price shown in the fourth column is expressed as a percentage of par, the bond closed at 93.25 percent, which translates to $932.50, down 0.5 percent from the previous close.

Coupon rates are generally set at levels that reflect the "going rate of interest" on the day a bond is issued. If the rates were set lower, investors simply would not buy the bonds at the $1,000 par value, so the company could not borrow the money it needed. Thus, bonds generally sell at their par values on

FIGURE 8-7

BellSouth Telecommunications 7%, 30-Year Bond: Market Value as Interest Rates Change

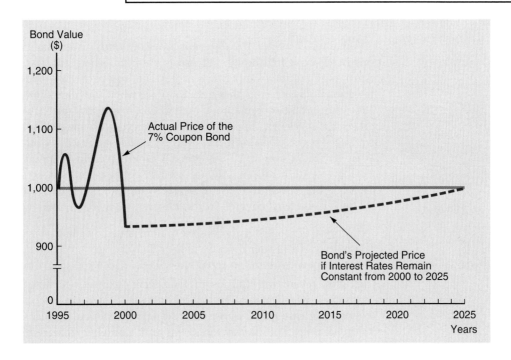

NOTE: The line from 2000 to 2025 appears linear, but it actually has a slight upward curve.

the day they are issued, but their prices fluctuate thereafter as interest rates change.

As shown in Figure 8-7, the BellSouth Telecommunications bonds initially sold at par. The bonds rose above par in 1995 when interest rates dipped below 7 percent, but then fell below par in 1996 when interest rates rose. Over the next four years this pattern was repeated: The price rose above par in 1997 and 1998 when interest rates fell, but the price fell again in 1999 and 2000 after another increase in interest rates. The dashed line in Figure 8-7 shows the projected price of the bonds, in the unlikely event that interest rates remain constant from 2000 to 2025. Looking at the actual and projected price history of these bonds, we see (1) the inverse relationship between interest rates and bond values and (2) the fact that bond values approach their par values as their maturiy date approaches.

SELF-TEST QUESTIONS

Why do most bond trades occur in the over-the-counter market?

If a bond issue is to be sold at par, how will its coupon rate be determined?

This chapter described the different types of bonds governments and corporations issue, explained how bond prices are established, and discussed how investors estimate the rates of return they can expect to earn. We also discussed the various types of risks that investors face when they buy bonds.

It is important to remember that when an investor purchases a company's bonds, that investor is providing the company with capital. Therefore, when a firm issues bonds, *the return that investors receive represents the cost of debt financing for the issuing company.* This point is emphasized in Chapter 10, where the ideas developed in this chapter are used to help determine a company's overall cost of capital, which is a basic component in the capital budgeting process.

The key concepts covered in this chapter are listed below:

- A **bond** is a long-term promissory note issued by a business or governmental unit. The issuer receives money in exchange for promising to make interest payments and to repay the principal on a specified future date.

- Some recent innovations in long-term financing include **zero coupon bonds,** which pay no annual interest but which are issued at a discount; **floating rate debt,** whose interest payments fluctuate with changes in the general level of interest rates; and **junk bonds,** which are high-risk, high-yield instruments issued by firms with very high debt ratios.

- A **call provision** gives the issuing corporation the right to redeem the bonds prior to maturity under specified terms, usually at a price greater than the maturity value (the difference is a **call premium**). A firm will typically call a bond if interest rates fall substantially below the coupon rate.

- A **sinking fund** is a provision that requires the corporation to retire a portion of the bond issue each year. The purpose of the sinking fund is to provide for the orderly retirement of the issue. A sinking fund typically requires no call premium.

- The **value of a bond** is found as the present value of an **annuity** (the interest payments) plus the present value of a lump sum (the **principal**). The bond is evaluated at the appropriate periodic interest rate over the number of periods for which interest payments are made.

- The equation used to find the value of an annual coupon bond is:

$$V_B = \sum_{t=1}^{N} \frac{INT}{(1 + k_d)^t} + \frac{M}{(1 + k_d)^N}.$$

An adjustment to the formula must be made if the bond pays interest **semiannually:** divide INT and k_d by 2, and multiply N by 2.

- The return earned on a bond held to maturity is defined as the bond's **yield to maturity (YTM).** If the bond can be redeemed before maturity, it is **callable,** and the return investors receive if it is called is defined as the **yield to call (YTC).** The YTC is found as the present value of the interest payments received while the bond is outstanding plus the present value of the call price (the par value plus a call premium).

- The longer the maturity of a bond, the more its price will change in response to a given change in interest rates; this is called **interest rate risk.** However, bonds with short maturities expose investors to high **reinvestment rate risk,** which is the risk that income will decline because cash flows received from a bond will be rolled over at a lower interest rate.

- Corporate and municipal bonds have **default risk.** If an issuer defaults, investors receive less than the promised return on the bond. Therefore, investors should evaluate a bond's default risk before making a purchase.

- There are many different types of bonds. They include **mortgage bonds, debentures, convertibles, bonds with warrants, income bonds,** and **purchasing power (indexed) bonds.** The return required on each type of bond is determined by the bond's riskiness.

- Bonds are assigned **ratings** that reflect the probability of their going into default. The highest rating is AAA, and they go down to D. The higher a bond's rating, the lower its risk and its interest rate.

Two related issues are discussed in detail in Appendixes 8A and 8B: zero coupon bonds and bankruptcy. In recent years many companies have used zeros to raise billions of dollars, while bankruptcy is an important consideration for both companies that issue debt and investors.

QUESTIONS

8-1 Is it true that the following equation can be used to find the value of an N-year bond that pays interest once a year?

$$V_B = \sum_{t=1}^{N} \frac{\text{Annual interest}}{(1 + k_d)^t} + \frac{\text{Par value}}{(1 + k_d)^N}.$$

8-2 "The values of outstanding bonds change whenever the going rate of interest changes. In general, short-term interest rates are more volatile than long-term interest rates. Therefore, short-term bond prices are more sensitive to interest rate changes than are long-term bond prices." Is this statement true or false? Explain.

8-3 The rate of return you would get if you bought a bond and held it to its maturity date is called the bond's yield to maturity. If interest rates in the economy rise after a bond has been issued, what will happen to the bond's price and to its YTM? Does the length of time to maturity affect the extent to which a given change in interest rates will affect the bond's price?

8-4 If you buy a *callable* bond and interest rates decline, will the value of your bond rise by as much as it would have risen if the bond had not been callable? Explain.

8-5 A sinking fund can be set up in one of two ways:
(1) The corporation makes annual payments to the trustee, who invests the proceeds in securities (frequently government bonds) and uses the accumulated total to retire the bond issue at maturity.
(2) The trustee uses the annual payments to retire a portion of the issue each year, either calling a given percentage of the issue by a lottery and paying a specified price per bond or buying bonds on the open market, whichever is cheaper.
Discuss the advantages and disadvantages of each procedure from the viewpoint of both the firm and its bondholders.

8-6 Indicate whether each of the following actions will increase or decrease a bond's yield to maturity:
a. A bond's price increases.
b. The company's bonds are downgraded by the rating agencies.

c. A change in the bankruptcy code makes it more difficult for bondholders to receive payments in the event a firm declares bankruptcy.

d. The economy enters a recession.

e. The bonds become subordinated to another debt issue.

8-7 Assume that you have a short investment horizon (that is, less than one year). You are considering two investments: a 1-year Treasury security and a 20-year Treasury security. Which of the two investments would you view as being more risky?

SELF-TEST PROBLEMS (SOLUTIONS APPEAR IN APPENDIX B)

ST-1
Key terms
Define each of the following terms:
a. Bond; Treasury bond; corporate bond; municipal bond; foreign bond
b. Par value; maturity date; original maturity
c. Coupon payment; coupon interest rate
d. Floating rate bond
e. Premium bond; discount bond
f. Current yield (on a bond); yield to maturity (YTM); yield to call (YTC)
g. Reinvestment rate risk; interest rate risk; investment horizon
h. Default risk
i. Mortgage bond
j. Debenture; subordinated debenture
k. Convertible bond; warrant; income bond; indexed, or purchasing power, bond
l. Call provision; sinking fund provision; indenture
m. Zero coupon bond; original issue discount (OID) bond
n. Junk bond; investment grade bonds

ST-2
Bond valuation
The Pennington Corporation issued a new series of bonds on January 1, 1978. The bonds were sold at par ($1,000), have a 12 percent coupon, and mature in 30 years, on December 31, 2007. Coupon payments are made semiannually (on June 30 and December 31).

a. What was the YTM of Pennington's bonds on January 1, 1978?
b. What was the price of the bond on January 1, 1983, 5 years later, assuming that the level of interest rates had fallen to 10 percent?
c. Find the current yield and capital gains yield on the bond on January 1, 1983, given the price as determined in part b.
d. On July 1, 2001, Pennington's bonds sold for $916.42. What was the YTM at that date?
e. What were the current yield and capital gains yield on July 1, 2001?
f. Now, assume that you purchased an outstanding Pennington bond on March 1, 2001, when the going rate of interest was 15.5 percent. How large a check must you have written to complete the transaction? This is a hard question! (Hint: $PVIFA_{7.75\%,13}$ = 8.0136 and $PVIF_{7.75\%,13}$ = 0.3789.)

ST-3
Sinking fund
The Vancouver Development Company has just sold a $100 million, 10-year, 12 percent bond issue. A sinking fund will retire the issue over its life. Sinking fund payments are of equal amounts and will be made *semiannually*, and the proceeds will be used to retire bonds as the payments are made. Bonds can be called at par for sinking fund purposes, or the funds paid into the sinking fund can be used to buy bonds in the open market.

a. How large must each semiannual sinking fund payment be?
b. What will happen, under the conditions of the problem thus far, to the company's debt service requirements per year for this issue over time?
c. Now suppose Vancouver Development set up its sinking fund so that *equal annual amounts*, payable at the end of each year, are paid into a sinking fund trust held by a bank, with the proceeds being used to buy government bonds that pay 9 percent interest. The payments, plus accumulated interest, must total $100 million at the end of 10 years, and the proceeds will be used to retire the bonds at that time. How large must the annual sinking fund payment be now?
d. What are the annual cash requirements for covering bond service costs under the trusteeship arrangement described in part c? (Note: Interest must be paid on Vancouver's outstanding bonds but not on bonds that have been retired.)
e. What would have to happen to interest rates to cause the company to buy bonds on the open market rather than call them under the original sinking fund plan?

STARTER PROBLEMS

8-1
Bond valuation

Callaghan Motors' bonds have 10 years remaining to maturity. Interest is paid annually, the bonds have a $1,000 par value, and the coupon interest rate is 8 percent. The bonds have a yield to maturity of 9 percent. What is the current market price of these bonds?

8-2
Financial calculator needed;
Yield to maturity

Wilson Wonders' bonds have 12 years remaining to maturity. Interest is paid annually, the bonds have a $1,000 par value, and the coupon interest rate is 10 percent. The bonds sell at a price of $850. What is their yield to maturity?

8-3
Financial calculator needed;
Yield to maturity and call

Thatcher Corporation's bonds will mature in 10 years. The bonds have a face value of $1,000 and an 8 percent coupon rate, paid semiannually. The price of the bonds is $1,100. The bonds are callable in 5 years at a call price of $1,050. What is the yield to maturity? What is the yield to call?

8-4
Current yield

Heath Foods' bonds have 7 years remaining to maturity. The bonds have a face value of $1,000 and a yield to maturity of 8 percent. They pay interest annually and have a 9 percent coupon rate. What is their current yield?

8-5
Financial calculator needed;
Bond valuation

Nungesser Corporation has issued bonds that have a 9 percent coupon rate, payable semiannually. The bonds mature in 8 years, have a face value of $1,000, and a yield to maturity of 8.5 percent. What is the price of the bonds?

8-6
Financial calculator needed;
Current yield and yield to maturity

A bond that matures in 10 years sells for $985. The bond has a face value of $1,000 and a 7 percent annual coupon.
a. What is the bond's current yield?
b. What is the bond's yield to maturity (YTM)?
c. Assume that the yield to maturity remains constant for the next 3 years. What will be the price of the bond 3 years from today?

EXAM-TYPE PROBLEMS

The problems included in this section are set up in such a way that they could be converted to multiple-choice exam problems.

8-7
Bond valuation

The Garraty Company has two bond issues outstanding. Both bonds pay $100 annual interest plus $1,000 at maturity. Bond L has a maturity of 15 years, and Bond S a maturity of 1 year.
a. What will be the value of each of these bonds when the going rate of interest is (1) 5 percent, (2) 8 percent, and (3) 12 percent? Assume that there is only one more interest payment to be made on Bond S.
b. Why does the longer-term (15-year) bond fluctuate more when interest rates change than does the shorter-term bond (1-year)?

8-8
Yield to maturity

The Heymann Company's bonds have 4 years remaining to maturity. Interest is paid annually; the bonds have a $1,000 par value; and the coupon interest rate is 9 percent.
a. What is the yield to maturity at a current market price of (1) $829 or (2) $1,104?
b. Would you pay $829 for one of these bonds if you thought that the appropriate rate of interest was 12 percent — that is, if k_d = 12%? Explain your answer.

8-9
Yield to call

Six years ago, The Singleton Company sold a 20-year bond issue with a 14 percent annual coupon rate and a 9 percent call premium. Today, Singleton called the bonds. The bonds originally were sold at their face value of $1,000. Compute the realized rate of return for investors who purchased the bonds when they were issued and who surrender them today in exchange for the call price.

8-10
Financial calculator needed;
Bond yields

A 10-year, 12 percent semiannual coupon bond, with a par value of $1,000, may be called in 4 years at a call price of $1,060. The bond sells for $1,100. (Assume that the bond has just been issued.)
a. What is the bond's yield to maturity?
b. What is the bond's current yield?
c. What is the bond's capital gain or loss yield?
d. What is the bond's yield to call?

8-11
Financial calculator needed;
Current yield and yield to maturity

A bond that matures in 6 years has an 8 percent coupon rate, semiannual payments, a face value of $1,000, and a 7.7 percent current yield. What is the bond's nominal yield to maturity (YTM)?

8-12
Financial calculator needed;
Yield to maturity

You just purchased a bond that matures in 5 years. The bond has a face value of $1,000, an 8 percent annual coupon, and has a current yield of 8.21 percent. What is the bond's yield to maturity (YTM)?

8-13
Financial calculator needed;
Current yield

A bond that matures in 7 years sells for $1,020. The bond has a face value of $1,000 and a yield to maturity of 10.5883 percent. The bond pays coupons semiannually. What is the bond's current yield?

8-14
Nominal interest rate

Lloyd Corporation's 14 percent coupon rate, semiannual payment, $1,000 par value bonds, which mature in 30 years, are callable 5 years from now at a price of $1,050. The bonds sell at a price of $1,353.54, and the yield curve is flat. Assuming that interest rates in the economy are expected to remain at their current level, what is the best estimate of Lloyd's nominal interest rate on new bonds?

PROBLEMS

8-15
Bond valuation

Suppose Ford Motor Company sold an issue of bonds with a 10-year maturity, a $1,000 par value, a 10 percent coupon rate, and semiannual interest payments.

a. Two years after the bonds were issued, the going rate of interest on bonds such as these fell to 6 percent. At what price would the bonds sell?

b. Suppose that, 2 years after the initial offering, the going interest rate had risen to 12 percent. At what price would the bonds sell?

c. Suppose that the conditions in part a existed — that is, interest rates fell to 6 percent 2 years after the issue date. Suppose further that the interest rate remained at 6 percent for the next 8 years. What would happen to the price of the Ford Motor Company bonds over time?

8-16
Bond reporting

Look up the prices of American Telephone & Telegraph's (AT&T) bonds in *The Wall Street Journal* (or some other newspaper that provides this information).

a. If AT&T were to sell a new issue of $1,000 par value long-term bonds, approximately what coupon interest rate would it have to set on the bonds if it wanted to bring them out at par?

b. If you had $10,000 and wanted to invest it in AT&T, what return would you expect to get if you bought AT&T's bonds?

8-17
Discount bond valuation

Assume that in February 1970 the Los Angeles Airport Authority issued a series of 3.4 percent, 30-year bonds. Interest rates rose substantially in the years following the issue, and as they did, the price of the bonds declined. Also, assume in February 1983, 13 years later, the price of the bonds had dropped from $1,000 to $650. In answering the following questions, assume that the bond requires annual interest payments.

a. Each bond originally sold at its $1,000 par value. What was the yield to maturity of these bonds when they were issued?

b. Calculate the yield to maturity in February 1983.

c. Assume that interest rates stabilized at the 1983 level and stayed there for the remainder of the life of the bonds. What would have been the bonds' price in February 1998, when they had 2 years remaining to maturity?

d. What was the price of the bonds the day before they matured in 2000? (Disregard the last interest payment.)

e. In 1983, the Los Angeles Airport bonds were classified as "discount bonds." What happens to the price of a discount bond as it approaches maturity? Is there a "built-in capital gain" on such bonds?

f. The coupon interest payment divided by the market price of a bond is called the bond's *current yield*. Assuming the conditions in part c, what would have been the current yield of a Los Angeles Airport bond (1) in February 1983 and (2) in February 1998? What would have been its capital gains yields and total yields (total yield equals yield to maturity) on those same two dates?

8-18
Yield to call

It is now January 1, 2002, and you are considering the purchase of an outstanding Racette Corporation bond that was issued on January 1, 2000. The Racette bond has a 9.5 percent annual coupon and a 30-year original maturity (it matures on December 31, 2029). There is a 5-year call protection (until December 31, 2004), after which time the bond can be called at 109 (that is, at 109 percent of par, or $1,090). Interest rates have declined since the bond was issued, and the bond is now selling at 116.575 percent of par, or $1,165.75. You want to determine both the yield to maturity and the yield to call for this bond. (Note: The yield to call considers the effect of a call provision on the bond's probable yield. In the calculation, we assume that the bond will be outstanding until the call date, at which time it will be called. Thus, the investor will have received interest payments for the call-protected period and then will receive the call price — in this case, $1,090 — on the call date.)

a. What is the yield to maturity in 2002 for the Racette bond? What is its yield to call?

b. If you bought this bond, which return do you think you would actually earn? Explain your reasoning.

c. Suppose the bond had sold at a discount. Would the yield to maturity or the yield to call have been more relevant?

8-19
Financial calculator needed;
Interest rate sensitivity

A bond trader purchased each of the following bonds at a yield to maturity of 8 percent. Immediately after she purchased the bonds interest rates fell to 7 percent. What is the percentage change in the price of each bond after the decline in interest rates? Fill in the following table:

	PRICE @ 8%	PRICE @ 7%	PERCENTAGE CHANGE
10-year, 10% annual coupon	————	————	————
10-year zero	————	————	————
5-year zero	————	————	————
30-year zero	————	————	————
$100 perpetuity	————	————	————

8-20
Financial calculator needed;
Bond valuation

An investor has two bonds in his portfolio. Each bond matures in 4 years, has a face value of $1,000, and has a yield to maturity equal to 9.6 percent. One bond, Bond C, pays an annual coupon of 10 percent; the other bond, Bond Z, is a zero coupon bond.

a. Assuming that the yield to maturity of each bond remains at 9.6 percent over the next 4 years, what will be the price of each of the bonds at the following time periods? Fill in the following table:

t	PRICE OF BOND C	PRICE OF BOND Z
0	————	————
1	————	————
2	————	————
3	————	————
4	————	————

b. Plot the time path of the prices for each of the two bonds.

SPREADSHEET PROBLEM

8-21
Bond valuation

Rework Problem 8-10 using a spreadsheet model. After completing parts a through d, answer the following related questions.

e. How would the price of the bond be affected by changing interest rates? (Hint: Conduct a sensitivity analysis of price to changes in the yield to maturity, which is also the going market interest rate for the bond. Assume that the bond will be called if and only if the going rate of interest *falls below* the coupon rate. That is an oversimplification, but assume it anyway for purposes of this problem.)

f. Now assume that the date is 10/25/2001. Assume further that our 12 percent, 10-year bond was issued on 7/1/2001, is callable on 7/1/2005 at $1,060, will mature on 6/30/2011, pays interest semiannually (January 1 and July 1), and sells for $1,100. Use your spreadsheet to find (1) the bond's yield to maturity and (2) its yield to call.

The information related to the cyberproblems is likely to change over time, due to the release of new information and the ever-changing nature of the World Wide Web. With these changes in mind, we will periodically update these problems on the textbook's web site. To avoid problems, please check for these updates before proceeding with the cyber-problems.

8-22

Bonds and their valuation

All bonds have some common characteristics, but they do not always have the same contractual features. Differences in contractual provisions, and in the underlying strength of the companies backing the bonds, lead to major differences in bonds' risks, prices, and expected returns. The risk investors are exposed to when buying a bond is in part gauged by bond rating agencies. The three major bond rating agencies are Moody's, Standard & Poor's, and Fitch's. Bonds are assigned quality ratings that reflect their probability of default. Changes in a firm's bond rating influence its ability to borrow long-term capital and the cost of that capital. Rating agencies review outstanding bonds on a periodic basis, occasionally upgrading or downgrading a bond because of changes in an issuer's circumstances. Visit **http://www.standardandpoors.com/ResourceCenter** and answer the following questions:

a. On what information are corporate issuer credit ratings based? To answer this question, click on "Ratings Definitions."

b. What do the following long-term issuer credit ratings mean: AAA, AA, A, BBB, CCC, and D?

c. Some debt issues have a plus (+) or minus (−) after their letter rating. What does the plus (+) or (−) signify?

d. How does Standard & Poor's assign ratings to short-term debt issues? Compare the A-1, A-2, A-3, B, and C ratings to each other.

e. What is CreditWatch?

f. For what other types of issues does Standard & Poor's offer ratings services?

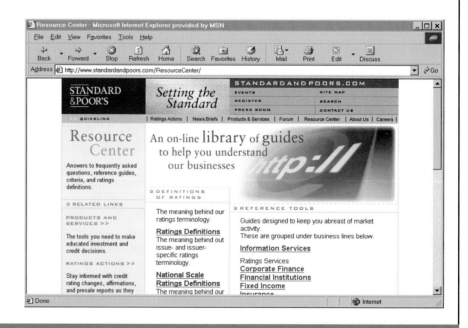

WESTERN MONEY MANAGEMENT INC.

8-23 **Bond Valuation** Robert Black and Carol Alvarez are vice-presidents of Western Money Management and codirectors of the company's pension fund management division. A major new client, the California League of Cities, has requested that Western present an investment seminar to the mayors of the represented cities, and Black and Alvarez, who will make the actual presentation, have asked you to help them by answering the following questions.

a. What are the key features of a bond?

b. What are call provisions and sinking fund provisions? Do these provisions make bonds more or less risky?

c. How is the value of any asset whose value is based on expected future cash flows determined?

d. How is the value of a bond determined? What is the value of a 10-year, $1,000 par value bond with a 10 percent annual coupon if its required rate of return is 10 percent?

e. (1) What would be the value of the bond described in part d if, just after it had been issued, the expected inflation rate rose by 3 percentage points, causing investors to require a 13 percent return? Would we now have a discount or a premium bond? (If you do not have a financial calculator, $PVIF_{13\%,10} = 0.2946$; $PVIFA_{13\%,10} = 5.4262$.)

(2) What would happen to the bond's value if inflation fell, and k_d declined to 7 percent? Would we now have a premium or a discount bond?

(3) What would happen to the value of the 10-year bond over time if the required rate of return remained at 13 percent, or if it remained at 7 percent? (Hint: With a financial calculator, enter PMT, I, FV, and N, and then change (override) N to see what happens to the PV as the bond approaches maturity.)

f. (1) What is the yield to maturity on a 10-year, 9 percent, annual coupon, $1,000 par value bond that sells for $887.00? That sells for $1,134.20? What does the fact that a bond sells at a discount or at a premium tell you about the relationship between k_d and the bond's coupon rate?

(2) What are the total return, the current yield, and the capital gains yield for the discount bond? (Assume the bond is held to maturity and the company does not default on the bond.)

g. What is *interest rate (or price) risk?* Which bond has more interest rate risk, an annual payment 1-year bond or a 10-year bond? Why?

h. What is *reinvestment rate risk?* Which has more reinvestment rate risk, a 1-year bond or a 10-year bond?

i. How does the equation for valuing a bond change if semiannual payments are made? Find the value of a 10-year, semiannual payment, 10 percent coupon bond if nominal $k_d = 13\%$. (Hint: $PVIF_{6.5\%,20} = 0.2838$ and $PVIFA_{6.5\%,20} = 11.0185$.)

j. Suppose you could buy, for $1,000, either a 10 percent, 10-year, annual payment bond or a 10 percent, 10-year, semiannual payment bond. They are equally risky. Which would you prefer? If $1,000 is the proper price for the semiannual bond, what is the equilibrium price for the annual payment bond?

k. Suppose a 10-year, 10 percent, semiannual coupon bond with a par value of $1,000 is currently selling for $1,135.90, producing a nominal yield to maturity of 8 percent. However, the bond can be called after 4 years for a price of $1,050.

(1) What is the bond's *nominal yield to call (YTC)?*

(2) If you bought this bond, do you think you would be more likely to earn the YTM or the YTC? Why?

l. Does the yield to maturity represent the promised or expected return on the bond?

m. These bonds were rated AA− by S&P. Would you consider these bonds investment grade or junk bonds?

n. What factors determine a company's bond rating?

o. If this firm were to default on the bonds, would the company be immediately liquidated? Would the bondholders be assured of receiving all of their promised payments?

ZERO COUPON BONDS

To understand how zeros are used and analyzed, consider the zeros that are going to be issued by Vandenberg Corporation, a shopping center developer. Vandenberg is developing a new shopping center in San Diego, California, and it needs $50 million. The company does not anticipate major cash flows from the project for about five years. However, Pieter Vandenberg, the president, plans to sell the center once it is fully developed and rented, which should take about five years. Therefore, Vandenberg wants to use a financing vehicle that will not require cash outflows for five years, and he has decided on a five-year zero coupon bond, with a maturity value of $1,000.

Vandenberg Corporation is an A-rated company, and A-rated zeros with five-year maturities yield 6 percent at this time (five-year coupon bonds also yield 6 percent). The company is in the 40 percent federal-plus-state tax bracket. Pieter Vandenberg wants to know the firm's after-tax cost of debt if it uses 6 percent, five-year maturity zeros, and he also wants to know what the bond's cash flows will be. Table 8A-1 provides an analysis of the situation, and the following numbered paragraphs explain the table itself.

TABLE 8A-1	**Analysis of a Zero Coupon Bond from Issuer's Perspective**

BASIC DATA

Maturity value	$1,000
k_d	6.00%, annual compounding
Maturity	5 years
Corporate tax rate	40.00%
Issue price	$747.26

ANALYSIS

	0 6%	1	2	3	4	5 Years
(1) Year-end accrued value	$747.26	$792.10	$839.62	$890.00	$943.40	$1,000.00
(2) Interest deduction		44.84	47.52	50.38	53.40	56.60
(3) Tax savings (40%)		17.94	19.01	20.15	21.36	22.64
(4) Cash flow to Vandenberg	+747.26	+17.94	+19.01	+20.15	+21.36	−977.36
After-tax cost of debt	3.60%					

Face value of bonds the company must issue to raise $50 million = Amount needed/Issue price as % of par

$$= \$50,000,000/0.74726$$

$$\approx \$66,911,000.$$

1. The information in the "Basic Data" section, except the issue price, was given in the preceding paragraph, and the information in the "Analysis" section was calculated using the known data. The maturity value of the bond is always set at $1,000 or some multiple thereof.

2. The issue price is the PV of $1,000, discounted back five years at the rate $k_d = 6\%$, annual compounding. Using the tables, we find PV = $1,000(0.7473) = \$747.30$. Using a financial calculator, we input N = 5, I = 6, PMT = 0, and FV = 1000, then press the PV key to find PV = $747.26. Note that $747.26, compounded annually for five years at 6 percent, will grow to $1,000 as shown by the time line on Line 1 in Table 8A-1.

3. The accrued values as shown on Line 1 in the analysis section represent the compounded value of the bond at the end of each year. The accrued value for Year 0 is the issue price; the accrued value for Year 1 is found as $747.26(1.06) = \$792.10$; the accrued value at the end of Year 2 is $747.26(1.06)^2 = \$839.62$; and, in general, the value at the end of any Year n is

$$\text{Accrued value at the end of Year n} = \text{Issue price} \times (1 + k_d)^n. \quad \text{(8A-1)}$$

4. The interest deduction as shown on Line 2 represents the increase in accrued value during the year. Thus, interest in Year 1 = $792.10 − $747.26 = $44.84. In general,

$$\text{Interest in Year n} = \text{Accrued value}_n - \text{Accrued value}_{n-1}. \quad \text{(8A-2)}$$

This method of calculating taxable interest is specified in the Tax Code.

5. The company can deduct interest each year, even though the payment is not made in cash. This deduction lowers the taxes that would otherwise be paid, producing the following tax savings:

$$\text{Tax savings} = (\text{Interest deduction})(\text{T}). \quad \text{(8A-3)}$$
$$= \$44.84(0.4)$$
$$= \$17.94 \text{ in Year 1.}$$

6. Line 4 represents cash flows on a time line; it shows the cash flow at the end of Years 0 through 5. At Year 0, the company receives the $747.26 issue price. The company also has positive cash inflows equal to the tax savings during Years 1 through 4. Finally, in Year 5, it must pay the $1,000 maturity value, but it gets one more year of interest tax savings. Therefore, the net cash flow in Year 5 is −$1,000 + $22.64 = −$977.36.

7. Next, we can determine the after-tax cost (or after-tax yield to maturity) of issuing the bonds. Since the cash flow stream is uneven, the after-tax yield to maturity is found by entering the after-tax cash flows, shown in Line 4 of Table 8A-1, into the cash flow register and then pressing the IRR key on the financial calculator. The IRR is the after-tax cost of zero coupon debt to the company. Conceptually, here is the situation:

$$\sum_{t=1}^{n} \frac{CF_n}{(1 + k_{d(AT)})^n} = 0. \quad \text{(8A-4)}$$

$$\frac{\$747.26}{(1 + k_{d(AT)})^0} + \frac{\$17.94}{(1 + k_{d(AT)})^1} + \frac{\$19.01}{(1 + k_{d(AT)})^2} + \frac{\$20.15}{(1 + k_{d(AT)})^3} + \frac{\$21.36}{(1 + k_{d(AT)})^4} + \frac{-\$977.36}{(1 + k_{d(AT)})^5} = 0.$$

The value $k_{d(AT)} = 0.036 = 3.6\%$, found with a financial calculator, produces the equality, and it is the cost of this debt. (Input in the cash flow register $CF_0 = 747.26$, $CF_1 = 17.94$, and so forth, out to $CF_5 = -977.36$. Then press the IRR key to find $k_d = 3.6\%$.)

8. Note that $k_d(1 - T) = 6\%(0.6) = 3.6\%$. As we will see in Chapter 10, the cost of capital for regular coupon debt is found using the formula $k_d(1 - T)$. Thus, there is symmetrical treatment for tax purposes for zero coupon and regular coupon debt; that is, both types of debt use the same after-tax cost formula. This was Congress's intent, and it is why the Tax Code specifies the treatment set forth in Table 8A-1.[1]

The purchaser of a zero coupon bond must calculate interest income on the bond in the same manner as the issuer calculates the interest deduction. Table 8A-2 shows the resulting tax payments for an investor in the 28 percent tax bracket who purchases the Vandenberg bond. Given this tax treatment, investors pay taxes in each year even though they don't receive any cash flows until the bond is sold or matures, a situation that many investors find unattractive. Consequently, because of the tax situation pension funds and other tax-exempt entities buy most zero coupon bonds. Individuals do, however, buy taxable zeros for their Individual Retirement Accounts (IRAs). Also, state and local governments issue "tax-exempt muni zeros" that are purchased by individuals in high tax brackets.

Not all original issue discount bonds (OIDs) have zero coupons. For example, Vandenberg might have sold an issue of five-year bonds with a 5 percent coupon at a time when other bonds with similar ratings and maturities were yielding 6 percent. Such bonds would have had a value of $957.88:

$$\text{Bond value} = \sum_{t=1}^{5} \frac{\$50}{(1.06)^t} + \frac{\$1,000}{(1.06)^5} = \$957.88.$$

If an investor had purchased these bonds at a price of $957.88, the yield to maturity would have been 6 percent. The discount of $1,000 - $957.88 = $42.12 would have been amortized over the bond's five-year life, and it would have been handled by both Vandenberg and the bondholders exactly as the discount on the zeros was handled.

Thus, zero coupon bonds are just one type of original issue discount bond. Any nonconvertible bond whose coupon rate is set below the going market rate at the time of its issue will sell at a discount, and it will be classified (for tax and other purposes) as an OID bond.

Shortly after corporations began to issue zeros, investment bankers figured out a way to create zeros from U.S. Treasury bonds, which at the time were issued only in coupon form. In 1982, Salomon Brothers bought $1 billion of 12 percent, 30-year Treasuries. Each bond had 60 coupons worth $60 each, which represented the interest payments due every six months. Salomon then in effect clipped the coupons and placed them in 60 piles; the last pile also contained the now "stripped" bond itself, which represented a promise of $1,000 in the year 2012. These 60 piles of U.S. Treasury promises were then placed with the trust

---

[1] Note too that we have analyzed the bond as if the cash flows accrued annually. Generally, to facilitate comparisons with semiannual payment coupon bonds, the analysis is conducted on a semiannual basis.

Analysis of a Zero Coupon Bond from Investor's Perspective

BASIC DATA

Maturity value	$1,000
k_d	6.00%, annual compounding
Maturity	5 years
Personal tax rate	28.00%
Issue price	$747.26

ANALYSIS

	0 6%	1	2	3	4	5 Years
(1) Year-end accrued value	$747.26	$792.10	$839.62	$890.00	$943.40	$1,000.00
(2) Interest income		44.84	47.52	50.38	53.40	56.60
(3) Tax payment (28%)		12.56	13.31	14.11	14.95	15.85
(4) Cash flow to investor	−747.26	−12.56	−13.31	−14.11	−14.95	+984.15
After-tax return	4.32%					

department of a bank and used as collateral for "zero coupon U.S. Treasury Trust Certificates," which are, in essence, zero coupon Treasury bonds. Treasury zeros are, of course, safer than corporate zeros, so they are very popular with pension fund managers. In response to this demand, the Treasury has also created its own "Strips" program, which allows investors to purchase zeros electronically.

Corporate (and municipal) zeros are generally callable at the option of the issuer, just like coupon bonds, after some stated call protection period. The call price is set at a premium over the accrued value at the time of the call. Stripped U.S. Treasury bonds (Treasury zeros) generally are not callable because the Treasury normally sells noncallable bonds. Thus, Treasury zeros are completely protected against reinvestment risk (the risk of having to invest cash flows from a bond at a lower rate because of a decline in interest rates).

PROBLEMS

8A-1
Zero coupon bonds

A company has just issued 4-year zero coupon bonds with a maturity value of $1,000 and a yield to maturity of 9 percent. The company's tax rate is 40 percent. What is the after-tax cost of debt for the company?

8A-2
Zero coupon bonds

An investor in the 28 percent bracket purchases the bond discussed in Problem 8A-1. What is the investor's after-tax return?

8A-3
Zero coupon bonds and EAR

Assume that the city of Tampa sold tax-exempt (muni), zero coupon bonds 5 years ago. The bonds had a 25-year maturity and a maturity value of $1,000 when they were issued, and the interest rate built into the issue was a nominal 10 percent, but with semi-annual compounding. The bonds are now callable at a premium of 10 percent over the accrued value. What effective annual rate of return would an investor who bought the bonds when they were issued and who still owns them earn if they are called today?

APPENDIX 8B

BANKRUPTCY AND REORGANIZATION

In the event of bankruptcy, debtholders have a prior claim to a firm's income and assets over the claims of both common and preferred stockholders. Further, different classes of debtholders are treated differently in the event of bankruptcy. Since bankruptcy is a fairly common occurrence, and since it affects both the bankrupt firm and its customers, suppliers, and creditors, it is important to know who gets what if a firm fails. These topics are discussed in this appendix.[1]

FEDERAL BANKRUPTCY LAWS

Bankruptcy actually begins when a firm is unable to meet scheduled payments on its debt or when the firm's cash flow projections indicate that it will soon be unable to meet payments. As the bankruptcy proceedings go forward, the following central issues arise:

1. Does the firm's inability to meet scheduled payments result from a temporary cash flow problem, or does it represent a permanent problem caused by asset values having fallen below debt obligations?

2. If the problem is a temporary one, then an agreement that stretches out payments may be worked out to give the firm time to recover and to satisfy everyone. However, if basic long-run asset values have truly declined, economic losses will have occurred. In this event, who should bear the losses?

3. Is the company "worth more dead than alive" — that is, would the business be more valuable if it were maintained and continued in operation or if it were liquidated and sold off in pieces?

4. Who should control the firm while it is being liquidated or rehabilitated? Should the existing management be left in control, or should a trustee be placed in charge of operations?

These are the primary issues that are addressed in the federal bankruptcy statutes.

Our bankruptcy laws were first enacted in 1898, modified substantially in 1938, changed again in 1978, and further fine-tuned in 1984. The 1978 Act, which provides the basic laws that govern bankruptcy today, was a major revi-

---

This appendix was coauthored by Arthur L. Herrmann of the University of Hartford.

[1] Much of the current work in this area is based on writings by Edward I. Altman. For a summary of his work, and that of others, see Edward I. Altman, "Bankruptcy and Reorganization," in *Handbook of Corporate Finance*, Edward I. Altman, ed. (New York: Wiley, 1986), Chapter 19.

sion designed to streamline and expedite proceedings, and it consists of eight odd-numbered chapters, the even-numbered chapters of the earlier Act having been deleted. Chapters 1, 3, and 5 of the 1978 Act contain general provisions applicable to the other chapters; Chapter 7 details the procedures to be followed when liquidating a firm; Chapter 9 deals with financially distressed municipalities; Chapter 11 is the business reorganization chapter; Chapter 13 covers the adjustment of debts for "individuals with regular income"; and Chapter 15 sets up a system of trustees who help administer proceedings under the Act.

Chapters 11 and 7 are the most important ones for financial management purposes. When you read in the paper that McCrory Corporation or some other company has "filed for Chapter 11," this means that the company is bankrupt and is trying to reorganize under Chapter 11 of the Act. If a reorganization plan cannot be worked out, then the company will be liquidated as prescribed in Chapter 7 of the Act.

The 1978 Act is quite flexible, and it provides a great deal of scope for informal negotiations between a company and its creditors. Under this Act, a case is opened by the filing of a petition with a federal district bankruptcy court. The petition may be either voluntary or involuntary — that is, it may be filed either by the firm's management or by its creditors. A committee of unsecured creditors is then appointed by the court to negotiate with management for a reorganization, that may include the restructuring of debt and other claims against the firm. (A "restructuring" could involve lengthening the maturity of debt, lowering the interest rate on it, reducing the principal amount owed, exchanging common or preferred stock for debt, or some combination of these actions.) A trustee may be appointed by the court if that is deemed to be in the best interests of the creditors and stockholders; otherwise, the existing management will retain control. If no fair and feasible reorganization can be worked out under Chapter 11, the firm will be liquidated under the procedures spelled out in Chapter 7.

FINANCIAL DECISIONS IN BANKRUPTCY

When a business becomes insolvent, a decision must be made whether to dissolve the firm through *liquidation* or to keep it alive through *reorganization*. To a large extent, this decision depends on a determination of the value of the firm if it is rehabilitated versus the value of its assets if they are sold off individually. The procedure that promises higher returns to the creditors and owners will be adopted. However, the "public interest" will also be considered, and this generally means attempting to salvage the firm, even if the salvaging effort may be costly to bondholders. For example, the bankruptcy court kept Eastern Airlines alive, at the cost of millions of dollars that could have been paid to bondholders, until it was obvious even to the judge that Eastern could not be saved. Note, too, that if the decision is made to reorganize the firm, the courts and possibly the SEC will be called upon to determine the fairness and the feasibility of the proposed reorganization plan.

Standard of Fairness

The basic doctrine of *fairness* states that claims must be recognized in the order of their legal and contractual priority. Carrying out this concept of fairness in a reorganization (as opposed to a liquidation) involves the following steps:

1. Future sales must be estimated.

2. Operating conditions must be analyzed so that the future earnings and cash flows can be predicted.

3. A capitalization (or discount) rate to be applied to these future cash flows must be determined.

4. This capitalization rate must then be applied to the estimated cash flows to obtain a present value figure, which is the indicated value for the reorganized company.

5. Provisions for the distribution of the restructured firm's securities to its claimants must be made.

Standard of Feasibility

The primary test of *feasibility* in a reorganization is whether the fixed charges after reorganization can be covered by cash flows. Adequate coverage generally requires an improvement in operating earnings, a reduction of fixed charges, or both. Among the actions that generally must be taken are the following:

1. Debt maturities are usually lengthened, interest rates may be scaled back, and some debt may be converted into equity.

2. When the quality of management has been substandard, a new team must be given control of the company.

3. If inventories have become obsolete or depleted, they must be replaced.

4. Sometimes the plant and equipment must be modernized before the firm can operate on a competitive basis.

LIQUIDATION PROCEDURES

If a company is too far gone to be reorganized, it must be liquidated. Liquidation should occur if a business is worth more dead than alive, or if the possibility of restoring it to financial health is so remote that the creditors would face a high risk of even greater losses if operations were continued.

Chapter 7 of the Bankruptcy Act is designed to do three things: (1) provide safeguards against the withdrawal of assets by the owners of the bankrupt firm, (2) provide for an equitable distribution of the assets among the creditors, and (3) allow insolvent debtors to discharge all of their obligations and to start over unhampered by a burden of prior debt.

The distribution of assets in a liquidation under Chapter 7 of the Bankruptcy Act is governed by the following priority of claims:

1. *Secured creditors, who are entitled to the proceeds of the sale of specific property pledged for a lien or a mortgage.* If the proceeds do not fully satisfy the secured creditors' claims, the remaining balance is treated as a general creditor claim. (See Item 9.)

2. *Trustee's costs to administer and operate the bankrupt firm.*

3. *Expenses incurred after an involuntary case has begun but before a trustee is appointed.*

4. *Wages due workers if earned within three months prior to the filing of the petition of bankruptcy.* The amount of wages is limited to $2,000 per person.

5. *Claims for unpaid contributions to employee benefit plans that were to have been paid within six months prior to filing.* However, these claims, plus wages in Item 4, are not to exceed the $2,000 per employee limit.

6. *Unsecured claims for customer deposits, not to exceed a maximum of $900 per individual.*

7. *Taxes due to federal, state, county, and any other government agency.*

8. *Unfunded pension plan liabilities.* Unfunded pension plan liabilities have a claim above that of the general creditors for an amount up to 30 percent of the common and preferred equity; any remaining unfunded pension claims rank with the general creditors.

9. *General, or unsecured, creditors.* Holders of trade credit, unsecured loans, the unsatisfied portion of secured loans, and debenture bonds are classified as *general creditors*. Holders of subordinated debt also fall into this category, but they must turn over required amounts to the holders of senior debt, as discussed later in this section.

10. *Preferred stockholders, who can receive an amount up to the par value of the issue.*

11. *Common stockholders, who receive any remaining funds.*

To illustrate how this priority system works, consider the balance sheet of Chiefland Inc., shown in Table 8B-1. The assets have a book value of $90 million. The claims are indicated on the right side of the balance sheet. Note that the debentures are subordinate to the notes payable to banks. Chiefland had filed for reorganization under Chapter 11, but since no fair and feasible reorganization could be arranged, the trustee is liquidating the firm under Chapter 7. The firm also has $15 million of unfunded pension liabilities.[2]

The assets as reported in the balance sheet in Table 8B-1 are greatly overstated; they are, in fact, worth about half of the $90 million at which they are carried. The following amounts are realized on liquidation:

Proceeds from sale of current assets	$41,950,000
Proceeds from sale of fixed assets	5,000,000
Total receipts	$46,950,000

---

[2] Under the federal statutes that regulate pension funds, corporations are required to estimate the amount of money needed to provide for the pensions that have been promised to their employees. This determination is made by professional actuaries, taking into account when employees will retire, how long they are likely to live, and the rate of return that can be earned on pension fund assets. If the assets currently in the pension fund are deemed sufficient to make all required payments, the plan is said to be *fully funded*. If assets in the plan are less than the present value of expected future payments, an *unfunded liability* exists. Under federal laws, companies are given up to 30 years to fund any unfunded liabilities. (Note that if a company were fully funded in 2001, but then agreed in 2002 to double pension benefits, this would immediately create a large unfunded liability, and it would need time to make the adjustment. Otherwise, it would be difficult for companies to agree to increase pension benefits.)

Unfunded pension liabilities, including medical benefits to retirees, represent a time bomb ticking in the bowels of many companies. If a company has a relatively old labor force, and if it has promised them substantial retirement benefits but has not set aside assets in a funded pension fund to cover these benefits, it could experience severe trouble in the future. These unfunded pension benefits could even drive the company into bankruptcy, at which point the pension plan would be subject to the bankruptcy laws.

TABLE 8B-1	Chiefland Inc.: Balance Sheet Just before Liquidation (Thousands of Dollars)		
Current assets	$80,000	Accounts payable	$20,000
Net fixed assets	10,000	Notes payable (to banks)	10,000
		Accrued wages, 1,400 @ $500	700
		U.S. taxes	1,000
		State and local taxes	300
		Current liabilities	$32,000
		First mortgage	6,000
		Second mortgage	1,000
		Subordinated debentures[a]	8,000
		Total long-term debt	$15,000
		Preferred stock	2,000
		Common stock	26,000
		Paid-in capital	4,000
		Retained earnings	11,000
		Total equity	$43,000
Total assets	$90,000	Total liabilities and equity	$90,000

[a] Subordinated to $10 million of notes payable to banks.

NOTE: Unfunded pension liabilities are $15 million; this is not reported on the balance sheet.

The allocation of available funds is shown in Table 8B-2. The holders of the first mortgage bonds receive the $5 million of net proceeds from the sale of fixed assets. Note that a $1 million unsatisfied claim of the first mortgage holders remains; this claim is added to those of the other general creditors. Next come the fees and expenses of administration, which are typically about 20 percent of gross proceeds; in this example, they are assumed to be $6 million. Next in priority are wages due workers, which total $700,000; taxes due, which amount to $1.3 million; and unfunded pension liabilities of up to 30 percent of the common plus preferred equity, or $12.9 million. Thus far, the total of claims paid from the $46.95 million is $25.90 million, leaving $21.05 million for the general creditors.

The claims of the general creditors total $42.1 million. Since $21.05 million is available, claimants will initially be allocated 50 percent of their claims, as shown in Column 2 of Table 8B-2, before the subordination adjustment. This adjustment requires that the holders of subordinated debentures turn over to the holders of notes payable all amounts received until the notes are satisfied. In this situation, the claim of the notes payable is $10 million, but only $5 million is available; the deficiency is therefore $5 million. After transfer of $4 million from the subordinated debentures, there remains a deficiency of $1 million on the notes. This amount will remain unsatisfied.

Note that 92 percent of the first mortgage, 90 percent of the notes payable, and 93 percent of the unfunded pension fund claims are satisfied, whereas a maximum of 50 percent of unsecured claims will be satisfied. These figures illustrate

DISTRIBUTION OF PROCEEDS ON LIQUIDATION

1. Proceeds from sale of assets		$46,950,000
2. First mortgage, paid from sale of fixed assets	$ 5,000,000	
3. Fees and expenses of administration of bankruptcy	6,000,000	
4. Wages due workers earned within three months prior to filing of bankruptcy petition	700,000	
5. Taxes	1,300,000	
6. Unfunded pension liabilities[a]	12,900,000	25,900,000
7. Available to general creditors		$21,050,000

DISTRIBUTION TO GENERAL CREDITORS

CLAIMS OF GENERAL CREDITORS	CLAIM[b] (1)	APPLICATION OF 50 PERCENT[c] (2)	AFTER SUBORDINATION ADJUSTMENT[d] (3)	PERCENTAGE OF ORIGINAL CLAIMS RECEIVED[e] (4)
Unsatisfied portion of first mortgage	$ 1,000,000	$ 500,000	$ 500,000	92%
Unsatisfied portion of second mortgage	1,000,000	500,000	500,000	50
Notes payable	10,000,000	5,000,000	9,000,000	90
Accounts payable	20,000,000	10,000,000	10,000,000	50
Subordinated debentures	8,000,000	4,000,000	0	0
Pension plan	2,100,000	1,050,000	1,050,000	93
	$42,100,000	$21,050,000	$21,050,000	

[a] Unfunded pension liabilities are $15,000,000, and common and preferred equity total $43,000,000. Unfunded pension liabilities have a prior claim of up to 30 percent of the total equity, or $12,900,000, with the remainder, $2,100,000, being treated as a general creditor claim.

[b] Column 1 is the claim of each class of general creditor. Total claims equal $42.1 million.

[c] From Line 7 in the upper section of the table, we see that $21.05 million is available for general creditors. This sum, divided by the $42.1 million of claims, indicates that general creditors will initially receive 50 percent of their claims; this is shown in Column 2.

[d] The debentures are subordinated to the notes payable, so $4 million is reallocated from debentures to notes payable in Column 3.

[e] Column 4 shows the results of dividing the amount in Column 3 by the original claim amount given in Column 1, except for the first mortgage, for which the $5 million received from the sale of fixed assets is included, and the pension plan, for which the $12.9 million is included.

the usefulness of the subordination provision to the security to which the subordination is made. Because no other funds remain, the claims of the holders of preferred and common stock are completely wiped out. Studies of bankruptcy liquidations indicate that unsecured creditors receive, on the average, about 15 cents on the dollar, whereas common stockholders generally receive nothing.

SOCIAL ISSUES IN BANKRUPTCY PROCEEDINGS

An interesting social issue arose in connection with bankruptcy during the 1980s — the role of bankruptcy in settling labor disputes and product liability suits. Normally, bankruptcy proceedings originate after a company has become so financially weak that it cannot meet its current obligations. However, provisions in the Bankruptcy Act permit a company to file for protection under Chapter 11 if *financial forecasts* indicate that a continuation of business under current conditions will lead to insolvency. These provisions were applied by Frank Lorenzo, the principal stockholder of Continental Airlines, who demonstrated that if Continental continued to operate under its then-current union contract, it would become insolvent in a matter of months. The company then filed a plan of reorganization that included major changes in its union contract. The court found for Continental and allowed the company to abrogate its contract. It then reorganized as a nonunion carrier, and that reorganization turned the company from a money loser into a money maker. (However, in 1990, Continental's financial situation reversed again, partly due to rising fuel prices, and the company once again filed for bankruptcy.) Under pressure from labor unions, Congress changed the bankruptcy laws after the Continental affair to make it more difficult to use the laws to break union contracts.

The bankruptcy laws have also been used to bring about settlements in major product liability suits, the Manville asbestos case being the first, followed by the Dalkon Shield case. In both instances, the companies were being bombarded by literally thousands of lawsuits, and the very existence of such huge contingent liabilities made continued operations virtually impossible. Further, in both cases, it was relatively easy to prove (1) that if the plaintiffs won, the companies would be unable to pay off the full amounts claimed, (2) that a larger amount of funds would be available if the companies continued to operate than if they were liquidated, (3) that continued operations were possible only if the suits were brought to a conclusion, and (4) that a timely resolution of all the suits was impossible because of the number of suits and the different positions taken by different parties. At any rate, the bankruptcy statutes were used to consolidate all the suits and to reach a settlement under which all the plaintiffs obtained more money than they otherwise would have gotten, and the companies were able to stay in business. The stockholders did not do very well because most of the companies' future cash flows were assigned to the plaintiffs, but, even so, the stockholders probably came out better than they would have if the individual suits had been carried through the jury system to a conclusion.

In the Johns-Manville Corporation case, the decision to reorganize was heavily influenced by the prospect of an imminent series of lawsuits. Johns-Manville, a profitable building supplier, faced increasing liabilities resulting from the manufacture of asbestos. When thousands of its employees and consumers were found to be exposed, Johns-Manville filed for Chapter 11 bankruptcy protection and set up a trust fund for the victims as part of its reorganization plan. Present and future claims for exposure were to be paid out of this fund. However, it was later determined that the trust fund was significantly underfunded due to more and larger claims than had been originally estimated.

We have no opinion about the use of the bankruptcy laws to settle social issues such as labor disputes and product liability suits. However, the examples do illustrate how financial projections can be used to demonstrate the effects of different legal decisions. Financial analysis is being used to an increasing extent in various types of legal work, from antitrust cases to suits against stockbrokers by disgruntled customers, and this trend is likely to continue.

PROBLEMS

8B-1
Bankruptcy distributions

The H. Quigley Marble Company has the following balance sheet:

Current assets	$5,040	Accounts payable	$1,080
Fixed assets	2,700	Notes payable (to bank)	540
		Accrued taxes	180
		Accrued wages	180
		Total current liabilities	$1,980
		First mortgage bonds	900
		Second mortgage bonds	900
		Total mortgage bonds	$1,800
		Subordinated debentures	1,080
		Total debt	$4,860
		Preferred stock	360
		Common stock	2,520
Total assets	$7,740	Total liabilities and equity	$7,740

The debentures are subordinated only to the notes payable. Suppose the company goes bankrupt and is liquidated, with $1,800 being received from the sale of the fixed assets, which were pledged as security for the first and second mortgage bonds, and $2,880 received from the sale of current assets. The trustee's costs total $480. How much will each class of investors receive?

8B-2
Bankruptcy distributions

Southwestern Wear Inc. has the following balance sheet:

Current assets	$1,875,000	Accounts payable	$ 375,000
Fixed assets	1,875,000	Notes payable	750,000
		Subordinated debentures	750,000
		Total debt	$1,875,000
		Common equity	1,875,000
Total assets	$3,750,000	Total liabilities and equity	$3,750,000

The trustee's costs total $281,250, and the firm has no accrued taxes or wages. The debentures are subordinated only to the notes payable. If the firm goes bankrupt, how much will each class of investors receive under each of the following conditions?

a. A total of $2.5 million is received from sale of the assets.
b. A total of $1.875 million is received from sale of the assets.

CHAPTER 9

Stocks and Their Valuation

SOURCE: Accessed January 11, 2000. © 2000 America Online, Inc. www.corp.aol.com/index.html

AOL TAKES INVESTORS ON AN EXCITING ROLLER COASTER RIDE

AMERICA ONLINE

A $10,000 investment in America Online (AOL) when it went public in 1992 would have grown to $10 million by November 1999! However, AOL's stock price has steadily declined throughout 2000 and early 2001. These ups and downs suggest that AOL's road to riches has been anything but smooth—its shareholders have had an exciting and often nerve-wracking roller coaster ride. At the beginning of 2001, AOL's investors are unsure whether the stock's long-run trend will be up or down but, if history is any guide, the movement will be swift, uneven, and large.

By virtually any measure, the stock market performed extraordinarily well up through 1999. From slightly less than 4,000 in early 1995, the Dow surged past 11,000 in 1999. To put this remarkable 7,000-point rise in perspective, consider that the Dow first reached 1,000 in 1965, then took another 22 years to hit 2,000, then four more years to reach 3,000, and another four to get to 4,000 (in 1995). Then, in just five years, it topped 11,000. Thus, in this five-year period investors made almost twice as much in the stock market as they made in the previous 70 years!

The recent bull market made it possible for many people to take early retirement, buy expensive homes, and afford large expenditures such as college tuition. Encouraged by this performance, more and more investors flocked to the market, and today more than 79 million Americans own stock. Moreover, a rising stock market makes it easier and cheaper for corporations to raise equity capital, which facilitates continued economic growth.

During this upswing some observers were concerned that many investors did not realize just how risky the stock market is. There is no guarantee that the market will continue to rise, and even in bull markets some stocks crash and burn. Indeed, after nearing the 12,000 mark in early 2000, the Dow declined later in the year to below 10,000 in the wake of concerns about corporate earnings, rising oil prices, and a weakening European currency. The drop in the once high-flying Nasdaq has been even more dramatic. After topping 5,000 in March 2000, the Nasdaq Composite Index fell more than 50 percent in the following year. By April 2001, the index stood around 1,700. While some analysts believe that these events suggest that the long bull market has finally run its course, others believe that these declines are only bumps in the road and that the long-run trend is still positive.

Note too that while all boats may rise with the tide, the same does not hold for the stock market — regardless of the trend, some individual stocks make huge gains while others suffer substantial losses. For example, during 2000, CIENA Corporation's stock rose from $28.75 to $81.38, but during this same period Priceline.com lost 97 percent of its value.

While it is difficult to predict prices, we are not completely in the dark when it comes to valuing stocks. After studying this chapter, you should have a reasonably good understanding of the factors that influence stock prices. With that knowledge — and a little luck — you may be able to find the next AOL or CIENA, and avoid being victimized by "irrational exuberance." ■

In Chapter 8 we examined bonds. We now turn to common and preferred stock, beginning with some important background material that helps establish a framework for valuing these securities.

While it is generally easy to predict the cash flows received from bonds, forecasting the cash flows on common stocks is much more difficult. However, two fairly straightforward models can be used to help estimate the "true," or intrinsic, value of a common stock: (1) the dividend growth model and (2) the total corporate value model. A stock should be bought if its intrinsic value exceeds its market price but sold if its price exceeds the intrinsic value.

The concepts and models developed here will also be used when we estimate the cost of capital in Chapter 10. In subsequent chapters, we demonstrate how the cost of capital is used to help make many important decisions, especially the decision to invest or not invest in new assets. Consequently, it is critically important that you understand the basics of stock valuation. ■

LEGAL RIGHTS AND PRIVILEGES OF COMMON STOCKHOLDERS

The common stockholders are the *owners* of a corporation, and as such they have certain rights and privileges as discussed in this section.

CONTROL OF THE FIRM

Its common stockholders have the right to elect a firm's directors, who, in turn, elect the officers who manage the business. In a small firm, the major stockholder typically assumes the positions of president and chairperson of the board of directors. In a large, publicly owned firm, the managers typically have some stock, but their personal holdings are generally insufficient to give them voting control. Thus, the managements of most publicly owned firms can be removed by the stockholders if the management team is not effective.

State and federal laws stipulate how stockholder control is to be exercised. First, corporations must hold an election of directors periodically, usually once a year, with the vote taken at the annual meeting. Frequently, one-third of the directors are elected each year for a three-year term. Each share of stock has one vote; thus, the owner of 1,000 shares has 1,000 votes for each director.[1] Stockholders can appear at the annual meeting and vote in person, but typically they transfer their right to vote to a second party by means of a **proxy.** Management always solicits stockholders' proxies and usually gets them. However, if earnings are poor and stockholders are dissatisfied, an outside group may solicit the proxies in an effort to overthrow management and take control of the business. This is known as a **proxy fight.**

The question of control has become a central issue in finance in recent years. The frequency of proxy fights has increased, as have attempts by one corporation to take over another by purchasing a majority of the outstanding stock. These actions are called **takeovers.** Some well-known examples of takeover battles include KKR's acquisition of RJR Nabisco, Chevron's acquisition of Gulf Oil, and the QVC/Viacom fight to take over Paramount.

Managers who do not have majority control (more than 50 percent of their firms' stock) are very much concerned about proxy fights and takeovers, and many of them are attempting to get stockholder approval for changes in their corporate charters that would make takeovers more difficult. For example, a number of companies have gotten their stockholders to agree (1) to elect only one-third of the directors each year (rather than electing all directors each year), (2) to require 75 percent of the stockholders (rather than 50 percent) to approve a merger, and (3) to vote in a "poison pill" provision that would allow the stockholders of a firm that is taken over by another firm to buy shares in the second firm at a reduced price. The poison pill makes the acquisition unattractive and, thus, wards off hostile takeover attempts. Managements seeking such changes generally cite a fear that the firm will be picked up at a bargain price, but it often appears that managers' concerns about their own positions might be an even more important consideration.

Management's moves to make takeovers more difficult have been countered by stockholders, especially large institutional stockholders, who do not want to see barriers erected to protect incompetent managers. To illustrate, the California Public Employees Retirement System (Calpers), which is one of the largest institutional investors, announced plans in early 1994 to conduct a proxy fight with several corporations whose financial performances were poor in Calpers' judgment. Calpers wants companies to give outside (nonmanagement) directors more clout and to force managers to be more responsive to stockholder complaints.

Prior to 1993, SEC rules prohibited large investors such as Calpers from getting together to force corporate managers to institute policy changes. However, the SEC changed its rules in 1993, and now large investors can work together to force management changes. This ruling has served to keep managers focused on stockholder concerns, which means the maximization of stock prices.

---

[1] In the situation described, a 1,000-share stockholder could cast 1,000 votes for each of three directors if there were three contested seats on the board. An alternative procedure that may be prescribed in the corporate charter calls for *cumulative voting*. Here the 1,000-share stockholder would get 3,000 votes if there were three vacancies, and he or she could cast all of them for one director. Cumulative voting helps small groups to get representation on the board.

THE PREEMPTIVE RIGHT

Preemptive Right
A provision in the corporate charter or bylaws that gives common stockholders the right to purchase on a pro rata basis new issues of common stock (or convertible securities).

Common stockholders often have the right, called the **preemptive right,** to purchase any additional shares sold by the firm. In some states, the preemptive right is automatically included in every corporate charter; in others, it is necessary to insert it specifically into the charter.

The purpose of the preemptive right is twofold. First, it enables current stockholders to maintain control. If it were not for this safeguard, the management of a corporation could issue a large number of additional shares and purchase these shares itself. Management could thereby seize control of the corporation and frustrate the will of the current stockholders.

The second, and by far the more important, reason for the preemptive right is to protect stockholders against a dilution of value. For example, suppose 1,000 shares of common stock, each with a price of $100, were outstanding, making the total market value of the firm $100,000. If an additional 1,000 shares were sold at $50 a share, or for $50,000, this would raise the total market value to $150,000. When total market value is divided by new total shares outstanding, a value of $75 a share is obtained. The old stockholders thus lose $25 per share, and the new stockholders have an instant profit of $25 per share. Thus, selling common stock at a price below the market value would dilute its price and transfer wealth from the present stockholders to those who were allowed to purchase the new shares. The preemptive right prevents such occurrences.

SELF-TEST QUESTIONS

Identify some actions that companies have taken to make takeovers more difficult.

What are the two primary reasons for the existence of the preemptive right?

TYPES OF COMMON STOCK

Classified Stock
Common stock that is given a special designation, such as Class A, Class B, and so forth, to meet special needs of the company.

Although most firms have only one type of common stock, in some instances **classified stock** is used to meet the special needs of the company. Generally, when special classifications are used, one type is designated *Class A*, another *Class B*, and so on. Small, new companies seeking funds from outside sources frequently use different types of common stock. For example, when Genetic Concepts went public recently, its Class A stock was sold to the public and paid a dividend, but this stock had no voting rights for five years. Its Class B stock, which was retained by the organizers of the company, had full voting rights for five years, but the legal terms stated that dividends could not be paid on the Class B stock until the company had established its earning power by building up retained earnings to a designated level. The use of classified stock thus enabled the public to take a position in a conservatively financed growth company without sacrificing income, while the founders retained absolute control during the crucial early stages of the firm's development. At the same time, outside in-

Founders' Shares
Stock owned by the firm's
founders that has sole voting
rights but restricted dividends for
a specified number of years.

vestors were protected against excessive withdrawals of funds by the original owners. As is often the case in such situations, the Class B stock was called **founders' shares.**

Note that "Class A," "Class B," and so on, have no standard meanings. Most firms have no classified shares, but a firm that does could designate its Class B shares as founders' shares and its Class A shares as those sold to the public, while another could reverse these designations. Still other firms could use stock classifications for entirely different purposes. For example, when General Motors acquired Hughes Aircraft for $5 billion, it paid in part with a new Class H common, GMH, which had limited voting rights and whose dividends are tied to Hughes's performance as a GM subsidiary. The reasons for the new stock were reported to be (1) that GM wanted to limit voting privileges on the new classified stock because of management's concern about a possible takeover and (2) that Hughes employees wanted to be rewarded more directly on Hughes's own performance than would have been possible through regular GM stock.

GM's deal posed a problem for the NYSE, which had a rule against listing a company's common stock if the company had any nonvoting common stock outstanding. GM made it clear that it was willing to delist if the NYSE did not change its rules. The NYSE concluded that such arrangements as GM had made were logical and were likely to be made by other companies in the future, so it changed its rules to accommodate GM. In reality, though, the NYSE had little choice. In recent years, the Nasdaq market has proven that it can provide a deep, liquid market for common stocks, and the defection of GM would have hurt the NYSE much more than GM.

SELF-TEST QUESTION

What are some reasons why a company might use classified stock?

THE MARKET FOR COMMON STOCK

Closely Held Corporation
A corporation that is owned by a
few individuals who are typically
associated with the firm's
management.

Publicly Owned Corporation
A corporation that is owned by a
relatively large number of
individuals who are not actively
involved in its management.

Some companies are so small that their common stocks are not actively traded; they are owned by only a few people, usually the companies' managers. Such firms are said to be *privately owned*, or **closely held, corporations,** and their stock is called *closely held stock.* In contrast, the stocks of most larger companies are owned by a large number of investors, most of whom are not active in management. Such companies are called **publicly owned corporations,** and their stock is called *publicly held stock.*

As we saw in Chapter 5, the stocks of smaller publicly owned firms are not listed on an exchange; they trade in the over-the-counter (OTC) market, and the companies and their stocks are said to be *unlisted.* However, larger publicly owned companies generally apply for listing on physical location exchanges, and they and their stocks are said to be *listed.* Many companies are first listed on Nasdaq or on a regional exchange, such as the Pacific Coast or Midwest exchanges. Once they become large enough to be listed on the "Big Board," many, but by no means all, choose to move to the NYSE. The largest company in the world in terms of market value, Microsoft, trades on the Nasdaq market, as do most other high-tech firms.

A recent study found that institutional investors owned about 46 percent of all publicly held common stocks. Included are pension plans (26 percent), mutual funds (10 percent), foreign investors (6 percent), insurance companies (3 percent), and brokerage firms (1 percent). These institutions buy and sell relatively actively, however, so they account for about 75 percent of all transactions. Thus, institutional investors have a heavy influence on the prices of individual stocks.

TYPES OF STOCK MARKET TRANSACTIONS

We can classify stock market transactions into three distinct types:

Secondary Market
The market in which "used" stocks are traded after they have been issued by corporations.

Primary Market
The market in which firms issue new securities to raise corporate capital.

Going Public
The act of selling stock to the public at large by a closely held corporation or its principal stockholders.

Initial Public Offering (IPO) Market
The market for stocks of companies that are in the process of going public.

1. *Trading in the outstanding shares of established, publicly owned companies: the secondary market.* Allied Food Products, the company we analyzed in earlier chapters, has 50 million shares of stock outstanding. If the owner of 100 shares sells his or her stock, the trade is said to have occurred in the **secondary market.** Thus, the market for outstanding shares, or *used shares*, is the secondary market. The company receives no new money when sales occur in this market.

2. *Additional shares sold by established, publicly owned companies: the primary market.* If Allied decides to sell (or issue) an additional 1 million shares to raise new equity capital, this transaction is said to occur in the **primary market.**[2]

3. *Initial public offerings by privately held firms: the IPO market.* Several years ago, the Coors Brewing Company, which was owned by the Coors family at the time, decided to sell some stock to raise capital needed for a major expansion program.[3] This type of transaction is called **going public** — whenever stock in a closely held corporation is offered to the public for the first time, the company is said to be going public. The market for stock that is just being offered to the public is called the **initial public offering (IPO) market.**

IPOs have received a lot of attention in recent years, primarily because a number of "hot" issues have realized spectacular gains — often in the first few minutes of trading. Consider the IPO of Red Hat, Inc., the open-source provider of software products and services. The company's underwriters set an offering price of $14 per share. However, because of intense demand for the issue, the stock's price rose more than 270 percent the first day of trading.

Table 9-1 lists the largest, the best performing, and the worst performing IPOs of 2000, and it shows how they performed from their offering dates through year-end 2000. As the table shows, not all IPOs are as well received as was Red Hat. Moreover, even if you are able to identify a

---

[2] Allied has 60 million shares authorized but only 50 million outstanding; thus, it has 10 million authorized but unissued shares. If it had no authorized but unissued shares, management could increase the authorized shares by obtaining stockholders' approval, which would generally be granted without any arguments.

[3] The stock Coors offered to the public was designated Class B, and it was nonvoting. The Coors family retained the founders' shares, called Class A stock, which carried full voting privileges. The company was large enough to obtain an NYSE listing, but at that time the Exchange had a requirement that listed common stocks must have full voting rights, which precluded Coors from obtaining an NYSE listing.

INDUSTRY PRACTICE

MARTHA STEWART TAKES ON THE WWF

During the week of October 18, 1999, both Martha Stewart Living Omnimedia Inc. and the World Wrestling Federation (WWF) went public in IPOs. This created a lot of public interest, and it led to media reports comparing the two companies. Both deals attracted strong investor demand, and both were well received. In its first day of trading, WWF's stock closed above $25, an increase of nearly 49 percent above its $17 offering price. Martha Stewart did even better — it closed a little above $37, which was 105 percent above its $18 offering price. This performance led CBS MarketWatch reporter Steve Gelsi to write an online report entitled, "Martha Bodyslams the WWF!"

Both stocks generated a lot of interest, but when the hype died down, astute investors recognized that both stocks have risk. Indeed, more than one year later, WWF had declined to around $15 per share, while Martha Stewart had fallen below $20 a share. As the accompanying chart shows, the performance of the two stocks has been quite similar, but both stocks have performed considerably worse than the overall market. Despite these setbacks, both stocks continue to have their devoted set of investors, which means that this is one battle that is far from over.

SOURCE: Steve Gelsi, "Martha Bodyslams the WWF," http://cbs.marketwatch.com, October 19, 1999 and http://finance.yahoo.com, February 26, 2001.

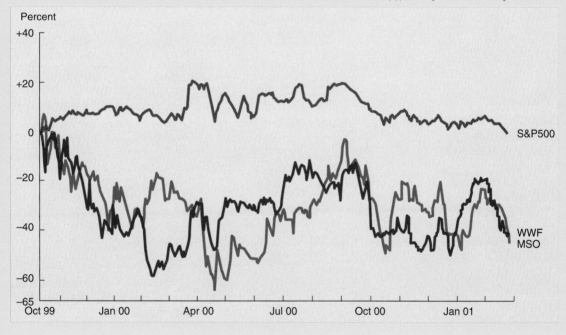

"hot" issue, it is often difficult to purchase shares in the initial offering. These deals are generally *oversubscribed*, which means that the demand for shares at the offering price exceeds the number of shares issued. In such instances, investment bankers favor large institutional investors (who are their best customers), and small investors find it hard, if not impossible, to get in on the ground floor. They can buy the stock in the after-market, but evidence suggests that if you do not get in on the ground floor, the average IPO underperforms the overall market over the long run.[4]

Indeed, the subsequent performance of Red Hat illustrates the risks that arise when investing in new issues. After its dramatic first day run-up,

---

[4] See Jay R. Ritter, "The Long-Run Performance of Initial Public Offerings," *Journal of Finance*, March 1991, Vol. 46, No. 1, 3–27.

TABLE 9-1

Initial Public Offerings in 2000

ISSUER	ISSUE DATE	OFFER PRICE	U.S. PROCEEDS (BILLIONS)	PERCENT CHANGE FROM OFFER	
				FIRST DAY	12/31/00
THE BIGGEST					
AT&T Wireless Group	4/27/00	$29.50	$9.03	+7.8%	−41.3%
Infineon Technologies	3/13/00	33.92	2.72	+126.5	+6.1
Metropolitan Life Insurance	4/5/00	14.25	2.50	+7.9	+145.6
TyCom	7/27/00	32.00	2.88	+15.6	−30.1
Genuity	6/28/00	11.00	1.91	−14.5	−54.0
China Unicom	6/21/00	19.99	1.57	+10.0	−26.3
John Hancock Financial Svcs	1/27/00	17.00	1.47	+3.7	+121.3
Southern Energy (Southern Co)	9/27/00	22.00	1.28	+31.8	+28.7
Turkcell	7/11/00	17.60	1.18	+0.1	−60.2
Corvis	7/28/00	36.00	1.14	+135.3	−33.9

ISSUER	ISSUE DATE	OFFER PRICE	U.S. PROCEEDS (MILLIONS)	PERCENT CHANGE FROM OFFER	
				FIRST DAY	12/31/00
THE BEST PERFORMERS					
Embarcadero Technologies	4/20/00	$10.00	$ 42.0	+60.0%	+350.0%
Krispy Kreme Doughnuts	4/5/00	21.00	63.0	+82.7	+295.2
First Horizon Pharmaceutical	5/31/00	8.00	30.4	+3.1	+284.4
Sonus Networks	5/25/00	7.67	115.0	+119.6	+229.3
Sun Life Finl Svcs of Canada	3/23/00	8.50	305.2	+10.3	+213.2
Stanford Microdevices	5/25/00	12.00	48.0	+28.1	+200.0
Praecis Pharmaceuticals	4/27/00	10.00	80.0	+10.0	+192.5
Ulticom	4/5/00	13.00	55.3	+53.9	+171.2
Community Health Systems	6/9/00	13.00	243.8	+5.3	+169.2
webMethods	2/11/00	35.00	165.0	+507.5	+167.0

ISSUER	ISSUE DATE	OFFER PRICE	U.S. PROCEEDS (MILLIONS)	PERCENT CHANGE FROM OFFER DATE	
				FIRST DAY	12/31/00
THE WORST PERFORMERS					
Pets.com	2/11/00	$11.00	$ 66.0	−34.1%	−99.1%
HealthGate Data	1/26/00	11.00	41.3	+6.8	−98.3
VarsityBooks.com	2/15/00	10.00	40.8	−1.3	−98.1
ImproveNet	3/16/00	16.00	44.2	−11.7	−97.7
Asiacontent.com	4/12/00	14.00	70.0	−21.4	−97.3
Uproar	3/17/00	33.88	84.7	−21.0	−97.1
Netpliance	3/17/00	18.00	144.0	+22.6	−97.1
Opus360	4/7/00	10.00	77.0	+25.0	−96.9
Savvis Communications	2/15/00	24.00	408.0	+0.0	−96.4
BusyBox.com	6/28/00	5.00	12.5	+11.3	−96.2

SOURCE: Kara Scannell, "IPO Rocket Lands as Investors Prefer Profits to Pipe Dreams," *The Wall Street Journal,* January 2, 2001, R6.

Red Hat's stock closed just above $54 per share. Demand for the stock continued to surge, and the stock's price reached a high of just over $300 in December 1999. Soon afterward, the company announced a two-for-one stock split. The split effectively cut the stock's price in half but it doubled the number of shares held by each shareholder. After adjusting for the split, the stock's price stood at $132 per share in early January 2000. However, from that point forward, Red Hat's stock has tumbled. At year-end 2000, the stock was trading below $14 per share, which is equivalent to $28 per share before the split.

Finally, it is important to recognize that firms can go public without raising any additional capital. For example, the Ford Motor Company was once owned exclusively by the Ford family. When Henry Ford died, he left a substantial part of his stock to the Ford Foundation. When the Foundation later sold some of this stock to the general public, the Ford Motor Company went public, even though the company raised no capital in the transaction.

SELF-TEST QUESTIONS

Differentiate between a closely held corporation and a publicly owned corporation.

Differentiate between a listed stock and an unlisted stock.

Differentiate between primary and secondary markets.

What is an IPO?

COMMON STOCK VALUATION

Common stock represents an ownership interest in a corporation, but to the typical investor, a share of common stock is simply a piece of paper characterized by two features:

1. It entitles its owner to dividends, but only if the company has earnings out of which dividends can be paid, and only if management chooses to pay dividends rather than retaining and reinvesting all the earnings. Whereas a bond contains a *promise* to pay interest, common stock provides no such promise — if you own a stock, you may *expect* a dividend, but your expectations may not in fact be met. To illustrate, Long Island Lighting Company (LILCO) had paid dividends on its common stock for more than 50 years, and people expected those dividends to continue. However, when the company encountered severe problems a few years ago, it stopped paying dividends. Note, though, that LILCO continued to pay interest on its bonds; if it had not, then it would have been declared bankrupt, and the bondholders could potentially have taken over the company.

2. Stock can be sold at some future date, hopefully at a price greater than the purchase price. If the stock is actually sold at a price above its purchase price, the investor will receive a *capital gain*. Generally, at the time people buy common stocks, they do expect to receive capital gains;

otherwise, they would not purchase the stocks. However, after the fact, one can end up with capital losses rather than capital gains. LILCO's stock price dropped from $17.50 to $3.75 in one year, so the *expected* capital gain on that stock turned out to be a huge *actual* capital loss.

DEFINITIONS OF TERMS USED IN STOCK VALUATION MODELS

Common stocks provide an expected future cash flow stream, and a stock's value is found in the same manner as the values of other financial assets — namely, as the present value of the expected future cash flow stream. The expected cash flows consist of two elements: (1) the dividends expected in each year and (2) the price investors expect to receive when they sell the stock. The expected final stock price includes the return of the original investment plus an expected capital gain.

We saw in Chapter 1 that managers seek to maximize the values of their firms' stocks. A manager's actions affect both the stream of income to investors and the riskiness of that stream. Therefore, managers need to know how alternative actions are likely to affect stock prices. At this point we develop some models to help show how the value of a share of stock is determined. We begin by defining the following terms:

D_t = dividend the stockholder *expects* to receive at the end of Year t. D_0 is the most recent dividend, which has already been paid; D_1 is the first dividend expected, and it will be paid at the end of this year; D_2 is the dividend expected at the end of two years; and so forth. D_1 represents the first cash flow a new purchaser of the stock will receive. Note that D_0, the dividend that has just been paid, is known with certainty. However, all future dividends are expected values, so the estimate of D_t may differ among investors.[5]

Market Price, P_0
The price at which a stock sells in the market.

P_0 = actual **market price** of the stock today.
$\hat{P}_t$ = expected price of the stock at the end of each Year t (pronounced "P hat t"). $\hat{P}_0$ is the **intrinsic,** or *theoretical,* **value** of the stock today as seen by the particular investor doing the analysis; $\hat{P}_1$ is the price expected at the end of one year; and so on. Note that $\hat{P}_0$ is the intrinsic value of the stock today based on a particular investor's estimate of the stock's expected dividend stream and the riskiness of that stream. Hence, whereas the market price P_0 is fixed and is identical for all investors, $\hat{P}_0$ could differ among investors depending on how optimistic they are regarding the

Intrinsic Value, $\hat{P}_0$
The value of an asset that, in the mind of a particular investor, is justified by the facts; $\hat{P}_0$ may be different from the asset's current market price.

---

[5] Stocks generally pay dividends quarterly, so theoretically we should evaluate them on a quarterly basis. However, in stock valuation, most analysts work on an annual basis because the data generally are not precise enough to warrant refinement to a quarterly model. For additional information on the quarterly model, see Charles M. Linke and J. Kenton Zumwalt, "Estimation Biases in Discounted Cash Flow Analysis of Equity Capital Cost in Rate Regulation," *Financial Management*, Autumn 1984, 15–21.

company. The caret, or "hat," is used to indicate that $\hat{P}_t$ is an estimated value. $\hat{P}_0$, the individual investor's estimate of the intrinsic value today, could be above or below P_0, the current stock price, but an investor would buy the stock only if his or her estimate of $\hat{P}_0$ were equal to or greater than P_0.

Since there are many investors in the market, there can be many values for $\hat{P}_0$. However, we can think of a group of "average," or "marginal," investors whose actions actually determine the market price. For these marginal investors, P_0 must equal $\hat{P}_0$; otherwise, a disequilibrium would exist, and buying and selling in the market would change P_0 until $P_0 = \hat{P}_0$ for the marginal investor.

Growth Rate, g
The expected rate of growth in dividends per share.

$g =$ expected **growth rate** in dividends as predicted by a marginal investor. If dividends are expected to grow at a constant rate, g is also equal to the expected rate of growth in earnings and in the stock's price. Different investors may use different g's to evaluate a firm's stock, but the market price, P_0, is set on the basis of the g estimated by marginal investors.

Required Rate of Return, k_s
The minimum rate of return on a common stock that a stockholder considers acceptable.

$k_s =$ minimum acceptable, or **required, rate of return** on the stock, considering both its riskiness and the returns available on other investments. Again, this term generally relates to marginal investors. The determinants of k_s include the real rate of return, expected inflation, and risk, as discussed in Chapter 6.

Expected Rate of Return, $\hat{k}_s$
The rate of return on a common stock that a stockholder expects to receive in the future.

$\hat{k}_s =$ **expected rate of return** that an investor who buys the stock expects to receive in the future. $\hat{k}_s$ (pronounced "k hat s") could be above or below k_s, but one would buy the stock only if $\hat{k}_s$ were equal to or greater than k_s.

Actual Realized Rate of Return, $\bar{k}_s$
The rate of return on a common stock actually received by stockholders in some past period. $\bar{k}_s$ may be greater or less than $\hat{k}_s$ and/or k_s.

$\bar{k}_s =$ **actual,** or **realized,** *after-the-fact* **rate of return,** pronounced "k bar s." You may *expect* to obtain a return of $\bar{k}_s = 15$ percent if you buy Exxon Mobil stock today, but if the market goes down, you may end up next year with an actual realized return that is much lower, perhaps even negative.

Dividend Yield
The expected dividend divided by the current price of a share of stock.

$D_1/P_0 =$ expected **dividend yield** on the stock during the coming year. If the stock is expected to pay a dividend of $D_1 = \$1$ during the next 12 months, and if its current price is $P_0 = \$10$, then the expected dividend yield is $\$1/\$10 = 0.10 = 10\%$.

Capital Gains Yield
The capital gain during a given year divided by the beginning price.

$\dfrac{\hat{P}_1 - P_0}{P_0} =$ expected **capital gains yield** on the stock during the coming year. If the stock sells for $\$10$ today, and if it is expected to rise to $\$10.50$ at the end of one year, then the expected capital gain is $\hat{P}_1 - P_0 = \$10.50 - \$10.00 = \$0.50$, and the expected capital gains yield is $\$0.50/\$10 = 0.05 = 5\%$.

Expected Total Return
The sum of the expected dividend yield and the expected capital gains yield.

Expected total return $= \hat{k}_s =$ expected dividend yield (D_1/P_0) plus expected capital gains yield $[(\hat{P}_1 - P_0)/P_0]$. In our example, the **expected total return** $= \hat{k}_s = 10\% + 5\% = 15\%$.

EXPECTED DIVIDENDS AS THE BASIS FOR STOCK VALUES

In our discussion of bonds, we found the value of a bond as the present value of interest payments over the life of the bond plus the present value of the bond's maturity (or par) value:

$$V_B = \frac{INT}{(1 + k_d)^1} + \frac{INT}{(1 + k_d)^2} + \cdots + \frac{INT}{(1 + k_d)^N} + \frac{M}{(1 + k_d)^N}.$$

Stock prices are likewise determined as the present value of a stream of cash flows, and the basic stock valuation equation is similar to the bond valuation equation. What are the cash flows that corporations provide to their stockholders? First, think of yourself as an investor who buys a stock with the intention of holding it (in your family) forever. In this case, all that you (and your heirs) will receive is a stream of dividends, and the value of the stock today is calculated as the present value of an infinite stream of dividends:

$$\text{Value of stock} = \hat{P}_0 = \text{PV of expected future dividends}$$

$$= \frac{D_1}{(1 + k_s)^1} + \frac{D_2}{(1 + k_s)^2} + \cdots + \frac{D_\infty}{(1 + k_s)^\infty}$$

$$= \sum_{t=1}^{\infty} \frac{D_t}{(1 + k_s)^t}. \tag{9-1}$$

What about the more typical case, where you expect to hold the stock for a finite period and then sell it — what will be the value of $\hat{P}_0$ in this case? Unless the company is likely to be liquidated or sold and thus to disappear, *the value of the stock is again determined by Equation 9-1*. To see this, recognize that for any individual investor, the expected cash flows consist of expected dividends plus the expected sale price of the stock. However, the sale price the current investor receives will depend on the dividends some future investor expects. Therefore, for all present and future investors in total, expected cash flows must be based on expected future dividends. Put another way, unless a firm is liquidated or sold to another concern, the cash flows it provides to its stockholders will consist only of a stream of dividends; therefore, the value of a share of its stock must be established as the present value of that expected dividend stream.

The general validity of Equation 9-1 can also be confirmed by asking the following question: Suppose I buy a stock and expect to hold it for one year. I will receive dividends during the year plus the value $\hat{P}_1$ when I sell out at the end of the year. But what will determine the value of $\hat{P}_1$? The answer is that it will be determined as the present value of the dividends expected during Year 2 plus the stock price at the end of that year, which, in turn, will be determined as the present value of another set of future dividends and an even more distant stock price. This process can be continued ad infinitum, and the ultimate result is Equation 9-1.[6]

---

[6] We should note that investors periodically lose sight of the long-run nature of stocks as investments and forget that in order to sell a stock at a profit, one must find a buyer who will pay the higher price. If you analyze a stock's value in accordance with Equation 9-1, conclude that the stock's market price exceeds a reasonable value, and then buy the stock anyway, then you would be following the "bigger fool" theory of investment — you think that you may be a fool to buy the stock at its excessive price, but you also think that when you get ready to sell it, you can find someone who is an even bigger fool. The bigger fool theory was widely followed in the summer of 1987, just before the stock market lost more than one-third of its value in the October 1987 crash. Many people think it is back in vogue now, in 2001.

Explain the following statement: "Whereas a bond contains a promise to pay interest, a share of common stock typically provides an expectation of, but no promise of, dividends plus capital gains."

What are the two parts of most stocks' expected total return?

How does one calculate the capital gains yield and the dividend yield of a stock?

CONSTANT GROWTH STOCKS

Equation 9-1 is a generalized stock valuation model in the sense that the time pattern of D_t can be anything: D_t can be rising, falling, fluctuating randomly, or it can even be zero for several years and Equation 9-1 will still hold. With a computer spreadsheet we can easily use this equation to find a stock's intrinsic value for any pattern of dividends. In practice, the hard part is getting an accurate forecast of the future dividends.

In many cases, the stream of dividends is expected to grow at a constant rate. If this is the case, Equation 9-1 may be rewritten as follows:[7]

$$\hat{P}_0 = \frac{D_0(1 + g)^1}{(1 + k_s)^1} + \frac{D_0(1 + g)^2}{(1 + k_s)^2} + \cdots + \frac{D_0(1 + g)^{\infty}}{(1 + k_s)^{\infty}}$$

$$= \frac{D_0(1 + g)}{k_s - g} = \frac{D_1}{k_s - g}. \tag{9-2}$$

Constant Growth (Gordon) Model
Used to find the value of a constant growth stock.

The last term of Equation 9-2 is called the **constant growth model,** or the **Gordon model** after Myron J. Gordon, who did much to develop and popularize it.

ILLUSTRATION OF A CONSTANT GROWTH STOCK

Assume that Allied Food Products just paid a dividend of $1.15 (that is, $D_0 = \$1.15$). Its stock has a required rate of return, k_s, of 13.4 percent, and investors expect the dividend to grow at a constant 8 percent rate in the future. The estimated dividend one year hence would be $D_1 = \$1.15(1.08) = \$1.24$; D_2 would be $1.34; and the estimated dividend five years hence would be $1.69:

$$D_t = D_0(1 + g)^t = \$1.15(1.08)^5 = \$1.69.$$

We could use this procedure to estimate all future dividends, then use Equation 9-1 to determine the current stock value, $\hat{P}_0$. In other words, we could find

---

[7] The last term in Equation 9-2 is derived in the Web/CD Extension to Chapter 5 of Eugene F. Brigham and Phillip R. Daves, *Intermediate Financial Management*, 7th ed. (Fort Worth, TX: Harcourt College Publishers, 2002). In essence, Equation 9-2 is the sum of a geometric progression, and the final result is the solution value of the progression.

FIGURE 9-1

Present Values of Dividends of a Constant Growth Stock where $D_0 = \$1.15$, $g = 8\%$, $k_s = 13.4\%$

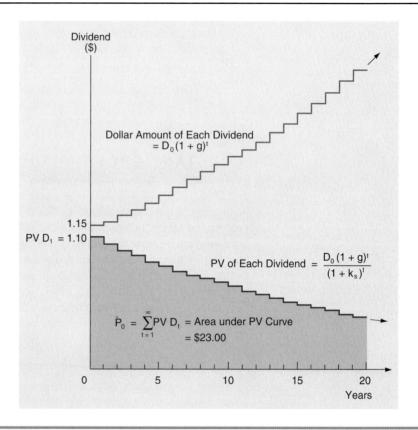

each expected future dividend, calculate its present value, and then sum all the present values to find the intrinsic value of the stock.

Such a process would be time consuming, but we can take a short cut—just insert the illustrative data into Equation 9-2 to find the stock's intrinsic value, $23:

$$\hat{P}_0 = \frac{\$1.15(1.08)}{0.134 - 0.08} = \frac{\$1.242}{0.054} = \$23.00.$$

Note that a necessary condition for the derivation of Equation 9-2 is that $k_s > g$. If the equation is used in situations where k_s is not greater than g, the results will be both wrong and meaningless.

The concept underlying the valuation process for a constant growth stock is graphed in Figure 9-1. Dividends are growing at the rate $g = 8\%$, but because $k_s > g$, the present value of each future dividend is declining. For example, the dividend in Year 1 is $D_1 = D_0(1 + g)^1 = \$1.15(1.08) = \$1.242$. However, the present value of this dividend, discounted at 13.4 percent, is $PV(D_1) = \$1.242/(1.134)^1 = \$1.095$. The dividend expected in Year 2 grows to $\$1.242(1.08) = \$1.341$, but the present value of this dividend falls to $1.043. Continuing, $D_3 = \$1.449$ and $PV(D_3) = \$0.993$, and so on. Thus, the expected dividends are growing, but the present value of each successive dividend is declining, because the dividend growth rate (8%) is less than the rate used for discounting the dividends to the present (13.4%).

If we summed the present values of each future dividend, this summation would be the value of the stock, $\hat{P}_0$. When g is a constant, this summation is equal to $D_1/(k_s - g)$, as shown in Equation 9-2. Therefore, if we extended the lower step function curve in Figure 9-1 on out to infinity and added up the present values of each future dividend, the summation would be identical to the value given by Equation 9-2, $23.00.

DIVIDEND AND EARNINGS GROWTH

Growth in dividends occurs primarily as a result of growth in *earnings per share (EPS)*. Earnings growth, in turn, results from a number of factors, including (1) inflation, (2) the amount of earnings the company retains and reinvests, and (3) the rate of return the company earns on its equity (ROE). Regarding inflation, if output (in units) is stable, but both sales prices and input costs rise at the inflation rate, then EPS will also grow at the inflation rate. Even without inflation, EPS will also grow as a result of the reinvestment, or plowback, of earnings. If the firm's earnings are not all paid out as dividends (that is, if some fraction of earnings is retained), the dollars of investment behind each share will rise over time, which should lead to growth in earnings and dividends.

Even though a stock's value is derived from expected dividends, this does not necessarily mean that corporations can increase their stock prices by simply raising the current dividend. Shareholders care about *all* dividends, both current and those expected in the future. Moreover, there is a trade-off between current dividends and future dividends. Companies that pay high current dividends necessarily retain and reinvest less of their earnings in the business, and that reduces future earnings and dividends. So, the issue is this: Do shareholders prefer higher current dividends at the cost of lower future dividends, the reverse, or are stockholders indifferent? As we will see in Chapter 14, there is no simple answer to this question. Shareholders prefer to have the company retain earnings, hence pay less current dividends, if it has highly profitable investment opportunities, but they want the company to pay earnings out if investment opportunities are poor. Taxes also play a role — since dividends and capital gains are taxed differently, dividend policy affects investors' taxes. We will consider dividend policy in detail in Chapter 14.

WHEN CAN THE CONSTANT GROWTH MODEL BE USED?

The constant growth model is often appropriate for mature companies with a stable history of growth. Expected growth rates vary somewhat among companies, but dividend growth for most mature firms is generally expected to continue in the future at about the same rate as nominal gross domestic product (real GDP plus inflation). On this basis, one might expect the dividends of an average, or "normal," company to grow at a rate of 5 to 8 percent a year.

Zero Growth Stock
A common stock whose future dividends are not expected to grow at all; that is, $g = 0$.

Note too that Equation 9-2 is sufficiently general to handle the case of a **zero growth stock**, where the dividend is expected to remain constant over time. If $g = 0$, Equation 9-2 reduces to Equation 9-3:

$$\hat{P}_0 = \frac{D}{k_s}. \tag{9-3}$$

This is essentially the same equation as the one we developed in Chapter 7 for a perpetuity, and it is simply the dividend divided by the discount rate.

SELF-TEST QUESTIONS

Write out and explain the valuation formula for a constant growth stock.

Explain how the formula for a zero growth stock is related to that for a constant growth stock.

EXPECTED RATE OF RETURN ON A CONSTANT GROWTH STOCK

We can solve Equation 9-2 for k_s, again using the hat to indicate that we are dealing with an expected rate of return:[8]

$$
\begin{array}{ccc}
\text{Expected rate} & \text{Expected} & \text{Expected growth} \\
\text{of return} & = \text{dividend} + & \text{rate, or capital} \\
& \text{yield} & \text{gains yield}
\end{array}
$$

$$\hat{k}_s = \frac{D_1}{P_0} + g. \tag{9-4}$$

Thus, if you buy a stock for a price $P_0 = \$23$, and if you expect the stock to pay a dividend $D_1 = \$1.242$ one year from now and to grow at a constant rate $g = 8\%$ in the future, then your expected rate of return will be 13.4 percent:

$$\hat{k}_s = \frac{\$1.242}{\$23} + 8\% = 5.4\% + 8\% = 13.4\%.$$

In this form, we see that $\hat{k}_s$ is the *expected total return* and that it consists of an *expected dividend yield*, $D_1/P_0 = 5.4\%$, plus an *expected growth rate or capital gains yield*, $g = 8\%$.

Suppose this analysis had been conducted on January 1, 2002, so $P_0 = \$23$ is the January 1, 2002, stock price, and $D_1 = \$1.242$ is the dividend expected at

---

[8] The k_s value in Equation 9-2 is a *required* rate of return, but when we transform to obtain Equation 9-4, we are finding an *expected* rate of return. Obviously, the transformation requires that $k_s = \hat{k}_s$. This equality holds if the stock market is in equilibrium, a condition that will be discussed later in the chapter.

the end of 2002. What is the expected stock price at the end of 2002? We would again apply Equation 9-2, but this time we would use the year-end dividend, $D_2 = D_1 (1 + g) = \$1.242(1.08) = \$1.3414$:

$$\hat{P}_{12/31/02} = \frac{D_{2003}}{k_s - g} = \frac{\$1.3414}{0.134 - 0.08} = \$24.84.$$

Now, notice that $24.84 is 8 percent greater than P_0, the $23 price on January 1, 2002:

$$\$23(1.08) = \$24.84.$$

Thus, we would expect to make a capital gain of $24.84 − $23.00 = $1.84 during 2002, which would provide a capital gains yield of 8 percent:

$$\text{Capital gains yield}_{2002} = \frac{\text{Capital gain}}{\text{Beginning price}} = \frac{\$1.84}{\$23.00} = 0.08 = 8\%.$$

We could extend the analysis on out, and in each future year the expected capital gains yield would always equal g, the expected dividend growth rate.
Continuing, the dividend yield in 2003 could be estimated as follows:

$$\text{Dividend yield}_{2003} = \frac{D_{2003}}{\hat{P}_{12/31/02}} = \frac{\$1.3414}{\$24.84} = 0.054 = 5.4\%.$$

The dividend yield for 2004 could also be calculated, and again it would be 5.4 percent. Thus, *for a constant growth stock*, the following conditions must hold:

The popular Motley Fool web site **http://www.fool.com/school/introductiontovaluation.htm** provides a good description of some of the benefits and drawbacks of a few of the more commonly used valuation procedures.

1. The dividend is expected to grow forever at a constant rate, g.
2. The stock price is expected to grow at this same rate.
3. The expected dividend yield is a constant.
4. The expected capital gains yield is also a constant, and it is equal to g.
5. The expected total rate of return, $\hat{k}_s$, is equal to the expected dividend yield plus the expected growth rate: $\hat{k}_s$ = dividend yield + g.

The term *expected* should be clarified — it means expected in a probabilistic sense, as the "statistically expected" outcome. Thus, if we say the growth rate is expected to remain constant at 8 percent, we mean that the best prediction for the growth rate in any future year is 8 percent, not that we literally expect the growth rate to be exactly 8 percent in each future year. In this sense, the constant growth assumption is a reasonable one for many large, mature companies.

SELF-TEST QUESTIONS

What conditions must hold if a stock is to be evaluated using the constant growth model?

What does the term "expected" mean when we say expected growth rate?

INDUSTRY PRACTICE

OTHER APPROACHES TO VALUING COMMON STOCKS

While the dividend growth and the corporate value models presented in this chapter are the most widely used methods for valuing common stocks, they are by no means the only approaches. Analysts often use a number of different techniques to value stocks. Two of these alternative approaches are described below.

THE P/E MULTIPLE APPROACH

Investors have long looked for simple rules of thumb to determine whether a stock is fairly valued. One such approach is to look at the stock's price-earnings (P/E) ratio. Recall from Chapter 3 that a company's P/E ratio shows how much investors are willing to pay for each dollar of reported earnings. As a starting point, you might conclude that stocks with low P/E ratios are undervalued, since their price is "low" given current earnings, while stocks with high P/E ratios are overvalued.

Unfortunately, however, valuing stocks is not that simple. We should not expect all companies to have the same P/E ratio. P/E ratios are affected by risk — investors discount the earnings of riskier stocks at a higher rate. Thus, all else equal, riskier stocks should have lower P/E ratios. In addition, when you buy a stock, you not only have a claim on current earnings — you also have a claim on all future earnings. All else

equal, companies with stronger growth opportunities will generate larger future earnings and thus should trade at higher P/E ratios. Therefore, Microsoft is not necessarily overvalued just because its P/E ratio is 32 at a time when the median firm has a P/E of 16. Investors believe that Microsoft's growth potential is well above average. Whether the stock's future prospects justify its P/E ratio remains to be seen, but in and of itself a high P/E ratio does not mean that a stock is overvalued.

Nevertheless, P/E ratios can provide a useful starting point in stock valuation. If a stock's P/E ratio is well above its industry average, and if the stock's growth potential and risk are similar to other firms in the industry, this may indicate that the stock's price is too high. Likewise, if a company's P/E ratio falls well below its historical average, this may signal that the stock is undervalued — particularly if the company's growth prospects and risk are unchanged, and if the overall P/E for the market has remained constant or increased.

One obvious drawback of the P/E approach is that it depends on reported accounting earnings. For this reason, some analysts choose to rely on other multiples to value stocks. For example, some analysts look at a company's price-to-cash-flow ratio, while others look at the price-to-sales ratio.

VALUING STOCKS THAT HAVE A NONCONSTANT GROWTH RATE

For many companies, it is inappropriate to assume that dividends will grow at a constant rate. Firms typically go through *life cycles*. During the early part of their lives, their growth is much faster than that of the economy as a whole; then they match the economy's growth; and finally their growth is slower than that of the economy.[9] Automobile manufacturers in the 1920s, computer software firms such as Microsoft in the 1990s, and Internet firms such as AOL in the 2000s are examples of firms in the early part of the cycle; these firms are

---

[9] The concept of life cycles could be broadened to *product cycle*, which would include both small startup companies and large companies like Procter & Gamble, which periodically introduce new products that give sales and earnings a boost. We should also mention *business cycles*, which alternately depress and boost sales and profits. The growth rate just after a major new product has been introduced, or just after a firm emerges from the depths of a recession, is likely to be much higher than the "expected long-run average growth rate," which is the proper number for a DCF analysis.

THE EVA APPROACH

In recent years, analysts have looked for more rigorous alternatives to the dividend growth model. More than a quarter of all stocks listed on the NYSE pay no dividends. This proportion is even higher on Nasdaq. While the dividend growth model can still be used for these stocks (see additional Industry Practice box, "Evaluating Stocks That Don't Pay Dividends"), this approach requires that analysts forecast when the stock will begin paying dividends, what the dividend will be once it is established, and the future dividend growth rate. In many cases, these forecasts contain considerable errors.

An alternative approach is based on the concept of economic value added (EVA), which we discussed back in Chapter 2. Also, recall from the Industry Practice box in Chapter 3 entitled, "Calculating EVA," that EVA can be written as:

$$\left(\begin{array}{c}\text{Equity}\\\text{Capital}\end{array}\right)\left(\text{ROE} - \begin{array}{c}\text{Cost of}\\\text{Equity Capital}\end{array}\right).$$

This equation suggests that companies can increase their EVA by investing in projects that provide shareholders with returns that are above their cost of capital, which is the return they could expect to earn on alternative investments with the same level of risk. When you buy stock in a company, you receive more than just the book value of equity — you also receive a claim on all future value that is created by the firm's managers (the present value of all future EVAs). It follows that a company's market value of equity can be written as:

$$\begin{array}{c}\text{Market Value}\\\text{of Equity}\end{array} = \begin{array}{c}\text{Book}\\\text{Value}\end{array} + \begin{array}{c}\text{PV of all}\\\text{future EVAs}\end{array}.$$

We can find the "fundamental" value of the stock, P_0, by simply dividing the above expression by the number of shares outstanding.

As is the case with the dividend growth model, we can simplify the above expression by assuming that at some point in time annual EVA becomes a perpetuity, or grows at some constant rate over time.[a]

---

[a] What we have presented here is a simplified version of what is often referred to as the Edwards-Bell-Ohlson (EBO) model. For a more complete description of this technique and an excellent summary of how it can be used in practice, take a look at the article, "Measuring Wealth," by Charles M.C. Lee in *CA Magazine*, April 1996, 32–37.

Supernormal (Nonconstant) Growth
The part of the firm's life cycle in which it grows much faster than the economy as a whole.

called **supernormal**, or **nonconstant**, **growth** firms. Figure 9-2 illustrates nonconstant growth and also compares it with normal growth, zero growth, and negative growth.[10]

In the figure, the dividends of the supernormal growth firm are expected to grow at a 30 percent rate for three years, after which the growth rate is expected to fall to 8 percent, the assumed average for the economy. The value of this firm, like any other, is the present value of its expected future dividends as determined by Equation 9-1. In the case in which D_t is growing at a constant rate, we simplified Equation 9-1 to $\hat{P}_0 = D_1/(k_s - g)$. In the supernormal case, however, the expected growth rate is not a constant — it declines at the end of the period of supernormal growth.

---

[10] A negative growth rate indicates a declining company. A mining company whose profits are falling because of a declining ore body is an example. Someone buying such a company would expect its earnings, and consequently its dividends and stock price, to decline each year, and this would lead to capital losses rather than capital gains. Obviously, a declining company's stock price will be relatively low, and its dividend yield must be high enough to offset the expected capital loss and still produce a competitive total return. Students sometimes argue that they would never be willing to buy a stock whose price was expected to decline. However, if the annual dividends are large enough to *more than offset* the falling stock price, the stock could still provide a good return.

FIGURE 9-2   **Illustrative Dividend Growth Rates**

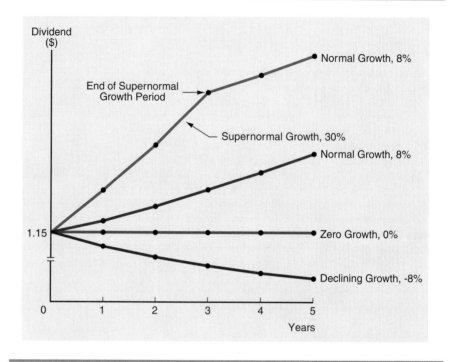

Because Equation 9-2 requires a constant growth rate, we obviously cannot use it to value stocks that have nonconstant growth. However, assuming that a company currently enjoying supernormal growth will eventually slow down and become a constant growth stock, we can combine Equations 9-1 and 9-2 to form a new formula, Equation 9-5, for valuing it. First, we assume that the dividend will grow at a nonconstant rate (generally a relatively high rate) for N periods, after which it will grow at a constant rate, g. N is often called the **terminal date,** or **horizon date.**

Terminal Date (Horizon Date)
The date when the growth rate becomes constant. At this date it is no longer necessary to forecast the individual dividends.

We can use the constant growth formula, Equation 9-2, to determine what the stock's **horizon,** or **terminal, value** will be N periods from today:

Horizon (Terminal) Value
The value at the horizon date of all dividends expected thereafter.

$$\text{Horizon value} = \hat{P}_N = \frac{D_{N+1}}{k_s - g}.$$

The stock's intrinsic value today, $\hat{P}_0$, is the present value of the dividends during the nonconstant growth period plus the present value of the horizon value:

$$\hat{P}_0 = \underbrace{\frac{D_1}{(1+k_s)^1} + \frac{D_2}{(1+k_s)^2} + \cdots + \frac{D_N}{(1+k_s)^N}}_{\substack{\text{PV of dividends during the} \\ \text{nonconstant growth period} \\ t = 1, \cdots N}} + \underbrace{\frac{D_{N+1}}{(1+k_s)^{N+1}} + \cdots + \frac{D_\infty}{(1+k_s)^\infty}}_{\substack{\text{PV of dividends during the} \\ \text{constant growth period} \\ t = N+1, \cdots \infty}}.$$

$$\hat{P}_0 = \underbrace{\frac{D_1}{(1 + k_s)^1} + \frac{D_2}{(1 + k_s)^2} + \cdots + \frac{D_N}{(1 + k_s)^N} +}_{\substack{\text{PV of dividends during the} \\ \text{nonconstant growth period} \\ t = 1, \cdots N}} \quad \underbrace{\frac{\hat{P}_N}{(1 + k_s)^N}.}_{\substack{\text{PV of horizon} \\ \text{value, } \hat{P}_N: \\ \frac{[(D_{N+1})/(k_s - g)]}{(1 + k_s)^N}.}} \quad (9\text{-}5)$$

To implement Equation 9-5, we go through the following three steps:

1. Find the PV of the dividends during the period of nonconstant growth.
2. Find the price of the stock at the end of the nonconstant growth period, at which point it has become a constant growth stock, and discount this price back to the present.
3. Add these two components to find the intrinsic value of the stock, $\hat{P}_0$.

Figure 9-3 can be used to illustrate the process for valuing nonconstant growth stocks. Here we assume the following five facts exist:

k_s = stockholders' required rate of return = 13.4%. This rate is used to discount the cash flows.

N = years of supernormal growth = 3.

g_s = rate of growth in both earnings and dividends during the supernormal growth period = 30%. This rate is shown directly on the time line. (Note: The growth rate during the supernormal growth period could vary from year to year. Also, there could be several different supernormal growth periods, e.g., 30% for three years, then 20% for three years, and then a constant 8%.)

g_n = rate of normal, constant growth after the supernormal period = 8%. This rate is also shown on the time line, between Periods 3 and 4.

D_0 = last dividend the company paid = $1.15.

The valuation process as diagrammed in Figure 9-3 is explained in the steps set forth below the time line. The value of the supernormal growth stock is calculated to be $39.21.

SELF-TEST QUESTIONS

Explain how one would find the value of a supernormal growth stock.

Explain what is meant by "terminal (horizon) date" and "horizon (terminal) value."

VALUING THE ENTIRE CORPORATION

In the previous three sections, we presented several equations for valuing a firm's common stock. These equations had one common element: They all

FIGURE 9-3

Process for Finding the Value of a Supernormal Growth Stock

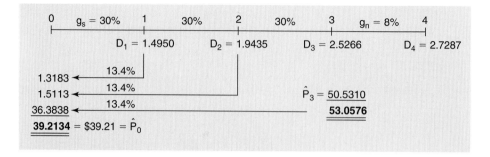

NOTES TO FIGURE 9-3:

Step 1. Calculate the dividends expected at the end of each year during the supernormal growth period. Calculate the first dividend, $D_1 = D_0(1 + g_s) = \$1.15(1.30) = \$1.4950$. Here g_s is the growth rate during the three-year supernormal growth period, 30 percent. Show the $1.4950 on the time line as the cash flow at Time 1. Then, calculate $D_2 = D_1(1 + g_s) = \$1.4950(1.30) = \$1.9435$, and then $D_3 = D_2(1 + g_s) = \$1.9435(1.30) = \$2.5266$. Show these values on the time line as the cash flows at Time 2 and Time 3. Note that D_0 is used only to calculate D_1.

Step 2. The price of the stock is the PV of dividends from Time 1 to infinity, so in theory we could project each future dividend, with the normal growth rate, $g_n = 8\%$, used to calculate D_4 and subsequent dividends. However, we know that after D_3 has been paid, which is at Time 3, the stock becomes a constant growth stock. Therefore, we can use the constant growth formula to find $\hat{P}_3$, which is the PV of the dividends from Time 4 to infinity as evaluated at Time 3.

First, we determine $D_4 = \$2.5266(1.08) = \$2.7287$ for use in the formula, and then we calculate $\hat{P}_3$ as follows:

$$\hat{P}_3 = \frac{D_4}{k_s - g_n} = \frac{\$2.7287}{0.134 - 0.08} = \$50.5310.$$

We show this $50.5310 on the time line as a second cash flow at Time 3. The $50.5310 is a Time 3 cash flow in the sense that the owner of the stock could sell it for $50.5310 at Time 3 and also in the sense that $50.5310 is the present value of the dividend cash flows from Time 4 to infinity. Note that the *total cash flow* at Time 3 consists of the sum of $D_3 + \hat{P}_3 = \$2.5266 + \$50.5310 = \$53.0576$.

Step 3. Now that the cash flows have been placed on the time line, we can discount each cash flow at the required rate of return, $k_s = 13.4\%$. We could discount each cash flow by dividing by $(1.134)^t$, where $t = 1$ for Time 1, $t = 2$ for Time 2, and $t = 3$ for Time 3. This produces the PVs shown to the left below the time line, and the sum of the PVs is the value of the supernormal growth stock, $39.21.

With a financial calculator, you can find the PV of the cash flows as shown on the time line with the cash flow (CFLO) register of your calculator. Enter 0 for CF_0 because you get no cash flow at Time 0, $CF_1 = 1.495$, $CF_2 = 1.9435$, and $CF_3 = 2.5266 + 50.531 = 53.0576$. Then enter I = 13.4, and press the NPV key to find the value of the stock, $39.21.

assumed that the firm is currently paying a dividend. But consider the situation of a startup company formed to develop and market a new product. Such a company generally expects to have low sales during its first few years as it develops and begins to market its product. Then, if the product catches on, sales will grow rapidly for several years. For example, Compaq Computer had just three employees when it was founded in 1982. Its first year was devoted to product development, so 1982 sales were zero. In early 1983, however, Compaq introduced its personal computer, and its 1983 sales hit $111 million, a record first-year volume for any new firm. Two years later, Compaq was included in *Fortune*'s 500 largest U.S. industrial firms. Obviously, Compaq was more successful than most new businesses, but growth rates of 100, 500, or even 1,000 percent are not uncommon during a firm's early years.

Growing sales require additional assets — Compaq could not have grown as it did without increasing its assets. Moreover, asset growth must be financed by increasing some liability and/or equity account. Small firms can often obtain some bank credit, but they must maintain a reasonable balance between debt and equity. Thus, additional bank borrowings require increases in equity, but small firms have limited access to the stock market. Moreover, even if they can sell stock, their owners are often reluctant to do so for fear of losing voting control. Therefore, the best source of equity for most small businesses is from retaining earnings, so most small firms pay no dividends during their rapid growth years. Eventually, most successful firms do pay dividends, with dividends growing rapidly at first but then slowing down as the firm approaches maturity.

Although most larger firms do pay a dividend, some firms, even highly profitable ones such as Microsoft, have never paid a dividend. How can the value of such a company be determined? Similarly, suppose you start a business, and someone offers to buy it from you. How could you determine its value, or that of any privately held business? Or suppose you work for a company with a number of divisions. How could you determine the value of one particular division that the company wants to sell? In none of these cases could you use the dividend growth model. However, you could use the **total company,** or **corporate value, model.**

Note too that the value of its stock is directly linked to a firm's total value. In the next section, we find the total value of the firm and then subtract the market value of the debt and preferred stock. We are then left with the total value of the common equity. We then divide by the number of shares outstanding to obtain an estimate of the value per share. That estimate should, in theory, be identical to the share value found using the discounted dividend model described earlier in the chapter.

While the total company model generally requires more data than the discounted dividend model, these data are often more reliable, particularly for companies that do not pay dividends and where future dividends are especially difficult to predict.

Total Company (Corporate Value) Model
A valuation model used as an alternative to the dividend growth model to determine the value of a firm, especially one that does not pay dividends or is privately held. This model discounts a firm's free cash flows at the WACC to determine its value.

THE CORPORATE VALUE MODEL

In Chapters 2 and 4 we explained that a firm's value is determined by its ability to generate cash flow, both now and in the future. Therefore, the market value of any company can be expressed as follows:

$$\text{Market value of company} = V_{\text{Company}} = \text{PV of expected future free cash flows}$$

$$= \frac{\text{FCF}_1}{(1 + \text{WACC})^1} + \frac{\text{FCF}_2}{(1 + \text{WACC})^2} + \cdots + \frac{\text{FCF}_\infty}{(1 + \text{WACC})^\infty}. \quad (9\text{-}6)$$

Now recall from Chapters 2 and 4 that free cash flow represents the cash generated in a given year minus the cash needed to finance the capital expenditures and operating working capital needed to support future growth. More specifically, we showed that free cash flow (FCF) can be expressed as follows:

$$FCF = NOPAT - \text{Net new investment in operating capital.}$$

The value of the firm is the present value of its future FCF. This question arises: Given the projected FCF, at what rate should those flows be discounted to find the value of the firm? Note first that free cash flow is the cash generated *before making any payments to common or preferred stockholders, or to bondholders, so it is the cash flow that is available to all investors.* Therefore, the FCF should be discounted at the company's weighted average cost of debt, preferred stock, and common stock, or the WACC.

To find a firm's value, we proceed as follows:

1. Assume that the firm will experience nonconstant growth for N years, after which it will grow at some constant rate.

2. Calculate the expected free cash flow (FCF) for each of the N nonconstant growth years, and find the PV of these cash flows.

3. Recognize that after Year N growth will be constant. Therefore, we can use the constant growth formula to find the firm's value at Year N. This "terminal value" is the sum of the PVs of the FCFs for N + 1 and all subsequent years, discounted back to Year N. Then, the Year N value must be discounted back to the present to find its PV at Year 0.

4. Now sum all the PVs, those of the annual free cash flows during the nonconstant period plus the PV of the terminal value, to find the firm's value.

Table 9-2 illustrates the free cash flow approach to estimating Allied Food's total corporate value. The figures represented in this valuation model are the product of an independent stock analyst. This analyst has reviewed Allied's financial statements, visited Allied's facilities, spoken to Allied's key personnel, and spoken to key figures outside the firm. On the basis of all the information gathered by this analyst, she has constructed the valuation model for Allied Food Products that is outlined in Table 9-2.

In her model, the analyst assumes that Allied's free cash flow will grow at a nonconstant rate for five years, after which time the company's free cash flow will grow at a constant rate of 7 percent a year. To construct her estimates of free cash flow for the first five years, she begins by forecasting the annual growth rate in sales. Recall from Chapter 4 that, in its own internal forecast, Allied's managers expect Allied's sales to grow 10 percent in 2002 to $3.3 billion. We see in Table 9-2 that this independent analyst also expects sales to increase by 10 percent in 2002. Looking further ahead, this analyst believes that Allied's sales will continue to grow, but at a slower rate — more specifically, she forecasts that annual sales growth will fall to 9 percent in 2003 through 2005 and then decline to 8 percent in 2006.

In addition to her sales forecast, the analyst has also forecasted that Allied's after-tax operating margin (NOPAT/Sales) will be 6.5 percent for each of the first five years. This forecasted margin exceeds the current operating margin, but the analyst believes that this is sustainable because of anticipated improvements in operating efficiency and favorable market conditions. The forecasted level of NOPAT for each year is obtained by simply multiplying the forecasted

	A	B	C	D	E	F	G	H
263								
264	(Time Line of Annual Free Cash Flows - millions of dollars)							
265					Years			
266				1	2	3	4	5
267	Key Input Data			2002	2003	2004	2005	2006
268	Sales growth rate			10.0%	9.0%	9.0%	9.0%	8.0%
269	After-tax operating margin				6.5%	6.5%	6.5%	6.5%
270	Operating capital growth rate				5.0%	5.0%	4.0%	4.0%
271	WACC			10%				
272	Tax rate			40%				
273	Long-run FCF growth rate			7.0%				
274								
275	*Free Cash Flows (Years 1-5)*							
276	Sales			$3,300.0	$3,597.0	$3,920.7	$4,273.6	$4,615.5
277	NOPAT			187.3	233.8	254.8	277.8	300.0
278	Net operating capital expenditures			180.0	189.0	198.5	206.4	214.6
279	FCF			$7.3	$44.8	$56.4	$71.4	$85.4
280	PV of FCFs			$6.6	$37.0	$42.4	$48.8	$53.0
281								
282	*Terminal Year Firm Value*							
283	Free Cash Flow - Year 6			$91.3		$TV_5 =$	FCF_6	
284	TV of Firm - Year 5			$3,044.6			$WACC - g$	
285	PV of Firm Terminal Value			$1,890.5				
286								
287	*Calculation of Firm Intrinsic Value*							
288	PV of FCFs (Years 1-5)			$187.8				
289	PV of Firm TV			$1,890.5				
290	Total corporate value			$2,078.3				
291	Less: MV of debt and pref			$904.0				
292	Value of common equity			$1,174.3				
293	Shares outstanding (millions)			50.0				
294	ESTIMATE OF STOCK PRICE			$23.49				

sales level by the forecasted after-tax operating margin. Note that while the analyst has assumed a constant operating margin for the first five years, the valuation model is flexible enough to allow for annual variations.

Next the analyst considers Allied's use of operating capital. Recall the free cash flow formula requires net capital expenditures and changes in operating working capital to be subtracted from NOPAT. The analyst has lumped these two variables into one category called net operating capital expenditures. In her valuation, the analyst assumes that operating capital will grow at 5 percent annually through 2004 and then will decline to 4 percent in 2005 and 2006. After 2006, the analyst believes that Allied's nonconstant growth pattern will cease and will be replaced by a long-run constant growth pattern that will enable free cash flow to grow by 7 percent per year.

In order to estimate the present value of the free cash flows, the analyst also needs to estimate the company's weighted average cost of capital (WACC). In Chapter 10, we will explain how to calculate the WACC, but for now just assume that Allied's WACC is 10 percent.

When we discount the first five free cash flows at 10 percent and sum them, we see that the present value of the free cash flows during the nonconstant growth period is $187.8 million. Next, we find the value of all the free cash flows beyond the nonconstant growth period, using a constant growth formula, just as we did with the supernormal growth stock in the previous section. This is the firm's value at Year N. It is called the terminal value, and it is calculated as follows:

$$\text{Terminal value} = V_{\text{Company at } t = N} = \text{FCF}_{N+1}/(\text{WACC} - g_{\text{FCF}}). \quad \text{(9-7)}$$

Here g_{FCF} is the constant rate at which free cash flows are expected to grow after Year N. For Allied, the nonconstant growth period is five years, so $N = 5$, and the constant growth rate for Year 6 and thereafter is 7 percent. As we see in Table 9-2, Allied's terminal value is $3,044.6 million. Note, though, that this is the value at the end of Year 5, so to find its value today we must discount this terminal value back for five years at the WACC. As Table 9-2 shows, the present value of the terminal value is $1,890.5 million. When we add this number to the $187.8 million calculated earlier for the present value of the free cash flows during the nonconstant growth period, we find Allied's total corporate value to be $2,078.3 million.

If Allied's total value on December 31, 2001, is $2,078.3 million, what is the value of its common equity? First, note that notes payable and long-term debt total $110 + $754 = $864 million, and these securities have first claim on assets and income. (Accounts payable and accruals were netted out earlier in the calculation of free cash flow.) Next, the preferred stock has a claim of $40 million, and it also ranks above common stock.[11] Therefore, the value left for common stockholders is $2,078.3 − $864 − $40 = $1,174.3 million. As a final step, we divide the value of the common equity by the 50 million shares outstanding to obtain the value per share: $1,174.3/50 = $23.49.

COMPARING THE TOTAL COMPANY AND DIVIDEND GROWTH MODELS

In principle, we should find the same intrinsic value for a stock using the total company model or the dividend growth model. In our Allied example, the estimates were close but not exactly the same — the dividend growth model predicted a price of $23.00 per share versus $23.49 using the total company model. Note too that both models' estimates were close to Allied's actual $23 stock price.

It is important to realize that stock value estimates are very sensitive to the assumptions used to generate them. This valuation model is very sensitive to the inputs used. For example, if the long-run constant growth rate for free cash flow was determined to be 6 percent (instead of 7 percent), the stock price estimate would change to $13.77. By contrast, if the long-run growth rate was 8 percent, the predicted stock price would be $42.92. (Note: You can use the spreadsheet model, 09MODEL.xls, that accompanies this chapter to verify all of these numbers.) For this reason, stock price valuations are heavily dependent on the analyst's inputs. Moreover, opinions about the value of a firm's stock price can vary widely amongst analysts.

---

[11] For our purposes here, we are assuming that the market and book values are the same for both long-term debt and preferred stock. If market conditions significantly changed after these securities were originally issued, the market and book values would be different. In that situation, we would use the market value of long-term debt and preferred stock.

In practice, the estimates of intrinsic value will often deviate considerably from the actual stock price. Such deviations occur because the forecaster's assumptions are different from those of the marginal investor in the marketplace. If the assumptions we used — about the initial cash flows, the long-term growth rate, the years before normal growth begins, and the WACC — differ from those of "the market," then the forecasted value will be above or below the actual price. The calculated value will be above the market price if the forecaster is more optimistic and below if he or she is less optimistic. If the forecaster has made the better assumptions, then eventually the market price will move toward the calculated value. If the analyst is wrong, convergence will not occur. It is dangerous to bet against the market, because "the market" reflects the judgments of millions of investors, some of whom may have better information than we do. However, if the analyst really can make a better-than-average forecast, then he or she can do well in the market.

Given all of this, does it matter whether you use the total company model or the dividend growth model to value stocks? Generally it does. For example, if you were a financial analyst estimating the values of mature companies whose dividends are expected to grow steadily in the future, it would probably be more efficient to use the dividend growth model. Here you would only need to estimate the growth rate in dividends, not the entire set of pro forma financial statements.

However, if a company is paying a dividend but is still in the high-growth stage of its life cycle, you would need to project the future financial statements before you could make a reasonable estimate of future dividends. Then, since you would have already estimated future financial statements, it would be a toss-up as to whether the total company model or the dividend growth model would be easier to apply. Intel, which pays a dividend of 8 cents versus earnings of about $1.50, is an example of a company where either model could be used.

Now suppose you were trying to estimate the value of a company that has never paid a dividend, such as Microsoft, or a new firm that is about to go public, or a division that GE or some other large company is planning to sell. In all of these situations, you would have no choice: You would have to estimate future financial statements and use the total company value model.

Actually, even if a company is paying steady dividends, much can be learned from the corporate value model, so analysts today use it for all types of valuations. The process of projecting future financial statements can reveal quite a bit about the company's operations and financing needs. Also, such an analysis can provide insights into actions that might be taken to increase the company's value, as we discussed in Chapter 4.

SELF-TEST QUESTIONS

Write out the equation for the corporate value model, and explain what it does.

Why might someone use the corporate model even though the dividend model could be used?

What are the steps for finding a firm's total value?

Why might the calculated intrinsic stock value differ from the stock's current market price? Which would be "correct"? What does "correct" mean?

EVALUATING STOCKS THAT DON'T PAY DIVIDENDS

The dividend growth model presented in the chapter assumed that the firm is currently paying a dividend. However, many firms, even highly profitable ones, such as Microsoft, have never paid a dividend. If a firm is expected to begin paying dividends in the future, we can modify the equations presented in the chapter and use them to determine the value of the stock.

A new business often expects to have low sales during its first few years of operation as it develops its product. Then, if the product catches on, sales will grow rapidly for several years. Sales growth brings with it the need for additional assets — a firm cannot increase sales without also increasing its assets, and asset growth requires an increase in liability and/or equity accounts. Small firms can generally obtain some bank credit, but they must maintain a reasonable balance between debt and equity. Thus, additional bank borrowings require increases in equity, and getting the equity capital needed to support growth can be difficult for small firms. They have limited access to the capital markets, and, even when they can sell common stock, their owners are reluctant to do so for fear of losing voting control. Therefore, the best source of equity for most small businesses is retained earnings, and for this reason most small firms pay no dividends during their rapid growth years. Eventually, though, successful small firms do pay dividends, and those dividends generally grow rapidly at first but slow down to a sustainable constant rate once the firm reaches maturity.

If a firm currently pays no dividend but is expected to pay dividends in the future, the value of its stock can be found as follows:

1. Estimate when dividends will be paid, the amount of the first dividend, the growth rate during the supernormal growth period, the length of the supernormal period, the long-run (constant) growth rate, and the rate of return required by investors.
2. Use the constant growth model to determine the price of the stock after the firm reaches a stable growth situation.
3. Set out on a time line the cash flows (dividends during the supernormal growth period and the stock price once the constant growth state is reached), and then find the present value of these cash flows. That present value represents the value of the stock today.

To illustrate this process, consider the situation for Marvel-Lure Inc., a company that was set up in 2000 to produce and market a new high-tech fishing lure. MarvelLure's sales are currently growing at a rate of 200 percent per year. The company expects to experience a high but declining rate of growth in sales and earnings during the next 10 years, after which analysts estimate that it will grow at a steady 10 percent per year. The firm's management has announced that it will pay no dividends for five years, but if earnings materialize as forecasted, it will pay a dividend of \$0.20 per share at the end of Year 6, \$0.30 in Year 7, \$0.40 in Year 8, \$0.45 in Year 9, and \$0.50 in Year 10. After Year 10, current plans are to increase the dividend by 10 percent per year.

MarvelLure's investment bankers estimate that investors require a 15 percent return on similar stocks. Therefore, we find the value of a share of MarvelLure's stock as follows:

$$P_0 = \frac{\$0}{(1.15)^1} + \cdots + \frac{\$0}{(1.15)^5}$$
$$+ \frac{\$0.20}{(1.15)^6} + \frac{\$0.30}{(1.15)^7}$$
$$+ \frac{\$0.40}{(1.15)^8} + \frac{\$0.45}{(1.15)^9} + \frac{\$0.50}{(1.15)^{10}}$$
$$+ \left(\frac{\$0.50(1.10)}{0.15 - 0.10} \right) \left(\frac{1}{(1.15)^{10}} \right)$$
$$= \$3.30.$$

The last term finds the expected price of the stock in Year 10 and then finds the present value of that price. Thus, we see that the dividend growth model can be applied to firms that currently pay no dividends, provided we can estimate future dividends with a fair degree of confidence. However, in many cases one can have more confidence in the forecasts of free cash flows, and in these situations it is better to use the corporate model.

STOCK MARKET EQUILIBRIUM

Recall that k_X, the required return on Stock X, can be found using the Security Market Line (SML) equation as it was developed in our discussion of the Capital Asset Pricing Model (CAPM) back in Chapter 6:

$$k_X = k_{RF} + (k_M - k_{RF})\, b_X.$$

If the risk-free rate of return is 8 percent, the required return on an average stock is 12 percent, and Stock X has a beta of 2, then the marginal investor will require a return of 16 percent on Stock X:

$$k_X = 8\% + (12\% - 8\%)\,2.0$$
$$= 16\%.$$

This 16 percent required return is shown as the point on the SML in Figure 9-4 associated with beta = 2.0.

The **marginal investor** will want to buy Stock X if its expected rate of return is more than 16 percent, will want to sell it if the expected rate of return is less than 16 percent, and will be indifferent, hence will hold but not buy or sell, if the expected rate of return is exactly 16 percent. Now suppose the investor's portfolio contains Stock X, and he or she analyzes the stock's prospects and concludes that its earnings, dividends, and price can be expected to grow at a constant rate of 5 percent per year. The last dividend was $D_0 = \$2.8571$, so the next expected dividend is

$$D_1 = \$2.8571(1.05) = \$3.$$

Our marginal investor observes that the present price of the stock, P_0, is $30. Should he or she purchase more of Stock X, sell the stock, or maintain the present position?

The investor can calculate Stock X's *expected rate of return* as follows:

$$\hat{k}_X = \frac{D_1}{P_0} + g = \frac{\$3}{\$30} + 5\% = 15\%.$$

This value is plotted on Figure 9-4 as Point X, which is below the SML. Because the expected rate of return is less than the required return, this marginal investor

Marginal Investor
A representative investor whose actions reflect the beliefs of those people who are currently trading a stock. It is the marginal investor who determines a stock's price.

FIGURE 9-4   **Expected and Required Returns on Stock X**

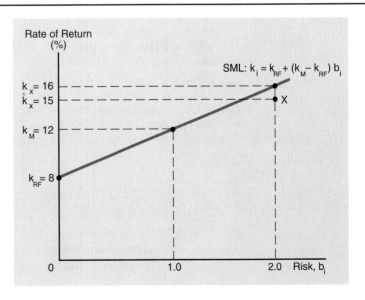

would want to sell the stock, as would most other holders. However, few people would want to buy at the $30 price, so the present owners would be unable to find buyers unless they cut the price of the stock. Thus, the price would decline, and this decline would continue until the stock's price reached $27.27, at which point the market for this security would be in **equilibrium,** defined as the price at which the expected rate of return, 16 percent, is equal to the required rate of return:

Equilibrium
The condition under which the expected return on a security is just equal to its required return, $\hat{k} = k$. Also, $\hat{P}_0 = P_0$, and the price is stable.

$$\hat{k}_X = \frac{\$3}{\$27.27} + 5\% = 11\% + 5\% = 16\% = k_X.$$

Had the stock initially sold for less than $27.27, say, at $25, events would have been reversed. Investors would have wanted to buy the stock because its expected rate of return would have exceeded its required rate of return, and buy orders would have driven the stock's price up to $27.27.

To summarize, in equilibrium two related conditions must hold:

1. A stock's expected rate of return as seen by the marginal investor must equal its required rate of return: $\hat{k}_i = k_i$.
2. The actual market price of the stock must equal its intrinsic value as estimated by the marginal investor: $P_0 = \hat{P}_0$.

Of course, some individual investors may believe that $\hat{k}_i > k$ and $\hat{P}_0 > P_0$, hence they would invest most of their funds in the stock, while other investors may have an opposite view and would sell all of their shares. However, it is the marginal investor who establishes the actual market price, and for this investor, we must have $\hat{k}_i = k_i$ and $P_0 = \hat{P}_0$. If these conditions do not hold, trading will occur until they do hold.

CHANGES IN EQUILIBRIUM STOCK PRICES

Stock prices are not constant — they undergo violent changes at times. For example, on October 19, 1987, the Dow Jones average dropped 508 points, and the average stock lost about 23 percent of its value on that one day. Some individual stocks lost more than 70 percent of their value. More recently, on October 27, 1997, the Dow Jones Industrials fell 554 points, which at the time was a 7.18 percent drop in value. To see how such changes can occur, assume that Stock X is in equilibrium, selling at a price of $27.27 per share. If all expectations were exactly met, during the next year the price would gradually rise to $28.63, or by 5 percent. However, many different events could occur to cause a change in the equilibrium price of the stock. To illustrate, consider again the set of inputs used to develop Stock X's price of $27.27, along with a new set of assumed input variables:

	VARIABLE VALUE	
	ORIGINAL	NEW
Risk-free rate, k_{RF}	8%	7%
Market risk premium, $k_M - k_{RF}$	4%	3%
Stock X's beta coefficient, b_X	2.0	1.0
Stock X's expected growth rate, g_X	5%	6%
D_0	$2.8571	$2.8571
Price of Stock X	$27.27	?

Now give yourself a test: How would the change in each variable, by itself, affect the price, and what is your guess as to the new stock price?

Every change, taken alone, would lead to an *increase* in the price. The first three changes all lower k_X, which declines from 16 to 10 percent:

$$\text{Original } k_X = 8\% + 4\%(2.0) = 16\%.$$
$$\text{New } k_X = 7\% + 3\%(1.0) = 10\%.$$

Using these values, together with the new g value, we find that $\hat{P}_0$ rises from $27.27 to $75.71.[12]

$$\text{Original } \hat{P}_0 = \frac{\$2.8571(1.05)}{0.16 - 0.05} = \frac{\$3}{0.11} = \$27.27.$$

$$\text{New } \hat{P}_0 = \frac{\$2.8571(1.06)}{0.10 - 0.06} = \frac{\$3.0285}{0.04} = \$75.71.$$

At the new price, the expected and required rates of return will be equal:[13]

$$\hat{k}_X = \frac{\$3.0285}{\$75.71} + 6\% = 10\% = k_X.$$

Evidence suggests that stocks, especially those of large companies, adjust rapidly to disequilibrium situations. Consequently, equilibrium ordinarily exists for any given stock, and required and expected returns are generally equal. Stock prices certainly change, sometimes violently and rapidly, but this simply reflects changing conditions and expectations. There are, of course, times when a stock continues to react for several months to favorable or unfavorable developments, but this does not signify a long adjustment period; rather, it simply indicates that as more new pieces of information about the situation become available, the market adjusts to them. The ability of the market to adjust to new information is discussed in the next section.

THE EFFICIENT MARKETS HYPOTHESIS

Efficient Markets Hypothesis (EMH)
The hypothesis that securities are typically in equilibrium — that they are fairly priced in the sense that the price reflects all publicly available information on each security.

A body of theory called the **Efficient Markets Hypothesis (EMH)** holds (1) that stocks are always in equilibrium and (2) that it is impossible for an investor to consistently "beat the market." Essentially, those who believe in the EMH note that there are 100,000 or so full-time, highly trained, professional analysts and traders operating in the market, while there are fewer than 3,000 major stocks. Therefore, if each analyst followed 30 stocks (which is about right, as analysts tend to specialize in the stocks in a specific industry), there would on

---

[12] A price change of this magnitude is by no means rare. The prices of *many* stocks double or halve during a year. For example, during 2000, CIENA Corporation, which designs, manufactures, and sells systems for fiberoptic communications networks, increased in value by 183.04 percent. On the other hand, Priceline.com, which pioneered a unique e-commerce pricing system, declined by 97.23 percent.

[13] It should be obvious by now that *actual realized* rates of return are not necessarily equal to expected and required returns. Thus, an investor might have *expected* to receive a return of 15 percent if he or she had bought Priceline.com or CIENA stock in 2000, but, after the fact, the realized return on CIENA was far above 15 percent, whereas that on Priceline.com was far below.

average be 1,000 analysts following each stock. Further, these analysts work for organizations such as Goldman Sachs, Merrill Lynch, Prudential Insurance, and the like, which have billions of dollars available with which to take advantage of bargains. In addition, as a result of SEC disclosure requirements and electronic information networks, as new information about a stock becomes available, these 1,000 analysts generally receive and evaluate it at about the same time. Therefore, the price of a stock will adjust almost immediately to any new development.

LEVELS OF MARKET EFFICIENCY

If markets are efficient, stock prices will rapidly reflect all available information. This raises an important question: What types of information are available and, therefore, incorporated into stock prices? Financial theorists have discussed three forms, or levels, of market efficiency.

Weak-Form Efficiency

The *weak form* of the EMH states that all information contained in past price movements is fully reflected in current market prices. If this were true, then information about recent trends in stock prices would be of no use in selecting stocks — the fact that a stock has risen for the past three days, for example, would give us no useful clues as to what it will do today or tomorrow. People who believe that weak-form efficiency exists also believe that "tape watchers" and "chartists" are wasting their time.[14]

For example, after studying the past history of the stock market, a chartist might "discover" the following pattern: If a stock falls three consecutive days, its price typically rises 10 percent the following day. The technician would then conclude that investors could make money by purchasing a stock whose price has fallen three consecutive days.

But if this pattern truly existed, wouldn't other investors also discover it, and if so, why would anyone be willing to sell a stock after it had fallen three consecutive days if he or she knows the stock's price is expected to increase by 10 percent the next day? In other words, if a stock is selling at $40 per share after falling three consecutive days, why would investors sell the stock if they expected it to rise to $44 per share one day later? Those who believe in weak-form efficiency argue that if the stock would really rise to $44 per share tomorrow, its price *today* would actually rise to somewhere near $44 per share immediately, thereby eliminating the trading opportunity. Consequently, weak-form efficiency implies that any information that comes from past stock prices is rapidly incorporated into the current stock price.

---

[14] Tape watchers are people who watch the NYSE tape, while chartists plot past patterns of stock price movements. Both are called "technicians," and both believe that they can tell if something is happening to the stock that will cause its price to move up or down in the near future.

Semistrong-Form Efficiency

The *semistrong form* of the EMH states that current market prices reflect all *publicly available* information. Therefore, if semistrong-form efficiency exists, it would do no good to pore over annual reports or other published data because market prices would have adjusted to any good or bad news contained in such reports back when the news came out. With semistrong-form efficiency, investors should expect to earn the returns predicted by the SML, but they should not expect to do any better unless they have good luck or information that is not publicly available. However, insiders (for example, the presidents of companies) who have information that is not publicly available can earn abnormal returns (returns higher than those predicted by the SML) even under semistrong-form efficiency.

Another implication of semistrong-form efficiency is that whenever information is released to the public, stock prices will respond only if the information is different from what had been expected. If, for example, a company announces a 30 percent increase in earnings, and if that increase is about what analysts had been expecting, the announcement should have little or no effect on the company's stock price. On the other hand, the stock price would probably fall if analysts had expected earnings to increase by more than 30 percent, but it probably would rise if they had expected a smaller increase.

Strong-Form Efficiency

The *strong form* of the EMH states that current market prices reflect all pertinent information, whether publicly available or privately held. If this form holds, even insiders would find it impossible to earn abnormal returns in the stock market.[15]

Many empirical studies have been conducted to test for the three forms of market efficiency. Most of these studies suggest that the stock market is indeed highly efficient in the weak form and reasonably efficient in the semistrong form, at least for the larger and more widely followed stocks. However, the strong-form EMH does not hold, so abnormal profits can be made by those who possess inside information.

IMPLICATIONS OF MARKET EFFICIENCY

What bearing does the EMH have on financial decisions? Since stock prices do seem to reflect public information, most stocks appear to be fairly valued. This does not mean that new developments could not cause a stock's price to soar or to plummet, but it does mean that stocks in general are neither overvalued nor

---

[15] Several cases of illegal insider trading have made the news headlines. These cases involved employees of several major investment banking houses and even an employee of the SEC. In the most famous case, Ivan Boesky admitted to making $50 million by purchasing stocks of firms he knew were about to merge. He went to jail, and he had to pay a large fine, but he helped disprove the strong-form EMH.

undervalued — they are fairly priced and in equilibrium. However, there are certainly cases in which corporate insiders have information not known to outsiders.

If the EMH is correct, it is a waste of time for most of us to analyze stocks by looking for those that are undervalued. If stock prices already reflect all publicly available information, and hence are fairly priced, one can "beat the market" only by luck, and it is difficult, if not impossible, for anyone to consistently outperform the market averages. Empirical tests have shown that the EMH is, in its weak and semistrong forms, valid. However, people such as corporate officers who have inside information can do better than the averages, and individuals and organizations that are especially good at digging out information on small, new companies also seem to do consistently well. Also, some investors may be able to analyze and react more quickly than others to releases of new information, and these investors may have an advantage over others. However, the buy-sell actions of those investors quickly bring market prices into equilibrium. Therefore, it is generally safe to assume that $\hat{k} = k$, that $\hat{P}_0 = P_0$, and that stocks plot on the SML.[16]

SELF-TEST QUESTIONS

For a stock to be in equilibrium, what two conditions must hold?

If a stock is *not* in equilibrium, explain how financial markets adjust to bring it into equilibrium.

What is the Efficient Markets Hypothesis (EMH)?

What is the difference among the three forms of the EMH: (1) weak form, (2) semistrong form, and (3) strong form?

What are the implications of the EMH for financial decisions?

---

[16] Market efficiency also has important implications for managerial decisions, especially those pertaining to common stock issues, stock repurchases, and tender offers. Stocks appear to be fairly valued, so decisions based on the premise that a stock is undervalued or overvalued must be approached with caution. However, managers do have better information about their own companies than outsiders, and this information can legally be used to the companies' (but not the managers') advantage.

We should also note that some Wall Street pros have consistently beaten the market over many years, which is inconsistent with the EMH. An interesting article in the April 3, 1995, issue of *Fortune* (Terence P. Paré, "Yes, You Can Beat the Market") argued strongly against the EMH. Paré suggested that each stock has a fundamental value, but when good or bad news about it is announced, most investors fail to interpret this news correctly. As a result, stocks are generally priced above or below their long-term values.

Think of a graph with stock price on the vertical axis and years on the horizontal axis. A stock's fundamental value might be moving up steadily over time as it retains and reinvests earnings. However, its actual price might fluctuate about the intrinsic value line, overreacting to good or bad news and indicating departures from equilibrium. Successful value investors, according to the article, use fundamental analysis to identify stocks' intrinsic values, and then they buy stocks that are undervalued and sell those that are overvalued.

Paré's argument implies that the market is systematically out of equilibrium and that investors can act on this knowledge to beat the market. That position may turn out to be correct, but it may also be that the superior performance Paré noted simply demonstrates that some people are better at obtaining and interpreting information than others, or have been lucky in the past.

TECHNOLOGY MATTERS

A NATION OF TRADERS

A recent story in *Fortune* profiled the dramatic revolution in the way investors trade stocks. Just a few years ago, the vast majority of investors bought and sold stocks by calling a full-service broker. The typical broker would place orders, maintain records, assist with stock selection, and provide guidance regarding long-run asset allocations. These services came at a price — when investors bought stocks, the commissions were often well in excess of $100 a trade.

While the full-service broker is far from dead, many are on the ropes. Now large and small investors have online access to the same type of company and market information that brokers provide, and they can trade stocks online at less than $10 a trade.

These technological changes, combined with the euphoria surrounding the long-running bull market, have encouraged more and more investors to become actively involved in managing their own investments. They tune in regularly to CNBC, and they keep their computer screens "at the ready" to trade on any new information that hits the market.

Online trading is by no means relegated to just a few investors — it now represents a significant percentage of all trades that occur. The *Fortune* article pointed out, for example, that in 1989 only 28 percent of households owned stock, while

10 years later this percentage had risen to 48 percent. Moreover, in 1999 there were 150 Internet brokerage firms versus only 5 three years earlier. Virtually nonexistent three years ago, today the percentage of stocks traded online is approximately 12.5 percent, and that number is expected to rise to nearly 30 percent in the next two or three years.

Changing technology is encouraging more and more investors to take control of their own finances. While this trend has lowered traditional brokers' incomes, it has reduced transaction costs, increased information, and empowered investors. Of course, concerns have been raised about whether individual investors fully understand the risks involved, and whether they have sound strategies in place for long-run investing once the current bull market ends.

Good or bad, most observers believe that online trading is here to stay. However, there will surely be a continuing, but changing, need for professional advisors and stockbrokers to work with the many investors who need guidance or who tire of the grind of keeping track of their positions.

SOURCE: Andy Serwer, Christine Y. Chen, and Angela Key, "A Nation of Traders," *Fortune* (Time Inc., 1999), 116–120.

ACTUAL STOCK PRICES AND RETURNS

Our discussion thus far has focused on *expected* stock prices and *expected* rates of return. Anyone who has ever invested in the stock market knows that there can be, and there generally are, large differences between *expected* and *realized* prices and returns.

Figure 9-5 shows how the market value of a portfolio of stocks has moved in recent years, and Figure 9-6 shows how total realized returns on the portfolio have varied from year to year. The market trend has been strongly up, but it has gone up in some years and down in others, and the stocks of individual companies have likewise gone up and down.[17] We know from theory that expected returns, as estimated by a marginal investor, are always positive, but in some years, as Figure 9-6 shows, actual returns are negative. Of course, even in bad years some individual companies do well, so "the name of the game" in

---

[17] If we constructed graphs like Figures 9-5 and 9-6 for individual stocks rather than for a large portfolio, far greater variability would be shown. Also, if we constructed a graph like Figure 9-6 for bonds, it would have the same general shape, but the bars would be smaller, indicating that gains and losses on bonds are generally smaller than those on stocks. Above-average bond returns occur in years when interest rates decline, and losses occur when interest rates rise sharply.

FIGURE 9-5   S&P 500 Index, 1968-2000

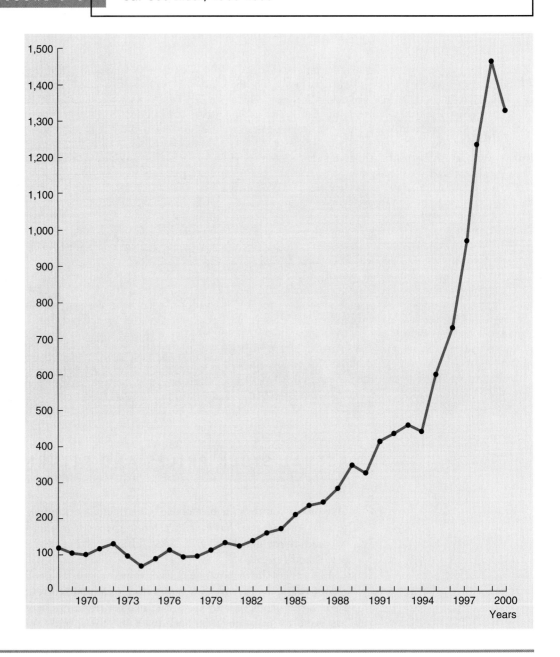

SOURCE: Data taken from various issues of *The Wall Street Journal,* "Stock Market Data Bank" section.

security analysis is to pick the winners. Financial managers attempt to take actions that will put their companies into the winners' column, but they don't always succeed. In subsequent chapters, we will examine the actions that managers can take to increase the odds of their firms doing relatively well in the marketplace.

FIGURE 9-6

S&P 500 Index, Total Returns: Dividend Yield + Capital Gain or Loss, 1968–2000

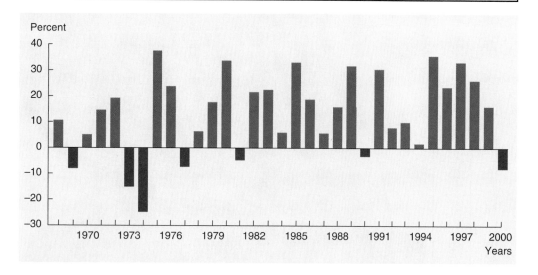

SOURCE: Data taken from various issues of *The Wall Street Journal*.

INVESTING IN INTERNATIONAL STOCKS

As noted in Chapter 6, the U.S. stock market amounts to only 40 percent of the world stock market, and this is prompting many U.S. investors to hold at least some foreign stocks. Analysts have long touted the benefits of investing overseas, arguing that foreign stocks both improve diversification and provide good growth opportunities. For example, after the U.S. stock market rose an average of 17.5 percent a year during the 1980s, many analysts thought that the U.S. market in the 1990s was due for a correction, and they suggested that investors should increase their holdings of foreign stocks.

To the surprise of many, however, U.S. stocks outperformed foreign stocks in the 1990s — they gained about 15 percent a year versus only 3 percent for foreign stocks. Figure 9-7 shows how stocks in different countries performed in 2000. The number in the left boxes indicates how stocks in each country performed in terms of its local currency, while the bold numbers to the right show how the country's stocks performed in terms of the U.S. dollar. For example, in 2000 Australian stocks rose by 5.72 percent, but the Australian dollar declined almost 16 percent versus the U.S. dollar. Therefore, if U.S. investors had bought Australian stocks, they would have made 5.72 percent in Australian dollar terms, but those Australian dollars would have bought 16 percent fewer U.S. dollars, so the effective return would have been −10.03 percent. So, the results of foreign investments depend in part on what happens to the exchange rate. Indeed, when you invest overseas, you are making two bets: (1) that foreign stocks will increase in their local markets and (2) that the currencies in which you will be paid will rise relative to the dollar.

Although U.S. stocks have outperformed foreign stocks in recent years, this by no means suggests that investors should avoid foreign stocks. Foreign

FIGURE 9-7 2000 Performance of the Dow Jones Global Stock Indexes

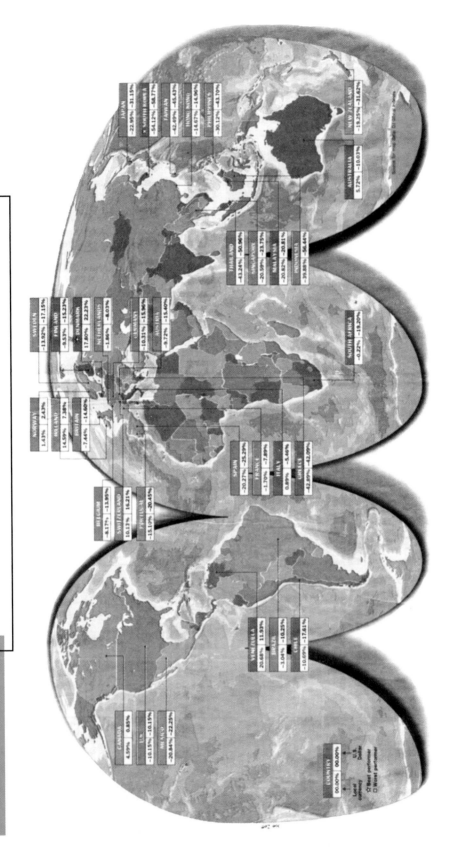

SOURCE: "Indexes Track Web Stocks Off a Cliff," *The Wall Street Journal*, January 2, 2001, R21.

GLOBAL PERSPECTIVES

INVESTING IN EMERGING MARKETS

Given the possibilities of better diversification and higher returns, U.S. investors have been putting more and more money into foreign stocks. While most investors limit their foreign holdings to developed countries such as Japan, Germany, Canada, and the United Kingdom, some have broadened their portfolios to include emerging markets such as South Korea, Mexico, Singapore, Taiwan, and Russia.

Emerging markets provide opportunities for larger returns, but they also entail greater risks. For example, Russian stocks rose more than 150 percent in the first half of 1996, as it became apparent that Boris Yeltsin would be reelected president. By contrast, if you had invested in Taiwanese stocks, you would have lost 30 percent in 1995 — a year in which most stock markets performed extremely well. More recently, rapidly declining currency values caused many Asian markets to fall more than 30 percent in 1997.

Stocks in emerging markets are intriguing for two reasons. First, developing nations have the greatest potential for growth. Second, while stock returns in developed countries often move in sync with one another, stocks in emerging markets march to their own drummers. Therefore, the correlation between U.S. stocks and those in emerging markets are generally lower than between U.S. stocks and those of other developed countries. Thus, correlation data suggest that emerging markets improve the diversification of U.S. investors' portfolios. (Recall from Chapter 6 that the lower the correlation, the better the diversification.)

On the other hand, stocks in emerging markets are often extremely risky, they are less liquid, they involve higher transaction costs, and most U.S. investors do not have ready access to information on the companies involved. To reduce these problems, mutual fund companies have created *country funds*, which invest in "baskets of stocks," for many emerging nations. Country funds avoid the problem of picking individual stocks, but as many investors have discovered recently, country funds do little to protect you in situations like the recent decline in Asian stock markets. There the entire market has fallen by more than 10 percent in a single day.

investments still improve diversification, and it is inevitable that there will be years when foreign stocks outperform domestic stocks. When this occurs, U.S. investors will be glad they put some of their money in overseas markets.

STOCK MARKET REPORTING

Figure 9-8, taken from a daily newspaper, is a section of the stock market page for stocks listed on the NYSE. For each stock, the NYSE report provides specific data on the trading that took place the prior day. Similar information is available for stocks listed on the Nasdaq and other exchanges.

Stocks are listed alphabetically, from AAR Industries to Zweig; the data in Figure 9-8 were taken from the top of the listing. We will examine the data for Abbott Laboratories, AbbotLab, shown toward the bottom of the table. The two columns on the left show the highest and lowest prices at which the stocks have sold during the past year; Abbott Labs has traded in the range from $29.38 to $55.00 during the preceding 52 weeks. The figure just to the right of the company's ticker symbol is the dividend; Abbott Labs had a current indicated annual dividend rate of $0.76 per share and a dividend yield (which is the current dividend divided by the closing stock price) of 1.4 percent. Next comes the ratio of the stock's price to its last 12 months' earnings (the P/E ratio), followed by the volume of trading for the day: 3,637,300 shares of Abbott Labs stock were traded on November 29, 2000. Following the volume come the high and low prices for the day, and then the closing price. On November 29, Abbott Labs traded as high as $55.88 and as low as $54.94, while the last trade was at $55.75. The last column gives the change from the closing price on the previous day. Abbott Labs' closing price was up $1.00 from the previous day's closing price.

FIGURE 9-8   Stock Market Transactions, November 29, 2000

Wednesday, November 29, 2000

52 WEEKS		STOCK	SYM	YLD		VOL				NET
HI	LO	STOCK	SYM	DIV	%	PE	100s	HI	LO	CLOSE	CHG

-A-A-A-

	HI	LO	STOCK	SYM	DIV	%	PE	100s	HI	LO	CLOSE	CHG
	28^{50}	9^{75}	AAR	AIR	.34	3.3	10	790	11^{13}	10^{13}	10^{44}	− 0^{56}
	30	19^{25}	ABM Indus	ABM	.62	2.1	16	116	28^{88}	28	28^{88}	+ 0^{38}
	26^{50}	19^{38}	ABN Am ADR	ABN	1.28e	6.0	...	1131	21^{50}	21^{13}	21^{25}	+ 0^{06}
▲	23^{50}	19^{19}	ABN Am pfA		1.88	8.0	...	993	23^{56}	23^{19}	23^{38}	+ 0^{25}
	22^{50}	18^{88}	ABN Am pfB		1.78	8.0	...	1075	22^{25}	22^{06}	22^{13}	+ 0^{06}
n	26^{25}	20^{25}	ACE CapTr		1.73e	6.9	...	20	25	24^{44}	24^{94}	+ 0^{56}
	42^{50}	14^{06}♣	ACE Ltd	ACL	.52	1.3	15	5183	40	38^{88}	39^{81}	+ 1^{06}
n	83^{75}	47^{69}	ACE LtdPRIDES		2.45e	3.0	...	155	80^{75}	80^{25}	80^{75}	+ 1^{44}
x	8^{06}	6^{31}	ACM GvtFd	ACG	.78	10.5	...	963	7^{50}	7^{44}	7^{44}	...
x	8	6^{25}	ACM OppFd	AOF	.72a	10.1	...	203	7^{25}	7^{13}	7^{13}	...
x	7^{69}	6^{19}	ACM SecFd	GSF	.78	10.8	...	1172	7^{31}	7^{25}	7^{25}	+ 0^{06}
x	6^{25}	5^{13}	ACM SpctmFd	SI	.60	10.1	...	382	6	5^{88}	5^{94}	...
▼x	9^{63}	6^{75}	ACM MgdDlr	ADF	1.02	15.0	...	279	6^{88}	6^{63}	6^{81}	+ 0^{06}
x	7^{19}	4^{56}	ACM MgdInco	AMF	.63	13.8	...	807	4^{69}	4^{56}	4^{56}	...
x	12^{75}	10^{13}	ACM MuniSec	AMU	.87	7.1	...	133	12^{31}	12^{19}	12^{19}	...
s	72^{81}	28^{78}♣	AES	AES	...		44	14644	56^{44}	55^{06}	55^{44}	− 0^{25}

⋮

	HI	LO	STOCK	SYM	DIV	%	PE	100s	HI	LO	CLOSE	CHG
	81^{50}	58^{25}	AXA ADS	AXA	2.16e	3.1	...	4506	70^{19}	69^{13}	70	+ 1^{81}
	56^{13}	25^{94}♣	AXA Fnl	AXF	.10	.2	34	29458	56	55^{56}	55^{63}	+ 0^{31}
	22^{94}	9	AZZ	AZZ	.16f	.9	11	49	17^{38}	17^{06}	17^{38}	+ 0^{19}
s	5^{94}	0^{44}	AamesFnl	AAM	...		dd	182	1	0^{88}	1	+ 0^{06}
x	18^{25}	11^{47}	AaronRent	RNT	.04	.3	12	77	15^{69}	15^{25}	15^{69}	− 0^{06}
	22^{25}	19	AbbeyNtl	SUA	1.75	7.9	...	85	22^{13}	21^{88}	22^{13}	+ 0^{19}
	23^{25}	19^{50}	AbbeyNtl 7 1/4%	SUD	1.81	8.0	...	130	22^{75}	22^{25}	22^{75}	+ 0^{31}
	25^{50}	22^{13}	AbbeyNtl pfA		2.19	9.1	...	72	24^{19}	23^{88}	23^{94}	+ 0^{06}
▲	55	29^{38}	AbbotLab	ABT	.76	1.4	32	36373	55^{88}	54^{94}	55^{75}	+ 1
	32^{56}	8	Abercrombie A	ANF			18	13231	28^{25}	26^{75}	28^{19}	+ 0^{19}
	13^{69}	7	Abitibi g	ABY	.40g	...	...	713	8^{81}	8^{56}	8^{69}	+ 0^{06}
	6^{25}	4^{38}♣	AcadiaRlty	AKR	.48	8.4	18	55	5^{75}	5^{69}	5^{69}	− 0^{13}
	7	2^{75}♣	AcceptIns	AIF	...		dd	257	5^{25}	5^{13}	5^{13}	− 0^{13}
	19^{56}	8	AckrlyGp	AK	.02	.2	2	122	9^{44}	9^{13}	9^{19}	− 0^{25}
	26^{88}	16^{31}	ACNielsen	ART			23	1651	23^{38}	23^{06}	23^{19}	− 0^{19}
s	5^{44}	1^{58}	Actuant A	ATU	...		5	459	3^{94}	3^{75}	3^{81}	+ 0^{06}
s	27^{04}	20^{17}♣	AdamsExp	ADX	1.85e	8.5	...	269	21^{81}	21^{50}	21^{81}	+ 0^{06}
	112	69^{55}	Adecco	ADO	.61e	.8	...	43	77^{45}	77^{01}	77^{05}	+ 1^{65}

NOTES: The "pf" following the stock name of the ABN Am listing tells us that this one is a preferred stock rather than a common stock. A "▲" preceding the columns containing a stock's 52-week high and low prices indicates that the price hit a new 52-week high, whereas a "▼" indicates a new 52-week low. An "x" preceding the columns containing the 52-week high and low prices indicates that the stock went ex-dividend that day; this means that someone who buys the stock will not receive the next dividend. An "s" preceding the 52-week high and low prices indicates that the stock was split within the past 52 weeks. (See Chapter 14 for a discussion of stock splits.) An "n" preceding the 52-week high and low prices indicates that the stock is newly issued within the past 52 weeks. An "f" following the dividend column indicates that the annual dividend was increased on the last declaration date. An "e" following the dividend column indicates that a dividend was declared or paid in the preceding 12 months, but there is no regular dividend rate. Other dividend indicators are also occasionally used. Finally, a "club" appearing before the company name indicates that *Journal* readers can obtain a copy of the company's annual report.

SOURCE: *The Wall Street Journal,* November 30, 2000, C5.

Explain why expected, required, and realized returns are often different.

What are the key benefits of adding foreign stocks to a portfolio?

When a U.S. investor purchases foreign stocks, what two things is he or she hoping will happen?

PREFERRED STOCK

Preferred stock is a *hybrid* — it is similar to bonds in some respects and to common stock in others. The hybrid nature of preferred stock becomes apparent when we try to classify it in relation to bonds and common stock. Like bonds, preferred stock has a par value and a fixed amount of dividends that must be paid before dividends can be paid on the common stock. However, if the preferred dividend is not earned, the directors can omit (or "pass") it without throwing the company into bankruptcy. So, although preferred stock has a fixed payment like bonds, a failure to make this payment will not lead to bankruptcy.

As noted above, a preferred stock entitles its owners to regular, fixed dividend payments. If the payments last forever, the issue is a perpetuity whose value, V_p, is found as follows:

$$V_p = \frac{D_p}{k_p}. \tag{9-8}$$

V_p is the value of the preferred stock, D_p is the preferred dividend, and k_p is the required rate of return. Allied Food Products has preferred stock outstanding that pays a dividend of $10 per year. If the required rate of return on this preferred stock is 10 percent, then its value is $100, found by solving Equation 9-8 as follows:

$$V_p = \frac{\$10.00}{0.10} = \$100.00.$$

In equilibrium the expected return, $\hat{k}_p$, is equal to the required return, k_p. Thus, if we know the current price of a preferred stock and its dividend, we can solve for the expected rate of return as follows:

$$\hat{k}_p = \frac{D_p}{V_p}. \tag{9-8a}$$

Some preferred stocks have a stated maturity date, say, 50 years. If Allied's preferred matured in 50 years, paid a $10 annual dividend, and had a required return of 8 percent, then we could find its price as follows: Enter N = 50, I = 8, PMT = 10, and FV = 100. Then press PV to find the price, V_p = $124.47. If k = I = 10%, change I = 8 to I = 10, and find V_p = PV = $100. If you know the price of a share of preferred stock, you can solve for I to find the expected rate of return, $\hat{k}_p$.

Most preferred stocks pay dividends quarterly. This is true for Allied Food, so we could find the effective rate of return on its preferred stock (perpetual or maturing) as follows:

$$EFF\% = EAR_p = \left(1 + \frac{k_{Nom}}{m}\right)^m - 1 = \left(1 + \frac{0.10}{4}\right)^4 - 1 = 10.38\%.$$

If an investor wanted to compare the returns on Allied's bonds and its preferred stock, it would be best to convert the nominal rates on each security to effective rates and then compare these "equivalent annual rates."

SELF-TEST QUESTIONS

Explain the following statement: "Preferred stock is a hybrid security."

Is the equation used to value preferred stock more like the one used to evaluate a bond or the one used to evaluate a "normal" common stock?

TYING IT ALL TOGETHER

Corporate decisions should be analyzed in terms of how alternative courses of action are likely to affect a firm's value. However, it is necessary to know how stock prices are established before attempting to measure how a given decision will affect a specific firm's value. This chapter showed how stock values are determined, and also how investors estimate the rates of return they expect to earn. The key concepts covered are summarized below.

- A **proxy** is a document that gives one person the power to act for another, typically the power to vote shares of common stock. A **proxy fight** occurs when an outside group solicits stockholders' proxies in an effort to vote a new management team into office.

- A **takeover** occurs when a person or group succeeds in ousting a firm's management and takes control of the company.

- Stockholders often have the right to purchase any additional shares sold by the firm. This right, called the **preemptive right,** protects the control of the present stockholders and prevents dilution of their stock's value.

- Although most firms have only one type of common stock, in some instances **classified stock** is used to meet the special needs of the company. One type of classified stock is **founders' shares.** This is stock owned by the firm's founders that carries sole voting rights but restricted dividends for a specified number of years.

- A **closely held corporation** is one that is owned by a few individuals who are typically associated with the firm's management.

- A **publicly owned corporation** is one that is owned by a relatively large number of individuals who are not actively involved in its management.

- Whenever stock in a closely held corporation is offered to the public for the first time, the company is said to be **going public.** The market for stock that is just being offered to the public is called the **initial public offering (IPO) market.**

■ The **value of a share of stock** is calculated as the **present value of the stream of dividends** the stock is expected to provide in the future.

■ The equation used to find the **value of a constant growth stock** is:

$$\hat{P}_0 = \frac{D_1}{k_s - g}.$$

■ The **expected total rate of return** from a stock consists of an **expected dividend yield** plus an **expected capital gains yield.** For a constant growth firm, both the expected dividend yield and the expected capital gains yield are constant.

■ The equation for $\hat{k}_s$, the **expected rate of return on a constant growth stock,** can be expressed as follows:

$$\hat{k}_s = \frac{D_1}{P_0} + g.$$

■ A **zero growth stock** is one whose future dividends are not expected to grow at all, while a **supernormal growth stock** is one whose earnings and dividends are expected to grow much faster than the economy as a whole over some specified time period and then to grow at the "normal" rate.

■ To find the **present value of a supernormal growth stock,** (1) find the dividends expected during the supernormal growth period, (2) find the price of the stock at the end of the supernormal growth period, (3) discount the dividends and the projected price back to the present, and (4) sum these PVs to find the current value of the stock, $\hat{P}_0$.

■ The **terminal,** or **horizon, date** is the date when individual dividend forecasts are no longer made because the dividend growth rate is assumed to be constant.

■ The **terminal value** is the value at the horizon date of all future dividends after that date.

■ The **total company,** or **corporate value, model** is a valuation model used in place of the dividend growth model to determine a firm's value, especially one that does not pay dividends or is privately held. This model discounts a firm's free cash flows at the WACC to determine its value.

■ The **marginal investor** is a representative investor whose actions reflect the beliefs of those people who are currently trading a stock. It is the marginal investor who determines a stock's price.

■ **Equilibrium** is the condition under which the expected return on a security as seen by the marginal investor is just equal to its required return, $\hat{k} = k$. Also, the stock's intrinsic value must be equal to its market price, $\hat{P}_0 = P_0$, and the market price is stable.

■ The **Efficient Markets Hypothesis (EMH)** holds (1) that stocks are always in equilibrium and (2) that it is impossible for an investor who does not have inside information to consistently "beat the market." Therefore, according to the EMH, stocks are always fairly valued ($\hat{P}_0 = P_0$), the required return on a stock is equal to its expected return ($k = \hat{k}$), and all stocks' expected returns plot on the SML.

- Differences can and do exist between expected and realized returns in the stock and bond markets—only for short-term, risk-free assets are expected and actual (or realized) returns equal.

- When U.S. investors purchase foreign stocks, they hope (1) that the stock prices will increase in the local market and (2) that the foreign currencies will rise relative to the U.S. dollar.

- **Preferred stock** is a hybrid security having some characteristics of debt and some of equity.

- Most preferred stocks are **perpetuities,** and the value of a share of perpetual preferred stock is found as the dividend divided by the required rate of return:

$$V_p = \frac{D_p}{k_p}.$$

- **Maturing preferred stock** is evaluated with a formula that is identical in form to the bond value formula.

QUESTIONS

9-1 Two investors are evaluating AT&T's stock for possible purchase. They agree on the expected value of D_1 and also on the expected future dividend growth rate. Further, they agree on the riskiness of the stock. However, one investor normally holds stocks for 2 years, while the other normally holds stocks for 10 years. On the basis of the type of analysis done in this chapter, they should both be willing to pay the same price for AT&T's stock. True or false? Explain.

9-2 A bond that pays interest forever and has no maturity date is a perpetual bond. In what respect is a perpetual bond similar to a no-growth common stock, and to a share of preferred stock?

9-3 If you bought a share of common stock, you would typically expect to receive dividends plus capital gains. Would you expect the distribution between dividend yield and capital gains to be influenced by the firm's decision to pay more dividends rather than to retain and reinvest more of its earnings?

9-4 Is it true that the following expression can be used to find the value of a constant growth stock?

$$\hat{P}_0 = \frac{D_0}{k_s + g}.$$

9-5 It is frequently stated that the primary purpose of the preemptive right is to allow individuals to maintain their proportionate share of the ownership and control of a corporation.
a. How important do you suppose this consideration is for the average stockholder of a firm whose shares are traded on the New York Stock Exchange?
b. Is the preemptive right likely to be of more importance to stockholders of publicly owned or closely held firms? Explain.

SELF-TEST PROBLEMS (SOLUTIONS APPEAR IN APPENDIX B)

ST-1
Key terms
Define each of the following terms:
a. Proxy; proxy fight; takeover
b. Preemptive right
c. Classified stock; founders' shares
d. Closely held corporation; publicly owned corporation
e. Secondary market; primary market
f. Going public; initial public offering (IPO) market
g. Intrinsic value ($\hat{P}_0$); market price (P_0)
h. Required rate of return, k_s; expected rate of return, $\hat{k}_s$; actual, or realized, rate of return, $\bar{k}_s$

i. Capital gains yield; dividend yield; expected total return; growth rate, g
j. Zero growth stock
k. Normal, or constant, growth; supernormal, or nonconstant, growth
l. Total company (corporate value) model
m. Terminal (horizon) date; horizon (terminal) value
n. Marginal investor
o. Equilibrium
p. Efficient Markets Hypothesis (EMH); three forms of EMH
q. Preferred stock

ST-2
Stock growth rates and valuation

You are considering buying the stocks of two companies that operate in the same industry; they have very similar characteristics except for their dividend payout policies. Both companies are expected to earn $6 per share this year. However, Company D (for "dividend") is expected to pay out all of its earnings as dividends, while Company G (for "growth") is expected to pay out only one-third of its earnings, or $2 per share. D's stock price is $40. G and D are equally risky. Which of the following is most likely to be true?
a. Company G will have a faster growth rate than Company D. Therefore, G's stock price should be greater than $40.
b. Although G's growth rate should exceed D's, D's current dividend exceeds that of G, and this should cause D's price to exceed G's.
c. An investor in Stock D will get his or her money back faster because D pays out more of its earnings as dividends. Thus, in a sense, D is like a short-term bond, and G is like a long-term bond. Therefore, if economic shifts cause k_d and k_s to increase, and if the expected streams of dividends from D and G remain constant, both Stocks D and G will decline, but D's price should decline further.
d. D's expected and required rate of return is $\hat{k}_s = k_s = 15\%$. G's expected return will be higher because of its higher expected growth rate.
e. If we observe that G's price is also $40, the best estimate of G's growth rate is 10 percent.

ST-3
Constant growth stock valuation

Ewald Company's current stock price is $36, and its last dividend was $2.40. In view of Ewald's strong financial position and its consequent low risk, its required rate of return is only 12 percent. If dividends are expected to grow at a constant rate, g, in the future, and if k_s is expected to remain at 12 percent, what is Ewald's expected stock price 5 years from now?

ST-4
Supernormal growth stock valuation

Snyder Computer Chips Inc. is experiencing a period of rapid growth. Earnings and dividends are expected to grow at a rate of 15 percent during the next 2 years, at 13 percent in the third year, and at a constant rate of 6 percent thereafter. Snyder's last dividend was $1.15, and the required rate of return on the stock is 12 percent.
a. Calculate the value of the stock today.
b. Calculate $\hat{P}_1$ and $\hat{P}_2$.
c. Calculate the dividend yield and capital gains yield for Years 1, 2, and 3.

STARTER PROBLEMS

9-1
DPS calculation

Warr Corporation just paid a dividend of $1.50 a share (i.e., $D_0 = \$1.50$). The dividend is expected to grow 5 percent a year for the next 3 years, and then 10 percent a year thereafter. What is the expected dividend per share for each of the next 5 years?

9-2
Constant growth valuation

Thomas Brothers is expected to pay a $0.50 per share dividend at the end of the year (i.e., $D_1 = \$0.50$). The dividend is expected to grow at a constant rate of 7 percent a year. The required rate of return on the stock, k_s, is 15 percent. What is the value per share of the company's stock?

9-3
Constant growth valuation

Harrison Clothiers' stock currently sells for $20 a share. The stock just paid a dividend of $1.00 a share (i.e., $D_0 = \$1.00$). The dividend is expected to grow at a constant rate of 10 percent a year. What stock price is expected 1 year from now? What is the required rate of return on the company's stock?

9-4
Preferred stock valuation

Fee Founders has preferred stock outstanding that pays a dividend of $5 at the end of each year. The preferred stock sells for $60 a share. What is the preferred stock's required rate of return?

9-5
Supernormal growth valuation

Hart Enterprises recently paid a dividend, D_0, of $1.25. The company expects to have supernormal growth of 20 percent for 2 years before the dividend is expected to grow at a constant rate of 5 percent. The firm's cost of equity is 10 percent.

a. What year is the terminal, or horizon, date?
b. What is the firm's horizon, or terminal, value?
c. What is the firm's intrinsic value today, $\hat{P}_0$?

EXAM-TYPE PROBLEMS

The problems included in this section are set up in such a way that they could be used as multiple-choice exam problems.

9-6
Corporate value model

Due to the highly specialized nature of the electronic industry, Barrett Industries invests a lot of money in R&D on prospective products. Consequently, it retains all of its earnings and reinvests them into the firm. (In other words, it does not pay any dividends.) At this time, Barrett does not have plans to pay any dividends in the near future. A major pension fund is interested in purchasing Barrett's stock, which is traded on the NYSE. The treasurer of the pension fund has done a great deal of research on the company and realizes that its valuation must be based on the total company model. The pension fund's treasurer has estimated Barrett's free cash flows for the next 4 years as follows: $3 million, $6 million, $10 million, and $15 million. After the fourth year, free cash flow is projected to grow at a constant 7 percent. Barrett's WACC is 12 percent, it has $60 million of total debt and preferred stock, and 10 million shares of common stock.
a. What is the present value of Barrett's free cash flows during the next 4 years?
b. What is the company's terminal value?
c. What is the total value of the firm today?
d. What is Barrett's price per share?

9-7
Corporate value model

Today is December 31, 2001. The following information applies to Vermeil Airlines:

■ After-tax, operating income [EBIT(1 − T)] for 2002 is expected to be $500 million.

■ The company's depreciation expense for 2002 is expected to be $100 million.

■ The company's capital expenditures for 2002 are expected to be $200 million.

■ No change is expected in the company's net operating working capital.

■ The company's free cash flow is expected to grow at a constant rate of 6 percent per year.

■ The company's cost of equity is 14 percent.

■ The company's WACC is 10 percent.

■ The market value of the company's debt is $3 billion.

■ The company has 200 million shares of stock outstanding.

Using the free cash flow approach, what should the company's stock price be today?

9-8
Corporate valuation

Dozier Corporation is a fast-growing supplier of office products. Analysts project the following free cash flows (FCFs) during the next 3 years, after which FCF is expected to grow at a constant 7 percent rate. Dozier's WACC is 13%.

Time	1	2	3
Free cash flow ($ millions)	−$20	$30	$40

a. What is Dozier's terminal, or horizon, value? (Hint: Find the value of all free cash flows beyond Year 3 discounted back to Year 3.)
b. What is the value of the firm today?
c. Suppose Dozier has $100 million in debt and 10 million shares of stock. What is the price per share?

9-9
Supernormal growth valuation

A company currently pays a dividend of $2 per share, $D_0 = \$2$. It is estimated that the company's dividend will grow at a rate of 20 percent per year for the next 2 years, then the dividend will grow at a constant rate of 7 percent thereafter. The company's stock has a beta equal to 1.2, the risk-free rate is 7.5 percent, and the market risk premium is 4 percent. What would you estimate is the stock's current price?

9-10
Constant growth rate, g

A stock is trading at $80 per share. The stock is expected to have a year-end dividend of $4 per share ($D_1 = \$4.00$), which is expected to grow at some constant rate g throughout time. The stock's required rate of return is 14 percent. If you are an analyst who believes in efficient markets, what would be your forecast of g?

9-11
Constant growth valuation

You are considering an investment in the common stock of Keller Corp. The stock is expected to pay a dividend of $2 a share at the end of the year ($D_1 = \$2.00$). The stock has a beta equal to 0.9. The risk-free rate is 5.6 percent, and the market risk premium is 6 percent. The stock's dividend is expected to grow at some constant rate g. The stock currently sells for $25 a share. Assuming the market is in equilibrium, what does the market believe will be the stock price at the end of 3 years? (That is, what is $\hat{P}_3$?)

9-12
Preferred stock rate of return

What will be the nominal rate of return on a preferred stock with a $100 par value, a stated dividend of 8 percent of par, and a current market price of (a) $60, (b) $80, (c) $100, and (d) $140?

9-13
Declining growth stock valuation

Martell Mining Company's ore reserves are being depleted, so its sales are falling. Also, its pit is getting deeper each year, so its costs are rising. As a result, the company's earnings and dividends are declining at the constant rate of 5 percent per year. If $D_0 = \$5$ and $k_s = 15\%$, what is the value of Martell Mining's stock?

9-14
Rates of return and equilibrium

The beta coefficient for Stock C is $b_C = 0.4$, whereas that for Stock D is $b_D = -0.5$. (Stock D's beta is negative, indicating that its rate of return rises whenever returns on most other stocks fall. There are very few negative beta stocks, although collection agency stocks are sometimes cited as an example.)

a. If the risk-free rate is 9 percent and the expected rate of return on an average stock is 13 percent, what are the required rates of return on Stocks C and D?

b. For Stock C, suppose the current price, P_0, is $25; the next expected dividend, D_1, is $1.50; and the stock's expected constant growth rate is 4 percent. Is the stock in equilibrium? Explain, and describe what will happen if the stock is not in equilibrium.

9-15
Supernormal growth stock valuation

Assume that the average firm in your company's industry is expected to grow at a constant rate of 6 percent and its dividend yield is 7 percent. Your company is about as risky as the average firm in the industry, but it has just successfully completed some R&D work that leads you to expect that its earnings and dividends will grow at a rate of 50 percent $[D_1 = D_0(1 + g) = D_0(1.50)]$ this year and 25 percent the following year, after which growth should match the 6 percent industry average rate. The last dividend paid (D_0) was $1.00. What is the value per share of your firm's stock?

9-16
Supernormal growth stock valuation

Microtech Corporation is expanding rapidly, and it currently needs to retain all of its earnings, hence it does not pay any dividends. However, investors expect Microtech to begin paying dividends, with the first dividend of $1.00 coming 3 years from today. The dividend should grow rapidly — at a rate of 50 percent per year — during Years 4 and 5. After Year 5, the company should grow at a constant rate of 8 percent per year. If the required return on the stock is 15 percent, what is the value of the stock today?

PROBLEMS

9-17
Preferred stock valuation

Ezzell Corporation issued preferred stock with a stated dividend of 10 percent of par. Preferred stock of this type currently yields 8 percent, and the par value is $100. Assume dividends are paid annually.

a. What is the value of Ezzell's preferred stock?

b. Suppose interest rate levels rise to the point where the preferred stock now yields 12 percent. What would be the value of Ezzell's preferred stock?

9-18
Constant growth stock valuation

Your broker offers to sell you some shares of Bahnsen & Co. common stock that paid a dividend of $2 *yesterday*. You expect the dividend to grow at the rate of 5 percent per year for the next 3 years, and, if you buy the stock, you plan to hold it for 3 years and then sell it.

a. Find the expected dividend for each of the next 3 years; that is, calculate D_1, D_2, and D_3. Note that $D_0 = \$2.00$.

b. Given that the appropriate discount rate is 12 percent and that the first of these dividend payments will occur 1 year from now, find the present value of the dividend stream; that is, calculate the PV of D_1, D_2, and D_3, and then sum these PVs.

c. You expect the price of the stock 3 years from now to be $34.73; that is, you expect $\hat{P}_3$ to equal $34.73. Discounted at a 12 percent rate, what is the present value of this expected future stock price? In other words, calculate the PV of $34.73.

d. If you plan to buy the stock, hold it for 3 years, and then sell it for $34.73, what is the most you should pay for it today?

e. Use Equation 9-2 to calculate the present value of this stock. Assume that g = 5%, and it is constant.

f. Is the value of this stock dependent upon how long you plan to hold it? In other words, if your planned holding period were 2 years or 5 years rather than 3 years, would this affect the value of the stock today, $\hat{P}_0$?

9-19
Return on common stock

You buy a share of The Ludwig Corporation stock for $21.40. You expect it to pay dividends of $1.07, $1.1449, and $1.2250 in Years 1, 2, and 3, respectively, and you expect to sell it at a price of $26.22 at the end of 3 years.

a. Calculate the growth rate in dividends.

b. Calculate the expected dividend yield.

c. Assuming that the calculated growth rate is expected to continue, you can add the dividend yield to the expected growth rate to get the expected total rate of return. What is this stock's expected total rate of return?

9-20
Constant growth stock valuation

Investors require a 15 percent rate of return on Levine Company's stock (k_s = 15%).

a. What will be Levine's stock value if the previous dividend was D_0 = $2 and if investors expect dividends to grow at a constant compound annual rate of (1) −5 percent, (2) 0 percent, (3) 5 percent, and (4) 10 percent?

b. Using data from part a, what is the Gordon (constant growth) model value for Levine's stock if the required rate of return is 15 percent and the expected growth rate is (1) 15 percent or (2) 20 percent? Are these reasonable results? Explain.

c. Is it reasonable to expect that a constant growth stock would have g > k_s?

9-21
Stock reporting

Look up the prices of American Telephone & Telegraph's (AT&T) stock in *The Wall Street Journal* (or some other newspaper that provides this information). (Hint: Its stock symbol is T.)

a. What was the stock's price range during the last year?

b. What is AT&T's current dividend? What is its dividend yield?

c. What change occurred in AT&T's stock price the day the newspaper was published?

d. If you had $10,000 and wanted to invest it in AT&T, what return would you expect to get if you bought AT&T's stock? (Hint: Think about capital gains when you answer this question.)

9-22
Supernormal growth stock valuation

It is now January 1, 2002. Wayne-Martin Electric Inc. (WME) has just developed a solar panel capable of generating 200 percent more electricity than any solar panel currently on the market. As a result, WME is expected to experience a 15 percent annual growth rate for the next 5 years. By the end of 5 years, other firms will have developed comparable technology, and WME's growth rate will slow to 5 percent per year indefinitely. Stockholders require a return of 12 percent on WME's stock. The most recent annual dividend (D_0), which was paid yesterday, was $1.75 per share.

a. Calculate WME's expected dividends for 2002, 2003, 2004, 2005, and 2006.

b. Calculate the value of the stock today, $\hat{P}_0$. Proceed by finding the present value of the dividends expected at the end of 2002, 2003, 2004, 2005, and 2006 plus the present value of the stock price that should exist at the end of 2006. The year-end 2006 stock price can be found by using the constant growth equation. Notice that to find the December 31, 2006, price, you use the dividend expected in 2007, which is 5 percent greater than the 2006 dividend.

c. Calculate the expected dividend yield, D_1/P_0, the capital gains yield expected in 2002, and the expected total return (dividend yield plus capital gains yield) for 2002. (Assume that $\hat{P}_0$ = P_0, and recognize that the capital gains yield is equal to the total return minus the dividend yield.) Also calculate these same three yields for 2007.

d. How might an investor's tax situation affect his or her decision to purchase stocks of companies in the early stages of their lives, when they are growing rapidly, versus stocks of older, more mature firms? When does WME's stock become "mature" in this example?

e. Suppose your boss tells you she believes that WME's annual growth rate will be only 12 percent during the next 5 years and that the firm's normal growth rate will be only 4 percent. Without doing any calculations, what general effect would these growth-rate changes have on the price of WME's stock?

f. Suppose your boss also tells you that she regards WME as being quite risky and that she believes the required rate of return should be 14 percent, not 12 percent. Again, without doing any calculations, how would the higher required rate of return affect the price of the stock, its capital gains yield, and its dividend yield? Again, assume that the firm's normal growth rate will be 4 percent.

Taussig Technologies Corporation (TTC) has been growing at a rate of 20 percent per year in recent years. This same growth rate is expected to last for another 2 years.
a. If $D_0 = \$1.60$, $k = 10\%$, and $g_n = 6\%$, what is TTC's stock worth today? What are its expected dividend yield and capital gains yield at this time?
b. Now assume that TTC's period of supernormal growth is to last for 5 years rather than 2 years. How would this affect its price, dividend yield, and capital gains yield? Answer in words only.
c. What will be TTC's dividend yield and capital gains yield once its period of supernormal growth ends? (Hint: These values will be the same regardless of whether you examine the case of 2 or 5 years of supernormal growth; the calculations are very easy.)
d. Of what interest to investors is the changing relationship between dividend yield and capital gains yield over time?

The risk-free rate of return, k_{RF}, is 11 percent; the required rate of return on the market, k_M, is 14 percent; and Upton Company's stock has a beta coefficient of 1.5.
a. If the dividend expected during the coming year, D_1, is \$2.25, and if g = a constant 5%, at what price should Upton's stock sell?
b. Now, suppose the Federal Reserve Board increases the money supply, causing the risk-free rate to drop to 9 percent and k_M to fall to 12 percent. What would this do to the price of the stock?
c. In addition to the change in Part b, suppose investors' risk aversion declines; this fact, combined with the decline in k_{RF}, causes k_M to fall to 11 percent. At what price would Upton's stock sell?
d. Now, suppose Upton has a change in management. The new group institutes policies that increase the expected constant growth rate to 6 percent. Also, the new management stabilizes sales and profits, and thus causes the beta coefficient to decline from 1.5 to 1.3. Assume that k_{RF} and k_M are equal to the values in part c. After all these changes, what is Upton's new equilibrium price? (Note: D_1 is now \$2.27.)

Suppose Chance Chemical Company's management conducts a study and concludes that if Chance expanded its consumer products division (which is less risky than its primary business, industrial chemicals), the firm's beta would decline from 1.2 to 0.9. However, consumer products have a somewhat lower profit margin, and this would cause Chance's constant growth rate in earnings and dividends to fall from 7 to 5 percent.
a. Should management make the change? Assume the following: $k_M = 12\%$; $k_{RF} = 9\%$; $D_0 = \$2.00$.
b. Assume all the facts as given above except the change in the beta coefficient. How low would the beta have to fall to cause the expansion to be a good one? (Hint: Set $\hat{P}_0$ under the new policy equal to $\hat{P}_0$ under the old one, and find the new beta that will produce this equality.)

SPREADSHEET PROBLEM

Rework Problem 9-23, parts a, b, and c, using a spreadsheet model. For part b, calculate the price, dividend yield, and capital gains yield as called for in the problem. After completing parts a through c, answer the following additional question using your spreadsheet model.
d. Suppose an alternative method of valuing TTC's stock has been proposed. It has been suggested that the free cash flow method be used to value the firm's stock. The firm has just introduced a new line of products that have been wildly successful. On the basis of this success and anticipated future success, the projected income statements resulted in the following free cash flow projections:

Year	1	2	3	4	5	6	7	8	9	10
FCF	\$5.5	\$12.1	\$23.8	\$44.1	\$69.0	\$88.8	\$107.5	\$128.9	\$147.1	\$161.3

In addition, the firm estimates its overall WACC has fallen to 9 percent. After the 10th year, TTC's financial planners anticipate that free cash flow will grow at a constant rate of 6 percent. TTC's balance sheet also shows that the market value of debt is \$1,200 million and that there are 20 million shares of common stock outstanding. Use the free cash flow method to value a share of TTC's stock.

9-27
Stock valuation

The information related to this cyberproblem is likely to change over time, due to the release of new information and the ever-changing nature of the World Wide Web. Accordingly, we will periodically update the problem on the textbook's web site. To avoid problems, please check for updates before proceeding with the cyberproblems.

In this cyberproblem, you will value the stock for Emerson Electric, a scientific and technical instrument company. While stock valuation is obviously important to investors, it is also vital to companies engaging in a merger or acquisition. Here, the process of stock valuation can often be quite subjective. Frequently, the opposing sides of a merger or acquisition will have vastly differing opinions of a firm's value.

For example, in 1994, part of AT&T's purchase of McCaw Cellular called for AT&T to acquire McCaw's 52 percent stake in LIN Broadcasting and purchase the remaining 48 percent at its fair value. LIN's advisors valued the stock at $162 a share, while AT&T estimated its value at $100 a share. The difference resulted in a whopping $1.6 billion. As this example demonstrates, stock valuation seems to be both art and science.

In this cyberproblem, you will use the dividend growth model's constant growth assumptions to value Emerson's stock. In addition, you will apply the concepts of risk and return by estimating the stock's required return from the CAPM model. In order to arrive at a value for Emerson Electric, you will gather and use information from a variety of sources, including **http://www.stocktrader.com** and **http://www.financialweb.com.**

a. To begin, you need to find an estimate of the risk-free rate of interest, k_{RF}. Use the web site **www.stocktrader.com** to find the 30-year Treasury bond rate, and use this interest rate as the risk-free rate. In addition, you need a value for the market risk premium; however, k_M is not directly observable. It can be estimated using index returns or consensus analyst estimates, but may not be entirely accurate. Nonetheless, studies indicate that historically the market risk premium ranges from 4 to 8 percent. For this cyberproblem, you will use an assumed market risk premium of 6.0 percent.

b. Find an estimate of Emerson Electric's beta using the web site **www. financialweb. com/rshIndex.asp.** Run a fundamental stock report for Emerson by clicking on

"Company Profiles and Fundamentals" and then entering Emerson's ticker symbol, EMR, in the symbol box on the next screen.

c. From data gathered in parts a and b, use the CAPM model to determine Emerson's required return.

d. Identify Emerson's current annual dividend and dividend growth rate. Use FinancialWeb's complete fundamental report to find this information.

e. The fundamental valuation of any financial asset is equal to the present value of all its anticipated future cash flows. For this reason, the current dividend does not interest us as much as the next annual dividend does. Calculate Emerson's next annual dividend, D_1.

f. Assuming a constant growth rate, use the DCF model to determine the expected price of one share of Emerson Electric stock.

g. Compare Emerson's expected value with its current market price. You can use **FinancialWeb.com** to obtain Emerson's current stock quote.

INTEGRATED CASE

MUTUAL OF CHICAGO INSURANCE COMPANY

9-28 Stock Valuation Robert Balik and Carol Kiefer are senior vice-presidents of the Mutual of Chicago Insurance Company. They are co-directors of the company's pension fund management division, with Balik having responsibility for fixed income securities (primarily bonds) and Kiefer being responsible for equity investments. A major new client, the California League of Cities, has requested that Mutual of Chicago present an investment seminar to the mayors of the represented cities, and Balik and Kiefer, who will make the actual presentation, have asked you to help them.

To illustrate the common stock valuation process, Balik and Kiefer have asked you to analyze the Bon Temps Company, an employment agency that supplies word processor operators and computer programmers to businesses with temporarily heavy workloads. You are to answer the following questions.

a. Describe briefly the legal rights and privileges of common stockholders.

b. (1) Write out a formula that can be used to value any stock, regardless of its dividend pattern.

(2) What is a constant growth stock? How are constant growth stocks valued?

(3) What happens if a company has a constant g that exceeds its k_s? Will many stocks have expected $g > k_s$ in the short run (that is, for the next few years)? In the long run (that is, forever)?

c. Assume that Bon Temps has a beta coefficient of 1.2, that the risk-free rate (the yield on T-bonds) is 7 percent, and that the required rate of return on the market is 12 percent. What is the required rate of return on the firm's stock?

d. Assume that Bon Temps is a constant growth company whose last dividend (D_0, which was paid yesterday) was $2.00 and whose dividend is expected to grow indefinitely at a 6 percent rate.

(1) What is the firm's expected dividend stream over the next 3 years?

(2) What is the firm's current stock price?

(3) What is the stock's expected value 1 year from now?

(4) What are the expected dividend yield, the capital gains yield, and the total return during the first year?

e. Now assume that the stock is currently selling at $30.29. What is the expected rate of return on the stock?

f. What would the stock price be if its dividends were expected to have zero growth?

g. Now assume that Bon Temps is expected to experience supernormal growth of 30 percent for the next 3 years, then to return to its long-run constant growth rate of 6 percent. What is the stock's value under these conditions? What is its expected dividend yield and capital gains yield in Year 1? Year 4?

h. Suppose Bon Temps is expected to experience zero growth during the first 3 years and then to resume its steady-state growth of 6 percent in the fourth year. What is the stock's value now? What is its expected dividend yield and its capital gains yield in Year 1? Year 4?

i. Finally, assume that Bon Temps' earnings and dividends are expected to decline by a constant 6 percent per year, that is, g = −6%. Why would anyone be willing to buy such a stock, and at what price should it sell? What would be the dividend yield and capital gains yield in each year?

j. Bon Temps embarks on an aggressive expansion that requires additional capital. Management decides to finance the expansion by borrowing $40 million and by halting dividend payments to increase retained earnings. The projected free cash flows for the next 3 years are −$5 million, $10 million, and $20 million. After the third year, free cash flow is projected to grow at a constant 6 percent. The overall cost of capital is 10 percent. What is Bon Temps' total value? If it has 10 million shares of stock and $40 million total debt, what is the price per share?

k. What does market equilibrium mean?

l. If equilibrium does not exist, how will it be established?

m. What is the Efficient Markets Hypothesis, what are its three forms, and what are its implications?

n. Phyfe Company recently issued preferred stock. It pays an annual dividend of $5, and the issue price was $50 per share. What is the expected return to an investor on this preferred stock?

PART **IV**

INVESTING IN LONG-TERM ASSETS: CAPITAL BUDGETING

CHAPTER **10** The Cost of Capital

SOURCE: IPIX™ Used with permission from Interactive Pictures Corporation. www.ipix.com.

CREATING VALUE AT GE

GENERAL ELECTRIC

In Chapter 2 we discussed the concept of EVA — Economic Value Added — which is used by an increasing number of companies to measure corporate performance. Developed by the consulting firm Stern Stewart & Company, EVA is designed to measure a corporation's true profitability, and it is calculated as after-tax operating profits less the annual after-tax cost of all the capital a firm uses.

The idea behind EVA is simple — firms are truly profitable and create value if and only if their income exceeds the cost of all the capital they use to finance operations. The conventional measure of performance, net income, takes into account the cost of debt, which shows up on financial statements as interest expense, but it does not reflect the cost of equity. Therefore, a firm can report positive net income yet still be unprofitable in an economic sense if its net income is less than its cost of equity. EVA corrects this flaw by recognizing that to properly measure performance, it is necessary to account for the cost of equity capital.

A variety of factors influence a firm's cost of capital. Some, such as the level of interest rates, state and federal tax policies, and the regulatory environment, are outside of the firm's control. However, the firm's financing and investment policies, especially the types of capital it uses and the types of investment projects it undertakes, have a profound effect on its cost of capital.

General Electric has long been recognized as one of the world's best-managed companies, and it has rewarded its shareholders with outstanding returns. Given its performance, it is not surprising that GE is always at or near the top of the list of companies in generating EVA. Thus, GE has been able to consistently find projects that earn more than their costs of capital.

Estimating the cost of capital for a company like GE is a fairly straightforward exercise, but it does require judgment. Since GE's capital comes largely from equity, its cost of capital depends to a large extent on the cost of its equity, which is in essence its shareholders' required return. One must recognize that when investors purchase GE stock, they are investing in a company that operates many different divisions throughout the world. Each division has a different level of risk, hence a different cost of capital. GE's appliance division's cost of capital is likely to be different than that of its NBC subsidiary, or than that of its aircraft engine division. Likewise, an overseas project may have different risks and thus a different cost of capital than an otherwise similar domestic project.

As we will see in this chapter, estimating a project's cost of capital is an important process, and one that requires judgment. Companies that manage this process well will probably produce positive economic value for their shareholders. ■

In the last two chapters, we discussed the values of and required rates of return on stocks and bonds. When companies issue stocks or bonds, they are raising capital for investment in various projects. Capital is a necessary factor of production, and like any other factor, it has a cost. This cost is equal to the marginal investor's required return on the security in question. With this in mind, we now consider the process of estimating the cost of capital.

The firm's primary objective is to maximize shareholder value, and companies can increase shareholder value by investing in projects that earn more than the cost of capital. For this reason, the cost of capital is sometimes referred to as a *hurdle rate:* For a project to be accepted, it must earn more than its hurdle rate.

Although its most important use is in capital budgeting, the cost of capital is also used for at least three other purposes: (1) It is a key input used to calculate a firm's or division's economic value added (EVA). (2) Managers estimate and use the cost of capital when deciding if they should lease or purchase assets. And (3), the cost of capital is important in the regulation of monopoly services provided by electric, gas, and telephone companies. These firms are natural monopolies in the sense that one firm can supply service at a lower cost than could two or more firms. Since it has a monopoly, your electric or telephone company could, if it were unregulated, exploit you. Therefore, regulators (1) determine the cost of the capital investors have provided to the utility and (2) then set rates designed to permit the company to earn its cost of capital, no more and no less.

It should be noted that the cost of capital models and formulas used in this chapter are the same ones we developed in Chapters 8 and 9, where we were concerned with the rates of return investors require on different securities. The same factors that affect investors' required rates of return also determine the cost of capital to a firm, so investors and corporate treasurers often use exactly the same models. ∎

THE LOGIC OF THE WEIGHTED AVERAGE COST OF CAPITAL

It is possible to finance a firm entirely with common equity. In that case, the cost of capital used to analyze capital budgeting decisions should be the company's required return on equity. However, most firms raise a substantial portion of their capital as debt, and many also use preferred stock. For these firms, the cost of capital must reflect the average cost of the various sources of funds used, not just the costs of equity.

Assume that Allied Food Products has a 10 percent cost of debt and a 13.4 percent cost of equity. Further, assume that Allied has made the decision to finance next year's projects with debt. The argument is sometimes made that the cost of capital for these projects is 10 percent because only debt will be used to finance them. However, this position is incorrect. If Allied finances a particular set of projects with debt, the firm will be using up some of its capacity for borrowing in the future. As expansion occurs in subsequent years, Allied will at some point find it necessary to raise additional equity to prevent the debt ratio from becoming too large.

To illustrate, suppose Allied borrows heavily at 10 percent during 2002, using up its debt capacity in the process, to finance projects yielding 11.5 percent. In 2003, it has new projects available that yield 13 percent, well above the return on 2002 projects, but it cannot accept them because they would have to be financed with 13.4 percent equity money. *To avoid this problem, Allied should be viewed as an ongoing concern, and the cost of capital used in capital budgeting should be calculated as a weighted average, or composite, of the various types of funds it generally uses, regardless of the specific financing used to fund a particular project.*

Ohio State University has a web site with video clips of business professionals discussing various topics of interest in finance. The site can be found at **http://fisher.osu.edu/fin/clips.htm.** The two video clips relevant to capital budgeting come from Steve Walsh, assistant treasurer of JCPenney: "How We Do Capital Budgeting" and "On the Cost of Capital and Debt." Be forewarned that these files are quite large and are best downloaded using a rapid Internet link.

SELF-TEST QUESTION

Why should the cost of capital used in capital budgeting be calculated as a weighted average of the various types of funds the firm generally uses, not the cost of the specific financing used to fund a particular project?

BASIC DEFINITIONS

Capital Component
One of the types of capital used by firms to raise money.

The items on the right side of a firm's balance sheet — various types of debt, preferred stock, and common equity — are called **capital components.** Any increase in total assets must be financed by an increase in one or more of these capital components.

The cost of each component is called the *component cost* of that particular type of capital; for example, if Allied can borrow money at 10 percent, its component cost of debt is 10 percent.[1] Throughout this chapter, we concentrate on these three major capital components: debt, preferred stock, and common equity. The following symbols identify the cost of each:

k_d = interest rate on the firm's new debt = before-tax component cost of debt. For Allied, k_d = 10%.

$k_d(1 - T)$ = after-tax component cost of debt, where T is the firm's marginal tax rate. $k_d(1 - T)$ is the debt cost used to calculate the weighted average cost of capital. For Allied, T = 40%, so $k_d(1 - T)$ = 10%(1 − 0.4) = 10%(0.6) = 6.0%.

k_p = component cost of preferred stock. For Allied, k_p = 10.3%.

k_s = component cost of common equity. It is identical to the k_s developed in Chapters 6 and 9 and defined there as the rate of return investors require on a firm's common stock. Equity capital is raised in two ways: (1) by retaining earnings (internal equity) or (2) by issuing new common stock (external equity). It is generally difficult to estimate k_s, but, as we shall see shortly, a reasonably good estimate for Allied is k_s = 13.4%.

WACC = the weighted average cost of capital. If Allied raises new capital to finance asset expansion, and if it is to keep its capital structure in balance (that is, if it is to keep the same percentage of debt, preferred stock, and common equity funds), then it must raise part of its new funds as debt, part as preferred stock, and part as common equity (with equity coming either from retained earnings or by issuing new common stock).[2] We will calculate WACC for Allied Food Products shortly.

These definitions and concepts are explained in detail in the remainder of the chapter. Later, in Chapter 13, we extend the analysis to determine the mix of securities that will minimize the firm's cost of capital and thereby maximize its value.

SELF-TEST QUESTION

Identify the firm's three major capital structure components, and give their respective component cost symbols.

After-tax Cost of Debt, $k_d(1 - T)$
The relevant cost of new debt, taking into account the tax deductibility of interest; used to calculate the WACC.

COST OF DEBT, $k_d(1 - T)$

The **after-tax cost of debt, $k_d(1 - T)$,** is used to calculate the weighted average cost of capital, and it is the interest rate on debt, k_d, less the tax savings that

---

[1] We will see shortly that there is both a before-tax and an after-tax cost of debt; for now, it is sufficient to know that 10 percent is the before-tax component cost of debt.

[2] Firms try to keep their debt, preferred stock, and common equity in optimal proportions; we will learn how they establish these "target" proportions in Chapter 13.

result because interest is deductible. This is the same as k_d multiplied by $(1 - T)$, where T is the firm's marginal tax rate:[3]

$$\text{After-tax component cost of debt} = \text{Interest rate} - \text{Tax savings}$$
$$= k_d - k_d T$$
$$= k_d(1 - T). \qquad (10\text{-}1)$$

In effect, the government pays part of the cost of debt because interest is deductible. Therefore, if Allied can borrow at an interest rate of 10 percent, and if it has a marginal federal-plus-state tax rate of 40 percent, then its after-tax cost of debt is 6 percent:

$$k_d(1 - T) = 10\%(1.0 - 0.4)$$
$$= 10\%(0.6)$$
$$= 6.0\%.$$

The reason for using the after-tax cost of debt in calculating the weighted average cost of capital is as follows. The value of the firm's stock, which we want to maximize, depends on *after-tax* cash flows. Because interest is a deductible expense, it produces tax savings that reduce the net cost of debt, making the after-tax cost of debt less than the before-tax cost. We are concerned with after-tax cash flows, and since cash flows and rates of return should be placed on a comparable basis, we adjust the interest rate downward to take account of the preferential tax treatment of debt.[4]

Note that the cost of debt is the interest rate on *new* debt, not that on already outstanding debt; in other words, we are interested in the *marginal* cost of debt. Our primary concern with the cost of capital is to use it for capital budgeting decisions — for example, would a new machine earn a return greater than the cost of the capital needed to acquire the machine? The rate at which the firm has borrowed in the past is irrelevant — we need the cost of *new capital.*

---

[3] The federal tax rate for most large corporations is 35 percent. However, most corporations are also subject to state income taxes, so the marginal tax rate on most corporate income is about 40 percent. For illustrative purposes, we assume that the effective federal-plus-state tax rate on marginal income is 40 percent. Also, note that the cost of debt is considered in isolation. The effect of debt on the cost of equity, as well as on future increments of debt, is ignored when the weighted cost of a combination of debt and equity is derived in this chapter, but it will be treated in Chapter 13, "Capital Structure and Leverage."

[4] The tax rate is *zero* for a firm with losses. Therefore, for a company that does not pay taxes, the cost of debt is not reduced; that is, in Equation 10-1, the tax rate equals zero, so the after-tax cost of debt is equal to the interest rate.

Strictly speaking, the after-tax cost of debt should reflect the *expected* cost of debt. While Allied's bonds have a promised return of 10 percent, there is some chance of default, so its bondholders' expected return (and consequently Allied's cost) is a bit less than 10 percent. For a relatively strong company such as Allied, this difference is quite small. As we discuss later in the chapter, Allied must also incur flotation costs when it issues debt, but like the difference between the promised and the expected rate of return, flotation costs are generally small. Finally, note that these two factors tend to offset one another — not including the possibility of default leads to an overstatement of the cost of debt, but not including flotation costs leads to an understatement. For all these reasons, k_d is generally a good approximation of the before-tax cost of debt capital.

Why is the after-tax cost of debt rather than the before-tax cost used to calculate the weighted average cost of capital?

Is the relevant cost of debt the interest rate on already *outstanding* debt or that on *new* debt? Why?

COST OF PREFERRED STOCK, k_p

Cost of Preferred Stock, k_p
The rate of return investors require on the firm's preferred stock. k_p is calculated as the preferred dividend, D_p, divided by the current price, P_p.

The component **cost of preferred stock** used to calculate the weighted average cost of capital, k_p, is the preferred dividend, D_p, divided by the current price of the preferred stock, P_p:[5]

$$\text{Component cost of preferred stock} = k_p = \frac{D_p}{P_p}. \qquad (10\text{-}2)$$

For example, Allied has preferred stock that pays a $10 dividend per share and sells for $97.50 per share in the open market. Therefore, Allied's cost of preferred stock is 10.3 percent:

$$k_p = \$10/\$97.50 = 10.3\%.$$

As we can see from Equation 10–2, calculating the cost of preferred stock is generally quite simple. This is particularly true when we consider the traditional, "plain vanilla" form of preferred stock that pays a fixed dividend in perpetuity. We mentioned, however, in Chapter 9 that some preferred stock has a fixed maturity date, and we described how to calculate the expected return on these issues. These expected returns would also represent the cost of preferred stock for these fixed-maturity issues. In some other instances, preferred stock may include an option to convert to common stock. In these cases, calculating the cost of preferred stock becomes considerably more complicated. We will leave these more complicated cases for advanced classes and restrict ourselves to "plain vanilla" preferred issues, such as the ones issued by Allied.

No tax adjustments are made when calculating k_p because preferred dividends, unlike interest on debt, are *not* deductible. Therefore, there are no tax savings associated with the use of preferred stock. However, as we discuss in the accompanying box entitled "Funny-Named Preferred-Like Securities," some companies have tried to come up with ways to issue securities that are similar to preferred stock but that are structured in ways that enable them to deduct the payments made on these securities.

Is a tax adjustment made to the cost of preferred stock? Why or why not?

---

[5] To be technically precise, we should make an adjustment for flotation costs, but in Allied's case those costs are not significant.

FUNNY-NAMED PREFERRED-LIKE SECURITIES

Wall Street's "financial engineers" are constantly trying to develop new securities with appeal to issuers and investors. One such new security is a special type of preferred stock created by Goldman Sachs in the mid-1990s. These securities trade under a variety of colorful names, including MIPS (modified income preferred securities), QUIPS (quarterly income preferred securities), and QUIDS (quarterly income debt securities). The corporation that wants to raise capital (the "parent") establishes a trust, which issues fixed-dividend preferred stock. The parent then issues bonds (or debt of some type) to the trust, and the trust pays for the bonds with the cash raised from the sale of preferred. At that point, the parent has the cash it needs, the trust holds debt issued by the parent, and the investing public holds preferred stock issued by the trust. The parent then makes interest payments to the trust, and the trust uses that income to make the preferred dividend payments. Because the parent company has issued debt, its interest payments are tax deductible.

If the dividends could be excluded from taxable income by corporate investors, this preferred would really be a great deal — the issuer could deduct the interest, corporate investors could exclude most of the dividends, and the IRS would be the loser. The corporate parent does get to deduct the interest paid to the trust, but IRS regulations do not allow the dividends on these securities to be excluded.

Because there is only one deduction, why are these new securities attractive? The answer is as follows: (1) Since the parent company gets to take the deduction, its cost of funds from the preferred is $k_p(1 - T)$, just as it would be if it used debt. (2) The parent generates a tax savings, and it can thus afford to pay a relatively high rate on trust-related preferred; that is, it can pass on some of its tax savings to investors to induce them to buy the new securities. (3) The primary purchasers of the preferred are low-tax-bracket individuals and tax-exempt institutions such as pension funds. For such purchasers, not being able to exclude the dividend from taxable income is not important. (4) Due to the differential tax rates, the arrangement results in a net tax savings. Competition in capital markets results in a sharing of the savings between investors and corporations.

A recent *SmartMoney Online* article argued that these hybrid securities are a good deal for individual investors for the reason set forth above and also because they are sold in small increments — often as small as $25. However, these securities are relatively complex, which increases their risk and makes them hard to value. There is also risk to the issuing corporations. The IRS has expressed concerns about these securities, and if at some point the IRS decides to disallow interest paid to the trusts, that will have a profound negative effect on the corporations that have issued them.

SOURCES: Kerry Capell, "High Yields, Low Cost, Funny Names," *Business Week*, September 9, 1996, 122; and Leslie Haggin, "SmartMoney Online: MIPS, QUIDS, and QUIPS," *SmartMoney Interactive*, April 6, 1999.

COST OF RETAINED EARNINGS, k_s

Cost of Retained Earnings, k_s
The rate of return required by stockholders on a firm's common stock.

k_e
The designation for the cost of common equity raised by issuing new stock, or external equity.

The costs of debt and preferred stock are based on the returns investors require on these securities. Similarly, the cost of common equity is based on the rate of return investors require on a company's common stock. Note, though, that new common equity is raised in two ways: (1) by retaining some of the current year's earnings and (2) by issuing new common stock. As we shall see, equity raised by issuing stock has a somewhat higher cost than equity raised as retained earnings due to the flotation costs involved with new stock issues. We use the symbol k_s to designate the **cost of retained earnings** and k_e to designate the cost of common equity raised by issuing new stock, or external equity.[6]

---

[6] The term *retained earnings* can be interpreted to mean either the balance sheet item "retained earnings," consisting of all the earnings retained in the business throughout its history, or the income statement item "addition to retained earnings." The income statement item is used in this chapter; for our purpose, *retained earnings* refers to that part of the current year's earnings not paid out in dividends, hence available for reinvestment in the business this year.

A corporation's management might misguidedly think that retained earnings are "free" because they represent money that is "left over" after paying dividends. While it is true that no direct costs are associated with capital raised as retained earnings, this capital still has a cost. The reason we must assign a cost of capital to retained earnings involves the *opportunity cost principle*. The firm's after-tax earnings belong to its stockholders. Bondholders are compensated by interest payments, and preferred stockholders by preferred dividends. All earnings remaining after interest and preferred dividends belong to the common stockholders, and these earnings serve to compensate stockholders for the use of their capital. Management may either pay out earnings in the form of dividends or else retain earnings and reinvest them in the business. If management decides to retain earnings, there is an *opportunity cost* involved — stockholders could have received the earnings as dividends and invested this money in other stocks, in bonds, in real estate, or in anything else. *Thus, the firm should earn on its retained earnings at least as much as the stockholders themselves could earn on alternative investments of comparable risk.*

What rate of return can stockholders expect to earn on equivalent-risk investments? First, recall from Chapter 9 that stocks are normally in equilibrium, with expected and required rates of return being equal: $\hat{k}_s = k_s$. Thus, we can assume that Allied's stockholders expect to earn a return of k_s on their money. *Therefore, if the firm cannot invest retained earnings and earn at least k_s, it should pay these funds to its stockholders and let them invest directly in other assets that do provide this return.*[7]

Whereas debt and preferred stocks are contractual obligations that have easily determined costs, it is difficult to measure k_s. However, we can employ the principles developed in Chapters 6 and 9 to produce reasonably good cost of equity estimates. Recall that if a stock is in equilibrium, then its required rate of return, k_s, must be equal to its expected rate of return, $\hat{k}_s$. Further, its *required* return is equal to a risk-free rate, k_{RF}, plus a risk premium, RP, whereas the *expected* return on a constant growth stock is the stock's dividend yield, D_1/P_0, plus its expected growth rate, g:

$$\text{Required rate of return} = \text{Expected rate of return}$$
$$k_s = k_{RF} + RP \quad = \quad D_1/P_0 + g = \hat{k}_s. \qquad (10\text{-}3)$$

Therefore, we can estimate k_s either as $k_s = k_{RF} + RP$ or as $k_s = D_1/P_0 + g$.

THE CAPM APPROACH

One approach to estimating the cost of common equity is to use the Capital Asset Pricing Model (CAPM) as developed in Chapter 6, proceeding as follows:

Step 1. Estimate the risk-free rate, k_{RF}, generally taken to be either the U.S. Treasury bond rate or the short-term (30-day) Treasury bill rate.

Step 2. Estimate the stock's beta coefficient, b_i, and use it as an index of the stock's risk. The i signifies the *i*th company's beta.

---

[7] Dividends and capital gains are taxed differently, with long-term capital gains being taxed at a lower rate than dividends for most stockholders. That makes it beneficial for companies to retain earnings rather than pay them out as dividends, and that, in turn, tends to lower the cost of capital for retained earnings. This point is discussed in detail in Chapter 14.

Step 3. Estimate the expected rate of return on the market, or on an "average" stock, k_M.

Step 4. Substitute the preceding values into the CAPM equation to estimate the required rate of return on the stock in question:

$$k_s = k_{RF} + (k_M - k_{RF})b_i. \qquad (10\text{-}4)$$

Equation 10-4 shows that the CAPM estimate of k_s begins with the risk-free rate, k_{RF}, to which is added a risk premium set equal to the risk premium on an average stock, $k_M - k_{RF}$, scaled up or down to reflect the particular stock's risk as measured by its beta coefficient.

To illustrate the CAPM approach, assume that $k_{RF} = 8\%$, $k_M = 13\%$, and $b_i = 0.7$ for a given stock. This stock's k_s is calculated as follows:

$$
\begin{aligned}
k_s &= 8\% + (13\% - 8\%)(0.7) \\
&= 8\% + (5\%)(0.7) \\
&= 8\% + 3.5\% \\
&= 11.5\%.
\end{aligned}
$$

Had b_i been 1.8, indicating that the stock was riskier than average, its k_s would have been

$$
\begin{aligned}
k_s &= 8\% + (5\%)(1.8) \\
&= 8\% + 9\% \\
&= 17\%.
\end{aligned}
$$

For an average stock when k_{RF} is 8 percent and the market risk premium is 5 percent,

$$k_s = k_M = 8\% + (5\%)(1.0) = 13\%.$$

It should be noted that although the CAPM approach appears to yield an accurate, precise estimate of k_s, there are actually several problems with it. First, as we saw in Chapter 6, if a firm's stockholders are not well diversified, they may be concerned with *stand-alone risk* rather than just market risk. In that case, the firm's true investment risk would not be measured by its beta, and the CAPM procedure would understate the correct value of k_s. Further, even if the CAPM method is valid, it is hard to obtain correct estimates of the inputs required to make it operational because (1) there is controversy about whether to use long-term or short-term Treasury yields for k_{RF}, (2) it is hard to estimate the beta that investors expect the company to have in the future, and (3) it is difficult to estimate the market risk premium.

BOND-YIELD-PLUS-RISK-PREMIUM APPROACH

Analysts who do not have confidence in the CAPM often use a subjective, ad hoc procedure to estimate a firm's cost of common equity: they simply add a judgmental risk premium of 3 to 5 percentage points to the interest rate on the firm's own long-term debt. It is logical to think that firms with risky, low-rated, and consequently high-interest-rate debt will also have risky, high-cost equity, and the procedure of basing the cost of equity on a readily observable debt cost utilizes this logic. For example, if an extremely strong firm such as BellSouth had bonds that yielded 8 percent, its cost of equity might be estimated as follows:

$$k_s = \text{Bond yield} + \text{Risk premium} = 8\% + 4\% = 12\%.$$

The bonds of a riskier company such as Continental Airlines might carry a yield of 12 percent, making its estimated cost of equity 16 percent:

$$k_s = 12\% + 4\% = 16\%.$$

Because the 4 percent risk premium is a judgmental estimate, the estimated value of k_s is also judgmental. Empirical work in recent years suggests that the risk premium over a firm's own bond yield has generally ranged from 3 to 5 percentage points, so while this method does not produce a precise cost of equity, it will "get us into the right ballpark."

DIVIDEND-YIELD-PLUS-GROWTH-RATE, OR DISCOUNTED CASH FLOW (DCF), APPROACH

In Chapter 9, we saw that both the price and the expected rate of return on a share of common stock depend, ultimately, on the dividends expected on the stock:

$$P_0 = \frac{D_1}{(1 + k_s)^1} + \frac{D_2}{(1 + k_s)^2} + \cdots$$

$$= \sum_{t=1}^{\infty} \frac{D_t}{(1 + k_s)^t}. \tag{10-5}$$

Here P_0 is the current price of the stock; D_t is the dividend expected to be paid at the end of Year t; and k_s is the required rate of return. If dividends are expected to grow at a constant rate, then, as we saw in Chapter 9, Equation 10-5 reduces to this important formula:

$$P_0 = \frac{D_1}{k_s - g}. \tag{10-6}$$

We can solve for k_s to obtain the required rate of return on common equity, which, for the marginal investor, is also equal to the expected rate of return:

$$k_s = \hat{k}_s = \frac{D_1}{P_0} + \text{Expected g}. \tag{10-7}$$

Thus, investors expect to receive a dividend yield, D_1/P_0, plus a capital gain, g, for a total expected return of $\hat{k}_s$, and in equilibrium this expected return is also equal to the required return, k_s. This method of estimating the cost of equity is called the *discounted cash flow, or DCF, method.* Henceforth, we will assume that equilibrium exists, and we will use the terms k_s and $\hat{k}_s$ interchangeably.

It is easy to determine the dividend yield, but it is difficult to establish the proper growth rate. If past growth rates in earnings and dividends have been relatively stable, and if investors appear to be projecting a continuation of past trends, then g may be based on the firm's historic growth rate. *However, if the company's past growth has been abnormally high or low, either because of its own unique situation or because of general economic fluctuations, then investors will not project the past growth rate into the future.* In this case, g must be estimated in some other manner.

Security analysts regularly make earnings and dividend growth forecasts, looking at such factors as projected sales, profit margins, and competitive factors. For example, *Value Line*, which is available in most libraries, provides growth rate forecasts for 1,700 companies, and Merrill Lynch, Salomon Smith Barney, and other organizations make similar forecasts. Therefore, someone making a cost of equity estimate can obtain several analysts' forecasts, average them, use the average as a proxy for the growth expectations of investors in general, and then combine this g with the current dividend yield to estimate $\hat{k}_s$ as follows:

$$\hat{k}_s = \frac{D_1}{P_0} + \text{Growth rate as projected by security analysts.}$$

Again, note that this estimate of $\hat{k}_s$ is based on the assumption that g is expected to remain constant in the future.[8]

Another method for estimating g involves first forecasting the firm's average future dividend payout ratio and its complement, the *retention rate*, and then multiplying the retention rate by the company's expected future rate of return on equity (ROE):

$$g = (\text{Retention rate})(\text{ROE}) = (1.0 - \text{Payout rate})(\text{ROE}). \qquad \textbf{(10-8)}$$

Intuitively, firms that are more profitable and retain a larger portion of their earnings for reinvestment in the firm will tend to have higher growth rates than firms that are less profitable and pay out a higher percentage of their earnings as dividends. Security analysts often use Equation 10-8 when they estimate growth rates. For example, suppose a company is expected to have a constant ROE of 13.4 percent, and it is expected to pay out 40 percent of its earnings and to retain 60 percent. In this case, its forecasted growth rate would be g = (0.60)(13.4%) = 8.0%.

To illustrate the DCF approach, suppose Allied's stock sells for $23; its next expected dividend is $1.24; and its expected growth rate is 8 percent. Allied's expected and required rate of return, hence its cost of retained earnings, would then be 13.4 percent:

$$\hat{k}_s = k_s = \frac{\$1.24}{\$23} + 8.0\%$$
$$= 5.4\% + 8.0\%$$
$$= 13.4\%.$$

This 13.4 percent is the minimum rate of return that management must expect to justify retaining earnings and plowing them back in the business rather than paying them out to stockholders as dividends. Put another way, since investors

---

[8] Analysts' growth rate forecasts are usually for five years into the future, and the rates provided represent the average growth rate over that five-year horizon. Studies have shown that analysts' forecasts represent the best source of growth rate data for DCF cost of capital estimates. See Robert Harris, "Using Analysts' Growth Rate Forecasts to Estimate Shareholder Required Rates of Return," *Financial Management*, Spring 1986.

Note also that two organizations — IBES and Zacks — collect the forecasts of leading analysts for most larger companies, average these forecasts, and then publish the averages. The IBES and Zacks data are available over the Internet through on-line computer data services.

have an *opportunity* to earn 13.4 percent if earnings are paid to them as dividends, then the company's *opportunity cost* of equity from retained earnings is 13.4 percent.

People experienced in estimating equity capital costs recognize that both careful analysis and sound judgment are required. It would be nice to pretend that judgment is unnecessary and to specify an easy, precise way of determining the exact cost of equity capital. Unfortunately, this is not possible — finance is in large part a matter of judgment, and we simply must face that fact.

SELF-TEST QUESTIONS

Why must a cost be assigned to retained earnings?

What three approaches are used to estimate the cost of common equity?

Identify some problems with the CAPM approach.

What is the reasoning behind the bond-yield-plus-risk-premium approach?

Which of the two components of the constant growth DCF formula, the dividend yield or the growth rate, is more difficult to estimate? Why?

COST OF NEW COMMON STOCK, k_e

Companies generally hire an investment banker to assist them when they issue common stock, preferred stock, or bonds. In return for a fee, the investment banker helps the company structure the terms and set a price for the issue, and then sells the issue to investors. The banker's fees are often referred to as *flotation costs*, and the total cost of capital should reflect both the required return paid to investors and the flotation fees paid to the investment banker.

As you can see in the accompanying box, "How Much Does It Cost to Raise External Capital?," flotation costs are often substantial, and they vary depending on the size and risk of the issuing firm and on the type of capital raised. So far, we have ignored flotation costs when estimating the component costs of capital, but some would argue that these costs should be included in a complete analysis of the cost of capital. [The counter-argument is that flotation costs are not high enough to worry about because (1) most equity comes from retained earnings, (2) most debt is raised in private placements and hence involves no flotation costs, and (3) preferred stock is rarely used.] A more complete discussion of flotation cost adjustments can be found in Eugene F. Brigham and Phillip R. Daves, *Intermediate Financial Management*, 7th ed., and other advanced texts, but we describe below two alternative approaches that can be used to account for flotation costs.

The first approach simply adds the estimated dollar amount of flotation costs for each project to the project's up-front cost. The estimated flotation costs are found as the sum of the flotation costs for the debt, preferred, and common stock used to finance the project. Because of the now-higher investment cost, the project's expected rate of return and NPV are decreased. For example, consider a one-year project that has an up-front cost (not including flotation costs) of $100 million. After one year, the project is expected to produce an inflow of $115 million. Therefore, its expected return is $115/$100 − 1 = 0.15 = 15%. However, if the project requires the company to issue new capital with an estimated $2 million of flotation costs, the total up-front cost is $102 million, and the expected rate of return is only $115/$102 − 1 = 0.1275 = 12.75%.

The second approach involves adjusting the cost of capital rather than increasing the project's cost. If the firm plans to continue to use the capital in the future, as is generally true for equity, then this second approach is better. The adjustment process is based on the following logic. If there are flotation costs, the issuing company receives only a portion of the total capital raised from investors, with the remainder going to the underwriter. When calculating the cost of common equity, the DCF approach can be adapted to account for flotation costs. For a constant growth stock, the **cost of new common stock, k_e,** can be expressed as:[9]

Cost of New Common Stock, k_e
The cost of external equity; based on the cost of retained earnings, but increased for flotation costs.

$$\text{Cost of equity from new stock issues} = k_e = \frac{D_1}{P_0(1 - F)} + g. \quad (10\text{-}9)$$

---

[9] Equation 10-9 is derived as follows:

Step 1. The old stockholders expect the firm to pay a stream of dividends, D_t, that will be derived from existing assets with a per-share value of P_0. New investors will likewise expect to receive the same stream of dividends, but the funds available to invest in assets will be less than P_0 because of flotation costs. For new investors to receive their expected dividend stream *without impairing the D_t stream of the old investors*, the new funds obtained from the sale of stock must be invested at a return high enough to provide a dividend stream whose present value is equal to the net price the firm will receive:

$$P_n = P_0(1 - F) = \sum_{t=1}^{\infty} \frac{D_t}{(1 + k_e)^t}. \quad (10\text{-}10)$$

Here D_t is the dividend stream to new (and old) stockholders, and k_e is the cost of new outside equity.

Step 2. When growth is constant, Equation 10-10 reduces to

$$P_n = P_0(1 - F) = \frac{D_1}{k_e - g}. \quad (10\text{-}10\text{a})$$

Step 3. Equation 10-10a can be rearranged to produce Equation 10-9:

$$k_e = \frac{D_1}{P_0(1 - F)} + g.$$

HOW MUCH DOES IT COST TO RAISE EXTERNAL CAPITAL?

A recent study by four professors provides some insights into how much it costs U.S. corporations to raise external capital. Using information from the Securities Data Company, they found the average flotation cost for debt and equity issued in the 1990s as presented below.

The common stock flotation costs are for non-IPOs. Costs associated with IPOs are even higher — flotation costs are about 17 percent of gross proceeds for common equity if the amount raised in the IPO is less than $10 million and about 6 percent if more than $500 million is raised. The data shown below include both utility and nonutility companies. If utilities were excluded, flotation costs would be somewhat higher.

SOURCE: Inmoo Lee, Scott Lochhead, Jay Ritter, and Quanshui Zhao, "The Costs of Raising Capital," *The Journal of Financial Research*, Vol. XIX, No. 1, Spring 1996, 59–74. Reprinted with permission.

AMOUNT OF CAPITAL RAISED (MILLIONS OF DOLLARS)	AVERAGE FLOTATION COST FOR COMMON STOCK (% OF TOTAL CAPITAL RAISED)	AVERAGE FLOTATION COST FOR NEW DEBT (% OF TOTAL CAPITAL RAISED)
2–9.99	13.28	4.39
10–19.99	8.72	2.76
20–39.99	6.93	2.42
40–59.99	5.87	1.32
60–79.99	5.18	2.34
80–99.99	4.73	2.16
100–199.99	4.22	2.31
200–499.99	3.47	2.19
500 and up	3.15	1.64

Flotation Cost, F

The percentage cost of issuing new common stock.

Here F is the percentage **flotation cost** required to sell the new stock, so $P_0(1 - F)$ is the net price per share received by the company.

Assuming that Allied has a flotation cost of 10 percent, its cost of new common equity, k_e, is computed as follows:

$$k_e = \frac{\$1.24}{\$23(1 - 0.10)} + 8.0\%$$

$$= \frac{\$1.24}{\$20.70} + 8.0\%$$

$$= 6.0\% + 8.0\% = 14.0\%.$$

Investors require a return of $k_s = 13.4\%$ on the stock. However, because of flotation costs the company must earn *more* than 13.4 percent on the net funds obtained by selling stock in order to give investors a 13.4 percent return on the money they put up. Specifically, if the firm earns 14 percent on funds obtained by issuing new stock, then earnings per share will remain at the previously expected level, the firm's expected dividend can be maintained, and, as a result, the price per share will not decline. If the firm earns less than 14 percent, then earnings, dividends, and growth will fall below expectations, causing the stock price to decline. If the firm earns more than 14 percent, the stock price will rise.

Retained Earnings Breakpoint
The amount of capital raised
beyond which new common stock
must be issued.

Because of flotation costs, dollars raised by selling new stock must "work harder" than dollars raised by retaining earnings. Moreover, since no flotation costs are involved, retained earnings have a lower cost than new stock. Therefore, firms should utilize retained earnings to the extent possible to avoid the costs of issuing new common stock. However, if a firm has more good investment opportunities than can be financed with retained earnings and debt supported by retained earnings, it may find it necessary to issue new common stock. The **retained earnings breakpoint** represents the total amount of financing that can be raised before the firm is forced to sell new common stock. This breakpoint can be calculated as follows:

$$\text{Retained earnings breakpoint} = \frac{\text{Addition to retained earnings}}{\text{Equity fraction}}. \qquad (10\text{-}11)$$

Allied's addition to retained earnings in 2002 is expected to be $68 million (see Table 4-3 in Chapter 4), and its capital structure consists of 45 percent debt, 2 percent preferred, and 53 percent equity. Therefore, its retained earnings breakpoint is $68/0.53 = $128 million. If Allied's capital budget called for spending exactly $128 million, then 0.45($128) = $57.6 million would be financed with debt, 0.02($128) = $2.6 million with preferred stock, and 0.53($128) = $67.8 million with equity raised from retained earnings. If Allied's capital budget exceeded the $128 million "breakpoint," the amount of equity required would exceed the amount of available retained earnings, so the company would have to obtain equity by issuing new, high-cost common stock.

It is important to recognize that this breakpoint is only suggestive — it is not written in stone. For example, rather than issuing new common stock, the company could use more debt (hence, less equity), or it could increase its additional retained earnings by reducing its dividend payout ratio. Both actions would increase the retained earnings breakpoint. In any event, firms that have a large number of good investment opportunities generally maximize their retained earnings by paying out a smaller percentage of income as dividends than firms with fewer good investment opportunities. We will discuss dividend policy in more detail in Chapter 14.

Flotation cost adjustments can also be made for preferred stock and debt. For preferred stock, the flotation-adjusted cost is the preferred dividend, D_p, divided by the net issuing price, P_n, the price the firm receives on preferred after deducting flotation costs. Similarly, if debt is issued to the public and flotation costs are incurred, the after-tax cost is found by calculating the after-tax yield to maturity, where the issue price is the bond's par value less the flotation expense.[10]

---

[10] More specifically, the solution value of k_d in this formula is used as the after-tax cost of debt:

$$M(1 - F) = \sum_{t=1}^{N} \frac{INT(1 - T)}{(1 + k_d)^t} + \frac{M}{(1 + k_d)^N}.$$

Here F is the percentage amount of the bond flotation cost, N is the number of periods to maturity, INT is the dollars of interest per period, T is the corporate tax rate, M is the maturity value of the bond, and k_d is the after-tax cost of debt adjusted to reflect flotation costs. If we assume that the bond in the example calls for annual payments, that it has a 20-year maturity, and that F = 2%, then the flotation-adjusted, after-tax cost of debt is 6.18 percent versus 6 percent before the flotation adjustment. Also see Eugene F. Brigham and Phillip R. Daves, *Intermediate Financial Management*, 7th ed. (Fort Worth, TX: Harcourt College Publishers, 2002), Chapter 9.

While flotation costs may seem high, their per-project cost is usually relatively small. For example, if a company issues common stock only once every 10 years, the flotation costs should be spread over all the projects funded during the 10-year period. If flotation costs are charged only during the years in which external capital is raised, a project evaluated during those years would appear worse than the same project analyzed in a year when no external capital is raised. Since flotation costs are not normally very important, unless stated otherwise, we will leave a detailed discussion of flotation costs to advanced finance courses.

SELF-TEST QUESTIONS

Explain briefly the two approaches that can be used to adjust for flotation costs.

Write out formulas that can be used to adjust the costs of debt and preferred for flotation costs.

Would firms that have many good investment opportunities be likely to have higher or lower dividend payout ratios than firms with few good investment opportunities? Explain.

COMPOSITE, OR WEIGHTED AVERAGE, COST OF CAPITAL, WACC

Target (Optimal) Capital Structure
The percentages of debt, preferred stock, and common equity that will maximize the firm's stock price.

Weighted Average Cost of Capital, WACC
A weighted average of the component costs of debt, preferred stock, and common equity.

As we shall see in Chapter 13, each firm has an optimal capital structure, defined as that mix of debt, preferred, and common equity that causes its stock price to be maximized. Therefore, a value-maximizing firm will determine its **optimal capital structure,** use it as a **target,** and then raise new capital in a manner designed to keep the actual capital structure on target over time. In this chapter, we assume that the firm has identified its optimal capital structure, that it uses this optimum as the target, and that it finances so as to remain on target. How the target is established will be examined in Chapter 13.

The target proportions of debt, preferred stock, and common equity, along with the costs of those components, are used to calculate the firm's **weighted average cost of capital, WACC.** To illustrate, suppose Allied Food has a target capital structure calling for 45 percent debt, 2 percent preferred stock, and 53 percent common equity (retained earnings plus common stock). Its before-tax cost of debt, k_d, is 10 percent; its after-tax cost of debt = $k_d(1 - T)$ = $10\%(0.6) = 6.0\%$; its cost of preferred stock, k_p, is 10.3 percent; its cost of common equity, k_s, is 13.4 percent; its marginal tax rate is 40 percent; and all of its new equity will come from retained earnings. We calculate Allied's weighted average cost of capital, WACC, as follows:

$$\text{WACC} = w_d k_d(1 - T) + w_p k_p + w_c k_s \qquad (10\text{-}12)$$

$$= 0.45(10\%)(0.6) + 0.02(10.3\%) + 0.53(13.4\%)$$

$$= 10.0\%.$$

INDUSTRY PRACTICE

WACC ESTIMATES FOR SOME LARGE U.S. CORPORATIONS

As noted in Chapter 2, the New York consulting firm of Stern Stewart & Company regularly estimates EVAs and MVAs for large U.S. corporations. To obtain these estimates, Stern Stewart must calculate a WACC for each company. The table below presents some recent WACC estimates as calculated by Stern Stewart for a sample of corporations, along with their long-term debt-to-total-capital ratios.

These estimates suggest that a typical company has a WACC somewhere in the 7.5 percent to 12.5 percent range and that the WACC varies considerably depending on (1) the company's risk and (2) the amount of debt it uses. Companies in riskier businesses, such as Intel, presumably have higher costs of common equity. Moreover, they tend not to use as much debt. These

two factors, in combination, result in higher WACCs than those of companies that operate in more stable businesses, such as BellSouth. We will discuss the effects of capital structure on WACC in more detail in Chapter 13.

Note that riskier companies may also have the potential for producing higher returns, and what really matters to shareholders is whether a company is able to generate returns in excess of its cost of capital, resulting in a positive EVA. Therefore, a high cost of capital is not necessarily bad if it is accompanied by projects with high rates of return.

SOURCE: "The 2000 Stern Stewart Performance 1000," http://www.sternstewart.com/performance/rankings.shtml; and *Value Line Investment Survey*, February 23, 2001.

COMPANY	WACC	BOOK VALUE DEBT RATIO[a]
General Electric	12.47%	1%
Coca-Cola	12.31	8
Intel	12.19	2
Motorola	11.65	19
Wal-Mart	10.99	36
Walt Disney	9.28	22
AT&T	9.22	20
Exxon Mobil	8.16	10
H.J. Heinz	7.78	55
BellSouth	7.41	39

[a] Long-term debt only.

Here w_d, w_p, and w_c are the weights used for debt, preferred, and common equity, respectively.

Every dollar of new capital that Allied obtains consists of 45 cents of debt with an after-tax cost of 6 percent, 2 cents of preferred stock with a cost of 10.3 percent, and 53 cents of common equity (all from additions to retained earnings) with a cost of 13.4 percent. The average cost of each whole dollar, WACC, is 10 percent.

Note that when calculating the firm's target capital structure, total debt includes both long-term debt and bank debt (notes payable). Recall from Chapter 2, that investor-supplied capital does not include other current liabilities such as accounts payable and accruals. Therefore, these other items are not included as part of Allied's capital structure.

Marginal Cost of Capital (MCC)
The cost of obtaining another dollar of new capital; the weighted average cost of the last dollar of new capital raised.

As long as Allied keeps its capital structure on target, and as long as its debt has an after-tax cost of 6 percent, its preferred stock costs 10.3 percent, and its common equity costs 13.4 percent, then its weighted average cost of capital will be WACC = 10%.[11] Each dollar the firm raises will consist of some long-term debt, some preferred stock, and some common equity, and the cost of the whole dollar will be 10 percent. Therefore, the WACC represents the **marginal cost of capital (MCC),** because it indicates the cost of raising an additional dollar.[12]

SELF-TEST QUESTIONS

Write out the equation for the weighted average cost of capital, WACC.

Is short-term debt included in the capital structure used to calculate WACC? Why or why not?

Why does the WACC at every amount of capital raised represent the marginal cost of that capital?

FACTORS THAT AFFECT THE COMPOSITE COST OF CAPITAL

The cost of capital is affected by a number of factors. Some are beyond a firm's control, but others are influenced by its financing and investment decisions.

---

[11] The 10 percent WACC assumed that Allied's equity capital came exclusively from retained earnings and had a cost of 13.4 percent. If Allied expanded so rapidly and required so much new capital that it had to issue new common stock at a cost of $k_e = 14\%$, then its WACC would rise to 10.3 percent:

$$\text{WACC} = w_d k_d (1 - T) + w_p k_p + w_c k_e$$

$$= 0.45(10\%)(0.6) + 0.02(10.3\%) + 0.53(14.0\%)$$

$$= 10.3\%.$$

The increase in the WACC would occur at the "retained earnings breakpoint" as discussed in the preceding section. However, as we noted, companies can and do change their dividend payout ratios and target capital structures if and when their capital budgets actually approach the breakpoint, so the breakpoint itself is flexible, not set in stone.

[12] As noted in Footnote 11, at times the marginal cost of capital will not remain constant but will instead increase as the firm raises more and more capital. This situation exists for large, established firms if they require so much capital that they are required to issue new common stock to the public. Note, though, that large firms rarely issue common stock — they typically obtain all the equity they need by retaining earnings. See Brigham and Daves, *Intermediate Financial Management,* 7th ed., Chapter 9.

FACTORS THE FIRM CANNOT CONTROL

The two most important factors that are beyond a firm's direct control are the level of interest rates and tax rates.

The Level of Interest Rates

If interest rates in the economy rise, the cost of debt increases because firms will have to pay bondholders more to obtain debt capital. Also, recall from our discussion of the CAPM that higher interest rates increase the costs of common and preferred equity capital. During the last decade, inflation, and consquently, interest rates in the United States declined significantly. This reduced the cost of capital for all firms, encouraging additional investment. Our lower interest rates also enabled U.S. firms to compete more effectively with German and Japanese firms, which in the past had enjoyed lower costs of capital than U.S. firms.

Tax Rates

Tax rates, which are largely beyond the control of an individual firm (although firms can and do lobby for more favorable tax treatment), have an important effect on the cost of capital. Tax rates are used in the calculation of the component cost of debt. In addition, there are other less apparent ways in which tax policy affects the cost of capital. For example, lowering the capital gains tax rate relative to the rate on ordinary income makes stocks more attractive, and that reduces the cost of equity. That would lower the WACC, and, as we will see in Chapter 13, it would also lead to a change in a firm's optimal capital structure (toward less debt and more equity).

FACTORS THE FIRM CAN CONTROL

A firm can directly affect its cost of capital through its capital structure policy, its dividend policy, and its investment (capital budgeting) policy.

Capital Structure Policy

Until now we have assumed that a firm has a given target capital structure, and we used weights based on that target structure to calculate the WACC. However, a firm can change its capital structure, and such a change can affect its cost of capital. The after-tax cost of debt is lower than the cost of equity. Specifically, if the firm decides to use more debt and less common equity, this change in the weights in the WACC equation will tend to lower the WACC. However, an increase in the use of debt will increase the riskiness of both the debt and the equity, and these increases in component costs will tend to offset the effects of the change in the weights. In Chapter 13, we will discuss this concept in more depth, and we will demonstrate that a firm's optimal capital structure minimizes its cost of capital.

Dividend Policy

As we indicated earlier, firms can obtain new equity either through retained earnings or by issuing new common stock, but because of flotation costs, new common stock is more expensive than retained earnings. For this reason, firms issue new common stock only after they have invested all of their retained earnings. Since retained earnings is income that has not been paid out as dividends, it follows that dividend policy can affect the cost of capital because it affects the level of retained earnings. As we will see in Chapter 14, firms take cost of capital effects into account when they establish their dividend policies.

Investment Policy

When we estimate the cost of capital, we use as the starting point the required rates of return on the firm's outstanding stock and bonds. Those cost rates reflect the riskiness of the firm's existing assets. Therefore, we have implicitly been assuming that new capital will be invested in assets of the same type and with the same degree of risk as is embedded in the existing assets. This assumption is generally correct, as most firms do invest in assets similar to those they currently operate. However, it would be incorrect if the firm dramatically changed its investment policy. For example, if a firm invests in an entirely new line of business, its marginal cost of capital should reflect the riskiness of that new business. To illustrate, ITT Corporation recently sold off its finance company and purchased Caesar's World, a casino gambling firm. This dramatic shift in corporate focus almost certainly affected ITT's cost of capital. Likewise, Disney's purchase of the ABC television network changed the nature and risk of the company in a way that might also influence its cost of capital. The effect of investment decisions on capital costs is discussed in detail in the next section.

SELF-TEST QUESTIONS

What two factors that affect the cost of capital are generally beyond the firm's control?

What policies under the firm's control are likely to affect its cost of capital?

Explain how a change in interest rates would affect each component of the weighted average cost of capital.

ADJUSTING THE COST OF CAPITAL FOR RISK

As noted above, the cost of capital is a key element in the capital budgeting process. As you will see in the next two chapters, a project should be accepted if and only if its estimated return exceeds its cost of capital. For this reason, the cost of capital is sometimes referred to as a "hurdle rate" — project returns must "jump the hurdle" to be accepted.

As we saw in Chapter 6, investors require higher returns for riskier investments. Consequently, a company that is raising capital to take on risky projects will have a higher cost of capital than a company that is investing in safer projects. Figure 10-1 illustrates the trade-off between risk and the cost of capital. Firm L is a low-risk business and has a WACC of 8 percent, whereas Firm H is exposed to high risks and has a WACC of 12 percent. Thus, Firm H will accept a typical project only if its expected return is above 12 percent. The corresponding hurdle rate for Firm L's typical project is only 8 percent.

It is important to remember that the cost of capital values at points L and H in Figure 10-1 represent the overall, or composite, WACCs for the two firms, and, thus, only represent the hurdle rate of a "typical" project for each firm. Different projects generally have different risks. Indeed, the hurdle rate for each project should reflect the risk of the project itself, not the risks associated

---

FIGURE 10-1	Risk and the Cost of Capital

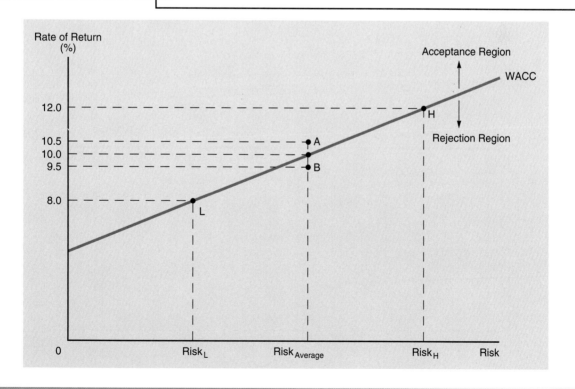

with the firm's average project as reflected in its composite WACC. For example, assume that Firms L and H are both considering Project A. This project has more risk than a typical Firm L project, but less risk than a typical Firm H project. As shown in Figure 10-1, Project A has a 10.5 percent expected return. At first, we might be tempted to conclude that Firm L should accept Project A because its 10.5 percent return is above Firm L's 8 percent WACC, while Firm H should turn down the project because its return is less than H's 12 percent WACC. However, this would be wrong. The relevant hurdle rate is the *project's WACC*, which is 10 percent, as read from the WACC line in Figure 10-1. Since the project's return exceeds its 10 percent cost, *both* firms should accept Project A.

Next, consider Project B. It has the same risk as Project A, but its expected return is 9.5 percent versus its 10 percent hurdle rate. Both firms should reject Project B. However, if they based their decisions on their overall WACCs rather than on the project-specific cost of capital, Firm L would accept Project B because its return is above L's 8 percent WACC. However, if Firm L's managers accept Project B, they would reduce their shareholders' wealth, because the project's return is not high enough to justify its risk. Applying a specific hurdle rate to each project insures that every project is evaluated properly.

Note that these same arguments apply to the cost of capital for a multidivisional firm. Consider Firm A in Figure 10-2. It has two divisions, L and H. Division L has relatively little risk, and if it were operated as a separate firm, its

---

FIGURE 10-2 | **Divisional Cost of Capital**

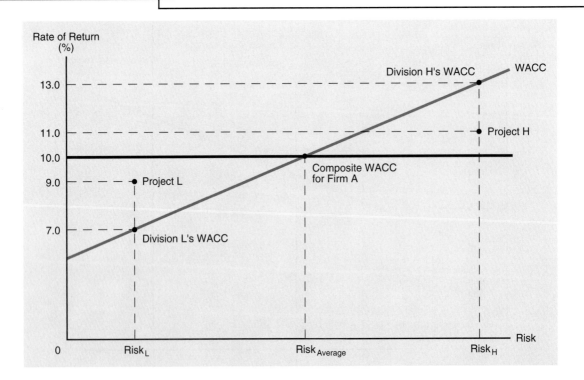

WACC would be 7 percent. Division H has a higher risk, and its divisional cost of capital is 13 percent. If the two divisions were of equal size, Firm A's composite WACC would be 0.50(7%) + 0.50(13%) = 10.0%. However, it would be a mistake to use this 10 percent WACC for either division. To see this point, assume that Division L is considering a relatively low-risk project with an expected return of 9 percent, while Division H is considering a high-risk project with an expected return of 11 percent. As shown in Figure 10-2, Division L's project should be accepted, because its return is above its risk-based cost of capital, whereas Division H's project should be rejected. If the 10 percent corporate WACC were used by each division, the decision would be reversed: Division H would incorrectly accept its project, and Division L would incorrectly reject its project. In general, failing to adjust for differences in risk would lead the firm to accept too many risky projects and reject too many safe ones. Over time, the firm would become more risky, its WACC would increase, and its shareholder value would suffer.

SELF-TEST QUESTIONS

Why is the cost of capital sometimes referred to as a "hurdle rate"?

How should firms evaluate projects with different risks?

Should divisions within the same firm all use the firm's composite WACC when considering capital budgeting projects? Explain.

ESTIMATING PROJECT RISK

Although it is intuitively clear that riskier projects should be assigned a higher cost of capital, it is often difficult to estimate project risk. First, note that three separate and distinct types of risk can be identified:

Stand-Alone Risk
The risk an asset would have if it were a firm's only asset and if investors owned only one stock. It is measured by the variability of the asset's expected returns.

1. **Stand-alone risk,** which is the project's risk disregarding the facts (a) that it is but one asset within the firm's portfolio of assets and (b) that the firm is but one stock in a typical investor's portfolio of stocks. Stand-alone risk is measured by the variability of the project's expected returns.

Corporate, or Within-Firm, Risk
Risk not considering the effects of stockholders' diversification; it is measured by a project's effect on uncertainty about the firm's future earnings.

2. **Corporate, or within-firm, risk,** which is the project's risk to the corporation, giving consideration to the fact that the project represents only one of the firm's portfolio of assets, hence that some of its risk effects on the firm's profits will be diversified away. Corporate risk is measured by the project's impact on uncertainty about the firm's future earnings.

Market, or Beta, Risk
That part of a project's risk that cannot be eliminated by diversification; it is measured by the project's beta coefficient.

3. **Market, or beta, risk,** which is the riskiness of the project as seen by a well-diversified stockholder who recognizes that the project is only one of the firm's assets and that the firm's stock is but one small part of the investor's total portfolio. Market risk is measured by the project's effect on the firm's beta coefficient.

Taking on a project with a high degree of either stand-alone or corporate risk will not necessarily affect the firm's beta. However, if the project has highly uncertain returns, and if those returns are highly correlated with returns on the firm's other assets and with most other assets in the economy, the project will have a high degree of all types of risk. For example, suppose General Motors decides to undertake a major expansion to build commuter airplanes. GM is not sure how its technology will work on a mass production basis, so there are great risks in the venture — its stand-alone risk is high. Management also estimates that the project will do best if the economy is strong, for then people will have more money to spend on the new planes. This means that the project will tend to do well if GM's other divisions do well and will tend to do badly if other divisions do badly. This being the case, the project will also have high corporate risk. Finally, since GM's profits are highly correlated with those of most other firms, the project's beta will also be high. Thus, this project will be risky under all three definitions of risk.

Of the three measures, market risk is theoretically the most relevant measure because it is the one reflected in stock prices. Unfortunately, market risk is also the most difficult to estimate. For this reason, most decision makers consider all three risk measures in a judgmental manner and then classify projects into subjective risk categories. Then, using the composite WACC as a starting point, **risk-adjusted costs of capital** are developed for each category. For example, a firm might establish three risk classes, then assign to average-risk projects the average (composite) cost of capital, to higher-risk projects an above-average cost, and to lower-risk projects a below-average cost. Thus, if a company's composite WACC estimate were 10 percent, its managers might use 10 percent to evaluate average-risk projects, 12 percent for those with high-risk, and 8 percent for low-risk projects. While this approach is better than not making any risk adjustments, these adjustments are subjective and somewhat arbitrary. Unfortunately, there is no perfect way to specify how much higher or lower we should go in setting risk-adjusted costs of capital. However, the CAPM approach as discussed in the next section generally produces reasonable results.

Risk-Adjusted Cost of Capital
The cost of capital appropriate for a given project, given the riskiness of that project. The greater the risk, the higher the cost of capital.

SELF-TEST QUESTIONS

What are the three types of project risk?

Which type of project risk is theoretically the most relevant? Why?

Explain the classification scheme many firms use when developing *subjective* risk-adjusted costs of capital.

USING THE CAPM TO ESTIMATE THE RISK-ADJUSTED COST OF CAPITAL

As an alternative to the subjective approach, firms can use the CAPM to directly estimate the cost of capital for specific projects or divisions. To begin, recall from Chapter 6 that the Security Market Line equation expresses the risk/return relationship as follows:

$$k_s = k_{RF} + (k_M - k_{RF})b_i.$$

As an example, consider the case of Erie Steel Company, an integrated steel producer operating in the Great Lakes region. For simplicity, assume that Erie uses only equity capital, so its cost of equity is also its corporate cost of capital, or WACC. Erie's beta = b = 1.1; k_{RF} = 8%; and k_M = 12%. Thus, Erie's cost of equity and hence its WACC is 12.4 percent:

$$k_s = WACC = 8\% + (12\% - 8\%)1.1$$
$$= 8\% + (4\%)1.1$$
$$= 12.4\%.$$

This suggests that investors should be willing to give Erie money to invest in average-risk projects if the company expects to earn 12.4 percent or more on this money. Here again, by average risk we mean projects having risk similar to the firm's existing assets. *Therefore, as a first approximation, Erie should invest in capital projects if and only if those projects have an expected return of 12.4 percent or more.*[13] Erie should use 12.4 percent as its hurdle rate for an average-risk project.

Suppose, however, that taking on a particular project would cause a change in Erie's beta coefficient, which, in turn, would change the company's cost of equity. For example, suppose Erie is considering the construction of a fleet of barges to haul iron ore, and barge operations have betas of 1.5 rather than 1.1. Since the firm itself may be regarded as a "portfolio of assets," and since the beta of any portfolio is a weighted average of the betas of its individual assets, taking on the barge project would cause the overall corporate beta to rise to somewhere between the original beta of 1.1 and the barge project's beta of 1.5. The exact value of the new beta would depend on the relative size of the investment in barge operations versus Erie's other assets. If 80 percent of Erie's total funds ended up in basic steel operations with a beta of 1.1 and 20 percent in barge operations with a beta of 1.5, the new corporate beta would be 1.18:

$$\text{New beta} = 0.8(1.1) + 0.2(1.5)$$
$$= 1.18.$$

This increase in Erie's beta coefficient would cause its stock price to decline *unless the increased beta were offset by a higher expected rate of return.* Specifically, taking on the new project would cause the overall corporate cost of capital to rise from the original 12.4 percent to 12.72 percent:

$$k_s = 8\% + (4\%)1.18$$
$$= 12.72\%.$$

Therefore, to keep the barge investment from lowering the value of the firm, Erie's overall expected rate of return must rise from 12.4 to 12.72 percent.

---

[13] Note that we assume that the firm uses only equity capital. If debt were used, the cost of capital must be a weighted average of the costs of debt and equity.

If investments in basic steel must earn 12.4 percent, how much must Erie expect to earn on the barge investment to cause the new overall expected rate of return to equal 12.72 percent? We know that if Erie undertakes the barge investment, it will have 80 percent of its assets invested in basic steel projects earning 12.4 percent and 20 percent in barge operations earning "X" percent, and the average required rate of return will be 12.72 percent. Therefore,

$$0.8(12.4\%) + 0.2X = 12.72\%$$
$$0.2X = 2.8\%$$
$$X = 14\%.$$

Since $X = 14\%$, we see that the barge project must have an expected return of 14 percent if the corporation is to earn its new cost of capital.

In summary, if Erie takes on the barge project, its corporate beta will rise from 1.1 to 1.18, its cost of capital will rise from 12.4 to 12.72 percent, and the barge investment must earn 14 percent if the company is to earn its new overall cost of capital.

This line of reasoning leads to the conclusion that if the beta coefficient for each project, b_p, could be determined, then a **project cost of capital, k_p,** for each individual project could be found as follows:[14]

Project Cost of Capital, k_p
The risk-adjusted cost of capital for an individual project.

$$k_p = k_{RF} + (k_M - k_{RF})b_p.$$

Thus, for basic steel projects with $b = 1.1$, Erie should use 12.4 percent as the cost of capital. The barge project, with $b = 1.5$, should be evaluated at a 14 percent cost of capital:

$$k_{Barge} = 8\% + (4\%)1.5$$
$$= 8\% + 6\%$$
$$= 14\%.$$

On the other hand, a low-risk project, such as a new distribution center with a beta of only 0.5, would have a cost of capital of 10 percent:

$$k_{Center} = 8\% + (4\%)0.5$$
$$= 10\%.$$

Figure 10-3 can be used to illustrate the CAPM approach for Erie Steel. Note the following points:

1. The SML is the same Security Market Line that we developed in Chapter 6. It shows how investors are willing to make trade-offs between risk as measured by beta and expected returns. The higher the beta risk, the higher the rate of return needed to compensate investors for bearing this risk.

---

[14] Note that the term k_p can also stand for the cost of preferred stock. Keep this dual usage of the term in mind to avoid confusion.

FIGURE 10-3

Using the Security Market Line Concept in Capital Budgeting

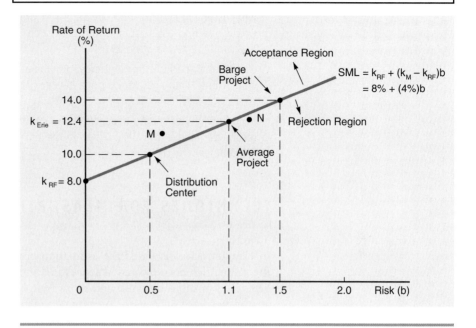

2. Erie Steel initially has a beta of 1.1, so its required rate of return on average-risk investments is 12.4 percent.

3. High-risk investments such as the barge line require higher rates of return, whereas low-risk investments such as the distribution center require lower rates. If Erie concentrates its new investments in either high- or low-risk projects as opposed to average-risk projects, its corporate beta will rise or fall from the current value of 1.1. Consequently, Erie's required rate of return on common stock would change from its current value of 12.4 percent.

4. If the expected rate of return on a given capital project lies *above* the SML, then the expected rate of return on the project is more than enough to compensate for its risk, and the project should be accepted. Conversely, if the project's rate of return lies *below* the SML, it should be rejected. Thus, Project M in Figure 10-3 is acceptable, whereas Project N should be rejected. N has a higher expected return than M, but the differential is not enough to offset its higher risk.

5. For simplicity, the Erie Steel illustration is based on the assumption that the company used no debt financing, which allows us to use the SML to plot the company's cost of capital. The basic concepts presented in the Erie illustration also hold for companies that use debt financing. As we discussed in previous chapters, the discount rate applied in capital budgeting is the firm's weighted average cost of capital. When debt financing is used, the project's cost of equity must be combined with the cost of debt to obtain the project's overall cost of capital.

What is meant by the term "average-risk project"? Based on the CAPM, how would one find the cost of capital for such a project, for a low-risk project, and for a high-risk project?

Complete the following sentence: An increase in a company's beta coefficient would cause its stock price to decline unless its expected rate of return . . .

Explain why you should accept a given capital project if its expected rate of return lies above the SML. What if the expected rate of return lies on the SML? Below the SML?

TECHNIQUES FOR MEASURING BETA RISK

In Chapter 6 we discussed the estimation of betas for stocks, and we indicated the difficulties encountered when estimating beta. The estimation of project betas is even more difficult, and more fraught with uncertainty. However, two approaches have been used to estimate individual assets' betas — the pure play method and the accounting beta method.

THE PURE PLAY METHOD

Pure Play Method
An approach used for estimating the beta of a project in which a firm (1) identifies several companies whose only business is to produce the product in question, (2) calculates the beta for each firm, and then (3) averages the betas to find an approximation to its own project's beta.

In the **pure play method,** the company finds several single-product companies in the same line of business as the project being evaluated and then averages those companies' betas to determine the cost of capital for its own project. For example, suppose Erie found three existing single-product firms that operate barges, and suppose also that Erie's management believes its barge project would be subject to the same risks as those firms. Erie could then determine the betas of those firms, average them, and use this average beta as a proxy for the barge project's beta.[15]

The pure play approach can only be used for major assets such as whole divisions, and even then it is frequently difficult to implement because it is often impossible to find pure play proxy firms. However, when IBM was considering going into personal computers, it was able to obtain data on Apple Computer and several other essentially pure play personal computer companies. This is often the case when a firm considers a major investment outside its primary field.

THE ACCOUNTING BETA METHOD

As noted above, it may be impossible to find single-product, publicly traded firms as required for the pure play approach. If that is the case, we may want

---

[15] If the pure play firms employ different capital structures than that of Erie, this fact must be dealt with by adjusting the beta coefficients. See Brigham and Daves, *Intermediate Financial Management,* 7th ed., Chapter 13, for a discussion of this aspect of the pure play method.

Accounting Beta Method
A method of estimating a project's beta by running a regression of the company's return on assets against the average return on assets for a large sample of firms.

to use the **accounting beta method.** Betas normally are found as described in Appendix 6A — by regressing the returns of a particular company's *stock* against returns on a *stock market index.* However, we could run a regression of the company's *accounting return on assets* against the *average return on assets* for a large sample of companies, such as those included in the S&P 400. Betas determined in this way (that is, by using accounting data rather than stock market data) are called *accounting betas.*

Accounting betas for a totally new project can be calculated only after the project has been accepted, placed in operation, and begun to generate output and accounting results — too late for the capital budgeting decision. However, to the extent management thinks a given project is similar to other projects the firm has undertaken in the past, some other project's accounting beta can be used as a proxy for that of the project in question. In practice, accounting betas are normally calculated for divisions or other large units, not for single assets, and divisional betas are then used to find the division's cost of capital.

SELF-TEST QUESTION

Describe the pure play and the accounting beta methods for estimating individual projects' betas.

SOME PROBLEM AREAS IN COST OF CAPITAL

A number of difficult issues relating to the cost of capital either have not been mentioned or were glossed over in this chapter. These topics are covered in advanced finance courses, but they deserve some mention now both to alert you to potential dangers and to provide you with a preview of some of the matters dealt with in advanced courses.

1. **Depreciation-generated funds.** The largest single source of capital for many firms is depreciation, yet we have not discussed the cost of funds from this source. In brief, depreciation cash flows can either be reinvested or returned to investors (stockholders *and* creditors). The cost of depreciation-generated funds is approximately equal to the weighted average cost of capital from retained earnings and low-cost debt. See Brigham and Daves, *Intermediate Financial Management,* 7th ed., Chapter 9, for a discussion.

2. **Privately owned firms.** Our discussion of the cost of equity was related to publicly owned corporations, and we have concentrated on the rate of return required by public stockholders. However, there is a serious question about how one should measure the cost of equity for a firm whose stock is not traded. Tax issues are also especially important in these cases. As a general rule, the same principles of cost of capital estimation apply to both privately held and publicly owned firms, but the problems of obtaining input data are somewhat different for each.

SMALL BUSINESS

THE COST OF EQUITY CAPITAL FOR SMALL FIRMS

The three equity cost-estimating techniques discussed in this chapter (DCF, Bond-Yield-plus-Risk-Premium, and CAPM) have serious limitations when applied to small firms. Consider first the constant growth model, $k_s = D_1/P_0 + g$. Imagine a small, rapidly growing firm, such as Bio-Technology General (BTG), which will not in the foreseeable future pay dividends. For firms like this, the constant growth model is simply not applicable. In fact, it is difficult to imagine any dividend model that would be of practical benefit for such a firm because of the difficulty of estimating dividends and growth rates.

The second method, which calls for adding a risk premium of 3 to 5 percent to the firm's cost of debt, can be used for some small firms, but problems arise if the firm does not have a publicly traded bond outstanding. BTG, for example, has no public debt outstanding, so we would have trouble using the bond-yield-plus-risk-premium approach for BTG.

The third approach, the CAPM, is often not usable, because if the firm's stock is not publicly traded, then we cannot calculate its beta. For the privately owned firm, we might use the "pure play" CAPM technique, which involves finding a publicly owned firm in the same line of business, estimating that firm's beta, and then using that beta as a replacement for the one of the small business in question.

To illustrate the pure play approach, again consider BTG. The firm is not publicly traded, so we cannot estimate its beta. However, data are available on more established firms, such as Genentech and Genetic Industries, so we could use their betas as representative of the biological and genetic engineering industry. Of course, these firms' betas would have to be subjectively modified to reflect their larger sizes and more established positions, as well as to take account of the differences in the nature of their products and their capital structures as compared to those of BTG. Still, as long as there are public companies in similar lines of business available for comparison, their betas can be used to help estimate the cost of capital of a firm whose equity is not publicly traded. Note also that a "liquidity premium" as discussed in Chapter 5 would also have to be added to reflect the illiquidity of the small, nonpublic firm's stock.

FLOTATION COSTS FOR SMALL ISSUES

When external equity capital is raised, flotation costs increase the cost of equity capital above that of internal funds. These flotation costs are especially significant for smaller firms, and they can have a major effect on capital budgeting decisions involving external equity funds. To illustrate, consider a firm that is expected to pay constant dividends forever, hence its growth rate is zero. In this case, if F is the percentage flotation cost, then the cost of equity capital is $k_e = D_1/[P_0(1 - F)]$. The higher the flotation cost, the higher the cost of external equity.

How big is F? Looking at the estimates presented earlier in the Industry Practice box entitled "How Much Does It Cost to Raise External Capital?," we see that small debt and equity issues have considerably higher flotation costs than large issues. For example, a non-IPO issue of common stock that raises more than $200 million in capital would have a flotation cost of about 3.5 percent. For a firm that is expected to provide a constant 15 percent dividend yield (that is, $D_1/P_0 = 15\%$), the cost of equity would be 15%/(1 − 0.04), or 15.6 percent. How-

3. **Small businesses.** Small businesses are generally privately owned, making it difficult to estimate their cost of equity. The Small Business box, entitled "The Cost of Equity Capital for Small Firms," discusses this issue.

4. **Measurement problems.** One cannot overemphasize the practical difficulties encountered when estimating the cost of equity. It is very difficult to obtain good input data for the CAPM, for g in the formula $k_s = D_1/P_0 + g$, and for the risk premium in the formula k_s = Bond yield + Risk premium. As a result, we can never be sure just how accurate our estimated cost of capital is.

5. **Costs of capital for projects of differing riskiness.** It is difficult to measure projects' risks, hence to assign risk-adjusted discount rates to capital budgeting projects of differing degrees of riskiness.

6. **Capital structure weights.** In this chapter, we have simply taken as given the target capital structure and have used it to calculate the cost of capital. As we shall see in Chapter 13, establishing the target capital structure is a major task in itself.

ever, a similar but smaller firm that raises less than $10 million would have a flotation cost of about 13 percent, which would result in a flotation-adjusted cost of equity capital of 15%/ $(1 - 0.13) = 17.2$ percent, or 1.6 percentage points higher. This differential would be even larger if an IPO were involved. Therefore, it is clear that a small firm would have to earn considerably more on the same project than a large firm. Small firms are therefore at a substantial disadvantage because of flotation cost effects.

THE SMALL-FIRM EFFECT

A number of researchers have observed that portfolios of small firms' stocks have earned higher average returns than portfolios of large firms' stocks; this is called the "small-firm effect." For example, over the time period 1926–1999, Ibbotson Associates finds that the average yearly return for the smallest stocks on the NYSE has been 17.6 percent. By contrast, over the same time period the largest NYSE stocks have had an average yearly return of 13.3 percent. On the surface it would seem to be advantageous to the small firm to provide average returns in the stock market that are higher than those of large firms. In reality, however, these higher returns suggest that smaller firms have a higher cost of equity captial.

What can explain the higher cost of capital for smaller firms? It may be argued that the stocks of smaller firms are riskier and less liquid than the stocks of larger firms, and this accounts for the differences in returns. Indeed, most academic research finds that both standard deviations of yearly returns and betas are higher for smaller firms than they are for larger firms. However, the returns for small firms are often still larger even after adjusting for the effects of their higher risks as reflected in their beta coefficients. In this regard, the small-firm effect is inconsistent with the CAPM. Some researchers have attempted to address this issue by including firm size as a predictor in their asset pricing models. For example, in Chapter 6 we mentioned that the multi-factor models recently developed by Fama and French include firm size as a key factor in explaining stock market returns.

Over the past few years there has been an interesting twist to the small-firm effect. In recent years, small firm stocks have tended to have *lower* returns than those of larger firms. Does this mean the small-firm effect has disappeared? Not necessarily. Remember from the Chapter 6 box entitled "Estimating the Market Risk Premium" that using historical returns to estimate expected future returns becomes problematic whenever the risk premium changes over time. It is possible that, in recent years, not only has the market risk premium itself changed but that the size premium has also changed.

While the small-firm effect continues to generate considerable discussion among both researchers and practitioners, most analysts conclude that smaller firms have higher capital costs than do otherwise similar large firms. In general, the cost of equity appears to be one or two percentage points higher for small firms (those with market values less than $20 million) than for large NYSE firms with similar risk characteristics. The manager of a small firm should take this factor into account when estimating his or her firm's cost of equity capital.

Although this listing of problems may appear formidable, the state of the art in cost of capital estimation is really not in bad shape. The procedures outlined in this chapter can be used to obtain cost of capital estimates that are sufficiently accurate for practical purposes, and the problems listed here merely indicate the desirability of refinements. The refinements are not unimportant, but the problems we have identified do not invalidate the usefulness of the procedures outlined in the chapter.

SELF-TEST QUESTION

Identify some problem areas in cost of capital analysis. Do these problems invalidate the cost of capital procedures discussed in the chapter?

We began this chapter by defining three capital components — debt, preferred stock, and common equity — and then estimating each component's cost of capital. After estimating the components' costs, we calculated a weighted average cost of capital (WACC). As we will see in the following two chapters, the WACC is a key element in the capital budgeting process. In this chapter we calculated the WACC assuming that the target capital structure is a given. In Chapter 13, we will discuss how firms determine their target capital structures and the effects of capital structure on the WACC. The key concepts covered in Chapter 10 are listed below:

- The cost of capital is sometimes referred to as a **hurdle rate.** For a project to increase shareholders' value, it must earn more than its hurdle rate.

- The cost of capital used in capital budgeting is a **weighted average** of the types of capital the firm uses, typically debt, preferred stock, and common equity.

- The **component cost of debt** is the **after-tax** cost of new debt. It is found by multiplying the cost of new debt by $(1 - T)$, where T is the firm's marginal tax rate: $k_d(1 - T)$.

- The **component cost of preferred stock** is calculated as the preferred dividend divided by the current price of the preferred stock: $k_p = D_p/P_p$.

- The **cost of retained earnings, k_s,** is the rate of return stockholders require on the company's common stock. There are two sources of equity capital: (1) internal equity generated through additions to retained earnings and (2) external equity obtained by issuing new shares of common stock.

- The cost of common equity can be estimated by three methods: (1) the **CAPM approach,** (2) the **bond-yield-plus-risk-premium approach,** and (3) the **dividend-yield-plus-growth-rate,** or **DCF, approach.**

- To use the **CAPM approach,** one (1) estimates the firm's beta, (2) multiplies this beta by the market risk premium to determine the firm's risk premium, and (3) adds the firm's risk premium to the risk-free rate to obtain the firm's cost of common equity: $k_s = k_{RF} + (k_M - k_{RF})b_i$.

- The **bond-yield-plus-risk-premium approach** calls for adding a risk premium of from 3 to 5 percentage points to the firm's interest rate on long-term debt: $k_s = $ Bond yield $+$ RP.

- To use the **dividend-yield-plus-growth-rate approach,** which is also called the **discounted cash flow (DCF) approach,** one adds the firm's expected growth rate to its expected dividend yield: $k_s = D_1/P_0 + g$.

- Companies generally hire an investment banker to assist them when they issue common stock, preferred stock, or bonds. In return for a fee, the investment banker helps the company with the terms, price, and sale of the issue. The banker's fees are often referred to as **flotation costs.** The total cost of capital should include not only the required return paid to investors but also the flotation fees paid to the investment banker for marketing the issue.

- Two alternative approaches can be used to account for flotation costs. The first approach adds the estimated dollar amount of flotation costs for each project to the project's up-front cost — this **lowers the project's expected rate of return.** An alternative approach is to **adjust the cost of equity.** When calculating the **cost of new common stock,** the DCF approach can be adapted to account for flotation costs. For a constant growth stock, this cost can be expressed as: $k_e = D_1/[P_0(1 - F)] + g$. Note that flotation costs cause k_e to be greater than k_s.

- **Flotation cost adjustments** can also be made for preferred stock and debt. The flotation-adjusted cost for preferred is calculated as D_p/P_n, where P_n is the price the firm receives on preferred after deducting flotation costs. For debt, the bond's issue price is reduced for flotation expenses and then used to solve for the after-tax yield to maturity.

- Each firm has an **optimal capital structure,** defined as the mix of debt, preferred stock, and common equity that minimizes its **weighted average cost of capital (WACC):**

$$WACC = w_d k_d (1 - T) + w_p k_p + w_c k_s.$$

- The WACC represents the **marginal cost of capital (MCC)** because it indicates the cost of raising an additional dollar.

- **Various factors affect a firm's cost of capital.** Some are determined by the financial environment, but the firm influences others through its financing, investment, and dividend decisions.

- A project's **stand-alone risk** is the risk the project would have if it were the firm's only asset and if the firm's stockholders held only that one stock. Stand-alone risk is measured by the variability of the asset's expected returns.

- **Corporate,** or **within-firm, risk** reflects the effects of a project on the firm's risk, and it is measured by the project's effect on the firm's earnings variability.

- **Market,** or **beta, risk** reflects the effects of a project on the riskiness of stockholders, assuming they hold diversified portfolios. Market risk is measured by the project's effect on the firm's beta coefficient.

- Most decision makers consider all three risk measures in a judgmental manner and then classify projects into subjective risk categories. Using the composite WACC as a starting point, *risk-adjusted costs of capital* are developed for each category. The **risk-adjusted cost of capital** is the cost of capital appropriate for a given project, given the riskiness of that project. The greater the risk, the higher the cost of capital.

- As an alternative to the subjective approach, firms can use the **CAPM** to directly estimate the risk-adjusted cost of capital for specific projects or divisions.

- The **pure play method** and the **accounting beta method** can be used to estimate betas for large projects or for divisions.

- The **hurdle rate** for each project should reflect the risk of the project itself, not the risks associated with the firm's average project as reflected in its composite WACC. Applying a specific hurdle rate to each project ensures that every project is evaluated properly.

- **Failing to adjust for differences in risk** would lead a firm to accept too many risky projects and reject too many safe ones. Over time, the firm would become more risky, its WACC would increase, and its shareholder value would suffer.

- The three equity cost-estimating techniques discussed in this chapter have **serious limitations** when applied to small firms, thus increasing the need for the small-business manager to use judgment.

- Stock offerings of less than $10 million have an average flotation cost of 13 percent, while the average flotation cost on large common stock offerings is about 4 percent. As a result, a small firm would have to earn considerably more on the same project than a large firm. Also, the capital market demands higher returns on stocks of small firms than on otherwise similar stocks of large firms — this is called the **small-firm effect.**

QUESTIONS

10-1 How would each of the following affect a firm's cost of debt, $k_d(1 - T)$; its cost of equity, k_s; and its weighted average cost of capital, WACC? Indicate by a plus (+), a minus (−), or a zero (0) if the factor would raise, lower, or have an indeterminate effect on the item in question. Assume other things are held constant. Be prepared to justify your answer, but recognize that several of the parts probably have no single correct answer; these questions are designed to stimulate thought and discussion.

	EFFECT ON		
	$k_d(1 - T)$	k_s	WACC
a. The corporate tax rate is lowered.	——	——	——
b. The Federal Reserve tightens credit.	——	——	——
c. The firm uses more debt; that is, it increases its debt/assets ratio.	——	——	——
d. The dividend payout ratio is increased.	——	——	——
e. The firm doubles the amount of capital it raises during the year.	——	——	——
f. The firm expands into a risky new area.	——	——	——
g. The firm merges with another firm whose earnings are countercyclical both to those of the first firm and to the stock market.	——	——	——
h. The stock market falls drastically, and the firm's stock falls along with the rest.	——	——	——

	EFFECT ON		
	$k_d(1 - T)$	k_s	WACC
i. Investors become more risk averse.	_____	_____	_____
j. The firm is an electric utility with a large investment in nuclear plants. Several states propose a ban on nuclear power generation.	_____	_____	_____

10-2 Distinguish among beta (or market) risk, within-firm (or corporate) risk, and stand-alone risk for a project being considered for inclusion in the capital budget. Of the three measures, which is theoretically the most relevant and why?

10-3 Suppose a firm estimates its cost of capital for the coming year to be 10 percent. What are reasonable costs of capital for evaluating average-risk projects, high-risk projects, and low-risk projects?

10-4 How should a manager determine the capital structure weights that are used to calculate the WACC?

10-5 Assume that there is an increase in the risk-free rate. What impact would this increase have on the cost of debt? What impact would this have on the cost of equity?

10-6 What are the likely effects of a policy in which a company fails to adjust for differences in risk when estimating the cost of capital for their various projects?

SELF-TEST PROBLEMS (SOLUTIONS APPEAR IN APPENDIX B)

ST-1
Key terms

Define each of the following terms:
a. After-tax cost of debt, $k_d(1 - T)$; capital component
b. Cost of preferred stock, k_p
c. Cost of retained earnings, k_s; cost of new common stock, k_e
d. Flotation cost, F; retained earnings breakpoint
e. Target (optimal) capital structure
f. Weighted average cost of capital, WACC
g. Marginal cost of capital, MCC
h. Stand-alone risk; corporate (within-firm) risk; market (beta) risk
i. Risk-adjusted cost of capital
j. Project cost of capital
k. Pure play method
l. Accounting beta method

ST-2
Marginal cost of capital

Lancaster Engineering Inc. (LEI) has the following capital structure, which it considers to be optimal:

Debt	25%
Preferred stock	15
Common equity	60
	100%

LEI's expected net income this year is $34,285.72, its established dividend payout ratio is 30 percent, its federal-plus-state tax rate is 40 percent, and investors expect earnings and dividends to grow at a constant rate of 9 percent in the future. LEI paid a dividend of $3.60 per share last year, and its stock currently sells at a price of $54 per share.

LEI can obtain new capital in the following ways:

- *Preferred:* New preferred stock with a dividend of $11 can be sold to the public at a price of $95 per share.
- *Debt:* Debt can be sold at an interest rate of 12 percent.

a. Determine the cost of each capital structure component.
b. Calculate the weighted average cost of capital.
c. LEI has the following investment opportunities that are typical average-risk projects for the firm:

PROJECT	COST AT t = 0	RATE OF RETURN
A	$10,000	17.4%
B	20,000	16.0
C	10,000	14.2
D	20,000	13.7
E	10,000	12.0

Which projects should LEI accept? Why?

STARTER PROBLEMS

10-1
Cost of common equity

Percy Motors has a target capital structure of 40 percent debt and 60 percent equity. The yield to maturity on the company's outstanding bonds is 9 percent, and the company's tax rate is 40 percent. Percy's CFO has calculated the company's WACC as 9.96 percent. What is the company's cost of common equity?

10-2
Cost of preferred stock

Tunney Industries can issue perpetual preferred stock at a price of $47.50 a share. The issue is expected to pay a constant annual dividend of $3.80 a share. What is the company's cost of preferred stock, k_p?

10-3
Cost of equity with and without flotation

Javits & Sons' common stock is currently trading at $30 a share. The stock is expected to pay a dividend of $3.00 a share at the end of the year (D_1 = $3.00), and the dividend is expected to grow at a constant rate of 5 percent a year. If the company were to issue external equity, it would incur a 10 percent flotation cost. What are the costs of internal and external equity?

10-4
Project selection

Midwest Water Works estimates that its WACC is 10.5 percent. The company is considering the following seven investment projects:

PROJECT	SIZE	RATE OF RETURN
A	$1 million	12.0%
B	2 million	11.5
C	2 million	11.2
D	2 million	11.0
E	1 million	10.7
F	1 million	10.3
G	1 million	10.2

Assume that each of these projects is just as risky as the firm's existing assets, and the firm may accept all the projects or only some of them. Which set of projects should be accepted?

The problems included in this section are set up in such a way that they could be used as multiple-choice exam problems.

10-5
After-tax cost of debt

Calculate the after-tax cost of debt under each of the following conditions:
a. Interest rate, 13 percent; tax rate, 0 percent.
b. Interest rate, 13 percent; tax rate, 20 percent.
c. Interest rate, 13 percent; tax rate, 35 percent.

10-6
After-tax cost of debt

The Heuser Company's currently outstanding 10 percent coupon bonds have a yield to maturity of 12 percent. Heuser believes it could issue at par new bonds that would provide a similar yield to maturity. If its marginal tax rate is 35 percent, what is Heuser's after-tax cost of debt?

10-7
Cost of preferred stock including flotation

Trivoli Industries plans to issue some $100 par preferred stock with an 11 percent dividend. The stock is selling on the market for $97.00, but Trivoli must pay flotation costs of 5 percent of the market price, so the net price the firm will receive is $92.15 per share. What is Trivoli's cost of preferred stock with flotation considered?

10-8
Cost of common equity with and without flotation

The Evanec Company's next expected dividend, D_1, is $3.18; its growth rate is 6 percent; and the stock now sells for $36. New stock (external equity) can be sold to net the firm $32.40 per share.
a. What is Evanec's cost of retained earnings, k_s?
b. What is Evanec's percentage flotation cost, F?
c. What is Evanec's cost of new common stock, k_e?

10-9
Weighted average cost of capital

The Patrick Company's cost of common equity is 16 percent. Its before-tax cost of debt is 13 percent, and its marginal tax rate is 40 percent. The stock sells at book value. Using the following balance sheet, calculate Patrick's after-tax weighted average cost of capital:

ASSETS		LIABILITIES AND EQUITY	
Cash	$ 120		
Accounts receivable	240		
Inventories	360	Long-term debt	$1,152
Plant and equipment, net	2,160	Equity	1,728
Total assets	$2,880	Total liabilities and equity	$2,880

10-10
WACC and percentage of debt financing

Hook Industries has a capital structure that consists solely of debt and common equity. The company can issue debt at 11 percent. Its stock currently pays a $2 dividend per share ($D_0 = $2), and the stock's price is currently $24.75. The company's dividend is expected to grow at a constant rate of 7 percent per year; its tax rate is 35 percent; and the company estimates that its WACC is 13.95 percent. What percentage of the company's capital structure consists of debt financing?

10-11
Weighted average cost of capital

Midwest Electric Company (MEC) uses only debt and equity. It can borrow unlimited amounts at an interest rate of 10 percent as long as it finances at its target capital structure, which calls for 45 percent debt and 55 percent common equity. Its last dividend was $2, its expected constant growth rate is 4 percent, and its stock sells at a price of $20. MEC's tax rate is 40 percent. Two projects are available: Project A has a rate of return of 13 percent, while Project B has a rate of return of 10 percent. All of the company's potential projects are equally risky and as risky as the firm's other assets.
a. What is MEC's cost of common equity?
b. What is MEC's WACC?
c. Which projects should MEC select?

10-12
After-tax cost of debt

A company's 6 percent coupon rate, semiannual payment, $1,000 par value bond that matures in 30 years sells at a price of $515.16. The company's federal-plus-state tax rate is 40 percent. What is the firm's component cost of debt for purposes of calculating the WACC? (Hint: Base your answer on the *nominal* rate.)

10-13

Cost of common equity and WACC

Patton Paints Corporation has a target capital structure of 40 percent debt and 60 percent common equity. The company's before-tax cost of debt is 12 percent and its marginal tax rate is 40 percent. The current stock price is $P_0 = \$22.50$; the last dividend was $D_0 = \$2.00$; and the dividend is expected to grow at a constant rate of 7 percent. What will be the firm's cost of common equity and its WACC?

PROBLEMS

10-14

Cost of common equity

The earnings, dividends, and stock price of Carpetto Technologies Inc. are expected to grow at 7 percent per year in the future. Carpetto's common stock sells for $23 per share, its last dividend was $2.00, and the company will pay a dividend of $2.14 at the end of the current year.

a. Using the discounted cash flow approach, what is its cost of common equity?
b. If the firm's beta is 1.6, the risk-free rate is 9 percent, and the average return on the market is 13 percent, what will be the firm's cost of common equity using the CAPM approach?
c. If the firm's bonds earn a return of 12 percent, what will k_s be using the bond-yield-plus-risk-premium approach? (Hint: Use the midpoint of the risk premium range.)
d. On the basis of the results obtained in parts a through c, what would you estimate Carpetto's cost of common equity to be?

10-15

Cost of common equity

The Bouchard Company's EPS was $6.50 in 2001 and $4.42 in 1996. The company pays out 40 percent of its earnings as dividends, and the stock sells for $36.

a. Calculate the past growth rate in earnings. (Hint: This is a 5-year growth period.)
b. Calculate the *next* expected dividend per share, D_1. ($D_0 = 0.4(\$6.50) = \$2.60$.) Assume that the past growth rate will continue.
c. What is the cost of retained earnings, k_s, for the Bouchard Company?

10-16

Calculation of g and EPS

Sidman Products' stock is currently selling for $60 a share. The firm is expected to earn $5.40 per share this year and to pay a year-end dividend of $3.60.

a. If investors require a 9 percent return, what rate of growth must be expected for Sidman?
b. If Sidman reinvests retained earnings in projects whose average return is equal to the stock's expected rate of return, what will be next year's EPS? [Hint: $g = (1 -$ Payout rate)(ROE).]

10-17

Weighted average cost of capital

The following tabulation gives earnings per share figures for the Foust Company during the preceding 10 years. The firm's common stock, 7.8 million shares outstanding, is now (1/1/02) selling for $65 per share, and the expected dividend at the end of the current year (2002) is 55 percent of the 2001 EPS. Because investors expect past trends to continue, g may be based on the earnings growth rate. (Note that 9 years of growth are reflected in the data.)

YEAR	EPS	YEAR	EPS
1992	$3.90	1997	$5.73
1993	4.21	1998	6.19
1994	4.55	1999	6.68
1995	4.91	2000	7.22
1996	5.31	2001	7.80

The current interest rate on new debt is 9 percent. The firm's marginal tax rate is 40 percent. Its capital structure, considered to be optimal, is as follows:

Debt	$104,000,000
Common equity	156,000,000
Total liabilities and equity	$260,000,000

a. Calculate Foust's after-tax cost of new debt and common equity. Calculate the cost of equity as $k_s = D_1/P_0 + g$.

b. Find Foust's weighted average cost of capital.

10-18

WACC and optimal capital budget

Adams Corporation has four investment projects with the following costs and rates of return:

	COST	RATE OF RETURN
Project 1	$2,000	16.00%
Project 2	3,000	15.00
Project 3	5,000	13.75
Project 4	2,000	12.50

The company estimates that it can issue debt at a before-tax cost of 10 percent, and its tax rate is 30 percent. The company also can issue preferred stock at $49 per share, which pays a constant dividend of $5 per year.

The company's stock currently sells at $36 per share. The year-end dividend, D_1, is expected to be $3.50, and the dividend is expected to grow at a constant rate of 6 percent per year. The company's capital structure consists of 75 percent common stock, 15 percent debt, and 10 percent preferred stock.

a. What is the cost of each of the capital components?

b. What is the WACC?

c. Which projects should the firm select if the projects are all of average risk?

10-19

CAPM approach to risk adjustments

Goodtread Rubber Company has two divisions: the tire division, which manufactures tires for new autos, and the recap division, which manufactures recapping materials that are sold to independent tire recapping shops throughout the United States. Since auto manufacturing fluctuates with the general economy, the tire division's earnings contribution to Goodtread's stock price is highly correlated with returns on most other stocks. If the tire division were operated as a separate company, its beta coefficient would be about 1.50. The sales and profits of the recap division, on the other hand, tend to be countercyclical, because recap sales boom when people cannot afford to buy new tires. The recap division's beta is estimated to be 0.5. Approximately 75 percent of Goodtread's corporate assets are invested in the tire division and 25 percent are invested in the recap division.

Currently, the rate of interest on Treasury securities is 9 percent, and the expected rate of return on an average share of stock is 13 percent. Goodtread uses only common equity capital, so it has no debt outstanding.

a. What is the new corporate beta?

b. What is the required rate of return on Goodtread's stock?

c. What is the cost of capital for projects in each division?

SPREADSHEET PROBLEM

10-20

Calculating the weighted average cost of capital

Here is the condensed balance sheet for Skye Computer Company (in thousands of dollars):

	2001
Current assets	$2,000
Net fixed assets	3,000
Total assets	$5,000

Current liabilities	$ 900
Long-term debt	1,200
Preferred stock	250
Common stock	1,300
Retained earnings	1,350
Total common equity	$2,650
Total liabilities and equity	$5,000

Skye Computer's earnings per share last year were $3.20; the stock sells for $55, and last year's dividend was $2.10. A flotation cost of 10 percent would be required to issue new common stock. Skye's preferred stock pays a dividend of $3.30 per share, and new preferred could be sold at a price to net the company $30 per share. Security analysts are projecting that the common dividend will grow at a rate of 9 percent per year. The firm can issue additional long-term debt at an interest rate (or before-tax cost) of 10 percent, and its marginal tax rate is 35 percent. The market risk premium is 5 percent, the risk-free rate is 6 percent, and Skye's beta is 1.516. In its cost of capital calculations, the company considers only long-term capital, hence it disregards current liabilities for this purpose.

a. Calculate the cost of each capital component, that is, the after-tax cost of debt, the cost of preferred stock, the cost of equity from retained earnings, and the cost of newly issued common stock. Use the DCF method to find the cost of common equity.

b. Now calculate the cost of common equity from retained earnings using the CAPM method.

c. What is the cost of new common stock, based on the CAPM? (Hint: Find the difference between k_e and k_s as determined by the DCF method, and add that differential to the CAPM value for k_s.)

d. If Skye Computer continues to use the same capital structure, what is the firm's WACC assuming (1) that it uses only retained earnings for equity and (2) that it expands so rapidly that it must issue new common stock?

e. Suppose Skye is evaluating three projects with the following characteristics:

- Each project has a cost of $1 million. They will all be financed using the target mix of long-term debt, preferred stock, and common equity. The cost of the common equity for each project should be based on the beta estimated for the project. All equity will come from retained earnings.

- Equity invested in Project A would have a beta of 0.5 and an expected return of 9.0 percent.

- Equity invested in Project B would have a beta of 1.0 and an expected return of 10.0 percent.

- Equity invested in Project C would have a beta of 2.0 and an expected return of 11.0 percent.

Analyze the company's situation and explain why each project should be accepted or rejected.

CYBER PROBLEM

The information related to the cyberproblems is likely to change over time, due to the release of new information and the ever-changing nature of the World Wide Web. With these changes in mind, we will periodically update these problems on the textbook's web site. To avoid problems, please check for these updates before proceeding with the cyberproblems.

10-21
The cost of capital — AT&T

Capital budgeting involves decisions about whether or not to invest in fixed assets, and it has a major influence on firms' future performances and values. Discounted cash flow analysis is used in capital budgeting, and a key element of this procedure is the discount rate used in the analysis. Capital must be raised to finance fixed assets, and this capital comes from debt, preferred stock, and common equity. Each of these capital components has a cost, and these cost rates, along with the target proportions of each, are used to calculate the firm's weighted average cost of capital, WACC. In this cyberproblem, you must obtain information from **www.att.com**, **www.marketguide.com**, and **www.stocktrader.com** to estimate AT&T's WACC.

a. How much interest-bearing short-term debt did AT&T have at the end of 1999, and what was the average cost of this debt? (Hint: Access AT&T's 1999 annual report, and look at "Debt Obligations," found in the Notes to the Consolidated Financial Statements.)

b. What was AT&T's actual capital structure at the end of 1999, based on its consolidated balance sheet? What portion of AT&T's capital structure did short-term debt, long-term debt, and stockholders' equity each represent in 1999? Short-term debt is defined as the total debt maturing within 1 year, and long-term debt is the figure given on the Consolidated Balance Sheet. Visit **www.marketguide.com** to compare your calculations with Marketguide's listed debt ratio.

c. Now recalculate AT&T's capital structure just using long-term capital, that is, long-term debt and common equity. Use your results from part b for this purpose. Calculate the long-term debt to total long-term capital ratio and the common equity to total long-term capital ratio.

d. Assume AT&T wants to issue fixed-rate 10-year bonds. If its investment bankers tell the firm that they can do so at a spread (premium) of 1.0 percent over the equivalent maturity Treasury security, what would be AT&T's before-tax cost of this long-term debt? (Hint: Use **www.stocktrader.com** to look at a yield curve of Treasury securities. The "Yield Curve" for the securities can be found on the right side of the screen.)

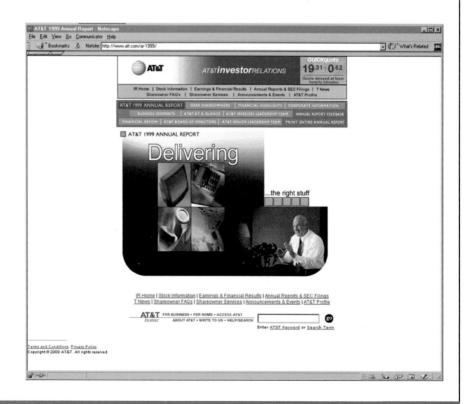

INTEGRATED CASE

COLEMAN TECHNOLOGIES INC.

10-22 Cost of Capital Coleman Technologies is considering a major expansion program that has been proposed by the company's information technology group. Before proceeding with the expansion, the company needs to develop an estimate of its cost of capital. Assume that you are an assistant to Jerry Lehman, the financial vice-president. Your first task is to estimate Coleman's cost of capital. Lehman has provided you with the following data, which he believes may be relevant to your task:

(1) The firm's tax rate is 40 percent.
(2) The current price of Coleman's 12 percent coupon, semiannual payment, noncallable bonds with 15 years remaining to maturity is $1,153.72. Coleman does not use short-term interest-bearing debt on a permanent basis. New bonds would be privately placed with no flotation cost.
(3) The current price of the firm's 10 percent, $100 par value, quarterly dividend, perpetual preferred stock is $111.10.

(4) Coleman's common stock is currently selling at $50 per share. Its last dividend (D_0) was $4.19, and dividends are expected to grow at a constant rate of 5 percent in the foreseeable future. Coleman's beta is 1.2, the yield on T-bonds is 7 percent, and the market risk premium is estimated to be 6 percent. For the bond-yield-plus-risk-premium approach, the firm uses a 4 percentage point risk premium.
(5) Coleman's target capital structure is 30 percent long-term debt, 10 percent preferred stock, and 60 percent common equity.

To structure the task somewhat, Lehman has asked you to answer the following questions.

a. (1) What sources of capital should be included when you estimate Coleman's weighted average cost of capital (WACC)?
 (2) Should the component costs be figured on a before-tax or an after-tax basis?
 (3) Should the costs be historical (embedded) costs or new (marginal) costs?

b. What is the market interest rate on Coleman's debt and its component cost of debt?

c. (1) What is the firm's cost of preferred stock?

   (2) Coleman's preferred stock is riskier to investors than its debt, yet the preferred's yield to investors is lower than the yield to maturity on the debt. Does this suggest that you have made a mistake? (Hint: Think about taxes.)

d. (1) Why is there a cost associated with retained earnings?

   (2) What is Coleman's estimated cost of common equity using the CAPM approach?

e. What is the estimated cost of common equity using the discounted cash flow (DCF) approach?

f. What is the bond-yield-plus-risk-premium estimate for Coleman's cost of common equity?

g. What is your final estimate for k_s?

h. Explain in words why new common stock has a higher percentage cost than retained earnings.

i. (1) What are two approaches that can be used to account for flotation costs?

   (2) Coleman estimates that if it issues new common stock, the flotation cost will be 15 percent. Coleman incorporates the flotation costs into the DCF approach. What is the estimated cost of newly issued common stock, taking into account the flotation cost?

j. What is Coleman's overall, or weighted average, cost of capital (WACC). Ignore flotation costs.

k. What factors influence Coleman's composite WACC?

l. Should the company use the composite WACC as the hurdle rate for each of its projects?

m. What are three types of project risk? How is each type of risk used?

n. What procedures are used to determine the risk-adjusted cost of capital for a particular project or division? What approaches are used to measure a project's beta?

o. Coleman is interested in establishing a new division, which will focus primarily on developing new Internet-based projects. In trying to determine the cost of capital for this new division, you discover that stand-alone firms involved in similar projects have on average the following characteristics:

- Their capital structure is 40 percent debt and 60 percent common equity.
- Their cost of debt is typically 12 percent.
- The beta is 1.7.

Given this information, what would your estimate be for the division's cost of capital?

CHAPTER 11

The Basics of Capital Budgeting

SOURCE: © George Hall/CORBIS

Boeing Co. had been struggling in recent years. In 1997, the 82-year-old company suffered its first loss in 50 years, and even though the overall market was rising, its stock fell from $60 per share to just under $30.

Boeing's troubles were not declining sales. In fact, sales doubled, from $23 billion in 1996 to more than $56 billion in 1998, as Boeing aggressively outbid its archrival Airbus for new business. However, Boeing's costs increased even faster than sales, and as a result, the company lost $178 million in 1997 and barely broke even in 1998.

Boeing has always had a strong engineering culture, but historically it paid little attention to financial performance. Managements could get away with such behavior in the past, but stockholders won't tolerate it today, as top-level firings at GM, IBM, and others attest. So, to turn things around, Boeing hired Deborah Hopkins in December 1998 as the company's chief financial officer (CFO). She had previously starred as a vice-president at Unisys and as CFO for General Motors Europe.

Hopkins, who was hired just after her 44th birthday, was Boeing's youngest senior executive and the company's highest-ranking woman. Known for her dynamic energy and strong communications skills, Hopkins quickly made her presence felt. She discovered that the company's accounting and financial practices were outmoded, making it hard to determine whether products were profitable. So, she immediately set out to devise better procedures for measuring and controlling costs.

After reviewing the company's $13 billion capital budget, Hopkins concluded that $2 billion of projects had little chance of ever being profitable, and another $1.6 billion were likely to only break even or generate modest profits at best. She developed a "value scorecard" and used it to help kill value-reducing projects and increase investments in profitable areas.

While everyone recognizes that it is difficult to improve overnight, analysts believe that Boeing is moving in the right direction. The company is once again profitable, and both its cash flow and operating margins have improved. Most importantly, the stock price has rebounded sharply, and the stock is once again trading above $60 per share.

Hopkins received considerable praise for her work at Boeing. For this reason, the markets were surprised and concerned when Hopkins announced in April 2000 that she was leaving Boeing to take a similar position at Lucent Technologies Inc. Indeed, Boeing's stock fell more than 5 percent the day of the announcement. Despite this setback, Boeing has continued to vastly outperform the market in the months following Hopkins' departure. At the same time, Hopkins has stepped into a tough situation at Lucent, where the once high-flying company has recently seen sharp declines in its stock price.

Boeing's new CFO, Michael Sears, appears to be continuing the policies that Hopkins put in place. In the future, each of Boeing's investment decisions will be based on a careful capital budgeting analysis. Hopkins will certainly try to impose the same type of discipline at Lucent. With this in mind as you read this chapter, think about how companies such as Boeing and Lucent use capital budgeting analysis to make better investment decisions. ■

PUTTING THINGS IN PERSPECTIVE

In the last chapter, we discussed the cost of capital. Now we turn to investment decisions involving fixed assets, or *capital budgeting*. Here the term *capital* refers to long-term assets used in production, while a *budget* is a plan that details projected inflows and outflows during some future period. Thus, the *capital budget* is an outline of planned investments in fixed assets, and **capital budgeting** is the whole process of analyzing projects and deciding which ones to include in the capital budget.

Capital Budgeting
The process of planning expenditures on assets whose cash flows are expected to extend beyond one year.

Our treatment of capital budgeting is divided into two chapters. This chapter gives an overview and explains the various techniques used in capital budgeting analysis. Chapter 12 goes on to explain how cash flows are estimated for projects, and it also considers techniques for estimating project risk. ■

IMPORTANCE OF CAPITAL BUDGETING

A number of factors combine to make capital budgeting perhaps the most important function financial managers and their staffs must perform. First, since the results of capital budgeting decisions continue for many years, the firm loses some of its flexibility. For example, the purchase of an asset with an economic life of 10 years "locks in" the firm for a 10-year period. Further, because asset expansion is based on expected future sales, a decision to buy an asset that is expected to last 10 years requires a 10-year sales forecast. Finally, a firm's capital budgeting decisions define its strategic direction, because moves into new products, services, or markets must be preceded by capital expenditures.

An erroneous forecast of asset requirements can have serious consequences. If the firm invests too much, it will incur unnecessarily high depreciation and other expenses. On the other hand, if it does not invest enough, two problems may arise. First, its equipment and computer software may not be sufficiently modern to enable it to produce competitively. Second, if it has inadequate capacity, it may lose market share to rival firms, and regaining lost customers requires heavy selling expenses, price reductions, or product improvements, all of which are costly.

Timing is also important — capital assets must be available when they are needed. Edward Ford, executive vice-president of Western Design, a decorative tile company, gave the authors an illustration of the importance of capital budgeting. His firm tried to operate near capacity most of the time. During a four-year period, Western experienced intermittent spurts in the demand for its products, which forced it to turn away orders. After these sharp increases in demand, Western would add capacity by renting an additional building, then purchasing and installing the appropriate equipment. It would take six to eight months to get the additional capacity ready, but by then demand had dried up — other firms with available capacity had already taken an increased share of the market. Once Western began to properly forecast demand and plan its capacity requirements a year or so in advance, it was able to maintain and even increase its market share.

Effective capital budgeting can improve both the timing and the quality of asset acquisitions. If a firm forecasts its needs for capital assets in advance, it can purchase and install the assets before they are needed. Unfortunately, many firms do not order capital goods until existing assets are approaching full-capacity usage. If sales increase because of an increase in general market demand, all firms in the industry will tend to order capital goods at about the same time. This results in backlogs, long waiting times for machinery, a deterioration in the quality of the capital equipment, and an increase in costs. The firm that foresees its needs and purchases capital assets during slack periods can avoid these problems. Note, though, that if a firm forecasts an increase in demand and then expands to meet the anticipated demand, but sales do not increase, it will be saddled with excess capacity and high costs, which can lead to losses or even bankruptcy. Thus, an accurate sales forecast is critical.

Capital budgeting typically involves substantial expenditures, and before a firm can spend a large amount of money, it must have the funds lined up — large amounts of money are not available automatically. Therefore, a firm contemplating a major capital expenditure program should plan its financing far enough in advance to be sure funds are available.

SELF-TEST QUESTIONS

Why are capital budgeting decisions so important?

Why is the sales forecast a key element in a capital budgeting decision?

GENERATING IDEAS FOR CAPITAL PROJECTS

The same general concepts that are used in security valuation are also involved in capital budgeting. However, whereas a set of stocks and bonds exists in the securities market, and investors select from this set, *capital budgeting projects are created by the firm.* For example, a sales representative may report that customers are asking for a particular product that the company does not now produce. The sales manager then discusses the idea with the marketing research group to determine the size of the market for the proposed product. If it appears that a significant market does exist, cost accountants and engineers will be asked to estimate production costs. If they conclude that the product can be produced and sold at a sufficient profit, the project will be undertaken.

A firm's growth, and even its ability to remain competitive and to survive, depends on a constant flow of ideas for new products, for ways to make existing products better, and for ways to operate at a lower cost. Accordingly, a well-managed firm will go to great lengths to develop good capital budgeting proposals. For example, the executive vice-president of one very successful corporation indicated that his company takes the following steps to generate projects:

> Our R&D department is constantly searching for new products and for ways to improve existing products. In addition, our executive committee, which consists of senior executives in marketing, production, and finance, identifies the products and markets in which our company should compete, and the committee sets long-run targets for each division. These targets, which are spelled out in the corporation's **strategic business plan,** provide a general guide to the operating executives who must meet them. The operating executives then seek new products, set expansion plans for existing products, and look for ways to reduce production and distribution costs. Since bonuses and promotions are based on each unit's ability to meet or exceed its targets, these economic incentives encourage our operating executives to seek out profitable investment opportunities.
>
> While our senior executives are judged and rewarded on the basis of how well their units perform, people further down the line are given bonuses and stock options for suggestions that lead to profitable investments. Additionally, a percentage of our corporate profit is set aside for distribution to nonexecutive employees, and we have an Employees' Stock Ownership Plan (ESOP) to provide further incentives. Our objective is to encourage employees at all levels to keep an eye out for good ideas, including those that lead to capital investments.

If a firm has capable and imaginative executives and employees, and if its incentive system is working properly, many ideas for capital investment will be advanced. Some ideas will be good ones, but others will not. Therefore, procedures must be established for screening projects, the primary topic of this chapter.

Strategic Business Plan
A long-run plan that outlines in broad terms the firm's basic strategy for the next five to ten years.

SELF-TEST QUESTION

What are some ways firms get ideas for capital projects?

PROJECT CLASSIFICATIONS

Analyzing capital expenditure proposals is not a costless operation — benefits can be gained, but analysis does have a cost. For certain types of projects, a relatively detailed analysis may be warranted; for others, simpler procedures should be used. Accordingly, firms generally categorize projects and then analyze those in each category somewhat differently:

1. **Replacement: maintenance of business.** One category consists of expenditures to replace worn-out or damaged equipment used in the production of profitable products. Replacement projects are necessary if the firm is to continue in business. The only issues here are (a) should this operation be continued and (b) should we continue to use the same production processes? The answers are usually yes, so maintenance decisions are normally made without going through an elaborate decision process.

2. **Replacement: cost reduction.** This category includes expenditures to replace serviceable but obsolete equipment. The purpose here is to lower the costs of labor, materials, and other inputs such as electricity. These decisions are discretionary, and a fairly detailed analysis is generally required.

3. **Expansion of existing products or markets.** Expenditures to increase output of existing products, or to expand retail outlets or distribution facilities in markets now being served, are included here. These decisions are more complex because they require an explicit forecast of growth in demand. Mistakes are more likely, so a more detailed analysis is required. Also, the go/no-go decision is generally made at a higher level within the firm.

4. **Expansion into new products or markets.** These are investments to produce a new product or to expand into a geographic area not currently being served. These projects involve strategic decisions that could change the fundamental nature of the business, and they normally require the expenditure of large sums of money with delayed paybacks. Invariably, a detailed analysis is required, and the final decision is generally made at the very top — by the board of directors as a part of the firm's strategic plan.

5. **Safety and/or environmental projects.** Expenditures necessary to comply with government orders, labor agreements, or insurance policy terms fall into this category. These expenditures are called *mandatory investments*, and they often involve *nonrevenue-producing projects*. How they are handled depends on their size, with small ones being treated much like the Category 1 projects described above.

6. **Other.** This catch-all includes office buildings, parking lots, executive aircraft, and so on. How they are handled varies among companies.

In general, relatively simple calculations, and only a few supporting documents, are required for replacement decisions, especially maintenance-type investments in profitable plants. A more detailed analysis is required for cost-reduction replacements, for expansion of existing product lines, and especially for investments in new products or areas. Also, within each category projects are broken down by their dollar costs: Larger investments require increasingly detailed analysis and approval at a higher level within the firm. Thus, whereas a plant manager may be authorized to approve maintenance expenditures up to $10,000 on the basis of a relatively unsophisticated analysis, the full board of directors may have to approve decisions that involve either amounts over $1 million or expansions into new products or markets. Statistical data are generally lacking for new-product decisions, so here judgments, as opposed to detailed cost data, are especially important.

Note that the term "assets" encompasses more than buildings and equipment. Computer software that a firm develops to help it buy supplies and materials more efficiently, or to communicate with customers, is also an asset. So is a customer base like that of AOL developed by sending out millions of free CDs to potential customers. And so is the design of a new computer chip, airplane, or movie. All of these are "intangible" as opposed to "tangible" assets, but decisions to invest in them are analyzed in the same way as decisions related to tangible assets. Keep this in mind as you go through the remainder of the chapter.

SELF-TEST QUESTION

Identify the major project classification categories, and explain how they are used.

SIMILARITIES BETWEEN CAPITAL BUDGETING AND SECURITY VALUATION

Once a potential capital budgeting project has been identified, its evaluation involves the same steps that are used in security analysis:

1. First, the cost of the project must be determined. This is similar to finding the price that must be paid for a stock or bond.

2. Next, management estimates the expected cash flows from the project, including the salvage value of the asset at the end of its expected life. This is similar to estimating the future dividend or interest payment stream on a stock or bond, along with the stock's expected sales price or the bond's maturity value.

3. Third, the riskiness of the projected cash flows must be estimated. This requires information about the probability distribution (riskiness) of the cash flows.

4. Given the project's riskiness, management determines the cost of capital at which the cash flows should be discounted.

5. Next, the expected cash inflows are put on a present value basis to obtain an estimate of the asset's value. This is equivalent to finding the present value of a stock's expected future dividends.

6. Finally, the present value of the expected cash inflows is compared with the required outlay. If the PV of the cash flows exceeds the cost, the project should be accepted. Otherwise, it should be rejected. (Alternatively, if the expected rate of return on the project exceeds its cost of capital, the project is accepted.)

If an individual investor identifies and invests in a stock or bond whose market price is less than its true value, the investor's wealth will increase. Similarly, if a firm identifies (or creates) an investment opportunity with a present value greater than its cost, the value of the firm will increase. Thus, there is a direct link between capital budgeting and stock values: The more effective the firm's capital budgeting procedures, the higher its stock price.

SELF-TEST QUESTION

List the six steps in the capital budgeting process, and compare them with the steps in security valuation.

CAPITAL BUDGETING DECISION RULES

Five key methods are used to rank projects and to decide whether or not they should be accepted for inclusion in the capital budget: (1) payback, (2) discounted payback, (3) net present value (NPV), (4) internal rate of return (IRR), and (5) modified internal rate of return (MIRR). We will explain how each ranking criterion is calculated, and then we will evaluate how well each performs in terms of identifying those projects that will maximize the firm's stock price.

We use the cash flow data shown in Figure 11-1 for Projects S and L to illustrate each method. Also, we assume that the projects are equally risky. Note that the cash flows, CF_t, are expected values, and that they have been adjusted to reflect taxes, depreciation, and salvage values. Further, since many projects require an investment in both fixed assets and working capital, the investment outlays shown as CF_0 include any necessary changes in net operating working

FIGURE 11-1 Net Cash Flows for Projects S and L

	EXPECTED AFTER-TAX NET CASH FLOWS, CF_t	
YEAR (t)	PROJECT S	PROJECT L
0[a]	($1,000)	($1,000)
1	500	100
2	400	300
3	300	400
4	100	600

Project S:

0	1	2	3	4
−1,000	500	400	300	100

Project L:

0	1	2	3	4
−1,000	100	300	400	600

[a] CF_0 represents the net investment outlay, or initial cost.

FIGURE 11-2   Payback Period for Projects S and L

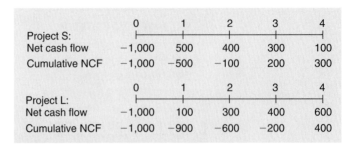

capital.[1] Finally, we assume that all cash flows occur at the end of the designated year. Incidentally, the S stands for *short* and the L for *long:* Project S is a short-term project in the sense that its cash inflows come in sooner than L's.

PAYBACK PERIOD

Payback Period
The length of time required for an investment's net revenues to cover its cost.

The **payback period,** defined as the expected number of years required to recover the original investment, was the first formal method used to evaluate capital budgeting projects. The payback calculation is diagrammed in Figure 11-2, and it is explained below for Project S.

1. Enter $CF_0 = -1000$ in your calculator. (You do not need to use the cash flow register; just have your display show −1,000.)
2. Now add $CF_1 = 500$ to find the cumulative cash flow at the end of Year 1. The result is −500.
3. Now add $CF_2 = 400$ to find the cumulative cash flow at the end of Year 2. This is −100.
4. Now add $CF_3 = 300$ to find the cumulative cash flow at the end of Year 3. This is +200.
5. We see that by the end of Year 3 the cumulative inflows have more than recovered the initial outflow. Thus, the payback occurred during the third year. If the $300 of inflows come in evenly during Year 3, then the exact payback period can be found as follows:

$$\text{Payback}_S = \text{Year before full recovery} + \frac{\text{Unrecovered cost at start of year}}{\text{Cash flow during year}}$$

$$= 2 + \frac{\$100}{\$300} = 2.33 \text{ years.}$$

Applying the same procedure to Project L, we find $\text{Payback}_L = 3.33$ years.

---

[1] The most difficult part of the capital budgeting process is estimating the relevant cash flows. For simplicity, the net cash flows are treated as a given in this chapter, which allows us to focus on the capital budgeting decision rules. However, in Chapter 12 we will discuss cash flow estimation in detail. Also, note that *working capital* is defined as the firm's current assets, and that *net operating working capital* is current assets minus non-interest-bearing liabilities.

FIGURE 11-3   Projects S and L: Discounted Payback Period

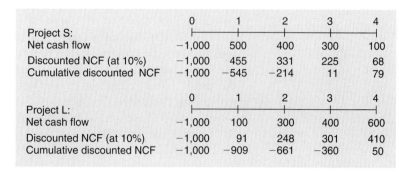

	0	1	2	3	4
Project S:					
Net cash flow	−1,000	500	400	300	100
Discounted NCF (at 10%)	−1,000	455	331	225	68
Cumulative discounted NCF	−1,000	−545	−214	11	79
	0	1	2	3	4
Project L:					
Net cash flow	−1,000	100	300	400	600
Discounted NCF (at 10%)	−1,000	91	248	301	410
Cumulative discounted NCF	−1,000	−909	−661	−360	50

The shorter the payback period, the better. Therefore, if the firm required a payback of three years or less, Project S would be accepted but Project L would be rejected. If the projects were **mutually exclusive,** S would be ranked over L because S has the shorter payback. *Mutually exclusive* means that if one project is taken on, the other must be rejected. For example, the installation of a conveyor-belt system in a warehouse and the purchase of a fleet of forklifts for the same warehouse would be mutually exclusive projects—accepting one implies rejection of the other. **Independent projects** are projects whose cash flows are independent of one another.

Some firms use a variant of the regular payback, the **discounted payback period,** which is similar to the regular payback period except that the expected cash flows are discounted by the project's cost of capital. Thus, the discounted payback period is defined as the number of years required to recover the investment from *discounted* net cash flows. Figure 11-3 contains the discounted net cash flows for Projects S and L, assuming both projects have a cost of capital of 10 percent. To construct Figure 11-3, each cash inflow is divided by $(1 + k)^t = (1.10)^t$, where t is the year in which the cash flow occurs and k is the project's cost of capital. After three years, Project S will have generated $1,011 in discounted cash inflows. Since the cost is $1,000, the discounted payback is just under three years, or, to be precise, 2 + ($214/$225) = 2.95 years. Project L's discounted payback is 3.88 years:

$$\text{Discounted payback}_S = 2.0 + \$214/\$225 = 2.95 \text{ years.}$$

$$\text{Discounted payback}_L = 3.0 + \$360/\$410 = 3.88 \text{ years.}$$

For Projects S and L, the rankings are the same regardless of which payback method is used; that is, Project S is preferred to Project L, and Project S would still be selected if the firm were to require a discounted payback of three years or less. Often, however, the regular and the discounted paybacks produce conflicting rankings.

Note that the payback is a type of "breakeven" calculation in the sense that if cash flows come in at the expected rate until the payback year, then the project will break even. However, the regular payback does not consider the cost of capital—no cost for the debt or equity used to undertake the project is reflected in the cash flows or the calculation. The discounted payback does consider capital costs—it shows the breakeven year after covering debt and equity costs.

Mutually Exclusive Projects
A set of projects where only one can be accepted.

Independent Projects
Projects whose cash flows are not affected by the acceptance or nonacceptance of other projects.

Discounted Payback Period
The length of time required for an investment's cash flows, discounted at the investment's cost of capital, to cover its cost.

An important drawback of both the payback and discounted payback methods is that they ignore cash flows that are paid or received after the payback period. For example, consider two projects, X and Y, each of which requires an up-front cash outflow of $3,000, so $CF_0 = -\$3,000$. Assume that both projects have a cost of capital of 10 percent. Project X is expected to produce cash inflows of $1,000 each of the next four years, while Project Y will produce no cash flows the first four years but then generate a cash inflow of $1,000,000 five years from now. Common sense suggests that Project Y creates more value for the firm's shareholders, yet its payback and discounted payback make it look worse than Project X. Consequently, both payback methods have serious deficiencies. Therefore, we will not dwell on the finer points of payback analysis.[2]

Although the payback method has some serious faults as a ranking criterion, it does provide information on how long funds will be tied up in a project. Thus, the shorter the payback period, other things held constant, the greater the project's *liquidity*. Also, since cash flows expected in the distant future are generally riskier than near-term cash flows, the payback is often used as an indicator of a project's *riskiness*.

NET PRESENT VALUE (NPV)

Net Present Value (NPV) Method
A method of ranking investment proposals using the NPV, which is equal to the present value of future net cash flows, discounted at the marginal cost of capital.

Discounted Cash Flow (DCF) Techniques
Methods for ranking investment proposals that employ time value of money concepts.

As the flaws in the payback were recognized, people began to search for ways to improve the effectiveness of project evaluations. One such method is the **net present value (NPV) method,** which relies on **discounted cash flow (DCF) techniques.** To implement this approach, we proceed as follows:

1. Find the present value of each cash flow, including both inflows and outflows, discounted at the project's cost of capital.
2. Sum these discounted cash flows; this sum is defined as the project's NPV.
3. If the NPV is positive, the project should be accepted, while if the NPV is negative, it should be rejected. If two projects with positive NPVs are mutually exclusive, the one with the higher NPV should be chosen.

The equation for the NPV is as follows:

$$NPV = CF_0 + \frac{CF_1}{(1+k)^1} + \frac{CF_2}{(1+k)^2} + \cdots + \frac{CF_n}{(1+k)^n}$$

$$= \sum_{t=1}^{n} \frac{CF_t}{(1+k)^t}. \qquad (11\text{-}1)$$

Here CF_t is the expected net cash flow at Period t, k is the project's cost of capital, and n is its life. Cash outflows (expenditures such as the cost of buying equipment or building factories) are treated as *negative* cash flows. In evaluating Projects S and L, only CF_0 is negative, but for many large projects such as the Alaska

---

[2] Another capital budgeting technique that was once used widely is the *accounting rate of return (ARR)*, which examines a project's contribution to the firm's net income. Although some companies still calculate an ARR, it really has no redeeming features, so we will not discuss it in this text. See Eugene F. Brigham and Phillip R. Daves, *Intermediate Financial Management*, 7th ed. (Fort Worth, TX: Harcourt College Publishers, 2002), Chapter 11. Yet another technique that we omit here is the *profitability index*, or *benefit/cost ratio*. Brigham and Daves also discuss this method.

Pipeline, an electric generating plant, or IBM's laptop computer project, outflows occur for several years before operations begin and cash flows turn positive. At a 10 percent cost of capital, Project S's NPV is $78.82:

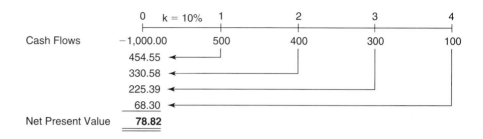

By a similar process, we find $NPV_L = \$49.18$. On this basis, both projects should be accepted if they are independent, but S should be chosen if they are mutually exclusive.

It is not hard to calculate the NPV as was done in the time line by using Equation 11-1 and a regular calculator, along with the interest rate tables. However, it is more efficient to use a financial calculator. Different calculators are set up somewhat differently, but they all have a section of memory called the "cash flow register" that is used for uneven cash flows such as those in Projects S and L (as opposed to equal annuity cash flows). A solution process for Equation 11-1 is literally programmed into financial calculators, and all you have to do is enter the cash flows (being sure to observe the signs), along with the value of k = I. At that point, you have (in your calculator) this equation:

$$NPV_S = -1,000 + \frac{500}{(1.10)^1} + \frac{400}{(1.10)^2} + \frac{300}{(1.10)^3} + \frac{100}{(1.10)^4}.$$

Notice that the equation has one unknown, NPV. Now, all you need to do is to ask the calculator to solve the equation for you, which you do by pressing the NPV button (and, on some calculators, the "compute" button). The answer, 78.82, will appear on the screen.[3]

---

[3] The *Technology Supplement* that accompanies this text explains this and other commonly used calculator applications. For those who do not have the *Supplement*, the steps for two popular calculators, the HP-10B and the HP-17B, are shown below. If you have another type of financial calculator, see its manual or the *Supplement*.

HP-10B:
1. Clear the memory.
2. Enter CF_0 as follows: 1000 +/− CFj.
3. Enter CF_1 as follows: 500 CFj.
4. Repeat the process to enter the other cash flows. Note that CF 0, CF 1, and so forth, flash on the screen as you press the CFj button. If you hold the button down, CF 0 and so forth, will remain on the screen until you release it.
5. Once the CFs have been entered, enter k = I = 10%: 10 I/YR .
6. Now that all of the inputs have been entered, you can press ■ NPV to get the answer, NPV = $78.82.

(footnote continues)

Most projects last for more than four years, and, as you will see in Chapter 12, most projects require many calculations to develop the estimated cash flows. Therefore, financial analysts generally use spreadsheets when dealing with capital budgeting projects. For Project S, this spreadsheet could be used (disregard for now the IRR on Row 6; we discuss it in the next section):

	A	B	C	D	E	F	G
1	Project S						
2	k =	10%					
3	Time	1	2	3	4	5	
4	Cash flow =	−1000	500	400	300	100	
5	NPV =	$78.82					
6	IRR =	14.5%					
7							

In *Excel*, the formula in Cell B5 is: **=B4+NPV(B2,C4:F4)**, and it results in a value of $78.82.[4] For a simple problem such as this, setting up a spreadsheet may not seem worth the trouble. However, in real-world problems there will be a number of rows above our cash flow line, starting with expected sales, then deducting various costs and taxes, and ending up with the cash flows shown on Row 4. Moreover, once a spreadsheet has been set up, it is easy to change input

---

(Footnote 3 continued)

7. If a cash flow is repeated for several years, you can avoid having to enter the CFs for each year. For example, if the $500 cash flow for Year 1 had also been the CF for Years 2 through 10, making 10 of these $500 cash flows, then after entering 500 **CFj** the first time, you could enter 10 **■ Nj** . This would automatically enter 10 CFs of 500.

HP-17B:

1. Go to the cash flow (CFLO) menu, clear if FLOW(0) = ? does not appear on the screen.
2. Enter CF_0 as follows: 1000 **+/−** **INPUT** .
3. Enter CF_1 as follows: 500 **INPUT** .
4. Now, the calculator will ask you if the 500 is for Period 1 only or if it is also used for several following periods. Since it is only used for Period 1, press **INPUT** to answer "1." Alternatively, you could press **EXIT** and then **#T?** to turn off the prompt for the remainder of the problem. For some problems, you will want to use the repeat feature.
5. Enter the remaining CFs, being sure to turn off the prompt or else to specify "1" for each entry.
6. Once the CFs have all been entered, press **EXIT** and then **CALC** .
7. Now enter k = I = 10% as follows: 10 **I%** .
8. Now press **NPV** to get the answer, NPV = $78.82.

[4] You could click the function wizard, f_x, then Financial, then NPV, and then OK. Then insert B2 as the rate and C4:F4 as "Value 1," which is the cash flow range. Then click OK, and edit the equation by adding B4. Note that you cannot enter the −$1,000 cost as part of the NPV range. It occurs at t = 0, but the *Excel* NPV function assumes that all cash flows occur at the end of the periods.

values to see what would happen if inputs are changed. For example, we could see what would happen if lower sales caused all cash flows to decline by $15, or if the cost of capital rose to 10.5 percent. It is easy to make such changes and then see the effects on NPV. See the model for this chapter, 11MODEL.xls.

Rationale for the NPV Method

The rationale for the NPV method is straightforward. An NPV of zero signifies that the project's cash flows are exactly sufficient to repay the invested capital and to provide the required rate of return on that capital. If a project has a positive NPV, then it is generating more cash than is needed to service its debt and to provide the required return to shareholders, and this excess cash accrues solely to the firm's stockholders. Therefore, if a firm takes on a project with a positive NPV, the position of the stockholders is improved. In our example, shareholders' wealth would increase by $78.82 if the firm takes on Project S, but by only $49.18 if it takes on Project L. Viewed in this manner, it is easy to see why S is preferred to L, and it is also easy to see the logic of the NPV approach.[5]

There is also a direct relationship between NPV and EVA (economic value added) — NPV is equal to the present value of the project's future EVAs. Therefore, accepting positive NPV projects should result in a positive EVA and a positive MVA (market value added, or the excess of the firm's market value over its book value). So, a reward system that compensates managers for producing positive EVA will lead to the use of NPV for making capital budgeting decisions.

Internal Rate of Return (IRR)

Internal Rate of Return (IRR) Method
A method of ranking investment proposals using the rate of return on an investment, calculated by finding the discount rate that equates the present value of future cash inflows to the project's cost.

IRR
The discount rate that forces the PV of a project's inflows to equal the PV of its costs.

In Chapter 8 we presented procedures for finding the yield to maturity, or rate of return, on a bond — if you invest in a bond, hold it to maturity, and receive all of the promised cash flows, you will earn the YTM on the money you invested. Exactly the same concepts are employed in capital budgeting when the **internal rate of return (IRR) method** is used. The **IRR** is defined as the discount rate that equates the present value of a project's expected cash inflows to the present value of the project's costs:

$$PV(\text{Inflows}) = PV(\text{Investment costs}),$$

or, equivalently, the rate that forces the NPV to equal zero:

$$CF_0 + \frac{CF_1}{(1 + IRR)^1} + \frac{CF_2}{(1 + IRR)^2} + \cdots + \frac{CF_n}{(1 + IRR)^n} = 0$$

$$NPV = \sum_{t=0}^{n} \frac{CF_t}{(1 + IRR)^t} = 0. \quad \textbf{(11-2)}$$

---

[5] This description of the process is somewhat oversimplified. Both analysts and investors anticipate that firms will identify and accept positive NPV projects, and current stock prices reflect these expectations. Thus, stock prices react to announcements of new capital projects only to the extent that such projects were not already expected. In this sense, we may think of a firm's value as consisting of two parts: (1) the value of its existing assets and (2) the value of its "growth opportunities," or projects with positive NPVs.

For our Project S, here is the time line setup:

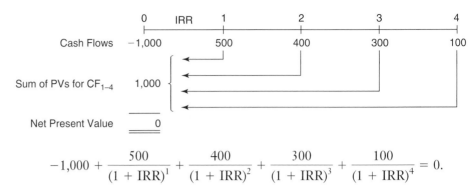

$$-1{,}000 + \frac{500}{(1 + \text{IRR})^1} + \frac{400}{(1 + \text{IRR})^2} + \frac{300}{(1 + \text{IRR})^3} + \frac{100}{(1 + \text{IRR})^4} = 0.$$

Thus, we have an equation with one unknown, IRR, and we need to solve for IRR.

Although it is easy to find the NPV without a financial calculator, this is *not* true of the IRR. If the cash flows are constant from year to year, then we have an annuity, and we can use annuity factors as discussed in Chapter 7 to find the IRR. However, if the cash flows are not constant, as is generally the case in capital budgeting, then it is difficult to find the IRR without a financial calculator. Without a calculator, you must solve Equation 11-2 by trial-and-error — try some discount rate (or PVIF factor) and see if the equation solves to zero, and if it does not, try a different discount rate, and continue until you find the rate that forces the equation to equal zero. The discount rate that causes the equation (and the NPV) to equal zero is defined as the IRR. For a realistic project with a fairly long life, the trial-and-error approach is a tedious, time-consuming task.

Fortunately, it is easy to find IRRs with a financial calculator. You follow procedures almost identical to those used to find the NPV. First, you enter the cash flows as shown on the preceding time line into the calculator's cash flow register. In effect, you have entered the cash flows into the equation shown below the time line. Note that we have one unknown, IRR, which is the discount rate that forces the equation to equal zero. The calculator has been programmed to solve for the IRR, and you activate this program by pressing the button labeled "IRR." Then the calculator solves for IRR and displays it on the screen. Here are the IRRs for Projects S and L as found with a financial calculator:[6]

$$\text{IRR}_\text{S} = 14.5\%.$$
$$\text{IRR}_\text{L} = 11.8\%.$$

It is also easy to find the IRR using the same spreadsheet we used for the NPV. With *Excel*, we simply enter this formula in Cell B6: **=IRR(B4:F4)**. For Project S, the result is 14.5 percent.[7]

---

[6] To find the IRR with an HP-10B or HP-17B, repeat the steps given in Footnote 3. Then, with an HP-10B, press ■ IRR/YR , and, after a pause, 14.49, Project S's IRR, will appear. With the HP-17B, simply press IRR% to get the IRR. With both calculators, you would generally want to get both the NPV and the IRR after entering the input data, before clearing the cash flow register. The *Technology Supplement* explains how to find IRR with several other calculators.

[7] Note that the full range can be specified with the IRR formula, because *Excel's* IRR function assumes that the first cash flow (the negative $1,000) occurs at t = 0. Note too that you can use the function wizard to find the IRR. This is convenient if you don't have the formula committed to memory.

Hurdle Rate
The discount rate (cost of capital) that the IRR must exceed if a project is to be accepted.

If both projects have a cost of capital, or **hurdle rate,** of 10 percent, then the internal rate of return rule indicates that if the projects are independent, both should be accepted — they are both expected to earn more than the cost of the capital needed to finance them. If they are mutually exclusive, S ranks higher and should be accepted, while L should be rejected. If the cost of capital is above 14.5 percent, both projects should be rejected.

Notice that the internal rate of return formula, Equation 11-2, is simply the NPV formula, Equation 11-1, solved for the particular discount rate that forces the NPV to equal zero. Thus, the same basic equation is used for both methods, but in the NPV method the discount rate, k, is specified and the NPV is found, whereas in the IRR method the NPV is specified to equal zero, and the interest rate that forces this equality (the IRR) is calculated.

Mathematically, the NPV and IRR methods will always lead to the same accept/reject decisions for independent projects. This occurs because if NPV is positive, IRR must exceed k. However, NPV and IRR can give conflicting rankings for mutually exclusive projects. This point will be discussed in more detail in a later section.

RATIONALE FOR THE IRR METHOD

Why is the particular discount rate that equates a project's cost with the present value of its receipts (the IRR) so special? The reason is based on this logic: (1) The IRR on a project is its expected rate of return. (2) If the internal rate of return exceeds the cost of the funds used to finance the project, a surplus remains after paying for the capital, and this surplus accrues to the firm's stockholders. (3) Therefore, taking on a project whose IRR exceeds its cost of capital increases shareholders' wealth. On the other hand, if the internal rate of return is less than the cost of capital, then taking on the project imposes a cost on current stockholders. It is this "breakeven" characteristic that makes the IRR useful in evaluating capital projects.

SELF-TEST QUESTIONS

What four capital budgeting ranking methods were discussed in this section? Describe each method, and give the rationale for its use.

What two methods always lead to the same accept/reject decision for independent projects?

What two pieces of information does the payback period convey that are not conveyed by the other methods?

COMPARISON OF THE NPV AND IRR METHODS

In many respects the NPV method is better than IRR, so it is tempting to explain NPV only, to state that it should be used to select projects, and to go on to the next topic. However, the IRR method is familiar to many corporate executives, it is widely entrenched in industry, and it does have some virtues.

Therefore, it is important for you to understand the IRR method but also to be able to explain why, at times, a project with a lower IRR may be preferable to a mutually exclusive alternative with a higher IRR.

NPV PROFILES

Net Present Value Profile
A graph showing the relationship between a project's NPV and the firm's cost of capital.

A graph that plots a project's NPV against cost of capital rates is defined as the project's **net present value profile;** profiles for Projects L and S are shown in Figure 11-4. To construct NPV profiles, first note that at a zero cost of capital, the NPV is simply the total of the project's undiscounted cash flows. Thus, at a zero cost of capital $NPV_S = \$300$, and $NPV_L = \$400$. These values are plotted as the vertical axis intercepts in Figure 11-4. Next, we calculate the projects' NPVs at three costs of capital, 5, 10, and 15 percent, and plot these values. The four points plotted on our graph for each project are shown at the bottom of the figure.[8]

Recall that the IRR is defined as the discount rate at which a project's NPV equals zero. Therefore, *the point where its net present value profile crosses the horizontal axis indicates a project's internal rate of return.* Since we calculated IRR_S and IRR_L in an earlier section, we can confirm the validity of the graph.

When we connect the data points, we have the net present value profiles.[9] NPV profiles can be very useful in project analysis, and we will use them often in the remainder of the chapter.

NPV RANKINGS DEPEND ON THE COST OF CAPITAL

Crossover Rate
The cost of capital at which the NPV profiles of two projects cross and, thus, at which the projects' NPVs are equal.

Figure 11-4 shows that the NPV profiles of both Project L and Project S decline as the cost of capital increases. But notice in the figure that Project L has the higher NPV at a low cost of capital, while Project S has the higher NPV if the cost of capital is greater than the 7.2 percent **crossover rate.** Notice also that Project L's NPV is "more sensitive" to changes in the cost of capital than is NPV_S; that is, Project L's net present value profile has the steeper slope, indicating that a given change in k has a larger effect on NPV_L than on NPV_S.

To see why L has the greater sensitivity, recall first that the cash flows from S are received faster than those from L. In a payback sense, S is a short-term project, while L is a long-term project. Next, recall the equation for the NPV:

$$NPV = \frac{CF_0}{(1+k)^0} + \frac{CF_1}{(1+k)^1} + \cdots + \frac{CF_n}{(1+k)^n}.$$

The impact of an increase in the cost of capital is much greater on distant than on near-term cash flows. To illustrate, consider the following:

---

[8] To calculate the points with a financial calculator, enter the cash flows in the cash flow register, enter I = 0, and press the NPV button to find the NPV at a zero cost of capital. Then enter I = 5 to override the zero, and press NPV to get the NPV at 5 percent. Repeat these steps for 10 and 15 percent. We did the calculations and made the graph with our *Excel* model. See 11MODEL.xls.

[9] Notice that the NPV profiles are curved — they are *not* straight lines. NPV approaches the t = 0 cash flow (the cost of the project) as the cost of capital increases without limit. The reason is that, at an infinitely high cost of capital, the PV of the inflows would be zero, so NPV at (k = ∞) is simply CF_0, which in our example is −$1,000. We should also note that under certain conditions the NPV profiles can cross the horizontal axis several times, or never cross it. This point is discussed later in the chapter.

FIGURE 11-4

Net Present Value Profiles: NPVs of Projects S and L at Different Costs of Capital

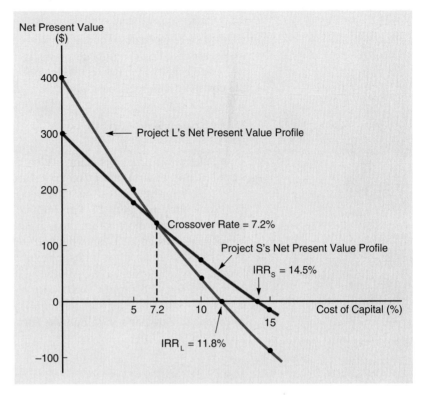

COST OF CAPITAL	NPV$_S$	NPV$_L$
0%	$300.00	$400.00
5	180.42	206.50
10	78.82	49.18
15	(8.33)	(80.14)

$$\text{PV of \$100 due in 1 year @k} = 5\%: \frac{\$100}{(1.05)^1} = \$95.24.$$

$$\text{PV of \$100 due in 1 year @ k} = 10\%: \frac{\$100}{(1.10)^1} = \$90.91.$$

$$\text{Percentage decline due to higher k} = \frac{\$95.24 - \$90.91}{\$95.24} = 4.5\%.$$

$$\text{PV of \$100 due in 20 years @ k} = 5\%: \frac{\$100}{(1.05)^{20}} = \$37.69.$$

$$\text{PV of \$100 due in 20 years @ k} = 10\%: \frac{\$100}{(1.10)^{20}} = \$14.86.$$

$$\text{Percentage decline due to higher k} = \frac{\$37.69 - \$14.86}{\$37.69} = 60.6\%.$$

Thus, a doubling of the discount rate causes only a 4.5 percent decline in the PV of a Year 1 cash flow, but the same doubling of the discount rate causes the PV of a Year 20 cash flow to fall by more than 60 percent. Therefore, if a project has most of its cash flows coming in the early years, its NPV will not decline very much if the cost of capital increases, but a project whose cash flows come later will be severely penalized by high capital costs. Accordingly, Project L, which has its largest cash flows in the later years, is hurt badly if the cost of capital is high, while Project S, which has relatively rapid cash flows, is affected less by high capital costs. Therefore, Project L's NPV profile has the steeper slope.

INDEPENDENT PROJECTS

If an *independent* project is being evaluated, then the NPV and IRR criteria always lead to the same accept/reject decision: if NPV says accept, IRR also says accept. To see why this is so, assume that Projects L and S are independent, and then look back at Figure 11-4 and notice (1) that the IRR criterion for acceptance for either project is that the project's cost of capital is less than (or to the left of) the IRR and (2) that whenever a project's cost of capital is less than its IRR, its NPV is positive. Thus, at any cost of capital less than 11.8 percent, Project L will be acceptable by both the NPV and the IRR criteria, while both methods reject the project if the cost of capital is greater than 11.8 percent. Project S — and all other independent projects under consideration — could be analyzed similarly, and it will always turn out that if the IRR method says accept, then so will the NPV method.

MUTUALLY EXCLUSIVE PROJECTS[10]

Now assume that Projects S and L are *mutually exclusive* rather than independent. That is, we can choose either Project S or Project L, or we can reject both, but we cannot accept both projects. Notice in Figure 11-4 that as long as the cost of capital is *greater than* the crossover rate of 7.2 percent, then (1) NPV_S is larger than NPV_L and (2) IRR_S exceeds IRR_L. Therefore, if k is *greater* than the crossover rate of 7.2 percent, the two methods both lead to the selection of Project S. However, if the cost of capital is *less than* the crossover rate, the NPV method ranks Project L higher, but the IRR method indicates that Project S is better. *Thus, a conflict exists if the cost of capital is less than the crossover rate.* NPV says choose mutually exclusive L, while IRR says take S. Which answer is correct? Logic suggests that the NPV method is better, because it selects the project that adds the most to shareholder wealth.[11]

There are two basic conditions that can cause NPV profiles to cross, and thus conflicts to arise between NPV and IRR: (1) when *project size (or scale) differences* exist, meaning that the cost of one project is larger than that of the other, or (2) when *timing differences* exist, meaning that the timing of cash flows

---

[10] This section is relatively technical, but it can be omitted without loss of continuity.

[11] The crossover rate is easy to calculate. Simply go back to Figure 11-1, where we set forth the two projects' cash flows, and calculate the difference in those flows in each year. The differences are $CF_S - CF_L = \$0, +\$400, +\$100, -\$100,$ and $-\$500,$ respectively. Enter these values in the cash flow register of a financial calculator, press the IRR button, and the crossover rate, $7.17\% \approx 7.2\%$, appears. Be sure to enter $CF_0 = 0$ or else you will not get the correct answer.

from the two projects differs such that most of the cash flows from one project come in the early years while most of the cash flows from the other project come in the later years, as occurred with our Projects L and S.[12]

When either size or timing differences occur, the firm will have different amounts of funds to invest in the various years, depending on which of the two mutually exclusive projects it chooses. For example, if one project costs more than the other, then the firm will have more money at t = 0 to invest elsewhere if it selects the smaller project. Similarly, for projects of equal size, the one with the larger early cash inflows — in our example, Project S — provides more funds for reinvestment in the early years. Given this situation, the rate of return at which differential cash flows can be invested is a critical issue.

The key to resolving conflicts between mutually exclusive projects is this: How useful is it to generate cash flows sooner rather than later? The value of early cash flows depends on the return we can earn on those cash flows, that is, the rate at which we can reinvest them. *The NPV method implicitly assumes that the rate at which cash flows can be reinvested is the cost of capital, whereas the IRR method assumes that the firm can reinvest at the IRR.* These assumptions are inherent in the mathematics of the discounting process. The cash flows may actually be withdrawn as dividends by the stockholders and spent on beer and pizza, but the NPV method still assumes that cash flows can be reinvested at the cost of capital, while the IRR method assumes reinvestment at the project's IRR.

Which is the better assumption — that cash flows can be reinvested at the cost of capital, or that they can be reinvested at the project's IRR? It can be demonstrated that the best assumption is that projects' cash flows are reinvested at the cost of capital.[13] Therefore, we conclude that *the best* **reinvestment rate assumption** *is the cost of capital, which is consistent with the NPV method.* This, in turn, leads us to prefer the NPV method, at least for a firm willing and able to obtain capital at a cost reasonably close to its current cost of capital.

We should reiterate that, when projects are independent, the NPV and IRR methods both lead to exactly the same accept/reject decision. However, *when evaluating mutually exclusive projects, especially those that differ in scale and/or timing, the NPV method should be used.*

MULTIPLE IRRs[14]

There is one other situation in which the IRR approach may not be usable — this is when projects with nonnormal cash flows are involved. A project has *normal* cash flows if it has one or more cash outflows (costs) followed by a series of

Reinvestment Rate Assumption

The assumption that cash flows from a project can be reinvested (1) at the cost of capital, if using the NPV method, or (2) at the internal rate of return, if using the IRR method.

---

[12] Of course, it is possible for mutually exclusive projects to differ with respect to both scale and timing. Also, if mutually exclusive projects have different lives (as opposed to different cash flow patterns over a common life), this introduces further complications, and for meaningful comparisons, some mutually exclusive projects must be evaluated over a common life. For a discussion of comparing projects with unequal lives refer to Eugene F. Brigham and Joel F. Houston, *Fundamentals of Financial Management*, 9th ed. (Fort Worth, TX: Harcourt College Publishers, 2001), Chapter 13 or Appendix 12D on the *Concise* web site.

[13] Again, see Brigham and Daves, *Intermediate Financial Management*, 7th ed., Chapter 11, for a discussion of this point.

[14] This section is relatively technical, but it can be omitted without loss of continuity.

cash inflows. If, however, a project calls for a large cash outflow sometime during or at the end of its life, then the project has *nonnormal* cash flows. Projects with nonnormal cash flows can present unique difficulties when they are evaluated by the IRR method, with the most common problem being the existence of **multiple IRRs.**

Multiple IRRs
The situation where a project has two or more IRRs.

When one solves Equation 11-2 to find the IRR for a project with nonnormal cash flows,

$$\sum_{t=0}^{n} \frac{CF_t}{(1 + IRR)^t} = 0, \qquad \textbf{(11-2)}$$

it is possible to obtain more than one solution value for IRR, which means that multiple IRRs occur. Notice that Equation 11-2 is a polynomial of degree n, so it has n different roots, or solutions. All except one of the roots are imaginary numbers when investments have normal cash flows (one or more cash outflows followed by cash inflows), so in the normal case, only one value of IRR appears. However, the possibility of multiple real roots, hence multiple IRRs, arises when the project has nonnormal cash flows (negative net cash flows occur during some year after the project has been placed in operation).

To illustrate this problem, suppose a firm is considering the expenditure of $1.6 million to develop a strip mine (Project M). The mine will produce a cash flow of $10 million at the end of Year 1. Then, at the end of Year 2, $10 million must be expended to restore the land to its original condition. Therefore, the project's expected net cash flows are as follows (in millions of dollars):

EXPECTED NET CASH FLOWS

YEAR 0	END OF YEAR 1	END OF YEAR 2
−$1.6	+$10	−$10

These values can be substituted into Equation 11-2 to derive the IRR for the investment:

$$NPV = \frac{-\$1.6 \text{ million}}{(1 + IRR)^0} + \frac{\$10 \text{ million}}{(1 + IRR)^1} + \frac{-\$10 \text{ million}}{(1 + IRR)^2} = 0.$$

When solved, we find that NPV = 0 when IRR = 25% and also when IRR = 400%.[15] Therefore, the IRR of the investment is both 25 and 400 percent. This

---

[15] If you attempted to find the IRR of Project M with many financial calculators, you would get an error message. This same message would be given for all projects with multiple IRRs. However, you can still find Project M's IRRs by first calculating NPVs using several different values for k and then plotting the NPV profile. The intersections with the X-axis give a rough idea of the IRR values. Finally, you can use trial-and-error to find the exact values of k that force NPV = 0.

Note, too, that some calculators, including the HP-10B and 17B, can find the IRR. At the error message, key in a guess, store it, and repress the IRR key. With the HP-10B, type 10 ■ STO ■ IRR, and the answer, 25.00, appears. If you enter as your guess a cost of capital less than the one at which NPV in Figure 11-5 is maximized (about 100%), the lower IRR, 25%, is displayed. If you guess a high rate, say, 150, the higher IRR is shown.

The IRR function in spreadsheets also begins its trial-and-error search for a solution with an initial guess. If you omit the initial guess, the *Excel* default starting point is 10 percent. Now suppose the values −1.6, +10, and −10 were in Cells A1:C1. You could use this *Excel* formula: **=IRR(A1:C1,10%)**, where 10 percent is the initial guess, and it would produce a result of 25 per-
(footnote continues)

FIGURE 11-5   NPV Profile for Project M

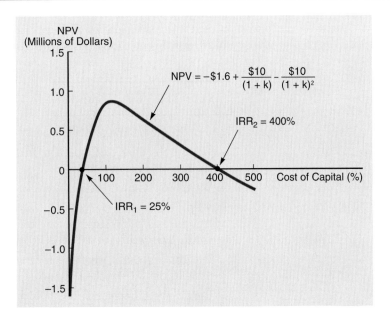

relationship is depicted graphically in Figure 11-5.[16] Note that no dilemma would arise if the NPV method were used; we would simply use Equation 11-1, find the NPV, and use this to evaluate the project. If Project M's cost of capital were 10 percent, then its NPV would be −$0.77 million, and the project should be rejected. If k were between 25 and 400 percent, the NPV would be positive.

One of the authors encountered another example of multiple internal rates of return when a major California bank *borrowed* funds from an insurance company and then used these funds (plus an initial investment of its own) to buy a number of jet engines, which it then leased to a major airline. The bank expected to receive positive net cash flows (lease payments plus tax savings minus interest on the insurance company loan) for a number of years, then several large negative cash flows as it repaid the insurance company loan, and, finally, a large inflow from the sale of the engines when the lease expired.

The bank discovered two IRRs and wondered which was correct. It could not ignore the IRR and use the NPV method since the lease was already on the books, and the bank's senior loan committee, as well as Federal Reserve bank examiners, wanted to know the return on the lease. The bank's solution called for calculating and then using the "modified internal rate of return" as discussed in the next section.

(Footnote 15 continued)

cent. If you used a guess of 150 percent, you would have this formula: **=IRR(A1:C1,150%)**, and it would produce a result of 400 percent.

[16] Does Figure 11-5 suggest that the firm should try to *raise* its cost of capital to about 100 percent in order to maximize the NPV of the project? Certainly not. The firm should seek to *minimize* its cost of capital; this will cause its stock price to be maximized. Actions taken to raise the cost of capital might make this particular project look good, but those actions would be terribly harmful to the firm's more numerous projects with normal cash flows. Only if the firm's cost of capital is high in spite of efforts to keep it down will the illustrative project have a positive NPV.

The examples just presented illustrate one problem, multiple IRRs, that can arise when the IRR criterion is used with a project that has nonnormal cash flows. Use of the IRR method on projects having nonnormal cash flows could produce other problems such as no IRR or an IRR that leads to an incorrect accept/reject decision. In all such cases, the NPV criterion could be easily applied, and this method leads to conceptually correct capital budgeting decisions.

SELF-TEST QUESTIONS

Describe how NPV profiles are constructed.

What is the crossover rate, and how does it affect the choice between mutually exclusive projects?

What two basic conditions can lead to conflicts between the NPV and IRR methods?

Why is the "reinvestment rate" considered to be the underlying cause of conflicts between the NPV and IRR methods?

If a conflict exists, should the capital budgeting decision be made on the basis of the NPV or the IRR ranking? Why?

Explain the difference between normal and nonnormal cash flows.

What is the "multiple IRR problem," and what condition is necessary for it to occur?

MODIFIED INTERNAL RATE OF RETURN (MIRR)[17]

In spite of a strong academic preference for NPV, surveys indicate that executives prefer IRR over NPV. Apparently, managers find it intuitively more appealing to evaluate investments in terms of percentage rates of return than dollars of NPV. Given this fact, can we devise a percentage evaluator that is better than the regular IRR? The answer is yes — we can modify the IRR and make it a better indicator of relative profitability, hence better for use in capital budgeting. The new measure is called the **modified IRR**, or **MIRR**, and it is defined as follows:

Modified IRR (MIRR)
The discount rate at which the present value of a project's cost is equal to the present value of its terminal value, where the terminal value is found as the sum of the future values of the cash inflows, compounded at the firm's cost of capital.

$$\text{PV costs} = \text{PV terminal value}$$

$$\sum_{t=0}^{n} \frac{COF_t}{(1 + k)^t} = \frac{\sum_{t=0}^{n} CIF_t(1 + k)^{n-t}}{(1 + MIRR)^n}$$

$$\text{PV costs} = \frac{TV}{(1 + MIRR)^n}. \tag{11-2a}$$

Here COF refers to cash outflows (negative numbers), or the cost of the project, and CIF refers to cash inflows (positive numbers). The left term is simply

---

[17] Again, this section is relatively technical, but it can be omitted without loss of continuity.

the PV of the investment outlays when discounted at the cost of capital, and the numerator of the right term is the compounded value of the inflows, assuming that the cash inflows are reinvested at the cost of capital. The compounded value of the cash inflows is also called the *terminal value*, or *TV*. The discount rate that forces the PV of the TV to equal the PV of the costs is defined as the MIRR.[18]

If the investment costs are all incurred at t = 0, and if the first operating inflow occurs at t = 1, as is true for the illustrative Projects S and L that we first presented in Figure 11-1, then this equation may be used:

$$\text{Cost} = \frac{\text{TV}}{(1 + \text{MIRR})^n} = \frac{\sum\limits_{t=1}^{n} \text{CIF}_t(1 + k)^{n-t}}{(1 + \text{MIRR})^n}. \qquad \text{(11-2b)}$$

We can illustrate the calculation with Project S:

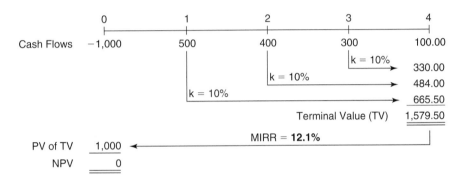

Using the cash flows as set out on the time line, first find the terminal value by compounding each cash inflow at the 10 percent cost of capital. Then enter N = 4, PV = −1000, PMT = 0, FV = 1579.5, and then press the I button to find MIRR$_S$ = 12.1%. Similarly, we find MIRR$_L$ = 11.3%.[19]

---

[18] There are several alternative definitions for the MIRR. The differences primarily relate to whether negative cash flows that occur after positive cash flows begin should be compounded and treated as part of the TV or discounted and treated as a cost. A related issue is whether negative and positive flows in a given year should be netted or treated separately. For a complete discussion, see William R. McDaniel, Daniel E. McCarty, and Kenneth A. Jessell, "Discounted Cash Flow with Explicit Reinvestment Rates: Tutorial and Extension," *The Financial Review*, August 1988, 369–385, and David M. Shull, "Interpreting Rates of Return: A Modified Rate of Return Approach," *Financial Practice and Education*, Fall 1993, 67–71.

[19] With some calculators, including the HP-17B, you could enter the cash inflows in the cash flow register (being sure to enter CF$_0$ = 0), enter I = 10, and then press the NFV key to find TV$_S$ = 1,579.50. The HP-10B does not have an NFV key, but you can still use the cash flow register to find TV. Enter the cash inflows in the cash flow register (with CF$_0$ = 0), then enter I = 10, then press ■ NPV to find the PV of the inflows, which is 1,078.82. Now, with the regular time value keys, enter N = 4, I = 10, PV = −1078.82, PMT = 0, and press FV to find TV$_S$ = 1,579.50. Similar procedures can be used with other financial calculators.

Most spreadsheets have a function for finding the MIRR. Refer back to our spreadsheet for Project S, with cash flows of −1,000, 500, 400, 300, and 100 in Cells B4:F4. You could use the *Excel* function wizard to set up the following formula: **=MIRR(B4:F4,10%,10%)**. Here the first 10 percent is the cost of capital used for discounting, and the second one is the rate used for compounding, or the reinvestment rate. In our definition of the MIRR, we assume that reinvestment is at the cost of capital, so we enter 10 percent twice. The result is an MIRR of 12.1 percent.

The modified IRR has a significant advantage over the regular IRR. MIRR assumes that cash flows from all projects are reinvested at the cost of capital, while the regular IRR assumes that the cash flows from each project are reinvested at the project's own IRR. Since reinvestment at the cost of capital is generally more correct, the modified IRR is a better indicator of a project's true profitability. The MIRR also solves the multiple IRR problem. To illustrate, with k = 10%, Project M (the strip mine project) has MIRR = 5.6% versus its 10 percent cost of capital, so it should be rejected. This is consistent with the decision based on the NPV method, because at k = 10%, NPV = −$0.77 million.

Is MIRR as good as NPV for choosing between mutually exclusive projects? If two projects are of equal size and have the same life, then NPV and MIRR will always lead to the same decision. Thus, for any set of projects like our Projects S and L, if $NPV_S > NPV_L$, then $MIRR_S > MIRR_L$, and the kinds of conflicts we encountered between NPV and the regular IRR will not occur. Also, if the projects are of equal size, but differ in lives, the MIRR will always lead to the same decision as the NPV if the MIRRs are both calculated using as the terminal year the life of the longer project. (Just fill in zeros for the shorter project's missing cash flows.) However, if the projects differ in size, then conflicts can still occur. For example, if we were choosing between a large project and a small mutually exclusive one, then we might find $NPV_L > NPV_S$, but $MIRR_S > MIRR_L$.

Our conclusion is that the MIRR is superior to the regular IRR as an indicator of a project's "true" rate of return, or "expected long-term rate of return," but the NPV method is still the best way to choose among competing projects because it provides the best indication of how much each project will increase the value of the firm.

SELF-TEST QUESTIONS

Describe how the modified IRR (MIRR) is calculated.

What is the primary difference between the MIRR and the regular IRR?

What advantages does the MIRR have over the regular IRR for making capital budgeting decisions?

What condition can cause the MIRR and NPV methods to produce conflicting rankings?

CONCLUSIONS ON CAPITAL BUDGETING METHODS

We have discussed five capital budgeting decision methods, comparing the methods with one another, and highlighting their relative strengths and weaknesses. In the process, we probably created the impression that "sophisticated" firms should use only one method in the decision process, NPV. However, virtually all capital budgeting decisions are analyzed by computer, so it is easy to calculate and list all the decision measures: payback and discounted payback, NPV, IRR, and modified IRR (MIRR). In making the accept/reject decision, most large, sophisticated firms such as IBM, GE, and Royal Dutch Petroleum calculate and consider all of the measures, because each one provides decision makers with a somewhat different piece of relevant information.

Payback and discounted payback provide an indication of both the *risk* and the *liquidity* of a project — a long payback means (1) that the investment dollars will be locked up for many years, hence the project is relatively illiquid, and (2) that the project's cash flows must be forecasted far out into the future, hence the project is probably quite risky. A good analogy for this is the bond valuation process. An investor should never compare the yields to maturity on two bonds without also considering their terms to maturity, because a bond's riskiness is significantly influenced by its maturity.

NPV is important because it gives a direct measure of the dollar benefit of the project to shareholders, so we regard NPV as the best single measure of *profitability*. IRR also measures profitability, but here it is expressed as a percentage rate of return, which many decision makers prefer. Further, IRR contains information concerning a project's "safety margin." To illustrate, consider the following two projects: Project S (for small) costs $10,000 and is expected to return $16,500 at the end of one year, while Project L (for large) costs $100,000 and has an expected payoff of $115,500 after one year. At a 10 percent cost of capital, both projects have an NPV of $5,000, so by the NPV rule we should be indifferent between them. However, Project S has a much larger margin for error. Even if its realized cash inflow were 39 percent below the $16,500 forecast, the firm would still recover its $10,000 investment. On the other hand, if Project L's inflows fell by only 13 percent from the forecasted $115,500, the firm would not recover its investment. Further, if no inflows were generated at all, the firm would lose only $10,000 with Project S, but $100,000 if it took on Project L.

The NPV provides no information about either of these factors — the "safety margin" inherent in the cash flow forecasts or the amount of capital at risk. However, the IRR does provide "safety margin" information — Project S's IRR is a whopping 65.0 percent, while Project L's IRR is only 15.5 percent. As a result, the realized return could fall substantially for Project S, and it would still make money. Finally, the modified IRR has all the virtues of the IRR, but (1) it incorporates a better reinvestment rate assumption, and (2) it avoids the multiple rate of return problem.

In summary, the different measures provide different types of information to decision makers. Since it is easy to calculate all of them, all should be considered in the decision process. For most decisions, the greatest weight should be given to the NPV, but it would be foolish to ignore the information provided by any of the methods.

SELF-TEST QUESTIONS

Describe the advantages and disadvantages of the five capital budgeting methods discussed in this chapter.

Should capital budgeting decisions be made solely on the basis of a project's NPV?

Harold Bierman published a survey of the capital budgeting methods used by the Fortune 500 industrial companies; here is a summary of his findings:[20]

1. Every single one of the responding firms used some type of DCF method. In 1955, a similar study reported that only 4 percent of large companies used a DCF method. Thus, large firms' usage of DCF methodology has increased dramatically in the last 40 years.

2. The payback period was used by 84 percent of Bierman's surveyed companies. However, no company used it as the primary method, and most companies gave the greatest weight to a DCF method. In 1955, surveys similar to Bierman's found that payback was the most important method.

3. Currently, 99 percent of the Fortune 500 companies use IRR, while 85 percent use NPV. Thus, most firms actually use both methods.

4. Ninety-three percent of Bierman's companies calculate a weighted average cost of capital as part of their capital budgeting process. A few companies apparently use the same WACC for all projects, but 73 percent adjust the corporate WACC to account for project risk, and 23 percent make adjustments to reflect divisional risk.

5. An examination of surveys done by other authors led Bierman to conclude that there has been a strong trend toward the acceptance of academic recommendations, at least by large companies.

A second 1993 study, conducted by Joe Walker, Richard Burns, and Chad Denson (WBD), focused on small companies.[21] WBD began by noting the same trend toward the use of DCF that Bierman cited, but they reported that only 21 percent of small companies used DCF versus 100 percent for Bierman's large companies. WBD also noted that within their sample, the smaller the firm, the smaller the likelihood that DCF would be used. The focal point of the WBD study was *why* small companies use DCF so much less frequently than large firms. WBD actually based their questionnaire on our box entitled "Capital Budgeting in the Small Firm" on pages 532 and 533, and they concluded that the reasons given in that box do indeed explain why DCF is used infrequently by small firms. The three most frequently cited reasons, according to the survey, were (1) small firms' preoccupation with liquidity, which is best indicated by payback, (2) a lack of familiarity with DCF methods, and (3) a belief that small project sizes make DCF not worth the effort.

The general conclusion one can reach from these studies is that large firms should and do use the procedures we recommend, and that managers of small firms, especially managers with aspirations for future growth, should at least understand DCF procedures well enough to make rational decisions about

---

[20] Harold Bierman, "Capital Budgeting in 1992: A Survey," *Financial Management*, Autumn 1993, 24.

[21] Joe Walker, Richard Burns, and Chad Denson, "Why Small Manufacturing Firms Shun DCF," *Journal of Small Business Finance*, 1993, 233–249.

TECHNIQUES FIRMS USE TO EVALUATE CORPORATE PROJECTS

Professors John Graham and Campbell Harvey of Duke University recently surveyed 392 chief financial officers (CFOs) about their companies' corporate practices. Of those firms, 26 percent had sales less than $100 million, 32 percent had sales between $100 million and $1 billion, and 42 percent exceeded $1 billion.

The CFOs were asked to indicate how frequently they use different approaches for estimating the cost of equity: 73.5 percent use the Capital Asset Pricing Model (CAPM), 34.3 percent use a multi-beta version of the CAPM, and 15.7 percent use the dividend discount model. The CFOs also use a variety of risk adjustment techniques, but most still choose to use a single hurdle rate to evaluate all corporate projects.

The CFOs were also asked about the capital budgeting techniques they use. Most use NPV (74.9 percent) and IRR (75.7 percent) to evaluate projects, but many (56.7 percent) also use the payback approach. These results confirm that most firms use more than one approach to evaluate projects.

The survey also found important differences between the practices of small firms (less than $1 billion in sales) and large firms (more than $1 billion in sales). Consistent with the earlier studies by Bierman and by Walker, Burns, and Denson (WBD) described in the text, Graham and Harvey found that small firms are more likely to rely on the payback approach, while large firms are more likely to rely on NPV and/or IRR.

SOURCE: John R. Graham and Campbell R. Harvey, "The Theory and Practice of Corporate Finance: Evidence from the Field," Forthcoming, *Journal of Financial Economics*, Vol. 60, No. 2–3.

using or not using them. Moreover, as computer technology makes it easier and less expensive for small firms to use DCF methods, and as more and more of their competitors begin using these methods, survival will necessitate increased DCF usage.

SELF-TEST QUESTIONS

What were Bierman's findings from his survey of capital budgeting methods used by the Fortune 500 companies?

How did WBD's findings differ from those of Bierman?

What general considerations can be reached from these studies?

THE POST-AUDIT

Post-Audit
A comparison of actual versus expected results for a given capital project.

An important aspect of the capital budgeting process is the **post-audit,** which involves (1) comparing actual results with those predicted by the project's sponsors and (2) explaining why any differences occurred. For example, many firms require that the operating divisions send a monthly report for the first six months after a project goes into operation, and a quarterly report thereafter, until the project's results are up to expectations. From then on, reports on the operation are reviewed on a regular basis like those of other operations.

The post-audit has two main purposes:

1. **Improve forecasts.** When decision makers are forced to compare their projections to actual outcomes, there is a tendency for estimates to

SMALL BUSINESS

CAPITAL BUDGETING IN THE SMALL FIRM

The allocation of capital in small firms is as important as it is in large ones. In fact, given their lack of access to the capital markets, it is often more important in the small firm, because the funds necessary to correct a mistake may not be available. Also, large firms allocate capital to numerous projects, so a mistake on one can be offset by successes with others. Small firms do not have this luxury.

In spite of the importance of capital expenditures to small business, studies of the way decisions are made generally suggest that many small firms use "back-of-the-envelope" analysis, or perhaps no analysis at all. For example, the Graham and Harvey study cited earlier in the box entitled "Techniques Firms Use to Evaluate Corporate Projects" points out that small firms are more likely to use simple rules such as payback, whereas large firms are more likely to rely on NPV and/or IRR. These findings confirm earlier results found by L. R. Runyon. Several years ago, Runyon studied 214 firms with net worths ranging from $500,000 to $1,000,000. He found that almost 70 percent relied upon payback or some other questionable criteria. Only 14 percent used a discounted cash flow analysis, and about 9 percent indicated that they used no formal analysis at all. Studies of larger firms, on the other hand, generally find that most analyze capital budgeting decisions using discounted cash flow techniques.

We are left with a puzzle. Capital budgeting is clearly important to small firms, yet these firms do not use the tools that have been developed to improve these decisions. Why does this situation exist? One argument is that managers of small firms are simply not well trained; they are unsophisticated. This argument suggests that the managers would use the more sophisticated techniques if they understood them better.

Another argument relates to the fact that management talent is a scarce resource in small firms. That is, even if the managers were exceptionally sophisticated, perhaps demands on them are such that they simply cannot take the time to use

elaborate techniques to analyze proposed projects. In other words, small-business managers may be capable of doing careful discounted cash flow analysis, but it would be irrational for them to allocate the time required for such an analysis.

A third argument relates to the cost of analyzing capital projects. To some extent, these costs are fixed; the costs of analysis may be larger for bigger projects, but not by much. To the extent that these costs are indeed fixed, it may not be economical to incur them if the project itself is relatively small. This argument suggests that small firms with small projects may in some cases be making the sensible decision when they rely on management's "gut feeling."

Note also that a major part of the capital budgeting process in large firms involves lower-level analysts' marshalling facts needed by higher-level decision makers. This step is less necessary in the small firm. Thus, a cursory examination of a small firm's decision process might suggest that capital budgeting decisions are based on snap judgment, but if that judgment is exercised by someone with a total knowledge of the firm and its markets, it could represent a better decision than one based on an elaborate analysis by a lower-level employee in a large firm.

Also, as Runyon reported in his study of manufacturing firms, small firms tend to be cash oriented. They are concerned with basic survival, so they tend to look at expenditures from the standpoint of their near-term effects on cash. This cash and survival orientation leads firms to focus on a relatively short time horizon, and this, in turn, may lead to an emphasis on the payback method. The limitations of payback are well known, but in spite of those limitations, the technique is popular in small business, as it gives the firm a feel for when the cash committed to an investment will be recovered and thus available to repay loans or for new opportunities. Therefore, small firms that are cash oriented and have limited managerial resources may find the payback method appealing. It represents a

improve. Conscious or unconscious biases are observed and eliminated; new forecasting methods are sought as the need for them becomes apparent; and people simply tend to do everything better, including forecasting, if they know that their actions are being monitored.

2. **Improve operations.** Businesses are run by people, and people can perform at higher or lower levels of efficiency. When a divisional team has made a forecast about an investment, its members are, in a sense, putting their reputations on the line. If costs are above predicted levels, sales below expectations, and so on, executives in production, sales, and other areas will strive to improve operations and to bring results into line with forecasts. In a discussion related to this point, one executive made this

compromise between the need for extensive analysis on the one hand and the high costs of analysis on the other.

Small firms also face greater uncertainty in the cash flows they might generate beyond the immediate future. Large firms such as AT&T and General Motors have "staying power" — they can make an investment and then ride out business downturns or situations of excess capacity in an industry. Such periods are called "shakeouts," and it is the smaller firms that are generally shaken out. Therefore, most small-business managers are uncomfortable making forecasts beyond a few years. Since discounted cash flow techniques require explicit estimates of cash flows through the life of the project, small-business managers may not take seriously an analysis that hinges on "guesstimate" numbers that, if wrong, could lead to bankruptcy.

THE VALUE OF THE FIRM AND CAPITAL BUDGETING

The single most appealing argument for the use of net present value in capital budgeting is that NPV gives an explicit measure of the effect the investment will have on the firm's value: If NPV is positive, the investment will increase the firm's value and make its owners wealthier. In small firms, however, the stock is often not traded in public markets, so its value cannot be observed. Also, for reasons of control, many small-business owners and managers may not want to broaden ownership by going public.

It is difficult to argue for value-based techniques when the firm's value itself is unobservable. Furthermore, in a closely held firm, the objectives of the individual owner-manager may extend beyond the firm's monetary value. For example, the owner-manager may value the firm's reputation for quality and service and therefore may make an investment that would be rejected on purely economic grounds. In addition, the owner-manager may not hold a well-diversified investment portfolio but may in-

stead have all of his or her eggs in this one basket. In that case, the manager would logically be sensitive to the firm's stand-alone risk, not just to its undiversifiable component. Thus, one project might be viewed as desirable because of its contribution to risk reduction in the firm as a whole, whereas another project with a low beta but high diversifiable risk might be unacceptable, even though in a CAPM framework it would be judged superior.

Another problem faced by a firm that is not publicly traded is that its cost of equity capital is not easily determined — the P_0 term in the cost of equity equation $k = D_1/P_0 + g$ is not observable, nor is its beta. Since a cost of capital estimate is required to use either the NPV or the IRR method, a small firm in an industry of small firms may simply have no basis for estimating its cost of capital.

CONCLUSIONS

Small firms make less extensive use of DCF techniques than larger firms. This may be a rational decision resulting from a conscious or subconscious conclusion that the costs of sophisticated analyses outweigh their benefits; it may reflect nonmonetary goals of small businesses' owner-managers; or it may reflect difficulties in estimating the cost of capital, which is required for DCF analyses but not for payback. However, nonuse of DCF methods may also reflect a weakness in many small firms. We simply do not know. We do know that small businesses must do all they can to compete effectively with big business, and to the extent that a small business fails to use DCF methods because its manager is unsophisticated or uninformed, it may be putting itself at a serious competitive disadvantage.

SOURCE: L. R. Runyon, "Capital Expenditure Decision Making in Small Firms," *Journal of Business Research*, September 1983, 389–397. Reprinted with permission.

statement: "You academicians worry only about making good decisions. In business, we also worry about making decisions good."

The post-audit is not a simple process — a number of factors can cause complications. First, we must recognize that each element of the cash flow forecast is subject to uncertainty, so a percentage of all projects undertaken by any reasonably aggressive firm will necessarily go awry. This fact must be considered when appraising the performances of the operating executives who submit capital expenditure requests. Second, projects sometimes fail to meet expectations for reasons beyond the control of the operating executives and for reasons that no one could realistically be expected to anticipate. For example, the 2000 runup in oil prices adversely affected many projects. Third, it is often difficult to separate the operating results of one investment from those of a larger system. Although some projects stand alone and permit ready identification of costs and revenues, the cost savings that result from a new computer, for example, may be very hard to measure. Fourth, it is often hard to hand out blame or praise because the executives who were responsible for launching a given investment have moved on by the time the results are known.

Because of these difficulties, some firms tend to play down the importance of the post-audit. However, observations of both businesses and governmental units suggest that the best-run and most successful organizations are the ones that put the greatest emphasis on post-audits. Accordingly, we regard the post-audit as being one of the most important elements in a good capital budgeting system.

SELF-TEST QUESTIONS

What is done in the post-audit?

Identify several purposes of the post-audit.

What are some factors that can cause complications in the post-audit?

USING CAPITAL BUDGETING TECHNIQUES IN OTHER CONTEXTS

The techniques developed in this chapter can help managers make a number of different types of decisions. One example is the use of these techniques when evaluating corporate mergers. Companies frequently decide to acquire other firms to obtain low-cost production facilities, to increase capacity, or to expand into new markets, and the analysis related to such mergers is conceptually similar to that related to regular capital budgeting. Thus, when AT&T decided to go into the cellular telephone business, it had the choice of building facilities from the ground up or acquiring an existing business. AT&T chose to acquire McCaw Cellular. In the analysis related to the merger, AT&T's managers used the techniques employed in regular capital budgeting analysis.

Managers also use capital budgeting techniques when deciding whether to downsize personnel or to sell off particular assets or divisions. Like capital budgeting, such an analysis requires an assessment of how the action will affect the firm's cash flows. In a downsizing, companies typically spend money (i.e., invest) in severance payments to employees who are no longer needed, but the companies then receive benefits in the form of lower future wage costs. When assets are sold, the pattern of cash flows is reversed from those in a typical capital budgeting decision — positive cash flows are realized at the outset, but the firm is sacrificing future cash flows that it would have received if it had continued to use the asset. So, when deciding whether it makes sense to shed assets, managers compare the cash received with the present value of the lost outflows. If the net present value is positive, the asset sale would increase shareholder value.

Most decisions should be based on whether they contribute to shareholder value, and that, in turn, can be determined by estimating the net present value of a set of cash flows. However, as you will see in the next chapter, the hardest part is coming up with reasonable estimates of those cash flows.

SELF-TEST QUESTION

Give some examples of other decisions that can be analyzed with the capital budgeting techniques developed in this chapter.

TYING IT ALL TOGETHER

This chapter has described five techniques (payback, discounted payback, NPV, IRR, and MIRR) that are used in capital budgeting analysis. Each approach provides the firm with a different piece of information, so in this age of computers, managers often look at a number of measures when evaluating corporate projects. However, NPV is the best single measure, and its use has been increasing over time.

We simplified things in this chapter. You were given a set of cash flows and a cost of capital, and you were then asked to evaluate the projects. The hard part, however, is estimating a project's cash flows and its risk, which affects its cost of capital. We will address these issues in the next chapter. Before proceeding, though, the key concepts covered are listed below.

- **Capital budgeting** is the process of analyzing potential fixed asset investments. Capital budgeting decisions are probably the most important ones financial managers must make.

- The **payback period** is defined as the number of years required to recover a project's cost. The regular payback method ignores cash flows beyond the payback period, and it does not consider the time value of money. The payback does, however, provide an indication of a project's risk and liquidity, because it shows how long the invested capital will be "at risk."

- The **discounted payback method** is similar to the regular payback method except that it discounts cash flows at the project's cost of capital. It considers the time value of money, but it ignores cash flows beyond the payback period.

- The **net present value (NPV) method** discounts all cash flows at the project's cost of capital and then sums those cash flows. The project is accepted if the NPV is positive.

- The **internal rate of return (IRR)** is defined as the discount rate that forces a project's NPV to equal zero. The project is accepted if the IRR is greater than the cost of capital.

- The NPV and IRR methods make the same accept/reject decisions for **independent projects,** but if projects are **mutually exclusive,** then ranking conflicts can arise. If conflicts arise, the NPV method should be used. The NPV and IRR methods are both superior to the payback, but NPV is superior to IRR.

- The NPV method assumes that cash flows will be reinvested at the firm's cost of capital, while the IRR method assumes reinvestment at the project's IRR. **Reinvestment at the cost of capital is generally a better assumption** because it is closer to reality.

- The **modified IRR (MIRR) method** corrects some of the problems with the regular IRR. MIRR involves finding the **terminal value (TV)** of the cash inflows, compounded at the firm's cost of capital, and then determining the discount rate that forces the present value of the TV to equal the present value of the outflows.

- Sophisticated managers consider all of the project evaluation measures because each measure provides a useful piece of information.

- The **post-audit** is a key element of capital budgeting. By comparing actual results with predicted results and then determining why differences occurred, decision makers can improve both their operations and their forecasts of projects' outcomes.

- Small firms tend to use the payback method rather than a discounted cash flow method. This may be rational, because (1) the **cost** of conducting a DCF analysis **may outweigh the benefits** for the project being considered, (2) **the firm's cost of capital cannot be estimated accurately,** or (3) the small-business owner may be considering **nonmonetary goals.**

Although this chapter has presented the basic elements of the capital budgeting process, there are many other aspects of this crucial topic. Some of the more important ones are discussed in the following chapter.

QUESTIONS

11-1 How is a project classification scheme (for example, replacement, expansion into new markets, and so forth) used in the capital budgeting process?

11-2 Explain why the NPV of a relatively long-term project, defined as one for which a high percentage of its cash flows are expected in the distant future, is more sensitive to changes in the cost of capital than is the NPV of a short-term project.

11-3 Explain why, if two mutually exclusive projects are being compared, the short-term project might have the higher ranking under the NPV criterion if the cost of capital is high, but the long-term project might be deemed better if the cost of capital is low. Would changes in the cost of capital ever cause a change in the IRR ranking of two such projects?

11-4 In what sense is a reinvestment rate assumption embodied in the NPV, IRR, and MIRR methods? What is the assumed reinvestment rate of each method?

11-5 "If a firm has no mutually exclusive projects, only independent ones, and it also has both a constant cost of capital and projects with normal cash flows in the sense that each project has one or more outflows followed by a stream of inflows, then the NPV and IRR methods will always lead to identical capital budgeting decisions." Discuss this statement. What does it imply about using the IRR method in lieu of the NPV method? If each of the assumptions made in the question were changed (one by one), how would these changes affect your answer?

11-6 Are there conditions under which a firm might be better off if it were to choose a machine with a rapid payback rather than one with a larger NPV?

11-7 A firm has $100 million available for capital expenditures. It is considering investing in one of two projects; each has a cost of $100 million. Project A has an IRR of 20 percent and an NPV of $9 million. It will be terminated at the end of 1 year at a profit of $20 million, resulting in an immediate increase in earnings per share (EPS). Project B, which cannot be postponed, has an IRR of 30 percent and an NPV of $50 million. However, the firm's short-run EPS will be reduced if it accepts Project B, because no revenues will be generated for several years.
   a. Should the short-run effects on EPS influence the choice between the two projects?
   b. How might situations like the one described here influence a firm's decision to use payback as a part of the capital budgeting process?

11-8 What does it mean for projects to be mutually exclusive? How should managers rank mutually exclusive projects?

11-9 Project X is very risky and has an NPV of $3 million. Project Y is very safe and has an NPV of $2.5 million. Assume that the two projects are mutually exclusive and that each of the net present value calculations takes into account the risk of the respective projects. Should the company accept Project X or Project Y? Explain.

SELF-TEST PROBLEMS (SOLUTIONS APPEAR IN APPENDIX B)

ST-1
Key terms

Define each of the following terms:
   a. Capital budget; capital budgeting; strategic business plan
   b. Regular payback period; discounted payback period
   c. Independent projects; mutually exclusive projects
   d. DCF techniques; net present value (NPV) method
   e. Internal rate of return (IRR) method; IRR
   f. Modified internal rate of return (MIRR) method
   g. NPV profile; crossover rate
   h. Nonnormal cash flow projects; normal cash flow projects; multiple IRRs
   i. Hurdle rate
   j. Reinvestment rate assumption
   k. Post-audit

ST-2
Project analysis

You are a financial analyst for Damon Electronics Company. The director of capital budgeting has asked you to analyze two proposed capital investments, Projects X and Y. Each project has a cost of $10,000, and the cost of capital for each project is 12 percent. The projects' expected net cash flows are as follows:

	EXPECTED NET CASH FLOWS	
YEAR	PROJECT X	PROJECT Y
0	($10,000)	($10,000)
1	6,500	3,500
2	3,000	3,500
3	3,000	3,500
4	1,000	3,500

   a. Calculate each project's payback period, net present value (NPV), internal rate of return (IRR), and modified internal rate of return (MIRR).
   b. Which project or projects should be accepted if they are independent?
   c. Which project should be accepted if they are mutually exclusive?
   d. How might a change in the cost of capital produce a conflict between the NPV and IRR rankings of these two projects? Would this conflict exist if k were 5 percent? (Hint: Plot the NPV profiles.)
   e. Why does the conflict exist?

STARTER PROBLEMS

11-1
Payback period

Project K has a cost of $52,125, its expected net cash inflows are $12,000 per year for 8 years, and its cost of capital is 12 percent. What is the project's payback period (to the closest year)? (Hint: Begin by constructing a time line.)

11-2
NPV

Refer to Problem 11-1. What is the project's NPV?

11-3
IRR

Refer to Problem 11-1. What is the project's IRR?

11-4
Discounted payback period

Refer to Problem 11-1. What is the project's discounted payback period?

11-5
MIRR

Refer to Problem 11-1. What is the project's MIRR?

11-6
NPV

Your division is considering two investment projects, each of which requires an up-front expenditure of $15 million. You estimate that the investments will produce the following net cash flows:

YEAR	PROJECT A	PROJECT B
1	$ 5,000,000	$20,000,000
2	10,000,000	10,000,000
3	20,000,000	6,000,000

What are the two projects' net present values, assuming the cost of capital is 10 percent? 5 percent? 15 percent?

11-7
Financial calculator required; NPV

Northwest Utility Corporation has a cost of capital of 11.5 percent, and it has a project with the following net cash flows:

YEAR	NET CASH FLOW
0	−$200
1	235
2	−65
3	300

What is the project's NPV?

EXAM-TYPE PROBLEMS

The problems included in this section are set up in such a way that they could be used as multiple-choice exam problems.

11-8
NPVs, IRRs, and MIRRs for independent projects

Edelman Engineering is considering including two pieces of equipment, a truck and an overhead pulley system, in this year's capital budget. The projects are independent. The cash outlay for the truck is $17,100, and that for the pulley system is $22,430. The firm's cost of capital is 14 percent. After-tax cash flows, including depreciation, are as follows:

YEAR	TRUCK	PULLEY
1	$5,100	$7,500
2	5,100	7,500
3	5,100	7,500
4	5,100	7,500
5	5,100	7,500

Calculate the IRR, the NPV, and the MIRR for each project, and indicate the correct accept/reject decision for each.

11-9

NPVs and IRRs for mutually exclusive projects

B. Davis Industries must choose between a gas-powered and an electric-powered fork-lift truck for moving materials in its factory. Since both forklifts perform the same function, the firm will choose only one. (They are mutually exclusive investments.) The electric-powered truck will cost more, but it will be less expensive to operate; it will cost $22,000, whereas the gas-powered truck will cost $17,500. The cost of capital that applies to both investments is 12 percent. The life for each type of truck is estimated to be 6 years, during which time the net cash flows for the electric-powered truck will be $6,290 per year and those for the gas-powered truck will be $5,000 per year. Annual net cash flows include depreciation expenses. Calculate the NPV and IRR for each type of truck, and decide which to recommend.

11-10

Capital budgeting methods

Project S costs $15,000 and is expected to produce cash flows of $4,500 per year for 5 years. Project L costs $37,500 and is expected to produce cash flows of $11,100 per year for 5 years. Calculate the two projects' NPVs, IRRs, and MIRRs, assuming a cost of capital of 14 percent. Which project would be selected, assuming they are mutually exclusive, using each ranking method? Which should actually be selected?

11-11

Present value of costs

The Costa Rican Coffee Company is evaluating the within-plant distribution system for its new roasting, grinding, and packing plant. The two alternatives are (1) a conveyor system with a high initial cost but low annual operating costs and (2) several forklift trucks, which cost less but have considerably higher operating costs. The decision to construct the plant has already been made, and the choice here will have no effect on the overall revenues of the project. The cost of capital for the plant is 9 percent, and the projects' expected net costs are listed below:

	EXPECTED NET CASH COSTS	
YEAR	CONVEYOR	FORKLIFT
0	($300,000)	($120,000)
1	(66,000)	(96,000)
2	(66,000)	(96,000)
3	(66,000)	(96,000)
4	(66,000)	(96,000)
5	(66,000)	(96,000)

a. What is the IRR of each alternative?
b. What is the present value of costs of each alternative? Which method should be chosen?

11-12

MIRR and NPV

Your company is considering two mutually exclusive projects, X and Y, whose costs and cash flows are shown below:

YEAR	X	Y
0	($1,000)	($1,000)
1	100	1,000
2	300	100
3	400	50
4	700	50

The projects are equally risky, and their cost of capital is 12 percent. You must make a recommendation, and you must base it on the modified IRR (MIRR). What is the MIRR of the better project?

11-13

NPV and IRR

A company is analyzing two mutually exclusive projects, S and L, whose cash flows are shown below:

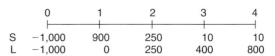

	0	1	2	3	4
S	−1,000	900	250	10	10
L	−1,000	0	250	400	800

The company's cost of capital is 10 percent, and it can get an unlimited amount of capital at that cost. What is the *regular IRR* (not MIRR) of the *better* project? (Hint: Note that the better project may or may not be the one with the higher IRR.)

11-14
MIRR
Project X has a cost of $1,000, and it is expected to produce a uniform cash flow stream for 10 years, i.e., the CFs are the same in Years 1 through 10, and it has a regular IRR of 12 percent. The cost of capital for the project is 10 percent. What is the project's modified IRR (MIRR)?

11-15
NPV and IRR
After discovering a new gold vein in the Colorado mountains, CTC Mining Corporation must decide whether to mine the deposit. The most cost-effective method of mining gold is sulfuric acid extraction, a process that results in environmental damage. To go ahead with the extraction, CTC must spend $900,000 for new mining equipment and pay $165,000 for its installation. The gold mined will net the firm an estimated $350,000 each year over the 5-year life of the vein. CTC's cost of capital is 14 percent. For the purposes of this problem, assume that the cash inflows occur at the end of the year.
a. What is the NPV and IRR of this project?
b. Should this project be undertaken, ignoring environmental concerns?
c. How should environmental effects be considered when evaluating this, or any other, project? How might these effects change your decision in part b?

11-16
NPV and IRR
John's Publishing Company, a new service that writes term papers for college students, provides 11-page term papers from a list of more than 500 topics. Each paper will cost $7.50 and is written by a graduate in the topic area. John's will pay $20,000 for the rights to all of the manuscripts. In addition, each author will receive $0.50 in royalties for every paper sold. Marketing expenses are estimated to be a total of $20,000 divided equally between Years 1 and 2, and John's cost of capital is 11 percent. Sales are expected as follows:

YEAR	VOLUME
1	10,000
2	7,000
3	3,000

a. What is the payback period for this investment? Its NPV? Its IRR?
b. What are the ethical implications of this investment?

11-17
NPV and IRR
Sharon Evans, who graduated from the local university 3 years ago with a degree in marketing, is manager of Ann Naylor's store in the Southwest Mall. Sharon's store has 5 years remaining on its lease. Rent is $2,000 per month, 60 payments remain, and the next payment is due in 1 month. The mall's owner plans to sell the property in a year and wants rents at that time to be high so the property will appear more valuable. Therefore, Sharon has been offered a "great deal" (owner's words) on a new 5-year lease. The new lease calls for zero rent for 9 months, then payments of $2,600 per month for the next 51 months. The lease cannot be broken, and Ann Naylor Corporation's cost of capital is 12 percent (or 1 percent per month). Sharon must make a decision. A good one could help her career and move her up in management, but a bad one could hurt her prospects for promotion.
a. Should Sharon accept the new lease? (Hint: Be sure to use 1 percent per month.)
b. Suppose Sharon decided to bargain with the mall's owner over the new lease payment. What new lease payment would make Sharon indifferent between the new and the old leases? (Hint: Find FV of the first 9 payments at t = 9, then treat this as the PV of a 51-period annuity whose payments represent the incremental rent during Months 10 to 60.)
c. Sharon is not sure of the 12 percent cost of capital — it could be higher or lower. At what *nominal cost* of capital would Sharon be indifferent between the two leases? (Hint: Calculate the differences between the two payment streams, and find the IRR of this difference stream.)

PROBLEMS

11-18
NPV and IRR
Cummings Products Company is considering two mutually exclusive investments. The projects' expected net cash flows are as follows:

	EXPECTED NET CASH FLOWS	
YEAR	PROJECT A	PROJECT B
0	($300)	($405)
1	(387)	134
2	(193)	134
3	(100)	134
4	600	134
5	600	134
6	850	134
7	(180)	0

   a. If you were told that each project's cost of capital was 12 percent, which project should be selected? If the cost of capital was 18 percent, what would be the proper choice?
   b. Construct NPV profiles for Projects A and B.
   c. What is each project's IRR?
   d. What is the crossover rate, and what is its significance?
   e. What is each project's MIRR at a cost of capital of 12 percent? At $k = 18\%$? (Hint: Consider Period 7 as the end of Project B's life.)

11-19
Timing differences

The Northwest Territories Oil Exploration Company is considering two mutually exclusive plans for extracting oil on property for which it has mineral rights. Both plans call for the expenditure of $12,000,000 to drill development wells. Under Plan A, all the oil will be extracted in 1 year, producing a cash flow at $t = 1$ of $14,400,000. Under Plan B, cash flows will be $2,100,000 per year for 20 years.
   a. Construct NPV profiles for Plans A and B, identify each project's IRR, and indicate the approximate crossover rate.
   b. Suppose a company has a cost of capital of 12 percent, and it can get unlimited capital at that cost. Is it logical to assume that it would take on all available independent projects (of average risk) with returns greater than 12 percent? Further, if all available projects with returns greater than 12 percent have been taken on, would this mean that cash flows from past investments would have an opportunity cost of only 12 percent, because all the firm could do with these cash flows would be to replace money that has a cost of 12 percent? Finally, does this imply that the cost of capital is the correct rate to assume for the reinvestment of a project's cash flows?

11-20
Scale differences

The Parrish Publishing Company is considering two mutually exclusive expansion plans. Plan A calls for the expenditure of $40 million on a large-scale, integrated plant that will provide an expected cash flow stream of $6.4 million per year for 20 years. Plan B calls for the expenditure of $12 million to build a somewhat less efficient, more labor-intensive plant that has an expected cash flow stream of $2.72 million per year for 20 years. Parrish's cost of capital is 10 percent.
   a. Calculate each project's NPV and IRR.
   b. Graph the NPV profiles for Plan A and Plan B. From the NPV profiles constructed, approximate the crossover rate.
   c. Give a logical explanation, based on reinvestment rates and opportunity costs, as to why the NPV method is better than the IRR method when the firm's cost of capital is constant at some value such as 10 percent.

11-21
Multiple rates of return

Eastern Electric is considering a project that has an up-front cost (at $t = 0$) of $150 million. The project is expected to generate positive cash flows of $800 million and $175 million at the end of Years 1 and 2, respectively. After the project is completed, the company expects to pay a cost of $900 million at $t = 3$ to clean up the land that is used for the project.
   a. Plot the project's NPV profile. (Hint: Calculate the project's NPV at $k = 0\%, 3\%, 5\%, 6\%, 10\%, 100\%, 400\%, 430\%,$ and 450%.)
   b. Using the NPV profile drawn in part a, estimate the project's two IRRs.
   c. Should the project be accepted at $k = 5\%$? If $k = 10\%$? Explain your reasoning.

11-22
Multiple rates of return

The Black Hills Uranium Company is deciding whether or not it should open a strip mine, the net cost of which is $2 million. Net cash inflows are expected to be $13 million, all coming at the end of Year 1. The land must be returned to its natural state at a cost of $12 million, payable at the end of Year 2.

a. Plot the project's NPV profile. (Hint: Calculate NPV at k = 0%, 10%, 80%, and 450%, and possibly at other k values.)

b. Should the project be accepted if k = 10%? If k = 20%? Explain your reasoning.

c. Can you think of some other capital budgeting situations in which negative cash flows during or at the other end of the project's life might lead to multiple IRRs?

d. What is the project's MIRR at k = 10%? At k = 20%? With this project, does the MIRR method lead to the same accept/reject decision as the NPV method? Does the MIRR method *always* lead to the same accept/reject decision as the NPV method? (Hint: Consider mutually exclusive projects that differ in size.)

11-23
Payback, NPV, and MIRR

Your division is considering two investment projects, each of which requires an up-front expenditure of $25 million. You estimate that the cost of capital is 10 percent and that the investments will produce the following after-tax cash flows (in millions of dollars):

YEAR	PROJECT A	PROJECT B
1	$ 5	$20
2	10	10
3	15	8
4	20	6

a. What is the regular payback period for each of the projects?

b. What is the discounted payback period for each of the projects?

c. If the two projects are independent and the cost of capital is 10 percent, which project or projects should the firm undertake?

d. If the two projects are mutually exclusive and the cost of capital is 5 percent, which project should the firm undertake?

e. If the two projects are mutually exclusive and the cost of capital is 15 percent, which project should the firm undertake?

f. What is the crossover rate?

g. If the cost of capital is 10 percent, what is the modified IRR (MIRR) of each project?

SPREADSHEET PROBLEM

11-24
Capital budgeting tools

Rework Problem 11-18, parts a through e, using a spreadsheet model. Then, answer the following related questions:

f. What is the regular payback period for these two projects?

g. At a cost of capital of 12 percent, what is the discounted payback period for these two projects?

CYBER PROBLEM

11-25
Capital budgeting — IBM

The information related to the cyberproblems is likely to change over time, due to the release of new information and the ever-changing nature of the World Wide Web. With these changes in mind, we will periodically update these problems on the textbook's web site. To avoid problems, please check for these updates before proceeding with the cyberproblems.

Capital budgeting is the process of evaluating potential projects and determining which are likely to be profitable and which are not. A company's capital budget is a function of its corporate strategy, and its effects are felt throughout the organization long after the actual decisions are made. Because of the size and importance of capital investments, companies must ensure that their capital budgeting decisions are based on good information and sound analysis. For a large, multinational corporation such as IBM, there are many challenges in the capital budgeting process. Use the "Financial Condition" section of the management discussion found in IBM's 1999 Annual Report (see **www.ibm.com/annualreport/1999**) to complete this exercise.

a. In addition to current operating performance, firms must never lose sight of their organizational goals and the need to maintain their distinctive competencies. For that reason, they must always be looking toward the future and ensuring success down the road. With that in mind, what major investments did IBM make in 1999 to fund future growth and increase shareholder value?

b. All firms face the fundamental question of where to raise capital. Multinational corporations' wider spheres of operations provide the opportunity to attract capital from a more diverse group of investors. How much debt, and at what interest rate, did IBM raise in the following countries: Japan, Canada, Germany, Switzerland, and Great Britain?

c. How does Standard & Poor's rate IBM's senior long-term debt, preferred stock, and commercial paper?

d. Briefly describe IBM's investment in new software research, development, and engineering. Did IBM amortize more or less capitalized software costs during 1999 as compared with 1998? Why was there a difference?

e. To identify the sources of specific risk, IBM uses sensitivity analysis to determine the effect of different market risk exposures on the fair value of some of its assets. What kind of financial instruments are subjected to this sensitivity analysis?

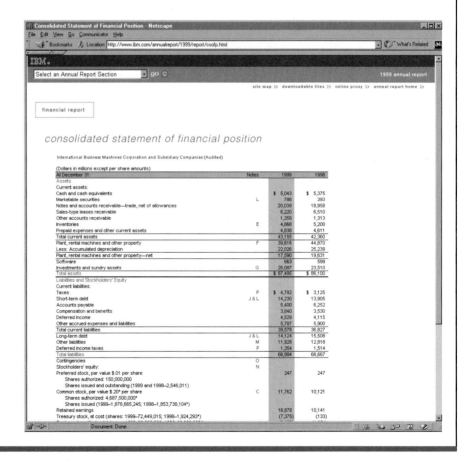

ALLIED COMPONENTS COMPANY

11-26 Basics of Capital Budgeting Assume that you recently went to work for Allied Components Company, a supplier of auto repair parts used in the after-market with products from DaimlerChrysler, Ford, and other auto makers. Your boss, the chief financial officer (CFO), has just handed you the estimated cash flows for two proposed projects. Project L involves adding a new item to the firm's ignition system line; it would take some time to build up the market for this product, so the cash inflows would increase over time. Project S involves an add-on to an existing line, and its cash flows would decrease over time. Both projects have 3-year lives, because Allied is planning to introduce entirely new models after 3 years.

Here are the projects' net cash flows (in thousands of dollars):

	EXPECTED NET CASH FLOW	
YEAR	PROJECT L	PROJECT S
0	($100)	($100)
1	10	70
2	60	50
3	80	20

Depreciation, salvage values, net operating working capital requirements, and tax effects are all included in these cash flows.

The CFO also made subjective risk assessments of each project, and he concluded that both projects have risk characteristics that are similar to the firm's average project. Allied's weighted average cost of capital is 10 percent. You must now determine whether one or both of the projects should be accepted.

a. What is capital budgeting? Are there any similarities between a firm's capital budgeting decisions and an individual's investment decisions?

b. What is the difference between independent and mutually exclusive projects? Between projects with normal and nonnormal cash flows?

c. (1) What is the payback period? Find the paybacks for Projects L and S.

   (2) What is the rationale for the payback method? According to the payback criterion, which project or projects should be accepted if the firm's maximum acceptable payback is 2 years, and if Projects L and S are independent? If they are mutually exclusive?

   (3) What is the difference between the regular and discounted payback periods?

   (4) What is the main disadvantage of discounted payback? Is the payback method of any real usefulness in capital budgeting decisions?

d. (1) Define the term *net present value (NPV)*. What is each project's NPV?

(2) What is the rationale behind the NPV method? According to NPV, which project or projects should be accepted if they are independent? Mutually exclusive?

(3) Would the NPVs change if the cost of capital changed?

e. (1) Define the term *internal rate of return (IRR)*. What is each project's IRR?

(2) How is the IRR on a project related to the YTM on a bond?

(3) What is the logic behind the IRR method? According to IRR, which projects should be accepted if they are independent? Mutually exclusive?

(4) Would the projects' IRRs change if the cost of capital changed?

f. (1) Draw NPV profiles for Projects L and S. At what discount rate do the profiles cross?

(2) Look at your NPV profile graph without referring to the actual NPVs and IRRs. Which project or projects should be accepted if they are independent? Mutually exclusive? Explain. Are your answers correct at any cost of capital less than 23.6 percent?

g. (1) What is the underlying cause of ranking conflicts between NPV and IRR?

(2) What is the "reinvestment rate assumption," and how does it affect the NPV versus IRR conflict?

(3) Which method is the best? Why?

h. (1) Define the term *modified IRR (MIRR)*. Find the MIRRs for Projects L and S.

(2) What are the MIRR's advantages and disadvantages vis-à-vis the regular IRR? What are the MIRR's advantages and disadvantages vis-à-vis the NPV?

i. As a separate project (Project P), the firm is considering sponsoring a pavilion at the upcoming World's Fair. The pavilion would cost $800,000, and it is expected to result in $5 million of incremental cash inflows during its 1 year of operation. However, it would then take another year, and $5 million of costs, to demolish the site and return it to its original condition. Thus, Project P's expected net cash flows look like this (in millions of dollars):

YEAR	NET CASH FLOWS
0	($0.8)
1	5.0
2	(5.0)

The project is estimated to be of average risk, so its cost of capital is 10 percent.

(1) What is Project P's NPV? What is its IRR? Its MIRR?

(2) Draw Project P's NPV profile. Does Project P have normal or nonnormal cash flows? Should this project be accepted?

12 Cash Flow Estimation and Risk Analysis

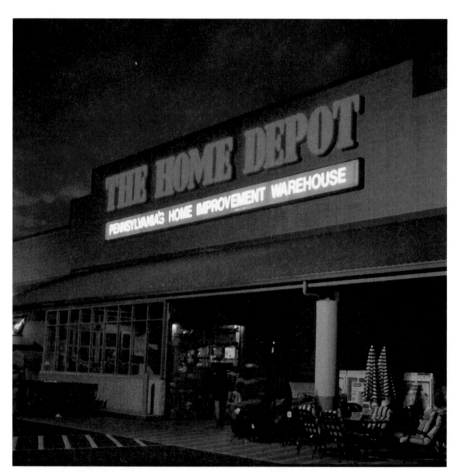

SOURCE: Andre Jenny/Unicorn Stock Photos

HOME DEPOT

Home Depot Inc. has grown phenomenally over the past decade, and it shows no sign of slowing down. At the beginning of 1990, it had 118 stores, and its annual sales were $2.8 billion. By early 2001, it had more than 1,000 stores, and its annual sales were in excess of $45 billion. Despite concerns of a slowing economy, the company expects to open another 200 stores in fiscal 2001.

Home Depot recently estimated that it costs, on average, $16 million to purchase land, construct a new store, and stock it with inventory. (The inventory costs about $5 million, but about $2 million of this is financed through accounts payable.) Each new store thus represents a major capital expenditure, so the company must use capital budgeting techniques to determine if a potential store's expected cash flows are sufficient to cover its costs.

Home Depot uses information from its existing stores to forecast new stores' expected cash flows. Thus far, its forecasts have been outstanding, but there are always risks that must be considered. First, store sales might be less than projected if the economy weakens. Second, some of Home Depot's customers might in the future bypass it altogether and buy directly from manufacturers

through the Internet. Third, new stores could "cannibalize," that is, take sales away from, existing stores. This last point was made in the July 16, 1999, issue of *Value Line:*

> The retailer has picked the "low-hanging fruit;" it has already entered the most attractive markets. To avoid "cannibalization" — which occurs when duplicative stores are located too closely together — the company is developing complementary formats. For example, Home Depot is beginning to roll out its *Expo Design Center* chain, which offers one-stop sales and service for kitchen and bath and other remodeling and renovation work . . .

The decision to expand requires a detailed assessment of the forecasted cash flows, including the risk that the forecasted level of sales might not be realized. In this chapter, we describe techniques for estimating a project's cash flows and their associated risk. Companies such as Home Depot use these techniques on a regular basis to evaluate capital budgeting decisions. ∎

The basic principles of capital budgeting were covered in Chapter 11. Given a project's expected cash flows, it is easy to calculate its payback, discounted payback, NPV, IRR, and MIRR. Unfortunately, cash flows are rarely just given — rather, managers must estimate them based on information collected from sources both inside and outside the company. Moreover, uncertainty surrounds the cash flow estimates, and some projects are riskier than others. In this chapter, we first develop procedures for estimating cash flows associated with capital budgeting projects. Then, we discuss techniques used to measure and take account of project risk. Finally, we introduce the concept of real options and discuss some general principles for determining the optimal capital budget. ■

ESTIMATING CASH FLOWS

The most important, but also the most difficult, step in capital budgeting is estimating projects' cash flows — the investment outlays and the annual net cash inflows after a project goes into operation. Many variables are involved, and many individuals and departments participate in the process. For example, the forecasts of unit sales and sales prices are normally made by the marketing group, based on their knowledge of price elasticity, advertising effects, the state of the economy, competitors' reactions, and trends in consumers' tastes. Similarly, the capital outlays associated with a new product are generally obtained from the engineering and product development staffs, while operating costs are estimated by cost accountants, production experts, personnel specialists, purchasing agents, and so forth.

It is difficult to accurately forecast the costs and revenues associated with a large, complex project, so forecast errors can be quite large. For example, when several major oil companies decided to build the Alaska Pipeline, the original cost estimates were in the neighborhood of $700 million, but the final cost was closer to $7 billion. Similar (or even worse) miscalculations are common in forecasts of product design costs, such as the costs to develop a new personal computer. Further, as difficult as plant and equipment costs are to estimate, sales revenues and operating costs over the project's life are even more uncertain. For example, several years ago, Federal Express developed an electronic delivery service system (ZapMail). It used the correct capital budgeting technique, NPV, but it incorrectly estimated the project's cash flows: Projected revenues were too high, projected costs were too low, and virtually no one was willing to pay the price required to cover the project's costs. As a result, cash flows failed to meet the forecasted levels, and Federal Express ended up losing about $200 million on the venture. This example demonstrates a basic truth —

if cash flow estimates are not reasonably accurate, any analytical technique, no matter how sophisticated, can lead to poor decisions. Because of its financial strength, Federal Express was able to absorb losses on the project, but the Zap-Mail venture could have forced a weaker firm into bankruptcy.

The financial staff's role in the forecasting process includes (1) obtaining information from various departments such as engineering and marketing, (2) ensuring that everyone involved with the forecast uses a consistent set of economic assumptions, and (3) making sure that no biases are inherent in the forecasts. This last point is extremely important, because managers often become emotionally involved with pet projects and also develop empire-building complexes, both of which lead to cash flow forecasting biases that make bad projects look good — on paper.

It is almost impossible to overstate the problems one can encounter in cash flow forecasts. It is also difficult to overstate the importance of these forecasts. Still, observing the principles discussed in the next several sections will help minimize forecasting errors.

SELF-TEST QUESTIONS

What is the most important step in a capital budgeting analysis?

What departments are involved in estimating a project's cash flows?

What is the financial staff's role in the forecasting process for capital projects?

IDENTIFYING THE RELEVANT CASH FLOWS

Relevant Cash Flows
The specific cash flows that should be considered in a capital budgeting decision.

The starting point in any capital budgeting analysis is identifying the **relevant cash flows,** defined as the specific set of cash flows that should be considered in the decision at hand. Analysts often make errors in estimating cash flows, but two cardinal rules can help you avoid mistakes: (1) Capital budgeting decisions must be based on *cash flows*, not accounting income. (2) Only *incremental cash flows* are relevant.

Recall from Chapter 2 that *free cash flow* is the cash flow available for distribution to investors. In a nutshell, the relevant cash flow for a project is the *additional* free cash flow that the company expects if it implements the project, that is, the cash flow above and beyond what the company could expect if it doesn't implement the project. The following sections discuss the relevant cash flows in more detail.

PROJECT CASH FLOW VERSUS ACCOUNTING INCOME

Recall that free cash flow is calculated as follows:

$$\text{Free cash flow} = \begin{array}{c}\text{After-tax}\\\text{operating income}\end{array} + \text{Depreciation} - \begin{array}{c}\text{Capital}\\\text{expenditures}\end{array} - \begin{array}{c}\text{Change in net}\\\text{operating}\\\text{working capital}\end{array}$$

$$= \text{EBIT}(1-\text{T}) + \text{Depreciation} - \begin{array}{c}\text{Capital}\\\text{expenditures}\end{array} - \left[\begin{array}{c}\Delta \text{ Current assets} -\\\Delta \text{ Spontaneous liabilities}\end{array}\right].$$

Just as a firm's value depends on its free cash flows, the value of a project depends on its free cash flow. We illustrate the estimation of project cash flow later in the chapter with a comprehensive example, but it is important for you to understand that project cash flow differs from accounting income.

Costs of Fixed Assets

Most projects require assets, and asset purchases represent *negative* cash flows. Even though the acquisition of assets results in a cash outflow, accountants do not show the purchase of fixed assets as a deduction from accounting income. Instead, they deduct a depreciation expense each year throughout the life of the asset.

Note that the full costs of fixed assets include any shipping and installation costs. When a firm acquires fixed assets, it often must incur substantial costs for shipping and installing the equipment. These charges are added to the price of the equipment when the project's cost is being determined. Then, the full cost of the equipment, including shipping and installation costs, is used as the *depreciable basis* when depreciation charges are being calculated. For example, if a company bought a computer with an invoice price of $100,000 and paid another $10,000 for shipping and installation, then the full cost of the computer (and its depreciable basis) would be $110,000. Note too that fixed assets can often be sold at the end of a project's life. If this is the case, then the after-tax cash proceeds represent a positive cash flow. We will illustrate both depreciation and cash flow from asset sales later in the chapter.

Noncash Charges

In calculating net income, accountants usually subtract depreciation from revenues. So, while accountants do not subtract the purchase price of fixed assets when calculating accounting income, they do subtract a charge each year for depreciation. Depreciation shelters income from taxation, and this has an impact on cash flow, but depreciation itself is not a cash flow. Therefore, depreciation must be added to net income when estimating a project's cash flow.

Changes in Net Operating Working Capital

Normally, additional inventories are required to support a new operation, and expanded sales tie additional funds up in accounts receivable. However, payables and accruals increase spontaneously as a result of the expansion, and this reduces the cash needed to finance inventories and receivables. The difference between the required increase in current assets and the spontaneous increase in current liabilities is the **change in net operating working capital.** If this change is positive, as it generally is for expansion projects, then additional financing, over and above the cost of the fixed assets, will be needed.

Toward the end of a project's life, inventories will be used but not replaced, and receivables will be collected without corresponding replacements. As these changes occur, the firm will receive cash inflows. As a result, the investment in operating working capital will be returned by the end of the project's life.

Change in Net Operating Working Capital
The increased current assets resulting from a new project minus the spontaneous increase in accounts payable and accruals.

Interest Expenses Are Not Included in Project Cash Flows

Recall from Chapter 11 that we discount a project's cash flows by its cost of capital, and that the cost of capital is a weighted average of the costs of debt, preferred stock, and common equity (WACC), adjusted for the project's risk. Moreover, the WACC is the rate of return necessary to satisfy all of the firm's investors — debtholders and stockholders. The discounting process *reduces* the cash flows to account for the project's capital costs. If interest charges were first deducted and then the resulting cash flows were discounted, this would double count the cost of debt. *Therefore, you should not subtract interest expenses when finding a project's cash flows.*

Note that this differs from the procedures used to calculate accounting income. Accountants measure the profit available for stockholders, so interest expenses are subtracted. However, project cash flow is the cash flow available for all investors, bondholders as well as stockholders, so interest expenses are not subtracted. All this is analogous to the procedures used in the corporate valuation model of Chapter 9, where the company's free cash flows are discounted at the WACC.[1]

INCREMENTAL CASH FLOWS

Incremental Cash Flow
The net cash flow attributable to an investment project.

In evaluating a project, we focus on those cash flows that occur if and only if we accept the project. These cash flows, called **incremental cash flows,** represent the change in the firm's total cash flow that occurs as a direct result of accepting the project. Three special problems in determining incremental cash flows are discussed next.

Sunk Costs

Sunk Cost
A cash outlay that has already been incurred and that cannot be recovered regardless of whether the project is accepted or rejected.

A **sunk cost** is an outlay that has already occurred, hence is not affected by the decision under consideration. Since sunk costs are not incremental costs, they should not be included in the analysis. To illustrate, in 2001, Northeast BankCorp was considering the establishment of a branch office in a newly developed section of Boston. To help with its evaluation, Northeast had, back in 2000, hired a consulting firm to perform a site analysis; the cost was $100,000, and this amount was expensed for tax purposes in 2000. Is this 2000 expenditure a relevant cost with respect to the 2001 capital budgeting decision? The answer is no — the $100,000 is a *sunk cost*, and it will not affect Northeast's future cash flows regardless of whether or not the new branch is built. It often turns out that a particular project has a negative NPV when all the associated costs, including sunk costs, are considered. However, on an incremental basis,

---

[1] An alternative approach to capital budgeting is to estimate the cash flows that are available for equity holders. Although this produces the same NPV as our approach, we do not recommend it because to apply it correctly requires that we determine the amount of debt and equity for every year of the project's life.

the project may be a good one because the *incremental cash flows* are large enough to produce a positive NPV on the *incremental investment.*

Opportunity Costs

A second potential problem relates to **opportunity costs,** which are cash flows that could be generated from an asset the firm already owns provided it is not used for the project in question. To illustrate, Northeast BankCorp already owns a piece of land that is suitable for the branch location. When evaluating the prospective branch, should the cost of the land be disregarded because no additional cash outlay would be required? The answer is no, because there is an *opportunity cost* inherent in the use of the property. In this case, the land could be sold to yield $150,000 after taxes. Use of the site for the branch would require forgoing this inflow, so the $150,000 must be charged as an opportunity cost against the project. Note that the proper land cost in this example is the $150,000 market-determined value, irrespective of whether Northeast originally paid $50,000 or $500,000 for the property. (What Northeast paid would, of course, have an effect on taxes, hence on the after-tax opportunity cost.)

Effects on Other Parts of the Firm: Externalities

The third potential problem involves the effects of a project on other parts of the firm, which economists call **externalities.** For example, some of Northeast's customers who would use the new branch are already banking with Northeast's downtown office. The loans and deposits, hence profits, generated by these customers would not be new to the bank; rather, they would represent a transfer from the main office to the branch. Thus, the net income produced by these customers should not be treated as incremental income in the capital budgeting decision. On the other hand, having a suburban branch would help the bank attract new business to its downtown office, because some people like to be able to bank both close to home and close to work. In this case, the additional income that would actually flow to the downtown office should be attributed to the branch. Although they are often difficult to quantify, *externalities* (which can be either positive or negative) should be considered.

When a new project takes sales from an existing product, this is often called **cannibalization.** Naturally, firms do not like to cannibalize their existing products, but it often turns out that if they do not, someone else will. To illustrate, IBM for years refused to provide full support for its PC division because it did not want to steal sales from its highly profitable mainframe business. That turned out to be a huge strategic error, because it allowed Intel, Microsoft, Compaq, and others to become dominant forces in the computer industry. Therefore, when considering externalities, the full implications of the proposed new project should be taken into account.

TIMING OF CASH FLOW

We must account properly for the timing of cash flows. Accounting income statements are for periods such as years or months, so they do not reflect exactly when during the period cash revenues or expenses occur. Because of the time value of money, capital budgeting cash flows should in theory be analyzed exactly as they occur. Of course, there must be a compromise between accuracy and feasibility. A time line with daily cash flows would in theory be most accurate, but daily cash flow estimates would be costly to construct, unwieldy to use, and probably no more accurate than annual cash flow estimates because we simply cannot forecast well enough to warrant this degree of detail. Therefore, in most cases, we simply assume that all cash flows occur at the end of every year. However, for some projects, it may be useful to assume that cash flows occur at mid-year, or even quarterly or monthly.

SELF-TEST QUESTIONS

Why should companies use project cash flow rather than accounting income when finding the NPV of a project?

How do shipping and installation costs affect the costs of fixed assets and the depreciable basis?

What is the most common noncash charge that must be added back when finding project cash flows?

What is net operating working capital, and how does it affect projects' costs in capital budgeting?

How does the company get back the dollars it invests in net operating working capital?

Explain the following terms: incremental cash flow, sunk cost, opportunity cost, externality, and cannibalization.

Give an example of a "good" externality, that is, one that makes a project look better.

EVALUATING CAPITAL BUDGETING PROJECTS

Up until this point, we have discussed several important aspects of cash flow analysis, but we have not seen how they affect capital budgeting decisions. Conceptually, these decisions are straightforward: A potential project creates value for the firm's shareholders if and only if the net present value of the incremental cash flows from the project is positive. In practice, however, estimating these cash flows can be difficult.

New Expansion Project
A project that is intended to increase sales.

Replacement Project
A project that replaces an existing asset with a new asset.

Incremental cash flows are affected by whether the project is a new expansion project or a replacement project. A **new expansion project** is defined as one where the firm invests in new assets to increase sales. Here the incremental cash flows are simply the project's cash inflows and outflows. In effect, the company is comparing what its value looks like with and without the proposed project. By contrast, a **replacement project** occurs when the firm replaces an existing asset with a new one. In this case, the incremental cash flows are the firm's *additional* inflows and outflows that result from investing in the new asset.

In a replacement analysis, the company is comparing its value if it acquires the new asset to its value if it continues to use the existing asset.[2]

Despite these differences, the basic principles for evaluating expansion and replacement projects are the same. In each case, the cash flows typically include the following items:

1. *Initial investment outlay.* The initial investment includes the up-front cost of fixed assets associated with the project plus any increases in net operating working capital.

2. *Operating cash flows over the project's life.* These are the incremental cash inflows over the project's economic life. Annual operating cash flows equal after-tax operating income plus depreciation. Recall (a) that depreciation is added back because it is a noncash expense and (b) that financing costs (including interest expense) are not included because they are accounted for in the discounting process.

3. *Terminal year cash flows.* At the end of a project's life, some extra cash flows are frequently received. These include the salvage value of the fixed assets, adjusted for taxes if assets are not sold at their book value, plus the return of the net operating working capital.

For each year of the project's life, the *net cash flow* is determined as the sum of the cash flows from each of the three categories. These annual net cash flows are then plotted on a time line and used to calculate the project's NPV and IRR.

We will illustrate the principles of capital budgeting analysis by examining a new project being considered by Brandt-Quigley Corporation (BQC), a large Atlanta-based technology company. BQC's research and development department has been applying its expertise in microprocessor technology to develop a small computer designed to control home appliances. Once programmed, the computer will automatically control the heating and air-conditioning systems, security system, hot water heater, and even small appliances such as a coffee maker. By increasing a home's energy efficiency, the computer can cut costs enough to pay for itself within a few years. Developments have now reached the stage where a decision must be made about whether or not to go forward with full-scale production.

BQC's marketing vice-president believes that annual sales would be 20,000 units if the units were priced at $3,000 each, so annual sales are estimated at $60 million. The engineering department has reported that the firm would need additional manufacturing capability, and BQC currently has an option to purchase an existing building, at a cost of $12 million, which would meet this need. The building would be bought and paid for on December 31, 2002, and for depreciation purposes it would fall into the MACRS 39-year class.

The necessary equipment would be purchased and installed late in 2002, and it would also be paid for on December 31, 2002. The equipment would fall into the MACRS 5-year class, and it would cost $8 million, including transportation

---

[2] For more discussion on replacement analysis decisions refer to the *Concise* web site or to Eugene F. Brigham and Phillip R. Daves, *Intermediate Financial Management*, 7th ed. (Fort Worth, TX: Harcourt College Publishers, 2002), Chapter 12.

and installation. Moreover, the project would also require an initial investment of $6 million in net operating working capital, which would also be made on December 31, 2002.

The project's estimated economic life is four years. At the end of that time, the building is expected to have a market value of $7.5 million and a book value of $10.908 million, whereas the equipment would have a market value of $2 million and a book value of $1.36 million.

The production department has estimated that variable manufacturing costs would be $2,100 per unit, and that fixed overhead costs, excluding depreciation, would be $8 million a year. Depreciation expenses would be determined in accordance with the MACRS rates (which are discussed in Appendix 12A).

BQC's marginal federal-plus-state tax rate is 40 percent; its cost of capital is 12 percent; and, for capital budgeting purposes, the company's policy is to assume that operating cash flows occur at the end of each year. Because the plant would begin operations on January 1, 2003, the first operating cash flows would occur on December 31, 2003.

Several other points should be noted: (1) BQC is a relatively large corporation, with sales of more than $4 billion, and it takes on many investments each year. Thus, if the computer control project does not work out, it will not bankrupt the company—management can afford to take a chance on the computer control project. (2) If the project is accepted, the company will be contractually obligated to operate it for its full four-year life. Management must make this commitment to its component suppliers. (3) Returns on this project would be positively correlated with returns on BQC's other projects and also with the stock market—the project should do well if other parts of the firm and the general economy are strong.

Assume that you are one of the company's financial analysts, and you must conduct the capital budgeting analysis. For now, assume that the project has the same risk as an average project, and use the corporate weighted average cost of capital, 12 percent.

ANALYSIS OF THE CASH FLOWS

Capital projects can be analyzed using a calculator, paper, and a pencil, or with a spreadsheet program such as *Excel*. Either way, you must set the analysis up as shown in Table 12-1 and go through the steps outlined in Parts 1 through 5 of the table. For exam purposes, you will probably have to work problems with a calculator. However, for reasons that will become obvious as you go through the chapter, in practice spreadsheets are virtually always used. Still, the steps involved in a capital budgeting analysis are the same regardless of whether you use a calculator or a computer to "get the answer."

Table 12-1, which is a printout from the CD-ROM file 12MODEL.xls, is divided into five parts: (1) Input Data, (2) Depreciation Schedule, (3) Net Salvage Values, (4) Projected Net Cash Flows, and (5) Key Output. There are also two extensions, Parts 6 and 7, that deal with risk analysis, which we will discuss later in the chapter when we cover sensitivity and scenario analyses. Note also that the table shows row and column indicators, so cells in the table have designations such as "Cell D33," which is the location of the cost of the building, found in Part 1, Input Data. If we deleted the row and column

TABLE 12-1				Analysis of a New (Expansion) Project Parts 1 and 2				

	A	B	C	D	E	F	G	H	I
29	Table 12-1. Analysis of a New (Expansion) Project								
30									
31	Part 1. Input Data (in thousands of dollars)								
32						Key Output: NPV	=		$5,166
33	Building cost (= Depreciable basis)			$12,000					
34	Equipment cost (= Depreciable basis)			$8,000		Market value of building in 2006			$7,500
35	Net Operating WC			$6,000		Market value of equip. in 2006			$2,000
36	First year sales (in units)			20,000		Tax rate			40%
37	Growth rate in units sold			0.0%		WACC			12%
38	Sales price per unit			$3.00		Inflation: growth in sales price			0.0%
39	Variable cost per unit			$2.10		Inflation: growth in VC per unit			0.0%
40	Fixed costs			$8,000		Inflation: growth in fixed costs			0.0%
41									
42	Part 2. Depreciation Schedule [a]				Years				Cumulative
43					1	2	3	4	Depr'n
44	Building Depr'n Rate				1.3%	2.6%	2.6%	2.6%	
45	Building Depr'n				$156	$312	$312	$312	$1,092
46	Ending Book Val: Cost - Cum. Depr'n				11,844	11,532	11,220	$10,908	
47									
48	Equipment Depr'n Rate				20.0%	32.0%	19.0%	12.0%	
49	Equipment Depr'n				$1,600	$2,560	$1,520	$960	$6,640
50	Ending Book Val: Cost - Cum. Depr'n				6,400	3,840	2,320	$1,360	
51									
52	[a] The indicated percentages are multiplied by the depreciable basis ($12,000 for the building and $8,000 for the equipment)								
53	to determine the depreciation expense for the year. See Appendix 12A for a review of MACRS depreciation rates.								

indicators, the table would look exactly like the setup for pencil-and-paper calculations.[3] Note also that the first row shown is Row 29; the first 28 rows contain information about the model that we omitted from the text.

Part 1, the Input Data section, provides the basic data used in the analysis. The inputs are really "assumptions"—thus, in the analysis we *assume* that 20,000 units can be sold at a price of $3 per unit.[4] Some of the inputs are known with near certainty—for example, the 40 percent tax rate is not likely to change. Others are more speculative—units sold and the variable cost percentage are in this category. Obviously, if sales or costs are different from the assumed levels, then profits and cash flows, hence NPV and IRR, will differ from their projected levels. Later in the chapter, we discuss how changes in the inputs affect the results.

---

[3] We first set up Table 12-1 as a "regular" table and did all the calculations with a calculator. We then typed all the labels into a spreadsheet and used the spreadsheet to do the calculations. The "answers" derived were identical. We show the spreadsheet version in Table 12-1, but the only visible difference is that it shows row and column indicators. If you have access to a computer, you might want to look at the model, which is on a file named 12MODEL.xls on the CD-ROM that accompanies this book.

[4] Recall that the sales price is actually $3,000, but for convenience we show all dollars in thousands.

TABLE 12-1

Analysis of a New (Expansion) Project
Part 3

	A	B	C	D	E	F	G	H	I
55	**Part 3 of Table 12-1. Net Salvage Values in 2006**								
56					**Building**	**Equipment**	**Total**		
57	Estimated Market Value in 2006				$7,500	$2,000			
58	Book Value in 2006[b]				10,908	1,360			
59	Expected Gain or Loss[c]				-3,408	640			
60	Taxes paid or tax credit				-1,363	256			
61	Net cash flow from salvage[d]				$8,863	$1,744	$10,607		
62									
63	[b] Book value equals depreciable basis (initial cost in this case) minus accumulated MACRS depreciation. For the								
64	building, accumulated depreciation equals $1,092, so book value equals $12,000 - $1,092 = $10,908. For the equipment,								
65	accumulated depreciation equals $6,640, so book value equals $8,000 - $6,640 = $1,360.								
66									
67	[c] Building: $7,500 market value - $10,908 book value = -$3,408, a loss. This represents a shortfall in depreciation								
68	taken versus "true" depreciation, and it is treated as an operating expense for 2006. Equipment: $2,000 market value -								
69	$1,360 book value = $640 profit. Here the depreciation charge exceeds the "true" depreciation, and the difference is called								
70	"depreciation recapture". It is taxed as ordinary income in 2006.								
71									
72	[d] Net cash flow from salvage equals salvage (market) value minus taxes. For the building, the loss results in a tax credit, so								
73	net salvage value = $7,500 - (-$1,363) = $8,863.								

Part 2, which calculates depreciation over the project's four-year life, is divided into two sections, one for the building and one for the equipment. The first row in each section gives the yearly depreciation rates as taken from Appendix 12A. The second row in each section gives the dollars of depreciation, found as the rate times the asset's depreciable basis, which, in this example, is the initial cost. The third row shows the book value at the end of Year 4, found by subtracting the accumulated depreciation from the depreciable basis.

Part 3 estimates the cash flows the firm will realize when it disposes of the assets. The first row shows the salvage value, which is the sales price the company expects to receive when it sells the assets four years hence. The second row shows the book values at the end of Year 4; these values were calculated in Part 2. The third row shows the expected gain or loss, defined as the difference between the sales price and the book value. As explained in notes c and d to Table 12-1, gains and losses are treated as ordinary income, not capital gains or losses.[5] Therefore, gains result in tax liabilities, and losses produce tax

---

[5] Note again that if an asset is sold for exactly its book value, there will be no gain or loss, hence no tax liability or credit. However, if an asset is sold for other than its book value, a gain or loss will be created. For example, BQC's building will have a book value of $10,908, but the company only expects to realize $7,500 when it is sold. This would result in a loss of $3,408. This indicates that the building should have been depreciated at a faster rate — only if depreciation had been $3,408 larger would the book and market values have been equal. So, the Tax Code stipulates that losses on the sale of operating assets can be used to reduce ordinary income, just as depreciation reduces income. On the other hand, if an asset is sold for more than its book value, as is the case for the equipment, then this signifies that the depreciation rates were too high, so the gain is called "depreciation recapture" by the IRS and is taxed as ordinary income.

TABLE 12-1

Analysis of a New (Expansion) Project
Part 4

	A	B	C	D	E	F	G	H	I
75	**Part 4 of Table 12-1. Projected Net Cash**						**Years**		
76	**Flows** (Time line of annual cash flows)				**0**	**1**	**2**	**3**	**4**
77					**2002**	**2003**	**2004**	**2005**	**2006**
78	*Investment Outlays at Time Zero*								
79	Building				($12,000)				
80	Equipment				(8,000)				
81	Increase in Net Operating WC				(6,000)				
82									
83	*Operating Cash Flows over the Project's Life*								
84	Units sold					20,000	20,000	20,000	20,000
85	Sales price					$3.00	$3.00	$3.00	$3.00
86									
87	Sales revenue					$60,000	$60,000	$60,000	$60,000
88	Variable costs					42,000	42,000	42,000	42,000
89	Fixed operating costs					8,000	8,000	8,000	8,000
90	Depreciation (building)					156	312	312	312
91	Depreciation (equipment)					1,600	2,560	1,520	960
92	Oper. income before taxes (EBIT)					8,244	7,128	8,168	8,728
93	Taxes on operating income (40%)					3,298	2,851	3,267	3,491
94	Net Operating Profit After Taxes (NOPAT)					4,946	4,277	4,901	5,237
95	Add back depreciation					1,756	2,872	1,832	1,272
96	Operating cash flow					$6,702	$7,149	$6,733	$6,509
97	*Terminal Year Cash Flows*								
98	Return of net operating working capital[e]								$6,000
99	Net salvage value								10,607
100	Total termination cash flows								$16,607
101									
102	Net Cash Flow (Time line of cash flows)				($26,000)	$6,702	$7,149	$6,733	$23,116
103									
104	[e] Net operating working capital will be recovered at the end of the project's operating life, in 2006, as inventories are								
105	sold off and receivables are collected.								

credits, that are equal to the gain or loss times the 40 percent tax rate. Taxes paid and tax credits are shown on the fourth row. The fifth row shows the after-tax cash flow the company expects when it disposes of the asset, found as the expected sales price minus the tax liability or plus the credit. Thus, the firm expects to net $8,863 from the sale of the building and $1,744 from the equipment, for a total of $10,607.

Next, in Part 4, we use the information developed in Parts 1, 2, and 3 to find the projected cash flows over the project's life. Five periods are shown, from Year 0 (2002) to Year 4 (2006). The cash outlays required at Year 0 are the negative numbers in the first column, and their sum, −$26,000, is shown at the bottom. Then, in the next four columns, we calculate the operating cash flows. We begin with sales revenues, found as the product of units sold and the sales

TABLE 12-1

Analysis of a New (Expansion) Project
Part 5

	A	B	C	D	E	F	G	H	I
107	Part 5 of Table 12-1. Key Output and Appraisal of the Proposed Project								
108									
109	Net Present Value (at 12%)			$5,166					
110	IRR			19.33%					
111	MIRR			17.19%			Years		
112					0	1	2	3	4
113	Cumulative cash flow for payback				(26,000)	(19,298)	(12,149)	(5,416)	17,700
114	Cum. CF > 0, hence Payback Year:				FALSE	FALSE	FALSE	FALSE	3.23
115	Payback found with Excel function =			3.23	See note below for an explanation of the Excel calculation.				
116	Check: Payback = 3 + 5,416/23,116 =			3.23	Manual calculation for the base case.				
117									
118	The Excel payback calculation is based on the logical IF function. Returns FALSE if the cumulative CF is negative or								
119	the actual payback if the cumulative CF is positive. Then, we use the MIN (minimum) function to find first year when								
120	payback is positive. The MIN function procedure is necessary for projects with longer lives, because then values, not the								
121	word FALSE, would appear in a number of cells. The MIN function picks the smallest number, which is the payback.								
122									
123	Based on the firm's 12% weighted average cost of capital, this project has a NPV of $5,166. Since the NPV is positive,								
124	we tentatively conclude that the project should be accepted. The IRR and MIRR confirm this decision because both								
125	exceed the cost of capital. Note, though, that no risk analysis has been conducted. It is possible that the firm's								
126	managers, after appraising the project's risk, might conclude that its projected return is insufficient to compensate								
127	for its risk, and reject it.								

price.[6] Next, we subtract variable costs, which were assumed to be $2.10 per unit. We then deduct fixed operating costs and depreciation to obtain taxable operating income, or EBIT. When taxes (at a 40 percent rate) are subtracted, we are left with net operating profit after taxes, or NOPAT. Note, though, that we are seeking cash flows, not accounting income. Sales are presumably for cash (or else receivables are collected promptly), and both taxes and all costs other than depreciation must be paid in cash. Therefore, each item in the "Operating Cash Flow" section of Part 4 represents cash *except depreciation*, which is a noncash charge. Thus, depreciation must be added back to obtain the project's cash flows from operations. The result is the row of operating cash flows shown toward the bottom of Part 4, on Row 96.

When the project's life ends, the company will receive the "Terminal Year Cash Flows" as shown in the column for Year 4 in the lower part of the table, on rows 98, 99, and 100. First, note that BQC invested $6,000 in net operating working capital — inventories plus accounts receivable — at Year 0.

---

[6] Notice that in Part 1, Input Data, we show a growth rate in unit sales, and inflation rates for the sales price, variable costs, and fixed costs. BQC anticipates that unit sales, the sales price, and costs will be stable over the project's life; hence, these variables are all set at zero. However, nonzero values can be inserted in the input section to determine the effects of growth and inflation. Incidentally, the inflation figures are all specific for this particular project — they do not reflect inflation as measured by the CPI. The expected CPI inflation is reflected in the WACC, and it is not expected to change over the forecast period.

As operations wind down in Year 4, inventories will be sold and not replaced, and this will provide cash. Similarly, accounts receivable will be collected and not replaced, and this too will provide cash. The end result is that the firm will recover its $6 million investment in net operating working capital during the last year of the project's life. In addition, when the company disposes of the building and equipment at the end of Year 4, it will receive cash as estimated in Part 3 of the table. Thus, the total terminal year cash flow amounts to $16,607 as shown on Row 100. When we sum the columns in Part 4, we obtain the net cash flows shown on Row 102. Those cash flows constitute a *cash flow time line*, and they are then evaluated in Part 5.

MAKING THE DECISION

Part 5 of the table shows the standard evaluation criteria—NPV, IRR, MIRR, and payback—based on the cash flows shown on Row 102. The NPV is positive, the IRR and MIRR both exceed the 12 percent cost of capital, and the payback indicates that the project will return the invested funds in 3.23 years. Therefore, on the basis of the analysis thus far, it appears that the project should be accepted. Note, though, that we have been assuming that the project is about as risky as the company's average project. If the project were judged to be riskier than average, it would be necessary to increase the cost of capital, which might cause the NPV to become negative and the IRR and MIRR to drop below the then-higher WACC. Therefore, we cannot make a final "go, no-go" decision until we evaluate the project's risk, the topic of the next section.

> **SELF-TEST QUESTIONS**
>
> What three types of cash flows must be considered when evaluating a proposed project?
>
> Define the following terms: new expansion project and replacement project.

INTRODUCTION TO PROJECT RISK ANALYSIS

Up to now we have simply assumed that projects will produce a given set of cash flows, and we then analyzed those cash flows to decide whether to accept or reject the project. Obviously, though, cash flows are not known with certainty. We now turn to risk in capital budgeting, examining the techniques firms use to determine a project's risk and then to decide whether its profit potential is worth the risk.

Recall from Chapter 10 that there are three distinct types of risk: stand-alone risk, corporate risk, and market risk. Given that the firm's primary objective is to maximize stockholder value, what ultimately matters is the risk that a project imposes on stockholders. Because stockholders are generally diversified, market risk is theoretically the most relevant measure of risk. Corporate risk is also important for these three reasons:

1. Undiversified stockholders, including the owners of small businesses, are more concerned about corporate risk than about market risk.

2. Empirical studies of the determinants of required rates of return (k) generally find that both market and corporate risk affect stock prices. This suggests that investors, even those who are well diversified, consider factors other than market risk when they establish required returns.

3. The firm's stability is important to its managers, workers, customers, suppliers, and creditors, as well as to the community in which it operates. Firms that are in serious danger of bankruptcy, or even of suffering low profits and reduced output, have difficulty attracting and retaining good managers and workers. Also, both suppliers and customers are reluctant to depend on weak firms, and such firms have difficulty borrowing money at reasonable interest rates. These factors tend to reduce risky firms' profitability and hence their stock prices, and this makes corporate risk significant.

For these three reasons, corporate risk is important even if a firm's stockholders are well diversified.

SELF-TEST QUESTIONS

What are the three types of project risk?

Why are (1) market and (2) corporate risk both important?

TECHNIQUES FOR MEASURING STAND-ALONE RISK

Why should a project's stand-alone risk be important to anyone? In theory, this type of risk should be of little or no concern. However, it is actually of great importance for two reasons:

1. It is easier to estimate a project's stand-alone risk than its corporate risk, and it is far easier to measure stand-alone risk than market risk.

2. In the vast majority of cases, all three types of risk are highly correlated — if the general economy does well, so will the firm, and if the firm does well, so will most of its projects. Because of this high correlation, stand-alone risk is generally a good proxy for hard-to-measure corporate and market risk.

The starting point for analyzing a project's stand-alone risk involves determining the uncertainty inherent in its cash flows. To illustrate what is involved, consider again Brandt-Quigley Corporation's appliance control computer project that we discussed above. Many of the key inputs shown in Part 1 of Table 12-1 are subject to uncertainty. For example, sales were projected at 20,000 units to be sold at a net price of $3,000 per unit. However, actual unit sales will almost certainly be somewhat higher or lower than 20,000, and the sales price will probably turn out to be different from the projected $3,000 per unit. *In* effect, the sales quantity and price estimates are really expected values based on probability distributions, as are many of the other values that were shown in Part 1 of Table 12-1. The distributions could be relatively "tight," reflecting small standard deviations and low risk, or they could be "flat," denoting a great deal of uncertainty about the actual value of the variable in question and thus a high degree of stand-alone risk.

The nature of the individual cash flow distributions, and their correlations with one another, determine the nature of the NPV probability distribution and, thus, the project's stand-alone risk. In the following sections, we discuss three techniques for assessing a project's stand-alone risk: (1) sensitivity analysis, (2) scenario analysis, and (3) Monte Carlo simulation.

SENSITIVITY ANALYSIS

Sensitivity Analysis
A risk analysis technique in which key variables are changed one at a time and the resulting changes in the NPV are observed.

Intuitively, we know that many of the variables that determine a project's cash flows could turn out to be different from the values used in the analysis. We also know that a change in a key input variable, such as units sold, will cause the NPV to change. **Sensitivity analysis** is a technique that indicates how much NPV will change in response to a given change in an input variable, other things held constant.

Sensitivity analysis begins with a *base-case* situation, which is developed using the *expected* values for each input. To illustrate, consider the data given back in Table 12-1, in which projected income statements for Brandt-Quigley's computer project were shown. The values used to develop the table, including unit sales, sales price, fixed costs, and variable costs, are the most likely, or base-case, values, and the resulting $5.166 million NPV shown in Table 12-1 is called the **base-case NPV.** Now we ask a series of "what if" questions: "What if unit sales fall 15 percent below the most likely level?" "What if the sales price per unit falls?" "What if variable costs are $2.50 per unit rather than the expected $2.10?" Sensitivity analysis is designed to provide the decision maker with answers to questions such as these.

Base-Case NPV
The NPV when sales and other input variables are set equal to their most likely (or base-case) values.

In a sensitivity analysis, each variable is changed by several percentage points above and below the expected value, holding all other variables constant. Then a new NPV is calculated using each of these values. Finally, the set of NPVs is plotted to show how sensitive NPV is to changes in each variable. Figure 12-1 shows the computer project's sensitivity graphs for six of the input variables. The table below the graph gives the NPVs that were used to construct the graph. The slopes of the lines in the graph show how sensitive NPV is to changes in each of the inputs: *the steeper the slope, the more sensitive the NPV is to a change in the variable.* From the figure and the table, we see that the project's NPV is very sensitive to changes in the sales price and variable costs, fairly sensitive to changes in the growth rate and units sold, and not very sensitive to changes in fixed costs and the cost of capital.

If we were comparing two projects, the one with the steeper sensitivity lines would be riskier, because for that project a relatively small error in estimating a variable such as unit sales would produce a large error in the project's expected NPV. Thus, sensitivity analysis can provide useful insights into the riskiness of a project.

Before we move on, we should note that spreadsheet computer programs such as *Excel* are ideally suited for performing sensitivity analysis. We used the model developed in Table 12-1 to conduct the analyses represented in Figure 12-1; it

FIGURE 12-1	Evaluating Risk: Sensitivity Analysis (Dollars in Thousands)

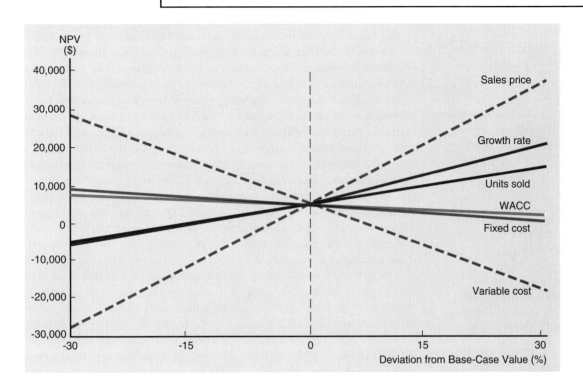

NPV AT DIFFERENT DEVIATIONS FROM BASE

DEVIATION FROM BASE CASE	SALES PRICE	VARIABLE COST/UNIT	GROWTH RATE	YEAR 1 UNITS SOLD	FIXED COST	WACC
−30%	($27,637)	$28,129	($5,847)	($4,675)	$9,540	$8,294
−15	(11,236)	16,647	(907)	246	7,353	6,674
0	5,166	5,166	5,166	5,166	5,166	5,166
15	21,568	(6,315)	12,512	10,087	2,979	3,761
30	37,970	(17,796)	21,269	15,007	792	2,450
Range	$65,607	$45,925	$27,116	$19,682	$8,748	$5,844

generated the NPVs and then drew the graphs. To conduct such an analysis by hand would be extremely time consuming.

SCENARIO ANALYSIS

Although sensitivity analysis is probably the most widely used risk analysis technique, it does have limitations. For example, we saw earlier that the computer project's NPV is highly sensitive to changes in the sales price and the variable cost per unit. Those sensitivities suggest that the project is risky. Suppose, however, that Home Depot or Circuit City was anxious to get the new computer product and would sign a contract to purchase 20,000 units per year for four years at $3,000 per unit. Moreover, suppose Intel would agree to provide the principal component at a price that would ensure that the variable cost per unit would not exceed $2,100. Under these conditions, there would be a zero probability of high or low sales prices and input costs, so the project would not be at all risky in spite of its sensitivity to those variables.

We see, then, that we need to extend sensitivity analysis to deal with the *probability distributions* of the inputs. In addition, it would be useful to vary more than one variable at a time so that we could see the combined effects of changes in the variables. **Scenario analysis** provides these extensions — it brings in the probabilities of changes in the key variables, and it allows us to change more than one variable at a time. In a scenario analysis, the financial analyst begins with the **base case**, or most likely set of values for the input variables. Then, he or she asks marketing, engineering, and other operating managers to specify a **worst-case scenario** (low unit sales, low sales price, high variable costs, and so on) and a **best-case scenario.** Often, the best case and worst case are defined as having a 25 percent probability of conditions being that good or bad, with a 50 percent probability that the base-case conditions will occur. Obviously, conditions could actually take on other values, but parameters such as these are useful to get people focused on the central issues in risk analysis.

The best-case, base-case, and worst-case values for BQC's computer project are shown in Table 12-2, along with plots of the data. If the product is highly successful, then the combination of a high sales price, low production costs, high first year sales, and a strong growth rate in future sales will result in a very high NPV, $144 million. However, if things turn out badly, then the NPV would be −$38.3 million. The graphs show the very wide range of possibilities, indicating that this is indeed a very risky project. If the bad conditions materialize, this will not bankrupt the company — this is just one project for a large company. Still, losing $38 million would certainly not help the stock price.

The project is clearly risky, and that suggests that its cost of capital is higher than the firm's WACC of 12 percent, which is applicable to an average-risk project. BQC generally adds 3 percentage points to the corporate WACC when it evaluates projects deemed to be risky, so it recalculated the NPV using a 15 percent cost of capital. That lowered the base-case NPV to $2,877,000 from $5,166,000. Thus, the project is still acceptable by the NPV criterion.

Scenario analysis provides useful information about a project's stand-alone risk. However, it is limited in that it considers only a few discrete outcomes (NPVs), even though there are an infinite number of possibilities. We briefly describe a more complete method of assessing a project's stand-alone risk in the next section.

MONTE CARLO SIMULATION

Monte Carlo simulation, so named because this type of analysis grew out of work on the mathematics of casino gambling, ties together sensitivities and input variable probability distributions. While Monte Carlo simulation is considerably more complex than scenario analysis, simulation software packages make this process manageable. Many of these packages are included as add-ons to spreadsheet programs such as *Microsoft Excel.*

In a simulation analysis, the computer begins by picking at random a value for each variable — sales in units, the sales price, the variable cost per unit, and

---

Scenario Analysis
A risk analysis technique in which "bad" and "good" sets of financial circumstances are compared with a most likely, or base-case, situation.

Base Case
An analysis in which all of the input variables are set at their most likely values.

Worst-Case Scenario
An analysis in which all of the input variables are set at their worst reasonably forecasted values.

Best-Case Scenario
An analysis in which all of the input variables are set at their best reasonably forecasted values.

Monte Carlo Simulation
A risk analysis technique in which probable future events are simulated on a computer, generating estimated rates of return and risk indexes.

| | | SALES | UNIT | VARIABLE | GROWTH | |
SCENARIO	PROBABILITY	PRICE	SALES	COSTS	RATE	NPV
Best case	25%	$3.90	26,000	$1.47	30%	$144,024
Base case	50	3.00	20,000	2.10	0	5,166
Worst case	25	2.10	14,000	2.73	−30	(38,315)

TABLE 12-2   Scenario Analysis (Dollars in Thousands)

Expected NPV = Sum, probability times NPV	$29,010
Standard deviation (calculated in *Excel* model)	$68,735
Coefficient of variation = Standard deviation/Expected NPV	2.37

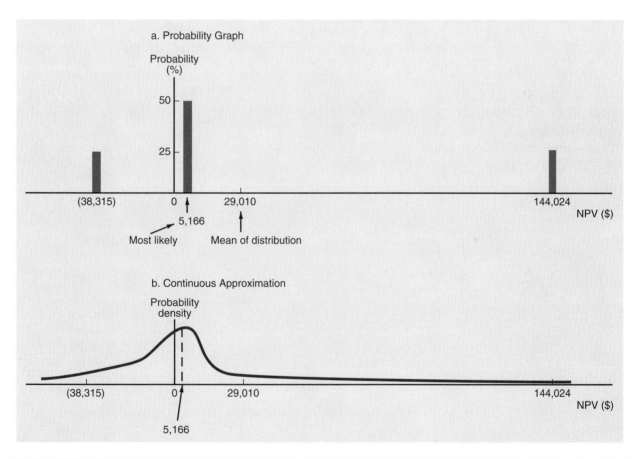

NOTE: The scenario analysis calculations were performed in the *Excel* model, 12MODEL.xls.

so on. Then those values are combined, and the project's NPV is calculated and stored in the computer's memory. Next, a second set of input values is selected at random, and a second NPV is calculated. This process is repeated perhaps 1,000 times, generating 1,000 NPVs. The mean and standard deviation of the set of NPVs is determined. The mean, or average value, is used as a measure of the project's expected profitability, and the standard deviation (or coefficient of variation) is used as a measure of the project's risk.

CAPITAL BUDGETING PRACTICES IN THE ASIA/PACIFIC REGION

A recent survey of executives in Australia, Hong Kong, Indonesia, Malaysia, the Philippines, and Singapore asked several questions about their companies' capital budgeting practices. The study yielded some interesting results, which are summarized here.

TECHNIQUES FOR EVALUATING CORPORATE PROJECTS

Consistent with evidence on U.S. companies, most companies in this region evaluate projects using IRR, NPV, and payback. IRR use ranged from 86 percent (in Hong Kong) to 96 percent (in Australia) of the companies. NPV use ranged from 81 percent (in the Philippines) to 96 percent (in Australia). Payback use ranged from 81 percent (in Indonesia) to 100 percent (in Hong Kong and the Philippines).

TECHNIQUES FOR ESTIMATING THE COST OF EQUITY CAPITAL

Recall from Chapter 10 that three basic approaches can be used to estimate the cost of equity: CAPM, dividend yield plus growth

rate (DCF), and cost of debt plus a risk premium. The use of these methods varied considerably from country to country (see Table A).

We noted in Chapter 11 that the CAPM is used most often by U.S. firms. (See the Industry Practice box in Chapter 11 entitled, "Techniques Firms Use to Evaluate Corporate Projects" on page 531.) Except for Australia, this is not the case for Asian/Pacific firms, who instead more often use the other two approaches.

TECHNIQUES FOR ASSESSING RISK

Finally, firms in these six countries rely heavily on scenario and sensitivity analyses to assess project risk. They also use decision trees (which we discuss later in this chapter) and Monte Carlo simulation, but less frequently than the other techniques (see Table B).

SOURCE: George W. Kester et al., "Capital Budgeting Practices in the Asia-Pacific Region: Australia, Hong Kong, Indonesia, Malaysia, Philippines, and Singapore," *Financial Practice and Education*, Vol. 9, No. 1, Spring/Summer 1999, 25–33.

TABLE A

METHOD	AUSTRALIA	HONG KONG	INDONESIA	MALAYSIA	PHILIPPINES	SINGAPORE
CAPM	72.7%	26.9%	0.0%	6.2%	24.1%	17.0%
Dividend yield plus growth rate	16.4	53.8	33.3	50.0	34.5	42.6
Cost of debt plus risk premium	10.9	23.1	53.4	37.5	58.6	42.6

TABLE B

RISK ASSESSMENT TECHNIQUE	AUSTRALIA	HONG KONG	INDONESIA	MALAYSIA	PHILIPPINES	SINGAPORE
Scenario analysis	96%	100%	94%	80%	97%	90%
Sensitivity analysis	100	100	88	83	94	79
Decision tree analysis	44	58	50	37	33	46
Monte Carlo simulation	38	35	25	9	24	35

HIGH-TECH CFOs

Recent developments in technology have made it easier for corporations to utilize complex risk analysis techniques. New software and higher-powered computers enable financial managers to process large amounts of information, so technically astute finance people can consider a broad range of scenarios using computers to estimate the effects of changes in sales, operating costs, interest rates, the overall economy, and even the weather. Given such analysis, financial managers can make better decisions as to which course of action is most likely to generate the optimal trade-off between risk and return.

Done properly, risk analysis can also take account of the correlation between various types of risk. For example, if interest rates and currencies tend to move together in a particular way, this tendency can be incorporated into the model. This can enable financial managers to better determine the likelihood and effect of "worst-case" outcomes.

While this type of risk analysis is undeniably useful, it is only as good as the information and assumptions that go into

constructing the models. Also, risk models frequently involve complex calculations, and they generate output that requires financial managers to have a fair amount of mathematical sophistication. However, technology is helping to solve these problems. New programs have been developed to present risk analysis output in an intuitive way. For example, Andrew Lo, an MIT finance professor, has developed a program that summarizes the risk, return, and liquidity profiles of various strategies using a new data visualization process that enables complicated relationships to be plotted along three-dimensional graphs that are easy to interpret. While some old-guard CFOs may bristle at these new approaches, younger and more computer-savvy CFOs are likely to embrace the technology. As Lo puts it: "The video-game generation just loves these 3-D tools."

SOURCE: Adapted from "The CFO Goes 3-D: Higher Math and Savvy Software Are Crucial," *Business Week*, October 28, 1996, 144, 150.

Monte Carlo simulation is useful, but it is a relatively complex procedure. Therefore, a detailed discussion is best left for advanced finance courses.

SELF-TEST QUESTIONS

List two reasons why, in practice, a project's stand-alone risk is important.

Differentiate between sensitivity and scenario analyses. What advantage does scenario analysis have over sensitivity analysis?

What is Monte Carlo simulation?

PROJECT RISK CONCLUSIONS

We have discussed the three types of risk normally considered in capital budgeting analysis — stand-alone risk, within-firm (or corporate) risk, and market risk — and we have discussed ways of assessing each. However, two important questions remain: (1) Should firms be concerned with stand-alone or corporate risk in their capital budgeting decisions, and (2) what do we do when the stand-alone, within-firm, and market risk assessments lead to different conclusions?

These questions do not have easy answers. From a theoretical standpoint, well-diversified investors should be concerned only with market risk and managers should be concerned only with stock price maximization, and these two factors should lead to the conclusion that market (beta) risk ought to be given virtually all the weight in capital budgeting decisions. However, if investors are not well diversified, if the CAPM does not operate exactly as theory says it should, or if measurement problems keep managers from having confidence in the CAPM approach in capital budgeting, it may be appropriate to give stand-alone and corporate risk more weight than financial theory suggests. Note also that the CAPM ignores bankruptcy costs, even though such costs can be substantial, and the probability of bankruptcy depends on a firm's corporate risk, not on its beta risk. Therefore, even well-diversified investors should want a firm's management to give at least some consideration to a project's corporate risk instead of concentrating entirely on market risk.

Although it would be nice to reconcile these problems and to measure project risk on some absolute scale, the best we can do in practice is to estimate project risk in a somewhat nebulous, relative sense. For example, we can generally say with a fair degree of confidence that a particular project has more or less stand-alone risk than the firm's average project. Then, assuming that stand-alone and corporate risk are highly correlated (which is typical), the project's stand-alone risk will be a good measure of its corporate risk. Finally, assuming that market risk and corporate risk are highly correlated (as is true for most companies), a project with more corporate risk than average will also have more market risk, and vice versa for projects with low corporate risk.[7]

> **SELF-TEST QUESTIONS**
>
> In theory, should a firm be concerned with stand-alone and corporate risk? Should the firm be concerned with these risks in practice?
>
> If a project's stand-alone, corporate, and market risk are highly correlated, would this make the task of measuring risk easier or harder? Explain.

INCORPORATING PROJECT RISK AND CAPITAL STRUCTURE INTO CAPITAL BUDGETING

Capital budgeting can affect a firm's market risk, its corporate risk, or both, but it is extremely difficult to quantify either type of risk. Although it may be possible to reach the general conclusion that one project is riskier than another, it is difficult to develop a really good *quantitative measure* of project risk. This makes it difficult to incorporate differential risk into capital budgeting decisions.

Risk-Adjusted Discount Rate
The discount rate that applies to a particular risky stream of income; the riskier the project's income stream, the higher the discount rate.

Two methods are used to incorporate project risk into capital budgeting. One is called the *certainty equivalent* approach. Here all cash flows that are not known with certainty are scaled down, and the riskier the flow, the lower its certainty equivalent value. The other method, and the one we focus on, is the **risk-adjusted discount rate** approach, under which differential project risk is dealt with by changing the discount rate. Average-risk projects are discounted

---

[7] For example, see M. Chapman Findlay III, Arthur E. Gooding, and Wallace Q. Weaver, Jr., "On the Relevant Risk for Determining Capital Expenditure Hurdle Rates," *Financial Management*, Winter 1976, 9–16.

at the firm's average cost of capital, higher-risk projects are discounted at a higher cost of capital, and lower-risk projects are discounted at a rate below the firm's average cost of capital. Unfortunately, there is no good way of specifying exactly *how much* higher or lower these discount rates should be. Given the present state of the art, risk adjustments are necessarily judgmental and somewhat arbitrary.

As a final consideration, capital structure must also be taken into account if a firm finances different assets in different ways. For example, one division might have a lot of real estate that is well suited as collateral for loans, whereas some other division might have most of its capital tied up in specialized machinery, which is not good collateral. As a result, the division with the real estate might have a higher *debt capacity* than the division with the machinery, hence an optimal capital structure that contains a higher percentage of debt. In this case, the financial staff might calculate the cost of capital differently for the two divisions.[8]

SELF-TEST QUESTION

How are risk-adjusted discount rates used to incorporate project risk into the capital budgeting decision process?

INCORPORATING REAL OPTIONS INTO THE CAPITAL BUDGETING DECISION

Capital budgeting analysis is in many respects straightforward. A project is deemed acceptable if it has a positive NPV, where the NPV is calculated by discounting the estimated cash flows at the project's risk-adjusted cost of capital. However, things often get more complicated in the real world. One complication is that many projects include a variety of embedded **real options** that dramatically affect their value. For example, companies often have to decide not only *if* they should proceed with a project, but also *when* they should proceed with the project. In many instances, this choice can radically affect the project's NPV.

Real Options
Involve real, rather than financial assets. They exist when managers can influence the size and riskiness of a project's cash flows by taking different actions during or at the end of a project's life.

DECISION TREES TO EVALUATE INVESTMENT TIMING OPTIONS

Decision Tree
A diagram that shows all possible outcomes that result from a decision. Each possible outcome is shown as a "branch" on the tree. Decision trees are especially useful to analyze the effects of real options in investment decisions.

Assume that BQC is considering a project that requires an initial investment of $5 million at the beginning of 2002 (or t = 0). The project will generate positive net cash flows at the end of each of the next four years (t = 1, 2, 3, and 4), but the size of the yearly cash flows will depend critically on what happens to market conditions in the future. Figure 12-2 illustrates two **decision trees** that diagram the problem at hand. As shown in the top section, Panel a, there is a 50 percent probability that market conditions will be strong, in which case the

---

[8] We will say more about the optimal capital structure and debt capacity in Chapter 13.

FIGURE 12-2   A Decision Tree for Analyzing the Timing of an Investment

BQC is considering a proposed expansion project. The project requires an initial investment of $5,000,000, and it has an economic life of four years. The project's yearly cash flows will depend on market conditions. BQC is deciding whether to turn down the project, to proceed with it today, or to wait a year before making the decision. Currently, there is a 50% probability that the market will be good and a 50% probability it will be bad. If the decision is postponed for a year, the market's condition will be known. Given the project's risk, all cash flows are discounted at 14%.

a. PROCEED WITH THE PROJECT TODAY

YEAR	2002	2003	2004	2005	2006		NPV	PROBABILITY OF MARKET CONDITION OCCURRENCE	PRODUCT (NPV × PROBABILITY)
	Market is good (50% probability)								
		+2.5M	+2.5M	+2.5M	+2.5M		$2,284,280.76	0.5	$1,142,140
Initial Investment:	−$5M								
		+1.5M	+1.5M	+1.5M	+1.5M		−629,431.54	0.5	−314,715
								Expected NPV =	$ 827,425
	Market is bad (50% probability)								

b. WAIT A YEAR TO SEE IF THE MARKET IS GOOD OR BAD, THEN INVEST ONLY IF THE MARKET IS GOOD

YEAR	2002	2003	2004	2005	2006	2007	NPV	PROBABILITY OF MARKET CONDITION OCCURRENCE	PRODUCT (NPV × PROBABILITY)
	Market is good (50% probability)								
		−5M	+2.5M	+2.5M	+2.5M	+2.5M	$2,284,280.76	0.5	$1,142,140
Wait: Spend $0									
		0	0	0	0	0	0	0.5	0
								Expected NPV =	$1,142,140
	Market is bad (50% probability)								

$$\text{Value of expected NPV in 2002} = \frac{\$1,142,140}{(1.14)} = \$1,001,877.$$

project will generate cash flows of $2.5 million at the end of each of the next four years. There is also a 50 percent probability that demand for the product will be weak, in which case the annual cash flows will be only $1.5 million.

Note that each branch of the decision tree is equivalent to a time line. Thus, the top line, which describes the payoffs under good conditions, has a cash flow of −$5 million at t = 0 and positive cash flows of $2.5 million for Years 1 through 4. BQC considers the project to have above-average risk, hence it will be evaluated using a 14 percent cost of capital. The NPV, if the market is strong, will turn out to be $2,284,280.76. On the other hand, if product demand is weak, the NPV will turn out to be −$629,431.54, so it will be a money loser.

The expected value for the project is found as a weighted average of the NPVs of the two possible outcomes, with the weights being the probabilities for each outcome. With a 50 percent probability for each branch, the expected value of the project, if it is undertaken today, is $827,425, as shown in the last column of Panel a in Figure 12-2. Since the project has a positive NPV, it appears that the company should proceed with it, even though there is a 50–50 chance that it will actually turn out to be a loser.

However, suppose BQC's managers can wait until next year, when more information will be available about market conditions, before making the decision. The best guess *today* is that the project has a 50–50 chance of generating $2.5 million or $1.5 million, hence ending up with a positive or a negative NPV. However, one year from now the company will be better able to estimate whether market conditions will be good or bad. To keep things simple, assume that if the company waits a year, the project's initial investment will still be $5 million, the annual cash flows will still be $2.5 or $1.5 million, but the firm will know for sure whether the market is strong or weak.

Should BQC proceed with the project today, or should it wait a year? In many respects, this decision is similar to choosing among mutually exclusive projects. When comparing two mutually exclusive projects that are both profitable, you should select the one with the highest net present value. In BQC's case, the mutually exclusive choice is between investing in the project today and waiting a year before deciding whether or not to make the investment. The company should select the strategy with the highest expected net present value.

If the company proceeds today, the project's estimated NPV is $827,425. If it waits a year, there is a 50 percent chance that the annual net cash flows will be $2.5 million, which at a 14 percent cost of capital, produces an NPV of $2,284,280.76. However, there is also a 50 percent chance that the annual net cash flows will be only $1.5 million, which translates into an NPV of −$629,431.54. However, under the "Wait" strategy, BQC would know which market condition existed, and it would make the decision to "Go" if conditions were good and make a "No Go" decision if they were bad. Under the No Go decision, no investment is made, hence the NPV will be zero. Thus, if BQC waits a year, there is a 50 percent probability the project will be undertaken, in which case the NPV will be $2,284,280.76, and there is a 50 percent probability the project will not be undertaken, in which case the NPV will be zero. This is illustrated in Panel b of Figure 12-2. As we see in the last column of Panel b in Figure 12-2, the expected NPV under the Wait option is $1,142,140.

Note, though, that all the cash flows under the Wait case are deferred for one year, hence the Wait case NPV is as of a year from now, in 2003 rather than 2002 as in the "Proceed Immediately" case. Therefore, to make the NPVs comparable, we must discount the Wait NPV back for one year to find the project's *value in today's dollars*. The PV of the Wait NPV, discounted at the 14 percent cost of capital, is shown in the lower right part of the figure to be $1,001,877. Since this number exceeds the NPV based on investing today, the analysis suggests that the company should wait to develop the project.

Note that we used 14 percent as the discount rate for both the Proceed Immediately and Wait analyses. Is this reasonable? Probably not. If we wait, we will have a much better idea of market demand. Indeed, in our simplified example, we have implicitly assumed that there is no uncertainty whatever about the cash flows if we wait a year. Therefore, it would be reasonable to discount the cash flows in Panel b of Figure 12-2 at a rate lower than 14 percent, which was the rate used for high-risk projects. A good case could be made for using 10 percent, the rate for low-risk projects, in the Wait case. Of course, a lower discount rate would cause the Wait NPV to be even higher, thus reinforcing the case for waiting.

Other Considerations

When making Proceed Immediately versus Wait decisions, financial managers need to consider several factors. First, if a firm like BQC decides to wait, it may lose any strategic advantages associated with being the first competitor to enter a new line of business, and this could alter the cash flows. On the other hand, as we saw in the above example, waiting enables the company to avoid costly mistakes. In general, the more uncertainty there is about future market conditions, the more attractive it becomes to wait, but this risk reduction can be offset by the loss of the "first mover advantage."

OTHER EXAMPLES OF EMBEDDED OPTIONS

Investment Timing Option
An option as to when to begin a project. Often, if a firm can delay a decision, it can increase a project's expected NPV.

In addition to the **investment timing option**, many projects also include a variety of other embedded strategic options. Some examples are given below.

Growth/Expansion Options

Growth/Expansion Option
If an investment creates the opportunity to make other potentially profitable investments that would not otherwise be possible, then the investment is said to contain a growth/expansion option.

Many projects, if undertaken, will enable the company to pursue other profitable projects down the road. These projects contain **growth/expansion options**. In some cases, a project that appears to have a negative NPV may still be attractive if it opens the door to new products or new markets. For example, many accounting, banking, and other types of firms have opened offices in Hong Kong, even though the offices do not appear to be profitable, because they want to prepare for possible entry into the vast China market. Likewise, motion picture producers may go ahead with a movie that they suspect may not fully cover its costs if they anticipate that there is some chance that the movie will lead to a profitable sequel. Similarly, a company may decide to build a larger headquarters facility than it currently needs because it recognizes that there is a chance it will want to expand headquarters staff over time.

Abandonment/Shutdown Options

Abandonment Option
The option of abandoning a project if operating cash flows turn out to be lower than expected. This option can both raise expected profitability and lower project risk.

After undertaking a project, managers may have the option to abandon or shut down the project if it is later found to be unprofitable. **Abandonment options** can reduce a project's loss potential, and this can both increase expected cash flows and reduce project risk. Therefore, including abandonment possibilities in the capital budgeting decision can increase a proposed project's expected NPV.

Coca-Cola's "New Coke" is an example of an abandonment situation. Shortly after its launch, it became apparent that the product would never be the money-maker Coke had anticipated. Note that Coca-Cola faced risks when it embarked on the project: Future operating cash flows and abandonment values might be lower than expected. Coca-Cola benefited by avoiding the "downside" losses that would have occurred due to the lower-than-anticipated operating cash flows by terminating the New Coke project. In general, the opportunity to abandon projects allows companies to limit downside losses.

Flexibility Options

Flexibility Option
The option to modify operations depending on how conditions develop during a project's life, especially the type of output produced or the inputs used.

It is often worth spending money today if it allows you to maintain flexibility over time. These investments contain **flexibility options**. For example, consider a situation where two competing technologies are vying to become the industry standard. Assume that BQC is developing a product whose design depends critically on which of the two competing technologies wins out. BQC might be better off spending more on product development if the added expenditures give the company the flexibility to use either technology. Similarly, a computer company might invest more in a plant to produce lap top computers if the extra investment meant that the plant would be flexible enough to produce desk top computers should demand turn out to be stronger in that segment of the market.

SELF-TEST QUESTIONS

What is a decision tree, and how is it used in capital budgeting?

Briefly illustrate an investment timing option.

Identify some examples of projects with embedded options.

Explain why the following statement is true: "In general, the more uncertainty there is about future market conditions, the more attractive it may be to wait."

THE OPTIMAL CAPITAL BUDGET

So far we have described various factors that managers consider when they evaluate individual projects. For planning purposes, managers also need to forecast the total amount of investment in order to determine how much capital must be raised. While every firm goes through this process in its own unique way, there are some commonly used procedures for estimating the optimal capital budget. We use Citrus Grove Corporation, a producer of fruit juices, to illustrate how this process works in practice.

Step 1. The financial vice-president obtains an estimate of her firm's overall composite WACC. As we discussed in Chapter 10, this composite WACC is based on market conditions, the firm's capital structure, and the riskiness of its assets. Citrus Grove's projects are roughly similar from year to year in terms of their risks.

Step 2. The corporate WACC is scaled up or down for each of the firm's divisions to reflect the division's capital structure and risk characteristics. Citrus Grove, for example, assigns a factor of 0.9 to its stable low-risk fresh citrus juice division, but a factor of 1.1 to its more exotic fruit juice group. Therefore, if the corporate cost of capital is determined to be 10.50 percent, the cost for the citrus juice division is $0.9(10.50\%) = 9.45\%$, while that for the exotic juice division is $1.1(10.50\%) = 11.55\%$.

Step 3. Financial managers within each of the firm's divisions estimate the relevant cash flows and risks of each of their potential projects. The estimated cash flows should explicitly consider any real options embedded in the projects, which includes any opportunities to repeat the project at a later date. Then, within each division, projects are classified into one of three groups — high risk, average risk, and low risk — and the same 0.9 and 1.1 factors are used to adjust the divisional cost of capital estimates. (A factor of 1 would be used for an average-risk project.) For example, a low-risk project in the citrus juice division would be assigned a cost of capital of 0.9(9.45%) = 8.51%, while a high-risk project in the exotic juice division would have a cost of 1.1(11.55%) = 12.71%.

Step 4. Each project's NPV is then determined, using its risk-adjusted cost of capital. The optimal capital budget consists of all independent projects with positive NPVs plus those mutually exclusive projects with the highest positive NPVs.

In estimating its optimal capital budget, we assumed that Citrus Grove will be able to obtain financing for all of its profitable projects. This assumption is reasonable for large, mature firms with good track records. However, smaller firms, new firms, and firms with dubious track records may have difficulties raising capital, even for projects that the firm concludes have positive NPVs. In such circumstances, the size of the firm's capital budget may be constrained. This circumstance is called **capital rationing.** In such situations capital is scarce, and it should be used in the most efficient way possible. Procedures are available for allocating capital so as to maximize the firm's aggregate NPV subject to the constraint that the capital rationing ceiling is not exceeded. However, due to its complexity, the details of this process are best left for advanced finance courses.

Capital Rationing
A situation in which a constraint is placed on the total size of the firm's capital budget.

The four steps outlined above also assume that the accepted projects have, on average, about the same debt-carrying capacity as the firm's existing assets. If this is not true, the corporate WACC determined in Step 1 will not be correct, and it will have to be adjusted.

The procedures discussed in this section cannot be implemented with much precision, but they do force the firm to think carefully about each division's relative risk, about the risk of each project within the divisions, and about the relationship between the total amount of capital raised and the cost of that capital. Further, the process forces the firm to adjust its capital budget to reflect capital market conditions. If the costs of debt and equity rise, this fact will be reflected in the cost of capital used to evaluate projects, and projects that would be marginally acceptable when capital costs were low would (correctly) be ruled unacceptable when capital costs become high.

SELF-TEST QUESTIONS

Explain how a financial manager might estimate his or her firm's optimal capital budget.

In estimating the optimal capital budget, what assumption is typically made concerning the amount of capital that can be raised?

What is capital rationing?

Throughout the book, we have indicated that the value of any asset depends on the amount, timing, and riskiness of the cash flows it produces. In this chapter, we developed a framework for analyzing a project's cash flows and risk. Given a set of inputs, we can use the techniques described back in Chapter 11 to evaluate whether projects should be accepted or rejected. In addition, in this chapter we briefly introduced real options and discussed the procedures for estimating the optimal capital budget.

- The most important (and most difficult) step in analyzing a capital budgeting project is **estimating the incremental after-tax cash flows** the project will produce.

- **Project cash flow** is different from accounting income. Project cash flow reflects: (1) **cash outlays for fixed assets,** (2) the **tax shield provided by depreciation,** and (3) cash flows due to **changes in net operating working capital.** Project cash flow does not include **interest payments.**

- In determining incremental cash flows, **opportunity costs** (the cash flows forgone by using an asset) must be included, but **sunk costs** (cash outlays that have been made and that cannot be recouped) are not included. Any **externalities** (effects of a project on other parts of the firm) should also be reflected in the analysis.

- **Cannibalization** occurs when a new project leads to a reduction in sales of an existing product.

- Capital projects often require an additional investment in **net operating working capital (NOWC).** An increase in NOWC must be included in the Year 0 initial cash outlay, and then shown as a cash inflow in the final year of the project.

- The incremental cash flows from a typical project can be classified into three categories: (1) **initial investment outlay,** (2) **operating cash flows over the project's life,** and (3) **terminal year cash flows.**

- Since stockholders are generally diversified, **market risk** is theoretically the most relevant measure of risk. Market, or beta, risk is important because beta affects the cost of capital, which, in turn, affects stock prices.

- **Corporate risk** is important because it influences the firm's ability to use low-cost debt, to maintain smooth operations over time, and to avoid crises that might consume management's energy and disrupt its employees, customers, suppliers, and community.

- **Sensitivity analysis** is a technique that shows how much a project's NPV will change in response to a given change in an input variable such as sales, other things held constant.

- **Scenario analysis** is a risk analysis technique in which the best- and worst-case NPVs are compared with the project's expected NPV.

- **Monte Carlo simulation** is a risk analysis technique that uses a computer to simulate future events and thus to estimate the profitability and riskiness of a project.

- The **risk-adjusted discount rate,** or **project cost of capital,** is the rate used to evaluate a particular project. It is based on the corporate WACC, which is increased for projects that are riskier than the firm's average project but decreased for less risky projects.

- **Real options** exist when managers can influence the size and riskiness of a project's cash flows by taking different actions during or at the end of the project's life.

- Many projects include a variety of **embedded options** that can dramatically affect the true NPV. Examples of embedded options include (1) the option to accelerate or delay a project, (2) "growth options" that might enable a firm to pursue other profitable future projects, (3) the option to abandon or shut down the project, and (4) "flexibility" options that allow a firm to modify its operations over time.

- Projects whose capital outlays are made in stages over several years are often evaluated using **decision trees.** Decision trees are also useful for identifying real options, which, in turn, may materially affect a project's true NPV.

- An **investment timing option** involves not only the decision of *whether* to proceed with a project but also the decision of *when* to proceed with it. This opportunity to affect a project's timing can dramatically change its estimated value.

- If an investment creates the opportunity to make other potentially profitable investments that would not otherwise be possible, then the investment is said to contain a **growth option.**

- The **abandonment option** is the ability to abandon a project if the operating cash flows and/or abandonment value turn out to be lower than expected. It reduces the riskiness of a project and increases its value.

- A **flexibility option** is the option to modify operations depending on how conditions develop during a project's life, especially the type of output produced or the inputs used.

- For planning purposes, managers need to forecast the total dollar amount that will be required to fund the acceptable projects, or the **total capital budget** for the planning period. They need this information to determine how much capital will have to be raised.

- **Capital rationing** occurs when management places a constraint on the size of the firm's capital budget during a particular period.

QUESTIONS

12-1 Operating cash flows rather than accounting profits are listed in Table 12-1. What is the basis for this emphasis on cash flows as opposed to net income?

12-2 Explain why sunk costs should not be included in a capital budgeting analysis, but opportunity costs and externalities should be included.

12-3 Explain how net operating working capital is recovered at the end of a project's life, and why it is included in a capital budgeting analysis.

12-4 Define (a) simulation analysis, (b) scenario analysis, and (c) sensitivity analysis. If AT&T were considering two investments, one calling for the expenditure of $200 million to develop a satellite communications system and the other involving the expenditure of $12,000 for a new truck, on which one would the company be more likely to use simulation analysis?

12-5 What factors should a company consider when it decides whether to invest in a project today or to wait until more information becomes available?

12-6 In general, do timing options make it more or less likely that a project will be accepted today?

12-7 If a company has an option to abandon a project, would this tend to make the company more or less likely to accept the project today?

SELF-TEST PROBLEMS (SOLUTIONS APPEAR IN APPENDIX B)

ST-1
Key terms

Define each of the following terms:
a. Relevant cash flow
b. Incremental cash flow; sunk cost; opportunity cost; externalities; cannibalization
c. Change in net operating working capital; new expansion project
d. Replacement project
e. Sensitivity analysis
f. Base-case NPV
g. Scenario analysis
h. Worst-case scenario; best-case scenario; base case
i. Monte Carlo simulation
j. Risk-adjusted discount rate
k. Real options; decision tree; investment timing option
l. Growth/expansion option; abandonment option; flexibility option
m. Capital rationing

ST-2
New project analysis

You have been asked by the president of Ellis Construction Company, headquartered in Toledo, to evaluate the proposed acquisition of a new earthmover. The mover's basic price is $50,000, and it will cost another $10,000 to modify it for special use by Ellis Construction. Assume that the mover falls into the MACRS 3-year class. (See Table 12A-2 for MACRS recovery allowance percentages.) It will be sold after 3 years for $20,000, and it will require an increase in net operating working capital (spare parts inventory) of $2,000. The earthmover purchase will have no effect on revenues, but it is expected to save Ellis $20,000 per year in before-tax operating costs, mainly labor. Ellis's marginal federal-plus-state tax rate is 40 percent.
a. What is the company's net investment if it acquires the earthmover? (That is, what are the Year 0 cash flows?)
b. What are the operating cash flows in Years 1, 2, and 3?
c. What is the terminal cash flow?
d. If the project's cost of capital is 10 percent, should the earthmover be purchased?
e. Suppose that the firm's management is unsure about the savings in before-tax operating costs and the earthmover's salvage value.
   (1) What is the earthmover's net present value if the savings in before-tax operating costs increase by 15 percent above the firm's original expectations? Would this change the firm's decision to acquire the earthmover from the decision made in part d?
   (2) What is the earthmover's net present value if the earthmover's salvage value increases by 10 percent above the firm's original expectations? Assume no other change in data from the original problem. Would this change the firm's decision to acquire the earthmover from the decision made in part d?
f. Suppose the firm's capital budgeting manager suggests that the firm do a scenario analysis for this project because of the sensitivities of both the equipment's cost savings and its salvage value. After an extensive analysis, he comes up with the following probabilities and values for the scenario analysis:

SCENARIO	PROBABILITY	BEFORE-TAX SAVINGS	SALVAGE VALUE
Worst case	30%	$15,000	$18,000
Base case	40	20,000	20,000
Best case	30	25,000	24,000

What is the project's expected net present value (NPV), the standard deviation of the NPV, and the coefficient of variation of the NPV?

ST-3

Corporate risk analysis

The staff of Heymann Manufacturing has estimated the following net cash flows and probabilities for a new manufacturing process:

	NET CASH FLOWS		
YEAR	P = 0.2	P = 0.6	P = 0.2
0	($100,000)	($100,000)	($100,000)
1	20,000	30,000	40,000
2	20,000	30,000	40,000
3	20,000	30,000	40,000
4	20,000	30,000	40,000
5	20,000	30,000	40,000
5*	0	20,000	30,000

Line 0 gives the cost of the process, Lines 1 through 5 give operating cash flows, and Line 5* contains the estimated salvage values. Heymann's cost of capital for an average-risk project is 10 percent.

a. Assume that the project has average risk. Find the project's expected NPV. (Hint: Use expected values for the net cash flow in each year.)

b. Find the best-case and worst-case NPVs. What is the probability of occurrence of the worst case if the cash flows are perfectly dependent (perfectly positively correlated) over time? If they are independent over time?

c. Assume that all the cash flows are perfectly positively correlated, that is, there are only three possible cash flow streams over time: (1) the worst case, (2) the most likely, or base, case, and (3) the best case, with probabilities of 0.2, 0.6, and 0.2, respectively. These cases are represented by each of the columns in the table. Find the expected NPV, its standard deviation, and its coefficient of variation.

d. The coefficient of variation of Heymann's average project is in the range 0.8 to 1.0. If the coefficient of variation of a project being evaluated is greater than 1.0, 2 percentage points are added to the firm's cost of capital. Similarly, if the coefficient of variation is less than 0.8, 1 percentage point is deducted from the cost of capital. What is the project's cost of capital? Should Heymann accept or reject the project?

STARTER PROBLEMS

12-1

Investment outlay

Truman Industries is considering an expansion project. The necessary equipment could be purchased for $9 million, and the project would also require an initial $3 million investment in net operating working capital. The company's tax rate is 40 percent. What is the project's initial investment outlay?

12-2

Operating cash flow

Eisenhower Communications is trying to estimate the first-year operating cash flow (at $t = 1$) for a proposed project. The financial staff has collected the following information:

Projected sales	$10 million
Operating costs (excluding depreciation)	7 million
Depreciation	2 million
Interest expense	2 million

The company faces a 40 percent tax rate. What is the project's operating cash flow for the first year ($t = 1$)?

12-3

Net salvage value

Kennedy Air Lines is now in the terminal year of a project. The equipment originally cost $20 million, of which 80 percent has been depreciated. Kennedy can sell the used equipment today to another airline for $5 million, and its tax rate is 40 percent. What is the equipment's after-tax net salvage value?

12-4
Optimal capital budget

Hampton Manufacturing estimates that its WACC is 12 percent if equity comes from retained earnings. However, if the company issues new stock to raise new equity, it estimates that its WACC will rise to 12.5 percent. The company believes that it will exhaust its retained earnings at $3,250,000 of capital due to the number of highly profitable projects available to the firm and its limited earnings. The company is considering the following seven investment projects:

PROJECT	SIZE	IRR
A	$ 750,000	14.0%
B	1,250,000	13.5
C	1,250,000	13.2
D	1,250,000	13.0
E	750,000	12.7
F	750,000	12.3
G	750,000	12.2

Assume that each of these projects is independent and that each is just as risky as the firm's existing assets. Which set of projects should be accepted, and what is the firm's optimal capital budget?

12-5
Optimal capital budget

Refer to Problem 12-4. Now assume that Projects C and D are mutually exclusive. Project D has an NPV of $400,000, whereas Project C has an NPV of $350,000. Which set of projects should be accepted, and what is the firm's optimal capital budget?

12-6
Risk-adjusted optimal capital budget

Refer to Problem 12-4. Assume again that each of the projects is independent but that management decides to incorporate project risk differentials. Management judges Projects B, C, D, and E to have average risk, Project A to have high risk, and Projects F and G to have low risk. The company adds 2 percentage points to the cost of capital of those projects that are significantly more risky than average, and it subtracts 2 percentage points from the cost of capital for those that are substantially less risky than average. Which set of projects should be accepted, and what is the firm's optimal capital budget?

EXAM-TYPE PROBLEMS

The problems included in this section are set up in such a way that they could be used as multiple-choice exam problems.

12-7
Scenario analysis

Worldwide Technologies encounters significant uncertainty in its sales volume and price with its primary product. The firm uses scenario analysis to determine an expected NPV, which it then uses in its capital budget. The base-case, best-case, and worst-case scenarios and probabilities are provided in the following table. What is this product's expected NPV, standard deviation, and coefficient of variation?

SCENARIO	PROBABILITY OF OUTCOME	UNIT SALES VOLUME	SALES PRICE	NPV (IN 000'S)
Worst case	0.30	10,800	$6,480	−$10,800
Base case	0.50	18,000	7,560	+23,400
Best case	0.20	23,400	7,920	+50,400

12-8
Scenario analysis

Huang Industries is considering a proposed project for its capital budget. The company estimates that the project's NPV is $12 million. This estimate assumes that the economy and market conditions will be average over the next few years. The company's CFO, however, forecasts that there is only a 50 percent chance that the economy will be average. Recognizing this uncertainty, she has also performed the following scenario analysis:

ECONOMIC SCENARIO	PROBABILITY OF OUTCOME	NPV
Recession	0.05	($70 million)
Below average	0.20	(25 million)
Average	0.50	12 million
Above average	0.20	20 million
Boom	0.05	30 million

What is the project's expected NPV, its standard deviation, and its coefficient of variation?

12-9
New project analysis

Holmes Manufacturing Company is considering the purchase of a new machine for $250,000 that will reduce manufacturing costs by $90,000 annually. Holmes will use the 3-year MACRS accelerated method to depreciate the machine, and it expects to sell the machine at the end of its 5-year operating life for $23,000. (See Table 12A-2 for MACRS recovery allowance percentages.) The firm will need to increase net operating working capital by $25,000 when the machine is installed, but required operating working capital will return to the original level when the machine is sold after 5 years. Holmes' marginal tax rate is 40 percent, and it uses a 10 percent cost of capital to evaluate projects of this nature.

a. What is the project's NPV?
b. Assume the firm is unsure about the savings to operating costs that will occur with the new machine's acquisition. Management believes these savings may deviate from their base-case value ($90,000) by as much as plus or minus 20 percent. What is the NPV of the project under both situations?
c. Suppose the firm's chief financial officer suggests that the firm do a scenario analysis for this project because of concerns raised about data assumptions, particularly the operating cost savings, the new machine's salvage value, and the net operating working capital (NOWC) requirement. After an extensive analysis, she arrives with the following probabilities and values for the scenario analysis:

SCENARIO	PROBABILITY	COST SAVINGS	SALVAGE VALUE	NOWC
Worst case	0.35	$ 72,000	$18,000	$30,000
Base case	0.35	90,000	23,000	25,000
Best case	0.30	108,000	28,000	20,000

What is the project's expected net present value, its standard deviation, and its coefficient of variation?

12-10
Investment timing option

Twain Hotels is interested in developing a new hotel in Tokyo. The company estimates that the hotel would require an initial investment of $20 million. Twain expects that the hotel will produce positive cash flows of $3 million a year at the end of each of the next 20 years. The project's cost of capital is 12 percent.

a. What is the project's net present value?
b. While Twain expects the cash flows to be $3 million a year, it recognizes that the cash flows could, in fact, be much higher or lower, depending on whether the Japanese government imposes a large hotel tax. One year from now, Twain will know whether the tax will be imposed. There is a 25 percent chance that the tax will be imposed, in which case the yearly cash flows will be only $2.4 million. At the same time, there is a 75 percent chance that the tax will not be imposed, in which case the yearly cash flows will be $3.2 million. Twain is deciding whether to proceed with the hotel today or to wait 1 year to find out whether the tax will be imposed. If Twain waits a year, the initial investment will remain at $20 million. Assume that all cash flows are discounted at 12 percent. Should Twain proceed with the project today or should it wait a year before deciding?

PROBLEMS

12-11
New project analysis

You have been asked by the president of your company to evaluate the proposed acquisition of a spectrometer for the firm's R&D department. The equipment's base price is $140,000, and it would cost another $30,000 to modify it for special use by your firm. The spectrometer, which falls into the MACRS 3-year class, would be sold after 3 years for $60,000. (See Table 12A-2 for MACRS recovery allowance percentages.) Use of the equipment would require an increase in net operating working capital (spare parts inventory) of $8,000. The spectrometer would have no effect on revenues, but it is expected to save the firm $50,000 per year in before-tax operating costs, mainly labor. The firm's marginal federal-plus-state tax rate is 40 percent.

a. What is the net cost of the spectrometer? (That is, what is the Year 0 net cash flow?)
b. What are the net operating cash flows in Years 1, 2, and 3?
c. What is the terminal cash flow?
d. If the project's cost of capital is 12 percent, should the spectrometer be purchased?

12-12
New project analysis

The Harris Company is evaluating the proposed acquisition of a new milling machine. The machine's base price is $108,000, and it would cost another $12,500 to modify it for special use by your firm. The machine falls into the MACRS 3-year class, and it would be sold after 3 years for $65,000. (See Table 12A-2 for MACRS recovery allowance percentages.) The machine would require an increase in net operating working capital (inventory) of $5,500. The milling machine would have no effect on revenues, but it is expected to save the firm $44,000 per year in before-tax operating costs, mainly labor. Harris's marginal tax rate is 35 percent.

a. What is the net cost of the machine for capital budgeting purposes? (That is, what is the Year 0 net cash flow?)
b. What are the net operating cash flows in Years 1, 2, and 3?
c. What is the terminal cash flow?
d. If the project's cost of capital is 12 percent, should the machine be purchased?

12-13
Risky cash flows

The Butler-Perkins Company (BPC) must decide between two mutually exclusive investment projects. Each project costs $6,750 and has an expected life of 3 years. Annual net cash flows from each project begin 1 year after the initial investment is made and have the following probability distributions:

PROJECT A		PROJECT B	
PROBABILITY	NET CASH FLOWS	PROBABILITY	NET CASH FLOWS
0.2	$6,000	0.2	$ 0
0.6	6,750	0.6	6,750
0.2	7,500	0.2	18,000

BPC has decided to evaluate the riskier project at a 12 percent rate and the less risky project at a 10 percent rate.

a. What is the expected value of the annual net cash flows from each project? What is the coefficient of variation (CV)? (Hint: $\sigma_B = \$5,798$ and $CV_B = 0.76$.)
b. What is the risk-adjusted NPV of each project?
c. If it were known that Project B's cash flows were negatively correlated with other cash flows of the firm whereas Project A's cash flows were positively correlated, how would this knowledge affect the decision? If Project B's cash flows were negatively correlated with gross domestic product (GDP), would that influence your assessment of its risk?

12-14
Scenario analysis

Your firm, Agrico Products, is considering the purchase of a tractor that will have a net cost of $36,000, will increase pre-tax operating cash flows before taking account of depreciation effects by $12,000 per year, and will be depreciated on a straight-line basis over 5 years at the rate of $7,200 per year, beginning the first year. (Annual cash flows will be $12,000, before taxes, plus the tax savings that result from $7,200 of depreciation.) The board of directors is having a heated debate about whether the tractor will actually last 5 years. Specifically, Elizabeth Brannigan insists that she knows of some tractors that have lasted only 4 years. Philip Glasgo agrees with Brannigan, but he argues that most tractors do give 5 years of service. Laura Evans says she has known some to last for as long as 8 years.

Given this discussion, the board asks you to prepare a scenario analysis to ascertain the importance of the uncertainty about the tractor's life. Assume a 40 percent marginal federal-plus-state tax rate, a zero salvage value, and a cost of capital of 10 percent. (Hint: Here straight-line depreciation is based on the MACRS class life of the tractor and is not affected by the actual life. Also, ignore the half-year convention for this problem.)

12-15
Abandonment value

The Scampini Supplies Company recently purchased a new delivery truck. The new truck costs $22,500, and it is expected to generate net after-tax operating cash flows, including depreciation, of $6,250 per year. The truck has a 5-year expected life. The expected year-end abandonment values (salvage values after tax adjustments) for the truck are given below. The company's cost of capital is 10 percent.

YEAR	ANNUAL OPERATING CASH FLOW	ABANDONMENT VALUE
0	($22,500)	—
1	6,250	17,500
2	6,250	14,000
3	6,250	11,000
4	6,250	5,000
5	6,250	0

a. Should the firm operate the truck until the end of its 5-year physical life; if not, what is its optimal economic life?
b. Would the introduction of abandonment values, in addition to operating cash flows, ever *reduce* the expected NPV and/or IRR of a project?

12-16
Investment timing option

The Bush Oil Company is deciding whether to drill for oil on a tract of land that the company owns. The company estimates that the project would cost $8 million today. Bush estimates that once drilled, the oil will generate positive net cash flows of $4 million a year at the end of each of the next 4 years. While the company is fairly confident about its cash flow forecast, it recognizes that if it waits 2 years, it would have more information about the local geology as well as the price of oil. Bush estimates that if it waits 2 years, the project would cost $9 million. Moreover, if it waits 2 years, there is a 90 percent chance that the net cash flows would be $4.2 million a year for 4 years, and there is a 10 percent chance that the cash flows will be $2.2 million a year for 4 years. Assume that all cash flows are discounted at 10 percent.
a. If the company chooses to drill today, what is the project's net present value?
b. Would it make sense to wait 2 years before deciding whether to drill?

SPREADSHEET PROBLEM

12-17
Issues in capital budgeting

Webmasters.com has developed a powerful new server that would be used for corporations' Internet activities. It would cost $10 million to purchase the equipment necessary to manufacture the server, and $3 million of net operating working capital would be required. The servers would sell for $24,000 per unit, and Webmasters believes that variable costs would amount to $17,500 per unit. The company's fixed costs would also rise by $1 million per year. It would take 1 year to purchase the required equipment and set up operations, and the server project would have a life of 4 years. Conditions are expected to remain stable during each year of the operating life; that is, unit sales, sales price, and costs would be unchanged. If the project is undertaken, it must be continued for the entire 4 years. Also, the project's returns are expected to be highly correlated with returns on the firm's other assets. The firm believes it could sell 1,000 units.

The equipment would be depreciated over a 5-year period, using MACRS rates as described in Appendix 12A. The estimated market value of the equipment at the end of the project's 4-year life is $500,000. Webmasters' federal-plus-state tax rate is 40 percent. Its cost of capital is 10 percent for average-risk projects, defined as projects with a coefficient of variation of NPV between 0.8 and 1.2. Low-risk projects are evaluated with a WACC of 8 percent, and high-risk projects are evaluated at 13 percent.

a. Develop a spreadsheet model and use it to find the project's NPV, IRR, and payback. (Hint: You might want to modify the model on file 12MODEL.xls rather than create an entirely new model.)

b. Now conduct a sensitivity analysis to determine the sensitivity of NPV to changes in the sales price, variable costs per unit, and number of units sold. Set these variables' values at 10 percent and 20 percent above and below their base-case values. Include a graph in your analysis.

c. Now conduct a scenario analysis. Assume that there is a 25 percent probability that "best-case" conditions, with each of the variables discussed in part b being 20 percent better than its base-case value, will occur. There is a 25 percent probability of "worst-case" conditions, with the variables 20 percent worse than base, and a 50 percent probability of base-case conditions.

d. If the project appears to be more or less risky than an average project, find its risk-adjusted NPV, IRR, and payback.

e. On the basis of information in the problem, would you recommend that the project be accepted?

CYBER PROBLEM

12-18

Issues in capital budgeting — Coca-Cola

The information related to this cyberproblem is likely to change over time, due to the release of new information and the ever-changing nature of the World Wide Web. Accordingly, we will periodically update the problem on the textbook's web site. To avoid problems, please check for updates before proceeding with the cyberproblems.

A company's capital budgeting program evolves from and is a function of its corporate strategy. The firm must evaluate itself and identify its place and direction in the business environment. Issues of liquidity and capital investment become primal

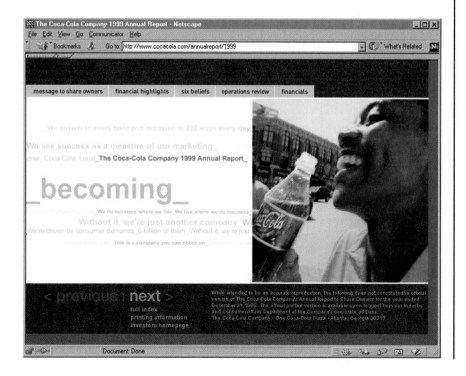

necessities as the firm strives to maximize shareholder value by generating free cash flows. To answer the following questions, first refer to Coca-Cola's 1999 annual report at **http://www.cocacola.com/annualreport/1999.** Click on message to shareowners, scroll down to the full index, and click on management's discussion and analysis.

a. How does Coca-Cola define its business?

b. Briefly discuss Coca-Cola's liquidity position and capital resources. How are these factors expected to influence Coca-Cola's ability to meet its financial targets?

c. How does Coca-Cola define free cash flow (FCF)? What was Coca-Cola's free cash flow in 1999?

d. How does the 1999 free cash flow compare with that in 1998? What are some reasons for the difference?

e. As a multinational corporation, Coca-Cola faces a number of additional risks, including exchange rate risk. How has Coca-Cola prepared for the European Union's new common currency, the Euro? What effect is the Euro expected to have on Coca-Cola's consolidated financial statements?

INTEGRATED CASE

ALLIED FOOD PRODUCTS

12-19 Capital Budgeting and Cash Flow Estimation After seeing Snapple's success with noncola soft drinks and learning of Coke's and Pepsi's interest, Allied Food Products has decided to consider an expansion of its own in the fruit juice business. The product being considered is fresh lemon juice. Assume that you were recently hired as assistant to the director of capital budgeting, and you must evaluate the new project.

The lemon juice would be produced in an unused building adjacent to Allied's Fort Myers plant; Allied owns the building, which is fully depreciated. The required equipment would cost $200,000, plus an additional $40,000 for shipping and installation. In addition, inventories would rise by $25,000, while accounts payable would go up by $5,000. All of these costs would be incurred at t = 0. By a special ruling, the machinery could be depreciated under the MACRS system as 3-year property.

The project is expected to operate for 4 years, at which time it will be terminated. The cash inflows are assumed to begin 1 year after the project is undertaken, or at t = 1, and to continue out to t = 4. At the end of the project's life (t = 4), the equipment is expected to have a salvage value of $25,000.

Unit sales are expected to total 100,000 cans per year, and the expected sales price is $2.00 per can. Cash operating costs for the project (total operating costs less depreciation) are expected to total 60 percent of dollar sales. Allied's tax rate is 40 percent, and its weighted average cost of capital is 10 percent. Tentatively, the lemon juice project is assumed to be of equal risk to Allied's other assets.

You have been asked to evaluate the project and to make a recommendation as to whether it should be accepted or rejected. To guide you in your analysis, your boss gave you the following set of questions.

a. Draw a time line that shows when the net cash inflows and outflows will occur, and explain how the time line can be used to help structure the analysis.

b. Allied has a standard form that is used in the capital budgeting process; see Table IC12-1. Part of the table has been completed, but you must replace the blanks with the missing numbers. Complete the table in the following steps:

(1) Fill in the blanks under Year 0 for the initial investment outlay.

(2) Complete the table for unit sales, sales price, total revenues, and operating costs excluding depreciation.

(3) Complete the depreciation data.

(4) Now complete the table down to operating income after taxes, and then down to net cash flows.

(5) Now fill in the blanks under Year 4 for the terminal cash flows, and complete the net cash flow line. Discuss net operating working capital. What would have happened if the machinery were sold for less than its book value?

c. (1) Allied uses debt in its capital structure, so some of the money used to finance the project will be debt. Given this fact, should the projected cash flows be revised to show projected interest charges? Explain.

(2) Suppose you learned that Allied had spent $50,000 to renovate the building last year, expensing these costs. Should this cost be reflected in the analysis? Explain.

(3) Now suppose you learned that Allied could lease its building to another party and earn $25,000 per year. Should that fact be reflected in the analysis? If so, how?

(4) Now assume that the lemon juice project would take away profitable sales from Allied's fresh orange juice business. Should that fact be reflected in your analysis? If so, how?

Allied's Lemon Juice Project (Total Cost in Thousands)

END OF YEAR:	0	1	2	3	4
I. INVESTMENT OUTLAY					
Equipment cost					
Installation					
Increase in inventory					
Increase in accounts payable	_____				
Total net investment	=======				
II. OPERATING CASH FLOWS					
Unit sales (thousands)			100		
Price/unit		$ 2.00	$ 2.00	_____	_____
Total revenues		_____	_____	_____	$200.0
Operating costs excluding depreciation			$120.0		
Depreciation		_____	_____	36.0	16.8
Total costs		$199.2	$228.0	_____	_____
Operating income before taxes				$44.0	
Taxes on operating income		0.3	_____		25.3
Operating income after taxes				$26.4	
Depreciation		79.2	_____	36.0	_____
Operating cash flow	$ 0.0	$ 79.7	=====	=====	$ 54.7
III. TERMINAL YEAR CASH FLOWS					
Return of net operating working capital					
Salvage value					
Tax on salvage value					_____
Total termination cash flows					=======
IV. NET CASH FLOWS					
Net cash flow	($260.0)	=====	=====	=====	$ 89.7
V. RESULTS					
NPV =					
IRR =					
MIRR =					
Payback =					

d. Disregard all the assumptions made in part c, and assume there was no alternative use for the building over the next 4 years. Now calculate the project's NPV, IRR, MIRR, and regular payback. Do these indicators suggest that the project should be accepted?

e. If this project had been a replacement rather than an expansion project, how would the analysis have changed?

Think about the changes that would have to occur in the cash flow table.

f. Assume that inflation is expected to average 5 percent over the next 4 years; that this expectation is reflected in the WACC; and that inflation will increase variable costs and revenues by the same percentage, 5 percent. Does it appear that inflation has been dealt with properly in the

TABLE IC12-2	Allied's Lemon Juice Project Considering Inflation (in Thousands)				
	YEAR				
	0	**1**	**2**	**3**	**4**
Investment in:					
Fixed assets	($240)				
Net operating working capital	(20)				
Unit sales (thousands)		100	100	100	100
Sales price (dollars)		$2.100	$2.205	$2.315	$2.431
Total revenues		$210.0	$220.5	$231.5	$243.1
Cash operating costs (60%)		126.0	132.3	138.9	145.9
Depreciation		79.2	108.0	36.0	16.8
Operating income before taxes		$ 4.8	($ 19.8)	$ 56.6	$ 80.4
Taxes on operating income (40%)		1.9	(7.9)	22.6	32.1
Operating income after taxes		$ 2.9	($ 11.9)	$ 34.0	$ 48.3
Plus depreciation		79.2	108.0	36.0	16.8
Operating cash flow		$ 82.1	$ 96.1	$ 70.0	$ 65.1
Salvage value					25.0
Tax on SV (40%)					(10.0)
Recovery of NOWC					20.0
Net cash flow	($260)	$ 82.1	$ 96.1	$ 70.0	$100.1
Cumulative cash flows for payback:	(260.0)	(177.9)	(81.8)	(11.8)	88.3
Compounded inflows for MIRR:		109.2	116.3	77.0	100.1
Terminal value of inflows:					402.6

NPV at 10% cost of capital = $15.0

IRR   = 12.6%

MIRR   = 11.6%

analysis? If not, what should be done, and how would the required adjustment affect the decision? You can modify the numbers in the table to quantify your results.

Although inflation was considered in the initial analysis, the riskiness of the project was not considered. The expected cash flows, considering inflation (in thousands of dollars), are given in Table IC12-2. Allied's overall cost of capital (WACC) is 10 percent.

You have been asked to answer the following questions.

g. (1) What are the three levels, or types, of project risk that are normally considered?
(2) Which type is most relevant?
(3) Which type is easiest to measure?
(4) Are the three types of risk generally highly correlated?

h. (1) What is sensitivity analysis?
(2) Discuss how one would perform a sensitivity analysis on the unit sales, salvage value, and cost of capital for the project. Assume that each of these variables deviates from its base-case, or expected, value by plus and minus 10, 20, and 30 percent. Explain how you would calculate the NPV, IRR, MIRR, and payback for each case.
(3) What is the primary weakness of sensitivity analysis? What are its primary advantages?

i. Assume that you are confident about the estimates of all the variables that affect the cash flows except unit sales. If product acceptance is poor, sales would be only 75,000 units a year, while a strong consumer response would produce sales of 125,000 units. In either case, cash costs would still amount to 60 percent of revenues. You believe that there is a 25 percent chance of poor acceptance, a 25 percent chance of excellent acceptance, and a 50 percent chance of average acceptance (the base case).

(1) What is the worst-case NPV? The best-case NPV?

(2) Use the worst-, most likely (or base), and best-case NPVs, with their probabilities of occurrence, to find the project's expected NPV, standard deviation, and coefficient of variation.

j. (1) Assume that Allied's average project has a coefficient of variation (CV) in the range of 1.25 to 1.75. Would the lemon juice project be classified as high risk, average risk, or low risk? What type of risk is being measured here?

(2) Based on common sense, how highly correlated do you think the project would be with the firm's other assets? (Give a correlation coefficient or range of coefficients, based on your judgment.)

(3) How would this correlation coefficient and the previously calculated σ combine to affect the project's contribution to corporate, or within-firm, risk? Explain.

k. (1) Based on your judgment, what do you think the project's correlation coefficient would be with respect to the general economy and thus with returns on "the market"?

(2) How would correlation with the economy affect the project's market risk?

l. (1) Allied typically adds or subtracts 3 percentage points to the overall cost of capital to adjust for risk. Should the lemon juice project be accepted?

(2) What subjective risk factors should be considered before the final decision is made?

m. In recent months, Allied's group has begun to focus on real option analysis.

(1) What is real option analysis?

(2) What are some examples of projects with embedded real options?

DEPRECIATION

Suppose a firm buys a milling machine for $100,000 and uses it for five years, after which it is scrapped. The cost of the goods produced by the machine must include a charge for the machine, and this charge is called *depreciation*. In the following sections, we review some of the depreciation concepts covered in accounting courses.

Companies often calculate depreciation one way when figuring taxes and another way when reporting income to investors: many use the *straight-line* method for stockholder reporting (or "book" purposes), but they use the fastest rate permitted by law for tax purposes. Under the straight-line method used for stockholder reporting, one normally takes the cost of the asset, subtracts its estimated salvage value, and divides the net amount by the asset's useful economic life. For an asset with a 5-year life, which costs $100,000 and has a $12,500 salvage value, the annual straight-line depreciation charge is ($100,000 − $12,500)/5 = $17,500. Note, however, as we discuss later in this appendix, that salvage value is *not* considered for tax depreciation purposes.

For tax purposes, Congress changes the permissible tax depreciation methods from time to time. Prior to 1954, the straight-line method was required for tax purposes, but in 1954 *accelerated* methods (double-declining balance and sum-of-years'-digits) were permitted. Then, in 1981, the old accelerated methods were replaced by a simpler procedure known as the Accelerated Cost Recovery System (ACRS). The ACRS system was changed again in 1986 as a part of the Tax Reform Act, and it is now known as the *Modified Accelerated Cost Recovery System (MACRS)*; a 1993 tax law made further changes in this area.

Note that U.S. tax laws are very complicated, and in this text we can only provide an overview of MACRS designed to give you a basic understanding of the impact of depreciation on capital budgeting decisions. Further, the tax laws change so often that the numbers we present may be outdated before the book is even published. Thus, when dealing with tax depreciation in real-world situations, current Internal Revenue Service (IRS) publications or individuals with expertise in tax matters should be consulted.

TAX DEPRECIATION LIFE

For tax purposes, the entire cost of an asset is expensed over its depreciable life. Historically, an asset's depreciable life was determined by its estimated useful economic life; it was intended that an asset would be fully depreciated at approximately the same time that it reached the end of its useful economic life. However, MACRS totally abandoned that practice and set simple guidelines that created several classes of assets, each with a more-or-less arbitrarily prescribed life called a *recovery period* or *class life*. The MACRS class life bears only a rough relationship to the expected useful economic life.

CLASS	TYPE OF PROPERTY
3-year	Certain special manufacturing tools
5-year	Automobiles, light-duty trucks, computers, and certain special manufacturing equipment
7-year	Most industrial equipment, office furniture, and fixtures
10-year	Certain longer-lived types of equipment
27.5-year	Residential rental real property such as apartment buildings
39-year	All nonresidential real property, including commercial and industrial buildings

A major effect of the MACRS system has been to shorten the depreciable lives of assets, thus giving businesses larger tax deductions and thereby increasing their cash flows available for investment. Table 12A-1 describes the types of property that fit into the different class life groups, and Table 12A-2 sets forth the MACRS recovery allowance percentages (depreciation rates) for selected classes of investment property.

Consider Table 12A-1 first. The first column gives the MACRS class life, while the second column describes the types of assets that fall into each category. Property in the 27.5- and 39-year categories (real estate) must be depreciated by the straight-line method, but 3-, 5-, 7-, and 10-year property (personal property) can be depreciated either by the accelerated method using the rates shown in Table 12A-2 or by an alternate straight-line method.[1]

As we saw earlier in the chapter, higher depreciation expenses result in lower taxes, hence higher cash flows. Therefore, since a firm has the choice of using the alternate straight-line rates or the accelerated rates shown in Table 12A-2, most elect to use the accelerated rates.

The yearly recovery allowance, or depreciation expense, is determined by multiplying each asset's *depreciable basis* by the applicable recovery percentage shown in Table 12A-2. Calculations are discussed in the following sections.

Half-Year Convention

Under MACRS, the assumption is generally made that property is placed in service in the middle of the first year. Thus, for 3-year class life property, the recovery period begins in the middle of the year the asset is placed in service and ends three years later. The effect of the *half-year convention* is to extend the recovery period out one more year, so 3-year class life property is depreciated over four calendar years, 5-year property is depreciated over six calendar years,

---

[1] As a benefit to very small companies, the Tax Code also permits companies to *expense*, which is equivalent to depreciating over one year, up to $20,000 of equipment for 2000 and $24,000 for 2001. Thus, if a small company bought one asset worth up to $20,000, it could write the asset off in the year it was acquired. This is called "Section 179 expensing." We shall disregard this provision throughout the book.

Recovery Allowance Percentage for Personal Property

OWNERSHIP YEAR	CLASS OF INVESTMENT			
	3-YEAR	5-YEAR	7-YEAR	10-YEAR
1	33%	20%	14%	10%
2	45	32	25	18
3	15	19	17	14
4	7	12	13	12
5		11	9	9
6		6	9	7
7			9	7
8			4	7
9				7
10				6
11				3
	100%	100%	100%	100%

NOTES:

a. We developed these recovery allowance percentages based on the 200 percent declining balance method prescribed by MACRS, with a switch to straight-line depreciation at some point in the asset's life. For example, consider the 5-year recovery allowance percentages. The straight line percentage would be 20 percent per year, so the 200 percent declining balance multiplier is $2.0(20\%) = 40\% = 0.4$. However, because the half-year convention applies, the MACRS percentage for Year 1 is 20 percent. For Year 2, there is 80 percent of the depreciable basis remaining to be depreciated, so the recovery allowance percentage is $0.40(80\%) = 32\%$. In Year 3, $20\% + 32\% = 52\%$ of the depreciation has been taken, leaving 48%, so the percentage is $0.4(48\%) \approx 19\%$. In Year 4, the percentage is $0.4(29\%) \approx 12\%$. After 4 years, straight-line depreciation exceeds the declining balance depreciation, so a switch is made to straight-line (this is permitted under the law). However, the half-year convention must also be applied at the end of the class life, and the remaining 17 percent of depreciation must be taken (amortized) over 1.5 years. Thus, the percentage in Year 5 is $17\%/1.5 \approx 11\%$, and in Year 6, $17\% - 11\% = 6\%$. Although the tax tables carry the allowance percentages out to two decimal places, we have rounded to the nearest whole number for ease of illustration.

b. Residential rental property (apartments) is depreciated over a 27.5-year life, whereas commercial and industrial structures are depreciated over 39 years. In both cases, straight-line depreciation must be used. The depreciation allowance for the first year is based, pro rata, on the month the asset was placed in service, with the remainder of the first year's depreciation being taken in the 28th or 40th year.

and so on. This convention is incorporated into Table 12A-2's recovery allowance percentages.[2]

Depreciable Basis

The *depreciable basis* is a critical element of MACRS because each year's allowance (depreciation expense) depends jointly on the asset's depreciable basis

---

[2] The half-year convention also applies if the straight-line alternative is used, with half of one year's depreciation taken in the first year, a full year's depreciation taken in each of the remaining years of the asset's class life, and the remaining half-year's depreciation taken in the year following the end of the class life. You should recognize that virtually all companies have computerized depreciation systems. Each asset's depreciation pattern is programmed into the system at the time of its acquisition, and the computer aggregates the depreciation allowances for all assets when the accountants close the books and prepare financial statements and tax returns.

and its MACRS class life. The depreciable basis under MACRS is equal to the purchase price of the asset plus any shipping and installation costs. The basis is *not* adjusted for *salvage value* (which is the estimated market value of the asset at the end of its useful life) regardless of whether accelerated or the alternate straight-line method is used.

Sale of a Depreciable Asset

If a depreciable asset is sold, the sales price (actual salvage value) minus the then-existing undepreciated book value is added to operating income and taxed at the firm's marginal tax rate. For example, suppose a firm buys a 5-year class life asset for $100,000 and sells it at the end of the fourth year for $25,000. The asset's book value is equal to $100,000(0.11 + 0.06) = $100,000(0.17) = $17,000. Therefore, $25,000 − $17,000 = $8,000 is added to the firm's operating income and is taxed.

Depreciation Illustration

Assume that Allied Food Products buys a $150,000 machine that falls into the MACRS 5-year class life and places it into service on March 15, 2002. Allied must pay an additional $30,000 for delivery and installation. Salvage value is not considered, so the machine's depreciable basis is $180,000. (Delivery and installation charges are included in the depreciable basis rather than expensed in the year incurred.) Each year's recovery allowance (tax depreciation expense) is determined by multiplying the depreciable basis by the applicable recovery allowance percentage. Thus, the depreciation expense for 2002 is 0.20($180,000) = $36,000, and for 2003 it is 0.32($180,000) = $57,600. Similarly, the depreciation expense is $34,200 for 2004, $21,600 for 2005, $19,800 for 2006, and $10,800 for 2007. The total depreciation expense over the six-year recovery period is $180,000, which is equal to the depreciable basis of the machine.

As noted above, most firms use straight-line depreciation for stockholder reporting purposes but MACRS for tax purposes. *For these firms, for capital budgeting, MACRS should be used.* The reason is that, in capital budgeting, we are concerned with cash flows, not reported income. Since MACRS depreciation is used for taxes, this type of depreciation must be used to determine the taxes that will be assessed against a particular project. Only if the depreciation method used for tax purposes is also used for capital budgeting will the analysis produce accurate cash flow estimates.

PROBLEM

12A-1
Depreciation effects

Cate Rzasa, great-granddaughter of the founder of Rzasa Tile Products and current president of the company, believes in simple, conservative accounting. In keeping with her philosophy, she has decreed that the company shall use alternative straight-line depreciation, based on the MACRS class lives, for all newly acquired assets. Your boss, the financial vice-president and the only nonfamily officer, has asked you to develop an exhibit that shows how much this policy costs the company in terms of market value. Rzasa is interested in increasing the value of the firm's stock because she fears a family stockholder revolt that might remove her from office. For your exhibit, assume that the company spends $100 million each year on new capital projects, that the projects have on average a 10-year class life, that the company has a 9 percent cost of debt, and that its tax rate is 35 percent. (Hint: Show how much the NPV of projects in an average year would increase if Rzasa used the standard MACRS recovery allowances.)

PART **V**

CAPITAL STRUCTURE
AND DIVIDEND POLICY

13 Capital Structure and Leverage

SOURCE: @ Photopia

DEBT: ROCKET BOOSTER OR ANCHOR?

GENERAL MILLS

When a firm expands, it needs capital, and that capital can come from debt or equity. Debt has two important advantages. First, interest paid is tax deductible, which lowers debt's effective cost. Second, debtholders get a fixed return, so stockholders do not have to share their profits if the business is extremely successful.

However, debt also has disadvantages. First, the higher the debt ratio, the riskier the company, hence the higher its cost of both debt and equity. Second, if a company falls on hard times and operating income is not sufficient to cover interest charges, its stockholders will have to make up the shortfall, and if they cannot, bankruptcy will result. Good times may be just around the corner, but too much debt can keep the company from getting there and thus can wipe out the stockholders.

Companies with volatile earnings and operating cash flows therefore limit their use of debt. On the other hand, companies with less business risk and more stable operating cash flows can take on more debt. General Mills, a consumer-goods company with such well-known brands as Cheerios, Wheaties, Betty Crocker, and Hamburger Helper, is a good example of a stable company that uses a lot of debt financing. Indeed, at the end of 1999, General Mills' capital structure as shown on its balance sheet was 90 percent debt and 10 percent equity.

At first glance, a 90 percent debt ratio seems extraordinarily high. In the past, there have been numerous examples of high debt pushing otherwise well-regarded companies into bankruptcy. For example, a few years ago, two of the nation's largest retailers, Federated Department Stores and R.H. Macy, were forced to declare bankruptcy as a result of their excessive use of debt.

With these examples in mind, some analysts are concerned that General Mills may have taken on too much debt. These concerns have recently increased. The company has issued more debt and has repurchased common stock, to the point where the company had negative equity on its year-end 2000 balance sheet. Moreover, these numbers do not reflect General Mills' recent plans to acquire Pillsbury assets from Diageo PLC. General Mills plans to finance the purchase by issuing more than $5 billion in stock. The terms of the deal also require General Mills to assume $5.14 billion of Pillsbury's debt.

Despite these concerns, General Mills' high debt ratio might be appropriate, given the stability of its basic business. After all, the consumption of Cheerios and Hamburger Helper has historically remained stable even during economic downturns. Moreover, if we examine General Mills' capital structure in more detail, it soon becomes apparent that there is more here than first meets the eye. According to its year-end 2000 balance sheet, General Mills had roughly $3.5 billion of total debt and its stockholders' equity was a negative $289 million. However, the market value of General Mills' equity is actually much higher than its book value. At year-end 2000, the market capitalization of the equity (which is simply the stock price times the number of shares outstanding) was approximately $11.6 billion. From a market value perspective, General Mills' capital structure ($3.5 billion of debt versus $11.6 billion of equity) is thus quite conservative, and it also helps explain why General Mills has an A-level bond rating.

General Mills and other companies can finance with either debt or equity. Is one better than the other? If so, should firms be financed either with all debt or all equity? If the best solution is some mix of debt and equity, what is the optimal mix? In this chapter, we discuss the key facets of the debt-versus-equity, or capital structure, decision. As you read the chapter, think about these concepts and consider how they can aid managers as they make capital structure decisions. ■

PUTTING THINGS IN PERSPECTIVE

WWW

Two video clips of Steve Walsh, Assistant Treasurer at JCPenney, talking about capital structure are available at **http:// fisher.osu.edu/fin/resources_ education/clips.htm**. The first clip on capital structure discusses the cost of capital and debt, while the second clip discusses optimal capital structure at JCPenney relative to the capital structure theory of Modigliani/Miller.

In Chapter 10, when we calculated the weighted average cost of capital for use in capital budgeting, we assumed that the firm had a specific target capital structure. However, the optimal capital structure may change over time, changes in capital structure affect the riskiness and cost of each type of capital, and all this can change the weighted average cost of capital. Moreover, a change in the cost of capital can affect capital budgeting decisions and, ultimately, the firm's stock price.

Many factors influence the capital structure decision, and, as you will see, determining the optimal capital structure is not an exact science. Therefore, even firms in the same industry often have dramatically different capital structures. In this chapter we first consider the effect of capital structure on risk, and then we use these insights to help answer the question of how firms should determine the mix of debt and equity used to finance their operations. ■

THE TARGET CAPITAL STRUCTURE

Target Capital Structure
The mix of debt, preferred stock, and common equity with which the firm plans to raise capital.

Firms should first analyze a number of factors, then establish a **target capital structure.** This target may change over time as conditions change, but at any given moment, management should have a specific capital structure in mind. If the actual debt ratio is below the target level, expansion capital should generally be raised by issuing debt, whereas if the debt ratio is above the target, equity should generally be issued.

Capital structure policy involves a trade-off between risk and return:

- Using more debt raises the risk borne by stockholders.
- However, using more debt generally leads to a higher expected rate of return on equity.

Higher risk tends to lower a stock's price, but a higher expected rate of return raises it. *Therefore, the optimal capital structure must strike a balance between risk and return so as to maximize the firm's stock price.*

Four primary factors influence capital structure decisions.

1. *Business risk*, or the riskiness inherent in the firm's operations if it used no debt. The greater the firm's business risk, the lower its optimal debt ratio.

2. The firm's *tax position.* A major reason for using debt is that interest is deductible, which lowers the effective cost of debt. However, if most of a firm's income is already sheltered from taxes by depreciation tax shields, by interest on currently outstanding debt, or by tax loss carry-forwards, its tax rate will be low, so additional debt will not be as advantageous as it would be to a firm with a higher effective tax rate.

3. *Financial flexibility*, or the ability to raise capital on reasonable terms under adverse conditions. Corporate treasurers know that a steady supply of capital is necessary for stable operations, which is vital for long-run success. They also know that when money is tight in the economy, or when a firm is experiencing operating difficulties, suppliers of capital prefer to provide funds to companies with strong balance sheets. Therefore, both the potential future need for funds and the consequences of a funds shortage influence the target capital structure — the greater the probable future need for capital, and the worse the consequences of a capital shortage, the stronger the balance sheet should be.

4. *Managerial conservatism or aggressiveness.* Some managers are more aggressive than others, hence some firms are more inclined to use debt in an effort to boost profits. This factor does not affect the true optimal, or value-maximizing, capital structure, but it does influence the manager-determined target capital structure.

These four points largely determine the target capital structure, but operating conditions can cause the actual capital structure to vary from the target. For example, Illinois Power has a target debt ratio of about 45 percent, but large losses associated with a nuclear plant forced it to write down its common equity, and that raised the debt ratio above the target level. The company is now trying to get its equity back up to the target level.

SELF-TEST QUESTIONS

What four factors affect the target capital structure?

In what sense does capital structure policy involve a trade-off between risk and return?

BUSINESS AND FINANCIAL RISK

In Chapter 6, when we examined risk from the viewpoint of a stock investor, we distinguished between *market risk*, which is measured by the firm's beta coefficient, and *stand-alone risk*, which includes both market risk and an element of risk that can be eliminated by diversification. Now we introduce two new dimensions of risk: (1) *business risk*, or the riskiness of the firm's stock if it uses no debt, and (2) *financial risk*, which is the additional risk placed on the common stockholders as a result of the firm's decision to use debt.[1]

Conceptually, the firm has a certain amount of risk inherent in its operations: this is its business risk. If it uses debt, then, in effect, it partitions its investors into two groups and concentrates most of its business risk on one class of investors — the common stockholders. However, the common stockholders will demand compensation for assuming more risk and thus require a higher rate of return. In this section, we examine business and financial risk within a stand-alone risk framework, which ignores the benefits of stockholder diversification.

BUSINESS RISK

Business Risk
The riskiness inherent in the firm's operations if it uses no debt.

Business risk in a stand-alone sense is a function of the uncertainty inherent in projections of a firm's return on invested capital (ROIC), defined as follows:

$$\text{ROIC} = \frac{\text{NOPAT}}{\text{Capital}} = \frac{\begin{array}{c}\text{Net income to}\\ \text{common stockholders}\end{array} + \begin{array}{c}\text{After tax}\\ \text{interest payments}\end{array}}{\text{Capital}}.$$

Here NOPAT is net operating profit after taxes and capital is the sum of the firm's debt and common equity. (We ignore preferred stock in this section.) If a firm uses no debt, then its interest payments will be zero, its capital will be all equity, and its ROIC will equal its return on equity, ROE:

$$\text{ROIC (zero debt)} = \text{ROE} = \frac{\text{Net income to common stockholders}}{\text{Common equity}}.$$

Therefore, the business risk of a *leverage-free* firm can be measured by the standard deviation of its ROE, σ_{ROE}.

To illustrate, consider Bigbee Electronics Company, a *debt-free (unlevered)* firm. Figure 13-1 gives some clues about the company's business risk. The top graph shows the trend in ROE from 1991 through 2001; this graph gives both security analysts and Bigbee's management an idea of the degree to which ROE has varied in the past and might vary in the future.

The lower graph shows the beginning-of-year subjectively estimated probability distribution of Bigbee's ROE for 2001, based on the trend line in the top section of Figure 13-1. As both graphs indicate, Bigbee's actual ROE in 2001 was only 8 percent, well below the expected value of 12 percent — 2001 was a bad year.

---

[1] Preferred stock also adds to financial risk. To simplify matters, we concentrate on debt and common equity in this chapter.

FIGURE 13-1

Bigbee Electronics: Trend in ROE, 1991–2001, and Subjective Probability Distribution of ROE, 2001

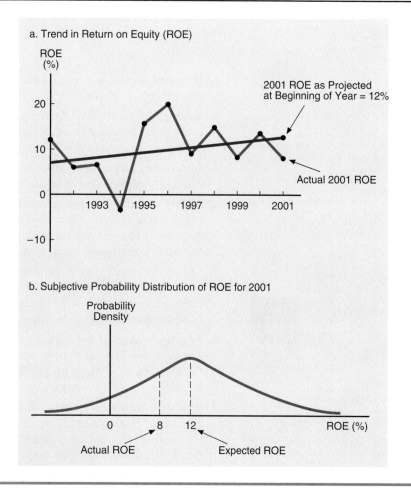

a. Trend in Return on Equity (ROE)

2001 ROE as Projected at Beginning of Year = 12%

Actual 2001 ROE

b. Subjective Probability Distribution of ROE for 2001

Actual ROE

Expected ROE

Bigbee's past fluctuations in ROE were caused by many factors — booms and recessions in the national economy, successful new products introduced both by Bigbee and by its competitors, labor strikes, a fire in Bigbee's main plant, and so on. Similar events will doubtless occur in the future, and when they do, the realized ROE will be higher or lower than the projected level. Further, there is always the possibility that a long-term disaster will strike, permanently depressing the company's earning power; for example, a competitor might introduce a new product that would permanently lower Bigbee's earnings. This uncertainty regarding Bigbee's future ROE, *assuming the firm uses no debt financing*, is defined as the company's *business risk*. Because Bigbee uses no debt, stockholders bear all of the company's business risk.

Business risk varies not only from industry to industry but also among firms in a given industry. Further, business risk can change over time. For example, the electric utilities were regarded for years as having little business risk, but a combination of events in recent years altered the utilities' situation, producing sharp declines in their ROEs and greatly increasing the industry's business risk.

Now, food processors and grocery retailers frequently are given as examples of industries with low business risk, while cyclical manufacturing industries such as autos and steel, as well as many small startup companies, are regarded as having especially high business risk.[2]

Business risk depends on a number of factors, the more important of which are listed below:

1. **Demand variability.** The more stable the demand for a firm's products, other things held constant, the lower its business risk.

2. **Sales price variability.** Firms whose products are sold in highly volatile markets are exposed to more business risk than similar firms whose output prices are more stable.

3. **Input cost variability.** Firms whose input costs are highly uncertain are exposed to a high degree of business risk.

4. **Ability to adjust output prices for changes in input costs.** Some firms are better able than others to raise their own output prices when input costs rise. The greater the ability to adjust output prices to reflect cost conditions, the lower the degree of business risk.

5. **Ability to develop new products in a timely, cost-effective manner.** Firms in such high-tech industries as drugs and computers depend on a constant stream of new products. The faster its products become obsolete, the greater a firm's business risk.

6. **Foreign risk exposure.** Firms that generate a high percentage of their earnings overseas are subject to earnings declines due to exchange rate fluctuations. Also, if a firm operates in a politically unstable area, it may be subject to political risks. See Chapter 16 for a further discussion.

7. **The extent to which costs are fixed: operating leverage.** If a high percentage of costs are fixed, hence do not decline when demand falls, then the firm is exposed to a relatively high degree of business risk. This factor is called *operating leverage*, and it is discussed at length in the next section.

Each of these factors is determined partly by the firm's industry characteristics, but each of them is also controllable to some extent by management. For example, most firms can, through their marketing policies, take actions to stabilize both unit sales and sales prices. However, this stabilization may require spending a great deal on advertising and/or price concessions to get commitments from customers to purchase fixed quantities at fixed prices in the future. Similarly, firms such as Bigbee Electronics can reduce the volatility of future input costs by negotiating long-term labor and materials supply contracts, but they may have to pay prices above the current spot price to obtain these contracts. Many firms are also using hedging techniques to reduce business risk, but the curious student may refer to Brigham and Houston's *Fundamentals of Financial Management*, 9th edition, Chapter 18, where hedging is discussed in more detail.

---

[2] We have avoided any discussion of market versus company-specific risk in this section. We note now (1) that any action that increases business risk in the stand-alone risk sense will generally also increase a firm's beta coefficient and (2) that a part of business risk as we define it will generally be company-specific, hence subject to elimination by diversification by the firm's stockholders.

OPERATING LEVERAGE

As noted above, business risk depends in part on the extent to which a firm builds fixed costs into its operations — if fixed costs are high, even a small decline in sales can lead to a large decline in ROE. So, other things held constant, the higher a firm's fixed costs, the greater its business risk. Higher fixed costs are generally associated with more highly automated, capital intensive firms and industries. However, businesses that employ highly skilled workers who must be retained and paid even during recessions also have relatively high fixed costs, as do firms with high product development costs, because the amortization of development costs is an element of fixed costs.

Operating Leverage
The extent to which fixed costs are used in a firm's operations.

If a high percentage of total costs are fixed, then the firm is said to have a high degree of **operating leverage.** In physics, leverage implies the use of a lever to raise a heavy object with a small force. In politics, if people have leverage, their smallest word or action can accomplish a lot. *In business terminology, a high degree of operating leverage, other factors held constant, implies that a relatively small change in sales results in a large change in ROE.*

Figure 13-2 illustrates the concept of operating leverage by comparing the results that Bigbee could expect if it used different degrees of operating leverage. Plan A calls for a relatively small amount of fixed costs, $20,000. Here the firm would not have much automated equipment, so its depreciation, maintenance, property taxes, and so on would be low. However, the total operating costs line has a relatively steep slope, indicating that variable costs per unit are higher than they would be if the firm used more operating leverage. Plan B calls for a higher level of fixed costs, $60,000. Here the firm uses automated equipment (with which one operator can turn out a few or many units at the same labor cost) to a much larger extent. The breakeven point is higher under Plan B — breakeven occurs at 60,000 units under Plan B versus only 40,000 units under Plan A.

Operating Breakeven
The output quantity at which ROE = 0, hence when EBIT = 0.

We can calculate the breakeven quantity by recognizing that **operating breakeven** occurs when ROE = 0, hence when earnings before interest and taxes (EBIT) = 0:[3]

$$EBIT = PQ - VQ - F = 0. \tag{13-1}$$

Here P is average sales price per unit of output, Q is units of output, V is variable cost per unit, and F is fixed operating costs. If we solve for the breakeven quantity, Q_{BE}, we get this expression:

$$Q_{BE} = \frac{F}{P - V}. \tag{13-1a}$$

Thus for Plan A,

$$Q_{BE} = \frac{\$20,000}{\$2.00 - \$1.50} = 40,000 \text{ units,}$$

and for Plan B,

$$Q_{BE} = \frac{\$60,000}{\$2.00 - \$1.00} = 60,000 \text{ units.}$$

---

[3] This definition of breakeven does not include any fixed financial costs because Bigbee is an unlevered firm. If there were fixed financial costs, the firm would suffer an accounting loss at the operating breakeven point. We will introduce financial costs shortly.

FIGURE 13-2 **Illustration of Operating Leverage**

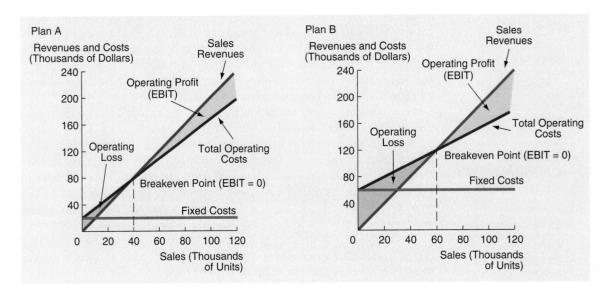

	PLAN A	PLAN B
Price	$2.00	$2.00
Variable costs	$1.50	$1.00
Fixed costs	$20,000	$60,000
Assets	$200,000	$200,000
Tax rate	40%	40%

				PLAN A				PLAN B		
DEMAND	PROBABILITY	UNITS SOLD	DOLLAR SALES	OPERATING COSTS	OPERATING PROFITS (EBIT)	NET INCOME	ROE	OPERATING COSTS	OPERATING PROFITS (EBIT)	NET INCOME	ROE
Terrible	0.05	0	$ 0	$ 20,000	($20,000)	($12,000)	−6.00%	$ 60,000	($ 60,000)	($36,000)	−18.00%
Poor	0.20	40,000	80,000	80,000	0	0	0.00	100,000	(20,000)	(12,000)	−6.00
Normal	0.50	100,000	200,000	170,000	30,000	18,000	9.00	160,000	40,000	24,000	12.00
Good	0.20	160,000	320,000	260,000	60,000	36,000	18.00	220,000	100,000	60,000	30.00
Wonderful	0.05	200,000	400,000	320,000	80,000	48,000	24.00	260,000	140,000	84,000	42.00
Expected value:		100,000	$200,000	$170,000	$30,000	$18,000	9.00%	$160,000	$ 40,000	$24,000	12.00%
Standard deviation:					$24,698		7.41%		$ 49,396		14.82%
Coefficient of variation:					0.82		0.82		1.23		1.23

NOTES: a. Operating costs = Variable costs + Fixed costs.

b. The federal-plus-state tax rate is 40 percent, so NI = EBIT(1 − Tax rate) = EBIT(0.6).

c. ROE = NI/Equity. The firm has no debt, so Assets = Equity = $200,000.

d. The breakeven sales level for Plan B is not shown in the table, but it is 60,000 units or $120,000.

e. The expected values, standard deviations, and coefficients of variation were found using the procedures discussed in Chapter 6.

FIGURE 13-3   Analysis of Business Risk

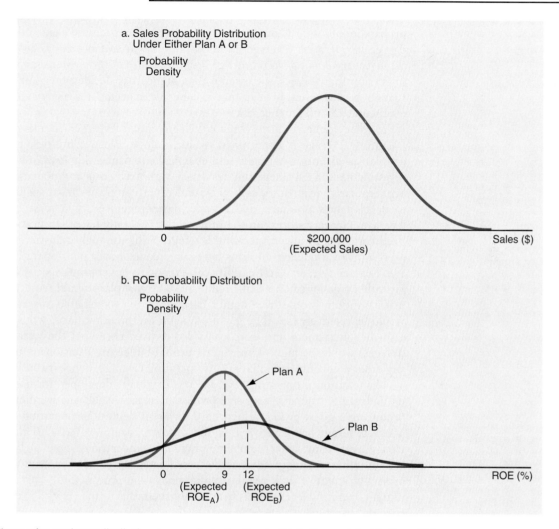

a. Sales Probability Distribution
Under Either Plan A or B

Probability
Density

0          $200,000   Sales ($)
        (Expected Sales)

b. ROE Probability Distribution

Probability
Density

Plan A

Plan B

0   9   12   ROE (%)
  (Expected (Expected
   ROE$_A$)   ROE$_B$)

NOTE: We are using continuous distributions to approximate the discrete distributions contained in Figure 13-2.

How does operating leverage affect business risk? *Other things held constant, the higher a firm's operating leverage, the higher its business risk.* This point is demonstrated in Figure 13-3, where we develop probability distributions for ROE under Plans A and B.

The top section of Figure 13-3 graphs the probability distribution of sales that was presented in tabular form in Figure 13-2. The sales probability distribution depends on how demand for the product varies, not on whether the product is manufactured by Plan A or by Plan B. Therefore, the same sales probability distribution applies to both production plans; this distribution has expected sales of $200,000, and it ranges from zero to about $400,000, with a standard deviation of $\sigma_{Sales} = \$98,793$.

We use the sales probability distribution, together with the operating costs at each sales level, to develop graphs of the ROE probability distributions under Plans A and B. These are shown in the bottom section of Figure 13-3. Plan B has a higher expected ROE, but this plan also entails a much higher probability of losses. Clearly, Plan B, the one with more fixed costs and a higher degree of operating leverage, is riskier. *In general, holding other factors constant, the higher the degree of operating leverage, the greater the firm's business risk.* In the discussion that follows, we assume that Bigbee has decided to go ahead with Plan B because they believe that the higher expected return is sufficient to compensate for the higher risk.

To what extent can firms control their operating leverage? To a large extent, operating leverage is determined by technology. Electric utilities, telephone companies, airlines, steel mills, and chemical companies simply *must* have large investments in fixed assets; this results in high fixed costs and operating leverage. Similarly, drug, auto, computer, and other companies must spend heavily to develop new products, and product-development costs increase operating leverage. Grocery stores, on the other hand, generally have significantly lower fixed costs, hence lower operating leverage. Still, although industry factors do exert a major influence, all firms have some control over their operating leverage. For example, an electric utility can expand its generating capacity by building either a gas-fired or a coal-fired plant. The coal plant would require a larger investment and would have higher fixed costs, but its variable operating costs would be relatively low. The gas-fired plant, on the other hand, would require a smaller investment and would have lower fixed costs, but the variable costs (for gas) would be high. Thus, by its capital budgeting decisions, a utility (or any other company) can influence its operating leverage, hence its business risk.

The concept of operating leverage was originally developed for use in capital budgeting. Mutually exclusive projects that involve alternative methods for producing a given product often have different degrees of operating leverage, hence different breakeven points and different degrees of risk. Bigbee Electronics and many other companies regularly undertake a type of breakeven analysis (the sensitivity analysis discussed in Chapter 12) for each proposed project as a part of their regular capital budgeting process. Still, once a corporation's operating leverage has been established, this factor exerts a major influence on its capital structure decision.

FINANCIAL RISK

Financial Risk
An increase in stockholders' risk, over and above the firm's basic business risk, resulting from the use of financial leverage.

Financial risk is the additional risk placed on the common stockholders as a result of the decision to finance with debt. Conceptually, stockholders face a certain amount of risk that is inherent in a firm's operations — this is its business risk, which is defined as the uncertainty inherent in projections of future operating income. If a firm uses debt (financial leverage), this concentrates the business risk on common stockholders. To illustrate, suppose 10 people decide to form a corporation to manufacture disk drives. There is a certain amount of business risk in the operation. If the firm is capitalized only with common equity, and if each person buys 10 percent of the stock, then each investor shares equally in the business risk. However, suppose the firm is capitalized with 50 percent debt and 50 percent equity, with five of the investors putting up their capital as debt and the other five putting up their money as equity. In this case, the five investors who put

AMOUNT BORROWED[a]	DEBT/ASSETS RATIO	INTEREST RATE, k_d, ON ALL DEBT
$ 20,000	10%	8.0%
40,000	20	8.3
60,000	30	9.0
80,000	40	10.0
100,000	50	12.0
120,000	60	15.0

[a] We assume that the firm must borrow in increments of $20,000. We also assume that Bigbee is unable to borrow more than $120,000, which is 60 percent of its $200,000 of assets, because of restrictions in its corporate charter.

Financial Leverage
The extent to which fixed-income securities (debt and preferred stock) are used in a firm's capital structure.

up the equity will have to bear all of the business risk, so the common stock will be twice as risky as it would have been had the firm been financed only with equity. Thus, the use of debt, or **financial leverage,** concentrates the firm's business risk on its stockholders. This concentration of business risk occurs because debtholders, who receive fixed interest payments, bear none of the business risk.

To illustrate the concentration of business risk, we can extend the Bigbee Electronics example. To date, the company has never used debt, but the treasurer is now considering a possible change in the capital structure. Changes in the use of debt will cause changes in earnings per share (EPS) as well as changes in risk — both of which will affect the company's stock price. To understand the relationship between financial leverage and EPS, first consider Table 13-1, which shows how Bigbee's cost of debt would vary if it used different percentages of debt. The higher the percentage of debt, the riskier the debt, hence the higher the interest rate lenders will charge.

For now, assume that only two financing choices are being considered — remaining at 100 percent equity, or shifting to 50 percent debt and 50 percent equity. We also assume that with no debt Bigbee has 10,000 shares of common stock outstanding and, if it changes its capital structure, common stock can be repurchased at the $20 current stock price. Now consider Table 13-2, which shows how the financing choice will affect Bigbee's profitability and risk.

First focus on Section I of Table 13-2, which assumes that Bigbee uses no debt. Since debt is zero, interest is also zero, hence pre-tax income is equal to EBIT. Taxes at 40 percent are deducted to obtain net income, which is then divided by the $200,000 of equity to calculate ROE. Note that Bigbee receives a tax credit if the demand is either terrible or poor (which are the two scenarios where net income is negative). Here we assume that Bigbee's losses can be carried back to offset income earned in the prior year. The ROE at each sales level is then multiplied by the probability of that sales level to calculate the 12 percent expected ROE. Note that this 12 percent is the same as we found in Figure 13-2 for Plan B.

Section I of Table 13-2 also calculates Bigbee's earnings per share (EPS) for each scenario under the assumption that the company continues to use no debt. Net income is divided by the 10,000 common shares outstanding to obtain

TABLE 13-2

Effects of Financial Leverage: Bigbee Electronics Financed with Zero Debt or with 50 Percent Debt

SECTION I. ZERO DEBT

Debt ratio	0%
Assets	$200,000
Debt	0
Equity	$200,000
Shares outstanding	10,000

DEMAND FOR PRODUCT (1)	PROBABILITY (2)	EBIT (3)	INTEREST (4)	PRE-TAX INCOME (5)	TAXES (40%) (6)	NET INCOME (7)	ROE (8)	EPS[a] (9)
Terrible	0.05	($ 60,000)	$0	($ 60,000)	($24,000)	($36,000)	−18.00%	($3.60)
Poor	0.20	(20,000)	0	(20,000)	(8,000)	(12,000)	−6.00	(1.20)
Normal	0.50	40,000	0	40,000	16,000	24,000	12.00	2.40
Good	0.20	100,000	0	100,000	40,000	60,000	30.00	6.00
Wonderful	0.05	140,000	0	140,000	56,000	84,000	42.00	8.40
Expected value:		$ 40,000	$0	$ 40,000	$16,000	$24,000	12.00%	$2.40
Standard deviation:							14.82%	$2.96
Coefficient of variation:							1.23	1.23

Assumptions: 1. In terms of its operating leverage, Bigbee has chosen Plan B. The probability distribution and EBIT are obtained from Figure 13-2.
2. Sales and operating costs, hence EBIT, are not affected by the financing decision. Therefore, EBIT under both financing plans is identical, and it is taken from the EBIT column for Plan B in Figure 13-2.
3. All losses can be carried back to offset income in the prior year.

[a] The EPS figures can also be obtained using the following formula, in which the numerator amounts to an income statement at a given sales level laid out horizontally:

$$EPS = \frac{(Sales - Fixed\ costs - Variable\ costs - Interest)(1 - Tax\ rate)}{Shares\ outstanding} = \frac{(EBIT - I)(1 - T)}{Shares\ outstanding}.$$

(note continues)

EPS. If the demand is terrible, the EPS will be −$3.60, but if demand is wonderful, the EPS will rise to $8.40. The EPS at each sales level is then multiplied by the probability of that sales level to calculate the expected EPS, which is $2.40 if Bigbee uses no debt. We also calculate the standard deviation of EPS and the coefficient of variation as indicators of the firm's risk at a zero debt ratio: $\sigma_{EPS} = \$2.96$, and $CV_{EPS} = 1.23$.[4]

Now let's look at the situation if Bigbee decides to use 50 percent debt financing, shown in Section II of Table 13-2, with the debt costing 12 percent. Demand will not be affected, nor will operating costs, hence the EBIT columns are the same for the zero debt and 50 percent debt cases. However, the company will now have $100,000 of debt with a cost of 12 percent, hence its inter-

[4] See Chapter 6 for a review of procedures for calculating the standard deviation and coefficient of variation. Recall that the advantage of the coefficient of variation is that it permits better comparisons when the expected values of EPS vary, as they do here for the two capital structures.

TABLE 13-2 | Continued

SECTION II. 50% DEBT

Debt ratio	50.00%
Assets	$200,000
Debt	$100,000
Interest rate	12.00%
Equity	$100,000
Shares outstanding	5,000

DEMAND FOR PRODUCT (1)	PROBABILITY (2)	EBIT (3)	INTEREST (4)	PRE-TAX INCOME (5)	TAXES (40%) (6)	NET INCOME (7)	ROE (8)	EPS[a] (9)
Terrible	0.05	($ 60,000)	$12,000	($ 72,000)	($28,800)	($43,200)	−43.20%	($8.64)
Poor	0.20	(20,000)	12,000	(32,000)	(12,800)	(19,200)	−19.20	(3.84)
Normal	0.50	40,000	12,000	28,000	11,200	16,800	16.80	3.36
Good	0.20	100,000	12,000	88,000	35,200	52,800	52.80	10.56
Wonderful	0.05	140,000	12,000	128,000	51,200	76,800	76.80	15.36
Expected value:		$ 40,000	$12,000	$ 28,000	$11,200	$16,800	16.80%	$3.36
Standard deviation:							29.64%	$5.93
Coefficient of variation:							1.76	1.76

For example, with zero debt and sales = $200,000, EPS is $2.40:

$$EPS_{D/A=0} = \frac{(\$200,000 - \$60,000 - \$100,000 - 0)(0.6)}{10,000} = \$2.40.$$

With 50 percent debt and sales = $200,000, EPS is $3.36:

$$EPS_{D/A=0.05} = \frac{(\$200,000 - \$60,000 - \$100,000 - \$12,000)(0.6)}{5,000} = \$3.36.$$

Refer to the tabular data given in Figure 13-2 to arrive at sales, fixed costs, and variable costs that are used in the equations above.

est expense will be $12,000. This interest must be paid regardless of the state of the economy — if it is not paid, the company will be forced into bankruptcy, and stockholders will probably be wiped out. Therefore, we show a $12,000 cost in Column 4 as a fixed number for all demand conditions. Column 5 shows pre-tax income, Column 6 the applicable taxes, and Column 7 the resulting net income. When the net income figures are divided by the equity investment — which will now be only $100,000 because $100,000 of the $200,000 total requirement was obtained as debt — we find the ROEs under each demand state. If demand is terrible and sales are zero, then a very large loss will be incurred, and the ROE will be −43.2 percent. However, if demand is wonderful, then ROE will be 76.8 percent. The probability-weighted average is the expected ROE, which is 16.8 percent if the company uses 50 percent debt.

Typically, financing with debt increases the expected rate of return for an investment, but debt also increases the riskiness of the investment to the owners of the firm, its common stockholders. This situation holds with our example —

FIGURE 13-4

ROE Probability Distributions for Bigbee Electronics, with and without Leverage

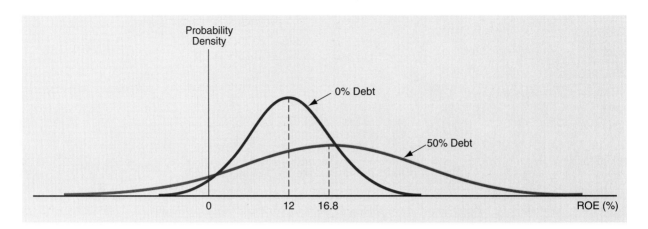

financial leverage raises the expected ROE from 12 percent to 16.8 percent, but it also increases the riskiness of the investment as measured by the coefficient of variation from 1.23 to 1.76.

Figure 13-4 graphs the data in Table 13-2. It shows in another way that using financial leverage increases the expected ROE, but that leverage also flattens out the probability distribution and increases the probability of a large loss, thus increasing the risk borne by stockholders.

We can also calculate Bigbee's EPS if it is financed with 50 percent debt. Once again EPS is calculated as net income divided by shares outstanding. With debt = 0, there would be 10,000 shares outstanding. However, if half of the equity were replaced by debt (debt = $100,000), there would be only 5,000 shares outstanding, and we must use this fact to determine the EPS figures that would result at each of the possible demand levels.[5] With a debt/assets ratio of 50 percent, the EPS figure would be −$8.64 if sales were terrible; it would rise to $3.36 if sales were normal; and it would soar to $15.36 if sales were wonderful.

The EPS distributions under the two financial structures are graphed in Figure 13-5, where we use continuous distributions rather than the discrete distributions contained in Table 13-2. Although expected EPS would be much higher if financial leverage were employed, the graph makes it clear that the risk of low, or even negative, EPS would also be higher if debt were used.

Another view of the relationships among expected EPS, risk, and financial leverage is presented in Figure 13-6. The tabular data in the lower section were calculated in the manner set forth in Table 13-2, and the graphs plot these data. Here we see that expected EPS rises until the firm is financed with 50 percent debt. Interest charges rise, but this effect is more than off-

---

[5] We assume in this example that the firm could change its capital structure by repurchasing common stock at its book value of $100,000/5,000 shares = $20 per share. However, the firm may actually have to pay a higher price to repurchase its stock on the open market. If Bigbee had to pay $22 per share, then it could repurchase only $100,000/$22 = 4,545 shares, and, in this case, expected EPS would be only $16,800/(10,000 − 4,545) = $16,800/5,455 = $3.08 rather than $3.36.

FIGURE 13-5

Probability Distributions of EPS with Different Amounts of Financial Leverage

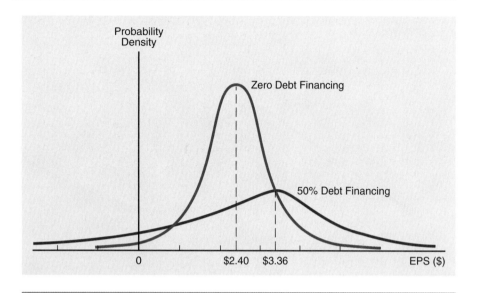

set by the declining number of shares outstanding as debt is substituted for equity. However, EPS peaks at a debt ratio of 50 percent, beyond which interest rates rise so rapidly that EPS falls in spite of the falling number of shares outstanding.

The right panel of Figure 13-6 shows that risk, as measured by the coefficient of variation of EPS, rises continuously, and at an increasing rate, as debt is substituted for equity.

We see, then, that using leverage has both good and bad effects: higher leverage increases expected earnings per share (in this example, until the D/A ratio equals 50 percent), but it also increases risk. Clearly, Bigbee's debt ratio should not exceed 50 percent, but where, in the range of 0 to 50 percent, should it be set? This issue is discussed in the following sections.

SELF-TEST QUESTIONS

What is business risk, and how can it be measured?

What are some determinants of business risk?

Why does business risk vary from industry to industry?

What is operating leverage?

How does operating leverage affect business risk?

What is financial risk, and how does it arise?

Explain this statement: "Using leverage has both good and bad effects."

FIGURE 13-6

Relationships among Expected EPS, Risk, and Financial Leverage

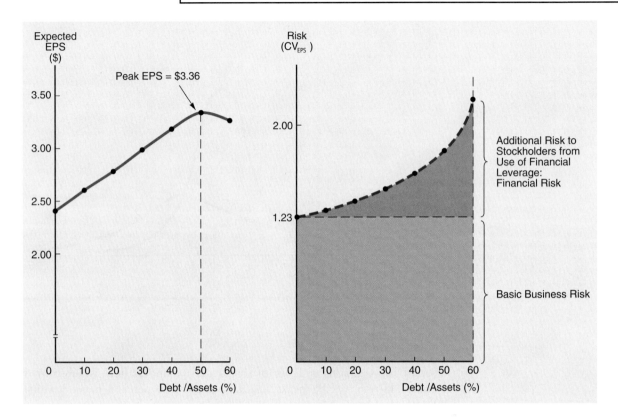

DEBT/ASSETS RATIO	EXPECTED EPS	STANDARD DEVIATION OF EPS	COEFFICIENT OF VARIATION
0%[a]	$2.40[a]	$2.96[a]	1.23[a]
10	2.56	3.29	1.29
20	2.75	3.70	1.35
30	2.97	4.23	1.43
40	3.20	4.94	1.54
50[a]	3.36[a]	5.93[a]	1.76[a]
60	3.30	7.41	2.25

[a] Values for D/A = 0 and D/A = 50 percent are taken from Table 13-2. Values at other D/A ratios were calculated similarly.

DETERMINING THE OPTIMAL CAPITAL STRUCTURE

As we saw in Figure 13-6, Bigbee's expected EPS is maximized at a debt/assets ratio of 50 percent. Does that mean that Bigbee's optimal capital structure calls for 50 percent debt? The answer is a resounding no — *the optimal capital struc-*

ture is the one that maximizes the price of the firm's stock, and this generally calls for a debt ratio that is lower than the one that maximizes expected EPS.

Recall from Chapter 9 that stock prices are positively related to expected dividends but negatively related to the required return on equity. Firms with higher earnings are able to pay higher dividends, so to the extent that higher debt levels raise expected earnings per share, leverage works to increase the stock price. However, higher debt levels also increase the firm's risk, and that raises the cost of equity and works to reduce the stock price. So, even though increasing the debt ratio from 40 to 50 percent raises EPS, the higher EPS is more than offset by the corresponding increase in risk.

WACC AND CAPITAL STRUCTURE CHANGES

Managers should choose the capital structure that maximizes the firm's stock price. However, it is difficult to estimate how a given change in the capital structure will affect the stock price. As it turns out, however, the capital structure that maximizes the stock price is also the one that minimizes the WACC. Because it is usually easier to predict how a capital structure change will affect the WACC than the stock price, many managers use the predicted changes in the WACC to guide their capital structure decisions.

Recall from Chapter 10 that when there is no preferred stock in a firm's capital structure, the WACC is defined as follows:

$$WACC = w_d(k_d)(1 - T) + w_c(k_s)$$
$$= (D/A)(k_d)(1 - T) + (E/A)(k_s).$$

In this expression, D/A and E/A represent the debt and equity ratios, and they sum to 1.0.

Note that in Table 13-3 an increase in the debt/assets ratio raises the costs of both debt and equity. [The cost of debt, k_d, is taken from Table 13-1, but multiplied by $(1 - T)$ to put it on an after-tax basis.] Bondholders recognize that if a firm has a higher debt ratio, this increases the risk of financial distress, and more risk leads to higher interest rates.

In practice, financial managers use the forecasting techniques described in Chapter 4 to determine how changes in the debt ratio will affect the current ratio, times-interest-earned ratio, and EBITDA coverage ratio. They then discuss their pro forma financial statements with bankers and bond rating agencies, who ask probing questions and may make their own adjustments to the firm's forecasts. The bankers and rating agencies then compare the firm's ratios with those of other firms in its industry, and end up with a rating and corresponding interest rate. Moreover, if the company plans to issue bonds to the public, the SEC requires that it inform investors what the coverages will be after the new bonds have been sold. Recognizing all this, sophisticated financial managers use their forecasted ratios to predict how bankers and other lenders will judge their firms' risks and thus determine their cost of debt. Thus, they can judge quite accurately the effects of capital structure on the cost of debt.

THE HAMADA EQUATION

An increase in the debt ratio also increases the risk faced by shareholders, and this has an effect on the cost of equity, k_s. This relationship is harder to quantify, but it can be done. To begin, recall from Chapter 6 that a stock's beta

TABLE 13-3

Bigbee's Stock Price and Cost of Capital Estimates with Different Debt/Assets Ratios

DEBT/ ASSETS (1)	DEBT/ EQUITY[a] (2)	A – T k_d (3)	EXPECTED EPS (AND DPS)[b] (4)	ESTIMATED BETA[c] (5)	$k_s = [k_{RF} + (k_M - k_{RF})b]$[d] (6)	ESTIMATED PRICE[e] (7)	RESULTING P/E RATIO (8)	WEIGHTED AVERAGE COST OF CAPITAL, WACC[f] (9)
0%	0.00%	4.8%	$2.40	1.50	12.0%	$20.00	8.33×	12.00%
10	11.11	4.8	2.56	1.60	12.4	20.65	8.06	11.64
20	25.00	5.0	2.75	1.73	12.9	21.33	7.75	11.32
30	42.86	5.4	2.97	1.89	13.5	21.90	7.38	11.10
40	**66.67**	**6.0**	**3.20**	**2.10**	**14.4**	**22.22**	**6.94**	**11.04**
50	100.00	7.2	3.36	2.40	15.6	21.54	6.41	11.40
60	150.00	9.0	3.30	2.85	17.4	18.97	5.75	12.36

[a] $D/E = \dfrac{D/A}{1 - D/A}$.

[b] Bigbee pays all of its earnings out as dividends, so EPS = DPS.

[c] The firm's unlevered beta, b_U, is 1.5. The remaining betas were calculated using the Hamada Equation, given the unlevered beta, tax rate, and D/E ratio as inputs.

[d] We assume that $k_{RF} = 6\%$ and $k_M = 10\%$. Therefore, at debt/assets equal to zero, $k_s = 6\% + (10\% - 6\%)1.5 = 6\% + 6\% = 12\%$. Other values of k_s are calculated similarly.

[e] Since all earnings are paid out as dividends, no retained earnings will be plowed back into the business, and growth in EPS and DPS will be zero. Hence, the zero growth stock price model developed in Chapter 9 can be used to estimate the price of Bigbee's stock. For example, at Debt/Assets = 0,

$$P_0 = \frac{DPS}{k_s} = \frac{\$2.40}{0.12} = \$20.$$

Other prices were calculated similarly.

[f] Column 9 is found by use of the weighted average cost of capital (WACC) equation developed in Chapter 10:

$$WACC = w_d k_d (1 - T) + w_c k_s$$
$$= (D/A)(k_d)(1 - T) + (1 - D/A)k_s.$$

For example, at D/A = 40%,

$$WACC = 0.4(10\%)(0.6) + 0.6(14.4\%) = 11.04\%.$$

We use book weights here, but market value weights would be theoretically better. See Eugene F. Brigham and Phillip R. Daves, *Intermediate Financial Management,* 7th ed. (Fort Worth, TX: Harcourt College Publishers, 2002), Chapter 9, for a discussion of this point.

is the relevant measure of risk for diversified investors. Moreover, it has been demonstrated, both theoretically and empirically, that beta increases with financial leverage. Indeed, Robert Hamada developed the following equation to specify the effect of financial leverage on beta:[6]

$$b = b_U[1 + (1 - T)(D/E)]. \tag{13-2}$$

---

[6] See Robert S. Hamada, "Portfolio Analysis, Market Equilibrium, and Corporation Finance," *Journal of Finance,* March 1969, 13–31. Note that Thomas Conine and Maurry Tamarkin have extended Hamada's work to include risky debt. See "Divisional Cost of Capital Estimation: Adjusting for Leverage," *Financial Management,* Spring 1985, 54–58. See also Brigham and Daves, *Intermediate Financial Management,* 7th ed. (Fort Worth, TX: Harcourt College Publishers, 2002), Chapter 15, for a more detailed discussion of the Hamada equation.

The Hamada equation shows how increases in the debt/equity ratio increase beta. Here b_U is the firm's unlevered beta coefficient, that is, the beta it would have if it has no debt. In that case, beta would depend entirely upon business risk and thus be a measure of the firm's "basic business risk." D/E is the measure of financial leverage used in the Hamada equation.[7]

Note that beta is the only variable under management's control in the cost of equity equation, $k_s = k_{RF} + (k_M - k_{RF}) b_i$. Both k_{RF} and k_M are determined by market forces that are beyond the firm's control. However, b_i is determined (1) by the firm's operating decisions as discussed earlier in the chapter, which affect b_U, and (2) by its capital structure decisions as reflected in its D/A (or D/E) ratio.

As a starting point, a firm can take its current beta, tax rate, and debt/equity ratio and calculate its **unlevered beta, b_U,** by simply transforming Equation 13-2 as follows:

Unlevered Beta, b_U
The firm's beta coefficient if it has no debt.

$$b_U = b/[1 + (1 - T)(D/E)]. \qquad (13\text{-}2a)$$

Then, once b_U is determined, the Hamada equation can be used to estimate how changes in the debt/equity ratio would affect the leveraged beta, b_i, and thus the cost of equity, k_s.

We can illustrate the procedure with Bigbee Electronics. First, we assume that the risk-free rate of return, k_{RF}, is 6 percent, and that the required return on an average stock, k_M, is 10 percent. Next, we need the unlevered beta, b_U. Because Bigbee has no debt, its D/E = 0. Therefore, its current beta of 1.5 is also its unlevered beta; hence $b_U = 1.5$. Now, with b_U, k_{RF}, and k_M specified, we can use the CAPM to estimate how much Bigbee's market beta would rise if it began to use financial leverage, hence what its cost of equity would be at different capital structures. These beta estimates are shown in Column 5 of Table 13-3.

Currently, based on Plan B and no debt, Bigbee has a beta of b = 1.5. Further, the risk-free rate is k_{RF} = 6% and the market risk premium is $k_M - k_{RF}$ = 10% − 6% = 4%. Therefore, Bigbee's current cost of equity is 12 percent as shown in Column 6:

$$k_s = k_{RF} + \text{Risk premium}$$
$$= 6\% + (4\%)(1.5)$$
$$= 6\% + 6\% = 12\%.$$

The first 6 percent is the risk-free rate, the second the risk premium. Because Bigbee currently uses no debt, it has no financial risk. Therefore, the 6 percent risk premium reflects only its business risk.

---

[7] Recall from Chapter 3 that the debt/equity ratio, D/E, is directly related to the D/A ratio:

$$\frac{D}{E} = \frac{D/A}{1 - D/A}.$$

For example, if the firm has $40 of debt and $60 of equity, then D/A = 0.4, E/A = 0.6, and

$$\frac{D}{E} = \frac{0.4}{1 - 0.4} = 0.4/0.6 = 0.6667.$$

Thus, any D/A ratio can be directly translated into a D/E ratio. Note also that Hamada's equation assumes that assets are reported at market values rather than accounting book values. This point is discussed at length in Brigham and Daves, *Intermediate Financial Management*, 7th edition, where the feedbacks among capital structure, stock prices, and capital costs are developed.

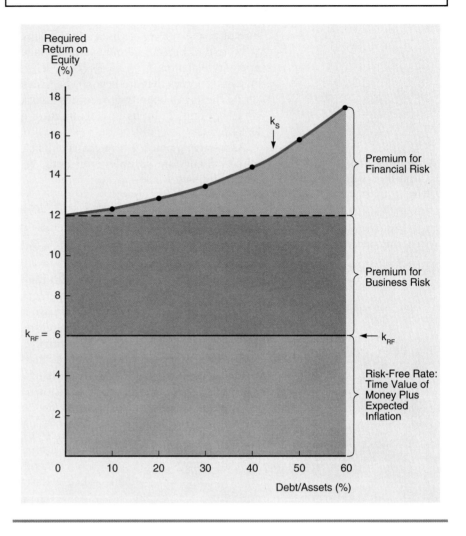

If Bigbee changes its capital structure by adding debt, this would increase the risk stockholders bear. That, in turn, would result in an additional risk premium. Conceptually, this situation would exist:

$$k_s = k_{RF} + \text{Premium for business risk} + \text{Premium for financial risk.}$$

Figure 13-7 (using data calculated in Column 6 of Table 13-3) graphs Bigbee's required return on equity at different debt ratios. As the figure shows, k_s consists of the 6 percent risk-free rate, a constant 6 percent premium for business risk, and a premium for financial risk that starts at zero but rises at an increasing rate as the debt ratio increases.

THE OPTIMAL CAPITAL STRUCTURE

Column 9 of Table 13-3 shows Bigbee's weighted average cost of capital, WACC, at different capital structures. Currently, it has no debt, so its capital structure is 100 percent equity, and at this point WACC = k_s = 12%. As Bigbee begins to use lower-cost debt, the WACC declines. However, as the debt ratio increases, the costs of both debt and equity rise, at first slowly but then at a faster and faster rate. Eventually, the increasing costs of the two components offset the fact that more low-cost debt is being used. At 40 percent debt, the WACC hits a minimum of 11.04 percent, and after that it rises with further increases in the debt ratio.

Note too that even though the component cost of equity is generally higher than that of debt, using only lower-cost debt would not maximize value because of the feedback effects of debt on the costs of debt and equity. If Bigbee were to issue more than 40 percent debt, it would then be relying more on the cheaper source of capital, but this lower cost would be more than offset by the fact that using more debt would raise the costs of both debt and equity. These thoughts were echoed in a recent Annual Report of the Georgia-Pacific Corporation:

> On a market-value basis, our debt-to-capital ratio was 47 percent. By employing this capital structure, we believe that our weighted average cost of capital is nearly optimized — at approximately 10 percent. Although reducing debt significantly would somewhat reduce the marginal cost of debt, significant debt reduction would likely increase our weighted average cost of capital by raising the proportion of higher-cost equity.

Finally, recall that the capital structure that minimizes the WACC is also the capital structure that maximizes the firm's stock price. In principle, we could use the stock valuation techniques described in Chapter 9 to predict how changes in capital structure would affect the stock price. This exercise is difficult, especially for firms that do not pay a dividend or whose cash flows are not constant over time. However, Bigbee pays out all of its earnings as dividends, so it plows none of its earnings back into the business and its growth in earnings and dividends per share are zero. Thus, in Bigbee's case we can use the zero growth stock price model developed in Chapter 9 to estimate the stock price at each different capital structure. These estimates are shown in Column 7 of Table 13-3. Here we see that the expected stock price first rises with financial leverage, hits a peak of $22.22 at a debt ratio of 40 percent, and then begins to decline. *Thus, Bigbee's optimal capital structure occurs at a debt ratio of 40 percent, and that debt ratio both maximizes its stock price and minimizes its WACC.*

The EPS, cost of capital, and stock price data shown in Table 13-3 are plotted in Figure 13-8. As the graph shows, the debt/assets ratio that maximizes Bigbee's expected EPS is 50 percent. However, the expected stock price is maximized, and the cost of capital is minimized, at a 40 percent debt ratio. *Thus, Bigbee's optimal capital structure calls for 40 percent debt and 60 percent equity.* Management should set its target capital structure at these ratios, and if the existing ratios are off target, it should move toward the target when new security offerings are made.

FIGURE 13-8 **Effects of Capital Structure on EPS, Cost of Capital, and Stock Price**

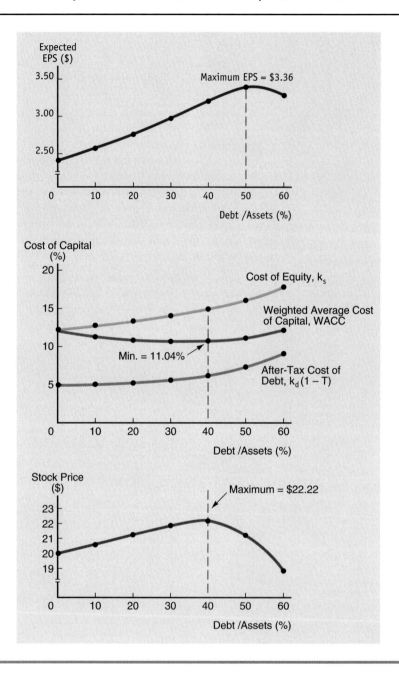

INDUSTRY PRACTICE

YOGI BERRA ON THE M&M PROPOSITION

When a waitress asked Yogi Berra (Baseball Hall of Fame catcher for the New York Yankees) whether he wanted his pizza cut into four pieces or eight, Yogi replied: "Better make it four. I don't think I can eat eight."[a]

Yogi's quip helps convey the basic insight of Modigliani and Miller. The firm's choice of leverage "slices" the distribution of future cash flows in a way that is like slicing a pizza. M&M recognize that if you fix a company's investment activities, it's like fixing the size of the pizza; no information costs means that everyone sees the same pizza; no taxes means the IRS gets none of the pie; and no "contracting" costs means nothing sticks to the knife.

So, just as the substance of Yogi's meal is unaffected by whether the pizza is sliced into four pieces or eight, the economic substance of the firm is unaffected by whether the liability side of the balance sheet is sliced to include more or less debt under the M&M assumptions.

[a]Lee Green, *Sportswit* (New York: Fawcett Crest, 1984), 228.

SOURCE: "Yogi Berra on the M&M Proposition," *Journal of Applied Corporate Finance,* Vol. 7, No. 4, Winter 1995, 6. Used by permission.

SELF-TEST QUESTIONS

What happens to the costs of debt and equity when the debt/assets ratio increases? Explain.

Using the Hamada equation, show the effect of financial leverage on beta.

Give the equation for calculating a firm's unlevered beta.

Using a graph and illustrative data, identify the premiums for financial risk and business risk at different debt levels. Do these premiums vary depending on the debt level? Explain.

Is expected EPS maximized at the optimal capital structure?

CAPITAL STRUCTURE THEORY

In the previous section, we showed how a firm might estimate its optimal capital structure. For a number of reasons, we would expect capital structures to vary considerably across industries. For example, pharmaceutical companies generally have very different capital structures than airline companies. Moreover, capital structures vary among firms within a given industry. What factors can explain these differences? In an attempt to answer this question, academics and practitioners developed a number of theories, and the theories have been subjected to empirical tests.

Modern capital structure theory began in 1958, when Professors Franco Modigliani and Merton Miller (hereafter MM) published what has been called the most influential finance article ever written.[8] MM proved, under a very

---

[8] Franco Modigliani and Merton H. Miller, "The Cost of Capital, Corporation Finance, and the Theory of Investment," *American Economic Review,* June 1958. Modigliani and Miller both won Nobel Prizes for their work.

restrictive set of assumptions, that a firm's value is unaffected by its capital structure. Put another way, MM's results suggest that it does not matter how a firm finances its operations, hence capital structure is irrelevant. However, MM's study was based on some unrealistic assumptions, including the following:

1. There are no brokerage costs.
2. There are no taxes.
3. There are no bankruptcy costs.
4. Investors can borrow at the same rate as corporations.
5. All investors have the same information as management about the firm's future investment opportunities.
6. EBIT is not affected by the use of debt.

Despite the fact that some of these assumptions are obviously unrealistic, MM's irrelevance result is extremely important. By indicating the conditions under which capital structure is irrelevant, MM also provided us with clues about what is required for capital structure to be relevant and hence to affect a firm's value. MM's work marked the beginning of modern capital structure research, and subsequent research has focused on relaxing the MM assumptions in order to develop a more realistic theory of capital structure. Research in this area is quite extensive, but the highlights are summarized in the following sections.

THE EFFECT OF TAXES

MM published a follow-up paper in 1963 in which they relaxed the assumption that there are no corporate taxes.[9] The Tax Code allows corporations to deduct interest payments as an expense, but dividend payments to stockholders are not deductible. This differential treatment encourages corporations to use debt in their capital structures. Indeed, MM demonstrated that if all their other assumptions hold, this differential treatment leads to a situation that calls for 100 percent debt financing.

However, this conclusion was modified several years later by Merton Miller (this time without Modigliani) when he brought in the effects of personal taxes.[10] He noted that all of the income from bonds is generally interest, which is taxed as personal income at rates going up to 39.6 percent, while income from stocks generally comes partly from dividends and partly from capital gains. Further, long-term capital gains are taxed at a rate of 20 percent, and this tax is deferred until the stock is sold and the gain realized. If stock is held until the owner dies, no capital gains tax whatever must be paid. So, on balance, returns on common stocks are taxed at lower effective rates than returns on debt.

Because of the tax situation, Miller argued that investors are willing to accept relatively low before-tax returns on stock relative to the before-tax returns on bonds. (The situation here is similar to that with tax-exempt municipal

---

[9] Franco Modigliani and Merton H. Miller, "Corporate Income Taxes and the Cost of Capital: A Correction," *American Economic Review* 53, June 1963, 433–443.

[10] Merton H. Miller, "Debt and Taxes," *Journal of Finance* 32, May 1977, 261–275.

bonds as discussed in Chapter 8 and preferred stocks held by corporate investors as discussed in Chapter 9.) For example, an investor might require a return of 10 percent on Bigbee's bonds, and if stock income were taxed at the same rate as bond income, the required rate of return on Bigbee's stock might be 16 percent because of the stock's greater risk. However, in view of the favorable treatment of income on the stock, investors might be willing to accept a before-tax return of only 14 percent on the stock.

Thus, as Miller pointed out, (1) the *deductibility of interest* favors the use of debt financing, but (2) the *more favorable tax treatment of income from stocks* lowers the required rate of return on stock and thus favors the use of equity financing. It is difficult to say what the net effect of these two factors is. Most observers believe that interest deductibility has the stronger effect, hence that our tax system still favors the corporate use of debt. However, that effect is certainly reduced by the lower long-term capital gains tax rate.

One can observe changes in corporate financing patterns following major changes in tax rates. For example, in 1993 the top personal tax rate on interest and dividends was raised sharply, but the capital gains tax rate was not increased. This could be expected to result in a greater reliance on equity financing, especially through retained earnings, and that has indeed been the case. The lowering of the long-term capital gains tax rate in 1997 has continued this trend.

THE EFFECT OF BANKRUPTCY COSTS

MM's irrelevance results also depend on the assumption that there are no bankruptcy costs. However, in practice bankruptcy can be quite costly. Firms in bankruptcy have very high legal and accounting expenses, and they also have a hard time retaining customers, suppliers, and employees. Moreover, bankruptcy often forces a firm to liquidate or sell assets for less than they would be worth if the firm were to continue operating. For example, if a steel manufacturer goes out of business, it might be hard to find buyers for the company's blast furnaces, even though they were quite expensive. Assets such as plant and equipment are often illiquid because they are configured to a company's individual needs and also because they are difficult to disassemble and move.

Note, too, that the *threat of bankruptcy*, not just bankruptcy per se, brings about these problems. Key employees jump ship, suppliers refuse to grant credit, customers seek more stable suppliers, and lenders demand higher interest rates and impose more restrictive loan covenants if potential bankruptcy looms.

Bankruptcy-related problems are more likely to arise when a firm includes more debt in its capital structure. Therefore, bankruptcy costs discourage firms from pushing their use of debt to excessive levels.

Bankruptcy-related costs have two components: (1) the probability of their occurrence and (2) the costs they would produce given that financial distress has arisen. Firms whose earnings are more volatile, all else equal, face a greater chance of bankruptcy and, therefore, should use less debt than more stable firms. This is consistent with our earlier point that firms with high operating leverage, and thus greater business risk, should limit their use of financial leverage. Likewise, firms that would face high costs in the event of financial distress should rely less heavily on debt. For example, firms whose assets are illiquid and thus would have to be sold at "fire sale" prices should limit their use of debt financing.

FIGURE 13-9   Effect of Leverage on the Value of Bigbee's Stock

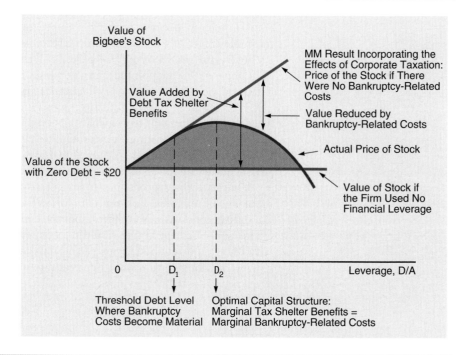

TRADE-OFF THEORY

The preceding arguments led to the development of what is called "the trade-off theory of leverage," in which firms trade off the benefits of debt financing (favorable corporate tax treatment) against the higher interest rates and bankruptcy costs. A summary of the trade-off theory is expressed graphically in Figure 13-9. Here are some observations about the figure:

1. The fact that interest is a deductible expense makes debt less expensive than common or preferred stock. In effect, the government pays part of the cost of debt capital, or, to put it another way, debt provides *tax shelter benefits*. As a result, using debt causes more of the firm's operating income (EBIT) to flow through to investors. Therefore, the more debt a company uses, the higher its value and stock price. Under the assumptions of the Modigliani-Miller with-taxes paper, a firm's stock price will be maximized if it uses virtually 100 percent debt, and the line labeled "MM Result Incorporating the Effects of Corporate Taxation" in Figure 13-9 expresses the relationship between stock prices and debt under their assumptions.

2. In the real world, firms rarely use 100 percent debt. The primary reason is that firms limit their use of debt to hold down bankruptcy-related costs.

3. There is some threshold level of debt, labeled D_1 in Figure 13-9, below which the probability of bankruptcy is so low as to be immaterial. Beyond

D_1, however, bankruptcy-related costs become increasingly important, and they reduce the tax benefits of debt at an increasing rate. In the range from D_1 to D_2, bankruptcy-related costs reduce but do not completely offset the tax benefits of debt, so the firm's stock price rises (but at a decreasing rate) as its debt ratio increases. However, beyond D_2, bankruptcy-related costs exceed the tax benefits, so from this point on increasing the debt ratio lowers the value of the stock. Therefore, D_2 is the optimal capital structure. Of course, D_1 and D_2 vary from firm to firm, depending on their business risk and bankruptcy costs.

4. While theoretical and empirical work supports the general shape of the curves in Figures 13-8 and 13-9, these graphs must be taken as approximations, not as precisely defined functions. The numbers in Figure 13-8 are shown out to two decimal places, but that is merely for illustrative purposes — the numbers are not nearly that accurate in view of the fact that the data on which the graph is based are judgmental estimates.

5. Another disturbing aspect of capital structure theory as expressed in Figure 13-9 is the fact that many large, successful firms, such as Intel and Microsoft, use far less debt than the theory suggests. This point led to the development of signaling theory, which is discussed below.

SIGNALING THEORY

Symmetric Information
The situation in which investors and managers have identical information about firms' prospects.

Asymmetric Information
The situation in which managers have different (better) information about firms' prospects than do investors.

MM assumed that investors have the same information about a firm's prospects as its managers — this is called **symmetric information.** However, in fact managers often have better information than outside investors. This is called **asymmetric information,** and it has an important effect on the optimal capital structure. To see why, consider two situations, one in which the company's managers know that its prospects are extremely favorable (Firm F) and one in which the managers know that the future looks unfavorable (Firm U).

Suppose, for example, that Firm F's R&D labs have just discovered a non-patentable cure for the common cold. They want to keep the new product a secret as long as possible to delay competitors' entry into the market. New plants must be built to make the new product, so capital must be raised. How should Firm F's management raise the needed capital? If the firm sells stock, then, when profits from the new product start flowing in, the price of the stock would rise sharply, and the purchasers of the new stock would make a bonanza. The current stockholders (including the managers) would also do well, but not as well as they would have done if the company had not sold stock before the price increased, because then they would not have had to share the benefits of the new product with the new stockholders. *Therefore, one would expect a firm with very favorable prospects to try to avoid selling stock and, rather, to raise any required new capital by other means, including using debt beyond the normal target capital structure.*[11]

Now let's consider Firm U. Suppose its managers have information that new orders are off sharply because a competitor has installed new technology that has improved its products' quality. Firm U must upgrade its own facilities, at a

---

[11] It would be illegal for Firm F's managers to personally purchase more shares on the basis of their inside knowledge of the new product. They could be sent to jail if they did.

high cost, just to maintain its current sales. As a result, its return on investment will fall (but not by as much as if it took no action, which would lead to a 100 percent loss through bankruptcy). How should Firm U raise the needed capital? Here the situation is just the reverse of that facing Firm F, which did not want to sell stock so as to avoid having to share the benefits of future developments. *A firm with unfavorable prospects would want to sell stock, which would mean bringing in new investors to share the losses!*[12]

The conclusion from all this is that firms with extremely bright prospects prefer not to finance through new stock offerings, whereas firms with poor prospects do like to finance with outside equity. How should you, as an investor, react to this conclusion? You ought to say, "If I see that a company plans to issue new stock, this should worry me because I know that management would not want to issue stock if future prospects looked good. However, management would want to issue stock if things looked bad. Therefore, I should lower my estimate of the firm's value, other things held constant, if it plans to issue new stock."

If you gave the above answer, your views are consistent with those of sophisticated portfolio managers of institutions such as Morgan Guaranty Trust, Prudential Insurance, and so forth. *In a nutshell, the announcement of a stock offering is generally taken as a* **signal** *that the firm's prospects as seen by its management are not bright.* This, in turn, suggests that when a firm announces a new stock offering, more often than not, the price of its stock will decline. Empirical studies have shown that this situation does indeed exist.[13]

What are the implications of all this for capital structure decisions? Since issuing stock emits a negative signal and thus tends to depress the stock price, even if the company's prospects are bright, a firm should, in normal times, maintain a **reserve borrowing capacity** that can be used in the event that some especially good investment opportunity comes along. *This means that firms should, in normal times, use more equity and less debt than is suggested by the tax benefit/bankruptcy cost trade-off model expressed in Figure 13-9.*

USING DEBT FINANCING TO CONSTRAIN MANAGERS

In Chapter 1 we stated that agency problems may arise if managers and shareholders have different objectives. Such conflicts are particularly likely when the firm's managers have too much cash at their disposal. Managers often use such cash to finance their pet projects or for perquisites such as nicer offices, corporate jets, and sky boxes at sports arenas, all of which may do little to maximize stock prices.[14] By contrast, managers with limited "free cash flow" are less able to make wasteful expenditures.

Firms can reduce excess cash flow in a variety of ways. One way is to funnel some of it back to shareholders through higher dividends or stock repurchases. Another alternative is to shift the capital structure toward more debt in the hope that higher debt service requirements will force managers to become

Signal
An action taken by a firm's management that provides clues to investors about how management views the firm's prospects.

Reserve Borrowing Capacity
The ability to borrow money at a reasonable cost when good investment opportunities arise. Firms often use less debt than specified by the MM optimal capital structure in "normal" times to ensure that they can obtain debt capital later if they need to.

---

[12] Of course, Firm U would have to make certain disclosures when it offered new shares to the public, but it might be able to meet the legal requirements without fully disclosing management's worst fears.

[13] Paul Asquith and David W. Mullins, Jr., "The Impact of Initiating Dividend Payments on Shareholders' Wealth," *Journal of Business*, January 1983, 77–96.

[14] If you don't believe corporate managers can waste money, read Bryan Burrough, *Barbarians at the Gate* (New York: Harper & Row, 1990), the story of the takeover of RJR-Nabisco.

more disciplined. If debt is not serviced as required, the firm will be forced into bankruptcy, in which case its managers would likely lose their jobs. Therefore, a manager is less likely to buy an expensive new corporate jet if the firm has large debt service requirements that could cost the manager his or her job.

A leveraged buyout (LBO) is one way to reduce excess cash flow. In an LBO debt is used to finance the purchase of a company's shares, after which the firm "goes private." Many leveraged buyouts, which were especially common during the late 1980s, were designed specifically to reduce corporate waste. As noted, high debt payments force managers to conserve cash by eliminating unnecessary expenditures.

Of course, increasing debt and reducing free cash flow has its downside: It increases the risk of bankruptcy. One professor has argued that adding debt to a firm's capital structure is like putting a dagger into the steering wheel of a car.[15] The dagger—which points toward your stomach—motivates you to drive more carefully, but you may get stabbed if someone runs into you, even if you are being careful. The analogy applies to corporations in the following sense: Higher debt forces managers to be more careful with shareholders' money, but even well-run firms could face bankruptcy (get stabbed) if some event beyond their control such as a war, an earthquake, a strike, or a recession occurs. To complete the analogy, the capital structure decision comes down to deciding how big a dagger stockholders should use to keep managers in line.

If you find our discussion of capital structure theory imprecise and somewhat confusing, you are not alone. In truth, no one knows how to identify precisely a firm's optimal capital structure, or how to measure the effects of capital structure on stock prices and the cost of capital. In practice, capital structure decisions must be made using a combination of judgment and numerical analysis. Still, an understanding of the theoretical issues presented here can help you make better judgments on capital structure issues.[16]

> ## SELF-TEST QUESTIONS
>
> Why does M&M's theory with taxes lead to 100 percent debt?
>
> How would an increase in corporate taxes affect firms' capital structure decisions? What about personal taxes?
>
> Explain how "asymmetric information" and "signals" affect capital structure decisions.
>
> What is meant by *reserve borrowing capacity,* and why is it important to firms?
>
> How can the use of debt serve to discipline managers?

---

[15] Ben Bernake, "Is There Too Much Corporate Debt?" Federal Reserve Bank of Philadelphia *Business Review*, September/October 1989, 3–13.

[16] One of the authors can report firsthand the usefulness of financial theory in the actual establishment of corporate capital structures. In recent years, he has served as a consultant to several of the regional telephone companies established as a result of the breakup of AT&T, as well as to several large electric utilities. On the basis of finance theory and computer models that simulated results under a range of conditions, the companies were able to specify "optimal capital structure ranges" with at least a reasonable degree of confidence. Without finance theory, setting a target capital structure would have amounted to little more than throwing darts.

CHECKLIST FOR CAPITAL STRUCTURE DECISIONS

In addition to the types of analysis discussed above, firms generally consider the following factors when making capital structure decisions:

1. *Sales stability.* A firm whose sales are relatively stable can safely take on more debt and incur higher fixed charges than a company with unstable sales. Utility companies, because of their stable demand, have historically been able to use more financial leverage than industrial firms.

2. *Asset structure.* Firms whose assets are suitable as security for loans tend to use debt rather heavily. General-purpose assets that can be used by many businesses make good collateral, whereas special-purpose assets do not. Thus, real estate companies are usually highly leveraged, whereas companies involved in technological research are not.

3. *Operating leverage.* Other things the same, a firm with less operating leverage is better able to employ financial leverage because it will have less business risk.

4. *Growth rate.* Other things the same, faster-growing firms must rely more heavily on external capital (see Chapter 4). Further, the flotation costs involved in selling common stock exceed those incurred when selling debt, which encourages rapidly growing firms to rely more heavily on debt. At the same time, however, these firms often face greater uncertainty, which tends to reduce their willingness to use debt.

5. *Profitability.* One often observes that firms with very high rates of return on investment use relatively little debt. Although there is no theoretical justification for this fact, one practical explanation is that very profitable firms such as Intel, Microsoft, and Coca-Cola simply do not need to do much debt financing. Their high rates of return enable them to do most of their financing with internally generated funds.

6. *Taxes.* Interest is a deductible expense, and deductions are most valuable to firms with high tax rates. Therefore, the higher a firm's tax rate, the greater the advantage of debt.

7. *Control.* The effect of debt versus stock on a management's control position can influence capital structure. If management currently has voting control (over 50 percent of the stock) but is not in a position to buy any more stock, it may choose debt for new financings. On the other hand, management may decide to use equity if the firm's financial situation is so weak that the use of debt might subject it to serious risk of default, because if the firm goes into default, the managers will almost surely lose their jobs. However, if too little debt is used, management runs the risk of a takeover. Thus, control considerations could lead to the use of *either* debt or equity, because the type of capital that best protects management will vary from situation to situation. In any event, if management is at all insecure, it will consider the control situation.

8. *Management attitudes.* Since no one can prove that one capital structure will lead to higher stock prices than another, management can exercise its own judgment about the proper capital structure. Some manage-

ments tend to be more conservative than others, and thus use less debt than the average firm in their industry, whereas aggressive managements use more debt in the quest for higher profits.

9. *Lender and rating agency attitudes.* Regardless of managers' own analyses of the proper leverage factors for their firms, lenders' and rating agencies' attitudes frequently influence financial structure decisions. In the majority of cases, the corporation discusses its capital structure with lenders and rating agencies and gives much weight to their advice. For example, one large utility was recently told by Moody's and Standard & Poor's that its bonds would be downgraded if it issued more bonds. This influenced its decision to finance its expansion with common equity.

10. *Market conditions.* Conditions in the stock and bond markets undergo both long- and short-run changes that can have an important bearing on a firm's optimal capital structure. For example, during a recent credit crunch, the junk bond market dried up, and there was simply no market at a "reasonable" interest rate for any new long-term bonds rated below triple B. Therefore, low-rated companies in need of capital were forced to go to the stock market or to the short-term debt market, regardless of their target capital structures. When conditions eased, however, these companies sold bonds to get their capital structures back on target.

11. *The firm's internal condition.* A firm's own internal condition can also have a bearing on its target capital structure. For example, suppose a firm has just successfully completed an R&D program, and it forecasts higher earnings in the immediate future. However, the new earnings are not yet anticipated by investors, hence are not reflected in the stock price. This company would not want to issue stock—it would prefer to finance with debt until the higher earnings materialize and are reflected in the stock price. Then it could sell an issue of common stock, retire the debt, and return to its target capital structure. This point was discussed earlier in connection with asymmetric information and signaling.

12. *Financial flexibility.* An astute corporate treasurer made this statement to the authors:

> Our company can earn a lot more money from good capital budgeting and operating decisions than from good financing decisions. Indeed, we are not sure exactly how financing decisions affect our stock price, but we know for sure that having to turn down a promising venture because funds are not available will reduce our long-run profitability. For this reason, my primary goal as treasurer is to always be in a position to raise the capital needed to support operations.
>
> We also know that when times are good, we can raise capital with either stocks or bonds, but when times are bad, suppliers of capital are much more willing to make funds available if we give them a secured position, and this means debt. Further, when we sell a new issue of stock, this sends a negative "signal" to investors, so stock sales by a mature company such as ours are not desirable.

Putting all these thoughts together gives rise to the goal of *maintaining financial flexibility*, which, from an operational viewpoint, means *maintaining adequate reserve borrowing capacity*. Determining an "adequate" reserve borrowing capacity is judgmental, but it clearly depends on the factors discussed in the chapter, including the firm's forecasted need for funds, predicted capital market conditions, management's confidence in its forecasts, and the consequences of a capital shortage.

SELF-TEST QUESTIONS

How does sales stability affect the target capital structure?

How do the types of assets used affect a firm's capital structure?

How do taxes affect the target capital structure?

How do lender and rating agency attitudes affect capital structure?

How does the firm's internal condition affect its actual capital structure?

What is "financial flexibility," and is it increased or decreased by a high debt ratio?

VARIATIONS IN CAPITAL STRUCTURES

As might be expected, wide variations in the use of financial leverage occur both across industries and among the individual firms in each industry. Table 13-4 illustrates differences for selected industries; the ranking is in descending order of the ratio of common equity to total capital, as shown in Column 1.[17]

Pharmaceutical and computer companies do not use much debt (their ratios of common equity to total capital are high) because the uncertainties inherent in industries that are cyclical, oriented toward research, or subject to huge product liability suits render the heavy use of debt unwise. The airline and utility companies, on the other hand, use debt relatively heavily. The utilities have traditionally used large amounts of debt, particularly long-term debt, because their fixed assets make good security for mortgage bonds, and also because their relatively stable sales make it safe for them to carry more debt than would be true for firms with more business risk.

Particular attention should be given to the times-interest-earned (TIE) ratio because it gives an indication of how safe the debt is and how vulnerable the company is to financial distress. TIE ratios depend on three factors: (1) the percentage of debt, (2) the interest rate on the debt, and (3) the company's profitability. Generally, the least leveraged industries, such as the pharmaceutical industry, have the highest coverage ratios, whereas the utility industry, which finances heavily with debt, has a low average coverage ratio.

Wide variations also exist among firms within given industries. For example, although the average ratio of common equity to total capital in 2000 for the pharmaceutical industry was 80 percent, Eli Lilly & Co. had a ratio of only 68.5 percent. Thus, factors unique to individual firms, including managerial attitudes, play an important role in setting target capital structures.

---

[17] Information on capital structures and financial strength is available from a multitude of sources. We used the *Dow Jones News Retrieval* system to develop Table 13-4, but published sources include *The Value Line Investment Survey, Robert Morris Association Annual Studies,* and *Dun & Bradstreet Key Business Ratios.*

GLOBAL PERSPECTIVES

TAKING A LOOK AT GLOBAL CAPITAL STRUCTURES

To what extent does capital structure vary across different countries? The following table, which is taken from a recent study by Raghuram Rajan and Luigi Zingales, both of the University of Chicago, shows the median debt ratios of firms in the largest industrial countries.

Rajan and Zingales also show that there is considerable variation in capital structure among firms within each of the seven countries. However, they also show that capital structures for the firms in each country are generally determined by a similar set of factors: firm size, profitability, market-to-book ratio, and the ratio of fixed assets to total assets. All in all, the Rajan-Zingales study suggests that the points developed in this chapter apply to firms all around the world.

SOURCE: Raghuram G. Rajan and Luigi Zingales, "What Do We Know about Capital Structure? Some Evidence from International Data," *The Journal of Finance*, Vol. 50, No. 5, December 1995, 1421–1460. Used with permission.

Median Percentage of Debt to Total Assets in Different Countries

COUNTRY	BOOK VALUE DEBT RATIO
Canada	32%
France	18
Germany	11
Italy	21
Japan	21
United Kingdom	10
United States	25

TABLE 13-4 — Capital Structure Percentages, 2000: Six Industries Ranked by Common Equity Ratios[a]

INDUSTRY	COMMON EQUITY RATIO[b] (1)	LONG-TERM DEBT RATIO (2)	TIMES-INTEREST-EARNED RATIO (3)	RETURN ON EQUITY (4)
Pharmaceuticals	80.00%	20.00%	13.4×	34.8%
Computers	71.43	28.57	11.7	18.2
Steel	65.79	34.21	2.4	6.8
Aerospace	57.47	42.53	4.2	11.6
Utilities	41.91	58.09	2.8	10.5
Airlines	40.82	59.18	3.7	10.5

NOTES:
[a]Capital structure ratios are calculated as a percentage of total capital, where total capital is defined as long-term debt plus equity, with both measured at book value.
[b] These ratios are based on accounting (or book) values. Stated on a market-value basis, the equity percentages would rise because most stocks sell at prices that are much higher than their book values.
SOURCE: *Dow Jones News Retrieval*, 2000. Data collected through November 27, 2000.

> **SELF-TEST QUESTION**

Why do wide variations in the use of financial leverage occur both across industries and among individual firms in each industry?

TYING IT ALL TOGETHER

In Chapter 10, we took the firm's financing choice as given and then calculated the cost of capital based on that capital structure. Then, in Chapters 11 and 12, we described capital budgeting techniques, which use the firm's cost of capital as input. Capital budgeting decisions determine the types of projects that the firm accepts, which affect the nature of the firm's assets and its business risk. In this chapter we reverse the process, taking the firm's assets and business risk as given and then seeking to determine the best way to finance those assets. More specifically, in this chapter we examined the effects of financial leverage on stock prices, earnings per share, and the cost of capital. The key concepts covered are listed below.

- A firm's **optimal capital structure** is that mix of debt and equity that maximizes the stock price. At any point in time, management has a specific **target capital structure** in mind, presumably the optimal one, although this target may change over time.

- Several factors influence a firm's capital structure. These include the firm's (1) **business risk,** (2) **tax position,** (3) need for **financial flexibility,** and (4) **managerial conservatism or aggressiveness.**

- **Business risk** is the riskiness inherent in the firm's operations if it uses no debt. A firm will have little business risk if the demand for its products is stable, if the prices of its inputs and products remain relatively constant, if it can adjust its prices freely if costs increase, and if a high percentage of its costs are variable and hence will decrease if sales decrease. Other things the same, the lower a firm's business risk, the higher its optimal debt ratio.

- **Financial leverage** is the extent to which fixed-income securities (debt and preferred stock) are used in a firm's capital structure. **Financial risk** is the added risk borne by stockholders as a result of financial leverage.

- **Operating leverage** is the extent to which fixed costs are used in a firm's operations. In business terminology, a high degree of operating leverage, other factors held constant, implies that a relatively small change in sales results in a large change in ROE.

- Robert Hamada used the underlying assumptions of the CAPM, along with the Modigliani and Miller model, to develop the **Hamada equation,** which shows the effect of financial leverage on beta as follows:

$$b = b_U [1 + (1 - T)(D/E)].$$

Firms can take their current beta, tax rate, and debt/equity ratio to arrive at their **unlevered beta,** b_U, as follows:

$$b_U = b/[1 + (1 - T)(D/E)].$$

- **Modigliani and Miller** and their followers developed a **trade-off theory of capital structure.** They showed that debt is useful because interest is **tax deductible,** but also that debt brings with it costs associated with actual or potential bankruptcy. Under MM's theory, the optimal capital structure strikes a balance between the tax benefits of debt and the costs associated with bankruptcy.

- An alternative (or, really, complementary) theory of capital structure relates to the **signals** given to investors by a firm's decision to use debt versus stock to raise new capital. A stock issue sets off a negative signal, while using debt is a positive, or at least a neutral, signal. As a result, companies try to avoid having to issue stock by maintaining a **reserve borrowing capacity,** and this means using less debt in "normal" times than the MM trade-off theory would suggest.

- A firm's owners may have it use a relatively large amount of debt to constrain the managers. **A high debt ratio raises the threat of bankruptcy,** which carries a cost but which also forces managers to be more careful and less wasteful with shareholders' money. Many of the corporate takeovers and leveraged buyouts in recent years were designed to improve efficiency by reducing the free cash flow available to managers.

Although it is theoretically possible to determine a firm's optimal capital structure, as a practical matter we cannot estimate it with precision. Accordingly, financial executives generally treat the optimal capital structure as a range — for example, 40 to 50 percent debt — rather than as a precise point, such as 45 percent. The concepts discussed in this chapter help managers understand the factors they should consider when they set the target capital structure ranges for their firms.

QUESTIONS

13-1 Explain why the following statement is true: "Other things the same, firms with relatively stable sales are able to carry relatively high debt ratios."

13-2 Why do public utilities pursue a different financial policy than retail firms?

13-3 Why is EBIT generally considered to be independent of financial leverage? Why might EBIT actually be influenced by financial leverage at high debt levels?

13-4 If a firm went from zero debt to successively higher levels of debt, why would you expect its stock price to first rise, then hit a peak, and then begin to decline?

13-5 Why is the debt level that maximizes a firm's expected EPS generally higher than the one that maximizes its stock price?

13-6 When the Bell System was originally broken up, the old AT&T was split into a new AT&T plus seven regional telephone companies. The specific reason for forcing the breakup was to increase the degree of competition in the telephone industry. AT&T had a monopoly on local service, long distance, and the manufacture of all the equipment used by telephone companies, and the breakup was expected to open most of these markets to competition. In the court order that set the terms of the breakup, the capital structures of the surviving companies were specified, and much attention was given to the increased competition telephone companies could expect in the future. Do you think the optimal capital structure after the breakup should be the same as the pre-breakup optimal capital structure? Explain your position.

13-7 Assume that you are advising the management of a firm that is about to double its assets to serve its rapidly growing market. It must choose between a highly automated production process and a less automated one, and it must also choose a capital structure for financing the expansion. Should the asset investment and financing decisions be jointly determined, or should each decision be made separately? How would these decisions affect one another? How could the leverage concept be used to help management analyze the situation?

13-8 Your firm's R&D department has been working on a new process that, if it works, can produce oil from coal at a cost of about $5 per barrel versus a current market price of $30 per barrel. The company needs $10 million of external funds at this time to complete the research. The results of the research will be known in about a year, and there is about a 50-50 chance of success. If the research is successful, your company will need to raise a substantial amount of new money to put the idea into production. Your economists forecast that although the economy will be depressed next year, interest rates will be high because of international monetary problems. You must recommend how the currently needed $10 million should be raised — as debt or as equity. How would the potential impact of your project influence your decision?

13-9 Explain how profits or losses will be magnified for a firm with high operating leverage as opposed to a firm with lower operating leverage.

13-10 What data are necessary to construct a breakeven analysis?

13-11 What would be the effect of each of the following on a firm's breakeven point?
a. An increase in the sales price with no change in unit costs.
b. A change from straight-line depreciation to the MACRS method with no change in the beginning amount of fixed assets.
c. A reduction in variable labor costs; other things are held constant.

13-12 If Congress considers a change in the Tax Code that will increase personal tax rates but reduce corporate tax rates, what effect would this Tax Code change have on the average company's capital structure decision?

13-13 Which of the following are likely to encourage a firm to increase the amount of debt in its capital structure?
a. The corporate tax rate increases.
b. The personal tax rate increases.
c. The firm's assets become less liquid.
d. Changes in the bankruptcy code make bankruptcy less costly.
e. The firm's earnings become more volatile.

SELF-TEST PROBLEMS (SOLUTIONS APPEAR IN APPENDIX B)

ST-1
Key terms
Define each of the following terms:
a. Target capital structure
b. Business risk; financial risk
c. Financial leverage; operating leverage; operating breakeven
d. Hamada equation; unlevered beta; signal
e. Symmetric information; asymmetric information
f. Trade-off theory; signaling theory
g. Reserve borrowing capacity

ST-2
Financial leverage
Gentry Motors Inc., a producer of turbine generators, is in this situation: EBIT = $4 million; tax rate = T = 35%; debt outstanding = D = $2 million; k_d = 10%; k_s = 15%; shares of stock outstanding = N_0 = 600,000; and book value per share = $10. Since Gentry's product market is stable and the company expects no growth, all earnings are paid out as dividends. The debt consists of perpetual bonds.
a. What are Gentry's earnings per share (EPS) and its price per share (P_0)?
b. What is Gentry's weighted average cost of capital (WACC)?
c. Gentry can increase its debt by $8 million, to a total of $10 million, using the new debt to buy back and retire some of its shares at the current price. Its interest rate on debt will be 12 percent (it will have to call and refund the old debt), and its cost of equity will rise from 15 percent to 17 percent. EBIT will remain constant. Should Gentry change its capital structure?

d. If Gentry did not have to refund the $2 million of old debt, how would this affect things? Assume that the new and the still outstanding debt are equally risky, with $k_d = 12\%$, but that the coupon rate on the old debt is 10 percent.

e. What is Gentry's TIE coverage ratio under the original situation and under the conditions in Part c of this question?

ST-3
Operating leverage and breakeven analysis

Olinde Electronics Inc. produces stereo components that sell for $P = \$100$. Olinde's fixed costs are $200,000; 5,000 components are produced and sold each year; EBIT is currently $50,000; and Olinde's assets (all equity financed) are $500,000. Olinde estimates that it can change its production process, adding $400,000 to investment and $50,000 to fixed operating costs. This change will (1) reduce variable costs per unit by $10 and (2) increase output by 2,000 units, but (3) the sales price on all units will have to be lowered to $95 to permit sales of the additional output. Olinde has tax loss carry-forwards that cause its tax rate to be zero. Olinde uses no debt, and its average cost of capital is 10 percent.

a. Should Olinde make the change?

b. Would Olinde's breakeven point increase or decrease if it made the change?

c. Suppose Olinde were unable to raise additional equity financing and had to borrow the $400,000 to make the investment at an interest rate of 10 percent. Use the Du Pont equation to find the expected ROA of the investment. Should Olinde make the change if debt financing must be used?

STARTER PROBLEMS

13-1
Breakeven quantity

A company estimates that its fixed operating costs are $500,000, and its variable costs are $3.00 per unit sold. Each unit produced sells for $4.00. What is the company's breakeven point? In other words, how many units must it sell before its operating income becomes positive?

13-2
Optimal capital structure

Jackson Trucking Company is trying to determine its optimal capital structure. The company's CFO believes the optimal debt ratio is somewhere between 20 percent and 50 percent. Her staff has compiled the following projections for the company's EPS and stock price for various debt levels:

DEBT RATIO	PROJECTED EPS	PROJECTED STOCK PRICE
20%	$3.20	$35.00
30	3.45	36.50
40	3.75	36.25
50	3.50	35.50

Assuming that the firm uses only debt and common equity, what is Jackson's optimal capital structure? At what debt ratio is the company's WACC minimized?

13-3
Unlevered beta

Harley Motors has $10 million in assets, which is financed with $2 million of debt and $8 million in equity. If Harley's beta is currently 1.2 and its tax rate is 40 percent, what is its unlevered beta, b_U?

EXAM-TYPE PROBLEMS

The problems included in this section are set up in such a way that they could be used as multiple-choice exam problems.

13-4
Breakeven analysis

The Shipley Corporation produces tea kettles, which it sells for $15 each. Fixed costs are $700,000 for up to 400,000 units of output. Variable costs are $10 per kettle.

a. What is the firm's gain or loss at sales of 125,000 units? Of 175,000 units?

b. What is the breakeven point? Illustrate by means of a chart.

13-5
Breakeven analysis

The Weaver Watch Company manufactures ladies' watches that are sold through discount houses. Each watch is sold for $25; the fixed costs are $140,000 for 30,000 watches or less; variable costs are $15 per watch.

a. What is the firm's gain or loss at sales of 8,000 watches? Of 18,000 watches?

b. What is the breakeven point? Illustrate by means of a chart.

c. What happens to the breakeven point if the selling price rises to $31? What is the significance of the change to the financial manager?

d. What happens to the breakeven point if the selling price rises to $31 but variable costs rise to $23 a unit?

13-6
Breakeven analysis

The following relationships exist for Shome Industries, a manufacturer of electronic components. Each unit of output is sold for $45; the fixed costs are $175,000; variable costs are $20 per unit.

a. What is the firm's gain or loss at sales of 5,000 units? Of 12,000 units?
b. What is the breakeven point?

13-7
Financial leverage effects

A company currently has assets of $5 million. The firm is 100 percent equity financed. The company currently has net income of $1 million, and it pays out 40 percent of its net income as dividends. Both net income and dividends are expected to grow at a constant rate of 5 percent per year. There are 200,000 shares of stock outstanding, and it is estimated that the current cost of capital is 13.40 percent.

The company is considering a recapitalization where it will issue $1 million in debt and use the proceeds to repurchase stock. Investment bankers have estimated that if the company goes through with the recapitalization, its before-tax cost of debt will be 11 percent, and the cost of equity will rise to 14.5 percent. The company has a 40 percent federal-plus-state tax rate.

a. What is the current share price of the stock (before the recapitalization)?
b. Assuming that the company maintains the same payout ratio, what will be its stock price following the recapitalization?

13-8
Financial leverage effects

The firms HL and LL are identical except for their leverage ratios and interest rates on debt. Each has $20 million in assets, earned $4 million before interest and taxes in 2001, and has a 40 percent federal-plus-state tax rate. Firm HL, however, has a leverage ratio (D/TA) of 50 percent and pays 12 percent interest on its debt, whereas LL has a 30 percent leverage ratio and pays only 10 percent interest on debt.

a. Calculate the rate of return on equity (net income/equity) for each firm.
b. Observing that HL has a higher return on equity, LL's treasurer decides to raise the leverage ratio from 30 to 60 percent, which will increase LL's interest rate on all debt to 15 percent. Calculate the new rate of return on equity for LL.

13-9
Financial leverage effects

The Neal Company wishes to calculate next year's return on equity under different leverage ratios. Neal's total assets are $14 million, and its federal-plus-state tax rate is 40 percent. The company is able to estimate next year's earnings before interest and taxes for three possible states of the world: $4.2 million with a 0.2 probability, $2.8 million with a 0.5 probability, and $700,000 with a 0.3 probability. Calculate Neal's expected return on equity, standard deviation, and coefficient of variation for each of the following leverage ratios, and evaluate the results:

LEVERAGE (DEBT/TOTAL ASSETS)	INTEREST RATE
0%	—
10	9%
50	11
60	14

13-10
Hamada equation

Cyclone Software Co. is trying to estimate its optimal capital structure. Cyclone's current capital structure consists of 25 percent debt and 75 percent equity; however, management believes the firm should use more debt. The risk-free rate, k_{RF}, is 5 percent, the market risk premium, $k_M - k_{RF}$, is 6 percent, and the firm's tax rate is 40 percent. Currently, Cyclone's cost of equity is 14 percent, which is determined on the basis of the CAPM. What would be Cyclone's estimated cost of equity if it were to change its capital structure from its present capital structure to 50 percent debt and 50 percent equity?

PROBLEMS

13-11
Risk analysis

a. Given the following information, calculate the expected value for Firm C's EPS. $E(EPS_A) = 5.10, and $\sigma_A = 3.61; $E(EPS_B) = 4.20, and $\sigma_B = 2.96; and $\sigma_C = 4.11.

PROBABILITY				
0.1	0.2	0.4	0.2	0.1
Firm A: EPS_A	($1.50)	$1.80	$5.10	$8.40	$11.70
Firm B: EPS_B	(1.20)	1.50	4.20	6.90	9.60
Firm C: EPS_C	(2.40)	1.35	5.10	8.85	12.60

b. Discuss the relative riskiness of the three firms' (A, B, and C) earnings.

13-12
Degree of leverage

Wingler Communications Corporation (WCC) supplies headphones to airlines for use with movie and stereo programs. The headphones, which use the latest in electronic components, sell for $28.80 per set, and this year's sales are expected to be 450,000 units. Variable production costs for the expected sales under present production methods are estimated at $10,200,000, and fixed production (operating) costs at present are $1,560,000. WCC has $4,800,000 of debt outstanding at an interest rate of 8 percent. There are 240,000 shares of common stock outstanding, and there is no preferred stock. The dividend payout ratio is 70 percent, and WCC is in the 40 percent federal-plus-state tax bracket.

The company is considering investing $7,200,000 in new equipment. Sales would not increase, but variable costs per unit would decline by 20 percent. Also, fixed operating costs would increase from $1,560,000 to $1,800,000. WCC could raise the required capital by borrowing $7,200,000 at 10 percent or by selling 240,000 additional shares at $30 per share.

a. What would be WCC's EPS (1) under the old production process, (2) under the new process if it uses debt, and (3) under the new process if it uses common stock?

b. At what unit sales level would WCC have the same EPS, assuming it undertakes the investment and finances it with debt or with stock? (Hint: V = variable cost per unit = $8,160,000/450,000, and $EPS = [(PQ - VQ - F - I)(1 - T)]/N$. Set $EPS_{Stock} = EPS_{Debt}$ and solve for Q.)

c. At what unit sales level would EPS = 0 under the three production/financing setups — that is, under the old plan, the new plan with debt financing, and the new plan with stock financing? (Hint: Note that $V_{Old} = $10,200,000/450,000$, and use the hints for part b, setting the EPS equation equal to zero.)

d. On the basis of the analysis in parts a through c, and given that operating leverage is lower under the new setup, which plan is the riskiest, which has the highest expected EPS, and which would you recommend? Assume here that there is a fairly high probability of sales falling as low as 250,000 units, and determine EPS_{Debt} and EPS_{Stock} at that sales level to help assess the riskiness of the two financing plans.

13-13
Financing alternatives

The Severn Company plans to raise a net amount of $270 million to finance new equipment and working capital in early 2002. Two alternatives are being considered: Common stock may be sold to net $60 per share, or bonds yielding 12 percent may be issued. The balance sheet and income statement of the Severn Company prior to financing are as follows:

The Severn Company: Balance Sheet as of December 31, 2001
(Millions of Dollars)

Current assets	$ 900.00	Accounts payable	$ 172.50
Net fixed assets	450.00	Notes payable to bank	255.00
		Other current liabilities	225.00
		Total current liabilities	$ 652.50
		Long-term debt (10%)	300.00
		Common stock, $3 par	60.00
		Retained earnings	337.50
Total assets	$1,350.00	Total liabilities and equity	$1,350.00

The Severn Company: Income Statement for Year Ended December 31, 2001 (Millions of Dollars)

Sales	$2,475.00
Operating costs	2,227.50
Earnings before interest and taxes (10%)	$ 247.50
Interest on short-term debt	15.00
Interest on long-term debt	30.00
Earnings before taxes	$ 202.50
Federal-plus-state taxes (40%)	81.00
Net income	$ 121.50

The probability distribution for annual sales is as follows:

PROBABILITY	ANNUAL SALES (MILLIONS OF DOLLARS)
0.30	$2,250
0.40	2,700
0.30	3,150

Assuming that EBIT is equal to 10 percent of sales, calculate earnings per share under both the debt financing and the stock financing alternatives at each possible level of sales. Then calculate expected earnings per share and σ_{EPS} under both debt and stock financing alternatives. Also, calculate the debt ratio and the times-interest-earned (TIE) ratio at the expected sales level under each alternative. The old debt will remain outstanding. Which financing method do you recommend?

13-14
Breakeven and operating leverage

a. Given the graphs shown at the top of the next page, calculate the total fixed costs, variable costs per unit, and sales price for Firm A. Firm B's fixed costs are $120,000, its variable costs per unit are $4, and its sales price is $8 per unit.
b. Which firm has the higher operating leverage at any given level of sales? Explain.
c. At what *sales level*, in units, do both firms earn the same operating profit?

13-15
WACC and optimal capital structure

Elliott Athletics is trying to determine its optimal capital structure, which now consists of only debt and common equity. The firm does not currently use preferred stock in its capital structure, and it does not plan to do so in the future. To estimate how much its debt would cost at different debt levels, the company's treasury staff has consulted with investment bankers and, on the basis of those discussions, has created the following table:

DEBT-TO-ASSETS RATIO (w_d)	EQUITY-TO-ASSETS RATIO (w_c)	DEBT-TO-EQUITY RATIO (D/E)	BOND RATING	BEFORE-TAX COST OF DEBT (k_d)
0.0	1.0	0.00	A	7.0%
0.2	0.8	0.25	BBB	8.0
0.4	0.6	0.67	BB	10.0
0.6	0.4	1.50	C	12.0
0.8	0.2	4.00	D	15.0

Elliott uses the CAPM to estimate its cost of common equity, k_s. The company estimates that the risk-free rate is 5 percent, the market risk premium is 6 percent, and its tax rate is 40 percent. Elliott estimates that if it had no debt, its "unlevered" beta, b_U, would be 1.2. On the basis of this information, what is the firm's optimal capital structure, and what would the weighted average cost of capital be at the optimal capital structure?

Firm A

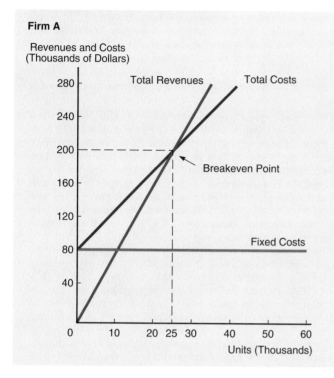

Revenues and Costs
(Thousands of Dollars)

Units (Thousands)

Firm B

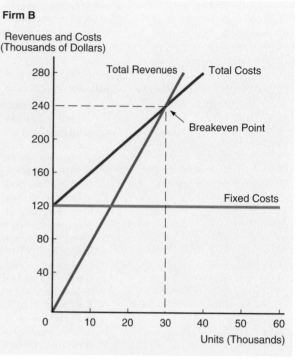

Revenues and Costs
(Thousands of Dollars)

Units (Thousands)

SPREADSHEET PROBLEM

13-16

WACC and optimal capital structure

Rework Problem 13-15 using a spreadsheet model. After completing the problem as it appears, answer the following related questions.

a. Plot a graph of the after-tax cost of debt, the cost of equity, and the WACC versus (1) the debt/assets ratio and (2) the debt/equity ratio.

b. Would the optimal capital structure change if the unlevered beta changed? To answer this question, do a sensitivity analysis of WACC on b_U for different levels of b_U.

CYBER PROBLEM

13-17

Applying the Hamada equation

The information related to this cyberproblem is likely to change over time, due to the release of new information and the ever-changing nature of the World Wide Web. Accordingly, we will periodically update the problem on the textbook's web site. To avoid problems, please check for updates before proceeding with the cyberproblems.

In Chapter 6, we introduced the concept of the Capital Asset Pricing Model (CAPM). The CAPM, as developed by Harry Markowitz and William Sharpe, contends that all stocks have an element of market risk. This market risk is materialized in the form of beta. We arrive at an asset's beta by running a linear regression of an asset's returns against market returns. However, we have never really addressed the matter of what drives beta.

In 1969, Robert Hamada published his paper, "Portfolio Analysis, Market Equilibrium, and Corporation Finance," wherein he combined the traditional CAPM and the Modigliani and Miller capital structure theory to create what is now called the "Hamada equation." The Hamada equation seeks to illustrate how increasing financial leverage increases a firm's risk and, by extension, the firm's beta.

In this cyberproblem, we use the Hamada equation to determine how useful it is when used in practice. Recall from the chapter that the Hamada equation is:

$$b = b_U [1 + (1 - T)(D/E)].$$

For this cyberproblem, you will need to access Quicken's web site at **http://www.quicken.com**.

a. Access Quicken's web site, and request a stock quote for Pfizer, Inc., whose stock symbol is PFE. When the quote appears, scroll down the page and look for "Fundamentals" on the left side of your screen. Click on that. Now, a large screen of data appears. First, record the 60-month beta for Pfizer. You should find the beta in the first section of the "Fundamentals" page, called "Price and Valuation." Next, scroll further down the "Fundamentals" page until you find the "Financial Strength" section. In this section, we see two kinds of debt-to-equity ratios: total debt to equity and long-term debt to equity. Because we are concerned with the long-term capital structure effects on beta, we will use the long-term debt-to-equity ratio. So, be sure to write that down, too.

b. From the "Fundamentals" page, request reports on the following companies: Merck & Co. (MRK), Heinz, HJ Co. (HNZ), Nabisco Holdings Company (NA), Southwest Airlines (LUV), American Airlines (AMR), Dow Chemical Co. (DOW), and DuPont (DD). Be sure to record the same information (the 60-month beta and the long-term debt-to-equity ratio) for these companies as we did for Pfizer, Inc. *Note, at this point we have two companies each from the chemical, drug, food, and airline industries.*

c. These data illustrate that those firms in different industries and even firms within the same industry have relatively different capital structures. Using the Hamada equation and data gathered in parts a and b, unlever the betas of these eight companies. For simplicity, assume the corporate tax rate is 40 percent for all of these companies.

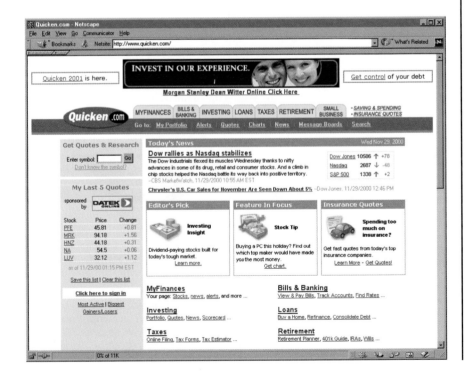

d. Compare the unlevered betas of the firms within the same industry. Are they consistent? Do they tend to support or contradict the theory behind the Hamada equation?

e. Now repeat this process for a new set of companies. Unlever the betas for Union Carbide (UK, chemical industry), Johnson & Johnson (JNJ, drug), General Mills (GIS, food), and Delta Airlines (DAL, airline).

f. Compare these firms' unlevered betas to their industry counterparts' unlevered betas calculated in part c. Do they seem consistent with your previous results? What conclusions can you make about using the Hamada equation in practice?

INTEGRATED CASE

CAMPUS DELI INC.

13-18 Optimal capital structure Assume that you have just been hired as business manager of Campus Deli (CD), which is located adjacent to the campus. Sales were $1,100,000 last year; variable costs were 60 percent of sales; and fixed costs were $40,000. Therefore, EBIT totaled $400,000. Because the university's enrollment is capped, EBIT is expected to be constant over time. Since no expansion capital is required, CD pays out all earnings as dividends. Assets are $2 million, and 80,000 shares are outstanding. The management group owns about 50 percent of the stock, which is traded in the over-the-counter market.

CD currently has no debt — it is an all-equity firm — and its 80,000 shares outstanding sell at a price of $25 per share, which is also the book value. The firm's federal-plus-state tax rate is 40 percent. On the basis of statements made in your finance text, you believe that CD's shareholders would be better off if some debt financing were used. When you suggested this to your new boss, she encouraged you to pursue the idea, but to provide support for the suggestion.

In today's market, the risk-free rate, k_{RF}, is 6 percent and the market risk premium, $k_M - k_{RF}$, is 6 percent. CD's unlevered beta, b_U, is 1.0. Since CD currently has no debt, its cost of equity (and WACC) is 12 percent.

If the firm were recapitalized, debt would be issued, and the borrowed funds would be used to repurchase stock. Stockholders, in turn, would use funds provided by the repurchase to buy equities in other fast-food companies similar to CD. You plan to complete your report by asking and then answering the following questions.

a. (1) What is business risk? What factors influence a firm's business risk?
   (2) What is operating leverage, and how does it affect a firm's business risk?

b. (1) What is meant by the terms "financial leverage" and "financial risk"?
   (2) How does financial risk differ from business risk?

c. Now, to develop an example that can be presented to CD's management as an illustration, consider two hypothetical firms, Firm U, with zero debt financing, and Firm L, with $10,000 of 12 percent debt. Both firms have $20,000 in total assets and a 40 percent federal-plus-state tax rate, and they have the following EBIT probability distribution for next year:

PROBABILITY	EBIT
0.25	$2,000
0.50	3,000
0.25	4,000

(1) Complete the partial income statements and the firms' ratios in Table IC13-1.
(2) Be prepared to discuss each entry in the table and to explain how this example illustrates the impact of financial leverage on expected rate of return and risk.

d. After speaking with a local investment banker, you obtain the following estimates of the cost of debt at different debt levels (in thousands of dollars):

AMOUNT BORROWED	DEBT/ASSETS RATIO	DEBT/EQUITY RATIO	BOND RATING	k_d
$ 0	0	0	—	—
250	0.125	0.1429	AA	8.0%
500	0.250	0.3333	A	9.0
750	0.375	0.6000	BBB	11.5
1,000	0.500	1.0000	BB	14.0

Now consider the optimal capital structure for CD.
(1) To begin, define the terms "optimal capital structure" and "target capital structure."

(2) Why does CD's bond rating and cost of debt depend on the amount of money borrowed?

(3) Assume that shares could be repurchased at the current market price of $25 per share. Calculate CD's expected EPS and TIE at debt levels of $0, $250,000, $500,000, $750,000, and $1,000,000. How many shares would remain after recapitalization under each scenario?

(4) Using the Hamada equation, what is the cost of equity if CD recapitalizes with $250,000 of debt? $500,000? $750,000? $1,000,000?

(5) Considering only the levels of debt discussed, what is the capital structure that minimizes CD's WACC?

(6) What would be the new stock price if CD recapitalizes with $250,000 of debt? $500,000? $750,000? $1,000,000? Recall that the payout ratio is 100 percent, so g = 0.

(7) Is EPS maximized at the debt level that maximizes share price? Why or why not?

(8) Considering only the levels of debt discussed, what is CD's optimal capital structure?

(9) What is the WACC at the optimal capital structure?

e. Suppose you discovered that CD had more business risk than you originally estimated. Describe how this would affect the analysis. What if the firm had less business risk than originally estimated?

f. What are some factors a manager should consider when establishing his or her firm's target capital structure?

g. Put labels on Figure IC13-1, and then discuss the graph as you might use it to explain to your boss why CD might want to use some debt.

h. How does the existence of asymmetric information and signaling affect capital structure?

TABLE IC13-1	**Income Statements and Ratios**					
	FIRM U			**FIRM L**		
Assets	$20,000	$20,000	$20,000	$20,000	$20,000	$20,000
Equity	$20,000	$20,000	$20,000	$10,000	$10,000	$10,000
Probability	0.25	0.50	0.25	0.25	0.50	0.25
Sales	$ 6,000	$ 9,000	$12,000	$ 6,000	$ 9,000	$12,000
Operating costs	4,000	6,000	8,000	4,000	6,000	8,000
Earnings before interest and taxes	$ 2,000	$ 3,000	$ 4,000	$ 2,000	$ 3,000	$ 4,000
Interest (12%)	0	0	0	1,200		1,200
Earnings before taxes	$ 2,000	$ 3,000	$ 4,000	$ 800	$	$ 2,800
Taxes (40%)	800	1,200	1,600	320		1,120
Net income	$ 1,200	$ 1,800	$ 2,400	$ 480	$	$ 1,680
Basic earning power (BEP = EBIT/Assets)	10.0%	15.0%	20.0%	10.0%	%	20.0%
ROE	6.0%	9.0%	12.0%	4.8%	%	16.8%
TIE	∞	∞	∞	1.7×	×	3.3×
Expected basic earning power		15.0%			%	
Expected ROE		9.0%			10.8%	
Expected TIE		∞			2.5×	
σ_{BEP}		3.5%			%	
σ_{ROE}		2.1%			4.2%	
σ_{TIE}		0			0.6×	

Relationship between Capital Structure and Stock Price

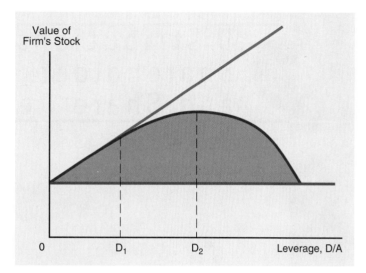

Distributions to Shareholders: Dividends and Share Repurchases

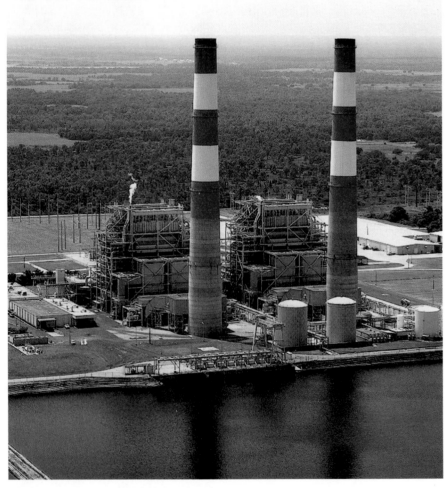

SOURCE: Cliff McBride/Tampa Tribune/Silver Image

FPL STUNS THE MARKET BY CHANGING ITS DIVIDEND POLICY

FPL GROUP

Profitable companies regularly face three important questions. (1) How much of its free cash flow should it pass on to shareholders? (2) Should it provide this cash to stockholders by raising the dividend or by repurchasing stock? (3) Should it maintain a stable, consistent payment policy, or should it let the payments vary as conditions change?

In this chapter we will discuss many of the issues that affect a firm's cash distribution policy. As we will see, most firms establish a policy that considers their forecasted cash flows and forecasted capital expenditures, and then try to stick to it. The policy can be changed, but this can cause problems because such changes inconvenience shareholders, send unintended signals, and convey the impression of dividend instability, all of which have negative implications for stock prices. Still, economic circumstances do change, and occasionally such changes require firms to change their dividend policies.

One of the most striking examples of a dividend policy change occurred in May 1994, when FPL Group, a utility holding company whose primary subsidiary is Florida Power & Light, announced a cut in its quarterly dividend from $0.62 per share to $0.42. At the same time, FPL stated that it would buy back 10 million of its common shares over the next three years to bolster its

stock price.[1] Here is the text of the letter sent to its stockholders in which FPL announced these changes:

Dear Shareholder,

Over the past several years, we have been working hard to enhance shareholder value by aligning our strategy with a rapidly changing business environment. . . . The Energy Policy Act of 1992 has brought permanent changes to the electric industry. Although we have taken effective and sometimes painful steps to prepare for these changes, one critical problem remains. Our dividend payout ratio of 90 percent — the percentage of our earnings paid to shareholders as dividends — is far too high for a growth company. It is well above the industry average, and it has limited the growth in the price of our stock.

To meet the challenges of this competitive marketplace and to ensure the financial strength and flexibility necessary for success, the Board of Directors has announced a change in our financial strategy that includes the following milestones:

■ A new dividend policy that provides for paying out 60 to 65 percent of prior years' earnings. This means a reduction in the quarterly dividend from 62 to 42 cents per share beginning with the next payment.

[1] For a complete discussion of the FPL decision, see Dennis Soter, Eugene Brigham, and Paul Evanson, "The Dividend Cut Heard 'Round the World: The Case of FPL," *Journal of Applied Corporate Finance,* Spring 1996, 4–15. Also, note that stock repurchases are discussed in a later section of this chapter.

- The authorization to repurchase 10 million shares of common stock over the next three years, including at least 4 million shares in the next year.
- An earlier dividend evaluation beginning in February 1995 to more closely link dividend rates to annual earnings.

We believe this financial strategy will enhance long-term share value and will facilitate both earnings per share and dividend growth to about 5 percent per year over the next several years.

Adding to shareholder wealth in this manner should be increasingly significant given recent changes in the tax law, which have made capital gains more attractive than dividend income.

. . . We take this action from a position of strength. We are not being forced into a defensive position by expectations of poor financial performance. Rather, it is a strategic decision to align our dividend policy and your total return as a shareholder with the growth characteristics of our company.

We appreciate your understanding and support, and we will continue to provide updates on our progress in forthcoming shareholder reports.

Several analysts called the FPL decision a watershed event for the electric utility industry. FPL saw that its circumstances were changing — its core electric business was moving from a regulated monopoly environment to one of increasing competition, and the new environment required a stronger balance sheet and more financial flexibility than was consistent with a 90 percent payout policy.

What did the market think about FPL's dividend policy change? The company's stock price fell by 14 percent the day the announcement was made. In the past, hundreds of dividend cuts followed by sharply lower earnings had conditioned investors to expect the worst when a company reduces its dividend — this is the signaling effect, which is discussed later in the chapter. However, over the next few months, as they understood FPL's actions better, analysts began to praise the decision and to recommend the stock. As a result, FPL's stock outperformed the average utility and soon exceeded the pre-announcement price. ■

PUTTING THINGS IN PERSPECTIVE

An excellent source of recent dividend news releases for major corporations is available at the web site of Corporate Financials Online at **http://www.cfonews.com/scs**. By clicking the down arrow of the "News Category" box to the left of the screen, students may select "Dividends" to receive a list of companies with dividend news. Click on any company, and you will see its latest dividend news.

Successful companies earn income. That income can then be reinvested in operating assets, used to acquire securities, used to retire debt, or distributed to stockholders. If the decision is made to distribute income to stockholders, three key issues arise: (1) How much should be distributed? (2) Should the distribution be as cash dividends, or should the cash be passed on to shareholders by buying back some of the stock they hold? (3) How stable should the distribution be; that is, should the funds paid out from year to year be stable and dependable, which stockholders would probably prefer, or be allowed to vary with the firms' cash flows and investment requirements, which would probably be better from the firm's standpoint? These three issues are the primary focus of this chapter, but we also consider two related issues, stock dividends and stock splits. ■

DIVIDENDS VERSUS CAPITAL GAINS: WHAT DO INVESTORS PREFER?

Target Payout Ratio
The percentage of net income paid out as cash dividends.

When deciding how much cash to distribute to stockholders, financial managers must keep in mind that the firm's objective is to maximize shareholder value. Consequently, the **target payout ratio**—defined as the percentage of net income to be paid out as cash dividends—should be based in large part on investors' preferences for dividends versus capital gains: do investors prefer (1) to have the firm distribute income as cash dividends or (2) to have it either repurchase stock or else plow the earnings back into the business, both of which should result in capital gains? This preference can be considered in terms of the constant growth stock valuation model:

$$\hat{P}_0 = \frac{D_1}{k_s - g}.$$

If the company increases the payout ratio, this raises D_1. This increase in the numerator, taken alone, would cause the stock price to rise. However, if D_1 is raised, then less money will be available for reinvestment, that will cause the expected growth rate to decline, and that will tend to lower the stock's price. Thus, any change in payout policy will have two opposing effects. Therefore, the firm's **optimal dividend policy** must strike a balance between current dividends and future growth so as to maximize the stock price.

Optimal Dividend Policy
The dividend policy that strikes a balance between current dividends and future growth and maximizes the firm's stock price.

In this section we examine three theories of investor preference: (1) the dividend irrelevance theory, (2) the "bird-in-the-hand" theory, and (3) the tax preference theory.

DIVIDEND IRRELEVANCE THEORY

Dividend Irrelevance Theory
The theory that a firm's dividend policy has no effect on either its value or its cost of capital.

It has been argued that dividend policy has no effect on either the price of a firm's stock or its cost of capital. If dividend policy has no significant effects, then it would be *irrelevant*. The principal proponents of the **dividend irrelevance theory** are Merton Miller and Franco Modigliani (MM).[2] They argued that the firm's value is determined only by its basic earning power and its business risk. In other words, MM argued that the value of the firm depends only on the income produced by its assets, not on how this income is split between dividends and retained earnings.

To understand MM's argument that dividend policy is irrelevant, recognize that any shareholder can in theory construct his or her own dividend policy. For example, if a firm does not pay dividends, a shareholder who wants a 5 percent dividend can "create" it by selling 5 percent of his or her stock. Conversely, if a company pays a higher dividend than an investor desires, the

[2] Merton H. Miller and Franco Modigliani, "Dividend Policy, Growth, and the Valuation of Shares," *Journal of Business*, October 1961, 411–433.

investor can use the unwanted dividends to buy additional shares of the company's stock. If investors could buy and sell shares and thus create their own dividend policy without incurring costs, then the firm's dividend policy would truly be irrelevant. Note, though, that investors who want additional dividends must incur brokerage costs to sell shares, and investors who do not want dividends must first pay taxes on the unwanted dividends and then incur brokerage costs to purchase shares with the after-tax dividends. Since taxes and brokerage costs certainly exist, dividend policy may well be relevant.

In developing their dividend theory, MM made a number of assumptions, especially the absence of taxes and brokerage costs. Obviously, taxes and brokerage costs do exist, so the MM irrelevance theory may not be true. However, MM argued (correctly) that all economic theories are based on simplifying assumptions, and that the validity of a theory must be judged by empirical tests, not by the realism of its assumptions. We will discuss empirical tests of MM's dividend irrelevance theory shortly.

BIRD-IN-THE-HAND THEORY

The principal conclusion of MM's dividend irrelevance theory is that dividend policy does not affect the required rate of return on equity, k_s. This conclusion has been hotly debated in academic circles. In particular, Myron Gordon and John Lintner argued that k_s decreases as the dividend payout is increased because investors are less certain of receiving the capital gains that are supposed to result from retaining earnings than they are of receiving dividend payments.[3] Gordon and Lintner said, in effect, that investors value a dollar of expected dividends more highly than a dollar of expected capital gains because the dividend yield component, D_1/P_0, is less risky than the g component in the total expected return equation, $k_s = D_1/P_0 + g$.

MM disagreed. They argued that k_s is independent of dividend policy, which implies that investors are indifferent between D_1/P_0 and g and, hence, between dividends and capital gains. MM called the Gordon-Lintner argument the **bird-in-the-hand** fallacy because, in MM's view, most investors plan to reinvest their dividends in the stock of the same or similar firms, and, in any event, the riskiness of the firm's cash flows to investors in the long run is determined by the riskiness of operating cash flows, not by dividend payout policy.

Bird-in-the-Hand Theory
MM's name for the theory that a firm's value will be maximized by setting a high dividend payout ratio.

TAX PREFERENCE THEORY

There are three tax-related reasons for thinking that investors might prefer a low dividend payout to a high payout: (1) Recall from Chapter 2 that long-term capital gains are taxed at a rate of 20 percent, whereas dividend income is taxed at effective rates that go up to 39.6 percent. Therefore, wealthy investors (who own most of the stock and receive most of the dividends) might prefer to have

---

[3] Myron J. Gordon, "Optimal Investment and Financing Policy," *Journal of Finance*, May 1963, 264–272; and John Lintner, "Dividends, Earnings, Leverage, Stock Prices, and the Supply of Capital to Corporations," *Review of Economics and Statistics*, August 1962, 243–269.

companies retain and plow earnings back into the business. Earnings growth would presumably lead to stock price increases, and thus lower-taxed capital gains would be substituted for higher-taxed dividends. (2) Taxes are not paid on the gain until a stock is sold. Due to time value effects, a dollar of taxes paid in the future has a lower effective cost than a dollar paid today. (3) If a stock is held by someone until he or she dies, no capital gains tax is due at all — the beneficiaries who receive the stock can use the stock's value on the death day as their cost basis and thus completely escape the capital gains tax.

Because of these tax advantages, investors may prefer to have companies retain most of their earnings. If so, investors would be willing to pay more for low-payout companies than for otherwise similar high-payout companies.

ILLUSTRATION OF THE THREE DIVIDEND POLICY THEORIES

Figure 14-1 illustrates the three alternative dividend policy theories: (1) Miller and Modigliani's dividend irrelevance theory, (2) Gordon and Lintner's bird-in-the-hand theory, and (3) the tax preference theory. To understand the three theories, consider the case of Hardin Electronics, which has from its inception plowed all earnings back into the business and thus has never paid a dividend. Hardin's management is now reconsidering its dividend policy, and it wants to adopt the policy that will maximize its stock price.

Consider first the data presented below the graph. Each row shows an alternative payout policy: (1) Retain all earnings and pay out nothing, which is the present policy, (2) pay out 50 percent of earnings, and (3) pay out 100 percent of earnings. In the example, we assume that the company will have a 15 percent ROE regardless of which payout policy it follows, so with a book value per share of $30, EPS will be 0.15($30) = $4.50 under all payout policies.[4] Given an EPS of $4.50, dividends per share are shown in Column 3 under each payout policy.

Under the assumption of a constant ROE, the growth rate shown in Column 4 will be g = (% Retained)(ROE), and it will vary from 15 percent at a zero payout to zero at a 100 percent payout. For example, if Hardin pays out 50 percent of its earnings, then its dividend growth rate will be g = 0.5(15%) = 7.5%.

Columns 5, 6, and 7 show how the situation would look if MM's irrelevance theory were correct. Under this theory, neither the stock price nor the cost of equity would be affected by the payout policy — the stock price would remain constant at $30, and k_s would be stable at 15 percent. Note that k_s is found as the sum of the growth rate in Column 4 plus the dividend yield in Column 6.

Columns 8, 9, and 10 show the situation if the bird-in-the-hand theory were true. Under this theory, investors prefer dividends, and the more of its earnings the company pays out, the higher its stock price and the lower its cost of equity.

---

[4] When the three theories were developed, it was assumed that a company's investment opportunities would be held constant and that if the company increased its dividends, its capital budget could be funded by selling common stock. Conversely, if a high-payout company lowered its payout to the point where earnings exceeded good investment opportunities, it was assumed that the company would repurchase shares. Transactions costs were assumed to be immaterial. We maintain those assumptions in our example.

FIGURE 14-1

**Dividend Irrelevance, Bird-in-the-Hand,
and Tax Preference Dividend Theories**

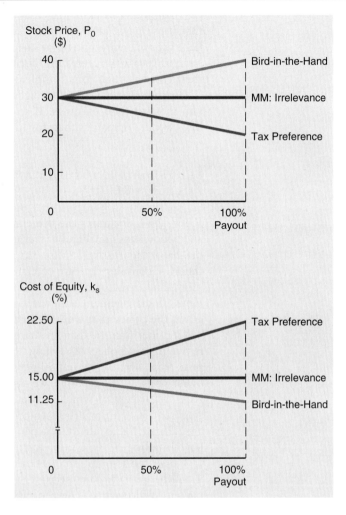

POSSIBLE SITUATIONS (ONLY ONE CAN BE TRUE)

ALTERNATIVE PAYOUT POLICIES				MM: IRRELEVANCE			BIRD-IN-THE-HAND			TAX PREFERENCE		
PERCENT PAYOUT (1)	PERCENT RETAINED (2)	DPS (3)	g (4)	P_0 (5)	D/P_0 (6)	k_s (7)	P_0 (8)	D/P_0 (9)	k_s (10)	P_0 (11)	D/P_0 (12)	k_s (13)
0%	100%	$0.00	15.0%	$30	0.0%	15.0%	$30	0.00%	15.00%	$30	0.0%	15.0%
50	50	2.25	7.5	30	7.5	15.0	35	6.43	13.93	25	9.0	16.5
100	0	4.50	0.0	30	15.0	15.0	40	11.25	11.25	20	22.5	22.5

NOTES:

1. Book value = Initial market value = $30 per share.

2. ROE = 15%.

3. EPS = $30(0.15) = $4.50.

4. g = (% retained)(ROE) = (% retained)(15%). Example: At payout = 50%, g = 0.5(15%) = 7.5%.

5. k_s = Dividend yield + Growth rate.

In our example, the bird-in-the-hand theory indicates that adopting a 100 percent payout policy would cause the stock price to rise from $30 to $40, and the cost of equity would decline from 15 percent to 11.25 percent.

Finally, Columns 11, 12, and 13 show the situation if the tax preference theory were correct. Under this theory, investors prefer companies that retain earnings and thus provide returns in the form of lower-taxed capital gains rather than higher-taxed dividends. If the tax preference theory were correct, then an increase in the dividend payout ratio from its current zero level would cause the stock price to decline and the cost of equity to rise.

The data in the table are plotted to produce the two graphs shown in Figure 14-1. The upper graph shows how the stock price would react to dividend policy under each of the theories, and the lower graph shows how the cost of equity would be affected.

USING EMPIRICAL EVIDENCE TO DECIDE WHICH THEORY IS BEST

These three theories offer contradictory advice to corporate managers, so which, if any, should we believe? The most logical way to proceed is to test the theories empirically. Many such tests have been conducted, but their results have been unclear. There are two reasons for this: (1) For a valid statistical test, things other than dividend policy must be held constant; that is, the sample companies must differ only in their dividend policies, and (2) we must be able to measure with a high degree of accuracy each firm's cost of equity. Neither of these two conditions holds: We cannot find a set of publicly owned firms that differ only in their dividend policies, nor can we obtain precise estimates of the cost of equity.

Therefore, no one can establish a clear relationship between dividend policy and the cost of equity. Investors in the aggregate cannot be seen to uniformly prefer either higher or lower dividends. Nevertheless, *individual* investors do have strong preferences. Some prefer high dividends, while others prefer all capital gains. These differences among individuals help explain why it is difficult to reach any definitive conclusions regarding the optimal dividend payout. Even so, both evidence and logic suggest that investors prefer firms that follow a *stable, predictable* dividend policy (regardless of the payout level). We will consider the issue of dividend stability later in the chapter.

SELF-TEST QUESTIONS

Explain the differences among the dividend irrelevance theory, the bird-in-the-hand theory, and the tax preference theory. Use a graph such as Figure 14-1 to illustrate your answer.

What did Modigliani and Miller assume about taxes and brokerage costs when they developed their dividend irrelevance theory?

How did the bird-in-the-hand theory get its name?

In what sense does MM's theory represent a middle-ground position between the other two theories?

What have been the results of empirical tests of the dividend theories?

DIVIDEND YIELDS AROUND THE WORLD

Dividend yields vary considerably in different stock markets throughout the world. In 1999 in the United States, dividend yields averaged 1.6 percent for the large blue chip stocks in the Dow Jones Industrials, 1.2 percent for a broader sample of stocks in the S&P 500, and 0.3 percent for stocks in the high-tech-dominated Nasdaq. Outside the United States, average dividend yields ranged from 5.7 percent in New Zealand to 0.7 percent in Taiwan. The accompanying table summarizes the dividend picture in 1999.

WORLD STOCK MARKET (INDEX)	DIVIDEND YIELD
New Zealand	5.7%
Australia	3.1
Britain FTSE 100	2.4
Hong Kong	2.4
France	2.1
Germany	2.1
Belgium	2.0
Singapore	1.7
United States (Dow Jones Industrials)	1.6
Canada (TSE 300)	1.5
United States (S&P 500)	1.2
Mexico	1.1
Japan Nikkei	0.7
Taiwan	0.7
United States (Nasdaq)	0.3

SOURCE: Alexandra Eadie, "On the Grid Looking for Dividend Yield Around the World," *The Globe and Mail,* June 23, 1999, B16. Eadie's source was Bloomberg Financial Services.

OTHER DIVIDEND POLICY ISSUES

Before we discuss how dividend policy is set in practice, we must examine two other theoretical issues that could affect our views toward dividend policy: (1) the *information content*, or *signaling*, *hypothesis* and (2) the *clientele effect*.

INFORMATION CONTENT, OR SIGNALING, HYPOTHESIS

When MM set forth their dividend irrelevance theory, they assumed that everyone — investors and managers alike — has identical information regarding the firm's future earnings and dividends. In reality, however, different investors have different views on both the level of future dividend payments and the uncertainty inherent in those payments, and managers have better information about future prospects than public stockholders.

It has been observed that an increase in the dividend is often accompanied by an increase in the price of a stock, while a dividend cut generally leads to a stock price decline. This could indicate that investors, in the aggregate, prefer dividends to capital gains. However, MM argued differently. They noted the well-established fact that corporations are reluctant to cut dividends, hence do not raise dividends unless they anticipate higher earnings in the future. Thus, MM argued that a higher-than-expected dividend increase is a "signal" to investors that the firm's management forecasts good future earnings.[5] Conversely, a dividend reduction, or a smaller-than-expected increase, is a signal that management is forecasting poor earnings in the future. Thus, MM argued that investors' reactions to changes in dividend policy do not necessarily show that investors prefer dividends to retained earnings. Rather, they argue that price changes following dividend actions simply indicate that there is an important **information, or signaling, content** in dividend announcements.

Information Content (Signaling) Hypothesis
The theory that investors regard dividend changes as signals of management's earnings forecasts.

Like most other aspects of dividend policy, empirical studies of signaling have had mixed results. There is clearly some information content in dividend announcements. However, it is difficult to tell whether the stock price changes that follow increases or decreases in dividends reflect only signaling effects or both signaling and dividend preference. Still, signaling effects should definitely be considered when a firm is contemplating a change in dividend policy.

CLIENTELE EFFECT

As we indicated earlier, different groups, or *clienteles*, of stockholders prefer different dividend payout policies. For example, retired individuals and university endowment funds generally prefer cash income, so they may want the firm to pay out a high percentage of its earnings. Such investors (and pension funds) are often in low or even zero tax brackets, so taxes are of no concern. On the other hand, stockholders in their peak earning years might prefer reinvestment, because they have less need for current investment income and would simply reinvest dividends received, after first paying income taxes on those dividends.

If a firm retains and reinvests income rather than paying dividends, those stockholders who need current income would be disadvantaged. The value of their stock might increase, but they would be forced to go to the trouble and expense of selling off some of their shares to obtain cash. Also, some institutional investors (or trustees for individuals) would be legally precluded from

---

[5] Stephen Ross has suggested that managers can use capital structure as well as dividends to give signals concerning firms' future prospects. For example, a firm with good earnings prospects can carry more debt than a similar firm with poor earnings prospects. This theory, called *incentive signaling*, rests on the premise that signals with cash-based variables (either debt interest or dividends) cannot be mimicked by unsuccessful firms because such firms do not have the future cash-generating power to maintain the announced interest or dividend payment. Thus, investors are more likely to believe a glowing verbal report when it is accompanied by a dividend increase or a debt-financed expansion program. See Stephen A. Ross, "The Determination of Financial Structure: The Incentive-Signaling Approach," *The Bell Journal of Economics*, Spring 1977, 23–40.

selling stock and then "spending capital." On the other hand, stockholders who are saving rather than spending dividends might favor the low dividend policy, for the less the firm pays out in dividends, the less these stockholders will have to pay in current taxes, and the less trouble and expense they will have to go through to reinvest their after-tax dividends. Therefore, investors who want current investment income should own shares in high dividend payout firms, while investors with no need for current investment income should own shares in low dividend payout firms. For example, investors seeking high cash income might invest in electric utilities, which averaged a 73 percent payout from 1996 through 2000, while those favoring growth could invest in the semiconductor industry, which paid out only 7 percent during the same time period.

To the extent that stockholders can switch firms, a firm can change from one dividend payout policy to another and then let stockholders who do not like the new policy sell to other investors who do. However, frequent switching would be inefficient because of (1) brokerage costs, (2) the likelihood that stockholders who are selling will have to pay capital gains taxes, and (3) a possible shortage of investors who like the firm's newly adopted dividend policy. Thus, management should be hesitant to change its dividend policy, because a change might cause current shareholders to sell their stock, forcing the stock price down. Such a price decline might be temporary, but it might also be permanent — if few new investors are attracted by the new dividend policy, then the stock price would remain depressed. Of course, the new policy might attract an even larger clientele than the firm had before, in which case the stock price would rise.

Clientele Effect

The tendency of a firm to attract a set of investors who like its dividend policy.

Evidence from several studies suggests that there is in fact a **clientele effect.**[6] MM and others have argued that one clientele is as good as another, so the existence of a clientele effect does not necessarily imply that one dividend policy is better than any other. MM may be wrong, though, and neither they nor anyone else can prove that the aggregate makeup of investors permits firms to disregard clientele effects. This issue, like most others in the dividend arena, is still up in the air.

SELF-TEST QUESTION

Define (1) information content and (2) the clientele effect, and explain how they affect dividend policy.

DIVIDEND STABILITY

As we noted at the beginning of the chapter, the stability of dividends is also important. Profits and cash flows vary over time, as do investment opportunities. Taken alone, this suggests that corporations should vary their dividends over time, increasing them when cash flows are large and the need for funds is low and lowering them when cash is in short supply relative to investment opportunities. However, many stockholders rely on dividends to meet expenses, and they would be seriously inconvenienced if the dividend stream were unstable. Further,

---

[6] For example, see R. Richardson Pettit, "Taxes, Transactions Costs and the Clientele Effect of Dividends," *The Journal of Financial Economics*, December 1977, 419–436.

reducing dividends to make funds available for capital investment could send incorrect signals to investors, who might push down the stock price because they interpreted the dividend cut to mean that the company's future earnings prospects have been diminished. Thus, maximizing its stock price requires a firm to balance its internal needs for funds against the needs and desires of its stockholders.

How should this balance be struck; that is, how stable and dependable should a firm attempt to make its dividends? It is impossible to give a definitive answer to this question, but the following points are relevant:

1. Virtually every publicly owned company makes a five- to ten-year financial forecast of earnings and dividends. Such forecasts are never made public — they are used for internal planning purposes only. However, security analysts construct similar forecasts and do make them available to investors; see *Value Line* for an example. Further, virtually every internal five- to ten-year corporate forecast we have seen for a "normal" company projects a trend of higher earnings and dividends. Both managers and investors know that economic conditions may cause actual results to differ from forecasted results, but "normal" companies expect to grow.

2. Years ago, when inflation was not persistent, the term "stable dividend policy" meant a policy of paying the same dollar dividend year after year. AT&T was a prime example of a company with a stable dividend policy — it paid $9 per year ($2.25 per quarter) for 25 straight years. Today, though, most companies and stockholders expect earnings to grow over time as a result of retained earnings and inflation. Further, dividends are normally expected to grow more or less in line with earnings. Thus, today a "stable dividend policy" generally means increasing the dividend at a reasonably steady rate.

   Dividend stability has two components: (1) How dependable is the growth rate, and (2) can we count on at least receiving the current dividend in the future? The most stable policy, from an investor's standpoint, is that of a firm whose dividend growth rate is predictable — such a company's total return (dividend yield plus capital gains yield) would be relatively stable over the long run, and its stock would be a good hedge against inflation. The second most stable policy is where stockholders can be reasonably sure that the current dividend will not be reduced — it may not grow at a steady rate, but management will probably be able to avoid cutting the dividend. The least stable situation is where earnings and cash flows are so volatile that investors cannot count on the company to maintain the current dividend over a typical business cycle.

3. Most observers believe that dividend stability is desirable. Assuming this position is correct, investors prefer stocks that pay more predictable dividends to stocks that pay the same average amount of dividends but in a more erratic manner. This means that the cost of equity will be minimized, and the stock price maximized, if a firm stabilizes its dividends as much as possible.

SELF-TEST QUESTIONS

What does the term "stable dividend policy" mean?

What are the two components of dividend stability?

ESTABLISHING THE DIVIDEND POLICY IN PRACTICE

In the preceding sections we saw that investors may or may not prefer dividends to capital gains, but that they do prefer predictable to unpredictable dividends. Given this situation, how should a firm determine the specific percentage of earnings that it will pay out as dividends? While policies undoubtedly vary from firm to firm, we describe in this section the steps that a typical firm takes when it establishes its target payout ratio.

SETTING THE TARGET PAYOUT RATIO: THE RESIDUAL DIVIDEND MODEL[7]

When deciding how much cash to distribute to stockholders, two points should be kept in mind: (1) The overriding objective is to maximize shareholder value, and (2) the firm's cash flows really belong to its shareholders, so management should refrain from retaining income unless they can reinvest it to produce returns higher than shareholders could themselves earn by investing the cash in investments of equal risk. On the other hand, recall from Chapter 10 that internal equity (retained earnings) is cheaper than external equity (new common stock). This encourages firms to retain earnings because they add to the equity base, increase debt capacity, and thus reduce the likelihood that the firm will have to issue common stock at a later date to fund future investment projects.

When establishing a dividend policy, one size does not fit all. Some firms produce a lot of cash but have limited investment opportunities — this is true for firms in profitable but mature industries where few opportunities for growth exist. Such firms typically distribute a large percentage of their cash to shareholders, thereby attracting investment clienteles that prefer high dividends. Other firms generate little or no excess cash but have many good investment opportunities — this is often true of new firms in rapidly growing industries. Such firms generally distribute little or no cash but enjoy rising earnings and stock prices, thereby attracting investors who prefer capital gains.

As Table 14-1 suggests, dividend payouts and dividend yields for large corporations vary considerably. Generally, firms in stable, cash-producing industries such as utilities, financial services, and tobacco pay relatively high dividends, whereas companies in rapidly growing industries such as computer and cable TV tend to pay lower dividends.

---

[7] The term "payout ratio" can be interpreted in two ways: (1) the conventional way, where the payout ratio means the percentage of net income to common paid out as cash dividends, or (2) the percentage of net income distributed to stockholders as dividends and through share repurchases. In this section, we assume that no repurchases occur. Increasingly, though, firms are using the residual model to determine "distributions to shareholders" and then making a separate decision as to the form of that distribution. Further, an increasing percentage of the distribution is in the form of share repurchases.

TABLE 14-1

Dividend Payouts

COMPANY	INDUSTRY	DIVIDEND PAYOUT	DIVIDEND YIELD
I. COMPANIES THAT PAY HIGH DIVIDENDS			
Pennzoil-Quaker States	Automotive consumer products	99%	6.3%
AGL Resources	Natural gas distribution	90	5.4
Flowers Ind.	Food processing	88	3.3
CSX Corp.	Rail transportation	86	4.8
Goodyear Tire	Tire and rubber	72	5.2
Alliance Cap. Mgmt.	Financial services	68	7.7
II. COMPANIES THAT PAY LITTLE OR NO DIVIDENDS			
McDonald's	Fast-food restaurants	15%	0.7%
Compaq Computer	Computers	11	0.5
Intel Corp.	Semiconductor	5	0.2
Delta Air Lines	Airline	3	0.2
Starbucks	Coffee retailer	0	0
Sun Microsystems	Computers	0	0

SOURCE: *Value Line Investment Survey,* CD-ROM, November 2000.

Residual Dividend Model
A model in which the dividend paid is set equal to net income minus the amount of retained earnings necessary to finance the firm's optimal capital budget.

For a given firm, the optimal payout ratio is a function of four factors: (1) investor's preferences for dividends versus capital gains, (2) the firm's investment opportunities, (3) its target capital structure, and (4) the availability and cost of external capital. The last three elements are combined in what we call the **residual dividend model.** Under this model a firm follows these four steps when establishing its target payout ratio: (1) It determines the optimal capital budget; (2) it determines the amount of equity needed to finance that budget, given its target capital structure; (3) it uses retained earnings to meet equity requirements to the extent possible; and (4) it pays dividends only if more earnings are available than are needed to support the optimal capital budget. The word *residual* implies "leftover," and the residual policy implies that dividends are paid out of "leftover" earnings.

If a firm rigidly follows the residual dividend policy, then dividends paid in any given year can be expressed as follows:

$$\text{Dividends} = \text{Net income} - \begin{array}{c}\text{Retained earnings required to help}\\ \text{finance new investments}\end{array}$$
$$= \text{Net income} - [(\text{Target equity ratio})(\text{Total capital budget})].$$

For example, suppose the target equity ratio is 60 percent and the firm plans to spend $50 million on capital projects. In that case, it would need $50(0.6) = $30 million of common equity. Then, if its net income were $100 million, its dividends would be $100 - $30 = $70 million. So, if the company had

$100 million of earnings and a capital budget of $50 million, it would use $30 million of the retained earnings plus $50 − $30 = $20 million of new debt to finance the capital budget, and this would keep its capital structure on target. Note that the amount of equity needed to finance new investments might exceed the net income; in our example, this would happen if the capital budget were $200 million. In that case, no dividends would be paid, and the company would have to issue new common stock in order to maintain its target capital structure.

Most firms have a target capital structure that calls for at least some debt, so new financing is done partly with debt and partly with equity. As long as the firm finances with the optimal mix of debt and equity, and provided it uses only internally generated equity (retained earnings), then the marginal cost of each new dollar of capital will be minimized. Internally generated equity is available for financing a certain amount of new investment, but beyond that amount, the firm must turn to more expensive new common stock. At the point where new stock must be sold, the cost of equity, and consequently the marginal cost of capital, rises.

To illustrate these points, consider the case of Texas and Western (T&W) Transport Company. T&W's overall composite cost of capital is 10 percent. However, this cost assumes that all new equity comes from retained earnings. If the company must issue new stock, its cost of capital will be higher. T&W has $60 million in net income and a target capital structure of 60 percent equity and 40 percent debt. Provided that it does not pay any cash dividends, T&W could make net investments (investments in addition to asset replacements from depreciation) of $100 million, consisting of $60 million from retained earnings plus $40 million of new debt supported by the retained earnings, at a 10 percent marginal cost of capital. If the capital budget exceeded $100 million, the required equity component would exceed net income, which is of course the maximum amount of retained earnings. In this case, T&W would have to issue new common stock, thereby pushing its cost of capital above 10 percent.[8]

At the beginning of its planning period, T&W's financial staff considers all proposed projects for the upcoming period. Independent projects are accepted if their estimated returns exceed the risk-adjusted cost of capital. In choosing among mutually exclusive projects, T&W chooses the project with the highest positive NPV. The capital budget represents the amount of capital that is required to finance all accepted projects. If T&W follows a strict residual dividend policy, we can see from Table 14-2 that the estimated capital budget will have a profound effect on its dividend payout ratio.

If T&W forecasts poor investment opportunities, its estimated capital budget will be only $40 million. To maintain the target capital structure, 40 percent of this capital ($16 million) must be raised as debt, and 60 percent ($24 million) must be equity. If it followed a strict residual policy, T&W would

---

[8] If T&W does not retain all of its earnings, its cost of capital will rise above 10 percent before its capital budget reaches $100 million. For example, if T&W chose to retain $36 million, its cost of capital would increase once the capital budget exceeded $36/0.6 = $60 million. To see this point, note that a capital budget of $60 million would require $36 million of equity — if the capital budget rose above $60 million, the company's required equity capital would exceed its retained earnings, thereby requiring it to issue new common stock.

TABLE 14-2

	T&W's Dividend Payout Ratio with $60 Million of Net Income When Faced with Different Investment Opportunities (Dollars in Millions)		

| | INVESTMENT OPPORTUNITIES | | |
	POOR	AVERAGE	GOOD
Capital budget	$40	$70	$150
Net income	$60	$60	$ 60
Required equity (0.6 × Capital budget)	24	42	90
Dividends paid (NI − Required equity)	$36	$18	−$ 30[a]
Dividend payout ratio (Dividend/NI)	60%	30%	0%

[a] With a $150 million capital budget, T&W would retain all of its earnings and also issue $30 million of new stock.

retain $24 million to help finance new investments, then pay out the remaining $36 million as dividends. Under this scenario, the company's dividend payout ratio would be $36 million/$60 million = 0.6 = 60%.

By contrast, if the company's investment opportunities were average, its optimal capital budget would rise to $70 million. Here it would require $42 million of retained earnings, so dividends would be $60 − $42 = $18 million, for a payout of $18/$60 = 30%. Finally, if investment opportunities are good, the capital budget would be $150 million, which would require 0.6($150) = $90 million of equity. T&W would retain all of its net income ($60 million), thus pay no dividends. Moreover, since the required equity exceeds the retained earnings, the company would have to issue new common stock in order to maintain the target capital structure.

Since investment opportunities and earnings will surely vary from year to year, strict adherence to the residual dividend policy would result in unstable dividends. One year the firm might pay zero dividends because it needed the money to finance good investment opportunities, but the next year it might pay a large dividend because investment opportunities were poor and it therefore did not need to retain much. Similarly, fluctuating earnings could also lead to variable dividends, even if investment opportunities were stable. Therefore, following the residual dividend policy would almost certainly lead to fluctuating, unstable dividends. Thus, following the residual dividend policy would be optimal only if investors were not bothered by fluctuating dividends. However, since investors prefer stable, dependable dividends, k_s would be higher, and the stock price lower, if the firm followed the residual model in a strict sense rather than attempting to stabilize its dividends over time. Therefore, firms should

1. Estimate the firm's earnings and investment opportunities, on average, over the next five or so years.
2. Use this forecasted information to find the residual model payout ratio and dollars of dividends during the planning period.
3. Then set a *target payout ratio* on the basis of the projected data.

Thus, firms should use the residual policy to help set their long-run target payout ratios, but not as a guide to the payout in any one year.

Companies do use the residual dividend model as discussed above to help understand the determinants of an optimal dividend policy, but they typically use a computerized financial forecasting model when setting the target payout ratio. Most larger corporations forecast their financial statements over the next five to ten years. Information on projected capital expenditures and working capital requirements is entered into the model, along with sales forecasts, profit margins, depreciation, and the other elements required to forecast cash flows. The target capital structure is also specified, and the model shows the amount of debt and equity that will be required to meet the capital budgeting requirements while maintaining the target capital structure.

Then, dividend payments are introduced. Naturally, the higher the payout ratio, the greater the required external equity. Most companies use the model to find a dividend pattern over the forecast period (generally five years) that will provide sufficient equity to support the capital budget without having to sell new common stock or move the capital structure ratios outside the optimal range. The end result might include a statement, in a memo from the financial vice-president to the chairman of the board, such as the following:

> We forecasted the total market demand for our products, what our share of the market is likely to be, and our required investments in capital assets and working capital. Using this information, we developed projected balance sheets and income statements for the period 2002–2006.
>
> Our 2001 dividends totaled $50 million, or $2 per share. On the basis of projected earnings, cash flows, and capital requirements, we can increase the dividend by 8 percent per year. This is consistent with a payout ratio of 42 percent, on average, over the forecast period. Any faster dividend growth rate (or higher payout) would require us to sell common stock, cut the capital budget, or raise the debt ratio. Any slower growth rate would lead to increases in the common equity ratio. Therefore, I recommend that the Board increase the dividend for 2002 by 8 percent, to $2.16, and that it plan for similar increases in the future.
>
> Events over the next five years will undoubtedly lead to differences between our forecasts and actual results. If and when such events occur, we will want to reexamine our position. However, I am confident that we can meet any random cash shortfalls by increasing our borrowings — we have unused debt capacity that gives us flexibility in this regard.
>
> We ran the corporate model under several recession scenarios. If the economy really crashes, our earnings will not cover the dividend. However, in all "reasonable" scenarios our cash flows do cover the dividend. I know the Board does not want to push the dividend up to a level where we would have to cut it under bad economic conditions. Our model runs indicate, though, that the $2.16 dividend can be maintained under any reasonable set of forecasts. Only if we increased the dividend to over $3 would we be seriously exposed to the danger of having to cut the dividend.
>
> I might also note that *Value Line* and most other analysts' reports are forecasting that our dividends will grow in the 6 percent to 8 percent range. Thus, if we go to $2.16, we will be at the high end of the range, which should give our stock a boost. With takeover rumors so widespread, getting the stock up a bit would make us all breathe a little easier.

Finally, we considered distributing cash to shareholders through a stock repurchase program. Here we would reduce the dividend payout ratio and use the funds so generated to buy our stock on the open market. Such a program has several advantages, but it would also have drawbacks. I do not recommend that we institute a stock repurchase program at this time. However, if our free cash flows exceed our forecasts, I would recommend that we use these surpluses to buy back stock. Also, I plan to continue looking into a regular repurchase program, and I may recommend such a program in the future.

This company has very stable operations, so it can plan its dividends with a fairly high degree of confidence. Other companies, especially those in cyclical industries, have difficulty maintaining in bad times a dividend that is really too low in good times. Such companies set a very low "regular" dividend and then supplement it with an "extra" dividend when times are good. General Motors, Ford, and other auto companies have followed the **low-regular-dividend-plus-extras** policy in the past. Each company announced a low regular dividend that it was sure could be maintained "through hell or high water," and stockholders could count on receiving that dividend under all conditions. Then, when times were good and profits and cash flows were high, the companies paid a clearly designated extra dividend. Investors recognized that the extras might not be maintained in the future, so they did not interpret them as a signal that the companies' earnings were going up permanently, nor did they take the elimination of the extra as a negative signal. In recent years, however, the auto companies and many other companies have replaced the "extras" in their low-regular-dividend-plus-extras policy with stock repurchases.

EARNINGS, CASH FLOWS, AND DIVIDENDS

We normally think of earnings as being the primary determinant of dividends, but in reality cash flows are more important. This situation is revealed in Figure 14-2, which gives data for Chevron Corporation from 1979 through 2000. Chevron's dividends increased steadily from 1979 to 1981; during that period both earnings and cash flows were rising, as was the price of oil. After 1981, oil prices declined sharply, pulling earnings down. Cash flows, though, remained well above the dividend requirement.

Chevron acquired Gulf Oil in 1984, and it issued more than $10 billion of debt to finance the acquisition. Interest on the debt hurt earnings immediately after the merger, as did certain write-offs connected with the merger. Further, Chevron's management wanted to pay off the new debt as fast as possible. All of this influenced the company's decision to hold the dividend constant from 1982 through 1987. Earnings improved dramatically in 1988, and the dividend has increased more or less steadily since then. Note that the dividend was increased in 1991 in spite of the weak earnings and cash flow resulting from the Persian Gulf War. More recently, in October 2000, Chevron announced that it plans to merge with Texaco. If the deal is ultimately completed, it will be interesting to see how this merger affects Chevron's future dividend policy.

Now look at Columns 4 and 6, which show payout ratios based on earnings and on cash flows. The earnings payout is quite volatile — dividends ranged

Low-Regular-Dividend-plus-Extras

The policy of announcing a low, regular dividend that can be maintained no matter what, and then when times are good paying a designated "extra" dividend.

FIGURE 14-2   Chevron: Earnings, Cash Flows, and Dividends, 1979–2000

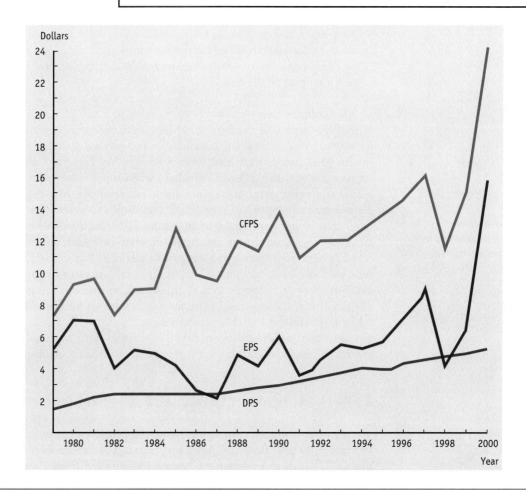

from 26 percent to 120 percent of earnings. The cash flow payout, on the other hand, is much more stable — it ranged from 19 percent to 44 percent. Further, the correlation between dividends and cash flows was 0.79 versus 0.53 between dividends and earnings. Thus, dividends clearly depend more on cash flows, which reflect the company's *ability* to pay dividends, than on current earnings, which are heavily influenced by accounting practices and which do not necessarily reflect the ability to pay dividends.

PAYMENT PROCEDURES

Dividends are normally paid quarterly, and, if conditions permit, the dividend is increased once each year. For example, Katz Corporation paid $0.50 per quarter in 2001, or at an annual rate of $2.00. In common financial parlance, we say that in 2001 Katz's *regular quarterly dividend* was $0.50, and its *annual dividend* was $2.00. In late 2001, Katz's board of directors met, reviewed pro-

YEAR (1)	DIVIDENDS PER SHARE (2)	EARNINGS PER SHARE (3)	EARNINGS PAYOUT (4)	CASH FLOW PER SHARE (5)	CASH FLOW PAYOUT (6)
1979	$1.45	$5.22	28%	$ 7.29	20%
1980	1.80	7.02	26	9.26	19
1981	2.20	6.96	32	9.61	23
1982	2.40	4.03	60	7.35	33
1983	2.40	5.15	47	8.93	27
1984	2.40	4.94	49	9.00	27
1985	2.40	4.19	57	12.76	19
1986	2.40	2.63	91	9.86	24
1987	2.40	2.13	113	9.47	25
1988	2.55	4.86	52	11.97	21
1989	2.80	4.16	67	11.33	25
1990	2.95	6.02	49	13.75	21
1991	3.25	3.69	88	11.28	29
1992	3.30	4.70	70	12.88	26
1993	3.50	5.60	63	13.12	27
1994	3.70	5.20	71	12.66	29
1995	3.85	6.02	64	13.36	29
1996	4.16	8.12	51	14.90	28
1997	4.56	9.66	47	16.70	27
1998	4.88	4.08	120	11.20	44
1999	4.96	6.28	79	15.04	33
2000	5.20	15.90	33	24.10	22

NOTE: For consistency, data have not been adjusted for a two-for-one split in 1994.

SOURCE: *Value Line Investment Survey*, various issues.

jections for 2001, and decided to keep the 2002 dividend at $2.00. The directors announced the $2 rate, so stockholders could count on receiving it unless the company experienced unanticipated operating problems.

The actual payment procedure is as follows:

Declaration Date
The date on which a firm's directors issue a statement declaring a dividend.

1. **Declaration date.** On the **declaration date** — say, on November 9 — the directors meet and declare the regular dividend, issuing a statement similar to the following: "On November 9, 2001, the directors of Katz Corporation met and declared the regular quarterly dividend of 50 cents per share, payable to holders of record on December 7, payment to be made on January 2, 2002." For accounting purposes, the declared dividend becomes an actual liability on the declaration date. If a balance sheet were constructed, the amount ($0.50) × (Number of shares outstanding) would appear as a current liability, and retained earnings would be reduced by a like amount.

Holder-of-Record Date
If the company lists the stockholder as an owner on this date, then the stockholder receives the dividend.

2. **Holder-of-record date.** At the close of business on the **holder-of-record date,** December 7, the company closes its stock transfer books and makes up a list of shareholders as of that date. If Katz Corporation is notified of the sales before 5 P.M. on December 7, then the new owner receives the dividend. However, if notification is received on or after December 8, the previous owner gets the dividend check.

Ex-Dividend Date
The date on which the right to the current dividend no longer accompanies a stock; it is usually two business days prior to the holder-of-record date.

Payment Date
The date on which a firm actually mails dividend checks.

3. **Ex-dividend date.** Suppose Jean Buyer buys 100 shares of stock from John Seller on December 4. Will the company be notified of the transfer in time to list Buyer as the new owner and thus pay the dividend to her? To avoid conflict, the securities industry has set up a convention under which the right to the dividend remains with the stock until two business days prior to the holder-of-record date; on the second day before that date, the right to the dividend no longer goes with the shares. The date when the right to the dividend leaves the stock is called the **ex-dividend date.** In this case, the ex-dividend date is two days prior to December 7, or December 5:

Dividend goes with stock: December 4
Ex-dividend date: December 5
                             December 6
Holder-of-record date: December 7

Therefore, if Buyer is to receive the dividend, she must buy the stock on or before December 4. If she buys it on December 5 or later, Seller will receive the dividend because he will be the official holder of record.

Katz's dividend amounts to $0.50, so the ex-dividend date is important. Barring fluctuations in the stock market, one would normally expect the price of a stock to drop by approximately the amount of the dividend on the ex-dividend date. Thus, if Katz closed at $30½ on December 4, it would probably open at about $30 on December 5.[9]

4. **Payment date**. The company actually mails the checks to the holders of record on January 2, the **payment date.**

SELF-TEST QUESTIONS

Explain the logic of the residual dividend model, the steps a firm would take to implement it, and why it is more likely to be used to establish a long-run payout target than to set the actual year-by-year payout ratio.

How do firms use planning models to help set dividend policy?

Which are more critical to the dividend decision, earnings or cash flow? Explain.

Explain the procedures used to actually pay the dividend.

Why is the ex-dividend date important to investors?

---

[9] Tax effects cause the price decline on average to be less than the full amount of the dividend. Suppose you were an investor in the 40 percent federal-plus-state tax bracket. If you bought Katz's stock on December 4, you would receive the dividend, but you would almost immediately pay 40 percent of it out in taxes. Thus, you would want to wait until December 5, to buy the stock if you thought you could get it for $0.50 less per share. Your reaction, and that of others, would influence stock prices around dividend payment dates. Here is what would happen:

1. Other things held constant, a stock's price should rise during the quarter, with the daily price increase (for Katz) equal to $0.50/90 = $0.005556. Therefore, if the price started at $30 just after its last ex-dividend date, it would rise to $30.50 on December 4.

(*footnote continues*)

Dividend Reinvestment Plan (DRIP)
A plan that enables a stockholder to automatically reinvest dividends received back into the stock of the paying firm.

During the 1970s, most large companies instituted **dividend reinvestment plans (DRIPs)**, whereby stockholders can automatically reinvest their dividends in the stock of the paying corporation.[10] Today most larger companies offer DRIPs, and although participation rates vary considerably, about 25 percent of the average firm's shareholders are enrolled. There are two types of DRIPs: (1) plans that involve only "old stock" that is already outstanding and (2) plans that involve newly issued stock. In either case, the stockholder must pay taxes on the amount of the dividends, even though stock rather than cash is received.

Under both types of DRIPs, stockholders choose between continuing to receive dividend checks or having the company use the dividends to buy more stock in the corporation. Under the "old stock" type of plan, if a stockholder elects reinvestment, a bank, acting as trustee, takes the total funds available for reinvestment, purchases the corporation's stock on the open market, and allocates the shares purchased to the participating stockholders' accounts on a pro rata basis. The transactions costs of buying shares (brokerage costs) are low because of volume purchases, so these plans benefit small stockholders who do not need cash dividends for current consumption.

The "new stock" type of DRIP invests the dividends in newly issued stock, hence these plans raise new capital for the firm. AT&T, Xerox, Union Carbide, and many other companies have had new stock plans in effect in recent years, using them to raise substantial amounts of new equity capital. No fees are charged to stockholders, and many companies offer stock at a discount of 3 percent to 5 percent below the actual market price. The companies offer discounts as a trade-off against flotation costs that would be incurred if new stock had been issued through investment bankers rather than through the dividend reinvestment plans.

One interesting aspect of DRIPs is that they are forcing corporations to re-examine their basic dividend policies. A high participation rate in a DRIP suggests that stockholders might be better off if the firm simply reduced cash dividends, which would save stockholders some personal income taxes. Quite a few firms are surveying their stockholders to learn more about their preferences and to find out how they would react to a change in dividend policy. A more rational approach to basic dividend policy decisions may emerge from this research.

(*Footnote 9 continued*)

2. In the absence of taxes, the stock's price would fall to $30 on December 5 and then start up as the next dividend accrual period began. Thus, over time, if everything else were held constant, the stock's price would follow a sawtooth pattern if it were plotted on a graph.

3. Because of taxes, the stock's price would neither rise by the full amount of the dividend nor fall by the full dividend amount when it goes ex-dividend.

4. The amount of the rise and subsequent fall would depend on the average investor's marginal tax rate.

See Edwin J. Elton and Martin J. Gruber, "Marginal Stockholder Tax Rates and the Clientele Effect," *Review of Economics and Statistics*, February 1970, 68–74, for an interesting discussion of all this.

[10] See Richard H. Pettway and R. Phil Malone, "Automatic Dividend Reinvestment Plans," *Financial Management*, Winter 1973, 11–18, for an old but still excellent discussion of the subject.

Note that companies start or stop using new stock DRIPs depending on their need for equity capital. Thus, both Union Carbide and AT&T recently stopped offering a new stock DRIP with a 5 percent discount because their needs for equity capital declined. However, about the same time Xerox began such a plan.

Some companies have expanded their DRIPs by moving to "open enrollment," whereby anyone can purchase the firm's stock directly and thus bypass brokers' commissions. Exxon Mobil not only allows investors to buy their initial shares at no fee but also lets them pick up additional shares through automatic bank account withdrawals. Several plans, including Exxon Mobil's, offer dividend reinvestment for individual retirement accounts, and some, such as U.S. West, allow participants to invest weekly or monthly rather than on the quarterly dividend schedule. In all of these plans, and many others, stockholders can invest more than the dividends they are foregoing—they simply send a check to the company and buy shares without a brokerage commission. According to First Chicago Trust, which handles the paperwork for 13 million shareholder DRIP accounts, at least half of all DRIPs will offer open enrollment, extra purchases, and other expanded services within the next few years.

SELF-TEST QUESTIONS

What are dividend reinvestment plans?

What are their advantages and disadvantages from both the stockholders' and the firm's perspectives?

SUMMARY OF FACTORS INFLUENCING DIVIDEND POLICY

In earlier sections, we described both the major theories of investor preference and some issues concerning the effects of dividend policy on the value of a firm. We also discussed the residual dividend model for setting a firm's long-run target payout ratio. In this section, we discuss several other factors that affect the dividend decision. These factors may be grouped into four broad categories: (1) constraints on dividend payments, (2) investment opportunities, (3) availability and cost of alternative sources of capital, and (4) effects of dividend policy on k_s. Each of these categories has several subparts, which we discuss in the following paragraphs.

CONSTRAINTS

1. **Bond indentures.** Debt contracts often limit dividend payments to earnings generated after the loan was granted. Also, debt contracts often stipulate that no dividends can be paid unless the current ratio, times-interest-earned ratio, and other safety ratios exceed stated minimums.

2. **Preferred stock restrictions.** Typically, common dividends cannot be paid if the company has omitted its preferred dividend. The preferred arrearages must be satisfied before common dividends can be resumed.

3. **Impairment of capital rule.** Dividend payments cannot exceed the balance sheet item "retained earnings." This legal restriction, known as the *impairment of capital rule*, is designed to protect creditors. Without the rule, a company that is in trouble might distribute most of its assets to stockholders and leave its debtholders out in the cold. (*Liquidating dividends* can be paid out of capital, but they must be indicated as such, and they must not reduce capital below the limits stated in debt contracts.)

4. **Availability of cash.** Cash dividends can be paid only with cash. Thus, a shortage of cash in the bank can restrict dividend payments. However, the ability to borrow can offset this factor.

5. **Penalty tax on improperly accumulated earnings.** To prevent wealthy individuals from using corporations to avoid personal taxes, the Tax Code provides for a special surtax on improperly accumulated income. Thus, if the IRS can demonstrate that a firm's dividend payout ratio is being deliberately held down to help its stockholders avoid personal taxes, the firm is subject to heavy penalties. This factor is generally relevant only to privately owned firms.

INVESTMENT OPPORTUNITIES

1. **Number of profitable investment opportunities.** If a firm typically has a large number of profitable investment opportunities, this will tend to produce a low target payout ratio, and vice versa if the firm's profitable investment opportunities are few in number.

2. **Possibility of accelerating or delaying projects.** The ability to accelerate or postpone projects will permit a firm to adhere more closely to a stable dividend policy.

ALTERNATIVE SOURCES OF CAPITAL

1. **Cost of selling new stock.** If a firm needs to finance a given level of investment, it can obtain equity by retaining earnings or by issuing new common stock. If flotation costs (including any negative signaling effects of a stock offering) are high, k_e will be well above k_s, making it better to set a low payout ratio and to finance through retention rather than through sale of new common stock. On the other hand, a high dividend payout ratio is more feasible for a firm whose flotation costs are low. Flotation costs differ among firms — for example, the flotation percentage is generally higher for small firms, so they tend to set low payout ratios.

2. **Ability to substitute debt for equity.** A firm can finance a given level of investment with either debt or equity. As noted above, low stock flotation costs permit a more flexible dividend policy because equity can be raised either by retaining earnings or by selling new stock. A similar situation holds for debt policy: If the firm can adjust its debt ratio without raising

costs sharply, it can pay the expected dividend, even if earnings fluctuate, by increasing its debt ratio.

3. **Control.** If management is concerned about maintaining control, it may be reluctant to sell new stock, hence the company may retain more earnings than it otherwise would. However, if stockholders want higher dividends and a proxy fight looms, then the dividend will be increased.

EFFECTS OF DIVIDEND POLICY ON k_s

The effects of dividend policy on k_s may be considered in terms of four factors: (1) stockholders' desire for current versus future income, (2) perceived riskiness of dividends versus capital gains, (3) the tax advantage of capital gains over dividends, and (4) the information content of dividends (signaling). Since we discussed each of these factors in detail earlier, we need only note here that the importance of each factor in terms of its effect on k_s varies from firm to firm depending on the makeup of its current and possible future stockholders.

It should be apparent from our discussion that dividend policy decisions are truly exercises in informed judgment, not decisions that can be quantified precisely. Even so, to make rational dividend decisions, financial managers must take account of all the points discussed in the preceding sections.

SELF-TEST QUESTIONS

Identify the four broad sets of factors that affect dividend policy.

What constraints affect dividend policy?

How do investment opportunities affect dividend policy?

How does the availability and cost of outside capital affect dividend policy?

OVERVIEW OF THE DIVIDEND POLICY DECISION

In many ways, our discussion of dividend policy parallels our discussion of capital structure: We presented the relevant theories and issues, and we listed some additional factors that influence dividend policy, but we did not come up with any hard-and-fast guidelines that managers can follow. It should be apparent from our discussion that dividend policy decisions are exercises in informed judgment, not decisions that can be based on a precise mathematical model.

In practice, dividend policy is not an independent decision — the dividend decision is made jointly with capital structure and capital budgeting decisions. The underlying reason for this joint decision process is asymmetric information, which influences managerial actions in two ways:

1. In general, managers do not want to issue new common stock. First, new common stock involves issuance costs — commissions, fees, and so on — and those costs can be avoided by using retained earnings to finance the

firm's equity needs. Also, as we discussed in Chapter 13, asymmetric information causes investors to view new common stock issues as negative signals and thus lowers expectations regarding the firm's future prospects. The end result is that the announcement of a new stock issue usually leads to a decrease in the stock price. Considering the total costs involved, including both issuance and asymmetric information costs, managers strongly prefer to use retained earnings as their primary source of new equity.

2. Dividend changes provide signals about managers' beliefs as to their firms' future prospects. Thus, dividend reductions, or worse yet, omissions, generally have a significant negative effect on a firm's stock price. Since managers recognize this, they try to set dollar dividends low enough so that there is only a remote chance that the dividend will have to be reduced in the future. Of course, unexpectedly large dividend increases can be used to provide positive signals.

The effects of asymmetric information suggest that, to the extent possible, managers should avoid both new common stock sales and dividend cuts, because both actions tend to lower stock prices. Thus, in setting dividend policy, managers should begin by considering the firm's future investment opportunities relative to its projected internal sources of funds. The firm's target capital structure also plays a part, but because the optimal capital structure is a *range*, firms can vary their actual capital structures somewhat from year to year. Since it is best to avoid issuing new common stock, the target long-term payout ratio should be designed to permit the firm to meet all of its equity capital requirements with retained earnings. In effect, managers should use the residual dividend model to set dividends, but in a long-term framework. Finally, the current dollar dividend should be set so that there is an extremely low probability that the dividend, once set, will ever have to be lowered or omitted.

Of course, the dividend decision is made during the planning process, so there is uncertainty about future investment opportunities and operating cash flows. Thus, the actual payout ratio in any year will probably be above or below the firm's long-range target. However, the dollar dividend should be maintained, or increased as planned, unless the firm's financial condition deteriorates to the point where the planned policy simply cannot be maintained. A steady or increasing stream of dividends over the long run signals that the firm's financial condition is under control. Further, investor uncertainty is decreased by stable dividends, so a steady dividend stream reduces the negative effect of a new stock issue, should one become absolutely necessary.

In general, firms with superior investment opportunities should set lower payouts, hence retain more earnings, than firms with poor investment opportunities. The degree of uncertainty also influences the decision. If there is a great deal of uncertainty in the forecasts of free cash flows, which are defined here as the firm's operating cash flows minus mandatory equity investments, then it is best to be conservative and to set a lower current dollar dividend. Also, firms with postponable investment opportunities can afford to set a higher dollar dividend, because in times of stress investments can be postponed for a year or two, thus increasing the cash available for dividends. Finally, firms whose cost of capital is largely unaffected by changes in the debt ratio can also afford to set a higher payout ratio, because they can, in times of stress, more easily issue additional debt to maintain the capital budgeting program without having to cut dividends or issue stock.

Firms have only one opportunity to set the dividend payment from scratch. Therefore, today's dividend decisions are constrained by policies that were set in the past, hence setting a policy for the next five years necessarily begins with a review of the current situation.

Although we have outlined a rational process for managers to use when setting their firms' dividend policies, dividend policy still remains one of the most judgmental decisions that firms must make. For this reason, dividend policy is always set by the board of directors—the financial staff analyzes the situation and makes a recommendation, but the board makes the final decision.

SELF-TEST QUESTION

Describe the dividend policy decision process. Be sure to discuss all the factors that influence the decision.

STOCK DIVIDENDS AND STOCK SPLITS

Stock dividends and stock splits are related to the firm's cash dividend policy. The rationale for stock dividends and splits can best be explained through an example. We will use Porter Electronic Controls Inc., a $700 million electronic components manufacturer, for this purpose. Since its inception, Porter's markets have been expanding, and the company has enjoyed growth in sales and earnings. Some of its earnings have been paid out in dividends, but some are also retained each year, causing its earnings per share and stock price to grow. The company began its life with only a few thousand shares outstanding, and, after some years of growth, each of Porter's shares had a very high EPS and DPS. When a "normal" P/E ratio was applied, the derived market price was so high that few people could afford to buy a "round lot" of 100 shares. This limited the demand for the stock and thus kept the total market value of the firm below what it would have been if more shares, at a lower price, had been outstanding. To correct this situation, Porter "split its stock," as described in the next section.

STOCK SPLITS

Stock Split
An action taken by a firm to increase the number of shares outstanding, such as doubling the number of shares outstanding by giving each stockholder two new shares for each one formerly held.

Although there is little empirical evidence to support the contention, there is nevertheless a widespread belief in financial circles that an *optimal price range* exists for stocks. "Optimal" means that if the price is within this range, the price/earnings ratio, hence the firm's value, will be maximized. Many observers, including Porter's management, believe that the best range for most stocks is from $20 to $80 per share. Accordingly, if the price of Porter's stock rose to $80, management would probably declare a two-for-one **stock split,** thus doubling the number of shares outstanding, halving the earnings and dividends per share, and thereby lowering the stock price. Each stockholder would have more

TECHNOLOGY MATTERS

LOOKING ONLINE FOR INFORMATION ON STOCK SPLITS AND STOCK REPURCHASES

Up-to-date information about changes in stock splits and stock repurchases is now just a few clicks away. While this information is reported on several web sites, a good place to get started is the Online Investor at **http://www.investhelp.com.** Online Investor's home page includes recent stock repurchase and stock split announcements at "Buybacks" and "Splits Center."

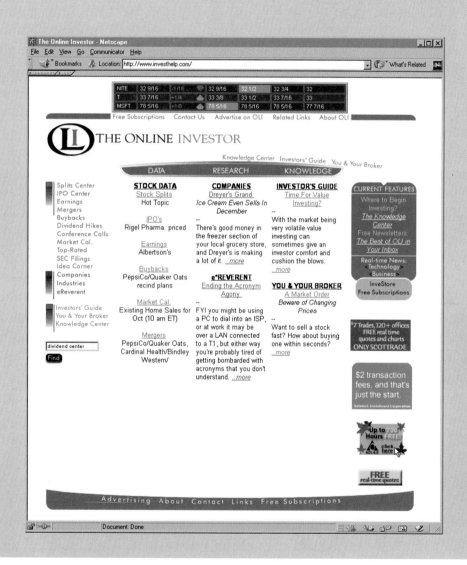

shares, but each share would be worth less. If the post-split price were $40, Porter's stockholders would be exactly as well off as they were before the split. However, if the stock price were to stabilize above $40, stockholders would be better off. Stock splits can be of any size — for example, the stock could be split two-for-one, three-for-one, one-and-a-half-for-one, or in any other way.[11]

STOCK DIVIDENDS

Stock Dividend
A dividend paid in the form of additional shares of stock rather than in cash.

Stock dividends are similar to stock splits in that they "divide the pie into smaller slices" without affecting the fundamental position of the current stockholders. On a 5 percent stock dividend, the holder of 100 shares would receive an additional 5 shares (without cost); on a 20 percent stock dividend, the same holder would receive 20 new shares; and so on. Again, the total number of shares is increased, so earnings, dividends, and price per share all decline.

If a firm wants to reduce the price of its stock, should it use a stock split or a stock dividend? Stock splits are generally used after a sharp price run-up to produce a large price reduction. Stock dividends used on a regular annual basis will keep the stock price more or less constrained. For example, if a firm's earnings and dividends were growing at about 10 percent per year, its stock price would tend to go up at about that same rate, and it would soon be outside the desired trading range. A 10 percent annual stock dividend would maintain the stock price within the optimal trading range. Note, though, that small stock dividends create bookkeeping problems and unnecessary expenses, so firms today use stock splits far more often than stock dividends.[12]

EFFECT ON STOCK PRICES

If a company splits its stock or declares a stock dividend, will this increase the market value of its stock? Several empirical studies have sought to answer this question. Here is a summary of their findings.[13]

---

[11] *Reverse splits*, which reduce the shares outstanding, can even be used. For example, a company whose stock sells for $5 might employ a one-for-five reverse split, exchanging one new share for five old ones and raising the value of the shares to about $25, which is within the optimal price range. LTV Corporation did this after several years of losses had driven its stock price below the optimal range.

[12] Accountants treat stock splits and stock dividends somewhat differently. For example, in a two-for-one stock split, the number of shares outstanding is doubled and the par value is halved, and that is about all there is to it. With a stock dividend, a bookkeeping entry is made transferring "retained earnings" to "common stock." For example, if a firm had 1,000,000 shares outstanding, if the stock price was $10, and if it wanted to pay a 10 percent stock dividend, then (1) each stockholder would be given one new share of stock for each 10 shares held, and (2) the accounting entries would involve showing 100,000 more shares outstanding and transferring 100,000($10) = $1,000,000 from "retained earnings" to "common stock." The retained earnings transfer limits the size of stock dividends, but that is not important because companies can always split their stock in any way they choose.

[13] See Eugene F. Fama, Lawrence Fisher, Michael C. Jensen, and Richard Roll, "The Adjustment of Stock Prices to New Information," *International Economic Review*, February 1969, 1–21; Mark S. Grinblatt, Ronald M. Masulis, and Sheridan Titman, "The Valuation Effects of Stock Splits and Stock Dividends," *Journal of Financial Economics*, December 1984, 461–490; C. Austin Barker, "Evaluation of Stock Dividends," *Harvard Business Review*, July–August 1958, 99–114; and Thomas E. Copeland, "Liquidity Changes Following Stock Splits," *Journal of Finance*, March 1979, 115–141.

1. On average, the price of a company's stock rises shortly after it announces a stock split or dividend.

2. However, these price increases are more the result of the fact that investors take stock splits/dividends as signals of higher future earnings and dividends than of a desire for stock dividends/splits per se. Since only companies whose managements think things look good tend to split their stocks, the announcement of a stock split is taken as a signal that earnings and cash dividends are likely to rise. Thus, the price increases associated with stock splits/dividends are probably the result of signals of favorable prospects for earnings and dividends, not a desire for stock splits/dividends per se.

3. If a company announces a stock split or dividend, its price will tend to rise. However, if during the next few months it does not announce an increase in earnings and dividends, then its stock price will drop back to the earlier level.

4. As we noted earlier, brokerage commissions are generally higher in percentage terms on lower-priced stocks. This means that it is more expensive to trade low-priced than high-priced stocks, and this, in turn, means that stock splits may reduce the liquidity of a company's shares. This particular piece of evidence suggests that stock splits/dividends might actually be harmful, although a lower price does mean that more investors can afford to trade in round lots (100 shares), which carry lower commissions than do odd lots (less than 100 shares).

What do we conclude from all this? From a pure economic standpoint, stock dividends and splits are just additional pieces of paper. However, they provide management with a relatively low-cost way of signaling that the firm's prospects look good. Further, we should note that since few large, publicly owned stocks sell at prices above several hundred dollars, we simply do not know what the effect would be if Microsoft, Xerox, Hewlett-Packard, and other highly successful firms had never split their stocks, and consequently sold at prices in the thousands or even tens of thousands of dollars. All in all, it probably makes sense to employ stock dividends/splits when a firm's prospects are favorable, especially if the price of its stock has gone beyond the normal trading range.[14]

SELF-TEST QUESTIONS

What are stock dividends and stock splits?

How do stock dividends and splits affect stock prices?

In what situations should managers consider the use of stock dividends?

In what situations should they consider the use of stock splits?

---

[14] It is interesting to note that Berkshire Hathaway, which is controlled by billionaire Warren Buffett, one of the most successful financiers of the twentieth century, has never had a stock split, and its stock sold on the NYSE for $65,000 per share in December 2000. But, in response to investment trusts that were being formed to sell fractional units of the stock, and thus, in effect, split it, Buffett himself created a new class of Berkshire Hathaway stock (Class B) worth about $1/30$ of a Class A (regular) share.

STOCK REPURCHASES

Several years ago, a *Fortune* article entitled "Beating the Market by Buying Back Stock" discussed the fact that during a one-year period, more than 600 major corporations repurchased significant amounts of their own stock. It also gave illustrations of some specific companies' repurchase programs and the effects of these programs on stock prices. The article's conclusion was that "buybacks have made a mint for shareholders who stay with the companies carrying them out."

In addition, we noted earlier that several years ago FPL cut its dividends but simultaneously instituted a program to repurchase shares of its stock. Thus, it substituted share repurchases for cash dividends as a way to distribute funds to stockholders. FPL is not alone — in recent years Philip Morris, GE, Disney, Citigroup, Merck, and more than 800 other companies took similar actions, and the dollars used to repurchase shares approximately matched the amount paid out as dividends.

Why are stock repurchase programs becoming so popular? The short answer is that they enhance shareholder value: A more complete answer is given in the remainder of this section, where we explain what a **stock repurchase** is, how it is carried out, and how the financial manager should analyze a possible repurchase program.

There are three principal types of repurchases: (1) situations where the firm has cash available for distribution to its stockholders, and it distributes this cash by repurchasing shares rather than by paying cash dividends; (2) situations where the firm concludes that its capital structure is too heavily weighted with equity, and then it sells debt and uses the proceeds to buy back its stock; and (3) situations where a firm has issued options to employees and then uses open market repurchases to obtain stock for use when the options are exercised.

Stock that has been repurchased by a firm is called *treasury stock*. If some of the outstanding stock is repurchased, fewer shares will remain outstanding. Assuming that the repurchase does not adversely affect the firm's future earnings, the earnings per share on the remaining shares will increase, resulting in a higher market price per share. As a result, capital gains will have been substituted for dividends.

Stock Repurchase
A transaction in which a firm buys back shares of its own stock, thereby decreasing shares outstanding, increasing EPS, and, often, increasing the stock price.

THE EFFECTS OF STOCK REPURCHASES

Many companies have been repurchasing their stock in recent years. Until the 1980s, most repurchases amounted to a few million dollars, but in 1985, Phillips Petroleum announced plans for the largest repurchase on record — 81 million of its shares with a market value of $4.1 billion. Other large repurchases have been made by Texaco, IBM, CBS, Coca-Cola, Teledyne, Atlantic Richfield, Goodyear, and Xerox. Indeed, since 1985, more shares have been repurchased than issued.

The effects of a repurchase can be illustrated with data on American Development Corporation (ADC). The company expects to earn $4.4 million in 2002, and 50 percent of this amount, or $2.2 million, has been allocated for distribution to common shareholders. There are 1.1 million shares outstanding, and the market price is $20 a share. ADC believes that it can either use the $2.2

INDUSTRY PRACTICE

STOCK REPURCHASES: AN EASY WAY TO BOOST STOCK PRICES?

Looking for a way to boost your company's stock price? Why not buy back some of your company's shares? That reflects the thinking of an increasing number of financial managers.

The buyback rage is in some ways surprising. Given the recent performance of the stock market, it has become quite expensive to buy back shares. Nevertheless, the market's response to a buyback announcement is usually positive. For example, in mid-1996 Reebok announced that it would buy back one-third of its outstanding shares, and on the announcement day, the stock price rose 10 percent. Reebok's experience is not unique. A recent study found (1) that the average company's stock rose 3.5 percent the day a buyback was announced and (2) that companies that repurchase shares outperform the market over a four-year period following the announcement.[a]

Why are buybacks so popular with investors? The general view is that financial managers are signaling to the investment community a belief that the stock is undervalued, hence that the company thinks its own stock is an attractive investment. In this respect, stock repurchases have the opposite effect of stock issuances, which are thought to signal that the firm's stock is overvalued. Buybacks also help assure investors that the company is not wasting its shareholders' money by invest-

ing in sub-par investments. Michael O'Neill, the CFO of BankAmerica, puts it this way: "We look very hard internally, but if we don't have a profitable use for capital, we think we should return it to shareholders."

Despite all the recent hoopla surrounding buybacks, many analysts stress that in some instances repurchases have a downside: If a firm's stock is actually overvalued, buying back shares at the inflated price will harm the remaining stockholders. In this regard, buybacks should not be viewed as a gimmick to boost stock prices in the short run, but should be used only if they are part of a well-thought-out strategy for investment and for distributing cash to stockholders. Indeed, buybacks do not always succeed — Disney, for example, announced a buyback in April 1996, and its stock price fell more than 10 percent in the next six months.

[a] David Ikenberry, Josef Lakonishok, and Theo Vermaelen, "Market Under-Reaction to Open Market Share Repurchases," *Journal of Financial Economics,* 1995, Vol. 39, 181–208.

SOURCE: Adapted from "Buybacks Make News, But Do They Make Sense?" *BusinessWeek,* August 12, 1996, 76.

---

million to repurchase 100,000 of its shares through a tender offer at $22 a share or else pay a cash dividend of $2 a share.[15]

The effect of the repurchase on the EPS and market price per share of the remaining stock can be analyzed in the following way:

1. Current EPS $= \dfrac{\text{Total earnings}}{\text{Number of shares}} = \dfrac{\$4.4 \text{ million}}{1.1 \text{ million}} = \$4$ per share.

2. P/E ratio $= \dfrac{\$20}{\$4} = 5\times.$

---

[15] Stock repurchases are generally made in one of three ways: (1) A publicly owned firm can simply buy its own stock through a broker on the open market. (2) It can make a *tender offer,* under which it permits stockholders to send in (that is, "tender") their shares to the firm in exchange for a specified price per share. In this case, it generally indicates that it will buy up to a specified number of shares within a particular time period (usually about two weeks); if more shares are tendered than the company wishes to purchase, purchases are made on a pro rata basis. (3) The firm can purchase a block of shares from one large holder on a negotiated basis. If a negotiated purchase is employed, care must be taken to ensure that this one stockholder does not receive preferential treatment over other stockholders or that any preference given can be justified by "sound business reasons." Texaco's management was sued by stockholders who were unhappy over the company's repurchase of about $600 million of stock from the Bass Brothers' interests at a substantial premium over the market price. The suit charged that Texaco's management, afraid the Bass Brothers would attempt a takeover, used the buyback to get them off its back. Such payments have been dubbed "greenmail."

INDUSTRY PRACTICE

BUYBACKS HAVE LOWERED DIVIDEND YIELDS

Dividend payouts and yields have fallen sharply over the past two decades. In 1980, the average large company paid out 55 percent of its earnings as dividends, and its dividend yield exceeded 5 percent. Today, the average payout is less than 40 percent, and the yield has dipped below 1.5 percent.

A number of theories have been offered to explain these results. First, declining dividend yields imply that stock prices have increased faster than dividends paid. Some analysts point to the low yields as evidence that the stock market is overvalued. Second, lower interest rates led to a decline in required stock returns. This increased stock prices, which, in turn, resulted in lower dividend yields. Third, over the past two decades the composition of the stock market has changed dramatically. In 1980, the market was dominated by oil, industrial, utility, and retail companies that paid high dividends. Today the market includes many high-tech companies that pay little or no dividends.

In addition, dividend yields have fallen because more and more companies now recognize the tax and other advantages of stock repurchases over dividends as a way of distributing cash to shareholders. Indeed, stock repurchases have tripled in recent years, and in each year since 1997 stock repurchases have exceeded cash dividends paid.

The popularity of stock repurchases led Federal Reserve Board economists Nellie Liang and Steve Sharpe to redefine a stock's "total yield." First, they developed a "net repurchases yield," calculated as the dollars per share spent on repurchases minus the cost of shares used to cover the exercise of stock options, divided by the stock price. Then, the stock's "total yield" is found as the sum of the traditional dividend yield plus the net repurchases yield.

Liang and Sharpe's estimated yields for the largest 144 companies in the S&P 500 during 1994–1998 are reported in the accompanying table. These data confirm the declining importance of dividends and the increasing importance of stock repurchases. They also indicate that total yields have been trending downward. Even after including stock repurchases, total yields are still only half of what the dividend yield alone was in 1980. Thus, no matter how you slice it, payouts to shareholders have declined. This is, of course, consistent with lower interest rates and a declining cost of equity capital.

SOURCE: Gene Epstein, "Soaring Buybacks Make Dividend Yield a Misleading Measure of a Stock's Value," *Barron's Online*, November 1, 1999.

YIELDS	1994	1995	1996	1997	1998
Dividend yield	2.76%	2.41%	2.06%	1.73%	1.41%
Repurchase yield	1.19	1.34	1.56	1.98	1.49
Total yield	3.95%	3.75%	3.62%	3.71%	2.90%
Percent of repurchases	30%	36%	43%	53%	51%

3. EPS after repurchasing 100,000 shares $= \dfrac{\$4.4 \text{ million}}{1 \text{ million}} = \$4.40$ per share.

4. Expected market price after repurchase $=$ (P/E)(EPS) $=$ (5)($4.40)

$$= \$22 \text{ per share.}$$

It should be noted from this example that investors would receive before-tax benefits of $2 per share in any case, either in the form of a $2 cash dividend or a $2 increase in the stock price. This result would occur because we assumed, first, that shares could be repurchased at exactly $22 a share and, second, that the P/E ratio would remain constant. If shares could be bought for less than $22, the operation would be even better for *remaining* stockholders, but the reverse would hold if ADC had to pay more than $22 a share. Furthermore, the P/E ratio might change as a result of the repurchase operation, rising if investors viewed it favorably and falling if they viewed it unfavorably. Some factors that might affect P/E ratios are considered next.

ADVANTAGES OF REPURCHASES

The advantages of repurchases are as follows:

1. Repurchase announcements are viewed as positive signals by investors because the repurchase is often motivated by management's belief that the firm's shares are undervalued.

2. The stockholders have a choice when the firm distributes cash by repurchasing stock — they can sell or not sell. With a cash dividend, on the other hand, stockholders must accept a dividend payment and pay the tax. Thus, those stockholders who need cash can sell back some of their shares, while those who do not want additional cash can simply retain their stock. From a tax standpoint, a repurchase permits both types of stockholders to get what they want.

3. A third advantage is that a repurchase can remove a large block of stock that is "overhanging" the market and keep the price per share down.

4. Dividends are "sticky" in the short run because managements are reluctant to raise the dividend if the increase cannot be maintained in the future — managements dislike cutting cash dividends because of the negative signal a cut gives. Hence, if the excess cash flow is thought to be only temporary, management may prefer to make the distribution in the form of a share repurchase rather than to declare an increased cash dividend that cannot be maintained.

5. Companies can use the residual model to set a *target cash distribution* level, then divide the distribution into a *dividend component* and a *repurchase component*. The dividend payout ratio will be relatively low, but the dividend itself will be relatively secure, and it will grow as a result of the declining number of shares outstanding. The company has more flexibility in adjusting the total distribution than it would if the entire distribution were in the form of cash dividends, because repurchases can be varied from year to year without giving off adverse signals. This procedure, which is what FPL employed, has much to recommend it, and it is a primary reason for the dramatic increase in the volume of share repurchases.

6. Repurchases can be used to produce large-scale changes in capital structures. For example, several years ago Consolidated Edison decided to repurchase $400 million of its common stock in order to increase its debt ratio. The repurchase was necessary because even if the company financed its capital budget only with debt, it would still have taken years to get the debt ratio up to the target level. Con Ed used the repurchase to produce a rapid change in its capital structure.

7. Companies that use stock options as an important component of employee compensation can repurchase shares and then use those shares when employees exercise their options. This avoids the issuance of new shares and a resulting dilution of earnings. Microsoft and other high-tech companies have used this procedure in recent years.

DISADVANTAGES OF REPURCHASES

Disadvantages of repurchases include the following:

1. Stockholders may not be indifferent between dividends and capital gains, and the price of the stock might benefit more from cash dividends than from repurchases. Cash dividends are generally dependable, but repurchases are not. Further, if many firms announced regular, dependable repurchase programs, the improper accumulation tax might become a threat.

2. The *selling* stockholders may not be fully aware of all the implications of a repurchase, or they may not have all the pertinent information about the corporation's present and future activities. However, firms generally announce repurchase programs before embarking on them to avoid potential stockholder suits.

3. The corporation may pay too high a price for the repurchased stock, to the disadvantage of remaining stockholders. If its shares are not actively traded, and if the firm seeks to acquire a relatively large amount of its stock, then the price may be bid above its equilibrium level and then fall after the firm ceases its repurchase operations.

CONCLUSIONS ON STOCK REPURCHASES

When all the pros and cons on stock repurchases have been totaled, where do we stand? Our conclusions may be summarized as follows:

1. Because of the lower capital gains tax rate and the deferred tax on capital gains, repurchases have a significant tax advantage over dividends as a way to distribute income to stockholders. This advantage is reinforced by the fact that repurchases provide cash to stockholders who want cash but allow those who do not need current cash to delay its receipt. On the other hand, dividends are more dependable and are thus better suited for those who need a steady source of income.

2. Because of signaling effects, companies should not vary their dividends — that would lower investors' confidence in the company and adversely affect its cost of equity and its stock price. However, cash flows vary over time, as do investment opportunities, so the "proper" dividend in the residual model sense varies. To get around this problem, a company can set its dividend at a level low enough to keep dividend payments from constraining operations and then use repurchases on a more or less regular basis to distribute excess cash. Such a procedure would provide regular, dependable dividends plus additional cash flow to those stockholders who want it.

3. Repurchases are also useful when a firm wants to make a large shift in its capital structure within a short period of time, wants to distribute cash from a one-time event such as the sale of a division, or wants to obtain shares for use in an employee stock option plan.

In an earlier edition of this book, we argued that companies ought to be doing more repurchasing and paying out less cash as dividends than they were. Increases in the size and frequency of repurchases in recent years suggest that companies have reached this same conclusion.

SELF-TEST QUESTIONS

Explain how repurchases can (1) help stockholders hold down taxes and (2) help firms change their capital structures.

What is treasury stock?

What are three procedures a firm can use to repurchase its stock?

What are some advantages and disadvantages of stock repurchases?

How can stock repurchases help a company operate in accordance with the residual dividend model?

TYING IT ALL TOGETHER

Once a company becomes profitable, it must decide what to do with the cash it generates. It may choose to retain cash and use it to purchase additional assets or to reduce outstanding debt. Alternatively, it may choose to return cash to shareholders. Keep in mind that every dollar that management chooses to retain is a dollar that shareholders could have received and invested elsewhere. Therefore, managers should retain earnings if and only if they can invest the money within the firm and earn more than stockholders could earn outside the firm. Consequently, high-growth companies with many good projects will tend to retain a high percentage of earnings, whereas mature companies with lots of cash but limited investment opportunities will have generous cash distributions.

This basic tendency has a major influence on firms' long-run distribution policies. However, as we saw in this chapter, in any given year several important situations could complicate the long-run policy. Companies with excess cash have to decide whether to pay dividends or repurchase stock. In addition, due to the importance of signaling and the clientele effect, companies generally find it desirable to maintain a stable, consistent dividend policy over time. The key concepts covered in this chapter are listed below.

- **Dividend policy** involves three issues: (1) What fraction of earnings should be distributed? (2) Should the distribution be in the form of cash dividends or stock repurchases? (3) Should the firm maintain a steady, stable dividend growth rate?
- The **optimal dividend policy** strikes a balance between current dividends and future growth so as to maximize the firm's stock price.

- Miller and Modigliani developed the **dividend irrelevance theory,** which holds that a firm's dividend policy has no effect on either the value of its stock or its cost of capital.

- The **bird-in-the-hand theory** holds that the firm's value will be maximized by a high dividend payout ratio, because investors regard cash dividends as being less risky than potential capital gains.

- The **tax preference theory** states that because long-term capital gains are subject to less onerous taxes than dividends, investors prefer to have companies retain earnings rather than pay them out as dividends.

- **Empirical tests** of the three theories **have been inconclusive.** Therefore, academicians cannot tell corporate managers how a given change in dividend policy will affect stock prices and capital costs.

- Dividend policy should take account of the **information content of dividends (signaling)** and the **clientele effect.** The information content, or signaling, effect relates to the fact that investors regard an unexpected dividend change as a signal of management's forecast of future earnings. The clientele effect suggests that a firm will attract investors who like the firm's dividend payout policy. Both factors should be considered by firms that are considering a change in dividend policy.

- In practice, most firms try to follow a policy of paying a **steadily increasing dividend.** This policy provides investors with stable, dependable income, and departures from it give investors signals about management's expectations for future earnings.

- Most firms use the **residual dividend model** to set the long-run target payout ratio at a level that will permit the firm to satisfy its equity requirements with retained earnings.

- A **dividend reinvestment plan (DRIP)** allows stockholders to have the company automatically use dividends to purchase additional shares of stock. DRIPs are popular because they allow stockholders to acquire additional shares without incurring brokerage fees.

- **Legal constraints, investment opportunities, availability and cost of funds from other sources,** and **taxes** are also considered when firms establish dividend policies.

- A **stock split** increases the number of shares outstanding. Normally, splits reduce the price per share in proportion to the increase in shares because splits merely "divide the pie into smaller slices." However, firms generally split their stocks only if (1) the price is quite high and (2) management thinks the future is bright. Therefore, stock splits are often taken as positive signals and thus boost stock prices.

- A **stock dividend** is a dividend paid in additional shares of stock rather than in cash. Both stock dividends and splits are used to keep stock prices within an "optimal" trading range.

- Under a **stock repurchase plan,** a firm buys back some of its outstanding stock, thereby decreasing the number of shares, which should increase both EPS and the stock price. Repurchases are useful for making major changes in capital structure, as well as for distributing excess cash.

14-1 How would each of the following changes tend to affect aggregate (that is, the average for all corporations) payout ratios, other things held constant? Explain your answers.
  a. An increase in the personal income tax rate.
  b. A liberalization of depreciation for federal income tax purposes — that is, faster tax write-offs.
  c. A rise in interest rates.
  d. An increase in corporate profits.
  e. A decline in investment opportunities.
  f. Permission for corporations to deduct dividends for tax purposes as they now do interest charges.
  g. A change in the Tax Code so that both realized and unrealized capital gains in any year were taxed at the same rate as dividends.

14-2 Discuss the pros and cons of having the directors formally announce what a firm's dividend policy will be in the future.

14-3 Most firms would like to have their stock selling at a high P/E ratio, and they would also like to have extensive public ownership (many different shareholders). Explain how stock dividends or stock splits may help achieve these goals.

14-4 What is the difference between a stock dividend and a stock split? As a stockholder, would you prefer to see your company declare a 100 percent stock dividend or a two-for-one split? Assume that either action is feasible.

14-5 "The cost of retained earnings is less than the cost of new outside equity capital. Consequently, it is totally irrational for a firm to sell a new issue of stock and to pay dividends during the same year." Discuss this statement.

14-6 Would it ever be rational for a firm to borrow money in order to pay dividends? Explain.

14-7 "Executive salaries have been shown to be more closely correlated to the size of the firm than to its profitability. If a firm's board of directors is controlled by management instead of by outside directors, this might result in the firm's retaining more earnings than can be justified from the stockholders' point of view." Discuss the statement, being sure (a) to discuss the interrelationships among cost of capital, investment opportunities, and new investment and (b) to explain the implied relationship between dividend policy and stock prices.

14-8 Modigliani and Miller (MM) on the one hand and Gordon and Lintner (GL) on the other have expressed strong views regarding the effect of dividend policy on a firm's cost of capital and value.
  a. In essence, what are the MM and GL views regarding the effect of dividend policy on the cost of capital and stock prices?
  b. How does the tax preference theory differ from the views of MM and GL?
  c. According to the text, which of the theories, if any, has received statistical confirmation from empirical tests?
  d. How could MM use the *information content*, or *signaling*, *hypothesis* to counter their opponents' arguments? If you were debating MM, how would you counter them?
  e. How could MM use the *clientele effect* concept to counter their opponents' arguments? If you were debating MM, how would you counter them?

14-9 More NYSE companies had stock dividends and stock splits during 1983 and 1984 than ever before. What events in these years could have made stock splits and stock dividends so popular? Explain the rationale that a financial vice-president might give his or her board of directors to support a stock split/dividend recommendation.

14-10 One position expressed in the financial literature is that firms set their dividends as a residual after using income to support new investment.
  a. Explain what a residual dividend policy implies, illustrating your answer with a table showing how different investment opportunities could lead to different dividend payout ratios.
  b. Think back to Chapter 13, where we considered the relationship between capital structure and the cost of capital. If the WACC-versus-debt-ratio plot were shaped like a sharp V, would this have a different implication for the importance of setting

dividends according to the residual policy than if the plot were shaped like a shallow bowl (or a flattened U)?

14-11 Indicate whether the following statements are true or false. If the statement is false, explain why.
a. If a firm repurchases its stock in the open market, the shareholders who tender the stock are subject to capital gains taxes.
b. If you own 100 shares in a company's stock and the company's stock splits two for one, you will own 200 shares in the company following the split.
c. Some dividend reinvestment plans increase the amount of equity capital available to the firm.
d. The Tax Code encourages companies to pay a large percentage of their net income in the form of dividends.
e. If your company has established a clientele of investors who prefer large dividends, the company is unlikely to adopt a residual dividend policy.
f. If a firm follows a residual dividend policy, holding all else constant, its dividend payout will tend to rise whenever the firm's investment opportunities improve.

SELF-TEST PROBLEMS   (SOLUTIONS APPEAR IN APPENDIX B)

ST-1
Key terms

Define each of the following terms:
a. Optimal dividend policy
b. Dividend irrelevance theory; bird-in-the-hand theory; tax preference theory
c. Information content, or signaling, hypothesis; clientele effect
d. Residual dividend model
e. Extra dividend
f. Declaration date; holder-of-record date; ex-dividend date; payment date
g. Dividend reinvestment plan (DRIP)
h. Stock split; stock dividend
i. Stock repurchase

ST-2
Alternative dividend policies

Components Manufacturing Corporation (CMC) has an all-common-equity capital structure. It has 200,000 shares of $2 par value common stock outstanding. When CMC's founder, who was also its research director and most successful inventor, retired unexpectedly to the South Pacific in late 2001, CMC was left suddenly and permanently with materially lower growth expectations and relatively few attractive new investment opportunities. Unfortunately, there was no way to replace the founder's contributions to the firm. Previously, CMC found it necessary to plow back most of its earnings to finance growth, which averaged 12 percent per year. Future growth at a 5 percent rate is considered realistic, but that level would call for an increase in the dividend payout. Further, it now appears that new investment projects with at least the 14 percent rate of return required by CMC's stockholders (k_s = 14%) would amount to only $800,000 for 2002 in comparison to a projected $2,000,000 of net income. If the existing 20 percent dividend payout were continued, retained earnings would be $1.6 million in 2002, but, as noted, investments that yield the 14 percent cost of capital would amount to only $800,000.

The one encouraging point is that the high earnings from existing assets are expected to continue, and net income of $2 million is still expected for 2002. Given the dramatically changed circumstances, CMC's management is reviewing the firm's dividend policy.
a. Assuming that the acceptable 2002 investment projects would be financed entirely by earnings retained during the year, calculate DPS in 2002, assuming that CMC uses the residual dividend model.
b. What payout ratio does your answer to part a imply for 2002?
c. If a 60 percent payout ratio is maintained for the foreseeable future, what is your estimate of the present market price of the common stock? How does this compare with the market price that should have prevailed under the assumptions existing just before the news about the founder's retirement? If the two values of P_0 are different, comment on why.
d. What would happen to the price of the stock if the old 20 percent payout were continued? Assume that if this payout is maintained, the average rate of return on the retained earnings will fall to 7.5 percent and the new growth rate will be

$$g = (1.0 - \text{Payout ratio})(\text{ROE})$$
$$= (1.0 - 0.2)(7.5\%)$$
$$= (0.8)(7.5\%) = 6.0\%.$$

STARTER PROBLEMS

14-1
Residual dividend model

Axel Telecommunications has a target capital structure that consists of 70 percent debt and 30 percent equity. The company anticipates that its capital budget for the upcoming year will be $3,000,000. If Axel reports net income of $2,000,000 and it follows a residual dividend payout policy, what will be its dividend payout ratio?

14-2
Stock split

Gamma Medical's stock trades at $90 a share. The company is contemplating a 3-for-2 stock split. Assuming that the stock split will have no effect on the market value of its equity, what will be the company's stock price following the stock split?

14-3
Stock repurchases

Beta Industries has net income of $2,000,000 and it has 1,000,000 shares of common stock outstanding. The company's stock currently trades at $32 a share. Beta is considering a plan in which it will use available cash to repurchase 20 percent of its shares in the open market. The repurchase is expected to have no effect on either net income or the company's P/E ratio. What will be its stock price following the stock repurchase?

EXAM-TYPE PROBLEMS

The problems included in this section are set up in such a way that they could be used as multiple-choice exam problems.

14-4
External equity financing

Northern Pacific Heating and Cooling Inc. has a 6-month backlog of orders for its patented solar heating system. To meet this demand, management plans to expand production capacity by 40 percent with a $10 million investment in plant and machinery. The firm wants to maintain a 40 percent debt-to-total-assets ratio in its capital structure; it also wants to maintain its past dividend policy of distributing 45 percent of last year's net income. In 2001, net income was $5 million. How much external equity must Northern Pacific seek at the beginning of 2002 to expand capacity as desired? Assume the firm uses only debt and common equity in its capital structure.

14-5
Residual dividend model

Petersen Company has a capital budget of $1.2 million. The company wants to maintain a target capital structure that is 60 percent debt and 40 percent equity. The company forecasts that its net income this year will be $600,000. If the company follows a residual dividend policy, what will be its payout ratio?

14-6
Residual dividend model

The Wei Corporation expects next year's net income to be $15 million. The firm's debt ratio is currently 40 percent. Wei has $12 million of profitable investment opportunities, and it wishes to maintain its existing debt ratio. According to the residual dividend model, how large should Wei's dividend payout ratio be next year? Assume the firm uses only debt and common equity in its capital structure.

14-7
Stock split

After a 5-for-1 stock split, the Strasburg Company paid a dividend of $0.75 per new share, which represents a 9 percent increase over last year's pre-split dividend. What was last year's dividend per share?

14-8
Residual dividend model

The Welch Company is considering three independent projects, each of which requires a $5 million investment. The estimated internal rate of return (IRR) and cost of capital for these projects is presented below:

Project H (High risk): Cost of capital = 16%; IRR = 20%.

Project M (Medium risk): Cost of capital = 12%; IRR = 10%.

Project L (Low risk): Cost of capital = 8%; IRR = 9%.

Note that the projects' cost of capital varies because the projects have different levels of risk. The company's optimal capital structure calls for 50 percent debt and 50 percent common equity. Welch expects to have net income of $7,287,500. If Welch bases its dividends on the residual model, what will its payout ratio be?

PROBLEMS

14-9
Dividends

Bowles Sporting Inc. is prepared to report the following income statement (shown in thousands of dollars) for the year 2002.

Sales	$15,200
Operating costs including depreciation	11,900
EBIT	$ 3,300
Interest	300
EBT	$ 3,000
Taxes (40%)	1,200
Net income	$ 1,800

Prior to reporting this income statement, the company wants to determine its annual dividend. The company has 500,000 shares of stock outstanding and its stock trades at $48 per share.
a. The company had a 40 percent dividend payout ratio in 2001. If Bowles wants to maintain this payout ratio in 2002, what will be its per-share dividend in 2002?
b. If the company maintains this 40 percent payout ratio, what will be the current dividend yield on the company's stock?
c. The company reported net income of $1.5 million in 2001. Assume that the number of shares outstanding has remained constant. What was the company's per-share dividend in 2001?
d. As an alternative to maintaining the same dividend payout ratio, Bowles is considering maintaining the same per-share dividend in 2002 that it paid in 2001. If it chooses this policy, what will be the company's dividend payout ratio in 2002?
e. Assume that the company is interested in dramatically expanding its operations and that this expansion will require significant amounts of capital. The company would like to avoid transactions costs involved in issuing new equity. Given this scenario, would it make more sense for the company to maintain a constant dividend payout ratio or to maintain the same per-share dividend?

14-10
Alternative dividend policies

In 2001 the Keenan Company paid dividends totaling $3,600,000 on net income of $10.8 million. 2001 was a normal year, and for the past 10 years, earnings have grown at a constant rate of 10 percent. However, in 2002, earnings are expected to jump to $14.4 million, and the firm expects to have profitable investment opportunities of $8.4 million. It is predicted that Keenan will not be able to maintain the 2002 level of earnings growth — the high 2002 earnings level is attributable to an exceptionally profitable new product line introduced that year — and the company will return to its previous 10 percent growth rate. Keenan's target capital structure is 40 percent debt and 60 percent equity.
a. Calculate Keenan's total dividends for 2002 if it follows each of the following policies:
  (1) Its 2002 dividend payment is set to force dividends to grow at the long-run growth rate in earnings.
  (2) It continues the 2001 dividend payout ratio.
  (3) It uses a pure residual dividend policy (40 percent of the $8.4 million investment is financed with debt and 60 percent with common equity).
  (4) It employs a regular-dividend-plus-extras policy, with the regular dividend being based on the long-run growth rate and the extra dividend being set according to the residual policy.
b. Which of the preceding policies would you recommend? Restrict your choices to the ones listed, but justify your answer.

c. Assume that investors expect Keenan to pay total dividends of $9,000,000 in 2002 and to have the dividend grow at 10 percent after 2002. The stock's total market value is $180 million. What is the company's cost of equity?

d. What is Keenan's long-run average return on equity? [Hint: g = (Retention rate) × (ROE) = (1.0 − Payout rate)(ROE).]

e. Does a 2002 dividend of $9,000,000 seem reasonable in view of your answers to parts c and d? If not, should the dividend be higher or lower?

14-11
Residual dividend model

Buena Terra Corporation is reviewing its capital budget for the upcoming year. It has paid a $3.00 dividend per share (DPS) for the past several years, and its shareholders expect the dividend to remain constant for the next several years. The company's target capital structure is 60 percent equity and 40 percent debt; it has 1,000,000 shares of common equity outstanding; and its net income is $8 million. The company forecasts that it would require $10 million to fund all of its profitable (i.e., positive NPV) projects for the upcoming year.

a. If Buena Terra follows the residual dividend model, how much retained earnings will it need to fund its capital budget?

b. If Buena Terra follows the residual dividend model, what will be the company's dividend per share and payout ratio for the upcoming year?

c. If Buena Terra maintains its current $3.00 DPS for next year, how much retained earnings will be available for the firm's capital budget?

d. Can the company maintain its current capital structure, maintain the $3.00 DPS, and maintain a $10 million capital budget without having to raise new common stock?

e. Suppose that Buena Terra's management is firmly opposed to cutting the dividend, that is, it wishes to maintain the $3.00 dividend for the next year. Also, assume that the company was committed to funding all profitable projects and was willing to issue more debt (along with the available retained earnings) to help finance the company's capital budget. Assume that the resulting change in capital structure has a minimal impact on the company's composite cost of capital, so that the capital budget remains at $10 million. What portion of this year's capital budget would have to be financed with debt?

f. Suppose once again that Buena Terra's management wants to maintain the $3.00 DPS. In addition, the company wants to maintain its target capital structure (60 percent equity, 40 percent debt) and maintain its $10 million capital budget. What is the minimum dollar amount of new common stock that the company would have to issue in order to meet each of its objectives?

g. Now consider the case where Buena Terra's management wants to maintain the $3.00 DPS and its target capital structure, but it wants to avoid issuing new common stock. The company is willing to cut its capital budget in order to meet its other objectives. Assuming that the company's projects are divisible, what will be the company's capital budget for the next year?

h. What actions can a firm that follows the residual dividend policy take when its forecasted retained earnings are less than the retained earnings required to fund its capital budget?

SPREADSHEET PROBLEM

14-12
Residual dividend model

Rework Problem 14-11 parts a through g, using a spreadsheet model.

The information related to this cyberproblem is likely to change over time, due to the release of new information and the ever-changing nature of the World Wide Web. Accordingly, we will periodically update the problem on the textbook's web site. To avoid problems, please check for updates before proceeding with the cyberproblems.

14-13
Dividend reinvestment plans

Dividend reinvestment plans (DRIPs) enable stockholders to automatically reinvest dividends received back into the stock of the paying firm. In addition, many DRIPs allow their shareholders the option to buy more shares directly from the company by just writing a check. The major advantage is that investors are able to avoid brokerage commissions. Although some plans require small service fees, these service fees usually pale in comparison to brokerage fees; however, the specific details of DRIPs will vary from plan to plan.

To learn about dividend reinvestment plans, you need to get back to basics. Let's find out what fools think about them, specifically the Motley Fool. For this cyberproblem, you will be going back to school with "Motley Fool's School," found at **http://www.fool.com/school.htm**.

From the "Fool's School" front page, scroll down to "Drip Investing" on the left side of your computer screen. This link will take you to the "Investing through DRIPs" section of the Fool's School. Make sure you also click on "starting a DRP" after reading the material on the first screen to answer the following questions:

a. According to the Fool, what are some of the advantages to DRIPs or DRPs, as the Fool refers to them?
b. What variation of the traditional dividend reinvestment plan does the Fool mention?

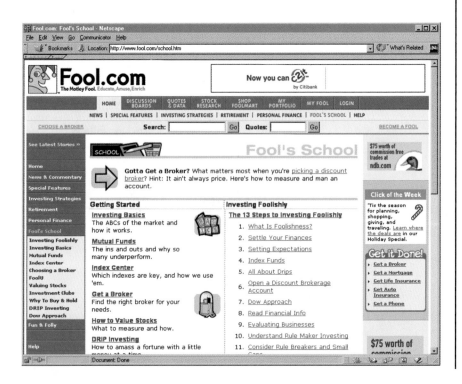

c. What effects can DRIPs have on participants' investing and consumption habits?
d. Describe the three kinds of DRIPs outlined by the Fool.
e. Describe Direct Investment Plans (DIPs). What are the pros and cons of this program?
f. What pros and cons does the Fool mention for DRIPs/Optional Cash Purchase Plans (OCPs)?

INTEGRATED CASE

SOUTHEASTERN STEEL COMPANY

14–14 Dividend policy Southeastern Steel Company (SSC) was formed 5 years ago to exploit a new continuous-casting process. SSC's founders, Donald Brown and Margo Valencia, had been employed in the research department of a major integrated-steel company, but when that company decided against using the new process (which Brown and Valencia had developed), they decided to strike out on their own. One advantage of the new process was that it required relatively little capital in comparison with the typical steel company, so Brown and Valencia have been able to avoid issuing new stock, and thus they own all of the shares. However, SSC has now reached the stage in which outside equity capital is necessary if the firm is to achieve its growth targets yet still maintain its target capital structure of 60 percent equity and 40 percent debt. Therefore, Brown and Valencia have decided to take the company public. Until now, Brown and Valencia have paid themselves reasonable salaries but routinely reinvested all after-tax earnings in the firm, so dividend policy has not been an issue. However, before talking with potential outside investors, they must decide on a dividend policy.

Assume that you were recently hired by Arthur Adamson & Company (AA), a national consulting firm, which has been asked to help SSC prepare for its public offering. Martha Millon, the senior AA consultant in your group, has asked you to make a presentation to Brown and Valencia in which you review the theory of dividend policy and discuss the following questions.

a. (1) What is meant by the term "dividend policy"?
  (2) The terms "irrelevance," "bird-in-the-hand," and "tax preference" have been used to describe three major theories regarding the way dividend policy affects a firm's value. Explain what these terms mean, and briefly describe each theory.
  (3) What do the three theories indicate regarding the actions management should take with respect to dividend policy?

  (4) Explain the relationships between dividend policy, stock price, and the cost of equity under each dividend policy theory by constructing two graphs such as those shown in Figure 14-1. Dividend payout should be placed on the X axis.
  (5) What results have empirical studies of the dividend theories produced? How does all this affect what we can tell managers about dividend policy?

b. Discuss (1) the information content, or signaling, hypothesis, (2) the clientele effect, and (3) their effects on dividend policy.

c. (1) Assume that SSC has an $800,000 capital budget planned for the coming year. You have determined that its present capital structure (60 percent equity and 40 percent debt) is optimal, and its net income is forecasted at $600,000. Use the residual dividend model approach to determine SSC's total dollar dividend and payout ratio. In the process, explain what the residual dividend model is. Then, explain what would happen if net income were forecasted at $400,000, or at $800,000.
  (2) In general terms, how would a change in investment opportunities affect the payout ratio under the residual payment policy?
  (3) What are the advantages and disadvantages of the residual policy? (Hint: Don't neglect signaling and clientele effects.)

d. What is a dividend reinvestment plan (DRIP), and how does it work?

e. Describe the series of steps that most firms take in setting dividend policy in practice.

f. What are stock repurchases? Discuss the advantages and disadvantages of a firm's repurchasing its own shares.

g. What are stock dividends and stock splits? What are the advantages and disadvantages of stock dividends and stock splits?

PART **VI**

WORKING CAPITAL MANAGEMENT AND MULTINATIONAL FINANCIAL MANAGEMENT

CHAPTER 15

Working Capital Management

SOURCE: © Greg Girard/Contact Press Images

DELL REVOLUTIONIZES WORKING CAPITAL MANAGEMENT

DELL COMPUTER

Dramatic improvements in computer technology and the growth in the Internet have dramatically transformed the computer industry. Some companies have succeeded while others have failed. Despite some recent setbacks, Dell Computer has clearly been one that has succeeded: Its sales have grown from roughly $5 billion in 1995 to more than $30 billion in 2000.

There are a lot of reasons behind Dell's remarkable success over the past decade. Perhaps the number one reason is the company's impressive success in managing its working capital, which is the focus of this chapter.

The key to Dell's success is its ability to build and deliver customized computers very quickly. Traditionally, manufacturers of custom-design products had two choices. They could keep a large supply of inventory on hand to meet customer needs, or they could make their customers wait for weeks while the customized product was being built. Dell uses information technology to revolutionize working capital management. First, it uses information technology to better coordinate with its suppliers. If a supplier wants to do business with Dell, it must be able to provide the necessary components quickly and cheaply. Suppliers that adapt and meet Dell's demands are rewarded with increased business, and those that don't lose their Dell business.

Second, Dell uses information technology to collect data that enables it to better customize products for its customers. For example, a recent *Fortune* article described how Dell has been able to capture most of the Ford Motor Company's PC business:

> Look at what the company does for one big customer, Ford Motor. Dell creates a bunch of different configurations designed for Ford employees in different departments. When Dell receives an order via the Ford Intranet, it knows immediately what type of worker is ordering and what kind of computer he or she needs. The company assembles the proper hardware and even installs the right software, some of which consists of Ford-specific code that's stored at Dell. Since Dell's logistics software is so sophisticated, it can do the customization quickly and inexpensively.

Sound working capital management is necessary if a company wants to compete in the information age, and the lessons taught by Dell extend to other industries. Indeed, Michael Dell, founder and CEO of Dell Computer, recently discussed in an interview with *The Wall Street Journal* how traditional manufacturers, such as the automobile companies, can use the experience of Dell to improve their operations. The article included Michael Dell's five points on how to build a better car:

1. Use the Internet to lower the costs of linking manufacturers with their suppliers and dealers.
2. Turn over to an outside specialist any operation that isn't central to the business.
3. Accelerate the pace of change, and get employees conditioned to accept change.
4. Experiment with Internet businesses. Set up trials to see what happens when customers can access information more easily, and in ways they never could before.
5. Think about what could be done with the capital that would be freed up by shedding excessive inventory and other redundant assets. ■

SOURCES: J. William Gurley and Jane Hodges, "A Dell for Every Industry," *Fortune,* October 12, 1998, 167–172; and Gary McWilliams and Joseph B. White, "Dell to Detroit: Get into Gear Online!" *The Wall Street Journal,* December 1, 1999, B1.

PUTTING THINGS IN PERSPECTIVE

About 60 percent of a typical financial manager's time is devoted to working capital management, and many students' first jobs will involve working capital. This is particularly true in smaller businesses, where most new jobs in the United States are being created.

Working capital policy involves two basic questions: (1) What is the appropriate amount of current assets for the firm to carry, both in total and for each specific account, and (2) how should current assets be financed? This chapter addresses current asset holdings and their financing.

As you will see in this chapter, sound working capital management goes beyond finance. Indeed, most of the ideas for improving working capital management often stem from other disciplines. For example, experts in business logistics, operations management, and information technology often work with the marketing group to develop a better way to deliver the firm's products. Where finance comes into play is in evaluating the profitability of alternative systems, which are generally costly to install. For example, assume that a firm's information technology and marketing groups decide that they want to (1) develop new software and (2) purchase computer terminals that will be installed in their customers' premises. Customers will then keep track of their own inventories and automatically order new supplies when inventory levels hit specified targets. The system will improve inventory management for both the manufacturer and its customers and also help "lock in" good customers.

Significant costs will be incurred to develop and install the new system, but if it is adopted, the company can meet its customers' needs better, and with smaller inventory, and also increase sales. In many respects, this scenario looks like a typical capital budgeting project — it has an up-front cost followed by a series of positive cash flows. The finance group can use the capital budgeting techniques described in Chapters 11 and 12 to evaluate whether the new system is worth the cost and also whether it should be developed in-house or purchased from an outside source. As with other chapters in this text, the textbook's CD-ROM contains an *Excel* file, 15MODEL.xls, that will guide you through the chapter's calculations. ■

WORKING CAPITAL TERMINOLOGY

We begin our discussion of working capital policy by reviewing some basic definitions and concepts:

Working Capital
A firm's investment in short-term assets — cash, marketable securities, inventory, and accounts receivable.

Net Working Capital
Current assets minus current liabilities.

Net Operating Working Capital
Current assets minus non-interest-bearing current liabilities.

1. **Working capital,** sometimes called *gross working capital*, simply refers to current assets used in operations.
2. **Net working capital** is defined as current assets minus current liabilities.
3. **Net operating working capital** is defined as current assets minus non-interest-bearing current liabilities. More specifically, net operating working capital is often expressed as cash and marketable securities, accounts receivable, and inventories, less accounts payable and accruals.[1]
4. The *current ratio*, which was discussed in Chapter 3, is calculated by dividing current assets by current liabilities, and it is intended to measure liquidity. However, a high current ratio does not ensure that a firm will have the cash required to meet its needs. If inventories cannot be sold, or if receivables cannot be collected in a timely manner, then the apparent safety reflected in a high current ratio could be illusory.
5. The *quick ratio*, or *acid test*, also attempts to measure liquidity, and it is found by subtracting inventories from current assets and then dividing by current liabilities. The quick ratio removes inventories from current assets because they are the least liquid of current assets. Therefore, the quick ratio is an "acid test" of a company's ability to meet its current obligations.
6. The best and most comprehensive picture of a firm's liquidity position is shown by its *cash budget*. This statement, which forecasts cash inflows and

---

[1] This definition assumes that cash and marketable securities on the balance sheet are at their normal long-run target levels and that the company is not holding any excess cash. Excess holdings of cash and marketable securities are generally not included as part of net operating working capital.

outflows, focuses on what really counts, namely, the firm's ability to generate sufficient cash inflows to meet its required cash outflows. We will discuss cash budgeting in detail later in the chapter.

7. **Working capital policy** refers to the firm's policies regarding (1) target levels for each category of current assets and (2) how current assets will be financed.

8. *Working capital management* involves both setting working capital policy and carrying out that policy in day-to-day operations.

Working Capital Policy
Basic policy decisions regarding (1) target levels for each category of current assets and (2) how current assets will be financed.

The term *working capital* originated with the old Yankee peddler, who would load up his wagon with goods and then go off on his route to peddle his wares. The merchandise was called working capital because it was what he actually sold, or "turned over," to produce his profits. The wagon and horse were his fixed assets. He generally owned the horse and wagon, so they were financed with "equity" capital, but he borrowed the funds to buy the merchandise. These borrowings were called *working capital loans*, and they had to be repaid after each trip to demonstrate to the bank that the credit was sound. If the peddler was able to repay the loan, then the bank would make another loan, and banks that followed this procedure were said to be employing "sound banking practices."

SELF-TEST QUESTIONS

Why is the quick ratio also called an acid test?

How did the term "working capital" originate?

Differentiate between net working capital and net operating working capital.

THE CASH CONVERSION CYCLE

As we noted above, the concept of working capital management originated with the old Yankee peddler, who would borrow to buy inventory, sell the inventory to pay off the bank loan, and then repeat the cycle. That concept has been applied to more complex businesses, where it is used to analyze the effectiveness of a firm's working capital management.

Firms typically follow a cycle in which they purchase inventory, sell goods on credit, and then collect accounts receivable. This cycle is referred to as the *cash conversion cycle*, and it is discussed in detail in the next section. Sound working capital policy is designed to minimize the time between cash expenditures on materials and the collection of cash on sales.

AN ILLUSTRATION

We can illustrate the process with data from Real Time Computer Corporation (RTC), which in early 2001 introduced a new minicomputer that can perform one billion instructions per second and that will sell for $250,000. RTC expects to sell 40 computers in its first year of production. The effects of this new product on RTC's working capital position were analyzed in terms of the following five steps:

1. RTC will order and then receive the materials it needs to produce the 40 computers it expects to sell. Because RTC and most other firms purchase materials on credit, this transaction will create an account payable. However, the purchase will have no immediate cash flow effect.

2. Labor will be used to convert the materials into finished computers. However, wages will not be fully paid at the time the work is done, so, like accounts payable, accrued wages will also build up.

3. The finished computers will be sold, but on credit. Therefore, sales will create receivables, not immediate cash inflows.

4. At some point before cash comes in, RTC must pay off its accounts payable and accrued wages. This outflow must be financed.

5. The cycle will be completed when RTC's receivables have been collected. At that time, the company can pay off the credit that was used to finance production, and it can then repeat the cycle.

Cash Conversion Cycle Model
Focuses on the length of time between when the company makes payments and when it receives cash inflows.

The **cash conversion cycle model,** which focuses on the length of time between when the company makes payments and when it receives cash inflows, formalizes the steps outlined above.[2] The following terms are used in the model:

Inventory Conversion Period
The average time required to convert materials into finished goods and then to sell those goods.

1. **Inventory conversion period,** which is the average time required to convert materials into finished goods and then to sell those goods. Note that the inventory conversion period is calculated by dividing inventory by sales per day. For example, if average inventories are $2 million and sales are $10 million, then the inventory conversion period is 73 days:

$$\text{Inventory conversion period} = \frac{\text{Inventory}}{\text{Sales per day}} \qquad (15\text{-}1)$$

$$= \frac{\$2,000,000}{\$10,000,000/365}$$

$$= 73 \text{ days.}$$

Thus, it takes an average of 73 days to convert materials into finished goods and then to sell those goods.[3]

Receivables Collection Period
The average length of time required to convert the firm's receivables into cash, that is, to collect cash following a sale.

2. **Receivables collection period,** which is the average length of time required to convert the firm's receivables into cash, that is, to collect cash following a sale. The receivables collection period is also called the *days*

---

[2] See Verlyn D. Richards and Eugene J. Laughlin, "A Cash Conversion Cycle Approach to Liquidity Analysis," *Financial Management*, Spring 1980, 32–38.

[3] Some analysts define the inventory conversion period as inventory divided by daily cost of goods sold. However, most published sources use the formula we show in Equation 15-1. In addition, some analysts use a 360-day year; however, unless stated otherwise, we will base all our calculations on a 365-day year.

sales outstanding (DSO), and it is calculated by dividing accounts receivable by the average credit sales per day. If receivables are $657,534 and sales are $10 million, the receivables collection period is

$$\frac{\text{Receivables}}{\text{collection period}} = \text{DSO} = \frac{\text{Receivables}}{\text{Sales}/365} \tag{15-2}$$

$$= \frac{\$657,534}{\$10,000,000/365} = 24 \text{ days.}$$

Thus, it takes 24 days after a sale to convert the receivables into cash.

Payables Deferral Period
The average length of time between the purchase of materials and labor and the payment of cash for them.

3. **Payables deferral period,** which is the average length of time between the purchase of materials and labor and the payment of cash for them. For example, if the firm on average has 30 days to pay for labor and materials, if its cost of goods sold are $8 million per year, and if its accounts payable average $657,534, then its payables deferral period can be calculated as follows:

$$\frac{\text{Payables}}{\text{deferral}} = \frac{\text{Payables}}{\text{Purchases per day}}$$
$$\text{period}$$

$$= \frac{\text{Payables}}{\text{Cost of goods sold}/365} \tag{15-3}$$

$$= \frac{\$657,534}{\$8,000,000/365}$$

$$= 30 \text{ days.}$$

The calculated figure is consistent with the stated 30-day payment period.[4]

Cash Conversion Cycle
The average length of time a dollar is tied up in current assets.

4. **Cash conversion cycle,** which nets out the three periods just defined and which therefore equals the length of time between the firm's actual cash expenditures to pay for productive resources (materials and labor) and its own cash receipts from the sale of products (that is, the length of time between paying for labor and materials and collecting on receivables). The cash conversion cycle thus equals the average length of time a dollar is tied up in current assets.

We can now use these definitions to analyze the cash conversion cycle. First, the concept is diagrammed in Figure 15-1. Each component is given a number, and the cash conversion cycle can be expressed by this equation:

$$\begin{array}{ccccccc} (1) & + & (2) & - & (3) & = & (4) \\ \text{Inventory} & & \text{Receivables} & & \text{Payables} & & \text{Cash} \\ \text{conversion} & + & \text{collection} & - & \text{deferral} & = & \text{conversion.} \\ \text{period} & & \text{period} & & \text{period} & & \text{cycle} \end{array} \tag{15-4}$$

To illustrate, suppose it takes Real Time an average of 73 days to convert raw materials to computers and then to sell them, and another 24 days to collect on receivables. However, 30 days normally elapse between receipt of raw

---

[4] Some sources define the payables deferral period as payables divided by daily sales.

FIGURE 15-1   The Cash Conversion Cycle Model

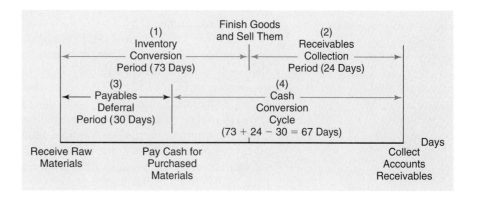

materials and payment for them. In this case, the cash conversion cycle would be 67 days:

Days in Cash Conversion Cycle = 73 days + 24 days − 30 days = 67 days.

To look at it another way,

Cash inflow delay − Payment delay = Net delay

(73 days + 24 days) −   30 days   = 67 days.

SHORTENING THE CASH CONVERSION CYCLE

Given these data, RTC knows when it starts producing a computer that it will have to finance the manufacturing costs for a 67-day period. The firm's goal should be to shorten its cash conversion cycle as much as possible without hurting operations. This would improve profits, because the longer the cash conversion cycle, the greater the need for external financing, and that financing has a cost.

The cash conversion cycle can be shortened (1) by reducing the inventory conversion period by processing and selling goods more quickly, (2) by reducing the receivables collection period by speeding up collections, or (3) by lengthening the payables deferral period by slowing down the firm's own payments. To the extent that these actions can be taken *without increasing costs or depressing sales*, they should be carried out.

BENEFITS

We can illustrate the benefits of shortening the cash conversion cycle by looking again at Real Time Computer Corporation. Suppose RTC must spend approximately $197,250 on materials and labor to produce one computer, and it takes about nine days to produce a computer. Thus, it must invest $197,250/9 = $21,917 for each day's production. This investment must be financed for 67 days — the length of the cash conversion cycle — so the company's working capital financing needs will be $67 \times \$21,917 = \$1,468,439$. If RTC could reduce the cash conversion cycle to 57 days, say, by deferring payment of its accounts payable an additional 10 days, or by speeding up either the production process or the collection of its receivables, it could reduce its working capital financing requirements by $219,170.

Recall that free cash flow (FCF) is equal to NOPAT minus net investments in operating capital. Therefore, if working capital decreases, FCF increases by that same amount. RTC's reduction in its cash conversion cycle would lead to an increase in FCF of $219,170. Notice also that reducing the cash conversion cycle reduces the ratio of net operating working capital to sales (NOWC/Sales). If sales stay at the same level, then the reduction in working capital is simply a one-time cash inflow. However, if sales are expected to grow, and if the NOWC/Sales ratio remains at its new level, then less working capital will be required to support the additional sales, leading to an increase in projected FCF for each future year.

The combination of the one-time cash inflow and the long-term improvement in working capital can add substantial value to companies. Two professors, Hyun-Han Shin and Luc Soenen, studied more then 2,900 companies during a recent 20-year period and found a strong relationship between a company's cash conversion cycle and its performance.[5] In particular, their results show that for the average company a 10-day improvement in the cash conversion cycle was associated with an increase in pre-tax operating profit from 12.76 to 13.02 percent. They also demonstrated that companies with a cash conversion cycle 10 days shorter than average also had an annual stock return that was 1.7 percentage points higher than that of an average company, even after adjusting for differences in risk. Given results like these, it's no wonder firms now place so much emphasis on working capital management!

SELF-TEST QUESTIONS

Define the following terms: inventory conversion period, receivables collection period, and payables deferral period. Give the equation for each term.

What is the cash conversion cycle? What is its equation?

What should the firm's goal be regarding the cash conversion cycle? Explain your answer.

What are some actions the firm can take to shorten its cash conversion cycle?

ALTERNATIVE CURRENT ASSET INVESTMENT POLICIES

The cash conversion cycle highlights the strengths and weaknesses of the company's working capital policy, which depend critically on current asset manage-

---

[5] See Hyun-Han Shin and Luc Soenen, "Efficiency of Working Capital Management and Corporate Profitability," *Financial Practice and Education*, Fall/Winter 1998, 37–45.

FIGURE 15-2

Alternative Current Asset Investment Policies
(Millions of Dollars)

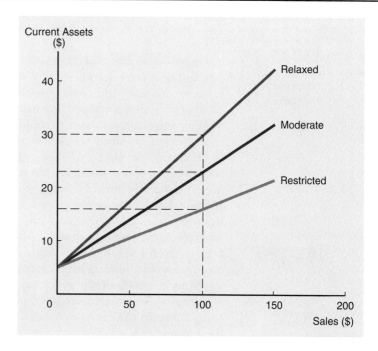

POLICY	CURRENT ASSETS TO SUPPORT SALES OF $100	TURNOVER OF CURRENT ASSETS
Relaxed	$30	3.3×
Moderate	23	4.3×
Restricted	16	6.3×

NOTE: The sales/current assets relationship is shown here as being linear, but the relationship is often curvilinear.

ment and the financing of current assets. In the remaining part of this chapter, we consider each of these items in more detail. We begin by describing alternative current asset investment policies, after which we consider a more detailed analysis of the various components of working capital. We conclude by discussing different strategies for financing current assets.

Figure 15-2 shows three alternative policies regarding the total amount of current assets carried. Essentially, these policies differ with regard to the amount of current assets carried to support any given level of sales, hence in the turnover of those assets. The line with the steepest slope represents a **relaxed current asset investment** (or "fat cat") **policy,** where relatively large amounts of cash, marketable securities, and inventories are carried, and where sales are stimulated by the use of a credit policy that provides liberal financing to customers and a corresponding high level of receivables.

Relaxed Current Asset Investment Policy
A policy under which relatively large amounts of cash, marketable securities, and inventories are carried and under which sales are stimulated by a liberal credit policy, resulting in a high level of receivables.

Conversely, with the **restricted current asset investment** (or "lean-and-mean") **policy,** the holdings of cash, securities, inventories, and receivables are minimized. Under the restricted policy, current assets are turned over more frequently, so each dollar of current assets is forced to "work harder." The **moderate current asset investment policy** is between the two extremes.

Under conditions of certainty — when sales, costs, lead times, payment periods, and so on, are known for sure — all firms would hold only minimal levels of current assets. Any larger amounts would increase the need for external funding without a corresponding increase in profits, while any smaller holdings would involve late payments to suppliers along with lost sales due to inventory shortages and an overly restrictive credit policy.

However, the picture changes when uncertainty is introduced. Here the firm requires some minimum amount of cash and inventories based on expected payments, expected sales, expected order lead times, and so on, plus additional holdings, or *safety stocks*, which enable it to deal with departures from the expected values. Similarly, accounts receivable levels are determined by credit terms, and the tougher the credit terms, the lower the receivables for any given level of sales. With a restricted current asset investment policy, the firm would hold minimal safety stocks of cash and inventories, and it would have a tight credit policy even though this meant running the risk of losing sales. A restricted, lean-and-mean current asset investment policy generally provides the highest expected return on this investment, but it entails the greatest risk, while the reverse is true under a relaxed policy. The moderate policy falls in between the two extremes in terms of expected risk and return.

Changing technology can lead to dramatic changes in the optimal current asset investment policy. For example, if new technology makes it possible for a manufacturer to speed up the production of a given product from 10 days to five days, then its work-in-progress inventory can be cut in half. Similarly, retailers such as Wal-Mart or Home Depot have installed systems under which bar codes on all merchandise are read at the cash register. The information on the sale is electronically transmitted to a computer that maintains a record of the inventory of each item, and the computer automatically transmits orders to suppliers' computers when stocks fall to prescribed levels. With such a system, inventories will be held at optimal levels; orders will reflect exactly what styles, colors, and sizes consumers are buying; and the firm's profits will be maximized.

MANAGING THE COMPONENTS OF WORKING CAPITAL

Working capital consists of four main components: cash, marketable securities, inventory, and accounts receivable. The first part of this chapter will focus on the issues involved with managing each of these components, while the remaining part will deal with their financing. As you will see, a common thread underlies all current asset management. For each type of asset, firms face a fundamental trade-off: Current assets (that is, working capital) are necessary to conduct business, and the greater the holdings of current assets, the smaller the danger of running out, hence the lower the firm's operating risk. However, holding working capital is costly — if inventories are too large, then the firm

FREE CASH FLOW, EVA, AND WORKING CAPITAL

Recall from Chapter 2 that a company's value depends on its free cash flow (FCF), defined as follows:

FCF = Net operating profit after taxes − Net investment in operating capital

= NOPAT − Net investment in operating capital

= [EBIT × (1 − T)] − [Capital this year − Capital last year].

If a company can reduce its inventories, its cash holdings, or its receivables, then its net investment in operating capital will decline. If these actions don't harm operating profit, then FCF will increase, which will lead to a higher stock price.

Economic Value Added (EVA) provides another useful way of thinking about working capital, particularly if a manager's compensation is linked to EVA. Recall from Chapter 2 that EVA is defined as follows:

EVA = NOPAT − (WACC × Total operating capital).

A reduction in working capital decreases total operating capital, which increases EVA. Many firms report that when division managers and other operating people begin to think in these terms, they often find ways to reduce working capital, especially if their compensation depends on their divisions' EVAs.

We can also think of working capital management in terms of ROE and the Du Pont equation:

$$ROE = \frac{Profit}{margin} \times \frac{Total\ assets}{turnover} \times \frac{Leverage}{factor}$$

$$= \frac{Net\ income}{Sales} \times \frac{Sales}{Total\ assets} \times \frac{Assets}{Equity}.$$

If working capital and hence total assets can be reduced without seriously affecting the profit margin, this will increase the total assets turnover and, consequently, ROE.

will have assets that earn a zero or even negative return if storage and spoilage costs are high. And, of course, firms must acquire capital to buy assets such as inventory, this capital has a cost, and this increases the downward drag from excessive inventories (or receivables or even cash). So, there is pressure to hold the amount of working capital to the minimum consistent with running the business without interruption.

SELF-TEST QUESTIONS

Identify and explain three alternative current asset investment policies.

What are the principal components of working capital?

What are the reasons for not wanting to hold too little working capital? For not wanting to hold too much?

What is the fundamental trade-off that managers face when managing working capital?

CASH MANAGEMENT

Approximately 1.5 percent of the average industrial firm's assets are held in the form of cash, which is defined as demand deposits plus currency. Cash is often called a "nonearning asset." It is needed to pay for labor and raw materials, to buy fixed assets, to pay taxes, to service debt, to pay dividends, and so on. However, cash itself (and also most commercial checking accounts) earns no interest. Thus, the goal of the cash manager is to minimize the amount of cash the firm must hold for use in conducting its normal business activities, yet, at the same time, to have sufficient cash (1) to take trade discounts, (2) to maintain its credit rating, and (3) to meet unexpected cash needs. We begin our analysis with a discussion of the reasons for holding cash.

REASONS FOR HOLDING CASH

Firms hold cash for two primary reasons:

Transactions Balance
A cash balance associated with payments and collections; the balance necessary for day-to-day operations.

Compensating Balance
A bank balance that a firm must maintain to compensate the bank for services rendered or for granting a loan.

Precautionary Balance
A cash balance held in reserve for random, unforeseen fluctuations in cash inflows and outflows.

Speculative Balance
A cash balance that is held to enable the firm to take advantage of any bargain purchases that might arise.

1. *Transactions.* Cash balances are necessary in business operations. Payments must be made in cash, and receipts are deposited in the cash account. Cash balances associated with routine payments and collections are known as **transactions balances.**

2. *Compensation to banks for providing loans and services.* A bank makes money by lending out funds that have been deposited with it, so the larger its deposits, the better the bank's profit position. If a bank is providing services to a customer, it may require the customer to leave a minimum balance on deposit to help offset the costs of providing the services. Also, banks may require borrowers to hold deposits at the bank. Both types of deposits are defined as **compensating balances.**[6]

Two other reasons for holding cash have been noted in the finance and economics literature: for *precaution* and for *speculation*. Cash inflows and outflows are unpredictable, with the degree of predictability varying among firms and industries. Therefore, firms need to hold some cash in reserve for random, unforeseen fluctuations in inflows and outflows. These "safety stocks" are called **precautionary balances,** and the less predictable the firm's cash flows, the larger such balances should be. However, if the firm has easy access to borrowed funds — that is, if it can borrow on short notice — its need for precautionary balances is reduced. Also, as we note later in this chapter, firms that would otherwise need large precautionary balances tend to hold highly liquid marketable securities rather than cash per se. Marketable securities serve many of the purposes of cash, but they provide greater interest income than bank deposits.

Some cash balances may be held to enable the firm to take advantage of bargain purchases that might arise; these funds are called **speculative balances.** However, firms today are more likely to rely on reserve borrowing capacity and/or marketable securities portfolios than on cash per se for speculative purposes.

The cash accounts of most firms can be thought of as consisting of transactions, compensating, precautionary, and speculative balances. However, we cannot calculate the amount needed for each purpose, sum them, and produce a total desired cash balance, because the same money often serves more than one purpose. For instance, precautionary and speculative balances can also be used

---

[6] In a 1979 survey, 84.7 percent of responding companies reported that they were required to maintain compensating balances to help pay for bank services. Only 13.3 percent reported paying direct fees for bank services. By 1996 those findings were reversed: only 28 percent paid for bank services with compensating balances, while 83 percent paid direct fees. So, while use of compensating balances to pay for services has declined, it is still a reason some companies hold so much cash.

to satisfy compensating balance requirements. Firms do, however, consider all four factors when establishing their target cash positions.

ADVANTAGES OF HOLDING ADEQUATE CASH AND NEAR-CASH ASSETS

In addition to the four motives just discussed, sound working capital management requires that an ample supply of cash and near-cash assets be maintained for several specific reasons:

Trade Discount
A price reduction that suppliers offer customers for early payment of bills.

1. It is essential that the firm have sufficient cash and near-cash assets to take **trade discounts.** Suppliers frequently offer customers discounts for early payment of bills. As we will see later in this chapter, the cost of not taking discounts is very high, so firms should have enough cash to permit payment of bills in time to take discounts.
2. Adequate holdings of cash and near-cash assets can help the firm maintain its credit rating by keeping its current and acid test ratios in line with those of other firms in its industry. A strong credit rating enables the firm both to purchase goods from suppliers on favorable terms and to maintain an ample line of low-cost credit with its bank.
3. Cash and near-cash assets are useful for taking advantage of favorable business opportunities, such as special offers from suppliers or the chance to acquire another firm.
4. The firm should have sufficient cash and near-cash assets to meet such emergencies as strikes, fires, or competitors' marketing campaigns, and to weather seasonal and cyclical downturns.

SELF-TEST QUESTIONS

Why is cash management important?

What are the two primary motives for holding cash?

What are the two secondary motives for holding cash as noted in the finance and economics literature?

THE CASH BUDGET[7]

The firm estimates its needs for cash as a part of its general budgeting, or forecasting, process. First, it forecasts sales, its fixed asset and inventory requirements, and the times when payments must be made. This information is combined with projections about when accounts receivable will be collected, tax

---

[7] We used an *Excel* spreadsheet to generate the cash budget shown in Table 15-1. It would be worthwhile to go through the model, 15MODEL.xls, which is on the CD-ROM that accompanies this text. This will give you a good example of how spreadsheets can be applied to solve practical problems.

Cash Budget
A table showing cash flows (receipts, disbursements, and cash balances) for a firm over a specified period.

payment dates, dividend and interest payment dates, and so on. All of this information is summarized in the **cash budget,** which shows the firm's projected cash inflows and outflows over some specified period. Generally, firms use a monthly cash budget forecasted over the next year, plus a more detailed daily or weekly cash budget for the coming month. The monthly cash budgets are used for planning purposes, and the daily or weekly budgets for actual cash control.

The cash budget provides more detailed information concerning a firm's future cash flows than do the forecasted financial statements. In Chapter 4, we developed Allied Food Products' 2002 forecasted financial statements. Allied's projected 2002 sales were $3,300 million, resulting in a net cash flow from operations of $162 million. When all expenditures and financing flows are considered, Allied's cash account is projected to increase by $1 million in 2002. Does this mean that Allied will not have to worry about cash shortages during 2002? To answer this question, we must construct Allied's cash budget for 2002.

To simplify the example, we will only consider Allied's cash budget for the last half of 2002. Further, we will not list every cash flow but rather focus on the operating cash flows. Allied's sales peak is in September, shortly after the majority of its raw food inputs have been harvested. All sales are made on terms of 2/10, net 40, meaning that a 2 percent discount is allowed if payment is made within 10 days, and, if the discount is not taken, the full amount is due in 40 days. However, like most companies, Allied finds that some of its customers delay payment up to 90 days. Experience has shown that payment on 20 percent of Allied's dollar sales is made during the month in which the sale is made — these are the discount sales. On 70 percent of sales, payment is made during the month immediately following the month of sale, and on 10 percent of sales payment is made in the second month following the month of sale.

The costs to Allied of foodstuffs, spices, preservatives, and packaging materials average 70 percent of the sales prices of the finished products. These purchases are generally made one month before the firm expects to sell the finished products, but Allied's purchase terms with its suppliers allow it to delay payments for 30 days. Accordingly, if July sales are forecasted at $300 million, then purchases during June will amount to $210 million, and this amount will actually be paid in July.

Such other cash expenditures as wages and lease payments are also built into the cash budget, and Allied must make estimated tax payments of $30 million on September 15 and $20 million on December 15. Also, a $100 million payment for a new plant must be made in October. Assuming that Allied's **target cash balance** is $10 million, and that it projects $15 million to be on hand on July 1, 2002, what will its monthly cash surpluses or shortfalls be for the period from July to December?

Target Cash Balance
The desired cash balance that a firm plans to maintain in order to conduct business.

The monthly cash flows are shown in Table 15-1. Section I of the table provides a worksheet for calculating both collections on sales and payments on purchases. Line 1 gives the sales forecast for the period from May through December. (May and June sales are necessary to determine collections for July and August.) Next, Lines 2 through 5 show cash collections. Line 2 shows that 20 percent of the sales during any given month are collected during that month. Customers who pay in the first month, however, take the discount, so the cash collected in the month of sale is reduced by 2 percent; for example, collections during July for the $300 million of sales in that month will be 20 percent times sales times 1.0 minus the 2 percent discount = (0.20)($300)(0.98) ≈ $59 million.

TABLE 15-1

Allied Food Products: Cash Budget (Millions of Dollars)

	MAY	JUN	JUL	AUG	SEP	OCT	NOV	DEC
I. COLLECTIONS AND PURCHASES WORKSHEET								
(1) Sales (gross)[a]	$200	$250	$300	$400	$500	$350	$250	$200
Collections								
(2) During month of sale: (0.2)(0.98)(month's sales)			59	78	98	69	49	39
(3) During first month after sale: 0.7(previous month's sales)			175	210	280	350	245	175
(4) During second month after sale: 0.1(sales 2 months ago)			20	25	30	40	50	35
(5) Total collections (2 + 3 + 4)			$254	$313	$408	$459	$344	$249
Purchases								
(6) 0.7(next month's sales)		$210	$280	$350	$245	$175	$140	
(7) Payments (prior month's purchases)			$210	$280	$350	$245	$175	$140
II. CASH GAIN OR LOSS FOR MONTH								
(8) Collections (from Section I)			$254	$313	$408	$459	$344	$249
(9) Payments for purchases (from Section I)			$210	$280	$350	$245	$175	$140
(10) Wages and salaries			30	40	50	40	30	30
(11) Lease payments			15	15	15	15	15	15
(12) Other expenses			10	15	20	15	10	10
(13) Taxes					30			20
(14) Payment for plant construction						100		
(15) Total payments			$265	$350	$465	$415	$230	$215
(16) Net cash gain (loss) during month (Line 8 − Line 15)			($ 11)	($ 37)	($ 57)	$ 44	$114	$ 34
III. LOAN REQUIREMENT OR CASH SURPLUS								
(17) Cash at start of month if no borrowing is done[b]			$ 15	$ 4	($ 33)	($ 90)	($ 46)	$ 68
(18) Cumulative cash: cash at start if no borrowing + gain or − loss (Line 16 + Line 17)			$ 4	($ 33)	($ 90)	($ 46)	$ 68	$102
(19) Target cash balance			10	10	10	10	10	10
(20) Cumulative surplus cash or loans outstanding to maintain $10 target cash balance (Line 18 − Line 19)[c]			($ 6)	($ 43)	($100)	($ 56)	$ 58	$ 92

[a] Although the budget period is July through December, sales and purchases data for May and June are needed to determine collections and payments during July and August.

[b] The amount shown on Line 17 for July, the $15 balance (in millions), is on hand initially. The values shown for each of the following months on Line 17 are equal to the cumulative cash as shown on Line 18 for the preceding month; for example, the $4 shown on Line 17 for August is taken from Line 18 in the July column.

[c] When the target cash balance of $10 (Line 19) is deducted from the cumulative cash balance (Line 18), a resulting negative figure on Line 20 (shown in parentheses) represents a required loan, whereas a positive figure represents surplus cash. Loans are required from July through October, and surpluses are expected during November and December. Note also that firms can borrow or pay off loans on a daily basis, so the $6 borrowed during July would be done on a daily basis, as needed, and during October the $100 loan that existed at the beginning of the month would be reduced daily to the $56 ending balance, which, in turn, would be completely paid off during November.

Line 3 shows the collections on the previous month's sales, or 70 percent of sales in the preceding month; for example, in July, 70 percent of the $250 million June sales, or $175 million, will be collected. Line 4 gives collections from sales two months earlier, or 10 percent of sales in that month; for example, the July collections for May sales are $(0.10)(\$200) = \$20$ million. The collections during each month are summed and shown on Line 5; thus, the July collections represent 20 percent of July sales (minus the discount) plus 70 percent of June sales plus 10 percent of May sales, or $254 million in total.

Next, payments for purchases of raw materials are shown. July sales are forecasted at $300 million, so Allied will purchase $210 million of materials in June (Line 6) and pay for these purchases in July (Line 7). Similarly, Allied will purchase $280 million of materials in July to meet August's forecasted sales of $400 million.

With Section I completed, Section II can be constructed. Cash from collections is shown on Line 8. Lines 9 through 14 list payments made during each month, and these payments are summed on Line 15. The difference between cash receipts and cash payments (Line 8 minus Line 15) is the net cash gain or loss during the month. For July there is a net cash loss of $11 million, as shown on Line 16.

In Section III, we first determine the cash balance Allied would have at the start of each month, assuming no borrowing is done. This is shown on Line 17. Allied will have $15 million on hand on July 1. The beginning cash balance (Line 17) is then added to the net cash gain or loss during the month (Line 16) to obtain the cumulative cash that would be on hand if no financing were done (Line 18). At the end of July, Allied forecasts a cumulative cash balance of $4 million in the absence of borrowing.

The target cash balance, $10 million, is then subtracted from the cumulative cash balance to determine the firm's borrowing requirements, shown in parentheses, or its surplus cash. Because Allied expects to have cumulative cash, as shown on Line 18, of only $4 million in July, it will have to borrow $6 million to bring the cash account up to the target balance of $10 million. Assuming that this amount is indeed borrowed, loans outstanding will total $6 million at the end of July. (Allied did not have any loans outstanding on July 1.) The cash surplus or required loan balance is given on Line 20; a positive value indicates a cash surplus, whereas a negative value indicates a loan requirement. Note that the surplus cash or loan requirement shown on Line 20 is a *cumulative amount*. Allied must borrow $6 million in July. Then, it has an additional cash shortfall during August of $37 million as reported on Line 16, so its total loan requirement at the end of August is $6 + $37 = $43 million, as reported on Line 20. Allied's arrangement with the bank permits it to increase its outstanding loans on a daily basis, up to a prearranged maximum, just as you could increase the amount you owe on a credit card. Allied will use any surplus funds it generates to pay off its loans, and because the loan can be paid down at any time, on a daily basis, the firm will never have both a cash surplus and an outstanding loan balance.

This same procedure is used in the following months. Sales will peak in September, accompanied by increased payments for purchases, wages, and other items. Receipts from sales will also go up, but the firm will still be left with a $57 million net cash outflow during the month. The total loan requirement at the end of September will hit a peak of $100 million, the cumulative cash plus the target cash balance. The $100 million can also be found as the $43 million needed at the end of August plus the $57 million cash deficit for September.

Sales, purchases, and payments for past purchases will fall sharply in October, but collections will be the highest of any month because they will reflect the high September sales. As a result, Allied will enjoy a healthy $44 million net cash gain during October. This net gain can be used to pay off borrowings, so loans outstanding will decline by $44 million, to $56 million.

Allied will have an even larger cash surplus in November, which will permit it to pay off all of its loans. In fact, the company is expected to have $58 million in surplus cash by the month's end, and another cash surplus in December will swell the excess cash to $92 million. With such a large amount of unneeded funds, Allied's treasurer will certainly want to invest in interest-bearing securities or to put the funds to use in some other way.

Here are some additional points about cash budgets:

1. For simplicity, our illustrative budget for Allied omitted many important cash flows that are anticipated for 2002, such as dividends and proceeds from stock and bond sales. Some of these are projected to occur in the first half of the year, but those that are projected for the July–December period could easily be added to the table. The final cash budget should contain all projected cash inflows and outflows, and it should be consistent with the forecasted financial statements.

2. Our cash budget does not reflect interest on loans or income from investing surplus cash. This refinement could easily be added.

3. If cash inflows and outflows are not uniform during the month, we could seriously understate the firm's peak financing requirements. The data in Table 15-1 show the situation expected on the last day of each month, but on any given day during the month, it could be quite different. For example, if all payments had to be made on the fifth of each month, but collections came in uniformly throughout the month, the firm would need to borrow much larger amounts than those shown in Table 15-1. In this case, we would prepare a cash budget that determined requirements on a daily basis.

4. Since depreciation is a noncash charge, it does not appear on the cash budget other than through its effect on taxable income, hence on taxes paid.

5. Since the cash budget represents a forecast, all the values in the table are *expected* values. If actual sales, purchases, and so on, are different from the forecasted levels, then the projected cash deficits and surpluses will also be incorrect. Thus, Allied might end up needing to borrow larger amounts than are indicated on Line 20, so it should arrange a line of credit in excess of that amount. For example, if Allied's monthly sales turn out to be only 80 percent of their forecasted levels, its maximum cumulative borrowing requirement will turn out to be $126 million rather than $100 million, a 26 percent increase from the expected figure.

6. Spreadsheet programs are particularly well suited for constructing and analyzing cash budgets, especially with respect to the sensitivity of cash flows to changes in sales levels, collection periods, and the like. We

INDUSTRY PRACTICE

THE GREAT DEBATE: HOW MUCH CASH IS ENOUGH?

"I hate cash on hand," says Fred Salerno, Bell Atlantic's CFO. According to a recent survey, Salerno has backed up his talk with actions. When rated on the number of days of operating expenses held in cash (DOEHIC), Bell Atlantic leads its industry with a DOEHIC of 6 days versus an industry average of 27. Put another way, Bell Atlantic has cash holdings equal to only 0.90 percent of sales as compared with an industry median cash/sales ratio of 5.20 percent.

A great relationship with its banks is a key to keeping low cash levels. Jim Hopwood, treasurer of Wickes, says, "We have a credit revolver if we ever need it." The same is true at Haverty Furniture, where CFO Dennis Fink says, "You don't have to worry about predicting short-term fluctuations in cash flow," if you have solid bank commitments.

Treasurer Wayne Smith of Avery Dennison says that their low cash holdings have reduced their net operating working capital to such an extent that their return on invested capital (ROIC)

is 3 percentage points higher than it would be if their cash holdings were at the industry average. He goes on to say that this adds a lot of economic value to their company.

Despite these and other comments about the advantages of low cash holdings, many companies still hold extremely large amounts of cash and marketable securities, including Procter & Gamble ($2.6 billion, 32 days DOEHIC, 7.1 percent cash/sales) and Ford Motor Company ($24 billion, 76 DOEHIC). When asked about the appropriate level of cash holdings, Ford CFO Henry Wallace refused to be pinned down, saying, "There is no answer for a company this size." However, it is interesting to note that Ford recently completed a huge stock repurchase, reducing its cash by about $10 billion.

SOURCE: S. L. Mintz, "Lean Green Machine," *CFO*, July 2000, 76–94.

could change any assumption, say, the projected monthly sales or the lag before customers pay, and the cash budget would automatically and instantly be recalculated. This would show us exactly how the firm's borrowing requirements would change if conditions changed. Also, with a spreadsheet model, it is easy to add features like interest paid on loans, interest earned on marketable securities, and so on. See 15MODEL.xls for the spreadsheet model we used to generate the cash budget for this chapter.

7. Finally, we should note that the target cash balance probably will be adjusted over time, rising and falling with seasonal patterns and with long-term changes in the scale of the firm's operations. Thus, Allied will probably plan to maintain larger cash balances during August and September than at other times, and as the company grows, so will its required cash balance. Also, the firm might even set the target cash balance at zero — this could be done if it carried a portfolio of marketable securities that could be sold to replenish the cash account, or if it had an arrangement with its bank that permitted it to borrow any funds needed on a daily basis. In that event, the cash budget would simply stop with Line 18, and the amounts on that line would represent projected loans outstanding or surplus cash. Note, though, that most firms would find it difficult to operate with a zero-balance bank account, just as you would, and the costs of such an operation would in most instances offset the costs associated with maintaining a positive cash balance. Therefore, most firms do set a positive target cash balance.

What is the purpose of a cash budget?

What are the three major sections of a cash budget?

Suppose a firm's cash flows do not occur uniformly throughout the month. What effect would this have on the accuracy of the forecasted borrowing requirements?

How could uncertainty be handled in a cash budget?

Does depreciation appear in a cash budget? Explain.

MARKETABLE SECURITIES

Marketable Securities
Securities that can be sold on short notice.

Realistically, the management of cash and marketable securities cannot be separated — management of one implies management of the other. In the first part of the chapter, we focused on cash management. Now, we turn to **marketable securities.**

Marketable securities typically provide much lower yields than operating assets. For example, recently DaimlerChrysler held approximately a $7 billion portfolio of short-term marketable securities that provided a much lower yield than its operating assets. Why would a company such as DaimlerChrysler have such large holdings of low-yielding assets?

In many cases, companies hold marketable securities for the same reasons they hold cash. Although these securities are not the same as cash, in most cases they can be converted to cash on very short notice (often just a few minutes) with a single telephone call. Moreover, while cash and most commercial checking accounts yield nothing, marketable securities provide at least a modest return. For this reason, many firms hold at least some marketable securities in lieu of larger cash balances, liquidating part of the portfolio to increase the cash account when cash outflows exceed inflows. In such situations, the marketable securities could be used as a substitute for transactions balances, for precautionary balances, for speculative balances, or for all three. In most cases, the securities are held primarily for precautionary purposes — most firms prefer to rely on bank credit to make temporary transactions or to meet speculative needs, but they may still hold some liquid assets to guard against a possible shortage of bank credit.

A few years ago before its merger with Daimler-Benz, Chrysler had essentially no cash — it was incurring huge losses, and those losses had drained its cash account. Then a new management team took over, improved operations, and began generating positive cash flows. By 2000, DaimlerChrysler's cash (and marketable securities) was up to about $7 billion. Management indicated, in various statements, that the cash hoard was necessary to enable the company to weather the next downturn in auto sales.

Although setting the target cash balance is, to a large extent, judgmental, analytical rules can be applied to help formulate better judgments. For example, years ago William Baumol recognized that the trade-off between cash and marketable securities is similar to the one firms face when setting the optimal level of inventory.[8] Baumol applied the EOQ inventory model to determine the optimal level of cash balances.[9] He suggested that cash holdings should be higher if costs are high and the time to liquidate marketable securities is long, but that those cash holdings should be lower if interest rates are high. His logic was that if it is expensive and time consuming to convert securities to cash, and if securities do not earn much because interest rates are low, then it does not pay to hold securities as opposed to cash. It does pay to hold securities if interest rates are high and the securities can be converted to cash quickly and cheaply.

To summarize, there are both benefits and costs associated with holding cash and marketable securities. The benefits are twofold: (1) the firm reduces transactions costs because it won't have to issue securities or borrow as frequently to raise cash; and (2) it will have ready cash to take advantage of bargain purchases or growth opportunities. The primary disadvantage is that the after-tax return on cash and short-term securities is very low. Thus, firms face a trade-off between benefits and costs.

Recent research supports this trade-off hypothesis as an explanation for firms' cash holdings.[10] Firms with high growth opportunities suffer the most if they don't have ready cash to quickly take advantage of an opportunity, and the data show that these firms do hold relatively high levels of cash and marketable securities. Firms with volatile cash flows are the ones most likely to run low on cash, so they are the ones that hold the highest levels of cash. In contrast, cash holdings are less important to large firms with high credit ratings, because they have quick and inexpensive access to capital markets. As expected, such firms hold relatively low levels of cash. Of course, there will always be outliers such as Ford, which is large, strong, and cash-rich, but volatile firms with good growth opportunities are still the ones with the highest cash balances, on average.

SELF-TEST QUESTIONS

Why might a company hold low-yielding marketable securities when it could earn a much higher return on operating assets?

Why would a low interest rate environment lead to larger cash balances?

How might improvements in telecommunications technology affect the level of corporations' cash balances?

---

[8] William J. Baumol, "The Transactions Demand for Cash: An Inventory Theoretic Approach," *Quarterly Journal of Economics*, November 1952, 545–556.

[9] A more complete description of the Economic Ordering Quantity (EOQ) model can be found in Eugene F. Brigham and Phillip R. Daves, *Intermediate Financial Management*, 7th ed. (Fort Worth, TX: Harcourt College Publishers, 2002), Chapter 22.

[10] See Tim Opler, Lee Pinkowitz, René Stulz, and Rohan Williamson, "The Determinants and Implications of Corporate Cash Holdings," *Journal of Financial Economics*, Vol. 52, 1999, 3–46.

INVENTORY

Inventories, which may be classified as (1) *supplies*, (2) *raw materials*, (3) *work-in-process*, and (4) *finished goods*, are an essential part of virtually all business operations. As is the case with accounts receivable, inventory levels depend heavily upon sales. However, whereas receivables build up *after* sales have been made, inventory must be acquired *ahead* of sales. This is a critical difference, and the necessity of forecasting sales before establishing target inventory levels makes inventory management a difficult task. Also, since errors in the establishment of inventory levels quickly lead either to lost sales or to excessive carrying costs, inventory management is as important as it is difficult.

Inventory management techniques are covered in depth in production management courses. Still, since financial managers have a responsibility both for raising the capital needed to carry inventory and for the firm's overall profitability, we need to cover the financial aspects of inventory management here.

Proper inventory management requires close coordination among the sales, purchasing, production, and finance departments. The sales/marketing department is generally the first to spot changes in demand. These changes must be worked into the company's purchasing and manufacturing schedules, and the financial manager must arrange any financing needed to support the inventory buildup. Lack of coordination among departments, poor sales forecasts, or both, can lead to disaster.

SELF-TEST QUESTIONS

Why is good inventory management essential to a firm's success?

What departments should be involved in inventory decisions?

INVENTORY COSTS

The twin goals of inventory management are (1) to ensure that the inventories needed to sustain operations are available, but (2) to hold the costs of ordering and carrying inventories to the lowest possible level. Table 15-2 gives a listing of the typical costs associated with inventory, divided into three categories: carrying costs, ordering and receiving costs, and the costs that are incurred if the firm runs short of inventory.

Inventory is costly to store; therefore, there is always pressure to reduce inventory as part of firms' overall cost-containment strategies. An article in *Fortune* highlights the fact that an increasing number of corporations are taking drastic steps to control inventory costs.[11] For example, Trane Corporation, which makes air conditioners, recently adopted just-in-time inventory procedures.

---

[11] Shawn Tully, "Raiding a Company's Hidden Cash," *Fortune*, August 22, 1994, 82–87.

TABLE 15-2

Costs Associated with Inventory

	APPROXIMATE ANNUAL COST AS A PERCENTAGE OF INVENTORY VALUE
I. CARRYING COSTS	
Cost of capital tied up	12.0%
Storage and handling costs	0.5
Insurance	0.5
Property taxes	1.0
Depreciation and obsolescence	12.0
Total	26.0%
II. ORDERING, SHIPPING, AND RECEIVING COSTS	
Cost of placing orders, including production and set-up costs	Varies
Shipping and handling costs	2.5%
III. COSTS OF RUNNING SHORT	
Loss of sales	Varies
Loss of customer goodwill	Varies
Disruption of production schedules	Varies

NOTE: These costs vary from firm to firm, from item to item, and also over time. The figures shown are U.S. Department of Commerce estimates for an average manufacturing firm. Where costs vary so widely that no meaningful numbers can be assigned, the term "Varies" is reported.

In the past, Trane produced parts on a steady basis, stored them as inventory, and had them ready whenever the company received an order for a batch of air conditioners. However, the company reached the point where its inventory covered an area equal to three football fields, and it still sometimes took as long as 15 days to fill an order. To make matters worse, occasionally some of the necessary components simply could not be located, while in other instances the components were located but found to have been damaged from long storage.

Then Trane adopted a new inventory policy — it began producing components only after an order is received, and then sending the parts directly from the machines that make them to the final assembly line. The net effect: Inventories fell nearly 40 percent even as sales increased by 30 percent.

However, as Table 15-2 indicates, there are costs associated with holding too little inventory, and these costs can be severe. Generally, if a business carries small inventories, it must reorder frequently. This increases ordering costs. Even more important, firms can miss out on profitable sales, and also suffer a loss of goodwill that can lead to lower future sales. So, it is important to have enough inventory on hand to meet customer demands.

Suppose IBM has developed a new line of notebook computers. How much inventory should it produce and have on hand when the marketing campaign is launched? If it fails to produce enough inventory, retailers and customers are likely to be frustrated because they cannot immediately purchase the highly advertised product. Rather than wait, many customers will purchase a notebook computer elsewhere. On the other hand, if IBM has too much inventory, it will

INDUSTRY PRACTICE

SUPPLY CHAIN MANAGEMENT

Herman Miller Inc. manufactures a wide variety of office furniture, and a typical order from a single customer might require work at five different plants. Each plant uses components from different suppliers, and each plant works on orders for many customers. Imagine all the coordination that is required. The sales force generates the order, the purchasing department orders components from suppliers, and the suppliers must order materials from their own suppliers. Then, the suppliers ship the components to Herman Miller, the factory builds the product, the different products are gathered together to complete the order, and then the order is shipped to the customer. If one part of that process malfunctions, then the order will be delayed, inventory will pile up, extra costs to expedite the order will be incurred, and the customer's goodwill will be damaged, which will hurt future sales growth.

To prevent such consequences, many companies are turning to a process called supply chain management (SCM). The key element in SCM is sharing information all the way from the point-of-sale at the product's retailer to the suppliers, and even back to the suppliers' suppliers. SCM requires special software, but even more important, it requires cooperation between the different companies and departments in the supply chain. This new culture of open communication is often difficult for many companies — they are reluctant to divulge operating information. For example, EMC Corp., a manufacturer of data storage systems, has become deeply involved in the design processes and financial controls of its key suppliers. Many of EMC's suppliers were initially wary of these new relationships. However, SCM has been a win-win situation, with increases in value for EMC and its suppliers.

The same is true at many other companies. After implementing SCM, Herman Miller was able to reduce its days of inventory on hand by a week, and to cut two weeks off of delivery times to customers. Herman Miller was also able to operate its plants at a 20 percent higher volume without additional capital expenditures. Heineken USA can now get beer from its breweries to its customers' shelves in less than six weeks, compared with 10 to 12 weeks before implementing SCM. As these and other companies have found, SCM increases free cash flows, and that leads to higher stock prices.

SOURCES: Elaine L. Appleton, "Supply Chain Brain," *CFO,* July 1997, 51–54; and Kris Frieswick, "Up Close and Virtual," *CFO,* April 1998, 87–91.

incur unnecessarily high carrying costs. In addition, computers become obsolete quickly, so if inventory levels are high but sales are mediocre, the company may have to discount the notebooks to sell them. Apart from reducing the profit margin on this year's line of computers, these discounts may push down computer prices in general, thereby reducing profit margins on the company's other products as well.

> ### SELF-TEST QUESTIONS
>
> What are the three categories of inventory costs?
>
> What are some components of inventory carrying costs?
>
> What are some components of inventory ordering costs?

RECEIVABLES MANAGEMENT

Firms would, in general, rather sell for cash than on credit, but competitive pressures force most firms to offer credit. Thus, goods are shipped, inventories

Account Receivable
A balance due from a customer.

are reduced, and an **account receivable** is created.[12] Eventually, the customer will pay the account, at which time (1) the firm will receive cash and (2) its receivables will decline. Carrying receivables has both direct and indirect costs, but it also has an important benefit — increased sales.

Receivables management begins with the decision of whether or not to grant credit. In this section, we discuss the manner in which receivables build up, and we also discuss several alternative ways to monitor receivables. A monitoring system is important, because without it receivables will build up to excessive levels, cash flows will decline, and bad debts will offset the profits on sales. Corrective action is often needed, and the only way to know whether the situation is getting out of hand is with a good receivables control system.

THE ACCUMULATION OF RECEIVABLES

The total amount of accounts receivable outstanding at any given time is determined by two factors: (1) the volume of credit sales and (2) the average length of time between sales and collections. For example, suppose Boston Lumber Company (BLC), a wholesale distributor of lumber products, opens a warehouse on January 1 and, starting the first day, makes sales of $1,000 each day. For simplicity, we assume that all sales are on credit, and customers are given 10 days to pay. At the end of the first day, accounts receivable will be $1,000; they will rise to $2,000 by the end of the second day; and by January 10, they will have risen to 10($1,000) = $10,000. On January 11, another $1,000 will be added to receivables, but payments for sales made on January 1 will reduce receivables by $1,000, so total accounts receivable will remain constant at $10,000. In general, once the firm's operations have stabilized, this situation will exist:

$$\frac{\text{Accounts}}{\text{receivable}} = \frac{\text{Credit sales}}{\text{per day}} \times \frac{\text{Length of}}{\text{collection period}} \qquad (15\text{-}5)$$

$$= \quad \$1,000 \quad \times \quad 10 \text{ days} \quad = \$10,000.$$

If either credit sales or the collection period changes, such changes will be reflected in accounts receivable.

Notice that the $10,000 investment in receivables must be financed. To illustrate, suppose that when the warehouse opened on January 1, BLC's shareholders had put up $800 as common stock and used this money to buy the goods sold the first day. The $800 of inventory will be sold for $1,000, so BLC's gross profit on the $800 investment is $200, or 25 percent. In this situation, the beginning balance sheet would be as follows:[13]

---

[12] Whenever goods are sold on credit, two accounts are created — an asset item entitled *accounts receivable* appears on the books of the selling firm, and a liability item called *accounts payable* appears on the books of the purchaser. At this point, we are analyzing the transaction from the viewpoint of the seller, so we are concentrating on the variables under its control, in this case, the receivables. We will examine the transaction from the viewpoint of the purchaser later in this chapter, where we discuss accounts payable as a source of funds and consider their cost.

[13] Note that the firm would need other assets such as cash, fixed assets, and a permanent stock of inventory. Also, overhead costs and taxes would have to be deducted, so retained earnings would be less than the figures shown here. We abstract from these details here so that we may focus on receivables.

Inventories	$800	Common stock	$800
Total assets	$800	Total liabilities and equity	$800

At the end of the day, the balance sheet would look like this:

Accounts receivable	$1,000	Common stock	$ 800
Inventories	0	Retained earnings	200
Total assets	$1,000	Total liabilities and equity	$1,000

To remain in business, BLC must replenish inventories. To do so requires that $800 of goods be purchased, and this requires $800 in cash. Assuming that BLC borrows the $800 from the bank, the balance sheet at the start of the second day will be as follows:

Accounts receivable	$1,000	Notes payable to bank	$ 800
Inventories	800	Common stock	800
		Retained earnings	200
Total assets	$1,800	Total liabilities and equity	$1,800

At the end of the second day, the inventories will have been converted to receivables, and the firm will have to borrow another $800 to restock for the third day.

This process will continue, provided the bank is willing to lend the necessary funds, until the beginning of the 11th day, when the balance sheet reads as follows:

Accounts receivable	$10,000	Notes payable to bank	$ 8,000
Inventories	800	Common stock	800
		Retained earnings	2,000
Total assets	$10,800	Total liabilities and equity	$10,800

From this point on, $1,000 of receivables will be collected every day, and $800 of these funds can be used to purchase new inventories.

This example makes it clear (1) that accounts receivable depend jointly on the level of credit sales and the collection period, (2) that any increase in receivables must be financed in some manner, but (3) that the entire amount of receivables does not have to be financed because the profit portion ($200 of each $1,000 of sales) does not represent a cash outflow. In our example, we assumed bank financing, but, as we discuss later in this chapter, there are many alternative ways to finance current assets.

MONITORING THE RECEIVABLES POSITION

Investors — both stockholders and bank loan officers — should pay close attention to accounts receivable management, for, as we shall see, one can be misled by reported financial statements and later suffer serious losses on an investment.

When a credit sale is made, the following events occur: (1) Inventories are reduced by the cost of goods sold, (2) accounts receivable are increased by the sales price, and (3) the difference is profit, which is added to retained earnings. If the sale is for cash, then the cash from the sale has actually been received by the firm, but if the sale is on credit, the firm will not receive the cash from the sale unless and until the account is collected. Firms have been known to encourage "sales" to very weak customers in order to report high profits. This could boost the firm's stock price, at least until credit losses begin to lower earnings, at which time the stock price will fall. Analyses along the lines suggested in the following sections will detect any such questionable practice, as well as any unconscious deterioration in the quality of accounts receivable. Such early detection could help both investors and bankers avoid losses.[14]

Days Sales Outstanding (DSO)

Suppose Super Sets Inc., a television manufacturer, sells 200,000 television sets a year at a price of $198 each. Further, assume that all sales are on credit with the following terms: if payment is made within 10 days, customers will receive a 2 percent discount; otherwise the full amount is due within 30 days. Finally, assume that 70 percent of the customers take discounts and pay on Day 10, while the other 30 percent pay on Day 30.

Days Sales Outstanding (DSO)
The average length of time required to collect credit sales.

Super Sets's **days sales outstanding (DSO),** sometimes called the *average collection period (ACP)*, is 16 days:

$$DSO = ACP = 0.7(10 \text{ days}) + 0.3(30 \text{ days}) = 16 \text{ days}.$$

Super Sets's *average daily sales (ADS)* is $108,493:

$$ADS = \frac{\text{Annual sales}}{365} = \frac{(\text{Units sold})(\text{Sales price})}{365} \qquad (15\text{-}6)$$

$$= \frac{200,000(\$198)}{365} = \frac{\$39,600,000}{365} = \$108,493.$$

Super Sets's accounts receivable, assuming a constant, uniform rate of sales throughout the year, will at any point in time be $1,735,888:

$$\text{Receivables} = (\text{ADS})(\text{DSO}) \qquad (15\text{-}7)$$

$$= (\$108,493)(16) = \$1,735,888.$$

Note also that its DSO, or average collection period, is a measure of the average length of time it takes Super Sets's customers to pay off their credit purchases, and the DSO is often compared with an industry average DSO. For example, if all television manufacturers sell on the same credit terms, and if the industry average DSO is 25 days versus Super Sets's 16 days, then Super Sets either has a higher percentage of discount customers or else its credit department is exceptionally good at ensuring prompt payment.

---

[14] Accountants are increasingly interested in these matters. Investors have sued several of the major accounting firms for substantial damages when (1) profits were overstated and (2) it could be shown that the auditors should have conducted an analysis along the lines described here and then reported the results to stockholders in their audit opinion.

Finally, note that if you know both the annual sales and the receivables balance, you can calculate DSO as follows:

$$\text{DSO} = \frac{\text{Receivables}}{\text{Sales per day}} = \frac{\$1,735,888}{\$108,493} = 16 \text{ days}.$$

The DSO can also be compared with the firm's own credit terms. For example, suppose Super Sets's DSO had been averaging 35 days. With a 35-day DSO, some customers would obviously be taking more than 30 days to pay their bills. In fact, if many customers were paying within 10 days to take advantage of the discount, the others must, on average, be taking much longer than 35 days. One way to check this possibility is to use an aging schedule as described in the next section.

Aging Schedules

An **aging schedule** breaks down a firm's receivables by age of account. Table 15-3 contains the December 31, 2001, aging schedules of two television manufacturers, Super Sets and Wonder Vision. Both firms offer the same credit terms, and both show the same total receivables. However, Super Sets's aging schedule indicates that all of its customers pay on time — 70 percent pay on Day 10 while 30 percent pay on Day 30. Wonder Vision's schedule, which is more typical, shows that many of its customers are not abiding by its credit terms — some 27 percent of its receivables are more than 30 days past due, even though Wonder Vision's credit terms call for full payment by Day 30.

Aging schedules cannot be constructed from the type of summary data reported in financial statements; they must be developed from the firm's accounts receivable ledger. However, well-run firms have computerized their accounts receivable records, so it is easy to determine the age of each invoice, to sort electronically by age categories, and thus to generate an aging schedule.

Management should constantly monitor both the DSO and the aging schedule to detect trends, to see how the firm's collection experience compares with its credit terms, and to see how effectively the credit department is operating in comparison with other firms in the industry. If the DSO starts to lengthen, or

TABLE 15-3	Aging Schedules			

	SUPER SETS		WONDER VISION	
AGE OF ACCOUNT (DAYS)	VALUE OF ACCOUNT	PERCENTAGE OF TOTAL VALUE	VALUE OF ACCOUNT	PERCENTAGE OF TOTAL VALUE
0–10	$1,215,122	70%	$ 815,867	47%
11–30	520,766	30	451,331	26
31–45	0	0	260,383	15
46–60	0	0	173,589	10
Over 60	0	0	34,718	2
Total receivables	$1,735,888	100%	$1,735,888	100%

if the aging schedule begins to show an increasing percentage of past-due accounts, then the firm's credit policy may need to be tightened.

Although a change in the DSO or the aging schedule should signal the firm to investigate its credit policy, a deterioration in either of these measures does not necessarily indicate that the firm's credit policy has weakened. In fact, if a firm experiences sharp seasonal variations, or if it is growing rapidly, then both the aging schedule and the DSO may be distorted. To see this point, note that the DSO is calculated as follows:

$$\text{DSO} = \frac{\text{Accounts receivable}}{\text{Sales}/365}.$$

Since receivables at a given point in time reflect sales in the last month or so, but sales as shown in the denominator of the equation are for the last 12 months, a seasonal increase in sales will increase the numerator more than the denominator, hence will raise the DSO. This will occur even if customers are still paying exactly as before. Similar problems arise with the aging schedule if sales fluctuate widely. Therefore, a change in either the DSO or the aging schedule should be taken as a signal to investigate further, but not necessarily as a sign that the firm's credit policy has weakened. Still, days sales outstanding and the aging schedule are useful tools for reviewing the credit department's performance.[15]

SELF-TEST QUESTIONS

Explain how a new firm's receivables balance is built up over time.

Define days sales outstanding (DSO). What can be learned from it? How is it affected by sales fluctuations?

What is an aging schedule? What can be learned from it? How is it affected by sales fluctuations?

CREDIT POLICY

The success or failure of a business depends primarily on the demand for its products — as a rule, the higher its sales, the larger its profits and the higher its stock price. Sales, in turn, depend on a number of factors, some exogenous but others under the firm's control. The major controllable determinants of demand are sales prices, product quality, advertising, and the firm's **credit policy.** Credit policy, in turn, consists of these four variables:

Credit Policy
A set of decisions that include a firm's credit period, credit standards, collection procedures, and discounts offered.

1. *Credit period*, which is the length of time buyers are given to pay for their purchases.

---

[15] See Brigham and Daves, *Intermediate Financial Management*, 7th ed., Chapter 22, for a more complete discussion of the problems with the DSO and aging schedule and ways to correct for them.

2. *Discounts* given for early payment, including the discount percentage and how rapidly payment must be made to qualify for the discount.

3. *Credit standards*, which refer to the required financial strength of acceptable credit customers.

4. *Collection policy*, which is measured by its toughness or laxity in attempting to collect on slow-paying accounts.

The credit manager is responsible for administering the firm's credit policy. However, because of the pervasive importance of credit, the credit policy itself is normally established by the executive committee, which usually consists of the president plus the vice-presidents of finance, marketing, and production.

SELF-TEST QUESTION

What are the four credit policy variables?

FINANCING CURRENT ASSETS

Up until this point, we have discussed the first step in working capital management — determining the optimal level for each type of current asset. Now we turn to the second step — financing those assets. We begin with a discussion of alternative financing policies. Some companies use current liabilities as a major source of financing for current assets, while others rely more heavily on long-term debt and equity. In the remaining parts of this chapter we consider the advantages and disadvantages of each policy. In addition, we describe the various sources of short-term financing — accruals, accounts payable, bank loans, and commercial paper.

ALTERNATIVE CURRENT ASSET FINANCING POLICIES

Permanent Current Assets
Current assets that a firm must carry even at the trough of its cycles.

Temporary Current Assets
Current assets that fluctuate with seasonal or cyclical variations in sales.

Most businesses experience seasonal and/or cyclical fluctuations. For example, construction firms have peaks in the spring and summer, retailers peak around Christmas, and the manufacturers who supply both construction companies and retailers follow similar patterns. Similarly, virtually all businesses must build up current assets when the economy is strong, but they then sell off inventories and reduce receivables when the economy slacks off. Still, current assets rarely drop to zero — companies have some **permanent current assets,** which are the current assets on hand at the low point of the cycle. Then, as sales increase during the upswing, current assets must be increased, and these additional current assets are defined as **temporary current assets.** The manner in which the permanent and temporary current assets are financed is called the firm's *current asset financing policy*.

MATURITY MATCHING, OR "SELF-LIQUIDATING," APPROACH

Maturity Matching, or "Self-Liquidating," Approach
A financing policy that matches asset and liability maturities. This is a moderate policy.

The **maturity matching,** or **"self-liquidating," approach** calls for matching asset and liability maturities as shown in Panel a of Figure 15-3. This strategy minimizes the risk that the firm will be unable to pay off its maturing obligations. To illustrate, suppose a company borrows on a one-year basis and uses the funds obtained to build and equip a plant. Cash flows from the plant (profits plus depreciation) would not be sufficient to pay off the loan at the end of only one year, so the loan would have to be renewed. If for some reason the lender refused to renew the loan, then the company would have problems. Had the plant been financed with long-term debt, however, the required loan payments would have been better matched with cash flows from profits and depreciation, and the problem of renewal would not have arisen.

At the limit, a firm could attempt to match exactly the maturity structure of its assets and liabilities. Inventory expected to be sold in 30 days could be financed with a 30-day bank loan; a machine expected to last for 5 years could be financed with a 5-year loan; a 20-year building could be financed with a 20-year mortgage bond; and so forth. Actually, of course, two factors prevent this exact maturity matching: (1) there is uncertainty about the lives of assets, and (2) some common equity must be used, and common equity has no maturity. To illustrate the uncertainty factor, a firm might finance inventories with a 30-day loan, expecting to sell the inventories and then use the cash to retire the loan. But if sales were slow, the cash would not be forthcoming, and the use of short-term credit could end up causing a problem. Still, if a firm makes an attempt to match asset and liability maturities, we would define this as a moderate current asset financing policy.

In practice, firms don't finance each specific asset with a type of capital that has a maturity equal to the asset's life. However, academic studies do show that most firms tend to finance short-term assets from short-term sources and long-term assets from long-term sources.[16]

AGGRESSIVE APPROACH

Students can access various types of historical interest rates, including fixed and variable rates, at the St. Louis Federal Reserve's FRED site. The address is **http://www.stls.frb.org/fred/**.

Panel b of Figure 15-3 illustrates the situation for a relatively aggressive firm that finances all of its fixed assets with long-term capital and part of its permanent current assets with short-term, nonspontaneous credit. Note that we used the term "relatively" in the title for Panel b because there can be different *degrees* of aggressiveness. For example, the dashed line in Panel b could have been drawn *below* the line designating fixed assets, indicating that all of the permanent current assets and part of the fixed assets were financed with short-term credit; this would be a highly aggressive, extremely nonconservative position, and the firm would be very much subject to dangers from rising interest rates as well as to loan renewal problems. However, short-term debt is often cheaper than long-term debt, and some firms are willing to sacrifice safety for the chance of higher profits.

---

[16] For example, see William Beranek, Christopher Cornwell, and Sunho Choi, "External Financing, Liquidity, and Capital Expenditures," *Journal of Financial Research*, Vol. 18, No. 2, 207–222.

FIGURE 15-3 Alternative Current Asset Financing Policies

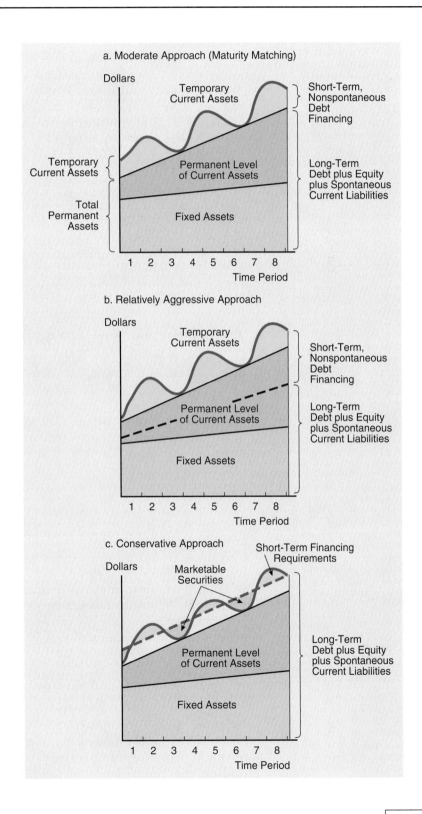

a. Moderate Approach (Maturity Matching)

b. Relatively Aggressive Approach

c. Conservative Approach

CONSERVATIVE APPROACH

Panel c of Figure 15-3 has the dashed line *above* the line designating permanent current assets, indicating that permanent capital is being used to finance all permanent asset requirements and also to meet some of the seasonal needs. In this situation, the firm uses a small amount of short-term, nonspontaneous credit to meet its peak requirements, but it also meets a part of its seasonal needs by "storing liquidity" in the form of marketable securities. The humps above the dashed line represent short-term financing, while the troughs below the dashed line represent short-term security holdings. Panel c represents a very safe, conservative current asset financing policy.

SELF-TEST QUESTIONS

What is meant by the term "permanent current assets"?

What is meant by the term "temporary current assets"?

What is meant by the term "current asset financing policy"?

What are three alternative current asset financing policies? Is one best?

ADVANTAGES AND DISADVANTAGES OF SHORT-TERM FINANCING

The three possible financing policies described above were distinguished by the relative amounts of short-term debt used under each policy. The aggressive policy called for the greatest use of short-term debt, while the conservative policy called for the least. Maturity matching fell in between. Although short-term credit is generally riskier than long-term credit, using short-term funds does have some significant advantages. The pros and cons of short-term financing are considered in this section.

SPEED

A short-term loan can be obtained much faster than long-term credit. Lenders will insist on a more thorough financial examination before extending long-term credit, and the loan agreement will have to be spelled out in considerable detail because a lot can happen during the life of a 10- to 20-year loan. Therefore, if funds are needed in a hurry, the firm should look to the short-term markets.

FLEXIBILITY

If its needs for funds are seasonal or cyclical, a firm may not want to commit itself to long-term debt for three reasons: (1) Flotation costs are higher for long-term debt than for short-term credit. (2) Although long-term debt can be repaid early, provided the loan agreement includes a prepayment provision, prepayment penalties can be expensive. Accordingly, if a firm thinks its need for funds will diminish in the near future, it should choose short-term debt. (3) Long-term loan agreements always contain provisions, or covenants, which constrain the firm's future actions. Short-term credit agreements are generally less restrictive.

COST OF LONG-TERM VERSUS SHORT-TERM DEBT

The yield curve is normally upward sloping, indicating that interest rates are generally lower on short-term debt. Thus, under normal conditions, interest costs at the time the funds are obtained will be lower if the firm borrows on a short-term rather than a long-term basis.

RISKS OF LONG-TERM VERSUS SHORT-TERM DEBT

Even though short-term rates are often lower than long-term rates, short-term credit is riskier for two reasons: (1) If a firm borrows on a long-term basis, its interest costs will be relatively stable over time, but if it uses short-term credit, its interest expense will fluctuate widely, at times going quite high. For example, the rate banks charge large corporations for short-term debt more than tripled over a two-year period in the 1980s, rising from 6.25 to 21 percent. Many firms that had borrowed heavily on a short-term basis simply could not meet their rising interest costs, and as a result, bankruptcies hit record levels during that period. (2) If a firm borrows heavily on a short-term basis, a temporary recession may render it unable to repay this debt. If the borrower is in a weak financial position, the lender may not extend the loan, which could force the firm into bankruptcy. Braniff Airlines, which failed during a credit crunch in the 1980s, is an example.

Another good example of the riskiness of short-term debt is provided by Transamerica Corporation, a major financial services company. Transamerica's former chairman, Mr. Beckett, described how his company was moving to reduce its dependency on short-term loans whose costs vary with short-term interest rates. According to Beckett, Transamerica had reduced its variable-rate (short-term) loans by about $450 million over a two-year period. "We aren't going to go through the enormous increase in debt expense again that had such a serious impact on earnings," he said. The company's earnings fell sharply because money rates rose to record highs. "We were almost entirely in variable-rate debt," he said, but currently "about 65 percent is fixed rate and 35 percent variable. We've come a long way, and we'll keep plugging away at it." Transamerica's earnings were badly depressed by the increase in short-term rates, but other companies were even less fortunate — they simply could not pay the rising interest charges, and this forced them into bankruptcy.

SELF-TEST QUESTION

What are the advantages and disadvantages of short-term debt over long-term debt?

SOURCES OF SHORT-TERM FINANCING

Statements about the flexibility, cost, and riskiness of short-term versus long-term debt depend, to a large extent, on the type of short-term credit that is actually used. There are numerous sources of short-term funds, and in the following sections we describe four major types: (1) accruals, (2) accounts payable (trade credit), (3) bank loans, and (4) commercial paper.

ACCRUALS

Firms generally pay employees on a weekly, biweekly, or monthly basis, so the balance sheet will typically show some accrued wages. Similarly, the firm's own estimated income taxes, Social Security and income taxes withheld from employee payrolls, and sales taxes collected are generally paid on a weekly, monthly, or quarterly basis, hence the balance sheet will typically show some accrued taxes along with accrued wages.

Accruals
Continually recurring short-term liabilities, especially accrued wages and accrued taxes.

These **accruals** increase automatically, or spontaneously, as a firm's operations expand. Further, this type of debt is "free" in the sense that no explicit interest is paid on funds raised through accruals. However, a firm cannot ordinarily control its accruals: The timing of wage payments is set by economic forces and industry custom, while tax payment dates are established by law. Thus, firms use all the accruals they can, but they have little control over the levels of these accounts.

SELF-TEST QUESTIONS

What types of short-term credit are classified as accruals?

What is the cost of accruals?

How much control do financial managers have over the dollar amount of accruals?

ACCOUNTS PAYABLE (TRADE CREDIT)

Trade Credit
Debt arising from credit sales and recorded as an account receivable by the seller and as an account payable by the buyer.

Firms generally make purchases from other firms on credit, recording the debt as an *account payable*. Accounts payable, or **trade credit,** is the largest single category of short-term debt, representing about 40 percent of the current liabilities of the average nonfinancial corporation. The percentage is somewhat larger for smaller firms: Because small companies often do not qualify for financing from other sources, they rely especially heavily on trade credit.[17]

---

[17] In a credit sale, the seller records the transaction as a receivable, the buyer as a payable. We examined accounts receivable as an asset earlier in this chapter. Our focus now is on accounts payable, a liability item. We might also note that if a firm's accounts payable exceed its receivables, it is said to be *receiving net trade credit*, whereas if its receivables exceed its payables, it is *extending net trade credit*. Smaller firms frequently receive net credit; larger firms generally extend it.

Trade credit is a "spontaneous" source of financing in the sense that it arises from ordinary business transactions. For example, suppose a firm makes average purchases of $2,000 a day on terms of net 30, meaning that it must pay for goods 30 days after the invoice date. On average, it will owe 30 times $2,000, or $60,000, to its suppliers. If its sales, and consequently its purchases, were to double, then its accounts payable would also double, to $120,000. So, simply by growing, the firm would spontaneously generate an additional $60,000 of financing. Similarly, if the terms under which it bought were extended from 30 to 40 days, its accounts payable would expand from $60,000 to $80,000. Thus, lengthening the credit period, as well as expanding sales and purchases, generates additional financing.

THE COST OF TRADE CREDIT

Firms that sell on credit have a *credit policy* that includes certain *terms of credit*. For example, Microchip Electronics sells on terms of 2/10, net 30, meaning that it gives its customers a 2 percent discount if they pay within 10 days of the invoice date, but the full invoice amount is due and payable within 30 days if the discount is not taken.

Note that the true price of Microchip's products is the net price, or 0.98 times the list price, because any customer can purchase an item at that price as long as the customer pays within 10 days. Now consider Personal Computer Company (PCC), which buys its memory chips from Microchip. One commonly used memory chip is listed at $100, so the "true" price to PCC is $98. Now if PCC wants an additional 20 days of credit beyond the 10-day discount period, it must incur a finance charge of $2 per chip for that credit. Thus, the $100 list price consists of two components:

$$\text{List price} = \$98 \text{ true price} + \$2 \text{ finance charge.}$$

The question PCC must ask before it turns down the discount to obtain the additional 20 days of credit from Microchip is this: Could we obtain credit under better terms from some other lender, say, a bank? In other words, could 20 days of credit be obtained for less than $2 per chip?

PCC buys an average of $11,923,333 of memory chips from Microchip each year at the net, or true, price. This amounts to $11,923,333/365 = $32,666.67 per day. For simplicity, assume that Microchip is PCC's only supplier. If PCC decides not to take the additional trade credit — that is, if it pays on the 10th day and takes the discount — its payables will average 10($32,666.67) = $326,667. Thus, PCC will be receiving $326,667 of credit from Microchip.

Now suppose PCC decides to take the additional 20 days credit and thus must pay the finance charge. Since PCC will now pay on the 30th day, its accounts payable will increase to 30($32,666.67) = $980,000.[18] Microchip will now be supplying PCC with an additional $980,000 − $326,667 = $653,333 of credit, which PCC could use to build up its cash account, to pay off debt, to

---

[18] A question arises here: Should accounts payable reflect gross purchases or purchases net of discounts? Generally accepted accounting principles permit either treatment if the difference is not material, but if the discount is material, then the transaction must be recorded net of discounts, or at "true" prices. Then, the higher payment that results from not taking discounts is reported as an additional expense called "discounts lost." *Thus, we show accounts payable net of discounts even if the company does not expect to take discounts.*

expand inventories, or even to extend credit to its own customers, hence increasing its own accounts receivable.

The additional trade credit offered by Microchip has a cost — PCC must pay a finance charge equal to the 2 percent discount it is foregoing. PCC buys $11,923,333 of chips at the true price, and the added finance charges increase the total cost to $11,923,333/0.98 = $12,166,666. Therefore, the annual financing cost is $12,166,666 − $11,923,333 = $243,333. Dividing the $243,333 financing cost by the $653,333 of additional credit, we find the nominal annual cost rate of the additional trade credit to be 37.2 percent:

$$\text{Nominal annual cost} = \frac{\$243,333}{\$653,333} = 37.2\%.$$

If PCC can borrow from its bank (or from other sources) at an interest rate less than 37.2 percent, it should take discounts and forgo the additional trade credit.

The following equation can be used to calculate the nominal cost, on an annual basis, of not taking discounts, illustrated with terms of 2/10, net 30:

$$\begin{matrix} \text{Nominal} \\ \text{annual} \\ \text{cost} \end{matrix} = \frac{\text{Discount percent}}{100 - \begin{matrix}\text{Discount}\\\text{percent}\end{matrix}} \times \frac{365 \text{ days}}{\begin{matrix}\text{Days credit is}\\\text{outstanding}\end{matrix} - \begin{matrix}\text{Discount}\\\text{period}\end{matrix}} \quad (15\text{-}8)$$

$$= \frac{2}{98} \times \frac{365}{20} = 2.04\% \times 18.25 = 37.2\%.$$

The numerator of the first term, Discount percent, is the cost per dollar of credit, while the denominator in this term, 100 − Discount percent, represents the funds made available by not taking the discount. Thus, the first term, 2.04%, is the cost per period for the trade credit. The denominator of the second term is the number of days of extra credit obtained by not taking the discount, so the entire second term shows how many times each year the cost is incurred, 18.25 times in this example.

The nominal annual cost formula does not take account of compounding, and in effective annual interest terms, the cost of trade credit is even higher. The discount amounts to interest, and with terms of 2/10, net 30, the firm gains use of the funds for 30 − 10 = 20 days, so there are 365/20 = 18.25 "interest periods" per year. Remember that the first term in Equation 15-8, (Discount percent)/(100 − Discount percent) = 0.02/0.98 = 0.0204, is the periodic interest rate. This rate is paid 18.25 times each year, so the effective annual cost of trade credit is

$$\text{Effective annual rate} = (1.0204)^{18.25} - 1.0 = 1.4459 - 1.0 = 44.6\%.$$

Thus, the 37.2 percent nominal cost calculated with Equation 15-8 understates the true cost.

Note, however, that the cost of trade credit can be reduced by paying late. Thus, if PCC could get away with paying in 60 days rather than in the specified 30 days, then the effective credit period would become 60 − 10 = 50 days, the number of times the discount would be lost would fall to 365/50 = 7.3, and the nominal cost would drop from 37.2 percent to 2.04% × 7.3 = 14.9%. The effective annual rate would drop from 44.6 to 15.9 percent:

$$\text{Effective annual rate} = (1.0204)^{7.3} - 1.0 = 1.1589 - 1.0 = 15.9\%.$$

Stretching Accounts Payable
The practice of deliberately paying late.

In periods of excess capacity, firms may be able to get away with deliberately paying late, or **stretching accounts payable.** However, they will also suffer a variety of problems associated with being branded a "slow payer." These problems are discussed later in the chapter.

The costs of the additional trade credit from forgoing discounts under some other purchase terms are shown below:

	COST OF ADDITIONAL CREDIT IF THE CASH DISCOUNT IS NOT TAKEN	
CREDIT TERMS	NOMINAL COST	EFFECTIVE COST
1/10, net 20	36.9%	44.3%
1/10, net 30	18.4	20.1
2/10, net 20	74.5	109.0
3/15, net 45	37.6	44.9

As these figures show, the cost of not taking discounts can be substantial. Incidentally, throughout the chapter, we assume that payments are made either on the *last day* for taking discounts or on the *last day* of the credit period, unless otherwise noted. It would be foolish to pay, say, on the 5th day or on the 20th day if the credit terms were 2/10, net 30.[19]

COMPONENTS OF TRADE CREDIT: FREE VERSUS COSTLY

Free Trade Credit
Credit received during the discount period.

Costly Trade Credit
Credit taken in excess of free trade credit, whose cost is equal to the discount lost.

On the basis of the preceding discussion, trade credit can be divided into two components: (1) **free trade credit,** which involves credit received during the discount period and which for PCC amounts to 10 days' net purchases, or $326,667, and (2) **costly trade credit,** which involves credit in excess of the free trade credit and whose cost is an implicit one based on the forgone discounts.[20] PCC could obtain $653,333, or 20 days' net purchases, of nonfree trade credit at a nominal cost of 37.2 percent. *Firms should always use the free*

---

[19] A financial calculator can also be used to determine the cost of trade credit. If the terms of credit are 2/10, net 30, this implies that for every $100 of goods purchased at the full list price, the customer has the choice of paying the full amount in 30 days or else paying $98 in 10 days. If a customer decides not to take the discount, then it is in effect borrowing $98, the amount it would otherwise have to pay, from Day 11 to Day 30, or for 20 days. It will then have to pay $100, which is the $98 loan plus a $2 financing charge, at the end of the 20-day loan period. To calculate the interest rate, enter N = 1, PV = 98, PMT = 0, FV = −100, and then press I to obtain 2.04 percent. This is the rate for 20 days. To calculate the effective annual interest rate on a 365-day basis, enter N = 20/365 = 0.05479, PV = 98, PMT = 0, FV = −100, and then press I to obtain 44.6 percent. The 20/365 = 0.05479, is the fraction of a year the "loan" is outstanding, and the 44.6 percent is the annualized cost of not taking discounts.

[20] There is some question as to whether any credit is really "free," because the supplier will have a cost of carrying receivables, which must be passed on to the customer in the form of higher prices. Still, if suppliers sell on standard terms such as 2/10, net 30, and if the base price cannot be negotiated downward for early payment, then for all intents and purposes, the 10 days of trade credit is indeed "free."

TECHNOLOGY MATTERS

THE INTERNET THREATENS TO TRANSFORM THE BANKING INDUSTRY

Everywhere you turn you see stories about how the Internet has changed business. Increasingly, businesses and individuals are using the Internet to research and then buy a wide variety of products and services. We discussed in earlier chapters how the Internet has dramatically transformed the brokerage industry. For example, Merrill Lynch, which was slow to respond to the Internet phenomenon, has become much more aggressive. It recently rolled out a new site for online trading, developed a procedure through which companies can issue securities online, and entered several partnerships with Internet-oriented businesses.

The same forces that led to Internet trading are also affecting other parts of the financial services industry. Commercial bankers recognize that while the Internet provides them with a whole host of new opportunities, it will also subject them to increased competition from nontraditional sources. For example, Internet upstart E-LOAN, whose products include mortgages, consumer loans, and small business loans, is currently the nation's leading online lender. While E-LOAN's volume is still relatively small, it represents the tip of the iceberg, because down the road technology companies such as Microsoft will probably enter the industry.

Despite these concerns, there are reasons to believe that the Internet's effect on traditional banking may be smaller and slower than its effect on the brokerage industry. Banking relationships often require close personal contact between the bank and its customers. Corporate borrowers may not want to use the Internet to completely replace the personal relationships they have established with their lenders. Likewise, a large number of customers still prefer to walk into a local branch to do their banking. At a minimum, however, the Internet will be used to supplement these personal relationships.

The traditional banks are not sitting on their hands. Mostly conservative by nature, commercial bankers have begun to slowly embrace the opportunities, and confront the threats, that arise from changing technology. Virtually every leading bank now has an Internet presence. In most cases, customers can see their balances, transfer money, and research the bank's various products. Several banking giants, including Chase, Citigroup, Wells Fargo, and Bank of America, are taking things a step further and spending a lot of money to develop a wider range of online banking products. These banks are hoping to use their size, brand name, and experience to become major players in online financial services. Another leading bank, Bank One, has followed a different strategy. It set up a completely separate bank with a distinct operation and brand name, Wingspan.com. Bank One hopes that its separate identity will enable Wingspan to develop a more entrepreneurial, web-savvy culture. However, it is fair to say that Wingspan's performance to date has been a disappointment. Its customer base is roughly half of what the company projected.

Despite the sluggish start, it may still be too early to tell which strategies will be successful. Either way, it is likely that the financial services industry will be very different in 10 years.

---

component, but they should use the costly component only after analyzing the cost of this capital to make sure that it is less than the cost of funds that could be obtained from other sources. Under the terms of trade found in most industries, the costly component is relatively expensive, so stronger firms will avoid using it.

We noted earlier that firms sometimes can and do deviate from the stated credit terms, thus altering the percentage cost figures cited earlier. For example, a California manufacturing firm that buys on terms of 2/10, net 30, makes a practice of paying in 15 days (rather than 10), but it still takes discounts. Its treasurer simply waits until 15 days after receipt of the goods to pay, then writes a check for the invoiced amount less the 2 percent discount. The company's suppliers want its business, so they tolerate this practice. Similarly, a Wisconsin firm that also buys on terms of 2/10, net 30, does not take discounts, but it pays in 60 rather than in 30 days, thus "stretching" its trade credit. As we saw earlier, both practices reduce the calculated cost of trade credit. Neither of these firms is "loved" by its suppliers, and neither could continue these practices in times when suppliers were operating at full capacity and had order backlogs, but these practices can and do reduce the costs of trade credit during times when suppliers have excess capacity.

┌─────────────────────────────┐
│ **SELF-TEST QUESTIONS**   │
└─────────────────────────────┘

What is trade credit?

What is the difference between free trade credit and costly trade credit?

What is the formula for finding the nominal annual cost of trade credit? What is the formula for the effective annual cost of trade credit?

How does the cost of costly trade credit generally compare with the cost of short-term bank loans?

SHORT-TERM BANK LOANS

Commercial banks, whose loans generally appear on balance sheets as notes payable, are second in importance to trade credit as a source of short-term financing for nonfinancial corporations.[21] The banks' influence is actually greater than it appears from the dollar amounts because banks provide *nonspontaneous* funds. As a firm's financing needs increase, it requests additional funds from its bank. If the request is denied, the firm may be forced to abandon attractive growth opportunities. The key features of bank loans are discussed in the following paragraphs.

MATURITY

Although banks do make longer-term loans, *the bulk of their lending is on a short-term basis* — about two-thirds of all bank loans mature in a year or less. Bank loans to businesses are frequently written as 90-day notes, so the loan must be repaid or renewed at the end of 90 days. Of course, if a borrower's financial position has deteriorated, the bank may refuse to renew the loan. This can mean serious trouble for the borrower.

PROMISSORY NOTE

Promissory Note
A document specifying the terms and conditions of a loan, including the amount, interest rate, and repayment schedule.

When a bank loan is approved, the agreement is executed by signing a **promissory note.** The note specifies (1) the amount borrowed; (2) the interest rate; (3) the repayment schedule, which can call for either a lump sum or a series of installments; (4) any collateral that might have to be put up as security for the loan; and (5) any other terms and conditions to which the bank and the borrower have agreed. When the note is signed, the bank credits the borrower's checking account with the funds, so on the borrower's balance sheet both cash and notes payable increase.

---

[21] Although commercial banks remain the primary source of short-term loans, other sources are available. For example, GE Capital Corporation (GECC) had several billion dollars in commercial loans outstanding. Firms such as GECC, which was initially established to finance consumers' purchases of GE's durable goods, often find business loans to be more profitable than consumer loans.

COMPENSATING BALANCES

Compensating Balance
A minimum checking account balance that a firm must maintain with a commercial bank, generally equal to 10 to 20 percent of the amount of loans outstanding.

Banks sometimes require borrowers to maintain an average demand deposit (checking account) balance equal to from 10 to 20 percent of the face amount of the loan. This is called a **compensating balance,** and such balances raise the effective interest rate on the loans. For example, if a firm needs $80,000 to pay off outstanding obligations, but if it must maintain a 20 percent compensating balance, then it must borrow $100,000 to obtain a usable $80,000. If the stated annual interest rate is 8 percent, the effective cost is actually 10 percent: $8,000 interest divided by $80,000 of usable funds equals 10 percent.[22]

As we noted earlier in the chapter, recent surveys indicate that compensating balances are much less common now than 20 years ago. In fact, compensating balances are now illegal in many states. Despite this trend, some small banks in states where compensating balances are legal still require their customers to maintain compensating balances.

INFORMAL LINE OF CREDIT

Line of Credit
An informal arrangement in which a bank agrees to lend up to a specified maximum amount of funds during a designated period.

A **line of credit** is an informal agreement between a bank and a borrower indicating the maximum credit the bank will extend to the borrower. For example, on December 31, a bank loan officer might indicate to a financial manager that the bank regards the firm as being "good" for up to $80,000 during the forthcoming year, provided the borrower's financial condition does not deteriorate. If on January 10 the financial manager signs a promissory note for $15,000 for 90 days, this would be called "taking down" $15,000 of the total line of credit. This amount would be credited to the firm's checking account at the bank, and before repayment of the $15,000, the firm could borrow additional amounts up to a total of $80,000 outstanding at any one time.

REVOLVING CREDIT AGREEMENT

Revolving Credit Agreement
A formal, committed line of credit extended by a bank or other lending institution.

A **revolving credit agreement** is a formal line of credit often used by large firms. To illustrate, in 2001 Texas Petroleum Company negotiated a revolving credit agreement for $100 million with a group of banks. The banks were formally committed for four years to lend the firm up to $100 million if the funds were needed. Texas Petroleum, in turn, paid an annual commitment fee of $\frac{1}{4}$ of 1 percent on the unused balance of the commitment to compensate the banks for making the commitment. Thus, if Texas Petroleum did not take down any of the $100 million commitment during a year, it would still be required to pay a $250,000 annual fee, normally in monthly installments of $20,833.33. If it borrowed $50 million on the first day of the agreement, the unused portion of the line of credit would fall to $50 million, and the annual fee would fall to $125,000. Of course, interest would also have to be paid on the money Texas Petroleum actually borrowed. As a general rule, the interest rate on "revolvers" is pegged to the prime rate, the T-bill rate, or some other market rate, so the

---

[22] Note, however, that the compensating balance may be set as a minimum monthly *average*, and if the firm would maintain this average anyway, the compensating balance requirement would not raise the effective interest rate. Also, note that these *loan* compensating balances are added to any compensating balances that the firm's bank may require for *services performed*, such as clearing checks.

cost of the loan varies over time as interest rates change.[23] Texas Petroleum's rate was set at prime plus 0.5 percentage point.

Note that a revolving credit agreement is very similar to an informal line of credit, but with an important difference: The bank has a *legal obligation* to honor a revolving credit agreement, and it receives a commitment fee. Neither the legal obligation nor the fee exists under the informal line of credit.

Often a line of credit will have a *clean-up clause* that requires the borrower to reduce the loan balance to zero at least once a year. Keep in mind that a line of credit typically is designed to help finance negative operating cash flows that are incurred as a natural part of a company's business cycle, not as a source of permanent capital. For example, the total annual operating cash flow of Toys "Я" Us is normally positive, even though its operating cash flow is negative during the fall as it builds up inventory for the Christmas season. However, Toys "Я" Us has large positive cash flows in December through February, as it collects on Christmas sales. Their bankers would expect Toys "Я" Us to use those positive cash flows to pay off balances that had been drawn against their credit lines. Otherwise, Toys "Я" Us would be using its credit lines as a permanent source of financing.

SELF-TEST QUESTION

Explain how a firm that expects to need funds during the coming year might make sure the needed funds will be available.

COMMERCIAL PAPER

Commercial Paper
Unsecured, short-term promissory notes of large firms, usually issued in denominations of $100,000 or more and having an interest rate somewhat below the prime rate.

Commercial paper is a type of unsecured promissory note issued by large, strong firms and sold primarily to other business firms, to insurance companies, to pension funds, to money market mutual funds, and to banks. At year-end 2000, there was approximately $1,615.3 billion of commercial paper outstanding, versus about $1,090.7 billion of bank loans. Much of this commercial paper outstanding is issued by financial institutions.

MATURITY AND COST

Maturities of commercial paper generally vary from one day to nine months, with an average of about five months.[24] The interest rate on commercial paper fluctuates with supply and demand conditions — it is determined in the

---

[23] Each bank sets its own prime rate, but, because of competitive forces, most banks' prime rates are identical. Further, most banks follow the rate set by the large New York City banks.

In recent years many banks have been lending to the very strongest companies at rates below the prime rate. As we discuss in the next section, larger firms have ready access to the commercial paper market, and if banks want to do business with these larger companies, they must match, or at least come close to, the commercial paper rate.

[24] The maximum maturity without SEC registration is 270 days. Also, commercial paper can only be sold to "sophisticated" investors; otherwise, SEC registration would be required even for maturities of 270 days or less.

marketplace, varying daily as conditions change. Recently, commercial paper rates have ranged from $1\frac{1}{2}$ to $3\frac{1}{2}$ percentage points below the stated prime rate, and about $\frac{1}{8}$ to $\frac{1}{2}$ of a percentage point above the T-bill rate. For example, on December 15, 2000, the average rate on three-month commercial paper was 6.35 percent, the stated prime rate was 9.50 percent, and the three-month T-bill rate was 5.84 percent.

USE OF COMMERCIAL PAPER

The use of commercial paper is restricted to a comparatively small number of very large concerns that are exceptionally good credit risks. Dealers prefer to handle the paper of firms whose net worth is $100 million or more and whose annual borrowing exceeds $10 million. One potential problem with commercial paper is that a debtor who is in temporary financial difficulty may receive little help because commercial paper dealings are generally less personal than are bank relationships. Thus, banks are generally more able and willing to help a good customer weather a temporary storm than is a commercial paper dealer. On the other hand, using commercial paper permits a corporation to tap a wide range of credit sources, including financial institutions outside its own area and industrial corporations across the country, and this can reduce interest costs.

SELF-TEST QUESTIONS

What is commercial paper?

What types of companies can use commercial paper to meet their short-term financing needs?

How does the cost of commercial paper compare with the cost of short-term bank loans? With the cost of Treasury bills?

USE OF SECURITY IN SHORT-TERM FINANCING

Secured Loan
A loan backed by collateral, often inventories or receivables.

Thus far, we have not addressed the question of whether or not short-term loans should be secured. Commercial paper is never secured, but other types of loans can be secured if this is deemed necessary or desirable. Other things held constant, it is better to borrow on an unsecured basis, since the bookkeeping costs of **secured loans** are often high. However, firms often find that they can borrow only if they put up some type of collateral to protect the lender, or that by using security they can borrow at a much lower rate.

Several different kinds of collateral can be employed, including marketable stocks or bonds, land or buildings, equipment, inventory, and accounts receivable. Marketable securities make excellent collateral, but few firms that need loans also hold portfolios of stocks and bonds. Similarly, real property (land and buildings) and equipment are good forms of collateral, but they are generally used as security for long-term loans rather than for working capital loans. Therefore, most secured short-term business borrowing involves the use of accounts receivable and inventories as collateral.

To understand the use of security, consider the case of a Chicago hardware dealer who wanted to modernize and expand his store. He requested a $200,000 bank loan. After examining his business's financial statements, the bank indicated that it would lend him a maximum of $100,000 and that the effective interest rate would be 12.1 percent. The owner had a substantial personal portfolio of stocks, and he offered to put up $300,000 of high-quality stocks to support the $200,000 loan. The bank then granted the full $200,000 loan, and at the prime rate of 9.5 percent. The store owner might also have used his inventories or receivables as security for the loan, but processing costs would have been high.[25]

SELF-TEST QUESTIONS

What is a secured loan?

What are some types of current assets that are pledged as security for short-term loans?

---

[25] The term "asset-based financing" is often used as a synonym for "secured financing." In recent years, accounts receivable have been used as security for long-term bonds, and this permits corporations to borrow from lenders such as pension funds rather than being restricted to banks and other traditional short-term lenders.

TYING IT ALL TOGETHER

This chapter discussed working capital management. In the first part of the chapter we discussed current assets. While there are unique factors relating to each component of working capital, two important themes are developed relative to current assets. First, current assets are necessary, but there are costs associated with holding them. Therefore, if a company can manage its current assets more efficiently and thereby operate with a smaller investment in working capital, this will increase its profitability. At the same time, though, a company will have problems if it reduces its cash, inventory, and receivables too much. Thus, the optimal current asset management policy is one that carefully trades off the costs and benefits of holding working capital.

Second, changing technology has enabled companies to streamline their working capital, which has improved their cash flow and profitability. Indeed, companies today that fail to manage their working capital efficiently are finding themselves at a greater and greater competitive disadvantage.

In the second part of this chapter, we examined different policies for financing current assets. In particular, we looked at the factors that affect the use of current liabilities versus long-term capital and the specific types of current liabilities. Some companies have very few current liabilities, while others rely heavily on short-term credit to finance current assets. In some cases, companies even use short-term debt to finance a portion of their long-term assets. The key concepts covered are listed below.

- **Working capital** refers to current assets, and **net working capital** is defined as current assets minus current liabilities. **Net operating working capital** is defined as current assets minus non-interest bearing current liabilities. **Working capital policy** refers to decisions relating to current assets and their financing.

- The **cash conversion cycle model** focuses on the length of time between when the company makes payments and when it receives cash inflows.

- The **inventory conversion period** is the average time required to convert materials into finished goods and then to sell those goods.

$$\text{Inventory conversion period} = \text{Inventory/Sales per day.}$$

- The **receivables collection period** is the average length of time required to convert the firm's receivables into cash, that is, to collect cash following a sale.

$$\text{Receivables collection period} = \text{DSO} = \text{Receivables/(Sales/365).}$$

- The **payables deferral period** is the average length of time between the purchase of materials and labor and the payment of cash for them.

$$\text{Payables deferral period} = \text{Payables/Purchases per day.}$$

- The **cash conversion cycle** equals the length of time between the firm's actual cash expenditures to pay for productive resources (materials and labor) and its own cash receipts from the sale of products (that is, the length of time between paying for labor and materials and collecting on receivables).

$$\begin{matrix} \text{Cash} & & \text{Inventory} & & \text{Receivables} & & \text{Payables} \\ \text{conversion} & = & \text{conversion} & + & \text{collection} & - & \text{deferral} \\ \text{cycle} & & \text{period} & & \text{period} & & \text{period} \end{matrix}.$$

- Under a **relaxed current asset policy,** a firm would hold relatively large amounts of each type of current asset. Under a **restricted current asset policy,** the firm would hold minimal amounts of these items.

- The **primary goal of cash management** is to reduce the amount of cash held to the minimum necessary to conduct business.

- The **transactions balance** is the cash necessary to conduct day-to-day business, whereas the **precautionary balance** is a cash reserve held to meet random, unforeseen needs. A **compensating balance** is a minimum checking account balance that a bank requires as compensation either for services provided or as part of a loan agreement. Firms also hold **speculative balances,** which allow them to take advantage of bargain purchases. Note, though, that borrowing capacity and marketable security holdings both reduce the need for precautionary and speculative balances.

- A **cash budget** is a schedule showing projected cash inflows and outflows over some period. The cash budget is used to predict cash surpluses and deficits, and it is the primary cash management planning tool.

- Firms can reduce their cash balances by holding **marketable securities,** which can be sold on short notice at close to their quoted prices. Marketable securities serve both as a substitute for cash and as a temporary investment for funds that will be needed in the near future. Safety is the primary consideration when selecting marketable securities.

- **Inventory** can be grouped into four categories: (1) supplies, (2) raw materials, (3) work-in-process, and (4) finished goods.

- The twin goals of **inventory management** are (1) to ensure that the inventories needed to sustain operations are available, but (2) to hold the costs of ordering and carrying inventories to the lowest possible level.

- **Inventory costs** can be divided into three types: carrying costs, ordering costs, and stock-out costs. In general, carrying costs increase as the level of inventory rises, but ordering costs and stock-out costs decline with larger inventory holdings.

- When a firm sells goods to a customer on credit, an **account receivable** is created.

- A firm can use an **aging schedule** and the **days sales outstanding (DSO)** to help keep track of its receivables position and to help avoid an increase in bad debts.

- A firm's **credit policy** consists of four elements: (1) credit period, (2) discounts given for early payment, (3) credit standards, and (4) collection policy.

- The basic objective of the credit manager is to increase profitable sales by extending credit to worthy customers and therefore adding value to the firm.

- **Permanent current assets** are those current assets that the firm holds even during slack times, whereas **temporary current assets** are the additional current assets that are needed during seasonal or cyclical peaks. The methods used to finance permanent and temporary current assets define the firm's **current asset financing policy.**

- A **moderate** approach to current asset financing involves matching, to the extent possible, the maturities of assets and liabilities, so that temporary current assets are financed with short-term nonspontaneous debt, and permanent current assets and fixed assets are financed with long-term debt or equity, plus spontaneous debt. Under an **aggressive** approach, some permanent current assets, and perhaps even some fixed assets, are financed with short-term debt. A **conservative** approach would be to use long-term capital to finance all permanent assets and some of the temporary current assets.

- The advantages of short-term credit are (1) the **speed** with which short-term loans can be arranged, (2) increased **flexibility,** and (3) the fact that short-term **interest rates** are generally **lower** than long-term rates. The principal disadvantage of short-term credit is the **extra risk** the borrower must bear because (1) the lender can demand payment on short notice and (2) the cost of the loan will increase if interest rates rise.

- **Short-term credit** is defined as any liability originally scheduled for payment within one year. The four major sources of short-term credit are (1) accruals, (2) accounts payable, (3) loans from commercial banks and finance companies, and (4) commercial paper.

- **Accruals,** which are continually recurring short-term liabilities, represent free, spontaneous credit.

- **Accounts payable,** or **trade credit,** is the largest category of short-term debt. Trade credit arises spontaneously as a result of credit purchases. Firms should use all the **free trade credit** they can obtain, but they should use **costly trade credit** only if it is less expensive than other forms of short-term debt. Suppliers often offer discounts to customers who pay within a stated discount period. The following equation may be used to calculate the nominal cost, on an annual basis, of not taking discounts:

$$\frac{\text{Nominal}}{\text{cost}} = \frac{\text{Discount percent}}{100 - \frac{\text{Discount}}{\text{percent}}} \times \frac{365 \text{ days}}{\frac{\text{Days credit is}}{\text{outstanding}} - \frac{\text{Discount}}{\text{period}}}.$$

- **Bank loans** are an important source of short-term credit. When a bank loan is approved, a **promissory note** is signed. It specifies: (1) the amount borrowed, (2) the percentage interest rate, (3) the repayment schedule, (4) the collateral, and (5) any other conditions to which the parties have agreed.

- Banks sometimes require borrowers to maintain **compensating balances,** which are deposit requirements set at between 10 and 20 percent of the loan amount. Compensating balances raise the effective interest rate on bank loans.

- A **line of credit** is an informal agreement between the bank and the borrower indicating the maximum amount of credit the bank will extend to the borrower.

- A **revolving credit agreement** is a formal line of credit often used by large firms; it involves a **commitment fee.**

- **Commercial paper** is unsecured short-term debt issued by large, financially strong corporations. Although the cost of commercial paper is lower than the cost of bank loans, it can be used only by large firms with exceptionally strong credit ratings.

- Sometimes a borrower will find that it is necessary to borrow on a **secured basis,** in which case the borrower pledges assets such as real estate, securities, equipment, inventories, or accounts receivable as collateral for the loan.

QUESTIONS

15-1 Assuming the firm's sales volume remained constant, would you expect it to have a higher cash balance during a tight-money period or during an easy-money period? Why?

15-2 What are the two principal reasons for holding cash? Can a firm estimate its target cash balance by summing the cash held to satisfy each of the two?

15-3 Is it true that when one firm sells to another on credit, the seller records the transaction as an account receivable while the buyer records it as an account payable and that, disregarding discounts, the receivable typically exceeds the payable by the amount of profit on the sale?

15-4 What are the four elements of a firm's credit policy? To what extent can firms set their own credit policies as opposed to having to accept policies that are dictated by "the competition"?

15-5   a. What is the days sales outstanding (DSO) for a firm whose sales are $2,920,000 per year and whose accounts receivable are $312,000?

           b. Is it true that if this firm sells on terms of 3/10, net 40, its customers probably all pay on time?

15-6   Is it true that if a firm calculates its days sales outstanding, it has no need for an aging schedule?

15-7   How does the seasonal nature of a firm's sales influence its decision regarding the amount of short-term credit to use in its financial structure?

15-8   What are the advantages of matching the maturities of assets and liabilities? What are the disadvantages?

15-9   From the standpoint of the borrower, is long-term or short-term credit riskier? Explain. Would it ever make sense to borrow on a short-term basis if short-term rates were above long-term rates?

15-10   If long-term credit exposes a borrower to less risk, why would people or firms ever borrow on a short-term basis?

15-11   "Firms can control their accruals within fairly wide limits; depending on the cost of accruals, financing from this source will be increased or decreased." Discuss.

15-12   Is it true that both trade credit and accruals represent a spontaneous source of capital for financing growth? Explain.

15-13   Is it true that most firms are able to obtain some free trade credit and that additional trade credit is often available, but at a cost? Explain.

15-14   The availability of bank credit is often more important to a small firm than to a large one. Why?

15-15   What kinds of firms use commercial paper? Could Mama and Papa Gus's Corner Grocery borrow using this form of credit?

15-16   Given that commercial paper interest rates are generally lower than bank loan rates to a given borrower, why might firms that are capable of selling commercial paper also use bank credit?

15-17   Suppose a firm can obtain funds by borrowing at the prime rate or by selling commercial paper.

           a. If the prime rate is 9.50 percent, what is a reasonable estimate for the cost of commercial paper?

           b. If a substantial cost differential exists, why might a firm like this one actually borrow some of its funds in each market?

SELF-TEST PROBLEMS   (SOLUTIONS APPEAR IN APPENDIX B)

ST-1
Key terms

Define each of the following terms:

    a. Working capital; net working capital; net operating working capital; working capital policy

    b. Cash conversion cycle model; inventory conversion period; receivables collection period

    c. Payables deferral period; cash conversion cycle

    d. Relaxed current asset investment policy; restricted current asset investment policy; moderate current asset investment policy

    e. Transactions balance; compensating balance; precautionary balance; speculative balance

    f. Cash budget; target cash balance

    g. Trade discounts

    h. Marketable securities

    i. Account receivable; days sales outstanding

    j. Aging schedule

    k. Credit policy; credit period; credit standards; collection policy; cash discounts

    l. Permanent current assets; temporary current assets

    m. Moderate current asset financing policy; aggressive current asset financing policy; conservative current asset financing policy

n. Maturity matching, or "self-liquidating," approach
o. Accruals
p. Trade credit; stretching accounts payable; free trade credit; costly trade credit
q. Promissory note; line of credit; revolving credit agreement
r. Commercial paper
s. Secured loan

ST-2
Working capital policy

The Calgary Company is attempting to establish a current assets policy. Fixed assets are $600,000, and the firm plans to maintain a 50 percent debt-to-assets ratio. The interest rate is 10 percent on all debt. Three alternative current asset policies are under consideration: 40, 50, and 60 percent of projected sales. The company expects to earn 15 percent before interest and taxes on sales of $3 million. Calgary's effective federal-plus-state tax rate is 40 percent. What is the expected return on equity under each alternative?

ST-3
Current asset financing

Vanderheiden Press Inc. and the Herrenhouse Publishing Company had the following balance sheets as of December 31, 2001 (thousands of dollars):

	VANDERHEIDEN PRESS	HERRENHOUSE PUBLISHING
Current assets	$100,000	$ 80,000
Fixed assets (net)	100,000	120,000
Total assets	$200,000	$200,000
Current liabilities	$ 20,000	$ 80,000
Long-term debt	80,000	20,000
Common stock	50,000	50,000
Retained earnings	50,000	50,000
Total liabilities and equity	$200,000	$200,000

Earnings before interest and taxes for both firms are $30 million, and the effective federal-plus-state tax rate is 40 percent.
a. What is the return on equity for each firm if the interest rate on current liabilities is 10 percent and the rate on long-term debt is 13 percent?
b. Assume that the short-term rate rises to 20 percent. While the rate on new long-term debt rises to 16 percent, the rate on existing long-term debt remains unchanged. What would be the return on equity for Vanderheiden Press and Herrenhouse Publishing under these conditions?
c. Which company is in a riskier position? Why?

STARTER PROBLEMS

15-1
Cash management

Williams & Sons last year reported sales of $10 million and an inventory turnover ratio of 2. The company is now adopting a new inventory system. If the new system is able to reduce the firm's inventory level and increase the firm's inventory turnover ratio to 5, while maintaining the same level of sales, how much cash will be freed up?

15-2
Receivables investment

Medwig Corporation has a DSO of 17 days. The company averages $3,500 in credit sales each day. What is the company's average accounts receivable?

15-3
Cost of trade credit

What is the nominal and effective cost of trade credit under the credit terms of 3/15, net 30?

15-4
Cost of trade credit

A large retailer obtains merchandise under the credit terms of 1/15, net 45, but routinely takes 60 days to pay its bills. Given that the retailer is an important customer, suppliers allow the firm to stretch its credit terms. What is the retailer's effective cost of trade credit?

15-5
Accounts payable

A chain of appliance stores, APP Corporation, purchases inventory with a net price of $500,000 each day. The company purchases the inventory under the credit terms of 2/15, net 40. APP always takes the discount, but takes the full 15 days to pay its bills. What is the average accounts payable for APP?

The problems included in this section are set up in such a way that they could be used as multiple-choice exam problems.

15-6
Receivables investment

McDowell Industries sells on terms of 3/10, net 30. Total sales for the year are $912,500. Forty percent of the customers pay on the 10th day and take discounts; the other 60 percent pay, on average, 40 days after their purchases.
a. What is the days sales outstanding?
b. What is the average amount of receivables?
c. What would happen to average receivables if McDowell toughened up on its collection policy with the result that all nondiscount customers paid on the 30th day?

15-7
Cost of trade credit

Calculate the nominal annual cost of nonfree trade credit under each of the following terms. Assume payment is made either on the due date or on the discount date.
a. 1/15, net 20.
b. 2/10, net 60.
c. 3/10, net 45.
d. 2/10, net 45.
e. 2/15, net 40.

15-8
Cost of trade credit

a. If a firm buys under terms of 3/15, net 45, but actually pays on the 20th day and *still takes the discount*, what is the nominal cost of its nonfree trade credit?
b. Does it receive more or less credit than it would if it paid within 15 days?

15-9
Cost of trade credit

Grunewald Industries sells on terms of 2/10, net 40. Gross sales last year were $4,562,500, and accounts receivable averaged $437,500. Half of Grunewald's customers paid on the 10th day and took discounts. What are the nominal and effective costs of trade credit to Grunewald's nondiscount customers? (Hint: Calculate sales/day based on a 365-day year; then get average receivables of discount customers; then find the DSO for the nondiscount customers.)

15-10
Effective cost of trade credit

The D. J. Masson Corporation needs to raise $500,000 for 1 year to supply working capital to a new store. Masson buys from its suppliers on terms of 3/10, net 90, and it currently pays on the 10th day and takes discounts, but it could forgo discounts, pay on the 90th day, and get the needed $500,000 in the form of costly trade credit. What is the effective annual interest rate of the costly trade credit?

PROBLEMS

15-11
Working capital investment

The Prestopino Corporation is a leading U.S. producer of automobile batteries. Prestopino turns out 1,500 batteries a day at a cost of $6 per battery for materials and labor. It takes the firm 22 days to convert raw materials into a battery. Prestopino allows its customers 40 days in which to pay for the batteries, and the firm generally pays its suppliers in 30 days.
a. What is the length of Prestopino's cash conversion cycle?
b. At a steady state in which Prestopino produces 1,500 batteries a day, what amount of working capital must it finance?
c. By what amount could Prestopino reduce its working capital financing needs if it was able to stretch its payables deferral period to 35 days?
d. Prestopino's management is trying to analyze the effect of a proposed new production process on the working capital investment. The new production process would allow Prestopino to decrease its inventory conversion period to 20 days and to increase its daily production to 1,800 batteries. However, the new process would cause the cost of materials and labor to increase to $7. Assuming the change does not affect the receivables collection period (40 days) or the payables deferral period (30 days), what will be the length of the cash conversion cycle and the working capital financing requirement if the new production process is implemented?

15-12
Cash conversion cycle

The Zocco Corporation has an inventory conversion period of 75 days, a receivables collection period of 38 days, and a payables deferral period of 30 days.
a. What is the length of the firm's cash conversion cycle?

b. If Zocco's annual sales are $3,421,875 and all sales are on credit, what is the firm's investment in accounts receivable?

c. How many times per year does Zocco turn over its inventory?

15-13

Working capital cash flow cycle

The Christie Corporation is trying to determine the effect of its inventory turnover ratio and days sales outstanding (DSO) on its cash flow cycle. Christie's 2001 sales (all on credit) were $150,000, and it earned a net profit of 6 percent, or $9,000. It turned over its inventory 5 times during the year, and its DSO was 36.5 days. The firm had fixed assets totaling $35,000. Christie's payables deferral period is 40 days.

a. Calculate Christie's cash conversion cycle.

b. Assuming Christie holds negligible amounts of cash and marketable securities, calculate its total assets turnover and ROA.

c. Suppose Christie's managers believe that the inventory turnover can be raised to 7.3 times. What would Christie's cash conversion cycle, total assets turnover, and ROA have been if the inventory turnover had been 7.3 for 2001?

15-14

Working capital policy

The Rentz Corporation is attempting to determine the optimal level of current assets for the coming year. Management expects sales to increase to approximately $2 million as a result of an asset expansion presently being undertaken. Fixed assets total $1 million, and the firm wishes to maintain a 60 percent debt ratio. Rentz's interest cost is currently 8 percent on both short-term and longer-term debt (which the firm uses in its permanent structure). Three alternatives regarding the projected current asset level are available to the firm: (1) a tight policy requiring current assets of only 45 percent of projected sales, (2) a moderate policy of 50 percent of sales in current assets, and (3) a relaxed policy requiring current assets of 60 percent of sales. The firm expects to generate earnings before interest and taxes at a rate of 12 percent on total sales.

a. What is the expected return on equity under each current asset level? (Assume a 40 percent effective federal-plus-state tax rate.)

b. In this problem, we have assumed that the level of expected sales is independent of current asset policy. Is this a valid assumption?

c. How would the overall riskiness of the firm vary under each policy?

15-15

Cash budgeting

Dorothy Koehl recently leased space in the Southside Mall and opened a new business, Koehl's Doll Shop. Business has been good, but Koehl has frequently run out of cash. This has necessitated late payment on certain orders, which, in turn, is beginning to cause a problem with suppliers. Koehl plans to borrow from the bank to have cash ready as needed, but first she needs a forecast of just how much she must borrow. Accordingly, she has asked you to prepare a cash budget for the critical period around Christmas, when needs will be especially high.

Sales are made on a cash basis only. Koehl's purchases must be paid for during the following month. Koehl pays herself a salary of $4,800 per month, and the rent is $2,000 per month. In addition, she must make a tax payment of $12,000 in December. The current cash on hand (on December 1) is $400, but Koehl has agreed to maintain an average bank balance of $6,000 — this is her target cash balance. (Disregard till cash, which is insignificant because Koehl keeps only a small amount on hand in order to lessen the chances of robbery.)

The estimated sales and purchases for December, January, and February are shown below. Purchases during November amounted to $140,000.

	SALES	PURCHASES
December	$160,000	$40,000
January	40,000	40,000
February	60,000	40,000

a. Prepare a cash budget for December, January, and February.

b. Now, suppose Koehl were to start selling on a credit basis on December 1, giving customers 30 days to pay. All customers accept these terms, and all other facts in the problem are unchanged. What would the company's loan requirements be at the end of December in this case? (Hint: The calculations required to answer this question are minimal.)

15-16

Cash budgeting

Helen Bowers, owner of Helen's Fashion Designs, is planning to request a line of credit from her bank. She has estimated the following sales forecasts for the firm for parts of 2002 and 2003:

May 2002	$180,000
June	180,000
July	360,000
August	540,000
September	720,000
October	360,000
November	360,000
December	90,000
January 2003	180,000

Collection estimates obtained from the credit and collection department are as follows: collections within the month of sale, 10 percent; collections the month following the sale, 75 percent; collections the second month following the sale, 15 percent. Payments for labor and raw materials are typically made during the month following the one in which these costs have been incurred. Total labor and raw materials costs are estimated for each month as follows:

May 2002	$ 90,000
June	90,000
July	126,000
August	882,000
September	306,000
October	234,000
November	162,000
December	90,000

General and administrative salaries will amount to approximately $27,000 a month; lease payments under long-term lease contracts will be $9,000 a month; depreciation charges will be $36,000 a month; miscellaneous expenses will be $2,700 a month; income tax payments of $63,000 will be due in both September and December; and a progress payment of $180,000 on a new design studio must be paid in October. Cash on hand on July 1 will amount to $132,000, and a minimum cash balance of $90,000 will be maintained throughout the cash budget period.
a. Prepare a monthly cash budget for the last 6 months of 2002.
b. Prepare an estimate of the required financing (or excess funds) — that is, the amount of money Bowers will need to borrow (or will have available to invest) — for each month during that period.
c. Assume that receipts from sales come in uniformly during the month (that is, cash receipts come in at the rate of 1/30 each day), but all outflows are paid on the 5th of the month. Will this have an effect on the cash budget — in other words, would the cash budget you have prepared be valid under these assumptions? If not, what can be done to make a valid estimate of peak financing requirements? No calculations are required, although calculations can be used to illustrate the effects.
d. Bowers produces on a seasonal basis, just ahead of sales. Without making any calculations, discuss how the company's current ratio and debt ratio would vary during the year assuming all financial requirements were met by short-term bank loans. Could changes in these ratios affect the firm's ability to obtain bank credit?

15-17	Suppose a firm makes purchases of $3.65 million per year under terms of 2/10, net 30,			
Cash discounts	and takes discounts.			

15-17
Cash discounts

Suppose a firm makes purchases of $3.65 million per year under terms of 2/10, net 30, and takes discounts.

a. What is the average amount of accounts payable net of discounts? (Assume that the $3.65 million of purchases is net of discounts — that is, gross purchases are $3,724,490, discounts are $74,490, and net purchases are $3.65 million.)

b. Is there a cost of the trade credit the firm uses?

c. If the firm did not take discounts but it did pay on the due date, what would be its average payables and the cost of this nonfree trade credit?

d. What would its cost of not taking discounts be if it could stretch its payments to 40 days?

15-18
Trade credit versus bank credit

The Thompson Corporation projects an increase in sales from $1.5 million to $2 million, but it needs an additional $300,000 of current assets to support this expansion. Thompson can finance the expansion by no longer taking discounts, thus increasing accounts payable. Thompson purchases under terms of 2/10, net 30, but it can delay payment for an additional 35 days — paying in 65 days and thus becoming 35 days past due — without a penalty because of its suppliers' current excess capacity problems. What is the effective, or equivalent, annual cost of the trade credit?

15-19
Bank financing

The Raattama Corporation had sales of $3.5 million last year, and it earned a 5 percent return, after taxes, on sales. Recently, the company has fallen behind in its accounts payable. Although its terms of purchase are net 30 days, its accounts payable represent 60 days' purchases. The company's treasurer is seeking to increase bank borrowings in order to become current in meeting its trade obligations (that is, to have 30 days' payables outstanding). The company's balance sheet is as follows (thousands of dollars):

Cash	$ 100	Accounts payable	$ 600
Accounts receivable	300	Bank loans	700
Inventory	1,400	Accruals	200
Current assets	$1,800	Current liabilities	$1,500
Land and buildings	600	Mortgage on real estate	700
Equipment	600	Common stock, $0.10 par	300
		Retained earnings	500
Total assets	$3,000	Total liabilities and equity	$3,000

a. How much bank financing is needed to eliminate the past-due accounts payable?

b. Would you as a bank loan officer make the loan? Why or why not?

15-20
Alternative financing arrangements

Suncoast Boats Inc. estimates that because of the seasonal nature of its business, it will require an additional $2 million of cash for the month of July. Suncoast Boats has the following 4 options available for raising the needed funds:

(1) Establish a 1-year line of credit for $2 million with a commercial bank. The commitment fee will be 0.5 percent per year on the unused portion, and the interest charge on the used funds will be 11 percent per annum. Assume that the funds are needed only in July, and that there are 30 days in July and 365 days in the year.

(2) Forgo the trade discount of 2/10, net 40, on $2 million of purchases during July.

(3) Issue $2 million of 30-day commercial paper at a 9.5 percent per annum interest rate. The total transactions fee, including the cost of a backup credit line, on using commercial paper is 0.5 percent of the amount of the issue.

(4) Issue $2 million of 60-day commercial paper at a 9 percent per annum interest rate, plus a transactions fee of 0.5 percent. Since the funds are required for only 30 days, the excess funds ($2 million) can be invested in 9.4 percent per annum marketable securities for the month of August. The total transactions cost of purchasing and selling the marketable securities is 0.4 percent of the amount of the issue.

a. What is the dollar cost of each financing arrangement?

b. Is the source with the lowest expected cost necessarily the one to select? Why or why not?

15-21
Cash budgeting

Rework Problem 15-16 using a spreadsheet model. After completing parts a through d, answer the following related question.

e. If its customers began to pay late, this would slow down collections and thus increase the required loan amount. Also, if sales dropped off, this would have an effect on the required loan. Do a sensitivity analysis that shows the effects of these two factors on the maximum loan requirement.

CYBER PROBLEM

The information related to this cyberproblem is likely to change over time, due to the release of new information and the ever-changing nature of the World Wide Web. Accordingly, we will periodically update the problem on the textbook's web site. To avoid problems, please check for updates before proceeding with the cyberproblems.

15-22
The cash conversion cycle in practice

The text identifies three principal components that jointly comprise the cash conversion cycle. The cash conversion cycle is defined as the average length of time a dollar is tied up in current assets, and it is determined by the interaction between the inventory conversion period, receivables collection period, and the payables deferral period. Ideally, a company wants to minimize the cash conversion cycle as much as possible. In some circumstances, a firm has a comparative advantage in working capital management because of the nature of its business. This cyberproblem looks at two competing booksellers. Barnes and Noble Inc. is a hybrid between the traditional brick and mortar retailer and the Internet retailer. However, approximately 85 percent of its revenues are generated in the traditional retail setting, which will lead us to consider it a traditional retail firm. Amazon.com, on the

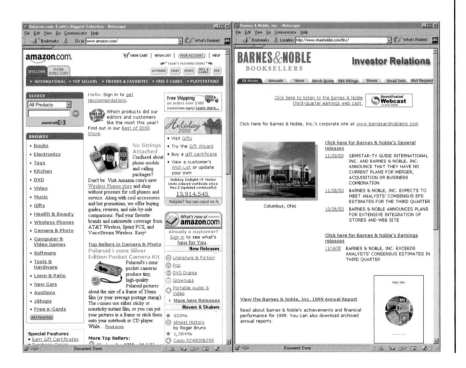

other hand, represents the new wave of Internet retailing. The success of Amazon.com has spawned the flood of specialty retailing into the Internet marketplace. We will look at the cash conversion cycles of these companies and their implications.

For this cyberproblem, you will be accessing information from the web sites for Barnes and Noble Inc. and Amazon.com at **http://www.shareholder.com/bks** and **http://www.amazon.com**, respectively.

a. Go to Barnes and Noble's web site, and click on "Annuals." Now that you are in the annual report gallery, click on "1999 Annual Report. (HTML version)" to view the 1999 annual report. Click on "1999 Financial Review" and then click on "Consolidated statements of Operations." From the income statement, write down the annual sales and cost of goods sold for 1999. Assuming a 365-day year, what are the average daily sales and purchases for Barnes and Noble Inc.?

b. Go back one screen and click on "Consolidated Balance Sheets." Write down the 1999 balances shown for the firm's inventories, accounts receivable, and accounts payable. Using this information plus that from part a, calculate its inventory conversion period, receivables collection period, and payables deferral period.

c. What is Barnes and Noble's cash conversion cycle?

d. Now, access Amazon's web site. Scroll to the bottom of the page, and click on "About Amazon.com." Next, click on "Investor Relations," and then click on "Annual Reports & Financial Documents." Click on 1999 Annual Report on Form 10-K, and scroll down until you see Amazon's Consolidated Statement of Operations. Find the annual sales and cost of goods sold. Again, assuming a 365-day year, calculate the average daily sales and purchases for Amazon.

e. Scroll up a page until you see Amazon's Consolidated Balance Sheets. Record 1999 balances for inventories, accounts receivable, and accounts payable. Use this information to calculate Amazon's inventory conversion period, receivables collection period, and payables deferral period.

f. Calculate Amazon's cash conversion cycle.

g. Compare the cash conversion cycles of Barnes and Noble and Amazon. What factors are responsible for these differences? Are these differences firm specific, or are they consequences of the nature of the businesses in which these firms operate?

h. Interpret your results. Explain in words what the cash conversion cycles you calculated mean for these companies.

SKI EQUIPMENT INC.

15-23 Working Capital Management Dan Barnes, financial manager of Ski Equipment Inc. (SKI), is excited, but apprehensive. The company's founder recently sold his 51 percent controlling block of stock to Kent Koren, who is a big fan of EVA (Economic Value Added). EVA is found by taking the after-tax operating profit and then subtracting the dollar cost of all the capital the firm uses:

$$EVA = EBIT(1 - T) - \text{Capital costs}$$
$$= EBIT(1 - T) - WACC(\text{Capital employed}).$$

If EVA is positive, then the firm is creating value. On the other hand, if EVA is negative, the firm is not covering its cost of capital, and stockholders' value is being eroded. Koren rewards managers handsomely if they create value, but those whose operations produce negative EVAs are soon looking for work. Koren frequently points out that if a company can generate its current level of sales with less assets, it would need less capital. That would, other things held constant, lower capital costs and increase its EVA.

Shortly after he took control of SKI, Kent Koren met with SKI's senior executives to tell them of his plans for the company. First, he presented some EVA data that convinced everyone that SKI had not been creating value in recent years. He then stated, in no uncertain terms, that this situation must change. He noted that SKI's designs of skis, boots, and clothing are acclaimed throughout the industry, but something is seriously amiss elsewhere in the company. Costs are too high, prices are too low, or the company employs too much capital, and he wants SKI's managers to correct the problem or else.

Barnes has long felt that SKI's working capital situation should be studied — the company may have the optimal amounts of cash, securities, receivables, and inventories, but it may also have too much or too little of these items. In the past, the production manager resisted Barnes' efforts to question his holdings of raw materials inventories, the marketing manager resisted questions about finished goods, the sales staff resisted questions about credit policy (which affects accounts receivable), and the treasurer did not want to talk about her cash and securities balances. Koren's speech made it clear that such resistance would no longer be tolerated.

Barnes also knows that decisions about working capital cannot be made in a vacuum. For example, if inventories could be lowered without adversely affecting operations, then less capital would be required, the dollar cost of capital would decline, and EVA would increase. However, lower raw materials inventories might lead to production slowdowns and higher costs, while lower finished goods inventories might lead to the loss of profitable sales. So, before inventories are changed, it will be necessary to study operating as well as financial effects. The situation is the same with regard to cash and receivables.

a. Barnes plans to use the ratios in Table IC15-1 as the starting point for discussions with SKI's operating executives. He wants everyone to think about the pros and cons of changing each type of current asset and how changes would interact to affect profits and EVA. Based on the Table IC15-1 data, does SKI seem to be following a relaxed, moderate, or restricted working capital policy?

TABLE IC15-1   **Selected Ratios: SKI and Industry Average**

	SKI	INDUSTRY
Current	1.75	2.25
Quick	0.83	1.20
Debt/assets	58.76%	50.00%
Turnover of cash and securities	16.67	22.22
Days sales outstanding (365-day basis)	45.63	32.00
Inventory turnover	4.82	7.00
Fixed assets turnover	11.35	12.00
Total assets turnover	2.08	3.00
Profit margin on sales	2.07%	3.50%
Return on equity (ROE)	10.45%	21.00%

b. How can one distinguish between a relaxed but rational working capital policy and a situation in which a firm simply has a lot of current assets because it is inefficient? Does SKI's working capital policy seem appropriate?

c. Assume that SKI's payables deferral period is 30 days. Now, calculate the firm's cash conversion cycle.

d. What might SKI do to reduce its cash and securities without harming operations?

In an attempt to better understand SKI's cash position, Barnes developed a cash budget. Data for the first 2 months of the year are shown in Table IC15-2. (Note that Barnes' preliminary cash budget does not account for interest income or interest expense.) He has the figures for the other months, but they are not shown in Table IC15-2.

e. Should depreciation expense be explicitly included in the cash budget? Why or why not?

f. In his preliminary cash budget, Barnes has assumed that all sales are collected and, thus, that SKI has no bad debts. Is this realistic? If not, how would bad debts be

TABLE IC15-2	SKI's Cash Budget for January and February					
	NOV	**DEC**	**JAN**	**FEB**	**MAR**	**APR**
I. COLLECTIONS AND PURCHASES WORKSHEET						
(1) Sales (gross)	$71,218	$68,212	$65,213	$52,475	$42,909	$30,524
Collections						
(2) During month of sale (0.2)(0.98)(month's sales)			12,781.75	10,285.10		
(3) During first month after sale (0.7)(previous month's sales)			47,748.40	45,649.10		
(4) During second month after sale (0.1)(sales 2 months ago)			7,121.80	6,821.20		
(5) Total collections (Lines 2 + 3 + 4)			$67,651.95	$62,755.40		
Purchases						
(6) (0.85)(forecasted sales 2 months from now)		$44,603.75	$36,472.65	$25,945.40		
(7) Payments (1-month lag)			44,603.75	36,472.65		
II. CASH GAIN OR LOSS FOR MONTH						
(8) Collections (from Section I)			$67,651.95	$62,755.40		
(9) Payments for purchases (from Section I)			44,603.75	36,472.65		
(10) Wages and salaries			6,690.56	5,470.90		
(11) Rent			2,500.00	2,500.00		
(12) Taxes						
(13) Total payments			$53,794.31	$44,443.55		
(14) Net cash gain (loss) during month (Line 8 − Line 13)			$13,857.64	$18,311.85		
III. CASH SURPLUS OR LOAN REQUIREMENT						
(15) Cash at beginning of month if no borrowing is done			$3,000.00	$16,857.64		
(16) Cumulative cash (cash at start, + gain or − loss = Line 14 + Line 15)			16,857.64	35,169.49		
(17) Target cash balance			1,500.00	1,500.00		
(18) Cumulative surplus cash or loans outstanding to maintain $1,500 target cash balance (Line 16 − Line 17)			$15,357.64	$33,669.49		

dealt with in a cash budgeting sense? (Hint: Bad debts will affect collections but not purchases.)

g. Barnes' cash budget for the entire year, although not given here, is based heavily on his forecast for monthly sales. Sales are expected to be extremely low between May and September but then increase dramatically in the fall and winter. November is typically the firm's best month, when SKI ships equipment to retailers for the holiday season. Interestingly, Barnes' forecasted cash budget indicates that the company's cash holdings will exceed the targeted cash balance every month except for October and November, when shipments will be high but collections will not be coming in until later. Based on the ratios in Table IC15-1, does it appear that SKI's target cash balance is appropriate? In addition to possibly lowering the target cash balance, what actions might SKI take to better improve its cash management policies, and how might that affect its EVA?

h. What reasons might SKI have for maintaining a relatively high amount of cash?

i. What are the three categories of inventory costs? If the company takes steps to reduce its inventory, what effect would this have on the various costs of holding inventory?

j. Is there any reason to think that SKI may be holding too much inventory? If so, how would that affect EVA and ROE?

k. If the company reduces its inventory without adversely affecting sales, what effect should this have on the company's cash position (1) in the short run and (2) in the long run? Explain in terms of the cash budget and the balance sheet.

l. Barnes knows that SKI sells on the same credit terms as other firms in its industry. Use the ratios presented in Table IC15-1 to explain whether SKI's customers pay more or less promptly than those of its competitors. If there are differences, does that suggest that SKI should tighten or loosen its credit policy? What four variables make up a firm's credit policy, and in what direction should each be changed by SKI?

m. Does SKI face any risks if it tightens its credit policy?

n. If the company reduces its DSO without seriously affecting sales, what effect would this have on its cash position (1) in the short run and (2) in the long run? Answer in terms of the cash budget and the balance sheet. What effect should this have on EVA in the long run?

In addition to improving the management of its current assets, SKI is also reviewing the ways in which it finances its current assets. With this concern in mind, Dan is also trying to answer the following questions.

o. SKI tries to match the maturity of its assets and liabilities. Describe how SKI could adopt either a more aggressive or more conservative financing policy.

p. What are the advantages and disadvantages of using short-term credit as a source of financing?

q. Is it likely that SKI could make significantly greater use of accruals?

r. Assume that SKI buys on terms of 1/10, net 30, but that it can get away with paying on the 40th day if it chooses not to take discounts. Also, assume that it purchases $506,985 of equipment per year, net of discounts. How much free trade credit can the company get, how much costly trade credit can it get, and what is the percentage cost of the costly credit? Should SKI take discounts?

s. Would it be feasible for SKI to finance with commercial paper?

CHAPTER 16

Multinational Financial Management*

SOURCE: © James Leynse/SABA

From the end of World War II until the 1970s, the United States dominated the world economy. However, that situation no longer exists. Raw materials, finished goods, services, and money flow freely across most national boundaries, as do innovative ideas and new technologies. World-class U.S. companies are making breakthroughs in foreign labs, obtaining capital from foreign investors, and putting foreign employees on the fast track to the top. Dozens of top U.S. manufacturers, including Dow Chemical, Colgate-Palmolive, Gillette, Hewlett-Packard, and Xerox, sell more of their products outside the United States than they do at home. Service firms are not far behind, as Citigroup, Disney, McDonald's, and Time Warner all receive more than 20 percent of their revenues from foreign sales.

The trend is even more pronounced in profits. In recent years, Coca-Cola and many other companies have made more money in the Pacific Rim and Western Europe than in the United States. However, like other companies, Coke has found that global investing also presents unique challenges and risks. Recent weakness in the Asian economy, along with a contamination scare in Belgium, have hurt the bottom line and put Coke on the defensive. Still, most analysts believe that these are only temporary setbacks and that Coke will continue to generate huge profits from its overseas operations in the years ahead.

Successful global companies such as Coca-Cola must conduct business in different economies, and they must be sensitive to the many subtleties of different cultures and political systems. Accordingly, they find it useful to blend into the foreign landscape to help win product acceptance and avoid political problems.

At the same time, foreign-based multinationals are arriving on American shores in ever greater numbers. Sweden's ABB, the Netherlands's Philips, France's Thomson, and Japan's Fujitsu and Honda are all waging campaigns to be identified as American companies that employ Americans, transfer technology to America, and help the U.S. trade balance. Few Americans know or care that Thomson owns the RCA and General Electric names in consumer electronics, or that Philips owns Magnavox.

The emergence of "world companies" raises a host of questions for governments. For example, should domestic firms be favored, or does it make no difference what a company's nationality is as long as it provides domestic jobs? Should a company make an effort to keep jobs in its home country, or should it produce where total production costs are lowest? What nation controls the technology developed by a multinational corporation, particularly if the technology can be used in military applications? Must a multinational company adhere to rules imposed in its home country with respect to its operations outside the home country? And if a U.S. firm such as Xerox produces copiers in Japan

---

* This chapter was coauthored with Professor Roy Crum of the University of Florida and Subu Venkataraman of Morgan Stanley Dean Witter.

and then ships them to the United States, should they be reflected in the trade deficit in the same way as Toshiba copiers imported from Japan? Keep these questions in mind as you read this chapter. When you finish it, you should have a better appreciation of both the problems facing governments and the difficult but profitable opportunities facing managers of multinational companies. ■

Managers of multinational companies must deal with a wide range of issues that are not present when a company operates in a single country. In this chapter, we highlight the key differences between multinational and domestic corporations, and we discuss the impact these differences have on the financial management of multinational businesses. ■

MULTINATIONAL, OR GLOBAL, CORPORATIONS

Multinational, or Global, Corporation
A firm that operates in an integrated fashion in a number of countries.

The term **multinational,** or **global, corporation** is used to describe a firm that operates in an integrated fashion in a number of countries. During the past 20 years, a new and fundamentally different form of international commercial activity has developed, and this has greatly increased worldwide economic and political interdependence. Rather than merely buying resources from and selling goods to foreign nations, multinational firms now make direct investments in fully integrated operations, from extraction of raw materials, through the manufacturing process, to distribution to consumers throughout the world. Today, multinational corporate networks control a large and growing share of the world's technological, marketing, and productive resources.

Companies, both U.S. and foreign, go "global" for six primary reasons:

1. *To broaden their markets.* After a company has saturated its home market, growth opportunities are often better in foreign markets. Thus, such homegrown firms as Coca-Cola and McDonald's are aggressively expanding into overseas markets, and foreign firms such as Sony and Toshiba now dominate the U.S. consumer electronics market. Also, as products become more complex, and development becomes more expensive, it is necessary to sell more units to cover overhead costs, so larger markets are critical. Thus, movie companies have "gone global" to get the volume necessary to support pictures such as *Titanic*.

2. *To seek raw materials.* Many U.S. oil companies, such as Exxon Mobil, have major subsidiaries around the world to ensure access to the basic resources needed to sustain the companies' primary business line.

3. *To seek new technology.* No single nation holds a commanding advantage in all technologies, so companies are scouring the globe for leading scientific and design ideas. For example, Xerox has introduced more than 80 different office copiers in the United States that were engineered and built by its Japanese joint venture, Fuji Xerox. Similarly, versions of the superconcentrated detergent that Procter & Gamble first formulated in Japan in response to a rival's product are now being marketed in Europe and the United States.

4. *To seek production efficiency.* Companies in high-cost countries are shifting production to low-cost regions. For example, GE has production and assembly plants in Mexico, South Korea, and Singapore, and even Japanese manufacturers are shifting some of their production to lower-cost countries in the Pacific Rim. BMW, in response to high production costs in Germany, has built assembly plants in the United States. The ability to shift production from country to country has important implications for labor costs in all countries. For example, when Xerox threatened to move its copier rebuilding work to Mexico, its union in Rochester agreed to work rule changes and productivity improvements that kept the operation in the United States. Some multinational companies make decisions almost daily on where to shift production. When Dow Chemical saw European demand for a certain solvent declining, the company scaled back production at a German plant and shifted its production to another chemical that had previously been imported from the United States. Relying on complex computer models for making such decisions, Dow runs its plants at peak capacity and thus keeps capital costs down.

5. *To avoid political and regulatory hurdles.* The primary reason Japanese auto companies moved production to the United States was to get around U.S. import quotas. Now Honda, Nissan, Toyota, Mazda, and Mitsubishi are all assembling vehicles in the United States. One of the factors that prompted U.S. pharmaceutical maker SmithKline and Britain's Beecham to merge was that they wanted to avoid licensing and regulatory delays in their largest markets, Western Europe and the United States. Now SmithKline Beecham can identify itself as an inside player in both Europe and the United States. Similarly, when Germany's BASF launched biotechnology research at home, it confronted legal and political challenges from the environmentally conscious Green movement. In response, BASF shifted its cancer and immune system research to two laboratories in Boston suburbs. This location is attractive not only because of its large number of engineers and scientists but also because the Boston area has resolved controversies involving safety, animal rights, and the environment. "We decided it would be better to have the laboratories located where we have fewer insecurities about what will happen in the future," said Rolf-Dieter Acker, BASF's director of biotechnology research.

6. *To diversify.* By establishing worldwide production facilities and markets, firms can cushion the impact of adverse economic trends in any single country. For example, General Motors softened the blow of poor sales in the United States during the 1990–1991 recession with strong sales by its European subsidiaries. In general, geographic diversification works because the economic ups and downs of different countries are not perfectly

FIGURE 16-1   **Direct Investment for the United States, 1982–1999**

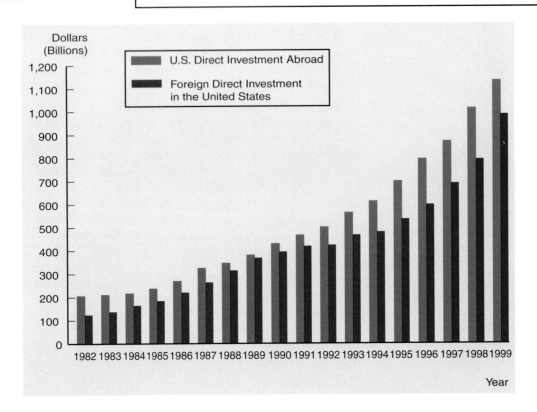

SOURCE: Sylvia E Bargas, "Direct Investment Positions for 1999, Country and Industry Detail," *Survey of Current Business,* July 2000, 57–68.

correlated. Therefore, companies investing overseas benefit from diversification in the same way that individuals benefit from investing in a broad portfolio of stocks.

Over the past 10 to 15 years, there has been an increasing amount of investment in the United States by foreign corporations, and in foreign nations by U.S. corporations. This trend is shown in Figure 16-1, and it is important because of its implications for eroding the traditional doctrine of independence and self-reliance that has been a hallmark of U.S. policy. Just as U.S. corporations with extensive overseas operations are said to use their economic power to exert substantial economic and political influence over host governments in many parts of the world, it is feared that foreign corporations are gaining similar sway over U.S. policy. These developments suggest an increasing degree of mutual influence and interdependence among business enterprises and nations, to which the United States is not immune.

The world economy is quite fluid. Here are a few of the recent events that have dramatically changed the international financial environment:

1. The disintegration of the former Soviet Union and the movement toward market economies in the newly formed countries have created a vast new market for international commerce.

2. The reunification of Germany, coupled with the collapse of communism in Eastern Europe, has created significant new opportunities for foreign investment.

3. The European Community and the European Free Trade Association have created a "borderless" region where people, capital, goods, and services move freely among the 19 nations without the burden of tariffs. This consolidation has led to the creation of a single "Eurocurrency" called the "Euro." (See the Global Perspectives box entitled, "The Euro: What You Need to Know.")

4. The North American Free Trade Agreement (NAFTA) has moved the economies of the United States, Canada, and Mexico much closer together, and made them more interdependent.

5. U.S. bank regulations have been loosened dramatically. One key deregulatory feature was the removal of interest rate ceilings, thus allowing banks to attract foreign deposits by raising rates. Another key feature was the removal of barriers to entry by foreign banks, which resulted in more cross-border banking transactions. Still, U.S. commercial and investment banks do not have as much freedom as foreign banks, which has led many U.S. banks to establish subsidiaries in Europe that can offer a wider range of services. All this has increased global competition in the financial services industry.

 The NAFTA (North American Free Trade Agreement) ensures that continued international investment will be made by U.S. corporations. An interesting report about the effect of NAFTA on the U.S. economy can be found on the United States Trade Representative's home page at **http://www.ustr.gov/naftareport/intro.htm**.

SELF-TEST QUESTIONS

What is a multinational corporation?

Why do companies "go global"?

MULTINATIONAL VERSUS DOMESTIC FINANCIAL MANAGEMENT

In theory, the concepts and procedures discussed in the first 15 chapters are valid for both domestic and multinational operations. However, six major factors distinguish financial management in firms operating entirely within a single country from firms that operate globally:

1. *Different currency denominations.* Cash flows in various parts of a multinational corporate system will be denominated in different currencies. Hence, an analysis of exchange rates must be included in all financial analyses.

GLOBAL PERSPECTIVES

THE EURO: WHAT YOU NEED TO KNOW

If you are puzzled about the details of European consolidation and what it means for investors, tourists, and companies doing business in Europe, then take a look at the following excerpt from an excellent article in The Wall Street Journal *that answers many of these questions. This article was written on January 4, 1999, the day the European consolidation went into effect. Note that since the date of this article, Greece has also joined the EMU.*

After 40 years of negotiating that began when European leaders signed the Treaty of Rome in 1957, EMU takes wing today. The 11 countries participating in economic and monetary union turned over control of their monetary policy to the new European Central Bank. Officially, the euro is now a currency. It can be used to buy, trade and sell.

It may at times seem arcane, but EMU is one of the greatest adventures Europe has ever embarked upon. Here's a cheat sheet on the euro, how it came to be, and what it means for Europe and for the U.S.:

Q. What is EMU?

A. It stands for economic and monetary union, the formal name for the system under which participating countries will share the same currency. It was debated for decades. Finally, in 1992, European Union countries signed the Maastricht Treaty, named after the town in the Netherlands where it was signed, that created the common currency and set up the criteria for countries to join.

Q. Why is Europe doing this?

A. Partly because it's one more step — albeit a giant one — in Europe's quest for closer political integration. But there are real economic reasons, too: A single currency is the logical consequence of a single European market, in which goods, people and services travel freely across national borders. A common currency eliminates exchange costs when you convert one European currency into another and eliminates the uncertainty associated with exchange-rate fluctuations.

Q. Why is the EMU considered to be so important?

A. Eleven sovereign nations have decided at once to do away with printing their own money, one of the most important prerogatives of a state, hand over their monetary policy to a supranational body and literally destroy their own currency. It means an end to the days when member European countries could devalue their currencies to gain competitiveness. And it makes Europe a force to be reckoned with on the world scene, even if it remains a collection of states, not a unified, federal state like the U.S.

Q. What will the common currency be called, and what's it worth?

A. The euro. It's worth $1.17 as of Jan. 1, but that's subject to the whims of the currency markets.

Q. When does it go into effect?

A. Technically, it began on Jan. 1. But practically, it starts today for paperless transactions. All cash transactions will continue to be in national currencies until Jan. 1, 2002, when euro bills and coins start circulating. Then, there will be a transition period of up to six months, when the euro will be used along with the national currencies.

Q. If euro notes and coins don't exist, what good is the currency?

A. Consumers and businesses can now open bank accounts, write checks and borrow money in euros. Travelers can buy euro travelers checks. Stocks and bonds will be quoted in euros.

Q. How do the euro-savvy refer to the bloc of 11 countries in the euro?

A. "Euroland" is the hottest. "Euro-zone" is common, but not as snappy.

Q. What happened this weekend?

A. The 11 euro countries locked in the exchange rates between their national currencies and the euro. The mark, the lira and the others will now trade at the same rate against the euro until they completely disappear in 2002. But the euro's value will vary day to day against the dollar and other non-member currencies in the exchange markets.

Q. Which countries are in EMU?

A. France and Germany, which together account for 55% of Euroland's output. Plus Italy, Spain and Portugal, the so-called Club Med countries, which squeaked in by the skins of their teeth. The other members are Finland, Ireland, Belgium, the Netherlands, Luxembourg, and Austria.

Q. What are the criteria for joining?

A. To be an EMU member, countries had to be a part of the European Union. They also had to meet five criteria:

1. Inflation during the year before joining couldn't exceed by more than 1.5 percentage points that of the three best-performing members.
2. Budget deficits must not exceed 3% of gross domestic product.

3. Government debt had to be about 60% of GDP or on a declining trend.

4. Long-term interest rates had to be within two percentage points of the three best-performing members.

5. Exchange rates had to be within the fluctuation margins provided by the European Monetary System.

Q. So who's not in EMU?

A. There are four remaining European Union countries that aren't in the single currency. Greece flunked all of the Maastricht criteria. Sweden, Britain and Denmark passed, but declined to join the party.

Q. Why would Britain not want to be in the single currency?

A. Many Brits don't trust the French or the Germans. They don't like the idea of linking their economic fate to a continent where they've lost so many lives at war. They fret about a further erosion of national sovereignty. And they really *hate* that their beloved queen would be banished from the euro's banknotes.

Q. So why do France and Germany want to be in the single currency?

A. Germany wants to make sure it never gets into another war with the rest of its neighbors. To prevent that, German leaders want to cement themselves to the continent economically, figuring it's harder to have conflict with countries when their economies are tied so tightly to your own. Helmet Kohl put it best. The single currency, he argued, "means the difference between peace and war."

France sees the euro as a way to dilute Germany's economic power and give itself a larger voice in European affairs.

The countries in the euro are also sick of playing second fiddle to America's dollar on world markets. They figure that by forming one monetary bloc, they'll have more clout than individually.

Q. What does the euro mean for America?

A. If Europe gets this right, Euroland will be a more nimble competitor, which could eventually cost jobs in the U.S. Europe has traditionally lagged behind the U.S. in privatization, deregulation and productivity. But now, partly to prepare for the euro, European countries and companies are streamlining to become more competitive.

And whatever happens to the euro will affect American exports abroad: If the euro is strong, this could help U.S. exports by making them seem cheaper on world markets than European goods; if the euro is weak, U.S. exports would be more expen-

sive, which could hurt the U.S. economy and further widen America's trade deficit.

But there's a silver lining: U.S. multinationals, already used to doing business in the vast U.S. market, are expected to do well in the new, continent-sized euro-zone.

Q. What's the impact on the dollar?

A. Some economists say the greenback's role as the world's most powerful currency is threatened by the euro. They argue that central banks and institutional investors will rebalance their portfolios by selling dollars and buying euros, which would weaken the dollar.

Q. What happens when I go to France on vacation?

A. Nothing much right now, although if you're that hot to use the new currency, you could get traveler's checks in euros. For the next three years, the euro will be used for paperless transactions. This means that if a boutique in Paris posts prices in euros, you may use your Visa card to pay for your Hermes scarf in euros. But you can't pay for it in cash in euros, because there won't be any euro bills or coins until 2002. In the meantime, banks in Euroland are required to let customers keep their accounts in either euros or the national currencies, and all interbank transfers will be done in euros.

Starting in 2002, you will have 10 years to get rid of your old francs, marks or lire by trading them in at the bank. After that, they're no longer valid.

And airline tickets will be priced in euros.

Q. Does this mean the days are over when it was cheaper to buy a round-trip Frankfurt–Paris–Frankfurt ticket than a Paris–Frankfurt–Paris ticket?

A. Well, those days are numbered. One of the big changes EMU will bring is price transparency in Europe. In the past, it was harder for European consumers to tell how much more expensive a bottle of aspirin was in Spain than in Belgium, because that aspirin was priced in both pesetas and Belgian francs. But with one currency that will change. A euro in Spain will be equal to a euro in Belgium, which should, the theory goes, prod companies toward more uniform pricing.

Q. What happens if I own a stock or bond in a European currency?

A. Stocks and bonds will be automatically redenominated in euros as of today, and their prices will now be listed in euros. European government-bond yields may vary slightly from country to country, depending on the perceived credit standing of the issuer.

(box continues)

Q. Who's going to manage the whole thing?

A. The European Central Bank, which will be based in Frankfurt. The ECB will set interest rates for Euroland and manage the monetary policies for the 11 countries. The ECB, Euroland's equivalent to America's Federal Reserve, has a tough job ahead of it. It must choose the right policy course for Europe's slowing economic growth. It must make sure Euroland governments adhere to agreed-on fiscal policy limits. It's got to win the public's confidence. And, perhaps most important, the ECB must guard its political independence from Euroland national governments who might try to use monetary policy to spur their own economies. The ECB also has to carry out foreign-exchange operations, manage the official reserves of Euroland, and promote the smooth operation of the payment systems.

Q. Who's going to head the ECB?

A. Wim Duisenberg, the former Dutch finance minister and head of the Dutch Central Bank, who comes from the same anti-inflation school as Hans Tietmeyer, the head of Germany's Bundesbank. That's probably a good thing, because the ECB has been modeled after the Bundesbank, which will stay in business but only have one representative participating in ECB interest-rate decisions.

Q. What's the biggest challenge facing the new single currency?

A. Unemployment. European countries have notoriously higher jobless rates than America, and Euroland is no exception: the projected 1998 unemployment rate for the 11 countries is 11.8%. While EMU shouldn't worsen unemployment in Europe, most economists don't think it will relieve unemployment, at least not in the short term, unless it contributes quickly to growth. But political pressure is building to use monetary policy to spur economic growth, and a high jobless rate will only increase that pressure.

What's more, Euroland has less labor-market flexibility than America. Americans in an economically sagging region routinely pack up and move to more prosperous parts of the country. Legally, Europeans from one European Union country can work in any other EU state. But inconsistent application of the law, along with general confusion and language differences, make it more difficult for people to leave home. Without labor mobility as an agent to counter unemployment, the euro could run into trouble.

Q. Can any of the Euroland countries bail out of EMU? Can they get kicked out?

A. Yes, and no. Remember, national governments joining EMU are surrendering control over their monetary policy to the ECB. If things don't go well, they could be pressured by domestic political forces at home to pull out so that they can once again use their monetary policy to try to fix their economy, though the complexity of such a move would be huge. And, while countries don't get booted if their fiscal policies don't stick to the Maastricht criterion, they can be fined under the so-called Growth and Stability Pact.

Q. What's the best way to remember who's in EMU?

A. Try following this guide now popular in the British newspapers.

The key to remember: **BAFFLING SIP:**

B — Belgium	S — Spain
A — Austria	I — Ireland
F — Finland	P — Portugal
F — France	
L — Luxembourg	
I — Italy	
N — Netherlands	
G — Germany	

SOURCE: Helene Cooper, "Europe Unites: The Launch of the Euro, The Euro: What You Need to Know," *The Wall Street Journal*, January 4, 1999, A5.

Who's in, Who's out of Europe's Currency

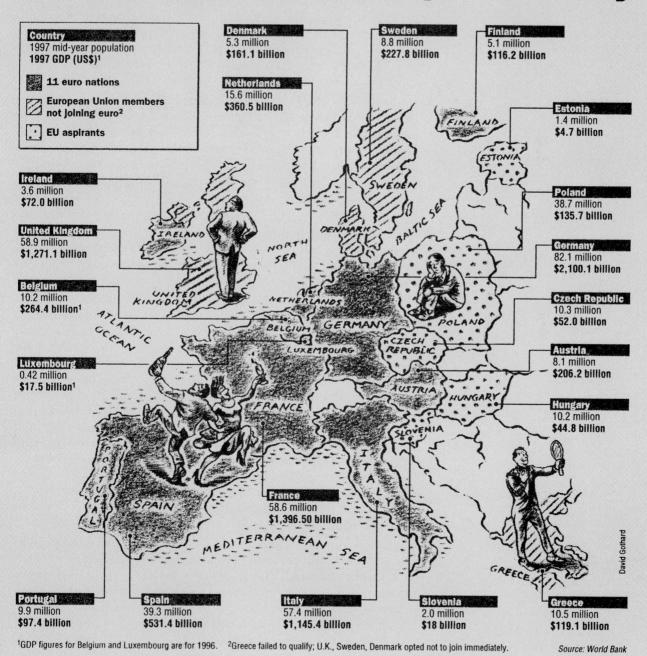

Country
1997 mid-year population
1997 GDP (US$)[1]

▨ 11 euro nations

▧ European Union members
not joining euro[2]

▫ EU aspirants

Denmark
5.3 million
$161.1 billion

Sweden
8.8 million
$227.8 billion

Finland
5.1 million
$116.2 billion

Netherlands
15.6 million
$360.5 billion

Estonia
1.4 million
$4.7 billion

Ireland
3.6 million
$72.0 billion

Poland
38.7 million
$135.7 billion

United Kingdom
58.9 million
$1,271.1 billion

Germany
82.1 million
$2,100.1 billion

Belgium
10.2 million
$264.4 billion[1]

Czech Republic
10.3 million
$52.0 billion

Luxembourg
0.42 million
$17.5 billion[1]

Austria
8.1 million
$206.2 billion

Hungary
10.2 million
$44.8 billion

France
58.6 million
$1,396.50 billion

Portugal
9.9 million
$97.4 billion

Spain
39.3 million
$531.4 billion

Italy
57.4 million
$1,145.4 billion

Slovenia
2.0 million
$18 billion

Greece
10.5 million
$119.1 billion

David Gothard

[1]GDP figures for Belgium and Luxembourg are for 1996.   [2]Greece failed to qualify; U.K., Sweden, Denmark opted not to join immediately.

Source: World Bank

Note: On January 1, 2001, Greece was admitted to the EMU.

2. *Economic and legal ramifications.* Each country has its own unique economic and legal systems, and these differences can cause significant problems when a corporation tries to coordinate and control its worldwide operations. For example, differences in tax laws among countries can cause a given economic transaction to have strikingly different after-tax consequences, depending on where the transaction occurs. Similarly, differences in legal systems of host nations, such as the Common Law of Great Britain versus the French Civil Law, complicate matters ranging from the simple recording of business transactions to the role played by the judiciary in resolving conflicts. Such differences can restrict multinational corporations' flexibility in deploying resources, and can even make procedures that are required in one part of the company illegal in another part. These differences also make it difficult for executives trained in one country to move easily to another.

3. *Language differences.* The ability to communicate is critical in all business transactions, and here U.S. citizens are often at a disadvantage because we are generally fluent only in English, while European and Japanese businesspeople are usually fluent in several languages, including English. Thus, they can invade our markets more easily than we can penetrate theirs.

4. *Cultural differences.* Even within geographic regions that are considered relatively homogeneous, different countries have unique cultural heritages that shape values and influence the conduct of business. Multinational corporations find that matters such as defining the appropriate goals of the firm, attitudes toward risk, dealings with employees, and the ability to curtail unprofitable operations vary dramatically from one country to the next.

5. *Role of governments.* Most financial models assume the existence of a competitive marketplace in which the terms of trade are determined by the participants. The government, through its power to establish basic ground rules, is involved in the process, but its role is minimal. Thus, the market provides the primary barometer of success, and it gives the best clues about what must be done to remain competitive. This view of the process is reasonably correct for the United States and Western Europe, but it does not accurately describe the situation in most of the world. Frequently, the terms under which companies compete, the actions that must be taken or avoided, and the terms of trade on various transactions are determined not in the marketplace but by direct negotiation between the host government and the multinational corporation. This is essentially a political process, and it must be treated as such. Thus, our traditional financial models have to be recast to include political and other noneconomic aspects of the decision.

6. *Political risk.* A nation is free to place constraints on the transfer of corporate resources and even to expropriate without compensation assets within their boundaries. This is *political risk*, and it tends to be largely a given rather than a variable that can be changed by negotiation. Political risk varies from country to country, and it must be addressed explicitly in any financial analysis. Another aspect of political risk is terrorism against U.S. firms or executives. For example, U.S. and Japanese executives have been kidnapped and held for ransom in several South American countries.

These six factors complicate financial management, and they increase the risks faced by multinational firms. However, the prospects for high returns, diversification benefits, and other factors make it worthwhile for firms to accept these risks and learn how to manage them.

SELF-TEST QUESTION

Identify and briefly discuss six major factors that complicate financial management in multinational firms.

EXCHANGE RATES

Exchange Rate
The number of units of a given currency that can be purchased for one unit of another currency.

The Bloomberg World Currency Values site provides up-to-the-minute foreign currency values versus the U.S. dollar, as well as a cross-currency table similar to that found in *The Wall Street Journal* for the world's major currencies. The site can be accessed at **http://www.bloomberg.com/markets/fxc.html.**

An **exchange rate** specifies the number of units of a given currency that can be purchased with one unit of another currency. Exchange rates appear in the financial sections of newspapers each day. Selected rates from *The Wall Street Journal* are given in Table 16-1. The values shown in Column 1 are the number of U.S. dollars required to purchase one unit of foreign currency; this is called a *direct quotation*. Direct quotations have a dollar sign in their quotation. Thus, the direct U.S. dollar quotation for the German mark is $0.4559, because one German mark could be bought for 45.59 cents. The exchange rates given in Column 2 represent the number of units of foreign currency that can be purchased for one U.S. dollar; these are called *indirect quotations*. Indirect quotations often begin with the foreign currency's equivalent to the dollar sign. Thus, the indirect quotation for the German mark is M2.1934. (The "M" stands for *Mark*, and it is equivalent to the symbol "$.") Normal practice in the United States is to use indirect quotations (Column 2) for all currencies other than British pounds, for which direct quotations are given. Thus, we speak of the pound as "selling at $1.44" but of the mark as "being at 2.19."

It is also a universal convention on the world's foreign currency exchanges to state all exchange rates except British pounds on a "dollar basis" — that is, as the foreign currency price of one U.S. dollar as reported in Column 2 of Table 16-1. Thus, in all currency trading centers, whether in New York, Frankfurt, London, Tokyo, or anywhere else, the exchange rate for the German mark would be displayed as M2.1934. This convention eliminates confusion when comparing quotations from one trading center with those from another.

We can use the data in Table 16-1 to show how one works with exchange rates. Suppose a U.S. tourist on holiday flies from New York to London, then to Paris, then on to Munich, and finally back to New York. When she arrives at London's Heathrow Airport, she goes to the bank to check the foreign exchange listing. The rate she observes for U.S. dollars is $1.4428; this means that £1 will cost her $1.4428. Assume that she exchanges $2,000 for $2,000/$1.4428 = £1,386.19 and enjoys a week's vacation in London, spending £786.19 while there and saving £600.

At the end of the week she travels to Dover to catch the Hovercraft to Calais on the coast of France and realizes that she needs to exchange her 600 remaining

TABLE 16-1 **Illustrative Exchange Rates**

	DIRECT QUOTATION: U.S. DOLLARS REQUIRED TO BUY ONE UNIT OF FOREIGN CURRENCY (1)	INDIRECT QUOTATION: NUMBER OF UNITS OF FOREIGN CURRENCY PER U.S. DOLLAR (2)
British pound	$1.4428	0.6931
Canadian dollar	0.6540	1.5291
Denmark krone	0.1196	8.3601
Dutch guilder	0.4046	2.4714
Euro	0.8917	1.1215
French franc	0.1359	7.3563
German mark	0.4559	2.1934
Italian lira	0.0004605	2,171.44
Japanese yen	0.009064	110.33
Mexican peso	0.1061	9.4220
Spanish peseta	0.005359	186.59
Swedish krona	0.1044	9.5810
Swiss franc	0.5883	1.6999

NOTE: Column 2 equals 1.0 divided by Column 1. However, rounding differences do occur.
SOURCE: *The Wall Street Journal,* December 7, 2000, C24.

British pounds for French francs. However, what she sees on the board is the direct quotation between pounds and dollars ($1.4428) and the indirect quotation between francs and dollars (FF7.3563). (For our purposes, we assume that the exchange rates in effect at the start of the trip remain in effect throughout our example. This is unrealistic for reasons explained later in this chapter.) The exchange rate between any two currencies is called a *cross rate*. Cross rates are actually calculated on the basis of various currencies relative to the U.S. dollar. For example, the cross rate between British pounds and French francs is computed as follows:

$$\text{Cross rate} = \frac{\text{Dollars}}{\text{Pound}} \times \frac{\text{Francs}}{\text{Dollar}} = \frac{\text{Francs}}{\text{Pound}}$$

$$= 1.4428 \text{ dollars per pound} \times 7.3563 \text{ francs per dollar}$$

$$= 10.6137 \text{ francs per pound.}$$

Therefore, for every British pound she would receive 10.6137 French francs, so she would receive $10.6137 \times 600 = 6,368.22 \approx 6,368$ francs.

When she finishes touring in France and arrives in Germany, she again needs to determine a cross rate, this time between French francs and German marks. The dollar-basis quotes she sees, as shown in Table 16-1, are FF7.3563 per dollar and M2.1934 per dollar. To find the cross rate, she must divide the two dollar-basis rates:

$$\text{Cross rate} = \frac{\dfrac{\text{Marks}}{\text{Dollar}}}{\dfrac{\text{Francs}}{\text{Dollar}}} = \frac{\text{Marks}}{\text{Franc}}$$

$$= \frac{\text{M2.1934 per \$}}{\text{FF7.3563 per \$}} = 0.2982 \text{ marks per franc.}$$

Then, if she had FF3,000 remaining, she could exchange them for 0.2982 × 3,000 = M894.60, or about 895 marks.

Finally, when her vacation ends and she returns to New York, the quotation she sees is M2.1934, which tells her that she can buy 2.1934 marks for a dollar. She now holds 50 marks, so she wants to know how many U.S. dollars she will receive for her marks. First, she must find the reciprocal of the quoted indirect rate,

$$\frac{1}{\text{M2.1934}} = \$0.4559,$$

which is the direct quote shown in Table 16-1, Column 1. Then she will end up with

$$\$0.4559 \times 50 = \$22.80.$$

In this example, we made three very strong and generally incorrect assumptions. First, we assumed that our traveler had to calculate all the cross rates. For retail transactions, it is customary to display the cross rates directly instead of a series of dollar rates. Second, we assumed that exchange rates remain constant over time. Actually, exchange rates vary every day, often dramatically. We will have more to say about exchange rate fluctuations in the next section. Finally, we assumed that there were no transactions costs involved in exchanging currencies. In reality, small retail exchange transactions such as those in our example usually involve fixed and/or sliding scale fees that can easily consume 5 or more percent of the transaction amount. However, credit card purchases minimize these fees.

Major business publications such as *The Wall Street Journal* regularly report cross rates among key currencies. A set of cross rates is given in Table 16-2. When examining the table, note the following points:

1. Column 1 gives indirect quotes for dollars, that is, units of a foreign currency that can be bought with one U.S. dollar. Examples: $1 will buy 7.3563 French francs or 2.1934 German marks. Note the consistency with Table 16-1, Column 2.

2. Other columns show number of units of other currencies that can be bought with one pound, one Swiss franc, etc. For example, the D-mark column shows that 1 D-mark will buy 0.69714 Canadian dollar, 3.3538 French francs, or 0.45591 U.S. dollar.

3. The rows show direct quotes, that is, number of units of the currency of the country listed in the left column required to buy one unit of the currency listed in the top row. The bottom row is particularly interesting, as it shows the direct quotes for the U.S. dollar. This row is consistent with Column 1 of Table 16-1. Note too that the values on the bottom row are reciprocals of the values in Column 1. Thus, in Column 1 of the United

TABLE 16-2   Key Currency Cross Rates

	DOLLAR	EURO	POUND	SFRANC	GUILDER	PESO	YEN	LIRA	D-MARK	FFRANC	CDNDLR
Canada	1.5291	1.3635	2.2062	0.8995	.61872	.16229	.01386	.00070	.69714	.20786	—
France	7.3563	6.5596	10.6137	4.3275	2.9766	.78076	.06668	.00339	3.3538	—	4.8109
Germany	2.1934	1.9559	3.1646	1.2903	.88751	.23280	.01988	.00101	—	.29817	1.4344
Italy	2171.4	1936.3	3133.0	1277.4	878.63	230.47	19.681	—	990.00	295.18	1420.1
Japan	110.33	98.38	159.18	64.904	44.643	11.710	—	.05081	50.301	14.998	72.154
Mexico	9.4220	8.4016	13.594	5.5427	3.8124	—	.08540	.00434	4.2956	1.2808	6.1618
Netherlands	2.4714	2.2037	3.5657	1.4539	—	.26230	.02240	.00114	1.1267	.33596	1.6162
Switzerland	1.6999	1.5158	2.4526	—	.68783	.18042	.01541	.00078	.77501	.23108	1.1117
United Kingdom	.69310	.6180	—	.4077	.28045	.07356	.00628	.00032	.31599	.09422	.45327
Euro	1.12150	—	1.6180	.65972	.45377	.11902	.01016	.00052	.51129	.15245	.73341
United States	—	.8917	1.4428	.58827	.40463	.10613	.00906	.00046	.45591	.13594	.65398

SOURCE: "Key Currency Cross Rates," *The Wall Street Journal,* December 7, 2000, C24.

Kingdom row, £0.69310 is equivalent to $1, so the reciprocal, 1/0.69310 = 1.4428, is shown in the last row (for the United States) under the pound column. In other words, one pound is worth $1.4428.

4. Now notice, by reading down the FFranc column, that one French franc was worth 0.29817 ≈ 0.2982 German mark. This is the same cross rate that we calculated for the U.S. tourist in our example.

The tie-in with the dollar ensures that all currencies are related to one another in a consistent manner. If this consistency did not exist, currency traders could profit by buying undervalued and selling overvalued currencies. This process, known as *arbitrage*, works to bring about an equilibrium wherein the same relationship described earlier would exist. Currency traders are constantly operating in the market, seeking small inconsistencies from which they can profit. The traders' existence enables the rest of us to assume that currency markets are in equilibrium and that, at any point in time cross rates are all internally consistent.

As a final point, you should recognize that the consolidation of the European market has had a profound impact on European exchange rates. The exchange rates for the currencies of each of the participating countries are now fixed relative to the **euro.** Consequently, the cross-exchange rates between the various participating currencies are also fixed. Note, however, that the value of the euro continues to fluctuate. Therefore, if the euro strengthens relative to the U.S. dollar, the value of the German mark and the French franc (and all other EMU countries' currencies) will also strengthen relative to the dollar. However, because the mark and the franc are fixed relative to the euro, each of the currencies will increase by the same proportion and the cross-exchange rate between the mark and the franc will remain constant. Recall that these individual currencies are scheduled to disappear after 2002, at which time the euro will be the sole currency for each of the participating countries. (See the Global Perspectives box, "The Euro: What You Need to Know.")

Euro

The official currency of the 12 countries participating in the EMU, the economic and monetary union. The exchange rates for the national currencies of each of the participating countries are fixed relative to the euro.

What is an exchange rate?

Explain the difference between direct and indirect quotations.

What is a cross rate?

THE INTERNATIONAL MONETARY SYSTEM

Every nation has a monetary system and a monetary authority. In the United States, the Federal Reserve is our monetary authority, and its task is to hold down inflation while promoting economic growth and raising our national standard of living. Moreover, if countries are to trade with one another, we must have some sort of system designed to facilitate payments between nations.

Fixed Exchange Rate System
The world monetary system in existence after World War II until 1971, under which the value of the U.S. dollar was tied to gold, and values of other currencies were pegged to the U.S. dollar.

From the end of World War II until August 1971, the world was on a **fixed exchange rate system** administered by the International Monetary Fund (IMF). Under this system, the U.S. dollar was linked to gold ($35 per ounce), and other currencies were then tied to the dollar. Exchange rates between other currencies and the dollar were controlled within narrow limits but then adjusted periodically. For example, in 1964 the British pound was adjusted to $2.80 for £1, with a 1 percent permissible fluctuation about this rate.

Fluctuations in exchange rates occur because of changes in the supply of and demand for dollars, pounds, and other currencies. These supply and demand changes have two primary sources. First, changes in the demand for currencies depend on changes in imports and exports of goods and services. For example, U.S. importers must buy British pounds to pay for British goods, whereas British importers must buy U.S. dollars to pay for U.S. goods. If U.S. imports from Great Britain exceeded U.S. exports to Great Britain, there would be a greater demand for pounds than for dollars, and this would drive up the price of the pound relative to that of the dollar. In terms of Table 16-1, the dollar cost of a pound might rise from $1.4428 to $2.0000. The U.S. dollar would be said to be *depreciating*, because a dollar would now be worth fewer pounds, whereas the pound would be *appreciating*. In this example, the root cause of the change would be the U.S. **trade deficit** with Great Britain. Of course, if U.S. exports to Great Britain were greater than U.S. imports from Great Britain, Great Britain would have a trade deficit with the United States.[1]

Trade Deficit
A situation in which a country imports more than it exports.

Changes in the demand for a currency, and the resulting exchange rate fluctuations, also depend on capital movements. For example, suppose interest rates in Great Britain were higher than those in the United States. To take advantage of the high British interest rates, U.S. banks, corporations, and even

---

[1] If the dollar value of the pound moved up from $1.44 to $2.00, this increase in the value of the pound would mean that British goods would now be more expensive in the United States. For example, a box of candy costing £1 in England would rise in price in the United States from about $1.44 to $2.00. Conversely, U.S. goods would become cheaper in England. For example, the British could now buy goods worth $2.00 for £1, whereas before the exchange rate change £1 would buy merchandise worth only $1.44. These price changes would, of course, tend to *reduce* British exports and *increase* imports, and this, in turn, would lower the exchange rate, because people in the United States would be buying fewer pounds to pay for English goods.

sophisticated individuals would buy pounds with dollars and then use those pounds to purchase high-yielding British securities. This buying of pounds would tend to drive up their price.[2]

Before August 1971, exchange rate fluctuations were kept within a narrow 1 percent limit by regular intervention of the British government in the market. When the value of the pound was falling, the Bank of England would step in and buy pounds to push up their price, offering gold or foreign currencies in exchange. Conversely, when the pound rate was too high, the Bank of England would sell pounds. The central banks of other countries operated similarly.

Devaluations and **revaluations** occurred only rarely before 1971. They were usually accompanied by severe international financial repercussions, partly because nations tended to postpone needed measures until economic pressures had built up to explosive proportions. For this and other reasons, the old international monetary system came to a dramatic end in the early 1970s, when the U.S. dollar, the foundation upon which all other currencies were anchored, was cut loose from the gold standard and, in effect, allowed to "float."

The United States and other major trading nations currently operate under a system of **floating exchange rates,** whereby currency prices are allowed to seek their own levels without much governmental intervention. However, the central bank of each country does intervene to some extent buying and selling its currency to smooth out exchange rate fluctuations.

Each central bank would like to keep its average exchange rate at a level deemed desirable by its government's economic policy. This is important, because exchange rates have a profound effect on the levels of imports and exports, which influence the level of domestic employment. For example, if a country is having a problem with unemployment, its central bank might try to lower interest rates, which would cause capital to flee the country to find higher rates, which would lead to the sale of the currency, which would cause a *decline* in the value of the currency. This would cause its goods to be cheaper in world markets and thus stimulate exports, production, and domestic employment. Conversely, the central bank of a country that is operating at full capacity and experiencing inflation might try to raise the value of its currency to reduce exports and increase imports. Under the current floating rate system, however, such intervention can affect the situation only temporarily, because market forces will prevail in the long run. In the case of the euro, each of the EMU currencies is fixed relative to the euro; however, the value of the euro still fluctuates. The 12 EMU countries have turned over control of their monetary policy to the new European Central Bank. Beginning in 2002, the national cur-

Devaluation

The process of officially *reducing* the value of a country's currency relative to other currencies.

Revaluation

The process of officially *increasing* the value of a country's currency relative to other currencies.

Floating Exchange Rates

A system under which exchange rates are not fixed by government policy but are allowed to float up or down in accordance with supply and demand.

---

[2] Such capital inflows would also tend to drive down British interest rates. If British rates were high in the first place because of efforts by the British monetary authorities to curb inflation, these international currency flows would tend to thwart that effort. This is one of the reasons domestic and international economies are so closely linked.

A good example of this occurred during the summer of 1981. In an effort to curb inflation, the Federal Reserve Board helped push U.S. interest rates to record levels. This, in turn, caused a flow of capital from European nations to the United States. The Europeans were suffering from a severe recession and wanted to keep interest rates down in order to stimulate investment, but U.S. policy made this difficult because of international capital flows. Just the opposite occurred in 1992, when the Fed drove short-term rates down to record lows in the United States to promote growth, while Germany and most other European countries pushed their rates higher to combat the inflationary pressures of reunification. Thus, investment in the United States was dampened as investors moved their money overseas to capture higher interest rates.

rencies of the countries in the EMU will be phased out, and only the euro will exist.

Exchange rate fluctuations can have a profound impact on international monetary transactions. For example, in 1985 it cost Honda Motors 2,380,000 yen to build a particular model in Japan and ship it to the United States. The model carried a U.S. sticker price of $12,000. Since the $12,000 sales price was the equivalent of (238 yen per dollar)($12,000) = 2,856,000 yen, which was 20 percent above the 2,380,000 yen cost, the automaker had built a 20 percent markup into the U.S. sales price. However, three years later the dollar had depreciated to 128 yen. Now if the model still sold for $12,000, the yen return to Honda would be only (128 yen per dollar)($12,000) = 1,536,000 yen, and the automaker would be losing about 35 percent on each auto sold. Therefore, the depreciation of the dollar against the yen turned a healthy profit into a huge loss. In fact, for Honda to maintain its 20 percent markup, the model would have to sell in the United States for 2,856,000 yen/128 yen per dollar = $22,312.50. This situation, which grew even worse, led Honda to build its most popular model, the Accord, in Marysville, Ohio.

The inherent volatility of exchange rates under a floating system increases the uncertainty of the cash flows for a multinational corporation. Because these cash flows are generated in many parts of the world, they are denominated in many different currencies. Since exchange rates can change, the dollar-equivalent value of a company's consolidated cash flows can also fluctuate. For example, Toyota estimates that each one-yen drop in the dollar reduces the company's annual net income by about 10 billion yen. This is known as *exchange rate risk*, and it is a major factor differentiating a global company from a purely domestic one.

Concerns about exchange rate risk have led to attempts to stabilize currency movements. Indeed, this concern was one of the motivating factors behind the European consolidation. As we indicated above, each participating country's currency is now pegged relative to the euro. Countries with **pegged exchange rates** establish a fixed exchange rate with some major currency, and then the values of the pegged currencies move together over time. Other countries have chosen to peg their currency to the U.S. dollar. For example, Kuwait pegs its currency to a composite of currencies that roughly represents the mix of currencies used by its trading partners to purchase its oil. In other instances, currencies are pegged because of traditional ties — for example, Chad, a former French colony, still pegs its currency to the French franc.[3]

Before closing our discussion of the international monetary system, we should note that not all currencies are **convertible**. A currency is convertible when the nation that issued it allows it to be traded in the currency markets and is willing to redeem it at market rates. This means that, except for limited central bank influence, the issuing government loses control over the value of its currency. However, a lack of convertibility creates major problems for international trade. For example, consider the situation faced by Pepsico when it wanted to open a chain of Pizza Hut restaurants in the former Soviet Union. The Russian ruble is not convertible, so Pepsico could not take the profits from its restaurants out of the Soviet Union in the form of dollars. There was no

Pegged Exchange Rate
Occurs when a country establishes a fixed exchange rate with another major currency; consequently, values of pegged currencies move together over time.

Convertible Currency
A currency that may be readily exchanged for other currencies.

---

[3] The International Monetary Fund reports each year a full listing of exchange rate arrangements in its *International Financial Statistics*.

mechanism to exchange the rubles it earned in Russia for dollars, so the investment in the Soviet Union was essentially worthless to the U.S. parent. However, Pepsico arranged to use the ruble profit from the restaurants to buy Russian vodka, which it then shipped to the United States and sold for dollars. Pepsico managed to work things out, but lack of convertibility significantly inhibits the ability of a country to attract foreign investment.

Current currency futures prices are available directly from the Chicago Mercantile Exchange (CME) on their web site at **http://www.cme.com/market/prices/currencies.html**. The quotes are updated every 10 minutes throughout the trading session. Updated currency spot and forward rates (from 1 to 12 months) are also provided by the Bank of Montreal Treasury Group at **http://www.bmo.com/economic/regular/fxrates.html**.

TRADING IN FOREIGN EXCHANGE

Importers, exporters, tourists, and governments buy and sell currencies in the foreign exchange market. For example, when a U.S. trader imports automobiles from Japan, payment will probably be made in Japanese yen. The importer buys yen (through its bank) in the foreign exchange market, much as one buys common stocks on the New York Stock Exchange or pork bellies on the Chicago Mercantile Exchange. However, whereas stock and commodity exchanges have organized trading floors, the foreign exchange market consists of a network of brokers and banks based in New York, London, Tokyo, and other financial centers. Most buy and sell orders are conducted by computer and telephone.[4]

SPOT RATES AND FORWARD RATES

Spot Rate
The effective exchange rate for a foreign currency for delivery on (approximately) the current day.

Forward Exchange Rate
An agreed-upon price at which two currencies will be exchanged at some future date.

The exchange rates shown earlier in Tables 16-1 and 16-2 are known as **spot rates,** which means the rate paid for delivery of the currency "on the spot" or, in reality, no more than two days after the day of the trade. For most of the world's major currencies, it is also possible to buy (or sell) currencies for delivery at some agreed-upon future date, usually 30, 90, or 180 days from the day the transaction is negotiated. This rate is known as the **forward exchange rate.**

For example, suppose a U.S. firm must pay 500 million yen to a Japanese firm in 30 days, and the current spot rate is 110.33 yen per dollar. Unless spot rates change, the U.S. firm will pay the Japanese firm the equivalent of $4.53 million (500 million yen divided by 110.33 yen per dollar) in 30 days. But if the spot rate falls to 100 yen per dollar, for example, the U.S. firm will have to pay the equivalent of $5 million. The treasurer of the U.S. firm can avoid this risk by entering

---

[4] For a more detailed explanation of exchange rate determination and operations of the foreign exchange market, see Mark Eaker, Frank Fabozzi, and Dwight Grant, *International Corporate Finance* (Fort Worth, TX: The Dryden Press, 1996).

TABLE 16-3

Selected Spot and Forward Exchange Rates
(Number of Units of Foreign Currency per U.S. Dollar)

		FORWARD RATES			
	SPOT RATE	30 DAYS	90 DAYS	180 DAYS	FORWARD RATE AT A PREMIUM OR DISCOUNT
British pound	0.6931	0.6926	0.6919	0.6910	Premium
Japanese yen	110.33	109.75	108.72	107.16	Premium
German mark	2.1934	2.1901	2.1846	2.1769	Premium

NOTES:

a. These are representative quotes as provided by a sample of New York banks. Forward rates for other currencies and for other lengths of time can often be negotiated.

b. When it takes more units of a foreign currency to buy one dollar in the future, the value of the foreign currency is less in the forward market than in the spot market, hence the forward rate is at a *discount* to the spot rate. Likewise, when it takes less units of a foreign currency to buy one dollar in the future, the value of the foreign currency is more in the forward market than in the spot market, hence the forward rate is at a premium to the spot rate.

SOURCE: *The Wall Street Journal,* December 7, 2000, C24.

into a 30-day forward exchange contract. This contract promises delivery of yen to the U.S. firm in 30 days at a guaranteed price of 109.75 yen per dollar. No cash changes hands at the time the treasurer signs the forward contract, although the U.S. firm might have to put some collateral down as a guarantee against default. Because the firm can use an interest-bearing instrument for the collateral, though, this requirement is not costly. The counterparty to the forward contract must deliver the yen to the U.S. firm in 30 days, and the U.S. firm is obligated to purchase the 500 million yen at the previously agreed-upon rate of 109.75 yen per dollar. Therefore, the treasurer of the U.S. firm is able to lock in a payment equivalent to $4.56 million, no matter what happens to spot rates. This technique, which is called "hedging," is discussed in more detail in Brigham and Houston's, *Fundamentals of Financial Management,* 9th edition, Chapter 18.

Forward rates for 30-, 90-, and 180-day delivery, along with the current spot rates for some commonly traded currencies, are given in Table 16-3. If one can obtain *more* of the foreign currency for a dollar in the forward than in the spot market, the forward currency is less valuable than the spot currency, and the forward currency is said to be selling at a **discount.** Conversely, if one can obtain *less* of the foreign currency for a dollar in the forward than in the spot market, the forward currency is more valuable than the spot currency, and the forward currency is said to be selling at a **premium.** Thus, because a dollar would buy *fewer* pounds, yen, and marks in the forward than in the spot market, the forward pounds, yen, and marks are selling at a premium.

Discount on Forward Rate
The situation when the spot rate is less than the forward rate.

Premium on Forward Rate
The situation when the spot rate is greater than the forward rate.

SELF-TEST QUESTIONS

Differentiate between spot and forward exchange rates.

Explain what it means for a forward currency to sell at a discount and at a premium.

INTEREST RATE PARITY

Interest Rate Parity
Specifies that investors should expect to earn the same return in all countries after adjusting for risk.

Market forces determine whether a currency sells at a forward premium or discount, and the general relationship between spot and forward exchange rates is specified by a concept called "interest rate parity."

Interest rate parity holds that investors should earn the same return on security investments in all countries after adjusting for risk. It recognizes that when you invest in a country other than your home country, you are affected by two forces — returns on the investment itself and changes in the exchange rate. It follows that your overall return will be higher than the investment's stated return if the currency in which your investment is denominated appreciates relative to your home currency. Likewise, your overall return will be lower if the foreign currency you receive declines in value.

Interest rate parity is expressed as follows:

$$\frac{\text{Forward exchange rate}}{\text{Spot exchange rate}} = \frac{(1 + k_h)}{(1 + k_f)}.$$

Here both the forward and spot rates are expressed in terms of the amount of home currency received per unit of foreign currency, and k_h and k_f are the periodic interest rates in the home country and the foreign country, respectively. If this relationship does not hold, then currency traders will buy and sell currencies — that is, engage in arbitrage — until it does hold.

To illustrate interest rate parity, consider the case of a U.S. investor who can buy default-free 90-day German bonds that promise a 4 percent nominal return. The 90-day interest rate, k_f, is 4%/4 = 1% because 90 days is 1/4 of a 360-day year. Assume also that the spot exchange rate is $0.4559, which means that you can exchange 0.4559 dollar for one mark, or 2.1934 marks per dollar. Finally, assume that the 90-day forward exchange rate is $0.4577, which means that you can exchange one mark for 0.4577 dollar, or receive 2.1846 marks per dollar exchanged, 90 days from now.

The U.S. investor can receive a 4 percent annualized return denominated in marks, but if he or she ultimately wants to consume goods in the United States, those marks must be converted to dollars. The dollar return on the investment depends, therefore, on what happens to exchange rates over the next three months. However, the investor can lock in the dollar return by selling the foreign currency in the forward market. For example, the investor could simultaneously

■ Convert $1,000 to 2,193.4 marks in the spot market.

■ Invest the 2,193.4 marks in 90-day German bonds that have a 4 percent annualized return or a 1 percent quarterly return, hence will pay (2,193.4)(1.01) = 2,215.33 marks in 90 days.

■ Agree today to exchange these 2,215.33 marks 90 days from now at the 90-day forward exchange rate of 2.1846 marks per dollar, or for a total of $1,014.07.

This investment, therefore, has an expected 90-day return of $14.07/$1,000 = 1.41%, which translates into a nominal return of 4(1.41%) = 5.64%. In this case, 4 percent of the expected 5.64 percent return is coming from the bond itself, and 1.64 percent arises because the market believes the mark will strengthen relative to the dollar. Note that by locking in the forward rate today, the investor has eliminated any exchange rate risk. And, since the German bond is assumed to be default-free, the investor is assured of earning a 5.64 percent dollar return.

Interest rate parity implies that an investment in the United States with the same risk as a German bond should have a return of 5.64 percent. Solving for k_h in the parity equation, we indeed find that the predicted interest rate in the United States is 5.64 percent.

Interest rate parity shows why a particular currency might be at a forward premium or discount. Note that a currency is at a forward premium whenever domestic interest rates are higher than foreign interest rates. Discounts prevail if domestic interest rates are lower than foreign interest rates. If these conditions do not hold, then arbitrage will soon force interest rates back to parity.

SELF-TEST QUESTION

Briefly explain interest rate parity, illustrating it with an example.

PURCHASING POWER PARITY

We have discussed exchange rates in some detail, and we have considered the relationship between spot and forward exchange rates. However, we have not yet addressed the fundamental question: What determines the spot level of exchange rates in each country? While exchange rates are influenced by a multitude of factors that are difficult to predict, particularly on a day-to-day basis, over the long run market forces work to ensure that similar goods sell for similar prices in different countries after taking exchange rates into account. This relationship is known as "purchasing power parity."

Purchasing Power Parity (PPP)
The relationship in which the same products cost roughly the same amount in different countries after taking into account the exchange rate.

Purchasing power parity (PPP), sometimes referred to as the *law of one price*, implies that the level of exchange rates adjusts so as to cause identical goods to cost the same amount in different countries. For example, if a pair of tennis shoes costs $150 in the United States and 100 pounds in Britain, PPP implies that the exchange rate be $1.50 per pound. Consumers could purchase the shoes in Britain for 100 pounds, or they could exchange their 100 pounds for $150 and then purchase the same shoes in the United States at the same effective cost, assuming no transaction or transportation costs. Here is the equation for purchasing power parity:

$$P_h = (P_f)(\text{Spot rate}),$$

or

$$\text{Spot rate} = \frac{P_h}{P_f}.$$

Here

P_h = the price of the good in the home country ($150, assuming the United States is the home country).

P_f = the price of the good in the foreign country (100 pounds).

GLOBAL PERSPECTIVES

HUNGRY FOR A BIG MAC? GO TO MALAYSIA!

Purchasing power parity (PPP) implies that the same product will sell for the same price in every country after adjusting for current exchange rates. One problem when testing to see if PPP holds is that it assumes that goods consumed in different countries are of the same quality. For example, if you find that a product is more expensive in Switzerland than it is in Canada, one explanation is that PPP fails to hold, but another explanation is that the product sold in Switzerland is of a higher quality and therefore deserves a higher price.

One way to test for PPP is to find goods that have the same quality worldwide. With this in mind, *The Economist* magazine occasionally compares the prices of a well-known good whose quality is the same in nearly 120 different countries: the McDonald's Big Mac hamburger.

The table on the next page provides information collected during 2000. The first column shows the price of a Big Mac in the local currency. Column 2 calculates the price of the Big Mac in terms of the U.S. dollar — this is obtained by dividing the local price by the actual exchange rate at that time. For example, a Big Mac costs 4.99 German marks in Munich. Given an exchange rate of 2.11 marks per dollar, this implies that the dollar price of a Big Mac is 4.99 marks/2.11 marks per dollar = $2.37.

The third column backs out the implied exchange rate that would hold under PPP. This is obtained by dividing the price of the Big Mac in each local currency by its U.S. price. For example, a Big Mac costs 39.50 rubles in Russia, and $2.51 in the United States. If PPP holds, the exchange rate should be 15.74 rubles per dollar (39.50 rubles/$2.51).

Comparing the implied exchange rate to the actual exchange rate in Column 4, we see the extent to which the local currency is under- or overvalued relative to the dollar. Given that the actual exchange rate at the time was 28.5 rubles per dollar, this implies that the ruble was 45 percent undervalued.

The evidence suggests that strict PPP does not hold, but the Big Mac test may shed some insights about where exchange rates are headed. The price of a Big Mac varies within the 11 countries of the EMU, but the average price within the EMU is 2.56 euros. The euro is undervalued by 5 percent. This is considerably less than many market analysts believe. The table shows Big Mac prices for the EMU's biggest member countries — ranging from the equivalent of $2.62 in France to $2.09 in Spain. Because their currencies are fixed to the euro, this gap can be narrowed only if prices fall in France or rise in Spain.

The currencies of the European countries that decided to stay outside the EMU are all overvalued. For example, the British pound is overvalued by 20 percent against the dollar and 27 percent against the euro. In contrast, most of the emerging market currencies are significantly undervalued against the dollar. The Big Mac 2000 test suggests that the pound and other non-euro currencies will fall over the next year or so, but that China's yuan will rise.

One last benefit of the Big Mac test is that it tells us the cheapest places to find a Big Mac. According to the data, if you are looking for a Big Mac, head to Malaysia, and avoid Israel.

SOURCE: Excerpted from "Big MacCurrencies," *The Economist*, April 29, 2000, 79. Reprinted by permission from *The Economist*.

	BIG MAC PRICES		IMPLIED EXCHANGE RATE BASED ON PPP[a] (3)	ACTUAL $ EXCHANGE RATE 4/25/00 (4)	LOCAL CURRENCY UNDER(−)/OVER(+) VALUATION[b](%) (5)
	IN LOCAL CURRENCY (1)	IN DOLLARS (2)			
United States[c]	$2.51	2.51	—	—	—
Argentina	Peso2.50	2.50	1.00	1.00	0
Australia	A$2.59	1.54	1.03	1.68	−38
Brazil	Real2.95	1.65	1.18	1.79	−34
Britain	£1.90	3.00	1.32[d]	1.58[d]	+20
Canada	C$2.85	1.94	1.14	1.47	−23
Chile	Peso1,260	2.45	502	514	−2
China	Yuan9.90	1.20	3.94	8.28	−52
Czech Rep	Koruna54.37	1.39	21.7	39.1	−45
Denmark	DKr24.75	3.08	9.86	8.04	+23
Euro area	€2.56	2.37	0.98[e]	0.93[e]	−5
France	FFr18.50	2.62	7.37	7.07	+4
Germany	DM4.99	2.37	1.99	2.11	−6
Italy	Lire4,500	2.16	1,793	2,088	−14
Spain	Pta375	2.09	149	179	−17
Hong Kong	HK$10.20	1.31	4.06	7.79	−48
Hungary	Forint339	1.21	135	279	−52
Indonesia	Rupiah14,500	1.83	5,777	7,945	−27
Israel	Shekel14.5	3.58	5.78	4.05	+43
Japan	¥294	2.78	117	106	+11
Malaysia	M$4.52	1.19	1.80	3.80	−53
Mexico	Peso20.90	2.22	8.33	9.41	−11
New Zealand	NZ$3.40	1.69	1.35	2.01	−33
Poland	Zloty5.50	1.28	2.19	4.30	−49
Russia	Ruble39.50	1.39	15.7	28.5	−45
Singapore	S$3.20	1.88	1.27	1.70	−25
South Africa	Rand9.00	1.34	3.59	6.72	−47
South Korea	Won3,000	2.71	1,195	1,108	+8
Sweden	SKr24.00	2.71	9.56	8.84	+8
Switzerland	SFr5.90	3.48	2.35	1.70	+39
Taiwan	NT$70.00	2.29	27.9	30.6	−9
Thailand	Baht55.00	1.45	21.9	38.0	−42

NOTES:

[a] Purchasing power parity: local price divided by price in the United States.

[b] Against dollar.

[c] Average of New York, Chicago, San Francisco, and Atlanta.

[d] Dollars per pound.

[e] Dollars per euro.

SOURCES: McDonald's; and *The Economist*.

Note that the spot market exchange rate is expressed as the number of units of home currency that can be exchanged for one unit of foreign currency ($1.50 per pound).

PPP assumes that market forces will eliminate situations in which the same product sells at a different price overseas. For example, if the shoes cost $140 in the United States, importers/exporters could purchase them in the United States for $140, sell them for 100 pounds in Britain, exchange the 100 pounds for $150 in the foreign exchange market, and earn a profit of $10 on every pair of shoes. Ultimately, this trading activity would increase the demand for shoes in the United States and thus raise P_h, increase the supply of shoes in Britain and thus reduce P_f, and increase the demand for dollars in the foreign exchange market and thus reduce the spot rate. Each of these actions works to restore PPP.

Note that PPP assumes that there are no transportation or transaction costs, or import restrictions, all of which limit the ability to ship goods between countries. In many cases, these assumptions are incorrect, which explains why PPP is often violated. An additional complication, when empirically testing to see whether PPP holds, is that products in different countries are rarely identical. Frequently, there are real or perceived differences in quality, which can lead to price differences in different countries.

Still, the concepts of interest rate and purchasing power parity are critically important to those engaged in international activities. Companies and investors must anticipate changes in interest rates, inflation, and exchange rates, and they often try to hedge the risks of adverse movements in these factors. The parity relationships are extremely useful when anticipating future conditions.

SELF-TEST QUESTION

What is meant by purchasing power parity? Illustrate it.

INFLATION, INTEREST RATES, AND EXCHANGE RATES

Relative inflation rates, or the rates of inflation in foreign countries compared with that in the home country, have many implications for multinational financial decisions. Obviously, relative inflation rates will greatly influence future production costs at home and abroad. Equally important, inflation has a dominant influence on relative interest rates and exchange rates. Both of these factors influence the methods chosen by multinational corporations for financing their foreign investments, and both have an important effect on the profitability of foreign investments.

The currencies of countries with higher inflation rates than that of the United States by definition *depreciate* over time against the dollar. Countries where this has occurred include Italy, Mexico, and all the South American nations. On the other hand, the currencies of Germany, Switzerland, and Japan, which have had less inflation than the United States, have *appreciated* against the dollar. *In fact, a foreign currency will, on average, depreciate or appreciate at a percentage rate approximately equal to the amount by which its inflation rate exceeds or is less than our own.*

Relative inflation rates also affect interest rates. The interest rate in any country is largely determined by its inflation rate. Therefore, countries currently experiencing higher rates of inflation than the United States also tend to have higher interest rates. The reverse is true for countries with lower inflation rates.

It is tempting for a multinational corporation to borrow in countries with the lowest interest rates. However, this is not always a good strategy. Suppose, for example, that interest rates in Germany are lower than those in the United States because of Germany's lower inflation rate. A U.S. multinational firm could therefore save interest by borrowing in Germany. However, because of relative inflation rates, the mark will probably appreciate in the future, causing the dollar cost of annual interest and principal payments on German debt to rise over time. Thus, *the lower interest rate could be more than offset by losses from currency appreciation.* Similarly, multinational corporations should not necessarily avoid borrowing in a country such as Brazil, where interest rates have been very high, because future depreciation of the Brazilian real could make such borrowing relatively inexpensive.

SELF-TEST QUESTIONS

What effects do relative inflation rates have on relative interest rates?

What happens over time to the currencies of countries with higher inflation rates than that of the United States? To those with lower inflation rates?

Why might a multinational corporation decide to borrow in a country such as Brazil, where interest rates are high, rather than in a country like Germany, where interest rates are low?

INTERNATIONAL MONEY AND CAPITAL MARKETS

One way for U.S. citizens to invest in world markets is to buy the stocks of U.S. multinational corporations that invest directly in foreign countries. Another way is to purchase foreign securities — stocks, bonds, or money market instruments issued by foreign companies. Security investments are known as *portfolio investments*, and they are distinguished from *direct investments* in physical assets by U.S. corporations.

From World War II through the 1960s, the U.S. capital markets dominated world markets. Today, however, the value of U.S. securities represents less than one-fourth the value of all securities. Given this situation, it is important for both corporate managers and investors to have an understanding of international markets. Moreover, these markets often offer better opportunities for raising or investing capital than are available domestically.

EURODOLLAR MARKET

Eurodollar
A U.S. dollar deposited in a bank outside the United States.

A **Eurodollar** is a U.S. dollar deposited in a bank outside the United States. (Although they are called Eurodollars because they originated in Europe, Eurodollars are really any dollars deposited in any part of the world other than the United States.) The bank in which the deposit is made may be a non-U.S. bank, such as Barclay's Bank in London; the foreign branch of a U.S. bank, such as Citibank's Paris branch; or even a foreign branch of a third-country bank, such as Barclay's Munich branch. Most Eurodollar deposits are for $500,000 or more, and they have maturities ranging from overnight to about one year.

The major difference between Eurodollar deposits and regular U.S. time deposits is their geographic locations. The two types of deposits do not involve different currencies — in both cases, dollars are on deposit. However, Eurodollars are outside the direct control of the U.S. monetary authorities, so U.S. banking regulations, including reserve requirements and FDIC insurance premiums, do not apply. The absence of these costs means that the interest rate paid on Eurodollar deposits can be higher than domestic U.S. rates on equivalent instruments.

Although the dollar is the leading international currency, British pounds, German marks, Swiss francs, Japanese yen, and other currencies are also deposited outside their home countries; these *Eurocurrencies* are handled in exactly the same way as Eurodollars.

Eurodollars are borrowed by U.S. and foreign corporations for various purposes, but especially to pay for goods exported from the United States and to invest in U.S. security markets. Also, U.S. dollars are used as an international currency, or international medium of exchange, and many Eurodollars are used for this purpose. It is interesting to note that Eurodollars were actually "invented" by the Soviets in 1946. International merchants did not trust the Soviets or their rubles, so the Soviets bought some dollars (for gold), deposited them in a Paris bank, and then used these dollars to buy goods in the world markets. Others found it convenient to use dollars this same way, and soon the Eurodollar market was in full swing.

Eurodollars are usually held in interest-bearing accounts. The interest rate paid on these deposits depends (1) on the bank's lending rate, as the interest a bank earns on loans determines its willingness and ability to pay interest on deposits, and (2) on rates of return available on U.S. money market instruments. If money market rates in the United States were above Eurodollar deposit rates, these dollars would be sent back and invested in the United States, whereas if Eurodollar deposit rates were significantly above U.S. rates, which is more often the case, more dollars would be sent out of the United States to become Eurodollars. Given the existence of the Eurodollar market and the electronic flow of dollars to and from the United States, it is easy to see why interest rates in the United States cannot be insulated from those in other parts of the world.

Interest rates on Eurodollar deposits (and loans) are tied to a standard rate known by the acronym *LIBOR*, which stands for *London Interbank Offer Rate*. LIBOR is the rate of interest offered by the largest and strongest London banks on dollar deposits of significant size. In December 2000, LIBOR rates were over a percentage point above domestic U.S. bank rates on time deposits of the same maturity — 5.44 percent for three-month CDs versus 6.62 percent for LIBOR CDs. The Eurodollar market is essentially a short-term market; most loans and deposits are for less than one year.

International Bond Markets

Any bond sold outside the country of the borrower is called an *international bond*. However, there are two important types of international bonds: foreign

Foreign Bond
A bond sold by a foreign borrower but denominated in the currency of the country in which it is sold.

Eurobond
A bond sold in a country other than the one in whose currency the bond is denominated.

bonds and Eurobonds. **Foreign bonds** are bonds sold by a foreign borrower but denominated in the currency of the country in which the issue is sold. For instance, Northern Telcom (a Canadian company) may need U.S. dollars to finance the operations of its subsidiaries in the United States. If it decides to raise the needed capital in the United States, the bond will be underwritten by a syndicate of U.S. investment bankers, denominated in U.S. dollars, and sold to U.S. investors in accordance with SEC and applicable state regulations. Except for the foreign origin of the borrower, this bond will be indistinguishable from those issued by equivalent U.S. corporations. Since Northern Telcom is a foreign corporation, however, the bond would be a foreign bond.

The term **Eurobond** is used to designate any bond issued in one country but denominated in the currency of some other country. Examples include a Ford Motor Company issue denominated in dollars and sold in Germany, or a British firm's sale of mark-denominated bonds in Switzerland. The institutional arrangements by which Eurobonds are marketed are different than those for most other bond issues, with the most important distinction being a far lower level of required disclosure than is usually found for bonds issued in domestic markets, particularly in the United States. Governments tend to be less strict when regulating securities denominated in foreign currencies, because the bonds' purchasers are generally more "sophisticated." The lower disclosure requirements result in lower total transaction costs for Eurobonds.

Eurobonds appeal to investors for several reasons. Generally, they are issued in bearer form rather than as registered bonds, so the names and nationalities of investors are not recorded. Individuals who desire anonymity, whether for privacy reasons or for tax avoidance, like Eurobonds. Similarly, most governments do not withhold taxes on interest payments associated with Eurobonds. If the investor requires an effective yield of 10 percent, a Eurobond that is exempt from tax withholding would need a coupon rate of 10 percent. Another type of bond — for instance, a domestic issue subject to a 30 percent withholding tax on interest paid to foreigners — would need a coupon rate of 14.3 percent to yield an after-withholding rate of 10 percent. Investors who desire secrecy would not want to file for a refund of the tax, so they would prefer to hold the Eurobond.

More than half of all Eurobonds are denominated in dollars. Bonds in Japanese yen, German marks, and Dutch guilders account for most of the rest. Although centered in Europe, Eurobonds are truly international. Their underwriting syndicates include investment bankers from all parts of the world, and the bonds are sold to investors not only in Europe but also in such faraway places as Bahrain and Singapore. Up until a few years ago, Eurobonds were issued solely by multinational firms, by international financial institutions, or by national governments. Today, however, the Eurobond market is also being tapped by purely domestic U.S. firms, because they often find that by borrowing overseas they can lower their debt costs.

INTERNATIONAL STOCK MARKETS

New issues of stock are sold in international markets for a variety of reasons. For example, a non-U.S. firm might sell an equity issue in the United States because it can tap a much larger source of capital than in its home country. Also, a U.S. firm might tap a foreign market because it wants to create an

STOCK MARKET INDICES AROUND THE WORLD

In Chapter 5, we described the major U.S. stock market indices. As discussed below, similar market indices also exist for each major world financial center. The accompanying figure compares four of the indices against the U.S. indices.

HONG KONG

In Hong Kong, the primary stock index is the Hang Seng. Created by HSI Services Limited, the Hang Seng index reflects the performance of the Hong Kong stock market. It is composed of 33 domestic stocks that account for about 70 percent of the market's capitalization. The largest stock in the index is HBSC Holdings, which alone accounts for 21 percent of the index's total market value.

GERMANY

The major indicator of the German stock market, the XETRA DAX, is comprised of 30 German blue chip stocks. These stocks are all listed on the Frankfurt exchange, and they are representative of the industrial structure of the German economy.

GREAT BRITAIN

The FT-SE 100 Index (pronounced "footsie") is the most widely followed indicator of equity investments in Great Britain. It is a value-weighted index composed of the 100 largest companies on the London Stock Exchange whose value is calculated every minute of trading.

JAPAN

In Japan, the principal barometer of stock performance is the Nikkei 225 Index. The index's value, which is calculated every minute throughout daily trading, consists of a collection of highly liquid equity issues thought to be representative of the Japanese economy.

CHILE

The Santiago Stock Exchange has three main share indices: the General Stock Price Index (IGPA), the Selective Stock Price Index (IPSA), and the INTER-10 Index. The IPSA, which reflects the price variations of the most active stocks, is composed of 40 of the most actively traded stocks on the exchange.

INDIA

Of the 22 stock exchanges in India, the Bombay Stock Exchange (BSE) is the largest, with more than 6,000 listed stocks and approximately two-thirds of the country's total trading volume. Established in 1875, the exchange is also the oldest in Asia. Its yardstick is the BSE Sensex, an index of 30 publicly traded Indian stocks that account for one-fifth of the BSE's market capitalization.

SPAIN

In Spain, the IBEX 35 is the official index for measuring equity market performance for continuously traded stocks. This index is composed of the 35 most actively traded securities on the Joint Stock Exchange System (comprising the four Spanish stock exchanges).

equity market presence to accompany its operations in that country. Large multinational companies also occasionally issue new stock simultaneously in multiple countries. For example, Alcan Aluminum, a Canadian company, recently issued new stock in Canada, Europe, and the United States simultaneously, using different underwriting syndicates in each market.

In addition to new issues, outstanding stocks of large multinational companies are increasingly being listed on multiple international exchanges. For example, Coca-Cola's stock is traded on six stock exchanges in the United States, four stock exchanges in Switzerland, and the Frankfurt stock exchange in Germany. Some 500 foreign stocks are listed in the United States — an example here is Royal Dutch Petroleum, which is listed on the NYSE. U.S. investors can also invest in foreign companies through *American Depository Receipts (ADRs)*, which are certificates representing ownership of foreign stock held in trust. About 1,700 ADRs are now available in the United States, with most of them traded on the over-the-counter (OTC) market. However, more and more

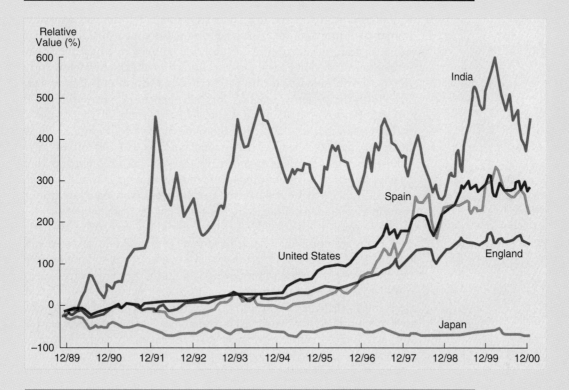

International Stock Indices — Compound Returns from
December 1989 through December 2000

SOURCE: Yahoo Finance historical quotes obtained from the web site at **http://finance.yahoo.com.**

ADRs are being listed on the New York Stock Exchange, including England's
British Airways, Japan's Honda Motors, and Italy's Fiat Group.

MULTINATIONAL CAPITAL BUDGETING

Up to now, we have discussed the general environment in which multinational firms operate. In the remainder of the chapter, we will see how international factors affect key corporate decisions. We begin with capital budgeting. Although the same basic principles of capital budgeting analysis apply to both foreign and domestic operations, there are some key differences. First, cash flow estimation is more complex for overseas investments. Most multinational firms set up separate subsidiaries in each foreign country in which they operate, and the relevant cash flows for the parent company are the dividends and royalties paid by the subsidiaries to the parent. Second, these cash flows must be converted into the parent company's currency, hence they are subject to exchange rate risk. For example, General Motors' German subsidiary may make a profit of 100 million marks in 2001, but the value of this profit to GM will depend on the dollar/mark exchange rate: How many *dollars* will 100 million marks buy?

Repatriation of Earnings
The process of sending cash flows from a foreign subsidiary back to the parent company.

Dividends and royalties are normally taxed by both foreign and home-country governments. Furthermore, a foreign government may restrict the amount of the cash that may be **repatriated** to the parent company. For example, some governments place a ceiling, stated as a percentage of the company's net worth, on the amount of cash dividends that a subsidiary can pay to its parent. Such restrictions are normally intended to force multinational firms to reinvest earnings in the foreign country, although restrictions are sometimes imposed to prevent large currency outflows, which might disrupt the exchange rate.

Whatever the host country's motivation for blocking repatriation of profits, the result is that the parent corporation cannot use cash flows blocked in the foreign country to pay dividends to its shareholders or to invest elsewhere in the business. Hence, from the perspective of the parent organization, *the cash flows relevant for foreign investment analysis are the cash flows that the subsidiary is actually expected to send back to the parent.* The present value of those cash flows is found by applying an appropriate discount rate, and this present value is then compared with the parent's required investment to determine the project's NPV.

In addition to the complexities of the cash flow analysis, *the cost of capital may be different for a foreign project than for an equivalent domestic project, because foreign projects may be more or less risky.* A higher risk could arise from two primary sources — (1) exchange rate risk and (2) political risk. A lower risk might result from international diversification.

Exchange Rate Risk
The risk that relates to what the basic cash flows will be worth in the parent company's home currency.

Exchange rate risk relates to the value of the basic cash flows in the parent company's home currency. The foreign currency cash flows to be turned over to the parent must be converted into U.S. dollars by translating them at expected future exchange rates. An analysis should be conducted to ascertain the effects of exchange rate variations, and, on the basis of this analysis, an exchange rate risk premium should be added to the domestic cost of capital to reflect this risk. It is sometimes possible to hedge against exchange rate fluctuations, but it may not be possible to hedge completely, especially on long-term projects. If hedging is used, the costs of doing so must be subtracted from the project's cash flows.

Political Risk
Potential actions by a host government that would reduce the value of a company's investment.

Political risk refers to potential actions by a host government that would reduce the value of a company's investment. It includes at one extreme the expropriation without compensation of the subsidiary's assets, but it also includes less drastic actions that reduce the value of the parent firm's investment in the

Selected Countries Ranked by Composite Risk

RANK	COUNTRY	POLITICAL RISK	FINANCIAL RISK	ECONOMIC RISK	COMPOSITE RISK
1	Luxembourg	92.0	42.0	45.4	89.7
4	Switzerland	85.0	46.0	42.8	86.9
9	United States	88.0	37.0	41.6	83.3
13	Canada	86.0	39.0	39.8	82.4
55	Panama	77.0	31.5	34.5	71.5
76	Peru	61.0	36.5	35.4	66.4
81	Israel	59.0	37.5	34.4	65.4
91	Venezuela	62.0	38.0	25.7	62.9
111	Colombia	51.0	35.5	27.9	57.2
140	Sierra Leone	35.0	8.0	21.5	32.3

NOTE: A total of 140 countries are ranked, but only 10 are shown here.
SOURCE: *International Country Risk Guide,* June 1999.

foreign subsidiary, including higher taxes, tighter repatriation or currency controls, and restrictions on prices charged. The risk of expropriation is small in traditionally friendly and stable countries such as Great Britain or Switzerland. However, in Latin America, Africa, the Far East, and Eastern Europe, the risk may be substantial. Past expropriations include those of ITT and Anaconda Copper in Chile, Gulf Oil in Bolivia, Occidental Petroleum in Libya, Enron Corporation in Peru, and the assets of many companies in Iraq, Iran, and Cuba.

Several organizations rate the political risk of countries. For example, The PRS Group, Inc., an independent company based in East Syracuse, New York, publishes the *International Country Risk Guide,* which contains individual ratings for political, financial, and economic risk, along with a composite rating for each country. Table 16-4 contains selected portions of its June 1999 report. The political variable — which is given 50 percent of the weight in the composite rating — includes factors such as government corruption and the gap between economic expectations and reality. The financial rating looks at such things as the likelihood of losses from exchange controls and loan defaults. The economic rating takes into account such factors as inflation and debt-service costs.

The best, or least risky, score is 100 for political factors and 50 each for the financial and economic factors, and the composite risk is a weighted average of the political, financial, and economic factors. The United States is ranked 9th, below Luxembourg, Singapore, Norway, Switzerland, Ireland, Finland, Netherlands, and Denmark. Sierra Leone, as shown in Table 16-4, is ranked last.

Note that companies can take several steps to reduce the potential loss from expropriation: (1) finance the subsidiary with local capital, (2) structure operations so that the subsidiary has value only as a part of the integrated corporate system, and (3) obtain insurance against economic losses from expropriation from a source such as the Overseas Private Investment Corporation (OPIC). In the latter case, insurance premiums would have to be added to the project's cost.

Students can obtain a sample copy of the *International Country Risk Guide* published by The PRS Group, Inc. at
http://www.prsgroup.com.

List some key differences in capital budgeting as applied to foreign versus domestic operations.

What are the relevant cash flows for an international investment — the cash flow produced by the subsidiary in the country where it operates or the cash flows in dollars that it sends to its parent company?

Why might the cost of capital for a foreign project differ from that of an equivalent domestic project? Could it be lower?

What adjustments might be made to the domestic cost of capital for a foreign investment due to exchange rate risk and political risk?

INTERNATIONAL CAPITAL STRUCTURES

Companies' capital structures vary among countries. For example, the Organization for Economic Cooperation and Development (OECD) recently reported that, on average, Japanese firms use 85 percent debt to total assets (in book value terms), German firms use 64 percent, and U.S. firms use 55 percent. One problem, however, when interpreting these numbers is that different countries often use very different accounting conventions with regard to (1) reporting assets on a historical- versus a replacement-cost basis, (2) the treatment of leased assets, (3) pension plan funding, and (4) capitalizing versus expensing R&D costs. These differences make it difficult to compare capital structures.

A recent study by Raghuram Rajan and Luigi Zingales of the University of Chicago attempts to control for differences in accounting practices. In their study, Rajan and Zingales used a database that covers fewer firms than the OECD but that provides a more complete breakdown of balance sheet data. They concluded that differences in accounting practices can explain much of the cross-country variation in capital structures.

Rajan and Zingales' results are summarized in Table 16-5. There are a number of different ways to measure capital structure. One measure is the average ratio of total liabilities to total assets — this is similar to the measure used by the OECD, and it is reported in Column 1. Based on this measure, German and Japanese firms appear to be more highly levered than U.S. firms. However, if you look at Column 2, where capital structure is measured by interest-bearing debt to total assets, it appears that German firms use *less* leverage than U.S. and Japanese firms. What explains this difference? Rajan and Zingales argue that much of this difference is explained by the way German firms account for pension liabilities. German firms generally include all pension liabilities (and their offsetting assets) on the balance sheet, whereas firms in other countries (including the United States) generally "net out" pension assets and liabilities on their balance sheets. To see the importance of this difference, consider a firm with $10 million in liabilities (not including pension liabilities) and $20 million in assets (not including pension assets). Assume that the firm has $10 million in pension liabilities that are fully funded by $10 million in pension assets. Therefore, net pension liabilities are zero. If this firm were in the United States, it

TABLE 16-5	Median Capital Structures among Large Industrialized Countries (Measured in Terms of Book Value)				
COUNTRY	TOTAL LIABILITIES TO TOTAL ASSETS (UNADJUSTED FOR ACCOUNTING DIFFERENCES) (1)	DEBT TO TOTAL ASSETS (UNADJUSTED FOR ACCOUNTING DIFFERENCES) (2)	TOTAL LIABILITIES TO TOTAL ASSETS (ADJUSTED FOR ACCOUNTING DIFFERENCES) (3)	DEBT TO TOTAL ASSETS (ADJUSTED FOR ACCOUNTING DIFFERENCES) (4)	TIMES INTEREST EARNED (TIE) RATIO (5)
Canada	56%	32%	48%	32%	1.55×
France	71	25	69	18	2.64
Germany	73	16	50	11	3.20
Italy	70	27	68	21	1.81
Japan	69	35	62	21	2.46
United Kingdom	54	18	47	10	4.79
United States	58	27	52	25	2.41
Mean	64%	26%	57%	20%	2.69×
Standard deviation	8%	7%	10%	8%	1.07×

SOURCE: Raghuram Rajan and Luigi Zingales, "What Do We Know about Capital Structure? Some Evidence from International Data," *The Journal of Finance*, Vol. 50, No. 5, December 1995, 1421–1460. Used with permission.

would report a ratio of total liabilities to total assets equal to 50 percent ($10 million/$20 million). By contrast, if this firm operated in Germany, both its pension assets and liabilities would be reported on the balance sheet. The firm would have $20 million in liabilities and $30 million in assets — or a 67 percent ($20 million/$30 million) ratio of total liabilities to total assets. Total debt is the sum of short-term debt and long-term debt and excludes other liabilities including pension liabilities. Therefore, the measure of total debt to total assets provides a more comparable measure of leverage across different countries.

Rajan and Zingales also make a variety of adjustments that attempt to control for other differences in accounting practices. The effect of these adjustments are reported in Columns 3 and 4. Overall, the evidence suggests that companies in Germany and the United Kingdom tend to have less leverage, whereas firms in Canada appear to have more leverage, relative to firms in the United States, France, Italy, and Japan. This conclusion is supported by data in the final column, which shows the average times-interest-earned ratio for firms in a number of different countries. Recall from Chapter 3 that the times-interest-earned ratio is the ratio of operating income (EBIT) to interest expense. This measure indicates how much cash the firm has available to service its interest expense. In general, firms with more leverage have a lower times-interest-earned ratio. The data indicate that this ratio is highest in the United Kingdom and Germany and lowest in Canada.

SELF-TEST QUESTION

Do international differences in financial leverage exist? Explain.

MULTINATIONAL WORKING CAPITAL MANAGEMENT

CASH MANAGEMENT

The goals of cash management in a multinational corporation are similar to those in a purely domestic corporation: (1) to speed up collections, slow down disbursements, and thus maximize net float; (2) to shift cash as rapidly as possible from those parts of the business where it is not needed to those parts where it is needed; and (3) to maximize the risk-adjusted, after-tax rate of return on temporary cash balances. Multinational companies use the same general procedures for achieving these goals as domestic firms, but because of longer distances and more serious mail delays, such devices as lockbox systems and electronic funds transfers are especially important.

Although multinational and domestic corporations have the same objectives and use similar procedures, multinational corporations face a far more complex task. As noted earlier in our discussion of political risk, foreign governments often place restrictions on transfers of funds out of the country, so although IBM can transfer money from its Salt Lake City office to its New York concentration bank just by pressing a few buttons, a similar transfer from its Buenos Aires office is far more complex. Buenos Aires funds are denominated in australs (Argentina's equivalent of the dollar), so the australs must be converted to dollars before the transfer. If there is a shortage of dollars in Argentina, or if the Argentinean government wants to conserve dollars to purchase strategic materials, then conversion, hence the transfer, may be blocked. Even if no dollar shortage exists in Argentina, the government may still restrict funds outflows if those funds represent profits or depreciation rather than payments for purchased materials or equipment, because many countries, especially those that are less developed, want profits reinvested in the country in order to stimulate economic growth.

Once it has been determined what funds can be transferred, the next task is to get those funds to locations where they will earn the highest returns. Whereas domestic corporations tend to think in terms of domestic securities, multinationals are more likely to be aware of investment opportunities all around the world. Most multinational corporations use one or more global concentration banks, located in money centers such as London, New York, Tokyo, Zurich, or Singapore, and their staffs in those cities, working with international bankers, know of and are able to take advantage of the best rates available anywhere in the world.

CREDIT MANAGEMENT

Like most other aspects of finance, credit management in the multinational corporation is similar to but more complex than that in a purely domestic business. First, granting credit is more risky in an international context because, in addition to the normal risks of default, the multinational corporation must also worry about exchange rate fluctuations between the time a sale is made and the time a receivable is collected. For example, if IBM sold a computer to a Japanese customer for 90 million yen when the exchange rate was 90 yen to the dollar, IBM would receive 90,000,000/90 = $1,000,000 for the computer. However, if it sold the computer on terms of net/6 months, and if the yen fell against the dollar so that one dollar would now buy 112.5 yen, IBM would end up realizing only 90,000,000/112.5 = $800,000 when it collected the receivable. Hedging can reduce this type of risk, but at a cost.

Offering credit is generally more important for multinational corporations than for purely domestic firms for two reasons. First, much U.S. trade is with poorer, less-developed nations, where granting credit is generally a necessary condition for doing business. Second, and in large part as a result of the first point, developed nations whose economic health depends on exports often help their manufacturing firms compete internationally by granting credit to foreign countries. In Japan, for example, the major manufacturing firms have direct ownership ties with large "trading companies" engaged in international trade, as well as with giant commercial banks. In addition, a government agency, the Ministry of International Trade and Industry (MITI), helps Japanese firms identify potential export markets and also helps potential customers arrange credit for purchases from Japanese firms. In effect, the huge Japanese trade surpluses are used to finance Japanese exports, thus helping to perpetuate their favorable trade balance. The United States has attempted to counter with the Export-Import Bank, which is funded by Congress, but the fact that the United States has a large balance of payments deficit is clear evidence that we have been less successful than others in world markets in recent years.

The huge debt that countries such as Korea and Thailand owe U.S. and other international banks is well known, and this situation illustrates how credit policy (by banks in this case) can go astray. The banks face a particularly sticky problem with these loans, because if a sovereign nation defaults, the banks cannot lay claim to the assets of the country as they could if a corporate customer defaulted. Note too that although the banks' loans to foreign governments often get most of the headlines, many U.S. multinational corporations are also in trouble as a result of granting credit to business customers in the same countries where bank loans to governments are on shaky ground.

By pointing out the risks in granting credit internationally, we are not suggesting that such credit is bad. Quite the contrary, for the potential gains from international operations far outweigh the risks, at least for companies (and banks) that have the necessary expertise.

INVENTORY MANAGEMENT

As with most other aspects of finance, inventory management in a multinational setting is similar to but more complex than for a purely domestic firm. First, there is the matter of the physical location of inventories. For example, where should Exxon Mobil keep its stockpiles of crude oil and refined products? It has refineries and marketing centers located worldwide, and one alternative is to keep items concentrated in a few strategic spots from which they can then be shipped as needs arise. Such a strategy might minimize the total amount of inventories needed and thus might minimize the investment in inventories. Note, though, that consideration will have to be given to potential delays in getting goods from central storage locations to user locations all around the world. Both working stocks and safety stocks would have to be maintained at each user location, as well as at the strategic storage centers.

Problems like the Iraqi occupation of Kuwait and the subsequent trade embargo, which brought with it the potential for a shutdown of production of about 25 percent of the world's oil supply, complicate matters further.

Exchange rates also influence inventory policy. If a local currency, say, the Danish krone, were expected to rise in value against the dollar, a U.S. company operating in Denmark would want to increase stocks of local products before the rise in the krone, and vice versa if the krone were expected to fall.

Another factor that must be considered is the possibility of import or export quotas or tariffs. For example, Apple Computer Company was buying certain memory chips from Japanese suppliers at a bargain price. Then U.S. chipmakers accused the Japanese of dumping chips in the U.S. market at prices below cost, so they sought to force the Japanese to raise prices.[5] That led Apple to increase its chip inventory. Then computer sales slacked off, and Apple ended up with an oversupply of obsolete computer chips. As a result, Apple's profits were hurt and its stock price fell, demonstrating once more the importance of careful inventory management.

As mentioned earlier, another danger in certain countries is the threat of expropriation. If that threat is large, inventory holdings will be minimized, and goods will be brought in only as needed. Similarly, if the operation involves extraction of raw materials such as oil or bauxite, processing plants may be moved offshore rather than located close to the production site.

Taxes have two effects on multinational inventory management. First, countries often impose property taxes on assets, including inventories, and when this is done, the tax is based on holdings as of a specific date, say, January 1 or March 1. Such rules make it advantageous for a multinational firm (1) to schedule production so that inventories are low on the assessment date, and (2) if assessment dates vary among countries in a region, to hold safety stocks in different countries at different times during the year.

Finally, multinational firms may consider the possibility of at-sea storage. Oil, chemical, grain, and other companies that deal in a bulk commodity that must be stored in some type of tank can often buy tankers at a cost not much greater — or perhaps even less, considering land cost — than land-based facilities. Loaded tankers can then be kept at sea or at anchor in some strategic location. This eliminates the danger of expropriation, minimizes the property tax problem, and maximizes flexibility with regard to shipping to areas where needs are greatest or prices highest.

This discussion has only scratched the surface of inventory management in the multinational corporation — the task is much more complex than for a purely domestic firm. However, the greater the degree of complexity, the greater the rewards from superior performance, so if you want challenge along with potentially high rewards, look to the international arena.

---

[5] The term "dumping" warrants explanation, because the practice is so potentially important in international markets. Suppose Japanese chipmakers have excess capacity. A particular chip has a variable cost of $25, and its "fully allocated cost," which is the $25 plus total fixed cost per unit of output, is $40. Now suppose the Japanese firm can sell chips in the United States at $35 per unit, but if it charges $40, it will not make any sales because U.S. chipmakers sell for $35.50. If the Japanese firm sells at $35, it will cover variable cost plus make a contribution to fixed overhead, so selling at $35 makes sense. Continuing, if the Japanese firm can sell in Japan at $40, but U.S. firms are excluded from Japanese markets by import duties or other barriers, the Japanese will have a huge advantage over U.S. manufacturers. This practice of selling goods at lower prices in foreign markets than at home is called "dumping." U.S. firms are required by antitrust laws to offer the same price to all customers and, therefore, cannot engage in dumping.

What are some factors that make cash management especially complicated in a multinational corporation?

Why is granting credit especially risky in an international context?

Why is inventory management especially important for a multinational firm?

TYING IT ALL TOGETHER

Over the past two decades, the global economy has become increasingly integrated, and more and more companies generate more and more of their profits from overseas operations. In many respects, the concepts developed in the first 15 chapters still apply to multinational firms. However, multinational companies have more opportunities but also face different risks than do companies that operate only in their home market. The chapter discussed many of the key trends affecting the global markets today, and it described the most important differences between multinational and domestic financial management. The key concepts are listed below.

- **International operations** are becoming increasingly important to individual firms and to the national economy. A **multinational,** or **global, corporation** is a firm that operates in an integrated fashion in a number of countries.

- Companies "go global" for six primary reasons: (1) **to expand their markets,** (2) **to obtain raw materials,** (3) **to seek new technology,** (4) **to lower production costs,** (5) **to avoid trade barriers,** and (6) **to diversify.**

- Six major factors distinguish financial management as practiced by domestic firms from that practiced by multinational corporations: (1) **different currency denominations,** (2) **different economic and legal structures,** (3) **languages,** (4) **cultural differences,** (5) **role of governments,** and (6) **political risk.**

- When discussing **exchange rates,** the number of U.S. dollars required to purchase one unit of a foreign currency is called a **direct quotation,** while the number of units of foreign currency that can be purchased for one U.S. dollar is an **indirect quotation.**

- **Exchange rate fluctuations** make it difficult to estimate the dollars that overseas operations will produce.

- Prior to August 1971, the world was on a **fixed exchange rate system** whereby the U.S. dollar was linked to gold, and other currencies were then tied to the dollar. After August 1971, the world monetary system changed to a **floating system** under which major world currency rates float with market forces, largely unrestricted by governmental intervention. The central bank of each country does operate in the foreign exchange market, buying and selling currencies to smooth out exchange rate fluctuations, but only to a limited extent.

- The consolidation of the European market has had a profound impact on European exchange rates. The exchange rates for the currencies of each of the participating countries are now fixed relative to the **euro.** Consequently, the cross rates between the various participating currencies are also fixed. However, the value of the euro continues to fluctuate.

- **Pegged exchange rates** occur when a country establishes a fixed exchange rate with a major currency. Consequently, the values of pegged currencies move together over time.

- A **convertible currency** is one that may be readily exchanged for other currencies.

- **Spot rates** are the rates paid for delivery of currency "on the spot," while the **forward exchange rate** is the rate paid for delivery at some agreed-upon future date, usually 30, 90, or 180 days from the day the transaction is negotiated. The forward rate can be at either a **premium** or a **discount** to the spot rate.

- **Interest rate parity** holds that investors should expect to earn the same return in all countries after adjusting for risk.

- **Purchasing power parity,** sometimes referred to as the *law of one price*, implies that the level of exchange rates adjusts so that identical goods cost the same in different countries.

- Granting credit is more risky in an international context because, in addition to the normal risks of default, the multinational firm must worry about **exchange rate changes** between the time a sale is made and the time a receivable is collected.

- Credit policy is important for a multinational firm for two reasons: (1) Much trade is with less-developed nations, and in such situations granting credit is a necessary condition for doing business. (2) The governments of nations such as Japan whose economic health depends upon exports often help their firms compete by granting credit to foreign customers.

- Foreign investments are similar to domestic investments, but political risk and exchange rate risk must be considered. **Political risk** is the risk that the foreign government will take some action that will decrease the value of the investment, while **exchange rate risk** is the risk of losses due to fluctuations in the value of the dollar relative to the values of foreign currencies.

- Investments in **international capital projects** expose firms to exchange rate risk and political risk. The relevant cash flows in international capital budgeting are the dollars that can be **repatriated** to the parent company.

- **Eurodollars** are U.S. dollars deposited in banks outside the United States. Interest rates on Eurodollars are tied to **LIBOR,** the London Interbank Offer Rate.

- U.S. firms often find that they can raise long-term capital at a lower cost outside the United States by selling bonds in the **international capital markets.** International bonds may be either **foreign bonds,** which are exactly like regular domestic bonds except that the issuer is a foreign company, or **Eurobonds,** which are bonds sold in a foreign country but denominated in the currency of the issuing company's home country.

QUESTIONS

16-1 Under the fixed exchange rate system, what was the currency against which all other currency values were defined? Why?

16-2 Exchange rates fluctuate under both the fixed exchange rate and floating exchange rate systems. What, then, is the difference between the two systems?

16-3 If the euro depreciates against the U.S. dollar, can a dollar buy more or fewer euros as a result?

16-4 If the United States imports more goods from abroad than it exports, foreigners will tend to have a surplus of U.S. dollars. What will this do to the value of the dollar with respect to foreign currencies? What is the corresponding effect on foreign investments in the United States?

16-5 Why do U.S. corporations build manufacturing plants abroad when they could build them at home?

16-6 Should firms require higher rates of return on foreign projects than on identical projects located at home? Explain.

16-7 What is a Eurodollar? If a French citizen deposits $10,000 in Chase Manhattan Bank in New York, have Eurodollars been created? What if the deposit is made in Barclay's Bank in London? Chase Manhattan's Paris branch? Does the existence of the Eurodollar market make the Federal Reserve's job of controlling U.S. interest rates easier or more difficult? Explain.

16-8 Does interest rate parity imply that interest rates are the same in all countries?

16-9 Why might purchasing power parity fail to hold?

16-10 What is the euro, and is its value fixed or fluctuating? What are the implications for the cross rates between the various participating currencies?

SELF-TEST PROBLEMS (SOLUTIONS APPEAR IN APPENDIX B)

ST-1
Key terms
Define each of the following terms:
a. Multinational corporation
b. Exchange rate; euro
c. Fixed exchange rate system; floating exchange rates
d. Trade deficit
e. Devaluation; revaluation
f. Exchange rate risk; convertible currency
g. Pegged exchange rates
h. Interest rate parity; purchasing power parity
i. Spot rate; forward exchange rate
j. Discount on forward rate; premium on forward rate
k. Repatriation of earnings; political risk
l. Eurodollar; Eurobond; international bond; foreign bond

ST-2
Cross rates
Suppose the exchange rate between U.S. dollars and EMU euros is Euro 1.1215 = $1.00, and the exchange rate between the U.S. dollar and the Canadian dollar is $1.00 = C$1.5291. What is the cross rate of euros to Canadian dollars?

STARTER PROBLEMS

16-1
Cross rates
A currency trader observes that in the spot exchange market, one U.S. dollar can be exchanged for 4.0828 Israeli shekel or for 111.23 Japanese yen. What is the cross-exchange rate between the yen and the shekel; that is, how many yen would you receive for every shekel exchanged?

16-2
Interest rate parity
Six-month T-bills have a nominal rate of 7 percent, while default-free Japanese bonds that mature in 6 months have a nominal rate of 5.5 percent. In the spot exchange market, one yen equals $0.009. If interest rate parity holds, what is the 6-month forward exchange rate?

16-3
Purchasing power parity

A television set costs $500 in the United States. The same set costs 725 euros. If purchasing power parity holds, what is the spot exchange rate between the euro and the dollar?

EXAM-TYPE PROBLEMS

The problems included in this section are set up in such a way that they could be used as multiple-choice exam problems.

16-4
Exchange rate

If British pounds sell for $1.50 (U.S.) per pound, what should dollars sell for in pounds per dollar?

16-5
Currency appreciation

Suppose that 1 Danish krone could be purchased in the foreign exchange market for 14 U.S. cents today. If the krone appreciated 10 percent tomorrow against the dollar, how many krones would a dollar buy tomorrow?

16-6
Cross exchange rates

Suppose the exchange rate between the U.S. dollar and the Swedish krona was 10 krona = $1.00, and the exchange rate between the dollar and the British pound was £1 = $1.50. What was the exchange rate between Swedish kronas and pounds?

16-7
Cross exchange rates

Look up the 3 currencies in Problem 16-6 in the foreign exchange section of a current issue of *The Wall Street Journal*. What is the current exchange rate between Swedish kronas and pounds?

16-8
Foreign investment analysis

After all foreign and U.S. taxes, a U.S. corporation expects to receive 3 pounds of dividends per share from a British subsidiary this year. The exchange rate at the end of the year is expected to be $1.60 per pound, and the pound is expected to depreciate 5 percent against the dollar each year for an indefinite period. The dividend (in pounds) is expected to grow at 10 percent a year indefinitely. The parent U.S. corporation owns 10 million shares of the subsidiary. What is the present value in dollars of its equity ownership of the subsidiary? Assume a cost of equity capital of 15 percent for the subsidiary.

16-9
Exchange gains and losses

You are the vice-president of International InfoXchange, headquartered in Chicago, Illinois. All shareholders of the firm live in the United States. Earlier this month, you obtained a loan of 5 million Canadian dollars from a bank in Toronto to finance the construction of a new plant in Montreal. At the time the loan was received, the exchange rate was 75 U.S. cents to the Canadian dollar. By the end of the month, it has unexpectedly dropped to 70 cents. Has your company made a gain or loss as a result, and by how much?

PROBLEMS

16-10
Exchange rates

Table 16-1 lists foreign exchange rates for December 6, 2000. On that day, how many dollars would be required to purchase 1,000 units of each of the following: British pounds, Canadian dollars, EMU euros, Japanese yen, Mexican pesos, and Swedish kronas?

16-11
Exchange rates

Look up the 6 currencies in Problem 16-10 in the foreign exchange section of a current issue of *The Wall Street Journal*.
a. What is the current exchange rate for changing dollars into 1,000 units of pounds, Canadian dollars, euros, yen, Mexican pesos, and Swedish kronas?
b. What is the percentage gain or loss between the December 6, 2000, exchange rate and the current exchange rate for each of the currencies in part a?

16-12
Results of exchange rate changes

Early in September 1983, it took 245 Japanese yen to equal $1. More than 17 years later, in December 2000 that exchange rate had fallen to 110 yen to $1. Assume the price of a Japanese-manufactured automobile was $9,000 in September 1983 and that its price changes were in direct relation to exchange rates.
a. Has the price, in dollars, of the automobile increased or decreased during the 17-year period because of changes in the exchange rate?
b. What would the dollar price of the automobile be in December 2000, again assuming that the car's price changes only with exchange rates?

16-13
Spot and forward rates

Chamberlain Canadian Imports has agreed to purchase 15,000 cases of Canadian beer for 4 million Canadian dollars at today's spot rate. The firm's financial manager, James Churchill, has noted the following current spot and forward rates:

	U.S. DOLLAR/CANADIAN DOLLAR	CANADIAN DOLLAR/U.S. DOLLAR
Spot	0.6930	1.4430
30-day forward	0.6935	1.4420
90-day forward	0.6944	1.4401
180-day forward	0.6957	1.4374

On the same day, Churchill agrees to purchase 15,000 more cases of beer in 3 months at the same price of 4 million Canadian dollars.
- a. What is the price of the beer, in U.S. dollars, if it is purchased at today's spot rate?
- b. What is the cost, in U.S. dollars, of the second 15,000 cases if payment is made in 90 days and the spot rate at that time equals today's 90-day forward rate?
- c. If the exchange rate for the Canadian dollar is 1.20 to $1 in 90 days, how much will Churchill have to pay for the beer (in U.S. dollars)?

16-14
Interest rate parity

Assume that interest rate parity holds and that 90-day risk-free securities yield 5 percent in the United States and 5.3 percent in Britain. In the spot market 1 pound equals 1.65 dollars.
- a. Is the 90-day forward rate trading at a premium or discount relative to the spot rate?
- b. What is the 90-day forward rate?

16-15
Interest rate parity

Assume that interest rate parity holds. In both the spot market and the 90-day forward market 1 Japanese yen equals 0.0086 dollar. The 90-day risk-free securities yield 4.6 percent in Japan. What is the yield on 90-day risk-free securities in the United States?

16-16
Purchasing power parity

In the spot market 7.8 Mexican pesos can be exchanged for 1 U.S. dollar. A compact disc costs $15 in the United States. If purchasing power parity (PPP) holds, what should be the price of the same disc in Mexico?

16-17
Purchasing power parity

A chair costs 500 euros. The same chair also costs 10,000 Japanese yen. If purchasing power parity (PPP) holds, what should be the exchange rate between the yen and the euro?

SPREADSHEET PROBLEM

16-18
Multinational financial management

Yohe Telecommunications is a multinational corporation that produces and distributes telecommunications technology. Although its corporate headquarters are located in Maitland, Florida, Yohe usually must buy its raw materials in several different foreign countries using several different foreign currencies. The matter is further complicated because Yohe usually sells its products in other foreign countries. One product in particular, the SY-20 radio transmitter, draws its principal components, Component X, Component Y, and Component Z, from Germany, France, and England, respectively. Specifically, Component X costs 165 German DM, Component Y costs 425 French francs, and Component Z costs 105 British pounds. The largest market for the SY-20 is in Japan, where it sells for 38,000 Japanese yen. Naturally, Yohe is intimately concerned with economic conditions that could adversely affect dollar exchange rates. You will find Tables 16-1, 16-2, and 16-3 useful for this problem.
- a. How much, in dollars, does it cost for Yohe to produce the SY-20? What is the dollar sale price of the SY-20?
- b. What is the dollar profit that Yohe makes on the sale of the SY-20? What is the percentage profit?
- c. If the U.S. dollar were to weaken by 10 percent against all foreign currencies, what would be the dollar profit for the SY-20?
- d. If the U.S. dollar were to weaken by 10 percent only against the Japanese yen and remained constant relative to all other foreign currencies, what would be the dollar and percentage profits for the SY-20?
- e. Using the forward exchange information from Table 16-3, calculate the return on 1-year securities in Germany, if the rate of return on 1-year securities in the U.S. is 4.9 percent.
- f. Assuming that purchasing power parity (PPP) holds, what would be the sale price of the SY-20 if it were sold in England rather than Japan?

The information related to this cyberproblem is likely to change over time, due to the release of new information and the ever-changing nature of the World Wide Web. Accordingly, we will periodically update the problem on the textbook's web site. To avoid problems, please check for updates before proceeding with the cyberproblems.

16-19

Multinational financial management—McDonald's

With more than 28,000 restaurants in over 100 countries, McDonald's is the largest and best-known global foodservice retailer. Built upon the Dick and Mac McDonald's concept of a quick-service restaurant and pioneered by Ray Kroc, McDonald's has evolved from a simple restaurant to a cultural icon and global empire. McDonald's has effectively fostered innovation and established itself as the premier entity in the fast-food industry. This cyberproblem looks at McDonald's presence abroad and the strategies it employs to maintain stability in an always-evolving foreign market.

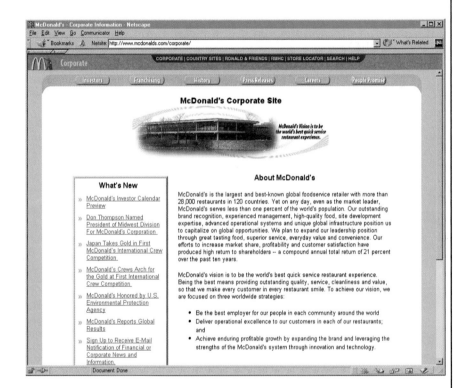

a. Access McDonald's investor relations web page at **http://www.mcdonalds.com/corporate/investor/index.html**. Click on the label, "Downloadable Financials," which is located under the "Financial Information" section on the left side of the web page. Click on "2000 McDonald's Corp. Downloadable Financial Information" and save the Excel file, mcd00ar.xls. Then, retrieve the file in Excel and click on the tab at the bottom of the spreadsheet labeled "Restaurants by Country." (There are a number of tabs below the spreadsheet, so you will have to use the right and left arrow keys near the bottom of your screen until the tab appears.) In the current year, what is the percentage of stores located outside of the United States? Over the past 5 years, what was the percentage increase in the number of stores in the United States? What was the percentage increase in Europe? What was the percentage increase in the Asia/Pacific region?

b. Click on the tab labeled, "FR-Segment & Geo. Info." For the most recent year, what percentages of the company's sales, operating income, and capital expenditures are for its stores outside of the United States? Over the past 2 years, which region has had the largest increase in sales? Which region has had the largest increase in capital expenditures?

c. Click on the tab labeled, "YIR-Returns; Debt; Currency Exp." Look at the Foreign Currency Exposures section. For which foreign currencies does McDonald's have the most exposure?

d. Finally, click on the tab labeled, "YIR-Avg. Annual Sales; Revenues." Scroll down to the sections entitled, "Average Annual Sales Per Restaurant" and "Average Annual Sales Per New Restaurant." Among the existing stores, are sales per restaurant higher inside or outside the United States? Among newly opened stores, are sales per restaurant higher inside or outside the United States?

INTEGRATED CASE

CITRUS PRODUCTS INC.

19-20 Multinational Financial Management Citrus Products Inc. is a medium-sized producer of citrus juice drinks with groves in Indian River County, Florida. Until now, the company has confined its operations and sales to the United States, but its CEO, George Gaynor, wants to expand into the Pacific Rim. The first step would be to set up sales subsidiaries in Japan and Australia, then to set up a production plant in Japan, and, finally, to distribute the product throughout the Pacific Rim. The firm's financial manager, Ruth Schmidt, is enthusiastic about the plan, but she is worried about the implications of the foreign expansion on the firm's financial management process. She has asked you, the firm's most recently hired financial analyst, to develop a 1-hour tutorial package that explains the basics of multinational financial management. The tutorial will be presented at the next board of directors meeting. To get you started, Schmidt has supplied you with the following list of questions.

a. What is a multinational corporation? Why do firms expand into other countries?

b. What are the six major factors that distinguish multinational financial management from financial management as practiced by a purely domestic firm?

c. Consider the following illustrative exchange rates.

	U.S. DOLLARS REQUIRED TO BUY ONE UNIT OF FOREIGN CURRENCY
Japanese yen	0.009
Australian dollar	0.650

(1) Are these currency prices direct quotations or indirect quotations?

(2) Calculate the indirect quotations for yen and Australian dollars.

(3) What is a cross rate? Calculate the two cross rates between yen and Australian dollars.

(4) Assume Citrus Products can produce a liter of orange juice and ship it to Japan for $1.75. If the firm wants

a 50 percent markup on the product, what should the orange juice sell for in Japan?

(5) Now, assume Citrus Products begins producing the same liter of orange juice in Japan. The product costs 250 yen to produce and ship to Australia, where it can be sold for 6 Australian dollars. What is the U.S. dollar profit on the sale?

(6) What is exchange rate risk?

d. Briefly describe the current international monetary system. How does the current system differ from the system that was in place prior to August 1971?

e. What is a convertible currency? What problems arise when a multinational company operates in a country whose currency is not convertible?

f. What is the difference between spot rates and forward rates? When is the forward rate at a premium to the spot rate? At a discount?

g. What is interest rate parity? Currently, you can exchange 1 yen for 0.0095 U.S. dollar in the 30-day forward market, and the risk-free rate on 30-day securities is 4 percent in both Japan and the United States. Does interest rate parity hold? If not, which securities offer the highest expected return?

h. What is purchasing power parity (PPP)? If grapefruit juice costs $2.00 a liter in the United States and purchasing power parity holds, what should be the price of grapefruit juice in Australia?

i. What impact does relative inflation have on interest rates and exchange rates?

j. Briefly discuss the international capital markets.

k. To what extent do average capital structures vary across different countries?

l. What is the impact of multinational operations on each of the following financial management topics?
(1) Cash management.
(2) Capital budgeting decisions.
(3) Credit management.
(4) Inventory management.

TABLE A-1 — Present Value of $1 Due at the End of n Periods

EQUATION:

$$PVIF_{i,n} = \frac{1}{(1 + i)^n}$$

FINANCIAL CALCULATOR KEYS:

n	i		0	1.0
N	**I**	**PV**	**PMT**	**FV**

TABLE
VALUE

PERIOD	1%	2%	3%	4%	5%	6%	7%	8%	9%	10%
1	.9901	.9804	.9709	.9615	.9524	.9434	.9346	.9259	.9174	.9091
2	.9803	.9612	.9426	.9246	.9070	.8900	.8734	.8573	.8417	.8264
3	.9706	.9423	.9151	.8890	.8638	.8396	.8163	.7938	.7722	.7513
4	.9610	.9238	.8885	.8548	.8227	.7921	.7629	.7350	.7084	.6830
5	.9515	.9057	.8626	.8219	.7835	.7473	.7130	.6806	.6499	.6209
6	.9420	.8880	.8375	.7903	.7462	.7050	.6663	.6302	.5963	.5645
7	.9327	.8706	.8131	.7599	.7107	.6651	.6227	.5835	.5470	.5132
8	.9235	.8535	.7894	.7307	.6768	.6274	.5820	.5403	.5019	.4665
9	.9143	.8368	.7664	.7026	.6446	.5919	.5439	.5002	.4604	.4241
10	.9053	.8203	.7441	.6756	.6139	.5584	.5083	.4632	.4224	.3855
11	.8963	.8043	.7224	.6496	.5847	.5268	.4751	.4289	.3875	.3505
12	.8874	.7885	.7014	.6246	.5568	.4970	.4440	.3971	.3555	.3186
13	.8787	.7730	.6810	.6006	.5303	.4688	.4150	.3677	.3262	.2897
14	.8700	.7579	.6611	.5775	.5051	.4423	.3878	.3405	.2992	.2633
15	.8613	.7430	.6419	.5553	.4810	.4173	.3624	.3152	.2745	.2394
16	.8528	.7284	.6232	.5339	.4581	.3936	.3387	.2919	.2519	.2176
17	.8444	.7142	.6050	.5134	.4363	.3714	.3166	.2703	.2311	.1978
18	.8360	.7002	.5874	.4936	.4155	.3503	.2959	.2502	.2120	.1799
19	.8277	.6864	.5703	.4746	.3957	.3305	.2765	.2317	.1945	.1635
20	.8195	.6730	.5537	.4564	.3769	.3118	.2584	.2145	.1784	.1486
21	.8114	.6598	.5375	.4388	.3589	.2942	.2415	.1987	.1637	.1351
22	.8034	.6468	.5219	.4220	.3418	.2775	.2257	.1839	.1502	.1228
23	.7954	.6342	.5067	.4057	.3256	.2618	.2109	.1703	.1378	.1117
24	.7876	.6217	.4919	.3901	.3101	.2470	.1971	.1577	.1264	.1015
25	.7798	.6095	.4776	.3751	.2953	.2330	.1842	.1460	.1160	.0923
26	.7720	.5976	.4637	.3607	.2812	.2198	.1722	.1352	.1064	.0839
27	.7644	.5859	.4502	.3468	.2678	.2074	.1609	.1252	.0976	.0763
28	.7568	.5744	.4371	.3335	.2551	.1956	.1504	.1159	.0895	.0693
29	.7493	.5631	.4243	.3207	.2429	.1846	.1406	.1073	.0822	.0630
30	.7419	.5521	.4120	.3083	.2314	.1741	.1314	.0994	.0754	.0573
35	.7059	.5000	.3554	.2534	.1813	.1301	.0937	.0676	.0490	.0356
40	.6717	.4529	.3066	.2083	.1420	.0972	.0668	.0460	.0318	.0221
45	.6391	.4102	.2644	.1712	.1113	.0727	.0476	.0313	.0207	.0137
50	.6080	.3715	.2281	.1407	.0872	.0543	.0339	.0213	.0134	.0085
55	.5785	.3365	.1968	.1157	.0683	.0406	.0242	.0145	.0087	.0053

PERIOD	12%	14%	15%	16%	18%	20%	24%	28%	32%	36%
1	.8929	.8772	.8696	.8621	.8475	.8333	.8065	.7813	.7576	.7353
2	.7972	.7695	.7561	.7432	.7182	.6944	.6504	.6104	.5739	.5407
3	.7118	.6750	.6575	.6407	.6086	.5787	.5245	.4768	.4348	.3975
4	.6355	.5921	.5718	.5523	.5158	.4823	.4230	.3725	.3294	.2923
5	.5674	.5194	.4972	.4761	.4371	.4019	.3411	.2910	.2495	.2149
6	.5066	.4556	.4323	.4104	.3704	.3349	.2751	.2274	.1890	.1580
7	.4523	.3996	.3759	.3538	.3139	.2791	.2218	.1776	.1432	.1162
8	.4039	.3506	.3269	.3050	.2660	.2326	.1789	.1388	.1085	.0854
9	.3606	.3075	.2843	.2630	.2255	.1938	.1443	.1084	.0822	.0628
10	.3220	.2697	.2472	.2267	.1911	.1615	.1164	.0847	.0623	.0462
11	.2875	.2366	.2149	.1954	.1619	.1346	.0938	.0662	.0472	.0340
12	.2567	.2076	.1869	.1685	.1372	.1122	.0757	.0517	.0357	.0250
13	.2292	.1821	.1625	.1452	.1163	.0935	.0610	.0404	.0271	.0184
14	.2046	.1597	.1413	.1252	.0985	.0779	.0492	.0316	.0205	.0135
15	.1827	.1401	.1229	.1079	.0835	.0649	.0397	.0247	.0155	.0099
16	.1631	.1229	.1069	.0930	.0708	.0541	.0320	.0193	.0118	.0073
17	.1456	.1078	.0929	.0802	.0600	.0451	.0258	.0150	.0089	.0054
18	.1300	.0946	.0808	.0691	.0508	.0376	.0208	.0118	.0068	.0039
19	.1161	.0829	.0703	.0596	.0431	.0313	.0168	.0092	.0051	.0029
20	.1037	.0728	.0611	.0514	.0365	.0261	.0135	.0072	.0039	.0021
21	.0926	.0638	.0531	.0443	.0309	.0217	.0109	.0056	.0029	.0016
22	.0826	.0560	.0462	.0382	.0262	.0181	.0088	.0044	.0022	.0012
23	.0738	.0491	.0402	.0329	.0222	.0151	.0071	.0034	.0017	.0008
24	.0659	.0431	.0349	.0284	.0188	.0126	.0057	.0027	.0013	.0006
25	.0588	.0378	.0304	.0245	.0160	.0105	.0046	.0021	.0010	.0005
26	.0525	.0331	.0264	.0211	.0135	.0087	.0037	.0016	.0007	.0003
27	.0469	.0291	.0230	.0182	.0115	.0073	.0030	.0013	.0006	.0002
28	.0419	.0255	.0200	.0157	.0097	.0061	.0024	.0010	.0004	.0002
29	.0374	.0224	.0174	.0135	.0082	.0051	.0020	.0008	.0003	.0001
30	.0334	.0196	.0151	.0116	.0070	.0042	.0016	.0006	.0002	.0001
35	.0189	.0102	.0075	.0055	.0030	.0017	.0005	.0002	.0001	*
40	.0107	.0053	.0037	.0026	.0013	.0007	.0002	.0001	*	*
45	.0061	.0027	.0019	.0013	.0006	.0003	.0001	*	*	*
50	.0035	.0014	.0009	.0006	.0003	.0001	*	*	*	*
55	.0020	.0007	.0005	.0003	.0001	*	*	*	*	*

*The factor is zero to four decimal places.

EQUATION:

$$PVIFA_{i,n} = \sum_{t=1}^{n} \frac{1}{(1+i)^t} = \frac{1 - \dfrac{1}{(1+i)^n}}{i} = \frac{1}{i} - \frac{1}{i(1+i)^n}$$

FINANCIAL CALCULATOR KEYS:

n	i		1.0	0
N	**I**	**PV**	**PMT**	**FV**
		TABLE VALUE		

NUMBER OF PERIODS	1%	2%	3%	4%	5%	6%	7%	8%	9%
1	0.9901	0.9804	0.9709	0.9615	0.9524	0.9434	0.9346	0.9259	0.9174
2	1.9704	1.9416	1.9135	1.8861	1.8594	1.8334	1.8080	1.7833	1.7591
3	2.9410	2.8839	2.8286	2.7751	2.7232	2.6730	2.6243	2.5771	2.5313
4	3.9020	3.8077	3.7171	3.6299	3.5460	3.4651	3.3872	3.3121	3.2397
5	4.8534	4.7135	4.5797	4.4518	4.3295	4.2124	4.1002	3.9927	3.8897
6	5.7955	5.6014	5.4172	5.2421	5.0757	4.9173	4.7665	4.6229	4.4859
7	6.7282	6.4720	6.2303	6.0021	5.7864	5.5824	5.3893	5.2064	5.0330
8	7.6517	7.3255	7.0197	6.7327	6.4632	6.2098	5.9713	5.7466	5.5348
9	8.5660	8.1622	7.7861	7.4353	7.1078	6.8017	6.5152	6.2469	5.9952
10	9.4713	8.9826	8.5302	8.1109	7.7217	7.3601	7.0236	6.7101	6.4177
11	10.3676	9.7868	9.2526	8.7605	8.3064	7.8869	7.4987	7.1390	6.8052
12	11.2551	10.5753	9.9540	9.3851	8.8633	8.3838	7.9427	7.5361	7.1607
13	12.1337	11.3484	10.6350	9.9856	9.3936	8.8527	8.3577	7.9038	7.4869
14	13.0037	12.1062	11.2961	10.5631	9.8986	9.2950	8.7455	8.2442	7.7862
15	13.8651	12.8493	11.9379	11.1184	10.3797	9.7122	9.1079	8.5595	8.0607
16	14.7179	13.5777	12.5611	11.6523	10.8378	10.1059	9.4466	8.8514	8.3126
17	15.5623	14.2919	13.1661	12.1657	11.2741	10.4773	9.7632	9.1216	8.5436
18	16.3983	14.9920	13.7535	12.6593	11.6896	10.8276	10.0591	9.3719	8.7556
19	17.2260	15.6785	14.3238	13.1339	12.0853	11.1581	10.3356	9.6036	8.9501
20	18.0456	16.3514	14.8775	13.5903	12.4622	11.4699	10.5940	9.8181	9.1285
21	18.8570	17.0112	15.4150	14.0292	12.8212	11.7641	10.8355	10.0168	9.2922
22	19.6604	17.6580	15.9369	14.4511	13.1630	12.0416	11.0612	10.2007	9.4424
23	20.4558	18.2922	16.4436	14.8568	13.4886	12.3034	11.2722	10.3711	9.5802
24	21.2434	18.9139	16.9355	15.2470	13.7986	12.5504	11.4693	10.5288	9.7066
25	22.0232	19.5235	17.4131	15.6221	14.0939	12.7834	11.6536	10.6748	9.8226
26	22.7952	20.1210	17.8768	15.9828	14.3752	13.0032	11.8258	10.8100	9.9290
27	23.5596	20.7069	18.3270	16.3296	14.6430	13.2105	11.9867	10.9352	10.0266
28	24.3164	21.2813	18.7641	16.6631	14.8981	13.4062	12.1371	11.0511	10.1161
29	25.0658	21.8444	19.1885	16.9837	15.1411	13.5907	12.2777	11.1584	10.1983
30	25.8077	22.3965	19.6004	17.2920	15.3725	13.7648	12.4090	11.2578	10.2737
35	29.4086	24.9986	21.4872	18.6646	16.3742	14.4982	12.9477	11.6546	10.5668
40	32.8347	27.3555	23.1148	19.7928	17.1591	15.0463	13.3317	11.9246	10.7574
45	36.0945	29.4902	24.5187	20.7200	17.7741	15.4558	13.6055	12.1084	10.8812
50	39.1961	31.4236	25.7298	21.4822	18.2559	15.7619	13.8007	12.2335	10.9617
55	42.1472	33.1748	26.7744	22.1086	18.6335	15.9905	13.9399	12.3186	11.0140

NUMBER OF PERIODS	10%	12%	14%	15%	16%	18%	20%	24%	28%	32%
1	0.9091	0.8929	0.8772	0.8696	0.8621	0.8475	0.8333	0.8065	0.7813	0.7576
2	1.7355	1.6901	1.6467	1.6257	1.6052	1.5656	1.5278	1.4568	1.3916	1.3315
3	2.4869	2.4018	2.3216	2.2832	2.2459	2.1743	2.1065	1.9813	1.8684	1.7663
4	3.1699	3.0373	2.9137	2.8550	2.7982	2.6901	2.5887	2.4043	2.2410	2.0957
5	3.7908	3.6048	3.4331	3.3522	3.2743	3.1272	2.9906	2.7454	2.5320	2.3452
6	4.3553	4.1114	3.8887	3.7845	3.6847	3.4976	3.3255	3.0205	2.7594	2.5342
7	4.8684	4.5638	4.2883	4.1604	4.0386	3.8115	3.6046	3.2423	2.9370	2.6775
8	5.3349	4.9676	4.6389	4.4873	4.3436	4.0776	3.8372	3.4212	3.0758	2.7860
9	5.7590	5.3282	4.9464	4.7716	4.6065	4.3030	4.0310	3.5655	3.1842	2.8681
10	6.1446	5.6502	5.2161	5.0188	4.8332	4.4941	4.1925	3.6819	3.2689	2.9304
11	6.4951	5.9377	5.4527	5.2337	5.0286	4.6560	4.3271	3.7757	3.3351	2.9776
12	6.8137	6.1944	5.6603	5.4206	5.1971	4.7932	4.4392	3.8514	3.3868	3.0133
13	7.1034	6.4235	5.8424	5.5831	5.3423	4.9095	4.5327	3.9124	3.4272	3.0404
14	7.3667	6.6282	6.0021	5.7245	5.4675	5.0081	4.6106	3.9616	3.4587	3.0609
15	7.6061	6.8109	6.1422	5.8474	5.5755	5.0916	4.6755	4.0013	3.4834	3.0764
16	7.8237	6.9740	6.2651	5.9542	5.6685	5.1624	4.7296	4.0333	3.5026	3.0882
17	8.0216	7.1196	6.3729	6.0472	5.7487	5.2223	4.7746	4.0591	3.5177	3.0971
18	8.2014	7.2497	6.4674	6.1280	5.8178	5.2732	4.8122	4.0799	3.5294	3.1039
19	8.3649	7.3658	6.5504	6.1982	5.8775	5.3162	4.8435	4.0967	3.5386	3.1090
20	8.5136	7.4694	6.6231	6.2593	5.9288	5.3527	4.8696	4.1103	3.5458	3.1129
21	8.6487	7.5620	6.6870	6.3125	5.9731	5.3837	4.8913	4.1212	3.5514	3.1158
22	8.7715	7.6446	6.7429	6.3587	6.0113	5.4099	4.9094	4.1300	3.5558	3.1180
23	8.8832	7.7184	6.7921	6.3988	6.0442	5.4321	4.9245	4.1371	3.5592	3.1197
24	8.9847	7.7843	6.8351	6.4338	6.0726	5.4509	4.9371	4.1428	3.5619	3.1210
25	9.0770	7.8431	6.8729	6.4641	6.0971	5.4669	4.9476	4.1474	3.5640	3.1220
26	9.1609	7.8957	6.9061	6.4906	6.1182	5.4804	4.9563	4.1511	3.5656	3.1227
27	9.2372	7.9426	6.9352	6.5135	6.1364	5.4919	4.9636	4.1542	3.5669	3.1233
28	9.3066	7.9844	6.9607	6.5335	6.1520	5.5016	4.9697	4.1566	3.5679	3.1237
29	9.3696	8.0218	6.9830	6.5509	6.1656	5.5098	4.9747	4.1585	3.5687	3.1240
30	9.4269	8.0552	7.0027	6.5660	6.1772	5.5168	4.9789	4.1601	3.5693	3.1242
35	9.6442	8.1755	7.0700	6.6166	6.2153	5.5386	4.9915	4.1644	3.5708	3.1248
40	9.7791	8.2438	7.1050	6.6418	6.2335	5.5482	4.9966	4.1659	3.5712	3.1250
45	9.8628	8.2825	7.1232	6.6543	6.2421	5.5523	4.9986	4.1664	3.5714	3.1250
50	9.9148	8.3045	7.1327	6.6605	6.2463	5.5541	4.9995	4.1666	3.5714	3.1250
55	9.9471	8.3170	7.1376	6.6636	6.2482	5.5549	4.9998	4.1666	3.5714	3.1250

EQUATION:

$$FVIF_{i,n} = (1 + i)^n$$

FINANCIAL CALCULATOR KEYS:

n	i	1.0	0	
N	I	PV	PMT	FV

TABLE
VALUE

PERIOD	1%	2%	3%	4%	5%	6%	7%	8%	9%	10%
1	1.0100	1.0200	1.0300	1.0400	1.0500	1.0600	1.0700	1.0800	1.0900	1.1000
2	1.0201	1.0404	1.0609	1.0816	1.1025	1.1236	1.1449	1.1664	1.1881	1.2100
3	1.0303	1.0612	1.0927	1.1249	1.1576	1.1910	1.2250	1.2597	1.2950	1.3310
4	1.0406	1.0824	1.1255	1.1699	1.2155	1.2625	1.3108	1.3605	1.4116	1.4641
5	1.0510	1.1041	1.1593	1.2167	1.2763	1.3382	1.4026	1.4693	1.5386	1.6105
6	1.0615	1.1262	1.1941	1.2653	1.3401	1.4185	1.5007	1.5869	1.6771	1.7716
7	1.0721	1.1487	1.2299	1.3159	1.4071	1.5036	1.6058	1.7138	1.8280	1.9487
8	1.0829	1.1717	1.2668	1.3686	1.4775	1.5938	1.7182	1.8509	1.9926	2.1436
9	1.0937	1.1951	1.3048	1.4233	1.5513	1.6895	1.8385	1.9990	2.1719	2.3579
10	1.1046	1.2190	1.3439	1.4802	1.6289	1.7908	1.9672	2.1589	2.3674	2.5937
11	1.1157	1.2434	1.3842	1.5395	1.7103	1.8983	2.1049	2.3316	2.5804	2.8531
12	1.1268	1.2682	1.4258	1.6010	1.7959	2.0122	2.2522	2.5182	2.8127	3.1384
13	1.1381	1.2936	1.4685	1.6651	1.8856	2.1329	2.4098	2.7196	3.0658	3.4523
14	1.1495	1.3195	1.5126	1.7317	1.9799	2.2609	2.5785	2.9372	3.3417	3.7975
15	1.1610	1.3459	1.5580	1.8009	2.0789	2.3966	2.7590	3.1722	3.6425	4.1772
16	1.1726	1.3728	1.6047	1.8730	2.1829	2.5404	2.9522	3.4259	3.9703	4.5950
17	1.1843	1.4002	1.6528	1.9479	2.2920	2.6928	3.1588	3.7000	4.3276	5.0545
18	1.1961	1.4282	1.7024	2.0258	2.4066	2.8543	3.3799	3.9960	4.7171	5.5599
19	1.2081	1.4568	1.7535	2.1068	2.5270	3.0256	3.6165	4.3157	5.1417	6.1159
20	1.2202	1.4859	1.8061	2.1911	2.6533	3.2071	3.8697	4.6610	5.6044	6.7275
21	1.2324	1.5157	1.8603	2.2788	2.7860	3.3996	4.1406	5.0338	6.1088	7.4002
22	1.2447	1.5460	1.9161	2.3699	2.9253	3.6035	4.4304	5.4365	6.6586	8.1403
23	1.2572	1.5769	1.9736	2.4647	3.0715	3.8197	4.7405	5.8715	7.2579	8.9543
24	1.2697	1.6084	2.0328	2.5633	3.2251	4.0489	5.0724	6.3412	7.9111	9.8497
25	1.2824	1.6406	2.0938	2.6658	3.3864	4.2919	5.4274	6.8485	8.6231	10.835
26	1.2953	1.6734	2.1566	2.7725	3.5557	4.5494	5.8074	7.3964	9.3992	11.918
27	1.3082	1.7069	2.2213	2.8834	3.7335	4.8223	6.2139	7.9881	10.245	13.110
28	1.3213	1.7410	2.2879	2.9987	3.9201	5.1117	6.6488	8.6271	11.167	14.421
29	1.3345	1.7758	2.3566	3.1187	4.1161	5.4184	7.1143	9.3173	12.172	15.863
30	1.3478	1.8114	2.4273	3.2434	4.3219	5.7435	7.6123	10.063	13.268	17.449
40	1.4889	2.2080	3.2620	4.8010	7.0400	10.286	14.974	21.725	31.409	45.259
50	1.6446	2.6916	4.3839	7.1067	11.467	18.420	29.457	46.902	74.358	117.39
60	1.8167	3.2810	5.8916	10.520	18.679	32.988	57.946	101.26	176.03	304.48

PERIOD	12%	14%	15%	16%	18%	20%	24%	28%	32%	36%
1	1.1200	1.1400	1.1500	1.1600	1.1800	1.2000	1.2400	1.2800	1.3200	1.3600
2	1.2544	1.2996	1.3225	1.3456	1.3924	1.4400	1.5376	1.6384	1.7424	1.8496
3	1.4049	1.4815	1.5209	1.5609	1.6430	1.7280	1.9066	2.0972	2.3000	2.5155
4	1.5735	1.6890	1.7490	1.8106	1.9388	2.0736	2.3642	2.6844	3.0360	3.4210
5	1.7623	1.9254	2.0114	2.1003	2.2878	2.4883	2.9316	3.4360	4.0075	4.6526
6	1.9738	2.1950	2.3131	2.4364	2.6996	2.9860	3.6352	4.3980	5.2899	6.3275
7	2.2107	2.5023	2.6600	2.8262	3.1855	3.5832	4.5077	5.6295	6.9826	8.6054
8	2.4760	2.8526	3.0590	3.2784	3.7589	4.2998	5.5895	7.2058	9.2170	11.703
9	2.7731	3.2519	3.5179	3.8030	4.4355	5.1598	6.9310	9.2234	12.166	15.917
10	3.1058	3.7072	4.0456	4.4114	5.2338	6.1917	8.5944	11.806	16.060	21.647
11	3.4785	4.2262	4.6524	5.1173	6.1759	7.4301	10.657	15.112	21.199	29.439
12	3.8960	4.8179	5.3503	5.9360	7.2876	8.9161	13.215	19.343	27.983	40.037
13	4.3635	5.4924	6.1528	6.8858	8.5994	10.699	16.386	24.759	36.937	54.451
14	4.8871	6.2613	7.0757	7.9875	10.147	12.839	20.319	31.691	48.757	74.053
15	5.4736	7.1379	8.1371	9.2655	11.974	15.407	25.196	40.565	64.359	100.71
16	6.1304	8.1372	9.3576	10.748	14.129	18.488	31.243	51.923	84.954	136.97
17	6.8660	9.2765	10.761	12.468	16.672	22.186	38.741	66.461	112.14	186.28
18	7.6900	10.575	12.375	14.463	19.673	26.623	48.039	85.071	148.02	253.34
19	8.6128	12.056	14.232	16.777	23.214	31.948	59.568	108.89	195.39	344.54
20	9.6463	13.743	16.367	19.461	27.393	38.338	73.864	139.38	257.92	468.57
21	10.804	15.668	18.822	22.574	32.324	46.005	91.592	178.41	340.45	637.26
22	12.100	17.861	21.645	26.186	38.142	55.206	113.57	228.36	449.39	866.67
23	13.552	20.362	24.891	30.376	45.008	66.247	140.83	292.30	593.20	1178.7
24	15.179	23.212	28.625	35.236	53.109	79.497	174.63	374.14	783.02	1603.0
25	17.000	26.462	32.919	40.874	62.669	95.396	216.54	478.90	1033.6	2180.1
26	19.040	30.167	37.857	47.414	73.949	114.48	268.51	613.00	1364.3	2964.9
27	21.325	34.390	43.535	55.000	87.260	137.37	332.95	784.64	1800.9	4032.3
28	23.884	39.204	50.066	63.800	102.97	164.84	412.86	1004.3	2377.2	5483.9
29	26.750	44.693	57.575	74.009	121.50	197.81	511.95	1285.6	3137.9	7458.1
30	29.960	50.950	66.212	85.850	143.37	237.38	634.82	1645.5	4142.1	10143.
40	93.051	188.88	267.86	378.72	750.38	1469.8	5455.9	19427.	66521.	*
50	289.00	700.23	1083.7	1670.7	3927.4	9100.4	46890.	*	*	*
60	897.60	2595.9	4384.0	7370.2	20555.	56348.	*	*	*	*

*FVIF > 99,999.

TABLE A-4 Future Value of an Annuity of $1 per Period for n Periods

EQUATION:

$$FVIFA_{i,n} = \sum_{t=1}^{n} (1 + i)^{n-t} = \frac{(1 + i)^n - 1}{i}$$

FINANCIAL CALCULATOR KEYS:

n	i	0	1.0	
N	**I**	**PV**	**PMT**	**FV**

TABLE
VALUE

NUMBER OF PERIODS	1%	2%	3%	4%	5%	6%	7%	8%	9%	10%
1	1.0000	1.0000	1.0000	1.0000	1.0000	1.0000	1.0000	1.0000	1.0000	1.0000
2	2.0100	2.0200	2.0300	2.0400	2.0500	2.0600	2.0700	2.0800	2.0900	2.1000
3	3.0301	3.0604	3.0909	3.1216	3.1525	3.1836	3.2149	3.2464	3.2781	3.3100
4	4.0604	4.1216	4.1836	4.2465	4.3101	4.3746	4.4399	4.5061	4.5731	4.6410
5	5.1010	5.2040	5.3091	5.4163	5.5256	5.6371	5.7507	5.8666	5.9847	6.1051
6	6.1520	6.3081	6.4684	6.6330	6.8019	6.9753	7.1533	7.3359	7.5233	7.7156
7	7.2135	7.4343	7.6625	7.8983	8.1420	8.3938	8.6540	8.9228	9.2004	9.4872
8	8.2857	8.5830	8.8923	9.2142	9.5491	9.8975	10.260	10.637	11.028	11.436
9	9.3685	9.7546	10.159	10.583	11.027	11.491	11.978	12.488	13.021	13.579
10	10.462	10.950	11.464	12.006	12.578	13.181	13.816	14.487	15.193	15.937
11	11.567	12.169	12.808	13.486	14.207	14.972	15.784	16.645	17.560	18.531
12	12.683	13.412	14.192	15.026	15.917	16.870	17.888	18.977	20.141	21.384
13	13.809	14.680	15.618	16.627	17.713	18.882	20.141	21.495	22.953	24.523
14	14.947	15.974	17.086	18.292	19.599	21.015	22.550	24.215	26.019	27.975
15	16.097	17.293	18.599	20.024	21.579	23.276	25.129	27.152	29.361	31.772
16	17.258	18.639	20.157	21.825	23.657	25.673	27.888	30.324	33.003	35.950
17	18.430	20.012	21.762	23.698	25.840	28.213	30.840	33.750	36.974	40.545
18	19.615	21.412	23.414	25.645	28.132	30.906	33.999	37.450	41.301	45.599
19	20.811	22.841	25.117	27.671	30.539	33.760	37.379	41.446	46.018	51.159
20	22.019	24.297	26.870	29.778	33.066	36.786	40.995	45.762	51.160	57.275
21	23.239	25.783	28.676	31.969	35.719	39.993	44.865	50.423	56.765	64.002
22	24.472	27.299	30.537	34.248	38.505	43.392	49.006	55.457	62.873	71.403
23	25.716	28.845	32.453	36.618	41.430	46.996	53.436	60.893	69.532	79.543
24	26.973	30.422	34.426	39.083	44.502	50.816	58.177	66.765	76.790	88.497
25	28.243	32.030	36.459	41.646	47.727	54.865	63.249	73.106	84.701	98.347
26	29.526	33.671	38.553	44.312	51.113	59.156	68.676	79.954	93.324	109.18
27	30.821	35.344	40.710	47.084	54.669	63.706	74.484	87.351	102.72	121.10
28	32.129	37.051	42.931	49.968	58.403	68.528	80.698	95.339	112.97	134.21
29	33.450	38.792	45.219	52.966	62.323	73.640	87.347	103.97	124.14	148.63
30	34.785	40.568	47.575	56.085	66.439	79.058	94.461	113.28	136.31	164.49
40	48.886	60.402	75.401	95.026	120.80	154.76	199.64	259.06	337.88	442.59
50	64.463	84.579	112.80	152.67	209.35	290.34	406.53	573.77	815.08	1163.9
60	81.670	114.05	163.05	237.99	353.58	533.13	813.52	1253.2	1944.8	3034.8

NUMBER OF PERIODS	12%	14%	15%	16%	18%	20%	24%	28%	32%	36%
1	1.0000	1.0000	1.0000	1.0000	1.0000	1.0000	1.0000	1.0000	1.0000	1.0000
2	2.1200	2.1400	2.1500	2.1600	2.1800	2.2000	2.2400	2.2800	2.3200	2.3600
3	3.3744	3.4396	3.4725	3.5056	3.5724	3.6400	3.7776	3.9184	4.0624	4.2096
4	4.7793	4.9211	4.9934	5.0665	5.2154	5.3680	5.6842	6.0156	6.3624	6.7251
5	6.3528	6.6101	6.7424	6.8771	7.1542	7.4416	8.0484	8.6999	9.3983	10.146
6	8.1152	8.5355	8.7537	8.9775	9.4420	9.9299	10.980	12.136	13.406	14.799
7	10.089	10.730	11.067	11.414	12.142	12.916	14.615	16.534	18.696	21.126
8	12.300	13.233	13.727	14.240	15.327	16.499	19.123	22.163	25.678	29.732
9	14.776	16.085	16.786	17.519	19.086	20.799	24.712	29.369	34.895	41.435
10	17.549	19.337	20.304	21.321	23.521	25.959	31.643	38.593	47.062	57.352
11	20.655	23.045	24.349	25.733	28.755	32.150	40.238	50.398	63.122	78.998
12	24.133	27.271	29.002	30.850	34.931	39.581	50.895	65.510	84.320	108.44
13	28.029	32.089	34.352	36.786	42.219	48.497	64.110	84.853	112.30	148.47
14	32.393	37.581	40.505	43.672	50.818	59.196	80.496	109.61	149.24	202.93
15	37.280	43.842	47.580	51.660	60.965	72.035	100.82	141.30	198.00	276.98
16	42.753	50.980	55.717	60.925	72.939	87.442	126.01	181.87	262.36	377.69
17	48.884	59.118	65.075	71.673	87.068	105.93	157.25	233.79	347.31	514.66
18	55.750	68.394	75.836	84.141	103.74	128.12	195.99	300.25	459.45	700.94
19	63.440	78.969	88.212	98.603	123.41	154.74	244.03	385.32	607.47	954.28
20	72.052	91.025	102.44	115.38	146.63	186.69	303.60	494.21	802.86	1298.8
21	81.699	104.77	118.81	134.84	174.02	225.03	377.46	633.59	1060.8	1767.4
22	92.503	120.44	137.63	157.41	206.34	271.03	469.06	812.00	1401.2	2404.7
23	104.60	138.30	159.28	183.60	244.49	326.24	582.63	1040.4	1850.6	3271.3
24	118.16	158.66	184.17	213.98	289.49	392.48	723.46	1332.7	2443.8	4450.0
25	133.33	181.87	212.79	249.21	342.60	471.98	898.09	1706.8	3226.8	6053.0
26	150.33	208.33	245.71	290.09	405.27	567.38	1114.6	2185.7	4260.4	8233.1
27	169.37	238.50	283.57	337.50	479.22	681.85	1383.1	2798.7	5624.8	11198.0
28	190.70	272.89	327.10	392.50	566.48	819.22	1716.1	3583.3	7425.7	15230.3
29	214.58	312.09	377.17	456.30	669.45	984.07	2129.0	4587.7	9802.9	20714.2
30	241.33	356.79	434.75	530.31	790.95	1181.9	2640.9	5873.2	12941.	28172.3
40	767.09	1342.0	1779.1	2360.8	4163.2	7343.9	22729.	69377.	*	*
50	2400.0	4994.5	7217.7	10436.	21813.	45497.	*	*	*	*
60	7471.6	18535.	29220.	46058.	*	*	*	*	*	*

*FVIFA > 99,999.

SOLUTIONS TO
SELF-TEST PROBLEMS

Note: Except for Chapter 1, we do not show an answer for ST-1 problems because they are verbal rather than quantitative in nature.

CHAPTER 1

ST-1 Refer to the marginal glossary definitions or relevant chapter sections to check your responses.

CHAPTER 2

ST-2 a.

EBIT	$5,000,000
Interest	1,000,000
EBT	$4,000,000
Taxes (40%)	1,600,000
Net income	$2,400,000

b.
$$NCF = NI + DEP$$
$$= \$2,400,000 + \$1,000,000 = \$3,400,000.$$

c.
$$NOPAT = EBIT\,(1 - T)$$
$$= \$5,000,000\,(0.6)$$
$$= \$3,000,000.$$

d.
$$OCF = NOPAT + DEP$$
$$= EBIT\,(1 - T) + DEP$$
$$= \$5,000,000\,(0.6) + \$1,000,000$$
$$= \$4,000,000.$$

e.
$$FCF = NOPAT - \text{Net investment in operating capital}$$
$$= \$3,000,000 - (\$25,000,000 - \$24,000,000)$$
$$= \$2,000,000.$$

f.
$$EVA = EBIT\,(1 - T) - (\text{Total operating capital})\,(\text{After-tax cost of capital})$$
$$= \$5,000,000\,(0.6) - (\$25,000,000)\,(0.10)$$
$$= \$3,000,000 - \$2,500,000 = \$500,000.$$

ST-3	HENDERSON'S TAXES AS A CORPORATION	2002	2003	2004
	Income before salary and taxes	$52,700	$90,000	$150,000
	Less: salary	(40,000)	(40,000)	(40,000)
	Taxable income, corporate	$12,700	$50,000	$110,000
	Total corporate tax	1,905[a]	7,500	26,150
	Salary	$40,000	$40,000	$ 40,000
	Less exemptions and deductions	(18,100)	(18,100)	(18,100)
	Taxable personal income	$21,900	$21,900	$ 21,900
	Total personal tax	3,285[b]	3,285	3,285
	Combined corporate and personal tax:	$ 5,190	$10,785	$ 29,435
	HENDERSON'S TAXES AS A PROPRIETORSHIP			
	Total income	$52,700	$90,000	$150,000
	Less: exemptions and deductions	(18,100)	(18,100)	(18,100)
	Taxable personal income	$34,600	$71,900	$131,900
	Tax liability of proprietorship	$ 5,190[c]	$14,432	$ 32,010
	Advantage to being a corporation:	$ 0	$ 3,647	$ 2,575

[a] Corporate tax in 2002 = (0.15)($12,700) = $1,905.

[b] Personal tax (if Henderson incorporates) in 2002 = (0.15)($21,900) = $3,285.

[c] Proprietorship tax in 2002 = (0.15)($34,600) = $5,190.

Notice that in 2002, both the corporate form of organization and the proprietorship form have the same tax liability; however, in 2003 and 2004, the corporate form has the lower tax liability. Thus, the corporate form of organization allows Henderson to pay the lowest taxes in each year. Therefore, on the basis of taxes over the 3-year period, Henderson should incorporate her business. However, note that to get additional money out of the corporation so she can spend it, Henderson will have to have the corporation pay dividends, which will be taxed to Henderson, and thus she will, sometime in the future, have to pay additional taxes.

CHAPTER 3

ST-2 Billingsworth paid $2 in dividends and retained $2 per share. Since total retained earnings rose by $12 million, there must be 6 million shares outstanding. With a book value of $40 per share, total common equity must be $40(6 million) = $240 million. Since Billingsworth has $120 million of debt, its debt ratio must be 33.3 percent:

$$\frac{\text{Debt}}{\text{Assets}} = \frac{\text{Debt}}{\text{Debt} + \text{Equity}} = \frac{\$120 \text{ million}}{\$120 \text{ million} + \$240 \text{ million}}$$

$$= 0.333 = 33.3\%.$$

ST-3 a. In answering questions such as this, always begin by writing down the relevant definitional equations, then start filling in numbers. Note that the extra zeros indicating millions have been deleted in the calculations below.

$$(1) \qquad \text{DSO} = \frac{\text{Accounts receivable}}{\text{Sales}/365}$$

$$40.55 = \frac{\text{A/R}}{\$1,000/365}$$

$$\text{A/R} = 40.55(\$2.7397) = \$111.1 \text{ million.}$$

(2) $$\text{Quick ratio} = \frac{\text{Current assets} - \text{Inventories}}{\text{Current liabilities}} = 2.0$$

$$= \frac{\text{Cash and marketable securities} + \text{A/R}}{\text{Current liabilities}} = 2.0$$

$$2.0 = \frac{\$100 + \$11.1}{\text{Current liabilities}}$$

$$\text{Current liabilities} = (\$100 + \$111.1)/2 = \$105.5 \text{ million.}$$

(3) $$\text{Current ratio} = \frac{\text{Current assets}}{\text{Current liabilities}} = 3.0$$

$$= \frac{\text{Current assets}}{\$105.5} = 3.0$$

$$\text{Current assets} = 3.0(\$105.5) = \$316.50 \text{ million.}$$

(4) $$\text{Total assets} = \text{Current assets} + \text{Fixed assets}$$

$$= \$316.5 + \$283.5 = \$600 \text{ million.}$$

(5) $$\text{ROA} = \text{Profit margin} \times \text{Total assets turnover}$$

$$= \frac{\text{Net income}}{\text{Sales}} \times \frac{\text{Sales}}{\text{Total assets}}$$

$$= \frac{\$50}{\$1,000} \times \frac{\$1,000}{\$600}$$

$$= 0.05 \times 1.667 = 0.0833 = 8.33\%.$$

(6) $$\text{ROE} = \text{ROA} \times \frac{\text{Assets}}{\text{Equity}}$$

$$12.0\% = 8.33\% \times \frac{\$600}{\text{Equity}}$$

$$\text{Equity} = \frac{(8.33\%)(\$600)}{12.0\%}$$

$$= \$416.50 \text{ million.}$$

(7) $$\text{Total assets} = \text{Total claims} = \$600 \text{ million}$$

$$\text{Current liabilities} + \text{Long-term debt} + \text{Equity} = \$600 \text{ million}$$

$$\$105.5 + \text{Long-term debt} + \$416.5 = \$600 \text{ million}$$

$$\text{Long-term debt} = \$600 - \$105.5 - \$416.5 = \$78 \text{ million.}$$

Note: We could have found equity as follows:

$$\text{ROE} = \frac{\text{Net income}}{\text{Equity}}$$

$$12.0\% = \frac{\$50}{\text{Equity}}$$

$$\text{Equity} = \$50/0.12$$

$$= \$416.67 \text{ million (rounding difference).}$$

Then we could have gone on to find current liabilities and long-term debt.

b. Kaiser's average sales per day were $\$1,000/365 = \$2.74$ million. Its DSO was 40.55, so A/R = 40.55($2.74) = $111.1 million. Its new DSO of 30.4 would cause

A/R = 30.4($2.74) = $83.3 million. The reduction in receivables would be $111.1 − $83.3 = $27.8 million, which would equal the amount of cash generated.

(1)
$$\text{New equity} = \text{Old equity} - \text{Stock bought back}$$
$$= \$416.5 - \$27.8$$
$$= \$388.7 \text{ million.}$$

Thus,

$$\text{New ROE} = \frac{\text{Net income}}{\text{New equity}}$$
$$= \frac{\$50}{\$388.7}$$
$$= 12.86\% \text{ (versus old ROE of } 12.0\%\text{).}$$

(2)
$$\text{New ROA} = \frac{\text{Net income}}{\text{Total assets} - \text{Reduction in A/R}}$$
$$= \frac{\$50}{\$600 - \$27.8}$$
$$= 8.74\% \text{ (versus old ROA of } 8.33\%\text{).}$$

(3) The old debt is the same as the new debt:

$$\text{Debt} = \text{Total claims} - \text{Equity}$$
$$= \$600 - \$416.5 = \$183.5 \text{ million.}$$
$$\text{Old total assets} = \$600 \text{ million.}$$
$$\text{New total assets} = \text{Old total assets} - \text{Reduction in A/R}$$
$$= \$600 - \$27.8$$
$$= \$572.2 \text{ million.}$$

Therefore,

$$\frac{\text{Debt}}{\text{Old total assets}} = \frac{\$183.5}{\$600} = 30.6\%,$$

while

$$\frac{\text{New debt}}{\text{New total assets}} = \frac{\$183.5}{\$572.2} = 32.1\%.$$

CHAPTER 4

ST-2 To solve this problem, we will define ΔS as the change in sales and g as the growth rate in sales, and then we use the three following equations:

$$\Delta S = S_0 g.$$
$$S_1 = S_0(1 + g).$$
$$\text{AFN} = (A^*/S_0)(\Delta S) - (L^*/S_0)(\Delta S) - MS_1(RR).$$

Set AFN = 0, substitute in known values for A^*/S_0, L^*/S_0, M, RR, and S_0, and then solve for g:

$$0 = 1.6(\$100g) - 0.4(\$100g) - 0.10[\$100(1 + g)](0.55)$$
$$= \$160g - \$40g - 0.055(\$100 + \$100g)$$
$$= \$160g - \$40g - \$5.5 - \$5.5g$$

$$\$114.5g = \$5.5$$

$$g = \$5.5/\$114.5 = 0.048 = 4.8\%$$

$$= \text{Maximum growth rate without external financing.}$$

ST-3 Assets consist of cash, marketable securities, receivables, inventories, and fixed assets. Therefore, we can break the A^*/S_0 ratio into its components — cash/sales, inventories/sales, and so forth. Then,

$$\frac{A^*}{S_0} = \frac{A^* - \text{Inventories}}{S_0} + \frac{\text{Inventories}}{S_0} = 1.6.$$

We know that the inventory turnover ratio is sales/inventories = 3 times, so inventories/sales = 1/3 = 0.3333. Further, if the inventory turnover ratio can be increased to 4 times, then the inventory/sales ratio will fall to 1/4 = 0.25, a difference of 0.3333 − 0.2500 = 0.0833. This, in turn, causes the A^*/S_0 ratio to fall from A^*/S_0 = 1.6 to A^*/S_0 = 1.6 − 0.0833 = 1.5167.

This change has two effects: First, it changes the AFN equation, and second, it means that Weatherford currently has excessive inventories. Because it is costly to hold excess inventories, Weatherford will want to reduce its inventory holdings by not replacing inventories until the excess amounts have been used. We can account for this by setting up the revised AFN equation (using the new A^*/S_0 ratio), estimating the funds that will be needed next year if no excess inventories are currently on hand, and then subtracting out the excess inventories that are currently on hand:

Present conditions:

$$\frac{\text{Sales}}{\text{Inventories}} = \frac{\$100}{\text{Inventories}} = 3,$$

so

$$\text{Inventories} = \$100/3 = \$33.3 \text{ million at present.}$$

New conditions:

$$\frac{\text{Sales}}{\text{Inventories}} = \frac{\$100}{\text{Inventories}} = 4,$$

so

$$\text{New level of inventories} = \$100/4 = \$25 \text{ million.}$$

Therefore,

$$\text{Excess inventories} = \$33.3 - \$25 = \$8.3 \text{ million.}$$

Forecast of funds needed, first year:

$$\Delta S \text{ in first year} = 0.2(\$100 \text{ million}) = \$20 \text{ million.}$$

$$\text{AFN} = 1.5167(\$20) - 0.4(\$20) - 0.1(0.55)(\$120) - \$8.3$$

$$= \$30.3 - \$8 - \$6.6 - \$8.3$$

$$= \$7.4 \text{ million.}$$

Forecast of funds needed, second year:

$$\Delta S \text{ in second year} = gS_1 = 0.2(\$120 \text{ million}) = \$24 \text{ million.}$$

$$\text{AFN} = 1.5167(\$24) - 0.4(\$24) - 0.1(0.55)(\$144)$$

$$= \$36.4 - \$9.6 - \$7.9$$

$$= \$18.9 \text{ million.}$$

CHAPTER 5

ST-2   a. Average = $(4\% + 5\% + 6\% + 7\%)/4 = 22\%/4 = 5.5\%$.

     b. $k_{\text{T-bond}} = k^* + IP = 2\% + 5.5\% = 7.5\%$.

     c. If the 5-year T-bond rate is 8 percent, the inflation rate is expected to average approximately $8\% - 2\% = 6\%$ during the next 5 years. Thus, the implied Year 5 inflation rate is 8 percent:

$$6\% = (4\% + 5\% + 6\% + 7\% + I_5)/5$$

$$30\% = 22\% + I_5$$

$$I_5 = 8\%.$$

CHAPTER 6

ST-2   a. The average rate of return for each stock is calculated simply by averaging the returns over the 5-year period. The average return for each stock is 18.90 percent, calculated for Stock A as follows:

$$k_{\text{Avg}} = (-10.00\% + 18.50\% + 38.67\% + 14.33\% + 33.00\%)/5$$

$$= 18.90\%.$$

The realized rate of return on a portfolio made up of Stock A and Stock B would be calculated by finding the average return in each year as k_A(% of Stock A) + k_B(% of Stock B) and then averaging these annual returns:

YEAR	PORTFOLIO AB'S RETURN, k_{AB}
1997	(6.50%)
1998	19.90
1999	41.46
2000	9.00
2001	30.65
	$k_{\text{Avg}} = \underline{\underline{18.90\%}}$

     b. The standard deviation of returns is estimated, using Equation 6-3a, as follows (see Footnote 5):

$$\text{Estimated } \sigma = S = \sqrt{\frac{\sum_{t=1}^{n} (\bar{k}_t - \bar{k}_{\text{Avg}})^2}{n - 1}}. \qquad (6\text{-}3a)$$

For Stock A, the estimated σ is 19.0 percent:

$$\sigma_A = \sqrt{\frac{(-10.00 - 18.9)^2 + (18.50 - 18.9)^2 + \cdots + (33.00 - 18.9)^2}{5 - 1}}$$

$$= \sqrt{\frac{1{,}445.92}{4}} = 19.0\%.$$

The standard deviation of returns for Stock B and for the portfolio are similarly determined, and they are as follows:

	STOCK A	STOCK B	PORTFOLIO AB
Standard deviation	19.0	19.0	18.6

     c. Since the risk reduction from diversification is small (σ_{AB} falls only from 19.0 to 18.6 percent), the most likely value of the correlation coefficient is 0.9. If the correlation coefficient were −0.9, the risk reduction would be much larger. In fact, the correlation coefficient between Stocks A and B is 0.92.

d. If more randomly selected stocks were added to a portfolio, σ_p would decline to somewhere in the vicinity of 20 percent; see Figure 6-8. σ_p would remain constant only if the correlation coefficient were +1.0, which is most unlikely. σ_p would decline to zero only if the correlation coefficient, r, were equal to zero and a large number of stocks were added to the portfolio, or if the proper proportions were held in a two-stock portfolio with r = −1.0.

ST-3 a.
$$b = (0.6)(0.70) + (0.25)(0.90) + (0.1)(1.30) + (0.05)(1.50)$$
$$= 0.42 + 0.225 + 0.13 + 0.075 = 0.85.$$

b.
$$k_{RF} = 6\%; RP_M = 5\%; b = 0.85.$$
$$k = 6\% + (5\%)(0.85)$$
$$= 10.25\%.$$

c.
$$b_N = (0.5)(0.70) + (0.25)(0.90) + (0.1)(1.30) + (0.15)(1.50)$$
$$= 0.35 + 0.225 + 0.13 + 0.225$$
$$= 0.93.$$
$$k = 6\% + (5\%)(0.93)$$
$$= 10.65\%.$$

CHAPTER 7

ST-2 a.

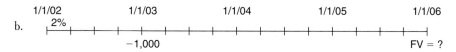

$1,000 is being compounded for 3 years, so your balance on January 1, 2006, is $1,259.71:

$$FV_n = PV(1 + i)^n = \$1,000(1 + 0.08)^3 = \$1,259.71.$$

Alternatively, using a financial calculator, input N = 3, I = 8, PV = −1000, PMT = 0, and FV = ? FV = $1,259.71.

b.

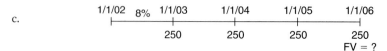

Use FVIF for 2%, 3 × 4 = 12 periods:

$$FV_{12} = \$1,000(FVIF_{2\%,12}) = \$1,000(1.2682) = \$1,268.20.$$

Alternatively, using a financial calculator, input N = 12, I = 2, PV = −1000, PMT = 0, and FV = ? FV = $1,268.24. (Note that since the interest factor is carried to only 4 decimal places, a rounding difference occurs.)

c.

As you work this problem, keep in mind that the tables assume that payments are made at the end of each period. Therefore, you may solve this problem by finding the future value of an annuity of $250 for 4 years at 8 percent:

$$FVA_4 = PMT(FVIFA_{i,n}) = \$250(4.5061) = \$1,126.53.$$

Alternatively, using a financial calculator, input N = 4, I = 8, PV = 0, PMT = −250, and FV = ? FV = $1,126.53.

d.

```
1/1/02  8%  1/1/03    1/1/04    1/1/05    1/1/06
  |----------+---------+---------+---------|
             ?         ?         ?         ?
                                      FV = 1,259.71
```

N = 4; I = 8; PV = 0; FV = 1259.71; PMT = ?; PMT = $279.56.

$$PMT(FVIFA_{8\%,4}) = FVA_4$$
$$PMT(4.5061) = \$1,259.71$$
$$PMT = \$1,259.71/4.5061 = \$279.56.$$

Therefore, you would have to make 4 payments of $279.56 each to have a balance of $1,259.71 on January 1, 2006.

ST-3 a. Set up a time line like the one in the preceding problem:

```
1/1/02  8%  1/1/03    1/1/04    1/1/05    1/1/06
  |----------+---------+---------+---------|
       PV = ?                           1,000
```

Note that your deposit will grow for 3 years at 8 percent. The fact that it is now January 1, 2002, is irrelevant. The deposit on January 1, 2003, is the PV, and the FV is $1,000. Here is the solution:

N = 3; I = 8; PMT = 0; FV = 1000; PV = ?; PV = $793.83.

$$FV_3(PVIF_{8\%,3}) = PV$$
$$PV = \$1,000(0.7938) = \$793.80 = \text{Initial deposit to accumulate } \$1,000.$$

(Difference due to rounding.)

b.

```
1/1/02  8%  1/1/03    1/1/04    1/1/05    1/1/06
  |----------+---------+---------+---------|
             ?         ?         ?         ?
                                      FV = 1,000
```

Here we are dealing with a 4-year annuity whose first payment occurs 1 year from today, on 1/1/03, and whose future value must equal $1,000. You should modify the time line to help visualize the situation. Here is the solution:

N = 4; I = 8; PV = 0; FV = 1000; PMT = ?; PMT = $221.92.

$$PMT(FVIFA_{8\%,4}) = FVA_4$$
$$PMT = \frac{FVA_4}{(FVIFA_{8\%,4})}$$
$$= \frac{\$1,000}{4.5061} = \$221.92 = \text{Payment necessary to accumulate } \$1,000.$$

c. This problem can be approached in several ways. Perhaps the simplest is to ask this question: "If I received $750 on 1/1/03 and deposited it to earn 8 percent, would I have the required $1,000 on 1/1/06?" The answer is no:

```
1/1/02  8%  1/1/03    1/1/04    1/1/05    1/1/06
  |----------+---------+---------+---------|
            −750       ?         ?       FV = ?
```

$$FV_3 = \$750(1.08)(1.08)(1.08) = \$944.78.$$

This indicates that you should let your father make the payments rather than accept the lump sum of $750.

You could also compare the $750 with the PV of the payments:

$$N = 4; I = 8; PMT = -221.92; FV = 0; PV = ?; PV = \$735.03.$$

$$PMT(PVIFA_{8\%,4}) = PVA_4$$

$$\$221.92(3.3121) = \$735.02 = \text{Present value}$$
$$\text{of the required payments.}$$

(Difference due to rounding.)

This is less than the $750 lump sum offer, so your initial reaction might be to accept the lump sum of $750. However, this would be a mistake. The problem is that when you found the $735.02 PV of the annuity, you were finding the value of the annuity *today*, on January 1, 2002. You were comparing $735.02 today with the lump sum of $750 1 year from now. This is, of course, invalid. What you should have done was take the $735.02, recognize that this is the PV of an annuity as of January 1, 2002, multiply $735.02 by 1.08 to get $793.82, and compare $793.82 with the lump sum of $750. You would then take your father's offer to make the payments rather than take the lump sum on January 1, 2003.

d.

$$N = 3; PV = -750; PMT = 0; FV = 1000; I = ?; I = 10.0642\%.$$

$$PV(FVIF_{i,3}) = FV$$

$$FVIF_{i,3} = \frac{FV}{PV}$$

$$= \frac{\$1,000}{\$750} = 1.3333.$$

Use the Future Value of $1 table (Table A-3 in Appendix A) for 3 periods to find the interest rate corresponding to an FVIF of 1.3333. Look across the Period 3 row of the table until you come to 1.3333. The closest value is 1.3310, in the 10 percent column. Therefore, you would require an interest rate of approximately 10 percent to achieve your $1,000 goal. The exact rate required, found with a financial calculator, is 10.0642 percent.

e.

$$N = 4; PV = 0; PMT = -186.29; FV = 1000; I = ?; I = 19.9997\%.$$

$$PMT(FVIFA_{i,4}) = FVA_4$$

$$\$186.29(FVIFA_{i,4}) = \$1,000$$

$$FVIFA_{i,4} = \frac{\$1,000}{\$186.29} = 5.3680.$$

Using Table A-4 in Appendix A, we find that 5.3680 corresponds to a 20 percent interest rate. You might be able to find a borrower willing to offer you a 20 percent interest rate, but there would be some risk involved — he or she might not actually pay you your $1,000!

f.

$$
\begin{array}{c}
\text{1/1/02} \quad 4\% \quad \text{1/1/03} \qquad \text{1/1/04} \qquad \text{1/1/05} \qquad \text{1/1/06} \\
\vert\!-\!-\!\vert\!-\!-\!\vert\!-\!-\!\vert\!-\!-\!\vert\!-\!-\!\vert\!-\!-\!\vert\!-\!-\!\vert \\
400 \quad ? \quad\ ? \quad\ ? \quad\ ? \quad\ ? \quad\ ? \\
\text{FV} = 1{,}000
\end{array}
$$

Find the future value of the original $400 deposit:

$$FV_6 = PV(FVIF_{4\%,6}) = \$400(1.2653) = \$506.12.$$

This means that on January 1, 2006, you need an additional sum of $493.88:

$$\$1{,}000.00 - \$506.12 = \$493.88.$$

This will be accumulated by making 6 equal payments that earn 8 percent compounded semiannually, or 4 percent each 6 months:

$$N = 6; I = 4; PV = 0; FV = 493.88; PMT = ?; PMT = \$74.46.$$

$$PMT(FVIFA_{4\%,6}) = FVA_6$$

$$PMT = \frac{FVA_6}{(FVIFA_{4\%,6})}$$

$$= \frac{\$493.88}{6.6330} = \$74.46.$$

Alternatively, using a financial calculator, input $N = 6$, $I = 4$, $PV = -400$, $FV = 1000$, and $PMT = ?$ $PMT = \$74.46$.

g.

$$\text{Effective annual rate} = \left(1 + \frac{i_{Nom}}{m}\right)^m - 1.0$$

$$= \left(1 + \frac{0.08}{2}\right)^2 - 1 = (1.04)^2 - 1$$

$$= 1.0816 - 1 = 0.0816 = 8.16\%.$$

h. There is a reinvestment rate risk here because we assumed that funds will earn an 8 percent return in the bank. In fact, if interest rates in the economy fall, the bank will lower its deposit rate because it will be earning less when it lends out the funds you deposited with it. If you buy certificates of deposit (CDs) that mature on the date you need the money (1/1/06), you will avoid the reinvestment risk, but that would work only if you were making the deposit today. Other ways of reducing reinvestment rate risk will be discussed later in the text.

ST-4 Bank A's effective annual rate is 8.24 percent:

$$\text{Effective annual rate} = \left(1 + \frac{0.08}{4}\right)^4 - 1.0$$

$$= (1.02)^4 - 1 = 1.0824 - 1$$

$$= 0.0824 = 8.24\%.$$

Now Bank B must have the same effective annual rate:

$$\left(1 + \frac{i}{12}\right)^{12} - 1.0 = 0.0824$$

$$\left(1 + \frac{i}{12}\right)^{12} = 1.0824$$

$$1 + \frac{i}{12} = (1.0824)^{1/12}$$

$$1 + \frac{i}{12} = 1.00662$$

$$\frac{i}{12} = 0.00662$$

$$i = 0.07944 = 7.94\%.$$

Thus, the two banks have different quoted rates — Bank A's quoted rate is 8 percent, while Bank B's quoted rate is 7.94 percent; however, both banks have the same effective annual rate of 8.24 percent. The difference in their quoted rates is due to the difference in compounding frequency.

CHAPTER 8

ST-2 a. Pennington's bonds were sold at par; therefore, the original YTM equaled the coupon rate of 12 percent.

b.
$$V_B = \sum_{t=1}^{50} \frac{\$120/2}{\left(1 + \frac{0.10}{2}\right)^t} + \frac{\$1,000}{\left(1 + \frac{0.10}{2}\right)^{50}}$$

$$= \$60(PVIFA_{5\%,50}) + \$1,000(PVIF_{5\%,50})$$
$$= \$60(18.2559) + \$1,000(0.0872)$$
$$= \$1,095.35 + \$87.20 = \$1,182.55.$$

Alternatively, with a financial calculator, input the following: N = 50, I = 5, PMT = 60, FV = 1000, and PV = ? PV = \$1,182.56.

c.
$$\text{Current yield} = \text{Annual coupon payment/Price}$$
$$= \$120/\$1,182.55$$
$$= 0.1015 = 10.15\%.$$

$$\text{Capital gains yield} = \text{Total yield} - \text{Current yield}$$
$$= 10\% - 10.15\% = -0.15\%.$$

d.
$$\$916.42 = \sum_{t=1}^{13} \frac{\$60}{(1 + k_d/2)^t} + \frac{\$1,000}{(1 + k_d/2)^{13}}.$$

Try $k_d = 14\%$:

$$V_B = \text{INT}(PVIFA_{7\%,13}) + M(PVIF_{7\%,13})$$
$$\$916.42 = \$60(8.3577) + \$1,000(0.4150)$$
$$= \$501.46 + \$415.00 = \$916.46.$$

Therefore, the YTM on July 1, 2001, was 14 percent. Alternatively, with a financial calculator, input the following: N = 13, PV = −916.42, PMT = 60, FV = 1000, and $k_d/2$ = I = ? Calculator solution = $k_d/2$ = 7.00%; therefore, k_d = 14.00%.

e.
$$\text{Current yield} = \$120/\$916.42 = 13.09\%.$$
$$\text{Capital gains yield} = 14\% - 13.09\% = 0.91\%.$$

f. The following time line illustrates the years to maturity of the bond:

Thus, on March 1, 2001, there were $13\frac{2}{3}$ periods left before the bond matured. Bond traders actually use the following procedure to determine the price of the bond:

(1) Find the price of the bond on the next coupon date, July 1, 2001.

$$V_{B\ 7/1/01} = \$60(PVIFA_{7.75\%,13}) + \$1,000(PVIF_{7.75\%,13})$$
$$= \$60(8.0136) + \$1,000(0.3789)$$
$$= \$859.72.$$

Note that we could use a calculator to solve for $V_{B\ 7/1/01}$ or we could substitute $i = 7.75\%$ and $n = 13$ periods into the equations for PVIFA and PVIF:

$$PVIFA = \frac{1 - \dfrac{1}{(1 + i)^n}}{i} = \frac{1 - \dfrac{1}{(1 + 0.0775)^{13}}}{0.0775} = 8.0136.$$

$$PVIF = \frac{1}{(1 + k)^n} = \frac{1}{(1 + 0.0775)^{13}} = 0.3789.$$

(2) Add the coupon, $60, to the bond price to get the total value, TV, of the bond on the next interest payment date: $TV = \$859.72 + \$60.00 = \$919.72$.

(3) Discount this total value back to the purchase date:

$$\text{Value at purchase date (March 1, 2001)} = \$919.72(PVIF_{7.75\%,4/6})$$
$$= \$919.72(0.9515)$$
$$= \$875.11.$$

Here

$$PVIF_{7.75\%,2/3} = \frac{1}{(1 + 0.0775)^{2/3}} = \frac{1}{1.0510} = 0.9515.$$

(4) Therefore, you would have written a check for $875.11 to complete the transaction. Of this amount, $20 = (\frac{1}{3})(\$60)$ would represent accrued interest and $855.11 would represent the bond's basic value. This breakdown would affect both your taxes and those of the seller.

(5) This problem could be solved *very* easily using a financial calculator with a bond valuation function, such as the HP-12C or the HP-17B. This is explained in the calculator manual under the heading, "Bond Calculations."

ST-3 a. $100,000,000/10 = $10,000,000 per year, or $5 million each 6 months. Since the $5 million will be used to retire bonds immediately, no interest will be earned on it.

b. The debt service requirements will decline. As the amount of bonds outstanding declines, so will the interest requirements (amounts given in millions of dollars):

SEMIANNUAL PAYMENT PERIOD (1)	SINKING FUND PAYMENT (2)	OUTSTANDING BONDS ON WHICH INTEREST IS PAID (3)	INTEREST PAYMENT[a] (4)	TOTAL BOND SERVICE (2) + (4) = (5)
1	$5	$100	$6.0	$11.0
2	5	95	5.7	10.7
3	5	90	5.4	10.4
.	.	.	.	.
.	.	.	.	.
.	.	.	.	.
20	5	5	0.3	5.3

[a] Interest is calculated as $(0.5)(0.12)$(Column 3); for example: interest in Period 2 = $(0.5)(0.12)(\$95) = \$5.7$.

The company's total cash bond service requirement will be $21.7 million per year for the first year. The requirement will decline by 0.12($10,000,000) = $1,200,000 per year for the remaining years.

c. Here we have a 10-year, 9 percent annuity whose compound value is $100 million, and we are seeking the annual payment, PMT. The solution can be obtained with a financial calculator. Input N = 10, I = 9, PV = 0, and FV = 100000000, and press the PMT key to obtain $6,582,009.

We could also find the solution using this equation:

$$\$100,000,000 = \sum_{t=1}^{10} PMT(1 + k)^t$$

$$= PMT(FVIFA_{9\%,10})$$

$$= PMT(15.193)$$

$$PMT = \$6,581,979 = \text{sinking fund payment.}$$

The difference is due to rounding the FVIFA to 3 decimal places.

d. Annual debt service costs will be $100,000,000(0.12) + $6,582,009 = $18,582,009.

e. If interest rates rose, causing the bond's price to fall, the company would use open market purchases. This would reduce its debt service requirements.

CHAPTER 9

ST-2 a. This is not necessarily true. Because G plows back two-thirds of its earnings, its growth rate should exceed that of D, but D pays higher dividends ($6 versus $2). We cannot say which stock should have the higher price.

b. Again, we just do not know which price would be higher.

c. This is false. The changes in k_d and k_s would have a greater effect on G; its price would decline more.

d. The total expected return for D is $\hat{k}_D = D_1/P_0 + g = 15\% + 0\% = 15\%$. The total expected return for G will have D_1/P_0 less than 15 percent and g greater than 0 percent, but $\hat{k}_G$ should be neither greater nor smaller than D's total expected return, 15 percent, because the two stocks are stated to be equally risky.

e. We have eliminated a, b, c, and d, so e should be correct. On the basis of the available information, D and G should sell at about the same price, $40; thus, $\hat{k}_s = 15\%$ for both D and G. G's current dividend yield is $2/$40 = 5%. Therefore, g = 15% − 5% = 10%.

ST-3 The first step is to solve for g, the unknown variable, in the constant growth equation. Since D_1 is unknown but D_0 is known, substitute $D_0(1 + g)$ as follows:

$$\hat{P}_0 = P_0 = \frac{D_1}{k_s - g} = \frac{D_0(1 + g)}{k_s - g}$$

$$\$36 = \frac{\$2.40(1 + g)}{0.12 - g}.$$

Solving for g, we find the growth rate to be 5 percent:

$$\$4.32 - \$36g = \$2.40 + \$2.40g$$

$$\$38.4g = \$1.92$$

$$g = 0.05 = 5\%.$$

The next step is to use the growth rate to project the stock price 5 years hence:

$$\hat{P}_5 = \frac{D_0(1 + g)^6}{k_s - g}$$

$$= \frac{\$2.40(1.05)^6}{0.12 - 0.05}$$

$$= \$45.95.$$

(Alternatively, $\hat{P}_5 = \$36(1.05)^5 = \$45.95$.)

Therefore, Ewald Company's expected stock price 5 years from now, $\hat{P}_5$, is $45.95.

ST-4   a. (1) Calculate the PV of the dividends paid during the supernormal growth period:

$$D_1 = \$1.1500(1.15) = \$1.3225.$$
$$D_2 = \$1.3225(1.15) = \$1.5209.$$
$$D_3 = \$1.5209(1.13) = \$1.7186.$$
$$PV\ D = \$1.3225(0.8929) + \$1.5209(0.7972) + \$1.7186(0.7118)$$
$$= \$1.1809 + \$1.2125 + \$1.2233$$
$$= \$3.6167 \approx \$3.62.$$

(2) Find the PV of Snyder's stock price at the end of Year 3:

$$\hat{P}_3 = \frac{D_4}{k_s - g} = \frac{D_3(1 + g)}{k_s - g}$$

$$= \frac{\$1.7186(1.06)}{0.12 - 0.06}$$

$$= \$30.36.$$

$$PV\ \hat{P}_3 = \$30.36(0.7118) = \$21.61.$$

(3) Sum the two components to find the value of the stock today:

$$\hat{P}_0 = \$3.62 + \$21.61 = \$25.23.$$

Alternatively, the cash flows can be placed on a time line as follows:

```
0    12%     1            2            3           4
├───────────┼────────────┼────────────┼───────────┤
  g = 15%                   g = 13%      g = 6%
          1.3225        1.5209       1.7186      1.8217
                                                   ↓
                                    30.3617  =  $1.8217
                                    32.0803     0.12 − 0.06
```

Enter the cash flows into the cash flow register, I = 12, and press the NPV key to obtain $P_0 = \$25.23$.

   b. $\hat{P}_1 = \$1.5209(0.8929) + \$1.7186(0.7972) + \$30.36(0.7972)$
$$= \$1.3580 + \$1.3701 + \$24.2030$$
$$= \$26.9311 \approx \$26.93.$$
(Calculator solution: \$26.93.)
$$\hat{P}_2 = \$1.7186(0.8929) + \$30.36(0.8929)$$
$$= \$1.5345 + \$27.1084$$
$$= \$28.6429 \approx \$28.64.$$
(Calculator solution: \$28.64.)

c. YEAR	DIVIDEND YIELD	+	CAPITAL GAINS YIELD	=	TOTAL RETURN
1	$\dfrac{\$1.3225}{\$25.23} \approx 5.24\%$		$\dfrac{\$26.93 - \$25.23}{\$25.23} \approx 6.74\%$		$\approx 12\%.$
2	$\dfrac{\$1.5209}{\$26.93} \approx 5.65\%$		$\dfrac{\$28.64 - \$26.93}{\$26.93} \approx 6.35\%$		$\approx 12\%.$
3	$\dfrac{\$1.7186}{\$28.64} \approx 6.00\%$		$\dfrac{\$30.36 - \$28.64}{\$28.64} \approx 6.00\%$		$\approx 12\%.$

CHAPTER 10

ST-2 a. Component costs are as follows:
Common:

$$k_s = \frac{D_1}{P_0} + g = \frac{D_0(1 + g)}{P_0} + g$$

$$= \frac{\$3.60(1.09)}{\$54} + 0.09$$

$$= 0.0727 + 0.09 \qquad\qquad = 16.27\%.$$

Preferred:

$$k_p = \frac{\text{Preferred dividend}}{P_p} = \frac{\$11}{\$95} \qquad = 11.58\%.$$

Debt at $k_d = 12\%$:

$$k_d(1 - T) = 12\%(0.6) \qquad\qquad = 7.20\%.$$

b. WACC calculation:

$$\text{WACC} = w_d k_d(1 - T) + w_p k_p + w_c k_s$$
$$\text{WACC} = 0.25(7.2\%) + 0.15(11.58\%) + 0.60(16.27\%) = 13.30\%.$$

c. LEI should accept Projects A, B, C, and D. It should reject Project E because its rate of return does not exceed the marginal cost of funds needed to finance it.

CHAPTER 11

ST-2 a. *Payback:*
To determine the payback, construct the cumulative cash flows for each project:

	CUMULATIVE CASH FLOWS	
YEAR	PROJECT X	PROJECT Y
0	($10,000)	($10,000)
1	(3,500)	(6,500)
2	(500)	(3,000)
3	2,500	500
4	3,500	4,000

$$\text{Payback}_X = 2 + \frac{\$500}{\$3,000} = 2.17 \text{ years.}$$

$$\text{Payback}_Y = 2 + \frac{\$3,000}{\$3,500} = 2.86 \text{ years.}$$

Net present value (NPV):

$$NPV_X = -\$10{,}000 + \frac{\$6{,}500}{(1.12)^1} + \frac{\$3{,}000}{(1.12)^2} + \frac{\$3{,}000}{(1.12)^3} + \frac{\$1{,}000}{(1.12)^4}$$
$$= \$966.01.$$

$$NPV_Y = -\$10{,}000 + \frac{\$3{,}500}{(1.12)^1} + \frac{\$3{,}500}{(1.12)^2} + \frac{\$3{,}500}{(1.12)^3} + \frac{\$3{,}500}{(1.12)^4}$$
$$= \$630.72.$$

Alternatively, using a financial calculator, input the cash flows into the cash flow register, enter I = 12, and then press the NPV key to obtain $NPV_X = \$966.01$ and $NPV_Y = \$630.72$.

Internal rate of return (IRR):
To solve for each project's IRR, find the discount rates that equate each NPV to zero:

$$IRR_X = 18.0\%.$$
$$IRR_Y = 15.0\%.$$

Modified internal rate of return (MIRR):
To obtain each project's MIRR, begin by finding each project's terminal value (TV) of cash inflows:

$$TV_X = \$6{,}500(1.12)^3 + \$3{,}000(1.12)^2$$
$$+ \$3{,}000(1.12)^1 + \$1{,}000 = \$17{,}255.23.$$
$$TV_Y = \$3{,}500(1.12)^3 + \$3{,}500(1.12)^2$$
$$+ \$3{,}500(1.12)^1 + \$3{,}500 = \$16{,}727.65.$$

Now, each project's MIRR is that discount rate that equates the PV of the TV to each project's cost, $10,000:

$$MIRR_X = 14.61\%.$$
$$MIRR_Y = 13.73\%.$$

b. The following table summarizes the project rankings by each method:

	PROJECT THAT RANKS HIGHER
Payback	X
NPV	X
IRR	X
MIRR	X

Note that all methods rank Project X over Project Y. In addition, both projects are acceptable under the NPV, IRR, and MIRR criteria. Thus, both projects should be accepted if they are independent.

c. In this case, we would choose the project with the higher NPV at k = 12%, or Project X.

d. To determine the effects of changing the cost of capital, plot the NPV profiles of each project. The crossover rate occurs at about 6 to 7 percent (6.2%). See the graph on the next page.

   If the firm's cost of capital is less than 6.2 percent, a conflict exists because $NPV_Y > NPV_X$, but $IRR_X > IRR_Y$. Therefore, if k were 5 percent, a conflict would exist.

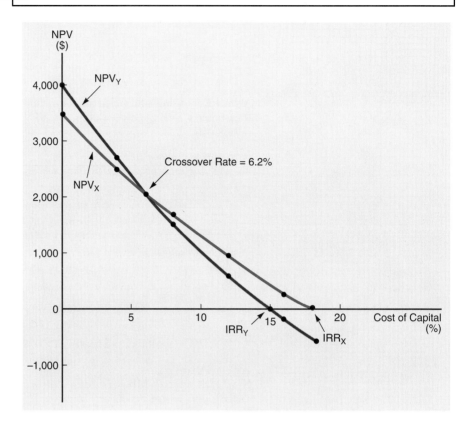

COST OF CAPITAL	NPV$_X$	NPV$_Y$
0%	$3,500	$4,000
4	2,545	2,705
8	1,707	1,592
12	966	631
16	307	(206)
18	5	(585)

Note, however, that when k = 5.0%, MIRR$_X$ = 10.64% and MIRR$_Y$ = 10.83%; hence, the modified IRR ranks the projects correctly, even if k is to the left of the crossover point.

e. The basic cause of the conflict is differing reinvestment rate assumptions between NPV and IRR. NPV assumes that cash flows can be reinvested at the cost of capital, while IRR assumes reinvestment at the (generally) higher IRR. The high reinvestment rate assumption under IRR makes early cash flows especially valuable, and hence short-term projects look better under IRR.

CHAPTER 12

ST-2 a. *Estimated investment requirements:*

Price	($50,000)
Modification	(10,000)
Change in net operating working capital	(2,000)
Total investment	($62,000)

b. *Operating cash flows:*

	YEAR 1	YEAR 2	YEAR 3
1. After-tax cost savings[a]	$12,000	$12,000	$12,000
2. Depreciation[b]	19,800	27,000	9,000
3. Depreciation tax savings[c]	7,920	10,800	3,600
Operating cash flow (1 + 3)	$19,920	$22,800	$15,600

[a] $20,000(1 − T).

[b] Depreciable basis = $60,000; the MACRS percentage allowances are 0.33, 0.45, and 0.15 in Years 1, 2, and 3, respectively; hence, depreciation in Year 1 = 0.33($60,000) = $19,800, and so on. There will remain $4,200, or 7 percent, undepreciated after Year 3; it would normally be taken in Year 4.

[c] Depreciation tax savings = T(Depreciation) = 0.4($19,800) = $7,920 in Year 1, and so on.

c. *Terminal cash flow:*

Salvage value	$20,000
Tax on salvage value[a]	(6,320)
Net operating working capital recovery	2,000
Termination cash flow	$15,680

[a] Sales price	$20,000
Less book value	4,200
Taxable income	$15,800
Tax at 40%	$ 6,320

Book value = Depreciable basis − Accumulated depreciation
= $60,000 − $55,800 = $4,200.

d. *Project NPV:*

$$\text{NPV} = -\$62,000 + \frac{\$19,920}{(1.10)^1} + \frac{\$22,800}{(1.10)^2} + \frac{\$31,280}{(1.10)^3}$$

$$= -\$1,547.$$

Alternatively, using a financial calculator, input the cash flows into the cash flow register, enter I = 10, and then press the NPV key to obtain NPV = −$1,547. Because the earthmover has a negative NPV, it should not be purchased.

e. (1) *Savings in before-tax operating costs increase 15 percent:*

	YEAR 1	YEAR 2	YEAR 3
1. After-tax cost savings[a]	$13,800	$13,800	$13,800
2. Depreciation	19,800	27,000	9,000
3. Depreciation tax savings	7,920	10,800	3,600
4. Operating cash flow (1 + 3)	$21,720	$24,600	$17,400
Terminal cash flows:			
5. After-tax salvage value			13,680
6. Net operating working capital recovery			2,000
Net cash inflows	$21,720	$24,600	$33,080

[a] $20,000(1.15)(1 − T).

Project NPV:

```
 0    10%    1         2         3
 +-----------+---------+---------+
-62,000    21,720    24,600    33,080
```

$$\text{NPV} = -\$62,000 + \frac{\$21,720}{(1.10)^1} + \frac{\$24,600}{(1.10)^2} + \frac{\$33,080}{(1.10)^3}$$

$$= \$2,930.$$

Alternatively, using a financial calculator, input the cash flows into the cash flow register, enter I = 10, and then press the NPV key to obtain NPV = $2,930. Because the savings have increased by 15 percent, the decision to purchase the earthmover has changed from that in part d. Since its NPV is positive, the earthmover would now be purchased.

e. (2) *Earthmover's salvage value increases by 10 percent above original expectations.* All other data remains unchanged.

	YEAR 1	YEAR 2	YEAR 3
1. After-tax cost savings	$12,000	$12,000	$12,000
2. Depreciation	19,800	27,000	9,000
3. Depreciation tax savings	7,920	10,800	3,600
4. Operating cash flow (1 + 3)	$19,920	$22,800	$15,600
Terminal cash flows:			
5. Salvage value[a]			22,000
6. Tax on salvage value[b]			(7,120)
7. Net operating working capital recovery			2,000
Net cash inflows	$19,920	$22,800	$32,480

[a] $20,000(1.10).

[b]
Sales price	$22,000
Less book value	4,200
Taxable income	$17,800
Tax at 40%	$ 7,120

Project NPV:

```
0     10%    1          2          3
├──────────┼──────────┼──────────┤
-62,000   19,920     22,800     32,480
```

$$\text{NPV} = -\$62,000 + \frac{\$19,920}{(1.10)^1} + \frac{\$22,800}{(1.10)^2} + \frac{\$32,480}{(1.10)^3}$$

$$= -\$645.$$

Alternatively, using a financial calculator, input the cash flows into the cash flow register, enter I = 10, and then press the NPV key to obtain NPV = -$645. Because the earthmover has a negative NPV, it should not be purchased. Thus, the decision is the same as in part d.

f. *Worst-case scenario:*

	YEAR 1	YEAR 2	YEAR 3
1. After-tax cost savings[a]	$ 9,000	$ 9,000	$ 9,000
2. Depreciation	19,800	27,000	9,000
3. Depreciation tax savings	7,920	10,800	3,600
4. Operating cash flow (1 + 3)	$16,920	$19,800	$12,600
Terminal cash flows:			
5. Salvage value[b]			18,000
6. Tax on salvage value[c]			(5,520)
7. Net operating working capital recovery			2,000
Net cash inflows	$16,920	$19,800	$27,080

[a] $15,000(1 − T).
[b] Given as $18,000.
[c]

Sales price	$18,000
Less book value	4,200
Taxable income	$13,800
Tax at 40%	$ 5,520

Project NPV:

```
0     10%    1          2          3
├──────────┼──────────┼──────────┤
-62,000   16,920     19,800     27,080
```

$$\text{NPV} = -\$62,000 + \frac{\$16,920}{(1.10)^1} + \frac{\$19,800}{(1.10)^2} + \frac{\$27,080}{(1.10)^3}$$

$$= -\$9,909.$$

Alternatively, using a financial calculator, input the cash flows into the cash flow register, enter I = 10, and then press the NPV key to obtain NPV = -$9,909.

Base-case scenario: The NPV was calculated in part d as -$1,547.

Best-case scenario:

	YEAR 1	YEAR 2	YEAR 3
1. After-tax cost savings[a]	$15,000	$15,000	$15,000
2. Depreciation	19,800	27,000	9,000
3. Depreciation tax savings	7,920	10,800	3,600
4. Operating cash flow (1 + 3)	$22,920	$25,800	$18,600
Terminal cash flows:			
5. Salvage value[b]			24,000
6. Tax on salvage value[c]			(7,920)
7. Net operating working capital recovery			2,000
Net cash inflows	$22,920	$25,800	$36,680

[a] $25,000(1 − T)$.
[b] Given as $24,000.
[c]
Sales price	$24,000
Less book value	4,200
Taxable income	$19,800
Tax at 40%	$ 7,920

Project NPV:

0 10% 1 2 3
−62,000 22,920 25,800 36,680

$$\text{NPV} = -\$62,000 + \frac{\$22,920}{(1.10)^1} + \frac{\$25,800}{(1.10)^2} + \frac{\$36,680}{(1.10)^3}$$
$$= \$7,717.$$

Alternatively, using a financial calculator, input the cash flows into the cash flow register, enter I = 10, and then press the NPV key to obtain NPV = $7,717.

SCENARIO	PROBABILITY	NPV
Worst case	30%	−$9,909
Base case	40	−1,547
Best case	30	7,717
	Expected NPV =	−$1,276

$$\sigma_{\text{NPV}} = [0.3(-\$9,909 - (-\$1,276)]^2 + 0.4\,[-\$1,547 - (-\$1,276)]^2 + 0.3\,[\$7,717 - (-\$1,276)]^2]^{1/2}$$
$$\sigma_{\text{NPV}} = [\$22,358,607 + \$29,376 + \$24,262,215]^{1/2}$$
$$\sigma_{\text{NPV}} = \$6,830.$$
$$\text{CV}_{\text{NPV}} = \frac{\$6,830}{-\$1,276} = -5.35.$$

ST-3   a. First, find the expected cash flows:

YEAR	EXPECTED CASH FLOWS			
0	0.2(−$100,000)	+ 0.6(−$100,000)	+ 0.2(−$100,000)	= ($100,000)
1	0.2($20,000)	+ 0.6($30,000)	+ 0.2($40,000)	= $30,000
2				$30,000
3				$30,000
4				$30,000
5				$30,000
5*	0.2($0)	+ 0.6($20,000)	+ 0.2($30,000)	= $18,000

```
0   10%  1       2       3       4       5
|--------+-------+-------+-------+-------|
-100,000 30,000  30,000  30,000  30,000  48,000
```

Next, determine the NPV based on the expected cash flows:

$$NPV = -\$100,000 + \frac{\$30,000}{(1.10)^1} + \frac{\$30,000}{(1.10)^2} + \frac{\$30,000}{(1.10)^3}$$
$$+ \frac{\$30,000}{(1.10)^4} + \frac{\$48,000}{(1.10)^5} = \$24,900.$$

Alternatively, using a financial calculator, input the cash flows into the cash flow register, enter I = 10, and then press the NPV key to obtain NPV = $24,900.

b. For the worst case, the cash flow values from the cash flow column farthest on the left are used to calculate NPV:

```
0   10%  1       2       3       4       5
|--------+-------+-------+-------+-------|
-100,000 20,000  20,000  20,000  20,000  20,000
```

$$NPV = -\$100,000 + \frac{\$20,000}{(1.10)^1} + \frac{\$20,000}{(1.10)^2} + \frac{\$20,000}{(1.10)^3}$$
$$+ \frac{\$20,000}{(1.10)^4} + \frac{\$20,000}{(1.10)^5} = -\$24,184.$$

Similarly, for the best case, use the values from the column farthest on the right. Here the NPV is $70,259.

If the cash flows are perfectly dependent, then the low cash flow in the first year will mean a low cash flow in every year. Thus, the probability of the worst case occurring is the probability of getting the $20,000 net cash flow in Year 1, or 20 percent. If the cash flows are independent, the cash flow in each year can be low, high, or average, and the probability of getting all low cash flows will be

$$0.2(0.2)(0.2)(0.2)(0.2) = 0.2^5 = 0.00032 = 0.032\%.$$

c. The base-case NPV is found using the most likely cash flows and is equal to $26,142. This value differs from the expected NPV of $24,900 because the Year 5 cash flows are not symmetric. Under these conditions, the NPV distribution is as follows:

P	NPV
0.2	($24,184)
0.6	26,142
0.2	70,259

Thus, the expected NPV is $0.2(-\$24,184) + 0.6(\$26,142) + 0.2(\$70,259) = \$24,900$. As is generally the case, the expected NPV is the same as the NPV of the expected cash flows found in part a. The standard deviation is $29,904:

$$\sigma^2_{NPV} = 0.2(-\$24,184 - \$24,900)^2 + 0.6(\$26,142 - \$24,900)^2$$
$$+ 0.2(\$70,259 - \$24,900)^2$$
$$= \$894,261,126.$$
$$\sigma_{NPV} = \sqrt{\$894,261,126} = \$29,904.$$

The coefficient of variation, CV, is $29,904/\$24,900 = 1.20$.

d. Since the project's coefficient of variation is 1.20, the project is riskier than average, and hence the project's risk-adjusted cost of capital is $10\% + 2\% = 12\%$. The project now should be evaluated by finding the NPV of the expected cash flows, as in part a, but using a 12 percent discount rate. The risk-adjusted NPV is $18,357, and, therefore, the project should be accepted.

CHAPTER 13

ST-2 a.

EBIT	$4,000,000
Interest ($2,000,000 × 0.10)	200,000
Earnings before taxes (EBT)	$3,800,000
Taxes (35%)	1,330,000
Net income	$2,470,000

$$EPS = \$2,470,000/600,000 = \$4.12.$$
$$P_0 = \$4.12/0.15 = \$27.47.$$

b.
$$Equity = 600,000 \times \$10 = \$6,000,000.$$
$$Debt = \$2,000,000.$$
$$Total\ capital = \$8,000,000.$$
$$WACC = w_d k_d (1 - T) + w_c k_s$$
$$= (2/8)(10\%)(1 - 0.35) + (6/8)(15\%)$$
$$= 1.63\% + 11.25\%$$
$$= 12.88\%.$$

c.

EBIT	$4,000,000
Interest ($10,000,000 × 0.12)	1,200,000
Earnings before taxes (EBT)	$2,800,000
Taxes (35%)	980,000
Net income	$1,820,000

Shares bought and retired:

$$\Delta N = \Delta Debt/P_0 = \$8,000,000/\$27.47 = 291,227.$$

New outstanding shares:

$$N_1 = N_0 - \Delta N = 600,000 - 291,227 = 308,773.$$

New EPS:

$$EPS = \$1,820,000/308,773 = \$5.89.$$

New price per share:

$$P_0 = \$5.89/0.17 = \$34.65\ versus\ \$27.47.$$

Therefore, Gentry should change its capital structure.

d. In this case, the company's net income would be higher by (0.12 − 0.10) ($2,000,000)(1 − 0.35) = $26,000 because its interest charges would be lower. The new price would be:

$$P_0 = \frac{(\$1,820,000 + \$26,000)/308,773}{0.17} = \$35.18.$$

In the first case, in which debt had to be refunded, the bondholders were compensated for the increased risk of the higher debt position. In the second case, the old bondholders were not compensated; their 10 percent coupon perpetual bonds would now be worth

$$\$100/0.12 = \$833.33,$$

or $1,666,667 in total, down from the old $2 million, or a loss of $333,333. The stockholders would have a gain of

$$(\$35.18 − \$34.65)(308,773) = \$163,650.$$

This gain would, of course, be at the expense of the old bondholders. (There is no reason to think that bondholders' losses would exactly offset stockholders' gains.)

e.
$$TIE = \frac{EBIT}{I}.$$

$$Original\ TIE = \frac{\$4,000,000}{\$200,000} = 20\ times.$$

$$New\ TIE = \frac{\$4,000,000}{\$1,200,000} = 3.33\ times.$$

ST-3 a. (1) Determine the variable cost per unit at present, using the following definitions and equations:

$$Q = units\ of\ output\ (sales) = 5,000.$$
$$P = average\ sales\ price\ per\ unit\ of\ output = \$100.$$
$$F = fixed\ operating\ costs = \$200,000.$$
$$V = variable\ costs\ per\ unit.$$
$$EBIT = P(Q) − F − V(Q)$$
$$\$50,000 = \$100(5,000) − \$200,000 − V(5,000)$$
$$5,000V = \$250,000$$
$$V = \$50.$$

(2) Determine the new EBIT level if the change is made:

$$New\ EBIT = P_2(Q_2) − F_2 − V_2(Q_2)$$
$$= \$95(7,000) − \$250,000 − \$40(7,000)$$
$$= \$135,000.$$

(3) Determine the incremental EBIT:

$$\Delta EBIT = \$135,000 − \$50,000 = \$85,000.$$

(4) Estimate the approximate rate of return on the new investment:

$$\Delta ROA = \frac{\Delta EBIT}{Investment} = \frac{\$85,000}{\$400,000} = 21.25\%.$$

Since the ROA exceeds Olinde's average cost of capital, this analysis suggests that Olinde should go ahead and make the investment.

b. The change would increase the breakeven point. Still, with a lower sales price, it might be easier to achieve the higher new breakeven volume.

$$\textit{Old: } Q_{BE} = \frac{F}{P - V} = \frac{\$200,000}{\$100 - \$50} = 4,000 \text{ units.}$$

$$\textit{New: } Q_{BE} = \frac{F}{P_2 - V_2} = \frac{\$250,000}{\$95 - \$40} = 4,545 \text{ units.}$$

c. The incremental ROA is:

$$ROA = \frac{\Delta Profit}{\Delta Sales} \times \frac{\Delta Sales}{\Delta Assets}.$$

Using debt financing, the incremental profit associated with the investment is equal to the incremental profit found in part a minus the interest expense incurred as a result of the investment:

$$
\begin{aligned}
\Delta Profit &= \text{New profit} - \text{Old profit} - \text{Interest} \\
&= \$135,000 - \$50,000 - 0.10(\$400,000) \\
&= \$45,000.
\end{aligned}
$$

The incremental sales is calculated as:

$$
\begin{aligned}
\Delta Sales &= P_2 Q_2 - P_1 Q_1 \\
&= \$95(7,000) - \$100(5,000) \\
&= \$665,000 - \$500,000 \\
&= \$165,000.
\end{aligned}
$$

$$ROA = \frac{\$45,000}{\$165,000} \times \frac{\$165,000}{\$400,000} = 11.25\%.$$

The return on the new equity investment still exceeds the average cost of capital, so Olinde should make the investment.

CHAPTER 14

ST-2 a.

Projected net income	$2,000,000
Less projected capital investments	800,000
Available residual	$1,200,000
Shares outstanding	200,000

$$DPS = \$1,200,000/200,000 \text{ shares} = \$6 = D_1.$$

b. $EPS = \$2,000,000/200,000 \text{ shares} = \$10.$

Payout ratio = DPS/EPS = $6/$10 = 60%, or

Total dividends/NI = $1,200,000/$2,000,000 = 60%.

c. $$\text{Currently, } P_0 = \frac{D_1}{k_s - g} = \frac{\$6}{0.14 - 0.05} = \frac{\$6}{0.09} = \$66.67.$$

Under the former circumstances, D_1 would be based on a 20 percent payout on $10 EPS, or $2. With $k_s = 14\%$ and $g = 12\%$, we solve for P_0:

$$P_0 = \frac{D_1}{k_s - g} = \frac{\$2}{0.14 - 0.12} = \frac{\$2}{0.02} = \$100.$$

Although CMC has suffered a severe setback, its existing assets will continue to provide a good income stream. More of these earnings should now be passed on to the shareholders, as the slowed internal growth has reduced the need for funds. However, the net result is a 33 percent decrease in the value of the shares.

d. If the payout ratio were continued at 20 percent, even after internal investment opportunities had declined, the price of the stock would drop to $2/(0.14 − 0.06) = $25 rather than to $66.67. Thus, an increase in the dividend payout is consistent with maximizing shareholder wealth.

Because of the diminishing nature of profitable investment opportunities, the greater the firm's level of investment, the lower the average ROE. Thus, the more money CMC retains and invests, the lower its average ROE will be. We can determine the average ROE under different conditions as follows:

Old situation (with founder active and a 20 percent payout):

$$g = (1.0 - \text{Payout ratio})(\text{Average ROE})$$
$$12\% = (1.0 - 0.2)(\text{Average ROE})$$
$$\text{Average ROE} = 12\%/0.8 = 15\% > k_s = 14\%.$$

Note that the *average* ROE is 15 percent, whereas the *marginal* ROE is presumably equal to 14 percent.

New situation (with founder retired and a 60 percent payout):

$$g = 6\% = (1.0 - 0.6)(\text{ROE})$$
$$\text{ROE} = 6\%/0.4 = 15\% > k_s = 14\%.$$

This suggests that the new payout is appropriate and that the firm is taking on investments down to the point at which marginal returns are equal to the cost of capital. Note that if the 20 percent payout was maintained, the *average* ROE would be only 7.5 percent, which would imply a marginal ROE far below the 14 percent cost of capital.

CHAPTER 15

ST-2 **The Calgary Company: Alternative Balance Sheets**

	RESTRICTED (40%)	MODERATE (50%)	RELAXED (60%)
Current assets	$1,200,000	$1,500,000	$1,800,000
Fixed assets	600,000	600,000	600,000
Total assets	$1,800,000	$2,100,000	$2,400,000
Debt	$ 900,000	$1,050,000	$1,200,000
Equity	900,000	1,050,000	1,200,000
Total liabilities and equity	$1,800,000	$2,100,000	$2,400,000

The Calgary Company: Alternative Income Statements

	RESTRICTED	MODERATE	RELAXED
Sales	$3,000,000	$3,000,000	$3,000,000
EBIT	450,000	450,000	450,000
Interest (10%)	90,000	105,000	120,000
Earnings before taxes	$ 360,000	$ 345,000	$ 330,000
Taxes (40%)	144,000	138,000	132,000
Net income	$ 216,000	$ 207,000	$ 198,000
ROE	24.0%	19.7%	16.5%

ST-3   a. and b.

Income Statements for Year Ended December 31, 2001 (Thousands of Dollars)

| | VANDERHEIDEN PRESS | | HERRENHOUSE PUBLISHING | |
	a	b	a	b
EBIT	$ 30,000	$ 30,000	$ 30,000	$ 30,000
Interest	12,400	14,400	10,600	18,600
Taxable income	$ 17,600	$ 15,600	$ 19,400	$ 11,400
Taxes (40%)	7,040	6,240	7,760	4,560
Net income	$ 10,560	$ 9,360	$ 11,640	$ 6,840
Equity	$100,000	$100,000	$100,000	$100,000
Return on equity	10.56%	9.36%	11.64%	6.84%

The Vanderheiden Press has a higher ROE when short-term interest rates are high, whereas Herrenhouse Publishing does better when rates are lower.

c. Herrenhouse's position is riskier. First, its profits and return on equity are much more volatile than Vanderheiden's. Second, Herrenhouse must renew its large short-term loan every year, and if the renewal comes up at a time when money is very tight, when its business is depressed, or both, then Herrenhouse could be denied credit, which could put it out of business.

CHAPTER 16

ST-2

$$\frac{\text{Euros}}{\text{C\$}} = \frac{\text{Euros}}{\text{US\$}} \times \frac{\text{US\$}}{\text{C\$}}$$

$$= \frac{1.1215}{\$1} \times \frac{\$1}{1.5291} = \frac{1.1215}{1.5291} = 0.7334 \text{ euro per Canadian dollar.}$$

ANSWERS TO END-OF-CHAPTER PROBLEMS

We present here some intermediate steps and final answers to selected end-of-chapter problems. Please note that your answer may differ slightly from ours due to rounding differences. Also, although we hope not, some of the problems may have more than one correct solution, depending upon what assumptions are made in working the problem. Finally, many of the problems involve some verbal discussion as well as numerical calculations; this verbal material is not presented here.

2-1 $1,000,000.

2-2 $3,600,000.

2-3 5.76%.

2-4 $22,859.50.

2-5 25%.

2-6 $9,000.

2-7 $20,000,000.

2-8 $2,500,000.

2-9 Tax = $107,855; NI = $222,145; Marginal tax rate = 39%; Average tax rate = 33.8%.

2-10 a. Tax = $3,575,000.
b. Tax = $350,000.
c. Tax = $105,000.

2-11 AT&T preferred stock = 5.37%.

2-12 Municipal bond; yield = 7%.

2-13 NI = $450,000; NCF = $650,000; OCF = $650,000.

2-14 a.

2-15 a. $2,400,000,000.
b. $4,500,000,000.
c. $5,400,000,000.
d. $1,100,000,000.
e. $400,000,000.

2-16 a. $584 million.
c. $1,520 million.

2-17 a. $2,400,000.

2-18 $2,500,000.

2-19 a. $90,000,000.
b. $NOWC_{01}$ = $192,000,000.
c. OC_{00} = $460,000,000.
d. FCF = $58,000,000.

2-21 Tax_{2002} = $0; Tax_{2004} = $12,000,000; Tax_{2005} = $32,000,000; Tax_{2006} = $0 and receive refund of $44,000,000 for 2004 and 2005 taxes.

2-22 a. 2002 advantage as a corporation = $826; 2003 advantage = $4,076; 2004 advantage = $5,226.

2-23 a. Personal tax = $25,553.
c. Disney yield = 5.52%; choose FLA bonds.
d. 25%.

3-1 CL = $2,000,000; Inv = $1,000,000.

3-2 AR = $800,000.

3-3 D/A = 58.33%.

3-4 TATO = 5; EM = 1.5.

3-5 M/B = 4.2667.

3-6 TIE = 2.25.

3-7 $\dfrac{NI}{S}$ = 2%; $\dfrac{D}{A}$ = 40%.

3-8 $262,500; 1.19×.

3-9 Sales = $2,592,000; DSO = 36.33 days.

3-10 TIE = 3.86×.

3-11 2.9867.

3-12 ROE = 23.1%.

3-13 7.2%.

3-14 a.

3-15 a. +5.54%.
b(2). +3.21%.
(3). +2.50%.

3-16 A/P = $90,000; Inv = $90,000; FA = $138,000.

3-17 a. Current ratio = 1.98×; DSO = 76.3 days; Total assets turnover = 1.7×; Debt ratio = 61.9%.

3-19 a. Quick ratio = 0.8×; DSO = 37.4 days; ROE = 13.1%; Debt ratio = 54.8%; P/CF = 2.0×.

4-1 AFN = $410,000.
4-2 AFN = $610,000.
4-3 AFN = $200,000.
4-4 5.01.
4-5 a. $5,555,555,556.
     b. 30.6%.
     c. $13,600,000.
4-6 a. $133.50 million.
     b. 39.06%.
4-7 $156 million.
4-8 a. NI = $200.16; N/P = $255.40;
        LTD = $705.40; C/S = $410.80.
     b. ROE = 8.09%; S/Inv = 10.29;
        PM = 4.41%.
4-9 a. $480,000.
     b. $18,750.
4-10 AFN = $360.
4-11 ΔS = $68,965.52.
4-12 a. $13.44 million.
     b. Notes payable = $31.44 million.
     c. Current ratio = 2.00×; ROE = 14.2%.
     d(1). −$14.28 million (surplus).
       (2). Total assets = $147 million; Notes payable = $3.72 million.
       (3). Current ratio = 4.25×; ROE = 10.84%.
4-13 Total assets = $33,534; AFN = $2,128.
4-14 a. 33%.
     b. AFN = $2,549.
     c. ROE = 13.06%.
4-15 a. AFN = $128,783.
     b. 3.45%.
4-16 a. AFN = $667.
     b. Increase in notes payable = $51; Increase in C/S = $368.

5-1 6%; 6.33%.
5-2 1.5%.
5-3 5.5%.
5-4 0.2%.
5-5 6.4%.
5-6 8.5%.
5-7 6.8%.
5-8 a. k_1 in Year 2 = 6%.
5-9 k_1 in Year 2 = 9%; Year 2 inflation = 7%.

5-10 1.5%.
5-11 6.0%.
5-12 a. k_1 = 9.20%; k_5 = 7.20%.
5-14 a. 8.20%.
     b. 10.20%.
     c. k_5 = 10.70%.

6-1 $\hat{k}$ = 11.40%; σ = 26.69%; CV = 2.34.
6-2 b_p = 1.12.
6-3 k_M = 11%; k = 12.2%.
6-4 k = 10.9%.
6-5 a. b = 1.
     b. k = 13%.
6-6 a. $\hat{k}_M$ = 13.5%; $\hat{k}_J$ = 11.6%.
     b. σ_M = 3.85%; σ_J = 6.22%.
     c. CV_M = 0.29; CV_J = 0.54.
6-7 a. $\hat{k}_Y$ = 14%.
     b. σ_X = 12.20%.
6-8 a. b_A = 1.40.
     b. k_A = 15%.
6-9 a. k_i = 15.5%.
     b(1). k_M = 15%; k_i = 16.5%.
     c(1). k_i = 18.1%.
6-10 b_N = 1.16.
6-11 b_p = 0.7625; k_p = 12.1%.
6-12 b_N = 1.1250.
6-13 4.5%.
6-14 a. CV_X = 3.5; CV_Y = 2.0.
     c. k_X = 10.5%; k_Y = 12%.
     d. Stock Y.
     e. k_p = 10.875%.
6-15 a. $0.5 million.
6-16 a. k_i = 6% + (5%)b_i.
     b. 15%.
     c. Indifference rate = 16%.
6-17 a. $\bar{k}_A$ = 11.30%.
     c. σ_A = 20.8%; σ_p = 20.1%.
6-18 a. b_X = 1.3471; b_Y = 0.6508.
     b. k_X = 12.7355%; k_Y = 9.254%.
     c. k_p = 12.04%.
6A-1 a. b = 0.62.
6A-2 a. b_A = 1.0; b_B = 0.5.
     c. k_A = 14%; k_B = 11.5%.

7-1 FV_5 = $16,105.10.
7-2 PV = $1,292.10.

7-3	n = 11.01 years.
7-4	n = 11 years.
7-5	i = 8.01%.
7-6	$FVA_5 = \$1,725.22$.
7-7	$FVA_{5 \text{ Due}} = \$1,845.99$.
7-8	$FVA_5 = \$1,725.22$.
7-9	PV = \$923.98; FV = \$1,466.24.
7-10	$i_{PER} = 2.25\%$; $i_{Nom} = 9\%$; EAR = 9.31%.
7-11	PMT = \$444.89; EAR = 12.6825%.
7-12	\$1,000 today is worth more.
7-13	a. 14.87%.
7-14	7.18%.
7-15	12%.
7-16	9%.
7-17	a. \$33,872.11. b. \$26,243.16 and \$0.
7-18	≈ 15 years.
7-19	6 years; \$1,106.01.
7-20	Contract 2; PV = \$10,717,847.14.
7-21	$PV_{7\%} = \$1,428.57$; $PV_{14\%} = \$714.29$.
7-22	\$893.16.
7-23	\$984.88 ≈ \$985.
7-24	57.2%.
7-25	a. FV = \$1,432.02. b. PMT = \$93.07.
7-26	$k_{Nom} = 15.19\%$.
7-27	PMT = \$36,948.95 or \$36,949.61.
7-28	a. \$18.56 million. b. \$86.49 million. c. PV = \$17.18 million; FV = \$80.08 million.
7-29	a. \$666,669.35. b. \$1,206,663.42.
7-30	\$353,171.50.
7-31	\$17,659.50.
7-32	\$35.
7-33	\$84.34.
7-34	a. \$530. d. \$445.
7-35	a. \$895.40. b. \$1,552.90. c. \$279.20. d. \$500.03; \$867.14.
7-36	a. ≈ 10 years. c. ≈ 4 years.
7-37	a. \$6,374.96. d(1). \$7,012.46.

7-38	a. \$2,457.84. c. \$2,000. d(1). \$2,703.62.
7-39	a. Stream A: \$1,251.25.
7-40	b. 7%. c. 9%. d. 15%.
7-41	a. \$881.17. b. \$895.42. c. \$903.06. d. \$908.35.
7-42	a. \$279.20. b. \$276.84. c. \$443.72.
7-43	a. \$5,272.32. b. \$5,374.07.
7-44	a. 1st City = 7%; 2nd City = 6.14%.
7-45	a. PMT = \$6,594.94.
7-46	a. \$917.21. c. \$118,837.32. b. 90.51%. d. \$163,540.19.
7-47	a. Z = 9%; B = 8%. b. Z = \$558.39; \$135.98; 32.2%; B = \$1,147.20; \$147.20; 14.72%.
7-48	a. \$61,203. b. \$11,020. c. \$6,841.

8-1	\$935.82.
8-2	12.48%.
8-3	YTM = 6.62%; YTC = 6.49%.
8-4	8.55%.
8-5	\$1,028.60.
8-6	a. 7.11%. b. 7.22%. c. \$988.46.
8-7	a. V_L at 5 percent = \$1,518.98; V_L at 8 percent = \$1,171.19; V_L at 12 percent = \$863.78.
8-8	a. YTM at \$829 ≈ 15%.
8-9	15.03%.
8-10	a. 10.37%. b. 10.91%. c. −0.54%. d. 10.15%.
8-11	YTM = 7.2%.
8-12	8.65%.
8-13	10.78%.
8-14	YTC = 6.47%.

8-15   a. $1,251.22.
        b. $898.94.

8-17   a. YTM = 3.4%.
        b. YTM $\approx$ 7%.
        c. $934.91.

8-18   a. YTM = 8%; YTC = 6.1%.

8-19   10-year, 10% coupon = 6.75%;
        10-year zero = 9.75%;
        5-year zero = 4.76%;
        30-year zero = 32.19%;
        $100 perpetuity = 14.29%.

8-20   a. C_0 = $1,012.79; Z_0 = $693.04;
          C_1 = $1,010.02; Z_1 = $759.57;
          C_2 = $1,006.98; Z_2 = $832.49;
          C_3 = $1,003.65; Z_3 = $912.41;
          C_4 = $1,000.00; Z_4 = $1,000.00.

8A-1   5.4%.

8A-2   6.48%.

8A-3   12.37%.

8B-1   A/P = $816; First mortgage = $900; Subordinated debentures = $684; P/S = $0.

8B-2   a. Trustee = $281,250; N/P = $750,000; A/P = $375,000; Subordinated debentures = $750,000; Equity = $343,750.
        b. Trustee = $281,250; N/P = $750,000; A/P = $318,750; Subordinated debentures = $525,000; Equity = $0.

9-1 D_1 = $1.5750; D_3 = $1.7364; D_5 = $2.1011.

9-2 P_0 = $6.25.

9-3 $\hat{P}_1$ = $22.00; k_s = 15.50%.

9-4 k_p = 8.33%.

9-5   b. $37.80.
       c. $34.09.

9-6   a. $24,112,308.
       b. $321,000,000.
       c. $228,113,612.
       d. $16.81.

9-7 $35.00.

9-8   a. $713.33 million.
       b. $527.89 million.
       c. $42.79.

9-9 $50.50.

9-10   g = 9%.

9-11 $\hat{P}_3$ = $27.32.

9-12   a. 13.3%.
        b. 10%.
        c. 8%.
        d. 5.7%.

9-13 $23.75.

9-14   a. k_C = 10.6%; k_D = 7%.

9-15 $25.03.

9-16 P_0 = $19.89.

9-17   a. $125.
        b. $83.33.

9-18   b. PV = $5.29.
        d. $30.01.

9-19   a. 7%.
        b. 5%.
        c. 12%.

9-20   a(1). $9.50.
         (2). $13.33.
        b(1). Undefined.

9-22   a. Dividend 2004 = $2.66.
        b. P_0 = $39.43.
        c. Dividend yield 2002 = 5.10%; 2007 = 7.00%.

9-23   a. P_0 = $54.11.

9-24   a. P_0 = $21.43.
        b. P_0 = $26.47.
        d. P_0 = $40.54.

9-25   a. New price = $31.34.
        b. beta = 0.49865.

10-1 k_s = 13%.

10-2 k_p = 8%.

10-3 k_s = 15%; k_e = 16.11%.

10-4   Projects A through E should be accepted.

10-5   a. 13%.
        b. 10.4%.
        c. 8.45%.

10-6   7.80%.

10-7   11.94%.

10-8   a. k_s = 14.83%.
        b. F = 10%.
        c. k_e = 15.81%.

10-9   WACC = 12.72%.

10-10 w_d = 20%.

10-11   a. k_s = 14.40%.
        b. WACC = 10.62%.
        c. Project A.

10-12   7.2%.

10-13 k_s = 16.51%; WACC = 12.79%.

10-14   a. 16.3%.
        b. 15.4%.
        c. 16%.

10-15
a. 8%.
b. $2.81.
c. 15.81%.

10-16
a. $g = 3\%$.
b. $EPS_1 = \$5.562$.

10-17
a. $k_d(1 - T) = 5.4\%$; $k_s = 14.6\%$.
b. WACC = 10.92%.

10-18
a. $k_d = 7\%$; $k_p = 10.20\%$; $k_s = 15.72\%$.
b. WACC = 13.86%.
c. Projects 1 and 2 will be accepted.

10-19
a. 1.25.
b. 14%.
c. $k_{TD} = 15\%$; $k_{RD} = 11\%$.

11-1 4.34 years.

11-2 NPV = $7,486.68.

11-3 IRR = 16%.

11-4 DPP = 6.51 years.

11-5 MIRR = 13.89%.

11-6 5%: $NPV_A = \$16,108,952$; $NPV_B = \$18,300,939$.
15%: $NPV_A = \$10,059,587$; $NPV_B = \$13,897,838$.

11-7 NPV = $174.90.

11-8 $NPV_T = \$409$; $IRR_T = 15\%$; $MIRR_T = 14.54\%$;
Accept; $NPV_P = \$3,318$; $IRR_P = 20\%$; $MIRR_P = 17.19\%$; Accept.

11-9 $NPV_E = \$3,861$; $IRR_E = 18\%$; $NPV_G = \$3,057$; $IRR_G = 18\%$; Purchase electric-powered forklift; it has a higher NPV.

11-10 $NPV_S = \$448.86$; $NPV_L = \$607.20$; $IRR_S = 15.24\%$; $IRR_L = 14.67\%$; $MIRR_S = 14.67\%$; $MIRR_L = 14.37\%$.

11-11 b. $PV_C = -\$556,717$; $PV_F = -\$493,407$; Forklift should be chosen due to lower cost.

11-12 $MIRR_X = 13.59\%$.

11-13 $IRR_L = 11.74\%$.

11-14 MIRR = 10.93%.

11-15 a. NPV = $136,578; IRR = 19.22%.

11-16 a. Payback = 0.33 year; NPV = $81,062.35; IRR = 261.90%.

11-17 a. No; $PV_{Old} = -\$89,910.08$; $PV_{New} = -\$94,611.45$.
b. $2,470.80.
c. 22.94%.

11-18 c. $IRR_A = 18.1\%$; $IRR_B = 24.0\%$.
e.(1). $MIRR_A = 15.10\%$; $MIRR_B = 17.03\%$.
(2). $MIRR_A = 18.05\%$; $MIRR_B = 20.49\%$.

11-19 a. $IRR_A = 20\%$; $IRR_B = 16.7\%$; Crossover rate = 16.07% ≈ 16%.

11-20 a. $NPV_A = \$14,486,808$; $NPV_B = \$11,156,893$;
$IRR_A = 15.03\%$; $IRR_B = 22.26\%$.

11-21 b. 5.6%; 434.2%.

11-22 d. 9.54%; 22.87%.

11-23 a. A = 2.67 years; B = 1.5 years.
b. A = 3.07 years; B = 1.825 years.
d. $NPV_A = \$18,243,813$; choose A.
e. $NPV_B = \$8,643,390$; choose B.
f. 13.53%.
g. $MIRR_A = 21.93\%$; $MIRR_B = 20.96\%$.

12-1 $12,000,000.

12-2 $2,600,000.

12-3 $4,600,000.

12-4 Accept A, B, C, D, and E; Capital budget = $5,250,000.

12-5 Accept A, B, D, and E; Capital budget = $4,000,000.

12-6 Accept B, C, D, E, F, and G; Capital budget = $6,000,000.

12-7 E(NPV) = $18,540,000; σ_{NPV} = $21,750,227.59; CV = 1.17.

12-8 E(NPV) = $3,000,000; σ_{NPV} = $23.622 million; CV = 7.874.

12-9
a. NPV = $37,035.13.
b. +20%: $77,975.63;
−20%: NPV = −$3,905.37.
c. E(NPV) = $34,800.21; σ_{NPV} = $35,967.84; CV = 1.03.

12-10
a. NPV = $2.4083 million.
b. Wait, NPV = $2.6131 million.

12-11
a. −$178,000.
b. $52,440; $60,600; $40,200.
c. $48,760.
d. NPV = −$19,549; Do not purchase.

12-12
a. −$126,000.
b. $42,518; $47,579; $34,926.
c. $50,702.
d. NPV = $10,841; Purchase.

12-13
a. Expected $CF_A = \$6,750$; Expected $CF_B = \$7,650$; $CV_A = 0.0703$.
b. $NPV_A = \$10,036.25$; $NPV_B = \$11,624.01$.

12-14 $NPV_5 = \$2,212$; $NPV_4 = -\$2,081$; $NPV_8 = \$13,329$.

12-15 a. No, $NPV_3 = \$1,307.29$.

12-16
a. NPV = $4.6795 million.
b. No, NPV = $3.2083 million.

12A-1 PV = $1,310,841.

13-1 Q_{BE} = 500,000.

13-2 30% debt and 70% equity.

13-3 b_U = 1.0435.

13-4 a(1). −$75,000.
(2). $175,000.
b. Q_{BE} = 140,000.

13-5 a(1). −$60,000.
b. Q_{BE} = 14,000.

13-6 a(2). $125,000.
b. Q_{BE} = 7,000.

13-7 a. P_0 = $25.
b. P_0 = $25.81.

13-8 a. ROE_{LL} = 14.6%; ROE_{HL} = 16.8%.
b. ROE_{LL} = 16.5%.

13-9 No leverage: ROE = 10.5%; σ = 5.4%; CV = 0.51; 60% leverage: ROE = 13.7%; σ = 13.5%; CV = 0.99.

13-10 k_s = 17%.

13-12 a. EPS_{Old} = $2.04; New: EPS_D = $4.74; EPS_S = $3.27.
b. 339,750 units.
c. $Q_{New, Debt}$ = 272,250 units.

13-13 Debt used: E(EPS) = $5.78; σ_{EPS} = $1.05; E(TIE) = 3.49×.
Stock used: E(EPS) = $5.51; σ_{EPS} = $0.85; E(TIE) = 6.00×.

13-14 a. FC_A = $80,000; V_A = $4.80/unit; P_A = $8.00/unit.

13-15 40% debt and 60% equity; WACC = 11.45%.

14-1 Payout = 55%.

14-2 P_0 = $60.

14-3 P_0 = $40.

14-4 $3,250,000.

14-5 Payout = 20%.

14-6 Payout = 52%.

14-7 D_0 = $3.44.

14-8 Payout = 31.39%.

14-9 a. $1.44.
b. 3%.
c. $1.20.
d. 33 1/3%.

14-10 a(1). $3,960,000.
(2). $4,800,000.
(3). $9,360,000.
(4). Regular = $3,960,000; Extra = $5,400,000.
c. 15%.
d. 15%.

14-11 a. $6,000,000.
b. $2.00; 25%.
c. $5,000,000.
e. 50%.
f. $1,000,000.
g. $8,333,333.

15-1 $3,000,000.

15-2 A/R = $59,500.

15-3 k_{Nom} = 75.26%; EAR = 109.84%.

15-4 EAR = 8.49%.

15-5 $7,500,000.

15-6 a. DSO = 28 days.
b. A/R = $70,000.

15-7 b. 14.90%.
d. 21.28%.

15-8 a. 45.15%.

15-9 Nominal cost = 14.90%; Effective cost = 15.89%.

15-10 14.91%.

15-11 a. 32 days.
b. $288,000.
c. $45,000.
d(1). 30.
(2). $378,000.

15-12 a. 83 days.
b. $356,250.
c. 4.87×.

15-13 a. 69.5 days.
b(1). 1.875×.
(2). 11.25%.
c(1). 46.5 days.
(2). 2.1262×.
(3). 12.76%.

15-14 a. ROE_T = 11.75%; ROE_M = 10.80%; ROE_R = 9.16%.

15-15 a. Feb. surplus = $2,000.

15-16 a. Oct. loan = $22,800.

15-17 a. $100,000.
c(1). $300,000.
(2). Nominal cost = 37.24%; Effective cost = 44.59%.

15-18 14.35%.

15-19 a. $300,000.

15-20 a(1). $27,260.
(3). $25,616.

16-1 27.2436 yen per shekel.

16-2 1 yen = $0.00907.

16-3 1 euro = $0.68966 or $1 = 1.45 euros.

16-4 0.6667 pound per dollar.

16-5 6.49351 krones.

16-6 15 kronas per pound.

16-8 $468,837,209.

16-9 +$250,000.

16-10

DOLLARS PER 1,000 UNITS OF:

POUNDS	CAN. DOLLARS	EUROS	YEN	PESOS	KRONAS
$1,442.80	$654.00	$891.70	$9.06	$106.10	$104.40

16-12 b. $20,045.45.

16-13 a. $2,772,003.
b. $2,777,585.
c. $3,333,333.

16-14 b. $1.6488.

16-15 $k_{\text{Nom-U.S.}}$ = 4.6%.

16-16 117 pesos.

16-17 20 yen per 1 euro, or 0.05 euro per 1 yen.

SELECTED EQUATIONS AND DATA

CHAPTER 2

Net cash flow = Net income − Noncash revenues + Noncash charges.

Net cash flow = Net income + Depreciation and amortization.

$$\text{Net operating} \atop \text{working capital} = {\text{All current} \atop \text{assets}} - {\text{All current liabilities that} \atop \text{do not charge interest}}.$$

$$\text{Net operating} \atop \text{working} \atop \text{capital} = \left({\text{Cash and} \atop \text{marketable} \atop \text{securities}} + {\text{Accounts} \atop \text{receivable}} + \text{Inventories} \right) - \left({\text{Accounts} \atop \text{payable}} + \text{Accruals} \right).$$

Total operating capital = Net operating working capital + Net fixed assets.

NOPAT = EBIT(1 − Tax rate).

Operating cash flow = NOPAT + Depreciation.

Free cash flow = Operating cash flow − Gross investment in operating capital.

Free cash flow = NOPAT − Net investment in operating capital.

MVA = Market value of stock − Equity capital supplied by shareholders
     = [(Shares outstanding)(Stock price)] − Total common equity.

EVA = NOPAT − After-tax dollar cost of capital used to support operations
    = (EBIT)(1 − T) − (Operating capital)(After-tax percentage cost of capital).

$$\text{Equivalent pre-tax yield} \atop \text{on taxable bond} = \frac{\text{Muni yield}}{1 - T}.$$

INDIVIDUAL TAX RATES FOR APRIL 2001

Single Individuals

IF YOUR TAXABLE INCOME IS	YOU PAY THIS AMOUNT ON THE BASE OF THE BRACKET	PLUS THIS PERCENTAGE ON THE EXCESS OVER THE BASE	AVERAGE TAX RATE AT TOP OF BRACKET
Up to $26,250	$ 0	15.0%	15.0%
$26,250–$63,550	3,937.50	28.0	22.6
$63,550–$132,600	14,381.50	31.0	27.0
$132,600–$288,350	35,787.00	36.0	31.9
Over $288,350	91,857.00	39.6	39.6

Married Couples Filing Joint Returns

IF YOUR TAXABLE INCOME IS	YOU PAY THIS AMOUNT ON THE BASE OF THE BRACKET	PLUS THIS PERCENTAGE ON THE EXCESS OVER THE BASE	AVERAGE TAX RATE AT TOP OF BRACKET
Up to $43,850	$ 0	15.0%	15.0%
$43,850–$105,950	6,577.50	28.0	22.6
$105,950–$161,450	23,965.50	31.0	25.5
$161,450–$288,350	41,170.50	36.0	30.1
Over $288,350	86,854.50	39.6	39.6

Corporate Tax Rates

IF A CORPORATION'S TAXABLE INCOME IS	IT PAYS THIS AMOUNT ON THE BASE OF THE BRACKET	PLUS THIS PERCENTAGE ON THE EXCESS OVER THE BASE	AVERAGE TAX RATE AT TOP OF BRACKET
Up to $50,000	$ 0	15.0%	15.0%
$50,000–$75,000	7,500	25.0	18.3
$75,000–$100,000	13,750	34.0	22.3
$100,000–$335,000	22,250	39.0	34.0
$335,000–$10,000,000	113,900	34.0	34.0
$10,000,000–$15,000,000	3,400,000	35.0	34.3
$15,000,000–$18,333,333	5,150,000	38.0	35.0
Over $18,333,333	6,416,667	35.0	35.0

CHAPTER 3

$$\text{Current ratio} = \frac{\text{Current assets}}{\text{Current liabilities}}.$$

$$\text{Quick, or acid test, ratio} = \frac{\text{Current assets} - \text{Inventories}}{\text{Current liabilities}}.$$

$$\text{Inventory turnover ratio} = \frac{\text{Sales}}{\text{Inventories}}.$$

$$\text{DSO} = \begin{matrix}\text{Days}\\\text{sales}\\\text{outstanding}\end{matrix} = \frac{\text{Receivables}}{\text{Average sales per day}} = \frac{\text{Receivables}}{\text{Annual sales}/365}.$$

$$\text{Fixed assets turnover ratio} = \frac{\text{Sales}}{\text{Net fixed assets}}.$$

$$\text{Total assets turnover ratio} = \frac{\text{Sales}}{\text{Total assets}}.$$

$$\text{Debt ratio} = \frac{\text{Total debt}}{\text{Total assets}}.$$

$$\text{D/E} = \frac{\text{D/A}}{1 - \text{D/A}}, \text{ and D/A} = \frac{\text{D/E}}{1 + \text{D/E}}.$$

$$\text{Debt ratio} = 1 - \frac{1}{\text{Equity multiplier}}.$$

$$\text{Times-interest-earned (TIE) ratio} = \frac{\text{EBIT}}{\text{Interest charges}}.$$

$$\text{EBITDA coverage ratio} = \frac{\text{EBITDA + Lease payments}}{\text{Interest + Principal payments + Lease payments}}.$$

$$\text{Profit margin on sales} = \frac{\text{Net income available to common stockholders}}{\text{Sales}}.$$

$$\text{Basic earning power ratio} = \frac{\text{EBIT}}{\text{Total assets}}.$$

$$\text{Return on total assets (ROA)} = \frac{\text{Net income available to common stockholders}}{\text{Total assets}}.$$

$$\text{ROA} = \left(\frac{\text{Profit}}{\text{margin}}\right)(\text{Total assets turnover}).$$

$$\text{Return on common equity (ROE)} = \frac{\text{Net income available to common stockholders}}{\text{Common equity}}.$$

$$\text{ROE} = \text{ROA} \times \text{Equity multiplier}$$

$$= \left(\frac{\text{Profit}}{\text{margin}}\right)\left(\frac{\text{Total assets}}{\text{turnover}}\right)\left(\frac{\text{Equity}}{\text{multiplier}}\right)$$

$$= \left(\frac{\text{Net income}}{\text{Sales}}\right)\left(\frac{\text{Sales}}{\text{Total assets}}\right)\left(\frac{\text{Total assets}}{\text{Common equity}}\right).$$

$$\text{Return on investors' capital} = \frac{\text{Net income + Interest}}{\text{Debt + Equity}}.$$

$$\text{Price/earnings (P/E) ratio} = \frac{\text{Price per share}}{\text{Earnings per share}}.$$

$$\text{Price/cash flow ratio} = \frac{\text{Price per share}}{\text{Cash flow per share}}.$$

$$\text{Book value per share} = \frac{\text{Common equity}}{\text{Shares outstanding}}.$$

$$\text{Market/book (M/B) ratio} = \frac{\text{Market price per share}}{\text{Book value per share}}.$$

$$\text{EVA} = \text{Net income} - [(\text{Cost of Equity Capital})(\text{Equity Capital})].$$

$$\text{EVA} = (\text{ROE} - \% \text{ Cost of Equity})(\text{Dollars of Equity Capital}).$$

CHAPTER 4

$$\text{AFN} = (A^*/S_0)\Delta S - (L^*/S_0)\Delta S - MS_1(RR).$$

$$\text{Full capacity sales} = \frac{\text{Actual sales}}{\text{Percentage of capacity at which fixed assets were operated}}.$$

$$\text{Target FA/Sales ratio} = \frac{\text{Actual fixed assets}}{\text{Full capacity sales}}.$$

Required level of FA = (Target FA/Sales ratio) (Projected sales).

CHAPTER 5

$k = k^* + IP + DRP + LP + MRP.$

$k_{RF} = k^* + IP.$

$$IP_n = \frac{I_1 + I_2 + \cdots + I_n}{n}.$$

CHAPTER 6

Dollar return = Amount received − Amount invested.

$$\text{Percentage return} = \frac{\text{Amount received} - \text{Amount invested}}{\text{Amount invested}}.$$

$$\text{Expected rate of return} = \hat{k} = \sum_{i=1}^{n} P_i k_i.$$

$$\text{Variance} = \sigma^2 = \sum_{i=1}^{n} (k_i - \hat{k})^2 P_i.$$

$$\text{Standard deviation} = \sigma = \sqrt{\sum_{i=1}^{n} (k_i - \hat{k})^2 P_i}.$$

$$CV = \frac{\sigma}{\hat{k}}.$$

$$\hat{k}_p = \sum_{i=1}^{n} w_i \hat{k}_i.$$

$$\sigma_p = \sqrt{\sum_{i=j}^{n} (k_{pj} - \hat{k}_p)^2 P_j}.$$

$$b_p = \sum_{i=1}^{n} w_i b_i.$$

$SML = k_i = k_{RF} + (k_M - k_{RF})b_i.$

$RP_i = (RP_M)b_i.$

$$b = \frac{Y_2 - Y_1}{X_2 - X_1} = \text{Slope coefficient in } \bar{k}_{it} = a + b \, \bar{k}_{Mt} + e_t.$$

CHAPTER 7

$FV_n = PV(1 + i)^n = PV(FVIF_{i,n}).$

$$PV = FV_n \left(\frac{1}{1 + i} \right)^n = FV_n(1 + i)^{-n} = FV_n(PVIF_{i,n}).$$

$$PVIF_{i,n} = \frac{1}{FVIF_{i,n}}.$$

$$FVIFA_{i,n} = [(1 + i)^n - 1]/i.$$

$$PVIFA_{i,n} = [1 - (1/(1 + i)^n)]/i.$$

$$FVA_n = PMT(FVIFA_{i,n}).$$

$$FVA_n \text{ (Annuity due)} = PMT(FVIFA_{i,n})(1 + i).$$

$$PVA_n = PMT(PVIFA_{i,n}).$$

$$PVA_n \text{ (Annuity due)} = PMT(PVIFA_{i,n})(1 + i).$$

$$PV \text{ (Perpetuity)} = \frac{\text{Payment}}{\text{Interest rate}} = \frac{PMT}{i}.$$

$$PV_{\text{Uneven stream}} = \sum_{t=1}^{n} CF_t \left(\frac{1}{1 + i}\right)^t = \sum_{t=1}^{n} CF_t(PVIF_{i,t}).$$

$$FV_{\text{Uneven stream}} = \sum_{t=1}^{n} CF_t (1 + i)^{n-t} = \sum_{t=1}^{n} CF_t(FVIF_{i,n-t}).$$

$$FV_n = PV\left(1 + \frac{i_{Nom}}{m}\right)^{mn}.$$

$$\text{Effective annual rate} = \left(1 + \frac{i_{Nom}}{m}\right)^m - 1.0.$$

$$\text{Periodic rate} = i_{Nom}/m.$$

$$i_{Nom} = APR = (\text{Periodic rate})(m).$$

$$FV_n = PV(e^{in}).$$

$$PV = FV_n(e^{-in}).$$

CHAPTER 8

$$V_B = \sum_{t=1}^{N} \frac{INT}{(1 + k_d)^t} + \frac{M}{(1 + k_d)^N}$$

$$= INT(PVIFA_{k_d,N}) + M(PVIF_{k_d,N}).$$

$$V_B = \sum_{t=1}^{2N} \frac{INT/2}{(1 + k_d/2)^t} + \frac{M}{(1 + k_d/2)^{2N}} = \frac{INT}{2}(PVIFA_{k_d/2,2N}) + M(PVIF_{k_d/2,2N}).$$

$$\text{Price of callable bond} = \sum_{t=1}^{N} \frac{INT}{(1 + k_d)^t} + \frac{\text{Call price}}{(1 + k_d)^N}.$$

$$\text{Current yield} = \frac{\text{Annual interest}}{\text{Bond's current price}}.$$

Accrued value at end of Year n = Issue price $\times (1 + k_d)^n$.

Interest in Year n = Accrued value$_n$ − Accrued value$_{n-1}$.

Tax savings = (Interest deduction)(T).

CHAPTER 9

$\hat{P}_0$ = PV of expected future dividends = $\displaystyle\sum_{t=1}^{\infty} \frac{D_t}{(1 + k_s)^t}$.

$\hat{P}_0 = \dfrac{D_0(1 + g)}{k_s - g} = \dfrac{D_1}{k_s - g}$.

$\hat{k}_s = \dfrac{D_1}{P_0} + g$.

For a constant growth stock, $P_n = P_0(1 + g)^n$.

Horizon value = $\hat{P}_N = \dfrac{D_{N+1}}{k_s - g}$.

$V_{\text{Company}} = \dfrac{FCF_1}{(1 + WACC)^1} + \dfrac{FCF_2}{(1 + WACC)^2} + \cdots + \dfrac{FCF_\infty}{(1 + WACC)^\infty}$.

$FCF = EBIT(1 - T) + \text{Depreciation} - \dfrac{\text{Capital}}{\text{expenditures}} - \dfrac{\text{Change in}}{\text{net operating}}$.
$\qquad\qquad\qquad\qquad\qquad\qquad\qquad\qquad\qquad\qquad\qquad\text{working capital}$

$V_p = \dfrac{D_p}{k_p}$.

$k_p = \dfrac{D_p}{V_p}$.

CHAPTER 10

After-tax component cost of debt = $k_d(1 - T)$.

Component cost of preferred stock = $k_p = \dfrac{D_p}{P_p}$.

$k_s = \hat{k}_s = k_{RF} + RP = D_1/P_0 + g$.

$k_s = k_{RF} + (k_M - k_{RF})b_i$.

k_s = Bond yield + Risk premium.

$k_e = \dfrac{D_1}{P_0(1 - F)} + g$.

$M(1 - F) = \displaystyle\sum_{t=1}^{N} \dfrac{INT(1 - T)}{(1 + k_d)^t} + \dfrac{M}{(1 + k_d)^N}$.

g = (Retention rate)(ROE) = (1.0 − Payout rate)(ROE).

$RE_{\text{Breakpoint}} = \dfrac{\text{Addition to retained earnings}}{\text{Equity fraction}}$.

$$WACC = w_d k_d (1 - T) + w_p k_p + w_c k_s.$$

$$k_p = k_{RF} + (k_M - k_{RF})b_p.$$

CHAPTER 11

$$\text{Payback} = \text{Year before full recovery} + \frac{\text{Unrecovered cost at start of year}}{\text{Cash flow during year}}.$$

$$NPV = CF_0 + \frac{CF_1}{(1 + k)^1} + \frac{CF_2}{(1 + k)^2} + \cdots + \frac{CF_n}{(1 + k)^n}$$

$$= \sum_{t=0}^{n} \frac{CF_t}{(1 + k)^t}.$$

$$IRR: CF_0 + \frac{CF_1}{(1 + IRR)^1} + \frac{CF_2}{(1 + IRR)^2} + \cdots + \frac{CF_n}{(1 + IRR)^n} = 0$$

$$\sum_{t=0}^{n} \frac{CF_t}{(1 + IRR)^t} = 0.$$

$$MIRR: \text{PV costs} = \text{PV terminal value}$$

$$\sum_{t=0}^{n} \frac{COF}{(1 + k)^t} = \frac{\sum\limits_{t=0}^{n} CIF_t(1 + k)^{n-t}}{(1 + MIRR)^n}$$

$$\text{PV costs} = \frac{TV}{(1 + MIRR)^n}.$$

CHAPTER 12

$$\text{Free cash flow} = EBIT(1 - T) + \text{Depreciation} - \frac{\text{Capital}}{\text{expenditures}} - \frac{\text{Change in}}{\text{net operating}}.$$
$$\text{working capital}$$

APPENDIX 12A

Recovery Allowance Percentages for Personal Property

OWNERSHIP YEAR	CLASS OF INVESTMENT			
	3-YEAR	5-YEAR	7-YEAR	10-YEAR
1	33%	20%	14%	10%
2	45	32	25	18
3	15	19	17	14
4	7	12	13	12
5		11	9	9
6		6	9	7
7			9	7
8			4	7
9				7
10				6
11				3
	100%	100%	100%	100%

CHAPTER 13

$$\text{Return on invested capital} = \frac{\text{NOPAT}}{\text{Capital}}.$$

$$EBIT = PQ - VQ - F.$$

$$Q_{BE} = \frac{F}{P - V}.$$

$$EPS = \frac{(S - FC - VC - I)(1 - T)}{\text{Shares outstanding}} = \frac{(EBIT - I)(1 - T)}{\text{Shares outstanding}}.$$

$$b = b_U [1 + (1 - T)(D/E)].$$

$$b_U = b/[1 + (1 - T)(D/E)].$$

$$D/E = \frac{D/A}{1 - D/A}.$$

$$k_s = k_{RF} + \text{Premium for business risk} + \text{Premium for financial risk}.$$

CHAPTER 14

$$g = (\text{Retention rate})(\text{ROE})$$
$$= (1 - \text{Payout rate})(\text{ROE}).$$

$$\text{Dividends} = \text{Net income} - [(\text{Target equity ratio})(\text{Total capital budget})].$$

CHAPTER 15

$$\frac{\text{Inventory conversion}}{\text{period}} = \frac{\text{Inventory}}{\text{Sales}/365}.$$

$$\frac{\text{Receivables collection}}{\text{period}} = DSO = \frac{\text{Receivables}}{\text{Sales}/365}.$$

$$\text{Payables deferral period} = \frac{\text{Payables}}{\text{Cost of goods sold}/365}.$$

$$\begin{matrix}\text{Inventory} \\ \text{conversion} \\ \text{period}\end{matrix} + \begin{matrix}\text{Receivables} \\ \text{collection} \\ \text{period}\end{matrix} - \begin{matrix}\text{Payables} \\ \text{deferral} \\ \text{period}\end{matrix} = \begin{matrix}\text{Cash} \\ \text{conversion.} \\ \text{cycle}\end{matrix}$$

$$A/R = \begin{matrix}\text{Credit sales} \\ \text{per day}\end{matrix} \times \begin{matrix}\text{Length of} \\ \text{collection period}\end{matrix}.$$

$$ADS = \text{Annual sales}/365 = \frac{(\text{Units sold})(\text{Sales price})}{365}.$$

$$\text{Receivables} = (ADS)(DSO).$$

$$\text{Nominal annual cost of payables} = \frac{\text{Discount percent}}{100 - \begin{matrix}\text{Discount} \\ \text{percent}\end{matrix}} \times \frac{365 \text{ days}}{\begin{matrix}\text{Days credit is} \\ \text{outstanding}\end{matrix} - \begin{matrix}\text{Discount} \\ \text{period}\end{matrix}}.$$

CHAPTER 16

$$\frac{\text{Forward exchange rate}}{\text{Spot exchange rate}} = \frac{1 + k_h}{1 + k_f}.$$

$$P_h = (P_f)(\text{Spot rate}).$$

$$\text{Spot rate} = \frac{P_h}{P_f}.$$